Foreword by Edward Woodward OBE

It is quite astounding how much our country has to offer the visitor these days. Whether you are after some time away from it all, a chance to delve into Britain's history, or the opportunity to walk amongst some of the many areas of outstanding natural beauty, rural or urban, we really do have it all, whether we get the chance to appreciate it or not!

I have stayed in most parts of Britain at one time or another. There is nothing more frustrating than the inevitable conversation shortly after you have returned from an area which makes you aware of what you have missed. You know the sort of thing; an assumption that you cannot possibly have visited such a town without seeing the superb orchards, ancient remains or perhaps modern shopping village. By then it is too late, and you silently vow to be much better prepared before future visits. I have made that promise many times, but seldom keep it!

I like the series of guides of which you are now holding a volume simply because they represent an attempt to give any visitor a comprehensive reference work for what can be found in a given area, but without sticking to dry facts alone. After all, what do you remember most about a particular visit, be it for work or holiday? Every town, city and village has its own atmosphere, its own stories from the past and present, and its own unique setting in our equally varied countryside. The most famous attraction may be the most remembered, but any two people will describe it differently, focusing on their own preferred details. When I hear mention of a particular town or city it is often a hotel room that comes to mind, or a certain street, theatre, or restaurant.

The authors of the Four Seasons Guides have put some real flavour into what they have written; a mixture of personal comment, recollection and opinion with solid base ingredients necessary to any guide book; relevant and up-to-date information about attractions, places to visit and stay in. So many places are covered, but each has retained some of its individuality even in the midst of such a multitude.

These are books into which you can dip now and then for a little entertainment or information. You may then find yourself reading for longer than you first intended, as one anecdote, piece of folklore or description leads into another. Any book which can make you smile at one moment, and at the next form a determination in your mind to visit somewhere new, must be a welcome addition to the bookshelf or travelling bag.

THE FOUR SEASONS
Bed & Breakfast
GREAT BRITAIN

Potted History, Interesting Attractions and Places to Visit
Great Venues, Great Food and Comfort, Great Value

*THE PERFECT COMPANION FOR
LOCALS – VISITORS – OVERSEAS GUESTS
A GUIDE YOU SHOULD NOT TO BE WITHOUT*

ISBN 0-9526555-4-3
Copyright Kingsley Media Ltd
All rights reserved

All Information is included in good faith and is believed to be correct at the time of going to press. No responsibility can be accepted for error.

The book is sold subject to the condition that it shall not by way of trade or other wise be lent, re-sold, hired out or otherwise circulated without the publisher's prior consent in any form of binding or cover other than that in which it is published and without similar condition including this condition being imposed on the subsequent purchaser.

Joy David's Choice

INTRODUCTION

Over a decade I have written many books about the regions of England and Wales and stayed and eaten in a myriad of hotels, guesthouses, inns and restaurants. Some have given me greater pleasure than others but everywhere there has always been a wonderful welcome. In addition I have seen glorious countryside, fabulous stately homes, exotic and beautiful gardens, castles, churches and cathedrals which have left me breathless with their beauty and architecture, all of which has made me realise just what Britain has to offer - a fact that seems to escape a lot of people who feel they have not had a holiday or a short break unless they leave these shores. I hope that what has given me so much pleasure may change their minds. For visitors from overseas I hope Joy David's Choice will encourage them to leave the familiar tourist beaten track and explore some of the lesser known places.

In this book I have endeavoured to put together a selection of some favourite bed and breakfast establishments, beloved vistas, exciting places to explore and the odd watering hole or two in which to refresh ones body rather than ones mind. In my choice I have covered a wide spectrum in order to ensure that financially there is a sensible choice - not everyone can, or wishes, to stay in a five star hotel, some prefer eating in pubs to restaurants. For myself I have frequently found as much, if not more, pleasure in staying in one of the Wolsey Lodges, that a more impersonal hotel. Here you are invited to stay with people in their own, very beautiful, homes and enjoy their conversation over a fabulous dinner. This choice will certainly not suit everyone but it gives me the opportunity of opening up new avenues for those who want to stay away. I have written the book county by county to make it user friendly and at the back you will find additional information which may prove of use to you, the reader.

My only regret about writing a book in this manner is that to really cover everything I have enjoyed with the written word and the drawings, would make it so vast you would need a fork lift truck to carry it about! However what cannot be included here will find its way into the new series of Regional books I hope to have published in the next two years.

Joy David

Joy David's Choice

Joy David's Choice

CONTENTS INCLUDES

Introduction   p. 3

Chapter 1	The West Country Devon & Cornwall, Somerset & Avon	p. 8
Chapter 2	Southern England Dorset, Wiltshire & Hampshire	p. 233
Chapter 3	The Home Counties, The Thames Valley & Greater London Including Surrey, Sussex, Kent Essex, Bucks, Beds, Berks	p. 332
Chapter 4	Central England Including Hereford, Worcestershire, Staffs, Shropshire, West Midlands, Warwickshire	p. 410
Chapter 5	The Mid-Shires Including Notts, Leicestershire, Lincolnshire, Derbyshire, Northamptonshire	p. 506
Chapter 6	Gloucester, Oxford & The Cotswolds	p. 520
Chapter 7	The North West Counties Including Lancashire, Cumbria, Cheshire, Merseyside, Greater Manchester	p. 556
Chapter 8	The North East Counties Including Yorkshire, Northumberland, Durham, Cleveland	p. 578
Chapter 9	East Anglia Including Norfolk, Suffolk, Cambridgeshire	p. 626
Chapter 10	Wales	p. 660
Chapter 11	Scotland	p. 770
	A-Z Index	p. 999
	Guide to Where to Eat & Drink	p. 847
	Guide to Places to Visit	p. 891
	Map	p. 1020

Joy David's Choice

Devon, Cornwall, Somerset and Avon

Chapter One

DEVON, CORNWALL, SOMERSET & AVON

CHAPTER 1

DEVON, CORNWALL, AVON & SOMERSET

INCLUDES

Penny Hill Farm	Alcomb, Minehead	p. 113
West Farm	Appledore	p. 135
Renson Mill	Ashwater	p. 136
Granary Cottage	Axminster	p. 127
Lea House	Axminster	p. 137
Manor House	Axminster	p. 138
Bradiford Cottage	Barnstaple	p. 139
Muddiford Inn	Barnstaple	p. 121
Outer Narracott	Barnstaple	p. 136
The Beeches	Barnstaple	p. 131
Della Rosa Guest House	Bath	p. 140
Oakleigh Guest House	Bath	p. 141
Parkside Guest House	Bath	p. 142
Redcar Hotel	Bath	p. 144
Siena Hotel	Bath	p. 145
The Old School House	Bathford, Bath	p. 146
Blagdon Manor Country Hotel	Beaworthy	p. 147
Garlands	Beer	p. 140
Langleigh House	Berrynarbour	p. 148
Burscott House	Bideford	p. 143
Lane Mill Farm	Bideford	p. 141
Newbridge Hotel	Bideford	p. 229
The Old Mill	Bideford	p. 149
Longaller Mill	Bishops Hull, Taunton	p. 150
Downrew House Hotel	Bishops Tawton	p. 151
Hawthorn House	Bishopswood	p. 152
Oaklands	Black Dog, Nr Crediton	p. 142
Hele House	Blue Anchor, Minehead	p. 143
Copperfield	Bodieve	p. 153
The Mowhay	Bodieve	p. 154
Helman Torr Cottages	Bodmin	p. 154
Loskeyle	Bodmin	p. 155
Skisdon	Bodmin	p. 156
Bottreaux House	Boscastle	p. 157
Lower Meadows House	Boscastle	p. 155
Westerings	Boscastle	p. 158
High Park	Bradworthy	p. 158
The Old Rectory	Bratton Clovelly	p. 159

Chapter One

Coppa Dolla Inn	**Broadhempston, Nr Totnes**	p. 160
Splatthayes	**Buckerell**	p. 161
Globe Inn	**Buckfastleigh**	p. 159
Brightland Apartments	**Bude**	p. 162
Langfield Manor	**Bude**	p. 163
Lopthorne	**Bude**	p. 164
Stratton Gardens Hotel	**Bude**	p. 165
The Inn On The Green	**Bude**	p. 166
Trebarn House	**Bude**	p. 167
Trelay Farm Cottages	**Bude**	p. 223
Treworgie Barton	**Bude**	p. 168
Winswood	**Bude**	p. 169
Halgarrack Cottage	**Camborne**	p. 161
Tregorran Hotel	**Carbis Bay**	p. 170
Cary Fitzpaine Farmhouse	**Cary Fitzpaine, Yeovil**	p. 166
The Horse Pond Inn & Motel	**Castle Cary**	p. 227
The Halfway House	**Cawsand Bay**	p. 171
The Mews	**Chagford**	p. 167
Hornsbury Mill	**Chard**	p. 172
Home Farm	**Churchstow, Nr Kingsbridge**	p. 171
The Hollies	**Clawton, Nr Holsworthy**	p. 173
Box Hedge Farm	**Coalpit Heath, Bristol**	p. 174
Rone House Hotel	**Combe Martin**	p. 174
Moxhill Farm	**Combwich, Nr Bridgwater**	p. 173
Windgate Farm	**Coombe Raleigh**	p. 175
Amber House	**Coxley, Wells**	p. 175
Bostona	**Crediton**	p. 176
Copper Oak Cottage	**Crediton**	p. 176
Great Leigh Farm	**Crediton**	p. 177
Beverly Farm	**Crewkerne**	p. 178
The George Hotel	**Crewkerne**	p. 102
Combas Farm	**Croyde**	p. 103
Knowles House	**Cullompton**	p. 103
Ford House	**Dartmouth**	p. 104
Cair Farm	**Deviock**	p. 105
The Barn	**Deviock**	p. 106
Cott Farm	**Dittisham, Nr Dartmouth**	p. 106
Treliddon Farm	**Downderry**	p. 107
Old Inn	**Drewsteignton**	p. 108
Manor Farm	**Dulcote, Wells**	p. 109
Higher Combe Farm	**Dulverton**	p. 109
Woodville House	**Dunster, Nr Minehead**	p. 110
Sir Walter Raleigh Inn	**East Budleigh**	p. 111
Black Ness Cottage	**East Cornworthy**	p. 112

Devon, Cornwall, Somerset and Avon

Channel Vista	**Exeter**	p. 112
Hill Farm	**Exeter**	p. 113
Sunnymead Guest House	**Exmouth**	p. 114
Camelot	**Falmouth**	p. 115
Ashcombe Farm	**Glastonbury**	p. 225
Dennis & Edna's Bed & Breakfast	**Glastonbury**	p. 116
Wick Hollow House	**Glastonbury**	p. 117
Swallows Rest	**Golberdon, Nr Callington**	p. 118
The Hungry Horse	**Harbetonford, Nr Totnes**	p. 118
Hartlake Farm	**Hartlake, Nr Glastonbury**	p. 119
Godolphin Bridge Hotel	**Hayle**	p. 119
Boak House	**Helston**	p. 120
Cobblers Cottage	**Helston**	p. 120
Sydney Farm	**Higher Halstock, Yeovil**	p. 131
Mildmay Colours	**Holbeton**	p. 122
Alfoxton Cottage	**Holford, Bridgwater**	p. 123
Court Barn Country House Hotel	**Holsworthy**	p. 124
Pheasantry	**Honiton**	p. 224
Yard Farm	**Honiton**	p. 104
Combe Lodge Hotel	**Ilfracombe**	p. 226
Seven Hills Hotel	**Ilfracombe**	p. 125
North Patchole Farmhouse	**Kentisbury Ford, Nr Barnstaple**	p. 126
Centry Farm	**Kingsbridge**	p. 127
Holmfield	**Kingsbridge**	p. 128
Lower Grimpstonleigh	**Kingsbridge**	p. 129
Marsh Mills	**Kingsbridge**	p. 130
Seamark Holiday Apartments	**Kingsbridge**	p. 131
The Hope And Anchor Inn	**Kingsbridge**	p. 132
The Sloop Inn	**Kingsbridge**	p. 133
Attworth	**Kingsteignton**	p. 134
Coleton Barton Farm	**Kingswear**	p. 195
The Old Mill	**Langport**	p. 196
Lynnwood Bed and Breakfast	**Lanlivery**	p. 197
Hall Farmhouse	**Lanteglos-by-Fowey**	p. 198
Chelsfield Farm	**Launceston**	p. 197
Glencoe Villa Guest House	**Launceston**	p. 199
Hurdon Farm	**Launceston**	p. 200
Courtyard Farm Cottages	**Lesnewth, Nr Boscastle**	p. 200
Millford Farm Cottages	**Lifton, Nr Launceston**	p. 201
Crylla Farm	**Liskeard**	p. 202
Linden Cottage	**Liskeard**	p. 202
Lower Trengale Farm	**Liskeard**	p. 203
Rosecraddoc Lodge	**Liskeard**	p. 204

Chapter One

Shenstone	**Liskeard**	p. 205
The Old Rectory		
Country House Hotel	**Liskeard**	p. 206
Tredinnick Farm	**Liskeard**	p. 204
Tregondale Farm	**Liskeard**	p. 207
Windermere House	**Looe**	p. 208
Lydford House Hotel	**Lydford**	p. 209
Ingleside Hotel	**Lynton**	p. 210
Sandrock Hotel	**Lynton**	p. 212
Hartland Quay Hotel	**Hartland Quay**	p. 213
Treleaven Farmhouse	**Mevagissey**	p. 208
Lovelynch Farm	**Milverton, Taunton**	p. 214
Alcombe House Hotel	**Minehead**	p. 211
Dollons House	**Minehead**	p. 215
Stockleigh Lodge	**Minehead**	p. 216
Cotehele Lodge	**Newquay**	p. 210
Fair Havens Holiday Flats	**Newquay**	p. 217
Trenance Lodge	**Newquay**	p. 218
Cleavelands St Mary	**Lustleigh**	p. 219
South Harton Farm	**Lustleigh**	p. 220
Warmhill Farm	**Newton Abbot**	p. 211
Yeolden House Hotel	**Northam**	p. 221
Smallicombe Farm	**North Leigh, Nr Colyton**	p. 222
Lower Clavelshay Farm	**North Petherton,**	
	Nr Bridgewater	p. 220
The Sunday School	**North Petherwin**	p. 64
Lower Nichols Nymet Farm	**North Tawton**	p. 64
Slade Barn	**Noss Mayo, Nr Plymouth**	p. 65
Easterbrook Farm Cottages	**Okehampton**	p. 65
Pitt Farm	**Ottery St Mary**	p. 66
Trevone Bay Hotel	**Padstow**	p. 67
The Old Mill Country House	**Padstow**	p. 68
Trenderway Farm	**Pelynt, Nr Polperro**	p. 69
Ednovean Farm Cottage	**Penzance**	p. 70
Lynwood Guest House	**Penzance**	p. 71
Wymering Guest House	**Penzance**	p. 71
The Queens Arms	**Pitminster**	p. 72
The Imperial Hotel	**Plymouth**	p. 73
The Watchers	**Polperro**	p. 66
Seaways Guest House	**Polzeath**	p. 74
Fairholme	**Port Isaac**	p. 75
St Andrews Hotel	**Port Isaac**	p. 76
Duchy House	**Princetown**	p. 77
Melon Cottage	**Radstock, Bath**	p. 78

Devon, Cornwall, Somerset and Avon

Holmehurst	**Redruth**	**p. 78**
Journey's End	**Ringmore, Nr Kingsbridge**	**p. 79**
Cant Farm	**Rock, Nr Wadebridge**	**p. 80**
Irondale House	**Rode, Bath**	**p. 81**
Higher Rodhuish Farm	**Rodhuish**	**p. 82**
The Harbour House	**Seaton**	**p. 76**
The Shrubbery Hotel	**Shepton Mallet**	**p. 83**
Groveside Guest House	**Sidmouth**	**p. 84**
Pinn Barton	**Sidmouth**	**p. 84**
Southern Cross Guest House	**Sidmouth**	**p. 85**
Willow Bridge Private Hotel	**Sidmouth**	**p. 86**
Still Cottage	**Somerton**	**p. 85**
Hollymount Cottage	**South Brent**	**p. 86**
The Grange Farmhouse	**St Agnes**	**p. 87**
Boskerris Hotel	**St Ives**	**p. 88**
Cobbles	**St Ives**	**p. 224**
Rivendell	**St Ives**	**p. 87**
Surfside Yellow House	**St Ives**	**p. 89**
The Count House	**St Ives**	**p. 89**
The Willows	**St Ives**	**p. 90**
Pheasant Hotel	**St Mary, Nr Ilminster**	**p. 91**
Dye Cottage	**St Neot, Nr Liskeard**	**p. 90**
London Inn	**St Neot, Nr Liskeard**	**p. 92**
Little Paddocks	**Stoke Gabriel**	**p. 93**
Apple Tree Hotel	**Stowey**	**p. 230**
Forde House	**Taunton**	**p. 228**
Bonrose	**Teignmouth**	**p. 93**
Knowle Manor	**Timberscombe, Nr Dunster**	**p. 94**
Bickleigh Cottage Hotel	**Tiverton**	**p. 95**
Challis	**Tiverton**	**p. 96**
Higher Western Restaurant	**Tiverton**	**p. 97**
Little Holwell	**Tiverton**	**p. 97**
Suite Dreams Country Hotel	**Torquay**	**p. 98**
Church Cottage	**Totnes**	**p. 100**
Durant Arms	**Totnes**	**p. 95**
Old Hazzard	**Totnes**	**p. 99**
Springfield House	**Totnes**	**p. 101**
The School House	**Totnes**	**p. 100**
The Port William	**Trebarwith Strand**	**p. 179**
Higher Dipford Farm	**Trull, Nr Taunton**	**p. 177**
Arrallas	**Truro**	**p. 180**
Pengelly Farmhouse	**Truro**	**p. 181**
Ventongimps Mill Barn	**Truro**	**p. 178**
Hillhead Farm	**Ugborough, Nr Ivybridge**	**p. 181**

Chapter One

Milton Manor Farm	**Upper Milton, Wells**	p. 182
Venterdon House	**Venterdon**	p. 182
Percys Restaurant with Rooms	**Virginstow**	p. 183
Greenham Hall	**Wellington**	p. 184
Mead Barn Cottages	**Welcombe**	p. 185
Bekynton House	**Wells**	p. 186
Home Farm	**Wells**	p. 187
The Ancient Gate House Hotel	**Wells**	p. 188
Anchor Lights	**West Looe**	p. 183
Westcliffe Hotel	**West Looe**	p. 185
Coombe Farm	**Widegates, Nr Looe**	p. 189
Trevaria Farm	**Widegates, Nr Looe**	p. 190
Kemps Farm	**Winsford, Minehead**	p. 191
Alpine House	**Wiveliscombe**	p. 192
Netherne	**Yarnscombe**	p. 188
Lydgate House Hotel	**Yelverton**	p. 193
The Forge	**Yelverton**	p. 191
Seeburg	**Yeovil**	p. 194

CHAPTER ONE

THE WEST COUNTRY
Devon, Cornwall, the Isles of Scilly, Somerset and Avon

Those of us lucky enough to live in this fabulous part of the world in which everyone of God's ingredients seems to have been made into a perfect cake, sometimes forget to look around us and see the stunning beauty of the coastline, the awesome and sometimes bleak grandeur of the moors -**Dartmoor, Exmoor and Bodmin Moor** -which all come within this Baileywick. The visitor does not make this mistake and as a result sometimes suffers from mental indigestion and the indecision that comes when the choice is great. I hope in this chapter to whet your appetite and encourage you to discover the West Country and all it has to offer.

Because you will inevitably reach **Bristol** first lets take a look at this fascinating city which owes much of its prosperity to navigation, the Avon estuary just before it reaches the sheltered Bristol Channel acting as a harbour, and a wide river to take cargoes inland. Trade was active from the early days of sail when ships left port for many parts of the world, bringing back exotic and unusual goods. The medieval woollen trade to Portugal, Spain and Ireland was at the beginning of a long period of importance for fine woollens in the region. More recent industries which have been at the centre of Bristol's success are papermaking, printing, flour milling, tobacco, engineering, chemical processing, and aircraft production. The city's wealth reached out into the surrounding area and can be seen in the status of buildings in many of the towns and villages..

One of the most impressive sights in Bristol is the **Clifton Suspension Bridge** built by Isambard Kingdom Brunel and completed in 1864, which crosses the Avon Gorge at a staggering 245 feet above the high water level. Brunel's work is much in evidence in this area, often associated with the Great Western Railway which was a feat of elegant engineering. His ship 'Great Britain', the world's first ocean-going, propellor-driven iron ship was built at Bristol in 1843 and following restoration after being marooned in the Falklands, is now on display here at the **Great Western Dock.**

Bristol has its own Cathedral and some of the oldest churches in the country. It also has a fabulous shopping centre which, in addition to the nationally known shops and department stores, are a wealth of small shops of all kinds selling antiques, designer clothes, books and many others.If you have some serious shopping to do the **Broadmead** shopping centre is the place to visit. There was an element of resistence to this project initially. Many believed that some of the buildings planned for demolition should be spared, however there comes a time when new and innovative schemes have to be introduced to prevent a place stagnating. Broadmead is a success, it contains virtually every major department store and literally hundreds of smaller shops many of which are housed undercover in the **Galleries**. It is mainly pedestrianised which makes shopping so much safer and easier especially for families with young children and the less able-bodied. Bristol is blessed with two good theatres, a thriving university and dozens of important art galleries and the exhibitions range from Old Masters to contemporary artists, ceramics, jewellery, sculpture, the list is infinite. So too is the variety of music which can be enjoyed throughout the city. **Colston Hall** offers performances which cannot fail to appeal to the most catholic of tastes. Where else could one expect to find The Bristol Bach Choir and Cambridge Baroque Camerata one week and ShirleyBassey the next?

You will find Bristol full of interesting old pubs, good eateries which in the case of the latter, cover virtually every ethnic variety one can think of. The hotels range from five star to the more modest Guest House but always with a good standard. Bristol makes a wonderful base from which to explore the countryside around Bristol which has been carefully preserved and nurtured and it is still possible to find places where wild flowers grow undisturbed and the best of these is the **Avon Gorge Nature Reserve**. This haven stretches along the West side of the Avon and it is one of the most important lowland limestone reserves in the country. Archeologists among you can see the Iron Age hill fort of Stockleigh camp which lies within the boundary.

There are many other attractions for nature lovers. It is possible to arrange a guided tour around the lovely **Long Ashton Cider Orchards** near **Abbots Leigh** and be reminded of the golden days of apple orchards and farmhouse cider in stone jars. The English Nature Warden will accompany you on seasonal walks through Leigh Woods and you are recommended to wear stout shoes and bring binoculars for an ornithological tour of Blaise.

Bath, a frisson of excitement courses through me whenever I think about this wonderful city. I treat it like an old friend but always with a decorum and an awareness that Beau Nash together with the Master of Ceremonies at the assembly and pump room insisted on the highest degree of civility and manners. Nonetheless it is always with a certain amount of impatience and eager anticipation that I seek out this incomparable city. I prefer to behave in the manner of an ostrich and bury my head in the sand when it comes to the outskirts or the 'new'Bath which arose because of indifferent planning. Thankfully, Georgian Bath still remains. It is not the individual buildings that make this city so wonderful but the whole architectural assembly. Take a walk down through Laura Place looking at the houses in which society used to dwell in its heyday when Bath was a fashionable watering hole, cross Argyle Street and so to Pulteney Bridge which spans the Avon. You could be forgiven for thinking you were in Florence as you cross this enchanting bridge which has small shops on either side of it not unlike the Ponte Vecchio. The Abbey must come high on your list of places to see. It is probably the most beautiful place in the city. There is more glass than stone in the walls which fill it with light. It is sometimes called the Lantern of the West. It is the West front that is its greatest glory. It looks down on the square where all the visitors gather outside the Roman Baths. The West door itself is heavily carved with heraldic shields set in a triple arch, and on each side are wonderful stone canopies covering ancient figures of St Peter and St Paul.

In Broad Street there is **The Bath Postal Museum**. The first known posting of a Penny Black, the world's first stamp took place from this historic building on the 2nd May 1840. The ground floor displays introduce the story of the letter writing and the carriage of mail throughout the ages. There are working machines and a life-size Victorian post office as well as children's activities room. The Museum opens every day from 11-5pm throughout the year and on Sundays from April to October 2-5pm. **The Victoria Art Gallery** in Bridge Street is a major venue for touring exhibitions of national importance. It also has a fine permanent display of European Masters, 18-20th century British paintings and drawings together with decorative art.

The Bath Boating Station in Forester Road, is a unique surviving Victorian boating station with tea gardens and licensed restaurant, a living museum with traditional wooden skiffs, punts and canoes for hire by hour or by day. A pleasant way for a family to spend a summers day on the river Avon. Abundant wildlife, kingfishers, heron, wild geese, moorhens, cormorants etc excites and delights birdwatchers. Punting is a speciality and you need have no fear if this demandingscience is foreign to you; there is tuition! You can find bed and breakfast here and somewhere to park your car - no easy matter in Bath.

If you have ever thought of viewing Bath from the air, may I suggest **Heritage Balloons**. The magic is inescapable and I promise that a trip in a hot-air balloon offers the adventure of a lifetime. From the air, the city of Bath and the surrounding countryside takes on an entirely new dimension. Only from the air can you truly appreciate the beauty of the designs of John Wood, the architect and his son, whose vision came to life in the shape of the **Royal Crescent** and **The Circus**. Flights take place early in the morning and early evening and the whole exercise lasts about three hours. In the oldest tradition of ballooning, each flight is celebrated with a glass or two of

Chapter One

chilled champagne. The take off site is Victoria Park and to book your flight which must be between March and October please ring 01225 318747.

The list is endless of exciting things to see and do. There is **The Roman Bath Museum** in the Pump Room, Abbey Churchyard. **Beckford's Tower and Museum** stands on the summit of Lansdown, with extensive views from its Belevedere, reached by 156 easy steps. **The Museum of Costume and Assembly Rooms** in Bennett Street tells the story of fashion over the last 400 years and is brought alive with one of the finest collections of its kind in the world. The displays include 200 dressed figures and up to a thousand other items of costume, accessories and jewellery to illustrate the changing styles in fashionable men's women's and children's clothes from the late 16th century to the present day. **Royal Crescent** which is popularly regarded as the climax of the **Palladian** achievement in this most classical of English cities is epitomised in **No 1 Royal Crescent** which provides one with an opportunity to see how a house in this wonderful crescent might have appeared when it was first built. **The American Museum** at **Claverton** has 18 period furnished rooms from the 17-19th centuries. The building of **Bath Museum** in the Countess of Huntingdon Chapel, The Vineyards, The Paragon is somewhere in which you will discover how one of the architectural masterpieces of Europe was created. At the same address is **The Museum of English Naive Art (1750-1900)**. This is the first museum of English folk painting, by travelling artists of the 18th and 19th century.

Without doubt one of the best ways of seeing Bath is on the splendid **Kennet and Avon Canal**. Run by the Bath and Dundas Canal Company you can join a boat at Brass Knocker Bottom, opposite the Viaduct Inn in Warminster Road, Monkton Combe. From this historic base near the famous Dundas Aqueduct in the beautiful Limpley Stoke Valley, five miles from Bath, attractive self-drive electric boats are available for the hour, day or evening hire. Picnicking becomes a delight or you can visit the canalside pubs and tea gardens along the delightful stretch between Bath and Bradford-on-Avon. You will find a number of these pubs also have bed and breakfast accommodation. The normal availability is from Easter until the end of September from 9am-5.30pm.

Advance booking is advisable. At Sydney Wharf you can join the **John Rennie**, named after the architect and engineer who designed the 87 mile long canal which joins the River Avon at Bath with the River Thames at Reading. This really is a magical cruise with the opportunity of dining on board. If you become addicted to travelling on the canal as many do you will see that there are stretches where it is obvious that work still needs to be done and more time and money spent, especially on the width and dredging but one has to remember that in the 1950s and 60s parts of the 'cut' were merely wet ditches and but for the totally voluntary work of the Kennet and Avon Canal Trust, would still remain un-navigable.

If you have time or the inclination to leave Bath for the surrounding countryside do go a little way up the A4 to **Bathford**, a pretty village, where The Old School House will look after you excellently.

There are various places that I enjoy visiting within easy reach of Bristol. **Badminton** is one of them. It is here on the Duke of Beaufort's estate that one of the great equestrian occasions of the years, the horse trials are held. People come from all around the world to spectate and to take part. It is also one of the rare times in the year when the great house is open to the public and the opportunity to see it should not be missed. It has always been a jealously guarded house by the Dukes of Beaufort and is hardly visible from the village. The trials are always held in April and frequently attended by members of the Royal Family. Indeed the Princess Royal was a winner here one year.

Chipping Sodbury was a 12th century property speculation! It lies on the edge of Old Sodbury parish and was primarily a market centre. The property developers laid out the plots in a regular pattern on each side of the road and so it has remained. It has some wonderful street names - Hatters Lane, Horse Street, Rouncival Street, Hounds Lane and Shoutinge Lane. It really is an attractive place in which to wander and while the population has grown, little has been built to its detriment.

The M4 with its unceasing traffic crosses the county a little to the south of Chipping Sodbury and just below that is **Marshfield**, surrounded by cornfields and at one time a place that supplied malt to Bristol and Bath. Those days have long gone but not so the attractive malthouses. The town thrived on the wool trade and many of the fine 17th and 18th century houses reflect the wealth of the citizens in that era. Its ancient traditions are carried on by the Marshfield Mummers, whose play is performed on Boxing Day each year. The play never varies in its presentation of the traditional conflict between Good and Evil.

Radstock will not please everybody but it is of great interest to the industrial archaeologist and to railway historians. Both of these industries were for many years the main providers of work and money in the town. The last coal mine closed in 1973 but well before that, great thought had been given to grassing and planting the batches - spoil tips for those who have not heard this word used in this context before - I always associate it with cooking and baking! Here **The Radstock, Midsomer Norton & District Museum** at Barton Meade House, Haydon, is an 18th century converted

Chapter One

barn and outbuildings standing in beautiful countryside in the former North Somerset Coalfield. You can see how a Victorian miner lived and worked with a re-constructed coalface and cottage. You can see where the colliery children went to school and where the family shopped at the co-op. There are displays covering 200 years of farming and railways, complete with a model layout. Everywhere there are reminders of the past including an early Methodist meeting room, blacksmith shop, and Saxon artefacts. Temporary exhibitions relating to local themes are held throughout the year. The tea room produces an excellent cup of tea but on a fine day you may prefer the picnic area. There is a souvenir shop and free car parking. It is only open at weekends on Saturdays from 10-4pm and Sundays and Bank Holidays from 2-5pm.

Going westwards you come to the **Chew Valley Lake**, a place of infinite beauty. It is a great place for anglers and for those who just want to stroll along its banks. Chew Valley has two villages worthy of note. **Chew Magna** and **Chew Stoke**. At Chew Magna you enter it by traversing one medieval bridge and leaving it by another.

Back on the main A368 you will come to **Blagdon** which also has a beautiful lake attracting tourists from afar for its trout fishing. It is also lucky enough to have a cosy and typically English village inn, **The Seymour Arms**.

You will either love or hate **Weston-Super-Mare**. There seem to be very few people who feel indifferently about it. There is no doubt that it has much to offer the visitor in every conceivable way. The question is where to start. I read one of the promotional brochures put out by the local Tourist Board and it describes the town as 'Miles of Smiles'. It is true that as a good family resort it has something to put a smile on every face whether young or not so young, with its attractive setting and choice of things to do and places to visit. The two miles of clean, golden sandy beach and the Grand Pier, with its large amusement centre and Blizzard white knuckle ride, certainly delight people. For those who enjoy leisure complexes you will not find a better one than **Tropicana Pleasure Beach** with its heated swimming pool, wave machine, water chutes and children's adventure equipment, based on a tropical fruit theme.

The Marine Lake should not be forgotten, here there is always shallow water for children to bathe and splash around in complete safety. I am not sure who is responsible for the flower displays in Weston but whoever it is does the town proud. The spacious beach lawns add a touch of charm to the seafront and the attractive parks and gardens around the resort have superb colourful displays. Just sitting and looking at them is joyous and therapeutic. You can ride in style along the Marine Parade daily during the season in a horse drawn Landau. It makes you feel very important and is quite delightful. If you have small children with you it will take them some time to be lured away from the land train which services the whole length of the promenade from April to September, weather permitting.

For those who want to walk with a purpose I would suggest collecting a series of leaflets published by the Civic Society which will help you follow trails around the town at your own pace. You will find them on sale at both the Tourist Information Centre and the Heritage Centre.

Three interesting museums should not be missed. **The International Helicopter Museum** at Weston Airport holds the world's largest collection of helicopters and autogyros, unique to Britain. You can see restoration work in progress and nobody seems to mind your asking questions in this friendly place. It is open from March-October daily from 10am-6pm and from November to March 10am-4pm. It is closed on Christmas Day, Boxing Day and New Years Day. **Woodspring Museum** is right in the town centre and is a re-creation of everyday life at the turn of the century. Having recently been to the dentist and suffered hardly at all, thank heavens, for I am a miserable coward, I was more than appreciative of the techniques used today when I saw a replica of an Edwardian dentist's surgery complete with the most horrendous implements. There are many displays and if you ever wondered what our Victorian ancestors did when they went to the seaside you can soon find out by examining one area of the museum which is devoted to this very subject. The Museum is open all the year round.

Clara's Cottage is another museum in its own way. This time it is a restored Weston seaside landlady's lodging of the 1890's which also includes the Peggy Nesbitt doll collection. It is open daily except Sundays from 10am-5pm and admission is free.

There are a host of delightful villages to be discovered and with the advent of the motorways which in many ways has been a blessing you can travel more easily from one place to another and they do not prevent you from slipping off at various junctions to explore. **Winterbourne** is one such place, although really it has become part of Bristol today. Its oldest part has managed to stay untouched. In the quiet area around the church are a few cottages, and the adjoining Winterbourne Court Farm. I like to think of Winterbourne when hat-making was a cottage industry and between 1770 and 1870 the whole place flourished with the trade brought to them because fashion dictated the wearing of beaver hats. The church too has a romantic story surrounding a knight whose effigy lies by the north wall. The knight is thought to be Hugo de Struden who eloped with a fair lady but was a bit of a rogue. He made a pact with the devil in return for certain favours. He

Chapter One

agreed that when he died he would not be carried into the church, buried in the churchyard, feet or head forward. He managed to cheat even on that and gave instructions that his coffin be carried in sideways and be buried in the wall. On one wall is a brass which I found fascinating. It is about 1370 and one of the Bardestone ladies whose family were lords of the manor. Her dress has pocket holes which show part of the girdle beneath. It is thought to be the oldest brass in the county.

And now for Somerset. The geology of Somerset is very noticeable: the low-lying and flat **Somerset Levels** in the centre of the county dotted with small round hills, through the middle of it running the Polden Hills, to the north the flat-topped Mendip Hills, to the south west the Blackdown Hills and to the west the Quantocks beyond which is Exmoor.

The miles of wet willow-lined Levels are some of the last surviving water meadows in Britain to be left undisturbed by modern farming. Once under the sea, the silt has provided rich soil and peat. Although much has been cut and used in garden composts, where it remains it provides a rare sight of endangered species of flora. Peat is a great preservative and many important finds of Neolithic, Bronze and Iron Age man have been made in the area. Many of the roads that cross this water-logged landscape are on timber Bronze Age causeway and medieval embankments, the suddenly rising hills in the flat landscape once islands in the water. **The Willows and Wetland Visitors Centre** which is at **Stoke Gregory** in the Sedgemoor area tells the story of the district and of traditional Somerset basket making from withies.

On the Levels, the fenland isle of **Athelney** is where King Alfred took refuge from the Vikings in the 9th century. Living as an outlaw he was hiding out in the hut of a herdsman's family when the cakes on the open hearth were burned. The wife, not knowing who he was blamed the King for not keeping an eye on the cooking! Thus came into being the story of Alfred burning the cakes.

Another story relating to food is that of 'Little Jack Horner'. The Abbot of Glastonbury, wishing to placate Henry VIII, sent him a pie containing the deeds of the manor house at **Mells**. The emissary was one Thomas Horner who opened the pie, put in his thumb and pulled out a plum.

Driving south west down the M5 from the Mendips towards Devon, every junction will lead you to attractive and interesting places.**Brent Knoll** can clearly be seen rising from the Levels. Likewise out of the levels, **Cadbury Hill**, with its Iron Age hill fort considered by some to be Arthur's Camelot. Not far from Brent Knoll is the pleasant town of **Burnham-on-Sea**, these days lived in by many commuters to Bristol. It has a laid back feel about it, no one seems to be in a hurry. You can walk for miles along the beach, enjoy the shops and find one or two very good hostelries. Its only drawback is its nearness to the less than pleasant site of **Hinckley Point**.

Bridgwater, now an industrial centre, was a busy port until Bristol overshadowed it. The town grew up around what was the best crossing point of a river which could not be forded. At the Norman Conquest it was held by a Saxon, Merleswain who lost it to Walter de la Douai. At that time it was known as Brugie but became the Bridge of Walter, hence its name today. By the 26thJune 1200, King John granted a Royal Charter giving borough status and permission to build a castle to protect the flourishing river port. The River Parrett has been used for commercial shipping since pre-Roman times and a relic of Phoenician ring money was discovered near the site of the old town bridge. In the 13th century the port was used as a victualling base for forays into Wales and Ireland, and by the 15th century had become a major port ranking 12th in the whole country. Woollen cloth was the principal export, the wool trade forming the basis of West Country wealth, and the main import was French wine.

It became the main point of entry and outlet for much of central and western Somerset, Taunton, Langport, Ilchester and even Yeovil sent, and received, goods through the estuary of the River Parrett and by the canal to Taunton and beyond.

The high ground of **Exmoor** to the west (part Somerset and part Devon) has a great variety of birds, rare plants and flowers, shaggy ponies and large herds of deer. This was at one time a royal hunting forest and still today the deer are hunted, but given refuge on land owned by Paul and Linda McCartney for that purpose as well as the sanctuary land owned by the League Against Cruel Sports. The moorland plateau rises to around 1,700 feet at Dunkery Beacon and terminates with the tallest cliffs in England, overlooking the Bristol Channel, designated as 'Heritage Coast'.

The subterranean rivers of the **Mendips**, have resulted in wonderful caves, potholes and gorges. At first sight the spectacular **Cheddar Gorge** and **Wookey Hole** with the many caves full of magnificent stalactites and stalagmites, must have been a wonderful experience for visitors. Now sadly it is marred by the sheer volume of people who come here - some 1.5million a year - which has resulted in overcrowding and too many tacky tourist trappings. However, the surrounding scenery of the Gorge is wondrous. It can be seen at its best from the vantage point on the **West Mendip Way**, a walk that starts at Wells Cathedral and concludes after 30 breathtaking miles at the Bristol Channel.

Chapter One

If you are a keen walker you will enjoy the 28 miles of the **Leland Trail** following in the footsteps of the 16th century John Leland, starting on the National Trust's Stourhead estate and crossing the quiet, southern Somerset countryside to another National Trust Property, Montacute House, and on to the high viewpoint of Ham Hill. The Gardens at **Stourhead** (just into Wiltshire) are best visited in the early summer, but at any time of the year the lake surrounded by classical temples and monuments are serenely beautiful. One of the loveliest evenings I have ever spent was at Stourhead on a summer's evening, listening to a concert whilst sitting by the lake enjoying a champagne picnic.These concerts are held quite regularly and are almost always with a theme. For example this year it was Chinese and one was expected to dress suitably for the occasion. **Montacute House**, not far from **Yeovil** is another of my favourite places. It is a fine example of Tudor domestic architecture which, although huge, is on a comfortable scale, set within early Jacobean gardens.

Montacute lies on the route of the Roman Fosse Way, one of the four Royal Roads, running from the south west to Lincolnshire. From this point you can follow the Fosse Way to another of the many fine houses in the region at **Cricket St Thomas Wildlife Park** now more associated with Noel Edmunds and Mr Blobby than the television programme with Penelope Keith, Peter Bowles and Angela Thorne, To the Manor Born. It is home to many rare and exotic species of animal and bird and recently also to a Heavy Horse Centre as well as being a place of enormous fun for children with an adventure park etc. At **Rode** is a 17 acre **Tropical Bird Garden.**

Who could resist turning off for Glastonbury and Wells with their wealth of history and beauty.**Glastonbury** is thought of as the cradle of English Christianity, but for me it is a place of legend, history, mystery and an overworked imagination. It may well have been the earliest Christian shrine but it is certainly the site of the richest monastery, and to this day still a place of pilgrimage. The Glastonbury legends are told again and again, and over the centuries have no doubt been embellished, but I never fail to feel excited by the thought of a visit here.

Towering over the town is **Glastonbury Tor**,possibly Arthur's Isle of Avalon, some 521 feet above sea level, and a landmark visible for miles around. St Michael's Tower on the summit is the remains of a 15th century church, the effort of climbing to which is rewarded by stunning views. First the home of primitive man, then a place of Christian pilgrimage, the Tor is still visited by thousands every year. I would advise you to walk up the Tor if it is possible because of the restricted availability of car parking nearby.

One of the legends told is of Christ coming here as a child with his merchant uncle, Joseph of Arimathea. Another is of Joseph coming here with the Holy Grail and yet another of the Apostle Philip sending missionaries from Gaul to establish a church, and one of those missionaries finding a church already here, dedicated by Christ himself. The undoubted Irish influence here is traced back to St Patrick who came first as an Abbot and to whom the lower church in Glastonbury is dedicated. Then there is the story of St Bridget from Kildare, Ireland, who left her bell and wallet behind at **Beckery** just one mile south west.

Glastonbury is so full of history. It was St Dunstan who laid the foundation of its spiritual and economic power. By the time of Domesday, Glastonbury owned an eighth of the county of Somerset covering much of the Somerset Levels, large parts of which were almost immediately drained to bring gain to the Abbot. It was Henry of Blois, Bishop of Winchester who built himself lodgings on such a grand scale that they would have made Buckingham Palace look small, who invited William of Malmesbury to write the history which has helped us develop the legends of Glastonbury over the centuries.

In 1189 when Royal support dried up and monks were thrown back on their own resources, they felt the Lord was smiling upon them when, as legend says, they were digging a grave for a monk, they found between the shafts of two ancient crosses, 16ft down in a wooden sarcophagus, the bones of a large man and a woman who must have been very beautiful; she certainly had long tresses - the story said these locks were totally preserved until one monk with straying hands touched them and they fell to dust. The monks were in no doubt that here were the remains of King Arthur and Queen Guinevere. Strangely however, William of Malmesbury had never mentioned Arthur in his 'History of Glastonbury' but the monks were adamant, and for them their acute need for money was immediately alleviated by this lovely, romantic idea. They never looked back!

Places to visit should include **The Somerset Rural Life Museum** with its relics from Somerset's past. **The Chalice Well** at the foot of the Tor. Set in attractive gardens, the waters of the well are claimed to have curative powers, and legend has it that Joseph of Arimathea hid the Chalice of the Holy Grail here. **The Lake Village Museum**, in the High Street, which displays many of the artefacts from an Iron Age settlement near Glastonbury. At **Westhay** is the **Peat Moors Visitor Centre**, where you can learn about the extraordinary history and natural history of the Somerset Levels. At the nearby village of **Meare** you can see the **Abbot's Fish House** dating back to the 14th century. This is where fish caught in the former Meare pool was dried, salted and stored by the monks of Glastonbury Abbey.

Chapter One

To the east of Glastonbury lies the village of **Boltonsborough**, the birthplace of St Dunstan. It was said that it was he who diverted the River Brue, sending it along the course of the little southward stream so that the village might have more power for its mill. Slightly to the north east of Glastonbury is **Shepton Mallet**, known almost entirely now for its permanenet showground which is the home of the Bath and West show and many others. The town is a wonderful mixture of old and new; a combination of ancient market town and modern industrial community nestling in a fold towards the western edge of the Mendip escarpment. Historically Shepton Mallet has always been strategically well placed; the Roman Fosse Way passes close by; the town's position on the River Sheppey led to its growth during the Midlle Ages as a centre for the wool trade, and enabling the brewing industry to be established. The town is not proud of one episode in its history. It happened in 1685 when the Market Cross was the scene for serveral executions of the unfortunate men of the Duke of Monmouth's 'Pitchfork Army' who were sentenced to death by that dreadful man, Judge Jeffreys.

Godney to the north west of Glastonbury is somewhere the monks used to call the Island of God; one of their seals has been found among the ruins of Glastonbury Abbey. It is older than any monk, older than christianity and in a field is Lake Village dating back to 250BC.

Wells is outstandingly beautiful and very special. A place that delights the eye and makes the heart beat faster. It is the smallest city in England with a population of just 9,400 but it is its Cathedral which gives it city standing. It is in fact Somerset's only city. It lies sheltered beneath the southern slopes of the Mendip Hills, and combines a wealth of historic interest and beautiful architecture with its role as a thriving market centre.

The swans at the **Bishop's Palace** have learnt to ring a bell when they are ready for lunch. The Palace is within the inner walls of the city which also enclose the Chapter House and Deanery as well as the **Cathedral.** What an enchanting place the city is with its narrow streets and lovely buildings. A place in which to spend many happy hours.

Amongst the many places to see around here are the two little villages of **Dulcote** on the Shepton Mallet road and **Coxley** on the A39

To me the little town of **Bruton** is one of the loveliest in Somerset.It has two parts, divided by the River Brue which meanders gently over stones and under a packhorse bridge. The part to the south which runs beneath and beyond the church is the oldest in Bruton, a Saxon religious centre which once had two churches, one founded by St Aldhelm. There was a mint here in the 10th century which opened up the way for the growth of a small town by the 11th century growing beyond the river around a market place near the present Patwell and Quaperlake streets. What attracts me most about this pretty place is the way in which the red roofed houses cling to each other in the winding and narrow streets. Standing on the little pack horse bridge sights of the past evoke all sorts of memories and the bonus is the entrancing peep across the valleys. The architecture of the town shows a rare continuity, through six centuries, of styles and techniques used where stone meets timber in Wessex. The regular form of the High Street is medieval town planning at its best. It includes the former Abbey Court House of the mid-15th century and Sexey's Hospital. Believe it or not this was established by a local stable lad who made his name and fortune and returned to Bruton to found this fine school. The school stands in a suburb called Lusty! Education is now the biggest business in Bruton.

When I have stayed in Bruton I have used it as a base for taking a look at some of the delightful places within easy reach. **Castle Cary** for example which is a charming, bustling place. Everything seems to be on a small scale. It has friendly shops, welcoming people, although you would be hard put to find much in the way of outstanding architecture It once had a castle with a motte and bailey structure but that has virtually gone, and its market hall was rebuilt in 1855 although there are some 17th century pillars. The church was largely rebuilt in 1855 also. There are some nice houses including the 18th century post office in Bailey Hill overlooking an intriguing lock-up of 1779. I am told it is frequently used as a threat of punishment to recalcitrant children!

Whenever I think about **Wincanton** to the east of Castle Cary, I think about horse racing. I have spent many happy hours on the course at various meetings. It is not a fashionable racecourse and is far less formal than its grander cousins but it is great fun. The town is frequently referred to as the 'Queen of the Vale' referring of course, to the Blackmore Vale. It is an interesting old town abounding in hotels and inns to suit all tastes, many of them survivors of the coaching era, when about seventeen coaches day stopped here on their journey from London to the cities of the west.

Going westwards there are two small towns that I have become attached to over the years. **Langport**, a town of narrow streets and full of antique shops, lies on the River Parrett. The old warehouses standing by the riverside bear witness to the time when the town was busy with waterborne trade coming from Wales via Bridgwater. It was once a walled town but all that remains of the wall is **The Hanging Chapel** -built over what was the East Gate. I used to think it had something to do with Judge Jeffreys but for once he is not responsible. Langport did play a decisive part in the Civil War though, in 1645 an important battle was fought on its outskirts, the site of

Chapter One

which can still be seen if you follow the B3155 to Somerton. You will find a side road leading to **Wagg** and **Huish Episcopi** with the small waterway of the Wagg Rhyne alongside. The Royalists were well positioned on the Langport side where there was a very narrow ford across the rhyne. Only four horsemen could cross it abreast, but Fairfax ordered his cavalry to charge and after a fierce battle the day was won. The Royalists were defeated, their morale broken and the end of the Civil War was in sight. **Somerton** is the other small town which claims to be the capital of ancient Wessex, and justifiably boasts much to entrance one for hours. The Church of St Michael has a roof that was created by the monks of Mulcheney from 7,000 fetter pieces. These monks obviously had a sense of humour: incorporated in the roof is a beer barrel playing on the name of Abbot Bere! If you wander down the leafy lane beside the church you will come into a delightful square of Georgian buildings, which has the misnomer of 'Cow Square' leading you into Broad Stret which was once called Pig Lane. There has to be a reason for these names, but I have found none.

One of England's smallest churches lies hidden in a wooded combe overlooking the Bristol Channel at **Culbone**, away from roads and cars. Nearby in a farmhouse Coleridge wrote 'Kubla Khan'.

Coleridge lived at **Nether Stowey** on the Quantocks at the end of the 18th century and his home is now open to the public. Here he wrote 'The Ancient Mariner'. The 'Rock of Ages'immortalised by Augustus Toplady in his hymn, was written at **Burrington Combe** on the Mendips. The village of Nether Stowey has a lovely old manor house begun in the time of Henry VII and left unfinished until Elizabeth's time, because somebody had carelessly executed the builder on Tower Hill for joining the Cornish men who marched to London protesting against taxation. **Coleridge Cottage** is open to the public from April to September, Tuesday to Thursday and Sunday from 2-5pm. It was here he was visited regularly by his friends William and Dorothy Wordsworth.

Close to Nether Stowey is the village of **Holford** where, according to Dorthy Wordsworth 'there is everything here, sea and woods wild as fancy are painted'. That is not the only pretty village within easy reach. **Combe Florey**, must come high on the list. It is stunningly beautiful and once was the home of the Reverend Sydney Smith and later the home of Evelyn Waugh.

Field Marshall Viscount Montgomery grew up in the village of **Halse**. I wonder if his child's eyes ever appreciated the beauty of the abundance of thatched cottages. Probably not, they would have been commonplace in his childhood. **Milverton** is a village that dates back to the Domesday study and boasts some glorious Georgian houses and a superb church. It was also the home of Thomas Young, whose work enabled the translation of Egyptian Hieroglyphics.

From here you are close to **Wiveliscombe**, not one of my favourite places but the church of St Andrew is outstandingly beautiful and has some fascinating catacombs. It was here that a safe haven was provided for many of the nation's treasures during World War II; a plaque inside the church records this.

Near to **Dulverton** on Exmoor the river Barle is crossed at **Tarr Steps** with huge, closely fitting stone slabs each weighing up to five tons. The age of the bridge is unknown but it was certainly used by packhorses during the height of the successful cloth trade. Wherever my travels take me I am always dumbfounded by the skill and ingenuity shown by the builders of our cathedrals and places like Tarr Steps, all without the assistance of any kind of machinery. Nearly always there is a story to tell and here we have the case of Tarr Steps supposedly being built by the Devil. He brought stones in his apron and dropped them in a sequence so he could cross the river. All this was done in just one night! It was for his exclusive use and he announced that he would destroy the first creature crossing it. A unfortunate cat attempted it and was torn to pieces. The animal's untimely death seems to have broken the spell, for a Parson then crossed in safety, exchanging niceties with the Devil en route! The Devil called the Parson a black crow to which the Parson replied that he was not blacker than the Devil. The woods and hills of Exmoor close around Dulverton on three sides, the Barle flows past its front doorsteps. It is a place steeped in history and one of tranquillity. In the church are two memorials to the Sydenhams who lived from 1540 to 1874 at Combe, a beautiful Tudor House. The life of the moor has made great literature and Dulverton is a name often found in books. Here Jan Ridd met Lorna Doone. Richard Jefferies watched the red deer. If you come to Dulverton in the spring take a walk in Burridge Woods which becomes totally carpeted with bluebells.

Winsford is arguably the prettiest village on Exmoor and it certainly has one of the most charming inns, **The Royal Oak Inn**, with an immaculately thatched roof, soft cream washed walls and a profusion of colourful hanging baskets on the outside. The pub dates from the 12th century and its open fireplaces and oak beams have been subtly combined with the modern facilities we all expect today. Winsford itself was described by W.H. Hudson in 1909 as 'fragrant, cool, grey green - immemorial peace - second to no English village in beauty, running waters, stone thatched cottages, hoary church tower.' Little has changed over the centuries. I believe there is still one lady in the village who has seen aeroplanes and cars but never a ship or a train because she has never left the village.

Chapter One

Simonsbath a few miles west of Winsford is an ideal stepping stone on your way to discover the wild, stark beauty of Exmoor. The quiet village is a wonderful foil for the exquisite scenery which surrounds it on every side.

I would never miss an opportunity to stay in **Dunster** which is charming with its impressive 17th century octagonal market hall by a wide main street, originally used for the sale of locally woven cloth. Here the **Gallox Bridge** which again used to carry pack-horses, has two ribbed arches, spanning the old mill stream in a picture-book setting. The medieval **Butter Cross** once stood in the high street but is now some way from the centre. **Dunster Castle** rises dramatically above the village and the sea. It dates from the 13th century and for over 600 years it has been the home of the Luttrell family. It now belongs to the National Trust and we are privileged to be able to visit it. The gardens and grounds are wonderful especially the terraces where rare shrubs grow. Dunster has a quiet unspoilt beach which is totally safe for children and has the great advantage of being the only beach on to which you can drive in Somerset. It also has one of the most valuable places for tourists, **The Exmoor National Park's Visitor Centre.**

The Visitor's Centre in Dunster is a must for any visitor. The town thrived in medieval times on the woollen industry. An eye-catching feature here draws attention to it. There are 30 metres of wool woven, exactly to the style of medieval cloth, from almost 30 miles of yarn, supplied by Craftsman's mark of Wellington, the proprietor of which, Morfudd Roberts, also supervised the production of the cloth. The yard was woven at **Coldharbour Mill** at **Uffculme**, itself a museum of wool production and well worth visiting. Setting up the loom took several days and involved tying many hundreds of knots by hand before weaving could start.

One length of cloth has been left in its natural, slightly grubby looking state. This would be virtually identical to the woollen cloth worn by the monks of nearby **Cleeve Abbey** in the 13th century. Further lengths of the unique reproduction medieval materials have been dyed by Gill Dalby, a local specialist in the use of vegetable dyes. Indigo was used to create the blue, madder, the red, and weld, the yellow. The invitation to the visitor very definitely is PLEASE TOUCH.

In 1500, many of the homes in Dunster would have had a spinning wheel where the housewife and the unmarried daughters would have toiled ceaselessly for all the daylight hours. Their efforts would have earned them little more than a penny a day. An independent weaver would have kept a team of about five or six women fully employed spinning yarn to meet his needs. This woven cloth was washed and taken out to the Castle Tor to be dried in the open air at the Tenteryarde. It was stretched on tenterframes by means of tenterhooks. Now you know where the expression ' to be on tenterhooks' comes from. I certainly did not know this before. Another term came into being as well. When using a spinning wheel, women (never men) drew fibres from the distaff. This women's work has resulted in the 'distaff side' to indicate the female side of a family.

Yeovil does not draw the visitor in the normal way but it should not be ignored. It has an excellent shopping centre, some good hostelries and is a good base from which to strike out into Dorset if one wishes - it is right on the boundary. One might say much the same of **Street** which was home to Clark's Shoes but now it has **The Shoe Museum** showing the history of shoes from Roman times to the present day. Housed in the oldest part of the original Clark's factory, the exhibits include documents and photographs, shoe buckles, fashion plates, hand tools and shoe machinery, as well of course, as shoes. There are also shoe-making demonstrations and 20 factory shops set within this small town made handsome by the Quaker Clark family who landscaped the factory buildings and built a school, a Quaker meeting house and even a temperance inn.

Not so far from Yeovil **Crewkerne** is a town whose streets converge in the market square. It has many old stone houses and four groups of almhouses but the church is the magnet. It is a grand cruciform church with glorious windows. The west front is almost cathedral like. Inside it is alittle disappointing but the width of the windows brings light to the lovely panelled roofs. Thirteen great stone angels stand holding up the enchanting nave roof. At Crewkerne is one of Somerset's most interesting and beautiful gardens, **Clapton Court**. It has ten acres with formal terraces, spacious lawns, rockery and water gardens. Recently designed is the gorgeous rose garden with arbors.Open March to October, Mondays to Fridays 10.30-5pm and Sundays from 2-5pm.

Another small town close to Chard and Crewkerne is **Ilminster**. Now bypassed it has been able to revert to its sleepy ways and is a nice place to visit. It has the immaculate **Shrubbery Hotel** for those wanting to be pampered. The superb crossing tower of the minster is reminiscent of the central tower at Wells Cathedral, with battlements and pinnacles. It is truly splendid.

Taunton is the county town of Somerset and a very busy place with so much to recommend it. Cricket lovers will know that it is Somerset's ground. There is horse-racing at regular intervals, It is a town of wide streets, a sprinking of medieval buildings even in the centre of the town, notably the timber-framed and gabled houses in Fore Street. It has super shops in well

Chapter One

laid out areas, much of it pedestrianised. Several old churches to visit including St Mary's which is a sure reflection of the town's prosperity, and many hostelries and restaurants. It is a place in which to mooch. At least three times in its history Taunton has supported the dissenter; in 1497 it proclaimed Perkin Warbeck king, and in the Civil War, Taunton backed Parliament and many of its population were killed or wounded in the Battle of Sedgemoor fighting for the Duke of Monmouth in 1685. The small team of professionals who run **The Brewhouse Theatre** will tell you that the theatre exists to present a wide range of arts and activities of the highest standard. The range is varied, drama, dance, opera, jazz and films make up the repertoire. It is recognised as one of the country's leading theatres and art centres. It provides hundreds of people with the opportunity to participate in the arts; either through workshops and courses or by joining forces with the hundreds of volunteers who help out.

If I am staying in Taunton I treat myself to a visit to **Poundisford Park**, three and a half miles souht of the town on the by-road between **Trull** and **Pitminster**. The Saxon deer park formed part of the estate granted to the Bishops of Winchester by King Ethelheard, around 730AD. It is still surrounded by the original bank or pale, hunted over by King John, and is the setting for this charming example of Tudor domestic architecture. It was built at the end of Henry VIII's reign by a merchant adventurer, and almost unaltered since. The cream walls, stone mullions and early glass give the house a comfortable and welcoming atmosphere. James I visited the house and his wife, Anne, stayed here. It was ransacked by the Royalists in the Civil War but otherwise it has been a peaceful family home, escaping implication in Monmouth's rebellion. It is open from the beginning of May until the middle of September. Ring for opening times 01823 421244.

A short distance from Taunton along the M5 is **Wellington** which has never quite got over the surprise at the honour bestowed upon it when the hero of the Battle of Waterloo decided to name this rural town for his Dukedom. The Duke of Wellington is believed only once to have visited the town but they have never forgotten. In his honour they built the monument standing high on the spur of the Blackdown Hills. This 175ft high construction looks not unlike Cleopatra's Needle when you see it, especially when it is floodlit at night. This compliment to the town brought them instant fame. The monument was meant to be crowned with a figure of the great man, and to be the centre of a group of cottages for Waterloo pensioners. Sadly, it was too expensive a scheme for the town which for years found the upkeep of the column, with its hundreds of steps, a big drain on the budget. There was great relief when it was taken over by the National Trust. Recently it had a face lift and looks beautiful in the glow of the floodlighting. I must warn you though that the climb up to it is daunting and not for the feeble.

The beautiful and timeless parish church in Wellington is descended mostly from the 13th and 14th centuries and the east window is about 700 years old. Sir John Popham lies here surrounded by his family. He was the man who sentenced Sir Walter Raleight to death. I am amazed he had the temerity when his own character was not without stain. He was reputed to have acquired the manor of Littlecote in Wiltshire as payment for acquitting the owner, William Darell after a sensational murder trial.

The Somerset coast is a must for anyone visiting the county. There is one corner of **Minehead** where a steep flight of steps takes you to the church of St Michael. It is quite charming and reminds me so much of **Clovelly**. Until you have been to Minehead you cannot appreciate what a delightful place it is. Protected by the hills which rise behind it, the houses have flowers climbing over their doors and walls. It is still a little old-fashioned which is part of its charm. It is the home of the **West Somerset Railway** where steam trains will take you on 20 miles of scenic delights. From the vale of Taunton Deane through the rolling Quantock Hills. Past the beaches of Blue Anchor Bay to Minehead or the reverse journey. There are nine restored stations at which you may break your journey, museums, displays and steam locos.

From Minehead there is so much to see and do. Few people can resist the beaches and the golden sands of **Blue Anchor.** Inland the tiny hamlet of **Alcombe** is the prettiest place and just down the road from Dunster is another delightful place, **Timberscombe**.

The little port of **Watchet** is somewhere that has a harbour so small that you wonder how any ship could safely manoeuvre in and out. The 15th century church stands above this miniature seaside town and has a 600 year old cross beside it. A family called Wyndham lived at Kentisford Farm near the church and a square 17th century pew bears their arms. One brass honours Florence Wyndham, an Elizabethan about whom a strange story is told. Whilst she was lying in her coffin in the church awaiting burial, a greedy sexton saw her rings and coveted them. He broke open her coffin and did it so roughly that she woke from her trance, went home and soon after gave birth to a child. History does not relate what happened to the sexton, was he a life saver or hung for being a thief?

Finally in this brief tour of Somerset we come to **Monksilver**, the home of that wonderful house **Combe Sydenham** with its fine Country Park. You must make sure you allow time to spend a day here. It was at Combe Sydenham that Francis Drake courted the beautiful daughter of the house, Elizabeth Sydenham, who finally agreed to marry him. The dashing Sir Francis then sailed away to fight more battles and chase the Spaniards. His voyages were so long and arduous that the lovely Elizabeth became

Chapter One

despondent believing that he would never return. Encouraged by her father she finally agreed to wed another suitor. The day of her wedding arrived and she was driven to **Stogumber** church for her marriage. As she alighted from her carriage a cannon ball fell at her feet. Her heart leapt in excitement. It had to be a sign that Drake was back in harbour.

She abandoned her unfortunate bridegroom and went home to await Drake. Drake came and they were married probably in this church. The cannon ball can be seen even today at Combe Sydenham, which experts believe to be a meteorite, in fact. It has become a symbol of good fortune for all those who touch it. It was this marriage that brought Buckland Abbey at Yelverton in Devon into Drake's possession. Their marriage lasted until Drake's death ten years later. Soon after shemarried Sir William Courtenay and became mistress of Powderham Castle in Devon. Her happiness lasted only a few months, until she too died.

Devon is a county of extremes. It has more roads than any other county in England which will lead you through highways and byways, sometimes amid leafy hedgerows teeming with plant and wildlife, sometimes along a coastline that is breathtaking or on the busy A38 which traverses the county to the borders of Cornwall and beyond. The roads will take you to the romantic and stark beauty of Dartmoor and Exmoor, the lush glory of the South Hams, the attractive resorts in Torbay, the spectacular coastline of North Devon, countless pretty villages tucked away and to the two cities of Exeter and Plymouth whose history goes back hundreds of years. It is a county that begs to be explored and will reward anyone who takes the time. It offers an abundance of stately homes, wildlife parks, museums, glorious sandy beaches, safe bathing, water sports and enough golf courses to inspire even the most ardent golfer. Fishing has always been part of Devonian life whether it be along the banks of flowing rivers or from a boat that will take you out from a sheltered harbour to spend hours of pleasure surrounded by the sparkling blue sea with the backdrop of the coast - it almost makes the catch unimportant!

Plymouth tucked away and separated from Cornwall by the River Tamar is a super centre for anyone wanting to tour the county and maybe pop over the border into Cornwall. It is a city which rose from the ashes after the German bombing in World War II. The bombing, horrific as it was, made way for a new city centre to grow, dispensing with the colourful old narrow streets that would have crucified modern commerce.There is no finer vantage point than Plymouth Hoe to take in the brilliance of Plymouth Sound on a sunlit day, its waters dotted with the white and often brightly coloured sails of the innumerable boating enthusiasts who flock to the Marinas and the Yacht Clubs here. Plymouth has been host to many people over the centuries. Catherine of Aragon first stepped ashore in Plymouth when she came to marry the unfortunate Prince Arthur and later Henry VIII. She would have seen a very different city from the one we know today. The narrow winding streets of the Barbican would have been unpaved. I doubt if any of the buildings now exist. Southside Street, now the main thoroughfare of the busy Barbican is first recorded in 1591. What an exciting place this city must have been in the time of Drake and Hawkins. It was from Plymouth that Drake sailed on the 19th July 1588 to defeat the Spanish Armada, and it was on Plymouth Hoe that he played his famous game of bowls. The construction of the Breakwater by Rennie (1812-1840) gave Plymouth one of the largest and safest harbours in Britain.

Plymouth is blessed with many attractions. **The Theatre Royal** is one of the finest in the country and provides theatrical entertainment from drama to comedy, ballet to opera. **The Pavilions**, a complex which offers ice skating, a swimming pool and a venue for concerts of all kinds from Shirley Bassey to the Bournemouth Symphony Orchestra is comparatively new. **Plymouth Dome** on **The Hoe** should be high on any visitors list and then there is the National Trust's **Saltram House** and across the river **Mount Edgcumbe**, given by the family to the city of Plymouth for the benefit of its people. A superb house and wonderful grounds stretching right round the coast to **Cawsand, Rame Head and Whitsand Bay**. Once across the river you are in fact in Cornwall but Cawsand, Rame and Whitsand Bay are favourite day visit places of Plymothians as well as the many visitors who discover the areas untold beauty. Cawsand and Kingsand are two villages separated by only a fluer de lys set in a wall. Delightful places, they have several good pubs including **The Halfway House** renowned for its food.

In the last twenty years Plymouth has grown almost out of recognition and taken under its wing several places which were at one time quiet villages.**Ivybridge** is a prime example. Here a rather sleepy community has found itself woken to life in the 20th century and the influx of massive new housing developments. Oddly this has not destroyed the village but allowed it to develop a community spirit that has found expression in the main street, now pedestrianised, where everyone seems to congregate from time to time either to shop or enjoy the various hostelries and restaurants. This main street now has major food stores and a big branch of Boots for example.

Several small places just outside Plymouth like to be thought of as part of the South Hams. **Noss Mayo** for one nestling on the opposite side of the River Yealm from **Newton Ferrers**. It is a different kettle of fish here because the river and the hinterland prevent either village from growing too large. Both are charming places offering pretty walks along the river, plenty of boating and yachting opportunities and a very pleasant way of life. Then

Chapter One

there is quiet, sleepy, **Holbeton** in pretty countryside with a splendid pub,**The Mildmay Colours. Ugborough** has great charm and a busy village square whilst **South Brent** just outside Ivybridge has become almost another commuter village for Plymouth.

Plymouth not only has its magnificent Plymouth Sound but in the hinterland lies **Dartmoor National Park**. Only a short drive from the city and you are up on the moor adapting your eyes from the blue of the sea to the haze and wondrous purple, green and brown colouring of the moor which seems to stretch endlessly with great beauty but at the same time is awesome. **Clearbrook**, on the edge of the moor might be your first stop outside Plymouth; a small hamlet in a nice setting complete with a good pub. **Yelverton** would certainly be your second.. A small community, with a nice church and tucked away at **Leg O'Mutton Corner, The Paperweight Centre** which has given me hours of pleasure over the years. No charge for going in there and certainly worth a visit.

There are many counties who envy Devon's good fortune in having **Exeter** as its county town. It has everything. The River Exe wends its gracious way through the heart of the city, stopping every now and again to prepare itself for the opening of the swing bridge which lets small coasters upstream for unloading. The jewel in the crown is the magnificent cathedral which dominates the city centre and dictates much of the lifestyle immediately around it. Exeter is Roman, Saxon and Norman; it has walls and a tower built by Athelstan, the first King of England, but most of all it is medieval. There are still miles of quaint streets and passageways, rambling walls, a plethora of churches and of course the cathedral bequeathed to us by many generations of the finest builders, apart from its Norman walls and towers. Of course the 20th century has crept in and much has had to be changed, but on the whole it has been done with the greatest care and dedication to the preservation of all that is good. Shopping is a pleasure, with the big stores living comfortably alongside medieval buildings. As in most county towns there are innumerable small shops which entice - most of them hidden away in enchanting alleyways. All the time you are wandering in and out of these alleyways you are probably getting closer and closer to the cathedral. Such is the dimension of its beauty that I find it hard to do it justice on paper. Gazing at the outside will give you hours of pleasure and probably an aching neck!

I love walking along the little Cathedral Close and Southernhay with its beautiful buildings, almost entirely occupied by professional people rather than residents. Perhaps I will walk in the garden of the 14th century Bishop's Palace, with its fine trees taking shade from the great walls of the cathedral. Certainly I will look at the Deanery where Catherine of Aragon stayed. Once inside the cathedral I am always mesmerised by the beauty around me. It is almost like being in a heaven in which modern man is allowed to go about in a peaceful, ordered existence which in no way lacks purpose. There is no strife, no threat of war, no anger, just a great sense of the presence of God in the most wonderful surroundings. If there is any cry for help at all it comes from the need to keep this treasure safe. The years are telling on it and constant war is waged against decay. It takes an immense amount of money which is mainly raised by the public. It is not only money that is needed, craftsmen are continually at work and some of them are getting very old. Finding replacements becomes quite a battle in itself.

Exeter is blessed with many fine churches, some of which are never used but most have stories attached to them. One entrance into the Close is by the tiny church of St Martin with its porch looking across to the Cathedral. It is quite easy to disregard this little gem because of the stunning beauty of the Elizabethan structure alongside, which was known as Moll's Coffee House. The tiers of windows lean out and are crowned by a little gallery. Its front reminds one of an old ship - not surprising because it was here that Drake used to meet his captains. Nothing much has changed since his time. The panelling is oak, almost black with age, and there is an intriguing gallery painted with 46 different coats of arms. The most fascinating sight though is the whole front of the low room, which is glass. I am told that there are no less than 230 panes and no two the same size.

Apart from the Cathedral, nothing can compare to the **Guildhall**, whose walls have stood for 650 years. It makes sure you will not miss it for it thrusts itself out into the busy main street, in amongst all the 20th century buildings. I can almost hear it saying 'I bet I will be here still when you are long gone.' Quite right too. Can you imagine C & A or Marks and Spencers still being there in 600 odd years? Inside it is quite lovely. The hall has a superb roof with gilded beams, from which hang dazzling candelabra. Displayed elsewhere are royal and other gifts that have been collected over the years, including a sword used by Nelson and some of the rarest seals in the land. One dates back to 1175 and is believed to be the oldest in the country.

From Exeter one can take a drive of about ten miles to **Exmouth**, the oldest seaside town in Devon. It is a cheerful resort with a good beach. Not the most attractive place architecturally, apart from the rather distinguished houses on the Beacon, where Lady Nelson lived at No.6 and Lady Byron at No 19. **Ottery St Mary** has an annual carnival. Nothing strange about that except here the young men rush through the main street rolling barrels of flaming tar, a sight worth beholding. **Otterton** has in its midst the **Domesday Mill**, somewhere every visitor should go. It is a collection of old buildings

Chapter One

with a flour mill still working. There are a lot of craft shops there and a very good wholefood restaurant.

Budleigh Salterton always makes me think of retired colonels! It is one of Devon's most charming and unspoilt places. There is a gentle brook running right through the street that houses the shops. The brook starts its run at Squabmoor, a drab name for such a beautiful spot adjoining Woodbury Common where Nigel Mansell owns the Woodbury Park Golf and Country Club. Enter the foyer there and you will see his famous Williams Renault Car as well as a McClaren. I had the pleasure of meeting and talking with Nigel Mansell very recently. The subject was not Formula One or Indycar racing but Woodbury Park which is a project in which he is totally involved and financially committed. He has done a wonderful job there. The golf course is a championship one and the clubhouse and its other buildings are unlike any other you will see. Superbly built and furnished, it is open to non-members who may come for the day if they wish, eat in the attractive conservatory restaurant, walk in the woods or on a summer's day sit on the terrace simply absorbing the stunning views. His advent to this area has been beneficial in every direction. Go and take a look you will not be disappointed and if you happen to be a golfer you will be stunned by what is on offer.

Like many beaches along this part of the coast, Budleigh Salterton is not blessed with golden sand but with pebbles that do not entice you to walk barefooted - but it is of no importance, the scenery makes up for any minor inconvenience.

Further along the coast you will come to one of my favourite parts of the Devon coast. Seemingly not quite of the 20th century,**Seaton, Sidmouth** and **Beer** have altered little since coming to prominence in Victorian times. Sheltered in Lyme Bay, all sharing shingle and pebble beaches and the dignity of yesteryears. These are not places to visit if you want a sophisticated life. Sidmouth springs to life for the annual Folk Festival which has become the Mecca for entrants from all over the world. The first time I saw it I could not believe that there were so many variations of Morris Dancing and Folk Singing, let alone the clacking Clog Dancer's. Seaton has that rare item today, a tramway. It is even more of a rarity to find a tramway working on an old railway line. Once run along the promenade at Eastbourne, and doomed when the promenade's extension was planned, the tram was rescued by the enthusiasts who care for it today - a considerable benefit for Devon. The hour's journey travelling the three miles aboard the double-decked tram, through the Axe and Coly valleys along the route of the old railway, will take you to **Colyton** one of the prettiest small towns in Devon. **Beer** is little more than a fishing village which attracts an influx of visitors in the summer, but unlike many similar seaside haunts, it does not die in winter. The community get together and a hundred and one activities spring up to occupy the winter months.

Axminster has a curiously shaped town centre dominated by the parish church of St Mary's. Inside the church you will be astounded by the magnificent carpeting. The pews are set well back so that one can admire this unexpected beauty. Then you realise that it is really quite natural as Axminster is the home of the carpet industry. One of the earliest Axminsters made in 1775, can ben seen in the Guildhall in which is also housed the original market charter dated 1210. Thomas Witty pioneered the carpet industry in Axminster having discovered the techniques from the Turks. His first carpets were produced in a little building alongside the church, and so important was the completion of each carpet that the church bells were rung in celebration.

Honiton is sometimes forgotten today. At one time it used to be a nightmare trying to drive through it when it was on the main road going to London. Now it is bypassed it is still busy but in the nicer way which allows the residents to enjoy their lives. Famed for lace of course, it also has one of the widest main streets in Britain. Two small places always please me close to Honiton. One is **Gittisham**, with its wide street, pale stone cottages, lovely old cob-and-thatch cottages, and its 500 year old church enshrining 500 years of the community's history. It also has a wonderful country house hotel, **Combe House**. The second is the tiny hamlet of **Buckerell** with another charming establishment **Splatthayes.**

Wandering about Devon is one of the pleasures of my life and I find myself equally enchanted with every corner. For those who like a resort atmosphere **Torbay** has to be the answer. It always gives one the feel of being on the French Riviera. The sea is a brilliant Mediterrannean blue coming ashore to sandy beaches and row upon row of sparkling white buildings which range from high class hotels to the many small guest houses. Torbay is made up of Torquay, Paignton and the old fishing port of Brixham. It welcomes visitors all the year round and most people who come out of season seem to prefer it when it is quieter.

Torquay has many admirers from all over the world who come to it for many different reasons.Many people decide to retire here because of the clement weather and the almost Riviera like atmosphere. There are those who come for conferences and seminars whose arrangers are delighted at the amenities the town and its hotels offer. Then there are the holiday makers who fill the resort at the height of the season and who come for the beaches,

Chapter One

the sun and all the fun of the fair. Finally there is the group of people who enjoy short breaks and perhaps come here two or sometimes three times during the year to enjoy the beauty and peace of the bay. For all of them there is much to do and not least, if they have any sense, to enjoy the charm of the little theatre at **Babbacombe** which runs a popular, true summer show which manages to keep running almost until Christmas.

    Paignton is renowned for having one of the best Zoos in the country. The town and sea front are gentle places generally. Flowers and rockeries along the promenade and a wonderful park, man-made out of marsh this century, are the outstanding features. Paignton is the sort of place that people of my age enjoy in the spring, autumn and even winter but who will probably avoid it like the plague in the height of the season.

    Brixham has always been the home of fishermen, whose houses perch on the side of the hills leading to Higher Brixham. Some are close to the harbour or open onto little streets or steps bringing their occupants to the seafront. Whilst tourism is not ignored it has always had to take a second place to the fishing industry and so the character of the town has changed little over the centuries. For me Brixham will always stay in my mind whenever I hear Henry Francis Lyte's wonderful hymn 'Abide with Me'. He was the vicar for over a quarter a century of the 19th century All Saints Church.

    It is a hymn that has been sung throughout the Christian world by people in times of great emotion. My father told me that in World War I it was sung by the men in the trenches and when they had finished the Germans would take it up from their dugouts. It has brought peace to thousands. Henry Lyte wrote it in the dusk after evening service. He did not know he had taken his last service in the church. He died not long afterwards. If you listen you will hear the bells of All Saints ring out his hymn every night.

    No one comes to Torquay without seeing **Cockington**. If you want to see it at its best go early in the morning, soon after sunrise, when it is still. Later it will be swamped with visitors and all you will remember will be the crowds and perhaps the thatched cottages. Seen early it is as if you were back in the 16th-17th century when Cockington was first built.

    Newton Abbot thankfully is by-passed today which makes it pleasanter to look at the town and much easier to reach other places such as **Ipplepen**, a village as old as time. Conan Doyle spent many a happy visit here with his friend Bertie Robinson who lived at Parkhill House. Exploring Dartmoor was one of his great pleasures and he used to be driven in a horse and carriage by the Robinson groom, one Harry Baskerville. Did you ever wonder where the title 'Hound of the Baskervilles' originated ? Now you know. No one ever denies the beauty of **Broadhempston** reached through a network of small lanes. Its church is 15th century with graceful arcades, old carved beams and bosses in the porch and roofs.

If you take the coastal road out of Torquay you will come to **Teignmouth** and **Dawlish** two unashamedly Victorian resorts of great charm. On the approach road to Teignmouth a turning off at **Shaldon** just before the bridge will take you to **Stoke-in-Teignhead**. It lies in one of Devon's combes by the mouth of the Teign. Full of pretty cottages and an old church which must have been here in Norman times. When you look at the mosaics in the sanctuary, you will wonder how so many years ago, such work was done by Italian craftsmen. Where did they stay, how did they cope with the language barrier and how long did their journey take?

Had you approached Teignmouth from Newton Abbot you would have passed by **Kingsteignton**, an ever growing place which has become almost a dormitory for Newton Abbot However one should always remember that this ancient village was thriving at the time of the Domesday Book..

Dawlish is close to **Powderham Castle**, one of the quiet glories of Devon, built between 1390 and 1420. It has been the home of the Courtenay family ever since. Sir Philip Courtenay was the first occupant, the sixth son of the second Earl of Devon, from whom the present Earl is directly descended. If you look at the castle you will see that every generation has made some form of alteration in order to keep up with the changes of their time. None of this has detracted from its beauty. A visit to Powderham will always remain in your mind as a red letter day.

Nearby Powderham is the little estuary village of **Starcross** on the west bank of the Exe. Essentially a residential community with the river as its key attraction it offers great sailing and at one time the oyster beds were a real source of income for the village, and today a shell industry is once more established.

The South Hams is one of the prettiest areas in the whole of Devon.**Modbury** built on the slopes of a valley with four main streets intersecting at right angles is full of nice buildings and many enchanting shops plus a sprinkling of good hostelries and the bonus of a free car park. The road from Modbury towards the sea winds its way towards **Kingsbridge** which rises sharply from the Salcombe estuary but before you get there you will find a turn to the right will take you to **Bigbury-on-Sea** with its enormous beach and the famous **Burgh Island**, which lies off the coast and is accessible by foot across the sand at low tide and by sea tractor from the car park at

Chapter One

high tide. A small, magical place which was first inhabited in 900AD. By the 14th century it had a thriving fishing community. There is only one cottage left today and that is now **The Pilchard Inn,** a delightful port of call after a walk across the sands. The island also has a spectacular hotel which is world famous and has a visitor's book with such illustrious names as Edward Prince of Wales, Mountbatten, Noel Coward etc. It went into decline after this era and was closed in 1955 and then brought to life by two exciting people, the Porters, who have restored it in the 1920's Art Deco style. Their love affair with the island and the hotel became almost a cult story with magazines and newspapers, so when they re-opened in March 1988, the word had spread across the world. People came from London, New York, Los Angeles and Europe, and loved every minute of their stay.

Kingsbridge is a charming place in its own right with a church that stands on massive 13th century arches. Apart from the excellent shopping facilities in the main street take a look at the **Cookworthy Museum of Rural Life**. Halfway between Kingsbridge and Totnes is the small village of **East Allington**, a quiet sort of place and most people coming here for the first time are amazed that it was one of the six villages evacuated during the Second World War to enable the Allied Forces to practise for a final invasion of Europe. Luckily, being on the outskirts of the D-Day rehearsal area, most of the houses remained undamaged and the residents were able to return home before the year was out. Another nice village close to Kingsbridge is **Churchstow** two miles to the north-west whose church of St Mary is a prominent landmark between the Avon valley and the sea inlet from Salcombe to Kingsbridge.

Ringmore is another very attractive village west of Kingsbridge. It has some interesting 16th to18th century buildings and the church of All Saints was built around 1300, although parts of it are Norman. The focal point of the village is the well-named hostelry **The Journey's End**.

The A381 takes you from Kingsbridge to **Dartmouth**, the undoubted 'show-stopper' of the South Hams. You approach the town from the top of a steep hill and if traffic permits I suggest you stop for a moment or two to catch the stunning panoramic view of the town and the river. The dramatic scenery is heightened by the tiers of houses which cling for dear life to the hillside overlooking the River Dart. It is always a busy and delightful place to be. You will see constant passenger and car ferries crossing the busy river to **Kingswear** on the other side.

Along the quayside at Dartmouth you will see notices advertising river trips up to **Totnes** and elsewhere. If you have time take to the water, for the trip covers some of the most beautiful scenery in the county. On a sunny day the brilliant blue of the water finds it hard to compete with the endless variation of greens to be seen in the trees and fields. You will see **Dittisham**, a village of thatched stone cottages winding through plum orchards and daffodil fields down to the river. From the quay by an old inn, a passenger ferry plies its trade, signalling its approach by ringing a large brass bell. It is the epitome of a peaceful English scene, but remember this river arguably the most beautiful in England, has been the means of bringing wealth to many places throughout our history.

If you were to continue up the river you would come to **Stoke Gabriel** tucked in the fold of the hills by the river. The village is a mixture of old and new but the essential character remains with the cobbled walk to the much loved church of St Mary and St Gabriel, the old cottages and the ancient yew. For centuries Stoke Gabriel has been the centre of the Dart salmon fishing industry. It is no longer a full time occupation but the netting rights are carefully guarded by those who own them. Visitors flock to the quay which is now a popular beauty spot. Rowing boats, sailing dinghies lie in a sheltered corner of the creek whilst there are many moorings for larger craft in the main river.

Salcombe delights every one who goes there with its colourful streets, vibrant river estuary and lively life style. It is full of good places to stay, places to eat, ferries to take you across the estuary to **East Portlemouth** where there are wonderful beaches. It is a paradise for anyone who enjoys being waterborne.

Totnes, first mentioned in the reign of Edgar about 959AD, was probably a small settlement. Today it is a busy, attractive town which is not much more than one beautiful street climbing up a hill by the River Dart. From choice I would always come to Totnes by river from Dartmouth but in a more mundane fashion this time I have taken the A3122 which is a pretty road and will take me to the village of **Harbertonford**, a village I never forget for several reasons. The first is the awkward bend as you approach it which puts some people off, but don't be. It is an interesting place with the restored **Crowdie Mill, The Malsters Arms** and the exciting **Hungry Horse.**

Every Tuesday morning in the summer **Totnes Elizabethan Society** members and local traders dress in Tudor costume to raise thousands of pounds for charity. It has become a world famous spectacle and celebrate's the town's 16th century heritage. There is much to see including **Bowden House**, the home of the British Photographic Museum with its large collection of vintage cameras, as well as antique weaponry, furniture and pictures. **The Devonshire Collection of Period Costume** in the High Street has a beautiful collection which is changed each season and is housed in one of the town's

Chapter One

loveliest Tudor merchant houses. **Totnes Castle** was built by theNormans over 900 years ago on an old Saxon stockade. It has spectacular views over Totnes and the Dart Valley. The courtyard is the biggest Norman courtyard in England - wonderful place for picnics. For me exploring the South Hams is a never ending treasure hunt with constantly different and unexpected clues to its beauty.

Changing route entirely, it is time to take a look at some of the places on **Dartmoor** which, when you are in Devon, is never far away. **Tavistock** one of the Stannary towns is a favourite haunt of mine. I love the sense of pride and stability. It has so much history which started a hundred years before the Conqueror, and was originally controlled by its Abbey.

You can seek out a great deal of the past in the fine medieval parish church, with its pinnacled tower, its wide nave, and countless gables that dominate the streets. It may well have been here that Francis Drake was taken to worship as a child for Tavistock was his home town, something one is never allowed to forget.

Many small villages surround Tavistock, all of which are worth seeing. On the Okehampton road there are two **Tavys, Mary and Peter**, the twins grew out of the settlement on either side of the River Tavy. Each has a church linked together by a bridle path and a little bridge over the river known as 'The Clam', an old name for a bridge. In **Mary Tavy** there is an excellent Vegetarian Restaurant,**The Stannary,** probably one of the best in the country. No one should miss seeing **Lydford Gorge**. Water pours off the moor onto the boulders of the gorge with a ferocity which would overshadow a witches cauldron. A mile or so away is **Lewtrenchard Manor**, the composer of great hymns, Sabine Baring-Gould's old home which is now a stunning country house hotel.

To the north of the moor is **Okehampton** with its romantic Castle, Okehampton seldom gets the recognition it deserves and is well worth taking a look at. **Chagford** is a sleepy market town that should also be on your list. It has grown up around the village square. Do visit **James Bowden & Sons**. It is an experience. Founded in 1862 it can only be called an emporium. This is a Stannary Town where tinners would come from miles around to have their precious metal weighed and given the King's Stamp before it was sold. Farmers too would come to sell their cattle and sheep and, in particular, their fleeces, for wool was an important industry. All this activity was watched over by the most distinctive of the town's many historic buildings: the old market house in the middle of the square.

Drewsteignton in addition to having a remarkable hostelry and charming thatched cottages, is home to the amazing **Castle Drogo**, the last castle to be built in this country. Julius Drewe was responsible for it and he got Sir Edward Lutyens to design it. The enchanted world of **Fingle Bridge** is just below Drewsteignton. You do not just simply arrive here, you have to seek it out. It is hidden away at the end of a long winding leafy lane that seems to descend forever, until suddenly there it is; a low pack horse bridge which dates back to Elizabethan times, if not earlier, straddling a river dancing and cavorting as it plays with the boulders strewn in the path. The paths leading away from the bridge were probably the way that merchants came with their laden pack-horses and the terrain was too difficult to develop further. We can count ourselves lucky that this was so, otherwise Fingle Bridge might not have survived the wear and tear of men and vehicles over the years. There are three Iron Age hill forts around Fingle Gorge. **Prestonbury** you can see clearly from the bridge. **Wooston** is down river and if you see it on a spring morning with the sun behind you, it is breathtaking. The third,**Cranbrook**, is higher up. At **Shilston** to the west is the best known of the cromlech or dolmens in Devon, with the odd name of **Spinster's Rock**. Legend has it that three spinsters put it in place, but fact says it is the remains of a Bronze Age megalithic tomb.

Moretonhampstead holds the key to so much that is beautiful. Within my lifetime it has changed considerably. Forty years ago it was a shopping centre for farmers and people living in outlying hamlets. It had everything a community needed. Today the butcher is still here and the chemist but the general store is no more and it is only recently that the baker has returned. It gets its livelihood mainly from tourists. The 'hampstead' part of its name has been added in the last century or so and most local people ignore it, calling the little town Moreton, derived from the Saxon Mor Tun. The 15th century church of St Andrew standing on high ground has tombstones in the porch in memory of two French officers who lived at Moreton during the Napoleonic Wars when they were on parole from their prison at Princetown. Four other villages in the vicinity should be looked at.**Doccombe, Dunsford, Bridford** and **Christow**, each has its own merits and all are part of the Dartmoor scene.

Close to Moreton is **Becky Falls**. High up in the solitude of Dartmoor you approach it through glorious woods. On one side of the road there is a car park, where, if you have any sense, you will don stout shoes or wellies, before making the descent alongside Becka brook, where the water cascades over and between massive boulders until with a roar it reaches its peak, and falls in sparkling torrents on its way to the sea. This enchanted world is at its best in November after the mid-winter rains.

Chapter One

Moments up the road is the isolated village of **Manaton**, with its green nestling beside the church. Mentioned in the Domesday book it seems to have been there for ever. Away to the south the great rocks known as **Bowerman's Nose** look like a petrified sentinel guarding the rugged hills, or a man with a sense of humour wearing a cardinal's hat playing God.

Whilst Manaton remains essentially Dartmoor, **Lustleigh** to the east has changed completely in the last two decades. There was a time when this rural community lived simply in the beautiful valley of the Wrey. They gained their livelihood from small holdings and cultivating productive vegetable gardens, seldom venturing away. A journey to Exeter was a once in a lifetime experience. Nowadays the 13th century church still stands. Look out for the mischievous carving of the small heads on top of the screen which was erected in Tudor times. The craftsman obviously had likes and dislikes; all the heads facing the chancel have a secret grin on their faces and those towards the nave, a scowl. There is a good pub, an excellent tearoom and village cricket still flourishes. At weekends you can sit and watch on a field, fringed with alders, and make believe that the noise and trauma of the 20th century does not exist. You must also explore all the little lanes and byways that surround Lustleigh and hide away some delightful places in which to stay. You will see more details about these hidden places in the dedicated pages at the back of this chapter.

Bovey Tracey is one of the Gateways to Dartmoor and has been important since the days of the Normans. It has charming, narrow streets and sits sedately overlooking the River Bovey. Perhaps not as peaceful as it once was it is still a delightful place to visit.

To describe the routes that one can take on the moor to get the greatest pleasure out of walking takes more space than I am permitted in this book. The Dartmoor Visitors Centre at **Princetown** will provide you with a comprehensive choice of books and pamphlets on the subject. The sort of things I look for are the old guide posts which are no more than pieces of granite standing onend. Each is marked with a letter. From Two Bridges one would be marked 'P' showing the direction of Princetown or 'M' for Moretonhampstead. It is primitive but effective. Frequently you will come across the remains of Bronze Age dwellings, just circles of stones which once were a hut. Sometimes you will see the remains of beehive huts. Not that they ever housed bees! They were used by medieval tinners for hiding their unsold tin, and other bits and pieces.

The clapper bridges are to be seen quite regularly over the streams that run through Dartmoor. **Postbridge** has one of the best examples. It is a tribute to the skill of the 14th century builders. You will see that all the bridges are made of huge slabs of granite balanced one upon the other. Built so well that they have withstood the onslaught of human feet, the insistent hammering of the river and the Dartmoor climate, for centuries.

Then there are the Dartmoor 'Letter Boxes'. If you know nothing about them; it is purely a fun thing that has developed over the years into quite a serious hobby. You seek out the position of the boxes, usually tucked away in a crag somewhere, quite well hidden. You then post your own cards and take out any that are already there, which then become your duty to post on. Inside the hiding place you will find a visitor's book for you to sign, a rubber stamp, and an indelible pad, and you have to stamp your cards with the Dartmoor Letter Boxes' own crest. One for instance, is to be found at Cranmere Pool, south west of Okehampton, another at Crow Tor.

Princetown is always an attraction albeit a macabre one because of the infamous Dartmoor Prison, built by French Prisoners of War. It is a threatening place and dominates this small village. Even on the sunniest of days it still looks formidable and extremely depressing. There is nothing depressing however about the lively **Plume of Feathers** where mine host is James Langton. This is a favourite watering hole for people from miles around and is equally popular with visitors who find the informality and fun infectious.

I am addicted to the road that runs from Two Bridges to Ashburton which has endless places of enchantment that run off it. Past **Dartmeet** and on to **Poundsgate, Widecombe-in-the-Moor** can be seen from miles away with its tall church tower built 400 years ago, by tin miners in thanksgiving for the thriving industry. It is dedicated to St Pancras and known as 'The Cathedral; on the Moor'. For centuries the village remained almost unknown and it was not until 1850, when the vicar decided to hold an annual fair and Sabine Baring-Gould popularised an old folk tune that made Widecombe become world famous. There will be few who do not know the old song 'As I was going to Widecombe Fair wi' Bill Brewer, Jan Stewer, Peter Davy, Uncle Tom Cobleigh an all.' If you are one of the few you may rest assured that someone in Widecombe will tell you the story of Uncle Tom Cobleigh and his grey mare. Whether he was fact or fiction is strenuously argued. What is a fact is that a Thomas Cobleigh was born in the nearby village of **Spreyton** in 1762 and died there in 1884. It could be that he brought his grey mare and his motley crew to Widecombe for the fair.

Buckland-in-the-Moor is enchanting with some of the loveliest thatched cottages I have ever seen. On a hill stands the 15th century church with carved bosses in the porch and old tiles under the tower. When you look up at the clock you will note that it does not have numerals. In their

Chapter One

places are the words 'My Dear Mother' and its bells chime out 'All things bright and beautiful'. There is no official explanation for this curiosity but legend has it that it was placed there by a man in memory of his mother. This remarkable lady, when told the news that her son had drowned at sea, refused to believe it. Every night she placed a candle in her window to guide him home. Her faith was rewarded. When she died this is how he repaid her constancy.

Holne is a little village of no more than 300 people. A busy community who have great links with **Ashburton**, a town of contrasts and beauty. In 1305 it was designated a Stannary Town. Tin mining and the wool industry brought it great wealth and with it the building of some fine houses. **Buckfast Abbey** must be one of your ports of call. Not during the day although it is beautiful then, but at night. Buckfast Abbey during Compline is magical. The monks come silently down the aisle, the only sound the swish of their long robes as they pass by, the only light, the bidding one high over the altar. As they reach their stalls, they push back the cowls from their heads and the service begins. Its simple message is chanted and reaches out to every corner of this great building. One cannot doubt that God is present.

In Mid-Devon I would include **Cullompton** and recommend you take a look at this old town with its interesting main street and fine parish church. Close by is the small village of **Kentisbeare** where you will be made very welcome at **Knowles House. Tiverton** is a place that grows on you. The prettiest way to approach this very old town is by the Exe valley road. It goes back to Saxon days when it had fords across the Exe and the Loman, and it is where these two meet that the town looks down from its high ground between the rivers. Right by the medieval gateway of Tiverton Castle is the 15th-century St Peter's Church. Its spacious windows glisten in the afternoon sunlight highlighting its pinnacles and battlemented parapets. The centuries have not destroyed the wonder of the carving on the outside walls. Look for a bear that creeps along a hollowed wall, a monkey holding fast to its baby and the proud lions which crouch on the buttresses. **Tiverton Castle** built by the Normans is still important to the town but it was the wool merchants who provided Tiverton with many of its finest buildings.

The rivers are not the only waterways in Tiverton. The reach of the **Grand Western Canal** has been lovingly and carefully restored and is now open to the public who can enjoy the gentle trip by horse drawn boat along this beautiful canal as far as **East Manley**.

The road that takes you from the very old town of **Crediton** with its ancient and very beautiful cathedral like church, to Tiverton takes you close to **Cadbury**, a small village amongst the hills, with wonderful views over the

Exe valley. The tall church tower which has stood for over 500 years dominates all around it at first sight, until you realise that it, in turn, is overshadowed by the mighty **Cadbury Castle**. Standing 700ft up, it is a fort of the ancient Britons. Nothing much left there now other than two ramparts enclosing a great space. It was here that General Fairfax pitched his camp in the Civil War.

So much beauty and history is crammed into the scenic village of **Bickleigh**. It has everything; a castle, a river flowing under a superb bridge, thatched cottages, an award-winning mill and two very good hostelries. Two other villages should not escape your attention.**Bampton** about 8 miles north of Tiverton should be visited if only to discover its ducks! **Holcombe Rogus** south of Bampton is the other. It is mentioned in the Domesday Book and has Holcombe Court where the lords of the manor from Tudor times were the Bluetts.Supposedly haunted it is said that tough American servicemen during World War II were frightened out of their wits by the persistent presence of an unknown ghost. Worth a nosey, I think.

North Devon is different again, wonderful countryside and a spectacular coast. Starting inland, the quiet market town of **Holsworthy** has two striking viaducts and a good pub. **Black Torrington** got its name because the stones in the nearby river turn black with iron oxide in the water.**Sheepwash** is a great base for anyone wanting to walk along the Torridge valley. Game fishing attracts keen anglers with salmon, sea trout and brown trout all providing excellent sportat different times of the season. Pony trekking and riding are available nearby. There are good golf courses and it is heaven for eager ornithologists. From here it is easy to visit **Rosemoor Garden** only a short journey from Sheepwash and one mile south of **Great Torrington.** Before moving on one should take a look at the sleepy village of **Hatherleigh** with the excellent **George Hotel** which is Heritage at its best.

In a sort of rectangle that has its base between Launceston in Cornwall, and Okehampton and its top end, in Holsworthy and Hatherleigh there are endless beautiful places and some stunning scenery. One of my favourites is **Ashwater** just off the Holsworthy-Launceston road which has one of the loveliest old manor houses, now a hotel, **Blagdon Manor** owned and run by two people who have restored the house, serve wonderful food and have a delightful sense of humour and a smaller but welcoming establishment, **Ransom Mill.**

Clawton a little further down the same main road is a small village with the River Claw running through it and is crossed by two small bridges. The village is very proud of two things, its Norman church and the exquisite **Court Barn Country House Hotel** which is one of the most peaceful places I have ever visited. Another is **Bratton Clovelly** which is rightly proud of its

Chapter One

late 14th century church which is one of the few remaining churches to possess wall paintings dating back to the 17th century. Don't be confused, as many visitors are, who arrive here looking for Clovelly with its steep cobbled hill leading down to the sea. One must say that most people are totally happy with what they find in Bratton Clovelly which has a great charm of its own. It used to be the home of the famous politician Alan Clarke, when he was MP for Plymouth. Then between Holsworthy and Hatherleigh is **North Tawton** which can be traced back to Roman times at least and in 1086 it was recorded in the Domesday Book as Tawland. It is a pleasant place which one would not associate with disaster but legend tells us De-Bathe Pool overflows (even in dry weather) immediately prior to some national disaster or bereavment. The inhabitants will confirm this by pointing out that the overflow happened just before the deaths of Nelson, Pitt, Wellington and King Edward VII, and when the First World War broke out! The legend has its roots in 1630 when it was spoken of by one Thomas Westcote.

Close to Holsworthy is **Bradworthy** where people born and bred in the village are known as 'Horniwinks'! Why? Because it is the local name for a species of plover, the pee-wit, which used to be found in large numbers on Bradworthy Moors. It was probably founded about AD700 and originally mentioned in the Domesday Book as the manor of 'Braurdina'. It has a splendid village green and at the centre of the village is the Square, the largest village square in the West Country.

In Great Torrington I am always reminded of its past. It was literally blown into history by the great explosion of eighty barrels of gunpowder. It happened in the Civil War, when General Fairfax marching from the east, took the Royalists by surprise, and captured the town. The prisoners were shut off for safety in the tower of the church. They were held in complete darkness and had no idea that they were scrambling about in what had been the arsenal of the Royalists. Somehow the powder was set alight and the ensuing explosion shattered the church, killed 200 men and nearly killed the General as well. Today Great Torrington is the home of the world famous **Dartington Glass**.

North west of Torrington is **South Molton**. This ancient sheep and cattle market town is on the edge of Exmoor. It dates back to the 12th century and until the middle of the 19th-century thrived as a centre of the wool trade.

Now for the coast. **Lynton** and **Lynmouth** are linked together by a remarkable Cliff Railway which opened in 1890. It climbs 500ft above sea level along a 900ft track and allows you to enjoy both villages without having the severe climb from one to the other. Both are attractive places and especially Lynmouth. The Napoleonic Wars were responsible for the rising popularity of the two villages. Restrictions on travelling abroad made people look for alternatives and here they found comfort and beauty. Shelley and Coleridge were regular visitors. The River Lyn runs through Lynton and tumbles over moss strewn rocks and boulders, through thickly wooded hills as it falls to the sea at Lynmouth.

The main road from Lynton will take you to **Combe Martin**, but there are some spectacular walks in between which should not be missed, nor should you leave out the little village of **Parracombe** which lies between steep hills and must have been one of the first places in Devon to have a Christian church, for 1450 years ago, St Petrock came here and built a little chapel of cob and wattles, with a roof of straw.

Combe Martin has one of the longest village streets in the whole of the country. It became part of history over 750 years ago when its silver mines produced the wherewithal to pay for the Hundred Years War. Just inland is the pretty village of **Berrynarbor** which lives a quiet life all of its own and has a first class hostelry. **Ilfracombe** is the next stop and as you drive from Combe Martin you will be bewitched by the panoramic and stunning views glimpsed only occasionally over the cliff to the sea. Wonderful scenery, a good beach and friendly pubs are good reasons for coming here.

The winding coast road takes you to the seaside villages of **Mortehoe,Woolacombe** and **Croyde** with their magnificent beaches beloved by surfers and families. They are all just big enough to have a life style of their own but small enough to remain intimate. From Woolacombe you can just see, far out to sea, **Lundy Island,** the granite haunt of pirates long ago and now chiefly the haunt of sea birds; the island stands out 400ft above the sea.

Baggy Point offers some outstanding walks and this may attract you to **Croyde** which is tucked away on the southern flank of the peninsula. **Saunton** three miles away is renowned for its Championship Golf Course.

A busy main road will lead you from here through **Braunton** and into **Barnstaple** which claims to be the oldest borough in England. Whilst it remains an interesting town, much of the old has given way to the new to allow it to develop as the business centre of North Devon. It has an excellent theatre. From Barnstaple to Bideford you have the choice of two roads. The main A339 or the small B3233. The latter allows you to take a look at the villages of **Fremlingham** and **Instow** on the banks of the River Taw as it comes out of the sea at **Bideford Bay**. From Instow a ferry trip across the river to **Appledore** is rewarding. It is here that the two great estuaries of the

Chapter One

Taw and the Torridge meet. Appledore is charming and picturesque. The little street running up from the quay is nothing short of beautiful.

Bideford is an excellent base for anyone who wants to explore the coast and villages between itself and **Hartland Point**. It is a friendly town looking over the river. Nothing ever changes in **Clovelly**. It is an artist's paradise. Cars are taboo. You leave your vehicle in the car park at the top of the village and descend down the cobbled street which tumbles for half a mile to the sea. On either side are old cottages with flowers and creepers climbing up their walls. The scenery is unforgettable. High above you trees reach for the skies whilst way below the sea sparkles in the sunshine. It is divorced from this world.

Hartland is a place that goes nowhere and makes a good place in which to end this rather hotch potch tour of Devon. Here we have **Hartland Abbey** which stirs the heart and soul of everyone who visits. It dates from the 12th century, is situated near the wild, desolate coastline, has monastic origins and has been lived in by the same family, although frequently inherited through the female line, since the Dissolution, when Henry VIII gave it to William Abbot, the Sergeant of his royal wine cellars. There are many lovely rooms and the grounds are outstanding. The Valley is still as beautiful as it must have been in the days of the Abbots. It is open to the public from May-September on Wednesdays, Bank Holiday Sundays and Mondays from 2-5.30pm. Dogs on leads are allowed in the grounds.

I have an unashamed love for **Cornwall** from whence my family stemmed. It is an incredible mixture of glorious coastline running up either side of the peninsula until it joins Devon across the Tamar, the Atlantic and the English Channel. In the middle of this sandwich are the mining villages which frankly would not be out of place in a sci-fi film and have frequently been used for this purpose. Mineral wealth below ground, shaped the destiny of Cornwall and the Cornish for hundreds of years, changing the landscape and creating these unique villages, harbours and quays. The National Trust now owns a third of the coastline of Cornwall, more than 100 miles of magnificent walking country including many spectacular stretches and popular holiday resorts.

The coastal villages have always been among the most picturesque and sought after for film makers and artists, some liking the softer south side and others the incredible, harsh beauty of North Cornwall. Whichever way you go you are never far from the sea and for this part of the chapter I am going to take you across the North Devon border into Cornwall at **Bude**.John Betjeman described this place of endless golden sands, 'the least rowdy resort in the county'.People come here to enjoy family holidays in the traditional manner, revelling in the sun, sea and sand. Surfers flock here because the Atlantic rollers rise to great heights and provide them with some superb rides. It is only in recent years that Bude has come to prominence. At the end of the last century it was not even on the map. Next door **Stratton** was the established market town where the famous Battle of Stamford Hill took place in 1643 when Sir Bevil Grenville defeated the Parliamentary forces led by the Earl of Stamford. Every year in May this battle is re-enacted by members of the Sealed Knot Society.

Drive down the A38 and turn off towards the coast on a signposted B road and you will come to **Boscastle** which must have been known to sailors since men first sailed the English seas. If you have a choice of roads, then to see Boscastle at its most spectacular, approach from **Camelford** on the B3266 where the road rises until you suddenly see the most glorious prospect over the Valency Valley and the Atlantic Ocean before you drive down the twisting road into the village.

There is no doubt that the little harbour is one of the oddest in the country. It has a medieval breakwater, a long greasy slipwater and a huge dog leg opening into the ocean. For those who pass the stone jetty and clamber over the slippery rocks, the sea opens out in front of them to a sight that is unforgettable. If the tide is right you will not be able to miss the famous blow-hole working and rumbling. It is a natural curiosity throwing out a cloud of spray with a deep rumble like a tiny volcano. I have heard it called the Devil's Bellows.

Thomas Hardy came here as a young architect to help in the restoration of the church where he met his wife, Emma Gifford. This was not a marriage made in heaven although it lasted over 30 years. Oddly enough after her death in 1912 Hardy returned to Cornwall and the memory of their early romance at Boscastle inspired him to write some of the greatest love poems ever.

There are some magical walks around here. You can walk inland or take the coastal path from the harbour to **Penally** and on to **Pentargen** or climb the lane linking Boscastle with **Lesnewth** and nearby **Minster** with its church in an almost theatrical setting with not a house in sight and tall trees forming a backdrop. In spring the whole of the floor of this imaginary stage is covered with a carpet of bluebells and daffodils. The walk along the coast from **Boscastle** to **Tintagel** is nothing short of stunning. When the sun is shining, the sea is unbelievably blue and laps the rocks with such gentleness that it is hard to visualise the fury that is whipped up on a stormy day when the wind drives the sea in. So powerful is the wind that is difficult to stand upright but the sight is awesome.

Chapter One

I lived in the village of **Tintagel** for a while in 1950 and I used to walk up the long hill to the 14th century church which is the oldest in Cornwall. It is set high on the Clebe Cliff exposed to the ravages of the Atlantic storms. Take a look at the gravestones and you will see that the force of the wind has bent them all in the same direction and some have had to be supported by little buttresses. One really does not know whether King Arthur ever set foot here but there is no doubt that Tintagel's most famous attraction is his castle. It is a romantic place identifiable as a settlement from AD400 in the time of the Celts. In the 12th century it became a royal castle but by the 1500s the central portion had been washed away by the erosion of the sea. Edward, the Black Prince is supposed to have stayed here and if you climb down the path that leads to the shingle beach you will find Merlin's cave where it is alleged King Arthur spent his childhood.

Soft golden sand is to be found at **Bosinney Cove** and **Benoath Cove** - havens for the bather and sun-worshipper. **Trebarwith Strand** with its sandy beach is a popular place for surfers. One needs to take care, the tide roars in here and it is not always safe.

Another castle that is worth seeing is **Launceston Castle** which dominates the market town of **Launceston**, and is an easy drive from either Tintagel or Boscastle. It is a small, busy town with friendly people and a wonderful parish church. Market day here is so busy, people come in from miles around including places like **North Petherwin** on the Bude road and **Lifton** just the other side of the Devon border going along the A30 towards Okehampton. Another place no distance away from Launceston is **Virginstowe** which you must seek out for its newly opened, superb restaurant with rooms, **Percy's**. An off shoot of one of the same in London it is a welcome advent to anyone who loves good food. **Camelford** closer to the coast and **Wadebridge** should both be on your visiting list. Between them they form the base of the triangle that takes in so many pretty places. I always enjoy the small village of **Port Isaac** with its charming, irregular steep streets with cottages that lead down to the harbour. It is a village that is the essence of a Cornish fishing port. The estuary of the River Camel divides **Rock** from **Padstow**. Each side of the estuary has its afficionados. One of the strange things about Rock is that it lost its church in the sand! Sand dunes on the banks of **Padstow Harbour** engulfed an ancient chapel and it was out of use for ages until the middle of the 19th century when it was restored. You can see it now as it stands on the sand with a fine view across to Padstow. **Padstow** has a charm of its own. It is a little town that has clung to its own ways and traditions for centuries. For most people Padstow will be synonymous with its curious May Day custom of welcoming summer with songs and dancing in the streets while a man in a mask dances in front of a **Hobby Horse.**

The National Trust own **Bedruthan Steps**. The climb down the steps is definitely demanding and worse on the way back but the reward far and away outweighs the puffing and panting of those of us more used to driving than walking.

Its not that I dislike **Newquay** that I am bypassing it this time. Purely a lack of space and this busy resort is known by everyone. It is an excellent place to stay with some of the best of Cornwall's many good beaches. Beloved by surfers and by those who like to take long walks acorss the cliffs and the beaches. A great place for a family holiday. I like some of the places nearby like **Trerice,** one of the few Elizabethan manor houses in Cornwall which have escaped extensive alterations. For 400 years the home of the Cornish Royalist Arundell family, this glorious house still retains most of its 16th century glass in the great hall window of twenty four lights, comprising 576 panes. It was acquired by the National Trust in 1953. **Perranporth** to the south with its sand dunes and vast beaches is always popular in the summer for family holidays and for day visitors especially at weekends.

St Ives provides a different vista and a different feel from the towns and villages we have just covered. It is the home of so many artists that it does not need me to paint in words how very attractive it is. It was much frequented by Whistler and Sickert who delighted in the light which has a high ultra violet content. The whole reach of **St Ives Bay** from **Navax Point** to **St Ives** is glorious. The sea always seems to be bluer here than anywhere else in Cornwall. The streets are narrow and it is the worst possible scenario for drivers. You are well advised to leave your car at **Lelant** and use the excellent Park and Ride service which operates with stops all along the bay. As you wander round the centre of St Ives you will find pretty aspects at every turn. Little houses jut out at funny angles and lead to other houses, until you have climbed steadily to **St Ives Head** under which the town snuggles, safely sheltered.

Hayle lies at the very beginning of St Ives Bay and for a long time has tried to shed its 'poor relation' image. Peter De Savery promised great reclamations for this little port but he withdrew in the main and now, less speedily than the people of Hayle would like, they are giving the whole place a great facelift themselves. It is a friendly spot and not a bad place to make your base for a holiday at this end of Cornwall.

Now we are approaching **Lands End** and the coast and hinterland change again. There are small villages like **Zennor** clinging to the cliff and further down **St Just** next, not to be confused with St Just in Roseland to which we will come shortly. Spring comes early here with the beauty of the hedgerows ablaze with wild flowers - autumn lingers and in winter, frost and

Chapter One

snow are rare visitors. But the exhiliration of facing up to the Atlantic gales is an experience you are unlikely to forget!

Sennen is America's nearest neighbour! It stands high above the sea with a deep cove into which the sun hardly ever shines in winter. There is an odd story about the little medieval church. A great stone stands outside and round it seven Saxon Kings dined and wined, so the story goes, and then continues to say that when another seven kings dine here the end of the world will come!

Once I used to be filled with an enormous excitement when I stood at **Land's End**, the very end of Britain. There was nothing there then except the land and the sea beyond. Now it has a smart hotel, endless attractions and restaurants - not the same at all.

If you take to the lanes from Penzance and drive to the coast a few miles away you will reach **Porthcurno, St Levan** and **Lamorna** right by the sea and so beautiful. Take a look at **Paul**, the last village in Cornwall to speak the Cornish language back in the early 1700's. Winding roads lead to the fishing village of **Newlyn**, beloved by artists and then to **Penzance**. This is a nice old town with a busy port and wide promenade. **The Scillonian** sails daily for the **Scilly Isles**, twenty eight miles south west of Lands End. Directly in front of the fishing village of **Marazion** is **St Michaels Mount** rising out of the sea in **Mounts Bay**. Originally the site of a Benedictine Chapel established by Edward the Confessor, this spectacular castle dates from the 14th-century. To get there you can walk across from Marazion when the tide is out, or during the summer months take the ferry at high tide. It is a wonderful experience and the gardens which seem to grow out of the rock, are unique. Because of the narrow passages within the castle, it is necessary to limit the number of visitors at any one time.

The Lizard will be our next port of call but en route one should take a look at **Helston**, famous for the annual Floral Dance which is performed through the town rather like the Hobby Horse in Padstow on the north coast. The Royal Navy have a presence at Helston. The air station at **Culdrose** is home to several squadrons of helicopters and it is a rare day when you do not see these ungainly creatures of the air, landing and taking off. The skill of the pilots is unmatched. Many a sailor and visitor has been saved from certain death by the efficiency of their rescue skills and their bravery.

It would be sad not to visit the remote and wildly beautiful villages of **Manaccan, St Keverne,** and **Coverack**. Manaccan hides itelf in its hilly slopes. No matter which way you approach it you have to come down or climb up hills. Indeed the whole coastline of The Lizard is on the descent. One incline goes to St Keverne, another down the pretty valley to **Gillian Creek** and yet another to the **Helford River.**

The sea has never been kind to St Keverne and if you wander in the churchyard you will see graves of 400 people who have drowned off this shore in ships brought to their doom on the dreaded **Manacles**. On a calm summer's day when the sea is a brilliant blue and the little church surrounded by palms and hydrangeas, it is hard to conjure up the harshness of this piece of the coast in the height of a storm. But be there when a storm is raging and you will never again doubt the power of the ocean. **Coverack** is more sheltered and is charming. From there you need to go inland a bit to pick up the lanes that will lead you down to **Ruan Minor** and **Cadgwith**, two delightful spots. I almost forgot **Mullion** which has graves of some Ancient Britons on the downs above the cove. The cove itself is enchanting and has an impressive cavern and the striking **Lion Rock**.

Falmouth and **Truro** have not always seen eye to eye. In 1663 Truro was punished for its role in the Civil War and the whole river from **Tregothan Boathouse** was given to the new Co-operative of Falmouth. It was hard on Truro and it took from then until 1709 to assert its rights over Falmouth harbour, a claim strongly contested by Falmouth, which was by then a port of some consequence and saw no reason for Truro to have any say in the matter. It took the courts to settle the matter. Each today is a delightful place in its own right. **Truro** is the county town of Cornwall and with its fine cathedral attracts many a visitor. The cathedral is not all that old, it celebrated its centenary only in the last decade. It gives the appearance of having been there for ever and certainly creates a focal point for the city. If you can take a short while to sit within its walls, taking stock of life, you will find it rewarding. You may be lucky enough to have chosen a time when evensong is being sung by the splendid choir. The music soars into the rafters and the whole church is uplifted.

Almost up the road from Truro on the west coast is **St Agnes**, a quiet place with a delightful cove unusual in shape and ideal for a family picnic. From Truro, the rivers leading to the great **Carrick Roads** wander through some of the most beautiful scenery in the world. There are pleasure boats that will take you on a voyage of discovery that is a never ending delight, right the way down to **Falmouth** and **St Mawes**.

Inland the road from Truro to St Mawes is almost like trying to find the pot of gold at the end of a rainbow. You seem to drive forever, sometimes through sumptuous scenery. And at others indifferent, in the way that Cornwall has of teasing those who seek to know all about her. Finally, less

Chapter One

than twelve miles from Truro you are rewarded by sought for treasure, **St Mawes**. Everything is beautiful here, the glory of the sea, the majesty of **St Mawes Castle**, and it is surrounded by the villages of **The Roseland**. No nothing to do with roses. In this instance Roseland means promontory or commonland.

St Just in Roseland is a famous beauty spot with its pretty church nestling against the banks of the river. It has curious stones inscribed with slightly mawkish sentiments lining the steep path through the churchyard down to the church. I heard it described once as 'the sort of churchyard one would be happy to be buried in'. The church is open daily and I would list it as a must for visitors.

On the other side of the Fal, **Pendennis Castle** guards the entrance to the Carrick Roads as it has done, together with **St Mawes Castle**, for hundreds of years. Both castles can be visited. The easy way to get across the river to **Falmouth** is to take the little passenger ferry or go further up the river and take your car across on the King Harry Ferry. The road from there will take you via **Perranorworthal** to Falmouth. From here you are within easy reach of the enchanting inlets of **Feock, Mylor,** and **Restronguet.** Wonderful places in which to wander and spend the most contented of days.

En route for Falmouth you will come to **Penryn**, now by-passed but it does not like being missed out. It always seems to me that it is resentful of Falmouth and puts on a sombre forbidding air. It is far older than Falmouth whom it considers a modern upstart but the problem really lies in the fact that Falmouth became the chosen port and they would not be far wrong, a fact only denied by the seafarers who have used the haven of the Carrick Roads for centuries. Tourism is clearly very important to **Falmouth** but for all that the town is a very busy port with ship repairing facilities and a dry dock which is capable of taking vessels up to 90,000 tons. It is a pleasant town with lovely gardens, beautiful beaches and a climate which permits palm trees to grow.

Before we go inland and take a look at **Camborne** and **Redruth**, lets take the A30 a little north of Redruth and seek the turning for **Chacewater**. It lies in the heart of the Cornish mines - most no longer working - and had the richest vein of copper in the world. It can boast the first steam pumping engine in a Cornish mine, made by James Watt. Today Chacewater is a pleasant rural village with some nice houses and a fine old pub **The Rambling Miner** in Fore Street. From the village it is simple to visit the famous **Wheal Jane** mine and the entrancing **Blissoe Valley.**

Camborne is famous world wide for its School of Mines but apart from that it is a busy market town. The fine medieval church is well worth visiting with a churchyard crammed full of interesting gravestones many with entertaining epitaphs. Near Camborne is **Magor Farm** where in this century, ruins of a Roman villa were found.

Redruth is almost joined to Camborne these days but it still has its separate existence. William Murdoch lived in one of the plain little houses here. It was he who gave us gas light and invented the locomotive. A Scot by birth he married a Redruth girl and it was their house which had the very first gaslight in the whole of the country.

If you find the tin-mining industry interesting, you will not want to miss **Cornish Engines** at **East Pool.** Here there are impressive relics of these great beam engines which were used for pumping water from over 2,000ft deep, and for winding men and ore. The engines exemplify the use of high pressure steam patented by the Cornish engineer, Richard Trevithick of Camborne in 1802. It is open Good Friday to the end of October, daily from 11-6pm or sunset if earlier.

High above Redruth stands **Carn Brea Castle,** silhouetted against the sky, and near it is a great column in memory of Francis Basset who did so much for Cornish miners. It is worthwhile making the effort to climb up the inside stairway of this monument which stands 90ft high. From the top you get the most amazing view of the whole of this mining area and the sight of more coastline than anywhere in the county.

Where did miners go if they had free time? **Gwennap Pit**. This was the place where they would listen to the stirring oratory of John Wesley preaching in this naturally tiered open-aired ampitheatre. In my imagination I can hear the great sound of the Wesley hymns resounding around the place from the glorious Cornish voices. John Wesley converted the Cornish to Methodism in their thousands.

St Austell is one of the busiest towns in Cornwall. It does not have a great deal to offer the visitor other than its fine church which stands among palm trees, rising from a beautifully manicured lawn, right in the heart of the town opposite the premier hostelry **The White Hart**. It has a tower well over five centuries old but the church's rarest possession is its massive Norman font with a bowl carved with extraordinary creatures and resting on columns ending in human faces.

As a base for a holiday St Austell is excellent because there are so many stunning places within easy reach.**Mevagissey** in **St Austell Bay**, is the

Chapter One

largest fishing port in the bay and probably one of the most photographed harbours in Cornwall. Colourful fishing boats still sail out from here and nothing can take away the charm of the whitewashed cottages as they cling to the steep sides of the roads to Fore Street, where attractive shops flank the inner harbour. **Gorran Churchtown** should not be missed. Just one and a half miles from Mevagissey. It has a pub,**The Barleysheaf**, built in 1837 by a Mr Kendall who, hearsay states, had it erected for his own use because he was barred from every other hostelry in the area! You are close here to the wild headland that sailors call **The Dodman** with its 550 years old tower, a massive structure rising 110ft; a famous landmark from the sea.

Fowey with its spectacular harbour is a place of discovery; narrow winding streets where flower decked houses and cottages jostle side by side with quaint little shops and pubs on the hillside that slopes down to the glory of the Fowey river. From the days of pirates and smugglers with their barges and brigantines brazenly at moorings, to the hundreds of colourful craft that now fill what is undoubtedly one of the most enchanting harbours in this country, time has changed very little.

Rising in Bodmin Moor, the River Fowey has always been the lifeblood of those towns and villages through which it flows on its way to the open sea at St Austell Bay. Directly oppositeFowey and reached by a ferry is **Bodinnick** and at its heart is **The Old Ferry Inn** which has one of the world's most picturesque views from its lounge right over the estuary, past Fowey and Polruan to the sea. It is a great place to stay and full of the atmosphere built up over the four hundred years of its existence.

I am always drawn to the small, and so far unspoilt, harbour village of **Charlestown** where the tiny entrance to the harbour defies belief that any vessel of size, let alone the big clay carrying ships can enter its sheltering arms, but they do and demonstrate this every day. It is the home of the **Shipwreck Museum** which is Britain's biggest exhibition of shipwreck artefacts.

Lostwithiel may not appeal to you because of its rather uninteresting main street but do not judge it by this. Explore this little town on foot and you will find much to please you. The majesty of the ruins of **Restormel Castle** watch over the town. The Castle is a delightful place to be, the ruins enhanced by magnificent rhododendrons, trees and shrubs. Built in the 13th century it was a ruin by the 16th. Lostwithiel was strongly Royalist **in** the Civil War and legend has it that Charles II was hidden in an oak at **Boconnoc**, hence the name of the excellent pub in Duke Street, **The Royal Oak**. Lostwithiel was once the capital of Cornwall. It is an ancient borough with a working community who will tell you that they do not put on a special face for holiday makers for a few weeks in the year, but aim to give the same friendly welcome all year round. It is an excellent centre for fishing, walking or just relaxing and enjoying the Cornish countryside. The 13th century church of St Bartholomew is worth a visit.

From Lostwithiel the river continues meandering past the lovely little church of **St Winnow** on the east bank, which dates mainly from the 15th century, although there are some remains of Norman and 13th century architecture. A little further on is the creek that leads up to the pretty waterside village of **Lerryn**, where once sailing ships came to discharge their cargoes of road-stone from the quarries at **St Germans**. Now it is so silted up that you must keep a watchful eye on the tide if you are water-borne. It might be worth being stranded if it gave you the opportunity to visit **The Ship Inn**, a delightful hostelry with good food, good beer and good company.

On the west bank is an even smaller village, **Golant**, much beloved by small boat owners. They come to enjoy the sailing but also to visit **The Fisherman's Arms** which you will find at the end of a road marked 'Road liable to flooding at high tide'. The pub overlooks the water but it is out of harm's way - even the pavement is 2ft high!

Almost in the centre of Cornwall is the old county town of **Bodmin** and if you take the road from St Austell to the town you will go through English China Clay country. Go via **Nanpean** and **Carthew** and you will come to **Wheal Martyn Museum**. This will give you an unforgettable insight into Cornwall's single largest industry. Great white, eerie mountains appear on all sides, evidence of the industry that has provided so much of Cornwall's employment. In Bodmin, the handsome church of **St Petrock** delights all who see it. It is the biggest in the county, 151ft long and 65ft wide. Mainly 15th century it has been much restored. On **Beacon Hill**, looking down on the town, is a column of granite rising 144ft high. It is in memory of Sir Walter Raleigh Gilbert, a brave soldier, and belonging to the family of Sir Humphrey Gilbert who was the step-brother of Sir Walter Raleigh. Bodmin has a lot to offer including **The Bodmin and Wenford Railway** which allows you to explore some of Cornwall's finest countryside from a steam-hauled Branch Line train. **The Light Infantry Museum** is opposite the station and **Bodmin Town Museum** is a short walk away from the town centre. **The Camel Trail** paths to Wadebridge and Padstow start near the historic Bodmin Goal.

Just outside Bodmin is **Washaway** where you will find **Pencarrow House**, the home of the Molesworth family and has been so since it was completed by Sir John Molesworth, the 5th baronet about 1770. Essentially a family home, it is a delight to explore. For Gilbert and Sullivan fans it is interesting to know that Sir Arthur Sullivan composed the music for Iolanthe

Chapter One

here. The Pencarrow Gardens cover some 50acres. Huge rhododendrons and camellias provide a wonderful display every Spring. There are several gardens within striking distance from here which should not be missed. At **Prideaux Place,Padstow**, there is a deer park and a newly restored garden overlooking the Camel estuary. **Lanhydrock** has rare trees and shrubs, the unique circular herbaceous garden and exceptional magnolias. **Lancarffe** at Bodmin has four and a half acres of sheer beauty and then there is the fabulous **Longcross Victorian Gardens** atTrelights, near Port Isaac, which is open all the year round from 10.30am until dusk. It has fascinating maze type walkways and one of the best cream teas anywhere.

One should always take a look at the many small villages virtually encircling Bodmin, **St Tudy** off the main Launceston road for one and on the other side **Lanlivery** which one used to pass on the main road and today it has reverted to a quiet backwater - an ideal spot in which to stay.

Had we started this tour of Cornwall from **Plymouth** crossing by the **Torpoint Ferry** we would have had a pleasant run through the small town of **Torpoint** and then on to **Anthony**, a small hamlet really which has a pub, **The Ring of Bells** in which the Duke of Edinburgh used to play skittles before his marriage. It also has one of the nicest, small stately homes, **Anthony House**, now belonging to the National Trust but also the family home of the Pole-Carews. Open to the public it is a pleasure to spend time there both in the house and the gardens which reach down to the River Tamar The ferry route takes you through leafy roads with offshoots to all sorts of villages including **Deviock** where there are two interesting places to stay. Reach the coast road and it will lead you to the small seaside villages of **Downderry** and **Seaton**..

The traffic from the ferry and from the **Tamar Bridge** which has made entering Cornwall so much easier, meet at **Trerulefoot**, having by-passed **Saltash** en route and passed the turn to the right which would have led you past the championship Golf course at **St Mellion** and thence to **Callington**, a small town at the cross roads between Dartmoor and the west coast. At Trerulefoot maybe you would have decided to carry on deeper into the county but for our journey we are cutting off to the east and through the pretty **Hessenford Valley** until you reach the quaint fishing villages of **East** and **West Looe**. Here the river meets the sea, picturesque houses climb the steep hills, fishermen set sail every day in their colourful boats and visitors set out with some of them to go shark fishing. For the less adventurous Looe itself is fascinating, full of good pubs, sandy beaches and a plethora of hotels from which to choose if you should decide to stay. If you drove out of Looe towards **Liskeard** you would have a short, but delightful drive arriving in another small town which has benefitted enormously from being by-passed. It has a big square, a market, lots of odd, wandering streets and some good hostelries. From Liskeard you might well go out towards **Sibleyback Lake,** the haunt of anglers or perhaps to one of the small villages like **St Neots** where **The London Inn** is where locals meet for good ale and visitors come to enjoy the banter and the good pub food.. The great thing about Liskeard is its central position allowing one to take off for almost anywhere in Cornwall.

Across the old bridge which divides East and West Looe you will find the road that will lead you to **Talland Bay,** surely the most beautiful stretch of smuggling coast in Cornwall! And from there on to the little fishing village of **Polperro** which is a visitor's dream come true. So small are thestreets that you have to leave your car at the top but the reward is a journey that will take you between houses that almost touch each other. They are quaint as are the shops and the pubs. Every road leads to the harbour and if one had to talk about somewhere that paints the picture of what the visitor imagines Cornwall is all about then **Polperro** has to be that place.

Chapter One

THE SUNDAY SCHOOL
Copthorne, North Petherwin,
Launceston, PL15 8NB
Tel: 01566 781539/552
Bookings: 10566785723

Copthorne is a quiet place, some distance out of North Petherwin which makes it all the more surprising to find a thriving Bistro with rooms, at the centre of the hamlet. Sharon Seal has converted the old Victorian Sunday School into a most attractive dwelling in which the Bistro plays a large part and the Bed and Breakfast Accommodation is excellent. There are three rooms all decorated in simple country style with patchwork covers, tea and coffee making facilities and colour television. One room is downstairs, and as well as its ensuite bathroom it has grab rails - ideal for anyone elderly or disabled. The Lounge is one of those rooms in which you can flop into a chair in front of the woodburner at anytime of the day - read, play a board game or just relax after enjoying a meal in the bistro. The imaginative food, cooked by Sharon who is an experienced chef, is all prepared from local produce and home-cooked. A children's menu is available. Bring your own wine - Sharon will be happy to chill and serve it for you. Different and delightful - a good place to stay.

USEFUL INFORMATION

OPEN: All year
CHILDREN: Welcome
CREDIT CARDS: Yes
LICENSED: May bring your own wine
ACCOMMODATION: 3 rooms
DISABLED ACCESS: One room on the ground floor with grab rails in bathroom

DINING ROOM: Excellent food. No food on Sunday nights. Sunday lunch 1st & 3rd Sunday in the month. Bistro open to non-residents Thurs, Fri & Sat. Booking essential
VEGETARIAN: Catered for
NO-SMOKING

LOWER NICHOLS NYMET FARM
North Tawton,
Devon EX20 2BW
Tel: 01363 82510

Situated on the A3072 halfway between Crediton and Okehampton, this comfortable fairly modern farmhouse is an ideal base for anyone wanting to explore and enjoy the magic and mystery of Devon. David and Jane Pyle who own the farm are genuinely interested in people and offer their guests warmth, comfort and good food. Wake to the early morning chorus of the birds and the glistening dew on the grass. The two bedrooms are both ensuite and charmingly furnished complete with a beverage tray. Jane produces hearty and healthy breakfasts, packed lunches, home-made clotted cream and candlelit dinners upon request. There is something incredibly peaceful about seeing the cows come in for milking and you are invited to walk on a marked trail with breath taking views over the red soil countryside.

USEFUL INFORMATION

OPEN: March to October inclusive

CHILDREN: Welcome
CREDIT CARDS: None taken
ACCOMMODATION: 2 ensuite rooms
Self-catering cottage available

DINING ROOM: Hearty healthy breakfast packed lunches, candlelit dinners upon request

DISABLED ACCESS: No
GARDEN: Walk on a marked trail
PETS: No

Devon, Cornwall, Somerset and Avon

SLADE BARN
Netton Farm, Noss Mayo,
Plymouth,
Devon PL8 1HA
Tel: 01752 872235

Take a break with a difference. A superb barn conversion, set in attractive gardens, where mellowed oak beams, and sunny conservatory create an atmosphere of peace and tranquillity and it's only minutes from one of Devons finest coastal walks. For the energetic there is a lovely indoor pool, games room and tennis court or perhaps croquet on the lawn. What more could you ask for?. I know! professional Reflexology by appointment on the premises! Sounds wonderful, doesn't it! This is such a good centre for seeing the West Country. Historic Plymouth, Dartmoor, beaches and many other attractions all within easy distances.

USEFUL INFORMATION
OPEN; All year
CHILDREN; Over 10 years
PETS; By arrangement
CREDIT CARDS; None taken
LICENSED; No
ACCOMMODATION; 3 rooms, 2 dbl, 1 single
DINING ROOM; Evening meal by arrangement
Tea and coffee on request
VEGETARIAN; By arrangement
DISABLED ACCESS; No
GARDEN; Yes

EASTERBROOK FARM COTTAGES
Exbourne,
Okehampton,
Devon EX20 3QY
Tel: 01837 851674

If you wish to retreat from the hustle and bustle of everyday life then this is the place. These self-contained cottages, dating back to 1580, have all the luxuries of modern living and still manage to keep their charm of a bygone age. With the main house being partially thatched and the cottages with their stone and cob walls, this is a very picturesque scene. The farm consists of 70 acres; half of which is hay and grazing land, the other half being recently planted as woodland. There are lots of animals here. Horses, dogs, cats, goats, ducks, geese and chickens. You are more than welcome to wander round the farm and exercise will be provided free of charge at certain times of the year; hay making being one and apple picking being another! This is an ideal retreat if you wish a farm holiday, but also if you want to explore the South West. You are only 5 miles from Dartmoor and the town of Okehampton and about 20 miles from Exmoor. There are plenty of local activities such as golf, fishing and walking but I must point out that a car is really an essential, even to get to the pub unless you are pretty fit!

USEFUL INFORMATION
OPEN; All year
CHILDREN; Welcome
CREDIT CARDS; None taken
LICENSED; No
ACCOMMODATION; 3 self-contained cottages
EVENING MEAL; By request (French cuisine)
VEGETARIAN; Catered for
DISABLED ACCESS; No
PETS; Horses by arrangement

Chapter One

PITT FARM
*Ottery St Mary,
Devon EX11 1NL
Tel: 01404 812439*

This attractive thatched framhouse dates back to 1566 and is a typical Devon Long House. The atmosphere is wonderful, welcoming and friendly. George and Sue Hansford aim to provide a memorable stay, something they definitely achieve. The rooms are furnished in keeping with the house, oak beams are everywhere and on cooler days the entrancing smell of log fires adds to the ambience. The comfortable beds ensure a good nights sleep and in the morning a delicious full English breakfast is served. Evening meals are available most evenings. Most of the produce used is home or locally grown. There are 6 bedrooms, two are ensuite, two have private bathrooms and two have use of public bathrooms. Childrens meals by arrangement. Ottery St Mary is one of the oldest and most historic towns in Devon and Pitt Farm is an ideal centre for a holiday or a short break.

USEFUL INFORMATION
OPEN: January-November
CHILDREN: Welcome, childrens meals
CREDIT CARDS: Only Amex
LICENSED: May bring your own
ACCOMMODATION: 6 rooms, 2 ensuite, 2 with private bathrooms, 2 use public bathrooms
DINING ROOM: Delicious full English breakfast, evening meals available
VEGETARIAN: Catered for
DISABLED ACCESS: No
GARDEN: Yes
PETS: No

THE WATCHERS
*The Warren, Polperro
Cornwall PL13 2RD
Tel: 01503 272296*

Polperro is probably one of the most picturesque villages you will come across. With its harbour and views out to the Eddystone Lighthouse, it is hard to surpass. Nestling in the hillside, the historic fishing village has a great deal to offer the visitor. The Watchers is a friendly guest house run by Patsy Wilcox who gives all her guests a warm welcome in her Cornish home. The Cornish are renowned for their friendliness, and Patsy is no exception. The bedrooms have been extremely well thought out with TV, tea and coffee, hairdryers and shaving points in each. All are en suite and a nice touch are the wine glasses for your own wine. Breakfast is truly traditional English with the addition of potato pancakes and omelettes. Believe me, after one of these, lunch is an unnecessary expense! Polperro is a great place for walking, as the coast and the scenery is outstanding. Obviously fishing is popular and Patsy is only too happy to help you organise this. But there is much more : Looe is close by and here you can shop to your heart's content or perhaps golf. The historic city of Plymouth is within access and a great day out can be spent here. Great accommodation in a fascinating village setting, with access to all the attractions you could possibly require.

USEFUL INFORMATION
OPEN : All year
CHILDREN : Welcome
PETS : Welcome
ACCOMMODATION : 2 rooms en suite
VEGETARIAN : Catered for
DISABLED ACCESS : No
CREDIT CARDS : None taken
GARDEN : Terraced, overlooking harbour.

Devon, Cornwall, Somerset and Avon

TREVONE BAY HOTEL
Dobbin Close, Trevone,
Padstow, Cornwall PL28 8QS

Tel: 01841 520243
Fax: 01841 521195

Trevone Bay Hotel has a large sun lounge from which you can watch the thrilling sight of the sun setting over the sea. That is just one of the many benefits when you stay in this immaculate and beautifully run hotel which is situated in the quiet village of Trevone, just a short walk from the beach and 2 miles from the picturesque fishing port of Padstow. Sue and Andrew Hamilton have owned the hotel since 1985 and have a number of guests who return to the hotel year after year, regarding it as home from home. The friendly and relaxed atmosphere rapidly makes those visiting for the first time feel at ease. The hotel is strictly non-smoking.

There are 13 attractive and comfortably furnished ensuite bedrooms. Family rooms are large enough to take a cot if needs be. Tea and coffee making facilities are provided in every room. The spacious dining room is light and airy and it is here you will enjoy a traditional English breakfast, substantial enough to keep you going all day, and in the evening a four course meal with a choice at each course and home-baked rolls, cooked by Sue. She is an imaginative cook and provides a very varied menu using local produce. Sue is willing to cater for special diets. The wine list is interesting and the prices very reasonable. It is in the bar that people tend to gather after dinner to enjoy a drink and the company of friends old and new. The bar is also open at lunchtime. The Soft Lounge is for those who want to be quiet or to enjoy conversation. Children will not disturb you because they can play happily in one of the two sun lounges, one of which has a colour television. The garden is another popular spot in which to enjoy the peace and tranquillity and there is also an activity frame for children. A drying room is available for surfers or walkers. There is ample parking. Because of its location the hotel is ideally situated for a variety of activities including walking the Coastal Path, birdwatching, sea, river and shark fishing, golfing, surfing, horse riding and sailing. There are some superb old churches and Pencarrow House and Garden, where Arthur Sullivan stayed and wrote music for the Gilbert and Sullivan operas. It would be hard not to enjoy a holiday or a short break at the Trevone Bay Hotel.

USEFUL INFORMATION

OPEN: Easter-October
CHILDREN: Welcome. Cots, Highchairs
CREDIT CARDS: Yes, 3% surcharge
LICENSED: Yes. Good wine list
DINING ROOM: English & Continental Varied menu
VEGETARIAN: Yes on request
DISABLED ACCESS: 1 flight of stairs

Chapter One

THE OLD MILL COUNTRY HOUSE
Little Petherick, Nr Padstow,
Wadebridge, Cornwall PL277QT

Tel: 01841 540388

Little Petherick is a sleepy village, full of pretty and interesting houses and none more so than The Old Mill, a 16th century converted corn mill. This Grade II listed building is set in its own gardens, next to a stream that dawdles into the Camel estuary. The area is renowned as a fine centre for sailing, wind surfing and water skiing and has many sandy beaches and coves as well as beautiful walks around the estuary and along the National Trust coastline.

The Old Mill, owned and run by a very hospitable couple, Michael and Pat Walker, is complete with waterwheel and retains its original character and charm with antique furniture and collections of genuine artifacts throughout. The house has seven attractive and well-appointed bedrooms, most of which are ensuite and each has delightful views of the local countryside. One of the nicest features of The Old Mill is that the kitchen is available for residents to see what excellent food is being served for breakfast. You are offered a selection of various breakfasts all freshly cooked and served to your individual table. Dinner is not available but there are many good eateries within easy reach. The Old Mill also has a well equipped self-catering, two bedroomed cottage in Padstow available all the year round.

Padstow is a picturesque fishing harbour, and its central location makes it the perfect centre for a touring holiday. Rugged coastline, golden beaches, plenty of sporting facilities all make this area extra special and for those who want to do nothing but relax, The Old Mill's stream side walled garden, or the terraced sun garden next to the waterwheel is ideal.

USEFUL INFORMATION

OPEN;*March-end October*
CHILDREN;*Not under 14 years*
CREDIT CARDS;*All major cards Except Switch & Diners*
LICENSED;*Yes*
ACCOMMODATION;*7 rooms Mainly ensuite*

DINING ROOM:*Excellent breakfast*
VEGETARIAN;*Upon request*
DISABLED ACCESS;*No*

PETS; *No*
GARDEN; *Yes*

TRENDERWAY FARM
Pelynt, Nr Polperro,
Cornwall PL13 2LY

Tel: 01503 272214

This lovely 16th century farmhouse surrounded by granite barns is one of those places one hopes to find but rarely does!. Lynne Tuckett, the owner has a flair for interior decoration and her four letting bedrooms - two in a converted barn - are as pretty and stylish as any first class hotel. Spacious bathrooms with shower cabinets are the icing on the cake. Everywhere is sumptuously furnished. There's a sitting room for guests and a sunny breakfast room in a conservatory. Breakfast is a feast with eggs direct from the farm's free-range chickens and sausages specially delivered by the local butcher. Deservedly Trenderway Farm was the winner of the Southeast Cornwall Tourism Quality Award. It is also AA Premier Selected QQQQQ and has the English Tourist Board's Highly Commended. Standing in 450 acres of farmland which is recorded in the Domesday Book, Trenderway could not be a better place to stay while you set out to experience the magic and fascination of Cornwall or just stay put and enjoy the peace and calm one seldom achieves today. There are no evening meals but Lynne will recommend a number of restaurants nearby and introduce you to the local 16th century Inn which is well worth your patronage.

USEFUL INFORMATION

OPEN: All year.
CHILDREN: No
CREDIT CARDS: None taken
ACCOMMODATION: 4 letting rooms

DINING ROOM: Wonderful breakfast
No evening meal available
DISABLED ACCESS: No
PETS: No

Chapter One

EDNOVEAN FARM COTTAGE
Perranuthnoe,
Nr Penzance,
Cornwall TR20 9LZ

Tel: 01736 710065

If you are looking for exceptional scenery on your holiday then look no further than Ednovean Farm Cottage, the surrounding views are breathtaking, from here you can see Mounts Bay, including St Michael's Mount, Penzance, Newlyn and Mousehole. The cottage was built around the 16th century, and is possibly mentioned in the Doomsday Book, it still retains many of the original features. The furnishings are a comfortable cottage style, warm and welcoming, there are two sitting rooms for your use, both with colour televisions. The simple but attractively decorated bedrooms, one double, one twin and a single, one being ensuite, have a tea and coffee tray, tissues and toiletries. There is a shower room and a bathroom next to the bedrooms. After a good nights sleep, you wake to those stunning views from your window, which sets you up for a really sumptuous, large English Breakfast with eggs from the farm chickens. There are no evening meals at Ednovean, but your hosts Adrian and Jo Marsham are happy to point you in the direction of some very good pubs, particularly The Victoria where they serve excellent food and fine ales. Ednovean is ideally situated for exploring the Cornish countryside and visiting the towns and villages nearby. The village of Perranuthnoe is on the South Coastal Path, and has a lovely sandy beach with rock pools, there are guided tours of the West Penwith area by mini bus, sea fishing, trout fishing, golf, riding, cycling and water-sports all within easy distance of this magnificent setting.

USEFUL INFORMATION

OPEN: *All year*
CHILDREN: *No*
CREDIT CARDS: *None taken*
LICENSED: *No*
ACCOMMODATION: *1dbl, 1 twin, 1 single, one being ensuite*

DINING ROOM: *Full English Breakfast*
VEGETARIAN: *Yes and Special Diets*
DISABLED ACCESS: *No*
GARDEN: *Extensive south facing with wonderful views*
PETS: *No*

LYNWOOD GUEST HOUSE
41 Morrab Road,
Penzance,
Cornwall TR18 4EX
Tel: 01736 36871
Tel/Fax: 01736 365871

100 yards from the Promenade is this modern comfortable guest house. The Victorian house has gained a reputation over the years for cleanliness and good food. The bedrooms are tastefully decorated with modern furniture and each has TV, tea and coffee. There is a residents lounge with TV, games, books and jigsaws. Lynwood is ideally situated in the town of Penzance, being 1 minute from the beach and 3 minutes from the town centre with it's shops, restaurants, museums and entertainments. Places to visit easily from Penzance are the Lizard and Land's End with it's amusements and shops. There is a fine tour detailing the history of Land's End with some spectacular legends re-enacted, with 3D imagery. There are lovely coastal walks around here and of course, you have St. Michael's Mount to visit. Trips to the Isle of Scilly can be arranged and there are plenty of museums and art galleries.

USEFUL INFORMATION
OPEN; All year
CHILDREN; Welcome
CREDIT CARDS; All major cards
LICENSED; No
ACCOMMODATION; 6 rooms
DINING ROOM; Good home cooking
VEGETARIAN; By arrangement
DISABLED ACCESS; No
GARDEN; No
PETS; By arrangement

WYMERING GUEST HOUSE
15 Regent Square, Penzance
Cornwall
Tel: 01736 62126

This small, select guest house is set in a peaceful little square just off the town centre. It is a delightful location with ample parking and you are still in easy reach of the beach, promenade and all other amenities. Penzance is a very attractive town with lots of small quaint antique shops. Quite the place for a good browse! For the more active there is the usual array of sports : surfing, diving, even kite flying and many more! Pamela and Terry Chinn who are the proprietors, welcome their guests warmly and there are always special rates for senior citizens. The rooms are of a high standard with TV, tea and coffee, and hand basins. Breakfast is full English and you are within minutes of the many restaurants in the town for an evening meal.

USEFUL INFORMATION
OPEN : All year
CHILDREN : Welcome
PETS : Welcome
CREDIT CARDS : None taken
LICENSED : No
ACCOMMODATION : 5 rooms
RESTAURANT : Not applicable
BAR FOOD : Not applicable
VEGETARIAN : Yes
DISABLED ACCESS : Not really
GARDEN : Front; very nice

Chapter One

THE QUEENS ARMS
*Pitminster, Nr. Taunton,
Somerset TA3 7AZ*

*Tel: 01823 421529
Fax: 01823 421635*

It is quite recently that David and Anita Rowden became the owners of The Queens Arms, which has an amazing history going back to 1036. Of course over the years there have been many changes and many improvements but none has detracted from the charm and antiquity of the inn. Food is available either in the restaurant or in the bar and the choice is mouthwatering. Of course there are the traditional favourites but every day there is something new that will tempt the most difficult palate. Watch for the daily specials on the blackboard. Vegetarians have a choice. In the friendly bar you will find usually a selection of five Real Ales amongst the wide range of drinks. The wine list in not vast but it has been carefully chosen to give one a choice of wines from around the world. The Queens caters for functions of all kinds from small conferences to wedding receptions and private parties. The menus for these occasions whether a finger buffet or a banquet are well thought out and provide delicious food at sensible prices.

The Queens has four charming letting rooms all ensuite and equipped with TV and tea and coffee making facilities. A first class traditional breakfast is provided complete with complimentary newspapers. Pitminster is on the edge of the Blackdown Hills and is an ideal base for anyone wanting to walk or explore this part of Somerset. Taunton is nearby and Bristol about an hours drive.

USEFUL INFORMATION

OPEN; *All year*
CHILDREN; *Welcome*
CREDIT CARDS; *All major cards*
LICENSED; *Yes*
ACCOMMODATION; *4 ensuite rooms*

RESTAURANT; *Superb food*
BAR FOOD; *Wide range. Specials*
VEGETARIAN; *Daily choice*
DISABLED ACCESS; *No facilities*
PETS; *Yes*

THE IMPERIAL HOTEL
Lockyer Street, The Hoe,
Plymouth,
Devon PL1 2QD

Tel: 01752 227311

Parking facilities are always important and this is amply catered for in this friendly, comfortable hotel in Lockyer Street which runs from just behind the Theatre Royal to The Hoe. Alan and Prue Jones are the resident proprietors of this elegant Victorian hotel which has been sympathetically modernised and now boasts twenty two bedrooms - sixteen ensuite - and five at ground level. Every room has colour television, radio, direct-dial telephone and tea/coffee making facilities. There is a large comfortable sitting room with a roaring log fire in winter months. The bar has a nautical flavour. Alan Jones spent many years afloat and travelled the world. He has a host of amusing tales of life at sea and you will not be unaware that he was the last cadet to scrub decks on the Cutty Sark!. The discipline and strict standards of life at sea have been adapted to the smooth running of the hotel. It has a charming informality but underneath there are certain rules which he is insistent are adhered to. For example, in the bar there is no swearing, no mobile telephones or drinking out of bottles. He has been known to ask people to leave the hotel because of offensive speech. No, he is not Captain Bligh, but a man who believes that women on their own should be able to sit in his bar without being offended and to stay in his hotel without fear of intimidation. You will see from the Visitor's Book how many people are regulars here. A happy place to stay with good food and good company.

USEFUL INFORMATION

OPEN: All year
CHILDREN: Welcome
CREDIT CARDS: all major cards
LICENSED: Yes
ACCOMMODATION: 22 rooms, 16 ensuite rooms available
PARKING: Ample

RESTAURANT: Good, varied choice
BAR FOOD: Available at lunchtime
VEGETARIAN: Upon request
DISABLED ACCESS: Yes. Ground floor
PETS: No

Chapter One

SEAWAYS GUEST HOUSE
Polzeath, Cornwall PL27 6SU

Tel: 01208 862382

Polzeath has alway attracted those who love its wide golden beach, safe bathing, surfing and panoramic views but it has much more to offer than that. For example there are some splendid cliff walks to 'the Rumps' and 'Pentire Head', also Lundy Bay. It is an area in which much wild life thrives and can be seen. Wadebridge is the nearest town about 7 miles away and Padstow is only a short distance away by ferry from Rock. Famous around the world for its May Day celebrations. St Enodoc Golf Course welcomes golfers, Boscastle, Tintagel and Port Isaac will enchant you whilst trips further inland will take you to the wild scenic beauty of Bodmin Moor. There is deep sea fishing, tennis, squash, pony-trekking, sailing, water ski-ing.

A wonderful place to spend a holiday and what could be better than enjoying a stay at the friendly, comfortable Seaways just 5 minutes from the sea. The house is well furnished and there is colour TV available for guests use at all time. Simple home-cooked meals are served in a pleasant dining room - Breakfast is a really substantial meal and an evening meal is available. Vegetarians are catered for. The six bedrooms, some of which are ensuite have everything you require. Children are very welcome and both cots and high chairs are provided if required. Seaways is not licensed but Pauline and Ken White, the owners, will cheerfully open your own wine or chill your beer. It is a truly informal, relaxed house where the Whites succeed in making their guests feel at home in a very short space of time. If you come by train to Bodmin Road you can be met - you really can have a great holiday here without a car.

USEFUL INFORMATION

OPEN: *All year*
CHILDREN: *Welcome. Cot & high chair*
CREDIT CARDS: *None taken*
LICENSED: *No. Please bring your own*
ACCOMMODATION: *6 rooms ensuite*
PETS: *No*

DINING ROOM: *Good English breakfast*
Evening meal by arrangement
VEGETARIAN: *Yes upon request*
DISABLED ACCESS: *Restricted*
GARDEN: *Yes*
PARKING: *Car parking space*

Devon, Cornwall, Somerset and Avon

FAIRHOLME
30 Trewtha Lane,
Port Isaac, Cornwall PL29 3RW

Tel: 01028 880397

Picturesque Port Isaac is both enchanting and romantic, a place famed for ships and smugglers with quaint white and colour-washed cottages, gardens bursting with colour and winding streets which provide entrancing views at every turn. Boats for sea fishing, and pleasure cruising are available and there is good safe bathing from the cliff-enclosed beach at Port Gaverne. It is a wonderful area with so much to explore and see but to enjoy all this you need somewhere to stay that completes the idyll. Fairholme right between Port Isaac and Port Gaverne is that place. Owned by Lynda von Lintzgy, the house is bright and airy, tastefully furnished and decorated with six bedrooms. There is one ensuite family room on the ground floor and five first floor bedrooms consist of one twin, three double and one family. One bedroom has a private bathroom and the others share a beautifully appointed bathroom. All bedrooms have colour television, tea making facilities, hot and cold running water and shaving points. The attractive residents' lounge has a luxury television, video recorder and comfortable seating that just asks you to relax. You are welcome to treat the house as your home and come and go as you please. Home-cooking, using local produce makes every meal an occasion. The breakfast is generous and the evening meal menu changes daily. Children are very welcome. Babies up to 3 years are only charged for meals. From 3-6 inclusive the discount is 50% and for those from 6-10 inclusive there is a 25% discount. Lynda von Lintzgy is an almost fanatical gardener and the result of her efforts is a wondrous garden with all sorts of plants from all over the world especially the Southern Hemisphere.

USEFUL INFORMATION

OPEN: *All year except Christmas*
CHILDREN: *Welcome. Special discounts*
CREDIT CARDS: *None taken*
LICENSED: *Yes. Residential license*
ACCOMMODATION: *6 some ensuite*
PETS: *By arrangement*

DINING ROOM: *Excellent home-cooked food*
VEGETARIAN: *Upon request*
DISABLED ACCESS: *No*
GARDEN: *Wonderful garden*
PARKING: *Yes*

Chapter One

ST ANDREWS HOTEL
Port Isaac,
North Cornwall PL29 3SG
Tel: 01208 880240
Fax: 01208 880240

Anyone not finding St Andrews Hotel the ideal spot for a holiday or a short break must be hard to please. It stands on the clifftops between Port Isaac and Port Gaverne and commands probably the most spectacular view in Port Isaac, across the Bay to Tintagel, Hartland Point, and beyond to Lundy Island. Philip and Joy Slack own and run the hotel in a relaxed and delightfully informal manner but underneath there is the firm hand of the professional ensuring that every detail is attended to. The attractively furnished ensuite bedrooms have TV and courtesy trays. The cosy bar enables you to have a drink in the sun lounge as the sun dips below the Atlantic horizon. Well known for it's great English breakfast. Snacks, cream teas and morning coffee complete the picture. Well behaved children and dogs are welcome. There is also a self catering apartment.

USEFUL INFORMATION

OPEN: March-October
DINING ROOM: Renowned for it's English breakfast.
Open to non-residents
CHILDREN: Welcome
DISABLED ACCESS: No
CREDIT CARDS: Yes, not Amex
GARDEN: For self-catering apart.
LICENSED: Yes
Sun terrace for hotel residents
ACCOMMODATION: Ensuite rooms,
Plus a self-catering apartment
PETS: Welcome

THE HARBOUR HOUSE
Self Catering Holiday Apartments
& Bed & Breakfast
1, Trevelyan Road,
Seaton, Devon EX12 2NL

Tel: 01297 21797

The first thing that strikes you as you arrive in Trevelyan Road alongside Axmouth Harbour, is the extraordinary sense of peace, almost as if you are shutting out the rest of the world. Strange in many ways because there is a lot of activity amongst the boats lying at anchor, some just returning and others setting sail. The pretty apartments which are available are delightfully appointed and are suitable for out of season holidays and short breaks (minimum - 3 nights). Bed linen is included in the price but please bring your own towels and tea towels. Harbour House also offers Bed and Breakfast in the three first floor bedrooms which all have colour TV, H&C and refreshment trays. A full English Breakfast is provided and Vegetarians can be catered for. Harbour House is just 100 yards from the beach and a short level walk along the Esplanade to the town centre.

USEFUL INFORMATION
OPEN; February-November   **CREDIT CARDS;** None taken
CHILDREN; Welcome   **DISABLED ACCESS;** Ground floor S/C
ACCOMMODATION; 3 apartments 3 rooms B&B **PETS;** No

Devon, Cornwall, Somerset and Avon

DUCHY HOUSE
Tavistock Road,
Princetown, Devon PL20 6QF

Tel: 01822 890552

This interesting non-smoking Victorian house built some one hundred and ten years ago has received many visitors over the years; it is even rumoured that Edward and Mrs Simpson stayed here. Whoever stays today will find that Hilary and Ernie Trimble are generous hosts with a genuine liking for people. Within their non-smoking house they have three huge, comfortable letting rooms, one of which is ensuite and each has a tea and coffee tray. Princetown can be bleak with the whole of the small town dominated by the forbidding presence of Dartmoor Prison but no one can ever doubt the warmth of the welcome at this house at whatever the time of year. Every room is decorated with classic papers and drapes. The relaxing residents lounge has TV and Video and a suite into which one just sinks - blissful after a busy day exploring Dartmoor. Incidentally there are drying and ironing facilities for those who need it. A fire is lit in one of the two fine fireplaces in the restaurant during the winter months which makes it appealing to non-residents as well as guests. A delightful room in which to eat the excellent freshly cooked breakfast each morning.

Part of Duchy House is run as Tea Rooms and has a tremendous reputation for its food, especially Sunday roasts which people travel miles to enjoy. A wide range of home-cooked food is served including snacks, light meals and a full lunch menu. If you have a sweet tooth you will rave about the superb range of desserts and cakes. Tea lovers will appreciate the fine selection of Twinings teas. There is a childrens menu and Vegetarian meals can be prepared to order. With so much to enjoy in the surrounding countryside this is a great place to stay or simply enjoy a super meal.

USEFUL INFORMATION

OPEN; All year for Bed & Breakfast except the first 3 weeks in November.
Tearooms: Summer 10.30-5.30pm
Winter: Fri-Sun and School holidays including Christmas Day 11.00-4.30pm

CHILDREN; Welcome
CREDIT CARDS; None taken

RESTAURANT; Home-cooked fare
VEGETARIAN; Available on request
DISABLED ACCESS; With assistance
GARDEN; Yes
PETS; Not in Tearooms.
B & B by arrangement
ACCOMMODATION; 3 rooms, 1 ensuite
LICENSED; Yes

Chapter One

MELON COTTAGE VINEYARD,
The Vineyard, Charlton,
Padstock,
Bath, BA3 5TN.
Tel : 01761 435090

This picturesque, cosy cottage which dates back to the 12th century, has views from the bedrooms which overlook the gardens and vineyard. What a pleasant sight to greet you upon awakening, in one of these beamed, simply furnished rooms! This family run bed & breakfast has a warm, informal atmosphere, and is a happy place to visit. The Pountneys who own this house make their own wine and are quite happy to be joined in the picking when in season! I am sure you will sample some of the 'fruit of your toil' and enjoy every minute! Virginia Pountney, your hostess, is well informed on the various activities in the area such as pony trekking, walking, golf and fishing, and will be only too happy to impart some of her local knowledge!

USEFUL INFORMATION

OPEN : All year except Xmas
CHILDREN : Welcome
PETS : Welcome by arrangement
LICENSED : No
CREDIT CARDS : None taken
ACCOMMODATION : 3 rooms; 2 dbl, 1 sgl.
DINING ROOM : Breakfast only
VEGETARIANS : Catered for
BAR SNACKS : Not applicable
DISABLED ACCESS : No
GARDEN : Yes, & vineyard

HOLMEHURST,
South Downs, Redruth,
Cornwall, TR15 2NW.
Tel : 01209 214415

Set in the beautiful Cornish countryside, with views over the hills and valleys of Carn Brea and Redruth, this guest house is in the perfect situation. Malcolm and Kath Dillon are the proprietors of what once was a farmhouse and have established a reputable business through their excellent talents and friendly manner! The former farmyard is now an exquisite garden which you can enjoy. A full English breakfast with a large choice of cereals is provided. Evening meal is optional and snacks are also available. Kath is a first class cook and the exceptional thing about this guest house is that there are no set rules! You can come and go as you please with a front door key as well as a bedroom key. The bedrooms are light, airy rooms with comfortable beds and wonderful views. If you happen to be a honeymoon couple then do not be surprised to find 'bubbly and flowers' in the room! All have TV and tea/coffee trays, hot and cold wash basins, and a hairdryer and iron will be provided upon request. This is an excellent base for seeing much of Cornwall and whatever your preference in relaxation, you will find it here!

USEFUL INFORMATION

OPEN : All year
CHILDREN : Welcome by arrangement
PETS : Welcome
LICENSED : No
CREDIT CARDS : None taken
ACCOMMODATION : 4 rooms; 1 dbl, 1 twin, 1 fml, 1 sgl. cots & highchairs on request.
DINING ROOM : Optional evening meal
VEGETARIANS : catered for
BAR SNACKS : Not applicable
DISABLED ACCESS : No
GARDEN : Attractive
SMOKERS : Welcome

78

JOURNEY'S END INN
Ringmore, Nr. Kingsbridge,
Devon TQ7 4HL

Tel: 01548 810205

Ringmore is a beautiful and unspoilt, thatched village in the heart of the South Hams countryside, a few minutes stroll from National Trust coastal paths and beaches. A 30 minute drive will take you to the walkers paradise of Dartmoor National Park, with its wonderful scenery, there is golf close by and fishing in the sea or river. Nestling very comfortably in all this is the Journeys End Inn, one of the oldest pubs in Devon. It started life in 1180 as a labourers cottage and was used to house men building the nearby church, it was then known as the New Inn. It was not until R.C. Sheriff stayed there in 1926 whilst writing his famous play 'Journey's End', that it acquired its present name. Today it is owned and efficiently run by James and Gillian Parkin, who look after you very well indeed, making you feel welcome and totally at home. All the attractively decorated bedrooms are ensuite, and are appointed with television and tea and coffee making facilities. The furnishing are in keeping with the age of the property enhancing the atmosphere. The food here is second to none, with an excellent breakfast to start the day well, and an evening meal to rush back for. The menu is interesting and varied, with regular 'Food Feature' weekends, and of course being close to the sea, fish is a real speciality. A short drive away is the old town of Kingsbridge with its lovely Georgian houses, and the delightful Elizabethan arcade. The Cookworthy Museum is housed in an old school which dates from 1673, here you can see several displays of local history. Dartmouth is another charming town to visit, with its Naval connection, the Britannia Royal Naval College stands proud above the town, there are delightful shops, restaurants and pubs. The 15th century Castle stands at the harbour entrance. The Journey's End Inn is a superb holiday location.

USEFUL INFORMATION

OPEN; *All year*
CHILDREN; *Welcome*
CREDIT CARDS; *Mastercard/Visa*
LICENSED; *Yes*
ACCOMMODATION; *Double and twin rooms with ensuite facilities*

DINING ROOM; *Excellent home-cooked fare Interesting and varied evening menu*
VEGETARIAN; *Catered for*
DISABLED ACCESS; *No but welcome*
GARDEN; *Seating for around 50*
PETS; *Welcome*

Chapter One

CANT COVE COTTAGES
*Cant Farm, Rock,
Nr Wadebridge, Cornwall PL27 6RL*

Tel: 01208 862841

70 acres of beautifully landscaped gardens and countryside overlooking the Camel Estuary. Facilities for golf, croquet and tennis. Whirlpool bath or sauna in accommodation. Tempted? These self-catering cottages are just delightful. Constructed partly from the original stone and partly from carefully selected local stone, these cottages look as if they have been there for centuries. Carefully rebuilding the cottages as they were, but adding triple glazing, central heating, log fires, fully equipped kitchens, has only enhanced the charm and quality. Each cottage has a private garden with summer furniture and BBQ area, and as I already stated, a whirlpool bath or sauna. Imagine returning after a hard day's walking and easing away those aches in a whirlpool bath. Wonderful! This is definitely top of the range accommodation and to verify this Cant Cove Cottages have been awarded '5 keys de luxe' by the English Tourist Board. This is the highest accolade possible, and it is truly deserved. There are six super cottages, one of which, 'The Orchard', is suitable for those of limited mobility, as it is all on one level. All cottages have power showers and the majority of bedrooms have their own facilities. The sizes of cottages range from those accommodating five to eight, and all are very spacious and immaculately cleaned and maintained. Without ever leaving the grounds there is plenty to do. The views are fantastic and there are wild life walks. Deer, foxes and badgers all abound on this land, and badger watching has become a great feature, with prizes for best photos! Bird watching is another great pastime, and if you are an artist of any degree then the views and surroundings are sure to 'inspire' you! North Cornwall is famous for its water sports and the Camel Estuary has them all. Sailing, windsurfing, water ski-ing, sea fishing and many more. The famous St Enodoc golf course is at Rock, and there is horse riding and walking along some of the most breathtaking coastline in Britain. Cant Cove Cottages have a lot to offer, whether it be a short weekend break or a longer holiday to rest and revitalise a busy life!

USEFUL INFORMATION

OPEN; All year
CHILDREN; Welcome
CREDIT CARDS; Visa/Mastercard
LICENSED; Not applicable
ACCOMMODATION; Self-catering

DINING ROOM; Not applicable
VEGETARIAN; Not applicable
DISABLED ACCESS; Some
GARDEN; 70 acres
PETS; No

IRONDALE HOUSE
67, High Street,
Rode,
Bath BA3 6PB

Tel/Fax: 01373 830730

Irondale House is an elegant detached late 18th century property situated in the centre of Rode, a small quiet village 10 miles south of Bath, and 2 minutes from open countryside. The standard of accommodation is very high, the large residents lounge is very airy and relaxing with a splendid plaster ceiling, and is furnished with mainly antiques. There are 2 double bedrooms with extra large beds, one is ensuite the other has use of a private bathroom, both have colour televisions and hair dryers and as much tea and coffee as you can drink available in the kitchen. Irondale has a wonderful walled garden with superb views towards the city of Bath. It is ideally placed for getting out and about, not far from the house is Rode Tropical Bird Gardens, with its open-air aviaries set amongst trees and lakes, with such wonderful birds as flamingos, peacocks and penguins. The elegant city of Bath steeped in history with plenty of museums, galleries, lovely shops and delightful tea rooms. For the more energetic there is golf and a driving range also riding, there are always plenty of maps and guides available from the Guest House. The AA have placed Irondale on their 'Highly Recommended' list so you can be assured of a comfortable place to stay and a very warm welcome from Jayne and Oliver Holder, the owners.

USEFUL INFORMATION

OPEN; All year
CHILDREN; Only over 12 years
CREDIT CARDS; Visa & MasterCard
LICENSED; No
ACCOMMODATION; 2 double rooms, 1 ensuite

DINING ROOM; Home-cooking, no Evening meal
VEGETARIAN; Catered for
DISABLED ACCESS; No
GARDEN; Beautiful walled with views
PETS; No

Chapter One

HIGHER RODHUISH FARM
Rodhuish, Nr Minehead,
Somerset TA24 6QL

Tel: 01984 640253

Higher Rodhuish is situated in the hamlet of Rodhuish, one and a half miles off the A39, surrounded by unspoilt countryside, on the edge of the Exmoor National Park and close to Dunster and Minehead. The Farmhouse itself provides excellent Bed and Breakfast in comfortable, friendly, centrally heated accommodation plus a breakfast that is memorable. Alan and Jennifer Thomas also have two cottages for those who prefer a self-catering holiday. Crown Cottage is semi-detached with good views of unspoilt countryside with private garden. It sleeps 5/6 people comfortably, has three bedrooms, a well equipped kitchen with electric cooker, fridge, washing machine and microwave. There is a Lounge with a woodburner, a Dining Room and Children's playroom. Colour TV and Night Storage Heaters are there as well. Payment is inclusive of electricity. Duvets and bed linen are supplied. Short breaks available with a minimum of 3 nights. 1, Crown Cottage is open all year.

Tacker Street Cottage, Roadwater is also semi-detached and sleeps six. This comfortable cottage is set in a delightful wooded valley with a large garden, one edge of which is bordered by woods and very close to a stream with a small wooden bridge, which must be crossed to reach the cottage from the lane. It has a modernised kitchen with woodburner, electric cooker, refrigerator and microwave. There is a Lounge, bathroom and three bedrooms. Heating is by electricity or open fire. 50p meter, immersion heater, colour TV. There is a car parking space nearby.

This is an ideal centre for touring coast and moors, there is superb walking, horse riding, mountain biking, bird watching. A delightful place for a relaxed, healthy holiday.

USEFUL INFORMATION

OPEN; *All year*
CHILDREN; *Welcome*
CREDIT CARDS; *None taken*
LICENSED; *No*

DINING ROOM; *Excellent farmhouse fayre*
VEGETARIAN; *Upon request*
DISABLED ACCESS; *No Facilities*
PETS; *Accepted*

THE SHRUBBERY HOTEL
Commercial Road,
Shepton Mallet, Somerset BA4 5BU

Tel: 01749 346671

This charming hotel is as welcoming to non-residents as it is to those who enjoy the luxury of staying here. It is one of those quiet places that manage to exist even amongst the hurly burly of a busy town like Shepton Mallet with its enormous Showground.

People come to The Shrubbery to enjoy both the ambience and the friendly welcome they get from Chris West and his efficient yet unobtrusive staff. There are 6 ensuite bedrooms, beautifully decorated with delightful drapes and bed linen, they are light and airy and well appointed with colour television, trouser press, hair dryer, direct dial telephone and a plentifully supplied tea and coffee tray. The Hotel was built around 1770 and retains much of its character, although the furnishings are modern, they compliment the Hotel immensely, giving it a very warm and comfortable atmosphere. Before a meal it is very pleasant to sit in the bar enjoying an aperitif whilst you peruse the interesting and frequently innovative menu - Chris spent some time in Spain and the dishes he enjoyed there have been a welcome addition to the menu. Excellently situated for touring and exploring the surrounding area. Golf, fishing, walking and information about other outdoor pursuits, are available from Chris. The Shrubbery is '3 Crowns Commended' and one of those places you would be ill advised to miss.

USEFUL INFORMATION

OPEN; All year
CHILDREN; Welcome
CREDIT CARDS; All major cards
LICENSED; Yes. Good wine list
ACCOMMODATION; 6 ensuite rooms
RESTAURANT; Superb & interesting
VEGETARIAN; Always a choice
DISABLED ACCESS; No, welcome
GARDEN; Yes with play area
PETS; Yes

Chapter One

GROVESIDE GUEST HOUSE
Vicarage Road,
Sidmouth, Devon EX10 8UQ
Tel:01395 513406

This Victorian house is well known for its hospitality and comfort. David and Brenda Pring have many years of experience in caring for people who come to stay which is evident in the smooth running of the establishment - something that only happens when you have professional people in charge. The house stands in its own grounds and is ideally situated for easy level access for the 2 minute walk to the town centre and four minutes to the sea front. Free parking space in which you may leave your car for the whole of your stay, is a godsend because Sidmouth does not have the easiest of parking facilities. Groveside has recently beenre-decorated and renovated with pretty drapes and wall papers. The comfortable lounge has a colour television, the 10 bedrooms, 7 of which are ensuite, are all attractively furnished and centrally heated as well as having televisions, shaver points and tea/coffee making facilities. Traditional English cooking is the order of the day both at breakfast and the optional evening meal.

USEFUL INFORMATION
OPEN; All year except Dec-Feb
DINING ROOM; Traditional English Non-smoking dining room
CHILDREN; Welcome
VEGETARIAN; Catered for
CREDIT CARDS; None taken
DISABLED ACCESS; No
LICENSED; No
GARDEN; Yes
ACCOMMODATION; 10 rooms 7 ensuite
PETS; No

PINN BARTON FARM
Peak Hill,
Sidmouth, Devon EX10 0NN
Tel/Fax: 01395 514004

Turn right at the seafront in Sidmouth, go up over Peak Hill and Pinn Barton is the first farm on the other side. A glorious position in an area of outstanding natural beauty, close to safe beaches and with lovely walks along the cliffs and around the farm. Highly recommended, the Sage family will welcome you warmly into their friendly, informal home. The house is open most of the year, centrally heated and all the bedrooms have an ensuite bathroom or shower. Each has TV, clock radio, hair dryers, tea/coffee making facilities. Facilities for ironing and a fridge are provided for the use of guests. A good farmhouse breakfast is served in plenty with a choice of menu. Each table has its own toaster. Bedtime drinks are served in the guest sitting room. The farmhouse is open all day and keys are provided so that you can return at anytime. Just 2 miles from Sidmouth where there are many eating places for an evening meal.

USEFUL INFORMATION
OPEN: Most of the year
DINING ROOM: Good farmhouse breakfast
CHILDREN: Welcome
VEGETARIAN: By arrangement
CREDIT CARDS: None taken
DISABLED ACCESS: No
ACCOMMODATION: Ensuite bedrooms
GARDEN: Large
PETS: By arrangement

Devon, Cornwall, Somerset and Avon

**SOUTHERN CROSS GUEST HOUSE
& TEA ROOMS**
Newton Poppleford,
Sidmouth,
Devon EX10 0DU
Tel: 01395 568439

This pretty, thatched Guest House and Tea Rooms was world famous long before its present owners, Angela Karande and John Blaymires acquired it. The previous owner for 38 years, Eileen McKenna was world renowned for her wonderful Cream Teas. Angela and John have carried on her tradition of serving large quantities of cream and Angela has already gained a reputation for her scones. The refurbishment that they have carried out within the house has made the pretty bedrooms even nicer to stay in. Two of the five bedrooms are now ensuite. The Grade II Listed house was built about 1700 and has enormous character with its timber beams. Although Southern Cross stands on the road that runs through Newton Poppleford, the house is peaceful and the garden a delightful place to enjoy a cream tea on a summers day. A Gift Shop well stocked with all sorts of things including local pottery provides visitors with a splendid opportunity to take something home which will remind them forever of one of the most charming Guest Houses and Tea Rooms in Southern England.

USEFUL INFORMATION

OPEN: All year
CHILDREN: Welcome
CREDIT CARDS: No
ACCOMMODATION: 5 rooms 2 ensuite
GARDEN: Delightful & open for teas and light lunches
RESTAURANT: Renowned for Cream Teas Also serves light lunches
VEGETARIAN: On request
LICENSED: No
DISABLED ACCESS: Not accommodation

STILL COTTAGE
North Street, Somerton,
Somerset TA11 7NY
Tel: 01458 272323

Still Cottage is a 300 year old Georgian town house which is located in the historic town of Somerton. This cottage is very attractive and furnished to extremely high standards. All of the furniture is antique and there are tea and coffee making facilities, wash basins and shaver points in each room. Breakfast is home cooked traditional and evening meals are optional by prior arrangement. The meals are served in the charming flag stoned breakfast room. There is a comfortable drawing room with TV for guests to use. Somerton is in a good position for visiting many areas of the West Country and there are plenty of local attractions within easy reach.

USEFUL INFORMATION

OPEN: All Year Round
CHILDREN: No
PETS: No
CREDIT CARDS: None Taken
ACCOMMODATION: 3 Rooms
EVENING MEAL: By Prior Arrangement
VEGETARIAN: By Arrangement
DISABLED ACCESS: No
GARDEN: Spacious, Well Kept

Chapter One

WILLOW BRIDGE
Milford Road,
Sidmouth,
Devon EX10 8DR
Tel/Fax: 01395 513599

Sidmouth has managed to escape the intrusion of the 20th century and remains a charming seaside town with predominantly Regency architecture. It nestles between two grand headlands and is surrounded by wonderful natural countryside. It is renowned for it's delightfully mild climate and offers a great variety of activities including golf, bowls, tennis and swimming in a modern heated indoor pool as well as in the sea. It's two beaches are suited to safe bathing, sailing and fishing. Local entertainment caters for all tastes with theatre, cinema, concerts, carnivals not to mention the very famous annual Folk Festival. Willow Bridge Hotel is a small private hotel in an enviable position. It is situated in a quiet corner plot with an award winning garden, overlooking the River Sid and the tranquil Byes Park, yet it is only a short easy walk to the Esplanade and town centre. It has it's own guests car park and a fine reputation for it's standard of comfort and a very warm welcome. All rooms are attractively furnished and prettily decorated and are ensuite with colour television, tea and coffee making facilities, radio alarm and hair dryers. The pretty dining room makes eating a pleasure, the varying menu offers traditional English fare as well as dishes from around the world. The wine list is well chosen and at sensible prices. The residents lounge offers you comfort and relaxation, with plenty of books and games which are available for your interest. The proprietors Brenda and David Smith aim to please and ensure that time spent at Willow Bridge is enjoyed by you in every way.

USEFUL INFORMATION

OPEN; All year
CHILDREN; Preferably over 7 years
CREDIT CARDS; None taken
LICENSED; Yes. Good wines
ACCOMMODATION; 6 ensuite
PETS; If well behaved
DINING ROOM; Excellent breakfast & Traditional evening meal
VEGETARIAN; Yes
DISABLED ACCESS; Not really
GARDEN; Yes

HOLLYMOUNT COTTAGE
Avonwick, South Brent,
Devon TQ10 9NA
Tel: 01364 73460

Hollymount Cottage nestles in behind Avonwick Church and lives up to the "cottage" image. Furnished in pine, this delightful cottage offers traditional home cooking of ample quantity and excellent quality! South Brent is really a picturesque area with rolling hills and scenic valleys but also within easy reach of towns such as the lovely Totnes with it's narrow quaint streets and excellent shops. Plenty of sport facilities are at hand with Ivybridge Leisure Centre nearby.

USEFUL INFORMATION

OPEN : All year
CHILDREN : Over 3yrs
PETS : No
CREDIT CARDS : None taken
LICENSED : No
ACCOMMODATION : 1 Fml room, consists of 1 dbl bed & bunk beds, with en suite facilities
RESTAURANT : Not applicable
BAR FOOD : Not applicable
VEGETARIAN : & special diets by arrangement
DISABLED ACCESS : No
GARDEN : Yes

THE GRANGE FARMHOUSE
Barkla Shop,
St Agnes, Cornwall TR5 0XN

Tel: 01872 552332

This is a small working farm run by the family together with the guest house. What is so good about it is the fact that guests are invited to participate if they wish in the joys of farming. You can watch the milking, feed the animals and chickens, mix with the calves and goats. The farmhouse is warm and comfortable, the smoke free bedrooms pleasantly furnished together with TV and a beverage tray. The family room which sleeps up to 6, has everything for a family with children from birth upwards. The bathrooms are equipped with shaver points and there is plenty of hot water. Breakfast which is cooked fresh on the Aga is served at a time convenient to you and served in a room overlooking the field where the cows and calves graze. Several beaches are within a short distance and the area is ideally situated for walking and visiting all parts of Cornwall including some famous Gardens.

USEFUL INFORMATION
OPEN: All year.
CHILDREN: welcome.
CREDIT CARDS: No
ACCOMMODATION; Double, twin, single, also family room sleeps up to 6 persons
DINING ROOM: Delicious breakfast Evening meal by arrangement
VEGETARIAN: Catered for
DISABLED ACCESS: Yes
GARDEN: Yes with barbecue
PETS: Yes

RIVENDELL GUEST HOUSE
7 Porthminster Terrace,
St Ives,
Cornwall TR26 2DQ
Tel: 01736 794923

Rivendell has all the charm and elegance which existed when it was built as a Victorian Captain's house. The owners, Barrie and Angela Walker have enhanced that charm by carefully bringing the house into the 20th century. Furnished in a stylish but comfortable manner, the rooms are spacious and high ceilinged and the food prepared by the resident chef is memorable. Stay here and you will not only receive excellent service but be at the heart of all sorts of outdoor pursuits for which St Ives is famous. Definitely a place not to be missed.

USEFUL INFORMATION
OPEN; All year.
CHILDREN; Welcome
CREDIT CARDS; None taken
LICENSED; No
ACCOMMODATION; 5dbl 1 twin 1fml. 1 sgl. All ensuite
DINING ROOM; Varying menu. High standard
BAR FOOD; Not applicable
VEGETARIAN; Yes & other diets by arrangement
DISABLED ACCESS; No
GARDEN; No

Chapter One

BOSKERRIS HOTEL
*Boskerris Road,
Carbis Bay,
St Ives,
Cornwall TR26 2NQ*

Tel: 01736 795295

Marie Monk and her son Spencer are the proud owners of this superb hotel situated on one and a half acres of ground overlooking Carbis Bay. Having taken over the hotel 10 years ago, Marie and Spencer have worked hard to improve the already high standards of the hotel, and the success of this is measured by the number of people who return year after year. All rooms are equipped with modern furniture and have TV, telephone and tea and coffee as standard. There is a large and comfortable lounge with adjoining cocktail bar where you can mix with the other guests, or there is a TV room where you can enjoy your favourite programmes in peace and quiet. The dining room, run by chef Colin Williams, is delightful with an everchanging menu which stimulates and surprises. Fresh local produce is used wherever possible with herbs from Colin's specially planted garden. There is a fine selection of wines to compliment the food. Outdoors there is a large heated swimming pool which overlooks the sea and is ideal to relax by. There is also a putting green and table tennis for those slightly more energetic. The gardens are superb and all due credit is given to the gardener David Brown. The Boskerris Hotel is in an ideal position overlooking St Ives harbour on one side and Godrey Head the other. A stroll along the cliff path will bring you to St Ives with it's wonderful artists quarter and quaint whitewashed cottages. There are numerous shops, restaurants and a visit to the harbour is a must. Many artists have worked here such as Whistler, and you can still see many today with their easels and paints, trying to capture this wonderful scenery. Cornwall is a stunning county with ample entertainment to please everyone. The historic houses, gardens and medieval castles are some of the best in the country. The legends and myths are many. There is fishing, golf, walking, surfing, sailing and much much more. What better way to spend a holiday than to visit this land of Celtic legends, and at the end of the day relax and be cosseted in this fabulous hotel.

USEFUL INFORMATION

OPEN; Easter-November
CHILDREN; Welcome
CREDIT CARDS; All major cards
LICENSED; Full
ACCOMMODATION; 19 rooms, 17 ensuite
PETS; By arrangement

DINING ROOM; Superb English fare
VEGETARIAN; Catered for
DISABLED ACCESS; 2 x Grnd floor bedrooms
GARDEN; Excellent

SURFSIDE YELLOW HOUSE
Godrevy Terrace,
St. Ives,
Cornwall TR26 1JA
Tel: 01736 793825

Surfside Guest House in St. Ives is a mid terraced Victorian house that once belonged to a ship's captain. This lovely home has panoramic views over Porthmoer and Porthminster beaches and is within sound of the sea and only 3 minutes walk from the town centre. It is also next to the famous St. Ives 'Tate Gallery' which was opened by Prince Charles. Art in all forms abounds in this town. St. Ives is a well known and excellent base for seeing the county of Cornwall. It is only 12 miles from Land's End with it's attractions and coastal walks. There is a seal sanctuary close by at Gweek where you can see the great work done by the vets and rescuers of these loveable creatures. The Cornish moors are also accessible with their rugged wild scenery and there are walks for all abilities. Frank and Chrissie Adams run this friendly house and look after their guests well. All rooms are well furnished and have TV, tea and coffee in each. There is a comfortable residents lounge and a dining room. Relax in these pleasant surroundings after a busy day sight seeing or enjoying the multitude of other activities available.

USEFUL INFORMATION
OPEN; All year
CHILDREN; Welcome, babysitting available
PETS; By arrangement
CREDIT CARDS; None taken
ACCOMMODATION; 6 rooms, 2 ensuite
EVENING MEAL; No
VEGETARIAN; Yes
DISABLED ACCESS; No
GARDEN; No, but patio with views over beaches, rooftops and harbour
Free parking available

THE COUNT HOUSE
Trenwith Square, St Ives
Cornwall TR26 1DJ
Tel: 01736 795369

The unusual name of this house comes from 1825 when it was built as a place where the tin miners were paid their wages. Throughout, there are exposed granite walls, old oak beams, pews and many other fascinating features. One of the bedrooms is ideal for that special occasion with it's four poster bed and jacuzzi. Ken and Cheryl Canning are wonderful hosts, only too happy to please and exuding a warm friendly welcome. All meals are prepared and served by Ken and Cheryl and there is an excellent 4 course evening meal which is optional. The bar, which depicts the Trenwith Mine and features mining throughout, is well stocked and specialises in quality wines. St Ives is a wonderful place in itself but is also excellent for seeing the glories of West Cornwall and taking home the memories of a unforgettable holiday.

USEFUL INFORMATION
OPEN : All year
CHILDREN : Over 12yrs
PETS : No
CREDIT CARDS : None taken
LICENSED : Yes
ACCOMMODATION : 9 rooms; all en suite.
RESTAURANT : English Fayre
BAR FOOD : Out of season
VEGETARIAN : Yes, as required
DISABLED ACCESS : Not really
GARDEN : Patio area with benches

Chapter One

THE WILLOWS,
5, Ayr Terrace,
St Ives, Cornwall TR26 1ED
Tel/Fax: 01736 794703
With Alastair and Lynn's previous extensive experience in the hotel trade it is not surprising to find that the fully licensed Willows Guest House, which overlooks the town of St Ives, offers an extremely high standard. In this turn of the century property all guest bedrooms are individually appointed and include colour television, clock alarm radio, tea and coffee making facilities, hair dryer and fresh flowers. The furnishings are modern and extremely tasteful, and most rooms afford a sea view. In the evenings enjoy a drink in the lounge. Dinner is not served, however light snacks and childrens meals are available on request and one can be assured of the best Cornish Cream Teas around. Local produce is used whenever possible to ensure freshness. The Willows is ideally situated being 5 minutes walk from the Tate Gallery, the Town Centre and Porthmeor Beach which boasts a blue flag ensuring cleanliness and safety particularly for the younger members of the family. Water sports include windsurfing and surfing. Further outdoor pursuits to be found locally include fishing, golf, riding and walking. Children are welcome but no pets. The Willows is a strictly non-smoking establishment.

USEFUL INFORMATION
OPEN; All year
CHILDREN; Welcome
CREDIT CARDS; None taken
LICENSED; Yes
ACCOMMODATION; 3dbl (1 ensuite shower) 1 twin, 1 single
DINING ROOM; Home-cooked fare
VEGETARIAN; Catered for
DISABLED ACCESS; No
GARDEN; Patio. Parking by arrangement
PETS; No

DYE COTTAGE
ST. Neot, Nr. Liskeard,
Cornwall PL14 6NG
Tel: 01579 321394

Described by a visitor as 'a dream house and location' Dye Cottage situated in the heart of the unspoilt village of St. Neot is a Grade II Listed 17th century cottage, with oak beams, slate floors and twisting staircases. Within easy reach of many places of interest, with signposted walks through quiet country lanes, cycle tracks for mountain bikes and riding and fishing nearby. Brian and Sue Williams offer one pretty double bedroom, with TV and tea/coffee making facilities and two single rooms. Visitors have their own lounge with television from which French windows will take you into the garden and down to the river, you are welcome to use the garden and summerhouse. You can sit on the terrace to read or sunbathe and perhaps watch the Sunday cricket match taking place just across the river. Excellent breakfast with home-made bread, fresh eggs and fruit from the garden when available. No evening meals but the London Inn, an old coaching inn opposite the cottage serves good food.

USEFUL INFORMATION
OPEN: All year
CHILDREN: Welcome
CREDIT CARDS: None taken
ACCOMMODATION: 3 rooms, 1double, 2 single
PETS: Yes
DINING ROOM: Delicious breakfast with home-made bread. No evening meal available
VEGETARIAN: If required
DISABLED ACCESS: No
GARDEN: Yes

THE PHEASANT HOTEL & RESTAURANT
Seavington St Mary, Nr Ilminster,
Somerset TA19 0QH

Tel: 01460 240502

    When you first see The Pheasant Hotel and Restaurant you are immediately struck by the beauty and charm of this delightful 17th century converted farmhouse. It is encompassed by exceptionally well tended gardens full of flowers, shrubs and trees, with sweeping lawns, where during the summer months chairs and tables are set, so you can relax and enjoy the peace and tranquillity of this stunning location. No wonder the BBC filmed some parts of 'Tothe Manor Born' here. The interior is just as pleasing, the bar has a beamed ceiling, a large inglenook fireplace where logs crackle and burn on chilly winters evenings, while you relax in comfort with your drink and peruse the menu. The restaurant also has oak beams, subtle decor, comfortable chairs, and tables covered in crisp clean linen with candles and fresh flowers. The lighting is gentle, enhancing the intimate atmosphere. It is in this delightful setting you are served excellent food, the chef is very talented, and has created an imaginative and varied menu to suit all tastes. The Pheasant also has several outstanding guest rooms, they have all been individually designed and tastefully furnished, offering an extremely high calibre of comfort and luxury. Each room has its own name, The Camelot has an elegant four-poster bed with colourful drapes and canopy. The Dorset is cottage in style with a wonderful original solid brass bedstead, and floral drapes and bed cover enhancing the light airy feel. The other rooms are just as beautiful. All have the privacy of an ensuite bathroom, colour television, direct dial telephone, hair dryer, trouser press, complimentary toiletries and a tea and coffee tray. Some of the suites have an additional room for an extra member of the family. There are two cottages in the grounds also offering superior accommodation.

    There is plenty to do in the area including golf, horse riding and walking, this is excellent cycling country, just what you need to work up a good appetite. There are several National Trust properties to visit. Cricket St Thomas is only a short drive away. The owners Mark and Tania Harris and Robert and Maureen Collinge work very hard to make The Pheasant what it is, a superb, comfortable, friendly Hotel with outstanding food.

USEFUL INFORMATION

OPEN; All year
CHILDREN; Welcome
CREDIT CARDS; All major cards except Diners
LICENSED; Yes
ACCOMMODATION; 8 luxurious rooms plus 2 cottages in the grounds
RESTAURANT; Outstanding A La Carte Menu, Sunday Lunches
VEGETARIAN; Very well catered for
DISABLED ACCESS; Yes
GARDEN; Beautiful with lawn and flowers
PETS; No

Chapter One

THE LONDON INN
St Neot,
Cornwall PL14 6NG

Tel: 01579 320263

Bodmin Moor, a vast area of some 80sq miles, granite tors and swirling mists give a sense of loneliness and mystery, and where the scenery hasn't changed for centuries. On the edge of this wilderness is the charming village of St Neot, where the close village community still exists. Adding to that sense of community is The London Inn, a favourite watering hole for locals and visitors alike, where a warm and friendly welcome is extended by the owner Stefan Jones. It is situated next to the church of St Aneatus, renowned for its impressive 16th and 17th century stained glass windows, one window depicts the Creation with stories of Adam and Eve. The London Inn is a 17th century Coaching House, and retains many of the original features with low oak beamed ceilings, exposed stone walls and fine open fire places. The guest rooms have been newly refurbished, and are beautifully appointed with hand built pine furniture by local craftsmen, and attractive linen and drapes. All rooms have ensuite facilities, television, direct dial telephone and a beverages tray. The rooms have also been fully sound insulated. The dining room has a reputation of its own, here you can dine on the finest Cornish fare at sensible prices. The menu is very comprehensive to suit all tastes, and is designed so that you can choose a quick and wholesome snack or a 3 course meal. There are also salads, sandwiches, a 'Well Behaved' children's menu and some sumptuous puddings. You will not leave here hungry! There is a small wine list to accompany your meal, you may also like to try one of the excellent local Casked Conditioned Ales, one of them is served in the House of Commons. Once you have entered the doors you will be drawn here again and again.

USEFUL INFORMATION

OPEN; Weekdays: 11.30-3.00pm
6.30-11.00pm. Sat & Sun: all day
CHILDREN; Welcome
CREDIT CARDS; All major cards
LICENSED; Yes
ACCOMMODATION; 3 ensuite rooms
in the Inn
PETS; In the bars but not in the restaurant area

RESTAURANT; Excellent varied
menu from snack to 3 course dinner
VEGETARIAN; Good choice
DISABLED ACCESS; Side access for
wheelchairs, but not in bedrooms
GARDEN; Yes with tables and chairs
to the side and front

Devon, Cornwall, Somerset and Avon

LITTLE PADDOCKS
Aish Road, Stoke Gabriel,
Nr Totnes, South Devon TQ9 6PX
Tel: 01803 782251

Little Paddocks in Stoke Gabriel is run by Rita and David Blackmore. This high quality ground floor bed and breakfast, offers excellent accommodation set in it's own grounds within an area of outstanding natural beauty. With very comfortable bedrooms, TV, tea and coffee as standard. Stoke Gabriel, close to the historical town of Totnes is a lovely village situated on the River Dart. It looks as if time has stood still with a fascinating church and reputedly 1000 year old yew tree. A wonderful place to stay and a perfect retreat for exploring the South West.

USEFUL INFORMATION
OPEN; All year except Christmas and New Year
CHILDREN; Over 14 years
CREDIT CARDS; None taken
LICENSED; No
ACCOMMODATION; 3 ensuite rooms
DINING ROOM; Traditional English breakfast
VEGETARIAN; Catered for
DISABLED ACCESS; Some
GARDEN; Yes
PETS; No

BONROSE
125 Coombe Vale Road,
Teignmouth,
Devon TQ14 9EN
Tel: 01626 772099

Joan Osborne is the owner of this family run guest house and ensures that her guests have everything to make them feel relaxed and at home. The house is only 10 minutes from the beach and town centre, and there are plenty of amenities, with the local bus service passing the door. The rooms are pleasant and bright with central heating, and there is a residents lounge and dining room. Breakfast is full English and evening meal is available. All year round Joan offers a discount for OAP's and children aged 3-10 years. Baby sitting is also available free of charge. There is plenty to see and do in this lovely area, each year on November 15th, 16th, and 17th is a Jazz Festival, where a good time is had by all.

USEFUL INFORMATION
OPEN; All year
CHILDREN; Welcome
CREDIT CARDS; None taken
LICENSED; No
ACCOMMODATION; 4 rooms, 1 double, 1 family, 1 twin, 1 single.
DINING ROOM; Traditional English fare
VEGETARIAN; Catered for
DISABLED ACCESS; No
GARDEN; Pleasant
PETS; Small dogs welcome

Chapter One

KNOWLE MANOR
Timberscombe, Nr Dunster,
Somerset TA24 6TZ

Tel: 01643 841342
Fax: 01643 841644

When you think of Somerset you automatically think of Exmoor the vast area of steep combes, rugged pasture and open spaces, where sheep, cattle and the famous ponies wander around wherever they please. There are many charming villages tucked away and none more so than Dunster, a medieval village with olde worlde houses and a Yarn Market dating back to the 17th century. Two miles from here is Knowle Manor where Sue Lamacraft and her family run a hotel and riding centre. Knowle Manor is steeped in history and is mentioned in the Domesday Book. The house itself is an artistic reproduction of a Jacobean style of architecture, and was part of a large estate which was broken down, and now comprises 80 acres. There are 18 rooms; 4 double, 3 twin, 1 single and 9 family, 12 of which are ensuite, all are very comfortable. Each room has a TV point for the use of portable televisions, which are available on request. Room service is available for which a charge is made. The furnishings are a mixture of antique and modern which blend well together. Breakfast is a good traditional full English meal, to set you up for the day. Vegetarians and special diets are also catered for. A delicious evening meal is served using fresh local ingredients wherever possible. Horse lovers will be in their element, however there are other activities and places of interest including Porlock, Dunster Castle and further afield Lynton and Lynmouth. There is also the West Somerset Railway, steam and diesel trains travel a 20 mile track from Minehead to Bishops Lydeard. The coast is just a short drive away. Whether you like horses or not, Sue and her family are looking forward to meeting you and welcoming you to their lovely home.

USEFUL INFORMATION

OPEN; All year
CHILDREN; Welcome
CREDIT CARDS; None taken
ACCOMMODATION; 18 rooms, 12 ensuite, 4 double, 3 twin, 1 single, 9 family
DINING ROOM; Traditional home-cooked fare
VEGETARIAN; Catered for + special diets
DISABLED ACCESS; No, but welcome
GARDEN; Yes
PETS; Yes

Devon, Cornwall, Somerset and Avon

BICKLEIGH COTTAGE HOTEL
*Bickleigh Bridge, Nr. Tiverton,
Devon EX16 8RJ*

Tel: 01884 855230

This beautiful hotel which is situated on the A396, four miles south of Tiverton has been in the Cochrane family since 1933 and is situated on the bank of the River Exe near Bickleigh Bridge, a landmark famous for its beauty. The original cottage was built in 1640, with additions in the 1970s and with recent refurbishments, most rooms have en suite facilities. The hotel is perfect for access to Exmoor and Dartmoor and also for Exeter city. If you are a walker then Mr & Mrs Cochrane are full of information regarding this pastime.

USEFUL INFORMATION

OPEN : April to October inc
CHILDREN : No
CREDIT CARDS : Visa / Master
LICENSED : Residents license
ACCOMMODATION : 8 rooms, 7 en suite
RESTAURANT : Set evening meal
BAR FOOD : No
VEGETARIAN : On request
DISABLED ACCESS : No
GARDEN : Cottage style with superb river frontage

DURANT ARMS
*Ashprington, Totnes,
Devon TQ9 7UP
Tel: 01803 732240*

A warm welcome awaits you at The Durant Arms in Ashprington where Graham and Eileen Ellis keep one of the happiest country inns in the South Hams, dating back to the early 18th century. The Durant's long-established reputation for fine food is well deserved. With an extensive A La Carte menu as well as a wide selection of bar meals, there is something for everyone, including vegetarians, both lunch times and evenings. The bar offers a wide selection of beer, wines and spirits with at least two Real Ales always available. The Durant is popular for bed and breakfast with two delightful ensuite bedrooms, each with central heating. In addition, an old barn in the garden has been converted into a delightful cottage with a comfortable lounge, bathroom and double bedroom. For larger parties there is an additional single bed in the bedroom and a single sofa bed in the lounge. Most guests enjoy dining at the inn but with its fitted kitchen the cottage is also available on a self-catering basis. In fine weather many visitors to the cottage enjoy their meals on its small terrace overlooking the colourful garden.

USEFUL INFORMATION

OPEN: All year. Closed on Christmas evening
CHILDREN: Welcome
CREDIT CARDS: All except Diners/Amex
ACCOMMODATION: 2 ensuite bedrooms in the inn plus 1 double ensuite in the cottage
DISABLED ACCESS: No special facilities but welcome
VEGETARIAN: Catered for
PETS: Welcome in the inn

Chapter One

CHALLIS
12 Lower Town, Sampford Peverell,
Tiverton, Devon EX16 7BJ

Tel: 01884 820620

Mary and Graeme Isaac are the justly proud owners of Challis, a fine Victorian house in the centre of the village of Sampford Peverell. It has much about it that gladdens the heart with direct access to the tow-path of the Grand Western Canal from the garden. Fishing is available and there are lovely walks deep into the Devonshire countryside along the canal tow-path. Sampford Peverell is only 5 minutes from the M5 (Junction 27) and has two local Inns which Mary and Graeme are happy to recommend for meals throughout the year. The market town of Tiverton is 6 miles distant and the cities of Exeter and Taunton just 16 miles away. The National Trust's properties Killerton and Knightshayes Court are within easy distance. Challis could not be a better base from which to explore the Moors or the North and South coastlines.

Inside this dignified house you will receive a very warm welcome. There is a great lack of formality which in no way detracts from the professional manner in which the house is run. All the bedrooms have central heating, colour TV, tea/coffee making facilities and wash basins with H & C. In addition one of the double rooms is fully ensuite with another double having a shower ensuite. Great to visit at anytime of the year the midweek or weekend breaks on offer out of season are incredibly good value. Whilst Graeme and Mary concentrate on Bed and Breakfast, they are quite willing to provide you with a well-cooked, home-made evening meal if you ask in advance. The peaceful garden, complete with garden furniture for your use, is delightful with access to the Grand Western Canal Towpath. There is ample parking and whilst the house is not licensed you are very welcome to bring your own wine.

USEFUL INFORMATION

OPEN: All year
CHILDREN: Welcome
CREDIT CARDS: None taken
ACCOMMODATION: 4 rooms, 1 ensuite
LICENSED: No
PETS: Welcome

DINING ROOM: Excellent breakfast
Evening meal by arrangement
VEGETARIAN: Upon request
DISABLED ACCESS: No
GARDEN: Yes with garden furniture

Devon, Cornwall, Somerset and Avon

HIGHER WESTERN RESTAURANT WITH ROOMS
Oakford, Tiverton,
Devon EX16 9JE
Tel: 013984 210

The charming 17th century Old World licensed restaurant situated on the Taunton/Barnstaple Holiday Route B3227, one and a half miles west of Oakford is owned and run by Colin and Christine Cook. In addition to the imaginative and excellent food, cooked to order, using local and their own produce, Colin and Christine also offer quality accommodation in 2 Family rooms and 1 Double. The bedrooms are all ensuite with TV and a beverage tray. It could not be a better place for anyone wanting to enjoy good food, well chosen wines and above all seeking peace and quiet. The coast at Minehead, Lynton and Lynmouth is not far off, there is fishing at Dulverton - the Cooks can arrange a licence. Horse riding at Ansty Farm is five miles away and there are wonderful walks on Exmoor for which Christine will supply you with information. Children are welcome. There is ample parking and cyclists can be sure of free, safe storage for their machines. Home-made bread and ice-cream, home produce, a full English breakfast just add to the reason for staying at Higher Western.

USEFUL INFORMATION
OPEN: All year
CHILDREN: Welcome
CREDIT CARDS: Visa/Mastercard
LICENSED: Yes
ACCOMMODATION: 2 family rooms, 1 double, all ensuite
DINING ROOM: Excellent food
DISABLED ACCESS: No
GARDEN: Ample parking
PETS: Yes

LITTLE HOLWELL
Collipriest, Tiverton,
Devon EX16 4PT
Tel: 01844 257590

This delightful 13th century farmhouse tucked away in the wonderful rolling hills of the Exe Valley is just one and half miles south of Tiverton. When you arrive at this warm and friendly house you are greeted with a cup of tea, just what you need after your journey. Little Holwell is a non-smoking house and is furnished in a traditional farmhouse style, it also has central heating and in the dining room there is a huge Inglenook fireplace. The bedrooms are very comfortable, all have wash hand basins, hair dryers, radios, tea and coffee making facilities and the most stunning views overlooking the deep valley and woodlands. The lady of the house Mrs. Ruth Hill-King will serve a large traditional English breakfast, in the evening there is an excellent home-cooked 3 course meal. Little Holwell is ideally placed for touring, there is plenty to do in the area including fishing, golf, riding, cycling, and wonderful walks on Exmoor and Dartmoor. This really is a peaceful location and a lovely setting for a holiday.

USEFUL INFORMATION
OPEN; All year except Christmas
CHILDREN; By prior arrangement
CREDIT CARDS; Accepted, not Diners/Amex
LICENSED; No
ACCOMMODATION; 3 rooms, 2 double, 1 family, 1 ensuite, NON SMOKING HOUSE
DINING ROOM; Excellent home-cooked fare, 3 course evening meal
VEGETARIAN; Catered for
DISABLED ACCESS; No
GARDEN; Yes
PETS; No

Chapter One

SUITE DREAMS HOTEL
Steep Hill,
Maidencombe, Torquay TQ1 4TS

Tel: 01803 313900

Many hotels are beautifully appointed but few have had so much care and attention paid to even the smallest detail to ensure perfection. Every room is named after a tree and all the interior furniture is finished in either walnut or cherry. You may well find yourself sleeping in The Oak Room, The Chestnut Room, Sycamore, Beech or the magnificent Magnolia. In addition to every room being ensuite there are additional touches like ironing boards which are skilfully hidden behind full length mirrors, a fridge, a hairdryer as well as a plentifully supplied beverage tray, TV and Direct Dial Phones. Add to this comfort a wonderful view over the sea or over unspoilt countryside, a terrace with chairs and tables where you can laze to your hearts content. Reserve Sycamore, Beech or the magnificent Magnolia, and you will find bay windows, patio doors and direct access onto the sun terrace.

Maidencombe is a delightfully secluded place with its own beach and just below the hotel is the Thatched Tavern, a old Devon freehouse with fragrant, flower filled gardens. Within easy distance there is riding, sailing, watersports and birdwatching while Torbay simply stretches out before your eyes with all it has to offer including excellent shops and theatres. Ken and Lorraine James are the owners who greet you with true Devonian hospitality. This cheerful couple are developing the catering at Suite Dreams and as from the Spring of 1997 delicious evening meals will be available as well as the sumptuous breakfast currently on offer. Vegetarians are catered for. Also in the Spring the hotel will be licensed and one can imagine nothing nicer than dining at a table overlooking the sea, enjoying the perfectly cooked meal and a wine from the well chosen list, and at the same time chatting over what you have seen during the day in this glorious part of Devon.

Children are very welcome and cots and highchairs are available. Pets too may come to Suite Dreams but only by prior arrangement. Whilst there are no specially adapted rooms for the disabled, some of the bedrooms are on the ground floor.

USEFUL INFORMATION

OPEN;All year
CHILDREN;Welcome
CREDIT CARDS;Visa/Master/Amex

RESTAURANT;From Spring 1997
VEGETARIAN;Always one dish
DISABLED ACCESS;Some ground floor rooms

LICENSED;From Spring 1997
ACCOMMODATION;6dbl 3tw 3 family all ensuite

GARDEN;Yes. Sun terrace

OLD HAZARD
Higher Plymouth Road,
Harberton, Totnes,
Devon TQ9 7LN

Tel: 01803 862495

Do you yearn to escape the hustle and bustle of modern day living? Then Old Hazard offers just this welcome opportunity. A delightful haven with the very best accommodation, run by Mike and Janet Griffiths, Old Hazard is a former farm and the site is mentioned in the Domesday Book. Two holiday units are offered, both furnished and equipped to a high standard and as clean as a new pin for every visitor. Sleeping 4/5 persons is the well proportioned Farmhouse Flat, situated on the 1st floor with access on this level, comprising large lounge/dining room, bathroom, kitchen/breakfast room and 2 bedrooms, 1 double and 1 twin with wash hand basin. The second option, The Linhay, an attractive and cosy cottage converted from an original barn sleeps 3 people in 2 pretty bedrooms, one double and one single, with convenient bathroom. An open plan lounge/kitchen leads from a small entrance hall with a stable door from parking area. Old Hazard is conveniently located just three miles from Totnes and within easy reach of the spectacular Dartmoor National Park where walking, horse riding and fishing are readily available. It is an easy drive to the South Devon coastline with it's abundance of activities, surfing, swimming and wonderful walks. Discover secluded coves and fascinating villages with many attractive inns and restaurants then retire to the peace and seclusion of Old Hazard. What could be better?

USEFUL INFORMATION

OPEN; All year
CHILDREN; Welcomed
CREDIT CARDS; None taken
LICENSED; Not applicable
ACCOMMODATION; 2 self-contained properties

DISABLED ACCESS; No, although level access Welcomed
GARDEN; Linhay has secluded private walled patio. Flat has lawned garden adjacent to open farmland and car parking
PETS; Yes, welcomed

**1 CHURCH COTTAGES &
THE OLD SCHOOL**

*Littlehempston,
Totnes,
Devon
TQ9 6LY*

Tel: 01803 862194 (1 Church Cottages)

Tel: 01803 862705 (The Old School)

The village of Littlehempston is well worth a visit with its old bridges, thatched cottages and very nice pub/restaurant. Accommodation here can be found either at The Old School or 1 Church Cottages, both of which are excellent and run in a very friendly manner.

The Old School has 1 double ensuite bedroom with a complimentary beverages tray. It also has a really friendly dog which will happily go for a walk with guests apart from when its dark, it's scared of the dark! The garden is very pleasant with quiet secluded areas.

1 Church Cottages is similarly situated but may be perhaps a little quieter. There are 2 bedrooms, 1 double and 1 twin both have wash hand basins and a tea and coffee tray.

There is also a bathroom for your use. A residents lounge with a TV. The garden again is very nicely done. Both owners are friends and help each with guests and all in all manage to portray a most friendly village atmosphere.

USEFUL INFORMATION

OPEN; *All year*
DINING ROOM; *Good home cooking*
CHILDREN; *Welcome at 1 Church Cottages*
VEGETARIAN; *Catered for*
CREDIT CARDS; *None taken*
DISABLED ACCESS; *Not really*
LICENSED; *No*
GARDEN; *Both very pleasant & spacious*
ACCOMMODATION; *The Old School has*
PETS; *No*
*1 double ensuite, 1 Church Cottages
has 2 rooms, 1 double, 1 twin*

SPRINGFIELD HOUSE
Tuckenhay, Totnes,
Devon TQ9 7EQ

Tel: 01803 732225
Fax: 01803 732843

Springfield House dates back to 1760 and is owned by the friendly Viv Whybrow. This is a delightful place which seems to excel in the hospitality industry. Everything has been very well thought out to ensure the comfort and relaxation of the guests. All rooms are traditionally furnished and have hair dryers, bath robes, tea and coffee as standard. Breakfast is served in your bedroom between 8 and 10am, and the choice is really excellent. From a Champagne breakfast to a New York breakfast, which includes fruit juice, home smoked salmon with cream cheese, chopped hard boiled eggs and fresh bagels, followed by oven fresh croissants and preserves. Does this sound delicious? Well this is only a sample of what is on offer. During the summer breakfast is also served in the garden or on the terrace overlooking the valley. The walled garden is private and very pleasant. There are views over Bow Creek to the River Dart beyond. Spend some time in the heated outdoor swimming pool or relax with a jacuzzi and sauna. There are some resident guests at the hotel who will be only too pleased to enjoy your company; four donkeys, a Shetland, four labradors and two peacocks. But be careful, they are inclined to invite themselves on a stroll to the local pub and are not very good at paying when its their round! There are two pubs in the hamlet of Tuckenhay, one of which is just at the bottom of Springfield's drive. Both are within walking distance and a pleasant evening can be spent at either. Viv will recommend come eating places, all in the local vicinity. Springfield is one of those charming informal places with an air of civilisation which has been appreciated by guests such as Sir Clement Freud, who praised it in his column in the Times. Tuckenhay is a river side hamlet located between the medieval town of Totnes and the ancient port of Dartmouth. It is an ideal location for touring, with the mystery and seduction of Dartmoor within access and many excellent beaches close by. The steam trains of Dart Valley are something not to be missed, or perhaps a trip on the River Dart appeals. Salcombe, Kingsbridge and Torbay are all a short drive away. Viv is only too happy to advise and help you plan your trips, and a more pleasant stay would be difficult to imagine.

USEFUL INFORMATION

OPEN; All year
DINING ROOM; Wonderful breakfasts
CHILDREN; Under 12 years by arrangement   Evening by arrangement
CREDIT CARDS; None taken   **VEGETARIAN**; Catered for
LICENSED; No   **DISABLED ACCESS**; Not really
ACCOMMODATION; 3 ensuite rooms   **GARDEN**; Yes with heated swimming
PETS; By arrangement   pool

THE GEORGE HOTEL,
Market Square,
Crewkerne,
Somerset TA18 7LP

Tel: 01460 73650

For over four hundred years The George Hotel has been welcoming travellers and in the friendly and capable hands of Lina and Frank Joyce that tradition is as strong as ever today. They bought the hotel in 1994 and have spent the last two years refurbishing it and providing the facilities that the modern day visitor demands. That they have done so without destroying the ambience of yesteryear says much for their caring concern. You will find the ten double or twin bedrooms are centrally heated with tea and coffee making facilities, direct dial telephone, colour television and hair dryer. Each room has either en-suite shower or full en-suite bathroom. In addition there is one en-suite single and two basic singles, all of which have most of the facilities enjoyed by the double rooms.

Both the George Bar and Lamplighters Bar are haunts for local people and a friendly place in which newcomers can enjoy a drink. They are well-stocked and include three Real Ales. Food is all important. The George Restaurant serves a full English Breakfast, Lunch and Dinner seven days a week and for those not able to eat at those times, hot and cold food is available all day. Table d'Hote and a la Carte Menus are available together with a range of bar meals, all of which may be eaten in the restaurant, bar or lounge. The pretty and very elegant Wedgewood ballroom is ideal for wedding receptions, parties, meeting or seminars. Complete with its own private bar, the room can seat up to 100 people or 150 plus for a buffet. The George is a great place and one of its many virtues is the sensible prices charged. From here there are endless places to visit offering something for every age group.

USEFUL INFORMATION

OPEN; *All year*
CHILDREN; *Welcome*
CREDIT CARDS; *All major cards*
LICENSED; *Yes. Full On*
ACCOMMODATION; *11 ensuite 2 basic rooms*

RESTAURANT; *Good food at sensible prices*
BAR MEALS; *Wide range, traditional*
VEGETARIAN; *Always a choice*
DISABLED ACCESS; *No special facilities*

COMBAS FARM
Croyde,
North Devon EX33 1PH
Tel: 01271 890398

This 17th century farmhouse nestling in it's own quiet valley where wildlife abounds, is such a pretty house over which a grape vine and wisteria ramble joyously. There is an attractive garden and orchard where children can play and a 'veggy' plot and greenhouse in which your host, Gwen Adams, grows vegetables, herbs and salad as well as some more unusual crops - all to be freshly picked and prepared for the delicious and memorable evening meals. There is a charming Lounge and Dining room with inglenook fireplaces, 2 Family (or twin) ensuite, 2 double with private bathroom, 1 childrens' (or small single) with H & C. A cot and a high chair are available and baby-sitting can be arranged. Morning tea, evening drinks and sandwich packs are available on request. English Tourist Board Commended Two Crowns. Golden sands, surfing, National Trust coastline and footpaths. The Tarka Trail, riding stables, tennis and golf are all nearby.

USEFUL INFORMATION
OPEN: March-December
CHILDREN: Welcome
CREDIT CARDS: None taken
ACCOMMODATION: 2 family (or twin) ensuite, 2 double with private bathroom, 1 childrens' (or small single) with H & C
DINING ROOM: Delicious memorable meals morning tea, evening drinks, sandwich packs
VEGETARIAN: Upon request
DISABLED ACCESS: No
GARDEN: Attractive with orchard
PETS: No dogs in the house

KNOWLES HOUSE
Broad Road,
Kentisbeare,
Cullompton,
Devon, EX15 2EU
Tel: 01884 266209

Knowles House is situated at the end of the Blackdown Hills, an area of outstanding natural beauty, midway between Broadhembury, a thatched village with the famous Drewe Arms Restaurant, and Kentisbeare. Kentisbeare is a pretty village whose church is worth a visit which in parts dates back to the 15th century. There is wonderful trout fishing within 4 miles and many other activities such as a gliding club within a mile. Exeter city is not far and there is certainly no shortage of things to do! The house itself which is run by Sally Merrett, dates back to the 1750s and has comfortable rooms with TV, tea and coffee provided. The 3 acres of gardens are mature woodland with an ornamental duck pond and many species of butterflies can be found here.

USEFUL INFORMATION
OPEN; All year
CHILDREN; Welcome
CREDIT CARDS; None taken
LICENSED; Not applicable
ACCOMMODATION; 3 rooms. 1 double, 1 twin both ensuite, 1 small childs room
PETS; Yes
RESTAURANT; Not applicable
BAR FOOD; Not applicable
VEGETARIAN; Catered for
DISABLED ACCESS; Not really but willing to help
GARDEN; Outdoor swimming pool

Chapter One

FORD HOUSE
44 Victoria Road,
Dartmouth,
Devon TQ6 9DX
Tel: 01803 834047

For that very special occasion why not consider a luxury holiday at Ford House, a Listed Regency house in the fascinating and olde worlde haven of Dartmouth in glorious Devon. The interior of this delightful property is enriched with unique quality furniture, wall coverings and drapes, which blend in total harmony. Bedrooms are deluxe, with ensuite bathroom and a collection of toiletries, many thoughtful extras are to be found in the guestrooms, fresh fruit and bottled water, fridge, radio clock alarm, hair dryer, clothes brush and shoe cleaning kit, direct dial telephone, colour television and a tea and coffee tray. The cuisine is outstanding with succulent dishes created and presented in elegant surroundings. Richard and Jayne Turner feature special mid-week breaks, and hold wine and food weekends for the discerning palate. There is private parking. The town and harbour of Dartmouth is within walking distance. Your hosts have a plethora of information relating to local facilities and outdoor pursuits, guaranteed to keep you occupied. The beauty of Dartmoor with its many quaint and interesting villages, wild life and glorious walks is not to be missed. There are many scenic coastal paths just waiting to be explored, and sunny sandy beaches on which to relax.

USEFUL INFORMATION

OPEN; Except 1st November through Easter
DINING ROOM; Outstanding cuisine, Open to non residents
CHILDREN; Welcome
VEGETARIAN; Catered for
CREDIT CARDS; Mastercard/Visa/Amex
DISABLED ACCESS; No
LICENSED; May bring your own wine
GARDEN; Yes and balconies
PETS; Yes
ACCOMMODATION; 3 ensuite rooms

YARD FARM
Upottery, Honiton,
Devon, EX14 9QP

Tel: 01404 861680

With easy access from the A30 this 14th century traditional Devon farmhouse sits in 94 acres overlooking the beautiful Otter Valley. The River Otter runs through the farmland so if you are a fisherman (or woman) then this is the place for you! It is a working farm with plenty of animals, children will love to make friends with Honey our pony. There is plenty to do in the area with beaches nearby and the market town of Honiton only 3 miles away, plus a swimming pool. The accommodation is light and airy with lots of character (especially those low doorways!) and breakfast is full English with evening meal by arrangement.

USEFUL INFORMATION

OPEN; May-October
RESTAURANT; Not applicable
CHILDREN; Most welcome
BAR FOOD; Not applicable
CREDIT CARDS; None taken
VEGETARIAN; Yes
LICENSED; No
DISABLED ACCESS; No
ACCOMMODATION; 3 rooms 1 double, 1 family, 1 single. All with colour TV, wash basin, heating, tea/coffee facilities
LAND; 94 acres
PETS; No

CAIR FARM,
Deviock,
Cornwall, PL11 3DN.

Tel : 01503 250320

Cair Farm is situated in that delightful part of the country near to the quaint village of Looe and the stunning scenery of south east Cornwall. The farm is a charming 17th century building, set in three acres of colourful gardens, including trout and carp ponds, and having beautiful country and sea views. Marcus and Stephanie Connell are your hosts, and offer a friendly welcoming ambience to all their guests. There are three superb bedrooms, all ensuite, and with the ever essential tea/coffee tray plus colour TV. Guests also have their own lounge and conservatory where it is ideal to sit and relax after a day's activities. The garden, including a very old butter well, is a lovely place to stroll round, and the peace and tranquillity of this haven will have you relaxed in no time! There is a fun pool ideal for children and adults, also table tennis and snooker facilities. Stephanie offers a good substantial country breakfast, with a variety of choices, and vegetarians are catered for. Evening meal is not available but there is plenty of selection in the area with a range of eating establishments and pubs. You are also welcome to bring back takeaway meals or the shark you have just caught. The Koi carp in the ponds are not for frying! Marcus and Stephanie offer great value for money and you will be pleasantly surprised with the standard and quality you receive.

This is a great location for exploring much of what Cornwall has to offer. Looe and Polperro have a lot to volunteer in the way of fishing, history and sightseeing, and you will be guaranteed some good outings to these locations. The cliffs and coves of the nearby coastline present great opportunities for the walker and also any with artistic tendencies. Be sure to have your camera to hand as the stunning vistas will have you exclaiming in delight. Children love the many safe, sandy beaches along here. Bodmin Moor is another place to explore with its moorland tors and haunting landscapes. At any time of year this is a beautiful spot and you are sure to enjoy your visit. There are three golf courses within easy reach; one being St.Mellion, of Benson & Hedges fame, and all within 20 minutes drive. The city of Plymouth with its superb shopping facilities, theatre and historic Barbican is also only a half hour drive away, and here you can follow in the footsteps of Sir Francis Drake or the Pilgrim Fathers.

Altogether a wonderful spot to have a break, whether it is summer or winter, you are sure to enjoy the hospitality offered, also the peace and tranquillity of the surrounding beauty.

USEFUL INFORMATION

OPEN : *May to September*
CHILDREN : *Welcome*
PETS : *Not normally*
LICENSED : *No*
CREDIT CARDS : *None taken*
DINING ROOM : *Excellent breakfast*
VEGETARIANS : *Catered for*
EVENING MEAL : *No*
DISABLED ACCESS : *No*
GARDEN : *Charming*
ACCOMMODATION : *3 rooms en suite: 1 dbl, 1 twin, 1 fml.*

Chapter One

THE BARN
Cair Farm,
Deviock,
Nr Downderry,
Cornwall PL11 3DN
Tel: 01503 250545

This comfortable converted barn run by George and Ann Burton is set in a spacious 2.5 acres with views looking out to sea. The furnishing is superb and there is even a private function room available for those social occasions or business meetings. Local facilities are very good with ample fishing, golf and pleasurable walks. All food is home-cooked and fresh, and if required you can arrange an evening meal. As this is a rural setting there is private hire or taxi service on site. Whatever your requirements you will find a warm welcome from George and Ann.

USEFUL INFORMATION

OPEN; All year
CHILDREN; Welcome
CREDIT CARDS; None taken
LICENSED; No
ACCOMMODATION; 3 rooms with separate bath/shower
DINING ROOM; Good home-cooked fare
VEGETARIAN; By arrangement
DISABLED ACCESS; Yes
GARDEN; Spacious with small swimming pool
PETS; Welcome

COTT FARM
Dittisham,
Nr Dartmouth,
Devon TQ6 0JQ
Tel: 01803 722249

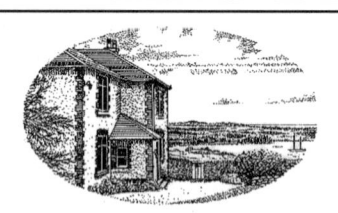

This turn of the century working farm set within attractive gardens with spectacular views over the River Dart, lies on the outskirts of the picturesque village of Dittisham. Immaculately presented rooms are tastefully decorated and furnished, enhanced by ensuite showers and wash basins, colour TV and tea and coffee making facilities as standard. There is also a main bathroom with separate wc. A full English breakfast prepared with fresh farm produce is certainly a pleasurable experience. Evening meal is not available but local restaurants of high quality abound in nearby Dartmouth and Dittisham. Country and coastal walks, cycling, golf, sailing, windsurfing and bird watching are all readily available.

USEFUL INFORMATION

OPEN; All year
CHILDREN; Welcome
CREDIT CARDS; None taken
LICENSED; No
ACCOMMODATION; 3 ensuite rooms
NO SMOKING in rooms
DINING ROOM; Full English breakfast
VEGETARIAN; Catered for
DISABLED ACCESS; No
GARDEN; Attractive well kept, superb views
PETS; By prior arrangement

Devon, Cornwall, Somerset and Avon

TRELIDDON FARM
*Downderry,
Torpoint,
Cornwall PL11 3DP
Tel: 01503 250288*

Just one mile from the garage in the seaside village of Downderry lies Treliddon Farm offering accommodation in basic, comfortable rooms with wash basins. It is one of those carefree houses in which you are welcome to go into the kitchen to make yourself tea or coffee and generally treat the farmhouse like home. A television in your bedroom is available if you need it and the view over the sea and moors from all the bedrooms is definitely a bonus. Steve and Susan Broad are genuinely welcoming people who will do everything within their power to ensure you have a good holiday. Steve can offer advice on Shark fishing from Looe or Trout from the river at Seaton. There are Sea Bass and Wreck fishing also from Looe. Golfers will find 4 courses within easy reach including the championship course at St Mellion. Walks abound along the Coastal Path and those belonging to the National Trust. Watersports, boat trips, splendid beaches are just the finishing touches. Most visitors enjoy looking at the very interesting antique furniture throughout the house - very much a talking point when you are enjoying a traditional, full English breakfast. Evening meals are only available in special circumstances, but Sue and Steve are happy to point you in the right direction to several restaurants and pubs within easy reach of the farmhouse. Access to farmland and animals.

USEFUL INFORMATION

OPEN; April-October
CHILDREN; Very welcome
CREDIT CARDS; None taken
ACCOMMODATION; 3 rooms not ensuite
PETS; Yes by arrangement
GARDEN; Yes + 150 acre farm
DINING ROOM; Full, traditional English breakfast. Evening meal in Special Circumstances
VEGETARIAN; Yes, if required
DISABLED ACCESS; No

Chapter One

OLD INN RESTAURANT WITH ROOMS
Drewsteignton,
Devon EX6 6QR

Tel: 01647 281276

On the edge of the Dartmoor National Park is the picture-book village of Drewsteignton. The church takes pride of place in the centre of the Square and is surrounded by thatched cottages, quaint shops and a wonderful restaurant. The Old Inn Restaurant is delightful, built in the 18th century it was originally the village inn serving both local community and travellers. Today it is a licensed restaurant with accommodation owned and excellently run by Margaret and Edward Butcher who succeed in making you feel welcome. The furnishings are elegant with many fascinating antiques including some genuine pre-World War 1 etchings of Ypres collected by the owners father and an extensive collection of beautiful decorative plates. The bedrooms are comfortable and warm, one of the double rooms has ensuite facilities, the other double and the twin share a bathroom. Colour television and a tea and coffee tray are standard, hair dryer, iron and ironing board are available on request. There is no need to rush when you stay here, after a leisurely breakfast, served as required, you are then free to explore this fascinating region, where some of the scenery will take your breath away. The Old Inn is surrounded by places of interest, you will definitely not get bored here. A mile away is Castle Drogo owned by the National Trust, it was designed by Lutyens and completed in 1930. Exeter with its wonderful Cathedral and lovely shops is only 13 miles away. There is also golf, fishing, riding and of course superb walks. You are sure to leave the Old Inn Restaurant feeling refreshed and totally relaxed.

USEFUL INFORMATION

OPEN; Closed January
CHILDREN; Welcome
CREDIT CARDS; Accepted
LICENSED; Yes
ACCOMMODATION; 3 rooms, 2 double, 1 twin, 1 ensuite
PETS; By prior arrangement only

DINING ROOM; Excellent home-cooked fare using fresh local produce
VEGETARIAN; Yes and Special Diets by prior arrangement
DISABLED ACCESS; Restaurant only
GARDEN; No

MANOR FARM
Dulcote,
Wells, Somerset
Tel: 01749 672125

A warm, West Country welcome awaits you at this country guest house, set in a charming corner of rural England. Previously a 17th century longhouse this house is now a lovingly restored family home which offers its guests sanctuary away from the bustle of everyday life. The rooms are well furnished with traditional English furniture and all efforts are made to ensure the comfort of each guest. The garden suite, although not fully converted for the disabled, does have wheelchair access and there is a private sitting room. Breakfasts are rather an indulgence with choices between English, continental and wholefood. The sunny dining room overlooks the orchard and I cannot think of a more relaxing way to start the day! The gardens are open to guests and with sheep, goats, chickens and ducks, the children are guaranteed a great time! Off season, when the weather is perhaps not so good, Ros Bufton, the owner, runs various weekend courses for your interest and amusement. One of these is a geological weekend, and another is a cookery course. So this is a holiday for all seasons! There are plenty of local facilities: fishing, golf, walking and you are never far away from the history and folklore of this majestic county.

USEFUL INFORMATION

OPEN : *All year*
CHILDREN : *Welcome*
PETS : *No*
ACCOMMODATION : *4 rooms*
EVENING MEAL : *Light supper by arrangement*
DISABLED ACCESS : *Some*
CREDIT CARDS : *None taken*
GARDEN : *With animals!*

HIGHERCOMBE FARM
Dulverton,
Somerset TA22 9PT
Tel: 01398 323616

Idyllically located Highercombe farm provides the perfect centre for those seeking a haven away from the stresses of modern day living and an insight into the peace and tranquillity one can find in the country. The farmhouse is luxurious and modern, with far reaching and commanding views over the 450 acre farm, which includes 100 acres of woodland and beyond to Exmoor and even Dartmoor. The furnishings are elegant and linens are colour co-ordinated. Each of the pretty bedrooms has colour TV, hair dryer and a tea and coffee tray. A comfortable and spacious lounge with inglenook fireplace and real log fire, colour TV and video is for the sole use of guests. Delicious farmhouse cooking with emphasis on home-made soups, pates, marmalade and bread, as well as using fresh local produce is assured. Vegetarian and special dietary needs are catered for by prior arrangement. Beef and sheep are reared on this working farm so there is always plenty going on, and your hosts Abigail Humphrey and Tom Flanagan, will be only to pleased to escort you on farm walks and to answer any questions you may have, or a farm drive can be arranged to observe the many wild animals that frequent the fields and woods, including deer. Should guests wish to partake in horse riding, clay pigeon shooting or shooting instruction, lake or sea fishing then arrangements can be made on your behalf.

USEFUL INFORMATION

OPEN; *Closed December*
CHILDREN; *Over 6 years*
CREDIT CARDS; *None taken*
ACCOMMODATION; *3 ensuite rooms*
GARDEN; *Extensive lawns and 450 acre farm, and woodlands*
DINING ROOM; *Excellent farmhouse cooking*
VEGETARIAN; *Yes and special diets with prior notice*
DISABLED ACCESS; *No*
PETS; *Welcome inc. grazing and barn for horses*

Chapter One

WOODVILLE HOUSE
*25 West Street, Dunster,
Nr. Minehead,
Somerset
TA24 6SN*

Tel: 01643 821228

Dunster has to be one of the most attractive villages in Somerset with its wide Main Street and 17th century Yarn Market. Exmoor is on the doorstep and no wonder it gave R.D. Blackmore inspiration for the book Lorna Doone, the scenery is breathtaking, it is barren and yet green, with wooded coombes and cattle, sheep and ponies roaming this natural wilderness. Back in Dunster is Woodville House, a Georgian Grade II listed house of impeccable taste. Owned and efficiently run by Mrs. Tymms, Woodville is a comfortable family home with a very warm and friendly atmosphere, it is well furnished and spotlessly clean. The homely bedrooms have exceptionally comfy beds along with a clock/radio, the drapes and linens are very attractive and pleasing, tea and coffee can be brought up on a tray as required. After an excellent sleep in those lovely beds Mrs. Tymms will serve a delicious full English or Continental breakfast, special diets and vegetarians are also catered for. Woodville House is set in the heart of Dunster Village close to the 13th century Castle, which is well worth a visit. The West Somerset Railway is also an attraction not to be missed where old steam engines run from Minehead to Bishop's Lydeard, stopping at several places on the way, delightful. You really will have plenty to do in this lovely part of Somerset.

USEFUL INFORMATION

OPEN; 1st March-End October
CHILDREN; No
CREDIT CARDS; None taken
ACCOMMODATION; 3 rooms, 1 double, 1 twin, 1 single
PETS; No

DINING ROOM; Full English or Continental breakfast. No evening meal, but choice of restaurants within walking distance
VEGETARIAN; Yes
DISABLED ACCESS; No
GARDEN; Courtyard, with parking facilities

SMOKING IN THE LOUNGE ONLY

THE SIR WALTER RALEIGH
High Street,
East Budleigh, Devon EX9 7ED

Tel: 01395 442510

This interesting, 16th century, thatched pub is so called in honour of Sir Walter Raleigh who was born at Hayes Barton, a fine Tudor farmhouse in Hayes Lane about a mile away. The villagers like to think that he quaffed a pint or two of ale in the pub. It is certainly a hostelry that is full of character and in keeping with the rest of this attractive village.

East Budleigh's church, All Saints, stands closeby. Apart from being of Saxon origin and renowned for its unique collection of bench ends, it also has memorials to the Reverend Ambrose Stapleton who was vicar from 1794-1852. He was a splendid preacher, a carer of the poor, but he is chiefly remembered for his involvement in the smuggling trade, reputedly allowing his vicarage to be used for hiding barrels of brandy!

Edward and Shirley Truman, the proprietors of the Sir Walter Raleigh certainly do not have any smuggled brandy in their cellars but nonetheless they have well kept ales and a fine menu which offers a wide range of tempting dishes at sensible prices. For those who want to stay in this part of Devon, the Trumans have three letting rooms which are full of olde worlde charm and you will be both comfortable and very welcome. Children need to be over fourteen years to stay here. Pets are not permitted. East Budleigh is a great base for exploring this glorious part of Devon and the Trumans will happily help you to plan your days.

USEFUL INFORMATION

OPEN; 11.30-3pm & 6-11pm
CHILDREN; Over 14 years
CREDIT CARDS; Mastercard/Visa
LICENSED; Full On
ACCOMMODATION; 3 rooms
GARDEN; No

RESTAURANT; Separate eating area
BAR FOOD; Wide range, home-cooked
VEGETARIAN; 5 dishes
DISABLED ACCESS; No. Loos awkward
PETS; No

Chapter One

BLACK NESS COTTAGE
East Cornworthy, Totnes,
Devon TQ9 7HQ
Tel: 01803 722467

If you are looking for a peaceful relaxing holiday then Black Ness Cottage, run by Judy and Tony Bryant, is the ideal rural location, midway between Totnes and Dartmouth. The house itself is 17th century and has been skilfully modernised and includes many original features. The bedrooms are beautifully furnished in pine with co-ordinating linen and curtains. All have TV, tea and coffee, complimentary toiletries and lovely views over the gardens and surrounding countryside. Breakfast is full English made with fresh local produce and includes home-made jams and marmalades. Packed lunches can also be arranged. Tony Bryant is a successful artist and much of his work can be seen around the house and perhaps purchased.

USEFUL INFORMATION

OPEN; All year except Christmas
CHILDREN; Over 12 years
CREDIT CARDS; None taken
LICENSED; No
ACCOMMODATION; 2 rooms, 1 double, 1 twin
DINING ROOM; Traditional English breakfast
VEGETARIAN; Catered for
DISABLED ACCESS; No
GARDEN; 1.5 acres with wildlife pond
PETS; By prior arrangement
NO SMOKING POLICY

CHANNEL VISTA GUEST HOUSE
Woodlands,
Combe Martin, Devon EX34 0AT
Tel/Fax: 01271 883514

This beautiful Victorian house standing in an elevated position at the west end of the village some 300 metres from the sea, beach and shops, makes a wonderful guest house. It is strictly non-smoking and apart from the health aspect one can fully understand that the owners, Lynda and Edward Norton have no wish to despoil their beautiful drapes, laundered sheets and linens or their elegant furniture with the smell of nicotine. The 6 immaculate, bright airy bedrooms are all ensuite and have TV. A plentiful beverage tray and pretty complimentary toiletries. You have only to read the glowing reports in the Visitors Book to know that everyone who stays here is delighted by the whole atmosphere and hospitality. Breakfast is a freshly cooked, generously portioned meal which starts off the day well and in the evening after a pre-dinner drink at the bar, dinner is a 5 course meal prepared using fresh meat and local produce. The dishes are a pleasing mixture of English and Italian. Combe Martin with its stunning coastline and so much happening around it is a great place for a holiday and no better place to stay in than Channel Vista which is ETB 3 Crown Commended.

USEFUL INFORMATION

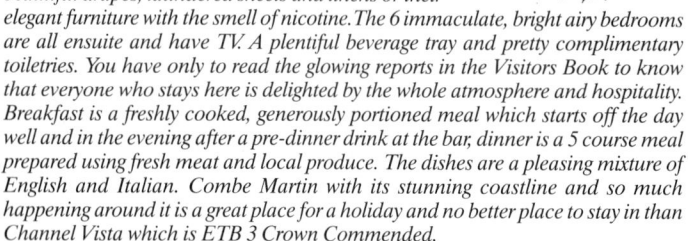

OPEN;All year
CHILDREN;Welcome, from 8 years upwards
CREDIT CARDS;Visa/Master/Euro
LICENSED;Yes
ACCOMMODATION;6 ensuite rooms
Including 1 suite
DINING ROOM;Good home-cooking
VEGETARIAN; Catered for
DISABLED ACCESS;No
GARDEN;No. Front terrace
PETS;No
No smoking house

HILL FARM
Hittisleigh, Exeter,
Devon EX6 6LQ
Tel: 01647 24149

Tucked away in the hill, this farm offers lovely views in all directions. Situated within easy reach of the A30 but not near enough to spoil the peace and tranquillity of the Devon countryside. Brian and Carol Howell invite guests to share their 17th century Farmhouse 'as family' if desired, and enjoy home-cooking in the farmhouse kitchen. The rooms offer comfort and individuality with character furnishings. The large beamed sitting room with inglenook, has games, shelves of books and television available. Within the large gardens there is a large outdoor heated swimming pool (heated May to Sept inclusive). Other facilities include table tennis, croquet and 50 acres of grass and woodland to explore. Hill Farm is close to Dartmoor National Park and centrally placed for North, South and West coasts. Historic Exeter with its beautiful Cathedral, fine shops, theatres and other varied amenities is approximately 15 miles away. For the country loving, the moors, walks, riding, fishing, golf, archery etc. are all to be found locally. Not to be missed - a friendly and quiet location for anybreak.

USEFUL INFORMATION

OPEN; All year
CHILDREN; Welcome
CREDIT CARDS; None taken
LICENSED; No
ACCOMMODATION; 5 rooms; 2 dbl (1 ensuite), 2 twin (1 ensuite), 1 ensuite fml
RESTAURANT; Not applicable
BAR FOOD; Not applicable
VEGETARIANS; By arrangement
DISABLED ACCESS; Partial
GARDEN; Yes
PETS; No

PENNY HILL FARM
Combeland Road, Alcombe,
Minehead, Somerset TA24 6BT
Tel: 01643 707806

There are views from this delightful bungalow across the Bristol Channel to Wales and also Exmoor. It is a working farm situated on the edge of Minehead with direct access on to the moor. Horses and a rare breed of cattle are farmed here, local horse riding can be arranged. Although it is in a rural setting with wonderful views, you are only 3 minutes from the pub and a little further from attractions such as ten pin bowling and cinemas. Something to keep in mind is that you are close to the West Somerset preserved steam railway. Local pursuits include fossil hunting, geology, sailing, windsurfing and many more too numerous to mention. The bungalow was built in the 1970s and is modernly furnished. A TV lounge with video is available for guests, and also houses a piano and many books and games. Breakfast is full English and made with good local produce.

USEFUL INFORMATION

OPEN; All year
CHILDREN; Welcome
PETS; Welcome
CREDIT CARDS; None taken
VEGETARIAN; Yes
DISABLED ACCESS; Some level access to house
GARDEN; Yes, patio with giant chess set!
ACCOMMODATION; 3 rooms, double ensuite

Chapter One

SUNNYMEAD GUEST HOUSE
74 Victoria Road,
Exmouth, Devon EX8 1DP

Tel: 01395 268413

Not only are Margaret and John Mewes the holders of the 'Good Service Award' a reflection of the excellent hospitality guests receive, but are the winners of the Exmouth 'Britain In Bloom' competition. Their delightful non-smoking Guest House is surrounded by hundreds of varieties of flowers grown in tubs and hanging baskets as well as in the garden. This very friendly Christian family run business, offers their guests comfortable and modern accommodation. Each bedroom has colour television, wash hand basins and tea and coffee making facilities. Ensuite bedrooms are limited so early booking is advisable. Delicious home cooking is a speciality, a wholesome traditional breakfast is served and an optional 3 course evening meal is available on weekday evenings only, provided they are booked in advance. The locality of Sunnymead is ideally situated on the level just 200 yards from the golden sandy beach of Exmouth and the splendid promenade. There is a variety of interesting shops and restaurants within the town. The wonderful Dartmoor National Park offers spectacular vistas and walks. Crealy Park is a wonderful day out for young and old alike. Bicton Park offers the visitor a taste of days gone by or a look to the future, or a train ride through the gardens and woods in the present.

USEFUL INFORMATION

OPEN; All year
CHILDREN; Welcome
CREDIT CARDS; None taken, cheques accepted with bankers card only
LICENSED; No
ACCOMMODATION; 6 rooms, 3 double, 1 twin, 1 single, 1 family, 2 ensuite Ground floor double ensuite

DINING ROOM; Full English breakfast, Optional evening meal - 3 course set menu on weekdays only
DISABLED ACCESS; No, but most welcome
GARDEN; Small front garden
PETS; No
NON-SMOKING HOUSE

CAMELOT
5 Avenue Road, Falmouth,
Cornwall TR11 4AZ

Tel: 01326 312480

Pat Rogers is your hostess at Camelot Guest House and provides a friendly, efficient service. This is evident in the number of visitors who return year after year to enjoy her hospitality. All the bedrooms are comfortably furnished with ensuite showers and w.c., colour television and complimentary tea/coffee making facilities as standard. There is a lounge to relax in, with games and books, where you can meet other guests and enjoy their company. The dining room is bright and sunny, and breakfast is a full traditional English meal. An evening meal can also be booked and is a good, home-cooked, four course dinner. There is a self-service bar for beverages and wine can be bought by the glass. Falmouth is an excellent resort with it's history and small narrow streets containing many shops of wide variety. There are four lovely beaches with water sports, and wonderful coastal walks along the headland. Falmouth harbour is renowned for it's sailing activities and a day could be spent just watching the comings and goings in this busy harbour, or experiencing one of the many boat excursions around the beautiful estuary. Museums, art galleries; Falmouth has it all, including a wonderful golf course with magnificent coastal views, and is also a great base to tour from. Pat has lots of information on things to do and is only too happy to help you plan your day.

USEFUL INFORMATION

OPEN; All year, except Christmas
CHILDREN; Welcome
CREDIT CARDS; None taken
ACCOMMODATION; 8 ensuite rooms plus a self-catering apartment for 2
PARKING; Private off road
DINING ROOM; Traditional home-cooking Evening meal by arrangement
LICENSED; Some, welcome to bring your own
DISABLED ACCESS; Not really
GARDEN; Yes, pretty

Chapter One

DENNIS AND ENA'S BED & BREAKFAST
46 & 46A High Street, Glastonbury,
Somerset BA6 9DX

Tel: 01458 832214

Built in 1840 this conveniently situated property standing on the High Street was originally called 'Somerset House' and was the dwelling house of the first Glastonbury Banker one H Stuckey of Stuckey Banker. The present day owners, Dennis and Ena, will make one feel very welcome and instantly at home in their modernly furnished home. Each bedroom is tastefully furnished and includes ensuite facilities, colour television and a tea and coffee tray. Full English breakfast and vegetarian dishes served. Dinner is not served, but there are many restaurants in the vicinity. Glastonbury is gloriously situated and an ideal centre for exploring the Mendip Hills and Cheddar Gorge with its breathtaking cliffs soaring to a height of almost 500ft, ideal for rock climbers, nature lovers and walkers. Bleadon Hill has magnificent views toward the Bristol Channel. Not far is the coastline including Burnam-on-Sea which offers golden sands, swimming, sailing, fishing and water ski-ing or Weston-Super-Mare with its piers and promenade, and at Brean Down is a Tropical Bird Garden. Local facilities include a swimming and fitness centre, golf, fishing and a theatre at nearby Street where films and live performances can be seen.

USEFUL INFORMATION

OPEN; *All year*
CHILDREN; *Welcome*
CREDIT CARDS; *Visa/Amex/ Mastercard/Diners*
LICENSED; *No*
ACCOMMODATION; *2 ensuite rooms*

DINING ROOM; *Home-cooked fare*
VEGETARIAN; *Catered for*
DISABLED ACCESS; *No, but welcome*
GARDEN; *No*
PETS; *Yes*

WICK HOLLOW HOUSE
8 Wick Hollow, Glastonbury,
Somerset BA6 8JJ

Tel: 01458 833595 Fax: 01458 834244

Sally Evans at Wick Hollow House which stands in glorious countryside, has a delightful self-contained annexe adjoining the main house on the ground floor. It has its own front door and entrance, to which you have a key so that you can come and go as you wish. It is ideal for a family with a large bedroom with a double bed and two single beds. A cot can also be provided if needs be. The room is attractively appointed and enhanced by the big picture window which provides a wonderful view. Leading off the bedroom is a spacious bathroom with bath, shower, basin and toilet. A similar view, looking over the extensive gardens with marvellous views of Chalice Hill, the Tor and a wealth of beautiful trees, can be had from the comfortable sitting room which has colour TV, a stereo, a bookcase with a variety of reading matter, and a dining table with seating for four. Sally provides a delicious, sustaining breakfast but no evening meal. There are many excellent pubs, cafes and restaurants in the area to which she will guide you - making sure you know which ones to avoid! Sally is also a mine of information about Glastonbury and places to visit which she will happily tell you about. Wick Hollow House is on the outskirts of Glastonbury with an easy 5-10 minute walk downhill to town. This is a no-smoking establishment.

USEFUL INFORMATION

OPEN; All year
CHILDREN; Welcome
CREDIT CARDS; None taken
PETS; Yes
ACCOMMODATION; Annexe adjoining house sleeps 4 in family room. Bookings also taken for twin, double or triple

DINING ROOM; Breakfast only
VEGETARIAN; Catered for
DISABLED ACCESS; Welcome. Certified Grade III
GARDEN; Yes

Chapter One

SWALLOWS REST
Golberdon, Nr Callington,
Cornwall PL17 7ND
Tel: 01579 383010

Swallows Rest is an attractive and comfortable house where you will receive a warm, friendly welcome from the owners Helena and Barry Scandrett. It offers excellent bed and breakfast accommodation with ensuite facilities and ample parking. It is situated in a beautiful rural setting at the edge of a small village, having panoramic views towards Bodmin Moor over the Lynher Valley. It is convenient for Plymouth and is within a short drive of both the North and South Cornish coast, or the airy spaces of Bodmin Moor and Dartmoor. Also nearby is the internationally famous St. Mellion Golf Course and Country Club. Packed lunches are available should you need them for your days activities.

USEFUL INFORMATION
OPEN; All year
RESTAURANT; Not applicable
CHILDREN; Welcome
VEGETARIAN; Can be accommodated
CREDIT CARDS; None taken
DISABLED ACCESS; No
LICENSED; No
GARDEN; Access to adjacent road
ACCOMMODATION; 1 dbl ensuite, **PETS**; Yes
1 twin ensuite and 1 single

THE HUNGRY HORSE
Harbertonford, Totnes,
Devon TQ9 7TA
Tel: 01803 732441

John and Caroline Tipper are the owners of this delightfully named accommodation and restaurant. They actually took over as the new owners in 1995, but Caroline's connection goes back 20 years working with the original owners. Obviously good experience, as the Hungry Horse is a delightful place to stay. All bedrooms are ensuite and have TV, tea and coffee in each. Breakfast is a full English traditional meal. Evening meals and Sunday roasts are served in the restaurant. As a guest, you are allowed a free bottle of house wine with your evening meal. This is per room - a very nice gesture. Evening meals are excellent, with an extremely varied menu. Local fish is rather a speciality. The Hungry Horse is set on the banks of the Harbourne River in the village of Harbertonford. Because of the mild climate in the South West this is an all year holiday. From the russets and golds of Autumn, to the sparkling blue of the sea in Summer. From toasting in front of a roaring log fire, to strolling the beach on a balmy evening. You have everything here. John and Caroline are only too happy to advise on the local pursuits which are varied and plentiful.

USEFUL INFORMATION
OPEN; All year
RESTAURANT; Excellent varied menu
CHILDREN; Welcome
VEGETARIAN; Catered for
CREDIT CARDS; Most major taken
DISABLED ACCESS; Not really
LICENSED; Full
GARDEN; With access to river shallows
ACCOMMODATION; 3 ensuite rooms
PETS; Welcome

118

Devon, Cornwall, Somerset and Avon

HARTLAKE FARM
Hartlake, Nr. Glastonbury,
Somerset BA6 9AB
Tel: 01458 835406

The engaging area surrounding the ancient town of Glastonbury where it is said rests the Holy Grail, is steeped in legend and history. Hartlake Farm is part of that history having been builtin the 17th century and is now a charming and comfortable guest house offering excellent facilities, and has been rewarded by the English Tourist Board with a '2 Crown Commended'. Bedrooms have ensuite bathrooms, tea and coffee making facilities and colour television. Furnishings are country cottage style, giving a warm and welcoming feel. Guests have the choice of either Continental or full English Breakfast. There are many places of interest ot visit including Cheddar Gorge, Wookey Hole, Castle Cary and Weston-Super-Mare with miles of shoreline from which to bathe, surf or sail.

USEFUL INFORMATION
OPEN; February-November   **DINING ROOM**; Good home-cooked fare
CHILDREN; Welcome   **VEGETARIAN**; Catered for
CREDIT CARDS; None taken   **DISABLED ACCESS**; Not really
LICENSED; No   **GARDEN**;Yes
ACCOMMODATION; 2 ensuite rooms   **PETS**; No

GODOLPHIN BRIDGE FARM
Townsend, Hayle,
Cornwall TR27 6AR
Tel: 01736 850873

Godolphin Bridge Farm is a 3 acre small holding where Louise and John have made a very comfortable home. The farmhouse is a late 18th century Listed Building once owned by the Duke of Leeds, and is attached to a converted barn. There are 3 ensuite bedrooms each with its own TV, tea and coffee making facilities, books and pot pouris to add that special touch. The farmhouse is furnished in a lovely modern cottage style which gives it a welcoming and friendly feeling. The breakfast is good English fare and can be served on the balcony or the patio in good weather. There is no evening meal but the local hostelries are only a few minutes away, there is no need to worry about being late back as you are given your own key. There is a large garden where delicious Cream Teas are served and for the more energetic a game of badminton on the farms own court. The garden also has a waterfall and river access. Trips can be arranged in small boats to see the local wildlife, birds and otters. There is plenty to do during your stay, the sandy beaches around Hayle are very safe for children, also a trip to the Hayle Paradise Park is well worth a visit. Godolphin House is only a 2 minute drive from where the Poldark series was filmed. You can fish, ride, windsurf, sail, play golf or walk the lovely coastal path and admire the wonderful scenery.

USEFUL INFORMATION
OPEN: All year   **DINING ROOM**: No evening meal
CHILDREN: Yes   except during Winter months Oct-Apr
CREDIT CARDS: None taken   **VEGETARIAN**: Yes
LICENSED: No   **DISABLED ACCESS**: No except for Cream Teas
ACCOMMODATION: 3 ensuite rooms   **GARDEN**: Yes with waterfall, river access
PETS: Yes

Chapter One

BOAK HOUSE
Coverack, Helston,
Cornwall TR12 6SH
Tel: 01326 280608

Sea views over the harbour, spectacular sunrises from a lovely summerhouse, all this and accommodation too! Wendy Watters runs this guest house which dates back to 1900. The accommodation is well furnished with TV, tea and coffee in each room. There are plenty of local pubs who specialise in serving local sea food delicacies. The coastal path is a lovely walk with hidden coves that take you by surprise. There is a wind surfing school, fishing, golf and many other activities; all within easy distances. This is an ideal situation for touring the southernmost tip of Cornwall.

USEFUL INFORMATION
OPEN; All year
DINING ROOM; Full English Breakfast
CHILDREN; Welcome
DISABLED ACCESS; No
CREDIT CARDS; None taken
GARDEN; Yes
LICENSED; No
PETS; Yes
ACCOMMODATION; 4 rooms, 2 double, 1 twin, 1 family

COBBLERS COTTAGE
Nantithet, Cury,
Helston, Cornwall TR12 7RB
Tel: 01326 241342

Captivating best describes this pristine 17th century cottage, known as Cobblers Cottage. Glorious hanging baskets, window boxes and pots abound with a riot of colour making this a truly welcoming sight. Hilary Lugg, the lady of the house, uses the saying 'this is our home, we aim to make you feel at home'. All the rooms are beautifully appointed with furnishings in keeping with the surroundings. Each bedroom has its own bathroom and shower, tea and coffee making facilities are as standard. The dining room with its beamed ceiling and superb reproduction furniture overlooking the garden, is a lovely setting to sit and enjoy the traditional English fare, specially prepared and using fresh home grown produce. This is truly an outstanding area situated as it is in the heart of the Lizard Peninsula. Beaches are within easy reach, as are many places of interest. Activities are numerous, swimming, surfing, fishing both river and sea, riding and of course the joy of coastal walking with spectacular sea views and enchanting and quaint fishing villages along the way. Helston, Falmouth and Penzance are within easy reach as is the Lizard and Lands End all worth a visit, and with the Isles of Scilly being a short hop away, why not make that a special day out.

USEFUL INFORMATION
OPEN; All year, keys supplied
DINING ROOM; Traditional home-cooked fare, optional evening meal
CHILDREN; Yes (no reductions)
CREDIT CARDS; None taken
VEGETARIAN; Catered for
LICENSED; No
DISABLED ACCESS; No, bookings considered
ACCOMMODATION; 3 ensuite rooms
GARDEN; Yes, beautiful with stream
PETS; No

SYDNEY FARM
Higher Halstock, Yeovil,
Somerset BA22 9QY
Tel: 01935 891249
Fax: 01935 891544

Sometimes an address can be confusing as in this case when Sydney Farm is in fact situated in Dorset! It does not matter where it is because it is a charming 18th century house which used to be the centre of a farm. It is as delightful inside as it is out, furnished with a harmonious mixture of antique and modern furniture. The two bedrooms are ensuite and well-appointed with very comfortable beds. A first class traditional English breakfast is served in the dining room or the conservatory, freshly cooked and to your choice. Vegetarians can be catered for. There is a garden to enjoy with the additional pleasure of a heated swimming pool and a games room. There is no evening meal but within two miles there are two pubs, both Egon Ronay recommended which serve delicious food. Alison Smith, your hostess, will help you plan your day if you wish; and advise you on the sporting activities nearby as well as the many interesting places to visit. Alison also has a self-catering 4 bed-roomed cottage, fully equipped, double glazed, centrally heated and with 2 bathrooms.

USEFUL INFORMATION

OPEN; March-October
CHILDREN; Over 8 years
CREDIT CARDS; None taken
ACCOMMODATION; 2 ensuite rooms
Self-catering 4 bed-roomed cottage

DINING ROOM; Excellent breakfast
VEGETARIAN; Yes
DISABLED ACCESS; No special facilities
GARDEN; Yes, plus heated pool
PETS; No

MUDDIFORD INN
Muddiford,
Barnstaple, Devon EX31 4EY
Tel: 01271 850243

Situated on the B3230 Barnstaple to Ilfracombe Road Muddiford Inn is probably one of the 'New Inns' established by Elizabeth I throughout the country. It is steeped in the atmosphere built up over the centuries. In addition to the very warm welcome you will get in the bars there is comfortable Bed and Breakfast accommodation, full Restaurant facilities, Bar Snacks, a large garden and ample Car Parking. People staying here enjoy the company of the locals in the bar and find the pub and excellent base for exploring the beaches and villages of North Devon. Woolacombe, Croyde, Ilfracombe, Combe Martin and Barnstaple are all less than ten miles away. The unpretentious menu offers well cooked food at sensible prices and includes a Childrens Menu. Daily Specials are shown on the Blackboard. Whilst favourite dishes appear frequently there are always one or two more adventurous ones and something for the vegetarians.

USEFUL INFORMATION

OPEN: All year
CHILDREN: Welcome
CREDIT CARDS: None taken
LICENSED: Yes
ACCOMMODATION: Comfortable rooms
GARDEN: Yes large, ample parking

RESTAURANT: Good food at sensible prices
Children's menu, Daily Specials blackboard
BAR MEALS: Yes
VEGETARIAN: Catered for
DISABLED ACCESS: No

MILDMAY COLOURS INN
Holbeton,
Devon PL8 1NA

Tel: 01752 830248
Fax: 01752 830540

In the reign of King James I in the year 1617 a manor house was built, today it is the Mildmay Colours Inn. Situated within the lovely picturesque village of Holbeton in the glorious county of Devon, close to Dartmoor and the coast. This fine establishment boasts its very own brewery and tours are available to have explained the intricacies involved in the art of beer making, with perhaps a sample, or enjoy a glass or two in one of the bars, of this fine 'real' ale. The chef ensures all tastes are catered for, including vegetarians, with delicious home-made dishes, using fresh local produce when available. The bar menu is extensive and a large 'Specials' blackboard changes daily. The 'Old Rent Collection Room', is now the delightful carvery restaurant. Here you can dine from the A La Carte menu, which is wide and varying. Theme Food Nights are a speciality for the connoisseur and are held on Wednesday, Friday, Saturday and Sunday. Opposite the Inn in this peaceful location can be found the accommodation. A conversion of 2 cottages has resulted in rooms furnished simply, but attractively, with colour co-ordinated linens. Each room has ensuite facilities plus, heaters, TV, clock radio and tea and coffee maker. Laundering and drying are available for hikers, walkers etc. Residents have their own key and may come and go as they please. Children are most welcome and are well catered for. It is regretted that disabled access is not available. Provision for you pets is by prior arrangement. Holbeton is in the invidious position of being close to the spectacular Dartmoor National Park, the coast and beaches of South Devon. With these wonderful venues available to the visitor, it is not surprising that pursuits are many and varied, walking, cycling, riding, fishing both river and sea and most water sports, and for the golf enthusiast there are many golf courses, including the well known St. Mellion Golf and Country Club. The staff will be only too happy to arrange riding and golf weekends and will lay on transport if requested. The historical city of Plymouth is certainly worth a visit, with its famous Hoe and Barbican from where the Mayflower set sail for the Americas. Open topped buses ensures the visitor a wonderful vantage point of the sights. There is the Theatre Royal where live shows can be enjoyed along with several cinemas.

USEFUL INFORMATION

OPEN; All year
CHILDREN; Welcome
CREDIT CARDS; All major cards/Switch
LICENSED; Yes
ACCOMMODATION; 9 ensuite rooms
PETS; By arrangement

RESTAURANT; A La Carte, carvery, Theme nights, open to non-residents
BAR FOOD; Extensive menu
VEGETARIAN; Catered for
DISABLED ACCESS; No
GARDEN; Yes

ALFOXTON COTTAGE
Holford, Bridgwater,
Somerset TA5 1SG

Tel: 01278 741418

This pretty cottage with its trailing creepers climbing the old stone walls was built sometime in the 18th century. From Alfoxton Cottage to the top of the Quantock Hills is just a few minutes walk and the rewarding scenery will give you views across the Bristol Channel to the Welsh Coast. It is a wonderful place to stay in order to be able to enjoy walking the heather clad moorland, exploring the deep tree lined combes, coming upon the wild red deer and noting the soaring buzzards. Exmoor National Park and many tourist attraction lie within a twenty mile radius. The cottage is situated at the end of a quiet lane with virtually no passing traffic - just right for a refreshing, relaxing break. The nearest main road (1 ½ miles away) is the A39 North Somerset Coast road (Exit 23 of M5 : 16 miles).

Angela and Richard Delderfield welcome you warmly into their home with its peaceful flower garden. They have three pretty cottage style bedrooms all with a wash hand basin. Downstairs, guests may relax in the comfortable lounge where log fires are lit on chilly evenings. The food is very special. Breakfast is sumptuous including eggs from their own hens, home-made bread and preserves. The four course dinner will be remembered long after you have left Alfoxton Cottage. The cooking is inspired and add to that fresh produce which comes from the garden whenever possible. Alfoxton Cottage is strictly non-smoking.

USEFUL INFORMATION

OPEN; March-November
CHILDREN; By arrangement
CREDIT CARDS; None taken
LICENSED; No. Table wine available
ACCOMMODATION; 3 rooms and two bathrooms
PETS; No

DINING ROOM; Super food from fresh produce, home-made bread etc.
VEGETARIAN; By arrangement
DISABLED ACCESS; No
GARDEN; Pretty cottage garden with summer-time seating
NON-SMOKING

Chapter One

COURT BARN COUNTRY HOUSE HOTEL
Clawton,
Holsworthy, Devon EX22 6PS

Tel: 01409 271219
Fax: 01409 271309

This area of the Duchy might almost be described as 'Hidden Cornwall'. It is certainly one of the least tourist troubled spots and provides those seeking a peaceful holiday with the ideal place. There can be nowhere within this delightful countryside better to stay than Court Barn at Clawton It was built as the 'Sanctuary' around the 16th century and the present house which was partly rebuilt in 1853 had its own chapel. The first impression as you turn into the leafy drive is one of peace - a respite from the world outside. Then you come to the house and its charm is immediate. Set in five acres of park-like grounds Court Barn is mellow and gracious, welcoming and friendly. Robert and Susan Wood who own and run the hotel strive to make people at home and relaxed. A crackling log fire in at least one of the lounges all year simply enhances the welcome.

There are eight en-suite bedrooms, each individually furnished with pretty drapes and decor. The bar is a meeting point at night before or after the excellent five-course dinner served in one of the two dining rooms where the tables gleam with sparkling glass and shining silver. The restaurant is furnished with antiques and it is here you will enjoy a perfectly served meal prepared from fresh, quality food accompanied by wines from the award winning list of 375 from around the world. In the morning the elegant breakfast room will provide you with a superb breakfast and at the same time allow you to assimilate, via the windows, the beauty of the 12th century Clawton church and perhaps tempt you to try your hand at croquet on the lawn outside. Afternoon tea is renowned at Clawton and recognised with a Tea Council award and the AA Rosette. Court Barn has endless accolades which are justly deserved. The astonishing thing is that its old-fashioned values of quality, comfort and hospitality are provided at prices of yesteryear!

Within easy reach there are Blue Flag beaches, nature trails, cycle trails, National Trust and National parks. Golf, riding, tennis, badminton, fishing, sailing and an indoor pool nearby are all readily available for the energetic.

USEFUL INFORMATION

OPEN;All year
CHILDREN;Welcome
CREDIT CARDS;All major cards
LICENSED;Yes. Award winning
ACCOMMODATION;8 ensuite rooms
RESTAURANT;Superb, quality food
BAR FOOD;Not applicable. Afternoon teas
VEGETARIAN;Catered for
DISABLED ACCESS;No facilities
GARDEN;5 acres

SEVEN HILLS HOTEL
Torrs Park, Ilfracombe,
Devon EX34 8AY

Tel: 01271 862207

Once a Victorian mansion house, the Seven Hills Hotel is a tastefully decorated, welcoming home run in a personal warm way. Frank and Ann Jackson are the owners and do everything possible to ensure an enjoyable stay. The rooms are decorated in a mixture of repro Victorian and modern furniture, and have co-ordinating wallpapers and linen. All are ensuite and are very comfortable. The bedrooms have views of the valley, the garden or sea, and have TV, tea and coffee as standard. Downstairs there are two residents lounges; one with TV for non-smokers and one with bar for smokers. Both are comfortable and cosy. The views are excellent as is that from the elegant dining room. Here you have home-cooked food 'straight from the Aga' to your table. Good, fresh local produce is used where possible and the menus are varied and exciting. Dinner is a five course meal at excellent prices. To go with this good meal are exclusive wines from all over the world and bottled ales. Breakfast is hearty with fruit juice and cereal, followed by a traditional English or Continental, with toast and tea or coffee. There is also a large private car park at the rear of the hotel, and there is ample parking for all guests. Ilfracombe has plenty to offer the visitor. Mid June sees the 'Victorian Festival' which includes a steam fair and traders in Victorian costumes. There is street entertainment and a holiday atmosphere throughout the town. There is also a reconstruction of 'The Battle of Ilfracombe' when French ships tried to invade and were repelled by the people of Ilfracombe. Highly entertaining! Away from this is still more. Sea fishing is popular, as is walking, with great coastal walks and those on Exmoor. There is the Tarka Trail of Tarka the Otter fame, and cycling trails on the moor. Golf is another popular pastime here and Frank and Ann would only be too happy to arrange a full golfing holiday. Water sports are in abundance and there is horse riding and much more. It is a good base for travel; the famous Shire Horse Centre is within access and a trip to Lundy Island is a must. There are many historical houses and beautiful gardens, coastal villages and towns. A great place with plenty of activities; energetic or otherwise.

USEFUL INFORMATION

OPEN; All year
CHILDREN; Over 5 years
CREDIT CARDS; None taken
LICENSED; Residents
ACCOMMODATION; 11 ensuite rooms
PETS; By arrangement

DINING ROOM; Excellent home-cooking. 5 course evening meal
VEGETARIAN; Catered for
DISABLED ACCESS; No
GARDEN; Great views

Chapter One

NORTH PATCHOLE FARMHOUSE
Kentisbury Ford, Barnstaple,
North Devon EX31 4NB

Tel: 01271 882029

The very name North Patchole conjures up a delightful image which is in no way discounted when the hamlet comes into view; it is charming and the mellow old farmhouse enhances the scene. You find Patchole by taking the road from Kentisbury Ford and bearing left onto the B3229 to Combe Martin turning immediately where it is signposted Patchole. Turn right at the only road in the hamlet and the farmhouse is on the corner on the left hand side. The 300 year old farmhouse which has immense character, is a traditional Devon longhouse set in 6 acres of land where Colin and Shirley Willoughby have a variety of farm animals including pigs, sheep, goats, ducks and hens. You may wonder how Patchole got its name! Legend has it that a large lady of the parish fell on the hills leaving a sizeable indentation which accounts for it!!

There is great freedom in staying here. You may come and go as you please, help feed the animals, wander around the farm fields or just laze in the attractive garden which has patio furniture for your use. Everything about the house is designed for comfort. There is a lounge with a woodburning stove, colour television and a good selection of books. The Snug Bar - the only room in the house where you may smoke - is just the place for a pre-dinner drink or coffee and liquers after. In the Dining Room with its inglenook and woodburning stove, you will be served delicious food. The Breakfast menu is varied with fresh eggs from the farms hens and ducks. The 4 course dinner is memorable. The Willoughbys use home farmed meat and locally produced fish and vegetables whenever possible. The menu changes every day, Outstandingly good are the starters and the delectable sweets.

The bedrooms have pretty drapes and bedlinen. Some have en-suite showers and wcs. They all have television, central heating, wash basins in vanity units, shaver points and tea/coffeemaking facilities.

USEFUL INFORMATION

OPEN; *All year*
CHILDREN; *Welcome*
CREDIT CARDS; *None taken*
LICENSED; *Yes*
ACCOMMODATION; *7 rooms some ensuite*
PETS; *Yes by prior arrangement*

DINING ROOM; *Varied Breakfast*
4 course dinner. Own produce
VEGETARIAN; *Catered for*
DISABLED ACCESS; *No*
GARDEN;
Yes + 6 acres smallholding

126

Devon, Cornwall, Somerset and Avon

CENTRY FARM
Kingsbridge, Devon
TQ7 2HF
Tel: 01548 852037

Everything about Centry Farm is beautiful from its setting, its exterior to the delightfully decorated and furnished interior. Pamela Lidstone is your host and it is she who has such an eye for colour and detail that ensures every one of the rooms pleases the eye and the comfort is second to none. There are two ensuite bedrooms with lovely views over the rolling South Hams countryside. Each room has hot drink facilities, radio/alarm, hair dryer, heater and electric blanket. The relaxing lounge has colour television and a separate dining room where a true, beautifully cooked farmhouse breakfast will be served to you. Evening meals are not available but there are many excellent local eateries. Definitely non-smoking. There is also a self-catering cottage adjoining the farmhouse which is attractively furnished and spotless. The large bedroom has a double and two single beds making it ideal for two or a family of four. It is fully equipped including a microwave and washer/dryer as well as colour television, convector heaters, iron and board, tea towels and cleaning materials are also provided. Kingsbridge has much to offer in its own right but it is the perfect base for exploring all the magical countryside and rivers of the South Hams.

USEFUL INFORMATION
OPEN;April-October inclusive
CHILDREN;Welcome
CREDIT CARDS;None taken
ACCOMMODATION;2 ensuite rooms
1 small self-catering cottage adjoining
PETS;No. This is a strictly non-smoking house
DINING ROOM;Delicious farmhouse breakfast
No evening meals
VEGETARIAN;Catered for
DISABLED ACCESS;No facilities
GARDEN;Extensive + 120 acre farm

GRANARY COTTAGE
Combpyne, Axminster,
Devon EX13 6SX

Tel: 01297 442856

Definitely off the beaten track in a secluded valley in tranquil countryside, nonetheless Granary Cottage is only 4 miles from the charming town of Lyme Regis. Drewe and Lyn Henley came to this attractive cottage in 1994 and they are happy to welcome you into their warm, comfortable friendly home. You will find it next door to the 13th century church but you are guaranteed there will be no more than 5 minutes of bells and those on Sundays only! The one double and 2 twin bedrooms are attractively furnished, the beds modern and each has TV and a beverage tray. One of the rooms is ensuite and the other two share a private bathroom. Breakfast is a sumptuous meal, freshly cooked to your order with several choices and both vegetarian and other diets can be catered for. Your hosts will be happy to help you plan your days if you wish. There is so much to see and do in this beautiful part of Devon, you are spoiled for choice.

USEFUL INFORMATION
OPEN;All year except Xmas
CHILDREN; Welcome
CREDIT CARDS; No
ACCOMMODTION;1dbl 2tw
DINING ROOM; Excellent breakfast only
VEGETARIAN;Yes + other diets
DISABLED ACCESS; No facilities
PETS; Yes

Chapter One

HOLMFIELD
West Charleton, Kingbridge,
South Devon TQ7 2AL

Tel: 01548 531650/857622 (work)

This handsome house standing in its own grounds and complete with a heated swimming pool and pool side barbecue for the use of guests, was recently converted from a farmhouse. It lies just 1.5 miles from the market town of Kingsbridge and between the Salcombe and Dart estuaries. From its South facing position there are magnificent unbroken views to the Salcombe Estuary. Holmfield is just a short walk from the shops, the Church and the pub. Everyone enjoys the relaxed and friendly atmosphere of Holmfield whether they stay in the three ensuite spacious and comfortably furnished bedrooms in the Main House or decide to use Holmfield Barn which sleeps 6 and Stable which sleeps 2-4 for a self-catering holiday. Most rooms in the Main House can accommodate extra beds and/or cot. Whichever you choose you are welcome to use the garden the barbecue and the pool. Breakfast is a first class meal with plenty of everything and vegetarians are catered for. There are no evening meals but Anne and Trevor Stockdale, the owners, are more than willing to suggest good eateries in the area.

The South Hams is renowned for its rolling hills, small, green, hedge lined fields, a rugged coastline and the beauty and splendour of the Salcombe and Dart Estuaries. The area has much to offer the visitor. There are miles of lovely walks to enjoy, including the spectacular National Trust coastal footpath. Holmfield is only a few minutes drive from Slapton Ley Field Centre and Nature Reserve. Sailing, windsurfing, fishing, riding, golf and other recreational activities are readily available.

USEFUL INFORMATION

OPEN: All year
CHILDREN: Welcome. Cots etc
CREDIT CARDS: All major cards
LICENSED: No
ACCOMMODATION: 3 ensuite rooms suitable for families. Self-catering accommodation for 6 and 2-4

DINING ROOM: Excellent breakfast
No evening meal
VEGETARIAN: Catered for
DISABLED ACCESS: No
GARDEN: Yes. Heated Pool
Poolside Barbecue
PETS: No

LOWER GRIMPSTONLEIGH
East Allington, Nr Kingsbridge,
Devon TQ9 7QH

Tel: 01548 521258 Fax: 01548 521329

A timeless charm is what you find at this tiny hamlet in the heart of Devon's South Hams. Mentioned in the Domesday Book, the house forms part of the original courtyard of Grimpstonleigh and is built of local stone. This pretty location has been used for filming a Victorian farm scene. It is very private, at the end of a lane and with no passing traffic. The charm of an old world farmstead with the ease of modern living. The house itself is furnished impeccably, in character antique and Chinese rosewood furniture. The bedrooms have beautiful vaulted beamed ceilings and are light, airy and comfortable. All have TV, tea and coffee, clock radios and hair dryers. There is a charming sitting room with a baby grand piano, and an open log fire which is wonderful for those winter evenings. Breakfast is a full English traditional meal with free range eggs, all served on fine bone china. Joy Jones, the owner, is known for her 'special suppers' and may be prevailed upon to arrange one for you. Outside the house is a dream. Across the lane a pond overflows into a ford, the smell of sweet roses fill the air, and there are plenty of walks right on you doorstep. Joy is an enthusiastic walker and has plenty of information on the area. Other local facilities include fishing, wild life and bird watching. A haven of peace and tranquillity not to be passed by.

USEFUL INFORMATION

OPEN; All year except Christmas and New Year
CHILDREN; Over 12 years
CREDIT CARDS; None taken
LICENSED; No
ACCOMMODATION; 2 ensuite rooms, 1 room with private bathroom
DINING ROOM; Excellent home cooking, including 'special suppers'
VEGETARIAN; Catered for
DISABLED ACCESS; Restricted
GARDEN; Beautiful
PETS; By arrangement
A NON-SMOKING HOUSE

Chapter One

MARSH MILLS
Aveton Gifford,
Kingsbridge, Devon TQ7 4JW

Tel/Fax: 01548 550549

Marsh Mills is a 5 acre working small holding with horses, goats, chickens, donkeys, sheep and ducks. It has a great deal of charm about it and not the least is the fine Georgian millhouse, which is adjacent to the remains of the original mill, now a granny flat. The whole atmosphere inside is reminiscent of the past, which adds to the pleasure of staying here. Only one ensuite bedroom, largely because of the need to retain the character of the old building. There is an enormous welcome from John and Maggie Newsham, who own it and work the small holding. Every room is comfortably furnished and has a wash basin, room heater and a plentifully supplied tea and coffee tray. There is a bathroom with plenty of hot water and an additional separate toilet.

After a peaceful night, you will come down to a true farmhouse breakfast with plenty of everything and all of it freshly prepared. There are no evening meals but with plenty of suitable eateries around to which the Newshams will guide you, some within easy walking distance, that will not cause any bother. If you want to spend a quiet day around the small holding you are very welcome and the secluded garden with views over the estuary is there for your use. From Salcombe sea fishing trips and sailing can be arranged. With coarse and trout fishing, wonderful walking country, beautiful beaches, Dartmoor closeby, as well as canoeing from Marsh Mills' own jetty, and birdwatching, there is always something to do.

USEFUL INFORMATION

OPEN: All year
CHILDREN: Welcome
CREDIT CARDS: None taken
LICENSED: No
ACCOMMODATION: 4 rooms
PETS: By arrangement

DINING ROOM: Excellent English breakfast. No evening meal
VEGETARIAN: Yes
DISABLED ACCESS: No
GARDEN: Yes
BROCHURE AVAILABLE

Devon, Cornwall, Somerset and Avon

SEAMARK
Thurlestone Sand, Kingsbridge,
South Devon TQ7 3JY

Tel: 01548 561300

Seamark stands on the point of the cliff-tops at Thurlestone and has unrivalled views over the seas; in the west to Bigbury and Plymouth and in the east to Hope Cove and Bolt Tail. It is worth coming here just for the magnificent sunsets. Thurlestone Sands, a large sandy beach, is below and you actually overlook the famous Thurlestone Rock. This is an ideal centre for bird watching, walking, fishing and many water sports. Seamark also has a wonderful recreational building complete with indoor heated swimming pool, sauna and well equipped games room. John and Trish Gange have equipped these apartments to a high standard and they are tastefully furnished and comfortable. You can either be self-contained or have bed and breakfast and if you are too tired after a hectic day on the beach then you can collect a meal for the evening from the main house which can be heated at your convenience. A superb idea!. There are gardens where children can play in safety and also a games room with a wide range of games, toys and books for all. John and Trish live on site and are always happy to help with further games or equipment.

USEFUL INFORMATION

OPEN; *All year*
CHILDREN; *Most welcome*
CREDIT CARDS; *None taken*
LICENSED; *Not applicable*
ACCOMMODATION; *5 cottages with 2 or 3 bedrooms*

DINING ROOM; *Not applicable*
VEGETARIAN; *Not applicable*
DISABLED ACCESS; *Poor*
GARDEN; *Large and level*
PETS; *Welcome*

THE BEECHES
Yarnscombe, Barnstaple
North Devon EX31 3LW
Tel: 01769 560714

Margaret Crocker runs a modern farmhouse on this small sheep farm on the outskirts of Yarnscombe. It has a hilltop position with fine views all round and is in unspoilt countryside. It offers comfortable accommodation and traditional home cooking. Evening meal can be arranged on request. The coasts and moors can be seen from the property, so you have plenty of choice. Whether you like walking or sunbathing (weather permitting) then this is the place! Within 9 miles you have the towns of Barnstaple, Torrington, Bideford and South Molton, so although this is a lovely rural location you are not far from the crowds if you wish! There are plenty of local activities with information on gardens, Royal Horticultural Society, Rosemoor being a great attraction, leisure centres, golf courses and much more.

Margaret will also arrange tours round her sheep farm detailing the various processes used. Very interesting and the children will love it!

USEFUL INFORMATION

OPEN : *All year*
CHILDREN : *Welcome*
CREDIT CARDS : *None taken*
LICENSED : *No*
ACCOMMODATION : *2 rooms.*

RESTAURANT : *Not applicable*
BAR FOOD : *Not applicable*
VEGETARIAN : *Catered for*
DISABLED ACCESS : *Not really*
GARDEN : *Pretty, with seating area.*

Chapter One

THE HOPE AND ANCHOR
Hope Cove, Kingsbridge,
Devon TQ7 0HQ

Tel: 01548 561294

You travel through some of Devon's most idyllic countryside to reach the rural fishing village of Hope Cove, a place that for years has attracted film and television programme makers. As you drive into the village square, you will see that The Hope and Anchor, a traditional inn, stands out as the focal point. Indeed it is the focal point of village life. Run by the Hall family for many years, it is Reg Hall who is now mine host. This cheerful, friendly man has gathered about him a staff who are equally friendly and purposeful in their desire to make visitors welcome. Of course there is local chatter at the bar but no stranger feels the barrier between 'them and us' which so often prevails in tight knit communities. Two large friendly bars open throughout the day, all year round and serve an excellent range of draught and bottled beers and ciders.

Food is all important and whether it is at lunch time when you eat excellent snacks in the bar, or the evenings when a well chosen, a la carte menu is available in the 'Upper Deck' restaurant, you will find there is a wide selection of tempting, beautifully cooked dishes. The Upper Deck is well known locally for the quality of the fresh fish and the succulence of the sumptuous steaks cooked to perfection to your taste. English fare is paramount but you will always find one or two dishes that have more than a hint of the Mediterranean about them. A sensibly priced wine list complements the food.

Built in the 1600s The Hope and Anchor is full of nooks and crannies and a delightful place tostay. There are 9 well appointed, comfortable bedrooms, all en-suite. The Residents Lounge is ideal for a little peace and quiet or to catch up on the news or your favourite television programme. The latter does take a back seat when there is so much to do in this exciting area. There is Golf at nearby Thurlestone, Fishing from Hope Cove, Riding in Marlborough, 3 miles away, good beaches, bathing and watersports. For those who enjoy walking the cliff paths and the countryside are spectacular.

USEFUL INFORMATION

OPEN; All year
CHILDREN; Welcome
C. CARDS; Visa/Euro/Access
LICENSED; Yes
ACCOMMODATION; 9 ensuite rooms

RESTAURANT; Upper Deck provides excellent Fish & Steaks in the evening
BAR FOOD; Snacks & other dishes lunch only
VEGETARIAN; Catered for
DISABLED ACCESS; Difficult

THE SLOOP INN
Bantham, Nr. Kingsbridge,
Devon TQ7 3AJ

Tel: 01548 560489/560215
Fax: 01548 561940

Situated in an area of great natural beauty in the beautiful and unspoilt South Hams is Bantham, a delightful village by the sea with wonderful white-washed thatched cottages, and pretty gardens. You can imagine in days of old, smugglers gathering in the local pub to share out the spoils, and that is indeed what went on in The Sloop Inn. In fact it was once owned by John Whiddon, a famous smuggler who would lure the unsuspecting ships onto the rocks using false lights. Today the pub is owned by Neil Girling and is everything a local village pub should be, beamed ceilings, stone-flagged floor and snug. The accommodation is warm and comfortable with 5 attractively furnished bedrooms complete with television, clock/radio, hair dryer, a tea and coffee tray and excellent ensuite facilities, most of the rooms have sea and river views. Breakfast is a traditional full English meal. Evening meals are not a problem, the Sloop Inn serves a delicious choice of high quality pub food recommended by Egon Ronay. An extensive wine list has wines from all over the world and 4 local ones. About 300 yards from the Inn is the beach, where children can play and build wonderful sand castles or spend hours with a net in the rock pools. Golf, fishing, riding and walking are all close by, not forgetting sailing, surfing, boating and swimming. This English Tourist Board '2 Crowns Commended' Inn also has self-catering accommodation. Not to be missed.

USEFUL INFORMATION

OPEN; *All year except Christmas*
CHILDREN; *Welcome*
CREDIT CARDS; *Only Debit Cards choice Delta/Switch*
LICENSED; *Full*
ACCOMMODATION; *5 ensuite rooms*
PETS; *Yes*

DINING ROOM; *Traditional English breakfast, Excellent high quality pub food*
VEGETARIAN; *Catered for, always a choice*
DISABLED ACCESS; *Limited access for wheelchairs*
GARDEN; *No, but 2 mins from the beach with access to open countryside*

Chapter One

ATTWORTH
*12 Crossley Moor Road,
Kingsteignton, Newton Abbot,
Devon TQ12 3LE*

Tel: 01626 69459

The saying 'never judge a book by its cover' is applicable to Attworth because the outside of the building does not have the sort of charm one might expect and the road it is in is full of uninspiring houses apart from one or two, but climb the steep steps to the front door, ring the bell and step inside to a most extraordinary home owned by two talented and delightful people Alec and Marcia Worth. They are both artists and sculptors and Alec is a keen and knowledgeable naturalist and wildlife photographer. Their home is full of their own paintings and sculptures all of which can do nothing but fascinate you. Apart from that they are such welcoming people that no one could feel anything but at home very rapidly. The three bedrooms are not ensuite but the spotless bathroom is within easy reach and there is plenty of hot water for baths. Tea and coffee facilities are in all the rooms. For anyone who would like a sketching or birdwatching holiday at Attworth you have two people who will willingly take you out to follow whatever pursuit you wish. They are patient souls who do not mind instructing the beginner at sketching, painting, or someone who has never been birdwatching before. If you would like to experience the wildlife of the area or the archaeology of Dartmoor, Alec can take you. Whichever activity you choose the Worths can cater for small groups of 4-6 people. The breakfast every morning is a delicious, sustaining meal and at night there are several pubs and restaurants close by. Attworth is centrally situated between the moor and the coast.

USEFUL INFORMATION

OPEN: *All year*
CHILDREN: *8 years & over*
CREDIT CARDS: *None taken*
ACCOMMODATION: *3 rooms not ensuite*
PETS: *No*
DINING ROOM: *Super breakfast. No evening meal*
VEGETARIAN: *Catered for*
DISABLED ACCESS: *No*
GARDEN: *Yes & stream*

WEST FARM,
Irsha Street,
Appledore, Devon EX39 1RY

Tel: 01237 425269

There are some houses that will for ever live in your memory and the Grade II listed West Farm is one of them. This circa 1600 house is stunning and has the added bonus of being a mere 20 paces from the sea. It is owned by Gail Sparkes, a lady who has vision and taste, and in her caring hands West Farm flourishes. It was originally part of a large farm but now only the house and the glorious walled garden together with a pretty courtyard, remain. The house is full of character and great architectural style. Undoubtedly it has manifestations of sounds and smells of the past from a very friendly ghost who is content to stay!

  Gail has furnished West Farm with classic antiques throughout. Every room has a wonderful colour scheme which enhances the beauty of the furniture. Not once however are you made to feel that this is a showpiece to be looked at and admired rather than lived in. The atmosphere is relaxed, welcoming and friendly. Fresh flowers and bowls of fruit are in all the rooms. The three bedrooms, one with a half tester the other 2 have twin beds all with top quality mattresses. Each room has TV, hairdryers plus complimentary toiletries and reading material. You get the feeling that unobtrusively you are being splendidly pampered!

  Breakfast and dinner in the beautiful dining room are meals to be savoured. Breakfast is delicious with a choice and the delight of having home-made preserves and condiments. The five coursedinner always includes local fish and meat as well as fresh vegetables. Gail has a deserved reputation for the quality of her food and for her wickedly tempting home-made cakes. West Farm is a member of the Wolsey Lodge Consortium. Appledore which is reputed to be England's most ancient fishing port, offers a wide range of activities for visitors including sailing, sea fishing, cycling, riding, golf at the Royal North Devon Golf Club and walking, especially along The Tarka Trail.

USEFUL INFORMATION

OPEN;*All year*   **DINING ROOM;***Super breakfast, 5 course dinner*
CHILDREN;*Not under 14*   **VEGETARIAN;***Options available. Special diets*
CREDIT CARDS;*None taken*   *By arrangement*
LICENSED;*Yes*   **DISABLED ACCESS;***Yes*
ACCOMMODATION; *3 ensuite rooms*
PETS;*No*   **GARDEN;***Beautiful walled garden & courtyard*

Chapter One

RENSON MILL
Ashwater, Devon
EX21 5ER

Tel/Fax: 01409 211665

Once a Devon Roundhouse, Renson Mill was skillfully converted in 1991 and is now the very attractive home of Geoffrey and Sonia Archer. You will find it 1 mile north of Ashwater village and eight miles north of the A30 at Stowford Cross intersection. Renson Mill is within easy access to many Devon and Cornish properties and gardens open to the public. Golf, fishing, riding, sailing and windsurfing are available within eight miles of the property. The Archers will meet trains at Exeter or flights at Exeter and Plymouth Airports. The charge is by arrangement. Geoffrey will also undertake to drive visitors in Devon and adjacent counties for an agreed fee. Every room is beautifully furnished in a cottage style with antique French Canadian Pine furniture. The Bed and Breakfast accommodation consists of a comfortable large twin-bedded room with bathroom ensuite and a small separate sitting room with television and fridge. Access to both rooms is directly from the courtyard. The sitting room may also be used as a separate single bedroom. Breakfast is a feast and the optional evening meal is cooked to Cordon Bleu standards - delicious and served with wine. No smoking indoors.

USEFUL INFORMATION

OPEN: All year
CHILDREN: No
CREDIT CARDS: None taken
ACCOMMODATION: Large twin-bedded room, sitting room could be a single bedroom
DINING ROOM: Superb breakfast
Optional Cordon Bleu evening meal
DISABLED ACCESS: No
GARDEN: Courtyard
NO SMOKING

OUTER NARRACOTT
Centery Lane, Bittadon
Barnstaple, Devon EX31 4HN
Tel: :01271 862951

Ralph and Anthea Burge are the owners of this excellent farmhouse. Formerly a working farm, Ralph and Anthea have now retired and enjoy having guests to stay. The rooms are to a very high standard and are furnished in a country style which suits this 200 year old house. There is also self catering accommodation in the form of a mobile home which once again is immaculate and to a high standard. The mobile home has its own garden space with room for BBQs and a laundry room is available. The gardens have been developed for the guests to relax in and many fine views can be enjoyed. There is plenty to do in the area. The town of Ilfracombe is a very pleasant 4 mile drive from the farm. The quay and harbour offer pleasure and fishing trips and there are lots of gift shops and places to eat. Just outside the town are many small coves and beaches to be enjoyed. This is a wonderful area for walking and there are plenty of short and long for any disposition. One worth mentioning specifically is the Tarka Trail; from the famous novel "Tarka the Otter" by Henry Williamson who resided for most of his working life in the area.

USEFUL INFORMATION

OPEN : April to October
CHILDREN : No
PETS : By arrangement
CREDIT CARDS : None taken
ACCOMMODATION : 3 rooms plus self catering.
BREAKFAST : Full English
VEGETARIAN : By arrangement
DISABLED ACCESS : No
GARDEN : Spacious

LEA HOUSE
Dalwood, Axminster,
East Devon, EX13 7DZ

Tel: 01404 831645

Anne and Edward's home is only a short distance (3/4 mile) from the A35 between Honiton and Axminster. It is situated on the outskirts of the pretty village of Dalwood which is set within the beautiful Blackdown Hills and with rolling countryside it is ideal country for walking.

Their attractive and spacious home is surrounded by a large garden which has interesting shrubs and banks of colourful flowers in summer. A swimming pool is tucked away in a wooded suntrap behind the house which guests are welcome to use when the weather is kind. The house is comfortably furnished with a dining room, a small quiet sitting-room and a large sitting room which guests are invited to share with their hosts. The upstairs bedrooms are all south facing and overlook the garden. They are brightly furnished in cottage pine and with pretty drapes. Each room has an en-suite shower or bathroom, plenty of hanging space, hairdryer and a tea/coffee making tray.

Each day begins with an interesting breakfast including cereals, fruits in season, followed by one of several cooked dishes and ending with croissants and toast with home made bread and preserves.

The popular towns of Beer, Branscombe, Sidmouth, Lyme Regis and Charmouth with its fossil cliffs, are all within 30 minutes drive. Further away, but still easily reached are the wild and beautiful areas of Dartmoor and Exmoor. The county towns of Exeter and Taunton are both nearby as are the National Trust properties of Killerton House, and Knighthayes.

USEFUL INFORMATION

OPEN; All year
CHILDREN; Yes
CREDIT CARDS; None taken
LICENSED; No
ACCOMMODATION; 3 ensuite rooms
PETS; Yes, with well behaved owners

DINING ROOM; Super breakfast
Evening meal by arrangement
VEGETARIAN; Yes
DISABLED ACCESS; No facilities
GARDEN; Yes. g pool in season

Chapter One

MANOR HOUSE
Combpyne, Axminster,
Devon EX13 6SX

Tel: 01297 445084

The history of this listed building is quite fascinating. It was a nunnery in the thirteenth century and has many historical connections. It is also mentioned in the Domesday Book which lists the owner in 1086, the present owners of the Manor have a list of owner/occupiers, which has been compiled by historians since that date. It is now a family home set in 3 acres of wooded gardens and is a haven for wildlife. Nicky and Donald Campbell are the owners and Donald is the chairperson of the local Conservation Society and obviously knows his stuff! You can actually join in conservation work if you desire, or Nicky can offer specialist help with most activities in the area. Fossil hunting on the proposed World Heritage coast at Charmouth and Monmouth Beach at Lyme Regis is available, bird watching for both the experienced and inexperienced, or even learn something of the local natural history with an experienced biologist. There are literary tours, (this is Jane Austen country) historical tours and garden tours. You can even have a tour to Thomas Hardy country. It is an ideal location for painting, drawing and photography. There is quite simply something for everyone here. This friendly home opens its arms to the visitor with its comfortable bedrooms and helpful hosts. Definitely a visit to remember.

USEFUL INFORMATION

OPEN; All year except Christmas to New Year
CHILDREN; Welcome
CREDIT CARDS; None taken
LICENSED; No
ACCOMMODATION; 3 rooms
DINING ROOM; English and Continental breakfast
VEGETARIAN; By arrangement
DISABLED ACCESS; No
GARDEN; Extensive and beautiful
PETS; By arrangement

Devon, Cornwall, Somerset and Avon

BRADIFORD COTTAGE
Halls Mill Lane, Bradiford,
Barnstaple, North Devon EX31 4DP

Tel: 01271 45039

    The 17th century Bradiford Cottage stands close to an old mill stream in the peaceful and scenic Bradiford Valley, yet it is only one mile from the centre of the old market town of Barnstaple. It could not be better for a relaxed holiday. From here the Atlantic coast is close and the moors of North Devon are superb for riding or walking. Directly from the Cottage a public footpath leadsto Blakewell Trout Farm, with the South West Coastal Path and the Tarka Trail nearby. For golfers the Royal North Devon, Ilfracombe, Saunton, Libbaton Golf Clubs and High Bullen at South Molton offer challenging courses. One can cycle, ride, sail enjoy watersports, fish or simply relax on the splendid sandy beaches a short drive away. The terrace with its garden furniture entices anyone who is feeling idle and not wanting to do anything but soak in the sun.

    Beautifully furnished, warm and comfortable, Bradiford Cottage is welcoming and has its own English Tourist Award, 1 Crown Commended.. There are four bedrooms upstairs, all with hand basins, with an adjoining wc/bathroom and separate wc/shower and one downstairs. Each bedroom is prettily but simply furnished and has a plentiful hostess tray. Tea and coffee is also available in the spacious sitting room during the evening. The bathroom is luxurious and complete with toiletries, fluffy towels and dressing gowns. Everything in fact for your comfort. Breakfast is a feast with a choice of a full English meal or Continental. There are no evening meals but Tony and Jane Hare will point you in the right direction towards the many good restaurants and pubs in the area. They can also provide free transport from the railway or bus station on your arrival. The mild weather in North Devon means one can enjoy a stay here as much in the winter and spring as in the summer.

    On the opposite side of the lane from Bradiford Cottage is Humes Farm which provides spacious self-catering accommodation for 10 people. The Barn, which has its own private entrance and garden sleeps 4 people and The Shippen with an alternative entrance sleeps 6. There are two other small cottages which sleep 2 people, All of them are centrally heated and fully equipped. Contact Jane and Tony for availability.

USEFUL INFORMATION

OPEN; *All year*
CHILDREN; *Welcome*
CREDIT CARDS; *None taken*
ACCOMMODATION; *4 bedrooms*
Self-catering cottages available

DINING ROOM; *Super breakfast*
VEGETARIAN; *Upon request*
DISABLED ACCESS; *No*
PETS;*Not in house but well behaved in Self-catering cottages.*

Chapter One

DELLA ROSA GUEST HOUSE
59 North Road, Combe Down,
Bath BA2 5DF

Tel: 01225 837193
Fax: 01225 835264

A friendly welcome can be expected at the Della Rosa Guest House, situated in a quiet suburb south of the River Avon and only 5 minutes drive from the golden stoned city of Bath. Accommodation offered includes single, double or family size bedrooms with ensuite shower and toilet facilities or private bathroom. Tastefully decorated with comfortable modern furnishings, all rooms have a tea and coffee tray and colour television. The residents lounge, which has been totally refurbished, is restful and cosy and is a charming room in which to relax. Jill and Bunny Harvey believe in providing their guests with a hearty and traditional English breakfast and this they do with special detail, using fresh local produce. Evening meals are not undertaken but there are several local hostelries serving good food. To the side of the property is ample parking space, there is also a small residents garden. Bath is a fascinating and elegant city steeped in history and affording visitors an abundance of interesting venues to explore. Local facilities and outdoor pursuits include fishing, horse riding, cycling and golf. There are many wonderful areas in which to walk and one of the most enjoyable is alongside the River Avon.

USEFUL INFORMATION
OPEN; All year   **DINING ROOM;** Hearty breakfast using local produce
CHILDREN; Welcome   **DISABLED ACCESS;** No
CREDIT CARDS; None taken   **GARDEN;** Small residents garden
ACCOMMODATION; 5 rooms,   **PETS;** Welcome
2 of which are ensuite

GARLANDS
Stovar Long Lane,
Beer, Devon EX12 3EA

Tel: 01297 20958
Fax: 01279 23869

Garlands is an excellent Edwardian house just outside the village of Beer. With views over the sea and Devonshire countryside, this is really an idyllic spot. All rooms are ensuite with TV, tea and coffee and the food is good English fare. Evening meal is available and there is a residents bar. Adjoining the main house is a cottage which is used for self-catering, and this too is furnished most attractively. You are within walking distance of the beach and there are many local pursuits available. This is quite a spectacular stretch of coastline and with the standard of accommodation, well worth a visit.

USEFUL INFORMATION
OPEN; All year   **DINING ROOM;** Good choice, 3 course evening meal
CHILDREN; Welcome   **VEGETARIAN;** By arrangement
CREDIT CARDS; All major   **DISABLED ACCESS;** Some on the ground floor
LICENSED; Residents   **GARDEN;** Excellent with complete access
ACCOMMODATION; 6 ensuite rooms   **PETS;** Dogs by arrangement

Devon, Cornwall, Somerset and Avon

OAKLEIGH HOUSE
19 Upper Oldfield Park,
Bath BA2 3JX
Tel: 01225 315698
Fax: 01225 448223

Oakleigh is a charming and elegant Victorian house in a quiet situation yet only 10 minutes from the centre of Bath, with lovely views of the city from the bedrooms. Each guest room has an ensuite bathroom and is superbly appointed with colour television, clock/radio, hair dryer, tea/coffee tray and complimentary toiletries. A cosy sitting room has been set aside for residents and here also the standard of furnishings is excellent. The spacious and stylish dining room is the perfect setting for one to enjoy a superb traditional English breakfast. A full vegetarian meal is available on request. Evening meals are not served, however there are many restaurants locally situated. Oakleigh has the RAC 'Highly Acclaimed' accolade, and the AA's '4Q Selected' award. A private car park is available for patrons. The Golden Stone of Bath is the facade for many museums, galleries, shops and the famous Roman Baths. The Bath Industrial Heritage Centre is well worth a visit as it traces the story of the 'Bath Stone' from which much of Bath has been built. Surrounding this delightful city are the beautiful Mendips and Cotswolds, with their many varied and interesting places to visit. Fishing, horse riding, cycling, tennis and extensive walking is available locally.

USEFUL INFORMATION
OPEN; All year except Christmas
CHILDREN; No
CREDIT CARDS; All major cards except Diners
ACCOMMODATION; 4 ensuite rooms
DINING ROOM; Excellent breakfast
VEGETARIAN; Very well catered for and Vegan
DISABLED ACCESS; No
GARDEN; Front only
PETS; No
NO SMOKING IN PUBLIC ROOMS

LANE MILL FARM
Wollfardisworthy,
Bideford, North Devon EX39 5PZ
Tel: 01237 431254

Three miles off the A39 and three quarters of a mile from the wonderfully named village of Woolfardisworthy, is Lane Mill Farm. It is a working beef farm with an assortment of smaller animals which guests can visit. The half acre landscaped garden includes an indoor heated swimming pool. The property offers very comfortable accommodation, simply but attractively furnished with pretty linens and wallpapers. The 2 bedrooms have ensuite shower rooms, tea and coffee making facilities, complimentary soaps and fine country views. There is a residents lounge/diner complete with colour television, here you will be served a full hearty English breakfast. Evening meals are available at your hosts, Gordon and Christina Leonard's own Restaurant and Inn, The Manor, in the village. The beautiful Devonshire countryside and glorious sandy beaches ensure a restful holiday time.

USEFUL INFORMATION
OPEN; Easter-end of October
CHILDREN; Welcome
CREDIT CARDS; None taken
LICENSED; No
ACCOMMODATION; 2 ensuite rooms, 1 double, 1 family
DINING ROOM; Full English breakfast
VEGETARIAN; Catered for
DISABLED ACCESS; No
GARDEN; Yes, with indoor heated swimming pool
PETS; Yes

Chapter One

PARKSIDE GUEST HOUSE
11 Marlborough Lane,
Bath BA1 2NQ
Tel: 01225 429444

Parkside is an Edwardian house situated in a wonderful location adjacent to Royal Victoria Park and the world famous Royal Crescent. A beautiful 10 minute stroll through the Park brings you to the city centre of Bath (a World Heritage City), or in the other direction to the Botanical Gardens. On entering the house one is aware of a genteel elegance. Furnishings are stylish and blend with the character. Bedrooms offer warmth and cosiness, each furnished in pastel shades, with colour television and a welcome tray. Most have ensuite facilities. Breakfast is taken in the Dining Room which overlooks an attractive city garden. Special emphasis is placed on the preparation and presentation of all meals with a menu choice for breakfast (traditional and vegetarian). Fresh local produce, free range eggs and wholefoods are used - sorry no sausages! Dinner is available by special arrangement, and imaginative courses are followed by coffee in the lounge which provides a relaxed atmosphere for conversation, reading or just planning the day's events. Bath is noted for it's historic Roman Baths (the only Hot Spring in Britain) and also it's beautiful Georgian architecture - Crescentson hillsides which glow in the sunlight. For shoppers there is a paradise of specialist shops - and for others the Museums and Exhibitions offer exciting interest, not to be missed.

USEFUL INFORMATION

OPEN; All year except Christmas week
CHILDREN; Not under 5 years
CREDIT CARDS; All major cards except Amex and Diners
ACCOMMODATION; 5 ensuite rooms
PETS; By prior arrangement only

DINING ROOM; English breakfast 3 course evening meal by prior arrangement
VEGETARIAN; Excellent choice, vegan
DISABLED ACCESS; No
GARDEN; Large garden with tables and chairs

OAKLANDS
Black Dog, Nr Crediton,
Devon
Tel: 01884 860645

This very modern house run by Janet Bradford offers spacious accommodation furnished to very high standards. Janet serves full traditional English breakfast but will also cater for vegetarians by arrangement. All rooms are fully equipped with TV and tea and coffee. The house is ideally situated in a lovely rural setting with access to local facilities such as fishing, golf and walking. There are two very good moors way walks from Ivybridge to Lynmouth and if after a hard day's activities you require sustenance then the Black Dog Inn is adjacent.

USEFUL INFORMATION

OPEN; All year
CHILDREN; Yes
CREDIT CARDS; No
LICENSED; Not applicable
ACCOMMODATION; 3 rooms, 2 ensuite 2 doubles, 1 twin

RESTAURANT; Not applicable
BAR FOOD; Not applicable
VEGETARIAN; Breakfast by arrangement
DISABLED ACCESS; No
GARDEN; Spacious

BURSCOTT HOUSE
3 Buttgarden Street,
Bideford, North Devon EX39 2AU
Tel: 01237 478262

A Grade II Listed Georgian town house built in 1729 is situated in the centre of the North Devon town of Bideford. Burscott House is run by Sheila Turner, who bids you a very warm welcome with a cup of tea and with the assurance that your stay will be a most enjoyable experience. All bedrooms are tasteful and most comfortable each with its own wash hand basin. A truly traditional English breakfast is served in the dining room which has the most glorious views of the River Torridge, over the river is the medieval Bideford Bridge with its 24 arches. The rugged and beautiful North Devon coastline offers the visitor a wide choice of activities. Instow, 3 miles away is the centre for yachting, and within a short drive the golden sands of Braunton and Saunton, where surfers and swimmers alike will enjoy the rollers. Appledore with its maritime history has a most interesting museum, with an insight into nautical accounts of yesteryear and well worth a visit. There is the South West Coastal Path where walkers will delight in the spectacular sea and coastal views, miles and miles of glorious breathtaking scenery.

USEFUL INFORMATION
OPEN; All year
CHILDREN; Welcome, over 7 years
CREDIT CARDS; None taken
LICENSED; No
ACCOMMODATION; 4 rooms
DINING ROOM; Full English breakfast
No evening meal
VEGETARIAN; Catered for
DISABLED ACCESS; No
GARDEN; No

HELE HOUSE
Carhampton Road, Blue Anchor,
Minehead, Somerset TA24 6LB
Tel: 01643 821967

With wonderful sea and coastal views this beautifully appointed guest house is welcoming indeed. The owners have ensured that public rooms and bedrooms are a delight. The bedrooms being ensuite include television, tea/coffee making facilities, hair dryer and complimentary soaps. The soft furnishings are co-ordinated and enhance these light airy rooms. In the evening light snacks or cold suppers are available. Vegetarians are catered for. Outdoor attractions are abundant in this area and include sea or river fishing, horse riding, cycling, walking, and golf. Regrettably there are no facilities for children or pets. Guests are requested not to smoke. There is ample off road parking.

USEFUL INFORMATION
OPEN: April-October
CHILDREN: No
CREDIT CARDS: None taken
LICENSED: No
ACCOMMODATION: 3 ensuite rooms
DINING ROOM: Full English breakfast
Light meals available in the evenings
VEGETARIAN: Catered for
DISABLED ACCESS: No
GARDEN: Yes *PETS:* No

Chapter One

THE REDCAR HOTEL & BENTLEY'S RESTAURANT
27-29 Henrietta Street,
Bath, Avon

Tel: 01225 469151 Fax: 01225 461424

Apart from the undoubted comfort and service of staying in a hotel of this calibre, there is the added pleasure in learning about its history. Its architect and designer, the redoubtable Sir William Pultney, who also designed Great Pultney Street, would no doubt be very surprised that the three houses numbers 2729 had changed from individual buildings into this elegant establishment which gives pleasure to visitors from all over the world, all the year round.

Centrally situated at the end of Laura Place, a street beloved by Regency society, The Redcar is versatile. It has 31 bedrooms each beautifully furnished and with every modern facility. It is an ideal venue for small conferences, where meetings can be held in quiet surroundings. It accommodates 70 people theatre style and 50 boardroom. The rooms are also excellent for a dinner dance or a wedding reception.

Bentley's Restaurant is somewhere that is popular with the residents of Bath. They know it is tranquil, delightfully appointed and it is somewhere that they can be sure of the freshest ingredients in all the interesting dishes that are produced by the Head Chef and his Brigade. Every dish on the A la Carte menu is a masterpiece and an excellent Table d'Hote menu is also available. The Bar is a meeting place for friends who want to enjoy comfort, a drink and probably indulge in one of the tasty lunchtime specials.

USEFUL INFORMATION

OPEN: All day, all year
CHILDREN: Welcome
CREDIT CARDS: All major cards
LICENSED: Full on
ACCOMMODATION: 31 rooms 22 ensuite

RESTAURANT: Superb food. A la Carte & Table d'Hote
BAR FOOD: Lunchtime Specials
VEGETARIAN: Always available
DISABLED ACCESS: No
GARDEN: Henrietta Park next door

SIENA HOTEL
24/25 Pulteney Road,
Bath BA2 4EZ

Tel: 01225 425495
Fax: 01225 469029

One of the loveliest hotels in Bath built within a walled garden enjoying exceptional views of the city and its medieval abbey, the Siena Hotel is a fine example of Victorian architecture. Internally it is elegantly decorated with superb classical furnishings exuding warmth and tranquillity. The ensuite bedrooms are sheer luxury with satellite colour TV, clock/radio, hospitality tray and hair dryers. Guests are served excellent home cuisine in the peaceful and intimate dining room overlooking the gardens, full English or Continental breakfast with home-made freshly baked bread, and vegetarian dishes are prepared and presented by the dedicated kitchen staff. With prior arrangement evening meals will be provided.

A delightful Lounge Bar serves a comprehensive range of alcoholic and soft drinks. Conference facilities are provided for up to 22 delegates and held in The Abbey Room, which has splendid stucco decoration in soft white and blue. The proprietors and staff endeavour to provide a first class and friendly service to compliment your stay in Bath. A private car park is provided. Bath is renowned for its superb shops and fascinating historical museums, galleries, houses and monuments. For those seeking outdoor sporting activities these are available locally and include fishing, cycling, golf and walking, particularly alongside the River Avon.

USEFUL INFORMATION

OPEN; All year except 2 weeks at Christmas
CHILDREN; Welcome, cots are available
CREDIT CARDS; All major cards
LICENSED; Yes
ACCOMMODATION; 15 ensuite rooms
RESTAURANT; Full English or Continental breakfast. Evening meal by prior arrangement
VEGETARIAN; Catered for
DISABLED ACCESS; 1 ground floor room with special ramped access
GARDEN; Walled with flowers, trees and lawns
PETS; By prior arrangement

Chapter One

THE OLD SCHOOL HOUSE
*Church Street, Bathford,
Bath, Avon BA1 7RR*

*Tel: 01225 859593
Fax: 01225 859590*

Bath is without doubt a most beautiful city, it has so much to offer in such pleasant surroundings, with fine Roman and Georgian buildings that blend so well. The splendour of the Abbey with its tower that soars up in the English 'Perpendicular' style to a height of 162ft, the decorative facade and lovely large windows. The Pump Room featured by Jane Austen, a handsome building where visitors may drink Bath water from the fountain; it is said to be very healthy, or you can relax have a cup of coffee and a Bath bun while you listen to classical music played by the resident trio. With museums and galleries and superb shops a stay here is a must.

Not far from this wonderful city of honey coloured Bath stone is the walled village of Bathford and nestling in this lovely little village is The Old School House the perfect bed and breakfast. Built 160 years ago it stands on the old Manor Court Barn site. For 140 years it was the village school, but today it is owned by Rodney and Sonia Stone, a very warm and friendly couple, who open their home for you to stay. The 4 pretty bedrooms all have an ensuite bathroom, TV, telephone and a tea and coffee tray. Two ground floor rooms aresuitable for less mobile. After a peaceful and relaxing sleep a full English breakfast is served in the dining room. There are many restaurants in Bath and the surrounding area for your evening meal, and excellent local pubs. Being in an area set aside for conservation, nature lovers will be in their element. Superbly positioned for touring the Cotswolds and Mendips and for visiting those elegant stately homes and gardens including Stourhead, Longleat, Lacock Abbey and Dyrham Park. There are fine walks along the Kennet and Avon Canal and through local Avon Trust Woodland where you can take in the beautiful views of the Avon Valley. The Old School House is 'Highly Commended' by the English Tourist Board and '5Q Premier Selected' by the AA. A stay at this lovely peaceful home is recommended.

USEFUL INFORMATION

OPEN; *All year*
CHILDREN; *Not really suitable*
CREDIT CARDS; *Visa/Mastercard*
ACCOMMODATION; *4 ensuite rooms*
NON SMOKING HOUSE

DINING ROOM; *Breakfast only*
DISABLED ACCESS; *Two ground floor rooms*
GARDEN; *Yes*
PETS; *No*

BLAGDON MANOR COUNTRY HOTEL
Ashwater,
Beaworthy,
Devon EX21 5DF

Tel: 01409 211224
Fax: 01409 211634

Tim and Gill Casey acquired Blagdon Manor four years ago and then set about restoring this wonderful old, typically Devonian, manor house to its former glory. It was a labour of love and determination with builders working inside and out for over eighteen months. The result is stunning and the atmosphere something very special. One can only suppose it was always a happy house and this sense of well being is still there today. Every room has been re-crated with floor coverings, drapes and beds all harmonising with the colour scheme appointed for that room. It is Gill who has this unerring ability to choose the right colours for every room. When you retire to bed you will appreciate the individual and attractive furnishings. The house varies in age with anything from the 12th century to the mid-1600s. Both Tim and Gill are gregarious people and genuinely enjoy meeting the people who beat a path to their door. Tim will tell you that most are 'Empty Nesters' or those whose children are grown up and the parents can escape for a break in the comfort provided by Blagdon Manor. Within the eight acres of grounds there is room to stroll and absorb the splendid views, to use the golfers' practice ground or to reveal the assertive side of ones nature on the croquet lawn.

As evening falls, the bar beckons with its enormous log fire or maybe you would prefer the peace of the library, a game of snooker or just the quiet of the drawing room. The highlight of the evening must be dinner. Guests dine together at a long table as though it were a dinner party, which encourages the art of conversation whilst enjoying the delicious and imaginative dishes cooked by Gill. It is a wonderful house and one cannot imagine anyone leaving there without the ardent desire to return as quickly as possible.

USEFUL INFORMATION

OPEN: All year
CHILDREN: Not suitable
CREDIT CARDS: Visa/Mastercard/Amex/Switch
LICENSED: Yes. Interesting wine list
ACCOMMODATION: 7 ensuite rooms
Facilities for small conferences. Self-catering cottage
DINING ROOM: Delicious, home-cooked and imaginative
VEGETARIAN: Upon request
DISABLED ACCESS: Not really
GARDEN: Beautiful + practice golf and croquet

Chapter One

LANGLEIGH HOUSE
*The Village,
Berrynarbor,
North Devon EX34 9SG
Tel: 0271 883410*

Berrynarbor is about one mile from the coastal resort of Combe Martin, with its own sheltered bay, and three miles from the larger seaside resort of Ilfracombe. The village is certainly one of the most attractive in Devon and has many times been adjudged winner of the 'Best Kept Village' competition. It remains nonetheless unscathed by commercialism and is a delightful place to make your base for a holiday or short break. In the centre of Berrynarbor is Langleigh House, almost opposite the 'Olde Globe' pub. Owned and run by Rod Skelly it is a friendly, relaxed guesthouse where people of all ages can feel at ease. There are few do's and don'ts and everything is done to ensure your stay is a happy and contented one.

Every room is light, airy and beautifully decorated and furnished with comfortable modern beds etc. Careful attention has been paid to the colour co-ordination both in drapes, papers and linen which lends charm throughout the house including the small, cosy lounge and the pleasant dining room which has excellent views as indeed there are from the back bedrooms. Every one of the six bedrooms, four of which are ensuite, has a TV, a tea and coffee tray as well as complimentary soaps and other touches. Breakfast is a feast but no evening meals are served, however the 12th century Olde Globe Inn has an excellent reputation for its food and facilities.

With sea fishing, local trout lakes, golf, walking on Exmoor and the coastal paths as well as cycling, riding and clay shooting, you will never be bored whilst staying at Langleigh House.

USEFUL INFORMATION

OPEN; *Easter to end October* **DINING ROOM;** *Traditional English Breakfast*
CHILDREN; *Welcome*   **VEGETARIAN;** *Catered for*
CREDIT CARDS; *All major cards not Diners/Amex*   **DISABLED ACCESS;** *No*
LICENSED; *No*   **GARDEN;** *Large, sloping gardens*
ACCOMMODATION; *6 rooms 4 ensuite*   **PETS;** *Yes.*
   Car parking

THE OLD MILL,
Buck's Mills, Bideford,
North Devon, EX39 5DY.

Tel : 01237 431701

Bucks Mill is a sleepy Devon village, nestling next to the sea, and with a wealth of fascinating history. It can be traced back to the Iron Age, and amazingly there is great detail of events since then. From history to ghost stories there is much known about the fortunes and mishaps of this tiny coastal village which has had it's share of heroes and devils, wrecks and even it's own Marie Celeste.

Today Bucks Mill is a holiday village with many of the cottages being let in the summer months to holiday makers. The Old Mill caters for bed & breakfast but can also boast a tearoom and a very fine restaurant. Rosemary and Ray Newport are the proprietors here and offer a high standard of hospitality and friendliness in their welcoming establishment. The Old Mill was originally a corn mill dating from 1605, and has now been refurbished and decorated in a charming country fashion. Many pictures and photographs decorate the walls giving you an insight into the history of the village. There are many antiques throughout, and the superb bedrooms offer eloquent accommodation with the modern essentials of colour TV, tea/coffee tray and toiletries.

During day time hours various light lunches and cream teas are served, and in the evening there is an excellent menu with strong Italian overtones and also traditional English dishes. Fresh lobster is something of a speciality in the summer months and there is a good wine list to compliment your meal. The Old Mill has a full license so a pre or even after dinner drink is available. This is a wonderful location to relax and enjoy nature, and with accommodation of a high standard and a welcoming atmosphere this must be the idyllic spot!

USEFUL INFORMATION

OPEN : B&B : All year
  Tearoom & Restaurant : March - Oct.
  10.30am to Dusk
  Evenings : 7-9pm.
CHILDREN : Welcome
PETS : No
CREDIT CARDS : None taken

RESTAURANT : Fine menu
VEGETARIAN : Catered for
DISABLED ACCESS : Some
LICENSED : Full
GARDEN : Superb
SMOKING : Yes
ACCOMMODATION : 4 rooms:
  1 twin, 2 dbl, 1 sgl.

Chapter One

LONGALLER MILL,
Bishops Hull, Taunton,
Somerset TA4 1AD

Tel: 01823 326071

It is a great privilege to stay in this enchanting historic watermill, spanning a leat of the River Tone. It is not only because of the interest in seeing much of the original machinery of the mill which was operational until 1964. This machinery is gradually being restored in the careful and loving hands of William and Jo Beaumont who genuinely enjoy their guests and make them very welcome. Now a grade 2 listed building Longaller has one charming double bedroom with a well appointed en suite shower room, colour TV and tea/coffee making facilities. The room has a happy mixture of traditional and antique furniture with fine views overlooking the orchard and millstream. Breakfast is a sumptuous meal in which the choice is yours. No evening meal is available but the Beaumonts will be delighted to recommend good places to you.

What is so special about Longaller Mill in addition to the excellent accommodation is the wealth of birdlife one can see as you gently wander along the riverbanks. You may well see herons, kingfishers, dippers, ducks, swans, cormorants and if you are up early, otters. There is a half mile of private coarse fishing, a cider orchard, and everywhere a sense of peace and quiet. Wonderful for re-charging ones batteries and for exploring the nearby Quantock, Blackdown and Exmoor hills, and it is within easy distance of the North and South Devon coasts, Exeter and Bath. There are a number of National Trust properties in the area, as well as some delightful gardens open to the public. William Beaumont has rare breeds of farm animals in which he is both very interested and very knowledgeable. He loves to talk about his achievments in this field and will be happy to show the animals to you.

USEFUL INFORMATION

OPEN; *All year except Nov/Feb inc*
CREDIT CARDS;*None taken*
LICENSED;*No*
ACCOMMODATION;*1dbl ensuite*
PETS;*By arrangement*

DINING ROOM; *Excellent breakfast*
VEGETARIAN;*Upon request*
DISABLED ACCESS;*No special facilities*
GARDEN;*5 acres. Private coarse fishing*

DOWNREW HOUSE
Bishops Tawton,
Devon EX32 0DY

Tel: 01271 42497/46673
Fax: 01271 23947

Tucked away in a quiet lane just off the A377 at Bishops Tawton, Downrew House has many superb qualities but perhaps above all it is the overwhelming sense of peace which strikes one. It is a house which has stood in 12 acres of meadowland and gardens for over 350 years. 500ft above sea level on the South facing slopes of Codden Hill just four miles from Barnstaple. Enlarged during the reign of Queen Anne, the main house, coach house and lodge are all integrated and look out over beautiful gardens to uninterrupted views of the surrounding countryside, extending to the South for over 20 miles. No more than twenty eight guests are ever accommodated at Downrew so you are assured of service of the highest order which at the same time is friendly and unobtrusive. The whole house has charm and warmth enhanced by the stylish and elegant furnishings and decor. It all looks beautiful but it is essentially a house to be lived in and enjoyed - not a museum piece. Comfortable armchairs by the fire, flowers and other touches entice one to be lazy, in fact there is so much to do within the grounds that one could be tempted not to go away from the house during your stay. The only contact with the outside world might be the local people who come to dine here knowing that they will be superbly fed on mouth watering cuisine in which only the finest ingredients are used.

In the Main House, the drawing room has views onto the garden and the dining room possesses an 18ft bow window overlooking miles of countryside, with Dartmoor in the far distance. Most people gather in the bar with its polished Delabole slate floor, for a drink before dinner. It is a cheery place and friendly enough to encourage conversation. There are four centrally heated, ensuite double bedrooms plus two family suites. The Coach House forms the third side of a square with the Main House and has six double bedrooms with en- suite bathrooms, colour television, radio and telephone. This building also contains a conference room, card room and solarium. The Lodge is fully self-contained, consisting of lounge, dining room, kitchen, bathroom, one double and one twin bedded room. Guests staying here have the use of all the Hotel facilities. A wonderful place in which to stay and one which will always demand a return visit.

USEFUL INFORMATION

OPEN;All year except January
CHILDREN;Welcome
CREDIT CARDS;All except Diners
LICENSED;Yes. Fine wine list
ACCOMMODATION;12 en suite rooms
GARDEN;12 acres enclosed gardens
Swimming pool

DINING ROOM;Superb cuisine
 Open to non-residents
VEGETARIAN;Special dishes to order
DISABLED ACCESS;3 rooms
Coach House & Dining Room, Lounge
PETS;Yes

Chapter One

HAWTHORNE HOUSE
Bishopswood, Nr Chard,
Somerset TA20 3RS

Tel:01460 234482

Bishopswood is a small hamlet nestling in the Blackdown Hills on the Somerset/Devon border. An area designated as being of Outstanding Natural Beauty, it is a wonderful place from which to set out to explore the footpaths and forest trails nearby or enjoy facilities for horse-riding, swimming and golf. Hawthorne House is ideal for anyone wanting to enjoy all this and much more including at least six national Trust Properties. Exmoor, Taunton Vale, Lyme Regis and the Quantock Hills are within 30 minutes drive. Roger and Sarah Newman-Coburn own and run Hawthorne House whose guests who can be sure of a great welcome and hospitality. The bedrooms are all decorated with Sanderson wallpapers with matching or co-ordinated curtains, linens etc. Two of the rooms are ensuite and the third has a private bathroom. A hostess tray in each room means you can make tea or coffee whenever you wish. Breakfast is served in the pretty conservatory with splendid views over the beautiful garden with its lawns, trees, shrubs and wildlife pond. Guests have the use of a comfortable lounge with colour T.V, board games and jigsaw puzzles. You are invited to relax on the terraces orthe garden and grounds which extend to about one acre, or stroll round the fields belonging to the house and in summer revel in the beauty of the wild flowers. Breakfast is an excellent meal either full English or Continental and with the added pleasure of home-made preserves. Dinner is by prior arrangement. Bring your own wine. A very happy house in which to stay. Hawthorne House is strictly non-smoking.

USEFUL INFORMATION

OPEN; All year
CHILDREN; Over 12 years
CREDIT CARDS; None taken

DINING ROOM; Delicious breakfast
Dinner by arrangement
VEGETARIAN; And special diets
by arrangement

LICENSED; No. Please bring your own
ACCOMMODATION; 2 ensuite 1 private bathroom
PETS; Well behaved by arrangement

DISABLED ACCESS; No

N.B. This is a Non-Smoking house

COPPERFIELD
Bodieve, Wadebridge,
Cornwall PL27 6EG

Tel: 01208 812264

The River Camel runs through the town of Wadebridge and alongside it is The Camel Trail, wonderful to walk or cycle as it stretches from Padstow to Bodmin, with superb scenery. About a mile from Wadebridge is the village of Bodieve where Mrs. Doris Jewel has her lovely Guest House. Copperfield was built around 1954 and is very comfortable, warm and welcoming. The 2 bedrooms, 1 double and 1 twin, are delightful each with their own separate bathroom, the modern style furniture is in keeping with house. A full and sumptuous English breakfast is served, there is no evening meal, but there are several good restaurants and pubs in Wadebridge and the surrounding area, Padstow is well known for its superb fish restaurants. Copperfield is a great place to stay as it is so central for touring and sightseeing. For those who are energetic and love the water, you will be spoilt for choice with some excellent surfing beaches, which are also safe for the children. Copperfield is six miles from Rock with its water ski-ing and sailing. The Cornish Shire Horse Centre is a must, with a show to start with where they talk about these wonderful heavy beasts. Land's End is only about an hours drive away with it's visitors centre, craft shops and England's last post box. With golf and fishing within easy reach you are assured a good holiday.

USEFUL INFORMATION

OPEN; Easter-end October
CHILDREN; Over 11 years
CREDIT CARDS; None taken
LICENSED; No
ACCOMMODATION; 2 rooms, 1 double, 1 twin, each with their own separate bathroom
DINING ROOM; Full English breakfast
VEGETARIAN; Catered for
DISABLED ACCESS; No, but welcome
GARDEN; Yes
PETS; No

Chapter One

THE MOWHAY
*Bodieve, Wadebridge,
Cornwall PL27 6EG
Tel: 01208 814078*

 The serenity and peace of this delightful Guest House is ideal for a relaxing sojourn, a short distance from some of the most spectacular coastal scenery in the country, and an area steeped in history and the land of King Arthur. This modern property standing in its own well tended gardens, is open all year. Bedrooms are well furnished and the decor pleasing to the eye and bed linen of excellent quality. Ensuite facilities are limited and so early booking advised. Colour television and tea/coffee tray are provided in each room. A delicious traditional breakfast is served, should an evening meal be required then prior notice is desirable, however there are local inns and restaurants offering varied menus within easy reach. Walking in this area is one of the top leisure pursuits and Bettie and Bill offer their guests the opportunity to enjoy 'one way' walks by providing their services driving you to or from your walk. The golden sandy beaches along the north Cornish coast are acclaimed for ideal surfing and swimming, boating and sea fishing. There are many delightful and fascinating fishing villages with narrow cobbled streets to explore including Tintagel, Rock and Port Isaac. Further afield is Looe, Mevagissey and Polperro.

USEFUL INFORMATION
OPEN; All year except Christmas   **DINING ROOM**; Full English breakfast
CHILDREN; Welcome   Evening meal with prior notice
CREDIT CARDS; None taken   **DISABLED ACCESS**; No but welcome
LICENSED; No   **GARDEN**; Yes, lovely
ACCOMMODATION; 3 rooms,   **PETS**; No
2 double, 1 twin with vanitory unit, 1 ensuite

HELMAN TOR COTTAGES
*Lanlivery,
Bodmin,
Cornwall PL30 5HT
Tel: 01208 872372*

 The five holiday cottages on this wonderful farm have been carefully converted from a range of old granite farm buildings which date back to the 1860s. The cottages are separated from the rest of the farm by a low wall and have their own car park and entrance lawn. Although there is easy access to both North and South coasts and to many of Cornwall's attractions, I believe you will not want to leave the 200 acres of this farm. There is an archeological site dating back to Neolithic times and a Bronze Age Hut Circle; there are Exmoor ponies, there are goats, there are ewes, there are wild flowers managed in conjunction with the Countryside Commission. Gill and Des Girdler are to be highly commended on this idyllic location which they have nurtured.

USEFUL INFORMATION
OPEN; All year   **RESTAURANT**; Not applicable
CHILDREN; Welcome   **VEGETARIAN**; Not applicable
CREDIT CARDS; None taken   **DISABLED ACCESS**; Some, with restrictions
LICENSED; No   **GARDEN**; Not applicable
ACCOMMODATION; Self-catering cottages

LOSKEYLE FARM
St Tudy, Bodmin
Cornwall PL30 3PW

Tel: 01208 851005

In a peaceful part of mid Cornwall and on the edge of Bodmin Moor, surrounded by unspoilt and almost undiscovered valleys, numerous footpaths linking villages and plenty of opportunities to visit the local Inns, Loskeyle Farm is everything one could wish for. Within 20 minutes the 'magic' of Cornwall is yours to behold with outstanding places to seek out. The views from the house are wonderful and the garden is there for your use. The farm has calves, hens and family pets. Accommodation is available from March to November inclusive and Sandra and Phil Menhinick have one double, one single and one family room with hot and cold water supply. All three have beverage facilities. Children are especially welcome and there are plenty of toys and games around the house. Babysitting is free on request. Excellent traditional breakfast and evening meal.

USEFUL INFORMATION

OPEN: March to November inclusive breakfast **CHILDREN:** Welcome
CREDIT CARDS: None taken
ACCOMMODATION: 3 rooms, 1 double, 1 single, 1 family
DINING ROOM: Excellent traditional and evening meal
DISABLED ACCESS: No
GARDEN: Yes
PETS: By arrangement

LOWER MEADOWS HOUSE
Penally Hill,
Boscatle, Cornwall PL35 0HF

Tel: 01840 250570

This non-smoking guest house is owned and run by a welcoming couple, John and Sylvia Wells who ensure that every one of their guests leaves determined to come back again as soon as possible. The house is modern, light and spacious and kept immaculately. The seven bedrooms, three of which are ensuite, are comfortably and attractively furnished and have Colour TV and a tea/coffee tray. The full English breakfast is freshly cooked and generously proportioned. No evening meal is available but there are many good pubs and restaurants in close proximity. Car parking is available and the Wells operate a fully licensed taxi service (between 10am and 10pm) offering it free of charge within a five mile radius for any one staying for two nights or more. A 20% discount is available for other journeys. Special break terms are available from November to the end of May.

USEFUL INFORMATION

OPEN: All year
CHILDREN: Welcome
CREDIT CARDS: None taken
ACCOMMODATION: 7 rooms, 3 ensuite
GARDEN: Yes
DINING ROOM: Delicious large breakfast No evening meal
VEGETARIAN: Catered for
DISABLED ACCESS: No
PETS: No

Chapter One

SKISDON
St Kew, Bodmin,
Cornwall PL30 3HB

Tel: 01208 841372

Skisdon is a Grade II listed country house in a quiet rural setting in a sheltered valley and only four miles from the coast. It is divided into six self-contained apartments of various sizes, providing holiday accommodation throughout the year. Two streams meet within the very large garden. There are magnificent trees and shrubs and extensive lawns plus ten acres of surrounding pasture and woodland; a paradise for children. St Kew Inn, a popular and interesting old pub, is 200 metres away and has a reputation for good food and the benefit of a family dining room and barbecue area in the garden. Wadebridge is 5 miles away and provides a good range of shops; St. Kew Highway, just one mile away, has a supermarket, a petrol station, and a post office. Skisdon is an ideal base for a holiday. Superb coastal scenery, unspoilt countryside, super beaches; endless activities locally available.

The apartments vary in size, one sleeping as many as seven people. Each is well furnished and well equipped. For example Japonica which sleeps 4/5 is a two bedroomed flat on the ground floor and can be directly intercommunicating with Clematis, a one bedroomed flat on the first floor. The conversion has been well thought out allowing access between apartments for larger families or groups. The 1996 price range is from £329-£105 which includes bed linen. The owners, who will give you more details, are Tom and Sandy Chadwick.

USEFUL INFORMATION

OPEN; All year
CHILDREN; Welcome
CREDIT CARDS; None taken
ACCOMMODATION; 6 self-catering apartments, varying in size

DISABLED ACCESS; No, but each case considered, please phone for more details
GARDEN; Yes
PETS; No

BOTTREAUX HOUSE HOTEL
Boscastle,
Cornwall

Tel: 01840 250231

This small, beautifully run private hotel is owned by Graham and Hazel Mee whose main purpose in life is to ensure that everyone who stays here leaves with memories that will long stay with them. It is a comfortably furnished and relaxed house in which the seven charmingly appointed bedrooms have everything that one requires.

The restaurant which welcomes non-residents is well kown locally for the quality of the food and the imaginative menu which includes succulent steaks and prime Stilton - the specialities of the house. From a knowledgeably chosen wine list there is a range of wines from all around the world which will produce something for everyones taste and pocket. Before dining the cosy bar tempts people to enjoy a drink whilst perusing the menu. While you are waiting for your meal take a look at the fascinating pictures signed by Group Captain Cheshire, Douglas Bader and Johnny Johnson and depicting aircraft of World War II.

Boscastle is charming and quaint in its own right with its very small, hidden harbour. Close by and near enough to walk to along the cliffs is Tintagel where the reputed ruins of King Arthur's Castle stand imposingly defying the inroads of the years and the weather. The views in every direction are magnificent.

USEFUL INFORMATION

OPEN;All year
CHILDREN;Welcome over 7 years
CREDIT CARDS;Access/Visa/Amex
LICENSED;Restaurant/Hotel Licence
ACCOMMODATION;7 rooms en-suite
GARDEN; No. Car Park.

RESTAURANT;Delicious food. Open to non-residents
BAR FOOD;Not applicable
VEGETARIAN;Excellent choice
DISABLED ACCESS; No. Difficult
PETS; Dogs by arrangement

Chapter One

WESTERINGS
*Forrabury, Boscastle,
Cornwall PL35 0DT
Tel: 01840 250389*

This 200 year old Georgian house was once a rectory, and has now been tastefully converted into luxury, spacious apartments. The house is in a conservation area above the harbour of Boscastle which is a National Trust property. Situated on the grounds are three self-contained bungalows and the old coach house has also been converted to accommodate guests. All apartments are fully furnished in a modern style, have central heating and are fully equipped for self-catering. A short walk takes you up on to the headland where the sea views are magnificent and there are many walks along the coast. A room book in your accommodation gives you plenty of ideas of the local facilities including fishing, golf and pony trekking. Boscastle itself is a most attractive village, with its 14th century cottages and the friendly Cornish people. It is perfect for touring and one can visit any part of the peninsula and return within the day. Relax and unwind in these congenial surroundings in splendid, rural Cornwall.

USEFUL INFORMATION

OPEN; All year
CHILDREN; Welcome
CREDIT CARDS; None taken
LICENSED; No
ACCOMMODATION; 3 apartments, Coach House and 3 bungalows
DINING ROOM; Not applicable
VEGETARIAN; Not applicable
DISABLED ACCESS; Not really
GARDEN; Very pleasant
PETS; Welcome

HIGH PARK
*Bradworthy,
Devon EX22 7SH
Tel: 01409 241492*

Five acres of garden and grounds surround this elegant and refined Victorian house, home to Marilyn and Michael Cook, who it is obvious has ensured that all their guests are truly spoilt and pampered. The pristine bedrooms are bright and airy and very welcoming. Furnishings are modern with king size beds, colour TV and tea and coffee making facilities. Each room has a private bathroom and the added bliss of fluffy white bathrobes. Stunning views of the Devonshire countryside can be enjoyed from all rooms, and throughout vases full of fresh flowers and bowls of fruit are an absolute delight. Delicious breakfasts are a wonderful start to the day and these are beautifully presented, home cooked and plenty of it. Evening meals are optional but highly recommended. The English Nature Moorland area adjacent to High Park is teeming with wildlife including, badgers, fox, rabbits and many more. This haven is home to numerous species of birds who share this habitat with sheep, cows and ponies. Being situated close to the North Devon coast outdoor activities are plentiful, long stretches of golden beaches offer surfing, swimming, fishing and spectacular coastal walks. Golf courses are close by.

USEFUL INFORMATION

OPEN; All year
CHILDREN; Welcome
CREDIT CARDS; None taken
LICENSED; No
ACCOMMODATION; 3 ensuite rooms, 1 double, 1 twin, 1 single
DINING ROOM; Excellent home-cooked fare, Optional evening meal
VEGETARIAN; Catered for
DISABLED ACCESS; No, but welcome
GARDEN; Yes, large lawns
PETS; Dogs but not indoors, kennels available

THE OLD RECTORY
Bratton Clovelly,
Devon EX20 4LA
Tel: 01837 871382

The Old Rectory, built around 1903, is a beautiful building set in 2.5 acres of lawn, gardens and paddock. Kept to immaculate standards, these grounds are a pleasure to wander round. The rooms are charmingly furnished in an antique style and have views over Dartmoor. Each has TV, tea and coffee, and radio. There are also laundry and drying facilities. A comfortable lounge is provided for the guests to relax in, and during the winter has a roaring log fire. The dining room is quite lovely and good English country breakfasts are served here. Your hosts, David and Eileen Arney can also be prevailed upon to give you a packed lunch if you are thinking of going for a trek on the moor or some other such activity. The house is in the pretty village setting of Bratton Clovelly. This old fashioned country village is delightful, with it's 13th century church (the stocks are on the porch!) and the Clovely Inn which is approximately 200 yards from the accommodation. There are plenty of facilities, with miles of coastland nearby, the rugged moors and lots of outdoor pursuits such as fishing, boating, bird watching, walking, horse riding and many more. An excellent centre for touring.

USEFUL INFORMATION

OPEN : *All year*
CHILDREN : *Welcome*
PETS : *Welcome*
ACCOMMODATION : *4 rooms*

VEGETARIAN : *Catered for*
DISABLED ACCESS : *No*
CREDIT CARDS : *None taken*
GARDEN : *Absolutely delightful.*

THE GLOBE INN,
123 Plymouth Road,
Buckfastleigh,
Devon, TQ11 0DA.
Tel : 01364 642223

The Globe Inn which dates back to 1600, is a good traditional inn with pool, darts, dominoes and cards. While playing these games in the cosy bar, you can indulge in some of the delicious real ales which are served. The menu is extensive, and is varied in its content, with reasonable prices throughout. Children are catered for, with a smaller menu for those smaller tummies! Frank and Vicki Brown are your friendly hosts, and offer great hospitality alongside good service. The accommodation consists of 4 rooms, well furnished in the traditional style of the pub, with T.V. tea & coffee tray, and vanity units, and with all other facilities available. A good night's rest here is followed by a hearty English breakfast sure to set you up for the day!

USEFUL INFORMATION

OPEN : *All year*
CHILDREN : *Welcome*
PETS : *Not in bedrooms*
LICENSE : *Full*
CREDIT CARDS : *All major*
ACCOMMODATION : *4 rooms; 1 fml, 1 dbl, 1 twin, 1 triple with 3 beds.*

RESTAURANT : *Good varied menu*
VEGETARIANS : *Well catered for*
BAR FOOD : *Excellent choice*
DISABLED ACCESS : *Not really*
GARDEN : *Pleasant courtyard*

Chapter One

COPPA DOLLA INN & RESTAURANT
Broadhempston, near Totnes,
Devon TQ9 6BD

Tel: 01803 812455

An odd name for an inn? Possibly but it takes its name from the Coppa Dolla farm mentioned in the Domesday Book, originally 'Coppede Ealdre' meaning an Alder tree with the centre top removed. Whatever its name it is one of the outstanding inns of Devon and stands in the small and beautiful village of Broadhempston tucked away in the heart of the South Devon countryside. Dartmoor is 20 minutes away and the coast 25 minutes. The Roman towns of Totnes and Newton Abbot are only a ten minute drive.

The charm of this delightful inn is undoubted but it is enhanced by the blissful absence of any form of machine or pool table. The bars are always busy and welcoming. For many a decade it has been the meeting place for the many farmers providing a welcoming buzz of conversation as you step through the door. There is a happy mixture of people who come to dine from all the local towns, Torquay and Plymouth. It is a perfect atmosphere in which to enjoy the top of the range cuisine, including an a la carte menu, varied home-cooked bar meals and snacks and a choice of six excellent Vegetarian dishes.

The Coppa Dolla has two first class apartments in which you can stay, each with a lounge, a bedroom and separate bathroom. Ideal if you want to explore the area or enjoy the fine wines which accompany the meals. The Coppa Dolla is a memorable experience.

USEFUL INFORMATION

OPEN;11.30-2.30pm & 6.30-11pm   **RESTAURANT;**Emphasis on fish, classic dishes
CHILDREN;In Dining areas only   **BAR FOOD;**First class choice
CREDIT CARDS;Visa/Access/Master   **VEGETARIAN;**6 dishes daily
LICENSED;Yes   **DISABLED ACCESS;**No, difficult
ACCOMMODATION;2 luxury apartments   **GARDEN;**Lovely garden, moorland views

Devon, Cornwall, Somerset and Avon

SPLATTHAYES
*Buckerell, Honiton,
East Devon EX14 0ER
Tel: 01404 850464*

Bed and breakfast with a difference is the most apt way to describe staying at the 16th century Splatthayes in the tiny East Devon village of Buckerell. This enchanting thatched house has 18th and 19th century additions but the overall impression is one of great antiquity with the tranquillity that seems to surround ancient buildings. However having said that, one has to say that the present atmosphere is undoubtedly enhanced by Splatthayes owners, Douglas Cowan and Mandy Dalton. Apart from being so comfortable and being able to enjoy some of the best cooking to be had in Devon, for example a breakfast of fresh eggs, crisp fruit and organic muesli, homemade rolls and a selection of preserves made by Doug who is the inspired cook in this establishment, dinner is another memorable experience. However the great difference between this and any other house is that one can come here for a 'Relaxation Break' of two nights with two breakfasts and two dinners and an aromatherapy or electro crystal therapy treatment under Mandy's skilled and trained hands. A wonderful place to stay for whatever reason with its beautiful beamed ceilings and huge open fire. No one could ever leave here without a sense of loss and a memory of the most relaxing stay.

USEFUL INFORMATION

OPEN; *All year except Christmas*
CHILDREN; *By prior arrangement*
CREDIT CARDS; *None taken*
PETS; *No*
ACCOMMODATION; *3 bedrooms*
**NON-SMOKING HOUSE*
DINING ROOM; *Wonderful home-made food, organic bread etc.*
VEGETARIAN; *Full choice + diets*
DISABLED ACCESS; *No*
GARDEN; *Beautiful, sheltered, enclosed*
SPECIALITIES; *Aromatherapy & electro crystal therapy treatments*

HALGARRACK COTTAGE
*Praze-an-Beeble, Camborne,
Cornwall TR14 0PH*

Tel: 01209 832300

Halgarrack Cottage is an 18th century barn which Brian and Valerie Makins have converted into an outstanding home, they have been rewarded for their efforts with an 'Approved' by the Cornwall Tourist Board. The house is traditionally furnished and has extensive views over the surrounding farmland. The double room for guests has TV, tea and coffee facilities and is ensuite. The area where this guest house is situated makes it an ideal base for touring Central and West Cornwall and there are also plenty of local pursuits to enjoy. These include water sports like windsurfing, fishing and many more outdoor activities such as golf or walking. The National Trust plays an important role in Cornwall and there are many delightful houses and gardens to visit.

USEFUL INFORMATION

OPEN; *All year*
CHILDREN; *No*
CREDIT CARDS; *None taken*
LICENSED; *Not applicable*
ACCOMMODATION; *1 double ensuite room*
PARKING
DINING ROOM; *Traditional fare*
VEGETARIAN; *By arrangement*
DISABLED ACCESS; *No*
GARDEN; *Yes, with open views*
PETS; *No*

Chapter One

BRIGHTLAND HOLIDAY APARTMENTS
Maer Lane, Crooklets,
Bude, Cornwall EX23 9EE

Tel: 01288 352738

Brightland Apartments are set in beautiful countryside, a short distance from the beach and picturesque town of Bude. This part of Cornwall is close to the Devon border and has much to offer; from rugged cliffs and coastal walks to quaint villages and the haunting beauty of the moors. The people of Cornwall are as special as their views, with their friendly, open ways and helpfulness to visitors. Bude itself is a water sport haven and many a surfing competition can be seen here. The beaches are good and provide an ideal playground for all the family, with plenty of good shops, restaurants and pubs in the town. There are numerous things to do in this area, all the water sports you can imagine, historical houses, gardens, deep sea fishing, golf and who could go to Cornwall without taking a stroll along a coastal path on a warm Summer's evening? The Brightland apartments are self-catering and are Cornish Registered Accommodation, they are modern and of a very high standard, and all have large south facing windows giving spectacular views over National Trust countryside and the Maer Lake Nature Reserve. Twelve apartments are available, depending on your needs, and are equipped with all necessary appliances. A really wonderful place for all the family and definitely a good base from which to visit the rest of Cornwall.

USEFUL INFORMATION

OPEN; All year
CHILDREN; Welcome
CREDIT CARDS; None taken
LICENSED; No
ACCOMMODATION; 12 Self-catering apartments
PETS; Welcome

DINING ROOM; Not applicable
VEGETARIAN; Not applicable
DISABLED ACCESS; By arrangement
GARDEN; Spacious and secluded, play area for the children overlooked by apartments, BBQ facilities

Devon, Cornwall, Somerset and Avon

LANGFIELD MANOR
Bude,
Cornwall EX23 8DP

Tel: 01288 352415

Langfield Manor run by Ann and Trevor Farbrother, is a fine Edwardian house siting in about an acre of delightful, sheltered, south facing gardens. The house has been carefully turned into seven individual, self catering apartments which cater for between two and six persons. Each apartment has it's own lounge/dining area and a fully equipped kitchen. There is a bar, for residents use, which is open most evenings, and a recreation room which includes a full size snooker table. Outside, the solar heated swimming pool is a great gathering place and the patio and gardens are a real suntrap, ideal for sunbathing or watching the great variety of bird life. This is a very informal place and has a great family atmosphere. With various pleasant fun evenings planned you cannot but makefriends amongst the other guests (or perhaps renew accquaintances from the previous year!) There is a BBQ most summer Friday nights and this is just like a house party. Bude has some of the finest beaches in Cornwall and the coastal walks are superb. For those who would rather be in the sea there is every watersport imaginable, from surfing, water skiing, sailing to fishing. There is a tropical leisure pool in the town for those who like it a little warmer! Golf, horse riding, bowling and much more is on your doorstep. Bude is a thriving seaside town with much to offer the visitor. The shops keep late hours and the variety is excellent. There are numerous restaurants to suit any pocket and pubs where you can choose to be entertained or just have a quiet drink. People always talk about the quality of light in Cornwall. It is something to do with the lower sun shining through the clean air from the Atlantic. Spring seems to come earlier, and autumn later, so this is the perfect place to take a late or early break. The climate is mild and the way of life unhurried. The friendly locals will always be happy to 'yarn' and you can enjoy a drink in front of a roaring open fire. Many attractions are still open and Langfield Manor caters for it's guests all year round.

USEFUL INFORMATION

OPEN : All year
CHILDREN : Welcome
PETS : Welcome
ACCOMMODATION : Self catering.

DISABLED ACCESS : No
CREDIT CARDS : None taken
GARDEN : Spacious with heated pool

Chapter One

LOPTHORNE FARM
Morwenstow, Bude,
Cornwall EX23 9PJ

Tel: 01288 331226

This 100 acres working farm with Sheep and Beef Cattle is situated 1 mile from the A39 on a country road overlooking fields and wooded valleys. Lopthorne offers a splendid farmhouse style breakfast and evening dinner served in an attractive dining room. Dinner is a delicious, home-cooked meal using fresh produce, home grown vegetables and fruits. There is a lounge with coloured TV, a wide selection of books and leaflets on local walks, maps and guides. Sun lounge, garden, lawns, ponds, conservation area with wild flower meadow to explore. Parking by the farm house. The 4 pretty bedrooms either have showers or are ensuite and each has tea/coffee facilities. There is a guest bathroom and two toilets. The house has full central heating, essential food hygiene and fire certificate held. Baby sitting by arrangement. There is much to do when you stay here, at anytime of the year from February to the end of November. Short breaks are very popular. Morwenstow has small sandy coves and rugged cliffs up to 400 feet high making the coastal path exhilarating walking with superb scenery. The sandy and surfing beaches at Bude and Widemouth Bay are 8 miles to the south, whilst the picturesque fishing village of Clovelly with its cobbled street is 10 miles to the north. You can fish, sea, coarse and lake, play golf, tennis at Bude, ride horses at Bude and Morwenstow, enjoy the superb Sports Centre at Bude and Holsworthy and the Indoor and Outdoor Swimming Pools.

USEFUL INFORMATION

OPEN: Feb-end of November
CHILDREN: Welcome
CREDIT CARDS: None taken
LICENSED: No. Bring your own
ACCOMMODATION: 2 dbl 2 twin. 2 ensuite
PETS: No
DINING ROOM: Farmhouse style and Old English food. Evening dinner
VEGETARIAN: By arrangement
DISABLED ACCESS: No
GARDEN: Yes. Car parking

STRATTON GARDENS HOTEL
Cot hill, Stratton,
Bude, Cornwall EX23 9DN

Tel/Fax: 01288 352500

Some houses have instant appeal and this is so with the Stratton Gardens Hotel. The 16th century building is home to Sandra and Tony Dixon who have made it one of the most relaxing places you will ever stay in. It has a peaceful atmosphere all of its own which no doubt started when it was a Christian Retreat for Monks and Nuns. The aura of peace that they created by the manner of their lives now provides a retreat for guests away from the noise, hustle and bustle of everyday life. The resident ghost, Clarissa, is a friendly soul who has no desire to escape from this ambience.

There are 5 charming bedrooms beautifully furnished - one has a four-poster and all have ensuite facilities. The rooms mainly look out over the well stocked country gardens at the rear which extend to about an acre in all. In the restaurant which has a character all its own, a sumptuous English breakfast is served and at night dinner cooked in the English style using all fresh produce, is memorable. The Dixon's are also happy to cater for functions and special occasions. The Hotel is non-smoking, licensed, open all the year round. Stratton is a conservation area, close to Bude's wonderful beaches and dramatic coastline.

USEFUL INFORMATION

OPEN: All year
CHILDREN: Not really
CREDIT CARDS: Yes
LICENSED: Yes
ACCOMMODATION: 5 ensuite rooms
PETS: No
RESTAURANT: Delicious, home-cooked In the English style
VEGETARIAN: By arrangement
DISABLED ACCESS: Difficult
GARDEN: Beautiful and well stocked

Chapter One

THE INN ON THE GREEN
Crooklets Beach, Bude,
Cornwall EX23 8NF
Tel: 01288 356013
Fax: 01288 356244

The aptly named 'Inn On The Green' overlooks the 4th hole of Bude's Seaside Links Course and specialises in golfing breaks, for the experienced or not so experienced, if you fall into thelatter category then personal tuition can be arranged with a PGA Professional Instructor. However the Inn caters for family holidays as well as being a splendid centre for those wanting to escape the hustle and bustle of city life. The superior bedrooms are decorated in soft colours which are very relaxing, four being very spacious with lovely views through large windows. The majority offer ensuite facilities and all have a tea/coffee tray and colour television. The furnishings are modern and compliment the Inn. The restaurant is comely and inviting and to tempt your appetite there is a wide ranging selection of superbly cooked dishes chosen from either the A La Carte or Table D'Hote menu and proudly served. A very comprehensive vegetarian menu is available with unusual and delicious dishes. The friendly and relaxed bar stocks an extensive range of alcoholic beverages including Real Ales. Outdoor activities are many and varied. Beaches are some of the finest in the area, with surfing, boating, fishing and coastal walks with breathtaking views.

USEFUL INFORMATION
OPEN; All year
CHILDREN; Welcome
CREDIT CARDS; All major cards except Diners
LICENSED; Yes
ACCOMMODATION; 20 rooms, 17 ensuite
RESTAURANT; Superb English cooking
VEGETARIAN; Comprehensive menu
DISABLED ACCESS; No
GARDEN; Sun terrace. The Inn situated on the edge of the golf course
PETS; No

CARY FITZPAINE FARMHOUSE
Cary Fitzpaine, Yeovil,
Somerset BA22 8JB
Tel: 01458 223250
Fax: 01458 223372

It is in the small hamlet of Cary Fitzpaine, about a mile from the village of Chalton Mackrell, that Andrew and Susie Crang have their farm. A 600 acre working farm devoted to sheep, cattle, arable and horses in the heart of Somerset. The superb Farmhouse is a Georgian manor built of local stone in about 1800, the furnishing are old and antique and are in keeping with the house. The bedrooms are large, bright and airy with wash basin and own bathroom, colourtelevision, a tea and coffee tray and for added comfort central heating. For the romantic at heart there is a four-poster bed. An excellent breakfast is served in the guest's dining room. Why not enjoy a stroll across the fields to the river that runs through the farm, watching out for the wildlife that collects around the water. There are many stately homes and gardens open to the public in the area, as well as Yeovilton Air Museum, Sparkford Car Museum, Wookey Hole and Cheddar Gorge. A truly wonderful place to stay.

USEFUL INFORMATION
OPEN; All year
CHILDREN; Welcome
CREDIT CARDS; None taken
LICENSED; No
ACCOMMODATION; 3 rooms,
DINING ROOM; Excellent full English breakfast No evening meal
VEGETARIAN; Catered for
DISABLED ACCESS; Not really
GARDEN; Yes with access to the farm

Devon, Cornwall, Somerset and Avon

TREBARN HOUSE
3 Barn Close,
Wainhouse Corner,
Bude, Cornwall
EX23 0BB

Tel: 01840 230743

Three miles from the coastline of North Devon and Cornwall is Trebarn House, surrounded by neatly tended lawns and having far reaching views over rolling countryside toward Bodmin Moor. This very modern house is efficiently managed by Mrs. Pat Lane. Furnishings are in keeping with the style of this up to date Guest House. Fresh flowers further enhance the interior and every effort has been made to ensure guests are well looked after. Bedrooms are comfortable and modernly furnished and each have a tea and coffee maker. Ensuite facilities are limited so ensure an early booking for that extra touch of privacy. Glorious golden sands are many along this coast and activities associated with it are prolific, boating, sailing, fishing, windsurfing, swimming and with exceptional coastal walks, days will be inspired. Horse riding and golf are within easy reach. From Bideford a boat ride to Lundy Island will delight the visitor, where grey seals are to be admired and dramatic cliffs soar 400ft above. The Island has a variety of wild goats, Soay sheep and deer. Among the fascinating and quaint villages to visit include Clovelly, Bideford, Great Torrington and Appledore, each having their own inherent personality.

USEFUL INFORMATION

OPEN; All year
CHILDREN; Welcome
CREDIT CARDS; None taken
LICENSED; No
ACCOMMODATION; 3 rooms, 1 twin, 1 double ensuite, 1 single
DINING ROOM; Full English breakfast
VEGETARIAN; Catered for
DISABLED ACCESS; No, but welcome
GARDEN; Yes, nice lawn
PETS; No

THE MEWS
Meldon Hall,
Chagford, Devon
TQ13 8EJ
Tel: 01647 433466

The conversion of this 1820 Coach House was completed in 1995 and is a very sympathetic restoration. All the rooms are light and airy with lovely floral fabrics and some restored furniture. There are flowers in all rooms either dried or fresh, and a nice touch is that the rooms have a year book where you can read other peoples comments and leave your own. Each room has tea and coffee facilities with a variety of biscuits and teas. Sandy and Gordon Jones have put much thought into this establishment and welcome all their guests warmly. Chagford is a pleasant town with plenty of pubs, restaurants and shops. There are plenty of local facilities with Castle Drogo being within walking distance and the cities of Plymouth and Exeter accessible.

USEFUL INFORMATION

OPEN : All year
CHILDREN : Over 10yrs
PETS : By arrangement
CREDIT CARDS : None taken
LICENSED : No
ACCOMMODATION : 3 rooms; 3 dbl.
RESTAURANT : Not applicable
BAR FOOD : Not applicable
VEGETARIAN : Yes
DISABLED ACCESS : No
GARDEN : Yes ; flowers, lawns and terraces

Chapter One

TREWORGIE BARTON
Crackington Haven,
Bude, Cornwall EX23 0NL

Tel/Fax: 01840 230233

You have only to arrive at Treworgie Barton, a lovely 16th century farmhouse, to realise you are in another world. It is a world at peace with itself yet showing all the glory and the ruggedness of nature from the sometimes ferocious North Cornish coast to the gentleness of the rolling farmland and natural woodland. Treworgie lies at the head of Millook valley and once belonged to the Prior of Launceston. It was annexed to the Duchy of Cornwall by Henry VIII in 1540, illegally sold by Elizabeth I in 1601 and repossessed by James I a few years later. It was not until the 1970's that Pam and Tony Mount came here and immediately enhanced the great ambience of this historic house. It is such a happy house and such a great place to stay whether for a holiday or perhaps one of the excellent winter breaks in which the Mounts invite you to escape from winter gloom or enjoy the spectacular outburst of life in the Spring. Having slept comfortably in one of the four pretty, attractively furnished, ensuite bedrooms you will come down to a breakfast that suits you. It may be a freshly poached egg on home-made granary toast or a hearty full English breakfast. Whatever it is it will be delicious as will be the optional superb four course dinner. Pam is a cook of the highest standard and her menus feature exciting originals and old favourites. Not licensed but you are welcome to bring your own. After breakfast you can embark on one of the Treworgie Barton Walks, planned carefully by Tony, wander round the farm or just relax at one of the many secluded coves.

USEFUL INFORMATION

OPEN: April-September
(Nov, Feb, Mar advanced booking only)
CHILDREN: Not under 10 years
CREDIT CARDS: None taken
LICENSED: No. Bring your own
ACCOMMODATION: 4 ensuite 1 fourposter

DINING ROOM: Delicious home-cooked fare. 4 course dinner optional
VEGETARIAN: By arrangement
DISABLED ACCESS: No
GARDEN: Yes + farm
PETS: No

WINSWOOD
Kilkhampton, Bude,
Cornwall, EX23 9QT

Tel: 01288 321699

This pretty 18th century Georgian Manor House with a porticoed entrance situated at the southern edge of the village of Kilkhampton, is the home of Jean and Peter Claris. They are a friendly and hospitable couple who work hard, and succeed, in ensuring that their guests have a memorable holiday. Everything is done to ensure that you are comfortable. The three bedrooms are attractively furnished, one double is ensuite and they all have handbasins and shaver points. Each room has a generously filled tea and coffee tray and the ensuite room has TV. The spacious dining room welcomes you for breakfast - a sumptuous meal which makes sure you are ready for the day ahead - and in the evening it is here that you can sit leisurely over a delicious evening meal with good home-cooking using wholefoods and local produce. Vegetarians are very welcome. The delightful and colourful garden becomes a venue for those wanting to sample a splendid Cream Tea at the weekends. There is ample parking space in the courtyard and behind the house.

The sands and surfing beaches of Bude are 5 miles away. Tamar Lakes Water Park 3 miles and Dartmoor National Park is only a short drive away. Fascinating small and very beautiful coves abound, there are walks in the Cornish countryside. Clovelly Golf Course is just 6 miles. Winswood is perfect for a holiday or short break.

USEFUL INFORMATION

OPEN: All year
CHILDREN: Welcome
CREDIT CARDS: None taken
LICENSED: No
ACCOMMODATION: 2 dbl (1 ensuite) 1 twin. All with hand basins & shaver points
GARDEN: Large. Tea Garden
DINING ROOM: Super breakfast. Evening meal optional. Tea Garden at weekends
VEGETARIAN: Very welcome
DISABLED ACCESS: Yes but no special facilities
PETS: Not permitted
PARKING: Ample

Chapter One

TREGORRAN HOTEL
Headland Road, Carbis Bay,
St Ives, Cornwall TR26 2NU

Tel: 01736 795889

St Ives is a very picturesque village with its stone cottages tumbling over each other in a maze of narrow cobbled streets, it is full of old world charm, with lots of little shops for those holiday nic-nacs, and others full of fine paintings. To really enjoy your visit here you need somewhere to stay and Tregorran Hotel is just the place, the Edwardian bungalow, with its Spanish style frontage is perched high on the cliff top and has been extended to provide 16 ensuite bedrooms, seven double, two twin and seven family rooms, four of these family rooms are on the ground floor and are wheelchair accessible. All these rooms are comfortably furnished most have sea views and all have television and tea and coffee making facilities. In the morning there is an A La Carte breakfast, in the evening there is an extensive four course dinner with a good selection of wines. Vegetarians and Special Diets are by arrangement. Children are most welcome and there are generous reductions. For a small charge babysitting can be arranged. The Tregorran has a residential license so you can relax in the lounge, which is decorated with an eastern flavour, with your drink, meet the other guests and take in the wonderful views. There is plenty for you to enjoy at the Tregorran, with a heated swimming pool, games room, gymnasium, bar games, and in the main season there is live entertainment. There is an enclosed garden with a patio and a pathway from here leads down to the beach. Away from the hotel there are lovely sandy beaches, Carbis Bay and Porthkidney Beaches are very safe, which is ideal for children, activities include golf, horse riding, sailing, windsurfing, water skiing and surfing, fresh water fishing and sea fishing. The McDermott family are looking forward to meeting you in there warm and friendly hotel.

USEFUL INFORMATION

OPEN: Easter-1st October
CHILDREN: Welcome. Special reduction
CREDIT CARDS: Visa/Master/Amex
LICENSED: Yes. Residential
ACCOMMODATION: 16 ensuite rooms accessible
PETS: By arrangement

RESTAURANT: A La Carte breakfast Traditional and Continental food
VEGETARIAN: By arrangement
DISABLED ACCESS: Not fully but 4 Family rooms are wheelchair
GARDEN: Yes + patio, lots of parking

THE HALFWAY HOUSE
Fore Street, Kingsand,
Cawsand Bay, Torpoint,
Cornwall PL10 1NA
Tel: 01752 822279
Fax: 01752 823146

This is a little part of Cornwall that looks as if time has passed it by. A thriving community but unspoilt by the trappings of modernisation. A friendly village with a number of pubs, restaurants and shops, and within easy access of many other activities such as pony trecking, canoeing, boat trips, golfing and of course walking. There are many walks here such as to Mount Edgecombe and to Rame Head along the coastal path with spectacular sea views. Again for a day's shopping, take the passenger ferry from nearby Cremyl into Plymouth and see the sights of this great naval town. The inn gets it's name because the stream behind used to be the border between Devon and Cornwall; hence Halfway. The inn now marks the boundary between the villages of Kingsand and Cawsand. The building stems from 1820 and has been a pub since 1850. David and Sarah Riggs have refurbished to a very high standard and it is both smart and welcoming. Food is of a very high standard and has been mentioned in Egon Ronay's 1995 guide to Pubs and Inns. A speciality is fresh local fish but there are also many other mouth watering dishes on the menu. There are real ales and good wines also available all served by pleasant unobtrusive staff.

USEFUL INFORMATION
OPEN : All year
RESTAURANT : High standard : fish orientated
CHILDREN : Welcome
BAR FOOD : Snack menu to full menu
CREDIT CARDS : All taken
VEGETARIAN : Always available
LICENSED : Full on
DISABLED ACCESS : No
PETS : Welcome
GARDEN : No, but only 200yds from beach
ACCOMMODATION : 5 rooms: 3 dble, 1 family, 1 sgle all with en suite

HOME FARM
Churchstow, Nr. Kingsbridge,
Devon TQ7 3QR
Tel: 01548 853469

Churchstow is situated 2 miles north west of Kingsbridge and is steeped in history, there has been a community or village in some form or another since at least 1239AD. It is here you will find the very pretty traditional farmhouse of Home Farm, owned and run by Mrs. Dot Reeves, a very warm and friendly person, who not only cares for her guests but also for the chickens and geese that live in her garden. The house is idyllic, there are 2 family bedrooms, one is ensuite the other has use of a shared bathroom, each room has a complimentary tea and coffee tray. Dot will serve an excellent home-cooked full English breakfast, you will also be able to indulge in some delicious non-pasteurised milk, all this is served in the lovely dining room, which also has a television for your use. With plenty to do in the area such as golf, fishing, riding and walking, there are lots of lovely sandy beaches, Dot will be more than happy to provide you with information.

USEFUL INFORMATION
OPEN; All year, except Christmas
DINING ROOM; Home-cooked full English breakfast, no evening meal
CHILDREN; Welcome
CREDIT CARDS; None taken
VEGETARIAN; Catered for
LICENSED; No
DISABLED ACCESS; No, but people welcome
ACCOMMODATION; 2 family rooms,
GARDEN; Yes

Chapter One

HORNSBURY MILL
Luxury Accommodation,
Restaurant & Working Mill,
Eleighwater,
Chard, Somerset TA20 3AQ

Tel: 01460 63317

Hornsbury Mill is signposted, and easy to find on the A358 between Ilminster and Chard. To come here is to experience a great sense of history, to have one's imagination whetted, to eat in the unusual Waterwheel Restaurant in delightful surroundings and if you decide to stay, then the fully refurbished luxury accommodation, set in its own grounds of four acres, is wonderful.

The Mill is a good example of an early 19th century corn mill. Built of local flint stone with fine Ham stone mullion windows, and with the majority of the timber parts made of elm wood, it is essentially a Somerset mill.

The 5 luxury ensuite bedrooms are beautifully appointed and complete with television, radio and tea and coffee making facilities. For those visiting the Mill there is a bar and a licensed restaurant, a view of the working waterwheel. It is open for coffee, light lunches and famous for its Cream Teas. Booking is advisable for Sunday lunches. Hornsbury Mill is open from 10am. There are ducks and wildfowl, leaping trout in the lake, a children's play area, the Watermill and Museum to see. It is truly delightful and ideally situated as a 'stopover' en route to or from the West Country.

USEFUL INFORMATION

OPEN; 7 days a week. **RESTAURANT;** A La Carte,
 Closed for 3 weeks in January   plus Chef's Weekly Choice
CHILDREN; Very welcome   **BAR FOOD;** Wide selection, unusual, reasonable
CREDIT CARDS; All except Diners   **VEGETARIAN;** Always available
LICENSED; Full On Licence   **DISABLED ACCESS;** Mobility room, toilets
ACCOMMODATION; 5 luxury ensuite **GARDEN;** Wonderful grounds. Play area

THE HOLLIES
*Clawton, Nr. Holsworthy,
North Devon
Tel: 01409 253770*

Graham and Rosemary Colwill are the friendly owners of this attractive house on a working farm. The house is 7 years old and is furnished in comfortable up to date standards. Traditional full English breakfast is provided and evening meals can be arranged. All rooms are en suite with TV, tea and coffee supplied as standard, and fresh flowers decorating the rooms. There is a spacious lounge with an interesting pianola and TV.

The house has very pleasant views of the neighbouring lake and vineyard and is set in the attractive North Devon countryside close to the Cornish border. It is placed in an ideal situation for touring Devon and Cornwall and is within easy reach of many coastal resorts. Bude which is only 9 miles away has a lovely beach and many attractive shops. Dartmoor National Park is close by and local facilities include lake fishing, walking, riding and many others. Graham and Rosemary are a hive of local information and are only too happy to help you plan your days.

USEFUL INFORMATION

OPEN: *All year (except Xmas day)*
CHILDREN: *Welcome*
PETS: *Welcome*
CREDIT CARDS: *None taken*
LICENSED: *No*
ACCOMMODATION: *4 rooms.*

RESTAURANT: *Not applicable*
BAR FOOD: *Not applicable*
VEGETARIAN: *By arrangement*
DISABLED ACCESS: *Not really*
GARDEN: *Yes, guests welcome*

MOXHILL FARM
*Combwich, Nr. Bridgwater,
Somerset
Tel: 01278 652285*

Moxhill Farmhouse offers its guests excellent accommodation in this rural setting. The farmhouse dates back to the 18th century and is traditional in its furnishings. All rooms are equipped to a high standard with TV, tea and coffee, and hairdryers. There is a lounge and dining room for residents, with books and games for those quiet evenings. Carol and Nigel Venner run a working dairy farm but are never too busy for their guests. Carol actually uses what spare time she has knitting and her delightful sweaters can be bought by visitors! Something original from Somerset! The farmhouse is an excellent base for walking in the Quantock Hills and with the beautiful countryside of West Somerset, the coastline and the Parrett Trail, there is ample entertainment all around you! Golf, fishing, bird watching and riding are just some of the outdoor pursuits within easy reach.

USEFUL INFORMATION

OPEN: *All year*
CHILDREN: *Welcome*
PETS: *Welcome*
CREDIT CARDS: *None taken*
ACCOMMODATION: *3 rooms; 1 dbl, 2 fml.*

RESTAURANT: *English and International cooking*
VEGETARIAN: *Yes*
DISABLED ACCESS: *No*
GARDEN: *Orchard & childrens play area*

Chapter One

**BOX HEDGE FARM
BED & BREAKFAST,**
Westerleigh Rd.,
Coalpit Heath,
Bristol, BS17 2UW.
Tel : 01454 250786

Box Hedge Farm Bed & Breakfast is a farmhouse sitting in 200 acres of rustic countryside, but still with easy access to Bath or Bristol, and the M4 & M5. You will be made to feel most welcome here by Marilyn Collins, who has a lovely home and welcomes her guests as good friends. The warm cosy atmosphere of the farm is enhanced by the good, wholesome farmhouse cooking, and the inviting bedrooms that cater for all your needs. The furnishings are excellent, and there is a very romantic, four poster bed in the double room! An evening meal is optional but I would advise booking in advance. Corporate entertainment is something I have heard of but not paid much attention to, until now. I never realised it could be so much fun! Abseiling, canoeing, caving, team games ...... the list goes on! This all happens at Box Hedge Farm - and lots more - quad bikes, bob cat, and archery! Whether you come here as part of a company for 'team building' or you just fancy 'having a go' then this is a really fun place.

USEFUL INFORMATION
OPEN : All year
DINING ROOM : Excellent home cooking
CHILDREN : Welcome
VEGETARIAN : Catered for
PETS : Under control
BAR MEALS : Not applicable
CREDIT CARDS : None taken
DISABLED ACCESS : Not really
LICENSED : No
GARDEN : Very large & pretty
ACCOMMODATION : 3 rooms; 1 dble, 1 fml, 1 sgl. all with private facilities.

RONE HOUSE HOTEL
Kings Street,
Combe Martin,
Devon EX34 OAD
Tel: 01271 883428

The hotel is set in the heart of the village of Combe Martin, an ideal resting place for touring and walking it's many famous paths. The aim of Theresa and Michael Harding, the new owners, who run this hotel is to make your stay memorable. Rone House is approximately a 10 minute walk from the sea. The bedrooms are comfortably furnished and have television and tea and coffee making facilities. There is an elegant dining room with a choice of traditional cooking and als a lounge and bar. The outdoor heated swimming pool is open Whitsun to October. Golf, horse riding and clay pigeon shooting are all available nearby, and there are also lovely scenic walks. All in all, a very good hotel with friendly, personal service, and a relaxed atmosphere.

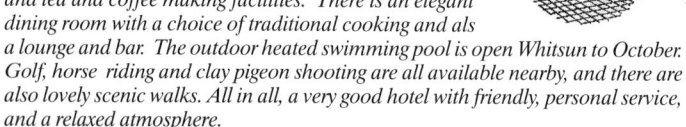

USEFUL INFORMATION
OPEN; April-October/November
DINING ROOM; Good home-cooked fare
CHILDREN; Welcome by arrangement
VEGETARIAN; Yes by arrangement
CREDIT CARDS; None taken
DISABLED ACCESS; No
LICENSED; Yes
GARDEN; Very attractive
ACCOMMODATION; 11 rooms, 8 ensuite
PETS; Yes by arrangement

WINDGATE FARM
Shippen, Combe Raleigh,
Honiton, Devon EX14 0UJ
Tel: 01404 42386

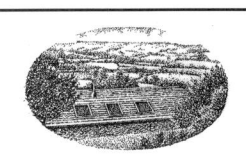

This Grade II Listed farmhouse dates partly from the 16th century and the remainder from the 18th. It is charming, full of atmosphere and a wonderful place to stay. The Shippen (Dairy Barn) and the old Cider Press Barn have both been imaginatively converted and now have comfortable, well furnished accommodation. There are three ensuite guest rooms, 1 double and 2 twin each with a tea and coffee tray and Television is also available if required. Elizabeth Batty, your host, is a friendly welcoming lady and a splendid cook who produces a substantial breakfast, freshly cooked using farm and local produce. A Vegetarian breakfast can be provided. Special 3 or 5 day breaks are available to include reflexology or aromatherapy at start and finish with talks plus activities on various subjects arranged to suit your needs, with (or if) prior notice is given, please ask for details. Small Business Conferences can be catered for. Combe Raleigh is well situated for anyone wanting to explore the magical beauty of Devon and there are many sporting activities within easy reach including Gliding at Dunkeswell. Honiton is an antique, lace and pottery centre within 20 minutes of the sea.

USEFUL INFORMATION
OPEN; All year
CHILDREN; Welcome
CREDIT CARDS; None taken
LICENSED; No, bring your own
ACCOMMODATION; 3 ensuite rooms
GARDEN; Yes
DINING ROOM; Subststantial breakfast using fresh local and farm produce
VEGETARIAN; Catered for
DISABLED ACCESS; Yes, but no special facilities at present
PETS; No

AMBER HOUSE
Coxley, Wells,
Somerset BA5 1QZ
Tel: 01749 679612

Amber House is a late Victorian former farmhouse which has open farmland to the rear with views over the hills. It is very nicely furnished in pine, and all bedrooms have wash basins, tea and coffee. There is a residents lounge/dining room with TV and games. Breakfast is full English and fresh local produce is used wherever possible. Vegetarian meals are also available. Cliff and Jenny Cooke are the owners of the establishment and give their guests a warm welcome. The village of Coxley is just 2 miles on the A39 from the historic city of Wells, 4 miles from Glastonbury and is a good centre for touring. There is a lot to do in the area; as I mentioned, Wells is only 2 miles away and there is a lot of architectural and historical interest in this fascinating city. Another is Bath with it's fine buildings and wonderful antique shops. Walking is very popular in this area, with excellent views all around you. Fishing, golf, cycling and riding are just some of the outdoor pursuits available. There are local vineyards which can be viewed (and maybe sampled?). A very pleasant example of the charming county of Somerset and what it has to offer the visitor.

USEFUL INFORMATION
OPEN; 24 hour access
CHILDREN; Welcome
CREDIT CARDS; None taken
LICENSED; No
ACCOMMODATION; 3 rooms, 2 double, 1 twin
DINING ROOM; Traditional English breakfast
VEGETARIAN; Catered for
DISABLED ACCESS; No
GARDEN; Very pleasant
PETS; No

Chapter One

BOSTONA
Zeal Monochorum,
Crediton, Devon
Tel: 01363 82527

The village of Zeal Monochorum is probably one of Devon's loveliest villages with it's thatched cottages and ancient church. Bill and Jan Moore, who run this excellent guest house, have much local knowledge, which they will cheerfully share with their guests.
This is a very pleasant family home with magnificent veiws over the moors. The rooms are light and airy and these friendly people have provided facilities such as TV, tea and coffee. The breakfast room again has fine views and there is a lovely garden with a terrace where you can eat, (weather permitting.)
A good base with plenty of local pursuits and although rural, just off the A3072.

USEFUL INFORMATION

OPEN: All Year
CHILDREN: Over 10 years
PETS: By Arrangement
CREDIT CARDS: None Taken
ACCOMMODATION: 3 Rooms
BREAKFAST: Full English
VEGETARIAN: Yes
DISABLED ACCESS: No
GARDEN: Very Pleasant

COPPER OAK COTTAGE
East Village
Crediton
EX17 4DW

Tel: 01363 772530

If your idea of a holiday is to forget it all, to relax and unwind in idyllic surroundings of fields, trees and wildflowers then look no further than Copper Oak Cottage, set in a peaceful hamlet this lovely old property built around 250 years ago has roses, honeysuckle and vines covering the front. The cottage has 3 bedrooms, and will sleep 5 comfortably, a camp bed and a cot areavailable. The cottage has been tastefully decorated throughout, and your needs catered for with a washing machine and dryer, microwave, ceramic hob and built-under electric oven, there is also an oil fired Rayburn for you to cook on as well as supplying the hot water. There is a modern bathroom with bath but no shower. All bed linen is provided but towels are not. In the lovely garden is a pond, if you ask Mrs. Georgina Edwards the owner, she will have it fenced off for your stay if you have small children. The location is ideal for painting, birdwatching, walking and riding. If you want to bring your horse there is a loose box. There is plenty of parking in the drive.

USEFUL INFORMATION

OPEN; May-Sept
CHILDREN; Welcome
CREDIT CARDS; None taken
ACCOMMODATION; 3 bedroomed cottage
DISABLED ACCESS; No
GARDEN; Yes, beautiful with pond and stream
PETS; Horses and dogs
PARKING; Yes

Devon, Cornwall, Somerset and Avon

GREAT LEIGH FARM
Crediton, Devon EX17 3QQ
Tel: 01647 24297

Two miles north of the A30, in a peaceful setting in the mid-Devon hills, Great Leigh Farm is ideally situated for touring Dartmoor and Exmoor National Parks and the North and South Devonshire coasts. Eleven miles west of the historic city of Exeter, the farm is also well placed as a stopover on the way to and from Cornwall. Great Leigh is a working sheep farm of eighty acres and guests are welcome to walk around the farm and enjoy the lovely views over the hills to Dartmoor. It is an 18th century Devon farmhouse full of character, the home of Mr and Mrs Barrie- Smith, a welcoming couple who create a relaxed atmosphere around them. There is a choice of two large bedrooms and two single bedrooms, two of which are ensuite. One double bedroom, on the ground floor, has its own toilet and wash basin. There is a large, comfortable lounge and a spacious dining room in which you will be served a truly great farmhouse breakfast and an optional evening meal of equal standard.

USEFUL INFORMATION
OPEN: All year
CHILDREN: Welcome at half price
CREDIT CARDS: None taken
LICENSED: May bring your own
ACCOMMODATION: 2 large bedrooms and 2 single rooms, 2 of which are ensuite
DINING ROOM: Truly great farmhouse breakfast, optional evening meal
DISABLED ACCESS: Limited, ground floor double bedroom with own basin & WC
GARDEN: 80 acres of farmland
PETS: No

HIGHER DIPFORD FARM
Trull, Taunton,
Somerset TA3 7NU

Tel: 01823 275770

This wonderful 600 year old farmhouse sits in the small hamlet of Trull just over 2 miles from the historic town of Taunton. The house is an old Longhouse with many features such as Elm beams and inglenook fireplaces. All rooms are equipped to very high standards with TV, tea and coffee making facilities, and all are ensuite. Fresh home-cooked food is a speciality and the full farmhouse breakfast includes free range eggs and local baked bread. The four course evening meal can be complimented by a jug of the famous local cider! There are lots of local facilities and this beautiful and fascinating county has much to offer the active or those who just want to take some time out to relax.

USEFUL INFORMATION
OPEN; All year/24 hour access
CHILDREN; Welcome
CREDIT CARDS; None taken
LICENSED; Full
ACCOMMODATION; 3 ensuite rooms
1 family, 1 double, 1 twin
DINING ROOM; Freshly prepared food with the emphasis on quality
VEGETARIAN; Catered for
DISABLED ACCESS; No
PETS; No

Chapter One

BEVERLY FARM
Hewish Lane, Crewkerne,
Somerset TA18 8RE
Tel: 01460 77742

Situated in the small town of Crewkerne is Beverly Farm, a charming guest house owned and run by Pam and Gary Rouse. The 60 year old house is set in 2 acres of grounds and gardens, and yet is only a 10 minute walk into the town. The house is attractively furnished in a modern style which compliment the surroundings and fresh flowers add that special touch. There are 2 double bedrooms, one being ensuite, the other has exclusive use of a bathroom. One of the rooms can be converted into a family room. After a good nights sleep, Pam will serve an excellent full English breakfast where she also caters for vegetarians and vegans. An evening meal can be arranged, if given plenty of notice. Somerset is a lovely county with rich and rolling farmland dotted with ancient market towns, as well as pretty villages full of immaculately kept gardens and thatched roofs. Beverly Farm has so much on the doorstep, Cricket St Thomas near Chard where young and old will have a wonderful time at this major theme park. Chard is the highest town in Somerset, it has lovely stone houses which line the High Street and 2 streams which flow through the town. The 'Ropemakers' town of Bridport is only 20 minutes drive away. Also fishing, golf, riding and lovely walks are all close by.

USEFUL INFORMATION
OPEN; All year except Christmas
CHILDREN; Welcome
CREDIT CARDS; None taken
LICENSED; No
ACCOMMODATION; 2 double rooms
1 ensuite, 1 double converts to family room
DINING ROOM; Excellent full English breakfast, evening meal by arrangement
VEGETARIAN; Yes, and vegan
DISABLED ACCESS; No, but welcome
GARDEN; Yes
PETS; No

VENTONGIMPS MILL BARN
Ventongimps,
Callestick
Truro,
Cornwall
Tel: 01872 573275

This Cornish Mill Barn next to 35 acres of nature reserve, has been tastefully converted into a country house. All the rooms are light and airy and have excellent furnishings. The house is surrounded by raised flower beds and there is a very pleasant sitting area overlooking the river. The house speciality is Portuguese cooking, compliments of Giselda Gibson, one half of the partnership that owns this property. Brian, the other half, will be able to give you details on the fishing available on their part of the river. Although this is a rural setting you are never far away from coastal villages and lovely coastal walks; nor are you far from Truro, a historic city, which is only 7 miles away.

USEFUL INFORMATION
OPEN : All year
CHILDREN : Welcome
PETS : No
CREDIT CARDS : None taken
LICENSED : Full license
ACCOMMODATION : 10 rooms; some en suite.
RESTAURANT : Portuguese cooking
BAR FOOD : No
VEGETARIAN : Yes
DISABLED ACCESS : Yes
GARDEN : Splendid

THE PORT WILLIAM INN
Trebarwith Strand,
North Cornwall
PL34 0HB

Tel: 01840 770230

Port William Inn was built about 300 years ago and is superbly placed, being only 50 yards from the sea overlooking Trebarwith Strand on the North Cornwall coast. This area of outstanding natural beauty, rugged coastline and sandy beaches, is a wonderful holiday location, with watersports being one of the main interests. Surfing around this area is of good quality as is windsurfing, the beach here is very safe and is ideal for young children, it has plenty of sand for those all important tools - the bucket and spade. If you are an outdoor person the worlds your oyster, with golf, sea fishing, riding and the wonderful South West Coastal Path, where you can walk for miles visiting some interesting places on the way, as well as admiring the breathtaking view, the camera will not stop clicking. The Inn's bedrooms have recently been tastefully refurbished with pine furniture and co-ordinated linens, the 6 rooms have ensuite baths with showers, tea and coffee making facilities, colour televisions, direct dial telephones, radios, hair dryers and stunning views of the beach and coastline. There is a room set aside for residents to sit down to a good home-cooked breakfast, either traditional or why not start the day with smoked haddock or wonderful Cornish kippers, that should set you up nicely for a busy time on the beach. The food at the Port William is well known, it specialises in good home-cooked dishes, the menu is varied and the food is good wholesome pub food using local produce especially local fish and shell fish. Vegetarians are well catered for with a good selection of dishes always on the menu. In the evening sit and relax in the bar with the locals, chat over a drink, why not try a glass of two of a local Cornish Ale, before heading up to bed to listen to the sound of the waves rolling up the beach as you drift off to sleep. Tintagel is the nearest town where you can wander around the shops or visit the ruins of a Celtic monestry and the castle of the Earl of Cornwall built in 1145. Another town close by is Camelford, this is reputed to be the site of King Arthur's 'Camelot', you can also visit the North Cornwall Museum which shows the different ways in which the Cornish live. No wonder the Port William has so many accolades including RAC 2 Star, AA QQQ, and 3 Crown Commended by the English Tourist Board, Peter Hale is looking forward to welcoming you so you can see for yourself.

USEFUL INFORMATION

OPEN; All year
CHILDREN; Welcome
CREDIT CARDS; All major cards, not Diners
LICENSED; Yes
ACCOMMODATION; 6 ensuite rooms
PETS; Yes

DINING ROOM; Good home-cooking
VEGETARIAN; Catered for
BAR FOOD; Yes
DISABLED ACCESS; No
GARDEN; No, over-looks the beach

Chapter One

ARRALLAS
Ladock,
Truro,
Cornwall TR4 4NP

Tel: 01872 510379
Fax: 01872 510200

Arrallas has two entrances - one from Ladock, the other from Summercourt. Please do not use the Ladock one - it is very difficult. To find us use the A30. After Bodmin keep on the A30 until you have passed exits to Indian Queens, Fraddon, Ladock and the first exit to Summercourt. Take the 2nd exit to Summercourt (and Chapel Town), turn right immediately, Arrallas is signed from opposite the Clock Garage (one and a half miles). When you arrive you will find a large double fronted house which is part of the Duchy of Cornwall Estate. It is a working arable farm adjoining 400 acres of Duchy Woodlands. Arrallas has been awarded '3 Crowns Highly Commended' by the English Tourist Board and 'QQQQQ' by the AA and you can see why. The property has 3 very attractive bedrooms, all are ensuite with colour TV, radios, hair dryers, alarm clocks, sewing kits and tea and coffee making facilities. The house has wonderful log fires in the winter and full central heating for those chilly days. Traditional English breakfast is served, with fresh fruit and yoghurt etc. for those with daintier appetites, the very popular evening meal is to order and optional, and on Sundays there are simple ordered suppers only at 7pm, all this served in the lovely dining room. Guests are more than welcome to bring their own wine when dining. After dinner you can relax in the drawing room with your coffee and enjoy the beautiful view. The furnishings are a mixture of antique and modern which compliment the house immensely. This is a real paradise for those who seek peace and seclusion with wonderful woodland, rolling countryside and wild life.

USEFUL INFORMATION

OPEN; February-October
CHILDREN; No
CREDIT CARDS; No
LICENSED; No, may bring your own
ACCOMMODATION; 3 rooms, 2 double, 1 twin, all ensuite

DINING ROOM; Delicious home cooking, evening meal, simple suppers on Sundays at 7pm
DISABLED ACCESS; No, but welcome
GARDEN; Yes
PETS; No

PENGELLY FARMHOUSE
St. Erme, Truro,
Cornwall
Tel: 01872 510245

A 230 acre working dairy farm, which offers quality and comfort in the accommodation at the farmhouse. The bedrooms are very nicely furnished in pine and have TV, tea and coffee in each. Breakfast is a choice between full English and continental, with vegetarians and diabetics catered for. There are several pubs and restaurants within 10 minutes drive which offer excellent meals for the evenings. As it is a dairy farm you can have home made clotted cream which is a treat not to be missed! Sue Hicks, the owner of this farm, is riding school trained and breeds horses. She is also the originator of the Cornish Foaling Bank, similar to the National Foaling Bank in Shropshire. Sue is happy to give out information on the local pursuits and there are many walks including those on the actual farm land. This is a good base for seeing Cornwall and access to the historic town of Truro and the great seaside town of Newquay can be easily had. There is much more to see in Cornwall, with the moors and villages, and the friendly people will help you enjoy a place which you will return to time and time again!

USEFUL INFORMATION
OPEN: All year
BREAKFAST: All catered for
CHILDREN: Welcome
DISABLED ACCESS: Not really but welcome
PETS: Responsible overtures listened to!
CREDIT CARDS: None taken
ACCOMMODATION: 2 rooms en suite
GARDEN: Yes

HILLHEAD FARM
Ugborough, Nr. Ivybridge,
Devon PL21 0HQ
Tel: 01752 892674

This 150 year old farmhouse has a lovely setting in the village of Ugborough. Jane Johns and her friendly family make this a most appealing place to stay. The food is all home prepared (and some home grown) and evening meal is optional. The rooms are furnished in a cottage antique style and are very pleasing. This is a working farm and there is fishing to be had, along with shooting. Many other outdoor pursuits can be enjoyed locally. Dartmoor is close to hand and many fine walks over the moors can be enjoyed. Again, you are not far from the historic town of Plymouth with it's famous Barbican and Hoe, and a host of shops to browse through. The Shire Horse Centre is close by and is a most enjoyable day for all the family. There is entertainment for every taste in a short distance of this pleasing accommodation.

USEFUL INFORMATION
OPEN: All year
RESTAURANT: Not applicable
CHILDREN: Welcome
BAR FOOD: Not applicable
PETS: Welcome
VEGETARIAN: By arrangement
CREDIT CARDS: None taken
DISABLED ACCESS: No
LICENSED: No
GARDEN: Yes
ACCOMMODATION: 3 rooms; 2 dbl, 1 twin.

Chapter One

MILTON MANOR FARM
*Old Bristol Road,
Upper Milton,
Wells,
Somerset BA5 3AH
Tel: 01749 673394*

History oozes from every crack in the Elizabethan Manor House. The property is Grade II Star Listed and is situated in an area designated as being of outstanding natural beauty. Facts about the Manor can be traced back to 1337. There is great character here, which is evident in all the rooms. The bedrooms are equipped with washbasins, tea and coffee and hot chocolate, and are good large rooms. There is a residents dining room and lounge, and guests are welcome to relax in the large garden. Breakfast is served at separate tables in the dining room and the menu is varied using good local produce. The 52 acres surrounding the house are used to raise beef cattle, and the views from the land are quite magnificent. You are only one mile away from the historic city of Wells and there is much in the area of interest. It is an excellent centre for reaching such places as Wookey Hole, Cheddar, Glastonbury and Clark's Village in Street. Bath is a good day out with its charming buildings and wealth of antique shops. Nearby you can participate in such pursuits as walking, fishing, caving, golf and riding. That is supposing you have managed to drag yourself away from the history of this fascinating house!

USEFUL INFORMATION
OPEN; 24 hour access   **DINING ROOM**; *Varied menu*
CHILDREN; *Welcome*   **VEGETARIAN**; *Catered for*
CREDIT CARDS; *None taken*   **DISABLED ACCESS**; *No*
LICENSED; *No*   **GARDEN**; *Extensive with a small pond*
ACCOMMODATION; *3 rooms,*   **PETS**; *No*
             the Manor is NON-SMOKING

VENTERDON HOUSE
*Venterdon, Callington,
Cornwall PL17 8PD
Tel: 01579 370179*

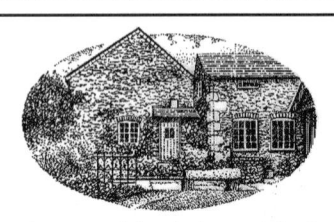

Self-catering accommodation here in a newly converted three bedroomed Grade II Listed Barn on three levels. Fully furnished in an antique cottage style in 1996. It has been done with great style and taste and much thought has gone into equipping the accommodation with everything needed to make a self-catering holiday a success, including a TV and video for wet days. The Listed attached main house dates from 1684 and is full of interest, as is the barn. The attractive garden with a well and fishponds is a sun trap, children are very welcome but dogs and other pets, regretfully, not. The barn is not suitable for disabled persons. The area surrounding Venterdon has the moors in one direction and the coast on the other, you can fish, walk on the moors, ride and take advantage of the specialist guided tours.

USEFUL INFORMATION
OPEN: *All year*   **DISABLED ACCESS**: *No*
CHILDREN: *Welcome*   **GARDEN**: *Yes*
CREDIT CARDS: *None taken*   **PETS**: *No*
ACCOMMODATION: *Self-catering barn*   *NO SMOKING*

Devon, Cornwall, Somerset and Avon

PERCY'S RESTAURANT WITH ROOMS,
Coombes Head, Virginstow,
Devon, EX21 5EA.
Tel : 01409 211236
Fax : 01409 211 275

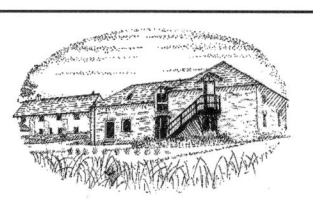

The 40 acre estate where Percy's is located, offers a haven of peace and tranquillity far from the busy outside world. Accommodation has been charmingly converted from courtyard stables dating back to 1782, and there are eight double rooms with either double or twin beds for your comfort. All rooms have stunning views over the quiet countryside, and are en suite with all facilities of colour TV, hairdryers and hospitality trays. A fresh fruit basket awaits your arrival, which has probably been hand picked from the orchards on the estate, and you are made immediately at home by the friendliness and courtesy of Tony and Tina Bricknell-Webb, your hosts. The restaurant is in the main farmhouse which dates back four to five hundred years, and is one of the finest in Devon. The ever changing menu is delightful with local fresh produce and innovative dishes to delight the palate. These are complimented by the excellent wine list, and by the unobtrusive but attentive staff. This is an experience you will be anxious to repeat, and one which is most memorable.

USEFUL INFORMATION
OPEN : All year
RESTAURANT : Modern English cuisine
CHILDREN : Welcome
SPECIAL DIETS : Catered for
PETS : By arrangement
DISABLED ACCESS : Yes
LICENSED : Yes
WINE LIST : Well selected
CREDIT CARDS : All major
GARDEN : 40 acres
ACCOMMODATION : 8 dbl rooms en suite   **NON SMOKING**

ANCHOR LIGHTS
The Quay,
West Looe,
Cornwall PL13 2BU
Tel: 01503 262334

This well appointed Guest House faces Looe Harbour and looks across the river to East Looe, a few minutes walk away over the bridge. The first thing you see as you arrive are the colourful hanging baskets and once over the doorstep a friendly welcome from Rachel Essam, the owner who has been here for many years and welcomes back visitors who have become friends, time and again. Spotlessly clean and furnished with a mixture of traditional and modern, all four bedrooms are ensuite with bath and shower, hair dryers, toiletries, radio alarms, central heating and a beverage tray. Breakfast is an enjoyable meal with a choice of dishes in a full English breakfast. Vegetarians are catered for. Anchor Lights is not licensed but you are welcome to bring your own. Parking is at a premium but you are permitted to park immediately outside on double yellow lines between 2200 and 1000am.

USEFUL INFORMATION
OPEN: Feb-Nov inc.
DINING ROOM: Home-cooked fare
CHILDREN: Welcome
VEGETARIAN: Catered for
CREDIT CARDS: None taken
DISABLED ACCESS: No
LICENSED: May bring your own
PETS: No
ACCOMMODATION: 4 ensuite rooms

Chapter One

GREENHAM HALL,
Greenham, Wellington,
Somerset TA21 0JJ

Tel: 01823 672603
Fax: 01823 672307

Post war shortages, and the freezing winter of 1947, led to the main wing of Greenham Hall being abandoned. Over the next twenty years it was used as a hay barn, floorboards doors and part of the staircase were removed, and many windows broken. In 1975 Caro Ayre and her husband Peter moved into two rooms of the main house and gradually worked on restoring the remainder. Almost a decade later they knew they were ready and very happy to share this former home of an Admiral, with guests giving them the opportunity to enjoy and benefit from the peaceful atmosphere that gives them so much pleasure. They will tell you that the worst complaint they have had from visitors has been that it is too quiet at night, which makes the birds' chorus in the morning almost deafening! The house is welcoming and friendly and the beautiful garden is a plant lovers' paradise and has a very large collection of perennials in it, with plenty of room for children to play unrestricted. Occasionally in the summer months Caro will give you tea in the garden - wonderfully therapeutic.

Greenham Hall is furnished throughout with a delightful collection of traditional and antique furniture. The seven bedrooms are warm, with pretty drapes and comfortable modern beds. Some of them are ensuite, one has a private bathroom and the others share plentiful bathroom facilities. The Sitting Room which is also where Breakfast is served has colour television for the use of guests. Breakfast is a delicious and substantial meal cooked to your choice. No evening meal but there are excellent meals available at many of the surrounding Pubs and Hotels - Caro will point you in the right direction. A light supper is available given sufficient notice. Children are very welcome and a cot is available although you are asked to bring the child's bedding. Baby sitting can be arranged. You are also welcome to bring your dog provided you have arranged this in advance of your arrival.

The area surrounding the small village of Greenham, through which the Grand Western Canal runs, provides super walking country for the energetic. There is Trout Fishing in the river Tone, several 18 hole Golf courses nearby at Tiverton and in the Taunton area as well as Equestrian centres in the area offering a choice of horses for beginners and expert riders. Both the North and South coast are within striking distance and there is a plethora of historic house including Combe Sydenham Hall, Gaulden Manor and Dunster Castle. You will not be bored, that is for sure.

USEFUL INFORMATION

OPEN; *All year*
CHILDREN; *Welcome. Cot available*
CREDIT CARDS; *None taken*
ACCOMMODATION; *7 rooms some ensuite*
PETS; *By arrangement*

DINING ROOM; *Breakfast only*
VEGETARIAN; *Upon request*
DISABLED ACCESS; *No facilities*
GARDEN; *Beautiful*

Devon, Cornwall, Somerset and Avon

MEAD BARN COTTAGES
Welcombe, Nr. Bideford,
North Devon

Tel: 01288 331721

The beauty of this area is hard to beat with its nearness to the coast and cliffs, and the lovely countryside. Mead Barns nestle in a hollow overlooking the sea, close to the Cornish border. It is reached by driving down a typical Devon lane with its high banks covered in wild flowers, and is peaceful and serene. There are plenty of activities in the area such as fishing, surfing and especially walking. The multitudes of coastal paths offer walks for all abilities. Hartland Forest is near by offering its golf and leisure facilities. As an area of outstanding beauty it is definitely worth a visit. The cottages are built of slate and stone dating back to the 1850's. The theme is pine throughout but each cottage has a different colour scheme which enhances its individuality. All modern facilities are present with fridges, freezers and microwaves amongst others. A laundry room is available to everyone and also a games room housing billiards, pool, table tennis and darts. The childrens' play area is excellent with swings and tennis courts. There is a B.B.Q. area with garden furniture for those balmy summer evenings.

USEFUL INFORMATION
OPEN: All Year   **DISABLED ACCESS:** No
CHILDREN: Welcome   **CREDIT CARDS:** None Taken
PETS: Welcome   **GARDEN:** Spacious and Individual
ACCOMMODATION: Self Catering Cottages

WESTCLIFF HOTEL
Hannafore, West Looe
Cornwall PL13 2DE
Tel: 01503 262500

Open all the year round this immaculately run hotel stands back a little from the hustle and bustle of Looe looking out over the sea with a rural setting in the background. An ideal place for anyone wanting to enjoy this beautiful coastline and to explore all the nooks and crannies that make up the ancient fishing village of Looe. Each room is attractively and comfortably furnished and although not ensuite has a wash basin and a tea/coffee tray. There is an excellent and plentiful English Breakfast and a delicious, home-cooked evening meal is available. Children under 5 are free and up to 15 years are charged half price. The friendly, well stocked bar is the meeting place for guests in the evenings. Jim and Jenny Petrie are your welcoming hosts.

USEFUL INFORMATION
OPEN: All year.   **DINING ROOM:** Delicious home-cooking.
CHILDREN: Welcome   Evening meal available
CREDIT CARDS: None taken   **PETS:** Welcome
LICENSED: Yes   **ACCOMMODATION:** Comfortable with wash basins

Chapter One

BEKYNTON HOUSE
7, St Thomas Street,
Wells, Somerset BA5 2UU

Tel/Fax: 01749 672222

Wells with its beautiful, small cathedral attracts visitors from all around the world who come to enjoy its architectural beauty and its very special atmosphere. An equally special atmosphere has been created by Desmond and Rosaleen Gripper at Bekynton House. The house is charming and every room has been furnished and decorated with taste and skill. The comfortably furnished lounge entices one to relax and in the light airy dining room with its high ceilings, attractively covered tables and pretty china, breakfast is served. This is a meal to savour with everything freshly cooked to order and in addition to the full English breakfast there are several other choices including a light Continental repast. The six bedrooms have all been equipped to ensure you have maximum comfort, 4 are ensuite, 2 with private bathrooms opposite, and every room has that blessing to the traveller, a well-stocked beverage tray as well as TV. The Grippers enjoy people and work hard to ensure that all their visitors enjoy their stay.

Wells is an excellent base for exploring both the city and the glorious countryside around as well as the numerous stately homes, famous gardens and wildlife parks. Walking is one of the great pleasures around here with bird watching, fishing and golf all within easy reach of Bekynton House. Not surprising that people return regularly to enjoy the Gripper's hospitality.

USEFUL INFORMATION

OPEN; All year
CHILDREN; Over 7 years
CREDIT CARDS; Mastercard/Visa
PETS; No
DINING ROOM; Excellent, freshly cooked Breakfast
VEGETARIAN; By arrangement
ACCOMMODATION; 6 rooms, 4 ensuite, 2 with private bathrooms opposite

HOME FARM
Stoppers Lane,
Upper Coxley,
Wells,
Somerset BA5 1QS
Tel: 01749 672434

This peaceful spot just 1.5 miles from the city of Wells is an old Somerset cider house that was converted pre war. The rooms are furnished in a country style to excellent standards, and all have TV, tea and coffee. The gardens are delightful being extremely well kept and spacious. A full English breakfast with plenty of choices gets you off to a good start, and vegetarians are catered for. Although there is not really facilities for the disabled, there is a ground floor room which can be used by prior arrangement. Pat Higgs is your friendly host who is quite informal and makes you feel very welcome indeed. The position of this farm in it's quiet location, makes this an ideal place to relax and unwind. If this is what you want, then Somerset is a great county to stroll around and enjoy the wonderful views. There is horse riding adjacent to Home Farm, and fishing and golf in the area. If on the other hand you prefer something more energetic, then the choice is unlimited. Somerset has more than its fair share of National Trust properties, with stately homes and magnificent gardens, or if you prefer wild life then Longleat is the place for you. The Fleet Air Arm Museum is within reach as is the lovely city of Bath. Lots of interesting places to visit and views that are difficult to surpass.

USEFUL INFORMATION

OPEN; All year except Christmas **DINING ROOM**; Traditional English breakfast
CHILDREN; Welcome **VEGETARIAN**; Catered for
CREDIT CARDS; None taken **DISABLED ACCESS**; Limited
LICENSED; No **GARDEN**; Spacious, extremely well kept
ACCOMMODATION; 7 rooms, 2 ensuite **PETS**; Dogs welcome

Chapter One

THE ANCIENT GATE HOUSE HOTEL
Sadler Street,
Wells, Somerset BA5 2RR

Tel: 01749 672029
Fax: 01749 670319

The hotel in the precincts of Wells Cathedral is probably one of the oldest in England. It is certainly one of the most interesting, with its well worn stone spiral staircase and quaint narrow passages. While having all of the modern conveniences, much thought has been taken to preserve the unique character and charm. Four of the bedrooms have wonderful four poster beds and others have testers. All the rooms have TV, tea and coffee making facilities and direct dial telephones. The hotel is Grade One Listed and is designated an Ancient Monument. No building of such historical importance is without its 'past' and this is 'apparent' in the Grey Lady and the Jilted Bride who have been known to visit the dining room and reception!

The Rugantino restaurant is open to the public and seats 45. Here you can be served authentic Italian food or traditional English table d'hote, all enhanced by a selection of wines, beers and spirits from the bar. There is a wonderful varied menu with many unusual and delicious starters and sweets. The garden is quite delightful, opening directly on to the cathedral green. Here you can sit on a balmy evening, sipping your drink and enjoying the history all around you.

USEFUL INFORMATION

OPEN;All year   *RESTAURANT;Italian & English cuisine*
CHILDREN;Welcome   *VEGETARIAN;Catered for*
CREDIT CARDS;All major cards   *DISABLED ACCESS;Restaurant only*
LICENSED;Yes   *GARDEN;Very pretty garden*
ACCOMMODATION;9 rooms; 7 ensuite   *PETS;Welcome*

NETHERNE
Clogshill Cross,
Yarnscombe, Barnstaple,
North Devon EX31 3LY

Tel: 01271 858297

Anyone choosing to stay at Netherne will find Janet and Chris Brice a mine of information about what to do in this picturesque area of North Devon. It is within easy reach of the coast and close to the Tarka Trail. The house is comfortable and homely, set in a peaceful secluded setting and surrounded on three sides by its own woodland. There are three bedrooms. All the rooms have central heating, colour TV and tea and coffee making facilities. Guests have the use of two bathrooms, both fitted with a shower and a bath. There is a sitting room for your use. Janet produces, in addition to a full English breakfast, delicious evening meals with traditional home-cooking including some delectable sweets. The house is not licensed but you are welcome to bring you own.

USEFUL INFORMATION

OPEN: All year   *DINING ROOM: Delicious home-cooking*
CHILDREN: Welcome   *VEGETARIAN: Catered for*
CREDIT CARDS: None taken   *DISABLED ACCESS: No*
LICENSED: May bring your own wine   *GARDEN: Yes, surrounded by woodland*
ACCOMMODATION: 3 bedrooms   *PETS: Welcome*

COOMBE FARM
Widegates, Nr Looe,
Cornwall PL13 1QN

Tel: 01503 240223
Fax: 01503 240895

This attractive ten-bedroomed country house is tucked away in ten and a half acres of lawns, meadows, woods and streams with magnificent views down an unspoilt wooded valley to the sea. Welcoming at anytime of the year it is a house to which many people return time and again. This is not only for the genuine welcome one gets from the owners, Alexander and Sally Low but because the house is beautifully run in a comfortable, informal style which denotes the true professional. Charmingly furnished with many antiques, paintings and interesting old objects, there are plants everywhere and in the cool weather wonderful open log fires in the lounge and dining room. This part of the world is often at its best out of season when the roads are less crowded and the majesty of the coastline is highlighted by the thundering seas. Coombe Farm is ideal not only for summer holidays but also for Spring and Autumn Breaks. Just imagine coming back to the warmth of this inviting house in winter after a brisk walk along the Cornish Coastal Path, knowing that a delicious four-course dinner served in the candlelit dining room awaits you!. Breakfast is another feast. The bedrooms all have country views and are equipped with shower and WC ensuite, colour TV, radio, hair dryer, tea and coffee making facilities and direct dial telephone. The three acres of lawns include croquet and a lovely swimming pool, heated in summer. There is plenty of space for children and a snug stone barn is det aside as a games room. Guests are very welcome to stay at Coombe Farm throughout the day and there is always someone available to make them refreshments. A truely delightful place.

USEFUL INFORMATION

OPEN: 1st March-31st October
CHILDREN: Very welcome (Min age 5 years)
CREDIT CARDS: All major cards
LICENCED: Yes, residential
ACCOMMODATION: 3 dbl 3 tw 4 family all ensuite
PETS: No except for Guide Dogs

DINING ROOM: Full English breakfast
Candlelit dinner
BAR FOOD: Refreshments available all day for guests
VEGETARIAN: Catered for
GARDEN: Yes, swimming pool, croquet
DISABLED ACCESS: Not as such but 5 ground floor rooms

Chapter One

TREVERIA FARM
*Widegates. Looe,
Cornwall PL13 1QR*

Tel/Fax: 01503 240237

Signs for the world famous Monkey Sanctuary will tell you that you are close to Treveria Farm. Both are off the B3253 close to Nomansland. Treveria is a gracious old farmhouse which nestles amongst the rolling landscape with stunning rural views and yet it is only 5 minutes by car from Looe and the sea. It is splendidly situated for anyone wanting to tour Devon and Cornwall and has the added bonus of many activities close by. You can fish, play golf, go horse riding or take part in water sports. There are super walks along the coastal footpath and a wealth of fascinating villages to explore. The National Trust have three properties within easy reach at Llanhydrock, Cotehele and Anthony House. The City of Plymouth steeped in history will delight many including shopaholics with its abundance of shops. A River Trip up the Tamar is another interesting outing allowing you to see what remains of the might of the Royal Navy as well as the beautiful river.

Treveria Farm has ensuite accommodation of an exceptionally high standard including one magnificent four-poster for the romantics. Every room has been stylishly and individually decorated with beautiful chintz and floral fabrics. Every room has Colour TV, Beveragemaking facilities, Radio Alarm Clocks and Hair dryers. It is in the sunny, bright and gracious Dining Room with its restored fireplace and lovely views, that you will be served what can only be described as a sumptuous breakfast with fresh eggs and milk Treveria is a non-smoking house. Janice Kitto is you host and it is she who has lovingly restored much of the fine antique furniture you see around you. There are many good eating places in Looe and Polperro for an evening meal.

USEFUL INFORMATION

OPEN: March-December
CHILDREN: No
CREDIT CARDS: None taken
LICENSED: No
ACCOMMODATION: 3 dbl ensuite
PETS: No
DINING ROOM: Traditional Breakfast or Continental
VEGETARIAN: Yes
DISABLED ACCESS: No
GARDEN: Yes + 200 acre farm

KEMPS FARM
Winsford,
Somerset TA24 7HT
Tel: 01643 851312

Gloriously placed for excursions into an area abounding in natural beauty is Kemps Farm set within 350 acres of farmland, which is home to an abundance of wildlife. This peaceful and cordial dwelling originally built 400 years ago was totally rebuilt in 1988, and offers guests a high standard of accommodation. The house is heated by electric radiators, with comfortable and modern furniture. All bedrooms are most tastefully furbished and decorated, one of which has ensuite facilities, with separate private bathroom for two other rooms. As one would expect of a farmhouse the home-cooking is second to none with a delicious breakfast to set one up for the day. On your return from your days outing, come home to a hearty and well presented evening meal, and later enjoy the warmth of the roaring wood burner. Stunning views from Kemps Farm, can be enjoyed from the garden which overlooks the River Exe, or watch the Red Deer play. Somerset enjoys not only some of the most breathtaking moorland and countryside, but the coastline close to Winsford offer visitors wonderful scenery and an opportunity for long coastal walks and exploring the many tiny villages with their thatched cottages and ancient monuments.

USEFUL INFORMATION

OPEN; *All year except Christmas*　**DINING ROOM**; *Full English breakfast*
CREDIT CARDS; *None taken*　*Evening meal - 3 course with cheese & biscuits*
ACCOMMODATION; *3 rooms,*　**VEGETARIAN**; *Catered for*
1 double, 1 twin, 1 ensuite　**DISABLED ACCESS**; *No, but welcome*
GARDEN; *Yes with views of River Exe*　**PETS**; *Yes, well behaved*

THE FORGE
Clearbrook House, Yelverton,
Devon PL20 6JD
Tel: 01822 853386

Judy Tracey is the owner of this 100 year old converted blacksmiths forge and keeps it to immaculate standards. It is separate from the main house and has its own private entrance. This accommodation is self-catering, but if you wish then breakfast can be served on a B&B basis. Evening meals can be taken at the excellent Skylark Inn next door or there are a number of local restaurants that Judy will recommend. Clearbrook is on the southern side of Dartmoor National Park and is ideal for exploring the moors. The coast is within easy reach and so is the historic city of Plymouth. A great base within easy access to all local amenities.

USEFUL INFORMATION

OPEN : *All year*　**RESTAURANT** : *Not applicable*
CHILDREN : *Not under 15yrs*　**BAR FOOD** : *Not applicable*
PETS : *No*　**VEGETARIAN** : *Yes*
CREDIT CARDS : *None taken*　**DISABLED ACCESS** : *Partial but no*
ACCOMMODATION : *1 twin room ensuite*　*wheelchairs*
with sitting room　**GARDEN** : *Yes*

Chapter One

ALPINE HOUSE
10 West Road,
Wiveliscombe,
Somerset TA4 2TF

Tel: 01984 623526

    Alpine House is an elegant and beautifully refurbished Victorian house on the outskirts of the village of Wiveliscombe. This imposing residence is owned and run by Indrani and Nevill Hewitt, a charming couple who work very hard to make you feel welcome and totally at home. There is everything here to make your stay an enjoyable and happy one. The beautifully decorated bedrooms are light and airy with superb views over open countryside at the front and the terraced garden at the rear. They are fully colour co-ordinated with a welcome tea and coffee tray and remote colour television, two of the rooms have ensuite bathrooms, one private bathroom, the other has a shower room. The rest of the house has locally made cane chairs, lovely pictures and Batik work from Sri Lanka and other exotic places. The dining room looks out across the cricket and rugby ground, and it is here Indrani serves breakfast, a choice of cereals, eggs, omelettes and full English can be had, evening meals are served by prior arrangement. The rear garden is quite a feature and must be seen to be believed, it is terraced and well stocked with a wide range of shrubs and plants. The area around Wiveliscombe is rich in attractions and activities including golf, fishing, riding and plenty of walking. This really is the ideal location to enjoy the West Country.

USEFUL INFORMATION

OPEN; All year
CHILDREN; No
CREDIT CARDS; Cash or Cheque preferred but will accept Visa/Access/Switch
ACCOMMODATION; 4 rooms, 3 double, 1 twin, 3 ensuite + 1 private facilities
GARDEN; Wonderful terraced garden
DINING ROOM; Choice of breakfast, Evening meal by arrangement
VEGETARIAN; Catered for
DISABLED ACCESS; Ground floor bed-room available, not suitable for wheelchairs
PETS; No
NON- SMOKING

LYDGATE HOUSE HOTEL
Postbridge,
Devon PL20 6TJ

Tel: 01822 880209
Fax: 01822 880202

This elegant house stands in an idyllic setting of 36 acres. Lydgate House faces due south and has superb views from almost every room. The East Dart River flows through the fields below the house. In some places it is deep enough for swimming and with a Water Authority licence you can fish the river for trout and salmon or try your luck in the four reservoirs nearby. What is particularly pleasing is that the house lies in a sheltered moorland valley at the end of a private lane some 400 metres fro the B3212. This provides the peace that one seeks for on a holiday in Dartmoor National Park. The village itself is a popular and very busy tourist spot, famous for its clapper bridge. The Dartmoor National Park organises a series of guided walks during the summer season; there's pony trekking all around and three golf courses within twelve miles.

The ensuite and centrally heated bedrooms have colour televisions, tea/coffee making facilities and hair driers. Downstairs the log fire in the sitting room where you will also find the bar, makes a focal point for visitors in the cooler months and the bar is always a gathering place for guests in the summertime. The simple but imaginative menu changes daily and has a variety of delicious dishes on offer, all home-cooked using produce from the hotel's garden and locally reared meat. There is always a vegetarian choice. The hotel has a very friendly, informal atmosphere and for anyone travelling on their own there is an especial welcome. You may book from any day for any length of time. Children are welcome and the charge is at the discretion of the management. Cots are available. Dogs are welcome and for them a charge of £2 a night is levied.

USEFUL INFORMATION

OPEN: Closed January & February
CHILDREN: Welcome. Cot available
CREDIT CARDS: Visa/Access
LICENSED: Yes
ACCOMMODATION: 8 ensuite rooms
PETS: Dogs welcome

DINING ROOM: Home-cooked fare using produce from garden & local meat
VEGETARIAN: Always a choice
DISABLED ACCESS: No
GARDEN: 37 acres

Chapter One

SEEBURG
138 Sherborne Road,
Yeovil, Somerset BA21 4HQ

Tel: 01935 472159
Fax: 01935 413066

    Unless you have stayed in this exceptionally friendly guest house you cannot possibly appreciate all that it has to offer. It is not that it is so different from other establishments which I am sure are equally well furnished, have equally comfortable beds and offer their guests just as good food. What is different to many places is that Chris and Val Abel are so flexible. If needs be they will shift rooms around to accommodate a family or some special circumstance. Whilst they naturally need to earn a living from running Seeburg, they have the good commonsense to be open to negotiations on their prices. All of this does not detract from the genuine welcome you receive. .

    Built in 1883 in the Edwardian era, the house is sturdy and yet has an elegance which is applicable to this age. The rooms are spacious with large windows. Every room is light and airy and decorated individually. There are 6 bedrooms, none of which are ensuite but there are three bathrooms with both baths and showers so this in no way causes a problem. Every room has television, direct dial telephone and a generously supplied tea and coffee tray - always a welcome sight for any traveller. The attractive dining room is where you will be served a substantial breakfast with several choices although if you prefer it you can have something lighter. Vegetarians are catered for by arrangement. For those who require an evening meal this can be arranged although Yeovil is not short of good eating places.

    Yeovil is right on the borders of Dorset and only five miles from the old town of Sherborne with its two castles and famous school. There are many National Trust properties within easy distance including Montacute. For the energetic there is fishing on the River Yeo, golf within 5 minutes walk, a dry ski slope, riding stables nearby and it is splendid walking countryside.

USEFUL INFORMATION

OPEN; All year
CHILDREN; Welcome
CREDIT CARDS;None taken
ACCOMMODATION; 6 rooms 3 bathrooms
PETS;By arrangement

DINING ROOM; Good traditional breakfast
Evening meals by arrangement.
VEGETARIAN;Upon request
DISABLED ACCESS; No
GARDEN; Yes. Private car parking at rear

COLETON BARTON FARM
*Brownstone Road, Kingswear,
Nr Dartmouth, Devon TQ6 0EQ*

Tel: 01803 752795

The emphasis here is on peace, tranquil surroundings and good food. The farm specialises in Aberdeen Angus cattle and all meats are home produced along with the season's vegetables. Food is wholesome, with local sea food, fattening puddings and a hearty breakfast that will keep you going all day. Coleton Barton Farm is set on the coastal path which runs between Kingswear and Paignton and all bedrooms have stunning views over the sea or Dartmoor. The rooms are pleasant and simple with pretty linens and curtains, and all have tea and coffee. The atmosphere is warm and friendly with Caroline Haddock making her guests feel at ease and at home. The farmhouse actually adjoins the sub-tropical gardens at Coleton Fishacre which really must be viewed, and there are plenty of walks in the area, be it cliff top or coastal paths. With Dartmoor beside you there is always the haunting beauty of the moor to be explored. Stabling and instruction is available should you want to bring you own horse, Caroline is a qualified instructor and experienced Event rider. For the train enthusiast there is the Dart Valley Railway, a lovely restored steam way, and there are water sports for all abilities. A really good location, giving peace and quiet but not too far away from a host of activities to suit everyone.

USEFUL INFORMATION

OPEN; All year
CHILDREN; Welcome
CREDIT CARDS; None taken
LICENSED; No
ACCOMMODATION; 3 rooms, 1 double, 1 family, 1 twin
DINING ROOM; Excellent wholesome cooking, 3 course dinner by arrangement
VEGETARIAN; Catered for
DISABLED ACCESS; No
GARDEN; 300 acre farm, plus lawns
PETS; Welcome

Chapter One

THE OLD MILL
Knole, Long Sutton,
Langport, Somerset TA10 9HY

Tel: 01458 241599 Fax: 01458 241710

As you drive up to The Old Mill you will be greeted by a charming property. The front of the house is covered with Clematis and other climbing plants and to the side is a huge waterwheel which adds such character. The Old Mill was built in approximately 1830 and is situated in the quiet idyllic hamlet of Knole. The gardens are very attractive with well kept lawned areas, trees, shrubs and flowers, and the stream flowing silently under the stone bridge. The English Tourist Board has awarded The Old Mill '2 Crowns Highly Commended' and you can understand why, the accommodation is very comfortable and homely. The 3 bedrooms are attractively furnished in a cottage style, 2 have ensuite facilities and the other has a private bathroom, they all have a television and a tea and coffee tray. There is a delightful lounge for guests which also has a TV. Paula Barber your host, serves up an excellent farmhouse style breakfast and plenty of it, the evening meal is country style with a touch of 'Cordon Bleu' and is by arrangement only. Guests are more than welcome to bring their own wine to have with their meal and Paula provides chilling facilities if needed. Somerset has an abundance of stately homes, gardens and places of interest as well as beautiful scenery and local history. So come and enjoy a stay at The Old Mill where Paula is looking forward to welcoming you.

USEFUL INFORMATION

OPEN; *All year*
CHILDREN; *Over 8 years or babes in arms*
CREDIT CARDS; *None taken*
LICENSED; *No, welcome to bring your own*
DINING ROOM; *Home-cooked fare*
VEGETARIAN; *Catered for*
DISABLED ACCESS; *No, but welcome*
GARDEN; *Yes*
PETS; *No*
ACCOMMODATION; *3 rooms, 2 doubles, 1 twin, 2 ensuite, 1 with private bathroom*

LYNNWOOD BED AND BREAKFAST
Lynnwood,
Lanlivery, Bodmin
Cornwall PL30 5BX
Tel: 01208 872326

This attractive, modern bungalow is set in 10 acres of landscaped gardens complete with a stream and abundant wildlife. Situated on 'The Saints Way' 5 miles from Fowey and 3 miles from the nearest beaches, it is ideal for those who enjoy walking, sailing and other water activities. Lynwood is also central for both golf with Carlyon Bay, Lostwithiel and Lanhydrock courses within a few miles and for garden enthusiasts being within easy reach of some of the Great Gardens of Cornwall such as Lanhydrock and Heligan. The standard throughout is very high, comfortably furnished with fresh flowers in every room. An excellent breakfast is served and other meals are by arrangement.

USEFUL INFORMATION
OPEN: All year.
CHILDREN: Welcome.
CREDIT CARDS: None taken
ACCOMMODATION: 1 dbl, 1 twin, 1 family room with adjacent bathroom
DINING ROOM: Excellent breakfast. Evening meal by arrangement
VEGETARIAN: Catered for
PETS: Welcome
Ample parking
NO SMOKING

CHELSFIELD FARM
Nr. Week St Mary,
Cornwall Pl15 8NU
Tel: 01566 785285

Bob and Pam Jones make you feel instantly welcome upon arrival at these attractive log cabins, set in the beautiful rolling countryside of the West Country. You are greeted by a welcome tray of tea and coffee with biscuits, and some fresh eggs and milk. The eggs are from the farm itself as Chelsfield is a registered organic farm, specialising in vegetables, fruit and free range eggs. The cabins themselves are set in 10 acres of conservation land surrounded by woodland, streams, ponds and wildlife habitat. Each cabin is tastefully furnished in cane and pine, and have all that is necessary for full comfort (including central heating). Cornwall has everything for the visitor and these cabins are only a short drive from many attractions. Enjoy the beaches and coves and coastal walks. Visit the historic town of Launceston with it's castle and steam railway. Try your hand at the many water sports available such as sailing, surfing or even microlites! There is an otter and deer sanctuary close by and golf courses a short drive away. What more could you ask? If you are a nature lover then you will be enchanted by this idyllic location.

USEFUL INFORMATION
OPEN : All year
CHILDREN : Welcome
PETS : By arrangement
CREDIT CARDS : None taken
LICENSED : No
ACCOMMODATION : 2 cabins; 3 farmland walks. Garden furniture & BBQ supplied bedrooms comprising 1 dbl, 1 twin & 1 bunkbed room (adult size).
RESTAURANT : Not applicable
BAR FOOD : Not applicable
VEGETARIAN : Not applicable
DISABLED ACCESS : Yes, assisted
GARDEN : Yes, with patio and BBQ areas and

HALL FARMHOUSE
Bodinnick,
Lanteglos-by-Fowey,
Cornwall PL23 1LX

Tel: 01726 870310
Fax: 01726 870050

Traditional farmhouse tucked away in an area of outstanding natural beauty with land overlooking Fowey Harbour and the sea. From Plymouth, cross the Tamar Bridge and follow the A38 to Dobwalls. Drive through the village and at the Y junction, controlled by traffic lights, take the left hand fork onto the A390 signposted to St Austell. After passing through the village of East Taphouse and a sharp bend to the right, take a left turning onto the B3359 signposted to Looe. Just part Shillamill Lakes and one mile short of Pelynt, turn sharp right, signposted Lerryn, Bodinnick and Polruan. Drive through Lanteglos Highway, continue for a mile and look for a left hand turning with a sign: Bodinnick Village Only. Take this turning and continue along a twisty Cornish lane for 350 metres. Hall is immediately to the front, before a sharp right hand bend in the road which then descends into Bodinnick village. Hall is very old and goes back to approximately 1170. It has that charm that age brings to a house - uneven floors, low ceilings and a welcoming atmosphere. Cleverly the comforts of modern life have been incorporated and the three letting bedrooms are all ensuite with TV and a beverage tray. Guests also enjoy a dedicated sitting room/breakfast room and a sun patio/garden. Margaret Shakerley will make you very welcome and make sure you have a superb farmhouse breakfast. An excellent pub in the village offers evening meals and there are many recommended restaurants across the river in Fowey. This is a wonderful base for anyone wanting to explore the incredible beauty of the area and especially its famous coastal walks.

USEFUL INFORMATION

OPEN: All year.
CHILDREN: Welcome.
CREDIT CARDS: None taken
ACCOMMODATION: 3 ensuite rooms
DINING ROOM: Superb farmhouse breakfast
No evening meal
VEGETARIAN: Catered for with notice
PETS: Dogs accepted

GLENCOE VILLA GUEST HOUSE
13, Race Hill,
Launceston, Cornwall PL15 9BB

Tel: 01566 775819/773012

Right in the heart of historical Launceston, Glencoe Villa - quite frequently known as simply 'Robinsons' after your host Gillian Robinson and her husband - is a 'back to front house'!. The front door is around the back amidst a plethora of hanging baskets, flowers, white garden furniture surrounded by low hung trees. The most obvious thing about Glencoe is the absence of any fuss. Gillian is a down to earth lady who has looked after guests for a long time and knows exactly what is needed to make anyone's stay enjoyable and memorable. The Victorian house was built by her grandfather and although the Robinsons have spent many years abroad, it has remained a family home. Gilllian has a fund on interesting and amusing anecdotes which are well worth listening to. Every room is typical of the Victorian age, spacious and with high ceilings. Two of the comfortable bedrooms have ensuite facilities and there are rooms suitable for couples or families, plus one twin and one double. All the bedrooms are strictly non-smoking. Every room has TV and tea and coffee making facilities and most have lovely views over the Tamar Valley. There is a lounge for the use of visitors. A beautifully cooked and generously portioned breakfast awaits you every morning. Glencoe is an ideal base at any time of the year with wonderful walks, fishing, riding, birdwatching and many historic and interesting places within easy reach.

USEFUL INFORMATION

OPEN: All year
CHILDREN: Welcome
CREDIT CARDS: Visa/MasterCard
ACCOMMODATION: 4 rooms mainly ensuite
PARKING: Yes
DINING ROOM: Super breakfast
VEGETARIAN: Catered for
DISABLED ACCESS: Downstairs
GARDEN: Yes
PETS: By arrangement

Chapter One

HURDON FARM
*Launceston,
Cornwall PL15 9LS
Tel: 01566 772955*

Margaret Smith and her daughter Nicola welcome guests to Hurdon Farm, with it's 18th century Georgian stone farmhouse set amongst 400 acres of mixed farmland. The house is very pleasant with large airy rooms and good facilities in each. Margaret and Nicola provide breakfast and evening meal (if required) and all the food is excellent. Flans, cakes puddings are all home made and have delightful names such as Sticky Toffee Pudding and Apple Dappy! Although not licensed, guests are welcome to bring their own wine or beer to compliment the food. A good centre for access to attractions in both Devon and Cornwall.

USEFUL INFORMATION
OPEN; All year   **DINING ROOM**; Excellent variety of food
CHILDREN; Welcome   **VEGETARIAN**; Catered for
CREDIT CARDS; None taken   **DISABLED ACCESS**; Not really
LICENSED; No, welcome to bring your own   **GARDEN**; Large with seating and pretty   **ACCOMMODATION**; 6 rooms, 3 double   thatched summer house
2 twin, 1 family   **PETS**; No

COURTYARD FARM COTTAGES
*Lesnewth, Nr. Boscastle,
Cornwall PL35 0HR
Tel: 01840 261256*

Courtyard Farm and cottages is set in a small hamlet, two and a half miles from the picturesque harbour of Boscastle. The self-catering cottages are converted from the original 17th century mill and farm buildings and retain character and atmosphere, many of the cottages overlook the Valency Valley and the sea. The cottages are equipped to a high standard and are key rated 2-4 by the English Tourist Board with a quality rating of Commended. The gardens have been lovingly cared for and there is a barbeque/picnic area. The lane to Boscastle is steep and winding and covered in wild flowers, bluebells in the Spring, cool and leafy in the Summer. As you descend down the valley you are followed by a babbling stream that meets the river at the bottom. Close to the cottages is St. Juliot's church where Thomas Hardy was married. There are 3 Shetland ponies, Toffee the oldest, is trained for driving and enjoys giving rides to the visiting children. A provisions pack can be ordered, complete with fresh home produced free range eggs. There is a good range of home-cooked foods and a beer and wine list. Clay pigeon shooting is on offer also creative workshops, with a crafts showroom, opening in 1997.

USEFUL INFORMATION
OPEN; All year   **FOOD**; Home-cooked food available
CHILDREN; Welcome   **DISABLED ACCESS**; No
CREDIT CARDS; Access & Visa   **GARDEN**; Delightful, with barbecue
LICENSED; Part, wines and beers   **PETS**; No
ACCOMMODATION; 7 self-catering cottages sleeping 2-8 persons

MILLFORD FARM COTTAGES
Lifton,
Devon PL16 0AT

Tel: 01566 783425

The Pound House and Gingerbread Cottage are set on Milford Farm; 200 acres of grazing meadows bounded by the rivers Thrushel and Wolf. Each cottage is unique with the Pound House adjacent to the main farmhouse, being a converted cider house and having spectacular views from the first floor living accommodation. Gingerbread Cottage sits in it's own private garden just off the main driveway and is surrounded by mature trees and shrubs. The really interesting thing about this farm is that it is the location of Dingles Steam Village which exhibits include fairground art and vintage machinery. This is most interesting with working traction engines, steam rollers and many more exhibits. There is also Mrs Dingle's Kitchen, where in season, you can obtain coffee, light snacks and cream teas. There is a play area for children, a gift shop and scenic walks and picnic spots along the banks of the rivers. If you are staying in accommodation at the farm then this is all free apart from a discounted entrance fee to the museum and adventure playground.

If this is not enough for you then Dartmoor is on your doorstep, the ancient market town of Tavistock is 9 miles away, Exeter and Plymouth are within easy access, as are the north and south coasts of Cornwall. Milford makes an ideal touring base with everything at your fingertips!

USEFUL INFORMATION

OPEN : All year
DINGLES STEAM VILLAGE : Easter to end Oct. 10am to 6pm - closed Fridays.
CHILDREN : Welcome
PETS : Gingerbread Cottage only
CREDIT CARDS : None taken
LICENSED : No
RESTAURANT : Access to cafe in season
BAR FOOD : Not applicable
VEGETARIAN : Not applicable
DISABLED ACCESS : No
PARKING : Each cottage up to 3 cars
GARDEN : Yes
ACCOMMODATION : 2 cottages :each sleep 6

Chapter One

CRYLLA FARM
Common Moor, Siblyback Lake,
Liskeard, Cornwall PL14 6ER

Tel: 01579 342473

Brian and Pearl Bunney who own Crylla Farm have a keen understanding of the needs of people on holiday. Their comfortable modern farmhouse is on the edge of the Moor and surrounded by well known walks and with extensive Lake views. Fishing and Windsurfing is readily available with tuition from someone nearby if needed. They will also collect you from Liskeard main line station and another plus is the lifts readily given to the pub and back as required!. There are three ensuite, centrally heated bedrooms each with a tea/coffee tray and a television if wanted. There is also TV and video in the attractively furnished lounge. There is a full farmhouse breakfast, half board is available and so too are delicious packed lunches. Vegetarians are catered for. Children are very welcome and so are pets. Whilst the house is not specifically equipped for the disabled, the house lends itself and your hosts are more than helpful.

USEFUL INFORMATION

OPEN: All year　　　　　　**DINING ROOM:** Delicious farmhouse breakfast
CHILDREN: Very welcome　　Evening meals available, packed lunches
CREDIT CARDS: None taken　**VEGETARIAN:** Catered for
ACCOMMODATION: 3 ensuite rooms　**DISABLED ACCESS:**
PETS: Welcome　　　　　　Not specifically equipped

LINDEN COTTAGE
Trewidland,
Nr. Looe, Cornwall PL14 4SS

Tel: 01503 240856

This pretty cottage is situated in the small hamlet of Trewidland surrounded by beautiful Cornish countryside and within easy distance of the sea and the moors. The cottage, built in the late 1700's emanates contentment and from time to time there are mysterious wafts of perfume - thought to be the presence of love. Whatever it is it underlines the very warm welcome you will experience in this happy house. Everywhere there is traditional furniture, the beds are very comfortable and the decor attractive. Wedgwood China and fine table linen graces the dining room in which you will be served a sumptuous English Breakfast. The bedrooms are delightful and warm with excellent quality bed linen and furnishings, they are well appointed with the luxury of ensuite facilities, colour television and a tea and coffee tray. Linden Cottage is strictly a non-smoking property. The cottage is not suitable for disabled people. There is a charming garden and plenty of parking space.

USEFUL INFORMATION

OPEN; March-October　　　**DINING ROOM;** Sumptuous English breakfast
CHILDREN; Unsuitable　　　**DISABLED ACCESS;** No
CREDIT CARDS; None taken　**GARDEN;** Yes, charming
ACCOMMODATION; Delightful cosy　**PETS;** Welcome by appointment
bedrooms

LOWER TRENGALE FARM
Liskeard,
Cornwall PL14 6HF

Tel: 01579 321019
Fax: 01579 321432

The welcome of home made cake with tea or coffee instantly makes you feel at ease at Lower Trengale Farm. The three self-catering cottages have been converted from an 18th century barn and offer a high quality of accommodation with comfortable furnishings and fabrics. Each cottage is fully equipped with dishwasher and microwave, and all have woodburning stoves which make them very cosy on those chilly days. The farm is set in 13 acres of peaceful farmland in a delightful setting overlooking a wooded valley and rolling countryside. A small flock of sheep graze the fields with ponies. Visitors enjoy all the friendly pets which include pot bellied pigs, goats, ducks and hens. The garden offers a BBQ and plenty of tables and chairs from which to enjoy the lovely views and the sight of the buzzards which circle high in the sky. There is a games room offering pool, table tennis, darts and a piano - as well as various games, toys and puzzles. A good choice of maps, books of local walks and various guides are also to be found. Home-cooked frozen dishes are available for guests to heat up, and twice a week a ready three course meal is offered. There is a laundry room and drying facilities for wet weather gear. During the off-season months the owner, Louise Kidd, a qualified teacher and local Adult Education tutor, runs several five day, full board, art/craftcourses. The classes are held in a purpose built workshop which is well-lit and heated. This is a great place for those dull wintry months in early Spring and late Autumn. Imagine at the end of the day in the workshop, coming back and relaxing in you cosy cottage with your feet up in front of a roaring log fire! When there are no courses being run the workshop makes a marvellous studio for painters to take advantage of. As if this was not enough, the farm is excellent for exploring Cornwall. Bodmin Moor is just 3 miles away with its magnificent walks and riding. Sibleyback Reservoir is 2 miles away where lessons in windsurfing and sailing are available. There are National Trust houses to visit, wonderful gardens, theme parks and fishing villages. There are coastal walks, boat trips and shark fishing within half an hour - not to mention a good choice of golf courses. Louise is only too happy to help with information and the storage of bicycles, boats, fishing gear or any other equipment you may have. It really is an excellent holiday - and if you are a nature lover then join in the nature watch for badgers, foxes and plenty more with a local gamekeeper. Is there any more you could ask from a country holiday?

USEFUL INFORMATION

OPEN; All year
CHILDREN; Most welcome
CREDIT CARDS; None taken
LICENSED; No
ACCOMMODATION; 3 self-contained cottages
EVENING MEAL; Set menu and frozen dishes
VEGETARIAN; Catered for
DISABLED ACCESS; No
GARDEN; Excellent, with separate play area
PETS; Strictly by arrangement

Chapter One

ROSECRADDOC LODGE
Liskeard,
Cornwall PL14 5BU
Tel: 01579 346768
Fax: 01579 346768

Roscraddoc Holiday Bungalows are set in an idyllic valley at the foot of Caradon Hill. The setting is wonderful in that the gardens and woodland are never dull with the different seasons of flowers and shrubs and also with the abundant wildlife, not including the ornamental ducks which may have occasion to visit you! The bungalows are all individually decorated to a high standard and there is everything a visitor could possibly need. Within a 2 minute walk is a bar and clubhouse, it is actually on a neighbouring property but welcomes visitors from Roscraddoc, serving bar meals and Sunday roasts. Because you are in such a central area there is more than ample to do if you wish. Both the south and the north coasts are easily accessible and also the moors of Bodmin and Dartmoor. For a day's shopping Plymouth is easily reached and the owners Louise and Richard are only too happy to give any further information you require.

USEFUL INFORMATION

OPEN; Mar-Dec inc.
CHILDREN; Welcome
CREDIT CARDS; None taken
LICENSED; No
ACCOMMODATION; 25 self-catering bungalows
GARDEN; Attractive and level
DINING ROOM; Not applicable
VEGETARIAN; Not applicable
DISABLED ACCESS; 2 specially adapted bungalows, carefully thought out and well fitted. Have been inspected and recommended for the disabled.
PETS; Welcome

TREDINNICK FARM
Duloe, Liskeard,
Cornwall PL14 4PJ
Tel: 01503 262997
Fax: 01503 265554

This Duchy farm accommodation is run by Angela Barrett who maintains very high standards and welcomes her guests warmly. The accommodation is self-catering, sleeping up to 10, and is attached to the farmhouse. This is actually a working farm and guests are most welcome to view the likes of cow milking. The nearest village is Duloe with a post office and shop, but even so you are never far from other major attractions such as Looe or Polperro. A lovely rural setting if you want to get away from it all, but not too far away. Ye Old Plough House Inn in Duloe serves very good food on those occasions you don't want to cater for yourself.

USEFUL INFORMATION

OPEN; Mar-Dec
CHILDREN; Welcome
CREDIT CARDS; None taken
LICENSED; No
ACCOMMODATION; Self-catering
RESTAURANT; Not applicable
VEGETARIAN; Not applicable
DISABLED ACCESS; No
GARDEN; Very nice, safe play area for children

SHENSTONE
Minions, Liskeard,
Cornwall PL14 5BL

Tel: 01579 363030
Fax: 01579 363530

This untouched corner of Cornwall delights all who discover it. Full of ruined mines with fascinating names like Gonamena, Phoenix United,. Archaeological sites from the Stone Age onwards, The Hurlers, Bronze Age stone circles, the Cheesewring rocks, Celtic crosses and many other monuments, can all be seen on fascinating walks in the area. A great place for a holiday and one can wholeheartedly recommend the warmth and hospitality of Shenstone. This traditional granite cottage was once 3 miners cottages, facing south it has remarkable views towards Caradon Hill (Cornwall's second highest point at 1212 feet). All you have to do is open the garden gate, step over the stream and climb to the top to enjoy some of the most spectacular scenery in Cornwall with Dartmoor to the East, Bodmin Moor to the North and the Cornish Coast to the South.

Inside Shenstone, the house is charming and beautifully furnished highlighting the old beams, the vast fireplace and the many attractive features of the building. There are two bedrooms, both ensuite with pretty drapes and decor, comfortable beds, TV and Tea Making Facilities. Upstairs is a twin-bedded room complete with beams and downstairs a double bedded room with a traditional fireplace. Both are exceptionally large and sunny. Breakfast is served in the Dining Room which is full of interesting pictures and has a large granite fireplace with the original clone ovens.. The food is excellent and enhanced by real coffee and home-made jams and marmalades.

USEFUL INFORMATION

OPEN; All year except Christmas
CHILDREN;Welcome
CREDIT CARDS;None taken
LICENSED;No
PETS; Yes
ACCOMMODATION;1dbl.1twin both ensuite

DINING ROOM;Breakfast only
BAR FOOD;Not applicable
VEGETARIAN;Upon request
DISABLED ACCESS;Limited
GARDEN;Yes

Chapter One

THE OLD RECTORY COUNTRY HOUSE HOTEL
St Keyne, Liskeard
Cornwall PL14 4 RL

Tel: 01579 342617

If one were to quote from the Bible 'The peace that passeth all understanding' it would be as applicable to the Old Rectory as it is in the biblical sense. The house is encompassed in an aura of peace and tranquillity, standing in a secluded setting in its own three acres of grounds and surrounded by farmland. The view from the grounds and the windows merely enhances the image. Built in the early 1800's this is a family run hotel with Pat and John Minifie at the helm. It combines the gracious charm of bygone days with cheery log fires on cooler evenings and the modern central heating to ensure your creature comfort. The furnishings and decor are in total harmony with the original architecture. Panelled doors, a black marble fireplace, a handsome staircase with barley-twist balusters, and velvet sofas add to the elegance.

There are eight ensuite bedrooms, tastefully decorated and all with tea/coffee making facilities and colour television. Two rooms have Four-Posters and there is a ground floor ensuite room to accommodate the disabled. A sumptuous breakfast and an a la carte dinner including traditional fine English cooking and the adventure of Continental cuisine complete the picture. St Keyne is delightfully 'off the beaten track' on the little used B3254 but it is only 5 miles from the picturesque fishing village of Looe and 3 miles from the market town of Liskeard. Safe beaches, wonderful walks, sailing, tennis, fishing, riding and golf are just some of the activities readily available.

USEFUL INFORMATION

OPEN: Closed at Christmas
CHILDREN: Over 12 years
CREDIT CARDS: All but Amex
LICENSED: Yes
ACCOMMODATION: 8 ensuite rooms
GARDEN: 3 acres
PETS: Well behaved with prior arrangement

DINING ROOM: Full English Breakfast
        A La Carte dinner
BAR FOOD: Not applicable
VEGETARIAN: Catered for on request
DISABLED ACCESS: One ground floor room suitable

TREGONDALE FARM
Menheniot, Liskeard,
Cornwall PL14 3RG

Tel/Fax: 01579 342407

In the peaceful heart of the Cornish countryside nestling in 200 acres of pasture and woodland lies Tregondale Farm, a member of the Cream of Cornwall Farm Holiday Group, is superbly situated, offering quality accommodation that one expects from this innovative group. Arthur Mee called the area 'Smiling Countryside'. Whichever direction you take all aspects of holiday excursions unfold before you. The south coast is softer than the north, Looe is 6 miles, Bodmin Moor lies in a westerly direction, within 15 minutes drive and back in Devon, Plymouth is less than half an hour, Dartmoor is easily found. This gracious farmhouse has everything. Guests are invited to take advantage of all amenities from this home, see the pedigree South Devon Cattle, long wool sheep, lambs in Spring all naturally reared situated in an attractive valley with rural views. The house is on the site of an old manor dating back to the Domesday Book and is set back into a beautiful walled garden, a swing and seesaw compliments an ancient Beech tree and with all its Cornish granite is idyllic to relax, providing a large tarmac parking area and an all weather tennis court for the energetic. The well planned Woodland Farm Trail will take you over styles, through the valley, wildflowers and wildlife abound. Activity Holidays including golf at local golf clubs with special rates, cycling, fishing, a wealth of country and coastal walks can be taken advantage of along with National Trust houses and gardens. Old as the house maybe it it has been refurbished to give all the creature comforts modern day visitors demand, filled with sunlight in the summer a superb inglenook fireplace in the pretty lounge acts as a magnet for guests in the winter months, a choice of three ensuite bedrooms all colour co-ordinated. Washing and drying facilities when required. A full English breakfast is served and delicious evening meals, with fresh home-grown produce, succulent meats and Cornish clotted cream, as there is no license you are welcome to bring your own!. Share all this tranquillity and self-cater in the charming character cottage and discover the beauty of Cornwall. Take note of the visitors book and you will see that people come back year after year.

USEFUL INFORMATION

OPEN: All year
CHILDREN: Welcome
CREDIT CARDS:: None taken
LICENSED: No
ACCOMMODATION: 3 dbl ensuite
GARDEN: Yes. Tennis court, Parking, swing, see-saw, woodland farm trail
DINING ROOM: Full English Breakfast
Evening meals by arrangement
VEGETARIAN: Catered for upon request
DISABLED ACCESS: No
PETS: In self catering cottage only
AMENITIES: Good village pub, shop and Post Office

Chapter One

WINDERMERE HOUSE
St Martins, Looe
Cornwall PL13 1NX
Tel: 01503 262035

Bed and breakfast in Windermere House is a delightful experience. Peter and Jenny Ashton, the owners, make your stay pleasant and warming, and leave you with a wish to return. The bedrooms are immaculately furnished in a traditional style, with exquisite bedding, and are en suite with TV, tea and coffee facilities. Peter and Jenny have their own free range chickens, so do have eggs for breakfast! Jenny is a qualified chef and an affiliate of the RoyalSociety of Health, so you can be assured of the quality of your meals. The dining room overlooks the gardens and has charming views of the sea. Breakfast is served on fine bone china and if you desire, you can have afternoon tea in the garden. To keep all the rooms fresh, Peter and Jenny operate a no smoking policy. Windermere is only one mile outside the picturesque port of Looe, which is situated in an area of outstanding natural beauty. This idyllic location with its peaceful hills and woods, rocky shores and busy harbours, offers plenty for the visitor. Looe has a wealth of restaurants and cosy pubs for the evenings, and the historic city of Plymouth is a short drive away. The perfect accommodation at any time of year in a rather special part of Cornwall.

USEFUL INFORMATION
OPEN : All year
CHILDREN : By arrangement
CREDIT CARDS : All major taken
ACCOMMODATION : 3 rooms en suite
VEGETARIAN : Catered for
DISABLED ACCESS : No
GARDEN : Pleasant

TRELEAVEN FARM HOUSE
Mevagissey, Cornwall PL26 6RZ

Tel: 01726 842413

Standing at the head of the valley overlooking Mevagissey, Treleaven is a comfortably modernised farmhouse to which Anne and Colin Hennah welcome you. It is a friendly, informal house and as ideal base from which to enjoy a holiday in Cornwall. Beautiful coastal and country walks as well as many sandy beaches are nearby and for those who love gardens, Treleaven is on the fringes of the Lost gardens of Heligan. In the grounds of Treleaven is a solar heated swimming pool, an 18 hole putting green and games barn. Laundry facilities are also available. All six attractively furnished bedrooms have toilet and shower ensuite, colour TV, tea/coffee making facilities and central heating. The farmhouse cooking using local produce is exceptionally good. Interesting and varied menus are offered every day. Cream Teas. No dinner on Sundays. The friendly licensed bar is a great meeting place at night.

USEFUL INFORMATION
OPEN: All year
CHILDREN: Welcome
CREDIT CARDS: Barclaycard/ Mastercard
LICENSED: Yes
ACCOMMODATION: 6 ensuite rooms
PETS: No
DINING ROOM: Excellent farmhouse cooking. Open to non-residents
DISABLED ACCESS: No
GARDEN: Yes, swimming pool, 18 hole putting green and games barn
Ample parking

LYDFORD HOUSE HOTEL
Lydford, Devon EX20 4AU

Tel: 01822 820347

This award winning hotel in 'One of Britain's Great Little Hotels'. It has charm and style in abundance and stands in eight acres of garden and pasture land, just outside the historic village of Lydford on the edge of Dartmoor. It is within the boundary of the National Park and enjoys the peace and quiet of the beautiful Devon countryside. Built for the artist William Widgery in 1880 it became a guest house at the turn of the century and then a licensed hotel in 1968. The Boulter family who own and run the hotel came here in 1972 and have steadily and carefully brought about many improvements for the benefit of their guests. Daughter Clare runs a Riding Stables in the Grounds and since 1984 son Simon has been the Manager. Everything about this house has a good feeling. It is kept in immaculate order but is nonetheless extremely relaxed and welcoming. In the spacious lounge there is a collection of William Widgery's paintings, a big log fire makes it cosy in winter and a small bar-lounge is behind the Cocktail Bar. Enjoy leisurely meals served to you by an efficient and unobtrusive staff. Breakfast is a splendid meal with fresh farm eggs, kippers, home-cooked ham and home-made marmalade. Morning coffee is available as well as snacks at Lunchtime and Afternoon Teas int eh Tea Room during the season. Sunday Lunch is served in the restaurant which is open to non-residents. The Table D'Hote Dinner is a three course meal of generous proportions with a wide choice at each course. Vegetarians and special diets can be catered for with prior notice. The Wine List compliments the menu. Sleep at night in comfortable beds in well appointed ensuite rooms and wake in the morning ready to explore the magic of the Moor, play golf, fish or take a look at the many picturesque villages. Residential Riding Holidays are available as are themed breaks at certain times of the year. A great hotel.

USEFUL INFORMATION

OPEN: All year
CHILDREN: Over 5 years
CREDIT CARDS: Visa/Master
LICENSED: Yes
ACCOMMODATION: 13 en suite rooms
RESTAURANT: Delicious home-cooked fare
VEGETARIAN: Upon request
DISABLED ACCESS: No special facilities
GARDEN: 8 acres
PETS: Yes in certain rooms

Chapter One

INGLESIDE HOTEL
Lynton,
North Devon EX35 6HW

Tel: 01598 752223

For a quarter of a century Clive and Lesley Horn have been welcoming guests at Ingleside, many have become friends over the years, not surprising to anyone who has stayed here and appreciated both the genuine welcome, the pleasant service and the comfort of the house. The Hotel stands high in its own grounds facing south overlooking the picturesque village of Lynton. A short private road brings you to the centre of Lynton where you are just a few minutes walk from the famous Cliff railway to Lynmouth. The side gate of the hotel leads you on to Hollerday Hill and the beautiful Valley of Rocks footpath. Built in 1895 as a gentleman's residence, the house has full central heating and all the modern comforts that the modern day traveller demands. The attractively furnished ensuite bedrooms all have television, clock radio, hair dryer and tea/coffee making facilities. The lounge has a warming log fire for chilly evenings and dinner is a candlelit affair which enhances the delicious and varied menu complemented by a well chosen wine list. Breakfast is a feast in its own right and plentiful enough to set you up for a day's exploring in this part of North Devon.

USEFUL INFORMATION

OPEN: Mid-March to early October
CHILDREN: 12 years +
CREDIT CARDS: Access/Visa/Master
LICENSED: Restaurant license
ACCOMMODATION: 7 rooms ensuite
PETS: Not permitted
GARDEN: Large. Patio. Car park

DINING ROOM: Traditional fare
Varied menu
BAR FOOD: Not applicable
VEGETARIAN: On request
DISABLED ACCESS: Level entrance but only suitable for those able to climb stairs to first floor.

COTEHELE LODGE
84 Tower Road,
Newquay, Cornwall TR7 1LY
Tel: 01637 873421

Situated close to all Newquay's amenities, approximately one minutes walk from the Golf Club, 3 minutes to Fistral Beach, the Harbour, the Town Centre and other beaches, Cotehele Lodge, built at the turn of the century, is an immaculately kept Family Guest House owned and run by Norman and Jean Drysdale. It is a friendly and welcoming place in which to stay for a holiday or short break. There are 6 bedrooms, 4 with ensuite facilities. Each room is comfortably furnished and has both TV and Satellite as well as a tea and coffee tray. Breakfast is a substantial meal, freshly cooked to order and the excellent optional evening meal varies every day. Vegetarians are catered for upon request.

USEFUL INFORMATION

OPEN: March to end October
CHILDREN: Welcome (up to 10 years half price)
CREDIT CARDS: None taken
ACCOMMODATION: 6 rooms, 4 ensuite
Private car parking

DINING ROOM: Substantial breakfast, optional evening meal
VEGETARIAN: Upon request
DISABLED ACCESS: Limited
PETS: No

ALCOMBE HOUSE HOTEL
Alcombe, Nr. Minehead
Somerset TA24 6BG

Tel: 01643 705130

    Alcombe House is a Georgian, Grade 2 listed house with 7 rooms for guests. It was built in 1843 by the Luttrell family of Dunster Castle, the village of which is less than a mile away. The rooms are all carefully furnished in delicate pastel shades and are light and airy. The lounge is furnished in wicker and cane with portraits and paintings by local artist Thelma Frost decorating the walls. One of the bedrooms has a historic visitor who "appears" from time to time! Friendly, of course! Valerie and Roger Kent are most concerned in supplying their guests with the comfort, attention and cuisine suitable to the standards of this house. Dinners are imaginative and served in a relaxed atmosphere. The menu is varied and uses fresh local produce wherever possible. The hotel is on a wonderful spot on the edge of Exmoor National Park with its many walks where herds of deer, badgers and birds of prey are seen frequently. Local facilities are good with fishing and golf, and many quaint villages and hamlets close to hand.

USEFUL INFORMATION

OPEN : All year
CHILDREN : Not suitable
PETS : By arrangement
CREDIT CARDS : All major cards
LICENSED : Full
ACCOMMODATION : 7 rooms en suite baths.
RESTAURANT : Imaginative good food
BAR FOOD : Not applicable
VEGETARIAN : and special diets
DISABLED ACCESS : No
GARDEN : Yes; afternoon tea if required

WARMHILL FARM
Hennock,
Newton Abbot,
South Devon TQ13 9QH
Tel: 01626 833229

    Warmhill Farmhouse is a 100 acre dairy farm on the slopes of the glorious Teign Valley, on the south eastern edge of the Dartmoor National Park. The farmhouse is situated on the edge of the farmyard and children are encouraged to help with the animals and milking. Visitors are free to walk over the farm which has an abundance of wild life and beautiful views over the valley. The village of Hennock which is a five minute walk away has a pub, a small shop and a church. The coast is within 10 miles and the wild expanses of Dartmoor 5 miles. The Cathedral city of Exeter is only 10 miles away. Riding, fishing, golf, walking and climbing are all readily available and there is a swimming pool and leisure centre six miles away. The farmhouse is a large, traditional beamed and thatched barn conversion, adjacent to the owners cottage. The original barn was built in the 16th century and many old features remain, it has spacious rooms and is comfortably furnished in keeping with the character of the property.

USEFUL INFORMATION

OPEN; All year
CHILDREN; Welcome
CREDIT CARDS; None taken
LICENSED; No
ACCOMMODATION; Self-catering
DISABLED ACCESS; No
GARDEN; Yes
PETS; Yes, up to 2 dogs

Chapter One

THE SANDROCK HOTEL
*Longmead,
Lynton, Devon EX35 6DH*

*Tel: 01598 753307
Fax:01598 752665*

At the entrance to the famous Valley of the Rocks, The Sandrock Hotel stands in a wonderful position. Hollerday Hill lies behind the hotel, and from there you can enjoy commanding views of the coast, from Countisbury Foreland and Lynmouth Bay to the east, to Lee and Woody Bays to the west. You will find shops, churches and post office within a few minutes walk. Lynmouth is ten minutes away via the sensational cliff railway. Buses run to all parts of North Devon, and motor boats will take you along the coast. For the energetic there is fishing, golf, superb walks, surfing, riding, tennis and bowls. The whole area is steeped in history and interest and will provide hours of delight for those who want to do no more than potter.

The hotel is almost the icing on the cake! It is a charming house with lots of nooks and crannies, furnished in a modern but comfortable manner with every room prettily draped and light and airy as so many of the houses built at the end of the last century were. Every bedroom, apart from the 2 singles, are ensuite and all of them are equipped with colour TV, direct dial telephones and a well supplied beverage tray. The food is excellent, good traditional English home-cooked fare with a choice at every meal and a changing menu. Vegetarians are catered for. The cosy bar is air-conditioned and the patio/terrace is a delightful place to enjoy a leisurely drink. Open to non-residents.

USEFUL INFORMATION

OPEN;*Closed Dec/Jan*   **DINING ROOM;***Good, traditional English cooking*
CHILDREN;*Welcome*   **VEGETARIAN;** *Catered for*
CREDIT CARDS;*Visa/Access/Switch/Amex* **DISABLED ACCESS;***No facilities*
LICENSED;*Yes*   **GARDEN;***No. Patio/Terrace*
ACCOMMODATION;*4dbl 3tw +family 2sgl all ensuite except singles*
PETS;*Yes - by arrangement*

HARTLAND QUAY HOTEL,
Hartland Quay, Bideford,
North Devon, EX39 6DU.

Tel : 01237 441281 / 441371

The Hartland Quay Hotel began it's business in 1887 when Thomas Oatway converted the existing buildings into the beginning of the comfortable hotel we see today. At that time the cost of a night's lodging was 2s, and a week could be had for 2 guineas. A guide book from the beginning of the century describes the hotel as 'excellent drainage and good water supply.' A little more description is necessary nowadays.....the above still stands...... but the hotel has many additional features and attractions.

Today the hotel is owned by Sir H.G.Stucley of Hartland Abbey, and managed by Philip and Nancy Johns, who has done so for the last 34 years, and has achieved an excellent reputation and status. Situated in an area of outstanding beauty on the lower slopes of a cliff facing the Atlantic Ocean, it is difficult to imagine a more beautiful spot. Legends of smugglers and wrecks are plenty in this area, where due to it's position (even today it is 25 miles from the nearest railway) seems as if time has passed it by. The scenery is stunning and this is a walker's paradise. Trout fishing is available to guests in the Speke stream while bass fishing is plentiful on the rocks below the cliffs! The Quay beach is safe for bathing and is a popular place for those guests with young families.

The hotel has 14 comfortable, cosy rooms, 10 of which are en suite, and all have colour TV, and a tea/coffee tray. The bar is a charming room with many interesting relics of wrecks salvaged from the rough seas, including the ;Green Ranger' of 1962, when many Hartland men played a large part in rescuing the crew. Food is available in both the bar and restaurant, and Nancy serves good English fayre at very reasonable prices. Vegetarians can be catered for and there is a children's menu on offer.

USEFUL INFORMATION

OPEN : Bar & Restaurant - All year
   Accommodation - Mid March - Mid Nov.
CHILDREN : Welcome
PETS : By arrangement
LICENSED : Full
CREDIT CARDS : All major
ACCOMMODATION : 14 rooms: 5 dbl, 5 twin, 2 sgl, 2 fml.

DINING ROOM : Good English fayre
VEGETARIANS : Catered for
BAR SNACKS : Good range
GARDEN : Yes
DISABLED ACCESS : Bar & restaurant

Chapter One

LOVELYNCH FARM,
Milverton, Taunton,
Somerset TA4 1NR

Tel: 01823 400268

Surrounded by gentle, rolling countryside, on the edge of Milverton, Lovelynch is one of the prettiest 15th century manor houses that you will see in England. It is small enough to be cosy and yet everywhere you turn, the character of the house stands out. The house is the focal point of the 200 acre farm run by the Loram family and everything about Lovelynch makes one feel at peace and able to withdraw from the stresses of everyday life. Come and stay here and you will be welcomed with the warmth and friendliness that will immediately put you at your ease. The farmhouse is furnished in keeping with its age, everywhere gleams with the care of years and the old world atmosphere is emphasised with exposed beams and log fires.. There are three very comfortable, spacious bedrooms, two of which are ideal for families. Therooms are not ensuite but there is a large bathroom with separate shower and plenty of hot water. Each room has TV and a beverage tray. The speciality of the house is the hearty English Breakfast, served in the charming dining room. There is no evening meal but there are several fine Inns offering hospitality and delicious local food. Mrs Loram will be happy to recommend somewhere as she will be to help you with your plans for touring this unspoilt corner of Somerset.

There is everything to make a great holiday or break. Exmoor and the Quantock Hills are nearby, you can ride, fish, sail, walk, play golf within easy distance and if you wish fish on the farm's private fishing lake. Taunton the county town of Somerset is 7 miles away and Wellington 4 miles. Accommodation for horses for those who wish to hunt or play Polo is available.

USEFUL INFORMATION

OPEN;*All year except Xmas*
CHILDREN; *Welcome*
CREDIT CARDS; *None taken*
LICENSED; *No*
ACCOMMODATION;*2fam. 1tw not ensuite*

BREAKFAST;*Hearty English Breakfast*
VEGETARIAN;*Upon request*
DISABLED ACCESS;*No special facilities*
PETS; *Yes*

DOLLONS HOUSE
Church Street, Dunster,
Minehead, Somerset TA24 6SH

Tel: 01643 821880

Dunster is probably the prettiest village in the Exmoor National Park and ideally suited for exploring the beautiful coastline, combes and moors of Exmoor, West Somerset and North Devon. Over a hundred years ago the Grade II listed building, Dollons House housed the village pharmacy, which as well as its potions, produced a marmalade of such high quality that they supplied the Houses of Parliament in London. The house is far older than its 19th century facade would suggest and is enchanting. Owned and run by Hannah and Humphrey Bradshaw, it is furnished with a happy marriage of antique and modern. The dining room is unique and a super place in which to eat the excellent, freshly cooked breakfast served every morning. The exclusive guests sitting room opens on to a 1st floor wooden verandah, above the very secluded garden with views of the church clock. The three bedrooms all have charming names. Tulips is spacious and pretty with a double bed, shower room, window seats and views of the castle. 'T' Bear Esq is a twin-bedded room with old pine furniture and just a few teddy bears! The shower room has a large mural of a honey bear. 'T' Bear also has window seats with views of the castle. Kates is at the back of the house overlooking the walled garden. There is a double bed with a 'Half Tester' effect and a large bathroom with both a shower and a bath. There are no evening meals and Dollons is strictly a _non-smoking_ house.

The ground floor of Dollons is run as a shop with the greatest variety of artificial flowers in the region, also many local and West Country crafts.

USEFUL INFORMATION

OPEN; *All year except Christmas and Boxing Day*
CHILDREN; *No. Not suitable*
CREDIT CARDS; *Mastercard/Visa*
GARDEN; *Yes*
ACCOMMODATION; *3 ensuite rooms*

DINING ROOM; *Excellent breakfast*
VEGETARIAN; *Catered for*
DISABLED ACCESS; *No*
PETS; *No*
NON-SMOKING

Chapter One

STOCKLEIGH LODGE,
Exford, Minehead,
Somerset, TA24 7PZ

Tel: 01643 831500
Fax: 01643 831595

What could be more beautiful than the heart of Exmoor, for the setting of this wonderful country lodge, run by the amiable Penny and John. Sitting in it's own wooded grounds, surrounded by the open moors, it is ideal for riding, walking, fishing and all outdoor sports. The stables on the grounds cater for all abilities of riding, and also have quality hunters available for hunting. Riding is a wonderful way to see the moor, and believe me, is not that painful! Penny and John are a mine of information regarding the local activities and are only too happy to share their knowledge.

The bedrooms are south facing and have a lovely sunny outlook, and are en suite or have their own private bathroom. All are comfortably furnished with complimentary tea and coffee, and are centrally heated for those winter breaks! Breakfast is an excellent meal; full English (including fish), and vegetarians are extremely well catered for. There is an optional three course evening meal, and both meals are served in the dining room overlooking the splendid, well kept garden. A packed lunch can be provided for those wishing to spend the day exploring the majestic countryside.

The drawing room is large and elegant with a grand piano and an open fire. Just sitting there on a winter's evening after an eventful day, with the hauntingly romantic moor all around makes me shiver deliciously, warm and content in the knowledge that someone will replace my drink when the glass is empty! Does sound good, doesn't it! This is not just the place for those wishing to relax or enjoy the moor, but is also ideal for business weekends or just a party of friends enjoying the company. You will feel welcome here no matter the occasion, and Penny and John will ensure that you and your friends will return again and again!

USEFUL INFORMATION

OPEN : *All year*
CHILDREN : *Welcome*
PETS: *Welcome*
CREDIT CARDS : *None taken*
LICENSED : *Residential*
ACCOMMODATION: *9 rooms; 7 dble, 1 sgl, 1 twin*
DINING ROOM : *Optional evening meal*
BAR MEALS : *Not applicable*
VEGETARIAN : *Well catered for*
DISABLED ACCESS :*No, but welcome*
GARDEN : *3 acres*

FAIR HAVENS HOLIDAY FLATS
89-91 Tower Road, Newquay,
Cornwall TR7 1LX
Tel: 01637 874005

What could be better than spending a holiday at Fair Havens Holiday Flats, these self-contained units sleep from 2-6 and are specially for young people. They are equipped with everything you need electric cooker, fridge, heaters, colour television, all crockery, cutlery, cooking utensils, vacuum cleaner and ironing board. All the electricity is metered, in the small flats the shower is also metered. All bed linen is supplied, but you are asked to bring your own towels. The units are ideally placed close to the town centre, where there are shops, banks and entertainment. There is a general grocers next door to the flats that is open everyday. Parking is in the street. Newquay is Cornwall's surfing capital, Fistral Beach being the main beach for competitions, with competitors from all over the world. Being near the coast water sports are very popular not just surfing, but also windsurfing, swimming, sailing and fishing. The beaches along this part of the coast are wonderful with plenty of room for everybody. If you fancy a game of golf you only have to go next door, not far from the flats you are able to go horse riding. What more could you want, an excellent location for an excellent holiday.

USEFUL INFORMATION
OPEN; All year
CHILDREN; No
CREDIT CARDS; No
LICENSED; Not applicable
ACCOMMODATION; 10 Self-contained flats, Electricity by meter
DINING ROOM; Not applicable
VEGETARIAN; Not applicable
DISABLED ACCESS; No
GARDEN; No, but line drying available
PETS; Yes, certain types
PARKING; On street

WARMHILL FARM
Hennock,
Newton Abbot,
South Devon TQ13 9QH
Tel: 01626 833229

Warmhill Farmhouse is a 100 acre dairy farm on the slopes of the glorious Teign Valley, on the south eastern edge of the Dartmoor National Park. The farmhouse is situated on the edge of the farmyard and children are encouraged to help with the animals and milking. Visitors are free to walk over the farm which has an abundance of wild life and beautiful views over the valley. The village of Hennock which is a five minute walk away has a pub, a small shop and a church. The coast is within 10 miles and the wild expanses of Dartmoor 5 miles. The Cathedral city of Exeter is only 10 miles away. Riding, fishing, golf, walking and climbing are all readily available and there is a swimming pool and leisure centre six miles away. The farmhouse is a large, traditional beamed and thatched barn conversion, adjacent to the owners cottage. The original barn was built in the 16th century and many old features remain, it has spacious rooms and is comfortably furnished in keeping with the character of the property.

USEFUL INFORMATION
OPEN; All year
CHILDREN; Welcome
CREDIT CARDS; None taken
LICENSED; No
ACCOMMODATION; Self-catering
DISABLED ACCESS; No
GARDEN; Yes
PETS; Yes, up to 2 dogs

Chapter One

**TRENANCE LODGE
RESTAURANT
AND HOTEL**
83, Trenance Road,
Newquay,
Cornwall TR7 2HW

Tel: 01637 876702
Fax: 01637 872034

Set in its own grounds in a quiet part of Newquay overlooking the picturesque Boating Lake and Trenance Gardens, Trenance Lodge is one of the most stylish small hotels and restaurants in the whole of Cornwall. It has everything to ensure one has a perfect holiday. The whole house is light and airy, every room is attractively and carefully appointed. The five comfortable bedrooms all have ensuite facilities with either bath or shower, heated towel rail and shaver points. Each room has colour TV, clock/radio alarm, hot drinks facility, writing desk and hair dryer. Trouser press and irons are available on request. A great place to stay with its secluded heated outdoor swimming pool, the highlight of your stay must be the superb food served in the charming restaurant which is open to non-residents. Trenance Lodge has a reputation for serving the very best seafood, steaks and poultry and the wine list has been chosen to complement the dishes, with wines from around the world, all reasonably priced. 50% of the restaurant is non-smoking. Vegetarian and other diets are catered for. Nothing could be more pleasant after a day out than to return to this charming establishment and dine in style, waited on by a skilled and unobtrusive staff. An excellent base for touring this beautiful and historic region, with a warm welcome assured.

USEFUL INFORMATION

OPEN: All year. Restaurant 7-10.30pm
CHILDREN: No
CREDIT CARDS: Visa/Mastercard
LICENSED: Yes. Good wine list
PETS: No
ACCOMMODATION: 5 ensuite rooms
RESTAURANT: Fine food frequently
VEGETARIAN: Catered for
DISABLED ACCESS: + assistance
GARDEN: Yes with heated pool
PARKING: Ample and safe

CLEAVELANDS ST MARY
Lustleigh, Nr Newton Abbot,
Devon TQ13 9SH

Tel: 01647 277349

Addresses can be confusing and this delightful house standing in idyllic surroundings bears no resemblance to its postal address. Go to Lustleigh and when you reach the cross roads in the village with the Post Office facing you, turn left and carry on until you come up to a steep T junction. Turn right and you will find the house about 500 yards up on the left hand side. The moment you turn into the drive you are in a world apart. In the early summer the rhododendrons of all colours are breathtakingly beautiful, trees stand gracefully making a backdrop for the stunning views. Viv and Val Bates acquired this house not long ago and have turned it into a charming, relaxed home into which they welcome their guests. Every room is different and as with all old houses it is full of nooks and crannies. The Library is full of books you are welcome to read, a grand piano stands in the sitting room asking to be played. Furnished with an eye to comfort, the bedrooms are ensuite and have TV as well as a beverage tray plentifully supplied with tea and coffee. Dinner using organic produce whenever possible, is available although there are many good eateries in the area and your hosts will willingly point you in the right direction. Cleavelands St Mary is a non-smoking house. The position of the house in this quiet, tranquil backwater, makes it an ideal base for anyone wanting to explore Dartmoor, go to the coast, play golf, fish, birdwatch and ride or just sit in the garden. You can see why this lovely house has been given an AA '4Q Selected' award and is '2 Crowns Commended' by the English Tourist Board.

USEFUL INFORMATION

OPEN: All year
CHILDREN: Over 8 years
CREDIT CARDS: Not at the moment
LICENSED: No. Please bring your own
ACCOMMODATION: 3 double
GARDEN: Yes

DINING ROOM: Traditional home-cooked Dinner by arrangement
VEGETARIAN: Upon request
DISABLED ACCESS: No facilities
PETS: Yes
NO SMOKING

Chapter One

SOUTH HARTON FARM
Lustleigh,
Newton Abbot, Devon TQ13 9SG
Tel: 01647 277216

The address of this enchanting farmhouse is misleading. The Lustleigh bit is correct but once having reached the village at the junction opposite the post office you need to turn left and follow the road up the hill to 'Rudge Cross' a steep 'T' junction. Turn right, signposted the Cleave, North Bovey. Follow this road for approximately 1 mile. South Harton drive entrance is on the left, proceed to the top of the drive go through the archway and there is the farmhouse. The house dates back to the 16th century and is typical of Devon thatched houses with open fireplaces, beamed ceilings and large rooms, but its much more than that. It wanders going up a few steps here and down some winding ones there, creating a charming, warm-hearted atmosphere which is enhanced by the friendliness of the owners, Mike and Myra Ellicott. There are stunning views and for birdwatchers it is heaven sent - woodpeckers strut about the patio and buzzards live in the trees. Fishing in the river and reservoir, inspiring walks and exploring Dartmoor or the coast will give you plenty to do. Mike Ellicott is more than willing to drop you off at the beginning of your walk and pick you up again at a designated point.

USEFUL INFORMATION

OPEN: All year
CHILDREN: Very welcome
CREDIT CARDS: No
ACCOMMODATION: 1 dbl ensuite + bath 1 twin ensuite shower room, 1 twin with adjoining bathroom
DINING ROOM: Good, wholesome Farmhouse fare
VEGETARIAN: By arrangement
DISABLED ACCESS: No
GARDEN: Farm, patio
PETS: Well behaved - by arrangement

LOWER CLAVELSHAY FARM
North Petherton,
Nr Bridgwater,
Somerset TA6 6PJ
Tel: 01278 662347

This 260 acre dairy farm in the beautiful Quantock Hills is run by Sue Milverton and her family. The farmhouse dates from the 17th century and retains some of the original features in it's stone fireplaces and beamed ceilings. The bedrooms are furnished in mainly antique style and have fine country views. A full English breakfast is served and if required, then an evening meal of good home-cooking with fresh local produce can be provided. There is also use of a small kitchen if required, in this delightful home. The farm is a haven for wild life such as buzzards, badgers, foxes and deer, and as it is a working farm there are cows, sheep, hens etc. Sue is perfectly happy for you to roam round the farm, watch the milking and if you want to feed the pigs or collect the eggs then all hands are welcome!. The area is great for fishing, riding, sailing, walking and more, and is ideal for The Quantock Hills, exploring Exmoor National Park or the wild North Devon coast and at the same time it is not far from the M5.

USEFUL INFORMATION

OPEN; All year
CHILDREN; Most welcome
CREDIT CARDS; None taken
LICENSED; No, welcome to bring your own
ACCOMMODATION; 3 rooms, 2 dbl, 1 family all with tea and coffee making facilities
DINING ROOM; Good home-cooked fare Evening meal can be provided
VEGETARIAN; Catered for
DISABLED ACCESS; No
GARDEN; Yes
PETS; Yes, if well behaved

YEOLDON HOUSE HOTEL
Durrant Lane,
Northam, Nr. Bideford,
North Devon EX39 2RL

Tel: 01237 474400

Yeoldon House has a refreshingly casual atmosphere and is one of the most hospitable hotels in North Devon. Owned by Kevin and Sue Jelley, the hotel is run superbly as one would expect from a couple who have years of experience in the business. You will find Yeoldon House set beside the River Torridge with lawns sloping down towards the river and from here you are within an hour's drive of many exceptional places to see and things to do. Almost on the doorstep you can take a trip to Lundy Island which offers some majestic scenery and outstanding sea bird and marine life. Exmoor holds Lorna Doone country which weaves a magic for many people. The picturesque village of Clovelly in which there are no cars enchants everyone who goes there. You can enjoy miles of Coastal Footpath, and for bathing and watersports there are some of the finest sandy beaches in the country.

Within the hotel one can relax in the comfortable lounge, chat over the day and enjoy a complimentary sherry before dinner. Both the lounge and the elegant 'Charters' restaurant look out over the lawns to the river. Everything about Yeoldon House has been carefully planned and that is especially true of the bedrooms which are all different. There are the cozy country style rooms, the grand four-poster room and the split level room with its own balcony and lounge area. All the rooms are ensuite and have several extra touches including TV, tea/coffee making facilities, and direct dial telephone.

'Charters' Restaurant is the perfect place in which to breakfast or dine. Imagine a breakfast that incorporates everything you enjoy most and add that to the stunning sight of the sun rising over the Torridge!. Dinner is memorable. Whilst you are in beautiful surroundings, it has an air of casual elegance in which you will feel comfortable in any attire. The hotel's talented chef obviously loves his job and creates some wonderful dishes using local fresh fish, meat and vegetables. Fresh baked bread and a garden salad are served with every meal. The desserts will tempt even those who have avowed not to indulge! Naturally the wine list lives up to the menu.

This thoroughly enjoyable hotel should not be missed.

USEFUL INFORMATION

OPEN; All year
Rest: 7 evenings & Sunday lunch
CHILDREN; Welcome
CREDIT CARDS; All major cards
LICENSED; Yes. Good wine list
ACCOMMODATION; 7dbl 3tw all ensuite

RESTAURANT; Imaginative, superb food
VEGETARIAN; Yes + other diets with notice
DISABLED ACCESS; Restaurant only
GARDEN; Extensive grounds
PETS; Yes

Chapter One

SMALLICOMBE FARM
*Northleigh, Colyton,
Devon EX13 6BU*

Tel: 01404 831310
Fax: 01404 831431

Occupying a superb location in an unspoilt valley where the rural scene has changed little since chronicled in the Domesday Book, Smallicombe Farm offers both catered and self-
catering accommodation, to a very high standard. The peaceful surroundings which give one the feeling of being away from the world belie the fact that you are only a short distance from historic Honiton and Colyton and the coast from Lyme Regis to Sidmouth. The Farm has 2 awards to its credit, one being the 'England for Excellence Award' from the English Tourist Board, and the other the 'Best Self-Catering Accommodation 1996' from the Holiday Care Service.

All the bedrooms are attractive and ensuite and have tea/coffee making facilities. There is one family suite on the first floor which sleeps 4 (5+cot). The double room has a colour television and refrigerator, and has lovely rural views. The ground floor twin room also has superb rural views. It has its own ensuite bathroom and its own living/dining room with colour television. A full English breakfast is served every day but alternatives can be make to suit you. In the evening there is an optional evening meal at a time you choose. Maggie Todd, the owner, cooks superbly and uses home produce or local fare. Special diets can be arranged with notice. For those who enjoy self-catering there are four venues. The Garden Flat which is a self-contained ground floor wing of the farmhouse, opens straight onto the garden. It will sleep 2-4. Cider Barrel and Granary are ground floor and each sleeps 4 + cot. These are recent barn conversions designed to accommodate both families and wheelchair bound disabled. Above is the Hay Loft which sleeps 8. All units are delightful and fully equipped with everything you need for a perfect holiday. Wonderful for holidays or short breaks.

USEFUL INFORMATION

OPEN: All year
CHILDREN: Welcome
CREDIT CARDS: None taken
LICENSED: No
ACCOMMODATION: 3 ensuite + 4 self-catering
PETS: No

DINING ROOM: Full English breakfast
                              Evening meals
VEGETARIAN: Yes but not vegan
DISABLED ACCESS: Yes. Award winning. Category 1
GARDEN: Yes

TRELAY FARM COTTAGES
Trelay, St Gennys
Bude, Cornwall EX23 0NJ

Tel: 01840 230378

Oliver and Andrea Tippett have converted the traditional Cornish farmstead of stone-built barns with slate roofs into six cottages. It has been done with care and imagination and the end result are cottages that will delight any visitor both visualy and becuase they are as beatifully appointed inside as they are full of character on the exterior. So often self catering accommodation lacks so much in the way of home comforts but this is not the case here. Each lounge has colour TV and fitted carpets. The kitchens have modern fitted units, toasters, coffee makers, ovenware and pretty china apart from the more mundane necesseties like cookers!

The garden of each cottage has something different to offer. For example, The Old Stable has a French door leading from the lounge to the sheltered, sunny lawn which is fenced in for children or pets. There is a patio of local slate slabs with a picnic table and a berbecue. Litle Trelay has an enclosed courtyard with tablkes and chairs and you are more than likely to be wlecomed by large families of house martins which return each year to muster under the eaves.

Trelay is a small working farm with sheep and some beef cattle. The setting is idyllic at the head of a wooded valley looking out over rolling countryside. From the fields, where visitors are welcome to walk, the views are superb across Bude Bay, along the coast of this unspoilt part of Cornwall. On a clear day Lundy Island can be seen. Trelay is 100 yards off the road, along the tarmac drive. The A39 at Wainhouse Corner is three quarters of a mile away, where ther is a general store, petrol station and country pub which serves food. Bude, with its splendid beaches, is only 8 miles away. Crackington Haven, which has a lovely sandy beach, is just two miles away. It is ideal for surfing or swimming or simply exploring the rock pools.

USEFUL INFORMATION

OPEN: All year   **CHILDREN**: Welcome, baby sitting by arrangement
CREDIT CARDS: None taken   **DISABLED ACCESS**: No special facilities
PETS: Welcome but some breeds not accepted.

Chapter One

PHEASANTRY
Combe Raleigh, Honiton,
Devon EX14 0TG
Tel: 01404 42130

The lovely house of Pheasantry is home to Dorothy Retter, who offers bed and breakfast accommodation to those visiting this lovely part of Devon. The house is in the quiet little hamlet of Combe Raleigh which is situated approximately one mile from the market town of Honiton. Dorothy offers comfortable accommodation in the form of one double and one twin bedded rooms, fully fitted with the essentials and with wash basins in each. Breakfast is a traditional English meal and vegetarians are catered for. This is a very pleasant location with a superb garden and views across open countryside.

There is plenty to do here with wonderful walks along the River Otter, and a National Trust wood to visit. Honiton has a market every Tuesday, and in addition has stalls in the High Street on Tuesday and Saturdays. The pottery and lace made here are well known, and for the children there is an excellent swimming pool in the town. Dorothy Retter will make you most welcome in her home, and you are sure to want to return again and again to this charming house in this appealing part of the country.

USEFUL INFORMATION
OPEN: Easter until end of October
CHILDREN: Welcome
CREDIT CARDS: None taken
LICENSED: No
ACCOMMODATION: 2 rooms, 1 double, 1 twin both with wash basins
DINING ROOM: Traditional breakfast
VEGETARIANS: Catered for
DISABLED ACCESS: No
GARDEN: Lovely
PETS: No

THE COBBLES
33 Back Road West, St Ives,
Cornwall TR26 1NL
Tel: 01736 798206

Baz and Wendy Searle are the owners of this fisherman's cottage in the heart of "the artist's paradise" in St Ives. This cottage is only 5 minutes from the Harbour and the sandy beaches, and a glut of restaurants, inns and shops, all within walking distance.

The cottage has a wonderful atmosphere with Baz and Wendy giving you all the local chat and information. Baz is an enthusiastic fisherman and can often provide fresh mackerel for breakfast!

USEFUL INFORMATION
OPEN : All year
CHILDREN : 12 And Over Welcome
PETS : Well behaved ones welcome
CREDIT CARDS : None taken
LICENSED : No
RESTAURANT : Not applicable
BAR FOOD : Not applicable
VEGETARIAN : Yes
DISABLED ACCESS : No
GARDEN : No
ACCOMMODATION : 3 rooms; 1 dbl, 1 twin, 1 sgl. All en suite with TV, tea and coffee and Central Heating.

ASHCOMBE FARM
West Pennard,
Nr. Glastonbury,
Somerset BA6 8ND
Tel: 01749 890153

Legend has it King Arthur and Guinevere are buried among the remains of the romantic 13th century abbey ruins in Glastonbury and it is also where the first seeds of English Christianity were sewn by Joseph of Arimathea. A few miles outside this historical town is West Pennard and it is here that Di and Peter Frayne have their farm. The Edwardian farmhouse is a substantial red brick property, with the front looking out over a well kept lawned garden with attractive borders and pots here and there full of flowers, it even has a disused well, hanging baskets complete a very pretty picture. The back looks out across delightful open countryside.

There are 3 bedrooms with television, a tea and coffee tray and the privacy of ensuite facilities. There is a comfortable residents lounge which is furnished with television, books and games for you to use at any time, here you plan your day out or rest after a hard days excursion. Di serves an excellent full English breakfast in the lovely dining room, an evening meal is not available, however, there is a delightful 'olde worlde' pub opposite the farmhouse. The area is not short of places to visit such as Glastonbury Tor and Abbey, Wells Cathedral, Wookey Hole Caves, Cheddar Gorge, the Fleet Air Arm Museum and Bath. So why not come and enjoy the warm and welcoming atmosphere of Ashcombe Farm.

USEFUL INFORMATION

OPEN; All year
CHILDREN; Welcome
CREDIT CARDS; None taken
LICENSED; No
ACCOMMODATION; 3 ensuite rooms
PETS; No

DINING ROOM; Full English breakfast, Evening meal is not available
VEGETARIAN; Catered for
DISABLED ACCESS; No
GARDEN; Lovely, well kept

Chapter One

COMBE LODGE HOTEL
Chambercombe Park,
Ilfracombe, Devon EX34 9QW

Tel:01271 864518
Fax: 01271 867628

    This small licensed, non-smoking hotel on the outskirts of Ilfracombe overlooks the sea and picturesque harbour. A pleasant place to stay for many reasons but especially for those who enjoy outdoor activities. Bryan Cath, the owner, an avid cyclist and walker himself has devised a series of 30 self-guided walking and 9 cycling routes based at the hotel. He takes you to the start of your chosen route with itinerary in hand and a packed lunch if you require in your bag, and then you go at your pace, have your picnic when you choose, in the sure knowledge that at the end the minibus will be waiting at a mutually pre-arranged time to bring you back again. Cycle rides are also carefully planned and take you through exciting country including the Tarka Trail. It makes for a wonderful holiday for those who like to be active but Combe Lodge is equally caring of people who just want to be at ease and relax. Within ten minutes walk are the rocky beaches of Rapparee Cove and Hele Bay. There are boat trips along the beautiful north Devon coast, across to Lundy Island and to the Welsh coast, all from the pretty harbour. Guests come from all over the world and Bryan receives letters of thanks and even Newsletters with tales of his guests adventures from as far afield as Wisconsin USA.
    The 8 bedrooms are mainly ensuite and some have lovely views over the harbour. There is a choice of room with or without TV but all of them have a generously supplied beverage tray with tea, coffee and drinking chocolate. The well stocked bar is the meeting place for those who like to enjoy a drink and a chat before a meal. Food is all important, especially when you have had a very active day. Breakfast is freshly cooked to order and generous and so too is the evening meal which is traditional home-cooked English with a hint of something special.

USEFUL INFORMATION

OPEN;*All year except Christmas*   **DINING ROOM;***Great breakfast. Traditional*
CHILDREN;*By arrangement*   *English home-cooked evening meal*
CREDIT CARDS;*Mastercard/Visa/Amex*   **VEGETARIAN:** *Wide option available*
LICENSED;*Yes*   **DISABLED ACCESS;***No*
GARDEN;*Yes*   **PETS;***Yes*

THE HORSE POND INN & MOTEL
The Triangle, Castle Cary,
Somerset BA7 7BD

Tel: 01963 350...
Fax: 01963 351

Castle Cary is one of those small characterful towns that abound in the South West. Sometimes as you wander round you might well be excused if you thought you were in a bygone age. Right in the centre is the 16th century Horse Pond Inn which has successfully combined the past with the requirements of this modern age. It is a great place for either the visitor wanting a base from which to explore the pleasures of this part of Somerset or for the business person who wants to escape from the frenetic every day world to spend a relaxing evening in a comfortable inn which has four very comfortable motel rooms, each with private bathroom, telephone, coffee and tea making facilities and the use of steam iron and board. There are another two attractive ensuite rooms in the inn itself.

Within The Horse Pond you will find welcoming and comfortable bars in which to relax and enjoy a good lunchtime meal or bar snack or an evening meal if you do not wish to dine in the charming restaurant with its excellent A la Carte menu. Wherever you choose to eat you will not be disappointed in the standard of the food or the service which is friendly and unobtrusive. Naturally there is a well chosen wine list with wines from around the world.

The Horse Pond has excellent facilities for conferences, seminars, weeding receptions and other occasions. Up to 160 guests can be catered for buffet style or 90 seated. One of the important factors is the attention to detail that is given to every occasion no matter how big or small, in order to make sure that the event runs smoothly.

USEFUL INFORMATION

OPEN: All year. Restaurant closed Mondays evenings
CHILDREN: Welcome
CREDIT CARDS: Switch/Master/Visa/Euro/JCB
ACCOMMODATION: 4 ensuite motel rooms 2 ensuite in inn

RESTAURANT: Delicious food
BAR FOOD: Wide range. Try the Horse Pond Chicken Special
VEGETARIAN: Daily choice
DISABLED ACCESS: No facilities
LICENSED: Yes

Chapter One

FORDE HOUSE
*9 Upper High Street, Taunton,
Somerset TA1 3PX*

Tel: 01823 279042

It is rare that one finds such an oasis of peace and tranquillity in a busy city but that is exactly what you will discover when you come to the 18th century Forde House which is within a few minutes walk of all amenities, including some fine restaurants and pubs and under 10 minutes from the M5 at Junction 25. Peter and Sheila Naylor have lovingly and carefully restored this period house bringing it to its present delightful standard. Whether you come to Taunton on business or for a holiday you will find the house relaxing. The rooms are all beautifully furnished and the garden is wonderful and a splendid place to sit and enjoy the sunshine or the peace of the early evening after a busy day.

All the bedrooms are spacious and charmingly furnished with full ensuite facilities. Each room is centrally heated, has colour TV clock/radio and tea and coffee making facilities. The dining room has a great atmosphere with its exposed beams and inglenook fireplace and the drawing room has a grand piano, a log fire and french windows into the large rear garden. Breakfast is delicious and more than enough to sustain the hungriest person. Everything is freshly cooked and you have a choice. A truly delightful house in which to stay.

USEFUL INFORMATION

OPEN: All year
DISABLED ACCESS: No special facilities
ACCOMMODATION: 2 double, 2 twin, 1 single, all ensuite
DINING ROOM: Traditional breakfast
VEGETARIAN: Catered for
PETS: No
GARDEN: Lovely garden. Ample parking

NEWBRIDGE HOTEL,
Northam, Bideford,
Devon, EX39 3QA.

Tel : 01237 474989

    The historic town of Bideford in North Devon is the perfect spot for this 1850s Georgian Hotel. Situated in 2 acres of gardens, this beautiful house has been extensively refurbished and tastefully decorated in keeping with the period of its building. Anthony Johnson is your friendly host, and is to be congratulated on the quality and standard of services provided. The ten bedrooms are all en suite, with TV, direct dialling, refreshments tray and full central heating. Each room is charmingly decorated and has period furniture throughout, and are snug and engaging in their character. The lounge is a comfortable, cosy room in which to relax and unwind after a day's entertainment, and perhaps discuss the next item on the agenda! Talking of 'agenda', this is a capital place for conferences, and even weddings or functions are eagerly catered for! The bar is fully licensed and 'mulling' over a glass of something may be the perfect end to the perfect day - if real ale is your forte then this is just the place, with a good selection for your scrutiny! The restaurant caters for breakfast, lunch and evening meal. This room is enticing in itself, with its crisp tablecloths, candles and pretty decor. The food is excellent; all freshly prepared and of the highest quality, with a varied menu to suit all tastes. There are some interesting items on the menu too, such as 'Surf & Turf', (haven't heard of this one!), which is a fillet of beef and pork grilled together with halibut and salmon, and served with a garlic sauce. It definitely makes the choice less difficult, doesn't it! - that's four items on the menu all in one! Sounds delicious, and is only one of a thoughtful, diverse array of dishes! A favourite must be Shark Steak which is described on the menu as being caught by 'a fast swimmer!' The service is good and each meal is served by friendly, cheerful staff, who are determined you will have a good time!
    Bideford is a great town with a historic port and market, and is a haven for yachting, wind surfing and all water sports. The art gallery is worth a visit to see its paintings, model ships, pewter and ceramics. There are many quality shops and a pleasant day can be spent strolling around this town. If you wish to venture further afield then you are only a stone's throw from Exmoor and Dartmoor, with that wild untamed beauty that only the moors seem to capture. The North Devon coast can be savage and rugged in places and has hardly changed since the time of smugglers and excise men! But then walking along cliff tops and sand dunes will quickly bring you to golden sandy beaches with the waves lapping the shoreline. The cities of Exeter and Plymouth are also within a car drive if you feel the need for a shopping spree! What more could you ask! A congenial host, good food and access to the beauty of one of England's prettiest counties!

USEFUL INFORMATION

OPEN : All year
CHILDREN : Welcome
PETS : No
LICENSED : Full
CREDIT CARDS : All major
ACCOMMODATION : 10 rooms en suite, 5 dbl, 4 twin, 1 fml. .

RESTAURANT : Excellent menu
VEGETARIANS : Catered for
BAR SNACKS : No
DISABLED ACCESS : Restaurant
GARDEN : 2 acres lawn & shrub

Chapter One

THE APPLE TREE HOTEL AND DE LOMMERD RESTAURANT
Keenthorne, Nr. Nether Stowey
Somerset TA5 1HZ

Tel: 01278 733238
Fax: 01278 732693

Extensive refurbishment has transformed the historic Apple Tree Inn into a hotel that is one of the finest in Somerset. There was a time when the height of its culinary capability was to offer afternoon tea. Now the food is renowned throughout Somerset. Whether you eat in the elegant, beautifully appointed De Lommerd Restaurant or would prefer to have a bar meal, the menu is outstanding. Luxurious is the only way to describe the twelve bedrooms with most of the rooms enjoying stunning views over the Quantocks and five overlooking the garden with facilities suitable for the disabled. Every room is en-suite with shower or bath, there is central heating, television, direct dial telephones and a plentiful supplied beverage tray. Breakfast is a substantial, freshly cooked traditional meal with several choices. The Apple Tree is open every day to residents and non-residents for Breakfast, Morning Coffee, Lunches and Dinners. Small conferences and weddings are also efficiently catered for.

The Apple Tree makes an ideal base from which to explore this part of Somerset. The nearby Quantock Hills have miles of walking and riding tracks. From the crests of the panoramic hills views allow you to gaze across the Bristol Channel to the islands of Flat Holm and Steep Holm and beyond to the Gower Coast and the Brecon Beacons. There are plentiful beaches within a few miles, excellent sea fishing close by and Steart, the famous nature reserve which houses the largest colony in Europe of Shell Duck.

USEFUL INFORMATION

OPEN: All Year
CHILDREN: Welcome
CREDIT CARDS: All
ACCOMMODATION: 12 ensuite rooms, 4 non smoking
PETS: No

RESTAURANT: Award Winning food
Open to non-residents. Breakfast, lunch, tea, dinner
BAR FOOD: Always a choise
DISABLED ACCESS: 5 ground floor rooms
GARDEN: Yes

Dorset, Wiltshire, Hampshire

Chapter Two

DORSET, WILTSHIRE, HAMPSHIRE

CHAPTER 2

DORSET, WILTSHIRE, HAMPSHIRE

INCLUDES

French Horn	**Alton**	p. 277
Broadwater	**Amport, Nr Andover**	p. 278
Lains Cottage	**Andover**	p. 279
Glen Derry	**Beech**	p. 279
Swaynesfirs Farm	**Bissett**	p. 280
Woodside Private Hotel	**Bournemouth**	p. 281
Lanscombes House Holiday Cottages	**Bridport**	p. 280
Bridge Farm	**Britford**	p. 282
Yewtree House	**Broughton**	p. 283
Manor Farm	**Burcombe**	p. 285
Chideock House Hotel	**Chideock**	p. 286
Bramleys	**Chippenham**	p. 284
Fairfield Farm	**Chippenham**	p. 287
Ashbourne Guest House	**Christchurch**	p. 288
Hazeldene	**Christchurch**	p. 286
Number 19	**Christchurch**	p. 288
The Homestead	**Christchurch**	p. 289
Three Gables	**Christchurch**	p. 291
Whiteways	**Cold Ashton**	p. 287
Lower Lynch House	**Corfe Castle, Nr Wareham**	p. 292
Coventry Lodge	**Corfe Mullen**	p. 290
Pickwick Lodge Farm	**Corsham**	p. 293
The Crudwell Court	**Crudwell, Nr Malmesbury**	p. 294
Castle Hotel	**Devizes**	p. 295
Orchard Cottage	**Devizes**	p. 296
The Old Farmhouse	**Dorchester**	p. 297
White Horse Inn	**Droxford**	p. 298
Coombe Cross House & Stables	**East Meon**	p. 299
Dunvegan Cottage	**East Meon**	p. 300
Alessandria Hotel & Giovannis Restaurant	**East Portland**	p. 301
Newnham House	**Emsworth**	p. 302
Sandy Corner	**Fordingbridge**	p. 289
Downshay Farm	**Harmans Cross, Swanage**	p. 290
16 Charleston Close	**Hayling Island**	p. 292
Paxcroft Cottages	**Hilperton, Trowbridge**	p. 303
The Coppers	**Holt, Trowbridge**	p. 293

Chapter Two

Maycroft	**Langton Matravers, Swanage**	p. 295
The Carpenters Arms	**Leigh, Nr Sherborne**	p. 304
Cliff Cottage Tea Gardens	**Lyme Regis**	p. 305
Devonia Guest House	**Lyme Regis**	p. 306
Coombe House	**Lyme Regis**	p. 297
St Michaels Hotel	**Lyme Regis**	p. 307
Pennavon House	**Lymington**	p. 308
Paddocks	**Marlborough**	p. 309
Longhope Guest House	**Melksham**	p. 306
Meltone House	**Mere**	p. 309
Peacehaven Guest House	**Merley, Wimborne**	p. 304
The Poachers Inn	**Piddletrenthide**	p. 310
Lewina Lodge Guest House	**Poole**	p. 311
Hazeland Wood	**Ratford, Calne**	p. 312
Pyesmead Farm	**Romsey**	p. 313
Castleavon Guest House	**Salisbury**	p. 314
Farthings	**Salisbury**	p. 310
The Gallery	**Salisbury**	p. 315
Websters	**Salisbury**	p. 316
Mitre Inn	**Shaftesbury**	p. 317
The Old Forge	**Shaftesbury**	p. 318
Wodonga	**Shaftesbury**	p. 319
The Mallow Guest House	**Southsea**	p. 320
Spiers Piece Farm	**Steeple Ashton, Trowbridge**	p. 321
Lower Fifehead Farm	**Sturminster Newton**	p. 322
The Deer Park	**Sturminster Newton**	p. 323
The Old Post Office	**Sturminster Newton**	p. 307
Yew House Farm	**Sturminster Newton**	p. 317
May Cottage	**Thruxton, Nr Andover**	p. 325
26 The Beeches	**Trowbridge**	p. 323
Herons Knoll	**Trowbridge**	p. 321
Ashcroft	**Wareham**	p. 313
Bradle Farm	**Wareham**	p. 323
Westpoint Tavern Hotel	**West Bay, Nr Bridport**	p. 326
Premier Hotel	**Weymouth**	p. 327
Brickworth Farmhouse	**Whiteparish, Salisbury**	p. 328
Thornhill Holt	**Wimborne**	p. 327
Twynham	**Wimborne**	p. 328
32 Hyde Street	**Winchester**	p. 329
Clovelly	**Winchester**	p. 326
Glen Rest	**Woodlands, Nr Lyndhurst**	p. 329

Chapter 2

SOUTHERN ENGLAND
Dorset, Wiltshire, Hampshire

Southern England covers many counties and each has its own characteristics and charm. If you asked me to name my favourite I would be hard put to choose and in fact I find that wherever I happen to be at the time means the most to me. My journey through these counties must be fleeting and you will have to forgive me if I leave out some of your favourite places. Each county would make a book in itself.

The whole of the region is crammed with history, from the abundant fossils on the Dorset coastline, to the hundreds of stone circles and monuments of early man. The Bronze Age settlements and Iron Age forts, and later sites of events so momentous that they have marked the course of history itself.

Dorset has that lovely sleepy feeling about it. It is both comforting and timeless with its smoothly-rounded hills and convexities which have a passive and ancient solidity that soothes and reassures. 'Here I stand and here I be' might well be the motto of a landscape that has sustained Man since his earliest days, from the cliffs, coves and shingle of the coast, the whin-clad heaths, the hills and dales and woodlands of the hinterland. The configuration is so attractive and so varied that it might almost be taken as an epitome of the scenery of Southern England.

It is an intensely rural county, averaging rather more than one acre per inhabitant and is not disturbed by motorways or major road works. There is only one major conurbation, that of **Poole** and **Bournemouth** with the remainder of the population residing mainly in the numerous small market towns and countless villages and hamlets whose names have a resounding ring out of all proportion to their size and present day standing: Rime Intrinsica, Melbury Osmond, Toller Porcorum, Chaldon Herring and Tarrant Gunville. The names, the people and the scenery have inspired writers and artists over the centuries.

In common with many other such rural areas, early settlements seem to have proliferated along the banks of streams and rivers, hence the numerous Winterbournes, Piddles, Puddles, Tarrants, Cernes, Chars and Weys. The great expanse of enclosed water that is Poole Harbour provided the county's earliest sheltered part, and one that remains of great economic importance to this day.

Chapter Two

My journey this time started in the extreme south-west in the delightful little town of **Lyme Regis** close to the boundary with Devonshire. Once an important harbour and protected from prevailing south-westerly winds by the massive breakwater known as the Cobb, Lyme Regis was granted its royal status by Edward I in 1284 during his wars against the French.

The town is enchanting, set on the shore surrounded by a backcloth of high steep hills and withhouses and shops set around narrow winding streets. It is a deservedly popular seaside resort, a role that replaced smuggling as a local, and profitable, pastime in the late 18th century. Jane Austen gives a vivid portrayal of the town in her novel 'Persuasion' written in 1815:

'..as there is nothing to admire in the buildings themselves, the remarkable situation of the town, the principal street almost hurrying into the water, the wall to the Cobb, skirting round the pleasant little bay, which in the season is animated with bathing machines and company, the Cobb itself, its old wonders and new improvements, with the very beautiful line of cliffs stretching out to the east of the town, are what the stranger's eye will seek; and a very strange stranger it must be, who does not see charms in the immediate environs of Lyme, to make him wish to know it better.'

I disagree with the eminent novelist's opinion of the local architecture, but wholeheartedly endorse the rest.

The wide main road through the village of **Charmouth** was first laid by the Romans on the foundations of an ancient pack-horse trail and after their departure it was favoured by the Saxons. The ancient highway became of increasing importance, linking the county towns of Exeter and Dorchester and the handsome Georgian and Regency buildings bear witness both to the popularity of the village as a coaching stop, and to the attractions of the area as a resort. Some of this history can be seen reflected in the displays at the **Charmouth Heritage Coast Centre**, together with exhibitions of fossils, geology and wildlife.

The lovely coast and inland scenery, combined with these small seaside communities, offers the holidaymaker a glimpse of more certain and simple pleasures and it is hardly surprising that families return year after year. Neighbouring **Chideock** has much the same atmosphere, albeit on a small scale; the houses here also line the hillside but the thatched cottage, rather than the grander Georgian and Victorian buildings of Charmouth, predominates. The happily named Duck Street leads to the tiny sea-side hamlet of **Seatown,** where the small River Winniford flows into the sea. The little beach is dominated by the highest cliff of the South Coast, **Golden Cap**,

618 feet above sea level. Now under the stewardship of the National Trust, the gorse clad cliff was the look-out post for an 18th century smuggling gang based in Chideock.

Apart from the obvious enjoyment to be had beside the sea, this western-most area of Dorset has a multitude of attractions inland; historic sites, lovely walks, pretty villages, friendly pubs and stately homes. **Whitchurch Canonicorum**, two miles inland from Charmouth has a link with those Viking raiders of long ago; the 13th century Church of St Candida and the Holy Cross contains the tomb of the saint, also known as St Wita, and who is thought to have been a Saxon woman slain in a raid.

Pilsdon Pen also bears evidence of an earlier culture with Iron Age earthworks to be found on the bare top of the highest hill in Dorset, at 909 feet a landmark for half the county and one that offers the most wonderful views.

Further north, **Thorncombe** clings to a steep hillside close to the border with Devon and Somerset, and between the village and the Somerset town of **Chard**, lie the lovely buildings of **Forde Abbey.** Started at the beginning of the 12th century, the Cistercian monastery was not fully completed for another 300 years. To avoid destruction at the Dissolution, the Abbot handed the Abbey over to the King. It has been a family home since the 17th century when Sir EdmundPrideaux, Attorney General to Cromwell, commissioned Inigo Jones to convert it into a private house. Set beside the River Axe in some 30 acres of beautiful gardens, the house and monastic buildings contain remarkable tapestries and furniture and pictures.

To the east, across the high rolling hills, lies the rambling village of **Broadwindsor**, reputedly the highest in Dorset, and close to the lovely wooded crest of **Lewesdon Hill**. Charles II stayed the night here after his failure to set sail from Charmouth; once again he had a narrow escape as the Parliamentarian soldiers were diverted by the site of one of their own camp-followers giving birth.

The principal market town for the area is **Beaminster**, a pleasant place which has had more than its share of bad luck, having been virtually destroyed by fire in 1644, 1684 and 1781; nevertheless it is a cheerful place where the little River Brit runs beside the main street with its handsome 18th century buildings.

Parnham House is world renowned as the home of John Makepeace furniture workshops, where innovative use of wood and the highest standards of woodworking skill reign supreme. The house dates from the Middle Ages,

Chapter Two

was rebuilt in Tudor times and further altered by the great Regency architect, John Nash. For 500 years it was the home of the Strode family, who are remembered in the church at Beaminster and within the park there is the grave of Lieutenant Rhodes-Moorhouse, the first airman to be awarded the Victoria Cross. The Makepeace family have restored both house and gardens and the result is superb.

Not far away is another house with lovely grounds, **Mapperton House** is perhaps the most beautiful manor house in Dorset and is set beside terraced gardens through which water gently flows. It is serene and timeless; qualities to be found throughout the county, but particularly in this region where the hills seemingly enfold and enclose minute communities guarding themselves against the intrusion of the modern world.

Now that **Bridport** has been by-passed it is much easier to enjoy this nice town with its very wide and handsome main street where no two buildings are quite alike, and the brick and stone Town Hall, complete with stately cupola, presides over all. To the east **Burton Bradstock**, a pretty village tucked away from the sea by a low ridge, lies close to the beginnings of the extraordinary **Chesil Beach.** One of the great wonders of England's coastline, the Beach is some 15 miles of blue-clay reef covered with an immense coating of shingle, more than 40 feet high in parts. No expert has yet produced a convincing theory as to why the pebbles get progressively smaller the further west along the Beach one goes. Behind Chesil Beach is The Fleet, a brackish and reed-filled lagoon.

North-east of Bridport, the narrow roads lead over the hills to **Powerstock**, a delightful village nestling beneath the 800foot high **Eggardon Hill**, where, from the massive earthen ramparts of an Iron Age fort on the top, excellent views are to be had of the surrounding countryside.

Returning southwards towards the fascination of Chesil Beach, the hilly country bounded by the A35 to the north and the Beach to the south has much to offer. **Kingston Russell** was the birthplace of Admiral Sir Thomas Masterman Hardy, Nelson's flag-captain at Trafalgar, and in whose arms Nelson died. A great seaman in his own right and passionately fond of his native county, particularly the village of **Portesham** where he spent much of his early life. The Hardy monument on neighbouring **Blackdown**, should not be confused with any memorial to Dorset'sgreatest author. The solid chimney like structure was erected to the memory of a great sailor and is still a notable landmark for those ships of the Royal Navy going about their lawful occasions in the Channel waters far below.

The gorse-laden heights overlooking the Beach are studded with reminders of far earlier civilisations; barrows, standing stones and circles mark the last resting places of forgotten tribal chieftains. **Abbotsbury** has a reminder of those pagan times in the survival of the ancient custom, Garland Day, held on May 13th. Thought to be a survival of sea-god worship, two garlands are carried through the village and one cast into the sea.

The village is one of the loveliest in the county, its narrow streets lined with mellow stone cottages, many of them thatched. Abbotsbury has had but three owners in its long history. First there was Orc, a steward of King Canute, and it was he and his wife Thola who established the Abbey. After the Dissolution, the village passed from the Church to the Strangways, Earls of Ilchester. The village suffered grievously during the Civil War; cottages were set alight, the Royalist Strangways' mansion was burnt to the ground and the pulpit of the parish church still bears bullet-holes received during a short but bloody battle, described by the Parliamentarian commander as being a 'hot bickering'. A masterful understatement

The Abbotsbury Sub Tropical Gardens have a wonderful display of rare and tender plants laid out around a walled garden with the added protection of a shelter-belt of trees. They were first laid out in 1760 and provide a stunning display of exotic blooms. **The Abbotsbury Swannery** dates back to the days when the monks reared swans for meat. Now the swanherd cares for around 1,000 mute swans, plus innumerable wildfowl, and his concern is that of a naturalist rather than that of an epicure.

Chesil Beach has long had a deserved reputation as a graveyard of ships and, together with the Fleet, as a haven for smugglers. This reputation was enhanced by the classic story of 'Moonfleet', which was written at the turn of the century by Meade Faulkner. It featured Fleet House, of Tudor origin and which is now the splendid **Moonfleet Manor Hotel.**

The eastern end of Chesil Beach runs into the massive rocky outcrop of **Portland**, the **'Gibraltar of Dorset'**, with its great harbour until recently one of the main bases for the Royal Navy, and narrow isthmus connecting to the ancient town and port of **Weymouth**. A seaport since Roman times, the small harbour is still busy with fishing boats, yachts and cross-channel ferries, . It is also a cheerful seaside resort, with a beautifully protected sandy beach and a fine esplanade, where the variety and irregularity of the buildings make for a view that is both comforting and good looking.

Portland has been a fortress since Roman times but it is perhaps best known for the high quality of the stone that has been quarried there since the 1700's. From this rocky hump, some four miles long and less than two

Chapter Two

miles wide, came stone for buildings as diverse as St Paul's Cathedral, London University and the United Nations Building.

The southern tip of Portland is known as **The Bill,** and is marked by a lighthouse which warns shipping not only of rocks but also the presence of a dangerous tidal race, where currents up to seven knots flow.

Economically, Portland's future is questionable. Stone is no longer a principal building materialand the naval presence has gone. There are many plans for its future and one hopes that the final outcome will be a happy and prosperous future for its friendly people.

Just north of Weymouth, to the west of the road to Dorchester lies the immense Stone Age hill fort of **Maiden Castle**, one of the largest in Europe. Dating back to 2000BC, the earthworks are truly impressive, covering some 47 acres, and stand as a still, silent tribute to the energies of the simple military engineers of long ago. **Dorchester,** the county town is fascinating. It has a colourful and sometimes violent past and its Roman origins are indicated by the layout of its main street, the square outlines of the town wall which ran where there are now tree-lined walks, and the remains of a magnificent villa behind County Hall, which reveals some of the original mosaics and the hypocaust, or central heating system. Just south of the town, at **Maumbury Rings**, an ancient 'henge' type monument of the stone circle variety was adapted by the Romans as an amphitheatre; it is a gruesome fact that the public gallows stood here until well into the 18th century. Judge Jeffreys opened his Bloody Assizes here trying those who were involved in the disastrous Monmouth Rebellion in 1685. The victims were involved frequently for no greater crime than being absent from their habitations from and at the time of the Rebellion. Those executed were hung, drawn and quartered, and their butchered bodies exhibited throughout the county as a grim warning.

Nearly 250 years later, the town was the scene of another famous 'trial' when six farm labourers from **Tolpuddle** were sentenced to seven years transportation for attempting to form a trade union.

It has to be said that today's town is far more just and friendly and wears its status as the county's capital far more lightly than many of its contemporaries. I feel this is partly to do with the character of Dorset and the fact that Dorchester is not a cathedral city; there is a light-hearted market town atmosphere with little of the dignity of the diocese. There is plenty to do and see including the excellent **Dorset County Museum** in West Street which has a section devoted to Dorset's most famous literary son, Thomas Hardy. Hardy was to Dorset as Wordsworth was to the Lakes, with much of their writing inextricably bound to their place of birth. Wessex was a long forgotten Saxon Kingdom until Hardy revived the title for use in his novel 'Far from the Madding Crowd' and many of the fictitious names in his writings refer to actual places. For instance, Dorchester is 'Casterbridge', Weymouth is 'Budmouth' and Sherborne 'Sherton Abbas.

Part of the charm of Dorchester is the fact that it is totally surrounded by the lovely rolling countryside. Nearby **Charminster** provides a link with the enterprising Spanish-speaking farmer, Squire Russell, for it was at **Wolferton House** that the future King of Castile stayed after his ship was driven into Weymouth by foul weather.

The modern traveller heads north along the A352, passing through the old and delightful village of **Cerne Abbas**. Lying in a chalk-lined valley and once more of a town than a village, the community's wealth was originally derived from the Benedictine Abbey, first established by the Saxon Ethelmaer, Earl of Cornwall, in 987 AD. The Dissolution brought the usual destruction and the only obvious remains are the handsome gatehouse, guest-house and tithe barns. The lovely 15th century church has a buttressed tower, a later Norman chancel and some early heraldic glass.

Cerne Abbas is probably best known for the enormous pagan figure of a priapic giant carved into the turf on the chalk hillside. His origins are unknown; local legend has a David and Goliath account of a local shepherd boy killing the giant while he slept on the hill, whereupon the villagersimmediately rushed up and marked the outline of the massive corpse, some 180feet from head to toe. He may be Neolithic or he may be the god, Hercules, carved by Roman Soldiers; no-one seems quite certain, although there is a strong belief that fertility is assured by spending the night on the giant phallus! Whatever the truth, the giant's outline still lies on the hillside, surrounded for miles around, by the stone pillars and earthen mounds of earlier and more superstitious times. In this rounded and hilly landscape, a turn away from the main road brings the traveller, by way of narrow twisting lanes, to tiny settlements and hamlets and one has the feeling that even in the 20th century, the ancient ways are given more than passing acknowledgment.

Mintern Gardens, at **Minterne Magna**, are a series of beautifully landscaped gardens which utilises lakes, cascades, streams and pools to show off a wonderful array of trees, shrubs and plants. Before reaching Sherborne, the road runs down to what Hardy called 'The Vale of Little Dairies' Blackmoor Vale. In comparison with the chalk downland grazing, this is rich, lush countryside and many dairies still survive, albeit somewhat larger than in Hardy's day.

Chapter Two

Who could not be enchanted by **Sherborne** which is rightly claimed as Dorset's loveliest town. It has charm, character, it abounds with fine buildings set beside curving little streets. The learned St Aldhelm founded the Abbey and School in the 8th century, and to our good fortune both have survived to this day, the school being re-founded by Royal Charter after the Dissolution. Sherborne Abbey as seen today dates principally from the 15th century although evidence of its Saxon and Norman Predecessors clearly remain. The delicate stone fan-vaulting is beautiful and intricate and the local yellow stone from which the building is constructed lends to a feeling of warmth and mellowness to the magnificent interior. The people of Sherborne showed great far sightedness when they bought 'the Abbey, the grounds about it, the lead, the bells and other fittings' for the sum of three hundred pounds. Many of the abbey's old monastic buildings have been incorporated into the school, which rambles around much of the southern half of the town with its numerous halls, houses and playing fields.

The town and the surroundings are full of the most marvellous treasures and attractions. **Sherborne Museum**, in the old Abbey gatehouse holds items of local interest, including Roman remains, a splendid 15th century wall-painting and a model of the town's original Norman castle. The actual castle was built between 1107 and 1135 by Roger, Bishop of Salisbury, and if the construction of a fortress seems a somewhat un-ecclesiastical act, it should be remembered that Bishops in those days were not 'all gas and gaiters'. Between 871 and 933AD three Bishops of Sherborne fell in battle against the Danes.

The castle passed into the ownership of Sir Walter Raleigh in 1597, but he was not to enjoy ownership for long, being indicted for treason in 1603. Nevertheless, he left his mark; evidently deciding that the massively-built stone castle offered little in the way of home comforts, he therefore initiated the building of a more suitable abode almost immediately adjacent to the grim fortress. Thus Sherborne has not one, but two 'castles'. **Sherborne Old Castle** and later **Sherborne Castle**. The old castle remained as a defensive position until the Civil War, when it was stormed by Parliamentarians under General Fairfax and destroyed. The new castle, originally known as The Lodge, is owned by the Digby family who have been there since Sir John Digby was awarded the estate by James I in recognition for his services as Ambassador to Spain - another Spanish-speaker made good! The Digbys utilised much of the ruins of the old castle to enlarge and enhance the house, and later employed Capability Brown to landscape the area around the two castles. The lake, waterfall and lovely gardens are the result, while the interior of the house is in restrained elegance, with notable collections of furniture and porcelain.

To the west of the town, close to the border with Somerset, lies another lovely home, **Compton House**. This 16th-century building is at the heart of an unique enterprise; for thirty years it has been the home of **Worldwide Butterflies**, where a variety of habitats provide the settings for butterflies and moths from all over the world. In conjunction with this amazing programme of conservation and breeding is **Lullingstone Silk Farm**, which has provided the silk used on many Royal occasions.

Just to the south is the intriguingly-named village of **Purse Caundle**. Amazingly this delightful community was described at the beginning of the century as a 'poor village... where most thatched roofs of the cottages have been replaced by corrugated iron, the churchyard of a ruinous condition...' All is now well, with the lovely 15th-century church possessed of an unusual panelled chancel arch, and the beautiful Elizabethan **Purse Caundle Manor** lying close beside the 'clear stream' that goes on to feed Sherborne lake. The manor has a most attractive garden, a great hall with minstrel's gallery, and an interior well, dug in case of siege!

Between Sherborne and Blandford Forum is **Sturminster Newton**, a truly lovely Minster town, cut in two by the gently flowing River Stour. It is full of picturesque cottages and has an ancient bridge which still bears a notice threatening to deport you if you cause damage! It really is a corner of rural England that seems to have remained unchanged. The little shops still have 19th century facades, the narrow roads cause a nightmare on market days but it is all taken in good part by the residents who would not change their delightful town for the world.

Continuing eastwards, the road leads on to Shaftesbury, but the unhurried traveller will find it well worth turning off and exploring the area around **Gillingham**, the county's most northerly town. Centuries ago there was a forest around these parts and at the time of Elizabeth I, it was recorded as being 'Her Majesty's Park and Forest of Gillingham, and Sir Walter Raleigh once held the honorary post of Forest Ranger.

South east of Gillingham, the land rises steeply to a 700foot plateau where stands the Saxon town of **Shaftesbury**. It is claimed that this ancient town contains more history in one square mile than any other settlement in ancient Wessex; a claim the visitor can well believe. For all that, it is far from being a fusty old museum of a town, being bright, lively and cheerful. Today as it has ever been it is an important market centre and has expanded to take advantage of its position and the talents of its population. Nevertheless, from both the physical and historical viewpoint it is extremely attractive and, in places like the steep cobbled Gold Hill with its wonderful views and varied architecture, quite enchanting. It has to be said though that particular view

Chapter Two

is oddly familiar to many since it is a favourite with art directors and has been used in television drama as well as numerous advertising campaigns.

The handsome Georgian appearance of **Blandford** owes everything to a great fire and two Bastards; the town was almost completely destroyed in 1731 and restored by two talented architects with that unfortunate name.

Stourpaine nestles at the foot of the great chalk hills, guarding what was once an important crossing of the River Stour. The country lanes meander to the south-west, climbing along the side of the steep chalk downs. Tucked into the lee, small villages and hamlets huddle against the hillside, which rises to its peak at **Bulbarrow Hill**, at 902 feet, the second highest in Dorset. It is alleged that both the Bristol Channel and the Isle of Wight are visible from this point.

Some three miles to the south-east, along a large tree-clad ridge, the road runs down into a steep narrow combe containing what must be the most unique village in Dorset, **Milton Abbas**. Essentially it is little more than a grass-lined street flanked on either side by twenty identical thatched cottages. There is a lake, a school and a pub, **The Hambro Arms**. The story behind this extraordinarily neat litle community begins with the founding of the Abbey in 932AD by King Athelstan. Later it became a Benedictine Monastery and was surrounded by a small market town that contained a famous brewery, a grammar school and numerous pubs. This was the state of affairs until 1786 when one, Joseph Damer, acquired the Abbey and its estates from the descendants of Henry VIII's lawyer who was awarded the Abbey (for a small consideration) at the time of the Dissolution for his servces in securing the said Monarch's divorce from Catherine of Aragon. Damer, afterwards Earl of Dorchester, proposed to build a great house on the site and objected to the rowdy presence of the small town. His solution was to buy up the entire town, lock, stock and barrel . This he accomplished over a period of twenty years demolishing each property as it fell vacant. Those who wished to stay in his employ were removed to the new village, built to a plan by the ever industrious Capability Brown. The house that Lord Dorchester built from the monastic buildings is now a school, but the Abbey Church remains and is a superb Gothic building dating from the 12th and 14th centuries.

The adjacent villages such as **Melcombe Bingham**, are every bit as attractive but rather more conventional; the 'toy town' effect of Milton Abbas takes a little time to get used to, but there is no denying its charm and fascination.

The River Piddle lends its name to the villages east of Dorchester known collectively as the Piddles and Puddles. **Tolpuddle** is celebrated for its association with the ill-treated farm workers of 1831. Public outcry forced the Government to pardon six men, but it took time for the message to reach Australia and one of the Martyrs only found out by sheer luck; four years later on a remote sheep station, he read of his pardon in an old and discarded newspaper!

Piddlehinton has a good Perpendicular church and two fine houses in **Glebe Court** and **Marston Manor**, while **Piddletrenthide's** church is of Norman origin with the village school sporting gates that once graced Westminster Abbey; the gift of a local man who became a famous London jeweller. **Puddletown** has a superb medieval church with box pews, a musician's gallery and tombs and memorials of the Martyn family.

Bovington Heath has been the site of an army camp since the First World War, and the **Tank Museum** must be the most complete collection of armoured fighting vehicles in existence, containing over 260 such vehicles from 23 countries. The narrow chalk ridge that divides the sea from heath has many notable beauty spots, the best known being the nearly circular **Lulworth Cove**. The coastline here has been carved into fantastic shapes by the ceaseless motion of the sea, and just to the west, a great natural arch of limestone projects out into the water at **Durdle Door.**

Corfe Castle was begun in the 1080's and expanded over the centuries. King John made much of the place, which is understandable given his undoubted unpopularity, any large, remote and easily defended castle must have been immensely appealing. He kept his crown, his ill-gotten treasure and his unfortunate prisoners at **Corfe**, few of whom were ever seen again.

The great white cliffs of **Durlston** guard the attractive little resort of **Swanage**, once the principal port for the shipping of Purbeck stone and marble. The sandy beach and sheltered waters of the Bay and that of neighbouring **Studland** make the area ideal for family holidays. Swanage is justlypopular and the town is attractive and welcoming; apart from watersports of every variety and the obvious attractions of the area, there is a fine parish church, built in the 13th century and sited next to the Millpond, the steam engines of **The Swanage Railway**, the **Tithe Barn Museum** and numerous pubs, hotels and restaurants.

The northern side of **Purbeck** is bounded by the huge natural expanse of **Poole Harbour**, whose perimeter, laid in a straight line , would stretch for some 95 miles.! The oldest community on the shores of this great lake-like harbour is **Wareham**, at the western end. The town suffered a terminal decline

Chapter Two

due to the silting up of the River Frome, attacks by pirates, plague and a succession of fires, the worst destroying over 140 buildings in 1762. The town fared no better in the Monmouth Rebellion with some of the citizens being brutally despatched by the dreadful Judge Jeffreys. It is hard to see what this most attractive and friendly little town ever did to encourage such a catalogue of disasters. It has two fine churches, plenty of interesting buildings, wonderful surroundings and in spite of the past, a remarkably cheerful atmosphere.

Poole has become almost as one with its neighbour to the east, **Bournemouth,** but still retains a strong streak of individuality; besides being a port it is a major residential centre, a light industrial centre and a recreational centre. There are two excellent museums, **The Waterfront Museum** and the **Guildhall Museum** and the delightfully restored **Scaplen's Court**, a medieval merchant's house. On the Quay, **Poole Pottery** has an international reputation, while the revamped and pedestrianised High Street has a modern indoor shopping centre and a wide variety of shops, pubs and restaurants. Within the harbour, boat trips are available to such attractions as **Brownsea Island**, a nature reserve and bird sanctuary where Baden Powell held his first scout camp. If the weather is unkind then the **Tower Park** is a vast indoor complex housing such diverse activities as bowling and ice-skating, together with water-slides, cinema, shops and restaurants.

Bournemouth is a town full of hotels and places to stay which concentrates on caring for tourists and business people. It is many things to many people depending on what you are looking for. Wonderful place for a quiet holiday with excellent beaches, pleasant walks along the cliffs and good entertainment in the theatre and concert hall. It has several attractive places around it including **Southbourne** and of course, the dignified **Christchurch** to the west - a wonderfully central position for anyone who wants to stay on the borders of Dorset and Hampshire.

Wimborne Minster is where the great twin towers of St Cuthberga stand on the site of an 8th century monastery. The church is a splendid amalgamation of ecclesiastical styles, from Norman to late Gothic, and contains many treasures, including an 800 year old font, a chained library, an Orrery or astronomical clock, and many interesting tombs and memorials. The town is an attraction in itself with an award winning local museum to tell its story in **The Priest's House Museum**. Other places of interest are the lovely **Knoll Gardens**, a six acre site of rare and exotic plants, and, to the south of the town, the Georgian **Merley House,** with its fascinating model toy collection, and **Merley Bird Gardens**, with avians ranging from parrots to penguins.

Kingston Lacy, a National Trust property has wonderful pictures and grounds and should be visited. Some half a dozen miles north of Wimborne lies **Wimborne St Giles**, on the edge of the old royal hunting grounds of **Cranborne Chase**. The Ashleys, Earls of Shaftesbury, have their seat here and the pleasant but ornate little church is full of their memorials. Many of the family were noted political reformers and philanthropists and the welcoming **Bull Inn** was built for workers on the estate. Another great political family are the Cecils, Marquesses of Salisbury, who's home has been at neighouring **Cranborne** since 1603. The fact that there was once a great Saxon Abbey on the site of the 13th century church and that William Conqueror gave the manor to his Queen, Matilda, shows the esteem that this attractive little village was once held in; perhaps because from 908AD to 1120, it was the seat of the Chase Court, which administered the hunting rights.

The deer that were once so prized by Saxon and Norman nobility still graze among the woods and coverts in this lovely part of the county. In the neat village which delights in the enchanting name of **Sixpenny Handley**, the cheerful **Roebuck Inn** is a reminder that the descendants of those noble animals are around; as too are the descendants of those who hunted them so long ago. Somehow, this seems only right in an ancient county possessed of timeless charm.

WILTSHIRE

The true inhabitants of South Wiltshire are unhurried rather than slow, thoughtful rather than thick. Their character has been shaped by the countryman's compromising attitude to the seasons and the weather, yet they don't lack for native wit. True Wiltshiremen are known as 'Moonrakers' after two of their number were challenged one moonlit night, raking the surface of a village pond with hay-rakes. Their explanation for this strange activity was that they were trying to retrieve 'they gurt yaller cheese' pointing to the reflection of the moon in the water. The interrogators rode away laughing and tapping their heads: but the last laugh was on them, for they were excisemen and unknown to them, the pond contained smuggled casks of brandy! There 'bain't no flies' on a Moonraker, as the over confident outsider can find to his cost. The story has echoes in other counties associated with the free-traders, but in Wiltshire it rings the truest.

My journey in Dorset ended on the edge of **Cranbourne Chase** which runs into the south-west of Wiltshire towards Salisbury. In medieval times much of this area was heavily afforested but now it is a region of chalkland divided by the valleys of the Ebble and the Nadder. The clearwaters flow by some of the most lovely little villages and hamlets in the county, often settlements of great antiquity that lie tucked into folds of the hills and protected by woodland. This is delightful country and an area that repays the peripatetic wanderer in full.

Ebbesbourne Wake is a rambling village to the south of **White Sheet Hill** (incidentally, there are two hills of this name in the area - this one is south of the Shaftesbury-Salisbury road and the other is near Mere, to the north). Thatched cottages cluster around what was once an important cattle drover's trail. Continuing eastwards via **Fifield Bavant** with its miniature Norman church, the valley floor begins to broaden by the time one reaches the 'capital' of the stream-set villages,**Broadchalke**. The Ebble provides nourishment for watercress beds and is splendid for trout fishing and brewing! On the northern side of White Sheet Hill where the bridleways are still a favourite with local riders, are the neighbouring villages of **Ansty** and **Swallowcliffe** close to which are two castles with the name of Wardour. Strictly speaking neither are true castles; **Old Wardour Castle** was more akin to the fortified chateaux of France and was a tower house of octagonal shape. Its defensive capability was proven in 1634, when the elderly Lady Blanche Arundell, commanding a force of twenty five men and some dozen or so womenfolk, held out against a besieging Parliamentarian force of 1,300. The siege lasted five days and nights and was ended when Lady Blanche negotiated an honourable surrender. The Parliamentarians reneged on the conditions, imprisoned the gallant defenders and looted the castle. When her son Lord Arundell heard the news, he became the besieger but at great cost: in order to force a conclusionto the siege, he was forced to blow up his own inheritance. In 1776, the family built a new house within sight of the romantic ruins of the old. **Wardour Castle** is a rather austere Palladian mansion designed by James Paine for the eighth Lord Arundell, which became a school after the Arundell family's tenure came to an end.

The surrounding countryside and villages are a delight to the curious visitor. **Chilmark**, where the best of the beautiful creamy limestone was quarried, has a wealth of lovely houses built of the same material; the stone being first utilised by the Romans and later in the construction of Salisbury Cathedral and then Wilton House. A stream running through the village is spanned by a delightful little stone bridge and the Early English church has a broad spire. The Teffonts, **Teffont Magna** and **Teffont Evias**, are charming. Many of the cottages in the latter have their own little stone bridges giving access across the stream from front door to street. To the south of the A30, at **Fovant**, there are some moving examples of 20th century graffiti; the huge regimental crests carved into the hillside by soldiers undergoing training during the First World War. Sad to reflect on how few returned to see their handiwork, and how few of those regiments have survived. **East Knoyle's** chief claim to fame is that it was the birthplace of Sir Christopher Wren who was far from being the only talented member of that family; the ornate plasterwork in the chancel of the parish church was designed by his father, the rector of the parish.

Close to the Somerset border, at **Mere**, is one of the finest churches in Wiltshire. St Michael the Archangel is an elegant blend of 13th and 15th century styles with fine decorative work and a 100foot tower which dominates the handsome small town. The undulating downlands to the north contain two of Wiltshire's most famous stately homes. The first is **Stourhead** where the famous gardens contain the source of the meandering River Stour. In 1714 the estate was sold to the Hoare family, goldsmiths and bankers, the old house was demolished and a handome Palladian mansion built in its place. However the chief glory of Stourhead are the grounds; the talented Henry Hoare was inspired by a Grand Tour of Europe and devised a delightful series of romantic gardens surrounding the lake, complete with temples and a grotto sheltering amongst the magnificent specimen trees.

The Hoare family continued to enhance both house and estate until, following the loss of their only son in the First World War, the late Sir Henry Hoare generously donated it to the National Trust. There is a sad but touching postscript to this story when Sir Henry and his wife, having given away their beloved home to which they had devoted most of their lives, died within two hours of each other.

The second great stately home stands just to the north and close to the Somerset border. **Longleat**, a palatial Elizabethan mansion set in wonderful grounds landscaped by the inimitable Capability Brown, is perhaps the best known such house in the country. Until the Dissolution it was the site of a medieval priory; the great house that replaced it was built by Sir John Thynne and has remained in the hands of the same family ever since. During the late 19th century it was redecorated in Italian Renaissance style with elaborately painted ceilings. Some idea of the scale of the house can be gained by the fact that it has seven libraries housing over 40,000 volumes! The late Marquess of Bath, faced with the horrendous problems of maintaining such a huge and elaborate building was the first peer to open his house on a business basis to the public,and as an added attraction, turned much of the surrounding estate into a fine Safari Park. Other entertainments, rallies and events have meant that these radical and pioneering measures have produced one of the country's premier tourist attractions.

Warminster is an appropriate name for the old town that plays host to a number of military establishments who exercise on the great open spaces of **Salisbury Plain**, immediately to the west. It is near the head of the third of the river valleys that run from the western county boundary back towards

Chapter Two

Salisbury. The river is the Wylye, one of the loveliest of the gin-clear chalk streams so beloved by trout fisherman and its valley was described in 1824 by William Cobbett as being 'Fine, very fine.'

Roughly halfway between Warminster and Salisbury is **Wylye** itself now thankfully by-passed. The river runs past an old mill and many of the cottages feature the checker-work stone and flint to be found throughout this part of Wiltshire.

Wiltshire takes its name from the West Saxons who settled in the valley at **Wilton**, the 'farmstead beside the banks of the Wylye'. Although now a small well-to-do town, Wilton was once capital of Saxon Wessex: Alfred founded an abbey here and there was also a royal palace. The Dissolution saw the Abbey in the hands of Sir William Herbert, first Earl of Pembroke, and the estates have remained in the possession of that family ever since. Sir William demolished the Abbey and asked his friend Hans Holbein to design him a house utilising much of the remains. It was a wonderful house. Elizabeth I held court here, Shakespeare's company first performed 'As You Like It' before James I, and Charles I declared that he did 'love Wilton above all places, and did come here every summer.' Sadly a great fire destroyed much of the house in 1647, but happily the great Inigo Jones was on hand to rebuild. The result is one of the most magnificent and dignified stately homes in the country.

The Pembrokes have a strong entrepreneurial streak and although Wilton has long been the centre for weaving, it was the eighth earl who established the famous Wilton reputation for carpets. He combined the local assets of plentiful wool from the sheep of Salisbury Plain with the talents and skills of French weavers, then renowned throughout the world for the superb quality of their work. Unfortunately, Louis XIV of France regarded his weavers as a national asset and guarded them accordingly; the earl was forced to adopt some underhand methods and smuggled a number of the coveted craftsmen out of France in a giant barrel of wine! **The Wilton Carpet Company** was established in 1655 and is still going strong. It has an excellent museum and shop.

Some pretty villages surround Wilton including **Barford St Martin** and **Burcombe**. It is well worth spending time seeking out the narrow lanes and B roads which will lead you to these and other delightful spots.

There is a triumvirate of ancient and important dwelling-places close to where the three valleys of the Wylye, Nadder and Ebble meet, and their histories are all intertwined. The oldest recorded site is that of **Old Sarum**, a 56 acre earthwork on a rise to the north of Salisbury. Of Iron Age origin, it was appropriated by the Romans and later became a Saxon fortified town, important enough for King Edgar to hold a Parliament there in 960AD and to have a mint. The Normans, probably by virtue of its raised and protected position, made a great to-do about the place, using it as an administrative headquarters and building a citadel and cathedral. It was here, in 1086, that William held council to establish the feudal system and to initiate the compilation of the Domesday Book. However, by the beginning of the 13th century all was not well within the ancient ramparts; friction between the soldiers and the clergy, coupled with cramped conditions and shortage of water led to Bishop Richard Poore seeking a new site for the cathedral. Naturally, he went first to Wilton, since it was the nearest community of size and importance, but the Abbess objected strongly to the thought of a rival religious foundation. Eventually Bishop Poore selected a site where the Wylye, Nadder and Avon met amongst lush green meadows. Legend has it that the spot was chosen by loosing an arrow from the ramparts of Old Sarum. The archer must have been an exceptional man, doubtless aided by a northerly gale, for the new site is some two miles from the old!

Under the direction of one Elias Dereham, rightly described as an 'incomparable artificer', building proceeded apace. The stone which has weathered over the centuries to a lovely greeny-grey was quarried and carted over the rutted lanes from Chilmark to New Sarum, or **Salisbury**, where the master-masons gave it its final shaping before it was hoisted into position. The building was completed in the remarkably short time of 40 years and is consequently an almost perfect example of Early English throughout. Almost certainly, Elias was aware of the problems that beset another cathedral, Winchester, which was also built on marshy ground and whose central tower had collapsed in 1107, for he left the construction of the elegant spire to his successors in the next century. By the time the people of Old Sarum, who appeared to have sided with the Bishop against the uncouth soldiers, had deserted the old hill-fort and settled around the new cathedral. There was nothing haphazard about this settlement; the new town was carefully planned from the start with the streets neatly laid out in a grid system which lasted almost untouched until the present century. There were numerous water-channels which led to the medieval nickname 'The Venice of England' and it may be that the drainage effect of these channels gave Bishop Wyvil and his architect, Richard of Farleigh, the confidence to add the audacious and elegant 404foot spire in 1334. Aware that vibration is the cause of collapse, the master-builder housed the peal of bells in a separate campanile. Over 400 years later, it was left to the 18th century architect James Wyatt to add, or rather subtract, the finishing touches. He was much criticised at the time for his ruthlessness, but it is to him that we owe the parity and beauty of what, externally, is the most beautiful cathedral in the country. Wyatt demolished the campanile, cleared away the jumble of tombstones in the graveyard and laid out the great sward of mown grass that surrounds the building. He removed much of the ornate that was within, including much of the early glass; the result is the austere Gothic nobility of the original craftsmen, who dared in those far off times to construct such a great and lofty edifice on marshy grounds; their decision must have been an act of faith in itself.

The great spire is a landmark from far and wide and every year thousands come to wonder and pay homage to those old master-builders. Glorious as the building is, with its great cloisters, massive Purbeck pillars, lovely choir vaulting, copy of Magna Carta and ancient clock (1386 - and still ticking!), it has to be said that part of its attraction lies in its incomparable setting. The Close is rectangular in shape, surrounded by an intact medieval wall, with a wonderful collection of buildings, houses, some contemporary with the great church, others fine examples of Queen Anne or Georgian. Three of these are not only fine examples of the architecture of their day but also excellent museums. A 13th century house, The Wardrobe, so named because it was once used for storing clothes belonging to the Bishop and his entourage, is now home to **The Museum of the Duke of Edinburgh's Royal Regiment.** It contains a fascinating collection of the historical items relating to 250 years of military history. The King's House is a 14th-century building housing the award-winning **Salisbury and South Wiltshire Museum** with a fine collection of archaeological and historical artefacts. The classic facade of **Mompesson House**, built in 1701, conceals a fine collection of glassware and furniture together with a delightful garden.

Salisbury is altogether a beautiful city and one which rewards the interested visitor with hours of pleasure. A Cathedral city always attracts the arts and Salisbury is no exception; there is a festival in September, music in the Cathedral and the Guildhall, exhibitions in the Arts Centre and live theatre at the excellent Playhouse. There is an attractive and well patronised racecourse whilst virtually all forms of recreation and sport are catered for in and around the city. You may find it easier to stay outside Salisbury and if you wish to I can recommend the hamlet of **Britford**, with the river running alongside and where **Bridge Farm** will open its welcoming arms to you.

The Avon runs south from Salisbury; passing the great estate of **Longford Castle**. The splendid mansion is a testament to one woman's ambition; she was Helena, wife of Sir Thomas Gorges, Governor of Hurst Castle during the reign of Elizabeth I. Hurst is on the Hampshire coast and during the battle of the Spanish Armada, a galleon was driven aground closeby. Lady Gorges prettily asked the Queen if she might have the wreck, omitting to inform her sovereign that the galleon was laden with silver! Consequently Sir Thomas' modest medieval manor-house was transformed into a large and imposing castle. Unusual in that it is triangular in shape with a tower at each corner; the castle is now the home of the Earl of Radnor, whose family have owned it since the 18th century.

The little town of **Amesbury** is always worth visiting for many reasons. It is one of the oldest continually-inhabited sites in the country and has a strong connection with the Arthurian legends. Legend has it that after the death of Arthur, Queen Guinevere became Abbess of Amesbury. Modern Amesbury is a friendly, bustling place, providing shopping facilities and accommodation for many of the modern military establishments that lie around it. The great expanse of Salisbury Plain to the north and west is the principal area where the weaponry and soldiers of today exercise to protect our civilisation - but surrounding Amesbury are the mysterious relics and memorials of civilisations of which we know little. The best known of these, of course is **Stonehenge**. Viewed from the main road, the stones appear insignificant against the sky-line; approach closer and they become massively impressive, the largest weighing some 50 tons. The image is so familiar to us we almost take it for granted until closer contact with its scale and brutal bulk begin to impress on our consciousness together with an almost indefinable sense of wonder and awe. Gazing at the marvellous circle of upright stones with their huge lintels, the question that comes to mind are Who, When, Why and How? The answers range from the wildly fanciful to the reasoned and scientific, but it must be admitted that even the soundest of answers is but theory and there are still great gaps in our knowledge when it comes to a matter of actual fact.

The high ground of the Plain is divided from the richer and lower soil of Northern Wiltshire by the road that runs from **Westbury** to **Upavon**. Protected by the bulk of the downland, numerous villages, hamlets and farmsteads are spread along the road. Solidly prosperous **Westbury** made its money from cloth-weaving, glove-making and later from foundries exploiting a seam of iron-ore that was discovered nearby. It is a nice town with an imposing Town Hall, fine Georgian houses and a nice little market place, but the chief attraction for most visitors lies on the hillside to the east of the town where a great White Horse is carved into the chalk downland. Some 160 feet high, the present shape was cut out of the turf in 1778 and overlies an earlier, somewhat oddly shaped animal of unknown origin. It is claimed that the original was made to commemorate King Alfred's victory over the Danes at the Battle of Ethandun in 878 A.D. This is by no means certain since no-one is sure where Ethandun actually is; no matter, the great horse is undoubtedly impressive and worth a visit. On the heights above is the 23 acre site of **Bratton Castle**, a massive and ancient earthwork hill-fort whose presence gives some credence to theories about that battle so long ago.

Chapter Two

Continuing eastwards, **Edington's** past is reflected in it's great church. Edington Priory was built between 1352 and 1361 and is therefore a fine example of the style known as Perpendicular. The Priory was the scene of a brutal and scandalous murder in 1449; at the time, the county was unsettled by the peasant's revolt, known as Jack Cade's Rebellion and the Bishop of Salisbury,one William Ayscough, felt Edington to be safer than his own cathedral. Sadly he was wrong, for the mob sought him out and dragged him from High Mass. At the top of the hill he ws savagely stoned to death. These days the church is widely known for its annual music festival.

Erlstoke has a connection with the legendary Dick Turpin for Tom Boulter, a highwayman whose exploits were often attributed to Turpin, stole a horse - and its name really was Black Bess!

Devizes lies not far to the north and close to the geographical heart of Wiltshire. It is a pleasant small market town. There are two attractive Norman churches and it has a thriving market. The town is an important centre for agriculture and light industry.

In medieval times it was second only to Salisbury in cloth-manufacturing and was one of the principal corn-markets in the West of England. There are a great many interesting and picturesque buildings including **The Bear Hotel**, an old coaching inn where, in the 18th century, the father of Sir Thomas Lawrence, the portrait painter, was once landlord. There is also the excellent **Devizes Museum**, which makes a speciality of displaying many of the Bronze Age finds taken from the county's innumerable sites.

Every year the Devizes to Westminster canoe race takes place using much of the old Kennet and Avon Canal which once linked London to Bristol. The Trust now administers the canal and has an exhibition centre on the wharf and, to the west of the town, at Caen Hill there is an amazing example of early 19th-century civil engineering where the canal is made to 'climb' the steep gradient by means of a flight of 16 locks.

The Vale of Pewsey runs between the high ground of the Plain to the south, and the even higher ground of the Marlborough Downs to the north. The Vale is some twelve miles long by five wide and contains some of the richest farmland in the country. The settlements between the hills are quiet and peaceful, their pasts containing no great historical dramas or events. The ecclesiastical architecture is particularly fine, probably as a result of agricultural wealth, and at **Chirton** there is one of the finest Norman churches in England. Built in 1170, it has a magnificent timber roof and fine decorative work, particularly around the doorway and the font.

The little town which lends its name to the Vale, **Pewsey**, is a friendly and cheerful place with good buildings and a fine statue of King Alfred gazing across the River Avon from the crossroads, a reminder of the time when the community was owned by Saxon Kings. The marketing and milling of corn and an iron foundry contributed to past wealth and every September there is a riotous celebration described as 'the Mother of West County carnivals'.

South of Pewsey, **Upavon** is situated at the foot of downland and overlooked by the extensive earthworks of **Casterley Camp**, a fortification dating from the first century A.D. To the east of the village is another, but more modern reminder of military activity in the area. **RAF Upavon** was one of the earliest purpose-built airfields in the country, constructed in 1912 to house the Central Flying School of the Royal Flying Corps.

The nobility who came to **Ludgershall** for sport would have looked to the preserves of the **Chute Forest** for their entertainment; the great medieval woodland spread from Hampshire through to Wiltshire and would have harboured huge herds of deer. The border between the two counties is hilly and broken and still contains large clumps of woodland. It is beautiful countryside, crossed by the **Chute Causeway**, a Roman road that is far from being perfectly straight and populated by a number of attractive little villages sheltering amongst the trees.

To the north-west, via the Causeway, is the pleasant village of **Burbage**, once totally surrounded by the **Savernake Forest**. Nearby **Wolfhall** was the home of the Seymours, hereditary wardens of another once vast forest, a favourite hunting ground for Norman kings. It was at Wolfhall tht Henry VIII met and courted Jane Seymour, his future queen who later died in childbirth. Half a mile from Burbage Wharf is the **Bruce Tunnel**, which is some 1500 feet long; horses were not used here since the boats were pulled through by hand using chains strung along the tunnel wall..

On the edge of Savernake is another of those ancient burial mounds known as **Barrows**; this particular one is believed to have been the last resting place of Maerla (in local legend, Merlin the Wizard) and the conjunction of names has been taken by the town that lies alongside, **Marlborough**. A handsome and popular town with fine, predominantly Georgian architecture lining the immensely wide main street. Where cars are parked down the middle of this street today, market stalls and livestock were tethered in the past; in fact, life in this cheerful town often seemed to be little short of one great long street party. A visitor in the 19th-century reported that there were '1333 partakers of conviviality seated at one long table from the market house to St Peter's Church, nearly half a mile'. Because of the town's past

Chapter Two

importance as a staging post on the main London to Bristol road, the modern 'partaker of conviviality' is well provided for at the many coaching inns that have survived.

The road to the west passes through small rural communities in the Downs, containing many a delight so typical of Wiltshire, sites where the historic and pre-historic sit peacefully side by side. **Fyfield** has a 13th-century church with a splendid 15th-century tower, complete with pinnacles and gargoyles. Half a mile away are the strange stones that comprise the **Devil's Den**, actually the remains of the stone-framed burial chamber that was once covered by a barrow, or mound. At first glance, **Avebury** appears little more than a picturesque downland village with an attractive grouping of part-Saxon church, the gabled Elizabethan **Avebury Manor**, thatched cottages and farmsteads - and then one notices the stones. Massive weather wrought lozenges of sandstone, many weighing more than 40 tons, stand upright in groups, around and amongst the village.

Avebury Stone Circle pre-dates Stonehenge by some two centuries and differs particularly in that the great stones are undressed; called sarsens (a local corruption of 'saracen' or foreign) they are found locally on Marlborough Downs. They surround the village, contained within the remains of a large earth ring, some 1200 feet across. Many are missing, having been broken up over the centuries for use in local houses and barns, but expert excavation has revealed their originl placement. The Stone Circle is by no means the only prehistoric site in the area and by no means the most mysterious. A 50 foot wide avenue of megaliths, nearly a mile long, once led to an older site, named the **Sanctuary**, near the village of **West Kennett**. The stones here have long vanished but, once again, patient archaeological detective work has established their positions. On the southern flank of Avebury is perhaps the strangest object of all, the vast conical earthwork of **Silbury Hill**; an earthen pyramid, 130 feet high whose base covers a staggering five and a half acres, large enough to fill Trafalgar Square and reach three quarters of the way up Nelson's Column. Described as ' the largest man-made mound in Europe' its purpose and origins are obscure; since the 18th century, shafts have been driven into its mighty bulk in search of burial chambers or similar but with no success. All that we know is that it was built over 4,000 years ago, that a million cubic yards of chalk were excavated and, given the simple tools of the period, would have taken 500 people ten years to build! Local legend has it that a certain King Sil or Zel, is somewhere beneath the mound buried upright on his horse and clad in a suit of golden armour.

Close by Silbuy Hill is **West Kennett Long Barrow**, a 350 foot long burial mound from around 3,500 BC while to the north is **Windmill Hill** a

Dorset, Wiltshire, Hampshire

series of concentric earthworks which was the home of a Neolithic race of farmers who were probably responsible for the long barrow. The excellent small **Alexander Keiller Museum** has many exhibits and finds relating to these ancient sites, and is named after the archaeologist who did so much to interpret the extraordinary works of so long ago. Nearby the splendid thatched Great Barn houses **The Museum of Wiltshire Folk Life**, with fascinating displays of rural crafts, skills, tools and equipment.

There is no doubt that it can be extremely breezy up on the downs and it has been suggested that specialised forms of miniature tornadoes or whirlwinds are responsible for a phenomona known as **Corn Circles**, strange geometric shapes that appear in the great cornfields around this area. Inevitably, fanciful theories have been produced linking the shapes with the ancient stone circles, or even with aliens from outer space. Undoubtedly, some are the work of hoaxers but others are not so easily explained although cosmic doodling seems highly unlikely.

The highest village in the county **Baydon** stands at 750feet and is set in the heart of race-horse training country, close to the famous **Lambourne Downs**. An ancient settlement its name may be derived from Mount Badon, the last of Arthur's twelve great battles against the invading Saxons in the 6th century. St Nicholas church has internal piers of chalk blocks, put in place some 700 years ago, which aptly illustrate the old Wiltshire dictum that chalk was an excellent building medium providing that it has 'a good hat and boots', a sound roof and foundations to keep out the damp.

The M4 motorway effectively chops off the flatter lands of the northern tip of the county and contains the great mass of **Swindon**, the largest industrial town in Wiltshire. It was the railway that brought prosperity to the town, particularly since the town became the centre of Brunel's Great Western Railway, affectionately referred to as 'God's wonderful railway'. By 1867, the town could boast that it was 'neatly and regularly built.... and is lighted by gas. The Mechanics Institute is a noble building, having a library with upward of 3,650 volumes, and is one of the finest institutions in the kingdom; lectures, concerts and dramatic performances are frequently given in it. A free recreation ground, with a permanent pavilion, has been established for the use of cricketers, of whom there are several clubs. At the factory locomotives for the whole line are manufactured. Such is the perfection to which the building of engines has arrived here that one engine per week can be turned out. Also about 330 tons of rails per week are turned out at the rolling mill, The works cover about eighteen acres of ground.....'

Although the great locomotive works have been phased out **Swindon** remains one of the principal termini for goods and passengers and the great days of the GWR are remembered in the **Great Western Railway Museum** in Farringdon Road, which has a comprehensive display of old locomotives and railway memorabilia. Just opposite is **The Railway Village House**, a perfectly restored foreman's house from the turn of the century. Both exhibits are situated within the area known as the Railway Village, a model community built by GWR for their workers.

The River Thames, although little more than a stream, takes a meander into the extreme north of Wiltshire, running under **Cricklade**, an ancient market town, important from Roman days onwards because it sits on the old Roman Road of Ermine Street.

An ecclesiastical establishment of great importance was situated at **Malmesbury**, a handsome small town, built on a rocky outcrop above the waters of the Avon. The abbey and the town flourished trading in wool and exploiting the rich agricultural land that lay around. It reached itsheyday in the 14th century when riches gained from the wool trade led to the Abbey having a spire higher than that of Salisbury. However pride comes before a fall, and at the end of the next century, that is precisely what happened; the spire collapsed and the great gilt ball that adorned its tip ' rolled unceremoniously down the High Street'. With the Dissolution the Abbey fell into the hands of an upwardly mobile clothier, one William Stumpe, who promptly filled the great building with weaving looms and cared nought for the great literary treasure house; manuscripts and parchment torn from books were put to varied uses, including making patterns for gloves, wrapping parcels, making bungs for beer-barrels and scouring guns. Stumpe went on to make a vast fortune, married his daughter off to the aristocracy, and perhaps to make amends for his earlier philistine behaviour, gave the great nave of the Abbey to the town as a parish church. What remains is lovely, with a splendid porch with fine, intricate Norman carving and a simple and elegant interior of the same period.

Malmesbury went on to establish itself as a centre of excellence in the manufacture of silk, gloves and lace and there are some fine Cotswold stone houses from the 17th and 18th century that bear testament to the wealth of those who dealt in these trades.

South of the M4 lies a mecca for tourists to this area of the county. **Castle Combe** is almost impossibly pretty, with its immaculate grouping of houses of golden Cotswold stone, thatch, and tile, trout-laden stream, church, old market cross, and manor house set below wooded hills, where a castle once stood. It looks like a film set, indeed it has been used as one, but its original prosperity came from weaving.

Chippenham was once the site of a Saxon palace, which would appear to have been a comfortable and hospitable establishment since the normally alert King Alfred was caught napping by the Danes, whilst spending Christmas here in 877 AD. Chippenham's greatest attraction to me is **Maude Heath's Causeway**. Maude was a market woman who, in the reign of Henry VII would make her way to **Chippenham** from her home in **Langley Burrell**, carrying heavy baskets full of eggs and butter. The roads in those far off days were generally appalling and the fact that most of the area was low-lying, boggy and riven with streams did not help matters. The good Maude was evidently industrious, far-sighted and charitable for, when she died, in 1474, she left all her savings to build and endow a cobbled footpath between Wick Hill and Chippenham Clift, linking the little villages of the Avon Valley with their principal market. She is commemorated not only by her Causeway, but also by a statue set high on a column on Wick Hill and by an inscription near Chippenham church which reads:

*'Hither extended Maude Heath's gift,
For where you stand is Chippenham's Clift'*

Going south west towards Bath from Chippenham you would come to the little town of **Corsham**. Nothing very exciting about it but it is a friendly place and a good base for anyone wanting to be close to the incomparable Bath but preferring to stay in the countryside. Just along the A420 from Chippenham and almost at the junction with the A46 is the small village of **Cold Ashton**, also worth a visit although just over the border from Wiltshire.

Due south you will come to another pretty place,**Melksham**. A quiet little town living up to Wiltshire's sleepy image. At one time however it had aspirations to be a Spa but did not succeed.Bath was already firmly established but it did mean that some very attractive Regency houses were built which can be seen today. It is a thriving market town and became prosperousfrom the Cloth Weaving Industry. You can see Weavers' Cottages in Canon Square and two Roundhouses in Lowbourne and Church Street where wool was stove-dried.

To the east of Chippenham is **Calne**. Once again weaving was the original basis of prosperity but when the Industrial Revolution ended that trade, it became famous for bacon-curing and the production of sausages and pies. This came about through the enterprise of a local family of butchers, the Harrises. At the time, the town was on the principal route for livestock being driven from the West to London and among the animals were large quantities of Irish pigs, having been off-loaded at Bristol. The Harris family realised that if they bought the pigs at Calne, before they became weary and lost weight on their long trot to London, then the pork would be of superior

Chapter Two

quality. From 1770 until the 1980's, their factory dealt with literally millions of those versatile beasts of whom it is said, 'everything can be used except the grunt.' Economic and regulatory factors conspired to close the factory and the only memorial to this once great business that made the name of Calne synonymous with bacon, is a bronze pig by the small shopping precinct.

Two miles to the south-west is the great estate of **Bowood**, home of the Marquesses of Lansdowne since 1754. Robert Adams spent eight years enlarging and improving Bowood House while Capability Brown was at work on the gardens and glorious parkland. The house has fine collections of sculpture, paintings and costumes. There is a Laboratory in which Dr Joseph Priestly discovered oxygen in 1774, a fine library and chapel, but undoubtedly the real glory is the setting, the wonderful park and gardens, over ninety acres of which are open to visitors.

Lacock Abbey was founded in 1232 by Ela, Countess of Salisbury, the grieving widow of William Longspee. An Augustinian order flourished there until the Dissolution, when it fell into the hands of one William Sharington, a man described as 'being of dubious character'. Fortunately, he also had excellent taste and did not go in for the usual large scale demolitions that most of the ecclesiastical property developers of that time seemed to enjoy. Indeed, such additions that he had made were very well-executed and in perfect harmony with the preserved Abbey. The Talbot family were next on the scene, but not without incident; Sir William's niece, Olivia, was being secretly courted by young John Talbot and in a scene reminiscent of Romeo and Juliet, she offered to leap from the battlements of the abbey church to join her suitor below.

The young man not believeing that she would jump told her to go ahead. The young Miss Sharrington, however was no simpering ninny and happily leapt into her lover's arms, flattening him to the ground. The story goes that 'she cried out for help, and he was with difficulty brought to life again. Her father told her that since she had made such a leap she should e'en marry him.' The Talbots were fine stewards of both Abbey and the village of **Lacock** and in 1944 Miss Matilda Talbot presented both, together with 284 acres of land to the National Trust. There is no building later than the 18th-century in the winding streets of grey stone and half-timbered cottages. The perpendicular church, dedicated to St Cyriac, has an elegant interior and beautiful east window. **The George** is one of the oldest continuously licensed pubs in England while **The Sign of the Angel** dates back to the 14th century. A stone barn contains a museum dedicated to William Fox-Talbot, pioneer of photography. One cannot help but wonder what he would think of his invention now as yet another coach-load of tourists arrive with motor-driven self-focussing cameras at the ready.

Another lovely house lies some six miles to the south-west at **Great Chalfield**. **Great Chalfield Manor** was built about 1480 by a prosperous wool-merchant, one Thomas Tropenell. Now under the care of the National Trust, the Manor is one of the loveliest houses of its era, lying in rich meadowlands on the edge of a moat.

Tropenell's wealth came from the same source as that of the neighbouring town of **Bradford-on-Avon** - wool. It is hard in these days of man-made fibres and multi-national fashion corporations to appreciate just how important fleece was to medieval life; suffice it to say that there were no other fibres that were so adaptable or so economical to produce and that the best wool came from the backs of English sheep raised on the chalk downlands. Until the early Middle Ages, wool was the country's principal export; later, with the development of the weaving trade, finished cloth, took that position. An indication of the little town's one time importance in this vital trade is the fact that the Yorkshire wool and textile town of Bradford was named after it.

It is a charming, picturesque town today with some wonderful buildings. The medieval Shambles is now a charming shopping area, full of antique shops and tea-rooms, light-years removed from its original purpose as the place where the town's slaughter-men worked. Wherever you go through the twisting winding streets there is always something to interest and delight.

To understand the history of **Trowbridge**, now the administrative centre of Wiltshire, a position gained by virtue of its old rail links, make a visit to **Trowbridge Museum** in the Civic Hall where the life and times of the community is well recorded.

Heading south and within sight of the White Horse at **Westbury**, the gentle countryside seems so peaceful and idyllic, the villages so friendly and welcoming that it is hard to imagine what life must have been like when that ancient Anglo-Saxon chronicler set down his despairing account of anarchy and misrule. Yet many of the small communities one drives through existed then and it is a tribute to the spirit and purpose of their habitants that they survived.

At **Hawkeridge**, there is a fine example of those characteristics that brought the countrymen and women of Wiltshire through the worst of times to the best of times. It is not the saga of a wealthy wool-merchant or rich clothier who became landed gentry, but a rather more modest account: in 1851, Mr Ephraim Dole and his wife Sarah invested their savings into converting three labourer's cottages into an ale-house. Nearly one hundred

Chapter Two

and fifty years later **The Royal Oak** is still going strong, complete with skittle-alley and dining room. Just goes to show that 'there ain't no flies on Wiltshire volk...'

HAMPSHIRE

Michael Drayton, a Warwickshire contemporary of Shakespeare, intended nothing derogatory in his description of one of England's finest counties. In ancient times, the thickly wooded downland of the northern part of the county must have been something of a procine paradise for the hirsute and thick-set wild boar, rootling amongst the myriad oaks in a never ending quest for acorns and other such delicacies. No true son of the county has ever objected to the sobriquet of Hampshire Hog, for the long vanished beast represented those qualities of independence, nimbleness and strength that has enabled the area to cope amd come to terms with both invasion and innovation.

Romans, Danes, Saxons and Normans found the rolling countryside much to their liking, whilst in recent times, industry and urban development have stamped their mark on the landscape. Nevertheless, adjacent to the roar of the motorway and the bustle of the conurbations, there exists a seemingly timeless world rich in history and bucolic charm. The Wild Boar of Hampshire, had he been somewhat less tasty and rather more intelligent, would still find much to please him.

An apt example of this happy balance is to be found in and around the county town of **Winchester.** The M3 noisily snakes it's way past to the east of the town, cutting a giant's furrowthrough the chalk downs. Motorways may not be the most attractive of man's creations, but they are far from being the worst; merely the 20th century equivalent of the railway bringing life and prosperity, even in these difficult times.

Winchester was once the capital of England until it was supplanted by Westminster (London). It is the county town of Hampshire and rich in historic associations and remains with a wealth of fine old architecture but it is not somewhere in which one feels trapped in a time-warp or historical 'experience'. The city bustles and flourishes; there is room for both tourist, citizen and trader. Much of the city centre has been set aside for pedestrians and it is a real pleasure to meander amongst the thoroughfares and narrow medieval streets, enjoying the wealth of shops and buildings, yet never being far from greenery or running water, for the River Itchen, one of the finest trout rivers, flows rapidly through the city towards the water-meadows to the south.

The great grey Cathedral dominates; at 556 feet, it is the longest medieval churh in Europe. Magnificent and awe-inspiring, it was founded in 1079 and consecrated in 1093. Over the centuries it has beome a graceful melange of styles, reflecting the energy, determination and skill of those who built 'to the greater glory of God'. The broad lawns and fine buildings of the Close set off the ancient Cathedral to perfection. To my mind, one of the greatest glories of English cathedral liturgy is to be found in it's music and Winchester's choristers are trained at the Pilgrim School, with its fine Pilgrim's Hall, worth visiting for its magnificent hammer-beamed roof that dates back to the early 14th century. I can remember reading that Sir Andrew Lloyd-Webber used to visit the Cathedral regularly when he lived nearby and found much inspiration for his own work from the music that poured out.

Education has long been an integral part of ecclesiastical life. In 1382, Bishop William of Wykeham founded **Winchester College** which is to be found south of the Close. 600 years later, the school is still going strong and using many of the same buildings. You will find a profusion of interesting museums to visit, good restaurants, old inns and shops. Although Winchester places a strong emphasis on preservation and heritage, its real charm comes from the fact that it possesses a past that is truly alive; clerics still tread the cloisters, scholars are still in the school-room and quadrangle, soldiers stamp the parade-ground, and traders hawk their wares in the market place.

Sport and recreation are strong in Hampshire traditions, the ethos of 'work hard, play hard' obviously appealing to the county character, yet even in play it is hard to escape a sense of the past. For example in the village of **Littleton**, to the north-east of Winchester has a recreation area which seems to accommodate an amazing range of sport including Cricket, Tennis, Bowls, Football and Croquet and closeby are some grassy mounds which are Bronze Age burial chambers dating from perhaps 1000 BC. As I watched children play, it was strange to reflect that those earthworks were created at about the same time King David ruled from Jerusalem.

Skirting the north of Winchester and heading east, I crossed the M3 and almost immediately found myself in fine countryside. Woods and coverts speckled the broad acres of rich plough and pasture through which ran the gin-clear waters of the Itchen. My first stop was at **Alresford** (pronounced Allsford), a delightful, predominantly Georgian town, whose fortunes were founded on the 14th-century wooltrade In more recent time, the inhabitants turned to the cultivation of watercress and because of the importance of the industry, the Mid-Hants Railway became known as **The Watercress Line**. A victim of Dr Beeching's now infamous cuts, the railway has been happily restored by dedicated individuals and is now one of Hampshire's most

Chapter Two

popular - and most useful - attractions. The steam railway runs via **Ropley, Medstead and Four Marks**, to the market town of **Alton**.

South of Alresford I came across another example of 'living history'. At **Tichborne**, the Tichborne Dole, in the form of a gallon of flour, bread or money has been handed out yearly to each deserving adult since the 12th century. It is said that the custom originated with the dying Lady Isabella who begged her husband Sir Roger Tichborne, to grant her enough land to care for the sick and the needy. In reply, Sir Roger, a chauvinist if ever there was one, took a flaming brand from the fire and told his sick wife that 'she could have as much land as she could crawl round before the flame was extinguished'.

Astonishingly she managed to cover some 23 acres before the flame burnt out, and the land thus enclosed is known to this day as The Crawles. Tradition has it that tragedy will befall the family if Lady Isabella's request for the Dole is ever ignored, and, astonishingly, on the few rare occasions that this has happened, the consequences have been singularly unpleasant.

Close by lie the small and attractive villages of **Hinton Ampner** and **Kilmeston**. The wonderful countryside provides a fitting setting for the handsome facade and beautiful gardens of **Hinton Ampner House**. The house, its origins going back to the Middle Ages, has been re-built several times - the last time as recently as 1960. Now in the care of the National Trust, the house is a tribute to the dedicated persistence of one man, Ralph Dutton, the last Lord Sherborne. In 1936 he lovingly restored the house and its contents. In 1940, he relinquished the house to a girl's school, and in 1960 he saw the house destroyed by fire. Undeterred, he started again to rebuild and refurbish and the house is now immaculately maintained and has fine displays of Regency furniture, pictures and paintings.

It is difficult when writing a guide to this part of the world to avoid the over-use of the word 'attractive'. So many of the small villages and hamlets nestling in the chalk downland catch the eye and are worthy of mention; not necessarily because they are linked with historical sites or notable personages, or because they possess a fine church or noble house, but simply because of their charm and character - their very individuality attracts. Six miles east along the A272, I turned south to visit **East Meon**, a village, which to me, represents the epitome of the Hampshire downland village. Old Izaak Walton fished the trout-rich waters of the River Meon, which rises from the chalk not far from the village to run under and beside the main street. The Norman church is one of the finest buildings of its type and set to perfection above the village in what was once a bishop's deer park.

I wandered roughly south-east from here to where the landscape is dominated by the imposing mass of **Butser Hill**. At nearly 900 feet, it is the highest point in the western end of the South Downs and is contained within **Queen Elizabeth Country Park**. Jointly administered by Hampshire County Council and the Forestry Commission, it is an admirable example of how an area can be successfully managed to incorporate a multitude of quite different interests. Recreation, forestry, conservation and education all take place within the 1,400 acres which is liberally strewn with nature trails, bridle ways and woodland walks I was fascinated by a modern reconstruction of an Iron Age farm of around 300BC, partly based on information gathered from local excavations. Crops of the period are grown here and it was intriguing to learn that the prehistoric varieties of wheat produce have nearly twice the protein content of today's. Not only that, but experiments have shown that yield per acres would have been not far off our modern figures - so much for selective breeding and generic engineering!

Petersfield is a handsome market town that has much to offer, but has suffered heavily since theintroduction of the internal combustion engine; too many people pass through and never stop to investigate. In a sense, it was ever thus since the town sits astride the main Portsmouth to London road and was an important coaching stop long before the car was invented. In the square, there is a heroic statue of William III on horseback, dressed for some odd reason as a Roman emperor.

North of the town, there is some of the finest scenery to be found in the South of England. Around **Steep**, and further north at **Selborne**, the remarkable landscape features great beech 'hangers', great clumps of mature trees hanging (hence the name) precipitously over almost sheer chalk inclines that run down to a base of greensand rock. Known as 'Little Switzerland', it is an area of great beauty and contrasts favourably with the more serene charms of the **Meon Valley**.

Selborne is, of course, the mecca for all English naturalists. It was the birthplace and home of Gilbert White (1720-93), four times curate of the church and author of that delightful classic 'The Natural History and Antiquities of Selborne'. Published in 1789, it is based on his forty years of observations of the wildlife, plants and habitat found in the immediate vicinity. The book, in the form of letters to the interested parties, has a singular freshness and charm which reflects the enthusiasm and character of the man. His old home, The Wakes, contains much relating to his studies, and also houses collections belonging to a later owner, the explorer Francis Oates, uncle of Captain Oates who perished with Scott on the expedition to the South Pole in 1912. The joint exhibitions are housed together as **Gilbert White's House and Garden and The Oates Exhibition**.

Chapter Two

Leaving the Selborne area, where the National Trust has done so much to preserve and maintain the landscape, other literary and botanical connections are to be found a few miles further north. At **Chawton, Jane Austen's House** provides an insight into the life led by the novelist and her family from 1809 to 1817, while she wrote or revised her six great novels. The delightful garden surrounding the house contains many old fashioned varieties of flowers and visitors are welcome to picnic on the lawns.

Nearby **Alton**, a busy and good looking market town, is home to the **Curtis Museum** named after William Curtis, the founder of the Botanical Magazine. As well as exhibits relating specifically to Curtis, the museum possesses excellent displays relating to local industry and crafts and all manner of historical exhibits including the exquisite **Alton Buckle**, a 1500 year old item of Saxon jewellery. There are also exhibitions of children's games, toys, silver and pottery. At **Beech**, just to the south of Alton you will find a quiet hamlet which offers hospitality at **Glen Derry**.

My next destination was amongst the big wooded downland that lies close to the border with Berkshire and to the south of Newbury. Trees fringe wide expanses of chalk soil either under cultivation or down to rich pasture. This is a county of quiet wealth and great estate, with small villages, hamlets and farms scattered across the countryside.

At **Highclere** a steep climb up **Beacon Hill** is worthwhile for the splendid view over the Downs. The summit is crowned by an Iron Age hill-fort and the grave of the fifth Earl of Caernarvon, who, with Howard Carter, led the expedition to find the tomb of Tutankhamun. The Earl's palatial home, **Highclere Castle** lies close to the foot of the hill surrounded by lovely parkland and laid out by the inimitable Capability Brown. The Castle, the largest mansion in the county, was rebuilt in the middle of the last century and is renowned for the richness and variety of its interior decoration.

On the subject of decoration, I recommend a visit to the **Sandham Memorial Chapel** at **Burghclere**, to view the paintings by Stanley Spencer (1891-1959). They are considered to be the most important of English murals. They reflect on the futility and horror of war and were painted between 1926 and 1932; the chapel was built in memory of Lieutenant H.W. Sandham who died in the First World War.

The largest of the 'Cleres' is **Kingsclere**, at the foot of **Watership Down** - made famous by the author Richard Adams. His hero was a rabbit, but for many years mine was a horse, the great Derby winner Mill Reef. He was trained at Kingsclere and throughout the area, studs and racing stables breed and train in an endeavour to produce another such equine star.

The most notable of Hampshire's rivers is The Test, and seven miles south of Highclere lies the attractive ancient town of **Whitchurch**. Here the fast running alkaline waters once served both sport and industry, providing power for silk-weaving and at nearby **Laverstock**, for the manufacture of bank-note paper. Both industries have survived and **The Silk Mill** is beautifully preserved and open to the public with a shop well worth visiting; not surprisingly the banknote contract with the Bank of England dates back to 1727 and continues to this day.

The nearby town of **Andover** is representative of much of the change occurring within the County in recent times. The area has been home to man since ancient times; at **Danebury**, together with some fascinating reconstructions and audio-visual displays. Andover was first recorded in 955AD and grew to become a prosperous market town and coaching centre but perhaps the most dramatic changes in the town's history occurred in the early 1960's when it became an overspill area from London. However, it must be said that Andover has not suffered quite so badly at the hands of the planners as have other such communities within Hampshire; the handsome town centre, with its market place, guildhall of 1825, fine Victorian parish church of St Mary's and numerous coaching inns, have survived. The coaches, with post horns blowing and horses snorting, no longer rumble down the high street, but it is nonetheless a cheerful and lively place.

Thatch is common throughout the area and doubtless owes its origins to the readily available supply of reed from along the river banks. The splendidly named Wallops, (the name means, rather disappointingly, 'valley of the stream') also have a wealth of thatched cottages. Strung along the valley of Wallop Brook, the three villages retain a wealth of character and tradition, with **Nether Wallop** being noted for its fine Saxon wall paintings in the church, **Over Wallop** for a magnificent 15th century font, and **Middle Wallop** for its **Museum of Army Flying**. This award winning museum houses a unique collection of flying machines, equipment and displays depicting the history of Army Aviation since the end of the last century, from balloons to kites to the latest in helicopters.

It is a truly lovely part of England with plenty of footpaths for the walker and bridleways for the rider. At **Stockbridge**, the Test flows under the London to Salisbury road and the wide main street reflects its past as a drover's town.

Income, and not an inconsiderable one at that, is unfortunately a necessity to enable one to fish much of the Test, and on the rare occasions that private stretches of river come on the market they change hands for quite astronomical sums. Even if you are not interested in the 'gentle art of

Chapter Two

the angle', a walk along the accessible sections of the river bank will offer a clue to the extraordinary costs involved. The water is alkaline, crystal clear and the brown trout thrive growingprodigiously within the food rich waters whilst the banks, feeder streams, wiers and sluice-gates are immaculately kept and maintained; skilled work on such a scale does not come cheap. Sadly, the river, like so many of its kind is under threat. The rapidly increasing populations of the new urban developments within the country require water for both domestic and industrial use and increased abstraction by the water companies mean a decrease in flow and greater threat of pollution.

I like the village of **Broughton** close to Stockbridge surrounded as it is by so much history - the hillfort of Woolbury for example from which there are stunning views.

My journey around North Hampshire ended close to where it began, just a few miles to the west of the ancient capital of Wessex. In 1201, a group of followers of St Augustinian established a priory in one of the most idyllic situations imaginable. **Mottisford Abbey** became a private house after the Dissolution and work over the centuries has resulted in the present handsome Georgian south front, perfectly complemented by the wonderful gardens that sweep down to the Test. Green lawns are shaded by great trees and the celebrated rose garden contains the National Trust's collection of old-fashioned roses. It has to be said that this is the most harmonious setting of any house in England - and one can well believe it.

The River Avon, noted for the variety of its fishing (particularly its fine, though sadly declining runs of salmon) runs southward, marking the eastern boundary of the county spur. The A338, from Salisbury to Bournemouth follows the river for much of its course, passing through the attractive towns of **Fordingbridge** and **Ringwood.** Ringwood is a cheerful market town. Tourism plays an important part of the town's economy and angling is a major attraction. Many of the hotels and inns cater especially for those enthusiasts who travel from all over the country to fish the Avon and its tributaries. It is popular too with those who love the diversity of sport to be found in the waters of the Avon. Because of its depth, the river offers unrivalled opportunities to both the game-fisherman after trout, salmon or grayling, and the coarse angler, pursuing the like of the chub, pike, dace and barbel.

The town lies on the western edge of another great area of natural beauty within this county of contrast - **The New Forest.** It is an area of over 90,000 acres of heath and mixed woodland with an abundance of wildlife. Paradoxically, it is the oldest of the forests of England but that is simply because the word 'forest' is of Norman origin; it means an area set aside for hunting and the New Forest was the first of these preserves to be created by William the Conqueror. Savage penalties were exacted on those who broke the forest laws; at one time a person could be blinded for merely disturbing deer, whilst death was the automatic penalty for poaching. The modern day visitor might like to be reassured that the passing of the centuries have seen extensive modification of these draconian measures: apart from occasional necessary culling the deer are left in peace while the tourist can wander freely through much of the beautiful country. There are three distinctive habitats within the forest boundaries. The high heath-lands, covered with heather and gorse together with Scots pine and birch, give a somewhat barren impression - particularly to the motorists travelling along the main east/west route of the A31. However the lower slopes and better-drained land provides true forest in the modern meaning; superb traditional woodland planted with oak, beech, yew and thorn, producing in the summer great sweeping canopies of foliage. Finally there is the marsh land where the white cotton-grass conceals the bogs and where the alder and willow grow.

Amongst this vegetation can be found all manner of wildlife, from grouse on the high heath to the four varities of deer (Red, Roe, Fallow and the tiny Sika) who favour the woodland. Domesticanimals, their numbers strictly controlled by the Verderers, graze amongst the trees and shrubs. These include cattle, pigs, donkeys and the celebrated New Forest ponies. Mention was first made of wild 'horses' at the time of King Canute (1017-35) while some believe them to be descendants of the Jennets, the small Spanish horses which swam ashore from the wrecks of the Spanish Armada in the 16th century. Many of them are employed in the numerous riding stables and schools to be found within the forest.

Leisure is the principal 'industry' of the New Forest and much has been done to encourage its development. Picnic area, camping sites, trails, drives and paths are to be found throughout, and hotels and boarding houses, inns and pubs all do their very best to make the visitor welcome.

'Badger's Wood' is the meaning of **Brockenhurst**, a village that grew in popularity with the arrival of the railway in 1847. It has a fine Norman church with many memorials; one of which is of particular local interest. 'Brusher'Mills, who died in 1905, earned his nickname because he brushed the cricket pitch at Balmer Lawn between innings. Of singular appearane, with a grey beard, long coat and furry hat, he made his living by catching snakes, mainly adders, with his bare hands. It is said he was never bitten because he drank a bottle of rum a day and never washed !! Undoubtedly, he would have approved of his other memorial in the village, a pub named **The Snake Catcher** - although I doubt whether the customers would have enjoyed his company.

Chapter Two

A couple of miles to the south of Brockenhurst lies **Boldre**, one of the best looking villages in the New Forest, where the thatched cottages spread out along the numerous country lanes. The church is a happy mixture of Norman and early English but is most celebrated for having been the living, from 1777 to 1804, of William Gilpin. Gilpin was a contemporary of Gilbert White, and like him, a writer and naturalist.

He must have been something of a saint, for he recorded, on first arriving in the parish, that the village was 'utterly neglected by the former pastor, and, exposed to every temptation of pillage and robbery from their proximity to the deer, the game, and the fuel of the forest, for these poor people were little better than a herd of banditti.' Thirty years later, the 'herd of banditti' clubbed together to erect a memorial within the church to Gilpin's memory, a tribute earned by remarkably few vicars in English village history. There is also a memorial to the ship's company of the battle-cruiser HMS Hood, sunk in May 1941; the 1,406 officers and men are remembered in an annual service.

In her eighteen years in commission HMS Hood frequently sailed through the narrow patch of water that guards the western entrance to the Solent. **Hurst Castle**, built at the end of a shingle spit less than a mile from the Isle of Wight, was built by Henry VIII with a formidable armament of 70 guns. It can be reached on foot from **Milford on Sea**, a small but popular resort, or by ferry from the little harbour of **Keyhaven**.

The mud flats and marshes run eastward to **Lymington**, an attractive market town whose popularity attests to its position by the water and close to the southern fringes of the New Forest. Now a popular yachting centre, its elegant streets lined with nautical boutiques and smart hostelries while every inch of shore-line appears dedicated to the parking of cars or the mooring of boats, it is hard to visualise this chic little town as being the great trading port that it once was. Its origins are ancient; it has to be one of the oldest charters in England, dating back to 1150.

Although the present facade of Lymington would appear smart and leisurely, its trading past has far from disappeared; the international reputation of its yacht designers, boat builders, sail makers and marine electronic manufacturers contribute significantly to the national export market, albeitin a less obvious manner than when the quays and warehouses bustled with rude life.

The only commercial shipping that survives comes from the operation of the Lymington-Yarmouth ferry and a handfulof fishing boats.

Some five miles to the north-east, set in the Forest and at the head of a lovely stretch of river, lies **Beaulieu** (the beautiful place), founded by the Cistercian monks more than 750 years ago. Now a ruin its remains are still singularly beautiful and well-kept. The second Lord Montagu did much to preserve and his successors have carried on the tradition in like manner. The present Lord Montagu took over the Abbey and retained only the Great Gate House (now known as Palace House), the porter's lodge, the cloisters, the lay brother's dormitory and the refectory, which has long served as the parish church.

Beaulieu apart from its attraction as the site of a great religious house, lovely situation and immaculate small village is also home to the splendid **National Motor Museum**, which was founded by the present Lord Montagu in memory of his father, a pioneer motorist. Downstream from Beaulieu lies the neat little community of **Bucklers Hard**, a single wide street of Queen Anne cottages that runs down to the river. Originally created by a Montagu for the importation and refining of sugar, political events in the West Indies made the development obsolete. Instead the site became one of the most famous naval shipyards in Britain, building many of the Royal Navy's most famous ships, including Nelson's favourite command, the Agamemnon. Today, yachts moor where the ships grew upon their slipways and **The Maritime Museum** at the top of the village recounts its past glories.

Exbury Gardens, on the opposite bank of the river, are made up of 200 acres of the most stunning displays of shrubs, trees and flowers. Particularly beautiful are the spring-time displays of the noted Rothschild collection of rhododendrons, azaleas, magnolias and camellias.

A meandering cross-country drive brings one back to the heart of the New Forest, to it's capital **Lyndhurst**. This pleasant little town is the administrative headquarters of the Forest; the Verderer's Court meets six times a year at the Queen's House which is also the headquarters of the Forestry Commission. At **The New Forest Museum and Visitor Centre**, an excellent introduction to the history, customs, traditions, flowers and fauna of the area is provided through the medium of displays and audio-visual presentations.

To my mind **Minstead** is the perfect New Forest village and it is here that Arthur Conan Doyle is buried. Although best known for his Sherlock Holmes stories, he also wrote many fine historical novels. His principal character in 'The White Company' becomes the spelndidly-titled Socman of Minstead, and Doyle obviously had much affection for the place for he and his wife spent several years there.

Chapter Two

Heading eastwards, after the peace and tranquillity of the forest glades, the heavy traffic rumbling towards **Southampton** comes as an unpleasant shock. The city, much of it modern , appears initially as an industrial sprawl, with pylons marching along the low marshy ground towards the tall cranes that indicate the presence of the docks. Further investigation of this unprepossessing facade is richly rewarding; Southampton is a city that rewards the inquisitive - its history is ancient and its treasures many.

Although the M27 and its associated developments are essential to the livelihood of this area ofthe country, there is no doubt that the great swathe of countryside that it occupies is lost to us forever; nevertheless charming pockets of rural calm are to be found with little trouble and often lie remarkably close to the motorway.

Equally, if you have small children in tow who are not enamoured of churches and museums, then there are plenty of suitable entertainments. Both forms of attractions can be found in close proximity to each other, just off Junction 2 of the M27. **Paultons Park** is 140 acres of gardens and woodland that was once part of a large estate and has now been transformed into a family leisure park with fairground rides, boating lake, aviary, pet's corner and numerous other features that appeal particularly to the young.

Of the many villages that put Southampton at the end of their address, I found **Droxford** on the A32 close to **Bishops Waltham**, a pleasant place, much of it Georgian. Here Izaak Walton, whose daughter married the rector of the village, spent many happy hours. The old hostelry **The White Horse**, has an extraordinary history going back some five hundred years. It is seldom that ladies are invited to visit the men's loos but here I was shown a huge forty foot well! It was used by Churchill and his staff when he was planning and making preparations for the D-Day landings of World War II. Apparently he approved of the food and that reputation has continued until today.

The River Test flows south through the town of **Romsey**, where it once provided the power for milling and water for the many breweries. The town grew around the building of **Romsey Abbey**, founded in 907AD by Edward the Elder for his daughter, Ethelflaeda. Sixty years later, it was re-founded as a Benedictine nunnery by King Edgar. The abbey church was begun in the early part of the 12th century and construction continued over the next hundred years; it is second only to Durham cathedral as the finest Norman building in England.

The North Aisle acted as the townspeople's church and they must have been more than fond of the building and its wonderful proportions because, at the Dissolution, they raised the sum of one hundred pounds to

Dorset, Wiltshire, Hampshire

save it. The conventual buildings were destroyed but the church was saved; a wonderful bargain which is recorded by the Bill of Sale being displayed inside.

The peaceful tranquillity of the abbey is a cheerful contrast to the bustling little market town surrounding it. Some idea of the town's history can be gained in the **King John's House**, a 13th century stone upper-hall house containing a small museum. Tudor, Georgian and Victorian domestic architecture are to be found throughout the town centre and the local Preservation Trust has done an excellent job.

Broadlands, to the south of the town, once belonged to the Abbey. The Palladian style mansion was remodelled for the Palmerston family (a statue of the third Viscount who became Prime Minister stands in Romsey market place) by Capability Brown, who also laid out the surrounding parkland. It was later the home of Earl Mountbatten until his tragic death, and the stables have been converted to an exhibition of his life and career.

From Romsey it is easy to visit the **Hillier Arboretum** at **Ampfield**, where a world renowned display of rare and beautiful plants is set in 160 acres together with a magnificent collection of trees and shrubs.

The reformer William Cobbett (1763-1835) farmed at **Botley** to the east of Southampton and described it as 'the most beautiful village in the world.' Much has changed since he penned those words but the large village still retains a rural atmosphere. An important market was held here for many years and at one time there were fourteen inns catering to the coach and carriage trade. Two of them still survive, **The Bugle** and **The Dolphin**, as does the mill, the only one in Hampshireto be listed in the Domesday Book and still working. Until the 1930's small trading vessels would come up the River Hamble to Botley to load timber and corn.

I think Cobbett would have approved of the **Upper Hamble Country Park** to the south of Botley. This is a clever blend of working farm and preserved wood and marshland: bridle paths and walkways allow almost unlimited access and the traditional farm buildings house livestock as well as displays of old farm machinery.

The lower reaches of the Hamble River must contain more yachts than any other waterway in the world. A forest of masts bristle upwards from the marinas and moorings that run the entire length of the river, from Swanwick Bridge to the rivermouth. At first sight it hardly seems possible for any of them to move, but on closer inspection a reasonably wide channel is revealed, running up the middle of the rows of moored pleasure craft.

Chapter Two

Like Lymington, the industry on and alongside the water is yachting and from the boatyards have come many notable vessels, including America's Cup yachts and record-breaking power boats. Two pubs, **The Jolly Sailors** at **Burlesden**, and **The Bugle** at **Hamble**, are ideally situated for eating and drinking and watching life on the river go by.

Both villages were once renowned for ship-building and The Elephant, Nelson's ship at the Battle of Copenhagen was built next to the Jolly Sailors; the boatyard still exists there and proudly carries the same name.

Of course, the name of Nelson will always be associated with one ship in particular, that of HMS Victory, both she and many other links with the Royal Navy are to be found less than ten miles to the east, at **Portsmouth**. 'Pompey', as it is affectionately known to both servicemen and natives alike, is situated on a peninsula that projects southwards between the two natural harbours of Portsmouth on the western side and Langstone to the east.

Like its civilian counterpart, Southampton, Portsmouth enjoys certain natural advantages: there is deep water throughout a large part of the harbour, the Isle of Wight offers shelter from much of the Channel weather and the narrow entrance is easily defended. These assets were first recognised by the Romans who ignored the site of present day Portsmouth and sailed right up to the top of the harbour, landing at what is now **Porchester**. Here they built **Porchester Castle**, the best preserved Roman fortress in northern Europe.

Undoubtedly the best place to start a tour of the city and its heritage is at **The Royal Dockyard** which houses three of the world's major maritime attractions as well as an excellent museum. Indisputably the most famous of the three is ,**HMS Victory**, Nelson's flagship at Trafalgar. Beautifully restored and maintained she still serves as Flagship to the Commander-in-Chief, Portsmouth. Once on board, it is not hard to imagine the appalling conditions in which officers and men lived and worked, fought and died. Close by are the impressive remains of the **Mary Rose**, complete with exhibits of thousands of artefacts salvaged from the ship. The third historical ship is **HMS Warrior**, who saw no battle action, but was the world's first steam-powered iron-hulled warship and was launched in 1860.

No visitor to the Dockyard should leave without viewing the excellent **Royal Naval Museum**, which contains much of interest relating to the Navy over the centuries. Other aspects of Naval and Military life are displayed in **Fort Nelson** near **Fareham**, the splendid **Royal Marines Museum** in Eastney Barracks on the Southsea front, **The D-Day Museum** which is adjacent to **Southsea Castle**, and **The Royal Naval Submarine Museum** across the water at **Gosport** (a good excuse to get afloat and see something of the harbour itself).

For those with young children, **Southsea**, the southern tip of the peninsula, has much to offer with its promenade, beach and common, which includes a boating lake and attractive gardens. Pleasure cruises around the Solent depart from **South Parade Pier** which, true to its Edwardian beginnings, offers entertainment seven nights a week. Alongside **Clarence Pier** the only hover-craft passenger service in the country runs to the Isle of Wight.

One tends to forget the virtues of **Hayling Island** especially for the holiday maker. It is a residential area as well as being the home of hotels, holiday parks and all the fun of the fair, especially for families.

North of Portsmouth one rapidly finds oneself back in the quiet charm of rural Hampshire. One moment it is all hustle and bustle with lorries, coaches and cars shooting past, while the next moment the scenery changes to narrow lanes, rolling green fields and small rural communities. A pleasant meandering drive westwards brings one to **Hambledon**, an isolated red-brick village celebrated as the early home of cricket,and in recent times for the fine vineyards planted on the chalk slopes behind the village. Cricket actually began some two miles to the north-east, on **Broadhalfpenny Down**, where Hambledon Cricket Club was the parent of the celebrated Marylebone Cricket Club. Hambledon's finest moment came in 1777; they played All-England and beat them by an innings and 168 runs. It is interesting to note that they played for the huge sum of one thousand pounds.

To the south of **Hambledon** is **East Meon** which to me represents the epitome of a Hampshire downland village. Izaak Walton fished the trout rich waters of the River Meon which rises from the chalk not far from the village to run under and beside the main street. A good and God-fearing man, he doubtless worshipped at East Meon Church, one of the finest Norman buildings of its type and set to perfection, built above the village which once was a bishop's deer park. The beautiful mellow stonework contains a Tournai marble font, wondefully carved and an unusual stained glass window depicting the patron saints of all the Allied Countries that took part in the First World War. The Court House, south east of the church is said to have been built about 1400 but the origins of the village are obviously far earlier, and reputedly it was the first community to be mentioned in the Domesday Book. Like all good villages it has an excellent hstelry, **Ye Olde George Inn.** It has charm, character and comfort complementing the warm welcome and excellent cuisine. Old Izaak may have been a Puritan but he

Chapter Two

was no kill joy and I have no doubt he would have enjoyed this inn. The furthest point east in Hampshire is **Emsworth** once upon a time noted for its oysters. Unfortunately in the beginning of the 19th century it was dealt a body blow, when oysters supplied for a banquet in Winchester were found to carry typhoid, resulting in a lot of deaths. Those days are long gone and this busy little place has become a yachting centre with excellent facilities for boat building.

It seems only fitting in this area of England so riddled with contrast to finish with ;'something completely different'. A little to the west is an area of gentle downland, once the site of a great estate belonging to the brother of Henry VIII's third wife, Jane Seymour. In this quintessentially English landscape, the visitor can come face to face with one of the world's rarest animals. Such exotica as Przewalski's horse, the snow leopard, or a scimitar-horned ibex are all to be foundwithin the confines of **Marwell Park**. The park is a charitable foundation that exists to promote breeding and conservation of rare animals that are threatened with extinction. It is both a zoo, as well as a scientific and educational trust with the administration housed in the Tudor facade of Marwell House. For the young and young-at-heart, it is a splendid place to visit and a fine example of the many and diverse attractions that South Hampshire has to offer.

THE FRENCH HORN
The Butts, Alton,
Hampshire GU34 1RT

Tel: 01420 83269

    Hampshire is a delightful county with wonderful scenery, small villages, historical houses, parks and gardens. It is part of the commuter belt, and after a hard days work there is nothing better than to know you are going home to the peace and tranquillity of this lovely part of the country. One particular town at the source of the River Wye is Alton, a charming place steeped in history. The church, St. Lawrences, is largely 15th century but has an extraordinary tower dating back to 1070. If you look closely you will be able to see bullet marks in the church door, there are from a battle that took place here during the Civil War. The Allen Gallery has a rather large collection of English ceramics and pottery on display that date from 1550 to the present day. The Curtis Museum is a must as it chronicles the day to day goings on of local life, there are wonderful displays of dolls and doll's houses, and of 19th century botany.
    It is in Alton you will come across a very nice hostelry known as The French Horn, itself steeped in history, the property dating back to 1746, when it was two cottages, it became a pub in the early 1800's. Many of the original features remain including in the main bar, the large beam that marked the wall between the two cottages, the huge fire place with its large bricks in the hearth, bread ovens and roasting spit, which is clothed in brasses and in the winter a log fire roars away. Nigel and Helen Collins extend a warm and friendly welcome as you walk in the door, the French Horn is comfortable and has a nice atmosphere. There are 2 delightful double bedrooms both have the luxury of ensuite facilities and are attractively furnished, for your convenience there is a hair dryer, colour television and a plentifully supplied tea and coffee tray. After an excellent nights sleep in your comfy bed, you descend to a delicious full English breakfast with all the trimmings. The menu at The French Horn is traditional with a wide and varied choice of good wholesome food. If you require information on golf, fishing and walking, Nigel and Helen will be only to pleased to help. The French Horn has been quoted as one of the 'best value for money' pubs in Hampshire by a national newspaper. It is deffinitely not to be missed.

USEFUL INFORMATION

OPEN; All year
CHILDREN; No
CREDIT CARDS; All major cards except Amex and Diners
LICENSED; Full
ACCOMMODATION; 2 ensuite rooms
PETS; No

RESTAURANT; Traditional menu, Daily Specials, value for money,
BAR FOOD; Same menu
VEGETARIAN; At least 5 choices
DISABLED ACCESS; Yes
GARDEN; Four available

Chapter Two

BROADWATER
Amport, Nr Andover,
Hampshire SP11 8AY

Tel/Fax: 01264 772240

The village of Amport lies close to Salisbury Plain and Stonehenge, in gently rolling downland with scattered woods and copses, hedgerows and trees, only one and a half hours from London. Steeped in history it is known from Neolithic and Bronze Age; burial mounds and flint implements found in the fields that man has lived here for over five thousand years. The name Amport is derived from the Norman 'Anne de Port' which was the seat of the Marquis of Winchester and Broadwater was the residence of the Estate Manager until 1870. The 17th century Grade II listed thatched house has a wonderful atmosphere and Carolyn Mallam, your host, will make you feel part of the family in the warm and friendly oak beamed rooms. You are free to come and go whenever you wish, the spacious bedrooms are both ensuite, each with its own character and that welcoming touch fresh flowers and a plentifully supplied hospitality tray. Guests have their own sitting room with traditional fireplace and colour TV. In the dining room, where you will be served a good full English breakfast, there is a wide range of books, maps and local information to help you plan your day. A cot, iron and hair dryer are available. A baby alarm and baby sitting can be arranged. No evening meals are served but there are several local pubs which all serve food. Broadwater is wonderfully situated for anyone wanting to explore anything from the Hawk Conservancy to Stourhead, Danebury Iron Age Hill Fort to Portsmouth and the Mary Rose; Salisbury and Winchester are but a pleasant drive away. There is an abundance of wonderful gardens in the area including Mottisfont (the rose specialists), Hollington Herb Garden, Tintinhull, East Lambrook to name but a few; Carolyn will provide you with a list of places, all within an hours distance.

USEFUL INFORMATION

OPEN; *All year*
CHILDREN; *Welcome*
CREDIT CARDS; *None taken*
PETS; *No*
ACCOMMODATION; *2 ensuite rooms*

DINING ROOM; *Full English breakfast*
VEGETARIAN; *Upon request*
DISABLED ACCESS; *No*
GARDEN; *Yes*

LAINS COTTAGE
Quarley, Andover,
Hampshire SP11 8PX
Tel/Fax: 01264 889697

The small village of Quarley in the Test Valley is some six miles west of Andover and just off the A303. It is an area of great beauty with a wealth of interesting pursuits including Horseracing at Salisbury and Newbury, Fishing in the Test and Avon Valley and Flying and Motor Racing at Thruxton circuit. In the midst of the village is the 17th century thatched house known as Lains Cottage set in an acre of cottage garden with ample parking. Angela Hicks is the owner and she has a great affinity with her guests providing an instant feeling of well being when they arrive. She will help you plan you daily outings and probably suggest the New Forest or the cathedral cities of Salisbury and Winchester or a visit to Stonehenge. Her home is charmingly furnished with great taste. There are single, double and twin bedrooms available, all attractively appointed and centrally heated with colour TV and tea and coffee making facilities. The double and twin rooms have an ensuite shower and toilet or bathroom. Breakfast is a memorable meal, freshly cooked to your choice and served in the delightful dining room. The garden entices people to relax and enjoy the sun. Without doubt people staying here will be totally relaxed, comfortable and contented.

USEFUL INFORMATION

OPEN; All year
CHILDREN; Over 8 years
CREDIT CARDS; None taken
PETS; No
ACCOMMODATION; All ensuite rooms
DINING ROOM; Breakfast only
VEGETARIAN; Upon request
DISABLED ACCESS; No
GARDEN; Yes

GLEN DERRY
52 Wellhouse Road, Beech,
Alton, Hampshire GU34 4AG
Tel: 01420 83235

Glen Derry is a haven of peace and tranquillity just outside the historic market town of Alton. Not difficult to find, you take the A339 Basingstoke road from Alton's town centre and continue a short way past the turning to Winchester and shortly afterwards you will see a signpost marked Beech. Turn left here and continue until you see a bus shelter on your right, turn right into Wellhouse Road and then, after 350 yards, right into Glenderry Drive. The house is at the top of the long drive. Glen Derry can take up to six guests in one double, one family (ground floor) and one twin bedroom and these rooms are so comfortable and Alison Griffiths so welcoming that you will feel quite at home. A delicious full English breakfast is served every morning and vegetarians are well looked after. Alison will pack lunches for you if you wish and an optional Snack Supper is available. This is Jane Austen country and there is much to see about this famous writer. Sporting facilities, including gliding and golf, are near at hand as well.

USEFUL INFORMATION

OPEN; All year
CHILDREN; Very welcome
CREDIT CARDS; None taken
LICENSED; No
ACCOMMODATION; 3 rooms
DINING ROOM; Excellent breakfast
VEGETARIAN; Catered for
DISABLED ACCESS; Yes, around side of house
GARDEN; Yes
PETS; No

SWAYNES FIRS FARM
Grimsdyke, Coombe Bissett,
Salisbury, Wiltshire SP5 5RF

Tel: 01725 519240

Swaynes Firs is a small but active farm where beef cattle are kept with horses and a large variety of poultry. To those with an interest in the past it is particularly interesting because The Grimsditch runs through the farm and is thought to have been constructed in the Bronze Age (1,000BC to 500BC) for farming purposes and as a tribal boundary ditch. It is also known locallyas Grims Dyke or Devils Ditch. The farm house is so attractive with its white bay windows and pretty colour schemes inside. The rooms are spacious and have lovely views overlooking the countryside. There are three bedrooms all ensuite and with beverage trays as well as television. The large dining room welcomes you when you come down to a plentiful breakfast, either traditional English or whatever you wish for. It is always cooked to order. No evening meals here but there are plenty of eating houses in the vicinity. The large garden has ornamental duck ponds which you can see from the dining room windows. There is a summerhouse and you will see Peacocks and Bantams strutting about the lawns whilst the geese and hens hold court in the adjacent paddocks. A happy house and one from which you can easily reach Salisbury Cathedral, Old Sarum, Wilton House, Stonehenge and many other historical and ancient sites.

USEFUL INFORMATION
OPEN; All year
CHILDREN; Welcome
CREDIT CARDS; None taken
LICENSED; No
ACCOMMODATION; 3 rooms ensuite
PETS; Yes
DINING ROOM; Full English breakfast with Options
VEGETARIAN; Catered for
DISABLED ACCESS; No
GARDEN; Yes, spacious with wildlife

LANSCOMBES HOUSE HOLIDAY COTTAGES
West Milton
Bridport
Dorset

Tel: 01308 485375

These holiday cottages are all part of a 200 year old barn and farm buildings which are arranged round a courtyard. They are all fully equipped and furnished to a high standard and have views over the hills and valleys of this area of outstanding natural beauty. Although in a rural setting, it is only 3 miles to the town of Bridport and 4 miles to the sea! There are activities to suit everyone from fossil hunting to golf and there are many places of interest to visit nearby. Carol and Carl Mansfield run a working farm here and there are many tame animals which children are welcome to help with!

USEFUL INFORMATION
OPEN : All year
CHILDREN : Welcome
PETS : Welcome
CREDIT CARDS : None taken
LICENSED : Not applicable
RESTAURANT : Not applicable
BAR FOOD : Not applicable
VEGETARIAN : Not applicable
DISABLED ACCESS : Not really
GARDEN : Set in 10 acres
ACCOM: Self catering holiday cottages; 2 sleeps 4, 1 sleeps 5, 1 sleeps 6.

Dorset, Wiltshire, Hampshire

WOODSIDE PRIVATE HOTEL,
29 Southern Road, Southbourne,
Bournemouth, Dorset BH6 3SR

Tel: 01202 427213

Ann and Jeff Eslick who own and run this select family managed Hotel have a wealth of experience behind them and know exactly how to ensure everyone of their guests has a good holiday. The Woodside has a tremendous reputation for its warm and friendly atmosphere and add to that its convenient situation within three minutes from all the amenities you require. Walks along the cliffs, testing your skill on the putting green, enjoying the beaches or exploring the array of shops which will entice you to spend, all make for pleasureable days. The paths to the beaches are sometimes steep but the readily available lifts make even this simple. If you want to take off on a coach tour, Southbourne has its own booking office and pick-up point for the daily tours.

Within the hotel you will find that the pleasant residents lounge hs a colour TV and a stock of books and games whilst the small Spanish style bar, which is well stocked with both alcoholic and non alcoholic beverages is a favourite gathering point each evening. You may smoke here and in the lounge but you are asked not to smoke in the bedrooms or the dining room during meals.

The attractive bedrooms, some of which are ensuite, and all have wash hand basins, are comfortable and have tea and coffee making facilities.

Food is all important on any holiday and here you may be sure of super home-cooking with a varied menu both at breakfast and dinner. Special diets can be catered for by prior arrangement. Packed lunches may be ordered. The wine list, whilst not vast, is well chosen and priced. Themoment you arrive you will be greeted with the offer of tea or coffee - very welcome after a journey.

USEFUL INFORMATION

OPEN; *All year*
CHILDREN; *Welcome*
CREDIT CARDS; *Visa/Access*
LICENSED; *Yes*
ACCOMMODATION; *Some ensuite*
DINING ROOM; *Home-cooked, varied.*
VEGETARIAN; *By prior arrangement*
DISABLED ACCESS; *No*
PETS; *No*
GARDEN; *No*

Chapter Two

BRIDGE FARM
Lower Road, Britford,
Salisbury, Wiltshire SP5 4DY

Tel: 01722 332376

This beautiful listed building was built in three stages, starting in 1724, the date of which is on the chimney on the North end of the house. Around 1840 it was approximately doubled in size and about 1880 it was extended by another one third, the part now used by guests. It has two listed barns in the entrance yard, both of historical interest and one of which is thatched and the other has the reputation of being the last genuine corn barn built in England. The Cheese House, now a private residence, was built in 1863 to house the Cheesemaker and store the cheese until sold. Add to this two Ancient Briton settlements on the higher land of the farm and a small river running through the garden which is a loop off the Hampshire Avon, cut as a canal for navigational purposes at the construction of 'water meadows' around the main river in 1691, when dams and weirs were constructed to raise water levels. Trout and Salmon spawn in the garden area regularly each year. What a fascinating place in which to stay! Your host, Norma Hunt can tell you much more about the property as well as directing you to all the interesting places to see nearby. There is excellent fishing, golf, horse riding, cycling and wonderful walking countryside.

The accommodation delights everyone who stays here. The bedrooms are situated in the Southern end and provide a separate entity from the rest of the house. The Breakfast Room overlooking the river is an authentic farmhouse kitchen in which you are served a superb breakfast, freshly cooked and to your choice. In this friendly kitchen you can also make tea whenever you feel so inclined. One of the talking points in the room is Norma's fascinating collection of over seventy cockerels from around the World. The comfortable siting room which is entirely for the use of guests has a colour television. Each bedroom has the name of a bird. The Kingfisher room has a king size double bed, The Pheasant bedroom has twin beds and The Dove a standard size double bed. All the rooms are individually decorated and are provided with hairdriers, wraps, fan heaters etc. There is a Shower Room and a Bathroom.

USEFUL INFORMATION

*OPEN;*All the year
*CHILDREN;*Welcome
CREDIT CARDS; None taken
*ACCOMMODATION;*2dbl 1 tw

*FARMHOUSE KITCHEN;*Excellent breakfast
No evening meals
*DISABLED ACCESS;*No
*PETS;*No

YEW TREE HOUSE
Broughton,
Hampshire SO20 8AA

Tel: 01794 301227

The atmosphere which pervades Yew Tree House is warm, friendly and exceptionally inviting. This charming Grade II Listed property in which it is said Dickens was a frequent visitor, is immaculately well presented and would certainly not be out of place featured in well known monthly magazines. The bedrooms are really special and ensuite facilities are available but limited. A fresh flower arrangement enhances each bedroom as well as a tea and coffee tray. The cuisine is specially supervised and complemented by the use of fresh produce. Guests wishing to dine are asked to kindly book in advance. Vegetarians are catered for. A walled garden is a feature of this lovely property and from here is afforded a splendid view of the 17th century dovecote.

There is so much to do and see in this glorious area, it is worth noting a few of the places to visit. The ancient capital of England - Winchester with its 11th century Cathedral and 'King Arthur's Round Table'. Jane Austen died here and is buried in the Cathedral; Hampshire is known as 'Jane Austen country'. Salisbury has wonderful architecture, here again the Cathedral dominates, it's 1386 clock is believed to be the oldest working clock. It was here they filmed 'Sense and Sensibility'. The National Motor Museum founded by Lord Montagu is easily accessible, as are a wealth of beautiful villages nearby.

USEFUL INFORMATION

OPEN; All year
CHILDREN; Very welcome
CREDIT CARDS; None taken
LICENSED; No, bring your own
ACCOMMODATION; 3 rooms, 1 ensuite 1 double, 1 twin, 1 single
PETS; No
DINING ROOM; Traditional English fare open to non-residents if meal is booked
VEGETARIAN; Catered for
DISABLED ACCESS; No
GARDEN; Beautiful walled with view of dovecote

Chapter Two

BRAMLEYS
73 Marshfield Road,
Chippenham,
Wiltshire SN15 1JR

Tel: 01249 653770

With Chippenham being close to the M4, it is an ideal base for business and pleasure. The houses here are built with the lovely warm stone from the Cotswolds, including Bramleys, a large Victorian Listed building close to the town centre. This delightful house with climbing roses clinging to the walls and trailing around the windows and front door, is a family run establishment owned by Mr. & Mrs. Swatton. They have created a wonderfully relaxed and friendly atmosphere which you notice as soon as you walk through the door.

The house is well furnished with lots of wood around and antique furniture, adding to the warmth. The 5 bedrooms are very comfortable having a wash basin, central heating, colour television, towels and tea and coffee making facilities. Breakfast is an excellent home-cooked affair and plenty of it, the plate positively groans with delicious food. Evening meals are by prior arrangement, if you prefer to eat out, there are plenty of good quality restaurants in the area. Whilst staying at Bramleys you will find lots to do, there are leaflets available so you can plan you day away. Choosing the right accommodation is important, you will be more than happy you chose Bramleys.

USEFUL INFORMATION

OPEN; All year
CHILDREN; Welcome
CREDIT CARDS; None taken
ACCOMMODATION; 5 rooms
3 twin, 1 single, 1 family

DINING ROOM; Delicious very large breakfast,
Evening meal by prior arrangement
VEGETARIAN; If required
DISABLED ACCESS; Not really
PETS; No
NON SMOKING HOUSE

MANOR FARM
*Burcombe, Salisbury,
Wiltshire*

*Tel: 01722 742177
Fax: 01722 744600*

    Manor Farm is an Edwardian farmhouse built around the 1700's, it is a very impressive property indeed, thick stone walls and lovely large windows overlook a very spacious walled garden which is full of trees, flowers, shrubs and lawned areas. The guest house is owned and managed by Sue Combes, who looks after your every need and ensures you have a pleasant and enjoyable stay. There are 3 charming rooms with one shower room and toilet, tea and coffee making facilities. The farmhouse is furnished in a traditional style which is of the finest quality. In the mornings you are served an excellent full English breakfast with several variations.

    From the house there is a walk around the 'Punchbowl' which takes about an hour, as you are walking you rise to about 600ft above sea level and on a clear day you are able to see Salisbury Cathedral, truely breathtaking. Salisbury itself is a wonderful city dominated by the Cathedral, its spire rises to 404ft the highest in England. The 13th century city stands on 4 rivers, and the library here contains the original Magna Carta. Wilton is a very interesting village to explore it was one of England's first manufacturing centres, Wilton House the home of the Earls of Pembroke, stands on the site of an old abbey which was founded by Alfred the Great. With fishing, golf, riding and walking this really is a marvellous place to stay.

USEFUL INFORMATION

OPEN; March-November
CHILDREN; Welcome
CREDIT CARDS; None taken
LICENSED; No
ACCOMMODATION; 3 rooms, 1 double, 1 twin, 1 single

DINING ROOM; Traditional English fare
VEGETARIANS; Catered for
DISABLED ACCESS; No
GARDEN; Spacious walled garden
PETS; No
NON SMOKING HOUSE

Chapter Two

CHIDEOCK HOUSE HOTEL
*Main Street, Chideock,
Dorset DT6 6JN*

Tel: 01297 489242

It is said that the ghosts of Chideock House "check out" each new owner, and once deemed suitable, leave them alone. Ann and George Dunn have passed the test and run this superb hotel without any "supernatural" help! High standards are evident throughout, from tissues and bottled water in the bedrooms to the a la carte dinner menu in the restaurant. There are two luxury bedrooms with king size beds, super fittings and even dressing gowns. Ann and George have some great ideas which make this the ideal place at any time of year. Xmas break is a time of celebration, murder mystery weekends, gastronomic experiences, (definitely for me!) and golfing breaks. As this is Thomas Hardy and Jane Austin country there are Wessex Weekends which include talks, visits and performances. The house itself has immense character and dates back to when the Cromwellian, General Fairfax, used it as his headquarters during the Civil War skirmishes. It was also here the famous Chideock Martyrs were tried, prior to their execution. The bathroom in one of the bedrooms is in the "priest hole" which was discovered 25 years ago in a fire. This is a charming hotel in the heart of a charming village which offers much rest and laughter to the traveller who decides to stay.

USEFUL INFORMATION

OPEN: All year
CHILDREN: Welcome
PETS: Welcome
CREDIT CARDS: Most major taken
ACCOMMODATION: 7 rooms; 6 ensuite
RESTAURANT: A la carte menu : Open to public
VEGETARIAN: Catered for
LICENSED: Yes
DISABLED ACCESS: No
GARDEN: Small but pleasant

HAZELDENE
*62 Hurn Road,
Christchurch, Dorset BH23 2RW
Tel: 01202 486299*

There are many good reasons why you should take advantage of staying at Hazeldene, a chalet bungalow built in the 1950's with guest accommodation on the first floor. Doreen Cook is the owner of this friendly house which is an excellent bed and breakfast establishment offering one double and one twin-bedded room both with vanity units and hot and cold water, a shared bathroom and a first class breakfast. Relax in the conservatory in total peace and quiet whilst watching the birds in the garden and the squirrels dancing across the lawn. In addition Doreen has a beautiful grand piano which she encourages her guests to play. Christchurch is an ideal base for touring Dorset and Hampshire and is equally convenient for the business person. You can be sure you will be comfortable and well cared for at Hazeldene.

USEFUL INFORMATION

OPEN; All year
CHILDREN; Welcome
ACCOMMODATION; 1 dbl, 1 twin
DINING ROOM; First class breakfast
DISABLED ACCESS; No
GARDEN; Yes. Bring back a bottle of wine and sit outside in the evening

FAIRFIELD FARM
Upper Wraxall, Chippenham,
Wiltshire SN14 7AG

Tel: 01225 891750
Fax: 01225 891050

WHITEWAYS
Nimlet, Cold Ashton,
Nr Chippenham, Wiltshire SN14 8SJ

Tel: 01225 891333

Upper Wraxall is a small village tucked away in Wiltshire, yet conveniently close to the M4, the town of Chippenham, and the city of Bath. This is where Mrs. Julie McDonough has her lovely house. Fairfield Farm was built in 1901, and is a very substantial property, with large windows that look out across the sizeable well tended garden with lovely flowers, shrubs and lawn, where barbecues and badminton take place in the summer. The large airy rooms are very pleasant, and attractively decorated throughout, with an added touch of fresh flowers.

The guests sitting room has a television and lovely comfy sofa and chairs to sink into and relax. The bedrooms, 1 double and 1 twin, have their own private facilities, clock radio, hair dryer and a complimentary tea and coffee tray. The dining room is particularly delightful and here you are served the most sumptuous farmhouse breakfast cook to perfection on the Aga. Vegetarians are catered for as well with yoghurts, fruit, cereals and plenty of toast. Evening meals are not available, but no need to worry, Chippenham has a wide variety of restaurants to choose from. A very warm and friendly atmosphere awaits you at this English Tourist Board '2 Crowns Commended' Farm.

From Fairfield Farm if you take the A420 to Bristol, then turn onto the A46 to Bath, you will come Cold Ashton, a village on the Gloucester/Wiltshire border, and a lovely bed and breakfast known as Whiteways. You are greeted with an extremely warm welcome from the owner Linda Pike. The house is charming with beautiful furnishings and delightfully decorated, the views are wonderful, you gaze out across rolling countryside. The 3 bedrooms are all ensuite with comfy beds, television and a beverages tray. Linda is a wonderful cook and serves a delicious traditional large full English breakfast, the plate groans. Being so close to Bath, evening meals can be taken in one of the many restaurants. The garden is lovely and well tended, here you can sit out and admire that superb view. A stay at Whiteways is a real treat and one not to be missed.

With the M4 so close you have plenty to choose from with regard to outing and activities, whichever guest house you decide to stay at, you can be assured a relaxed and enjoyable break.

USEFUL INFORMATION

OPEN; All year
CHILDREN; Welcome
CREDIT CARDS; None taken
ACCOMMODATION; Fairfield Farm- has 1 double, 1 twin, both ensuite.
Whiteways- has 1 double, 2 twin, all ensuite
Special Rate: Two nights or more

DINING ROOM; Both guest houses serve excellent home-cooked fare. No evening meal
VEGETARIAN; Catered for
DISABLED ACCESS; Not really at either
GARDEN; Beautiful gardens
PETS; No

Chapter Two

ASHBOURNE GUEST HOUSE
47 Stour Road, Christchurch,
Dorset BH23 1LN
Tel: 01202 475574

Dorset is such a lovely county with pretty well kept villages, wonderful countryside and impressive towns, none more so than Christchurch, it is mostly Edwardian although the plan of the streets is from Saxon times, here also is a memorial to Shelley the great poet. With Christchurch being so close to the coast, watersports feature quite a lot, with sailing, yachting, surfing and water ski-ing. This is where Barbara Hamilton has her lovely guest house, situated at the end of a row of large properties, this very attractive detached house is inviting indeed. There are 8 bedrooms, 5 of which are ensuite, they all have central heating, televisions, tea and coffee making facilities, hair dryers and radio alarms. The modern furnishings compliment the house as does the decor, this all goes to create a relaxed and enjoyable atmosphere, where you feel at home in this friendly house. The spacious lounge/diner which overlooks the charming walled garden, is where you will be served delicious home-cooked meals prepared by Barbara. An evening meal is by arrangement, also by prior arrangement is an early breakfast, packed lunches and flasks. Children are welcome and there are reduced rates for them. There is a local Priory, within walking distance which is very active in the arts. Ashbourne is also central for day trips, shopping, fishing, golf and walking.

USEFUL INFORMATION
OPEN; *All year*
CHILDREN; *Welcome, with reduced rates*
CREDIT CARDS; *None taken*
LICENSED; *No*
ACCOMMODATION; *8 rooms, 5 ensuite*
PETS; *Yes, by arrangement*
DINING ROOM; *Traditional home-cooked fare, evening meal by arrangement*
VEGETARIAN; *Catered for*
DISABLED ACCESS; *No*
GARDEN; *Pleasant walled, very quiet*

'NUMBER 19'
19 Friars Road, Friars Cliff,
Christchurch, Dorset BH23 4EB

Tel: 01425 273323
International: +44 1425 273323

With the sea close by and stunning cliff walks at hand, the reason for choosing to stay at 'Number 19' is re-inforced. Many people from all over the world have enjoyed the hospitality of Howard Gage's charming house which was built almost fifty years ago. Inside it is furnished to a very high standard both for its aesthetic appeal and for comfort. The bedrooms are well appointed and the beds are very comfortable. For those wanting a quiet moment or two the garden patio with its attractive furniture is there for your use. Breakfast has been designed to please everyone. The traditional English breakfast is one you will long remember and the Continental breakfast includes ham, cheese and jam. This is a wonderful area for exploration and for the attractions that are offered by nearby Bournemouth.

USEFUL INFORMATION
OPEN; *All year*
CHILDREN; *Welcome*
CREDIT CARDS; *None taken*
GARDEN; *Large, secluded with patio furniture*
DINING ROOM; *Traditional English or Continental breakfasts. No evening meals*
VEGETARIAN; *Upon request*
DISABLED ACCESS; *1 ground floor room with nearby WC*

Dorset, Wiltshire, Hampshire

THE HOMESTEAD
114, Stoney Lane, Burton,
Christchurch, Dorset BH23 7LD

Tel: 01202 473023

The Homestead is the perfect name for this wonderful double fronted red brick house, with lovely leaded light windows. The house is approximately 100 years old and substantially built, with a very warm and welcoming atmosphere. Jenny Haine and her husband are a very friendly couple who aim to make your stay here a happy one. The furnishings throughout are modern and of excellent quality, there are 3 bedrooms, 2 double and 1 twin, one of the rooms being ensuite, all have TVs and a tea and coffee tray. The whole house is 'non-smoking'. You are served a large full English breakfast which will set you up for the day, evening meal is not available, but this is no hardship as there are an array of restaurants and pubs within the surrounding area. The Homestead has a lovely garden, which you are welcome to use. You will be kept very busy with all sorts of activities and outings, the area is teeming with things to do, golfing, walking, visiting museums, and of course being so near the coast there is sailing, water ski-ing, surfing and swimming. There are several country houses and gardens to visit. Avon Forest Country Park is a must with 580 acres of heath and woodland, a visitors centre, guided walks and wildlife displays.

USEFUL INFORMATION

OPEN; All year
CHILDREN; Welcome
CREDIT CARDS; None taken
LICENSED; No
ACCOMMODATION; 3 rooms, 1 ensuite
Non-smoking

DINING ROOM; Full English breakfast
No evening meal
VEGETARIAN; Catered for
DISABLED ACCESS; No
GARDEN; Yes
PETS; Yes

SANDY CORNER
Ogdens North, Fordingbridge,
Hampshire SP6 2QD
Tel: 01425 657295

If you want to stay in a peaceful location in the New Forest with superb open views across undulating moorland in a house that is friendly and welcoming, then you will not do better than to choose Sandy Corner. Built in about 1930 it is mellow and pretty, sitting in its own garden surrounded by trees and shrubbery. The house is comfortable with large centrally-heated bedrooms - one is on the ground floor with its own bathroom. Breakfast in the sunny dining room is generous and traditional with choices. Evening meals, home-cooked, are by arrangement.

Only two and a half miles from Fordingbridge and with a village shop and two pubs nearby as well as fishing in the River Avon, golf, riding and wonderful walks in countryside that abounds with wild life, Sandy Corner is an excellent base for a holiday or for a short break at any time of the year.

USEFUL INFORMATION

OPEN;All year
CHILDREN;No
CREDIT CARDS;None taken
ACCOMMODATION;2dbl 1 tw
2 ensuite 1 private bathroom
PETS;Well-behaved dogs welcome

DINING ROOM;Full English breakfast
Evening meals by arrangement
VEGETARIAN;By arrangement
GARDEN;Spacious

Non-smoking house

Chapter Two

DOWNSHAY FARM
*Haycrafts Lane, Harmans Cross,
Swanage, Dorset BH19 3EB
Tel: 01929 480316*

Situated on the southern slope of the valley, halfway between Swanage and Corfe Castle is this working dairy farm. Offering very high standard accommodation, Martin and Justine Pike have the ideal retreat for a quiet holiday. The house is Victorian, and is over 100 years old. Each bedroom has tea and coffee and there is a family room with TV. The local Swanage Steam Train is within easy walking distance and there are many footpaths from the farm to the bays and headlands of the coastline. The list of outdoor pursuits is quite unending, with many water sports as well as golf, riding, fishing and bird watching. This quiet rural part of Dorset has many attractions to offer it's visitors.

USEFUL INFORMATION

OPEN : Easter to October
CHILDREN : Welcome
PETS : No
ACCOMMODATION : 2 rooms ; 1 fml, 1 dbl or twin
VEGETARIAN : By arrangement
DISABLED ACCESS : No
CREDIT CARDS : None taken
GARDEN : Very pleasant

COVENTRY LODGE
*Sleight Lane,
Corfe Mullen,
Wimborne,
Dorset BH21 3HL
Tel: 01202 694197*

Coventry Lodge is to be found in Corfe Mullen near Wimborne, a large town on the south coast of Dorset. This county is very pretty with many delightful features, quiet country lanes leading to attractive villages and open spaces, the coast with the sea and safe sandy beaches, where you can take part in the many water sports on offer such as sailing, surfing, windsurfing and swimming. Coventry Lodge was built in the 1800's and is a large impressive property furnished with lovely antiques. The 3 bedrooms, 2 doubles and 1 twin, have colour television and tea and coffee making facilities, they are comfortable and individually furnished to a very high standard. After a very peaceful and relaxing sleep, you are served a full English breakfast in the marvellous country kitchen, evening meal is not available, however there are plenty of eateries within easy reach. Susanne and Michael Parkin are looking forward to welcoming you to their warm and friendly home.

USEFUL INFORMATION

OPEN; All year
CHILDREN; Welcome
CREDIT CARDS; None taken
LICENSED; No
ACCOMMODATION; 3 rooms, 2 double, 1 twin, 1 ensuite
DINING ROOM; Full English breakfast
Evening meal not available
VEGETARIAN; Catered for
DISABLED ACCESS; Not really
GARDEN; Yes welcome to browse
PETS; No

Dorset, Wiltshire, Hampshire

THREE GABLES
*11, Wickfield Avenue,
Christchurch, Dorset BH23 1JB*

Tel: 01202 481166

The aptly named Three Gables is a delightful modern double fronted property situated in a quiet residential road yet within 3 minutes walk of the High Street or the Quay, which certainly catches the eye with its mock Tudor facade, large bay leaded light windows, brightly coloured hanging baskets adorn either side of the main entrance, and spacious off road parking is available. The proprietress Mrs. Natalie Gill can be justly proud of the 'Commended' accolade bestowed on her by the English Tourist Board. She is obviously aware of the importance of presentation as this is reflected as soon as one enters this lovely house. Delightful is the word to describe the bedrooms, the bed linen and curtains being of excellent quality, the furniture modern. Each room has that all important ensuite facility and to complete the picture colour television, radio alarm, and tea and coffee makers are included. Breakfast is guaranteed to satisfy the heartiest of appetites a comprehensive selection is offered. Christchurch is an excellent centre for either long or short stays and is within easy reach of many of the wonderful tourist area's. Christchurch itself is an Edwardian town and here you will find a memorial to the poet Shelley, an ancient Priory Church and a Water Mill dating back to Saxon times. Christchurch is a mecca for anglers (game, coarse or sea) and of course a very well known area for sailing and boating. Bournemouth with its miles of sandy beaches and promenade, not forgetting its two Piers, is but a short drive. The activities and places are many and varied, including museum, galleries, theatres and cinemas. There aresome 2000 acres of gardens and parks to be wandered. The shopping centre of Bournemouth has an abundance of shops and a wide variety of restaurants to suit all tastes. The New Forest is a must for the nature lovers amongst you, here in the oldest of England's forests flora and fauna are in abundance, roaming free in this natural habitat are the ponies and deer. There is also a Butterfly Farm with its spectacularly coloured butterflies housed within very large greenhouses filled with tropical plants, visit the Aviary or Dragonfly Park or spoil yourself with a ride through the cool wooded glades in a horse drawn carriage. A visit to the Motor Museum for all car enthusiasts is not to be missed, this venue is situated in the lovely Georgian village of Beaulieu. Here also is the Palace House the home of Lord Montagu, the owner of the now famous Motor Museum where vehicles from a by-gone age up to modern times will enthral.

USEFUL INFORMATION

OPEN; *All year*
CHILDREN; *By arrangement*
CREDIT CARDS; *None taken*
ACCOMMODATION; *5 ensuite rooms*
PETS; *No*
PARKING; *Spacious off road*

DINING ROOM; *English fare, comprehensive choice*
VEGETARIAN; *Catered for by arrangement*
DISABLED ACCESS; *Limited ground floor rooms*
GARDEN; *Cultivated walled and private*

Chapter Two

LOWER LYNCH HOUSE
Kingston Hill, Corfe Castle,
Nr. Wareham, Dorset BH20 5LG

Tel: 01929 480089

Corfe Castle is a delightful village with very friendly inhabitants and part of the community is Lower Lynch House built about the middle of the 19th century and once two cottages before they were knocked together. The house has great character probably enhanced by the shining slate floors. It is Bron Burt's home and it is here she welcomes you to stay in one of her two charming bedrooms. Both are beautifully and tastefully furnished and have either private facilities or are ensuite. There are some houses in which one instantly feels relaxed and this is one of them. Breakfast is served in the Breakfast Room, and if you keep quiet while you are enjoying the freshly cooked meal you may well see the wild deer creep into the garden and have their own breakfast - Bron's roses! Adjacent to the main house is a cottage which Bron uses for self-catering - although guests there are welcome to have breakfast with her. The cottage is as well furnished as the house and will sleep two in a four poster. It is fully equipped, has central heating and would make an ideal base for anyone wanting to enjoy this part of Dorset. There are so many places of interest closeby which will fill your days no matter what time of the year.

USEFUL INFORMATION

OPEN; All year
CHILDREN; Yes Over 5 years
CREDIT CARDS; None taken
PETS; No
ACCOMMODATION; 2 ensuite rooms, 1 self-catering cottage sleeps 2
DINING ROOM; Excellent breakfast, no evening meal
VEGETARIAN; Catered for
GARDEN; Yes
DISABLED ACCESS; No facilities

16 CHARLSTON CLOSE
Off West Lane, Hayling Island,
Hampshire

Tel: 01705 462527

Hayling Island is approached by the B3023, it is a marshy island shaped like and upside down 'T', there you will find Sophia Maguire's Guest House. Furnished to a very high standard with 3 ensuite rooms all with television. In the morning you will be served a good home-cooked full English breakfast, vegetarians are catered for by arrangement. With no evening meal you will be able to go out and about to the many restaurants and pubs in the surrounding area, Langstone is worth a visit, a Medieval fishing port with picturesque waterside inns. You don't have to go to far to enjoy yourself with a beach close by there is also golf, fishing, walking and watersports. The area is a painters paradise.

USEFUL INFORMATION

OPEN; All year
CHILDREN; From 7 years
CREDIT CARDS; None taken
LICENSED; No
ACCOMMODATION; 3 ensuite rooms
DINING ROOM; English home-cooking
VEGETARIAN; By arrangement
DISABLED ACCESS; No
GARDEN; Beautiful and cultivated
PETS; No

PICKWICK LODGE FARM
Guyers Lane, Corsham,
Wiltshire SN13 0PS

Tel: 01249 712207
Fax: 01249 701904

Charles Dickens was so inspired by the beautiful Wiltshire village of Pickwick, next to the town of Corsham, that he named his first successful novel 'The Pickwick Papers' after it. It is in this pretty village that Gill Stafford and her family live and work their farm. Pickwick Lodge Farm has sheep, cattle and ponies and is surrounded by wonderful countryside, with fields of barley and wheat. The Grade II Listed farmhouse has been 'Highly Commended' by the English Tourist Board, it was built around 1650 and extended in Victorian times. There are 2 bedrooms, the double is ensuite and the double/twin/family room has a private shower, all rooms have television, radio, hair dryer, tea and coffee tray and comfortable arm chairs. A traditional full English breakfast using the best local produce is served in the Breakfast Room by Gill. Pickwick Lodge Farm is ideally situated for exploring this beautiful part of England. There is something for everyone, stately homes and gardens, boat trips, golf and delightful river walks. Whatever you do, a stay at Pickwick Lodge Farm is certain to be a happy and relaxing one.

USEFUL INFORMATION
OPEN; *All year except Christmas and New Year*
CHILDREN; *Welcome*
CREDIT CARDS; *None taken*
LICENSED; *No*
ACCOMMODATION; *2 Rooms*
PETS; *No*

DINING ROOM; *Excellent full English breakfast with plenty of choice including fish*
VEGETARIAN; *Catered for*
DISABLED ACCESS; *No, but welcome*
GARDEN; *Lovely, with garden furniture for your use on request*

THE COPPERS
21B Leigh Road, Holt,
Trowbridge, West Wiltshire
BA14 6PW
Tel: 01225 783174

The Coppers Guest House is a pretty bungalow situated in the lovely village of Holt. It is a quiet and peaceful location with picturesque views over open fields. Accommodation is modern with TV, tea and coffee and many other facilities in each bedroom. Jill and John McCann are very amiable hosts and can provide lots of information about the surrounding area. The Courts, a National Trust Home, is in the village of Holt and is well worth viewing. Many other attraction are within visiting distance, Bath, Lacock, Stonehenge, Salisbury and Longleat House and Safari Park to name but a few. There are also plenty of inns close by which provide all manner of meals and have facilities for children. For the energetic there is golf and horse riding, and for the adventurous ballooning by arrangement.

USEFUL INFORMATION
OPEN; *All year*
CHILDREN; *Welcome*
CREDIT CARDS; *None taken*
LICENSED; *No*
ACCOMMODATION; *2 rooms 1 double, 1 family*

DINING ROOM; *Evening meal by arrangement*
VEGETARIAN; *Catered for*
DISABLED ACCESS; *Not fully adapted but able to provide some facilities*
GARDEN; *Pleasant*
PETS; *Welcome*

Chapter Two

CRUDWELL COURT HOTEL & RESTAURANT
Crudwell, Nr Malmesbury,
Wiltshire SN16 9EP

Tel: 01666 577194
Fax: 01666 577853

The happy marriage of the peace of a 17th Century Rectory with the comfort of a 20th Century English Country House Hotel has produced an establishment in a class of its own. It stands in 3 acres of Cotswold walled gardens with well established grounds, a lily pond, a heated swimming pool and a garden gate leading through to the village church. Crudwell is a quiet backwater just three miles from the old town of Malmesbury, not far from Cirencester and only 70 minutes by train from Paddington. What a wonderful place to stay! Its gracious rooms are furnished with style and grace with great consideration for comfort, the colour schemes are soft and pretty giving one the sense of warmth and space. The house has a lovely flagstone entrance hall, plenty of comfortable sofas and chairs in which to settle and enjoy the books and newspapers put out for you to read.

Fifteen spacious, individually decorated bedrooms overlook the garden and all have bathrooms and extremely comfortable beds. Additionally the rooms are equipped with remote control television, radios, direct dial telephones and tea and coffee making facilities. Crudwell Court is open to non-residents and has a great reputation locally for its superb cuisine and carefully chosen wines. You dine in the beautiful panelled dining room which overlooks the church and the floodlit walled garden. It is an atmosphere that tempts the palate and you will find yourself spoilt for choice with an award winning menu. Every dish is freshly prepared to order and only fresh seasonal produce is used in the kitchen. It is a gastronomic experience to dine here. With an owner who cares deeply about people and a beautifully trained staff Crudwell Court should be high on your list of places to be.

For those who wish to be active there are excellent walks, riding, a 9 or an 18 hole golf course nearby and clay pigeon shooting.

USEFUL INFORMATION

OPEN;*All year*
CHILDREN;*Welcome*
CREDIT CARDS;*All major cards*
LICENSED;*Yes. Fine wine list*
ACCOMMODATION;*15 ensuite rooms*
PETS;*Permitted*

RESTAURANT;*Award winning menu*
Open to non-residents
VEGETARIAN;*Several dishes*
DISABLED ACCESS;*No facilities*
GARDEN;*3 acres. Walled garden.*
Swimming Pool

THE CASTLE HOTEL
New Park Street, Devizes,
Wiltshire SN10 1DS

Tel: 01380 729300

Conveniently situated in the centre of Devizes, The Castle Hotel has been a landmark here since 1768 and is a favourite watering hole for locals. Guests will be delighted with the quality of the soft furnishings and the spacious and well decorated bedrooms each with private bath or shower. Remote control colour television, baby listening device, direct dial telephones, radio and a welcome tray are provided in every room. Professional but friendly and courteous service is evident in the well stocked comfortable bar. An extensive menu offers excellent home-cooked food, with Sunday lunches a speciality and Daily Specials all served in the charming restaurant. If you feel the need for a relaxing get away from it all rest, then why not take advantage of the special rate bargain breaks on offer at the Castle. A Conference Room is available for meetings and small gatherings. The rolling Marlborough Downs stretch toward the Vale of Pewsey extending a fascinating variety of interesting locations to visit. In the vicinity of Devizes is the Kennet and Avon Canal with its many species of wildlife and long leisurely walks. Rode Tropical Bird Gardens are certainly worth a visit.

USEFUL INFORMATION
OPEN; All year. Closed from Christmas Eve-Boxing Day
CHILDREN; Welcome
CREDIT CARDS; Mastercard/Visa/Amex
LICENSED; Yes
ACCOMMODATION; 18 ensuite rooms
RESTAURANT; Home-cooked fare. Evening meals, Sunday lunches and Daily Specials
VEGETARIAN; Catered for
DISABLED ACCESS; No
GARDEN; No
PETS; Yes

MAYCROFT
Old Malthouse Lane,
Langton Matravers,
Swanage, Dorset
BH19 3HH

Tel: 01929 424305

Maycroft is a lovely Victorian house at the top of Langton village. The rooms are all delightfully furnished with TV, tea and coffee as standard. A full traditional English breakfast is served, with vegetarians catered for. There is ample parking for all guests in the drive way. Maycroft is ideally situated for a quiet relaxing holiday in this quaint village, or as a base for touring the area. It is within easy reach of the amenities of the Isle of Purbeck, and has magnificent views over the valley and towards the sea. Local pursuits include fishing, golf, walking, riding and sailing.

USEFUL INFORMATION
OPEN : March to November
CHILDREN : Over 5 years
PETS : No taken
ACCOMMODATION : 2 rooms ; 1 dbl, 1 twin.
VEGETARIAN : Catered for
DISABLED ACCESS : No
CREDIT CARDS : None
GARDEN : Pleasant

Chapter Two

ORCHARD COTTAGE
Stert, Devizes,
Wiltshire SN10 3JD

Tel: 01380 723103

Devizes is an historic town, it boasts two 12th century churches, has many 16th century timber buildings and wonderful Georgian properties. Being so close tot he Kennet and Avon Canal there is an interesting display which charts the canal's story, all housed in a large warehouse. As you travel out of Devizes on the A342, take the road signposted Stert, you will enter a small village, and here down a quite lane is Orchard Cottage, the most magnificent thatched property owned by Roger Martin. Surrounded by a very well kept and profusely stocked garden with shrubs, trees, flowers and a large lawn with extensive views.

This wonderful cottage is certainly a place where one can relax and unwind in the peace and tranquillity. The interior is charming, with a large comfortable sitting room and dining room with an inglenook fireplace adding to the ambiance. The 2 bedrooms, one double and one twin, are attractively decorated with comfy beds, wash hand basin, television and a welcome tea and coffee tray. After an excellent nights sleep you are served a delicious full English breakfast in the elegant dining room, all seated around the lovely Tudor Table.

For your days out there are many things to do, Broadleas is close, where you can wander around the gardens which are full of unusual plants. Stonehenge with its ancient stones for sun worship and the delightful town of Avebury are both within easy reach. The charming City of Bath with all it has to offer. Once you stay at Orchard Cottage it will be awfully difficult to leave.

USEFUL INFORMATION

OPEN; All year
CHILDREN; Over 6 years
CREDIT CARDS; None taken
ACCOMMODATION; 2 rooms,
1 double, 1 twin both with wash basins
PETS; No
DINING ROOM; Full English breakfast, evening meal not available
VEGETARIAN; Catered for
DISABLED ACCESS; No
GARDEN; Wonderful with extensive views

Dorset, Wiltshire, Hampshire

THE OLD FARMHOUSE
Buckland Newton,
Dorchester DT2 7DJ
Tel: 01300 345549

If you are looking for seclusion, peace and quiet, somewhere off the beaten track, then you must come and stay at The Old Farmhouse. This English Tourist Board '2 Crowns Commended' house is delightful with open views of the countryside, excellent for walking, riding and bird watching. The property is about 200 years old and retains many of the original features, the rooms are comfortable with attractive antique pine furniture. Every care has been taken in the bedrooms to provide a pleasant stay they are light and airy with television, hair dryer, complimentary toiletries to use in the superb ensuite bathrooms, and a tea and coffee tray. The residents lounge is very cosy with an enormous open fire place, just the room to come back to after a long day out. The pleasant dining room has a collection of antique hand painted plates and is where you are served an excellent breakfast, either traditional or Continental with a selection of teas and coffees, home-made jams, marmalade and bread. Evening meal is by arrangement only. Alan and Clare Phipps are cat lovers and have 4 lovely, friendly and active cats who adore being cuddled. Ideally situated for touring and exploring the Dorset and Somerset countryside and close enough for a trip to the coast. You are assured a warm and friendly welcome at The Old Farmhouse.

USEFUL INFORMATION
OPEN; All year
DINING ROOM; Excellent home-cooked fare evening meal by arrangement
CHILDREN; By arrangement only
CREDIT CARDS; None taken
VEGETARIAN; Catered for
LICENSED; No
DISABLED ACCESS; No
ACCOMMODATION; 3 ensuite rooms, 2 double, 1 twin
GARDEN; Large with paddock
PETS; No
NO SMOKING

COOMBE HOUSE
41 Coombe Street,
Lyme Regis, Dorset DT7 3PY
Tel: 01297 443849

Lyme Regis is a charming place which delights visitors both for its history, it cobbled streets and of course, The Cobb, made famous by Jeremy Irons and Meryl Streep in the film 'The French Lieutenant's Woman'. Coombe Street is in the oldest part of the town and in its midst is Coombe House, 150 metres from the sea, south facing, on level ground and quite delightful. Dympna Duncan the owner, has one double and one twin room, both ensuite to which she invites guests. Each room has a TV and a hospitality tray. They are beautiful rooms furnished with great taste, in the double room there are wheeler chairs and tables and antique stripped wood wardrobes. Both rooms have large bay windows and it is sitting in front of the window you will be brought your breakfast comprising of fresh fruit, cereal, fresh local bread, boiled eggs, home-made jams and marmalades, coffee or tea. It is such a civilised way in which to start the day. Dympna does not serve evening meals but she will happily recommend goodplaces to eat. She will also tell you about her very well equipped self-catering unit in which you might be interested for future use.

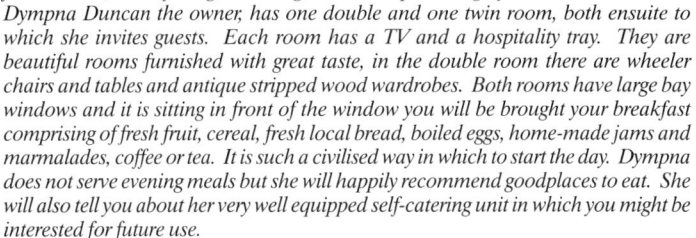

USEFUL INFORMATION
OPEN; All year
CREDIT CARDS; No
CHILDREN; Welcome
ACCOMMODATION; 2 ensuite rooms, 1 double, 1 twin
DISABLED ACCESS; No

Chapter Two

THE WHITE HORSE INN,
South Hill, Droxford,
Hampshire SO32 2PB

Tel: 01489 877490

This must rank as one of the best country inns in Hampshire. It was built in the 16th century and has looked after the needs of travellers over the centuries and at no time has this been better than the present day when Paul and the Young family are mine hosts. It is the friendliest and most welcoming of places whether you drop in for a drink, enjoy an excellent meal or stay in the comfortable accommodation. The bedrooms are charming and have colour TV, complimentary tea/coffee etc. The beds are comfortable, the nights quiet and when you come down in the morning refreshed after a peaceful night's sleep you will find a breakfast that you will not forget in a hurry. Freshly cooked to order it is delicious and substantial. In fact The White Horse is well known locally for the excellence of its food both at lunchtime and in the evening. Home-made pies are the speciality with delicious fillings such as Steak in Guinness. Fish platters are very popular subject to availability and every day there are 'Specials' on the board from which you can choose some of the perennial favourites or indulge in something more exotic. We have been told that the Portuguese Sardines in Garlic Butter are the best our informant has ever tasted! For those who have no time for a meal there are freshly cut, well-filled sandwiches, Ploughmans and salads. Vegetarians always have a choice and for the sweet-toothed some delectable desserts. Everything about The White Horse is right including the prices.

USEFUL INFORMATION

OPEN;All year
Closed Xmas & Boxing Day
CHILDREN; In family room or Rest.
CREDIT CARDS;All major cards
LICENSED;Yes
ACCOMMODATION;3 rooms 1 ensuite
1 basic double 1 basic twin

RESTAURANT;Wide range, good food
BAR MEALS; Excellent choice
VEGETARIAN;Several choices
DISABLED ACCESS;Yes but not to bedrooms
PETS;By arrangement
GARDEN;Patio

Dorset, Wiltshire, Hampshire

COOMBE CROSS HOUSE & STABLES
East Meon, Nr Petersfield,
Hampshire GU32 1HQ

Tel: 01730 823298
Fax: 01730 823515

Coombe Cross House is situated in the very picturesque village of East Meon close to the South Downs, in fact the South Downs Way almost goes through the grounds of the property. This is not just a guest house but a must for anyone interested in horses, Rozanne and Alan Bulmer are a very horse orientated family and are very much involved in the horse world. Horse owners are very welcome to bring their own horses to stay and ride through the most wonderful countryside, the house is surrounded by 10 acres of gardens and paddocks. This superb early Georgian house is very pleasing to the eye, built in red brick with lovely windows looking out onto the lawns. There are 3 bedrooms, 2 of which have ensuite bathrooms, the other has a wash hand basin, the rooms are light and airy and exquisitely furnished with antiques and pieces that compliment the surroundings, they also have colour televisions available on request, tea and coffee making facilities and the views are stunning. The breakfast is traditional English fare, with a wide choice, all of which is prepared by Rozanne. Vegetarians are catered for by arrangement as is an evening meal. This part of Hampshire is very pretty indeed, the village of East Meon itself is charming, the River Meon which starts here wends its way through the centre underneath no less than 8 bridges, it is a very active village having two shops, a Norman Church with a magnificent font in black Tournai marble carved with scenes from the garden of Eden, the Creation, Temptation and Expulsion. Two pubs, The Izaak Walton, who used to fish in the River Meon, he was described as the 'complete angler' and The George, both are very pleasant and serve very nice meals, the former serves a scrumptious cream tea. Another excellent inn is the Bat and Ball in Hambledon, it is full of cricketing memorabilia as the village was the scene of the first ever game of cricket, the cricket club founded in 1760 evolved the laws of the modern game. There are plenty of good walks from Coombe Cross and many other sporting activities including golf and fishing. This area has an abundance of places to visit, why not try Hollycombe Steam Collection, where everything to do with steam is on show, or there is the Romany Museum near Selborne with its crafts, workshops and history of Romany life. Whatever you decide to do you can be assured that your stay at Coombe Cross House will be a happy and friendly one.

USEFUL INFORMATION

OPEN; All year
CHILDREN; Over 10 years
CREDIT CARDS; None taken
LICENSED; No
ACCOMMODATION; 3 rooms, 2 ensuite
PETS; No

DINING ROOM; Traditional English fare
Evening meal by arrangement
VEGETARIAN; Catered for
DISABLED ACCESS; No
GARDEN; Spacious, wonderful views

Chapter Two

DUNVEGAN COTTAGE
Frogmore Lane, East Meon,
Petersfield, Hampshire GU32 1QJ

Tel/Fax: 01730 823213

In a quiet country lane about half a mile from the centre of the picturesque village of East Meon, which is mentioned in the Domesday Book, is Dunvegan Cottage, set in a 3 acre garden surrounded by open fields and wonderful views over the South Downs. The main house was built about 200 years ago, later an extension was added especially for the purpose of Bed and Breakfast. There are four first floor ensuite bedrooms, one double, two twin, and one family, and two ground floor bedrooms, one twin and one family, these rooms share a bathroom. They are also very suitable for wheelchair users as there are no steps. All the bedrooms are beautifully furnished and have the benefit of colour TV, central heating, tea and coffee making facilities, and shaver points in the bathrooms. There is a very comfortable breakfast/sitting room for your use which has easy chairs, tables and a colour television, it presents a warm and welcoming atmosphere. Guests also have the use of the conservatory/entrance hall. Breakfast is substantial with a wide choice of cereals, full English, toast, home-made marmalade and local honey, the produce is fresh and local, breakfast is served between 8.00-10.00am, but should you require it earlier it can be arranged the night before. Vegetarian and special diets are catered for. There is no evening meal, but Monique Aldridge, your hostess, will be more than willing to help you decide where to eat. Walkers will be in their element as the South Downs Way passes within one and a half miles of the house, and with lots of footpaths criss-crossing one another there is ample opportunity for long or short walks. Dunvegan is also on the border of West Sussex. The local pubs, the Izaak Walton and Ye Olde George Inn, both offer a variety of meals and both cater for children. The village of East Meon is so pretty, with the River Meon meandering through the village centre and under no less than eight bridges, the different types of houses from different eras give the village its charm. There are three shops selling a wide range of everyday items, a post office and a blacksmiths. Petersfield, a small market town is four miles away, is very quaint and was once the staging post from London to Portsmouth, the Red Lion was a coaching inn, it is also one of the few towns to still retain its twice-weekly market, it has a variety of shops, restaurants and pubs. Dunvegan is in the perfect position for exploring the wonderful countryside around Hampshire and West Sussex, with so many gardens to visit and hopefully give inspiration for your own!. Another excellent place to visit is Queen Elizabeth Country Park, it has everything to give an enjoyable day out. Monique will, if given some notice, pack a lunch for you and what better place to eat it, surrounded by fields and woods.

USEFUL INFORMATION

OPEN; All year
CHILDREN; Welcome
CREDIT CARDS; None taken
LICENSED; No
ACCOMMODATION; 6 rooms, 4 ensuite
DINING ROOM; Full English breakfast
No evening meal
VEGETARIAN; Catered for
DISABLED ACCESS; Yes, 2 ground floor rooms
GARDEN; Yes, spacious 3 acres
PETS; Yes, by arrangement

ITALY ON PORTLAND
ALESSANDRIA HOTEL &
GIOVANNI'S ITALIAN RESTAURANT
71 Wakeham, Easton,
Portland, Weymouth,
Dorset DT5 1HW

Tel: 01305 822270/820108
Fax: 01305 820561

There are seventeen spacious rooms in this friendly hotel owned and run by Giovanni Bisogno and Rose Cliffe, in the manner that is special to Italians. Most of the bedrooms are ensuite, all of them are very comfortable, well appointed and have tea and coffee welcome trays, colour and Sky television and nice extras like shower gel. All the family rooms are just that with plenty of space to move about in. Giovanni is a talented chef and so the food is especially good and if you dine in Giovanni's restaurant you will have a memorable meal cooked by him, in which he uses fresh produce and organically grown vegetables and salads from the hotel's garden.

Portland is a special place which offers the visitor some wonderful bird watching, diving at its best because of the varied marine life and wrecks. For the angler there are many casting sites, offering the opportunity to catch a wide selection of salt water fish. There are many buildings of historical interest on Portland; three castles, cottages and houses, a local museum, an art gallery and working and disused stone quarries. There are also two disused windmills. With Lighthouses, sailing, windsurfing and stunning views you can never be dull on Portland and certainly you will remember with affection your time at the Alessandria Hotel.

USEFUL INFORMATION

OPEN; All year. Restaurant evenings only

CHILDREN; Welcome
CREDIT CARDS; All major cards
LICENSED; Yes, good wine list

RESTAURANT; Superb, innovative food
VEGETARIAN; Always a choice
DISABLED ACCESS; Yes
ACCOMMODATION; 17 mainly ensuite rooms

Chapter Two

NEWNHAM HOUSE
Queen Street, Emsworth,
Hampshire PO10 7BL

Tel: 01243 373469/379838
Fax: 01243 379855

In this popular area of sailing excellence is the charming town of Emsworth in the County of Hampshire, situated in Queen Street is a collection of splendid Georgian houses of individual design, one of these being Newnham House. Built in 1760 this property is now a Grade II Listed building featuring many interesting architectural details. Mrs. Sally Macleay welcomes her guests with an assurance of true hospitality. The attractive guest rooms are furnished to a very high standard a feature of which is the quality antique furniture. Each room has its own tea/coffee making facilities, radio, TV and 2 have private bathroom. A full English breakfast is served, however an evening meal is available by prior arrangement only. Vegetarians too are catered for. This area is very well serviced by various forms of transport, the airport is in nearby Eastleigh and trains at either Portsmouth or Southampton, also the frequent local bus service. Sailing is the main leisure pursuit in the locality and Emsworth has a 240 berth marina with all relevant services, a sailing school and 2 large sailing clubs and being on the water surfing, swimming and fishing are very popular pastimes. The great City of Portsmouth with its sea faring history is brimful of interesting places to visit. The Royal Naval Museum with its displays of Naval history, the Mary Rose exhibition and many more go aboard the HMS Victory for an insight into ships of yesteryear. She is still in commission to this day as a Flagship. On the edge of the South Downs is the 'Glorious Goodwood' Race Course and Goodwood House which hosts many equestrian events. Within a short distance is Chichester renowned for its theatre and arts festivals, this is a delightful town and offers the visitor avariety of interests. For those interested in 'Those Magnificent Men in their Flying Machines' and the exploits of World War II, pilots and their planes, the nearby town of Tangmere has a museum dedicated to the intrepid Lysander Pilots and a reconstruction of the famous Dambusters Raid. Bognor Regis is a pleasant drive from Emsworth via the A259, this sedate and dignified resort is renowned for its safe bathing and glorious sandy beach. The Roman Palace at Fishbourne is only 5 miles away.

USEFUL INFORMATION

OPEN; All year
CHILDREN; Welcome
CREDIT CARDS; None taken
LICENSED; No
ACCOMMODATION; 4 rooms, 2 with private bathroom
DINING ROOM; Traditional home-cooked English fare, Evening meal by arrangement
VEGETARIAN; Catered for
DISABLED ACCESS; No
GARDEN; Walled with lovely flowers
PETS; Yes

Dorset, Wiltshire, Hampshire

PAXCROFT COTTAGES
Devizes Road, Hilperton,
Trowbridge, Wiltshire BA14 6JB

Tel: 01225 765838 (or 350830)

Jill and Stuart Matthews own Paxcroft Cottage, a modern house built in the 1970s in the village of Hilperton, just outside the market town of Trowbridge which is the administrative centre of Wiltshire. There are 3 bedrooms, 1 double, 1 twin and 1 family, although they are not ensuite, 2 of the rooms have wash hand basins and there is a bathroom and shower room exclusive for guests use. There is a residents lounge for you to relax in and maybe watch some television. A morning tray is provided but tea and coffee are available at any other reasonable time. The furnishings are modern and compliment the house, with fresh flowers to add that finishing touch. Breakfast is good home-cooked English fare. There are extensive views of the Wiltshire countryside. Paxcroft, which has been 'Commended' by the English Tourist Board, is a wonderful base for touring, there is so much to see in this region, Bradford-on-Avon with it's houses built of Bath stone between the 16th and 18th centuries, here also is a lovely meadow walk which eventually leads to one of the largest tithe barns in England built in the 14th century. For lovers of canals the Kennet & Avon is nearby with the famous flight of 29 locks at Devizes. For ancient monuments the standing stones at Stonehenge and Avebury are also close, as are the famous National Trust village of Lacock and world renowned Bath with it's museums and shops. Longleat is not far with landscaped gardens designed by Capability Brown and the famous lions wandering around. There is also fishing, golf, riding, canoeing, gliding and car racing at Castle Coombe, all within easy reach.

USEFUL INFORMATION

OPEN; All year
CHILDREN; Welcome
CREDIT CARDS; None taken
LICENSED; No
ACCOMMODATION; 3 rooms, 1 double, 1 twin, 1 family

DINING ROOM; Home-cooking, Evening meal by prior arrangement
VEGETARIAN; Catered for
DISABLED ACCESS; No
GARDEN; Yes
PETS; No

Chapter Two

THE CARPENTERS ARMS
Leigh, Nr Sherborne,
Dorset, DT9 6HJ.

Tel : 01935 872438

George and Sally Taylor are the friendly owners of this superb country inn which dates back to the 1800s. Beautifully furnished, catering to every need, this is the perfect place to 'while away' some of that ever needed but ever diminishing leisure time, and relax in these congenial surroundings. The food here is excellent with a reasonably priced and varied menu catering for all; anything from a beautifully prepared sirloin steak with whisky, cream and pate sauce, to a vegetarian Westcountry Hotpot, consisting of butter beans and vegetables steeped in a cider and cream sauce! There are some very good bar snacks too, and a variety of refreshing real ales. The bedrooms are all equipped with TV, direct dial telephone and the life saving tea & coffee, and are decorated and furnished in a tasteful manner, which aids a pleasant, restful night's slumber. There is a conservatory which looks out onto cages of animals plus an aviary with zebra finches. The patio has soft concealed lighting, making a very charming setting for your meal. All the country activities are available here, but you also are within a reasonable distance to Yeovil and Sherborne, should the desire for some 'town life' overtake you!

USEFUL INFORMATION
OPEN : All year
RESTAURANT : Tasteful menu with excellent variety
CHILDREN : Welcome
VEGETARIAN : Well catered for
PETS : Guide dogs welcome
DISABLED ACCESS : Not to bedrooms
Other dogs on leash in public bar
CREDIT CARDS : All major
GARDEN : Beer garden
LICENSED : Full
BAR FOOD : Excellent
ACCOMMODATION : 3 rooms; 2 dbl, 1 twin, either en suite or private facilities.

PEACEHAVEN GUEST HOUSE
282 Sopwith Crescent, Merley,
Wimborne, Dorset BH21 1XL
Tel: 01202 880281

Peacehaven Guest House reflects its name exactly. This lovely bungalow situated in a quiet road on the outskirts of Wimborne is surrounded by an attractive garden, full of flowers, shrubs and hanging baskets. Peacehaven is immaculate, comfortable and warm, owned and run by Margaret and Len Justice who offer a friendly welcome. The standard of accommodation is high, the cost bedrooms have attractive linen and curtains, television and a tea and coffee tray. The generous breakfast is full English with options for vegetarians. A lovely area to stay with so much to do and see, steeped in local history. Close to Bournemouth, Poole, Wareham and the New Forest. Fishing, golf, water sports, coastal and country walks, are all close by. So come and enjoy a relaxing stay at Peacehaven.

USEFUL INFORMATION
OPEN; All year
DINING ROOM; Generous full English breakfast
CHILDREN; Welcome
VEGETARIAN; Catered for
CREDIT CARDS; None taken
DISABLED ACCESS; No
LICENSED; No
GARDEN; Very attractive
ACCOMMODATION; 2 rooms,
PETS; No
1 double, 1 twin
NO SMOKING

CLIFF COTTAGE TEA GARDEN AND FISH RESTAURANT
Cobb Road, Lyme Regis,
Dorset DT7 3JP

Tel: 012974 3334

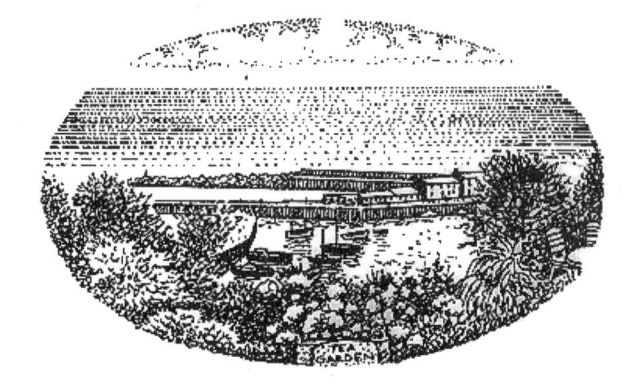

Even if the food were not superb it would be worth visiting Cliff Cottage just for the staggeringly beautiful views over Lyme Bay, the rugged coastline to Black Ven and beyond. Cliff Cottage is situated on the cliff overlooking the harbour called 'The Cobb' made famous in the film of John Fowle's classic novel 'The French Lieutenant's Woman'. John Fowle himself resides high above the Cobb. The house is charming in its own right with pretty cottage style furniture. Upstairs there are 3 comfortable bedrooms, one of which is ensuite and with tea/coffee making facilities. In addition to these there is a chalet which sleeps 2 adults. **_Bed and Breakfast is available._**

The Tea Gardens perched beneath the cliffs, in three quarters of an acre form a sun-trap between the picture postcard town and Cobb. They are ablaze with colours of every hue throughout the summer and decked with baskets brimming with begonias, geraniums and fuschia. It is the most restful and refreshing places to be. Cliff Cottage is the only restaurant in Lyme Regis that serves only fish caught and cooked in the same day. Everything is home-produced and the menu shows how varied the preparation of fish can be. There are always seven different and exciting salads using home grown herbs. Many more things are on the menu including savoury dishes such as home-made mackerel pate with buttered toast, super Ploughmans and fresh crab and prawn salads. Delicious teas with freshly baked home-made scones and delectable cakes are served every day. No one should miss tasting the Dorset Applecake with its lashings of clotted cream.

USEFUL INFORMATION

OPEN: *All year except Dec, Jan, Feb*
CHILDREN: *Welcome*
CREDIT CARDS: *None taken*
LICENSED: *Yes*
ACCOMMODATION: *4 rooms 2 ensuite*
PETS: *Yes*

DINING ROOM: *Delicious, home-cooked fare. Speciality fish*
VEGETARIAN: *Yes*
DISABLED ACCESS: *No*
GARDEN: *Beautiful overlooking sea*

Chapter Two

DEVONIA GUEST HOUSE
Woodmead Road, Lyme Regis,
Dorset DT7 3AB
Tel: 01297 442869

Sue and Roy Gapper who own this friendly Guest House belong to a family who have been serving the pretty town of Lyme Regis, known as the Pearl of Dorset, since the 1900's when Roy's great grandparents provided Cream Teas in 'Landslips Cottage'. They have a wealth of local knowledge which they are happy to share with their guests. Devonia stands in the quiet outskirts of Lyme but is only five minutes walk from the town and the beach. There are views over Lyme Bay as far as Portland Bill and from the rear bedrooms the scene is rural. Apart from being so picturesque Lyme Regis gained fame some years ago with the making of the film 'The French Lieutenant's Woman' from a book written by the classic author John Fowles who is a Lyme resident. All the bedrooms have ensuite or private bathroom with full tea and coffee making facilities, hair dryer and remote control - TV's and radio alarm clocks. Private parking at the side of the house has security lighting fitted. Breakfast and dinner are substantial meals with a comprehensive choice and a vegetarian meal if required. An early breakfast is available upon request.

USEFUL INFORMATION
OPEN; All year
CHILDREN; Welcome
CREDIT CARDS; None Taken
LICENSED; No
ACCOMMODATION; Family, double, twin and single all ensuite
DINING ROOM; Excellent, comprehensive breakfast. Evening meal optional
VEGETARIAN; Upon request
DISABLED ACCESS; No
GARDEN; Yes
PETS; No

LONGHOPE GUEST HOUSE
9 Beanacre Road, Melksham,
Wiltshire SN12 8AG
Tel: 01225 706737

Longhope Guest House is a large Victorian house standing in its own grounds just a quarter of a mile from the town centre of Melksham. This English Tourist Board '2 Crowns' property is comfortable and with a very friendly atmosphere, the lady of the house, Mrs. Diana Hyatt, will really look after you during your stay. There are 7 delightful bedrooms, all have the luxury of ensuite facilities, television and a tea and coffee tray. The furnishing are modern and are in keeping with the house. Diana serves an excellent full English breakfast, vegetarians are also catered for. Longhope is ideally placed for touring and sightseeing, your days will certainly be filled with houses, gardens, towns and villages to visit. If that is not enough there is fishing, golf, walking and other outdoor pursuits, and after your hard day it is reassuring to know you have this superb guest house to come home to.

USEFUL INFORMATION
OPEN; All year
CHILDREN; Welcome
CREDIT CARDS; None taken
LICENSED; No
ACCOMMODATION; 7 ensuite rooms 2 double, 2 twin, 2 family, 1 single
DINING ROOM; Excellent full English breakfast
VEGETARIAN; Catered for
DISABLED ACCESS; No, but welcome
GARDEN; Yes
PETS; No

ST MICHAEL'S HOTEL
Pound Street, Lyme Regis,
Dorset DT7 3HZ
Tel: 01297 442503

Lyme Regis is full of attractive architecture and amongst it in Pound Street is the elegant Georgian St Michael's Hotel which in spite of having all the 20th century comforts has retained the charm and atmosphere of a bygone age. The hotel has superb unspoilt views of the coastal scenery of Lyme Bay and is within easy walking distance of the town where the narrow streets, and cobbled lanes will enchant you. The beach, the sea and the famed Cobb are closeby. No one who ever saw Jeremy Irons and Meryl Streep in 'The French Lieutenant's Woman' will ever forget the Cobb. Jane Austen was another frequent visitor to Lyme and it was here she sited her novel 'Persuasion'. Inside the hotel you will find warmth and comfort as well as a genuine welcome from the Perrams who own St Michaels. The hotel is quietly and efficiently run with the wishes of the guests of paramount importance. Every bedroom is attractively appointed and all are ensuite or have private bathrooms. There are eleven rooms in all, each equipped with a TV and a beverage tray and one of the nice touches is that towels are changed every day. Enjoy a drink in the well appointed Cellar Bar, or indeed the Lounge and Sun Lounge. Breakfast in the non-smoking dining room is a generous meal, freshly cooked to order. A happy place for a holiday.

USEFUL INFORMATION
OPEN; All year
CHILDREN; Welcome
CREDIT CARDS; Visa/Master/Access
LICENSED; Yes
ACCOMMODATION; 7dbl 1tw 3 fam
Ensuite or private bathrooms
DINING ROOM; Excellent breakfast
VEGETARIAN; Catered for
DISABLED ACCESS; No
GARDEN; Yes with sun terrace
PETS; Yes. Not allowed in Public Rooms Or unattended in the bedrooms

THE DEER PARK,
Lydlinch, Sturminster Newton,
Dorset, DT10 2HW.

Tel : 01258 472472

This is a good country pub with skittle alley, darts and a pool table. Now that I've set the scene I will confuse the picture by telling you that the pub dates back to 1600, but has a very modern view with ostrich steak and kangaroo on the menu!! Clive and Nel Frampton are your hosts in this wonderful, atmospheric old inn, and cater to their guests with hospitality and friendliness. The bedrooms are comfortably furnished, are en suite and have T.V., and tea and coffee trays. The restaurant caters for a variety of tastes along with traditional English and fresh fish dishes. I've never actually tried ostrich but I am assured that it is a wonderful dish, and I am told kangaroo is just as tasty! All menus are very reasonably priced and worth trying! This is a lovely rural setting for a relaxing holiday, or for those wishing to pursue active outdoor sports. The city of Salisbury is within driving distance and is a delightful place to explore.

USEFUL INFORMATION
OPEN : All year
CHILDREN : Welcome
PETS : Welcome
LICENSED : Full
CREDIT CARDS : All major
ACCOMMODATION : 2 rooms en suite, both dbl.
DINING ROOM : Varied menu
VEGETARIANS : Catered for
BAR MEALS : Good menu
DISABLED ACCESS : Some
GARDEN : Yes

Chapter Two

PENNAVON HOUSE
Lower Pennington Lane,
Lymington, Hampshire SO41 8AL

Tel: 01590 673984

Set amidst spacious and cultivated grounds on the outskirts of Lymington is Pennavon House. This capacious and friendly family home assures the visitor a most warm and friendly welcome which will tempt you to 'bide-a-while', which is certainly what the Pot Bellied Pigs who have a permanent home in the gardens would say if only they could talk!. Antique furniture and pretty soft furnishings enhance the aesthetically pleasing bedrooms, which are bright and sunny being south facing and overlooking the countryside. There is full central heating for the cooler parts of the day. Each room has either its own shower facilities or an adjacent bathroom. Colour television, clock alarm and beverages tray all go to make your stay a comfortable one. On cold evenings enjoy the pleasure of a glorious open fire whilst relaxing in the large and very cosy sitting room. Breakfast is a veritable feast with an excellently cooked full English style meal accompanied by all the trimmings and for those who wish to enjoy an extra snooze then breakfast can be arranged to suit, within reason of course. Those with a preference for a vegetarian meal can be assured of a fine selection. The delightful town of Lymington is just one mile away with plenty to offer, shops, pubs and restaurants, and a Saturday market full of varied merchandise to tempt the prospective buyer. From the Pier there are daily sailings by the Isle of Wight ferry to Yarmouth, a wonderful day out with plenty of new and exciting places to visit. The wonderful area of the New Forest is home to an abundance of wild life creatures, glorious walks through cool wooded green leafy glades and home to the native ponies and deer is within a short drive. The motor museum, a history of automobiles through the century is at Beaulieu, the home of Lord Montague, the owner of this fascinating collection. The Georgian town of Lymington is within the North Solent Nature Reserve, where bird watching and walking is prevalent, both can be enjoyed along the sea shore and further inland. First and foremost this area is renowned for its sailing and boating and there are several yacht clubs and marinas. Fishing to is enjoyed by many and if it is peace and quiet you are seeking then there are plenty of secluded inlets to while away the hours. Golf and riding are readily available locally.

USEFUL INFORMATION

OPEN; All year
CHILDREN; Welcome
CREDIT CARDS; None taken
LICENSED; No
ACCOMMODATION; 2 double/family/twin, 2 ensuite
DINING ROOM; Excellent full English breakfast, no evening meal
VEGETARIAN; Catered for
GARDEN; Yes, spacious
PETS; No

PADDOCKS
Cardigan Road, Marlborough,
Wiltshire SN8 1LB
Tel: 01672 515280

Paddocks is a fine imposing character property located within its own beautifully tended grounds incorporating a hard tennis court. It offers a unique style of bed and breakfast accommodation, in two luxuriously appointed self-contained suites. Suite one consists of a spacious sitting room with open fireplace and oak beams with staircase leading to a double bedroom and Victorian style bathroom. Suite two, which can also be used on a self-catering basis, comes in the form of a flatlet, with small sitting room incorporating galley kitchen, double bedroom and ensuite shower room. The decor and furnishings have been carefully selected giving a feeling of relaxed comfort, with both suites benefiting from colour TV and tea/coffee making facilities. There is an extensive breakfast menu, catering for appetites large and small and also as an added treat, your hostess, Sue Brockwell, serves breakfast to you within the suite. Dinner is not served, but there is a good selection of bistros, winebars and restaurants within walking distance in Marlborough's famous High Street. Marlborough and the surrounding area has much to offer visitors. Ancient villages, historic houses, quaint antique and bric-a-brac shops, the magnificent Savernake Forest and the beauty of the Kennet and Avon Canal waits to be explored.

USEFUL INFORMATION
OPEN; All year except Christmas
CHILDREN; By arrangement
CREDIT CARDS; None taken
ACCOMMODATION; 2 luxurious suites
GARDEN; Yes
DINING ROOM; Full English breakfast
No Evening meal
VEGETARIAN; Catered for
DISABLED ACCESS; No, but welcome

MELTONE HOUSE
The Causeway, Shaftesbury Road,
Mere, Wiltshire BA12 6BW
Tel: 01747 861383

Mere is a small village in Wiltshire not far from the A303 yet surrounded by lovely countryside. On arrival at this newly built property you are greeted with tea or coffee and home-made cake, what better way to start your stay. Infact Mrs. Melody Parfitt loves cooking and all the food is excellent with home-made jams, marmalade and bread. The breakfast is a real treat with choices such as cereals, yoghurts and a traditional full English meal. Vegetarians are also catered for and if you let Melody know in advance she says you will be overwhelmed by the choice. Meltone House was built in 1991 of local stone and is very comfortable and attractively decorated, with 3 delightful bedrooms. Two are ensuite, all have colour television, hair dryer and tea and coffee making facilities. The large garden is very pretty. Your days here will be filled with outings both near and far, there is also fishing, golf, clay pigeon shooting and lovely walks. Once here you will not want to leave.

USEFUL INFORMATION
OPEN; All year
CHILDREN; Welcome, over 8 years
CREDIT CARDS; None taken
LICENSED; No
ACCOMMODATION; 2 ensuite rooms, 2 double, 1 single
DINING ROOM; Delicious home-cooked fare
VEGETARIAN; Catered for, wonderful choice
DISABLED ACCESS; Not really
GARDEN; Very attractive
PETS; No

Chapter Two

THE POACHERS INN
Piddletrenthide,
Dorset DT2 7QX

Tel: 01300 348358

As you travel through the captivating county of Dorset, past all the attractive house which wouldn't look out of place on a chocolate box. Why not take the B3143 to the small village of Piddletrenthide and there you will come across the most wonderful country inn, a successfully family run pub where guests are regarded as friends. The English Tourist Board '3 Crowns Commended' Poachers Inn is absolutely charming. The 12 bedrooms have been well appointed and have the comfort and privacy of ensuite facilities, central heating, colour television, shaver point, hair dryer, radio, telephone and a tea and coffee tray. For the romantic at heart there are 2 rooms with 4 poster beds. You are free to come and go as you please, as access to your room is independent of the Inn. The extensive garden is superb with flowers, shrubs and trees and an outdoor heated swimming pool for guests use only April-September. A full English or Continental breakfast is served in the dining room. There is easy access to Dorchester, Weymouth, Sherborne, Bournemouth and the New Forest. Golf, fishing, water sports, cycling, riding and walking are also easily accessible. A stay at the Poachers Inn is not to be missed.

USEFUL INFORMATION

OPEN; All year
CHILDREN; Welcome
CREDIT CARDS; Visa and Access
LICENSED; Full
ACCOMMODATION; 12 ensuite rooms 9 double, 2 family 1 twin
PETS; Yes
DINING ROOM; Excellent home-cooked fare, Traditional and Continental breakfast
VEGETARIAN; Catered for
DISABLED ACCESS; Yes
GARDEN; Extensive, heated outdoor swimming pool (guests only), fish pond & b-b-q

FARTHINGS
9 Swaynes Close, Salisbury,
Wiltshire SP1 3AE
Tel: 01722 330749

Salisbury is a charming 13th century city with it's magnificent Cathedral situated on the rivers Avon, Bourne, Naddar and Wylye. The black-and-white half timber houses line the streets. **Farthings** is a comfortable city house, although only a 5 minute walk from the centre of Salisbury with its many shops, you feel you are right out in the countryside. The house is very nicely decorated and has a warm and welcoming atmosphere, where you can feel at ease to relax and enjoy yourself. There are 4 bedrooms, 2 double/twin and 2 singles. The doubles have their own private facilities, all the rooms have a tea and coffee tray. There is no evening meal but Salisbury abounds with restaurants and pubs to suit every taste including vegetarians. Gill not only looks after her guests, but also has green fingers, the garden is a real feature with shrubs and lots of pretty flowers. Farthings is an excellent place to stay.

USEFUL INFORMATION

OPEN; All year
CHILDREN; Not really
CREDIT CARDS; None taken
LICENSED; No
ACCOMMODATION; 4 rooms,
DINING ROOM; Traditional English breakfast
VEGETARIAN; Catered for
DISABLED ACCESS; Not really
GARDEN; Feature, very attractive
PETS; No

310

LEWINA LODGE GUEST HOUSE
225 Bournemouth Road, Parkstone,
Poole, Dorset BH14 9HH

Tel: 01202 742295

Finding somewhere to stay that fits ones budget and at the same time offers very comfortable accommodation is not always easy but here at Lewina Lodge is the answer. Rosemarie and George Robertson have created, within the walls of their own home, a happy place for visitors to stay. Whilst it is furnished to a very high standard it is the sort of house in which children will fit. Parents will not have to constantly watch them to see what they are doing and promptly say 'don't'! Cots are available incidentally and there are reduced rates for children sharing with adults. Every bedrooms have colour TV, Hot and Cold washbasins, Tea and Coffee making facilities, Duvets and Towels and there is plenty of hot water for baths.

The Robertsons do not serve evening meals but they will willingly point you in the direction of some very good eateries locally. Take-Aways may be eaten in the Dining Room between 7-9pm. Poole is quite cosmopolitan and there are ethnic restaurants as well as the take-aways and the British Feast, Fish and Chips. In the light, airy dining room you will be served a freshly cooked, full English breakfast although a Continental version is available if you would prefer it. The walled garden is available for residents and is a pretty place in which to sit and relax.

Lewina Lodge is AA Listed '2Q' and is situated close to the town centre of Poole which is ideal for anyone wanting to explore Bournemouth with its splendid beaches or take a look at the beauty and magic of the New Forest. The Robertsons will make you very welcome.

USEFUL INFORMATION

OPEN; *All the year*
DINING ROOM;*Breakfast only. Take-aways may be eaten here between 7-9pm*
CHILDREN;*Welcome*
VEGETARIAN;*Catered for*
CREDIT CARDS;*None taken*
DISABLED ACCESS;*No*
LICENSED;*No*
PETS; *No*
ACCOMMODATION;*2dbl 2tw 2fam*
GARDEN;*Yes, walled. Ample parking*

Chapter Two

HAZELAND WOOD
Ratford, Calne,
Wiltshire SN11 9JX

Tel: 01249 821839

A superb modern home entrenched amid 50 acres of private woodland and pasture is Hazeland Wood, the farm home of David and Maureen Bowyer. Here are bred Aberdeen Angus cattle and Suffolk Punch heavy horses, on which David is somewhat of an authority. Guests are encouraged to meander through the grounds where wild life abounds, Roe deer, fox and badgers are very often to be seen. It is the ideal setting for bird watchers among those to frequent this area are the Kingfisher, game birds and fascinating birds of prey. Game shooting takes place on the property. Running through the grounds is the River Marden and guests are offered half a mile of private coarse fishing or day tickets at the local Trout lakes. Warm and friendly is the welcome you will receive, every effort has been afforded to ensure guests enjoy this relaxed and informal setting. The bedrooms are light and airy with countryside views. Furnishings a combination of some modern and some in country style antique, but suitably blended. A well equipped bathroom serves the letting room. Various diets are catered for including coeliac, diabetic and vegetarian. A hearty country style breakfast is a wonderful way to start the day, these are prepared and produced in the traditional manner and served in the delightful surroundings of the dining room. Should you require an evening meal this can be provided by prior arrangement. Guests have personal use of the comfortable lounge which has colour TV and video, and in the chill winter evenings a crackling log fire, and warm air central heating ensures a feeling of cosiness. The nearby town of Calne has a good selection of shops, cafes and restaurants. There are many country public houses offering home cooked fare with wide and varied menus. The Wiltshire Downs has so much to offer visitors in addition to the superb scenery; cycling, horse riding, fishing, walking and golf. Marlborough with its famous public school, antique and art shops. Pewsey is a large village with manyinteresting walks and Scotchel Nature Reserve. Bradford-on-Avon where the houses are built of Bath stone dating back to the 16th century, very quaint and picturesque. Often noted as being one of England's prettiest villages is Castle Combe, used many times in filming and well worth visiting. The seat of the Marquess of Bath is home to the Longleat Safari Park, situated south east of Calne and close to the town of Frome.

USEFUL INFORMATION

OPEN; All year
CHILDREN; Yes over 5 years
CREDIT CARDS; None taken
LICENSED; No
ACCOMMODATION; 3 rooms, 2 double, 1 twin all with private bathroom

DINING ROOM; Traditional English breakfast, Evening meal by arrangement
VEGETARIAN; Catered for, also special diets
DISABLED ACCESS; No
GARDEN; 50 acres
PETS; Welcome

PYESMEAD FARM
Plaitford, Romsey,
Hampshire SO 51 6EE

Tel: 01794 323386

Pyesmead Farm could not be better situated to provide anyone with a base for a wonderful holiday or short break. The glorious New Forest is on the doorstep, Salisbury with its stunning cathedral, Stonehenge, Romsey with its lovely abbey and Broadlands, former home of Lord Mountbatten, Winchester with its famous Cathedral and Grand Hall which houses King Arthur's Round Table are all within easy reach. Portsmouth well known for its long standing Naval history is home to HMS Victory and Southsea sea front has the D-Day Museum. The history of the car can be seen at the motor museum in the Georgian village of Beaulieu. Beaches, swimming, sailing, fishing, cycling and walking are ready accessible and so too are Hilliers Arboretum and Exbury Gardens famous for its Azaleas. If this were not enough then Pyesmead Farm has private lakes for fishing which are well stocked with coarse fish and in a lovely setting and has also an indoor heated swimming pool.. This working farm is owned and run by Christina and David Pybus who encourage visitors of all ages to become actively involved with the animals. Indoors the comfortable farmhouse is charmingly furnished and has three attractive and well appointed bedrooms which have either ensuite or private bathroom facilities. You will feel very at home here and come down each morning refreshed after a peaceful night's sleep, to a full English breakfast which will set you up for the day.

USEFUL INFORMATION

OPEN; All year
CHILDREN; Yes
CREDIT CARDS; None taken
LICENSED; No
ACCOMMODATION; 3 rooms ensuite or private facilities
DINING ROOM; Excellent breakfast
DISABLED ACCESS; No
GARDEN; Yes & access to the farm
PETS; By arrangement

ASHCROFT
64 Furzebrook Road, Stoborough,
Wareham, Dorset

Tel: 01929 552392

Ashcroft is a family run guest house situated just south of Wareham. All the bedrooms are comfortable and furnished to a very high standard in a modern style. Each has TV, tea and coffee. Eileen and Nick Cake are the friendly owners and do all that is possible to make your stay most pleasant. The lounge dining room overlooks the patio and mature gardens, and guests are welcome to relax here. Breakfast is English style using home grown produce where possible. This is an excellent base for enjoying the surrounding countryside and is close to Wareham, an interesting Saxon town.

USEFUL INFORMATION

OPEN: All year
CHILDREN: Welcome
PETS: Welcome
ACCOMMODATION: 3 bedrooms : 2 en suite
EVENING MEAL: By arrangement
VEGETARIANS: Catered for
CREDIT CARDS: None taken
DISABLED ACCESS: No
GARDEN: Half an acre

Chapter Two

CASTLEAVON,
Wyndham Road,
Sailsbury, Wiltshire SP1 3AA

Tel: *01722 339087*

This beautifully maintained Victorian terraced house is the home of Christine Coppack who has two rooms which she lets for bed and breakfast but she will also cook you a delicious evening meal if you arrange it in advance. Christine's attitude to her guests is that she will do anything within her power to make their stay a happy one. That she has a number of people who return to Castleavon regularly is no surprise. The comfortable double-bedded room which has a childrens bed available if needed, is furnished in a style suited to the age of the house and so too is the twin bedded-room but here there is something unusual - two 3ft6inch mahogany beds which certainly enhance a night's sleep. Both rooms have TV. A Beverage tray which includes tea, coffee, Horlicks and chocolate biscuits, dressing gowns, hairdryers, radio alarms and toiletries. Whilst the rooms are not ensuite, this poses no problem because there is a privately shared bathroom with plenty of piping hot water. Another thoughtful touch is the Information pack left in the bedrooms which tells you about local eateries, interesting places to visit, bus time tables etc. Breakfast served in the sunny dining room offers a traditional home-cooked full English meal with comprehensive options including omelettes, home-made fishcakes and kippers. Packed lunches are available if ordered the previous day. Refreshments and snacks are on offer until 10.30pm. A laundry service is there too at a cost of two pounds, fifty pence a load. Whilst this is not an entirely non-smoking house, smokers are requested to use the lounge if they want a cigarette.

USEFUL INFORMATION

OPEN;All year   **DINING ROOM;**Full English breakfast with options
CHILDREN;Welcome   **DISABLED ACCESS;**No special facilities
CREDIT CARDS;None taken   **PETS;**Welcome
LICENSED;No   **ACCOMMODATION;**1dbl 1 tw. Not ensuite

THE GALLERY
36 Wyndham Road, Salisbury,
Wiltshire SP1 3AB

Tel/Fax: 01722 324586

The Gallery is a delightful if somewhat unusual name for a guest house which might in the first instance be intriguing enough to encourage you to stay there. Having made that decision for whatever reason you will find yourself staying in a small family-run bed and breakfast house where your hosts, Rina and David Musselwhite, work hard to ensure everyone of their guests has a comfortable and happy stay. Material comforts are very important, and they abound here, but equally important is the happy atmosphere which the Musselwhite's have created in this attractive, strictly non-smoking house. The house is just ten minutes' walk from the city centre and the stunning Salisbury Cathedral, the museum, a leisure centre and swimming pool. Salisbury just begs to be explored and you are ideally placed for visiting all the other Wiltshire attractions such as Avebury and Stonehenge stone circles. The Musselwhites have put together, and placed in every bedroom, an excellent city walk together with a map which explains a great deal about the architecture of Salisbury and will give you hours of enjoyment.

The Gallery is open all the year round and within its welcoming walls you will find each en-suite bedroom is attractively furnished and has beds that will ensure a good night's sleep. There is colour television as well as a beverage tray which not only has tea and coffee but hot choclate as well. When you come down in the morning it will be to the tantalising smell of freshly brewed coffee and the unmistakable aroma of grilled bacon. Breakfast served in the spacious dining room is a delicious home-cooked meal offering the traditional English breakfast dish and lots of other choices including smoked mackerel and creamed mushrooms. Fruit and herb teas are also available as well as the usual beverages. No evening meals are served but a tempting assortment of hot and cold snacks are always available at very reasonable prices up to 9pm. Great idea if you do not feel like dining out.

USEFUL INFORMATION

OPEN;All the year
CHILDREN;Over 12 years
CREDIT CARDS;None taken
LICENSED;No
ACCOMMODATION;3 ensuite rooms
GARDEN;Yes

DINING ROOM;Delicious breakfast
Home-cooked hot & cold snacks until 9pm
VEGETARIAN;Yes + other diets by arrangement
DISABLED ACCESS;No
PETS;No

Chapter Two

WEBSTERS
11 Hartington Road,
Salisbury, Wiltshire SP27 LG

Tel/Fax: 01722 339779

This pretty Victorian house stands at the end of a terrace with a courtyard that has an array of tubs and hanging baskets full of colourful flowers which catch the eye and delight the nostril in the summer months. Mary and Peter Webb are the owners and they have designed and planned the house to provide their guests with every comfort. Selected 4Q's, AA Listed and Commended by the English Tourist Board, their four bedrooms are all en suite and attractively appointed with Colour TV and a hospitality tray well stocked with tea and coffee. There are full disabled facilities which conform to the ETB Category and Holiday Care Service. The whole house has an air of well being, totally relaxing and friendly.

Breakfast is served in the spacious dining room and is a meal to remember. Everything is freshly cooked and there are several options to the full English breakfast with plenty of toast and home-made preserves as well as freshly brewed coffee and piping hot tea. Evening meals are available with prior notice. Websters is one of those houses that remains cool in summer but radiates warmth in winter which is when a good many people take advantage of the short breaks available. Salisbury is always fascinating at anytime of the year and attracts visitors to the city and the stunning cathedral in their millions. But it is not only to see Salisbury that people come to stay at Websters, sometimes it is people on business who appreciate the pleasant informality of the house and sometimes it is visitors who want to explore the whole area including Old Sarum and Stonehenge. So many places of interest are within easy reach and for those who enjoy walking, the renowned and established walks from 'Broken Bridges to the Race Plain' or 'Old Road over Fovant Badges' are prime favourites. Your hosts will happily provide you with more information. Golf and fishing are readily available and if you wish to take a Pleasure Flight, Old Sarum Flying Club will happily oblige.

USEFUL INFORMATION

OPEN;*All year*
CHILDREN;*Over 12 years old*
CREDIT CARDS; *None taken*
LICENSED; *No*
ACCOMMODATION;*4 ensuite rooms*

DINING ROOM;*Excellent breakfast*
VEGETARIAN;*Catered for*
DISABLED ACCESS;*Full facilities*
PETS;*No*

THE MITRE INN,
23 High St., Shaftsbury,
Dorset, SP7 8JE.

Tel : 01747 852488

Shaftsbury is a small, pleasant town ideally situated for visiting Salisbury, Bath or Bournemouth, but giving you the benefit of country living! Anything is possible here, with all country sports available in addition to the delights of the nearby cities. History abounds, with scenic beauty (that makes the shutter finger of even the most amateur photographer itch!), shopping or simply relaxing, you can have whatever you wish. Pam and Pete Jones further pamper to those wishes! Their lovely country town inn has good food, good ale and comfortable beds, cheerful hosts and good service. What more could you want! The inn dates back to the 17th/18th century and is decorated in good taste in an appropriate style. The bedrooms are very comfortable with all facilities, and many have fine views over Blackmore Vale. The food is traditional English and is also available at lunch and evening meal times. Everything here is 'just right' including prices!

USEFUL INFORMATION
OPEN : All year
RESTAURANT : Good traditional food
CHILDREN : Welcome (also in restaurant)
VEGETARIANS : Catered for
PETS : No
BAR FOOD : Good quality
LICENSED : Yes
DISABLED ACCESS : Yes, but not
CREDIT CARDS : All major
GARDEN : Pleasant bedrooms
ACCOMMODATION : 5 rooms; all with wash basins, TV, tea/coffee tray, 1 with shower, 3 dbl rooms, 2 twin rooms.

THE OLD POST OFFICE
Hinton St. Mary, Sturminster Newton,
Dorset DT10 1NG

Tel: 01258 472366

The beautiful Blackmore Vale in the heart of Dorset where the pace of life is slower, gives you time to enjoy the hills and country lanes, to relax and unwind and admire this 'forgotten county of Dorset'. To do all this why not stay at The Old Post Office in the pretty village of Hinton St Mary near Sturminster Newton, the small market town is real Thomas Hardy country. The 19th century property used to be the former post office, general store, dairy and bakery but today it has 3 most attractive and comfortable bedrooms, furnished in keeping with the character of the house, a complimentary tea and coffee tray and wash hand basins. No one goes hungry here with good home-cooked fare using local produce where possible, and home-made marmalade. There is guest's lounge with books, games, radio, television and laden with maps and guide books. Sally and Boyd Sofield look forward to welcoming you to their delightful home.

USEFUL INFORMATION
OPEN; All year
DINING ROOM; Traditional home-cooking using local produce
CHILDREN; Welcome
CREDIT CARDS; None taken
VEGETARIAN; Catered for
LICENSED; No
DISABLED ACCESS; No
ACCOMMODATION; 3 rooms, 2 ensuite, 1 double, 1 family, 1 twin
GARDEN; Yes
PETS; Yes, well behaved dogs

Chapter Two

THE OLD FORGE,
*Fanners Yard, Compton Abbas,
Shaftesbury, Dorset SP7 0NQ.*

Tel/Fax: 01747 811881

The Old Forge is a fascinating place for many reasons apart from providing excellent Bed and Breakfast accommodation. It dates back approximately to 1700 and is a building full of local history. It was formally used as the local estate wheelwright and carriage builder. The blacksmiths forge lies just across the yard and has been restored as a museum of a traditional Dorset rural blacksmith. The Old Forge Car Restoration is another enterprise carried out in a converted lorry shed where Tim Kerridge, who with his wife Lucy owns the property, restores Post-war classics. There is also The Wheelwright's Cottage, a charming, non-smoking, ground-floor cottage adjoined to the main house with its own courtyard and parking. It has an open plan sitting room/kitchen with log burning stove. Double bedroom leading onto single bedroom and a bathroom. The whole cottage is decorated with country antiques and paintings by local artists and has Colour TV. It is English Tourist Board 3 keys Commended.

Within The Old Forge there are three delightful rooms for bed and breakfast accommodation. The Green Room is a spacious lofty, ensuite family room, The Blue Room is a pretty cottage bedroom with a pine double bed and a bathroom just adjacent The Sweet Pea Room is a charming single bedroom with a bathroom just adjacent and because these two latter rooms share the same bathroom they are not let out at the same time unless it is to one family. All the rooms have wash basins and beverage trays. The Dining/Sitting room with log burning stove, board games, local maps, TV etc is where a delicious farmhouse or continental breakfast is served consisting of local organic sausage and bacon, free range eggs, home-made marmalade, local honey, croissants, tea and real coffee. A substantial meal that will set you up for the day and ready to explore this area of outstanding natural beauty which is ideally placed for Hardy's Wessex with many walks, Cranborne Chase, Kingston Lacy, Stourhead, Corfe Castle and Brownsea Island, all within easy distance. The Old Forge is a strictly non-smoking house.

USEFUL INFORMATION

OPEN; *All year except Xmas Day*
CHILDREN; *Welcome*
CREDIT CARDS; *None taken*
ACCOMMODATION; *3 rooms + self-catering cottage*

DINING ROOM; *English or Continental Breakfast. No evening meal*
VEGETARIAN; *Catered for*
DISABLED ACCESS; *No special facilities*

WODONGA
Wincombe Lane,
Shaftesbury,
Dorset SP7 8PJ

Tel: 01747 854258

This modern non-smoking house has an attractive garden and parking space - an all important factor in Shaftesbury where parking is at a premium. Owned by Mr and Mrs Henstridge it is the epitome of comfort. There are two rooms for guests, one double and one twin-bedded, both with hand basins, television and a plentifully supplied hostess tray. The rooms are not ensuite but there is a bathroom with a shower solely for the use of guests. The Henstridges are keen gardeners and have won the Shaftesbury section of the Britain in Bloom Floral competition, Best Guest House Winner 1995. They are happy to share their garden with you. Mrs Henstridge is a particularly good cook and every breakfast is a memorable event, You can choose whatever you wish to go with your full English Breakfast or have something lighter if you prefer it. Evening meals are available with prior notice.

Shaftesbury is delightful in its own right with its famous Gold Hill cobbled street and it is an excellent base to explore both Dorset and Wiltshire with their splendid mixture of old market towns, the magnificent Salisbury Cathedral, several National Trust Properties and Gardens. It is a walkers paradise and for those who prefer outdoor games, there is a good golf course seven miles away from Wodonga.

USEFUL INFORMATION

OPEN; All year
CHILDREN;Welcome
CREDIT CARDS; None taken
ACCOMMODATION; 1dbl 1twin
GARDEN;Yes. Award winning
DINING ROOM; Excellent English Breakfast
   Evening meals with prior notice
VEGETARIAN; Catered for
DISABLED ACCESS; No special facilities
PETS; No

Chapter Two

THE MALLOW GUEST HOUSE
82, Whitewell Road, Southsea,
Hampshire PO4 0QS

Tel: 01705 293892

Portsmouth is a very busy port with the Isle of Wight hovercraft and Ferry terminals and the Continental Ferry Port, also the Royal Naval Base. There is never a dull moment with plenty to do and see. Portsmouth's Historic Dockyard is open to the public where you will be able to visit historical ships such as Mary Rose, HMS Victory and HMS Warrior. There is also the Royal Naval Museum where you can see the story of Britain's Royal Navy covering over 800 years. You can take a harbour boat trip where you will see today's modern Warships, and after all that if you feel hungry you can visit the Tradewinds Restaurant for a hearty meal or just a snack. On Southsea front is the famous D-Day Museum with the sights and sounds of that day in June when the Allies invaded the Normandy beaches, also the 272ft Overlord Embroidery which shows the Normandy landings. Still on Southsea front is the Pyramid Centre, a leisure complex with warm pools, a wave machine and water slides.

With all this going on you will need somewhere to stay and The Mallows Guest House is just the place, the Edwardian building is situated in a quiet residential area of Southsea and has an established reputation for cleanliness and hospitality. This 1 Crown Commended establishment is furnished to a very high standard, it has 7 rooms, 3 double, 1 twin, a single and a family, one of the rooms is ensuite the others having wash hand basin with H and C, there are 2 private showers. The bedrooms also boast colour televisions with satellite link and tea and coffee making facilities. There is a comfortable lounge for your use or you can have a drink and relax in the attractive bar, before you make your way into the pleasant pine dining room for your traditional home-cooked evening meal prepared by the owner Jayne Gentle. Vegetarian foods are a speciality and special diets are also catered for. After a good nights sleep its down for a full English breakfast which is served from 6.00am for those who wish to set off early. If you ask, Jayne will prepare a packed lunch for you, sandwiches and bar snacks are always available. The Mallows Guest House is ideally situated for exploring the Hampshire countryside and visiting such places as Butser Ancient Farm, which is a replica of an Iron Age farm, the Queen Elizabeth Country Park set in 1400 acres of wonderful downland and woodlands where you can walk, ride and picnic.

USEFUL INFORMATION
OPEN; *All year*
CHILDREN; *Welcome*
CREDIT CARDS; *All major cards but not Amex or Switch*
LICENSED; *Yes*
ACCOMMODATION; *7 rooms, 1 ensuite*
DINING ROOM; *Traditional home cooking*
BAR FOOD; *Sandwiches and snacks*
VEGETARIAN; *Speciality of the House*
DISABLED ACCESS; *No*
GARDEN; *Yes*
PETS; *Yes*

SPIERS PIECE FARM
Steeple Ashton, Trowbridge,
Wiltshire BA14 6 HG

Tel: 01380 870266

Spiers Piece Farm is a lovely Georgian house with Victorian extensions. Jill Awdry is the owner and keeps this house in immaculate condition. There is great character here and this is obvious throughout. The house is in a private road which is extremely quiet and tranquil with views over open country and Salisbury Plain. This is a working farm which specialises in live stock and arable farming. Breakfast is a hearty affair designed to last most of the day and there are good local pubs where an evening meal can be enjoyed. The bedrooms are very pleasant and have tea and coffee in each. There is a residents lounge with comfortable chairs, TV and plenty of games. Although the setting for this farm is so peaceful and quiet, you are within easy access for touring. Bath, Stonehenge, Stourhead and Longleat are just some of the attractions you could visit, with many more available. Local pursuits are also numerous with fishing, golf, hang gliding, riding and cycling. Walking is a great pursuit and with the stunning views a really pleasant pastime. This is a lovely location for a relaxing holiday but also a great touring centre to visit the many attractions in the area.

USEFUL INFORMATION
OPEN: All Year
CHILDREN: Welcome
PETS: Small Dogs By Arrangement But None in House
VEGETARIANS: Catered For
DISABLED ACCESS: No
CREDIT CARDS: None Taken
GARDEN: Large and Sunny
ACCOMMODATION: 3 Rooms - 2 Double, 1 Twin

HERONS KNOLL
18 Middle Lane, Trowbridge,
Wiltshire BA14 7LG
Tel: 01225 752593

On the outskirts of Trowbridge in the beautiful county of Wiltshire is a lovely guest house, Herons Knoll. Mrs. Parry is the owner, and a diligent one at that, she is a friendly person, who succeeds in making you feel welcome and at ease. Herons Knoll is only 30 years old, but has a real homely atmosphere, the furnishings are modern and comfortable. There are 3 bedrooms, a double, a twin and a single, they are not ensuite, however the delightful bathroom is adjacent. Each room has a colour television and a radio/alarm. If you require a hot drink, Mrs. Parry will gladly make one for you. After a really good nights sleep, you make your way down to the dining room, where you will be served a substantial full English breakfast. An evening meal is available with prior notice. Trowbridge is only 12 miles from the lovely City of Bath with all it has to offer, including museums, galleries, the superb Abbey with its intricate facade and 162ft tower, delightful buildings and of course those wonderful shops, a shopaholics dream! Salisbury Plain has lots of wide open space and interesting quaint little villages. Longleat is only a short drive away. Mrs. Parry will also assist with information on fishing, golf and other outdoor pursuits.

USEFUL INFORMATION
OPEN; All year
CHILDREN; Over 10 years
CREDIT CARDS; None taken
ACCOMMODATION; 3 guest rooms
GARDEN; Yes
DINING ROOM; Full English breakfast Evening meal with prior notice
VEGETARIAN; Catered for
DISABLED ACCESS; No

LOWER FIFEHEAD FARM
Fifehead St Quinton,
Sturminster Newton,
Dorset DT10 2AP

Tel/Fax: 01258 817335

Lower Fifehead farm built of a mellow stone in the early 18th century, is ideally positioned in the glorious county of Dorset where many beauty spots are just waiting to be explored. This listed building offers various forms of accommodation part of which is a two bedroomed cottage, modernly furnished with one double bedroom and a 2nd bedroom with bunk beds. It is fully equipped with electric cooker, microwave, fridge and modern units and fully carpeted, centrally heated and with colour television. There is also a one bedroomed flat with ensuite bathroom, lounge/dining and large kitchen again fully equipped as above.

And finally bed and breakfast where one is made to feel most welcome. Bedrooms are tastefully furnished, ensuite facilities are available. All rooms have a tea/coffee tray. A resident's lounge with a colour television is available for guests all day. Full English breakfast is served with various choices. Vegetarians are catered for, and where possible fresh locally produced ingredients are used. Farm tours are available around this interesting 400 acre dairy farm, and Mrs. Jill Miller will happily arrange a fishing trip for guests. Horse riding is by arrangement locally and a nearby golf course will satisfy the needs of the enthusiast. As for ramblers and walkers there are many glorious walks. Lower Fifehead Farm has the English Tourist Board '2 Crowns Recommended' award for bed and breakfast and '3 Keys Recommended' award for self-catering.

USEFUL INFORMATION

OPEN; *All year except Christmas*
CHILDREN; *Welcome*
CREDIT CARDS; *None taken*
ACCOMMODATION; *B&B 3 rooms, 2 double, 1 twin. Self-catering 2 bedroomed cottage. One bedroomed self-contained flat*

DINING ROOM; *Breakfast only*
VEGETARIAN; *Catered for*
DISABLED ACCESS; *No but welcome*
GARDEN; *Yes with tables outside*
PETS; *Only in self-catering cottage*

BRADLE FARM
Church Knowle, Wareham,
Dorset BH20 5NU
Tel: 01929 480712

Gillian Hole is your hostess at this friendly working farm 2.5 miles from Corfe Castle. The coast at Kimmeridge is only 1.5 miles away, and there are beautiful walks here and on the Purbeck Hills. This is not a dull place, although it is a very rural setting, as Poole and Bournemouth are only 30 minutes drive away, and there are many other attractions close by. The views are quite stunning and there are bird watching reserves at hand. The house is 150 years old and is built of local Purbeck stone. It is very spacious and airy, and is furnished traditionally to a very high standard. Breakfast is home cooked, fresh produce and is served in the dining room where you can also enjoy a cup of coffee or tea, and a slice or homemade cake at any time of the day! The lounge has an open log fire for those cosy off season breaks. Gillian does not serve evening meals but instead has an arrangement with the local pub one mile away. This works very well as The New Inn has an excellent menu and caters well for children. A delightful place to stay with a warm family atmosphere.

USEFUL INFORMATION
OPEN: All year
CHILDREN: Welcome
PETS: No
ACCOMMODATION: 3 rooms en suite
VEGETARIANS: Catered for
DISABLED ACCESS: No
GARDEN: 550 acres
CREDIT CARDS: None taken.

---

26 THE BEECHES
Hilperton Road, Trowbridge,
Wiltshire BA14 7HG

Tel: 01225 760760

26 The Beeches is where Mrs Staples has her charming Guest House. This English Tourist Board 'Listed. Commended' property was built approximately 18 years ago and is situated in a quiet cul-de-sac surrounded by fields where the cows graze quite happily amid the peace and tranquillity. The furniture is modern with delightful co-ordinated soft furnishings, adding to the amiable atmosphere created by Mrs Staples, a warm and friendly person who goes out of her way to make your stay a very pleasant one. There are two comfortable bedrooms sharing a bathroom, one double and a single, each having a clock radio and a welcome tea and coffee tray. The double also has a colour television. In the morning you are served a traditional English breakfast, then after a hard days sightseeing you can return to an enjoyable three course evening meal, at a very reasonable price. If you are a walker then 26 The Beeches is the place for you, there are some lovely walks especially along the canal. You are sure to enjoy yourselves at this very appealing Guest House.

USEFUL INFORMATION
OPEN: All year
CHILDREN: Welcome
CREDIT CARDS: None taken
ACCOMMODATION: 2 rooms, 1 double, 1 single. Shared bathroom
PETS: Yes if prior notice given
DINING ROOM: Traditional English breakfast, 3 course evening meal at a very reasonable price
VEGETARIAN: Catered for
DISABLED ACCESS: Not really
GARDEN: Yes

Chapter Two

YEW HOUSE FARM
*Marnhull, Sturminster Newton,
Dorset DT10 1ND*

Tel: 01258 820412

    For anyone wanting a good base from which to explore Salisbury, Shaftesbury and the market town of Sturminster Newton, which offers both a warm welcome and great comfort as well as a super traditional breakfast with a comprehensive choice, could not do better than opt to stay with Gil Espley in her very attractive cottage. Here is a new house that has been lovingly and charmingly furnished with beautiful antiques and other pieces which live in harmony with the surroundings. Probably one of the most interesting features of the house is the gallery with its wooden pillars which leads to the tastefully furnished bedrooms. The spacious landing is furnished with a comfortable armchair and every wall has interesting pictures and paintings.
    There are three en-suite bedrooms, two doubles and one twin-bedded room. They all have television and a plentifully supplied beverage tray - such a boon for the traveller. What strikes one especially is the restful and peaceful atmosphere; a place in which to relax and recharge ones batteries before rejoining the stresses of the 1990's. One comes down to breakfast in the morning having had a comfortable night's sleep and ready to enjoy the delicious food before setting off for a day of exploration or perhaps business meetings. Evening meals are not served but thereare many good pubs and restaurants within striking distance; Gil will happily recommend somewhere for you to eat.
    You will never be at a loss for something to see or do when you stay in this part of Dorset. The villages are delightful, the coast is not too far away and there is a wealth of National Trustproperties to visit.For the energetic golf and fishing are available within easy reach and there are some wonderful walks.

USEFUL INFORMATION

OPEN; *March-October*   **DINING ROOM**; *Excellent breakfast. No evening meal*
CHILDREN; *Over 12 years*   **VEGETARIAN**; *Catered for upon request*
CREDIT CARDS; *None taken*   **DISABLED ACCESS**; *No*
ACCOMMODATION; *3 ensuite*   **PETS**; *No*

MAY COTTAGE
Thruxton, Nr Andover,
Hampshire SP11 8LZ

Tel: 01264 771241
Fax: 01264 771770
Mobile: 0468 242166

    May Cottage is a beautiful building, with the oldest part dating back to 1740. It is home of Mr & Mrs Biddolph who both have had some previous experience in the hotel industry, Mr Biddolph being in the London hotel business for 15 years, and Fiona herself cooking directors lunches for many years. There are four guest rooms, tastefully decorated and furnished in old English furniture, with the ever essential tea/coffee tray, colour TV, central heating and use of a hair dryer. Guests have their own pleasant sitting area and dining room. May Cottage is at present awaiting a rating from the English Tourist Board after the area manager spent some two hours being suitably impressed by the facilities on offer! A full English breakfast is available with vegetarians catered for on request. An evening meal is also obtainable by arrangement and is a satisfying home cooked meal.

    Fiona and her husband are friendly, amiable hosts and ensure an informal, warm atmosphere for all their guests. It is set in a quiet country village with a post office and old inn, but is still within easy distance of areas of interest with cities like Salisbury and Winchester, and many National Trust and stately homes such as Wilton House and Montisfont Abbey & gardens. Locally there are outdoor pursuits such as golf and walking, and you are sure to enjoy this quiet, tranquil setting in a lovely part of the country. The English Tourist Board has deservedly given May Cottage a '2 Crowns Commended' award.

USEFUL INFORMATION

OPEN: All year except Christmas and New Year
CHILDREN: Over 12 years welcome
CREDIT CARDS: None taken
LICENSED: No
ACCOMMODATION: 4 rooms, 3 twin (2 ensuite, 1 private bathroom), 1 single
DINING/SITTING ROOM: Full English b/fast. Evening meal by arrangement
VEGETARIAN: Catered for on request
DISABLED ACCESS: No
GARDEN: Yes
PETS: No
A NON SMOKING ESTABLISHMENT

Chapter Two

WESTPOINT TAVERN HOTEL
The Esplanade, West Bay,
Nr Bridport, Dorset, DT6 4HG
Tel: 01308 423636

West Bay is situated on one of the most spectacular stretches of West Country coastline and the famous Golden Cap, the highest point on the South Coast provides a magnificent background to the 18 mile stretch of Chesil Beach. The Westpoint Tavern is situated right on the Esplanade with views from all rooms of the sea or harbour. The rooms are to a very high standard with TV, tea and coffee. The restaurant, which seats up to 60, offers good all round English food, with steaks being something of a speciality. There is a childrens menu and offers good value for money. Areas are named as parts of ships; the Captain's Quarters or Lower Deck, being examples. Quite fun, and with the friendly staff is an enjoyable place to stay. Around the bay there is a wealth of activities from watching the busy harbour with it's fishing boats to playing a round of golf on the clifftop golf club. Could be quite a problem if you lose your ball! There are a host of small shops and restaurants on the Esplanade and some fascinating history and countryside to discover close by.

USEFUL INFORMATION

OPEN; All year
CHILDREN; Welcome
PETS; No
CREDIT CARDS; Access/Visa
LICENSED; Full (real ales)
ACCOMMODATION; 5 rooms

RESTAURANT; Good food, reasonable price friendly service
BAR FOOD; Snacks served
VEGETARIAN; By arrangement
DISABLED ACCESS; Not really
GARDEN; Yes, patio with sun loungers

CLOVELLY
11 Gordon Avenue, Highcliffe,
Winchester, Hampshire SO23 8QE
Tel: 01962 867826

Hampshire is dominated by two great cities Winchester, the Saxon and Norman capital of England, and Southampton which was once a busy Norman Maritime centre. It is in Winchester you will find Clovelly, a very nice Victorian end terrace town house. Doreen Allingham runs her guest house in a professional and efficient manner, making sure her guests needs are catered for. There are 2 bedrooms, 1 double, a room with bunk beds and a bedroom downstairs, if needed, with a put-u-up bed, each has television, a tea and coffee tray with sweets and fresh fruit. All the bedrooms have private facilities. The house is very comfortable and really nice throughout, the furnishing compliment the house adding to the warm and friendly atmosphere. Doreen serves a very full English breakfast, it really keeps you going all day. Evening meals are not available, but with only a 10-12 minute walk into Winchester you are sure to find somewhere to eat, to suit your taste and pocket. Children are welcome, if you require a carrycot one can be arranged in advance. Clovelly has a very pretty garden with masses of flowers, plants and hanging baskets. If staying for a short break, there are many interesting places to visit and activities to take part in. Clovelly is a thoroughly nice place to stay.

USEFUL INFORMATION

OPEN; All year
CHILDREN; Welcome
CREDIT CARDS; None taken
ACCOMMODATION; 2/3 rooms, 1 with bunk beds, 1 double

DINING ROOM; Very full English breakfast
Evening meal not available
VEGETARIAN; Catered for
DISABLED ACCESS; Not really
GARDEN; Wonderful, full of flowers

Dorset, Wiltshire, Hampshire

PREMIER HOTEL
*121 The Esplanade, Weymouth,
Dorset DT4 7EH*

Tel: 01305 786144

The prestigious sea front location of the Premier Hotel offers an all embracing view across Weymouth Bay. A warm and friendly atmosphere pervades this efficiently run Hotel, Sue and Mike Beaumont endeavour to ensure their guests relax and feel at home. Recently re-decorated and with new carpets and bed linen the modern bedrooms with ensuite facilities to double/twin and family rooms, are comfortable and welcoming and offer colour TV and a tea/coffee tray. Breakfast is a typical traditional English meal, with a wide choice to suit all tastes, vegetarians are well catered for. The dinner menu is varied and comprehensive. A residents bar is available as well as a comfortable lounge with colour television. Car parking is situated in the street to the rear of the Hotel, as well as public car parks. The Premier is central to all amenities including coach and rail stations, also the town centre with its many interesting shops, tea houses and restaurants. The sheltered sandy beach is ideal for children and boating in the bay is safe. There are many and varied outdoor pursuits in the area and Mike will be only to happy to supply the information.

USEFUL INFORMATION

OPEN; 1st Mar-31 Oct
CHILDREN; Welcome
CREDIT CARDS; Visa
LICENSED; Yes
ACCOMMODATION; 14 rooms

RESTAURANT; Traditional English Fare
VEGETARIAN; Catered for
DISABLED ACCESS; No but welcome
GARDEN; No
PETS; No

THORNHILL
*Holt, Wimborne,
Dorset BH21 7DJ*

Tel: 01202 889434

Thornhill is a wonderful thatched house, surrounded by trees, shrubs and flowers. Built in the 1940's it has a warm and friendly atmosphere, John and Sara certainly know how to look after their guests and make them feel at home. You will feel very comfortable in your delightful bedroom, where you have the luxury of private facilities, a tea and coffee tray complete with biscuits and sweets, and for that special touch fresh flowers. There is a separate lounge with colour television. Breakfast is a traditional meal, John and Sara will be happy to recommend a restaurant or pub to suit your needs, as an evening meal at Thornhill is not available. The garden is very impressive, John will be more than delighted to talk to you about the unusual plants and shrubs as he shows you around. You maybe lucky enough to see rabbits, squirrels and deer which often frequent the garden. If you are feeling energetic why not have a game of tennis on Thornhill's hard court, otherwise just come here, relax and let the world pass you by. Wonderful.

USEFUL INFORMATION

OPEN; All year
CHILDREN; No
CREDIT CARDS; None taken
LICENSED; No
ACCOMMODATION; 3 rooms with private facilities, 1 double, 1 twin, 1 single

DINING ROOM; Full English breakfast, Evening meal not available
VEGETARIAN; Catered for
DISABLED ACCESS; Not really
GARDEN; Lovely plants and shrubs
PETS; No

Chapter Two

BRICKWORTH FARMHOUSE
Whiteparish, Salisbury,
Wiltshire SP5 2QE
Tel: 01794 884663

Whiteparish lies between Salisbury and Romsey and is known to have existed in the 9th century, although some pre-historic remains have been found. The village derives its name from the white chalk ground it is built on, consists of houses and farms, a shop, a church and 4 pubs. One of the properties is Brickworth Farmhouse, a Grade II Listed house built around 1725, it is set in 5 acres of land, which provides a lovely walled garden, an orchard and a 3 acre paddock. The house itself is imposing and built in red brick. It has 4 appealing bedrooms furnished in a cottage style with lots of pine and lovely comfortable quilts, the two double rooms and family room are ensuite, the single room has a private bathroom. The breakfast at Brickworth is traditional English or Continental using fresh produce, much of it home grown, all served with toast made from home-made bread, the eggs are free range from the chickens that roam the orchard, topped off with either Earl Grey tea or freshly brewed coffee, what better way to start the day. Sue Barry, your hostess, is a registered tourist guide and is more than willing to help you plan your ideal excursion to Salisbury, Romsey, Winchester and Bath to name but a few. There are also wonderful gardens and houses to visit. A warm and friendly welcome awaits you at this family home.

USEFUL INFORMATION
OPEN; All year
CHILDREN; By arrangement
CREDIT CARDS; None taken
LICENSED; No
ACCOMMODATION; 4 rooms, 2 double 1 family, 1 single, 3 ensuite
DINING ROOM; Traditional English fare
VEGETARIAN; Catered for
DISABLED ACCESS; By arrangement
GARDEN; cultivated walled plus orchard
PETS; No

TWYNHAM
67 Poole Road, Wimborne,
Dorset BH21 1QB
Tel: 01202 887310

Wimborne is dominated by the twin-towered Minster, its different architecture reveals 1000 years of history. There are many archeological and historical sites in this area. In this fascinating town is Twynham a substantially built late Victorian house, owned and efficiently run by Mr. & Mrs. Rendell. The AA '3Q' and English Tourist Board 'Listed' property is gracious living with a comfortable family house atmosphere. The 3 bedrooms are delightful they are light and airy with vanity units and wash hand basins, hair dryer, clock radio, complimentary toiletries, television and a tea and coffee tray all provided for your use. The front rooms have views of open pastureland and the River Stour Valley. There is an extra shower and toilet available. The full English breakfast is served in the lovely conservatory at a time to suit you. The charming dining room has very elegant furniture. There is a delightful garden with lovely lawns and flowers. Twynham is ideally located for Bournemouth, Christchurch, Poole and the New Forest.

USEFUL INFORMATION
OPEN; All year except Christmas Day
CHILDREN; Welcome
CREDIT CARDS; None taken
LICENSED; No
ACCOMMODATION; 3 rooms,
DINING ROOM; Full English breakfast
VEGETARIAN; Cater for
DISABLED ACCESS; No
GARDEN; Delightful with lawn and flowers
PETS; No, except Guide Dogs

MRS. S. TISDALL
32 Hyde Street, Winchester,
Hampshire SO23 7DX

Tel: 01962 851621

Until the late 12th century Winchester was the ancient Royal capital of Saxon Wessex and of England. Today it is a very impressive city with lovely shops, Military Museums, art galleries and the wonderful Cathedral started in 1079 for William the Conqueror. Jane Austen's tomb is here and Winchester College, one of Britain's oldest public schools, founded by William of Wykeham in 1382. 10 minutes walk from the centre of town is Hyde Street where Mrs. Tisdall has her 18th century guest house. This lovely old town house is a real home from home where guests are treated as friends, the furnishings are comfy and you are able to feel at ease. The bedrooms are light and airy with a wash basin, television and tea and coffee making facilities. The family room has 3 single beds, which can be let as a twin.

A small folding bed is available for use by a child in either the double or family room. There is a relaxing lounge for guests. This is a non-smoking house. A full English breakfast is prepared and served by Mrs. Tisdall. Evening meals are not available, but you will not go hungry as there is a wide choice of eateries within easy reach. 32 Hyde Street is also convenient for the railway station. Getting out and about is no problem, the area is teeming with attractions and activities, which should keep you busy for days.

USEFUL INFORMATION

OPEN; All year
CHILDREN; Welcome
CREDIT CARDS; None taken
ACCOMMODATION; 2 rooms,
1 double, 1 family, private facilities
DINING ROOM; Delicious breakfast only
VEGETARIAN; Catered for
DISABLED ACCESS; Not really
GARDEN; Yes
PETS; No
NO SMOKING

Chapter Two

GLEN REST,
Bourne Road, Woodlands,
Southampton SO40 7GR

Tel: 01703 812156

The first sight of the 'cottage style' Glen Rest gives one a feeling of peace and tranquillity. It is set in a pretty garden with ample off road parking and because Rosemary and Rob Sawyer only have two letting rooms you are assured of personal attention which is charming and helpful but unobtrusive. The bedrooms which can be either double, twin or family, share a private bathroom and they are very comfortably furnished complete with TV and a beverage tray. You are made to feel at home and welcome to use the garden whenever you wish. Breakfast is served in the attractive dining room and is freshly cooked to your choice. There is plenty of everything and vegetarians are catered for if required. No evening meals are available but Rosemary and Rob will suggest eating places to you in the forest which can be anything from standard English to exotic Oriental cuisine. In the interests of safety and hygiene you are requested not to smoke in the house. Open all the year and centrally heated Glen Rest makes an ideal place to stay at anytime of the year.

The village of Woodlands is only 5 minutes from junction 1 of the M27 and just ten minutes from Lyndhurst, the capital of the New Forest. This makes Glen Rest so convenient for forays into the picturesque New Forest , convenient for the coast, excellent for walking, riding, golf and fishing and other activities and is only a 30 minute drive from Winchester, Salisbury and Portsmouth with Bournemouth 45 minutes and Southampton 15 minutes away.

USEFUL INFORMATION

OPEN; *All year*
CHILDREN; *Welcome*
CREDIT CARDS; *None taken*
LICENSED; *No*
ACCOMMODATION; *2 rooms not ensuite*
DINING ROOM; *Breakfast only*
VEGETARIAN; *Catered for*
DISABLED ACCESS; *No*
GARDEN; *Yes*
PETS; *No*

The Home Counties

Chapter Three

THE HOME COUNTIES, THE THAMES VALLEY & GREATER LONDON

including SURREY, SUSSEX, KENT, ESSEX, BUCKINGHAMSHIRE, BEDFORDSHIRE & BERKSHIRE

The Home Counties

CHAPTER 3

THE HOME COUNTIES, THE THAMES VALLEY & GREATER LONDON
including SURREY, SUSSEX, KENT, ESSEX, BUCKINGHAMSHIRE, BEDFORDSHIRE & BERKSHIRE

INCLUDES

Stream Cottage	**Albury**	p. 379
Gadbrook Old Farm House	**Betchworth**	p. 380
Westholme Guest House	**Bognor Regis**	p. 381
White Barn	**Bosham**	p. 382
Holly House	**Chelwood Gate**	p. 383
The Cottage Guest House	**Chichester**	p. 384
Easton House	**Chichester**	p. 385
Hatpins	**Chichester**	p. 386
Riverside Lodge	**Chichester**	p. 387
St Andrews Lodge	**Chichester**	p. 388
Cedar House Restaurant	**Cobham**	p. 389
Ryegate House	**Colchester**	p. 390
Thorington Hall	**Colchester**	p. 391
Longcroft House	**Ditchling**	p. 392
St Marks Guest House	**Dover**	p. 392
King John Lodge	**Etchingham**	p. 393
Highwray	**Farnham**	p. 394
Mill Lane Lodge	**Farnham**	p. 395
Timbers	**Halstead**	p. 396
Nightingales	**Lewes**	p. 398
Durrants Hotel	**London**	p. 399
Eleven Cadogan Gardens	**London**	p. 400
Number Sixteen	**London**	p. 401
The Goring Hotel	**London**	p. 402
The Portobello	**London**	p. 403
Uptown Reservations	**London**	p. 404
Hurtwood Inn Hotel	**Peaslake**	p. 405
Abbeygail Guest House	**Ramsgate**	p. 384
Windy Brow	**Reading**	p. 397
Barn Cottage	**Reigate**	p. 408
Fiddlers Oast	**Rye**	p. 407

Chapter Three

CHAPTER 3

THE HOME COUNTIES, THE THAMES VALLEY & GREATER LONDON
Including **SURREY, SUSSEX, KENT, ESSEX, BUCKINGHAMSHIRE, BEDFORDSHIRE and BERKSHIRE**

The Chilterns, dividing Oxfordshire and Buckinghamshire, with their centuries old beechwoods were the home at one time of hundreds of 'bodgers', wood turners making chair legs with manual lathes, and whittlers of clothes pegs. The area is one of outstanding beauty, the mainly small buildings a mixture of brick with knapped flints. Where the Chilterns meet the Berkshire Downs and the river has created the **Goring Gap** through the chalk, the ancient **Icknield Way** and **Ridgeway** come together.

The Ridgeway runs along the Berkshire Downs (now in Oxfordshire) heading towards Stonehenge and Avebury although the ancient road pre-dates the great monuments. Being away from modern roads, the Ridgeway provides for peaceful walking or horseriding with extensive open views. Towards the west of its Oxfordshire section the Ridgeway passes by the **White Horse of Uffington**, nearly 40 feet high, cut through the turf into the chalk. If you leave a horse and a coin in the nearby **Wayland Smith's Cave**, rumour has it that by the morning the horse will have been shod. Here too is **Dragon Hill**, said to be where St George slayed the dragon.

Over the Berkshire Downs from Oxfordshire is the Royal County of Berkshire itself, now a small county with, sadly, much of its Iron Age and Roman history obscured by recent development. For all that it is an interesting county and the whole is really overshadowed by the majesty of **Windsor Castle**. This enormous fortress which dominates **Windsor**, is the largest inhabited castle in the world. It has been one of the principal residences of the sovereigns of England since the days of William the Conqueror, who built it. When you come to examine it closely you will see that almost every monarch since William's time has taken a hand in rebuilding. For our present Sovereign Lady, Queen Elizabeth II, the rebuilding has been forced upon her by the devastating fire just five years ago which destroyed much of value, although the works of art, furniture and books were saved by a human chain passing the priceless masterpieces gently down the line, hand to hand - hands that included the Queen, the Duke of York and many local people. The damage has now been restored and the castle is as magnificent and awe inspiring as ever. Three wards or enclosures make up Windsor Castle. The Round Tower in the Middle Ward was built by Henry II to replace the wooden

The Home Counties

Norman fortress. George IV added its upper half in 1828-32. The Lower Ward contains St Georges Chapel and the Upper Ward has the State Apartments.

Within the Castle, parts of which are open to the public, you must not miss the 15th and 16th century St Georges Chapel. It boasts some of the finest fan vaulting in the world, the helmets and banners of knights, the tombs of Henry VII and Charles I and a memorial to Prince Albert. The State Apartments also must not be missed. These magnificently furnished rooms on the precipitous north flank of the castle are still used on official occasions. On a quite different scale is the world's most famous **Doll's House** designed by Sir Edwin Lutyens in the 1920's for Queen Mary.

Everywhere in Windsor there are Royal connections. Indeed the town grew up because of the presence of the castle. It is a delightful town with a good theatre, attractive shops, fine museums and a beautiful parish church built in 1820 on the site of an earlier church. The building was supervised by Jeffrey Wyatt who later, as Sir Jeffrey Wyatville, designed the Castle's Waterloo Chamber for George IV.

Eton is always inextricably mixed with Windsor but it is a little town in its own right. It has always had a fascination for people especially because of the world famous school, Eton College.Each year on the 4th June Eton College celebrates its founding by Henry IV in 1440 with a firework display on the river. Also in June is Ascot Week when royalty, the gentry and celebrities as well as other racegoers, many of them in huge flamboyant hats, attend the meetings at **Ascot Racecourse**.

There are some wonderful drives along the River Thames to small towns and villages, **Maidenhead, Taplow,** amongst many. I always enjoy visiting **Cookham**, the home of the artist Sir Stanley Spencer (1891-1959). He loved his birthplace with an intensity that shows in his paintings. Cookham High Street, the parish church, the River Thames, the meadows, are all recognisable in his works. It is fitting that Cookham should be the home of the **Stanley Spencer Gallery**. It stands in the centre of Cookham in the former Wesleyan Chapel to which he was taken as a child by his mother. Pride of place is held by the immense, unfinished Christ Preaching at Cookham Regatta. There are some touching reminders of this talented man; his spectacles, easel, palettes, sunshade, and folding chair, and even a baby's push chair that he used to carry his equipment when he was off on a painting expedition.

Reading is a town that tends to be omitted from Guide Books but this should not be so. It is a busy place and has much to interest the visitor

Chapter Three

and if you are looking for somewhere comfortable to stay which will provide you with a base in order to discover all that this fascinating area has to offer then **Windy Brow** in Reading is the answer. Two good places to visit within easy distance of Reading are **Swallowfield Park** off the B3349 and just 6 miles south-east of the town. The house was built in 1690 for the 2nd Earl of Clarendon and then considerably altered in the 18th century when the redbrick stables were added. The house has great charm and the beautifully landscaped gardens are a delight. Covering 4 acres they contain a variety of flowering shrubs and roses, as well as many fine specimen trees. You can wander along an ancient yew-tree walk, muse by the small lake and revel in the banks of massed rhododendrons in season. Open May-Sept, Wednesday and Thursday afternoons. The second is the **R.E.M.E Museum** at **Arborfield** off the A327 5 miles south of Reading. Here you can study the history and many-sided work of the Royal Electrical Mechanical Engineers, your understanding helped by the life sized tableaux and large model dioramas.Formed in 1942, the corps came into being to support the rapid growth of military technology from the outset of the Second World War. Today it is still busy repairing army aircraft and seagoing ships, electronic equipment and so on. This is all reflected in this interesting museum, which also contains displays on R.E.M.E activities worldwide. Open all year. Monday to Friday. Free admission.

Over the Thames from Windsor and beyond the town of **Slough**, Berkshire joins the tall narrow county of **Buckinghamshire** on its short southern boundary. At this point Buckinghamshire is low and leafy, rising sharply further north to the Chilterns with its thick beechwoods, then further north still becoming a land of streams and marshes.

A prehistoric boundary known as **Grim's Ditch** runs across the Chilterns near to **Great Hampden** and nearby are two crosses cut through the turf into the chalk. Not as exciting as the White Horse of Uffingham but nonetheless intriguing.

The Chilterns are renowned for the many footpaths and there are walks both short and long, but rarely strenuous, that can take advantage of the scenery, giving just occasional glimpses through the trees of distant views. The **North Bucks Way** starting near **Wendover** on the Chilterns escarpment takes walkers down to **Wolverton** in the Vale of Aylesbury. On the North Bucks Way can be found the **Quainton Railway Centre** with trains in steam on the last Sunday of each month. The ancient trees of **Burnham Beeches** east of **Maidenhead** form a beautiful area which was bought for the people by the City of London in 1879. At one time this area was also home to Romany gypsies, now long gone.

Along the Thames, Buckinghamshire has some attractive towns such as **Marlow** which is particularly beautiful. This was the home of the poet Percy B. Shelley and Mary Shelley of 'Frankenstein' fame. The poet William Cowper spent the second half of his life in **Olney** where the **Cowper Museum** celebrates his works, including 'Amazing Grace' which was written here.

Stoke Poges church is where Thomas Gray wrote his 'Elegy written in a country Churchyard' and at **Beaconsfield** lived G.K. Chesterton and Enid Blyton who it is believed was inspired by the **Bekonscot Model Village** with tiny houses spread over a large garden. Milton lived in**Chalfont St Giles** when he fled from London to escape the plague and in addition to a small museum, his cottage is now open to visitors.

Near Beaconsfield the small town of **Jordans** was home to William Penn, the founder of Pennsylvania and he is buried at the small 17th century **Quaker Meeting House. The Mayflower Barn**, also open to the public, incorporates beams taken from the Mayflower after the Pilgrim Fathers sailed to America in 1620.

Hughenden Manor near **High Wycombe** was the home of Benjamin Disraeli and the house still contains much of his furniture and other belongings. Today's Prime Minister has a country residence southwest of **Wendover**, a Tudor house known as **Chequers**, presented to the nation for just this purpose during World War I.

From pretty, small villages such as **Hambleden** to modern towns like **Milton Keynes,** Buckinghamshire has absorbed a large increase in population in the latter part of this century, yet outside these conurbations retains its character as a rural area.

Bedfordshire to the north east is very much more rural, a green and peaceful county where water meadows flank the River Great Ouse and the rolling downs climb towards the mighty Chilterns. John Bunyan was born in the village of **Elstow** in 1628. Later he was imprisoned for his religious views in the county town of **Bedford**. Both places have much to remind us of this great man. **Elstow Moot Hall** is a beautiful brick and timber building built about 1500. Its purpose to house the goods for the famous May Fair at Elstow. It was also used as a court house and it has been suggested that Bunyan might have had Elstow Fair in mind when he described the worldly 'Vanity Fair' in the Pilgrim's Progress. The Hall belonged to the nuns of Elstow Abbey and after the abbey was dissolved at the Reformation, the Moot Hall continued as a court house. For centuries it was neglected until in 1951 it was restored. The upper floor has been opened up to display the superb medieval roof, with massive beams and graceful uprights.

Chapter Three

Two miles south west of **Dunstable**, the rolling hills of **Dunstable Downs** form the northern end of the Chilterns chalk escarpment and from them there are wide views over the Vale of Aylesbury and beyond. Thousands of years ago they were a highway for prehistoric man, who trudged along the Icknield Way (now the B489) at their foot. In a 300 acre area the ground has been left untreated by chemical weedkillers or fertilisers and the result is stunning. Rare plant species flourish, including fairy flax and chalk milkwort. Little muntjac deer browse among the scrub, and whinchats and grasshopper warblers dart over the hillside.

At **Whipsnade Heath** there is a reminder of the First World War. Here is the Tree Cathedral, in a sun dappled grove, laid out to a plan of nave, transepts and chapels. It was planted in the 1930's by Edmund Kell Blyth in memory of his fallen friends. Quite moving and very beautiful.

Nearby on top of the downs, more than 2,000 animals roam over 500 acres of **Whipsnade Park Zoo**, in conditions as nearly as wild as climate and safety will permit.

If you are a narrow gauge railway enthusiast you will want to visit **Leighton Buzzard Narrow Gauge Railway.** An average speed of five and a half miles an hour might not seem much by to-day's standards but it is quite enough for the locomotives of the Leighton Buzzard Railway which was built to carry sand from the quarries north of the town to the main London and North Western Railway. Due to be scrapped at the end of the 1960's, it was saved by a band of enthusiasts who have acquired steam and diesel engines from as far away as India and the Cameroons, constructed rolling stock, and built an engine shed for maintenance.

Market gardening flourishes around the town of **Biggleswade** set amidst highly productive arable land, showing the diversity of one of the smallest counties in England. Near here you can visit **The Swiss Garden**, a beautifully restored 19th century garden with fine trees. An intricate French garden features in a park that was laid out in the 18th century and partly re-landscaped by Capability Brown around **Wrest Park House** at **Silsoe**, modelled on the French chateaux style. The history of gardening through the ages can be seen here in a setting which includes some splendid water features.

Judging by its huge popularity, no visit to Bedfordshire would be complete without a tour around the splendid **Woburn Abbey**, home of the Dukes of Bedford, with its stately parklands, complete with wild animals, boat trips, art galleries and shops.

The Home Counties

Hertfordshire, along with the extinct county of Middlesex, made up the Northern Home Counties and it is here that the mix of grand country houses and new towns is in greatest contrast - or greatest harmony depending on your viewpoint. **Letchworth** was the first of the new 'Garden Cities', created as early as 1903 in a bid to bring better housing to ordinary people. Its **First Garden City Museum** tells the story of the somewhat radical social ideas which were held by those who originally created this town as well as those who lived here. **Welwyn Garden City** followed in 1920 and several other new towns, often around old town or village centres, sprung up in the post-war period of the 1950's.

I have to admit that for me Hertfordshire is principally **St Albans** with its fine cathedral in which thousands of years of worship have continued on the site of St Alban's martyrdom. Many centuries ago Alban was the first Christian martyr in this country and his shrine has always attracted pilgrims in search of spiritual and physical healing. It is a beautiful place which emanates strength.

You feel as if the Almighty is reaching out for you and endeavouring to pour into your soul the fortitude shown by St Alban, and at the same time give you hope for the present and peace eternal. The history of the cathedral is well documented and you will do no better than to purchase the beautifully presented, colourful Pitkin Guide to St Albans Cathedral which will cost you about two pounds and be a constant reminder of your visit.

Almost surrounded by motorways, St Albans is easy to reach and having done so you drive into quieter realms and begin to realise that you are going to discover in this one place, which offers the unusual combination of the dignity of a Cathedral City and the intimacy of a rural markettown, the full span of British history. For a moment or two the sense of history is overwhelming. St Albans is full of museums, beautifully laid out and providing easily digested information.

A totally different atmosphere you will find at **The Mosquito Aircraft Museum** in Salisbury Hall, **London Colney**. The historic site of the moated Salisbury Hall, mentioned in the Domesday Book, was chosen by the de Havilland Aircraft Company in 1939 to develop in secret the wooden, high speed, unarmed bomber, the Mosquito; with 41 variants of the type of the most versatile aircraft of the war. This began the museum's long association with Salisbury Hall making it the oldest Aircraft Museum in the country. Visitors to the museum soon discover that it can offer more than a collection of static aircraft. Close inspection of the exhibits provide a unique hands-on experience. Members are always on hand to assist the visitor and demonstrate the working displays. With a varied programme of regular events that include

Chapter Three

flying displays, vintage car and motor cycle rallies and model exhibitions, there is always something to appeal to all ages.

From the air to the ground. **The Royal National Rose Society** at Chiswell Green, St Albans on the outskirts of the town, invites you to enjoy the world famous 'Gardens of the Rose' at the Society's showground where there is a collection of some 30,000 roses of all types.

The 12 acres of gardens are a marvellous spectacle for the casual visitor and fascinating to the rose enthusiast. The gardens are being continuously developed - in particular by associating roses with a great many other plants - to create greater interest for visitors and to stimulate ideas leading to more adventurous gardening.

The British Rose Festival is a spectacular national event held every year in July. It includes a magificent display of roses organised by the Society and the British Rose Growers Association on an excitingly new and different theme each year. The competition is for the leading national amateur rose exhibitors and floral artists. All the best of British roses can be seen at this unique show.

Of particular interest in this county for vegetarians will be **Shaw's Corner** at **Ayot St Lawrence. Sir George Bernard Shaw,** playwright and critic, vegetarian and humanist, lived here for the second half of his long and active life. His vegetarian ideals were based on both moral and health grounds, proclaiming that 'Animals are our fellow creatures. I feel a strong kinship with them.; The house has been kept exactly as it was at the time of his death in 1950.

The many houses on a truly grand scale include **Hatfield House** originally home to the Bishops of Ely and later to Henry VIII's children and other members of the Royal family, **Brocket Hall** which was the home of Lord Melbourne and Lady Caroline Lamb, **Moor Park,** the historic home of Cardinal Wolsey later transformed into a Palladian mansion and now a golf club. and **Basing House** home of William Penn founder of Pennsylvania.

Sadly others have fared less well, such as the Castle at **Bishop's Stortford** now just a mound, and another earthworks with just a little masonry which was the Castle at Berkhamsted, presented by William the Conqueror to his brother, later visited by Thomas a Becket, Chaucer and three of Henry VIII's wives and involuntarily visited for a long term, by King John of France. Another was Ware Park which originally housed the 'Great Bed of Ware' mentiond by Shakespeare in his plays, now in the Victoria and Albert Museum.

Near **Ware** at **Amwell** is one of the most unexpected of museums in Britain, a **Lamp-Post Museum.**

Similarly bordering on the outer suburbs of London, the county of **Surrey** has a very high population, much of it in large villages or small towns, and all of it spread out in pleasant green surroundings.

The well know geographical feature of the **Hogs Back** is a part of the North Downs and other high points such as **Leith Hill** with its view of 13 counties, and **Box Hill** offer outstanding panoramic views. On the high point of **Chatley Heath** stands a tower which was part of the communication system, sending messages from London to Portsmouth in less than one minute in the days before telegraph.

Box Hill overlooks some of the prettiest of scenery along the River Mole. Despite its rather unpoetic name it is probably the river most written about in poetry, by Spencer, Milton, Pope and others, and the riverside village of **Brockham** is said to have given the name of 'brock' to the badger, many of which used to live here.

The riverside meadows of **Runnymede** are famous as being the site of King John's signing of (actually fixing his seal to) the Magna Carta in 1215. The memorial buildings at Runnymede were designed by Sir Edward Lutyens.

Architecture from the early part of this century can also be seen to great effect at **Whiteley.** Built according to the will of William Whiteley who left one million pounds for the creation of this retirement village for staff of Whiteley's Department Store. Surrey contains other fine recent buildings such as the **Yvonne Arnaud Theatre** at **Guildford**, as well as **Guildford Cathedral**, started in 1936 but not consecrated until 1962 due to the intervening war. With its position high on Stag Hill on the edge of the town it makes a magnificent spectacle. Close to Guildford at **Peaslake,** one of the most out of the way villages in the county, tucked away on the slopes of Hurt Wood, is the **Hurtwood Inn Hotel,** and at **Albury, Stream Cottage,** the most peaceful of places to stay. Both are great bases for anyone wanting to stay in and around Guildford. A mill and a church in Albury were recorded in the Domesday Book. The great architect Pugin influenced much of the style of building and his famous chimneys are still in evidence today.

Surrey has several special gardens, the most important of which is **Wisley Gardens,** for over 80 years the show gardens of the Royal Horticultural Society and a source of inspiration for all kinds of gardeners. There are features at their best at each time of the year; the Alpine Meadow in spring,

Chapter Three

the rhododendron-clad Battleston Hill in early summer, and for winter the Orchid House with its naturalistic 'rainforest setting'. Wisley is full of fascinating shapes, textures, sounds and smells, and the special garden for disabled people enables all those with a handicap to take full advantage of them all. There are occasional guided walks and the RHS also runs a series of courses, some of them on aspects of gardening, others on flower arranging or botanical painting. The Information Centre is reputed to sell the most extensive range of horticultural and botanical books in the world, and the range of plants for sale, is staggering with something like 8,500 varieties, many of them far from common-or-garden.

Peppermint used to be an important crop in **Banstead**. The watercress beds at **Abinger Hammer,** fed by underground springs are one of the claims to minor fame for the village, and its history as a centre for the iron industry is another. The iron working made use of a hammer mill (hence the name) driven by the stream.

Loseley Park between **Godalming** and **Guildford** is a splendid Elizabethan house, the home of the More-Molyneux family from the 16th century to the present day. The family farms 1,400 acres around the house, and it is here that Loseley ice-cream and yoghurt is made. All Loseley dairy products are free from artificial additives and they also grow organic crops. However the farm tour shows little of the dairy aspect and does incorporate other farm animals.

One of the most interesting of the many towns in Surrey is **Farnham**, an attractive small market town with elegant Georgian housing and with some interesting literary associations including Sir Walter Scott, Swift and William Cobbett (who described the beauty spot of **Hindhead** as 'the most villainouse spot God ever made') There are several historic houses open to the public in and around the town.

Mystery surrounds **Shalford Mill**, an early 18th century water mill which was in full use until 1914 when it fell into some disrepair. It was acquired by the 'Ferguson's Gang some years later and after restoration was given to the National Trust. The 'Gang' members used code names such as 'Bill Stickers' and none of their identities has ever been known.

Surrey has become one of the most popular commuter counties for London. It might well have destroyed its character but it has not and there are some truly charming towns with fine churches, good shops and excellent hotels and eateries. Between **Reigate** and **Dorking** at **Betchworth** is **Gadbrook Old Farm House** where the hospitality on offer highlights the welcoming attitude of the county. Betchworth is a quiet place through which the River

Mole wanders peacefully. It has a good hostelry, **The Dolphin Inn** and some attractive 16th century cottages untouched by any fake restoration. In Reigate itself an equal welcome awaits anyone who stays at **Barn Cottage.**

Anyone who loves horse racing will be familiar with **Epsom** and its famous downs on which The Derby is run. **Leatherhead, Woking, Walton-on-Thames** and **Esher** all have character. I probably have an unfair liking for **Weybridge** where I lived for a while enjoying the busy little town, its river, its shops and hostelries and finding out about some very good eateries within easy distance like the **Cedar House Restaurant** at **Cobham.**

Ending on a happy and smiling note, **Cranleigh Church** is believed to hold the inspiration for Lewis Carroll's Cheshire Cat, a grinning cat head carved on the transept arch.

London, how can anyone possibly cover the majesty, the excitement and the sprit in this probably the greatest of all capital cities, in one part of a chapter? I am not even going to try because suffice it to say there is so much literature available to the visitor, and totally up to date data, that any in put of mine would be trivial. I know that the years I spent living in London were probably the most exciting of my life. I lived just behind Oxford Street in Montague Square, and so I was in the heart if the West End. Theatreland was only a short distance, and I think I saw every play, musical, opera and ballet that was performed. It was a mental and visual experience that is unrepeatable and for which I will always be grateful that I had sufficient money to do it. The London stage attracts the very best theatre in the world.

Strangely enough when I lived in the great metropolis I seldom visited any of the tourist attractions like the Tower of London unless I had visitors staying with me. It was American friends from Texas who really made me take notice of things and places which I had come to take for granted. Something I will always be grateful for and I would urge you to see as much as you can whether it is from the river, on foot or maybe using one of the splendid sightseeing buses. It is frequently the unexpected vista that enchants or the sun glistening on the waters of the RiverThames**,** throwing odd lights onto familar buildings. The Houses of Parliament, Lambeth Palace, the great Savoy Hotel all seen from the river look totally different. You can take boat trips the length of the river and it is more than rewarding. It will leave you with indelible memories.

London is crammed with excellent museums, most of them in **South Kensington**, and no visitor should miss the splendid **Victoria and Albert Museum**. On **Butler's Wharf** is Britain's first **Tea and Coffee Museum**, featuring hundreds of different coffee grinders and machines, over 1,000

Chapter Three

teapots, teabags, prints, photographs, maps and drawings documenting the history of tea and coffee drinking over the past 350years. There are even tea bushes growing in the museum!

Visitors to **Greenwich's Fan Museum** are introduced to fans and their history through displays which also show their making and the materials used. There are some exquisite examples of 18th and 19th century fans in an elegant Georgian setting, in this, the first and only museum dedicated to the art and craft of fan making.

Just a few of the other exceptional museums around London are the **Bank of England Museum** with the history of the bank, displays of gold and banknotes: **The Design Museum** in the Docklands which has collections of well designed, mass production items along with a series of special exhibitions; **Dickens' House Museum** where the great man lived: **Florence Nightingale Museum** telling the story of her life and work, the **Freud Museum** in Sigmund Freud's last home. **The Guinness World of Records** with lifesize models and electronic displays to show the biggest, fastest etc. **Kew Bridge Steam Museum** with its unique collection of impressive, working steam pumping engines; and the **London Diamond Centre** where you can see the diamonds being cut and polished.

An extraordinary museum, if you can call it a museum, is to be found at **18 Folgate Street** in the heart of what was the Huguenot rag trade district of **Spitalfields**. The house is opened a few times a week by the owner who lives there as the house was when it was built in the 18th century, perfect in every detail of decor and, of course, with only candle and gas power. However those intending to visit are requested to 'telephone' for details!

The underground **Cabinet War Rooms** feature a Transatlantic Telephone Room and another 20 historic rooms which were operational during the 2nd World War. Very closeby in **Horseguard's Parade**, and also underground is **Henry VIII's Wine Cellar** which can only be seen by appointment, on a Saturday afternoon.

At **Wimbledon** is what must surely be the only **Lawn Tennis Museum** in the world. It is open during the Wimbledon Tennis season to ticket holders.

Also at Wimbledon, as part of the **Polka's Children Theatre**, is a toy and puppet exhibition. In Scala Street in central London, **Pollock's Toy Museum** displays not just Pollock's card cut-out theatres but puppets, dolls' houses and teddies of the past. The **London Toy and Model Museum** covers a similar subject, in Craven Hill in **Bayswater.** Somewhat different, but on the theme of puppets, is the **Spitting Image Rubberworks** in **Covent Garden.**

Also in Covent Garden, displays of work on an environmental theme are often held at the **London Ecology Centre**, founded on World Environment Day in 1985. The Centre's focus is the Information Service for the general public, a forum for environmental organisations and a single point of contact for the channelling of enquiries. Its 'London Sustainable Development Network'collects information on examples of good environmental practice which it then publicises to those interested. The offices of the Bat Conservation Trust and the Environmental Film Festival are also within the Centre, as is a Meditation Centre.

Covent Garden is an exciting development of mainly shops, cafes and small museums, several of them quite specialised and unique, mixed with street entertainment and an electric atmosphere, in what was the old fruit and vegetable market. No longer are there flower girls to be found under the portico of St Paul's church, but although the area has changed considerably since those days it has retained its lively spirit.

A short walk from Covent Garden via the Aldwych brings you to **Fleet Street,** another part of London now much changed. For centuries until just recently, Fleet Street was the home of all the important national newspapers, now most have moved, mainly to the **Docklands.** The other association with this area, that of the legal profession, continues. Although different, the charm of the old pubs and alleys persists, with much of its history on view such as the **Pepys Exhibition** within the **Prince Henry's Room**, and the **Wig and Pen** where lawyers and journalists have traditionally met, but Sweeney Todd's Barber Shop and the Pie Shop on the other side of St Dunstan's Church are no longer there. In the Strand, **Twinings** tea shop is said to be the longest established shop on its original site and also claims to be the narrowest. The names of the streets and alleys sum up something of their past history, with Wine Office Court and Old Cheshire Cheese.

An aerial view of London will show that much of it is covered in green. Not only are there large numbers of private gardens, but there are hundreds of public gardens and parks right up to the size of **Richmond Park**, which with deer roaming wild, really does seem to be a bit of the countryside within London. In **Westminster** the pretty **College Garden** with its **Little Cloister** is only occasionally open to the public. It is said to be the oldest garden of its type in England.

London probably has the most varied and best restaurants in the world - the French would not agree with me! It would be invidious to choose any one place in which to eat but because I know **The Portobello Hotel** and discovered that **Julie's Restaurant** was under the same management, it therefore gave me a sound reason for going there. If the standard was

Chapter Three

anything like that of the Portobello I would not be disappointed - and I was not. What an astonishing place. A labyrinthe fantasy warren made up of five rooms decorated in different styles, housed in three terraced houses and an ex builder's yard. The five rooms are Gothic; with chairs salvaged from nearby St Paul's Church; Forge, decorated in pink with an original forge as a set-piece; Back, with a pulpit and huge oval table that required a wall to be demolished to fit it in (this is the stag party room where the Prince of Wales, Mark Phillips, Mark Knopfler and Sting bade farewell to bachelordom;) The Garden, which has a removable canvas roof, and the Conservatory. Each room can be reserved for parties. The theatrical look evokes the novels of Jules Verne, but makes a congenial atmosphere for stars who want to let their hair down. It is a calm, romantic place and uncrowded. Somewhere to enjoy dinner by downlighters and candles. At Lunch, most customers are on business, usually from the local fashion and record industries. In the evenings, locals and stars alike enjoy the intimate atmosphere and well-known absence of paparazzi. You may see anyone from Joanna Lumley eating Vegetarian to Princess Margaret, Sean Connery, Roger Moore, Kenneth Branagh, Madonna - a never ending list. When booking, regulars specify rooms and then tables. George Michael for example, likes Table F6 in the Forge, somewhere to see and be seen! Sunday Brunch goes on from 12.30-7.30pm, there is a Morning Coffee Menu and delicious, imaginative food throughout. You will find Julie's at 135 Portland Road, W11. Tel:0171 229 8331 and Julie's Bar at 137 Portland Road, W11. Tel: 0171 727 7985.

Where to stay? Well, the list is endless but I have chosen a small selection of places that I can personally recommend having either stayed there or had friends who have. I have already mentioned the excellent **Portobello** at 22 Stanley Gardens. It gets its name from the thriving Notting Hill Portobello Market although Stanley Gardens is a quiet street. **The Goring Hotel** is a distinguished, dignified establishment, privately owned and run immaculately. It is delightful, has beautiful gardens, which provide the view for many of the bedrooms, some balconied. Next the old family hotel in George Street, **Durrants**. It has been owned by the Miller family for over 70 years and provides a service that meets the needs of today's travellers in an atmosphere of yesteryear.

To find a tranquil haven in the heart of London is a godsend. **Number Sixteen, Sumner Place**, in South Kensington is just that. The premises just ooze warmth and a sense of being in your own private dwelling cared for by an efficient and friendly staff. Another such place is **11 Cadogan Gardens, Sloane Square.** Which was the first exclusive Town House Hotel ever. It is set in a tree-lined square in the heart of Chelsea, just a few minutes walk from Sloane Square, close to Harrods and the shopping delights of Knightsbridge and the Kings Road.

If you feel in the mood to pamper yourselves and live a little in the past then go to **The Waldorf Hotel** in Aldwych. Taking tea and dancing the afternoon away in the magical terraced **Palm Court** is a truly unique experience, popular with Londoners and visitors alike. Held every Saturday and Sunday, the tea dance has also become a favourite pre-theatre venue - The Waldorf's location on the Aldwych, in the heart of theatreland, makes most theatres within easy walking distance. Afternoon tea at **The Ritz** in **Piccadilly** is another thrilling experience, quite different but equally memorable. Wonderful service, exquisitely thin sandwiches, delicious cakes and pastries and the lush greenery of St James Park outside the tall elegant windows. Both The Waldorf and The Ritz will long be remembered.

The ancient walled **Chelsea Physic Garden**, just along from the Chelsea Royal Hospital with its red-coated pensioners, was only the second botanical garden to be opened in Britain. It is a serene and beautiful place. It was the seed of a cotton plant taken from here that resulted in America's successful cotton industry.

The most famous London garden is undoubtedly **Kew Gardens**, and indeed it is accepted as being the finest botanic garden and plant research centre in the world, aimed at creating a better future for our planet. It consists of 300 acres of magnificent tranquil gardens alongside the River Thames in West London, with 6 acres under glass from the exquisite Victorian Palm House to the stunning new Princess of Wales Conservatory. There are buildings too, including Kew Palace and **Queen Charlotte's Cottage**. One of the most unusual features is the Pagoda, completed in 1762 as a surprise for Princess Augusta, the Dowager Princess of Wales, who had founded the gardens only a few years earlier. The ten storey octagonal structure reaches a height of 50 metres, and was at the time the most accurate imitation of a Chinese building in Europe, (although to be accurate it should have had an odd number of storeys). Vistas through the garden enable the Pagoda to be seen in superb settings. The 18th century Kew Gardens was just a tiny portion of that seen today, having the Richmond estate added to it early in the 19th century, with some of the areas coming more recently into cultivation.

In addition to the nine exceptional glass houses, the dozen other buildings, the many special garden features and the wonderful parkland of the three arboreta, work goes on behind the scenes to preserve endangered plant species and to conserve habitats. The 44,000 different types of plants at Kew represent one in six of known species (it is believed that there are many plant species still undiscovered and work too continues in this direction), with 13 species extinct in the wild and 1,000 threatened. The botanists at Kew now have some 6 million preserved specimens which through their research could be found to contain important medicines, fuels or food.

Chapter Three

Another very important although less well known garden is in **Enfield**. The National Gardening Centre at **Capel Manor** is actually not just a garden but a College for the study of landscape and garden maintenance and management, a Countryside Centre predominantly used by schools, and it incorporates 'Which? Magazine's' demonstration garden. The gardens extend over 25 acres and illustrate many different designs, styles and periods, from formal images to habitats for attracting wildlife.

In the centre of London, next to Lambeth Palace, is the **Museum of Garden History**, run by the Tradescant Trust. The Trust was founded less than 20 years ago to save the historic church of St Mary at Lambeth from demolition. There they establised the Museum of Garden History as a centre for plant displays, lectures and exhibitions. The Tradescants, father and son, were royal gardeners in the 17th century and brought back from their frequent travels many of the plants which we know, making them still today possibly the best known name in plant collecting. The plants were propagated in their famous 60 acres garden in Lambeth. Development of the garden is ongoing, with some exciting plans for the future.

Kent has long been known as the 'Garden of England' and the rich soils continue to provide abundant crops. The view of Kent as a county of hop fields dotted with oast houses is certainly inaccurate in certain parts, although a great many of the oast houses have now been converted into dwellings. The largest collection of oast houses in the world, dating from the Victorian era, are to be found at the **Whitbread Hop Farm** which is near **Paddock Wood**. You won't actually see beer being produced but you can see **The Hop Story Exhibition** as well as the **Whitbread Shire Horse Centre** and many other attractions.

As well as hop gardens, orchards feature frequently in this fertile landscape in the area known as 'The Weald' which actually covers about half of the county's total area in the south west. Further to the north is the North Downs, a high chalk ridge which ends at the White Cliffs of Dover, possibly the best known British landscape, seen from the ship and from air by many thousands of visitors each year. The highest point is known as Shakespeare's Cliff, having featured in King Lear.

Very different landscapes can be found in some coastal districts, such as the pretty meadows of the **Isle of Sheppey** in the north and next to it the **Isle of Grain** with the country's largest heronry, and **Romney Marsh** in the south, where the flat open marshes appear sumptuous in the bright summer light but truly desolate by winter. The Marsh was created by the Romans who constructed the Rhee Wall to claim the land from the sea. Although the sea is retreating, the small town of Old Romney once on the coast now stands well inland and even **New Romney** further out is now dilocated. In the centre of the marsh stands St Thomas Becket Church, with no village or even hamlet nearby. Several other communities have gradually become more distant from the sea such as **Sandwich** once a Cinque Port and now almost two miles from the coast. Although not necessarily as close to the water as they once were, an amazingly large number of castles and other fortified buildings can be seen around the coastal area, built because Kent, being the closestpart of Britain to foreign soil, has been subject to many invasions, and attempted invasions, over thousands of years.

Kent can also show signs of very much earlier occupation with flints found from the Old Stone Age and dwellings from around 6,000BC. **Kit's Coty House** and **Little Kit's Coty House**, taken from the Celtic for 'tomb in the woods' are two Neolithic burial chambers near **Aylesford**. It was in what is now Kent that the Romans first arrived, and later the Angles, the Saxons and the Jutes all came to these shores. **Dover** is now the busiest of the ferry ports with frequent trips to Calais, which can actually be seen on clear days. Increases to the 'friendly' invasion via the long planned Channel Tunnel are now a reality. Dover has always been of historical importance. Apart from being an ancient port linking Britain with the Continent, it was once the walled Roman town of Dubris, and the start of the Roman Road, Watling Street.

One particular rare Roman structure is the lighthouse, or 'pharos' which stands within Dover Castle, overlooking the White Cliffs. The castle reflects much of the county's history in one, being a mixture of many dates with its history in the Iron Age and the current buildings being part Roman, part Saxon and extensively Norman, with some later additions. Actually additions is possibly the wrong word to use for the most recent alterations to Dover Castle: tunnels were excavated within the White Cliffs to counter the threat of invasion by Napoleon, and during the Second World War these became a secret operational centre. It was from here that the evacuation from Dunkirk was masterminded. The expected Napoleonic invasion was also responsible for the construction of artillery towers such as the **Dymchurch Martello Tower** which formed a chain of strongholds around the coast.

The whole of the Kent coastline, many of the castles and several other historic sites are included on the **Saxon Shore Way**, a 143 mile walk, which links in the middle at **Dover** with the **North Downs Way**, following the crest of the North Downs and in places incorporating the **Pilgrims' Way** linking **Canterbury** with Winchester in Hampshire. The Pilgrim's Way is actually far older than the name would imply, and was probably first used by the Neolithic peoples.

Chapter Three

If one wanted to choose somewhere that spelt out beauty, history, heritage and national pride then **Canterbury** would probably top the poll. Canterbury was welcoming pilgrims 900 years ago and even then it was an ancient city. Three hundred years later Chaucer brought attention to it with his Canterbury Tales. The Cathedral dominates the city and is the spiritual centre for Christians who belong to the Church of England in many countries but the non-believers in the tenets of the Anglican Church are as much addicted to its beauty as anyone else. Thomas a Becket who was murdered within its walls by four knights who heeded Henry II's plea to rid him of ' this low born priest' has been revered as a martyr ever since that gruesome day. The martyrdom of Thomas a Becket is a well known fact and within days of his murder it turned Canterbury into a place of pilgrimage. He was canonised in 1173 and a year later a remorseful King Henry himself made the pilgrimage in an act of penance. The pilgrims were to help make Canterbury one of the richest and most magnificent churches of medieval times.

You may think Canterbury Cathedral holds the record for the number of steps one climbs up and down during your tour of the building. There are steps up the chancel, steps down to the transept and a flight of steps ascending to the pulpitum. It is a journey of never ending thrills, stunning architecture, glorious glass and always this awareness that the Almighty is gazing upon us.

Canterbury springs to everyone's mind when you talk about Kent but the county has much more to offer. Fifteen minutes to the north you come to **Whitstable** long renowned for its oysters. Here there is good fishing, bathing from a shingle beach and good yachting facilities. A spit of land known as 'The Street' juts out about a mile and a half into the sea and provides a pleasant promenade at lowtide. The Castle dates mainly from the 19th century but has a 15th century brick tower originally used as a look out post. Its parkland is open to the public.

To the east the seaside resorts of **Westgate on Sea** and **Margate** have been popular for generations. The former is less boisterous than the latter but both have their adherents who would not go anywhere else. I cannot say that it is a holiday that would appeal to me but the countryside and the sea are both beautiful and you see a lot of happy, smiling faces, so who am I to judge!

Broadstairs just round the North Foreland is a different kettle of fish. Here is a Regency resort which has not changed much since the society of those times put their stamp on it. It has miles of sheltered and sandy bays and to the north stand the chalk cliffs and lighthouses of the North foreland,

The Home Counties

with wide views over the Thames Estuary. Bleak House is now a Dickens Museum containing early editions of his books, pictures, photographs and some personal items. Nearby Dickens House which also contains a museum was immortalised as the home of Betsy Trotwood in 'David Copperfield' written while Dickens was living in Broadstairs. In June every year a Dickens Festival is held, when the local people throng the streets in costumes of the period.

Down past the busy ferryport of **Ramsgate**, **Sandwich** and **Deal**, one comes to the beautiful St Margaret's Bay, part of the South Foreland Heritage Coast. Here at **West Cliff** is the stunning **Wallets Court Hotel** with the tiny church of St Peters opposite. It is a fascinating hotel in its own right but add that to the history of the bulding which first gets its mention in the Domesday Book and you cannot help being enthralled.

The garden at Wallet's is open to the rolling fields and the bracing sea air with its regularly swirling mists. It now contains a rather unusual treehouse, an all weather tennis court, and a recently restored granary on Kentish straddle stones. During your wanderings you might visit the tiny church of St Peter where the Gibbon family who restored the house in the early 17th century, are all buried, or take a stroll up Pond Lane to a local vantage point. St Margaret's Bay has provided great inspiration for many writers, poets and artists over the years. The quintessential Englishman Noel Coward and also the man who created James Bond, Ian Fleming who both lived in the Bay at one time. One can lie there in the long grass for hours listening to the skylarks and watching the traffic on the Channel. On a clear day you can even see the French coastline which lies just over twenty miles away.

The next part of my travels takes me to the 'Garden Coast' encompassing **Folkestone, Hythe and Romney Marsh** which offers me endless pleasure both in the beautiful countryside, the sea and the history of the area together with the monaticism of the Romney Marshes. You will see from the list of attractions in the back of this book that there is so much to see and so varied that it must please everyone whatever age.

The M20 will take me to the busy town of **Ashford** and to the small medieval village of **Woodchurch** dating from the 11th century. There is a delightful house here in which you can stay. **Prospect House** overlooks the large village green where cricket and football are played in season.It is a wonderful house built in 1789 but could possibly be older judging from its very oldbeams in places. An old redbrick wall surrounds the house on two sides and the other sides are hedges. On warm summer days guests frequently have breakfast outside or sit in the shade of a large apple tree for tea. The

Chapter Three

owners Fiona Adams-Cairns and her South African husband are widely travelled, welcoming and excellent hosts. Look at the visitors book and you will find comments such as 'Every night is a dinner party'. An hours drive will take you to Glyndebourne, Canterbury, of course, Dover Castle, the moated Leeds Castle, Churchill's home, Chartwell and some wonderful gardens including Sissinghurst.

Royal Tunbridge Wells is beyond Sissinghurst to the west from Ashford. This is a town that delights the eye. A distinguished spa at one time especially among persons of fashion in the 18th century, though the waters can still be drunk. Samuel Pepys and John Evelyn both visited and Beau Nash left Bath to become the master of Tunbridge Wells ceremonies in 1735. However it was Lord North who had made the waters popular a hundred years earlier. Charles I's wife, Henrietta Maria came here after the birth of their son, the future Charles II in 1630. This was when the building of the town began. The Pantiles, the spa's oldest street was started in 1700. How beautiful this elegant arcade is enhanced by lime trees; its Italianate pillars supporting diverse frontages and a music balcony. The tiles were laid because Princess Anne - later to become Queen - threatened not to return after her son slipped on the original walk. Today flagstones have replaced almost all the tiles.

The town is blessed with many parks and gardens and a fine common with outcrops of weathered sandstone rocks. Such rocks are typical of the area, the source of its mineral waters, and an attraction for climbers: the nearby High Rocks, the Toad Rocks on Rushall Common; Bowles Rocks, Eridge, Harrison's Rocks, Groombridge and the Happy Valley. There are many places to visit including a leisurely cruise around **Bewl Water,** Southern Water's beautiful reservoir at Lamberhurst. This is the largest area of inland water in south east England and set in most attractive countryside. Also at Lamberhurst is **Scotney Castle Garden**, one of England's most romantic gardens, surrounding the ruins of a 14th century moated castle. Rhododendrons, azaleas, waterlilies and wisteria flower in profusion.

Groombridge Place Gardens and **Enchanted Forest** provide another stunning day out. Surrounded by breathtaking parkland this mystical medieval site includes the famous Grade I Listed 17th-century walled gardens set against the backdrop of the classical moated mansion and Enchanted Forest, which have inspired writers, artists and connoisseurs of beauty for hundreds of years.

To the north of Tunbridge Wells is **Tonbridge**, a prosperous market town at the navigable extremity of the River Medway, where it diverges into formidable streams. A settlement that has been strategically important since

Anglo Saxon and probably Roman times. The River Walk along the Medway, through willow-lined meadows gives a fine view of **Tonbridge Castle**. Its Norman to 13th century ruins, on a site defended since 1088, are substantial: the shell of the keep, curtain walls, round-towered gatehouse. Some of Tonbridge's 18th century houses are built of castle stone. It is an exciting place to visit and you are invited to travel back over 700 years to join the Lords of Tonbridge Castle and experience a vivid recreation of the sights, sounds and excitement of 13th century life.

Penshurst Place and Gardens, near Tonbridge must be visited. The beautiful medieval stately home of Viscount de L'Isle, with its magnificent Baron's Hall dates from 1341. The splendid gardens were first laid out in the 16th century. Two of the loveliest castles in Kent and some would say in the world, are **Leeds Castle** 4 miles east of Maidstone and **Hever Castle** near Edenbridge, the childhood home of Anne Boleyn. Both will provide you with hours of delight and will remain in your memory for years to come.

The Medway towns must not be forgotten. They have always been places of great interest. Made up of Strood, Gillingham, Chatham and Rochester, they are steeped in history and none more so than the ancient cathedral city of **Rochester** on the lower reaches of the Medway. It is a major port and an industrial centre and such a busy place but Rochester's older buildings are clustered around the Cathedral and in the High Street where they were confined by medieval walls. The city is closely associated with the novelist Charles Dickens, and features more often in his books than any other place, apart from London, although Portsmouth, where he was born, has The Charles Dickens Birthplace Museum. Many great cities have been built around a river and Rochester is no exception.

Chatham has had a long and distinguished history and until recent years been inextricably involved in the life of Her Majesty's Royal Navy. Those days are gone but a visit to **The Historic Dockyard** will give you at least five hours of absorbing interest. There are no less than 47 Scheduled Ancient Monuments, forming the most completely preserved Georgian dockyard in the world, dry docks, and covered slips, timber mast houses and seasoning sheds, huge storehouses and the quarter mile long working ropery stand beside the elegant Commissioner's house and garden, officers' terrace and dockyard church. Now a living, working museum, this tells of the lives of the dockyard craftsmen whose skills - from carpentry and caulking to rigging and forging - made the British fleet the finest in the world. No one can fail to be fascinated by what they see. With seven main attractions plus skills and crafts in action, it is not surprising visitors stay an average of 5 hours.

Chapter Three

Kent has so much beauty to offer in every direction. Its name 'The Garden of England' is fully justified. I constantly promise myself that the next time I come here I will spend more time - however long I stay it is never long enough.

I lived in Suffolk for a while on the Shotley Peninsula looking over the River Stour to **Harwich**. This allowed me to become happily familiar with the corner of Essex that includes the old Roman town of **Colchester**, and the glorious **Dedham Vale** as well as many of the smaller villages including **Wix** between Harwich and Colchester, bypassed by the A120 which is a direct route to London. It is a place surrounded by local beauty spots like **Mistley** where one of Great Britain's largest population of mute swans live and the twin 'Mistley Towers' stand the only remains of Robert Adams ecclesiastical work in England.

New Farm House is very much part of Wix and the owners, Pat and George Mitchell offer comfort, friendliness with good farmhouse cooking. They have a good reputation both in this country and abroad which is confirmed by the number of overseas visitors who return annually. The house is only 10 minutes drive from Parkeston Quay at Harwich from which Car and Passenger ferries depart for the continental ports of the Hook of Holland, Denmark, Germany and Sweden which makes it an ideal and convenient place to stay overnight before embarking for, or returning from, the Continent.

Colchester is Britain's oldest recorded town and has 2,000 years of fascinating history and heritage to discover. It is a history involving the Romans, the Saxons and the Normans which has been interpreted and displayed using the most exciting and up-to-date methods in the town's museums. Colchester Oysters were famous in Roman days and are still so today, but as a fishing and trading port, the town is no longer significant. It is significant however for the 1000 acres of public gardens and parks. You should not fail to walk in the glorious park surrounding the Castle which was built by William the Conqueror in 1076 and a visit to its museum is highly recommended.

The Vale of Dedham is somewhere very special and immortalised by John Constable. This north-east corner of Essex is where the River Stour forms the boundary with Suffolk and is an area of outstanding scenic beauty. It is still possible to stroll through the meadows and along the river banks with their abundance of flora and fauna, or explore the delightful villages with their impressive medieval churches and old pubs. It is constantly changing scenery. From **Bures** to **Harwich** the river loses its quiet willow-lined banks enclosing the gently flowing water, home to colourful ducks, elegant swans and moorhens and becomes tidal flats beyond Manningtree and the dominant east coast. Many places in Essex have been entrapped by the ever stretching tentacles of London but there are still delightful places, **Halstead** is one with a delightful establishment in which to stay at **Timbers**. It is a small town built about a hill overlooking the River Colne. The wide High Street has some charming gabled shops and houses.

Sussex now known as two counties **West Sussex** and **East Sussex** is a part of England that is totally delightful. **West Sussex** takes in an area bounded to the west by the Hampshire border, to the north with that of Surrey with an imaginary eastern division runnng south from the new urban mass of Crawley down to meet the coast at **Angmering-on-Sea**. As an introduction to the whole it serves well: there are great estates and houses, high hills where sheep graze and skylarks sing, ancient villages and hamlets nestling in natural folds and large stands of mature woodland, the remnants of mighty tracts of forest which once covered much of the county. Balanced against this rustic idyll are modern developments, new roads and a population that has expanded rapidly over the last few decades. Better communications and an increase in personal wealth has meant an influx of commuters, together with a large amount of light industry attracted to the area since the Second World War; all this is to the good, even if the aesthetics occasionally offend. Employment and prosperity has done much to preserve the rural charm that so attracted the likes of Belloc, even though that charm can often seem synthetic. But consider; the thatched farm-labourer's cottage with roses climbing over the porch would be no more than a weed-ridden mound of rubble if left to purely local concern. Estates, councils, and conservation bodies have but limited budgets and must spend accordingly; a tumbledown cottage of uncertain ancestry has no priority in their scheme of things, and few private landowners have sufficiency of cash to modernise such places to the standards that today's agricultural worker rightly expects. It is the outsider, the commuter, weekender or retiree who has the money and the determination to conserve. There are many students of the countryside and its vernacular architecture who grumble a great deal about the 'chocolate-box' or 'stockbroker-belt' image of many of these small rural communities, but to my mind it is better that it should be thus than down-at-heel and crumbling or worse, abandoned. One may raise an eyebrow at a satellite dish or an ill-advised conservatory - but doubtless our more affected ancestors reacted in like manner when confronted with innovations such as glazed windows or inside sanitation.

The newcomer rarely receives thanks and seldom praise for his efforts. However, those who have chosen Sussex in which to settle and 'improve' have made a wise choice for the natives have long been known for their pragmatic and friendly attitude to the outsider, whether Roman, Saxon,

Chapter Three

Norman or modern city worker. It is a county with an almost magical ability to absorb, adapt and change almost seemlessly. Throughout its long history, it has been directly affected by great politcal and economic upheavals, yet, when the dust has settled and the shouting died away, the essential Sussex still remains; quietly welcoming the visitor to its tranquil beauty.

My own tour began in the cathedral city of **Chichester**, just a few miles to the east of the border with Hampshire. Other than the cathedral spire, little of the city's fine heritage can be glimpsed from the outskirts by the passing traveller, who sees a flat countryside bounded to the north by the distant South Downs. This fertile land used for growing a wide variety of crops, is also home to numerous light industrial estates that seem to fringe the northern edge of the by-pass. Chichester is no grand cathedral city. Its scale is domestic and it has the air of a prosperous market town, friendly, unpretentious with nothing to intimidate. Even the lovely cathedral seems to stand at the pavement's edge without benefit of grand close or walled surround. No great avenues or parades, merely a sensible crossroads of four main streets running out in the direction of the cathedral points and the areas in between being filled with a happy warren of lanes, narrow alleyways and delightful little squares. Modern development has inevitably led to the introduction of pedestrian precincts, shopping arcades and car parks but happily the process has not been over-intrusive and the human scale remains. The cruciform layout owes much to the Romans who found the area of fertile plain to their liking when they arrived in AD43.

The lovely interior of this Norman cathedral contains some startlingly modern decorative art.The most obvious is John Piper's huge representative tapestry hanging behind the high altar, there is also a window by Chagall, a painting by Graham Sutherland and numerous other contemporary works including a pulpit of concrete and steel. George Bell was bishop from 1929 to 1958 and it was he who introduced the concept of modern art into the cathedral. A bold move, but one that added new dimensions of colour and life that had been effectively missing since the Parliamentarians destroyed so much of the decorative work during the Civil War.

The Pallants is a charming area of principally Georgian redbrick and once under the exclusive jurisdiction of the Archbishop of Canterbury. **Pallant House** built in 1713, is the finest of these buildings and has a link with the cathedral as it contains a fine collection of modern art, the bequest of the late Dean, Doctor Walter Hussey. There is also a wonderful collection of porcelain and a beautifully reconstructed small garden in keeping with the period of the house. It is both museum and gallery and succeeds in either sphere.

An old granary houses the excellent **Chichester Museum** while nearby stands **St Marys Hospital**, built as an infirmary and converted in the 1600's into eight small dwellings for old people. It has been little altered since and it is often held up as an example of excellent planning for the needs of the elderly. Further north of this area is **Priory Park**, a large open space named after the Franciscan Priors who established themselves here in the early 13th-century. The choir of their church survives as a museum and within the bounds of the Park is a grassy mound that once was the site of Chichester Castle, dismantled around the time of Henry III.

Chichester is representative of much of the county in that its prosperity comes from the ability to adapt without losing its essential character. As the visitor can see, ancient and modern co-exist happily and one of the principal examples of this is to be found in Oaklands Park to the north of the old city walls. **The Chichester Festival Theatre** was constructed in the 1960's and now has an international reputation, attracting audiences from all over the world to see productions of the highest quality. The city also has a major Arts Festival, inaugurated all but a quarter of a century ago which takes place every July.

To the west is **Fishbourne** where **The Fishbourne Roman Palace and Museum** is one of the most important Roman relics in Britain and contains much of the remains of a magnificent first century villa. For todays visitor, apart from this gem, there is an interesting if slightly eccentric pub, **The Woolpack Inn** where you will be fed at sensible prices.

Just west of Fishbourne lies one of the jewels of the Sussex shore, the small Saxon village of **Bosham** (pronounced 'Bozzum'). Lying at the top of an arm of Chiechester Harbour, this is a delightful little community jumbled around the waters of Bosham Creek. Canute had a palace here and it was on the foreshore that he was reputed to have commanded the tide to retreat. Anyone able to work such a miracle would undoubtedly be in much demand at the **Anchor Bleu**, a cosy pub by the creek, where the unwary motorist is frequently caught out by the rapidly rising tide which can cover the shore road. The Anchor is the sole survivor of several small pubs which once traded in the tiny and attractive High Street.

Northwards to the very border with Hampshire I was off to visit **Stansted Park** near Rowlands Castle. Ancient woodland, once part of the Forest of Bere, sets off this most decorative Wren-style house, which is full of treasures. There is an extraordinary and highly decorative chapel which owes its appearance to a previous owner of the house who spent most of his time trying to convert Jews to Christianity.

Chapter Three

From here head across the country to the B2147, a splendid Downland drive where thick woodland alternates with pasture and plough, and the road steadily climbs to the crest of the chalk hills. The Mardens, West, North, Up and East are all worth a diversion to visit the small churches and to admire the way in which the little communities seem to typify the essential SouthDown village. If you feel like stretching your legs, the **Stoughton Down Forest Walk** can be found to the south of East Marden.

Uppark is a National Trust property which was partially destroyed by fire in 1989 and is now restored to its former glory. It has the most handsome facade, the gardens are by Humphrey Repton and the views are breathtaking. Uppark has had a number of owners since it was built at the end of the 17th century and the most colourful of these must have been the splendidly rakish Sir Henry Featherstonhaugh. He was in his early twenties when he inherited the house and in no time at all it housed his mistress, the beautiful Emma Hart. Before long she had left the rackety Sir Harry to marry the diplomat Sir William Hamilton and later achieved further notoriety by becoming Lord Nelson's mistress. Her former lover never forgot her though, and when she fell on hard times after Nelson's death in 1805, Sir Henry helped her out. His own life of debauchery and scandal continued until 1810 when he quarrelled with the Prince Regent and retired from London life to lead the life of a country squire. However, he was far from finished with the world of scandal and gossip, for at the age of seventy, he shocked the fashionabe world by marrying his head dairymaid. He remained happily married until his death at the ripe old age of ninety-two.

The steep hill that runs down into **South Harting** is said to have deterred the Duke of Wellington when the house was offered to him after the Napoleonic Wars; the necessity for constant replenishment of horses was his excuse. The church here is unusual in that the short spire is clad in copper that has oxidised to a brilliant green; inside there are fine timbers in the roof and a sporting reminder of old Sir Harry from Uppark in the form of a grieving woman and a somewhat woebegone spaniel. In his time he would undoubtedy have patronised **The Ship Inn**, a suitably atmospheric establishment in the main street. You may think it odd that an inland pub should have a marine name. It was really because the pub was constructed of ship's timbers, a sort of 'quidpro quo' for the local timber being commandeered to build new ships for His Majesty's Navy. The Ship has been mentioned by the poet Hilaire Belloc and also appears in one of Nevil Shute's novels when the hero took tea in what was then the upstairs tearooms.

The country to the north of Chichester is both varied and well endowed with numerous attractions, both natural and man-made. From West Stoke a delightful walk takes one up to the escarpment of **Kingley Vale**, now under the administraion of the Nature Conservancy Council. The Vale is most notable for its ancient yew-woods, dark, dense and silent.

A cheerful and lively contrast to the mythical, perhaps Druidical, stillness of Kingley Vale can be found in the nearby village of **Lavant**, where the 17th-century pub, **The Earl of March**, dispenses good food and hospitality. The pub's name is the honorary title given to the eldest sons of the Dukes of Richmond, owners of the famous estate of Goodwood. **Goodwood House**, set in lovely parkland, lies a couple of miles to the east. A handsome, porticoed central section is flanked by two wings of flint construction with green-domed towers. As originally designed, this is only part of what would have been a truly palatial building and some idea of the projected scale can be gained by inspecting the enormous stable-block, which was completed before money for the main house ran out. The house contains numerous treasures including Old Master portraits, tapestries, porcelain and furniture, but to me, the real attraction of Goodwood is the magnificent setting and the fact that the 12,000 acre estate is a diverse working entity. Agriculture, forestry and recreation go hand in hand; the small airfield is surrounded by a once famous motor racing track (now used for club events and testing), and there is a golf course and a country park. The first Duke purchased the original Tudor house as a hunting lodge and, above all, it was the passion for all things equine that the Duke and his successors made the estate world famous. Today, international dressage competitions, horse trials and the principal attraction of 'Glorious Goodwood', Goodwood races, bring enthusiasts and competitors from all over the globe.

The Selsey Peninsula the home of everything horticultural and agricultural for centuries has produced grain, vegetables, fruit and flowers for generations, and its rich soil is keenly exploited. Nevertheless it is an attractive area with small villages and reed-fringed rivulets, popular with holiday makers and yachtsmen. On the western side it is bounded by Chichester Harbour and the yachting centres of Dell Quay (once the original port of Chichester), Birdham, and Itchenor, neat and trim beside the water. On the westernmost tip, close to the popular sands of East Head, is the small resort of **West Wittering**. Sounding rather like the title of an old BBC radio comedy, the village is attractive with a most welcoming pub, **The Lamb Inn** and a church that is definitely 'organic'in that it is a happy mixture of period and styles. A walk along the seaward shore reveals some massive chunks of wave-smoothed rock, geological analysis shows they are probably originated in the Channel Islands, detritus from an Ice Age glacier.

At the beginning of the chapter, I made mention of the fact that the great majority of country cottages owe their survival to the wealthy newcomer, at **Singleton** there is an exception to this at the **Weald and Downland Open**

Chapter Three

Air Museum. This is a collection of vernacular buildings from all over the county that have been painstakingly re-erected and restored to as near their original condition as possible. Cottages, mills and farm buildings are grouped attractively, and the site is brought alive by the presence of the rural crafts of the period - wheelwrights, potters, sawyers and charcoal burners. To inspect some of these 'idyllic' rural dwellings is to receive a salutary lesson; no sanitation or glazing and the 'central heating' being literally central- merely a fire in the middle of the earth floor!

Some five miles to the north, 20th century comfort is to be found in 16th century surroundings.**The Crown** at **Midhurst** is everything a small country town inn should be - warmly hospitable and full of character. The town is equally charming with a cheerful and prosperous air, good brick and half-timbered buildings from across the centuries line the streets around the centre. Its origins as a market town since the early 13th century are reflected in names such as Sheep Lane, Wood Lane, Duck Lane and Knockhundred Row. A curfew bell is still rung at eight o'clock every evening; a tradition that was begun when a lone traveller was lost in the mist one night and the tolling of the Midhurst bell led him to safety. In gratitude the man bequeathed a piece of land to enable the bell to be rung in perpetuity.

Cowdray is the name given to the large estate that virtually surrounds Midhurst and the great fire-blackened ruins of **Cowdray House** can be seen to the east of the town. It was begun in 1530, at the instigation of Shakespeare's patron, the Earl of Southampton and then passed to Viscount Montague, who had received Battle Abbey from Henry VIII. Legend has it that the last monk to leave the Abbey cursed Montague prophesying that his family would perish by fire and water, It was an effective although somewhat slow-acting curse, the house was burnt down in 1793 and shortly afterwards, the then Viscount was drowned in Switzerland and his two sons at Bognor. The remains of the house have a tragic splendour and a look round gives an indication as to why it was once compared to Hampton Court as an example of courtly Tudor splendour. The estate however, has flourished in the hands of the present owners, the Pearson family, and the great Park with its immense oaks, is internationally known as a venue for polo, From Midhurst, a pleasant drive takes one north towards the gentler hills of the Surrey border, although to the east of the main road lies **Blackdown**, the highest point in Sussex at 919ft. It was a favourite beauty spot of Tennyson's who described the view as 'green Sussex fading into the blue, with one grey glimpse of the sea'. The character of the countryside changes; it becomes more intimate with wood and copse interspersed by streams and small fields. The soil is healthy and acid with huge banks of rhododendrons hanging over some of the small lanes.

The Home Counties

The third of Sussex's great estates is centred on **Petworth**, a lovely, if cramped, little town, which has the reputation of being the centre of the antiques trade. It has a number of interesting 16th and 17th century buildings set around winding narrow streets and a small market place with a simple arcaded Town Hall from the 18th century. The town's condensed effect comes from being huddled against the east wall of **Petworth House** which with its 700 acre deer park, dominates both town and surrounding countryside. The house is now looked after by the National Trust.

To the east, the A283 runs close to the pretty village of **Fittleworth**, once the home of Sir Edward Elgar, and where the coach-horses were once changed in the 14th century **Swan Inn**. A little further along the main road passing over the medieval bridge at **Stopham**, is the 'longest village in Sussex' **Pulborough'** settled since Neolithic times and lying beside a flood plain of the river Arun, was once an important Roman encampment guarding Stane Street, which runs from Chichester to London.

In the hamlet of **Hardham**, a mile or so to the south, the little Norman church contains a wonderful set of wall paintings, rendered around 1100, they rank amongst the most important treasures of their kind in England. The South Down Way is some 80 miles of bridle and footpath that runs along the crest, affording riders and walkers views of some of the most lovely scenery in the country. South-west of Hardham, the Way runs close to **The Bignor Roman Villa**, site of an enormous farmstead andhouse, where the wonderful Roman mosaics, discovered in 1811, are displayed in a covered area.

The wealth and importance of Sussex in earlier times are also seen in three other major attractions that lie not far away to the east.**Amberley**, a truly lovely village seated at the foot of downland overlooking grazing marshes, was considered of such strategic importance in the 14th-century that the then Bishop of Chichester built a massive castle, the remains of which surround the ancient manor house. The name Amberley is reputed to mean 'fields yellow with buttercups' and the setting is exquisite.

The nearby **Amberley Chalk Pits Museum** contains fascinating displays of bygone Sussex industries, crafts and skills. Further to the east is **Parham House,** one of the loveliest of Tudor mansions, set in a deer park with a church standing on the lawns, all that is left of a medieval village. Parham was built on the site of an earlier house that belonged to the Abbey of Westminster and was rebuilt around 1580 for Sir Thomas Palmer, a wealthy mercer, or textile merchant. Surrounded by beautiful gardens, the house contains some wonderful treasures, including needlework said to have been done by Mary, Queen of Scots, and her ladies in waiting, while imprisoned.

Chapter Three

Arundel is the home of the premier Duke and Earl Marshal of England, the Duke of Norfolk, and it undoubtedly looks the part. Norman streets wind up from the fast flowing River Arun towards the immense turreted mass of **Arundel Castle**. With a great, grey cathedral thrusting alongside,

Trees and hills provide a backdrop to a sight that has the air of a Gothic fairytale. The castle's owners have nearly always been Catholics and the fourth Duke of Norfolk's son, Philip Howard, was canonized in 1970, he kept faith although persecuted and imprisoned during the reign of Elizabeth I. His remains are interred in the Cathedral of Our Lady and St Philip, which was designed in 1879 by A.J. Hansom, of Hansom Cab fame.. It is a large but not particularly distinguished building unlike the Parish Church of St Nicholas, a Perpendicular construction of the 14th century, which is unique in containing the Catholic Fitzalan Chapel, divided from the Protestant main body by a screen. The town itself has a great deal of charm, with some handsome buildings of timber, flint and brick crowding the narrow, steep streets.

The Arun flows into the sea at **Littlehampton**, a cheerful little portion of 'Sussex by the Sea', a popular family resort with all the usual attractions of an Engish sea-side town. Originally a small fishing settlement in Saxon times (mullet being the local delicacy, then as now) the arrival of the railway in 1863 helped develop the small port into resort status. However medieval Littlehampton was a far cry from the cheerful unpretentious town of today; stone from the vast quarries of Caen was landed here and some of Henry VIII's warships were constructed on the banks of the Arun.

Remains of a far more ancient industry are to be found in the downs to the east of **Findon**. A pick made from an antler, has been carbon-dated to 4000BC, and was one of the tools used by Neolithic flint miners of **Cissbury Ring**. Artefacts from these mines have been found all over Western Europe and it is no exaggeration to describe the area as 'the Sheffield of Flint' but Cissbury is better known for its enormous earthworks, built around 280BC during the Iron Age.

Findon today is renowned for its racehorse stables which have produced strings of winners including the famous Aldaniti and it is common to see champion jockey and Classic trainer Josh Gifford in the village. In the High Street **Findon Manor** standing in its own grounds is a charming hotel owned and run by Mike and Jan Parker-Hare whose welcoming presence adds to the pleasure of staying in this comfortable and friendly house. Excellent food, beautiful ensuite bedrooms and ample parking are just additional reasons why one should bide awhile.

Not far to the north lies an even better vantage point which must be the most famous landmark in Sussex. **Chanctonbury Ring** is a great clump of beeches planted around the remains of Neolithic earthworks. Although many of the beeches were blown down in the October 1987 storm, by a freak of nature it was principally the inner trees that suffered and not those on the perimeter. Although it is a stiffish walk, the views over the magnificent rolling hills are wonderful. The site has mystical significance; the Romans built a temple here and witches used to meet her on Midsummer's Eve.

Two very popular resorts lie along this coast. Just south of Chichester is **Bognor Regis**, beloved by King George V. Here the beaches are clean, the bathng safe and the people friendly. **Worthing** is a quiet, dignified resort which is all the more surprising when one knows that the lively 'London by the Sea' Brighton, is only a few miles along the coast. It has long been a place where people wanting a quiet, refreshing break, have found comfort and relaxation. Worthing has theatres, cinemas and first class shops as well as many good hotels, guest houses and restaurants. There is a wide variety of indoor and outdoor sporting activity. The town's location on the south coast provides an ideal base for exploring the beautiful Sussex Downs and the many pretty villages.

Until the River Adur silted up in the 14th-century,**Steyning** was a busy port. It was at the head of the Adur estuary and the task of guarding this strategic site fell to the lot of **Bramber.** Derived from the Saxon 'Brymmburh', meaning a fortified hill, there remains only a fragment of the grim Norman keep that kept watch atop the steep hill. The castle, which was torn down by the Parliamentarian forces after the Civil War, guarded not only the approaches to Steyning but also a great stone bridge that crossed the Adur. Th wardens of this bridge were monks and their home was the wonderful **St Mary's House,** one of the finest timber-framedbuildings in the county. Set in lovely gardens, the house contains finely panelled rooms, including the Painted Room, said to have been decorated for a visit by Elizabeth I. The Virgin Queen was not the only Royal visitor for Charles II hid here on his way to France.

Bramber had a colourful history; pitched battles were fought in the street between tariff-collectors and ships' crews during the 11th and 12th centuries, the Knights Templar owned Chapel House (now part of St Marys) until they were ruthlessly supressed for 'unlawful acts and gross immorality'. in 1312, and the Benedictine Order which succeeded them was also accused of much the same charges in 1539. Finally in the era of the 'rotten boroughs' Bramber was described as the 'most rotten' - with eighteen voters returning two MPs! Things are distinctly quieter nowadays; the village has a unique little museum, **The House of Pipes**, devoted to what could best be described

Chapter Three

as 'Smokiana' and an excellent hotel and restaurant **The Old Tollgate**, which cleverly combines old and new in an attractive setting.

The vagaries of the sea which turned Steyning into a market town were to benefit **Shoreham**, a town that is a thriving port and with a history stretching back to Roman times. The modern part of Shoreham harbour is an enclosed dock, the largest between Southampton and Dover, handling a tonnage nearly as great as the latter. Shoreham itself, a friendly and busy town, is on the western edge of the harbour by the mouth of the Adur, an area popular with small boats and sailing dinghies. Shoreham Harbour is a recent innovation; the old port was on the eastern side of the estuary and was of major importance from Saxon times until around the beginning of the 15thcentury. The little port saw great military expeditions setting out for the French Wars whilst trade with that same country continued. From an historical point of view, this has been an almost continuous process; in 1347, soldiers left from here to capture Calais and throughout the centuries, the campaigns continued, culminating in the D-Day invasion in 1944. Hopefully, this process is now at an end although the trading aspect still continues and it is worth noting that one of the principal imports in the 14th century was wine - a commodity still brought into Shoreham today.

To the south lies the ruins of **Knepp Castle**, built by the Broase family from Bramber in the 11th century. A new, and private castle was built by John Nash in 1809. **West Grinstead** should not be confused with its larger, but far distant relation **East Grinstead**. They lie some 17 miles apart and whereas East Grinstead is a town, West Grinstead is little more than a hamlet. The great house of West Grinstead Park was demolished many years ago, but the battlemented stables, once headquarters of the National Stud can still be seen. The real attraction of the village is the Church of St George, tucked away at the end of a lane overlooking the river. Once again the homely exterior belies the treasures inside. There are several brasses, one to a knight who fought at Agincourt, and a number of classical-style monuments. The pews have the names of local farms carved on them and there is a large scale parish map showing where these lie; the names are redolent of the Wealden countryside, Priors Bine, Thistleworth, Hobshorts, Sunt and Figland.

Lower Beeding is separated, like the Grinsteads, from **Upper Beeding**, by several miles of countryside. Also, for some unaccountable reason, Lower Beeding is well to the north and higher than Upper! However, the real reason to visit has nothing to do with the somewhat eccentric nomenclature, but to see the wonderful gardens at **Leonardslee**. The Loder family have lived here since 1889 and have created magnificent woodland gardens within a deep valley. Streams and ponds lead the visitor past magnificent trees and shrubs, including world famous displays of rhododendrons, azaleas and camellias.

Although springtime is obviously the most spectacular, the gardens are a year-round attraction with deer, and, believe-it-or-believe-it-not, wallabies living semi-wild among the trees and grassy banks.

Leonardslee takes its name from the surrounding forest of St Leonard, where the Saint, a French hermit is reputed to have slain a dragon. The blood from St Leonard's wound dripped on the ground, where lilies-of-the-valley immediately spring up. Later, the hermit, who must have been more than a touch grouchy, banned nightingales from the forest, on the grounds that they disturbed his meditations. Whatever the truth, it is a fact that lilies grow there and the nightingale is never heard.......

Horsham is not unlike Chichester, in that it has a sensible arrangement of streets in the centre based on the cardinal points. The market town stands on the western edge of St Leonard's Forest, and although it has become a commuter town, modernisation has not spoilt the charm tobe found around the Carfax, the old centre (the word means a crossroads), and in particular the Causeway, a delightful tree-lined street of mainly 17th century houses. **Causeway House**, a lovely late Tudor building houses the fascinating **Horsham Museum.** In the Middle Ages, the town was renowned for the manufacture of horseshoes, crossbows and quarrels, and in the early 19th-century it had a bloody reputation as an Assize town. Those who escaped the gallows were sentenced to transportation and it is a sad reflection of the times that so many place names in Australia owe their origin to this harsh penalty.

Just south of the town is **Christ's Hospital School**, and the pupils can often be seen walking around in their distinctive uniform of dark blue coat, white neck-band and yellow stockings. The dress is based on the Tudor uniform worn by those who attend the original school established by Edward IV in 1553. The school moved from London to Horsham in 1902.

The iron works that once were found all over the Weald used water to drive the bellows and trip-hammers, and many of these mill, or hammer ponds still exist. There is one at **Warnham**, a well kept village just off the A24, which was once the home of the poet Shelley, and who was reputed to have sailed model boats on the pond. **The Warnham War Museum**, outside the village on the A24, contains an impressive collection of relics and memorabilia from the two World Wars.

Ignore the bland New Town of **Crawley** and neighbouring **Gatwick Airport**. Noisy and busy places. It is much pleasanter to take the network of minor roads that skirt around the north of Crawley towards the Surrey border. **Charlwood** is only ten minutes away from the busy airport yet retains a pleasant and calm rural air, The Norman church has a fine chancel screen,

Chapter Three

re-coloured and gilded in 1858, and a number of memorials to the Saunders family, including a good brass of 1553. In Rosemary Lane is the 18th century village prison, a small squat brick building. Of the same period but much nicer and more welcoming, is the attractive white-painted frontage which houses the excellent **Limes Bistro**.

South of Crawley, close to the small community of **Handcross**, are the lovely National Trust Gardens at **Nymans**. There are a whole series of quite different gardens set in 30 acres around the gaunt but romantic shell of a burnt-out house. The gardens are both formal and informal yet not in the least overpowering. Nymans has been described as a domestic garden on a grand scale rather than a grand garden on a domestic scale. Without a doubt, this is a truly Sussex garden.

Place names are often a delight, the Saxon word of 'Cucufelda' meaning a field full of cuckoos, is said to be the origination of **Cuckfield**, a friendly village on the western outskirts of **Haywards Heath**. The two communities have a common link in that their prosperity was based on transport; Cuckfield was a major coaching centre and in 1828 it was recorded that over 50 coaches were passing through every day, on the London to Brighton run. Naturally, this trade employed vast numbers of people such as grooms, wheelwrights, harness makers and smiths, to say nothing of the staff employed by the coaching inns, such as **The Kings Head**, a favourite of George IV then Prince of Wales, and deservedly popular to this day. Although a coach service ran until as late as the first World War, the advent of the railway in the middle of the 19th century effectively killed off this lucrative and colourful trade almost overnight. However by refusing to accommodate this new fangled innovation, Cuckfield lost the financial rewards but retained its rural charm, while nearby the hamlet of Haywards Heath rapidly expanded into the commuting and shopping centre of today.

The other community to refuse the benefits of steam was **Lindfield**, on the opposite side of Haywards Heath. Although the financial penalties must have been severe at the time, the village's loss has been Sussex's gain; this is truly picturesque, situated on a gentle slope with the village pond at the bottom and the church with its tall spire, at the top. The houses are nearly all a delight, ranging from Tudor through to Georgian. There is a wonderful story concerning Church House, which was once a pub called the Tiger Inn; apparently the ale it served to the bellringers in 1588, triumphantly signalling the defeat of the Spanish Armada, was so strong that it caused them to crack a bell and all the ropes.

Hickstead, is internationally famous in the equestrian world as the home of the **All England Show Jumping Ground**, although there is rumour

366

that the owner Douglas Bunn does not want to carry on. It would be a pity because the arena, with its grandstand, and supporting facilities is set in an attractive area just to the west of the A23 and close to the pleasant little village of **Sayers Common**.

The rear escarpment of the South Downs, the last geographical obstacle before breaching the coast is breached by the **Devil's Dyke**, where the devil is said to have tried to dig a giant ditch through the downs in order to let the sea through. His intention was to flood the lower Weald and drown the churches, but he was foiled by a woman holding a candle. The Devil, who could only work in the dark, mistook the light for the rising sun and fled.

It's well worth a diversion to the east, to skirt the hills on their northern side and to visit **Newtimber Place**. Although the busy traffic rushes by within a few hundred yards, the moated house, built in 1681, is close to perfection with mellow brick and flint facade. The steep woodlands of Newtimber Hill, together with the dewponds, are owned and maintained by the National Trust.

The up-and-down route to the east takes one through the village of **Pycombe**, best known as a centre of the crook-maker's craft; an ornately carved shepherd's crook was once both badge of office and indispensable tool of Downland shepherds, The road to **Layton** takes one past some odd chimney-like structures which are just that; ventilators for the steam trains that once ran through the chalk hills.

The tunnel entrance near the village is an imposing Victorian Gothic affair with turrets and battlements, with a small house actually built over the entrance itself. One cannot help feeling inhabitants must be extremely fond of railways! Clayton's other claim to fame is the simple little village church with its marvellous wall paintings that are thought to have been created as early as 1080. They portray scenes such as The Last Judgment and the Fall of Satan, with the centrepiece of Christ in Judgment over the pre-Norman chancel arch.

High above the village stand two well-loved landmarks, a pair of windmills christened Jack and Jill. A mile or so to the east, one of the highest vantage points of the South Downs gives some wonderful views. **Ditchling Beacon** stands at 813 feet above sea-level, towering over the village of **Ditchling** that lies on the lee of the Downs. Artists such as Sir Frank Brangwyn and Eric Gill lived here and the village has some lovely buildings; the best-known being **Wing's Place**, said to have been given by Henry VIII to Anne of Cleves.

Chapter Three

South of the Downs is truly 'Sussex by the Sea' and **Brighton**, its capital, the best known and loved town in the country- although there is really nothing of Sussex about the place since the influences that created it are distinctly metropolitan in tone. Invasion, Royal patronage, scandal, outrageous architecture, culture, sport and tragedy have combined in equal parts to create a town with a history both rackety and respectable. Like the favourite aunt of fiction, Brighton is settling into quiet and prosperous middle age although a fondness for eccentric dress and garish make-up hint at a lowly beginning and a picaresque past.

Brighton owes its fame - or notoriety - to its discovery by the Prince Regent, son of George III. An afficionado of the newly invented 'dirty-weekend' (A Brighton speciality in the years to come), and obviously in need of Dr Russell's glandular treatment, he instigated the construction of the **Royal Pavilion**. In this extraordinary Indo-Chinese confection he secretly married his favourite mistress Maria Fitzherbert, a Catholic. Naturally, this was in direct contravention of the Act of Succession and the Royal Marriages Act and was thus doomed to end in politic divorce, nevertheless, His Royal Highness, later George IV, set the tone for the centuries ahead.

If the Royal Pavilion was, not to put too fine a point on it, outrageous, then much of the other contemporary development was in restrained, albeit fashionable form. Great crescents and squares, in classical Regency style, were built to house the cognoscenti and their households, and the town expanded into the neighbouring borough of Hove. The popularity of Brighton grew steadily and with the advent of the railway in the 1840's the town was brought within the reach of almost everybody. Hotels and boarding houses sprang up to cater for this new trade, and the three miles of sea-front were provided with elegant, wide promenades, splendid piers, amusements and fairgrounds. That great British instituition, the Seaside Holiday, was now firmly established, along with that redoubtable figure, the Seaside Landlady.

The visitor is spoilt for choice, where to go and what to see ? -perhaps the best plan is to establish a base-camp, and Brighton is renowned for the quality and range of its accommodation to make it eay for you.

Seaford was the principal port of this area until a series of events caused the mouth of the River Ouse to be diverted to **Newhaven**. Now it is a quiet and prosperous seaside town. From Seaford Head where there was once a Roman cemetery, there is a fine view of the **Seven Sisters**, the dramatic vertical chalk cliffs that mark the end of the South Downs. At their far end stands the towering bulk of **Beachy Head**; on a clear day the seaward view extends over 60 miles from the 536foot cliff.

Between Seaford Head and the first of the Sisters, Haven Brow, lies **Cuckmere Haven** where the meandering River Cuckmere runs into the Channel. This was a favourite haunt of those Sussex gentlemen averse to paying import duty; in particular, of the Alfriston Gang, a notorious bunch of cut-throat smugglers who terrorised the area for years. Almost hidden by the tall cliffs and with the river winding its way inland through marsh and tall reed, the Haven and surrounding area attract a wide range of flora and fauna, and 700 acres of marsh and Downland to the east of the river have been turned into the **Seven Sisters Country Park**. This includes a unique mini zoo, **The Living World**, which displays marine creatures, reptiles and insects.

Close to the river, to the north of the secluded and idyllic village of **Westdean**, is the lovely **Charleston Manor**. The house dates in parts, back to Norman times and is reputed to have been built for William the Conqueror's cup-bearer. Later additions are Tudor and Georgian with medieval dovecote. This splendid mixture is handsomely set off by a remarkable garden, created by the artist Sir Oswald Birley (1880-1952). The rich alluvial soil has been planted in terraces divided by low yew hedges to give an effect that it is a delightful combination of English and European.

Some three miles further up the river valley and set amidst lush water-meadows is **Alfriston**, once the smuggler's headquarters. Stanton Collins, the leader of the gang, lived in the Market Cross Inn, otherwise known as **The Smugglers Inn**. By a trick of fate, he was eventually caught and sentenced to transportation - but for sheep-stealing not smuggling!

The Star Inn dates from the 15th century, when it was probably built to house pilgrims on their way to visit the shrine of St Richard at Chichester. There are some splendid medieval carvings on the timbered facade, including one of a basilisk being slain by St Michael. There is also a small **Heritage Centre** and **Blacksmith's Museum**, housed in the Old Forge in Sloe Lane.

Drusillas Park, to the north of the village, has been a favourite with families for over 60 years;a winning combination of children's zoo, gardens, workshops, amusements and restaurants. Attached to this is the rather more grown up attraction of **The English Wine Centre**, which has its own vineyard and museum.

Wilmington's attraction is obvious; carved into the chalkface of the downs above the village is the outline of a giant, with a staff in either hand. No one knows the origin of **The Long Man of Wilmington**, first recorded as late as 1779; it has been variously suggested that he was a Bronze Age Chieftain, or the Saxon King Harold, or even an advertisement to guide

Chapter Three

pilgrims to **Wilmington Priory**. The Priory fell on hard times well before the Dissolution and became a farmhouse which now houses a museum specialising in bygone agricultural equipment. The little church next door is overshadowed by a huge and ancient yew, which probably dates back to when the priory was completed.

At **West Firle**, **Firle Place**, a Tudor mansion extensively remodelled in the 18th century, has been the home of the Gage family for 500 years. Set amongst wooded parkland beneath the 700 foot Firle Beacon, the house contains a fine collection of paintings and furniture. The family includes Henry VIII's Comptroller of Calais, a Governor of Massachussetts and the importer of the greengage, and the 13th century village church has a fine family chapel, containing amongst other memorials and brasses, an exquisitely-carved alabaster memorial to Sir John and Lady Phillipa Gage, and a window by John Piper, commemorating the sixth Viscount Gage. The village pub, **The Ram Inn**, dating from 1540 is well worth a visit.

North of the main road lies another handsome house, **Glynde Place**, also a mix of Tudor and Georgian architecture. The house was built for William Morley whose descendants Colonel Herbert Morley was one of the Parliamentarian judges at the trial of Charles I, although he refused to sign the death-warrant. The house contains much of interest, including collections of Bronzes, needlework and a small aviary. The small parish church is in the Wren style, not unlike a miniature version of St Paul's Covent Garden.

Glyndebourne, which was also a Morley home is world renowned for the quality of its opera. For over 50 years, opera lovers have flocked here to listen to the music and to enjoy picnicking in full evening dress during the long interval. Glyndebourne now has a new, purpose built Opera House which is thrilling audiences. There is a solid, respectable charm about **Lewes** with the old houses clustered around the castle on the hill, and its steep narrow streets and alleyways. **Anne of Cleves House**, Southover, once belonged to Henry VIII's 'Flander's Mare' and is an excellent place to begin a tour of the town since it is also a museum containing items of local and country life and history.

That early 'Hooray Henry' the Prince Regent, often stayed at **Southover Grange** in Keere Street and doubtless this was where the coaching wager was laid. A wager in which the Prince Regent drove a coach and four down Keere Street, a street which is narrow and precipitous. Did he win - I imagine so!

Simon de Montfort spent the night before the Battle of Lewes in prayerful vigil at the church of St Mary and St Andrew, **Fletching**. The village's name probably originated with the medieval industry of arrow making; a fletcher is the name given to such craftsmen. Edward Gibbon (1737-94), the historian and author, of 'The Decline and Fall of the Roman Empire' spent the last months of his life staying at **Sheffield Park**. The battlemented lodge and gateway lie just across the road from the church where Gibbon is buried.

The Park, landscaped by both Capability Brown and Humphrey Repton and now administered by the National Trust, was at one time as renowned for its cricket as for its beauty; the Australians used to play their first tour game here before Arundel became the venue and the Lord Sheffield of the day was such an enthusiast that he played on the lakes in the park when they were frozen over, and once aboard his yacht off the coast of Spitzbergen! James Wyatt built the lovely Gothic Revival house in the 1770's and it is perfectly complemented by the superb landscape with rare trees and shrubs arranged around five lakes, set at different levels and linked by cascades.

One of the finest steam railways in the country is **The Bluebell Railway** which has its southern depot, headquarters and museum close to the park entrance. Named after the flowers which grow along the length of the line, this famous railway has operated steam locomotives to **Horsted Keynes** for over thirty years, and it is a sheer delight to chuff gently through the wooded Sussex countryside.

Uckfield grew with the advent of the railway although originally it was a small village at the intersection of the London to Brighton turnpike and the more ancient pilgrim's route from Winchester to Canterbury. **Framfield** has a church that is long and low and built in 1288. An attractive village square with a number of pretty tile-hung houses face the church which seems to have been severely damaged by fire in 1509, while the tower collapsed in 1667, and was not replaced for two centuries. According to one authority, Framfield once fielded a cricket team of 15 men whose combined ages added up to 1,000 years - sadly they could find no suitably aged opponents.

Ashdown Forest is a mere shadow of what it once was when it was a mighty blanket of woodland that filled the valley between the North and South Downs. In the three heather thatched barns of the **Ashdown Forest Centre** at **Wych Cross**, you can learn all about its history and see what is going on in the conservation work alongside the natural process of regeneration.

In the old days the area was favoured by outlaws such as cutthroats, highwaymen and, of course, smugglers. **West Hoathly**, high on the ridge at the westernmost end of the forest, and once a centre of the iron industry, was a great favourite of the unofficial import brigade.

Sensibly **The Cat Inn**, was their headquarters and the church tower, their look out post. The 15th century **Priest's House**, with its roof of massive Horsham stone, is now a museum, and a fine Norman church and manor face each other across the street. With proper Sussex contempt for geographical exactitude, East Hoathly is some 15 miles to the south...

Across the border with Surrey is the attractive Wealden village of **Lingfield** with its 15th century buildings and fine race-course. Eastwards the Sussex border runs with that of Kent, and at **Hammerwood Park** there are strong links with the capital of the United States. Benjamin Latrobe, who also designed the Capitol and the White House in Washington DC, built Hammerwood in 1792. As the name implies, Hammerwood was an iron-working community, as was the nearby village of **Cowden**. Today's visitor will find this hard to believe when gazing at the community of half-timbered houses nestling amongst the hills. Nevertheless, to the west of the village are the 30 reed-fringed acres of Furnace Pond, which gives some indication of the size of the industry in times past.

Returning south towards the forest, the B2026 passes through the River Medway and enters the immaculate and substantial village of **Hartfield** with its weatherboarded stone, brick and tile-hung cottages. The church with a magnificent spire, acting as a landmark for miles around, has a most unusual lych-gate, half under the projecting floor of a fine little timber cottage. There is something cosy and comforting about this part of Sussex, and that feeling is engendered, together with childhood memories, by the sight of a small wooden bridge over a stream; this is the bridge where Winnie-the-Pooh and Christopher Robin first dropped twigs into the water, thus inventing the immortal game of 'Pooh-sticks'. Somehow fiction becomes reality in this timeless part of the Andredsweald.

The easternmost area of Sussex stretches along the coast from Eastbourne to Rye. It is lower lying than the country to the west, a pleasant, welcoming and varied landscape where small winding lanes take the visitor past farms, hamlets and villages which possess an almost timeless air. Deer browse in the shelter of thickets and wood, while fat fleecy sheep graze in gentle rolling pasture and ancient meadows. Well pruned orchards are laid out with military precision and along the Kentish border, the coned towers of oast houses denote hop-growing. Although the vast majority of these buildings seem to have been converted into what an estate agent's love of abbreviation would describe as a 'des-res', the hop is still grown to flavour our ale.

If Brighton is 'London by the Sea' then **Eastbourne** is more akin to 'Bath by the Sea'; refined, elegant and restrained, it has a three mile seafront with its terraced parades and fountained gardens. In contrast to other South coast resorts, one is immediately struck by the absence on the front of shops and the more raucous form of entertainment and amusement emporiums. At night, with gardens and fountains floodlit, the effect can be breathtaking. After having seen the sweeping grandeur of the front, with the sea breaking gently on the shingle and sand beach it no longer seems unusual or incongruous that Claude Debussy should have written his greatest orchestral work 'La Mer' while staying here in 1905.

Martello towers are to be seen from the shore road leading eastwards but at **Pevensey** there are traces of an older and greater fortification. The Saxon Shore Forts were built by the Romans and at Pevensey they constructed the fortress of Adnerida to repel the northern invaders. When the Romans departed, the Romano-British took the fortress over, but after a six month siege in 491AD, the Saxons took the castle and slaughtered every inhabitant. It is said that the Saxons never inhabited Anderida because of the savage deeds done that day and that the village was thus created. They took the name of the fortress and applied it to the vast hinterland of forest - Andreadswald, the Forest of Andred later known as The Weald. For such a small and seemingly insignificant community, Pevensey has had a long, important and violent history. Nearly six hundred years after the Saxon massacre, the long ships of William of Normandy loomed out of the Channel haze and grounded in the creeks and inlets of what was then a swamp natural harbour. This was the beginning of the Norman Conquest; Pevensey was where they landed and where they consolidated their position before moving on to capture Hastings and ultimately, to defeat Harold at Battle. **Pevensey Castle's** Roman curtain walls still stand, along with the 11th and 13th-century gatehouse and keep.

The Pevensey Levels is the name given to the low lying area of marsh inland from the town, once a region of shallow dykes and creeks until silting and storms filled the watery shallows. At the head of this area stands the striking shape of **Herstmonceaux Castle**, built of Flemish brick in 1440. By the time it was finished the introduction of the cannon had made that form of medievalfortress redundant; nevertheless,it is a satisfying, solid structure that could grace any romance involving knights in armour and damsels in distress. When it was finished it had a window for every day of the year and a chimney for every week; it was restored after decades of decay in 1913 and occupied by the Royal Observatory until recently.

Turning southwards towards the shore, **Bexhill** is the next coastal town to the east. Its history is not dissimilar to that of Eastbourne, a small

Chapter Three

village developed by the major landowner as a resort. The landowner was Lord De la Warr, who in 1885 began by building on his land that lay between the original village and the sea. Perhaps because it was a latecomer to the resort scene, Bexhill never achieved the size and status of its fellows and still retains something of a village atmosphere. However the town has led the way on many occasions. It had the first mixed bathing in the country in 1901 and followed this piece of daring by holding the first Motor Race in 1902. The De La Warr Pavilion is the town's best known building; a grade one listed architectural masterpiece designed in 1933 by the German Erich Mendelsohn. Overlooking the sea, it houses an 1100 seat theatre, restaurants, bars and function rooms. In delightful contrast to the sweeping modern design are the neighbouring Edwardian designs of Marine Arcade and Marina Court Avenue with their passing resemblance to Brighton's Royal Pavilion.

Hastings in common with other towns on this once troubled shore, has had an epic history; a past that is not easy to divine at first sight of this cheerful and easy-going seaside resort. The town was one of the Cinque Ports, a confederation that supplied the medieval monarchs with ships and men in time of war in exchange for certain privileges, such as the right to hold their own courts and to keep the revenue from fines. The other ports were Sandwich, Dover, Romney and Hythe, all in Kent. Until the 12th century, Hastings was a rich and powerful town, but then events both natural and political conspired to drastically reduce its importance.

The first was the loss of Normandy in 1204, which led to a considerable reduction in trade and the partial dismantling of the castle by King John, who feared it might be seized by the French. Great storms during the 13th century led to the loss and silting up of the harbour. In addition during the Hundred Years War (1338-1453) the French attacked and razed the town four times. Although Henry III restored the castle, erosion by the sea and subsequent collapse of the cliff-face led to its collapse and abandonment. West Hill Cliff Railway takes the modern visitor to the top of the hill where the ruins lie. There is an audio-visual presentation called 'The 1066 Story' while nearby St Clements Caves, which honeycomb the hill, contain an entertainment entitled 'the Smuggler's Adventure.'

From the 14th century onwards smuggling, fishing and boat building appear to have been the principal occupation of the inhabitants, who managed these occupations from an unprotected shingle beach. Immediately below the East Cliff is an area known as the Stade, from the Saxon word meaning a landing place. To this day, boats are still drawn up the shingle by winch to lie alongside the extraordinary tall net-sheds. These structures date from Tudor times and were built in this odd manner for two remarkably good reasons. The small base area meant paying less ground rent, and the tall height meant the fishermen could work out of doorways on the mast and rigging as well as the hull. The nearby fishmarket is also of historic interest; by local custom the auctioneer starts with a high price and works down, leaving the bidder just one chance to buy. Along the quaintly named Rock-a-Nore road there is also a Fishermen's Museum, Shipwreck Heritage Centre and an aquarium, the Sea-Life Centre.

To complete the story of Hastings it is important to head north-west to **Battle**, where Harold met William at what is known as the Battle of Hastings, although it actually took place some six miles from the town at Senlac Hill on October 14th 1066. After Harold's defeat, William vowed to build an abbey with the high altar on the spot where Harold fell. The abbey, dedicated to StMartin, was consecrated in 1094 and the town grew up around its walls.

The town is delightful, with a mainly Georgian High Street running up from the Abbey with a number of arched entrances between buildings acting as a reminder of the days when coaches needed to pull into yards of inns. Incidentally I stayed a night or two in the village of **Etchingham** just off the A21 to the north, while I explored this wonderful area. I found Etchingham fascinating and was particularly attracted to its beautiful church built in 1387 which is lovely in its simplicity. Certainly worth a visit.

Returning to the coast east of Hastings, the A259 takes one past the oldest windmill in Sussex, dating from 1670 at **Ickleham**, and on to **Winchelsea**, sometimes described as ;'the smallest town in England'. It is really no more than a small village, although it still boasts a mayor and corporation. Peaceful and utterly charming in the late 20th century, its past is every bit as bloodthirsty and tragic as any of the ancient towns of the Sussex Shore, having been destroyed by storm, razed by French raids and de-populated by the plague.

The original town, part of the Cinque Ports confederation, was set below Igham Hill on a shingle spit, and was the principal Cross-Channel port. The violent storms of 1250 destroyed much of the town, and, under the direction of Edward I, a new community was built on the hill, 'where the only coneys did dwell', the rabbits quickly lost possession of the area, for another storm in 1287 washed away the remainder of the old town, and construction of the new, neatly laid out in grid pattern, continued apace. However, further disasters were to strike; the French attacked Winchelsea seven times in the 14th and 15th centuries, while over the same period, the harbour was gradually silting up to the extent that the coastline today lies nearly two miles to the south of the town.

Chapter Three

Roses and wisteria cling to the attractive remains of England's first planned town since Roman times. Although the town was never completed, the existing buildings are a delight. The Church of St Thomas the Martyr was largely destroyed in one of the French raids but what remains is wonderful; the original building was of cathedral-like proportions although all that is left is the chancel and a ruined transept.

Looking eastwards across the flats where the River Brede wanders is arguably one of the most beautiful small towns in Britain, **Rye**. Like its neighbour, it also suffered at the hands of the sea and the French but survived through a combination of good fortune and the tenaciousness of its citizens. Julius Caesar noted that they were 'fierce and hostile' and the citizens of the little town had no compunction about turning to piracy and smuggling when times were hard. The town stands on a hill-top now two miles from its harbour mouth. Its narrow cobbled streets probably have a greater concentration of old houses and more of the atmosphere of a 16th-century town than anywhere else in the country. The waters of three rivers, the Tillingham, the Brede and the Rother combine to scour a channel through the marshy flats to the sea, and small craft can still make their way up on the tide to lie alongside the ancient wharves under the town.

Although the town is a major tourist attraction, it is still very much a working community and there is no feeling of being 'preserved in the Aspic of Time'. Rye is a market town and still retains a fishing fleet. There are boatyards, chandlers and marine engineers alongside the more obvious attractions of antique shops and craft galleries. Rye Harbour lies some two miles south, the road going over bleak and flat countryside. Some measure of the shore's vagaries can be seen by thefact that **Camber Castle**, built in the 1530's to protect the Harbour entrance, is now stranded well inland. Rye Harbour consists of a few houses, a pub and a stark Victorian church with a tragic memorial to the crew of the lifeboat, all drowned in full view of their families earlier this century.

North of the town is **Rye Foreign**. There are two theories as to the origin of this strange name and both equally convincing since they are based on fact. The first is that the Manor of Rye was given by King Canute to the Abbey of Fecamp in Normandy. This was fine until King John lost Normandy in 1204; a legal and political wrangle then began which was not resolved until Henry III negotiated the town's return to crown governance. However, one small area was not returned - hence Rye Foreign. The other theory is that most of the French Protestant refugees, the Hugenots, who settled in Rye during the 17th century, chose to live in their own community on the edge of the town - hence Rye Foreign. Take your pick!

The Home Counties

Just north of Rye Foreign is the pretty village of **Peasmarsh** one of many delightful villages around to discover and several interesting historical buildings including **Bateman's** at **Burwash**, an attractive village of little more than one street. Bateman's is best known for being the home of Rudyard Kipling from 1902 until his death in 1936. It contains many of his manuscripts and personal possessions. At the bottom of the lovely garden, a restored watermill grinds flour alongside a water turbine that once provided electricity for the house.

Robertsbridge is a small town on the River Rother with a large number of Wealden Hall houses, built as a result of prosperity in the 14th and early 15th century. In 1794 Horace Walpole when visiting the area, found that one of the inns was full of smugglers and another full of excise men, and a pitched battle at nearby **Silverhill** resulted in victory for the smugglers and the death of a captain of dragoons.

A splendid eccentric, 'Mad Jack' Fuller is buried in the pyrmidal mausoleum in **Brightling** churchyard; he declined to be buried conventionally as he had a fear of being eaten by his relatives -' the worms would eat me, the ducks would eat the worms and my relatives would eat the ducks'. Legend has it that he was buried sitting in an armchair, holding a bottle of claret. Far from mad he was an MP and a great benefactor, a patron of Turner, and a builder of numerous follies, such as the obelisk on Brightling Beacon, most of which were constructed to alleviate unemployment. An exception is the Sugar Loaf at **Dallington**. The story goes that Fuller, over a good dinner, bet a substantial sum of money that he could see the distinctive spire of Dallington church from his home at Brightling. On returning home from the meal, he found to his consternation that he was wrong, he immediately summoned help and had the folly built overnight in a field, so that from a distance it resembled the tip of a spire!

Finally to **Hailsham** where the cattle market once attracted drovers from as far away as Wales, and is still one of the most important in Sussex. A couple of miles to the west, **Michelham Priory** stands in beautiful grounds surrounded by a moat, founded in 1229, the Augustinian Priory had a fairly uneventful history until it was dissolved in 1536. Two thirds of the buildings, including the church, were destroyed and the remainder, together with the estate, became a large working farm belonging to the Pelham and Sackville families. Now the buildings belong to the Sussex Archaeological Society and are run as a fascinating and lively museum with numerous events being held in and around the Priory and its grounds. There are displays of crafts and separate museums related to skills such as that of the wheelwright, blacksmith and rope-maker. The last named is an industry still continued in Hailsham, which also made the special ropes used for executions.

Chapter Three

Perhaps one of these gruesome products dispatched the evil Lord Dacre who murdered a gamekeeper at Hellingly in 1541. He was hung at Tyburn after Henry VIII refused his plea for clemency. The evil deed occurred close to the magnificent **Horselunges Manor**, a moated timber-framed manor house built in the late 15th-century. The unusual name is thought to be a corruption of two of the original owners, Herst and Lyngyver.

The pretty little village has a Saxon churchyard, probably dating from the 8th century, although the church was built much later, around 1190. Appropriately for a village whose appearance and history represents much that is best about Sussex, the village inn bears the name of the county's heraldic bird, **The Golden Martlet**.

STREAM COTTAGE
The Street,
Albury,
Nr. Guildford,
Surrey GU5 9AG

Tel: 01483 202228
Fax: 01483 202793

Today Guildford is a modern business and shopping centre, in medieval times it was a stop over for pilgrims travelling to and from Canterbury. It is a mixture of past and present architecture, from the surviving keep of Henry II Castle to the modern Cathedral which was started in 1936 and completed in 1961. A few miles south east of this fascinating city is Albury, where you step back in time in this very old and quaint village. It is in The Street where you come across a charming property built around the 1500's, Stream Cottage. It is owned by Norman and Mel Thomas, who not only find the time to look after their guests and tend to their every need, they also run their business, Albury Saddlery, which is attached to the cottage.

The cottage has 3 very comfortable bedrooms all have the luxury of ensuite facilities, colour television and a well supplied tea and coffee tray. Breakfast is a real feast, Norman cooks a very full English breakfast with all the trimmings, along with cereal, fresh fruit and toast, it is all served in the delightful dining room which has a superb beamed ceiling, lovely wooden furniture and fresh flowers. The guests sitting room is just as charming with comfortable floral seats, open fire place, beamed ceiling and lots of pictures, which all go to create a comfortable and relaxing atmosphere. Surrey is not short of things to do, so all in all you are sure to have an excellent stay.

USEFUL INFORMATION

OPEN; All year
CHILDREN; Welcome
CREDIT CARDS; Yes all major cards
ACCOMMODATION; 3 ensuite rooms
1 double/family, 2 twin
DINING ROOM; Excellent breakfast with choices
DISABLED ACCESS; Not really
GARDEN; Very nice rear garden with seats and barbecue
PETS; Not really

Chapter Three

GADBROOK OLD FARM
Wellhouse Lane,
Betchworth,
Surrey RH3 7HH

Tel/Fax: 01737 842183

There are many charming properties around the county of Surrey none more so than Gadbrook Old Farm, this wonderful red brick house was built 500 years ago and is indeed picturesque. Set in its own secluded grounds near the villages of Betchworth and Brockham which are both close to the A25 and the M25 which makes Gadbrook ideal for business with Heathrow 45 minutes and Gatwick 15 minutes away, and pleasure with the beautiful countryside. The house itself is superb with lots of farmhouse features including inglenook fireplaces, oak beams and lovely traditional and antique furniture, matching the age of the property. There are 2 bedrooms, one double with private facilities and one ensuite twin room, both are extremely comfortable and are complete with a welcoming tea and coffee tray. Television are available.

Breakfast is served by Jeanette Bibby, the lady of the house, in the delightful dining room where you can partake in a traditional full English or Continental meal. Evening meals are by prior arrangement, packed lunches are also available for those away days. If you do not wish to eat in, there are several good pubs and restaurants in the area. Gadbrook has the most wonderful garden complete with a pond where you can feed the ducks and relax in the peace and tranquillity of it all. There are lots of lovely small villages to explore in Surrey so your days will certainly be filled. Gadbrooks offer additional services such as transfers to and from Gatwick Airport and short term car parking.

USEFUL INFORMATION

OPEN; *All year*
CHILDREN; *Welcome*
CREDIT CARDS; *None taken*
ACCOMMODATION; *2 rooms, 1 double with private facilities, 1 ensuite twin*
DINING ROOM; *Full English or Continental breakfast, evening meal by arrangement*
DISABLED ACCESS; *Not really*
GARDEN; *Beautiful with pond*
PETS; *Within reason*

WESTHOLME GUEST HOUSE
111 Aldwick Road,
Bognor Regis, West Sussex PO21 2NY

Tel: 01243 868207

    Bognor Regis remains one of the pleasantest resorts in the country and has managed to dodge the advent of the noisier tourist element allowing people who come here the opportunity to enjoy thesheer pleasure of the sea, shore, front, the gardens and many other quietly acceptable pastimes. One of the things you notice about Bognor is the profusion of flowers in the colourful beds and in the gardens of the houses. None more so than the front garden of Westholme Guest House which in addition to the flowerbeds edging the lawns, has a wealth of tubs and hanging baskets which delight the eye.

    This attractive modern house is the home of the Coopers who are a welcoming couple who cannot do enough for you. Their home is comfortably furnished with traditional oak chairs and tables, flowers and pretty ornaments add to the pleasure of the rooms. The bedrooms have been carefully appointed to give guests the maximum comfort and peace. Each room has pretty drapes, excellent beds, TV and that boon to the traveller, a well supplied tea/coffee and chocolate tray. The rooms are not ensuite but each has a wash basin and the bathroom has plenty of hot water. Breakfast is cooked freshly to your order and can be either a full English Breakfast or something lighter. No evening meals are served but Bognor has several good eating places which the Coopers will be happy to recommend to you.

    Bognor is a great area for those who enjoy fishing, golf, cycling and walking. The historical city of Portsmouth with its wonderful maritime museums is only 30 minutes away.

USEFUL INFORMATION

OPEN; *All year*
CHILDREN; *Welcome*
CREDIT CARDS; *None taken*
ACCOMMODATION; *1 double 2 twin*

DINING ROOM; *First class breakfast*
VEGETARIAN; *Catered for*
DISABLED ACCESS; *Downstairs beds*
PETS; *Not permitted*

Chapter Three

WHITE BARN
Crede Lane, Bosham,
West Sussex PO18 8NX

Tel: 01243 573113
Fax: 01243 573113

The village of Bosham, to the local people is pronounced 'Bozzum', is very attractive with lovely cottages topped with thatch, little lanes to stroll along and all surrounded by creeks belonging to the harbour of Chichester. Sailors will be in their element as sailing and boating are the main pastimes. In the Saxon church of Holy Trinity there is a copy of the panel of The Bayeux tapestry featuring the church, and King Harold is said to have prayed here before going into the Battle of Hastings in 1066. In this idyllic setting is White Barn owned and very well run by Sue and Tony Trotman. White Barn is not actually a barn but an architecturally designed single storey house, standing in the peace, tranquillity and privacy of a former orchard, at the end of a private road. The house is very impressive with much open plan, making it light, airy and spacious. The furnishings are original in design, with lots of pine. The bedrooms have been well thought out, especially the family complex with adjoining rooms, one having twin beds the other has children's bunk beds and resembles a ships cabin. The 'Honeysuckle' is a twin bedded room, and a beamed studio in the garden is another double. All these rooms are ensuite with shaver points, tea and coffee making facilities, colour television and overlook the garden. The house is very warm and comfortable with a welcoming atmosphere, making it very easy to relax here. Sue and Tony are very good at making you feel at home. The sitting room has a colour television and a crackling log fire on chilly evenings, there are also leaflets and local guides to peruse so you can plan your day trips. The dining area overlooks the landscaped garden and a small patio. It is in this room you are served a sumptuous breakfast, a full English meal with all the trimmings cooked superbly on the Aga. Sue is an excellent cook and takes great care in the preparation and presentation of food, she always combines the finest ingredients creating irresistible dishes with her own individual flair. To compliment Sue's wonderful food you are more than welcome to bring you own wine.

White Barn is ideally situated for visiting the surrounding area, being just 3 miles from the historic city of Chichester in one direction and to the Royal Naval port of Portsmouth, with all it has to offer in the other, with plenty to see in between; Goodwood, Arundel and of course the lovely countryside of Hampshire and West Sussex. You are assured of a wonderful warm and happy stay with super food. You couldn't ask for more.

USEFUL INFORMATION

OPEN; All year
CHILDREN; Welcome, over 10 years
CREDIT CARDS; Mastercard/Visa
ACCOMMODATION; 3 ensuite rooms
1 double, 1 family, 1 twin
PETS; No

DINING ROOM; Excellent home-cooked fare using fresh local produce
VEGETARIAN; Catered for
DISABLED ACCESS; No
GARDEN; Yes

HOLLY HOUSE
Chelwood Gate,
Sussex RH17 7LF

Tel: 01825 740484

Holly House is a rather attractive 19th century country guest house, with a superb garden of approximately one acre with ponds and a swimming pool. It is owned and excellently run by Mrs. D Birchell who welcomes you to her warm and friendly establishment. The house itself is very pleasant and attractively decorated throughout with antique furniture. The 5 bedrooms have colour television and tea and coffee making facilities. Breakfast is served in the beautiful conservatory overlooking the lovely garden, it is a traditional meal with all the trimmings. A meal in the evening can be taken at the local pub which has a varied menu catering for all tastes from traditional to the exotic. There are also plenty of restaurants in the surrounding area. Places of interest abound with something for everyone.

Chelwood Gate is a small village on the Ashdown Forest not far from Horsted Keynes, which is a station on the Bluebell Railway Line, where steam trains chug up and down to Sheffield Park. There is also a collection of locomotives and rolling stock dating between 1865 and 1958. Sheffield Park is 120 acres of trees and shrubs designed by Capability Brown in 1775 with five lakes, lovely walks and stunning views. Lewes and Royal Tunbridge Wells are interesting shopping centres.

USEFUL INFORMATION

OPEN; All year
CHILDREN; Welcome
CREDIT CARDS; None taken
LICENSED; No
ACCOMMODATION; 5 rooms, 2 double and 1 twin are ensuite, 1 twin and 1 single share a bathroom, both of the twin rooms can become doubles

DINING ROOM; Traditional breakfast
VEGETARIAN; Catered for
DISABLED ACCESS; 2 gnd flr rooms but not suitable for wheelchair users
GARDEN; Lovely with ponds & swimming pool
PETS; Yes

Chapter Three

THE COTTAGE GUEST HOUSE
*22b Westhampnett Rd, Chichester,
West Sussex,
PO19 4HW.
Tel: 01243 774979*

On the north side of historic Chichester lies the 100 year old cottage of Lynn and Arthur Smith. This friendly couple offer good accommodation in modern, cosy rooms that have T.V. and that ever essential tray of tea and coffee. Breakfast is full English traditional (with free range eggs), and vegetarians are welcome by prior arrangement.

Lynn and Arthur are members of the cycle touring club, so are very well informed on the surrounding countryside (especially the hills!). There is a great deal in the area with Chichester itself; the Cathedral with it's 177ft spire, the Chichester Festival Theatre (one of the best in the country) and Goodwood House; the seat of the Dukes of Richmond and Gordon. South Downe Way has some great walks and there are many more of those bracing outdoor activities, all around you.

USEFUL INFORMATION

OPEN : All year
CHILDREN : Welcome
CREDIT CARDS : None taken
LICENSED : No
ACCOMMODATION : 1 dble, 1 twin, bathroom shared by both rooms.

DINING ROOM : Breakfast only
BAR MEALS : Not applicable
VEGETARIAN : By arrangement
DISABLED ACCESS : By request
GARDEN : Yes: private.

ABBEYGAIL GUEST HOUSE
*17 Penshurst Road, East Cliff,
Ramsgate,
Kent, CT11 8EG.
Tel : 01843 594154*

The seaside town of Ramsgate is home to sandy beaches, cliffs and a pleasant town centre. Abbeygail Guest House is owned and run by Hazel and John Nash, your amiable hosts who are intent on you enjoying your stay with them! This is a very charming house with warm spacious bedrooms fully equipped with TV, tea/coffee tray and central heating. Hazel and John welcome all ages and can supply cots and various other equipment if needed. There is also access for the disabled, if they have some assistance, as there are some bedrooms on the ground floor. Breakfast is full English fayre, or continental if desired. An evening meal canbe provided if booked in advance, and if packed lunches are required this can also be arranged. There is much to see and do in the area- lots of information leaflets and timetables available. Hazel and John speak fluent French and German, and with the ferry port so close, this is ideal for our continental visitors!

USEFUL INFORMATION

OPEN : All year
CHILDREN : Most welcome
PETS : No
LICENSED : No
CREDIT CARDS : None taken
ACCOMMODATION : 10 rooms; 2 dbl, 2 twin, 3 sgl & 3 fml.

DINING ROOM : Good English fayre
VEGETARIANS : Catered for
DISABLED ACCESS : Assisted
BAR SNACKS ; Not applicable
GARDEN : Yes

EASTON HOUSE,
*Chidham Lane, Chidham,
Chichester,
West Sussex, PO18 8TF*

Tel & Fax : 01243 572514

    Chidham is probably the last unspoilt village on Chichester Harbour, sitting on the Chidham Peninsula. This is an exceptional setting for any house, but Easton House is simply idyllic! It quite literally oozes character, charm and ambience and I haven't even mentioned your hostess, Mary Hartley! Built as a farm in 1580, it has retained much of it's original character with timberbeams, lintels and framework showing, and picked out in a delightful way. Every little detail for comfort has been thought of, and there is a homely, welcoming feeling pervading the house. After a day's activities, you will feel as if you are coming home.

    Breakfast is full English traditional and 'designed to cope with any day!' The bedrooms are of a very high standard and charmingly furnished. Mary is an ardent musician and there is a Bechstein piano available if you wish to 'tinkle the ivories'. She is quite happy to arrange a musical evening should you wish to participate.

    The harbour is 5 minutes walk from the house, with the boats bobbing on the water (you'll wish you had brought your paints and brushes!) Walking is a joy here as you have everything you could want from a view, and you are close enough to Chichester to be able to spend a day visiting this engaging city.

USEFUL INFORMATION

OPEN : *All year*
CHILDREN : *Discount for under 10yrs*
PETS : *No*
LICENSED : *No*
CREDIT CARDS : *None taken*
ACCOMMODATION : *2 rooms; 1 dbl, 1 twin.*

DINING ROOM : *Breakfast only*
VEGETARIANS : *Well catered for*
BAR FOOD : *Not applicable*
DISABLED ACCESS : *No*
GARDEN : *Spacious & well kept*

Chapter Three

HATPINS
Bosham Lane,
Old Bosham, Chichester,
Sussex PO18 8HG

Tel: 01243 572644

Hatpins will appeal to anyone who appreciates a much loved home which has been beautifully furnished and decorated throughout. Mary Waller who owns this strictly non-smoking house was a former designer of hats and wedding dresses. This talent has now had a change of direction and instead of sowing wedding dresses she use s lovely fabrics to make drapes, pillows and bed covers. Every room in the house has something of her work and this combined with a natural gift for decorating makes Hatpins both delightful to stay in and the equal of any sophisticated manor house hotel. Mary is a very hospitable lady and she works hard to ensure her guests have a memorable stay and want to come back again. The bedrooms have exceptionally comfortable beds and are either ensuite or have a private bathroom. In addition there is the luxury of a sauna.. Each bedroom has colour television and a hostess tray. Breakfast is a delicious meal in which fresh produce is used. You can choose from several variations of a full English breakfast or opt for something lighter. There are no evening meals but you will find many good places in which to eat within easy distance.

Bosham is a delight in its own right especially Old Bosham with its narrow lanes wending their way down to the waterfront. The old church is fascinating and is depicted in the Bayeux Tapestry. The cathedral city of Chichester with its fascinating harbour is closeby. One can spend hours here exploring the cathedral, the shops and the museums. Goodwood House the home of the Duke of Richmond is a few miles inland. Throughout the year there are many events held here. The famous racecourse has several meetings a year. Sculpture at Goodwood is a changing collection of contemporary sculpture. There are Classic Car meetings and much more. Portsmouth is no distance either and here you can visit the HMS Victory and the Mary Rose. Certainly Hatpins makes a perfect base for a holiday or for a short break.

USEFUL INFORMATION

OPEN; All year
CHILDREN; By arrangement
CREDIT CARDS; None taken
ACCOMMODATION; 2 en suite +1 with Private bathroom. Sauna
PETS; No

DINING ROOM; First class breakfast
No evening meals
VEGETARIAN; Upon request
DISABLED ACCESS; No
GARDEN; Yes
A STRICTLY NON-SMOKING HOUSE

RIVERSIDE LODGE,
7 Market Avenue, Chichester,
West Sussex PO19 1JH

Tel: 01243 783164

In the heart of historic Chichester lies Riverside Lodge, a charming cottage built of traditional brick and flint. It was constructed just after the 1st World War by a member of the Halsted family whose origins go back as far as 1649, when they were a major part of the city's economy. They were prominent with their ownership of iron foundries, and at least one member of this family held the post of City Mayor. Riverside Lodge is now owned by Jan Tregear and she must be complimented on the enchanting aspects of her home, and applauded on the beautiful appointment of this secluded house in the heart of an extremely historic environment.

Accommodation on the first floor is a double room furnished in a delightful cottage style, with the ever needed tea and coffee being complimentary, and a T.V. On the ground floor is a self-contained suite with double bedroom, sitting room, kitchen and of course ensuite facilities. Jan supplies a hearty traditional English breakfast, and if you prefer Continental or vegetarian, then she will oblige. This is served in the pleasant dining room, overlooking the garden. Jan asks that you refrain from smoking indoors as it 'badly affects her husband's health'.

Chichester has a great deal to offer and days can be spent just exploring the city. It dates back to Roman occupation between 1st and 2nd century AD and the Cathedral has a 177ft spire which is visible at sea. The pennant from Sir Francis Chichester's Gypsy Moth is here in the cathedral, along with a wonderful altar tapestry designed by John Piper.

USEFUL INFORMATION

OPEN; *All year, except Christmas*
CHILDREN; *By special arrangement*
PETS; *No*
CREDIT CARDS; *None taken*
ACCOMMODATION; *2dbl rooms both Ensuite, one with self-catering options*

DINING ROOM; *Breakfast only*
VEGETARIAN; *Catered for*
DISABLED ACCESS; *No*
GARDEN; *Pleasant garden*

Chapter Three

ST ANDREWS LODGE
Chichester Road, Selsey,
Chichester, West Sussex
PO20 0LX

Tel: 01243 606899
Fax: 01243 607826

This wholesome establishment situated on the Manhood Peninsula lies 7 miles south of the ancient city of Chichester close to the sea and beaches and a short distance from the scenic South Downs. An abundance of attractions are situated within the area guaranteed to gratify visitors whatever their interests, making St Andrews Lodge the perfect base to establish oneself. Here you can rest assured that you every need is catered for by a caring and friendly hostess, whose aim is to provide her guests with comfort and a home from home ambiance. The neat and tidy garden laid mostly to lawn is favoured with a patio area with sun loungers and garden furniture. Overlooking the garden is the large and very restful lounge, with colour television and for those wishing to read or chat, a quiet area has been set aside. There is a cosy log fire for the winter evenings. Residents can enjoy the facilities of the small licenced bar where you may smoke, however smoking is not permitted in the bedrooms. All ensuite bedrooms are well appointed with their own individual style and pretty colour co-ordinated quality soft fabrics, offering a tea and coffee tray, colour television, radio and hair dryer. There are ground floor bedrooms with wheelchair accessibility and for guests unable to manipulate the stairs. The property benefits from full central heating. There is plenty of secure car parking space. The cuisine is worthy of a special mention, dishes are creative and prepared using fresh produce. One is spoilt for choice regarding breakfast which is wholesome and delicious. Prior arrangement is requested for evenings meals which come highly recommended and vegetarian diets are catered for. Mrs. Valma Kennedy has been awarded a 'Grade 1 Excellent Wheelchair Access' by the English Tourist Board, '3 Crown Commended' and AA '4Q Selected' and one can understand why. St Andrews Lodge is well situated being close to the coast with water sports, including boating, surfing, swimming and fishing and a choice of three beaches. Golf and horse riding can also be arranged locally. Along the coast from Selsey is a 1000 acre reserve at Pagham, which is home to many species of birds, butterflies and moths. Bognor Regis still retains some of the sedate charms of years gone by and benefits from a long stretch of beach and safe bathing. Chichester is renowned for its historical interest and the Festival Theatre which presents a yearly summer season of thespian delights. Museums, country houses, fascinating villages, parks and gardens are all within easy driving distance.

USEFUL INFORMATION

OPEN; All year
CHILDREN; Welcome
CREDIT CARDS; All except Switch
LICENSED; Yes
ACCOMMODATION; 9 guest rooms, all ensuite
DINING ROOM; Delicious home-cooking. Evening meal by prior arrangement - highly recommended
VEGETARIAN; Catered for
DISABLED ACCESS; Excellent facilities, awarded
GARDEN; Yes, spacious
PETS; Yes by arrangement

**THE CEDAR HOUSE
RESTAURANT & HOTEL,**
Mill Road, Cobham,
Surrey, KT11 3AL.

Tel : 01932 863424
Fax : 01932 862023

Cedar House, built in the 15th century, is a magnificent medieval house which is Grade II listed, and contains many of the original features. The partners who run this charming hotel are James Lunn and Clive Rothwell, who incidentally, first met when they were based at the same squadron in the RAF! This partnership definitely works as can be seen and appreciated in this outstanding venture. The house has considerable elegance, and everywhere is some sign of its great past. Some rooms are Jacobean and there is also an association with Lord Horatio Nelson, who stayed here on his way to Portsmouth where he was to take on the might of the French and Spanish navies. There are six bedrooms, all en suite, with colour TV, tea/coffee tray, direct dial and room service. These are large, bright, individually styled rooms with comfortable beds and period furniture throughout. After a refreshing night in one of these fine rooms come down to breakfast in the graceful dining room with its minstrel gallery, inglenook fireplace, timbered ceiling and stunning leaded window overlooking the main entrance of the house. Cedar House has an excellent reputation for food and is ideal for luncheon, dinner or private functions. There are two Queen Anne rooms, beautifully decorated, which are ideal for that intimate dinner party, family function or even business seminar. The menus are both innovative and original with some mouth watering dishes, and an appropriately varied wine list to match. Sunday Lunch gives a great choice for a set price, with starters such as 'Grilled medallions of goats cheese in a hazelnut crust, served with a salad of summer leaves dressed in walnut oil', and to follow perhaps 'Breast of chicken in a leek & roquefort cheese sauce served with seasonal vegetables & roast potatoes'. Sounds delicious, doesn't it. The desserts are a dream with choices such as 'Sticky toffee pudding with a toffee sauce' or 'Orange caramel cream on a fruit syrup'. The problem would be deciding which to exclude! A drink in the old orchard whilst choosing your menu is just one way to 'set the tone' of this enjoyable, friendly experience and to make the most of all that Cedar House has to offer.

1997 sees the addition of an extension in the form of the Coach House annexe, which will add a further five bedrooms to the hotel. This will give further accommodation for those wishing to sample the delights of this restaurant & hotel, and to relish the many attributes of the area in the way of fishing, golf, walking, riding, shooting and much, much more. It is an ideal location for those travelling from London or any of it's airports, and is worth taking a little extra time just to savour the experience of a lifetime.

USEFUL INFORMATION

OPEN : All year
CHILDREN : Welcome
PETS : No
LICENSED : Full
CREDIT CARDS : All major
ACCOMMODATION : 6 rooms en suite : 4dbl, 2 twin.

RESTAURANT : Fine new English food
VEGETARIANS : Catered for
BAR SNACKS : No
DISABLED ACCESS : To restaurant
GARDEN : Extensive grounds

Chapter Three

RYEGATE HOUSE
Stoke-by-Nayland,
Colchester, CO6 4RA

Tel: 01206 263679

Lying to the North of Colchester the Dedham Vale, well known as Constable Country, encompasses the River Stour from Nayland to Flatford. This beautiful vale has inspired many an artist with its watermills, quiet serene streams edged with willows and gently rolling meadows and fields. As you explore this picturesque area you will discover the delights of the riverside villages of Nayland, Dedham, Stratford-St-Mary and Flatford. On the Northern flank lies the charming village of Stoke-by-Nayland where you will find shops, restaurants, public houses, a post office, garage and St. Mary's Church, whose majestic tower dominates the skyline and overlooks the entire area.

Here too you will find Ryegate House, an English Tourist Board '2 Crown Highly Commended' Bed and Breakfast establishment, owned and efficiently run by Margaret and Albert Geater, a very accommodating couple, who extend a warm and friendly welcome to you. The house itself is delightful, reminiscent of a traditional Suffolk farmhouse, exceptionally well kept with emphasis placed on cleanliness and attention to detail. The building is surrounded by a well tended garden with ample private off-road parking. The furnishings are comfortable and in total keeping with the house. The guest's sitting room is very welcoming with comfortable relaxing chairs, colour television and countryside views. The bedrooms, two double and one twin, are very well appointed with central heating, colour co-ordinated soft furnishings, ensuite facilities, colour television, radio alarm, shaver point and a complimentary tea and coffee tray. Breakfast is served in the dining room where the outlook is across the garden to an old orchard left to nature. Here you can enjoy a full English, Continental or vegetarian meal. Evening meals are not available in house, but an excellent dinner or supper can easily be obtained from one of the restaurants or public houses in the village.

The surrounding area has much to offer the visitor. The market towns of Sudbury and Hadleigh with their historical backgrounds and ancient buildings. Many picturesque Suffolk villages and Long Melford with its baronial halls and plethora of antique shops. Lavenham, the jewel in the crown and only a short distance away, regarded as the finest medieval village in England. Colchester, Britain's oldest recorded town, steeped in history and worthy of more than one days exploration. The unspoilt Suffolk coast and the ports of Felixstowe and Harwich are within easy reach and with fishing, golf and plenty of walking nearby, Ryegate House is a delightful place to stay.

USEFUL INFORMATION

OPEN; All year except Christmas Evening **CHILDREN;** Over 10 years
CREDIT CARDS; None taken
ACCOMMODATION; 3 ensuite rooms
GARDEN; Yes

DINING ROOM; Choice of breakfast. meal is not available
VEGETARIAN; Catered for
DISABLED ACCESS; No
PETS; Small well behaved dogs

THORINGTON HALL,
Stoke-by-Nayland, Colchester,
Suffolk CO6 4SS.
Tel : 01206 337329

Thorington Hall is a 17th century house owned by the National Trust and home to Deirdre Wollaston and her family. Deirdre provides a full English breakfast and caters for vegetarians. Tea, coffee and various drinks are also served upon request. The rooms are airy and spacious, furnished simply but very comfortably. This is a friendly establishment, with guests looked after as part of the family, and situated in an area of outstanding beauty and steeped in history. This house boasts many fine original features such as the beautiful carved oak staircase (circa 1640), windows with original 17th century catches, oak panelling in one bedroom, and early 18th century English tiles depicting Biblical scenes in another. Externally, the spectacular tall chimney stack with star caps, and the warm, ochre walls of traditional Suffolk colour - this is maintained by the National Trust and traditionally painted using lime-based paint.

This is Constable country, and as such you may find yourself presented at any time with a familiar looking landscape or scene. Thorington Hall is one that you may be intimate with, having hung in the Tate Gallery in London during the last major Constable exhibition. The delightful story is that Deirdre's daughter visited the exhibition and saw the drawing labelled in the catalogue as 'unidentified manor house' and immediately recognised it! Deirdre's husband then wrote to the owners, who kindly provided a photograph of the drawing, which now has pride of place hanging in the sitting room. The drawing has since been bought by a Canadian collector who specialises in Constable's works, and has the finest private collection of his paintings and drawings. Nearby, in the nucleus of Constable country, is Flatford Mill, where Constable painted the famous Hay Wain, shown in Paris and much admired by the French. Flatford Mill is also a National Trust property, and although there are no original works here, there is an abundance of interesting information and guide books, indicating the exact spots where many of his famous works were executed. Good examples of his works can be found in Ipswich Museum (Christchurch Mansion).

Colchester is only 8 miles away and is an intriguing city to visit. In addition to being a good shopping area, there is history here, and a day out here would definitely be attractive. The Holy Trinity Church, (probably Anglo-Saxon), which was largely built from Roman materials, is now a rural crafts museum and very interesting. The Roman walls and the Norman castle are two of the most interesting attractions. It is thought that the castle was built by the same architect as the White Tower in London, and is definitely as impressive and even larger. The building houses the municipal museum and contains much interesting material from Roman and medieval times.

There are many beautiful towns and villages in the surrounding area too, these prospered from the medieval wool trade, which allowed many charming timbered houses and large churches to be built. A fine example of this is the town of Lavenham with it's half timbered buildings, both late medieval and Tudor. Kersey is one of the prettiest villages having a lovely site on a sheep hill with a stream at the bottom. There are a host of places to eat in this area, many craft shops and even local vineyards keeping alive an ancient tradition.

Deirdre Wollaston runs an excellent establishment, at the heart of an interesting and varied part of the country, and you will certainly be 'entertained' by the mixed wealth of pursuits available in the area which cater to all who visit.

USEFUL INFORMATION

OPEN : All year
CHILDREN : Welcome
PETS : If well behaved
LICENSED : No
CREDIT CARDS : None taken
DINING ROOM : Breakfast only
VEGETARIANS : Catered for
BAR SNACKS : Not applicable
DISABLED ACCESS : No
GARDEN : Yes
ACCOMMODATION : 4 rooms: 2 dbl/twin (with WC&basin) 1 sgl, 1 fml.

Chapter Three

LONGCROFT HOUSE
Beacon Road,
Ditchling,
East Sussex BN6 8UZ

Tel: 01273 842740

Nestling near the foot of Ditchling Beacon is Longcroft House, set in two and a half acres of garden and paddock, between a vineyard and the centre of the village. This very comfortable house, where you are offered tea and coffee in bed in the morning, is relaxing indeed. The 3 delightful bedrooms all with own private/ensuite facilities and colour television, and for the romantic at heart, there is one room with a four-poster bed. Evening meals are available at your request and are a gastronomic delight. You are welcome to bring you own wine, although dinners include some complimentary wine. Longcroft is quite close to the South Downs Way, where walkers and horse riders will be in their element, infact Robert and Helen Scull, your hosts, are more than happy to offer the facilities of the adjacent paddock for horses at certain times of the year, or livery facilities nearby. Fishing and golf are all withing easy reach, so come and be pampered at this excellent country house.

USEFUL INFORMATION
OPEN; All year
CHILDREN; By arrangement
CREDIT CARDS; None taken
LICENSED; No, but may bring your own
ACCOMMODATION; 2 ensuite rooms, 1 with private facilities
DINING ROOM; Excellent gourmet cuisine
VEGETARIAN; Catered for
DISABLED ACCESS; Not really
GARDEN; Yes with pond, plus paddock
PETS; No

ST.MARK'S GUEST HOUSE,
23 Castle Street, Dover,
Kent, CT16 1PT.
Tel : 01304 201894

Dover is a clean, tidy town, busy with its cosmopolitan range of people, travelling to and fro the continent! St.Mark's Guest House is in the heart of the town, really ideal for those people travelling by ferry. It offers a good night's rest in pleasant surroundings and is very good value for money! Mark Emanuele is your host and presents a good -natured, friendly attitude towards his guests. The bedrooms are cosy and inviting, and have TV and tea/coffee trays. Breakfast is a consuming affair, with quantities guaranteed to 'keep you going' and can either be English or continental. Although Mark does not cater for an evening meal, you are in the centre of town where some very good pubs and restaurants can be found. If you wish to spend a few days seeing Dover and the surrounding area, this is the ideal place to stay. There are lovely coastal walks (home of the White Cliffs!) and an evening stroll along the sea front is definitely recommended!

USEFUL INFORMATION
OPEN : All year
CHILDREN : Welcome
PETS : No
LICENSED : No
CREDIT CARDS : All major
ACCOMMODATION : 6 rooms; 2 dbl en suite, 2 fml en suite, 2 twin.
DINING ROOM : Good hearty breakfast
VEGETARIANS : Catered for
BAR SNACKS : Not applicable
DISABLED ACCESS : Not really
GARDEN : No

KING JOHN'S LODGE,
Sheepstreet Lane, Etchingham,
Sussex, TN19 7AZ.

Tel : 01580 819232

Sitting on the Kent/Sussex borders, this delightful 14th century house still retains much of its Jacobean origins. The present owners, Jill and Richard Cunningham, have endeavoured to maintain the charm of its history, while ensuring that every modern comfort is available. Stone and inglenook fireplaces, original leaded lights in stone mullion windows, richly beamed rooms, all enhance the atmosphere, and add to the ambience of this charming house. The bedrooms are attractively furnished, and have that essential tea/coffee tray, and each is either en suite or has it's own private bathroom. There is a private sitting room where guests can relax after a day's activities, or the garden is a delight with it's magnificent views over the countryside. The grounds amount to 4 acres, and there is a wild garden with a rosewalk, and a secret garden where you could spend some time in the tranquillity and peace. For those garden lovers, plants are on sale along with garden statuary, urns, troughs and fountains. There is also a tennis court, swimming pool and that very 'English' game of croquet can be played on the lawn.

Breakfast is full English and is served in the Elizabethan breakfast room, or on the terrace in milder weather. Dinner can also be arranged, but there are also many excellent pubs and restaurants in the surrounding area where a good meal can be enjoyed at reasonable prices.

This is a wonderful location for 'getting away' but within easy distances of many interesting places. Situated between Tunbridge Wells and Rye it is a haven for visiting castles, gardens and even Rudyard Kipling's home 'Batemans'. Sports available include golf, fishing and riding.

This is a really superb home from home with outstanding service and friendly hosts, and supplying memories that will have you returning again and again to this wonderful part of the world.

USEFUL INFORMATION

OPEN : All year   **DINING ROOM** : Good English fayre
CHILDREN : Welcome   **VEGETARIANS** : Catered for
ACCOMMODATION : 3 rooms: 1 dbl, 1 twin, 1 fml.

Chapter Three

HIGH WRAY,
73 Lodge Hill Road, Farnham,
Surrey, GU10 3RB.

Tel : 01252 715589

High Wray is a 1923 country house of high standards and excellent accommodation, and with Warren and Alexine Crawford as your friendly hosts, you are welcomed as part of the family! The house stands high up in 3 acres of grounds and has extensive views over the forests to the south. The grounds themselves are superb, with gardens, woodlands and a vegetable plot. Guests are welcome to wander round the peaceful, quiet gardens and relish the tranquillity of the land around them. In the actual house there is accommodation of one twin room and a single room, both with tea/coffee tray and a guest bathroom. Furnishings are comfortable and elegant, and both rooms have wonderful views over the countryside. An associated wing behind the house, **Audubon House**, provides superior accommodation for the disabled. All rooms are on the ground floor and include a twin room, a double en suite, and a single room. The doorways are wide and there is plenty of space for the movement of wheelchairs, and bathrooms have the appropriate grab rails for ease. Breakfast is a traditional affair, and you are welcome to join the family in an evening meal, if advance notice is given. As all food is home cooked, with home grown vegetables and free range eggs, it is a splendid country meal! Warren and Alexine are anxious that you should enjoy your stay with them, and with the warmth and amicable greeting they extend, there is very little doubt of anything else! The dining room is full of family portraits, which make for very interesting conversation, and the charming drawing room has a TV and piano for those cosy evening get togethers!

Farnham has a great deal to offer as a town, both historically and culturally, and the surrounding countryside offers the opportunity for many outdoor sports and activities.

USEFUL INFORMATION

OPEN : All year
CHILDREN : Welcome (cot available)
PETS : Welcome
LICENSED : No
CREDIT CARDS : None taken
DINING ROOM: Splendid food
VEGETARIANS : Catered for
BAR SNACKS : Not applicable
DISABLED ACCESS : Purpose built
GARDEN : Large, well maintained
ACCOMMODATION : 5 rooms: 3 with access for disabled, 2 twin, 1 dbl, 2 sgl.

MILL LANE LODGE
Mill Lane, Crondall,
Farnham, Surrey GU10 5RP

Tel: 01252 850230

Addresses can sometimes be deceiving and none more so than Mill Lane Lodge, the postal address is Surrey but in fact the property is in Hampshire. This very impressive red brick and timber house was built around 300 years ago, it has an old heavy wooden front door whichgives it a sense of security. The outside is charming, a well kept large garden front and back with lots of trees, shrubs and lawns. The inside is just as charming the double bedroom having vaulted ceiling, antique and reproduction furniture add to the character of the house. The 3 bedrooms are exceptional with delightful soft furnishings and comfortable beds, one double and twin ensuite and the single has private facilities. Sarah Matlock, the lady of the house, will serve an excellent breakfast in the lovely dining room. A four course evening meal is available by arrangement with tempting delights such as fish and shellfish and English type fare, you may like to bring a bottle of wine to compliment it. If you would rather eat out then the village pub serves excellent food. Mill Lane Lodge has its own heated indoor swimming pool available May-October, shower, W.C. and changing room within the pool complex. Meals can also be served around the pool. Getting about is not a problem, with so much to do in the area your days will certainly be filled. Golf course with driving range within walking distance. Easy drive to London Heathrow Airport.

USEFUL INFORMATION

OPEN; All year
CHILDREN; Welcome from 4 years
CREDIT CARDS; None taken
LICENSED; No, welcome to bring own
ACCOMMODATION; 3 rooms
1 double, 1 twin, 1 single
Swimming pool with changing room
PETS; By arrangement

DINING ROOM; Excellent breakfast
4 course evening meal by arrangement
VEGETARIAN; Upon request
DISABLED ACCESS; Ground floor ensuite
room by request, but not fully disabled
GARDEN; Yes, lovely, easy access
NO SMOKING HOUSE

Chapter Three

TIMBERS
*Cross End, Pebmarsh,
Halstead,
Essex CO9 2NT*

Tel: 01787 269330

Between the market town of Braintree and Sudbury, where the famous painter Thomas Gainsborough was born, is Halstead. Situated in the Colne Valley it boasts a wonderful water mill, which was originally built for corn, but was then converted in 1825 by Samuel Courtauld and used for silk weaving. The Brewery Chapel Museum is also in this charming town. A bit off the beaten track near the village of Pebmarsh, is Timbers, a delightful bungalow owned by Celia Rice, who looks after her guests very well indeed, making them feel at home. The bungalow has recently been refurbished with new carpets and curtains throughout, the lovely furniture enhances the cosy atmosphere.

Celia has one guest room, a large family room complete with ensuite facilities, colour television and a tea and coffee tray. The views are beautiful across open countryside. In the morning you are treated to the most delicious very full English breakfast, the plate groans! After breakfast it is time to get out and about, for the train enthusiast there is the East Anglian Railway Museum, where you are transported back in time to the age of steam, and the Colne Valley Railway where you can travel along a restored line. There are country houses, museums, fishing, golf and lovely walks especially along the 'Stour Valley'.

USEFUL INFORMATION

OPEN; 1st March-30th November
CHILDREN; Welcome, over 5 years
CREDIT CARDS; None taken
ACCOMMODATION; 1 ensuite family room
PETS; Yes, if friendly!
DINING ROOM; Very full English breakfast. No evening meal
DISABLED ACCESS; Please phone
GARDEN; Yes

WINDY BROW
204 Victoria Road,
Wargrave, Reading,
Berkshire RG10 8AJ

Tel: 01189 403336

Wargrave is a small village between the city of Reading, noted for its University and being the base for industry, and Henley-on-Thames which is famous for the Royal Regatta held in July, when it swells with people all with one thing in common, rowing. Heather Carver lives in this village in her beautiful red brick Victorian house, which she generously shares with her guests. Windy Brow was built in 1880 and is a substantial property with a superb conservatory overlooking the garden, a delightful well kept lawn with lots of lovely plants, shrubs and flowers, the whole house is surrounded by trees giving it a rural feeling.

Heather has furnished her house very well with lovely antique and pine furniture, the rooms are large, airy and comfortable, adding to the positively friendly atmosphere. The bedrooms, 4 in all, have TV and a tea and coffee tray. There is a ground floor ensuite room suitable for the disabled, the others share a bathroom and shower. Heather serves a fine full English breakfast, evening meals are not available so why not try the local pubs for a traditional meal, or you can go further afield. Windy Brow is an ideal base for touring with Windsor 11 miles, Henley 3 miles, Oxford 40 minutes and even London is only 40 minutes away. You are sure to have a great stay here. Windy Brow is Listed with the English Tourist Board.

USEFUL INFORMATION

OPEN; All year
CHILDREN; By arrangement
CREDIT CARDS; None taken
ACCOMMODATION; 4 rooms, 2 twin, 2 single, 1 twin is ensuite
DINING ROOM; Breakfast only
DISABLED ACCESS; 1 gnd floor ensuite twin
GARDEN; Yes, delightful well kept
PETS; No

Chapter Three

NIGHTINGALES
*The Avenue, Kingston,
Lewes, Sussex BN7 3LL*

*Tel: 01273 475673
E.Mail J.Hudson @ sussex. ac.uk*

Nightingales is as charming as its name. This quiet bungalow in the South Downs village of Kingston is set in beautiful gardens which are part of the National Gardens Scheme and bring delight to visitors when they open to the public twice a year. Geoff and Jean Hudson have devoted years to the planning and planting to achieve today's stunning result. The half acre is sloping and informal and has a wide range of plants including shrub roses and hardy geraniums. There is a conservatory with Mediterranean and tropical plants.

The same loving care has gone into furnishing and equipping the bungalow which is a happy blend of antique and modern. You will receive a very warm welcome at Nightingales reinforced by Ben, their waggy black Labrador. The two centrally heated guest bedrooms with their pretty curtains are either ensuite or have a private bathroom. Each has a beverage tray complete with tea, coffee, chocolate and Duchy biscuits, and there is a decanter of sherry. Both rooms have Vi-Spring beds, colour TV,radio and clock, reading lamps, chairs and original pictures. The ensuite room has a writing table with an antique writing slope containing writing paper and local greeting cards to buy. A shoe cleaning kit is available and there is even a torch and hot water bottles!

Breakfast is a wonderful meal with apricots and yoghurt, organic free range eggs, bacon and sausages from a local butcher. There is a comprehensive choice and there are fresh flowers and a newspaper on the Victorian table. No evening meals but the 15th century local pub serves very good food at reasonable prices. Guests have a complete run of the house and the garden. Above all, apart from being a very special place in which to stay, it is so peaceful and must make even the most tense person relax.

This area of Sussex is great for those who want to walk on the South Downs or explore the county town of Lewes. If you are feeling energetic you can play golf or tennis or go horseriding. Fishing is available. If you enjoy opera you will find that Nightingales is ideally situated for a visit to Glyndebourne. Geoff and Jean also have a holiday flat in the bungalow for those who would prefer a self-catering holiday. (ETB Highly Commended)

USEFUL INFORMATION

OPEN; *All year*
CHILDREN; *Yes*
CREDIT CARDS; *All major cards*
LICENSED; *No*
ACCOMMODATION; *1ensuite twin 1double with private bathroom.*
PAYPHONE

DINING ROOM; *Excellent breakfast Free range eggs. Local produce. No evening meal*
VEGETARIAN; *Catered for*
DISABLED ACCESS; *Yes*
GARDEN; *Superb. National Gardens Scheme*

DURRANTS HOTEL
George Street,
London W1H 6BJ

Tel: 0171 935 8131
Fax: 0171 487 3510

Durrants Hotel has been owned by the Miller family for over 70 years and provides a service that meets the needs of today's travellers in an atmosphere of yesteryear. This quintessentially English hotel has been awarded the 'Which Hotel Guide' Best London Hotel for Value on two consecutive years and offers quality, individual style, and fine service in the heart of London. Durrants is situated off Manchester Square and is close to theatreland, Harley Street and Mayfair. With the Wallace Collection directly opposite and West End shopping within walking distance, it is ideally situated for both business and pleasure.

The whole of the hotel is elegant and beautifully appointed. Every room has character. Reached off narrow sloping corridors with creaking floorboards, each bedroom is individually furnished with its own private bathroom or shower, and every modern comfort. Pine-panelled walls, brass-labelled post box, an impressive staircase and a frock-coated concierge make one believe that one has stepped back in time. The rooms used for private parties, conferences and meetings are almost all panelled and look stunning when the tables are laid. With such a good reputation it is almost an impertinence to talk about the food. Suffice it to say that the kitchen is run by masters of their craft who produce delicious and superbly presented dishes from around the world but with the main emphasis on traditional and modern English cuisine. The service comes from a staff, including the head waiter, who have been at Durrants for years. It is caring, efficient and unobtrusive.

Hard to believe that Durrants was once a country inn, but one is reminded by the faithful recreation in the cosy hunting themed bar, with its brass tables and cast-iron coal burning fireplace, and in the intimate surrounding of the restaurant. There are conference facilities for up to 100 non-residents.

USEFUL INFORMATION

OPEN: All year. 24 hours
CHILDREN: Welcome, family rooms
CREDIT CARDS: Mastercard/Amex/Visa
LICENSED: Full on
ACCOMMODATION: 19 sgl, 40 twn, 30 dbl, 3 family, 3 suites
GARDEN: No. Dogs not permitted

RESTAURANT: Intimate, mainly traditional English
BAR FOOD: Available
VEGETARIAN: Always dishes on menu
DISABLED ACCESS: Wheelchair 3 steps. 7 ground floor bedrooms

Chapter Three

ELEVEN CADOGAN GARDENS
Sloane Square, Chelsea,
London SW3 2RJ

Tel: 0171 730 3426 Fax: 0171 730 5217

Eleven Cadogan Gardens was the first of the exclusive private Town House hotels in London. It is set in a tree-lined square in the heart of Chelsea, just a few minutes walk from Sloan Square, close to Harrods and the shopping delights of Knightsbridge and Kings Road, a seven minute taxi ride to the Roman Catholic Westminster Cathedral at Victoria and 25 minutes to St Paul's Cathedral or Westminster Abbey.

The hotel was established by an eccentric Swiss gentleman in the summer of 1949 for his friends and 'such ladies and gentlemen as can furnish me with acceptable introductions'. It has been the London home to discerning visitors throughout the intervening years. With its own health and beauty spa at No 1 Synergy, just a few doors away it provides a haven of peace and tranquillity amid the hustle and bustle of the city. Guests have free use of the facilities.

There are 60 beautifully appointed rooms including 5 suites. Each has its ensuite bathroom and every modern comfort. There is a boardroom large enough to take 12 people and a Chauffeur driven limousine service.

Not surprisingly the service is impeccable, discreet and efficient. From the moment of arrival when the butler meets you at the door it is the epitome of Victorian hospitality. Room service is around the clock and can provide light meals and refreshments in a moment. The chauffeur driven limousine service is fantastic for those wanting to take in some sightseeing or a little shopping.

USEFUL INFORMATION

OPEN: 24 hours
CHILDREN: Yes. No special facilities
CREDIT CARDS: Amex/Visa/Diners/Mastercard
LICENSED: Liquor licence
ACCOMMODATION: 60 ensuite rooms including 5 suites

RESTAURANT: Room service only
BAR FOOD: No Bar
VEGETARIAN: Always a veg. dish of the day
DISABLED ACCESS: None
GARDEN: Deck chairs can be arranged in the communal gardens opposite

NUMBER SIXTEEN
*16 Sumner Place,
London SW7 3EG*

Tel: 0171 589 5232 Fax: 0171 584 8615

To find a quiet, tranquil haven in the heart of London, close to the shops, restaurants and theatres, is a godsend and almost unheard of. Number Sixteen Sumner Place in South Kensington is that place. The elegant 'Town House Hotel' comprises of 4 Victorian houses side by side in a quiet thoroughfare. The premises just ooze warmth and a sense of being in your own private dwelling cared for by an efficient and friendly staff.

The whole of Number Sixteen is decorated and furnished with exquisite good taste. Guests are invited to pour themselves a drink from the 'Honour Bar' in the relaxed surroundings of the lounge, a perfect setting in which to meet friends or business associates. The comfortable informality of the drawing room will encourage you to curl up in front of the blazing fire with a book or magazines thoughtfully provided.

The conservatory opens onto a secluded garden which has been tended with green fingers and loving care. It is no wonder that Number Sixteen is an award-winner. In 1991 it won the prestigious 'Spencer Trophy' and the 'London in Bloom' award. Both are well deserved, and only serve to confirm that there are few better places to stay in the metropolis than in the embracing comfort of this excellent hotel. Our American friends will tell you that in addition to the pleasure they get from staying in such an elegant environment, they think the sumptuous English breakfast is memorable.

USEFUL INFORMATION

OPEN: All year
CHILDREN: Over 12 years
CREDIT CARDS: All major cards
LICENSED: Residential Licence
ACCOMMODATION: Elegant, spacious ensuite rooms
RESTAURANT: Hotel and Breakfast only
BAR FOOD: Not applicable
VEGETARIAN: Not applicable
DISABLED ACCESS: No. Willing to assist
GARDEN: Secluded. Award-winning

Chapter Three

THE GORING HOTEL
Beeston Place, Grosvenor Gardens,
London SW1W 0JW

Tel: 0171 396 9000
Fax: 0171 834 4393
Telex 919166

For three generations the Goring family have harmonised traditional standards of hotel keeping with progressive management. They are proud to operate two of the very best privately-owned hotels in England, The Goring Hotel in London and The Spa Hotel in Tunbridge Wells. A warm and dignified atmosphere, excellent service and outstanding facilities in either of the hotels make them a wise choice. Here in London, The Goring is to be found in a quiet haven ideally located, adjacent to Buckingham Palace and within walking distance of the Royal Parks, London's principal shopping areas and the heart of the West End and theatreland. The Houses of Parliament and Westminster Abbey are close by.

Within the hotel there are seventy eight bedrooms, individually designed and decorated. They are luxuriously appointed and some have enchanting balconies; the ideal place to have breakfast overlooking the lawns and flower beds. Room service is available twenty four hours a day, with valeting and evening maid service. The traditional elegance of the lovely restaurant makes it popular for both lunch and dinner. Guests may enjoy excellent food accompanied by some of the best wines in London which are chosen by George Goring and William Coupe. The Private Dining Rooms will accommodate between four and one hundred guests for Breakfast, Luncheons, Dinners, Cocktail Parties and Wedding Receptions. These rooms are ideal for small private parties, board meetings or formal luncheons. The GardenBar is an excellent venue for friends or business associates to meet and enjoy a glass of champagne overlooking the beautiful Goring garden. The charming Garden Lounge is the place to relax over a pot of coffee, or enjoy the delights of warm scones and fresh cream with a Traditional English afternoon tea. Since the 2nd March 1910 when O.R. Goring opened the hotel; the first in the world with private bathroom and central heating in every bedroom, each guest has contributed something to the character, warmth and homeliness of this fine hotel which the Goring family run with the longstanding General Manager, William Cowpe. They genuinely enjoy making their guests feel at home and now have the pleasure of being able to welcome the children and grandchildren of families they have known for generations.

USEFUL INFORMATION

OPEN: *All year. 24 hours*
CHILDREN: *Welcome*
CREDIT CARDS: *All major cards*
LICENSED: *Full. Fine wines*
ACCOMMODATION: *78 ensuite rooms*
GARDEN: *Yes, lawns and flowerbeds*

RESTAURANT: *Traditional, elegant, superb food*
BAR FOOD: *Yes. 24 hr Room service*
VEGETARIAN: *Selection of dishes daily*
DISABLED ACCESS: *Yes*

THE PORTOBELLO
22 Stanley Gardens,
London W11 2NG

Tel: 0171 727 2777
Fax: 0171 792 9641

This exciting hotel is not quite the run of the mill. Originally two whitewashed town houses in a quiet street, within easy reach of the heart of London's West End and Theatres, it gets its name from Notting Hill's lively Portobello Market. You cannot fail to see it amidst the pretty porticoed terrace; luscious green bay trees stand guard at the entrance. Inside the furnishings, mainly antique, are set off with the help of elegant arched windows, wrought iron, ceiling mouldings and trompe l'oeil wall-beading. The atmosphere is wonderful and although it may appear totally laid back, this is an exceptionally well-kept and efficiently run hotel.

The bedrooms all have a lot of character although if you are happy to spend a little more money, one of the special rooms - Room 16 for example, is an indulgent choice with its round bed, oriental gold and flower wallpaper and Victorian shower bath on legs. Every room is well equipped and there is 24 hour room service. There is no access to the communal gardens behind but from the lounge it is very restful to look out at the floral displays and the well kept grass. This is a room that is nothing short of splendid with its Victorian antiques, abundant greenery and deep seated chairs. Downstairs from reception is a conservatory style bar and restaurant room which looks out to a pretty seashell wall-mosaic and a little fountain. The menu is not vast but it does have some interesting dishes - monkfish and wild mushroom pie for example. The nicest thing about The Portobello is its warmth. You feel welcome and important - very good for the ego.

USEFUL INFORMATION

OPEN: All year except 23 Dec-2 Jan
CHILDREN: Welcome
CREDIT CARDS: Mastercard/Amex/Diners/Visa
LICENSED: Yes
ACCOMMODATION: 7 suites, 5 dbl, 3 twn, 9 sgl

RESTAURANT: Small but interesting menu
BAR FOOD: Not applicable
VEGETARIAN: Always a choice
DISABLED ACCESS: Wheelchair. 2 ground floor rooms
GARDEN: Not applicable

Chapter Three

UPTOWN RESERVATIONS

50 Christchurch Street, Chelsea,
London SW3 4AR

Tel: 0171 351 3445

Fax: 0171 351 9383

This unique reservation service is reserved for those who prefer to stay in the comfort of a very nice home rather than the more impersonal hotel. Uptown reservations has a carefully chosen number of clients from all walks of life, from peers of the realm to actors and actresses who welcome guests on a bed and breakfast basis to their homes which are all in the heart of London; Mayfair, Knightsbridge, Chelsea and so on.

Every house has been inspected by the agency and everyone is delightful. You have the freedom to come and go as you please, enjoy the beauty of the house you are staying in and know that you will be both extremely comfortable and provided with a first class breakfast.

This leaves you with the opportunity to explore London's wide variety of restaurants at lunchtime and for dinner. You will find that none of the establishments on Uptown Reservations list is ever advertised publicly; in other words you will not be provided with a brochure from which to select a venue. When you ring to book accommodation, various houses will be offered to you to suit your requirements and you will never be disappointed.

The reason is a simple one - security. The houses are all so beautifully furnished, frequently with valuable antique furniture and paintings, that the risk would be to great. You will be agreeably surprised at the cost of staying in these elegant properties and having once decided to use this service you will no doubt be eager to book again.

USEFUL INFORMATION

OPEN: All year
CHILDREN: No
CREDIT CARDS: Yes with agency
ACCOMMODATION: Rooms ensuite
DINING ROOM: Breakfast only
DISABLED ACCESS: Not suitable
PETS: No

The Home Counties

THE HURTWOOD INN HOTEL
*Peaslake, Nr. Guildford,
Surrey GU5 9RR*

*Tel 01306 730851
Fax: 01306 731390*

    Guildford has a very modern shopping centre, and has also become a large business centre, there is plenty going on here with museums, theatres and exhibitions. If you are happy with the hustle and bustle this is the place for you, but if you prefer a more tranquil and peaceful setting, then take the A25 to Gomshall, then the turning opposite the petrol filling station and follow the road straight through to Peaslake and you will find a piece of heaven, TheHurtwood Inn Hotel. The village of Peaslake is picturesque indeed and quite deservedly has won an award, it is named after a small stream which has its origins here call 'Pise Lacu'. Adjacent to the village is The Hurtwood, a 4,000 acre privately owned forest, an excellent area for ramblers and riders. The Hurtwood Inn Hotel is absolutely charming and a classic example of architecture during the 1920's. The furnishings and decor have been thoughtfully chosen to complement the property. Ian and Susan Best, and their son Simon, work very hard and have assembled a hand picked team of people to ensure that each guest has personal and individual attention, and that their stay is a relaxed and happy one. The 15 guest rooms, are exquisitely furnished and tastefully decorated, they are spacious, light and airy. All have the privacy of ensuite facilities, direct dial telephone, colour television and complimentary tea and coffee tray. There is a very comfortable lounge and bar where you can relax, meet with friends and family or have a light snack from the comprehensive and delicious Bar Menu.

    The superb restaurant with oak panelling and an intimate atmosphere is known as Oscars, and has a reputation all of its own for simply excellent food and service. The talented Head Chef is Paul Jameson, who with his staff, create the most mouthwatering dishes. For a small private party you can also enjoy a perfect meal in the Garden Suite. The wine list is very comprehensive and has been carefully selected to complement every dish.

    The Hotel garden is delightful and during the summer months you are able to soak up the peace and quiet. Chairs and tables are also positioned at the front, and here you can sit and watch the world go by. The Hotel has facilities for conferences and this coupled with the convenience of the M25 makes it an ideal location for the business person. This really is a very special Hotel in idyllic surroundings, and one definitely not to be missed.

USEFUL INFORMATION

OPEN; *All year*
CHILDREN; *Welcome*
CREDIT CARDS; *Mastercard/Visa/ Switch/Amex*
LICENSED; *Full, comprehensive wine list*
ACCOMMODATION; *15 ensuite rooms*

RESTAURANT; *Superb A La Carte menu*
BAR FOOD; *Delicious bar snacks*
VEGETARIAN; *Excellent many choices*
DISABLED ACCESS; *Restaurant & lounge bar*
GARDEN; *Beautiful*
PETS; *Yes*

Chapter Three

BARN COTTAGE,
*Church Road, Leigh,
Reigate,
Surrey, RH2 8RF.*

Tel : 01306 611347

Remember the last time you flew away on holiday? Up at some unearthly hour of the night, last minute checks on everything, load the car, drive all the way down the motorway, drop the family off at the doors, drive to your parking space, then try and find your family again! All that rush....rush....rush! Totally worn out and probably stressed out too! Well next time consider travelling down earlier...much earlier...and stay at Barn Cottage, just 10 minutes from Gatwick Airport. . It is a beautifully converted 17th century barn owned and run by Pat and Mike Comer, who have provided every imaginable ease for their guests. This is an attractive property, set in private, luscious gardens containing a tennis court and swimming pool. There are two double bedrooms beautifully furnished in an antique style, with country curtains and bed covers to match. Children are most welcome, and Pat will provide cot, high chair or whatever is necessary. The lounge is a sunny room with an open fire, most suitable for those cooler evenings, when you wish to relax in the utmost comfort at the end of the day. Again it is a charming room with peach and cream colours lending a most welcoming softness to the beautiful beamed ceiling and white walls, so suitable for this country room. The dining room is another delight with excellent furnishings, beamed walls and ceiling, and that added touch of charm... plates on the walls and place settings to enchant! Breakfast is a hearty English affair, and an evening meal can be arranged. Pat and Mike grow all their own vegetables so obviously cater well for vegetarians!

Leigh is an appealing, unspoilt Surrey village. It is only 30 minutes from London and Pat and Mike offer transport to and from Gatwick, and also Redhill Station to London. Opposite the house is an ancient church and nearby is The Plough Inn, a listed building. Dorking and Brighton are just a car ride away, and there are many national Trust houses, including 'Chartwell' the house of Churchill. This is a wonderful setting, so close to the city, yet so rural, with lots to do and friendly accommodation to satisfy the most fastidious!

USEFUL INFORMATION

OPEN : All year except Xmas
CHILDREN : Most welcome
PETS : By arrangement
LICENSED : No
CREDIT CARDS : None taken
ACCOMMODATION : 2 rooms; 1 dbl, 1 twin.

DINING ROOM : Evening meal by arrangement
VEGETARIANS : Catered for
BAR MEALS : Not applicable
DISABLED ACCESS : No
GARDEN : Large with swimming pool & tennis

FIDDLERS OAST,
Watermill Lane, Beckley,
Nr Rye,
East Sussex, TN31 6SH.

Tel / Fax : 01797 252394

Stand very still and just listen! What do you hear? Glorious silence! The beautiful rural setting of this converted Oast House (used for drying hops) is a haven from the outside world. 2 acres of secluded gardens and woodland surround the house and screen it from the outside world - you could almost be in a time warp! Nick and Ruth Wynn are your friendly hosts, and are determined with their informal ways, that you have the most enjoyable and relaxing holiday possible! There is quite a sense of humour in this house; you can tell by the information leaflet in your room -'Nick might be known as The Beast of Beckley'- I'd like to hear the story behind that one! Or the fact that pets are welcome with 'well behaved owners' leads me to believe that a touch of the 'Monty Pythons' might be at large here! It all sounds great fun and immediately allows one to relax and feel at home. There are three double rooms en suite with tea/coffee trays, fridges and most of the earthly comforts you could require. All are beautifully furnished to a very high standard, and are most comfortable and inviting. Breakfast is a huge English affair which eliminates the need for lunch, and is local produce where possible, using local sausage and free range eggs. If you require something lighter then a continental breakfast is available, but the huge English is definitely recommended. The house is non smoking but Nick and Ruth do not mind you smoking on the balcony or outside - just not in the rooms. Children again are very welcome (with the obligatory well behaved adults!) and are well catered for. Nick and Ruth have two of their own, so are aware of the difficulties than can sometimes be had in bed and breakfast establishments. Sadly, there is no evening meal available,- these people lead busy lives - but there are many local pubs which Nick and Ruth will recommend to you, giving details of prices and various menus, and whether or not they cater for children.

Beckley is an ideal location if you have to stop on your way to catch a ferry, or perhaps the Channel Tunnel which is only 45 minutes away. On the other hand, a longer break is necessary to appreciate all within this area. You are only a car journey from a host of sights and activities, but have the added luxury of residing in a quiet, peaceful, relaxing environment! Canterbury, a beautiful city, is within driving distance, as is 1066 country, (Battle of Hastings, King Harold with the arrow in his eye etc....) Bodiam Castle, gardens and many more delightful pastimes. If walking is your pleasure, then a stroll through the leafy lanes will charm you with every step. What more could you ask for? A delightful house, with friendly, congenial hosts!

USEFUL INFORMATION

OPEN : All year
CHILDREN : Most welcome
PETS : Most welcome (with well behaved owners)
LICENSED : No
CREDIT CARDS : Most major
ACCOMMODATION : 3 rooms en suite; 3 dbl.
DINING ROOM : Huge English breakfast
VEGETARIANS : Catered for
BAR SNACKS : Not applicable
DISABLED ACCESS : No
GARDEN : Secluded with woodlands

Chapter Three

Central England

Chapter Four

**CENTRAL ENGLAND, HEREFORDSHIRE,
WORCESTERSHIRE,
STAFFORDSHIRE, SHROPSHIRE,
WEST MIDLANDS & WARWICKSHIRE**

Central England

CHAPTER 4

CENTRAL ENGLAND, HEREFORDSHIRE, WORCESTERSHIRE, STAFFORDSHIRE, SHROPSHIRE, WEST MIDLANDS & WARWICKSHIRE

INCLUDES

Hansley Cross Cottage	**Alton**	p. 455
Boars Head Hotel	**Bishops Castle**	p. 456
Croft Guest House	**Bransford**	p. 455
Hampton House	**Bridgnorth**	p. 457
Hannigans Farm	**Bridgnorth**	p. 458
Oldfield Cottage	**Bridgnorth**	p. 459
Barn House	**Broadway**	p. 460
Brook House	**Broadway**	p. 461
Leasow House	**Broadway**	p. 462
Tudor Cottage	**Broadway**	p. 463
The White House Hotel	**Cannock Chase**	p. 464
Belvedere	**Church Stretton**	p. 463
Court Farm	**Church Stretton**	p. 465
Woolston Farm	**Church Stretton**	p. 466
Little Lightwood Farm	**Cotheridge**	p. 467
Hesterworth Holidays	**Craven Arms**	p. 468
Slindon House Farm	**Eccleshall**	p. 469
Sandrene	**Eckington**	p. 470
Church House	**Evesham**	p. 471
Felton House	**Felton**	p. 472
Broughton Manor	**Hackett**	p. 473
The Swan at Hay Hotel	**Hay on Wye**	p. 474
Ruxton Farm	**Kings Caple**	p. 476
Kilmory	**Ledbury**	p. 467
Mill Cottage	**Ledbury**	p. 476
Moor Court Farm	**Ledbury**	p. 477
Preston Priory	**Ledbury**	p. 478
The Hopton Arms	**Ledbury**	p. 479
Wall Hills Country Guest House	**Ledbury**	p. 480
Heath House	**Leominster**	p. 481
Highfield	**Leominster**	p. 477
Ladymeadow Farm	**Leominster**	p. 469
The Compasses Hotel	**Leominster**	p. 482
Corndene	**Ludlow**	p. 483

Chapter Four

Lower Hayton Grange	**Ludlow**	**p. 484**
The Bull Hotel	**Ludlow**	**p. 485**
Brickbarn Farm	**Malvern Wells**	**p. 486**
Clevelands	**Malvern Wells**	**p. 470**
The Old Vicarage	**Malvern Wells**	**p. 502**
The Vauld House Farm	**Marden**	**p. 473**
Longville Arms	**Much Wenlock**	**p. 487**
Albynes	**Nordley**	**p. 488**
Line Farm	**Orleton**	**p. 489**
Bron Heulog	**Oswestry**	**p. 490**
The Leeze Guest House	**Rochester**	**p. 491**
Hillcrest Guest House	**Sherborne Hill**	**p. 492**
Ascott House Farm	**Shipston-on-Stour**	**p. 493**
The Citadel	**Shrewsbury**	**p. 495**
Danally House Hotel	**Stafford**	**p. 496**
Hollinhurst Farm	**Stoke on Trent**	**p. 497**
Caldewell	**Stoulton**	**p. 479**
Hardwick Guest House	**Stratford-upon-Avon**	**p. 498**
Newbold Nurseries	**Stratford-upon-Avon**	**p. 494**
Willow Corner	**Stratford-upon-Avon**	**p. 486**
Winton House	**Stratford-upon-Avon**	**p. 499**
The Old Rectory	**Tamworth**	**p. 494**
Tiltridge Farm	**Upton-upon-Severn**	**p. 500**
Westward Guest House	**Uttoxeter**	**p. 501**
The Crown Inn	**Wentnor**	**p. 503**
Dearnford Hall	**Whitchurch**	**p. 493**
Rhydspence Inn	**Whitney on Wye**	**p. 504**
Burgage House	**Worcester**	**p. 491**

CHAPTER 4

CENTRAL ENGLAND, HEREFORDSHIRE, WORCESTERSHIRE, STAFFORDSHIRE, SHROPSHIRE, WEST MIDLANDS & WARWICKSHIRE

Pulchra Terra Dei Donum' (This fair land is the Gift of God) is the county motto of Hereford and the more I see of this beautiful land, the truer I know that statement to be. Although Hereford is joined to Worcester for administrative purposes, the charactrs of the two counties have little in common. A perfect illustraion of this is gained from the viewpoint atop the Herefordshire Beacon in the Malvern Hills. To the east lie the rich fertile lowlands of Worcestershire through which the Severn and Avon wander, whilst to the west, the undulating wooded scenery of Herefordshire extends to the lowering ridge of the **Black Mountains**, some forty miles away.

The M50 motorway is a western spur of the M5 and runs some five miles into Herefordshire before ending at **Ross-on-Wye**, a delightful market town overlooking the River Wye. Agriculture, light industry and tourism form the basis of the local economy and Ross (from the Welsh ros, meaning a spit of land) is ideally situated for exploring the glorious country of the Wye Valley. Its friendly and welcoming atmosphere owes much to the example set by the town's best loved inhabitant, John Kyrle (1637-1724). Trained as a lawyer, he inherited a small fortune and never practiced, preferring to spend his time and money on good works and acts of great public generosity. He died, a bachelor, at the age of 89, having given all his money away but never incurred a debt. He is remembered as the 'Man of Ross' and among his many philanthropies were the provision of a town water supply, a causeway enabling the bridge to be used when flooding occurred, and a walled public garden, known as Kyrle's Prospect. He built a summer house in the grounds of his home, now known as **Kyrle House**, and paid the poor and unemployed to find horse's teeth from animals killed in a nearby cavalry skirmish during the Civil War; these were set into mortar to create a mosaic in the shape of a swan. A much loved man.

The little town on its steep rocky outcrop has been a favourite with visitors since the early Victorian era when, as now, the attractions of the surrounding countryside and the excellent salmon fishing brought people back year after year. Hotels, pubs and restaurants are plentiful. I was impressed by the enthusiasm and high standards to be found.

Chapter Four

The Lost Street Museum is a charming and very well thought out museum in the form of an arcade of Edwardian shops containing all manner of period items including amusement machines, musical boxes, toys, costumes and gramophones. An unusual local industry is candle-making and **Ross-on-Wye Candlemakers** open their workshop to the public in old Gloucester Road. Two gardens are worth visiting. **Hill Court Gardens and Garden Centre** to the east of the town and **How Caple Court Gardens** to the north, are a gardener's delight.

At **Symonds Yat West**, the Jubilee Park offers a wide range of family entertainment, including a maze, craft shops and a butterfly farm. **The Herefordshire Rural Heritage Museum**, set in an attractive rural location, houses one of the country's largest collections of historic farm machinery and agricultural implements. About three miles downstream in the wooded Doward Hills above the river is **King Arthurs Cave** where excavations have revealed that its occupancy by man dates back nearly 60,000 years! Five miles south of Ross and upstream from Symonds Yat are the romantic and massively impressive ruins of **Goodrich Castle**.

Goodrich is an entertaining though somewhat scattered little village and the 12th century castle is sited on a high, rocky spur overlooking a crossing of the river. Square in shape with a tower at each corner and surrounded by a moat hewn out of the red rock, Goodrich was besieged by Parliamentarians under the command of Colonel Birch, in 1646. Legend has it that Birch's niece, Alice, was inside the castle with her Royalist lover, and that they were both drowned in the Wye whilst trying to escape. Her shrieks of distress can still be heard on stormy nights when the river is in spate.

Heading north-east from Ross on the A449 and lying close to the eastern border of the county, is the attractive village of **Much Marcle**, blessed with a fine church of 13th-century origins, **St Bartholomews** and two historic houses. Just over four miles further along the A440 is the delightful ancient market town of **Ledbury**. Set by the old cross-roads to Tewkesbury, Hereford, Gloucester and Malvern, it has been inhabited since around 1500BC. The church of **St Michael and All Angels**, Herefordshire's premier parish church was built on an earlier Saxon foundation and has a Norman chancel and west door, and a magnificent medieval north chapel. The wide main street, flanked by many half-timbered houses including the Elizabethan **Feathers Inn** was the scene of a desperate charge by Prince Rupert's cavalry during the Civil War, when a Parliamentarian force was routed. Bullets are still embedded in the church door and in the walls of **The Talbot** in New Street. Church Lane, cobbled and narrow, offers a delightful period view of St Michaels and opens out into a small close with some handsome houses surrounding the church.

The south-eastern quarter of Herefordshire is the main hop-growing region, and hopyards, with their trellis work of poles, wires and strings can be seen throughout the area. At **Bishop Frome**, on the Ledbury to Bromyard road, **The Hop Pocket Hop Farm** is open to visitors interested in a form of cultivation that is regrettably in decline. Drying kilns, hop-picking machines and the hopyards are all open to inspection.

Further information on the history and practices of hop-growing can be found at the Bromyard Heritage Centre along with other displays relating to matters of local interest. **Bromyard** sits in a natural bowl, amongst rolling downland and was one of the most important towns in Herefordshire long before the Norman clerks started to compile the Domesday Book. It had a Saxon church in 840AD and the present church of **St Peter** was probably built onthe same site in about 1160. The town's wealth came principally from its market and local agriculture - later came an added bonus in the form of its geographical position halfway between Worcester and Hereford which led to its development as a coaching centre. Notable amongst the inns catering to the trade was **The Falcon** whose postboys wore a smart uniform of white hats, breeches and yellow jackets. Somehow I cannot believe they stayed smart for very long.

The River Teme wriggles through the three counties of Herefordshire, Worcestershire and Shropshire in the area around **Tenbury Wells**. A borough since 1248, Tenbury has remained an attractive small market town surrounded by hopyards and apple orchards. Hopes of fame and fortune came its way in the 19th century with the discovery of saline springs - but the town lacked an entrepreneur of the quality of Doctor Wall at Malvern and the spa never became fasionable. The incongruous Pump Rooms survive known locally as the 'Chinese Temple' because of the style of architecture.

Leominster (pronounced 'Lemster') a thriving market town, lies nine miles to the south-west and is Herefordshire's second largest town, set amongst a gentle landscape of fields, hills and meadows where river, stream and brook wander. The town's fortunes were based on the fine quality of the wool from the local breed of sheep, the Ryeland, an animal that thrives on the poorer grazing to be found on the neighbouring hills and the less fertile outcrops of sandy soil from which the name is derived. The demand for this wool was so great that at one time the fleece was known as 'Lempster Ore'.

Cider orchards along the road heading south to **Hereford** hint at one of the city's major industries. Bulmer's have been making cider in Hereford for well over a century and their premises in Plough Lane are open for tours and samplings. The contrast with modern automated production techniques with those of yesteryear are enormous, and a visit to **The Cider Museum and King Offa distillery**, in Ryelands Street, is a real eye-opener.

Any town or city engaged in the convivial pursuit of brewing or distilling has a rather jolly atmosphere, and Hereford is no exception, although its early history would suggest otherwise. Never free of strife until the end of the Civil War in 1651, the city suffered numerous attacks and sieges over the preceding centuries, yet during that time, managed to become one of the most thriving medieval cities in England, a centre for both trade and scholarship.

Items relating to the turbulent past, as well as to more peaceful interests such as bee-keeping, can be seen in **The Hereford City Museum and Art Gallery**, in Broad Street. The modern military presence in the city is restricted to the **Herefordshire Regimental Museum** at the TA Centre in Harold Street, and to the discreet gentlemen of the SAS, at Bradbury Lines. Hereford is rich in museums; apart from those already mentiond, there are the **Bulmer Railway Centre**, for steam enthusiasts, **The Churchill Gardens Museum**, displaying fine furniture, costumes, andpaintings of the late 18th and 19th centuries, **The St John Medieval Museum** containing armour and other relics relating to the order of St John, and **The Old House**, built in 1621 and beautifully furnished in period.

The medieval visitors to the city-scholars, men-at-arms, and traders - would have had their numbers swelled by large numbers of pilgrims, visiting **The Cathedral of St Mary the Virgin and St Ethelbert the King**. The cathedral was begun in the 7th century - in fact, the appointment of the first Bishop of Hereford dates back to that time. A large proportion of the Norman masonry work survives, particularly inside, but the siege and structural collapse in the 17th and 18th centuries led to extensive rebuilding and renovation. For all this, it is still a wonderfully handsome building, quite small compared to most cathedrals, and full of many unique treasures. Chief amongst these is the Mappa Mundi, a map of the world drawn around 1290 and of great importance because it shows us how the scholars of that time saw their world, both in spiritual, as well as geographical terms. The medieval draughtsmanship is superb with all manner of beasts, both fabulous and familiar. The cathedral also has a notable collection of manuscripts and early printed material in the Chained Library, including the 8th century Anglo-Saxon gospels still used when Hereford bishops are sworn in.

The choral traditions of the cathedral are long and the origins of the magnificent Three Choirs Festival can be traced back to an 18th-century chancellor, Thomas Bisse. To listen to soaring music in such surroundings is surely close to 'the rudiments of Paradise'.

Central England

The south-western region of Herefordshire and the Welsh Borders was known as **Archenfield** and stretched from the western back of the Wye to the long ridge of the Black Mountains, twenty miles away. It remained a Welsh enclave in England for around six centuries until well after the Conquest. Many of the laws and customs remained peculiarly Welsh until as recently as the present century. An attractive, yet sparsely populated region, with few large villages but a wealth of churches, which point to the fact that this area had possibly the longest history of continuous Christianity in England.

Welsh Newton is still the scene of a yearly pilgrimage since the graveyard contains the last of Herefordshire's many saints. John Kemble, who was canonised as recently as 1970, was a Jesuit priest who administered to the many catholics in the area, including the wife and daughter of the man who arrested him for complicity in the Popish Plot. An innocent and greatly loved man, he was executed in the most barbaric manner at Hereford, in August 1679. He was eighty years old.

At **Kilpeck**, just off the A465 from Hereford, is the most famous of Archenfield churches, Saint Mary and St David. Saxon work remains in the north-east wall of the nave but the church is principally Norman and the local red sandstone from which it was built has survived the weathers of time remarkably well. The real glory of the little church is its carvings; work of skilled masons who are sometimes referred to as the Herefordshire School, and who flourished during the 12th century. Behind the church can be found the remains, little more than a stump, of Kilbeck Castle, built around the same time that the carvers were indulging their strange fantasies with hammer and chisel. King John visited here a number of times, and it is recorded that a pretty widow, Joan de Kilpeck offered him a bribe of fifty marks and a palfrey (a small horse) if he would allow her to marry whom she pleased.

It was to the men of Archenfield that England looked in time of strife. From this area came the medieval equivalent of the machine-gun; the long bow, made from yew, and in the hands of a master, capable of piercing through the mailed thigh of a horseman and nailing him to the saddle at fifty paces or more. More importantly the next arrow would be on its way within seconds, whereas the cross-bowman would still be tensioning his weapon. Once the major disputes between English and Welsh were settled, it was the bowmen of Archenfield who led the armies in attack and held the rear in retreat.

Men-at-arms of higher rank, but of common experience, are remembered amongst the high, sheep grazing hills of **Garway**. These were

Chapter Four

the Knights Templar, Soldiers of Christian belief and noble birth who wore a red sign of the cross on simple white surcoats that covered their armour. Formed to protect pilgrims on the long and dangerous journeys to and from Jerusalem, they showed great bravery during the Crusades and later founded numerous religious houses throughout Europe. Garway was one of their estates and the church of **St Michael** is one of only six Templar foundations left in England. It seems strange to think of those grim monastic soldiers, used to the blazing sun and the desert battles with the Saracens, ending their days on these damp hillsides. The place is moving in its simplicity and well worth the meandering drive south.

The Golden Valley gets its name from a justifiable piece of linguistic confusion on the part of the Normans; they muddled the Welsh 'dwyr' meaning water with their own 'd'or' meaning gold - hence Golden Valley and the **River Dore**. Also Abbey Dore, a mile or so from **Ewyas Harold Castle** (pronounced Yewas) on the west side of the valley. This was a great Cistercian monastery until the Dissolution. The remains were carefully restored under the direction of the first Viscount Scudamore, and he and his craftsmen did a most excellent job. The present building possesses a simple grandeur and contains good glass, some interesting glazed tiles, and a knightly effigy of the grandson of the founder of the Abbey, Robert de Clifford.

Michaelchurch Escley sits tight under the lee of the Black Mountains, truly a dark and brooding mass, frequently blue or purple in tint. From these slopes the Celtic warriors of long ago would rush in ambush, only to vanish into the woods and hills when ambush threatened. The trout laden waters of **Escley Brook** run parallel to those of the Monnow, into which it eventually merges, and the area is border country at its best - remote and beautiful.

The road running north alongside the Monnow passes through **Crasswall** with **Hay Bluff**, the source of the river rising high over the hamlet. The Order of the Grandmontines, an offshoot of the Cistercian order and named after their founding house in Limoges had their abbey here. The remote situation must have suited an order which emphasised strict discipline and reliance on alms and agricultural labour.

The road continues northward, climbing to around 1500 feet, before dropping down through the steep, wooded slopes and into Wales at **Hay-on-Wye**. Hay changed hands several times in its turbulent early years, being burnt down five times, which may account for the fact that there are the remains of two castles in the small town. Hay is known worldwide for its bookshops. Second-hand books in their millions line the shelves of the castle, the cinema, a garage and shops that once catered for the more mundane demands of the local populace. Rare first editions and fine leather bindings lie in close proximity to heaps of dog-eared paperbacks and bundles of yellowing magazines. Sleepy little Hay woke up to the fact that it is now a tourist attraction in its own right - thanks to the wonderfully eccentric, but undoubtedly shrewd local entrepreneur, Richard Booth, who started the whole idea.

Turning back from Hay towards Hereford, it is worth taking a detour to view the remains of Clifford Castle, whose ivy-clad ruins tower over a shallow bend in the Wye. It was built by Walter de Clifford in the early 1200's and first saw action not long after when it was captured, not by Celt or fellow Norman Marcher Lord, but by Henry III. This unfortunate episode was as a result of Henry's request that Walter's debts be paid off. Walter's reply was to make the King's Messenger 'eat the King's writ, waxe and all', so the incensed Henry promptly sacked the castle. The 'Fair Rosamund'; an earlier Clifford who was the mistress of Henry II, was probably born here. The King kept her hidden from the jealous Queen Eleanor, but eventually the Queen found Rosamund and forced her to drink poison. The Mortimers succeeded the Cliffords, so the old fortress was held by two of the greatest Marcher families.

Weobley (pronounced Wedbley) is where the first tough Hereford strain of cattle, dark red with white faces, bellies and hocks, were first bred on the Garnstone Estate. The village was evidently one of the more successful Norman settlements. Only the castle's earthworks remain today, but Weobley;s prosperity is indicated by the wealth of half-timbered housing and the large parish church. Weobley is the place where the expression 'pot walloper' was first coined; the term referred to Shropshire tenants of the Marquess of Bath who had the right to vote in local elections - providing they had set up thir cooking fires in the main street the previous night. Needless to say, during the corrupt political era of the 18th century, His Lordship took full advantage of this strange custom to ensure the successful return of his chosen candidates.

The half-timbered black and white theme is continued at **Eardisland** to the north of the A44. A picture postcard village by the banks of the Arrow, the enchanting Mill Stream Cottage was once the village school and was built in the 1700's at a cost of fifty pounds! Close by was the site of an ancient British settlement, now the site of Burton Court, a Georgian house of 14th-century origins which houses a fascinating collection of European and Oriental costumes and curios, together with natural history displays, ship models and a working model fairground.

Chapter Four

Almost next door to Earidland is the beautiful and unspoilt village of **Pembridge** with a wealth of 13th and 14th century buildings and none more beautiful than **The New Inn** which is a hostelry of warmth and atmosphere acquired over the centuries. Everything about it reeks of history. It was the Court House before it became an inn and even after that one room was used to administer the majesty of the law. It has two ghosts who refuse to leave!

It does seem extraordinary that in such an area, outstanding in its natural beauty, combining peace and solitude with the scenery of the hills, woods and rivers, should have been the scene of so much strife - yet reminders lie all around. Wigmore Castle has a connection with Brampton Bryan in that it was briefly owned by the Harleys before being dismantled by Parliamentarian troops, but it was first built by William Fitz-Osborn, Earl of Hereford, and then owned by the Mortimer family. The castle is impressively and strongly sited on a ridge in a most commanding position. It was to this great fortress that Prince Edward fled, before rallying his forcs against Simon de Montfort (he had been imprisoned at Hereford and escaped by the simple ruse of challenging his captors to race their horses. When the animals were exhausted, the cunning Prince produced a fresh beast that had been kept hidden by a sympathiser and disappeared in the proverbial cloud of dust.

Of this great family who held the castle, perhaps the most astute and savage of the Marcher Lords, little remains but a tablet in the nearby gatehouse, where once stood an Augustinian Abbey. 'In this Abbey lies the remains of the noble family of Mortimer who founded it in 1179 and ruled the Marches of Wales for 400 years.' Henry VIII took little notice, even though his mother was a Mortimer, and the tombs vanished with the Abbey. Their name is, however, commemorated a little further down the road where the A4110 intersects the B4362. This innocent looking junction in the valley of the River Lugg, was the scene in 1461 of 'an obstinate bloody and decisive battle'. Four thousand men died at what is now known as Mortimer's Cross; the first defeat to be inflicted on the Lancastrians by Edward, Duke of York - himself half a Mortimer, and later to become Edward IV. Before the fight began an extraordinary sight was seen in the sky - three suns appeared. We now know that this phenomenon is caused by the refraction of light through particles in the atmosphere, and is called a parhelion, but to the superstitious medieval warriors it appeared as an omen, a sign from God. The Yorkists took the three suns to represent the triumvirate of Edward, Duke of York, Richard, Duke of Gloucester and George, Duke of Clarence, and the ' sun in splendour' became a favourite heraldic badge with the House of York.

Turn to the east at Mortimer's Cross, and you will come to three large houses lying within a few miles of each other, the firstof which acted as a rendezvous for the Yorkist forces. The Croft family have lived at Croft Castle since the time of Domesday, with the exception of 177 years - due to some unfortunate debts incurred by an 18th century Croft - and still live there, although the house and the estate is administered by the National Trust. In its present guise the castle is a massive but handsome house with turrets at each cornr, and stands in beautiful parkland with an avenue of Spanish chestnut trees - said by some to have been grown from chestnuts carried in a galleon of the Spanish Armada. For all its troubled history, it is a wonderfully peaceful and attractive home. A strong feeling of continuity and service hangs in the air; as exemplified by the memorials in the little church to two more recent members of the family. Both the tenth and eleventh baronets, father and sone, were killed while serving with the Herefordshire Regiment in the First and Second World Wars, nearly eight hundred years after their ancestor, Jasper de Croft, was knighted during the Crusades.

The other two house stand almost side-by-side to the east of the Leominster to Ludlow road. the smallest is **Eye Manor**, a neat restoration house, built for a slave-trader and plantation owner from Barbados, with the exotic name of Sir Ferdinando Georges. Known as the 'King of the Black Market', he spent a good deal of his ill-gotten gains on the interior decoration, particularly the ornate and well-crafted plasterwork.

Berrington Hall has links with Moccas Court and Brampton Bryan, for the estate once belonged to the Cornewells, who sold it to the Harleys in 1775. Thomas Harley, a prosperous banker, employed Henry Holland, later responsible for the original Brighton Pavilion, to design the house, and Holland's father-in-law, Capability Brown, to lay out the grounds. They succeeded splendidly and Berrington is surely one of the most attractive and elegant Georgian houses in the country. Berrington Hall is now run by the National Trust but from 1901, it belonged to Lord Cawley. and there is a moving memorial in the Norman church at Eye to his three sons, all killed in the First World War.

It is tragic, that they, like their neighbours the Crofts and so many other thousands of Herefordshire's sons and daughters, could not have been laid to rest in the soil of their birth, the land that Henry James described as 'The copse-chequered slopes of rolling Hereford, white with the blossom of apples.'

Chapter Four

WORCESTERSHIRE

This is an area of richness and contrast in terms of agricultural wealth, historical association and scenic beauty. The dark fertile soils of the Vale of Evesham produce the finest vegetables and fruits while farmers throughout the region happily indulge in the old-fashioned concept of mixed farming with seeming success. Orchards, arable fields and pasture lie happily grouped together while on the ancient western hills, contented sheep graze on both enclosed and common land. Man's presence on this rich, dark earth dates back to paleolithic times and its fertility was appreciated by Celt, Roman, Saxon and Norman as it is by the agricultural industrialists of today. Paradoxically, such pastoral splendour has also been the stage for savage blood-letting and the scene for king making and king-breaking. The power of the Barons was smashed at Evesham in 1265. **Tewkesbury** saw the Lancastrian claim defeated by the Yorkist Edward IV in 1471 and nearly two centuries later, Cromwell's greatest victory over the Royalists was at Worcester in 1651. Such viscious yet decisive battles, seem strangely at odds amongst such a gentle landscape where rivers meander through a countryside of quiet moderation and simple continuity; violence appears ill-suited to rolling hills and broad blossom strewn plains, lacking the bleak heathland or craggy peaks normally associated with such savageries.

The venerable Cathedral City of **Worcester** is capital to the region and reflects much of the contrasts to be found within the region as a whole with historical associations, architectural contrast and industrial, as opposed to agricultural wealth; yet even its industry has a bucolic air to it, for the black smoke and noisome forges of the industrial revolution have little place in the manufacture of gloves, Royal Worcester porcelain, or that secret blend of 'brown vinegar, walnut ketchup, anchovey essence, soy sauce, cayenne, and shallot's' known world-wide as Worcestershire sauce.

I am extremely fond of the city for it has much of interest and has always been a welcoming and friendly face, but it has to be said that the twentieth century has not treated it kindly. William Cobbett (1763-1835) described Worcester as 'One of the cleanest and handsomest towns I ever saw, indeed I do not recollect to have seen any one equal to it'. Sadly his description no longer tallies; ring-roads, multi-story car parks, power stations and other civic developments have changed forever what was once 'the noblest Georgian townscape in the Midlands'. Nevertheless, there remains much that is good and visitors will find their time amply repaid.

The Cathedral of Christ and the Blessed Virgin Mary contains much of interest, particularly if you have a sharp eye. The craftsmen of old were noted not only for their skills but often for their sense of humour, notably when it came to decoration: the 14th century choir stalls have a fine set of misericords (a rather grand name for a hinged support) and these represent a perfect riot of carver's fantasies - biblical characters, mythical beasts, scenes from both court and everyday life and even a wolf saying grace before devouring his victim! Memorials to the famous and the not-so-famous are scattered throughout but the real glory of the building, like so many of its kind, is in the construction and harmony of the interior which was skillfully overhauled in the last century by the famous Victorian architect, Sir George Gilbert Scott. Scott was responsible for many such restorations and was something of a workaholic, indeed he was so busy that he once telegraphed his London office from Manchester, with the perplexed request 'Why am I here?'

The Cathedral stands on a rise overlooking the River Severn and the Worcestershire County Cricket Ground, where traditionally, touring Test teams play their first county matches. Ornamental gardens cluster around the Watergate at the bottom of the rise where a ferry once ran when the city was walled and a tablet onthe gate records the impressive heights gained by the river during floods.

It is a splendidly English backdrop, ideally suited to our summer game but in 1651 the area now dedicated to peaceful recreation would have seen the Royalist forces stumbling in retreat before Cromwell's invincible Model Army. The clash of steel and thunder of guns rang out where leather meets willow today. Relics, displays and mementoes of the Battle Worcester and other aspects of the Civil War are to be found in the Commandery, a fine 15th-century timber-framed building built on the site of an earlier hospital founded by St Wulfstan, and in the baroque 18th century Guildhall with its sumptious assembly rooms. The City Museum and Art Gallery attracts many people and apart from much of general local interest contains the Regimental Museum of the Worcestershire Regiment, who rejoiced in the stomach-turning nickname of the 'Vein-Openers'! Their heroism in battle earned them the approbation of Wellington who called them ;'the best regiment in his army', while the city's loyalty to the Crown was recognised by Charles II, who gave it the motto 'May the faithful city flourish'. Music is an important part of Worcester life and every third year it plays host to the world's oldest musical celebration, the Three Choirs Festival, which was started in 1717. The other cathedral cities involved are Hereford and Gloucester.

There is a great deal to see and do in Worcester not least Spetchley Park which is an early 19th century museum with a deer park and splendid formal gardens that are open to the public. Greyfriars, a splendid half-timbered building (Tudor with later addition) has been fully restored under the aegis of the National Trust and has a delightful walled garden. The five

Chapter Four

hundred year old Tudor House Museum is close by and has fascinating displays of social history while in Severn Street, the Dyson Perrins Museum contains examples of Royal Worcester porcelain dating back to 1751 and includes the dinner service made for the Prince and Princess of Wales.

The River Avon almost entirely encircles **Evesham**, a town which owes its beginnings to a vision of the Madonna seen by a local swine-herd called Eoves. Egwin, Bishop of Worcester, established a monastery on the site in 704 and became its first abbot. The Abbey rapidly became an important place of pilgrimage and a town grew round the site. The original shrine of Eoves'vision increased in importance with the canonisation of Egwin and then, 560 years after the Abbey's foundation came the battle which would lead to a third shrine within its precincts. The Barons, led by Simon de Montfort, fell out with Henry III over the interpretation of the Magna Carta and a short but bloody war resulted. The Barons held Henry captive after defeating him in battle but had failed to hold on to his son, who later became Edward I.

The Battle of Evesham, which took place on the 4th August 1265, resulted in a crushing defeat for the Barons and was an astonishing feat of arms by the young prince who had left Worcester on the morning of August 2nd, marched to Kenilworth and captured it, then turned to the south to approach Evesham on the morning of the 4th - sixty miles in forty-eight hours, not forgetting the hand-to-hand combat on the way! De Montfort'sbody was dismembered but the trunk was buried before the High Altar of the Abbey where it soon became the shrine of a man the common people considered a folk-hero, and who is remembered today as the 'Father of Parliaments'. The Abbey grew evermore wealthy and two churches were built outside the monastic grounds to cater for the townsfolk and the pilgrims respectively, and these churches, dedicated to St Lawrence and to All Saints, still remain. The Abbey was pulled down during the Dissolution and the principal remains include the magnificent Perpendicular bell-tower, built by the last rightful abbot, Clement Lichfield who is also remembered in both churches.

The Almonry Museum chronicles much of Evesham's history and, although the town is a busy marketing and light industrial centre, its fascinating history is reflected in the ancient buildings and streets. It is also very much a town of, rather than by, the river since the Severn, has acted as a means of both defence and transport in times past and recreation today.

The Vale of Evesham was described by the American writer Henry James, as 'the dark, rich, hedgy flats of Worcestershire'. Since he wrote those world in 1875, the majority of the hedgs have long gone in the pursuit of intensive cultivation of fruit and vegetables. All manner of varieties are grown in the fertile tilth including such exotics as asparagus and peppers, but it is the fruit that gives the area its greatest glory - albeit for only a short time. Generally around late March and early May, depending on the climate, the area becomes almost magical with blossom from cherries, apples, pears and plums. There are well marked Spring Blossom Trails that can be followed by car, bike or on foot and it is one of the most wonderful sights that the English countryside has to offer. It is nothing less than a total transformation and there are many who come back year after year to view the splendour. It is an interesting fact that although local farmers had appreciated the fertility of the vale's soil for centuries, it was left to a foreigner to reveal its true potential. Francesco Bernardi was a Genoese envoy in the 17th century who settled in the Vale after a dispute with his country. He spent the enormous sum of thirty thousand pounds to begin, in effect, the local industry of market gardening.

Pershore is the second town of the Vale and was once the 'third town' of the county after Worcester and Droitwich. A handsome town with a predominance of seemingly Georgian architecture (many are facades built onto older buildings) it lies to the north of Bredon Hill amongst water meadows beside the Avon's meanderings. It too has an Abbey although considerably more survives than that of neighbouring Evesham. Pershore Abbey is still a magnificent building although much reduced in size, it has a splendid pinnacled tower supported on high Norman arches and a wonderful vaulted roof to the choir with much fine carving. The original religious settlement dates back as far as 689 but depradations from Danish pirates and disbelieving Saxons meant that little of import was established until the Benedictines founded a monastery dedicated to King Alfred's granddaughter, St Eadburgh. Over the centuries the Abbey grew, surviving setbacks like the fire in 1288 which led to the rebuilding of the present tower, until the Dissolution of the Monasteries when thefaithful citizens of Pershore bought the monastic part of the buildings for their own use at a cost of four hundred pounds. Pershore's prosperity, like Evesham, is strongly linked to the surrounding fertile lanmd and to the River Avon which for many years enabled agricultural produce to be sent downstream to Bristol, including the famous Pershore Plums.

The Lower and Upper Avon Navigation Trusts have done tremendous work in restoring the numerous locks and weirs dating back to the 17th century that enable the river to be fully navigable. The advent of the railways meant that many of these riverine structures fell into disrepair and the work done by the Trusts has been extensive and of benefit to all. I recommend a boat trip to appreciate not only the beauty of this unique part of England but also to see and appreciate the work that has been and is being done.

Chapter Four

To the south-west lies another small town of considerable appeal whose fortunes have also been linked to a river: **Upton upon Severn.** The Severn is stronger and more direct than the meandering Avon and for many years Upton possessed the only bridge across the river between Gloucester and Worcester and was such an important meeting place for river craft that what became known as the 'Bridge of Parliament' was held there. Obviously the bridge was of major tactical importance during the Civil War and the Royalists, based at Worcester, blew out two of the spans to prevent an outflanking movement - but in vain. Due to the negligence of a sentry, a small party of Roundheads crept across the plank that had been left across the gap and barricaded themselves in the church, resisting all efforts to displace them until relieved by their own cavalry which had crossed at an unguarded ford. Upton fell to the Parliamentarians and the church was partially destroyed. There is a romanitc sequel to this brief but savage skirmish; that evening Cromwell himself arrived to congratulate his men and saw, at an upstairs window, a beautiful girl in obvious distress. He asked her name and was told it was a Miss Morris whereupon he pardoned her brother whom he had just condemned to be shot. It is nice to know that Old Ironsides had the human touch.

Upton-upon-Severn is a charming little town where such a story seems eminently believable. The medieval church tower survives, crowned with a copper covered cupola and is now used as an heritage centre, whilst in the churchyard can be found the well known epitaph:

> 'Beneath this stone, in hope of Zion,
> Doth lie the landlord of the Lion,
> his son keeps on the business still,
> Resigned unto the heavenly will.

Apt lines for a town that has a greater number of pubs per head of resident population than most - probably as a result of the old river traffic. Incidentally **The White Lion Hotel** is still thriving and is a delightful place to stay. All the pubs do a roaring trade during the many Summer events that take place here, such as The Steam Rally, The Water Festival, and The Jazz and Folk Festivals.

Worcestershire's greatest natural glories are to be found to the west of the Severn. **The Malverns** are perhaps the originators of that well-known phrase 'as old as the hills' for this ridge of pre-Cambrian rock is more than 500 million years old. The name means 'the bare hills' and they rise gently from fertile soils and woodlands to stand guardians against the prevailing winds.Although of no great height (the highest point is only 1394 feet) their appearance is impressive in contrast to the lowlands from which they spring, and the infinite permutations of light and shade sweeping over their bracken-strewn slopes and barren summits have inspired musicians, poets and artists over the centuries. Walking the beautiful hills is one of the great pleasures of staying in The Malverns. The name is not only applied to the hills but to the straggle of six distinct settlements often referred to collectively as Malvern. These are **Little Malvern**, **Malvern Wells**, **Malvern Link**, **Great Malvern**, **North Malvern** and **West Malvern**.

Little Malvern is the smallest and southernmost of the Malverns nestling cosily in the lee of steeper slopes. The church of St Giles is all that remains of a larger priory church and was treated roughly by the Parliamentarians during th Civil War who removed the misericords and damaged some of the beautiful 15th century glass. They also left a sword behind in the graveyard which is now kept in a glass case. Next to the church is **Little Malvern Court**, parts of which date back to the 12th century and which was the refectory of Prior's Hall of the original monastic foundaion. Long a family home, it contains a priest-hole, a magnificent 14th century roof and a number of treasures including a travelling trunk and silk quilt belonging to Catherine of Aragon.

The shifting play of light and shadow on the ancient hills, sometimes dramatic, more often subtle and complex is nowhere better artistically represented than in the wonderful music of Sir Edward Elgar. It seems only right that this man of Worcestershire whose genius was acknowledged worldwide, but who remained a countryman at heart, should be buried, together with his wife and daughter, in the quiet peace of the Malverns at St Wulfstan's Roman Catholic Church.

The strict contemplative life of a monastic order would seem ideally suited to this region and Malvern Priory Church is the sole, but impressive remnant of a large priory which dates back to 1088. Unfortunately the monastic order was not always strict or contemplative for, in 1282, the prior was accused of adultery with twenty two women! Although the conventual buildings (the living quarters) were nearly all pulled down in the Dissolution, the church was retained by the payment of twenty pounds (in two instalments) - a wonderful bargain for a building which externally is a fine example of Perpendicular architecture with a light and airy interior which includes a six-bay Norman nave of the early 1100's. The 15th century stained glass is wonderfully complimented by some beautiful tiles of the same period, together with a fine set of misericords. Once again the humour of the old craftsmen has been given full sway, for example, there are three mice hanging a cat and a drunkard being beaten by his wife, to name but two. The Malvern Museum is housed in the other surviving part of the prior, the Abbey Gateway.

Chapter Four

Great Malvern surrounds the church and is essentially 18th and early 19th century in character and is a product of the period's preoccupation with spa waters. There are distinct parallels with life today; our preoccupation with health, diet, fitness and beauty has led to the establishment of fashionable 'health farms' while the Georgian and Victorians had their spas and hydros.

Perhaps the only difference being the emphasis our ancestors placed on ailments affecting digestion - hardly surprising when one considers the amount they ate! Four meals a day, breakfast, lunch, dinner and supper were the norm, even for the lower middle classes and a menu from a local hotel, now defunct, offers the following delights:

Caviare
Soups: Mulligatawny or Julienne
Fish: Brill or Stewed Eels
Entrees: Salmi of Wild Duck or Chicken Cream
Roast: Sirloin of Beef or Haunch of Mutton
Sweets: Orange Fritters, Benedictine Souffle or Ices
Savouries: Angel on Horseback or Cheese Straws

All this was accompanied by copious quantities of the appropriate wines and liquers and eaten in tight restricting clothing; well-laced whalebone corsets being de riguer for the women and the vainer men. Consequently, anyone offering relief from such embarassing disorders as 'Constipation, Flatulence, Diarrhoea and Indigestion or similar ailments arising from Impure Blood or Disordered Stomach' was undoubtedly on to a winner.

The first entrepreneur to exploit the area's water was the founder of the Royal Worcester Porcelain Works, one Doctor John Wall. He had, however, one slight problem in extolling the curative properties of the liquid: it tasted pleasantly fresh and sparkling - quite the reverse of the generally foul-flavoured, mineral rich fluids experienced at other fashionable resorts. Doctor Wall was evidently made of sterner stuff and had a marketing ability that would have made him a target for all major executive recruitment agencies were he still alive today.

'Malvern Water, said Doctor Wall,
is famed for containing nothing at all.'

This was the essence of the campaign and it worked! His premise was quite simply, that since the water was so pure, the cure was effected faster ' as it could pass more rapidly through the vessels of the body.'

Central England

The town quickly became fashionable and hotels, pump rooms and lodging houses were built. The Victorians added a further refinement by introducing a form of 'water-cure' that was horrific by anyone's standards. This consisted of being wrapped tightly in cold wet sheets for hours on end, having hundreds of gallons of icy water dropped on you from a great height, cold baths, long walks, a strict diet and naturally nothing but water to drink. Recreation was strictly controlled with even reading being banned as 'too demanding'. It was a wonder that anyone survived; nevertheless, the resort attracted the likes of the Royal Family, Gladstone, Florence Nightingale, Macaulay, Carlyle, Wordsworth and Charles Darwin.

The waters have not been forgotten and are bottled and exported all over the world by Cadbury Schweppes, while the awful Victorian water treatments have been replaced by the delights of a 'water activity centre'. The Splash an indoor complex complete with water-slide, wave-making machine and 'beach'. Above all Malvern are the hills, and to walk their eight mile length and savour the amazing views, is to see England at its very best. The Malvern Hills Conservators were set up by Parliament in 1884 to protect the common land from commercial exploitation and they have done their job wonderfully well. There are more than twenty six miles of footpaths, together with a number of discreet car-parks so that the hills can be enjoyed by all.

To the north, at the end of a lane in meadows bordering the Severn, lies the village of **Grimley**. Apart from some gravel pits and a number of farms, this would seem a quiet prosaic country community. However, in the churchyard lies Sir Samuel Baker (1821-93) an African explorer of renown, discovrer of Lake Nyanza and the Murchison Falls, big-game hunter and colonial administrator, While at neighbouring **Thorngrove** lived an even more exotic character, in the shape of Lucien Bonaparte. He was the younger brother of Napoleon and offended the Emperor by marrying the ex-wife of a planter. Napoleon offered Lucien the Kingdoms of Spain and Naples if he would renounce the woman, but Lucein refused and, in trying to escape to America, was captured by the British. He evntually settled with his wife in this remote corner of Worcestershire, where they happily whiled away the remaining war years by writing turgid epic poetry together.

At **Wichenford** the National Trust has restored a marvellous 17th century half-timbered Dovecote and the nearby **Wichenford Court** is said to play host to two female ghosts, both members of the Washbourne family. One stalks around holding a bloody dagger aloft (she was reputed to have murdered a French prince) and the other plays a harp whilst sitting in a silver boat drawn by white swans. Makes a change from grey ladies and headless horsemen!

Chapter Four

The landscape of Worcestershire reveals many gems whether man-made or natural. The glorious blossom, the ancient buildings and the views from the hills - even in the most mundane little corner there is always something to interest and delight.

SHROPSHIRE

Shropshire is such a wonderful mixture of countryside, architecture, agriculture and industry. It has wonderful places to visit, history which is fascinating and at times awe inspiring, stately homes, gardens and all manner of other attractions. I cannot tell you as much about the county as I would wish but I hope it is enough to encourage you to come here.

The temptation when you come to South Shropshire, is to seek out immediately places like Ludlow, a place of historical romance and one of the most beautiful country towns in England. This is what I have always done in the past but this time I was invited to stay with friends in **Telford**, a new town that is light years ahead. My friends had moved there with reluctance when a new posting for the husband made it imperative. To their surprise they have found living in this new town a good experience. Some of their enthusiasm rubbed off on me and I, too, was agreeably surprised at the great effort that has been made to make it a 'green and pleasant land'. For example, over a million trees, plants and shrubs have been planted throughout the town. The park is a mixture of landscaped and natural scenery complete with a lake at the side of which is an amphitheatre and a sports arena. The town offers all sorts of facilities and seems to me to be full of young and enthusiastic people who enjoy what it has to offer.

One of the reasons that made my friends happy with Telford was the unique range of top class sporting facilities, with everything from golf and tennis to skiing provided in a range of superb modern sports centres. In addition to the National Sports Centre at nearby **Lilleshall**, Telford has six fully equipped sports and leisure centres of its own. The Telford Ice Rink is one of the finest in the Midlands, and it is the home of one of the country's top ice hockey teams.

Newport is only eight miles to the north-east of Telford and is as different as chalk from cheese. Here I found a pleasant, unspoilt market town, centred around the broad, elegant High Street, a street just asking to be explored. The town has a large and graceful church, **St Nicholas**, standing on an island site in the middle of the High Street. There is a font from the year of the Restoration, a coffin lid carved quite wonderfully 700 years ago, and a list of rectors going back to the Normans.

Central England

The most famous son of Newport was the wise and extraordinary man, Sir Oliver Lodge, who experimented in wireless and sent wireless telegrams long before Marconi. He interested himself in all sorts of things from the mysterious problems of telepathy to the conquering of fog.

Just 3 miles north of Junction 3 on the M54 is **Weston Park** on the A5 at **Weston-under-Lizard**. This classic 17th century stately house is the historic home of the Earls of Bradford. The interior has been superbly restored and holds one of the country's finest collection of paintings, with originals by many of the great masters. There are fine tapestries from the famous 18th-century makers Gobelin and Aubusson, letters from Disraeli which provide a fascinating commentary on Victorian history. It is quite wonderful. It is used all the year round for Conferences, Banquets, Product Launches, Wedding Receptions and for very special 'Dine and Stay' gourmet evenings which are open to the public. These are truly wonderful occasions and will long stay in your memory. If you are interested ring 01952 76207 and askabout dates.

From Weston Park it is only a short distance to **Boscobel House**, in which Charles Stuart sought refuge after his defeat at Worcester. As I drove along the quiet road I wondered if the King had wished he was just a simple Shropshire man, secure in his everyday life rather than a hunted royal. The Giffords of Chillington owned Boscobel and as staunch catholics they had honeycombed the house with hiding places for priests. If you see the house today many of them still exist. One will be pointed out to you as the kings hiding place, reached by a short flight of stairs leading to the cheese room.

William Penderel tenanted Boscobel and he was one of the six brothers who were loyal supporters of the Stuart cause. However it was not Boscobel which hid Charles Stuart but **Whiteladies**, where Humphrey Penderel lived. Here, he left all his retinue but Lord Richard Wilmot and became a countryman wearing a coarse shirt, darned stockings, a leather doublet with pewter buttons, a ragged coat and breeches, a battered old hat and rough boots. He darkened his face and his hands with soot and accompanied only by Richard, he crept out, avoiding troops that he knew to be in the neighbourhood. He was attempting to make his way over the Severn into Wales, stopping at Madeley, the home of Francis Woolf. The journey was fraught with danger and at one stage he and Richard were chased by a miller and a number of soldiers. The journey became so perilous that the only thing they could do was to return to Boscobel. The only way to do this was to swim across the river but Richard could not swim. Charles helped him over but by this time the King's feet were so blistered and torn and his boots so full of grit, that he felt he could not go on. It was Richard who kept him going and at last they reached the safety of Boscobel. Here Charles's

Chapter Four

feet were doctored, he was given a change of stockings and his boots were dried. Outside the house was a great oak and into this Charles climbed. He slept during the day but woke to the sound of Cromwell's men searching for him in the wood. There was a price of a thousand pounds on the king's head: something all the Penderels knew about but such was their loyalty that not one of them even thought for a moment about betraying him. They would have died in his cause if need be. For two or more days and nights Charles stayed at Boscobel, sleeping in the hole beneath the trapdoor in the cheese room until finally it was thought safe enough for them to set out on the long journey which would eventually end in France.

You must visit **Tong**. It is only a small village but the magnificent 14th-century church of **St Bartholomew** would not be out of place in a city. It is frequently referred to as 'the Cathedral of the West Midlands'. Just north of the village, off the A41, you can see a peculiar pyramid-shaped building set back a few hundred yards from the road. It is called the **Egyptian Aviary**, and it is a bizarre hen-house designed by a celebrated eccentric, George Durant in the early 19th century.

The whole of the **Ironbridge Gorge** is one big real life museum that tells you every chapter of the fascinating story, on the spot, where it happened. There is no place anywhere like it in the world. Make sure you allow yourself plenty of time to enjoyit.

The Severn flows through this deep gorge and the houses cling to the hillsides looking as though a puff of wind would blow them into the swirling river, but they have been there for hundreds of years and are as much a part of this incredible place as the Museums. The chief distinction is, of course, the bridge, believed to be the first iron bridge ever built. It was built by Abraham Darby of Coalbrookdale in 1777. It is 196ft long with one span of 100 feet and two smaller ones, the total weight of iron being 380tons. So much for the statistics, worth knowing but fading almost into insignificance alongside the many things to be seen.

Over 250 years ago the Severn Gorge witnessed momentous events which culminated in the Industrial Revolution and it was the fortunate combination of coal, iron, water power and transport, all concentrated in this Shropshire Valley, which sparked off the series of events which affected all of us. Of the many places to visit perhaps **Rosehill House**, one of the elegant mansions where the Darby family lived in the 18th and 19th centuries, is probably my favourite. It is sheer pleasure to wander through the beautifully restored rooms with original period furniture. The house gives you an understanding of how a wealthy ironmaster would have lived.

In total contrast is **Carpenter's Row**, a terrace of workers' houses built by the company in the late 18th century. There is nothing grand about them. Four cottages have been restored and furnished to recreate a home from different periods between 1780 and 1930. Carpenters' Row is open to small groups by special appointment only. You will find many more places listed under 'Attractions' at the back of the book.

After the strenuous activity in Ironbridge it might be as well to take a look at **Broseley** across the Gorge. This was the great urban centre of the Coalbrookdale coalfield during the Industrial revolution. The ironmaster, John Wilkinson, built his furnace here, and in its heyday it was a rival to Coalbrookdale itself as a centre of the iron industry. John Wilkinson was the man who had the idea of building iron barges. He persevered in spite of being laughed at and he had the last laugh when, on one summer's day in 1787, the first iron barge was launched on the Severn. From this the idea of an iron ship was born and Broseley was its birthplace. John Wilkinson was so dedicated to the use of iron that he asked to be buried in an iron coffin!

Much Wenlock cries out to be visited; it is a lovely old market town full of history. Arthur Mee describes it as somewhere that' sleeps in the hills, dreaming of all that has been, stirring with the memory of warrior kings and the ancient strife of the Border valleys, and inspired by the natural spectacle of Wenlock Edge.

The steep wooded escarpment known as **Wenlock Edge**, runs for 16 miles and provides as series of spectacular viewpoints across to the Stretton Hills and the Long Mynd. It is essentially a geological phenomenon; the rock, Wenlock limestone, was formed more than 400 million years ago in a tropical sea. It developed as a barrier reef built up largely from the skeletons and shells of sea creatures.

Three miles north east of Much Wenlock, on the B4378 you will come to **Buildwas Abbey**. Standing in a beautiful situation on the banks of the River Severn quite close to Ironbridge Gorge, it is a worthwhile place to visit. It must be one of the country's finest ruined abbeys. Dating back over 800years to Norman times it is surprising that so much is still standing today. The imposing walls of the abbey church with 14 wonderful Norman arches remain. It was probably completed in 1200 with Norman and Early English architecture remaining virtually unaltered since the Dissolution in the 1530s.

When you are in Telford, Wellington, Ironbridge or Much Wenlock you should make the effort to reach the summit of **The Wrekin**. It is a curiosity and one of the most distinctive landmarks in the Shropshire Hills. The Wrekin is 1335 foot high, rising sharply from the flatness of the surrounding

Chapter Four

countryside. It is the site of the ancient Iron Age hill fort and it has been the focus of local legends and superstitions for hundred of years. My favourite is that the hill was formed by a giant who had quarrelled with the people of Shrewsbury. The giant was determined to punish the townsfolk and set off with a huge spadeful of earth to bury the whole town. On the way he met a cobbler by the roadside carrying a sack of shoes to be mended. The cobbler thought the giant was up to no good so he persuaded him that Shrewsbury was too far to walk, showing him the whole bag of shoes he had worn out with walking the enormous distance from the town. The giant decided the cobbler was right: he ditched the spadeful of earth on the spot - and the Wrekin was formed.

Bridgnorth is two towns in one perched dramatically on a steep cliff above the River Severn. It is naturally beautiful and quite unlike anywhere else inEngland. This picturesque market town has High Town and Low town linked by the famous Cliff Railway, which climbs up a hair raising incline. The only other I know like it is the Cliff railway which joins Lynton and Lynmouth in Devon. There is something reminiscent of old italian towns as you climb the Stoneway steps cut sheer through the rocks, or wander about the maze of old half-timbered buildings and elegant 18th-century houses. one of these is the curious 17th century Town Hall. this timber framed building is built on an arched sandstone base partly across the roadway in the middle of the high street. AZt the east end of the street is The North gate, the only remaining one of five gates in the town's fortifications. there is a Museum over the arches.

Bridgnorth castle is famous for its leaning tower which is 17 degrees out of straight. the leaning Tower of Pisa is only 5 degrees! It has survived safely for 850 years. the castle grounds are now a public park where you can admire a splendid view over the river and Low town. Take time out to discover this delightful town and it many interesting buildings which include the **Church of St Mary Magdalene, Bishop Percy's House** and the **Bridgnorth Costume and Childhood Museum.**

Ludlow beckoned and I happily answered the call. Here is a town that has few equals. Its river rings it like a moat and to walkabout its castle and streets is quite thrilling. We are lucky to claim it as part of England because it is almost on the Welsh border. It became a fortress from which Wales's unruly and mutinous tribes were eventually knocked into submission. **The Church of St Laurence** soars upwards and vies with the castle for supremacy. It is an outstandingly beautiful Perpendicular church with an earlier foundation, twice restored in the 19th century. The church is open in summer from 9-5pm and in winter until 4pm.

The most exciting culinary event in Ludlow was the recent arrival of the celebrated international chef, Shaun Hill who opened a superb restaurant, **The Merchants House** in Lower Curve Street. This black and white timbered building invites you to enter its modest front door and inside you will find two rooms, with covers for only twenty people. It is the epitome of charm and stylish simplicity. Shaun produces food to dream about and together with his delightful wife Anja, they have quickly created an atmosphere that will make anyone remember and savour with sheer pleasure a meal here.

There are some beautiful places to visit between Ludlow and Shrewsbury. one of my favourite haunts is **Stokesay Castle**. It stands just off the Ludlow-Shrewsbury road half a mile south of Craven Arms. There is a car park up the signposted lane and past the church, only a few yards from this romantic ruin. The marvellous state of preservation does give a very clear idea of the conditions in which well-to-do medieval families lived. It is one of the earliest fortified manor houses in England with the oldest parts dating from the 12th century and the Great Hall from the 13th. It is an extraordinary structure with massive stone towers topped with a timber-framed house.

The A49 going towards Shrewsbury will take you to **Little Stretton** which must be one of the most beautiful villages in Shropshire complete with a little thatched church and its big neighbour, **Church Stretton** is somewhere else you should visit. Houses dot the valley and climb the slopes. To the west is the great moorland ridge of the Longmynd rising nearly 1700feet, with the beautiful Cardingmill Valley below and the prehistoric Portway running along the top. To the east are the rugged Caradoc Hills with Watling Street at the foot, and the banks and trenches of Caer Caradoc's stronghold 1500ft up.

The strange cross-shaped church goes back 850 years and in the old churchyard is a stone of 1814 to Ann Cook which says:

> 'On a Thursday she was born
> On a Thursday made a bride
> On a Thursday broke a leg
> And on a Thursday died.'

Thursday was not a lucky day for Ann Cook!

Bishops Castle to the west and surrounded by the beauty of the South Shropshire hills, was plundered by Royalists during the Civil War in 1645 but somehow missed out the inn, **The Boars Head Hotel**, in which Roundheads were slaking their thirst.

Chapter Four

Here you are on the edge of the Clun Forest, a delightful place and if you have ever read A.E. Housman's 'A Shropshire Lad' you will know his description of the Cluns, he thought it a quiet area:

'Clunton and Clunbury
Clungunford and Clun.
Are the quietest places
Under the sun.'

And so to **Shrewsbury** where once again A.E. Housman says it all:

'High the vanes of Shrewsbury gleam
Islanded in Severn stream;
The bridges from the steepled crest
Cross the water, east to west.'

It is almost an island with its castle standing in a narrow strait and more than half-a dozen bridges crossing to and fro. It has old black and white houses, half-timbered of the Elizabethan era, fine brick buildings of the 17th century and wonderfully elegant Queen Anne and Georgian town houses, narrow streets and alleyways with strange names - Grope Lane, Shoplatch, Dogpole, Wyle Cop and Pride Hill. Everywhere oozes history and clamours for your attention.

There are people who may tell you that North Shropshire is dull. That is absolutely untrue; it may be flatter than the south but within it you will discover it has miles of gentle green countryside, reed fringed meres, the excitement of the Shropshire Union and Llangollen Canals, red sandstone hills, a wealth of small villages and five historic market towns, **Oswestry, Ellesmere, Whitchurch, Wem** and **Market Drayton**.

Oswestry is on the Shropshire side of the border with Wales and has very strong ties with the Principality. Apart from being a charming market town to explore it is equally splendid to wander the hilly, sparsely populated border country. This is a town that has much to offer ; you could well stay here for a month and still not have seen everything. Market days are full of life with one of the busiest street markets in the county. Over 120 traders set up their stalls with every imaginable kind of product and produce. The Market days are all the year round on Wednesdays with an additional market on Saturdays in the summer. There is ample car parking near the town centre.

Canals are very important to the way of life in this part of Shropshire and provide so much more than just water transport. Following the canal or 'the cut' is a wonderful way of exploring North Shropshire whether you have a boat or not. The towpath is a splendid, traffic free footpath on the level for miles albeit in some places it is distinctly rough going and very muddy. You are rewarded though by the wildlife that abounds on the water, in the bankside vegetation, and along the hedges. You can learn so much from the canal which tells its own story of our industrial and architectural heritage.

At **Whittington** you will meet with the **Llangollen Canal**, which wends its way across the country right up into Cheshire where it joins the main Shropshire Union Canal close to **Nantwich**. Whittington is a very large village in the centre of which is Whittington Castle. All that you can see today of this important border castle is the magnificent gatehouse and the moat. It is a delightful place to visit, with a childrens play area, ducks to feed and a tearoom in which to relax. The village is reputed to have been the birthplace of Dick Whittington, the famous Lord Mayor of London and cat owner!

From here I went north a little until I came to **Chirk** where it is the only way to cruise from England into Wales. This is quite a place with a lot of history, right on the border of Shropshire and Clwyd; it has withstood the slings and arrows of outrageous fortune. **Chirk Castle** which belongs to the National Trust, is a place you must visit and you should make sure you get to **Llanrhaedr Falls**, another of the seven wonders of Wales. They are stunning.

The Shropshire Union Canal, a popular waterway for pleasure craft, has played a great part in the history of **Ellesmere**, and the **Old Wharf** with its warehouse and crane is a reminder of a prosperous period for the development of the town when it was a centre of plans for a link to the River Mersey (at what was to become Ellesmere Port).

This was nearly 200 years ago when some of Britain's leading industrialists first met to discuss the project. Thomas Telford included. Circumstances caused them to build instead a most attractive canal from Llangollen's Horseshoe Falls to Hurleston junction near Nantwich.

Wem is a town that still manages to preserve more of the old market town atmosphere than most others. It is delightful and dates back before the Conquest in 1066. In fact it is the only town mentioned in the Domesday Book which can race descendants from before and after the Conquest. The fire of 1677 destroyed many of the ancient houses and it suffered for its staunch support of the Protestant Cause in the Civil War, being th first town to declare for Parliament and hence became the prime target for the Royalists of Whitchurch and Shrewsbury who laid siege to it for a long period without success. The church dates from the 14th century and has an uncommon doorway of that period, and a Perpendicular style upper tower.

Chapter Four

Whitchurch is the most ancient of the market towns dating from 60AD when it was founded as a garrison for the Roman legions marching between Chester and Wroxeter. Many Roman artefacts and buildings have been found in the town centre notably in 1967 and 1977, and Pepper Street, High Street and Bluegates occupy the same situation as the Roman streets.

Market in name and market by nature, ideally you should come to **Market Drayton** on a Wednesday and join in the bustling bargain hunting tradition that has been going on for over 750years. Since the Norman Conquest, this seemingly sleepy and isolated town has been the scene of revolt, riot, murder, adventure and trade; its links have extended worldwide. Clive of India was born here and he will never be forgotten. You will find much to enjoyincluding the celebrated product of local bakers' shops - Gingerbread Men, which come in a range of novelty shapes and packages, all faithful to recipes over 200 years old. A true taste of history.

You must find time to travel 6 miles down the A53 to **Hodnet** where the **Hodnet Hall Gardens** covering 60 acres, are unrivalled for their beauty and natural valley setting. The magnificent trees, lawns and lakes provide a background to an ever changing seasonal colour and interest. Between April and July the rhododendrons are fantastic. The gardens are famous nationally and have been the subject of several TV and radio programmes. This was a visit to remember among the very happy recollections I have of this county.

STAFFORDSHIRE

With limited time to spend in Staffordshire I decided to devote my time to a few places which interest me and in so doing hopefully stir in the reader a desire to see more of this most versatile and handsome county.

Thomas Telford's sixty-six mile canal was built to link the industrial city of Birmingham with the great port of Livrpool and was originally named the Birmingham and Liverpool Junction Canal. Looking at the peaceful waters running straight through the lovely countryside, it is difficult to see them as the 17th and 18th century equivalent of our motorways - yet that is what they were. Quiet tree-fringed stretches where the tranquillity is only disturbed by the quacking of the mallard and the puttering of an occasional leisure boat, were once bustling highways where entire generations of families lived their lives afloat. Goods of every concievable kind were carried by boat, together with passengers and even livestock, and a community such as **Gnosall**, situated beside both canal and major road, would have been important as a distribution centre. The popularity of the canals can be understood when one realises the appalling state of the majority of roads which were virtually impassable except by packhorse. Almost overnight the waterways enabled vast quantities of raw materials and finished goods to be moved quickly and economically - thus contributing enormously to the prosperity of the nation as a whole.

It is easy to forget the logistics involved in such a venture, as our own century place an enormous reliance on powerful and sophisticated machinery to construct the roads and motorways - today's equivalent of the canal systems. Labour in enormous numbers had to be accommodated, fed and paid during the building of such projects; to drive the great waterways through the heart of our country relied chiefly upon the speed and expertise of men aided with little more than picks, shovels and wheelbarrows.The problems were not over once the canal was built, for there was the continuous problem of maintenance - reinforcing banks, clearing weed, surfacing towpaths, breaking ice in winter and all the more skilled work involving locks, their gates and associated machinery.

Failure in any of these departments could lead to blockage of the canal, or worse still, to loss of water, leaving boats and their cargoes stranded for days, even weeks. Gangs ofmen were allocated a length of canal to maintain, and many spent their lives working to keep the waterway running. Close to the aqueduct carrying the 'Shroppy' across the attractive countryside at **Shebdon**, is **The Wharf Inn**, once headquarters for a maintenance gang of 'lengthmen'. These gangs were noted for the prodigious amounts of food and drink they could consume - the Wharf obviously did a good job in these departments and carries on the tradition by catering to today's visitor with the same cheerful generosity.

Shebdon is close to the Shropshire border, a mile or so to the north of the A519 which runs through **Eccleshall**. The beauty of the surrounding undulating and wooded countryside, together with the architecture and charm of this small town make it one of the most attractive communities in Staffordshire. Pronounced 'Eccle-shawl', it has a long history dating back to a Roman settlement and over the centuries became an important strategic, ecclesiastic and market centre. Soldiers, bishops and traders have all gone but their legacy remains in the buildings they left behind. **Eccleshall Castle** was the principal residnce of the Bishops of Lichfield for 600 years. Bishop Muschamp was granted a licence to fortify his house in 1200 and this led to the construction of the castle. Interesting to note that bureaucracy ruled even then, and one wonders whether there is still a department deep in the bowels of Whitehall dealing with requests of this nature. **The Church of the Holy Trinity** has been described as one of the finest 13th-century churches in the country. Restored in 1868, it is a tall, light and lofty building of considerable grace and contains the tombs of five of the Bishops of Lichfield.

Chapter Four

Stone is a thriving and good-looking town. Two local stories account for the name; some say it comes from a cairn of stones that marked the graves of two Christian Mercian princes murdered by their pagan father, while others maintain it derives from a mineral-rich local stream that petrifies plant life. Whatever the truth, the area has been inhabited for a long time - as shown by the number of fine stone axe-heads found locally. A market town which did well out of the Canal era (the River Trent and the Trent and Mersey Canal run parallel south of the town), Stone produced two notable figures; Admiral John Jervis, later Earl St Vincent (1735-1823) and the water colourist Peter de Wint (1748-1849). The neat 18th-century Gothic Church of St Michael, with its galleries and box pews contains a memorial to the Admiral who lies with other members of his family in a small palladian-style Mausoleum.

South down the A34 is the county town of **Stafford**, the city constructed on the site of a hermitage built by St Pertelin some 1200 years ago. Commercial development has left the town surprisingly untouched - apart from the jutting intrusion of a few tower blocks. Stafford still wears the bucolic air of a country town, even though it has been an imporant manufacturing centre for centuries; manufacturing internal combustion engines and electrical equipment since the beginning of the present century. Nevertheless its ancient heritage is on proud display for all to admire. Here you have **Stafford Castle** built in 1070, an impressive example of an early Norman fortress. The central building in Stafford is the late Georgian Shire Hall, a most handsome building that fits the part well, while not too far away is a positive triumph of the timber house builders art, **The High House**. Built in 1595 for a wool mnerchant, John Dorrington, it is the largest timber-framed town house in the country. Nor must one forget **Chetwynd House**, a handsome Georgian building that is now the Post Office. Here the ebullient playwright, theatre-manager and MP for Stafford, Richard Brinsley Sheridan, would stay on visits to his constituency.

Due west of Stafford, on the very tip of Cannock Chase, is **Shugborough Estate**, ancestral home of the camera-wielding Earl of Lichfield. A beautiful mansion, dating back to 1693, and set within a magnificent 900 acre estate. Shugborough contains fine collections of 18th-century ceramics, silver, paintings and French furniture. **The Staffordshire County museum** is housed in the old servants quarters and there are splendid recreations of life behind the 'green baize door'. Shugborough Park Farm is a working agricultural museum where rare breeds are kept, horse drawn machinery used and an old mill grinds corn.

Whether you arrive by canal or car, **Cannock Chase** remains the greatest attraction of the region. As its name implies it was once a Royal hunting ground, but Richard I, in need of funds, sold it to the Bishops of Lichfield. In those times it was a much larger area, extending from the River Penk in the west to the Trent in the east, with Stafford to the north and including Wolverhampton and Walsall to the south. Now it is around 26 square miles of forest and heath land that have been declared an 'area of outstanding natural beauty'. Medieval industrial activities meant the loss of much of the native oakwoods while the southern part was given over to coalpits, but these activities have long ceased and the deer and wildlife have returned to their natural habitat. The highest point is at **Castle Ring** with wonderful views over the countryside and the site of an Iron Age hill fort, dating from around 500BC.

Close to the eastern side of Cannock Chase lies the ancient city of **Lichfield** with its unique **Cathedral of St Mary and St Chad**, a magnificent red sandstone structure with three spires, known as 'the Ladies of the Vale'. The Cathedral is considered the Mother-church of the Midlands and is the third building on the site since it was consecrated in 700AD by St Chad. The present structure is a magnificent example of Early-English and Decorated work, a triumph of medieval craftmanship. The surrounds of the cathedral are equally beautiful with attractive houses of the 14th and 15th centuries surrounding the green lawns of **Vicar's Close.**

Uttoxeter is the mecca for Midlands horse racing fans. This cheerful little market town (every Wednesday since 1309) has three different ways of pronouncing its name - 'Uxeter', 'Utcheter' or 'U-tox-eter' - and its name has been spelt in seventy-seven different ways since it was first recorded in the Domesday Book as Wotochesede. The town evidently suffers no neuroses and goes about its quiet business, waking up for market days and race meetings. There is a tendency to think of the **Peak District** as belong exclusively to Derbyshire, but natural physical features have a distressing habit of ignoring man-made boundaries, and there is more than a little truth in the local boast that 'the best parts of Derbyshire are in Staffordshire'. This is fascinating countryside, almost cosy in scale one minute and then possessed of a wild grandeur, the next. North-east of **Oakmoor**, through the hills and dales, lies one of the most beautiful valleys in the region, The Manifold Valley. The village of **Ilam**, standing at the southern end, makes a good starting point for exploring the area, and the old mansion Ilam Hall, is now a Youth hostel. The valley is relatively flat at this point but becomes increasingly deep and narrow as one journeys northwards. The River Manifold has a disconcerting habit of disappearing underground and at Ilam Hall it re-emerges from its subterranean journey from **Darfur Crags.**

Chapter Four

Obviously this beautiful area has long been a favourite with those who love what is described in the glossy-brochure trade as 'the great outdoors' even if writers of such hyperbole rarely get nearer to the fresh air than kicking the cat out last thing at night! Over three hundred years ago, two learned gentlemen, close friends and 'Brothers of the Angle' rambled the length and breadth of the glorious river valleys in pursuit of the shy brook trout. Izaak Walton and Charles Cotton could discuss the classical poetry of Homer or the merits of a fishing lure with equal facility and enthusiasm, and had a particular fondness for the river that runs down the border between Staffordshire and Derbyshire, the Dove.

Cotton, who was to contribute a chapter on the art of fly-fishing in Walton's 'Compleat Angler' was a poet and author in his own right who lived at **Beresford Hall** near **Alstonfield**. The Hall was pulled down in the 1800's but the fishing lodge by the river still survives, and the village church still contains the Cotton family pew.

Longnor is a tiny market town in the farthermost corner of north-eastern Staffordshire on the same road the intrepid Greyhound rattled its way across the rutted potholes over the moors. The road may have improved, but Longnor is little altered; good looking 18th-century facades and a square with a small Market Hall dated 1873. Stone lined streets and alleyways with determined little houses of the same material give a sense of dogged continuity.

Wandering westwards one comes across the highest village in England, set close by the high road from Leek to Buxton. The oddly named **Flash** claims the title at 1,158 feet above sea level. A Nepalese would doubtless fall off his mountain laughing, but it is a respectable height for our 'sceptr'd isle' and probably just as cold in winter as the Himalayas.

'The Metropolis of the Moorland' was how one writer described **Leek**, though Doctor Johnson was not so charitable ' An old church but a poor town'. nowadays it is a neat mill town standing in magnificent countryside. Like so many of its kind Leek has a cheerful and generous nature and welcomes visitors; particularly on Wednesdays when the old cobbled market square is thronged with stalls and the air filled with cheerful banter. There are asurprisingly large number of antique shops and many of the mills have their own shops.

The great canal-builder, Brindley, started his working life as a mill-wright and the Brindley Mill in Mill Street, tells the sotry of his life and graphically demonstrates the many facets of this one, important craft. One of his later works was the Caldon Canal which runs with the River Chernet in the valley alongside the hillside of Cheddleton. Cheddleton Flint Mill ground up flints from Kent and Sussex for use in the pottery industry, and the waterwheels and grinding equipment are on display, together with other items associated with the trade, including a restored canal barge. The canal's successor, the railway, is also commemorated at the Cheddleton Railway Centre, with displays, mementoes, engines and other paraphernalia set in and around the attractive Victorian station.

The two different forms of transport were obviously of major importance to the development of the industries of the north-western sector of the county, Newcastle-under-Lyme and Stoke-on-Trent lie side by side, geographically close yet separate in terms of history and character.

Coming from the east, the first is **Stoke-on-Trent**, a combination of the six communities of Tunstall, Burslem, Hanley, Longton, Stoke and Fenton - known the world over as The Potteries. The companies based here, both large and small, have a world-wide market for their products and their heritage dates back many centuries. Wherever fine china-ware is used and appreciated, such as Spode, Copeland, Minton, Coalport, Royal Doulton and Wedgwood are revered and respected.

The Potteries have the flavour of a rural area; a feeling of continuity and a sense of tradition. The same family names crop up time and time again and, even in these difficult times, there is a pride in the past and has made enormous efforts to clean up the detritus of yesteryear and make Stoke an attractive place in which to work and live. Trentham Gardens cover 800 acres of parklands, gardens and lakes with numerous sporting facilities. Festival Park, is an amazing 23 acre complex which includes a sub-tropical aquatic playground with flumes, water slides and rapids.

The architecture is predominantly Victoria red-brick since the city was in a constant state of development, but there are exceptions; the Minton family brought over French artists to decorate their wares and built them ornate Italianate villas - their sense of geography being obviously inferior to their business acumen.

Newcastle-under-Lyme is the oldest of the two cities, dating back to its incorporation as a borough in 1180, at a time when the neighbouring Potteries were hamlets or villages. Although Stoke-on-Trent and Newcastle have grown into each other, they still retain their separate identities; the delicate craft of the Potteries being complemented by the ruder skills of the iron workers and colliers of their older neighbour. Modern Newcastle is an attractive town with much good architecture and is host toKeele University. Markets and a Fair date from medieval times.

Chapter Four

Staffordshire is a little-known county of remarkable contrast, interest and beauty that will repay the curious a thousandfold.

WARWICKSHIRE

This other Eden, demi-paradise, This fortress built by Nature for herself....'

These lines from Richard II conjure up images of a rural idyll and doubtless the beautiful countryside around Stratford-upon-Avon did much to inspire Warwickshire's most famous son. More than two centuries later, Shakespeare's affection for his native county was to be echoed in the words of the eminent novelist, Henry James, who described Warwickshire as 'the core and centre of the English world; mid-most England, unmitigated England... the genius of pastoral Britain'. James was an American and his words have done much to encourage his fellow countryman and women to visit this quintessentially English region Although the twentieth century has left its mark with evidence of industrialisation, the construction of motorways and some of the less appealing manifestations of the intensive tourist industry, there is still much of gentle grace and beauty beloved by both men; turn off the coach-laden main roads and one can enjoy pastoral scenery little changed since the Bard's day or, turning away from a modern shopping precinct, one can delight in architectural gems that would have been equally familiar to the great playwright and his contemporaries.

If Warwickshire can be described as the Heartland of England then the Avon must be its principal artery in that its waters have provided the means of irrigation, transport and power. **Stratford-upon-Avon** is without doubt the central tourist attraction of the county - perhaps of the entire country. Shakespeare may be synonymous with Stratford, but the town was of importance long before his birth (reputedly on St George's Day, 23rd April 1564) and had its beginnings as a Roman camp, and a Saxon monastic settlement. The name Stratford simply means 'a ford where the street crosses the river' and a market was first recorded in 1196. King John granted the right to hold a three-day fair in 1214 and in 1553 the town was incorporated as a borough and, regardles of Shakespeareama, Stratford is still an attractive and prosperous market town. the central part of the town which contains its chief attractions is arranged along the north bank of the Avon with three streets running parallel to the river and three at right angles, the names being unchanged since before Shakespeare's time. The predominant style of architecture is Tudor/Jacobean half-timbering, much of it genuine but with more than the occasional false facade; nevertheless the overall effect is pleasing and the town is an attraction in its own right.

Holy Trinity church, lying beside the banks of the Avon, is an excellent place to start exploring the town, for it is a dignified and graceful building that reflects both the early importance and history of the town as well as being the last resting place of England's greatest dramatist. The proportions and spaciousness are almost cathedral-like and the church was granted collegiate status by Henry V in the year of Agincourt (1415) and remained as an important theological centre until the Reformation in the 16th century. Throughout the building there are numerous memorials to many local worthies and associations and the former Lady Chapel is almost entirely given over to the Cloptons who contributed much to the growth and development of Warwickshire and to Stratford-upon-Avon in particular. They, like many of their medieval neighbours, made their fortune from the wool-trade and Sir Hugh Clopton is doubly remembered for having built the multi-arched bridge upstream from Holy Trinity and for being a Lord Mayor of London in 1492.

William Shakespeare died at the age of fifty-two on St George's Day, April 23rd 1616 and is buried, along with his wife Anne and other members of his family, in the chancel, and every year, on the anniversary of his death, the whole area around the tomb is covered with floral tributes from all over the world. We sometimes forget how great a man he was and just how much his works are appreciated throughout the world; he would not be forgotten even if he had been buried in an unmarked grave and perhaps this is best summed up by the epitaph written by his friend and contemporary, Ben Jonson:

'Thou art a monument without a tomb,
And art alive still, while thy book doth live,
And we have wits to read, and praise to give.'

At the age of eighteen Shakespeare married Anne Hathaway and it is believed he earned his living at this time as a schoolmaster although a year or so later after his marriage he left for London. However he was to return to Stratford at regular intervals and, with the prospering of his fortunes, he purchased **New Place** in 1597 and twelve years later settled there permanently with his family. That the house no longer exists is ascribed to the fact that a later owner, the Reverend Francis Gaskell, irritated by the rating assessments and constant pestering by Shakesperean enthusiasts was moved to pull down the entire house! That there is nothing new about the pressures that can be caused by tourism is evidenced by the fact that the demolition took place in 1759. The foundations have been preserved together with a beautifully re-created Elizabethan garden. The entrance is by way of **Nash's House**, once the home of Thomas Nash, who married Shakespeare's grand-daughter, and now containing what is effectively the town museum.

Chapter Four

Quite rightly, Stratford-upon-Avon is home to the **Royal Shakespeare Theatre**. Originally known as the Memorial Theatre, it was designed by Miss Elizabeth Scott, a niece of the great Victorian architect Sir Gilbert Scott, and was opened by Edward, Prince of Wales in 1932. Considered controversial and innovative when first built, it stands massively beside the river and is a wonderful place to spend an evening being entertained by one of the greatest companies in the world. In the **Bancroft Gardens**, adjacent to the theatre is the impressive Shakespeare Monument, cast from sixty-five tons of bronze which shows the dramatist seated on a plinth surrounded by four of his principal characters (Hamlet, Lady Macbeth, Falstaff and Prince Hal.) Also in close proximity to the theatre are the **Other Place**, a small intimatetheatre which presents a wide range of drama, and the **Black Swan Inn**, a favourite theatrical haunt that is better known as the Dirty Duck.

On the whole the town copes well with its immense number of visitors and has developed an infrastructure that operates extremely efficiently but it should be appreciated that Stratford-upon-Avon is perhaps the country's premier tourist attraction. A little planning will pay dividends in enabling you to enjoy your visit and the **Tourist Information Centre** at **Bridgefoot**, Stratford-upon-Avon (Tel: 01789293127) can provide considerable help and advice including details of guided tours.

Kenilworth will always haunt me because of the extraordinary and impressive sight of tall windows rising beside a massive fireplace in the ruins of the 14th-century Great Hall of Kenilworth Castle. Looking at it my imagination runs riot and I see the arrival of Queen Elizabeth I and her entourage to attend a lavish banquet in her honour. The whole castle would have been alive and busy. No doubt Her Majesty and her followers would have to be housed and their individual staffs cared for. On one occasion she stayed fifteen days. Quite wonderful. You will see the red-sandstone castle keep standing four-square on a grassy slope, aloof from the bustling market town below, serene in its own world. Though its towers are crumbling and its windows as blank as sightless eyes, it still retains the imposing strength and grandeur that made it one of England's chief strongholds in Norman times.

Approach it on foot across the causeway that leads from the car park on the south side and you will see that much of the castle's outer wall still stands. Beyond it is the Norman Keep standing dignified and alone, separated from the ravages of war, time and weather from the buildings added to it in later centuries. Only the walls remain of th great banqueting hall built by John of Gaunt in the 14th century and little more of the buildings added by Robert Dudley, Earl of Leicester in the 16th century.

The castle has not been lived in since the Restoration and the best preserved parts are Dudley's gatehouse, which was designed to impress distinguished visitors and still impresses with its tall corner towers and battlemented parapets. Then there are the stables built of dressed stone with a timbered upper storey. The Roundheads held the castle during the Civil War and destroyed the keep's north wall after the war.

Shipston-on-Stour dating from Saxon times has the flavour of other days about it. The streets are lined wih houses and inns of the Georgian period built when the woollen industry made Shipston a more prosperous place than now. It is charming with weathered roofs of Cotswold tiles, quaint little dormers and handsome doorways with old brass knockers. I came here to visit the **George Hotel** which dates back to the 15th century and a fireplace in the Front lobby dates to 1508. Queen Victoria stayed here before she became Queen and in more recent times it has been the haunt of famous racing people, actors and writers including George Bernard Shaw.

The Grand Union Canal and the River Avon make their way through **Royal Leamington Spa**, whose tree-lined avenues, riverside walks and wealth of handsomely proportioned architecture are laid out in a grid pattern. Named after the River Leam, a tributary of the Avon, Leamington (or Leamington Priors as it was then known.) was little more than a hamlet until the beginning of the 19th century when the fame of curative powers of the local spring-water became more widely known. Speculators and developers created the town we see today at the most astonishing speed; some idea of the rapid development that took place may be gained from the fact that in 1801 there were 315 inhabitants and yet by 1841 there were 13,000! As the town rapidly expanded, the rich and fashionable flocked in to see and be seen, to promenade, to take the waters and indulge in entertainments. One writer declared the town to be the 'King of Spas' and Queen Victoria, shortly after coming to the throne in 1837, granted the prefix 'Royal'. The locals must have been somewhat bemused since the original use for the salty waters was for seasoning meat and curing rabid dogs! Although the town has expanded further since the 19th century, much of the architectural interest has been retained around the centre and the original source of prosperity, the spring water, can still be sampled at the **Royal Pump Room and Baths**. This elegant building designed in the classical style with a colonnade, was first opened in 1814; the waters are described as being a mild aperient (a polite word for laxative), and 'particularly recommended in cases of gout, chronic and muscular rheumatism, lumbago, sciatica, inactivity of the liver and the digestive system, anaemia, chlorisis and certain skin disorders'.

The town is blessed with many parks and gardens, perhaps the best known being **The Jephson Gardens** whose entrance lodge faces the Pump

Chapter Four

Room. Originally planned as an arboretum, these spacious gardens contain mature specimens of many unusual trees together with magnificent floral displays, a lake and two fountains modelled on those at Hampton Court. The gardens were named after Dr Henry Jephson who did much to promote the curative effects of the waters as well as much Charitable work.

Warwickshire is a wonderful county - enjoy it.

THE WEST MIDLANDS

It seems only fitting that the West Midlands, like so many of its products, should be of modern invention, being an amalgamation of the most heavily industrialised areas of Staffordshire, Warwickshire and Worcestershire. created in 1974, the region covers an area of 347 square miles and incorporates the cities of Coventry and Birminghams with a population in the millions.

It is an area preoccupied with production, effectively created by the Industrial Revolution and vastly expanded by the insatiable demands of Empire. It has been touched by the dread hands of War and Recession, yet continues to thrive, producing goods and providing services that are in demand all over the world. Thousands of its acres have disappeared under industrial and suburban sprawl and it is soil scarred and riven by roads, motorways, canals, mines and railways, yet there is still much of beauty and a great deal of value. It can be both depressingand inspiring but if the poet's vision of the 'Heart of England' referred to the rural charm and historical assests of neighbouring Warwickshire then the West Midlands is where the pulse can be felt.

Droitwich in the south west of the region, was probably a Roman centre for the salt and mineral trade which was well developed by the time of the Domesday Book. The town lies on the western side of the M5 and the production of salt continued until quite recently. It was in the 1830's that John Corbett, the Droitwich Salt-King rose to prominence by modernising and developing the salt-mines and workings, particularly around **Stoke Prior** where he achieved the astonishing feat of turning the annual output of salt from 26,000 tons to 200,000 tons. Very much a man of his period, he had started life as the son of a bargee and at the peak of success controlled a vast empire. He built himself an ornate home, now an hotel, the **Chateau Impney**. He was an enlightened employer providing his workers with gardens, schools, a dispensary and cottages.

The many rivers, streams and canals that vein the entire Midland region mean that angling is one of the most popular local past-times and **Redditch** has been providing fish hooks for generations, as well as many other items of fishing tackle. The hooks are a natural adjunct to the town's chief industry and claim to fame, that of being the headquarters of the needle-making industry, indeed **The National Needle Museum** is situated here.

Between **Bromsgrove** and **Kidderminster** lies the pretty village of **Chaddesley Corbett** with its fine timbered houses and church dedicated to St Cassian, a schoolmaster who was condemned to death by his own pupils! The building is a good example of 14th-century architecture on an earlier base and has a handsome 12th-century carved font. Nearby are **Chaddesley Woods** with nature trail and reserve and **Harvington Hall**, a late medieval moated manor house which has a number of ingenious priestholes.

Weaving and carpet-making built up the wealth of **Kidderminster** and the industry continues to this day. I do not know whether this trade is particularly renowned for its friendly spirit but certainly the town's good natured atmosphere is as tangible today as it was over two hundred years ago when one John Brecknall established a charity to provide every child or unmarried person living in Church Street with a plum cake every Midsummer's Eve.

Stourport-on-Severn is unusual in that it is almost entirely a product of the Industrial Revolution, and an attractive one at that. The canal systems of the Midlands were the fore-runners of the Victorian's railway networks and our own motorways, opening up the country's industrial centres to national and international trade and Stourport was created as a 'new town' around the point where the Staffordshire-Worcestershire canal ran into the River Severn. Neat rows of cottages were built tidily around the central basin, which is almost an inland port, and the town still has a pleasant late-Georgian feel to it, although it has grown considerably since the days when the hard-working and often hard-driving bargees would gather to exchange cargoes, swap horses and gossip.

A couple of miles to the north-west lies **Bewdley** which also contains many fine Georgian houses but also architecture of earlier periods. It also rose to prosperity because of water-born traffic but that of the pre-canal era utilising the natural facilities of the River Severn in the 15th and 16th centuries. It was also a centre for weaving, manufacturing saltpeter, brass, horn goods, and cap-making (apparently this trade was so important that at one time the citizens of Bewdley were compelled to wear caps on pain of a fine).

Chapter Four

The image of grime, poverty and pollution in the Midlands may be out-moded now but it has a basis in truth and particularly applied to that area known as the Black Country, banded by **Wolverhampton** to the north and **Stourbridge** to the south and so-called because of the region's numerous open-cast coal mines and smoke-belching factories. Thomas Carlyle, visiting in 1824 described it as; '...a frightful scene...a dense cloud of pestilential smoke hangs over it forever.. and at night the whole region burns like a volcano spitting fire from a thousand tubes of brick.

But oh the wretched thousands of mortals who grind out their destiny there!' Paradoxically, from this vision of hell on earth came skills and objects of beauty that were to be admired and coveted the world over and a tough, warm hearted people proud of their heritage. The mining has gone, along with the old style furnaces but many of the skills, trades and industries survive albeit in a cleaner more efficient, and pleasant surroundings. Stourbridge was, and still is, a great centre for the glass-making industry. Familiar names such as Royal Brierley, Stuart and Thomas Webb still produce glassware of the finest quality. To see how glass is made and the incredible standards and varieties that are available, go and visit the **Broadfield House Glass Museum** in **Kingswinford**. The factories themselves welcome visitors and I particularly enjoyed the Stuart Crystal factory with its amazing glass cone; a brick structure like an elongated beehive which housed the furnaces and the glass-makers.

As with so much of the region, canals played a large part in the growth of industry and the **Stourbridge Branch Canal and Wharf** is worth visiting to see the old restored Bonded warehouses and canal company offices and also to take a trip on one of the boats.

Industrial, political and social history all combine at **Dudley** in the heart of the Black Country, together with varied architecture and attractions. The ruined castle, standing on a wooden rise above the busy industrial town, dates back to the 11th century although the basic structure that we can see today is principally 14th century. **Dudley Castle** has had a checkered history and was first destroyed in 1175 when the then owner made the tactical error of backing Prince Henry in the revolt against his father, Henry II. A century later, rebuilding began but proceeded slowly; one of the reasons being the unpopulatiry of the bullying and dishonest John de Somery, whose forcible taxations and reluctance to settle debts led to a natural disinclination on the part of the locals to help with construction.

The Dudley family took over during the reign of Henry VIII, but John Dudley followed in the footsteps of his predecessor by backing Lady Jane Grey for the throne and paid the supreme penalty. The family fortunes, like those of the castle, must have declined somewhat for in 1585 a report was submitted that the castle was unfit for Mary, Queen of Scots to visit - and she was a prisoner at the time! The massive ruins still stand and are well worth a visit especially as they are now part of the well known **Dudley Zoo**.

You should make the effort to visit the **Black Country Museum** at Tipton Road. An open-air site, it is essentially a reconstruction of a 19th century Black Country village complete with canal, mine, houses and factories where all the skills and crafts are demonstrated. Its authenticity can be judged from the fact that special permission had to be sought to contravene the regulations of the Clean Air Act so that cottages could burn coal!

Working museums are always fascinating with their emphasis on ancient skills and crafts and to the north-east of the Black Country can be found at the **Walsall Leather Centre Museum**. Leather working developed alongside the specialist metal trades in stirrups, bits, buckles and spurs with hides being provided by the sheep and cattle of Shropshire anbd Warwickshire and bark for tanning coming from the surrounding oak forests. Saddlery and tack manufacture are still local trades to this day, surviving amongst the more high-tec industries of the 20th century. **Walsall** is proud of its past and possesses a charter dating from the early 13th century and yet has always taken a progressive and enlightened approach to its own affairs, having been one of the first towns in the country to have its own police force, library and cottage hospital.

As I drove south to **Birmingham** I reflected on the facilities offered by **The National Exhibition Centre, The International Convention Centre and The National Indoor Arena**. These impressive and still expanding buildings are equipped to the highest standards and play host to a multitude of events as diverse as opera, international athletics and Cruft's Dog Show as well as numerous conferences and trade shows which attract several million people a year representing some 95 countries! Nevertheless these massive centres are not alone and it is typical of Birmingham's ability to react to market demand that numerous other conference venues are available from five-star hotels to stately homes, together with an impressive infrastructure that covers everything necessary, such as accommodation, travel, leisure facilities and marketing. Perhaps more than any other skill, it is this ability in the market place that has brought Birmingham from being a 'vill of ten adults and value at £1' in 1086 to to-day's priceless 65,000 acre metropolis of one million inhabitants.

The city is constantly changing and intensely alive so it is difficult to know where to start in order to give you some idea of this vibrant place. Perhaps the best place is the **Birmingham Museum of Science and Industry** in Newhall Street which amongst many other fascinating exhibits features

Chapter Four

the world's oldest working steam engine. For an insight into an early example of mass-production allied to social concern (plus a thoroughly enjoyable time) visit **Cadbury World** at **Bournville** - a must for every chocoholic! Old skills still relevant today can be seenin the **Jewellery Quarter** in **Hockley** whilst the network of canals provide a unique opportunity to explore the many waterways that wander through the city - Brum has more miles of canals than Venice!

The rural area lying between Birmingham and Coventry is well worth exploring containing a number of villages and small towns of interest such as **Knowle**, with its timbered buildings, Guildhall and church with beautifully carved chancel screen. **Temple Balsall** is a unique and historic hamlet which owes its origins to the Knights Templars, a religious order of knights who fought in the Crusades. They are remembered in the lovely 13th-century church which reflects much of the pageantry of those long-past times and in the village's name whilst charity and kindness of a later period is marked by the almshouses that were founded in 1670 by Lady Katherine Leveson. **Hampton-in-Arden**, a mile or so to the north, slopes down to the River Blythe, where there is a fine pack horse bridge built for salt-traders. The village has connections with Shakespeare, being the setting for 'As You Like It' and with the Peel family; Sir Robert Peel (1788-1875) founded the Metropolitan Police Force and was twice prime minister.

The region's second city is **Coventry** and although smaller than Birmingham is much older, originating in the 7th century. It was the centre of the old cloth-weaving industry from the 14th to the 17th century, was the fourth city in England in importance and from its iron-worker's skills developed the engineeering expertise which led it to become the centre of the British motor industry. The city's proud past was very nearly wiped out on November 14th 1940, when German bombers destroyed 40 acres of the city centre, killing or wounding 1500 inhabitants. The fire-gutted ruins of St Michael's Cathedral remains as a moving memorial and a charred cross made from the remains of two oak beams was set up in the ruined church with the words 'Father Forgive' inscribed on the wall behind. Immediately adjacent is the new cathedral designed by Sir Basil Spence and consecrated in 1962. It contains works by Graham Sutherland, John Piper, Jacob Epstein and many others and the whole is a moving testimony to the faith and optimism of the people of Coventry.

Re-building of the city centre began shortly after the war and the occasion was marked by the erection of a statue to one of Coventry's earliest notable citizens, Lady Godiva, who is best remembered for having ridden naked through the streets in order to persuade her husband, Leofric, to reduce the heavy taxes that he had imposed upon the townsfolk. History records that Leofric relented but I doubt that today's inland Revenue would take much notice!

Although the city centre is now a bustling modern development some notable remnants of the city's medieval past escaped the Blitz and are well worth a visit. **The Guildhall** contains some splendid glass, wonderful carvings, the Arras tapestry and a minstrel's gallery with a display of medieval armour. Mary, Queen of Scots was once incarcerated in its tower. **Bond's Hospital** and **Ford's Hospital** are both 16th-century almshouses and are still used as such while **Spon Street** is a rec-constructedmedieval cul-de-sac with ancient houses enjoying a new lease of life as shops and galleries. The 14th-century **Whitefriar's Gate** is a renovated Carmelite friary housing a number of exhibitions including a charming **Toy Museum**. The immediate past has not been forgotten and in Hales Street can be found the **Museum of British Road Transport**, which includes the Land Speed record holder, Thrust II, while at nearby **Baginton** there is the **Midlands Air Museum**.

One of our greatest novelists who made much use of this area of the Midlands in her books was Marian Evans (1819-80), better known under her pen-name of George Eliot. She was born north of Coventry at **Nuneaton** where her father was steward at nearby **Arbury Hall**, a fine example of Gothick Revival built onto an earlier Elizabethan house and with a porch and stables that were designed by Sir Christopher Wren. There are fine landscaped gardens and the stables are now home to **The Pinkerton Collection of Cycles and Motorcycles.**

Tamworth, once capital of the ancient Saxon Kingdom of Mercia is a pleasant town with some attractive architecture but surrounded by modern development; nevertheless the town is well worth visiting, particularly for its splendid castle. The predecessors of **Tamworth Castle** were destroyed by the Danes in 874 and 943AD but the present structure has stood firm since Norman times and, apart from the odd ghost, has an almost homely feel about it! A Jacobean manor house was built within the circular keep and occupation has been continuous until recent times. There is now a museum in the castle and the attractive grounds are open to the public and include a garden for the blind and disabled.

Tamworth is like so much of the region with modern development and ancient heritage happily co-existing; forward-looking yet concerned with the older values of a caring and friendly society. The West Midlands is continually evolving to meet the challenges of tomorrow whilst acknowledging the traditions and achievments of the past.

Chapter Four

HANSLEY CROSS COTTAGE
Cheadle Road,
Alton,
Staffordshire ST10 4DH

Tel: 01538 702189

Close to the well known pleasure and theme park of Alton Towers is Hensley Cross Cottage, an ideal base from which to visit the many varied and interesting venues in this area. Guests enjoy the warm and cordial hospitality shown by Jean Ditchfield, who is only too delighted to offer information and details of local facilities, which include fishing, golf and walking. Bedrooms are in keeping with the modern property, they are fresh and attractive in appearance and have colour television and tea and coffee making facilities. A splendid home cooked breakfast greets guests in the tastefully decorated dining room. Various choices are available and vegetarians are catered for by prior arrangement.

USEFUL INFORMATION

OPEN; All year
CHILDREN; Welcome
CREDIT CARDS; None taken
LICENSED; No
ACCOMMODATION; 2 rooms, 1 family, 1 double/twin

DINING ROOM; Excellent home-cooked fare
Evening meal by arrangement
VEGETARIAN; Catered for by arrangement
DISABLED ACCESS; Yes, specialises
GARDEN; Spacious for your use
PETS; Yes

CROFT GUEST HOUSE
Bransford,
Worcester WR6 5JD

Tel: 01886 832227

Croft Guest House is a pleasant country house sitting in the Worcestershire Countryside. Run by Ann and Brian Porter, it is a friendly, well maintained home which dates back to the 16th and 18th centuries. The furnishings are good and all bedrooms have tea and coffee facilities and wash basins. Some are ensuite. The emphasis is on good English food, using home grown or local produce where possible. There is also a sauna and jacuzzi in which to relax. This is a very rural setting but with plenty of local pursuits around you. One which Ann and Brian organise is a wood turning course which lasts for 1 or 2 days. A very interesting skill which is not easily available. A selection of Brian's work is on sale.

USEFUL INFORMATION

OPEN; All year
CHILDREN; Welcome
CREDIT CARDS; Access/Visa
LICENSED; Residents
ACCOMMODATION; 5 rooms, 3 ensuite

DINING ROOM; Good English fare
VEGETARIAN; By arrangement
DISABLED ACCESS; No
GARDEN; In excellent order
PETS; Dogs welcome

Chapter Four

THE BOARS HEAD HOTEL
Church Street,
Bishop's Castle, Shropshire SY9 5AE

Tel: 01588 638521

Granted its first licence in 1642 the Boars Head escaped unscathed in 1645 when, during the Civil War, Royalists plundered the town. Somehow they missed out the inn in which the Roundheads were slaking their thirst! You will find the hotel in the heart of Bishop's Castle; a wonderful area, surrounded by the unspoilt beauty of the South Shropshire hills. Close to the border towns of Ludlow, Shrewsbury, Welshpool and Newtown, Bishop's Castle has many annual events. The most notable are the Agricultural Show, the lively Carnival and the festive Christmas lights - the latter is a good reason for spending a break at the Boars Head, enjoying the fun and at the same time visiting places like Ludlow to seek out the unusual Christmas present.

Inside the exposed beams and a roaring log fire in winter all add to the happy atmosphere. The bars serve Real Ale, the wine list is cosmopolitan and the beautifully cooked food is mainly traditional English. You can dine in style in Trotters Restaurant or eat informally in a pleasant dining area in the main bar. Here, in addition to daily specials, there are a range of home-made soups, fresh sandwiches, crispy Ploughmans lunches and many other dishes. For Vegetarians there are never less than three items on the menu. The 4 ensuite, well appointed bedrooms, some with exposed beams, are in the converted stable block.

USEFUL INFORMATION

OPEN; All year
CHILDREN; Yes. Cots, Highchairs, Menu
CREDIT CARDS; All major cards
LICENSED; Yes. Good wine list
PETS; Yes
RESTAURANT; Exciting menu
BAR FOOD; Wide range, home-cooked
VEGETARIAN; Always a choice
DISABLED ACCESS; Yes
ACCOMMODATION; 4 ensuite rooms

HAMPTON HOUSE,
Hampton Loade,
Chelmarsh,
Nr. Bridgnorth, Shropshire WV16 6BN
Tel: 01746 861436

To find this interesting 16th century farmhouse, travel the Highley/ Bridgnorth Road (B4555) and take the turn for Hampton Loade, Reservoir and River Severn. The signpost tells you that this is going to be an attractive place to be and upon your arrival you will not be disappointed. Here you have a farmhouse full of character and with many features dating back to the 16th century including original inglenook fireplaces and a wealth of beamed rooms. Hampton House is ideally situated for a visit or to be used as a base to explore South Shropshire. Overlooking the Severn Valley, the farm is also 300 yards off the Hampton Loade Railway Station, 400 yards from the banks of the Severn and close to the Chelmarsh Reservoir and Nature Reserve, not forgetting the passenger ferry across the Severn from Hampton Loade. It is a walkers paradise who revel in the Clee Hills, Stretton Hills or Wenlock Edge. For the less energetic the historic market town of Bridgnorth which begs to be explored, is only 6 miles away. It boasts the only Inland Cliff Railway now working in Britain. Quaint Much Wenlock is 14 miles off and the world renowned Ironbridge 18 miles. Ludlow, one of England's prettiest towns is 22 miles and Shrewsbury, the county town of Shropshire, just 28 miles. Hampton House farm consists of a livestock enterprise including a beef suckler herd and Texel sheep. You are cordially invited to tour the farm.

Within the house you will find a great welcome. It is warm and comfortable with 3 delightful guest bedrooms all with their own private bathrooms, radios, tea and coffee making facilities. You will be fed a delicious breakfast in the atmospheric dining hall with its exposed beams. In addition to the Dining Hall there is a spacious, comfortable sitting room. This is a strictly non-smoking house and you will not find a television anywhere. A thoroughly nice place to stay.

USEFUL INFORMATION

OPEN; All year
CHILDREN; Over 12 years
CREDIT CARDS;No
ACCOMMODATION; 3 ensuite rooms
PETS; No
DINING HALL;Excellent farmhouse breakfast
VEGETARIAN; Upon request
DISABLED ACCESS; No
GARDEN; Extensive

HANNIGANS FARM
Morville, Bridgnorth,
Shropshire WV16 4RN

Tel: 01746 714332

There is only one bedroom for guests in this charming 18th century house part of an arable farm, and one must consider it a privilege to stay here. Not because it is outstandingly different from other places but because Fiona Thompson who owns it and is your hostess, is a remarkable woman of many talents, not the least of which is producing her own honey and making extra special Beeswax for polishing antique furniture. In point of fact the bedroom which is ensuite is in a converted stone barn which has been done with great style and a good eye for colour. As it is all at ground level it would be suitable for wheelchairs. Television and tea/coffee making facilities are both there for your enjoyment. The farm is supplied with spring water and one wonders if this is the reason why the breakfast cup of tea tastes so especially good. Breakfast is a true farmhouse meal which is served in the main house but can be in your room if you wish. There are no evening meals but there are good restaurants, excellent pub food and a variety of other eateries within easy distance.

Although Hannigans is a mite isolated - for many people this will prove a definite bonus - it is nonetheless within easy reach of such places as the Ironbridge Gorge Museum and the Severn Valley Railway. Ludlow and Shrewsbury, both awash with history and fascinating towns, are within half an hours drive. An ideal place for a break at anytime of the year.

USEFUL INFORMATION

OPEN; All year
CHILDREN; No
CREDIT CARDS; No
ACCOMMODATION; 1 self-contained room ensuite
PETS;No
DINING ROOM; Traditional farmhouse breakfast
VEGETARIAN; By arrangement
DISABLED ACCESS;Yes
GARDEN; Yes

OLDFIELD COTTAGE
Oldfield, Bridgnorth,
Shropshire WV16 6AQ

Tel: 01746 789257

This delightful cottage parts of which date to about 1540 is the home of Eileen Reynolds whose pleasure in meeting people is evident the moment you arrive at Oldfield Cottage. The strictly non-smoking cottage is attractively furnished throughout and retains much of its original character with exposed beams, and open log fire and has 2 pretty ensuite bedrooms, complete with TV and coffee/tea making facilities, which are completely self-contained in a tastefully converted stable building with glorious views. Breakfast is served in the main house. Very convenient for those who enjoy their privacy and yet still have the benefit of not having to prepare meals. You will find Breakfast is a hearty meal in which much home produce is used. Evening meals of an equal standard can be arranged.

The large garden with lovely views over the surrounding farm-land is a great place to relax and revel in the peace and quiet. You will find the cottage situated a quarter of a mile from the B3464 Bridgnorth to Ludlow road and 4 miles from the ancient town of Bridgnorth. Oldfield Cottage makes a great base from which to explore the surrounding countryside and the fascinating towns and villages within easy reach. If you are looking for a good pub for an evening meal or a drink, Eileen recommends the local Pheasant Inn which offers an excellent range of home cooked inexpensive evening meals.

USEFUL INFORMATION

OPEN; All year
CHILDREN; Welcome
CREDIT CARDS; None taken
ACCOMMODATION; 2 twin rooms ensuite
GARDEN; Yes

DINING ROOM; Traditional breakfast
Evening meals by arrangement
VEGETARIAN; Upon request
DISABLED ACCESS; Yes
PETS; By arrangement

Chapter Four

BARN HOUSE
152 High Street,
Broadway, Worcestershire WR12 7AJ

Tel: 01386 858633

Barn House is a large 17th century building which has that wonderful mellow stone that only the Cotswolds produce. It is gracious, elegant and looks as though it has been there for ever amidst its 16 acres of Gardens and Paddocks. The house offers 5 charming double and twin bedded rooms beautifully and comfortably furnished with attractive colour co-ordinated drapes and bed covers. Each room has radio, television and a tea and coffee tray. There are log fires everywhere and the Barn Rooms with it's fabulous log fire and the adjacent library and drawing room are all open for guests to use as are the 16 acres of gardens, walks, orchards and flower gardens. The Stables and Paddocks could accommodate people who are coming to the area for show or hunting with a little bit of notice and subject to a satisfactory agreement over cost and facilities. Two largeout door kennels are available for animals used to such accommodation and which would not create a nuisance to neighbours by excessive barking. The large heated swimming pool fully tiled with underwater lights in it's own accommodation has it's own changing rooms and is open from March 1st to October 1st. each year. A delicious breakfast is served every day. Good places in which to eat abound in the Broadway area and subject to the availability of a driver it is possible to take people out in the evenings and collect them. A truly delightful place to stay, the owner Jane Ricketts can also offer 1 and 2 bedroom cottages in Broadway and surrounding villages.

USEFUL INFORMATION

OPEN; All year
CHILDREN; Well behaved welcome
CREDIT CARDS; None taken
ACCOMMODATION; 5 bedrooms
PETS; Outside kennels

DINING ROOM; Delicious breakfast. Dinner by arrangement
VEGETARIAN; Upon request
DISABLED ACCESS; No

BROOK HOUSE
Station Road, Broadway,
Worcestershire WR12 7DE

Tel: 01386 852313

Broadway is the most appealing village. It has lovely warm stone buildings with pretty antique shops full of curios. The 16th century hostelry the Lygon Arms was a resting place for Cromwell. Not far from Broadway you will come across the Museum of Toys, which has approximately 800 teddy bears in its collection. In this attractive village is Brook House a late 19th century property of immense charm, although the furnishings are modern it does not take away any of the character. The 5 guest rooms provide a very comfortable place to stay, 2 of the rooms are ensuite, they all have TV and a complimentary tea and coffee tray. A well kept house with fresh flowers add that special touch. Breakfast is a traditional full English and plenty of it, there is no evening meal, however, there are plenty of restaurants and pubs in the surrounding vicinity. The area here abounds with things to do and places to go. The local railway station is a great tourist attraction. It is a restored section of the old Cheltenham to Honeybourne line. At Toddington you can take an 8 mile round trip to Winchcombe. Barnfield Cider Mill is well worth a visit. For the energetic there is fishing, golf, riding and plenty of walking in the wonderful countryside.

USEFUL INFORMATION

OPEN; All year except Christmas
CHILDREN; Welcome
CREDIT CARDS; None taken
LICENSED; No
ACCOMMODATION; 5 rooms, 2 ensuite, 2 double, 1 family, 1 twin, 1 single

DINING ROOM; Good home-cooking
No evening meal
VEGETARIAN; Catered for
DISABLED ACCESS; No
GARDEN; Yes
PETS; Yes

Chapter Four

LEASOW HOUSE
Laverton Meadows, Broadway,
Worcestershire WR12 7NA

Tel: 01386 584526

    Built in the early part of the 17th century, this traditionally furnished and friendly Cotswold stone farmhouse is ideally situated on the periphery of the escarpment in open countryside. Hosts Barbara and Gordon Meekings, offer a very warm and friendly welcome to all their guests, many of whom converge from all parts of the world to soak up the glorious atmosphere of this picturesque and scenic area. The accommodation is a sheer delight offering spacious and tastefully decorated ensuite bedrooms, each with its own individual style and complimented by subtle and pastel shaded soft furnishings, colour TV, direct dial telephone and tea and coffee making facilities are included. Beamed ceilings are prominent and none more so than in the delightfully furnished dining room. The perfect setting for your hosts to display their culinary prowess which are expertly executed. True traditional English fare is served and vegetarians very well catered for. A complimentary drinks tray is offered to guests in the sophisticated library with its comfortable leather suites and excellent selection of books, the perfect setting for a relaxed evening. Your hosts wish to ensure that your stay will be as relaxed and informal as possible and guests will be given their own key, ensuring no limitations on coming or going. A most comprehensive and informative book has been compiled for visitors explaining all there is to know about this area, ordinance survey maps and guide books may be borrowed. There are many places of interest to visit either by car or on foot, and where better to start than the local village of Broadway. A short distance from Leasow House you will find a 12 acre grass and woodland Nature Trail from which there are superb views. There is an excellent selection of local pubs and eateries offering a variety of cuisines including English, Greek and Indian. Buckland, Stanton and Stanway are delightful villages for a great 'walking' day out, and Stanway House has an outstanding Jacobean Manor with a magnificent 14th century tithe barn, well worth a visit. Stow-on-the-Wold has a veritable myriad of antique shops and art galleries set around a market square. The town of Bourton-on-the-Water with the River Winrush flowing through the main street, plenty to do here with a motor museum, gardens, houses, exotic birds and a superb model village recreated in fine detail. Further local facilities to be found nearby include National Trust properties, golf, horse riding and fishing.

USEFUL INFORMATION

OPEN; All year
CHILDREN; Welcome
CREDIT CARDS; Yes, not Diners
LICENSED; None taken
ACCOMMODATION; 7 ensuite rooms
DINING ROOM; Excellent home cooking
VEGETARIAN; Catered for
DISABLED ACCESS; Yes
GARDEN; Large cultivated garden
PETS; Yes

TUDOR COTTAGE
High Street, Broadway,
Worcestershire WR12 7DT
Tel: 01386 852674

Each room in this enchanting 17th century cottage has its own very definite character. Partly due to the age of the building it is full of interest but much of its charm has been enhanced by the loving care given to it by Jane and Frank Allen, the owners. It is not easy to instal the comforts that we require today in such an old house but very skilfully each of the three bedrooms has been made ensuite and is delightful with traditional colour co-ordinated drapes and covers. One of the rooms has a splendid fourposter and all have TV, Radio, Hair dryers and a well-stocked beverage tray. Breakfast is served in a pretty dining room where everything comes to the table freshly cooked and to your choice. Plentiful coffee and tea, many fresh fruit dishes, lashings of toast, butter and preserves make it a meal to remember. Broadway is very special in its own right and is also so conveniently placed for all sorts of other places of interest in the Cotswolds. Whilst the summer months are wonderful, many people find the peace of autumn and winter days more relaxing. Tudor Cottage is open all the year round except for Christmas and its warmth and comfort would be particularly good for the out of season months.

USEFUL INFORMATION
OPEN; All year except Christmas
CHILDREN; Welcome
CREDIT CARDS; None taken
ACCOMMODATION; 3 ensuite rooms
DINING ROOM; Super breakfast
No evening meal
DISABLED ACCESS; No
PETS; Welcome

BELVEDERE
Burway Road, Church Stretton,
Shropshire SY6 6DP
Tel/Fax: 01694 722232

This highly recommended Guest House has a host of awards, English Tourist Board '3 Crowns Commended', RAC 'Acclaimed' and the AA '4Q Selected', its reputation goes before it. Belvedere Guest House is an impressive turn of the century 3 storey property surrounded by beautiful gardens and clothed in Ivy. Don and Rita Rogers have created a warm and friendly house with a relaxed and informal atmosphere, giving an excellent service. There are 12 guest bedrooms with television, hair dryer, clock/radio and a tea and coffee tray. 6 of the rooms have ensuite facilities. There are 3 separate toilet and shower rooms and a bathroom. Also for your use are 2 reading rooms with a large selection of books and a television lounge. A full English breakfast is served in the dining room. Packed lunches are available for your days outing. Evening meal is by arrangement, and the Belvedere's residential licence means that you may enjoy a glass of wine or beer with your meal. Countryside around the Guest House is scenic indeed, a few minutes walk away and you are strolling along an unspoilt valley. Golf, fishing, riding, cycling and for a real thrill gliding, are all available and within easy reach.

USEFUL INFORMATION
OPEN; All year
CHILDREN; Welcome, cots available
CREDIT CARDS; Access and Visa
LICENSED; Residential
ACCOMMODATION; 12 rooms, 6 ensuite, 4 double, 3 twin, 3 single, 2 family
DINING ROOM; Good home-cooking, evening meal by arrangement, + packed lunches
VEGETARIAN; Catered for
DISABLED ACCESS; No
GARDEN; Yes
PETS; Yes, by arrangement

Chapter Four

THE WHITE HOUSE HOTEL & RESTAURANT
*Marquis Drive, Off Penkridge Bank Road,
Hednesford, Cannock Chase,
Staffordshire WS12 4 PR*

Tel: 01543 422712

Located in an area of outstanding natural beauty and with a long and colourful history, The White House is one of the most exciting hotel finds for miles around. It stands in the heart of Cannock Chase and yet it remains within easy reach of the road and rail network: marvellous for people on business and absolutely right for visitors wanting to discover this fascinating part of Staffordshire. Visitors find the hotel especially good because when they have finished a trip to one of the nearby towns and shopping areas, afternoon tea provides a welcome relaxation back at the hotel. Strolling across the Chase is another favourite pastime and certainly manages to develop an appetite for one of the White House's excellent lunches. Becoming more and more popular is the 'Weekend Special' offered by the hotel when two people for the small cost of one hundred and sixty five pounds, can arrive on Friday evening, enjoy dinner, sleep in one of the luxury bedrooms, enjoying breakfast and an excellent dinner on Saturday night, leaving after Sunday breakfast.

Run professionally by people who know their business and do not compromise on standards, yet at the same time create a welcoming, relaxed atmosphere, the interior of The White House is constantly being upgraded and extended to offer even better facilitities than it has now, if th at is possible. The reception rooms, restaurant and bar are attractively furnished and the food in the restaurant is well known locally for its high standard. The chef is clearly talented and mixes the menu with Continetal and traditional English dishes. Vegetarians are catered for and other diets can be arranged upon request. The Marquis Suite and the Syndicate room are used constantly for conferences, small meetings and private parties. Like everything else at The White House, the facilities are excellent and careful attention is paid to the needs of delegates. Phase two of the alterations in the hotel will see a garden added as well as more luxury bedrooms. Certainly a hotel to put on your list of places to stay.

USEFUL INFORMATION

OPEN; All year
CHILDREN; Yes
CREDIT CARDS; All major
LICENSED; Yes
ACCOMMODATION; 6 ensuite rooms

RESTAURANT; Innovative menu. Open to non-Residents
VEGETARIAN; Yes + other diets by arrangement
DISABLED ACCESS; Yes. Ground floor
PETS; No

COURT FARM
Gretton, Church Stretton,
Shropshire SY6 7HU

Tel: 01694 771219

Church Stretton became a health resort in the late 19th century, the wealth helped to build the wonderful half-timbered houses. As you travel along the B4371 south, you arrive in the village of Hope Bowdler, here follow the signs for Cardington, the hamlet of Gretton is just outside the village, surrounded by glorious countryside, and here you will find Court Farm. A working farm of some 325 acres, farming beef cattle, sheep and cereals, it is owned and worked by the Norris family. The family have lived in the area for over 500 years, Barbara says the continuity reflects the sense of rural tradition that is a feature of the Court Farm atmosphere, and what an atmosphere. It is warm, friendly and relaxing. A complimentary tea awaits as you arrive at this delightful farm. The furnishings are traditional farmhouse, which all go to enhance this 16th/17th century stone built Tudor property. The bedrooms are charming and are exquisitely furnished with period pieces, the double room has a magnificent brass bed and a private bathroom. The twin rooms are both ensuite. A single room is also available. All the rooms are well appointed with shaver point, hair dryer, television, radio, complimentary toiletries and bathrobes, there is also a tea and coffee tray. The guests sitting room is very cosy with an inglenook fireplace, television and comfortable sofa and chairs. All meals are prepared by Barbara using fresh local ingredients and home-grown produce. Breakfast is a hearty full English meal with several choices. Evening meals are by arrangement, the 3 course menu combines the best of English food with some continental dishes. Both meals are served in the attractive dining room.

Court Farm also has a self-contained luxurious barn conversion adjacent to the farmhouse. It has a lovely oak timbered gallery, staircase and landing. The bedroom, bathroom, sitting room and kitchen are all beautifully appointed with high quality furnishings and antique furniture. The Stable Suite can accommodate up to 4 people on a self-catering basis or for bed and breakfast. The superb rural location is perfect for touring, walking, horse riding and painting with such wonderful scenery, you are sure to leave here reluctantly, but rested and refreshed. The award by the English Tourist Board of '3 Crown Highly Commended' is rightly deserved.

USEFUL INFORMATION

OPEN; February-November
CHILDREN; Over 14 years
CREDIT CARDS; None taken
ACCOMMODATION; 3 ensuite rooms Plus a self-catering cottage sleeping up to 4
DINING ROOM; Traditional farmhouse cooking. Fresh local produce, home grown
DISABLED ACCESS; No
GARDEN; Mature and landscaped
PETS; No
NO SMOKING

Chapter Four

WOOLSTON FARM
Church Stretton,
Shropshire SY6 6QD

Tel: 01694 781201

Woolston Farm is a charming 17th century, red brick, Victorian farmhouse, home to Joanna and Max Brereton. This is a working farm with about 350 acres used for mixed farming of sheep, cattle and arable. With all this in mind, Joanna and Max still find the time to make their guests feel welcome and at home in their delightful, warm, informal surroundings. Children are very welcome here, and they are permitted to walk round the farm seeing the various animals and the homes they inhabit. For the more 'adult' visitor there is freshwater fishing available on the farm, and extensive walks in the beautiful countryside all around, mean that you will never have a dull moment here! It is an ideal situation for painting, horse riding and really, all outdoor sports.

The house itself is furnished in period style with pretty country farmhouse additions making this a real home from home. Add this to the friendly, relaxed atmosphere and you are sure to find yourself returning again and again, as so many of their guests do! There are three spacious bedrooms, two of which are ensuite, and all having outstanding panoramic views over the pretty Wistanstow village. Breakfast is a hearty farmhouse affair with vegetarians catered for. An evening meal can be arranged, but there is also a good local village pub which serves an agreeable variety of food and ales (the pub brews its own beer!) What more can one ask?

USEFUL INFORMATION

OPEN: Easter-Oct inc.
CHILDREN: Most welcome
CREDIT CARDS: None taken
LICENSED: No
ACCOMMODATION: 3 rooms, 2 ensuite 2 double, 1 twin

DINING ROOM: Evening meal by arrangement
VEGETARIAN: Catered for
DISABLED ACCESS: No
GARDEN: With seating area
PETS: By arrangement

LITTLE LIGHTWOOD FARM
Lightwood Lane,
Cotheridge, Worcestershire WR6 5LT

Tel: 01905 333236

Here you have a choice and either will give you a wonderful place in which to stay for a holiday or for a short break. Little Lightwood Farm is owned and run by Richard and Vee Rodgers and on the bed and breakfast front they offer you the choice of three attractive and well-appointed ensuite bedrooms all with TV and a plentiful tea and coffee tray. Breakfast is a typical Farmhouse meal complete with fresh eggs as well as the addition of fresh fruit and cheese. The latter is actually made on the farm and is a process the Rodgers are happy to show you. The second option is either a chalet or one of the two detached bungalows - all equally well furnished and equipped with all that you need to give you a contented stay.

Little Lightwood Farm is an excellent base from which to set off each day to discover the delights of one of Englands least spoiled counties. The glorious Malvern Hills are only 8 miles away and from there you get tremendous views over the Teme Valley. The two great cathedrals of Worcester and Hereford are within easy distance and so are many other fascinating places. Locally there is fishing, riding, golf, walking and swimming. A great place to stay at any time of the year.

USEFUL INFORMATION
OPEN; All year
DINING ROOM; Traditional farmhouse breakfast
CHILDREN; 'Welcome
DISABLED ACCESS; No
CREDIT CARDS; None taken
PETS; No
ACCOMMODATION; 3 ensuite rooms 1 chalet. 2 detached bungalows
GARDEN; Yes. Wonderful views

KILMORY
Bradlow, Ledbury,
Herefordshire HR8 1JF
Tel: 01531 631951

This beautiful bungalow, built from brick that blends into the Malvern Hills, sits in an acre of garden with magnificent, breathtaking views of the hills. The gardens themselves are wonderful with lawns, shrubs, borders and terraces. There is a patio built in the higher part where you can just relax and enjoy the view. All rooms are very nicely furnished with TV, tea and coffee as standard. Breakfast is a sumptuous affair with many choices and is served in the elegant guest dining room. This lovely rural setting is ideal for touring and you are sure to enjoy your stay!

USEFUL INFORMATION
OPEN: All Year
BREAKFAST: Traditional English
CHILDREN: Over 14yrs.
VEGETARIAN: Yes
PETS: No
DISABLED ACCESS: Yes-easy access
CREDIT CARDS: None Taken
GARDEN: Beautifully Kept
ACCOMMODATION: 2 rooms en suite - This is a **NO SMOKING** home!

Chapter Four

HESTERWORTH HOLIDAYS
*Hesterworth, Hopesay,
Craven Arms,
Shropshire SY7 8EX*

Tel: 01588 660487

    Shropshire is full of small villages and hamlets in some of England's most beautiful countryside, one of these small villages is Hopesay. It lies in an area of outstanding natural beauty in theShropshire hills. In this charming place is Hesterworth a very elegant Victorian house built around a 150 years ago, encompassed by trees, fields, stream, pond and garden amounting to 12 acres. This stunning property emanates peace, tranquillity and friendliness, reiterated by your host Sheila Davies. The house is divided into very attractive cottages/flats, and can be used as self-catering accommodation or bed and breakfast. Each cottage is named after a local hill and has a character of its own, they are comfortably furnished, fully carpeted they also have colour television, and a tea and coffee tray. Three of the flats are in the house, five are next to the house situated around a small courtyard, and three are beyond the courtyard, each sleeping between 2 and 8 persons. They all have sitting rooms, well equipped kitchens, bathrooms and bedrooms. One of the cottages has wide doorways to make wheelchair access easy, and another is on the ground floor. Meals can be ordered and delivered to your accommodation on arrival, there are at least 7 delicious dishes to choose from, all served with potatoes and vegetables, plus 3 desserts. The large dining room is where you are served a delicious full English or Continental breakfast, and evening meals, at a reasonable price, can also be taken in here. Hesterworth is licensed and they have a particularly fine range of wines at competitive prices.

    If you like castles, country houses and gardens, then Hesterworth is the place for you. This is a wonderful centre for the walker, birdwatcher or those who simply love the countryside. The grounds and gardens are magnificent and guests are more than welcome to wander around, or use the grass badminton court. As you drive up the leafy lane towards the house and catch your first glimpse of it, you will be more that satisfied with your choice. It will be a lot harder driving back the other way to go home.

USEFUL INFORMATION

OPEN; All year
CHILDREN; Very welcome
CREDIT CARDS; None taken
LICENSED; Yes
ACCOMMODATION; 11 cottages/ flats for self-catering and Bed & Breakfast

DINING ROOM; Delicious breakfast. 2 or 3 course evening meal available.
DISABLED ACCESS; Two ground floor cottage and one with wide doors for wheelchair access
GARDEN; With grass badminton court,
PETS; By arrangement

SLINDON HOUSE FARM
Slindon, Eccleshall,
Staffordshire ST21 6LX
Tel: 01782 791237

Slindon House Farm is a working farm run by Mr & Mrs Bonsall and their family. The large farmhouse is impressive indeed and is a welcoming sight as you approach up the long gravel driveway, there is a safe parking area infront of the house. The house was built approximately 200-250 years ago of red brick and has lovely Georgian windows which look out across open countryside. Slindon is a typical farmhouse with large comfortable rooms and high ceilings with a few squeaky floorboards to add to the character. The furnishings are antique or old English and compliment the house immensely. The 2 bedrooms, 1 of which is ensuite, are attractive and cosy, they both have tea and coffee making facilities and those wonderful views of fields and trees. There is a lounge with a colour television for your use. In the mornings Helen will serve an excellent farmhouse full English breakfast, and if arranged beforehand an evening meal will beprovided. Not far from the farm is the 13th century Eccleshall Castle with its 9 sided tower set amongst the ruins, the moat walls surround the lovely formal gardens. Cannock Chase is well worth a visit, the country park is full of fallow and red deer, which wander around the forest. There are canal trips from Stone, and Royal Doulton and Wedgwood Museums in Stoke. The Bonsall family are looking forward to meeting you at their warm and friendly home.

USEFUL INFORMATION

OPEN; All year
CHILDREN; Welcome
CREDIT CARDS; None taken
LICENSED; No
ACCOMMODATION; 2 rooms, 1 doubl, 1 twin, 1 ensuitee
DINING ROOM; Farmhouse cooking
VEGETARIAN; Catered for
DISABLED ACCESS; No
GARDEN; Spacious
PETS; No

LADYMEADOW FARM
Luston, Leominster,
Herefordshire HR6 OAS

Tel: 01568 780262

Ladymeadow Farm is an impressive sight as you approach up the private drive, this large substantial house, which is part half-timbered and part mellow brick, was built in 1650 and retains a lot of it's original character. Ladymeadow is a 290 acre working beef and arable farm, which guests are very welcome to look around. The bedrooms of the farmhouse are furnished in a traditional style as are the guest lounge and dining room. Breakfast is a traditional English meal and plenty of it. The beamed rooms have splendid views over the peaceful countryside. Janet and Reg Ruell are members of the Caravan Club, and provide a site for 5 caravans in their lovely orchard.

USEFUL INFORMATION

OPEN; All year except Christmas
CHILDREN; Welcome
CREDIT CARDS; None taken
LICENSED; No
ACCOMMODATION; 3 rooms
DINING ROOM; Traditional English fare
VEGETARIAN; Catered for
DISABLED ACCESS; Not really
GARDEN; Very pleasant
PETS; No

Chapter Four

SANDRENE
Tewkesbury Road, Eckington,
Nr. Pershore, Worcestershire
WR10 3AW
Tel: 01386 750756

A quiet homely country retreat offering a relaxed and informal atmosphere in comfortable and cheerful surroundings with glorious views over a rural landscape. Mrs. Andrews is a very experienced landlady and well aware of the demands of guests and therefore caters accordingly. The house was built some 5 years ago and is encompassed by delightful and well manicured gardens with ample parking space. The bedrooms are beautifully furnished in golden pine with lovely private bathrooms, and each room enjoys colour TV, radio and a tea and coffee tray. Full English breakfast, well presented, will set you up for the day. Evening meals are not served but locally available are a variety of inns and restaurants, two within a couple of minutes walk. Situated close to the River Avon, fishing and boating are accessible with extensive riverside and country walks, horse riding and golf. Being on the borders of the Cotswolds there are countless places of interest to visit nearby. Tewkesbury and Pershore are only a 10 minute drive and Cheltenham, Evesham and Worcester are but a 20 minute drive away. A full range of leaflets on where to go, what to see etc. are always kept in the rooms.

USEFUL INFORMATION
OPEN; All year
CHILDREN; Welcome
CREDIT CARDS; None taken
ACCOMMODATION; 1 double room with private bath/shower, 1 single room with private shower. Plus cot and Z-bed available for children
DINING ROOM; Breakfast only
DISABLED ACCESS; No
GARDEN; Yes very pretty
PETS; Yes

CLEVELANDS
41 Alexandra Road, Malvern,
Worcestershire WR14 1HE

Tel: 01684 572164

The Malvern Hills seem to descend into the back garden of this elegant Edwardian house, set in a quiet wooded residential area of Malvern where the views are good. The rooms all have Victorian/Edwardian style furnishings and are well equipped. They are extremely comfortable and airy, and there is a fine TV lounge and dining room. Breakfast is Traditional English, but Margaret Stocks (joint owner) is more than happy to cater for special diets and vegetarians. Malvern Town is an excellent centre for both business and pleasure, within easy access to road and railway, and Clevelands provides the perfect setting after a busy day's activities.

USEFUL INFORMATION
OPEN; All year
CHILDREN; Welcome
CREDIT CARDS; None taken
LICENSED; No
ACCOMMODATION; 3 rooms, 1 twin, 2 singles
DINING ROOM; Traditional English fare
VEGETARIAN; Catered for
DISABLED ACCESS; No
GARDEN; Excellent condition
PETS; No

CHURCH HOUSE
Greenhill Park Road,
Evesham,
Worcester WR11 4NL

Tel: 01386 40498

'...one of the authors favourite Bed and Breakfast is the Church House at Evesham...' Harvey Elliot, Travel Correspondent, The Times. '...Church House a beautiful Victorian country home...so superior in service, atmosphere and furnishings that I would like to recommend it to other travellers...'. Recommendations like these are typical of many heaped upon Veronica and Michael Shaw, reflecting the huge popularity of this gracious country home. Sitting atop Greenhill overlooking the historic Avonside town of Evesham, it is an ideal centre for discovering the magnetism of this area. Built in the Victorian era all the rooms are spacious and the furniture is antique in keeping with the age of the property, and yet it provides the creature comforts of the modern day being centrally heated. Each bedroom is beautifully appointed with ensuite shower/bathrooms, colour TV, tea and coffee tray, hair dryers and additional small indulgences, all guaranteed to make your stay that little bit special. The dining room offers a delicious breakfast selection freshly prepared including local produce when available. Log fires add a wonderful atmosphere to this home. Also fluent French and Spanish are spoken by Veronica. Local facilities are varied and many, the angler is well catered for, and for those wishing to indulge in a round of golf your hosts will point you in the right direction. Many historical places of interest are to be found, Worcester offers a wealth of history including the Cathedral dated from the 11th century. The Dyson Perrins Museum is a wonderful insight to local porcelain from the 18th century to present day, and a visit to the Tudor House Museum is a fascinating sojourn. Bradfield House Glass Museum near Dudley displaying glass making from Roman times and still with a glass theme, there is the Brierley Crystal and Edinburgh Crystal factory, all situated in the same area. Bournville created by the Cadbury Brothers is now the residence of Cadbury World and if you like chocolate you'll love this venue. Spanning centuries is a collection of historic buildings includes a chain making shop and a working windmill, this fascinating assemblage is to be found at Avoncroft on the A38 near Bromsgrove. South east of Evesham are the glorious golden stone villages of the Cotswolds, wonderful walks, fascinating antique shops and a divergence of interesting and informative pleasures. In and around Bourton-on-the-Water for instance is a model village, birdland and perfumery. Close to Burford and on the A361 is the Cotswold Wildlife Park.

USEFUL INFORMATION

OPEN; All year
CHILDREN; Welcome
CREDIT CARDS; None taken
LICENSED; No
ACCOMMODATION; 3 rooms, 1 twin, 1 single, 1 double/family all ensuite

DINING ROOM; Full traditional breakfast with variations
VEGETARIAN; Catered for
DISABLED ACCESS; No
GARDEN; Yes
PETS; Within reason

Chapter Four

FELTON HOUSE
Felton,
Herefordshire HR1 3PH

Tel: 01432 820366

Felton House has immense character, in a tranquil setting of beautiful gardens, set in the rich agricultural land of Herefordshire. With views to the Welsh hills, the Victorain/Edwardian character of this house settles nicely in the Herefordshire countryside and Welsh borderlands. For 5,000 years there have been people living in Felton; evidenced by the Bronze Age Woodhenge, the recording in the Domesday Book of 1086, and the church which has been maintained since 1556. Felton House was built in 1851 with the Verger's Cottage (now let for holidays) soon after. The house actually forms the heart of Felton with the rest being made up of 6 farms and cottages. There are approximately 80 people in the parish! Marjorie and Brian Roby arrived in 1977 and have restored the house to it's former glory. Everything is in keeping with it's Victorian/Edwardian heritage and has been thoughtfully and immaculately renovated. Brian takes charge of the gardens, which are just over 3 acres in size, and has extensively remodelled them, planting trees and shrubs, making it a haven of quiet spots where visitors can sit and relax. There is a garden stage which was used between 1919 and 1939 to produce Shakespeare's plays. Actors were local characters including farm labourers and inn keepers daughters. This interesting history is all recorded in the stained glass windows of the local church. Felton House is one of those places you return to time and time again, and recommend to friends. This has everything to do with the hospitality extended by Marjorie and Brian who do all they possibly can to make you welcome. You sleep in an 18th century four-poster bed or an Edwardian brass bed or even a Victorian mahogany half tester! Most rooms have either private bathrooms or ensuite shower rooms, and complimentary refreshments are provided. These can also be taken in the garden room, the sitting room, the library or the garden. The dining room is a beautiful relaxing room where breakfast is served and has a history all of it's own. You would have to stay at least two weeks to sample everything on the menu. All tastes are catered for; from full English to Continental to vegetarian. Local fresh produce is used where possible. The local inns, one within walking distance, serve excellent evening meals. A unique service which just rounds off the delights of this country house is the free route planning service that Marjorie and Brian offer. Whether your interest be castles, antiques, food, golf or any other, they will give helpful advice and plan your day (or whole holiday) as you require. This is an excellent holiday retreat with service and surroundings difficult to surpass.

USEFUL INFORMATION

OPEN; All year
CHILDREN; Welcome, babysitting service
CREDIT CARDS; None taken
LICENSED; No
ACCOMMODATION; 4 rooms
DINING ROOM; Breakfasts for all tastes
VEGETARIAN; Catered for
DISABLED ACCESS; Restricted
GARDEN; 3 acres, beautifully kept
PETS; Welcome

BROUGHTON MANOR
Mill Lane, Broughton Hackett,
Worcester WR7 4BB

Tel: 01905 381504

Unusually Broughton Manor is a house built purposely for Bed and Breakfast. Built on the site of an old Brickworks it was designed by the owner Hilary Morgan and is now a part of a working farm with hundreds of sheep. It is a truly delightful place and you will find Hilary Morgan both charming and helpful. Strictly non-smoking, all the rooms are light and airy and two of the three bedrooms are ensuite whilst the other has a private bathroom. All the rooms have colour TV and tea/coffee making facilities. Hair dryers, irons, shoe cleaning materials are all available. There is a large comfortable lounge and a separate dining area in which a super, sustaining breakfast is served every day. Staying here cannot be too highly recommended and many people return for more than one visit. It is not unusual to find more than one nationality staying here. Apart from the happy atmosphere of the house it does have the virtue of being set in such a delightful spot. Local footpaths wend their way alongside the Bowbrook River which leads into the Avon. Its not unusual to see kingfishers near the local weir and sometimes foxes venture onto the lawns. Within easy reach one can play golf, go Clay Pigeon shooting or ride. Fishing is available within 100 yards. Whilst no evening meal is available the local pub is within a few minutes walk, and there are numerous excellent eating houses in the locality.

USEFUL INFORMATION
OPEN; All year   **DINING ROOM;** Full English breakfast
CHILDREN; By arrangement   **VEGETARIAN;** Catered for
CREDIT CARDS; None taken   **DISABLED ACCESS;** No
ACCOMMODATION; 3 rooms 2 ensuite 1 private bathroom
N.B. This is a non-smoking establishment.

THE VAULD HOUSE FARM
The Vauld, Nr. Marden,
Herefordshire HR1 3HA
Tel: 01568 797347

Vauld House Farm is a beautiful farmhouse in a rural setting with very attractive gardens. There are ducks and moorhens in the lake which is shaded by a cascading weeping willow. The accommodation is of excellent regency style with comfortable bedrooms and a pleasant lounge. Food is served in the beamed, period furnished, dining room which overlooks the garden and a full English breakfast starts the day. Evening meal is optional and is an imaginative four course dinner using seasonal local produce. There is also self catering accommodation which has been thoughtfully renovated and although having every modern facility, has not lost the charm of an age gone by.

USEFUL INFORMATION
OPEN: All Year   **RESTAURANT:** English Farmhouse Cuisine
CHILDREN: Welcome   **VEGETARIAN:** Yes
PETS: By Arrangement   **DISABLED ACCESS:** Yes
CREDIT CARDS: None Taken   **GARDEN:** Extremely Nice
ACCOMMODATION: Self Catering and Farmhouse

Chapter Four

THE SWAN AT HAY HOTEL,
Church Street,
Hay on Wye, Hereford HR3 5DQ

Tel: 01497 821188
Fax: 01497 821424

For centuries this corner of Hay has been the site of the town's principal coaching inn. The present building stems from 1821. Today this elegant building has been transformed under the careful hands of Rosemary and Colin Vaughan who came here in 1987 and have spent the ensuing years making The Swan a luxurious 3 star hotel with every modern facility one could wish for. At the same time nothing but praise can be showered upon them for managing to retain everything that was good from the past. Eighteen ensuite bedrooms are equipped with colour television and radio, tea and coffee making facilities, hair dryer and safe. The colour schemes are charming and each room is individually furnished. After a superb night's sleep you come down to start the day with one of The Swan's legendary Welsh breakfasts.

Food is all important and is prepared in the hotel by chefs who obviously love their jobs. The Cygnet Restaurant, beautifully appointed, has a delicious a la carte menu whilst less formal meals are served in the Mallard Room. Whichever menu you choose to have including the separate vegetarian choice has an emphasis on fine food prepared with care. The addition of home-made bread and cakes, fresh local produce and garden herbs ensures that every meal is memorable. You will find the Drakes Bar where the locals meet, friendly and the lounge restful.

Hay On Wye, known as the 'Book Town' with dozens of antiquarian bookshops, a maze of streets and alleys little changed from medieval times, is a market town on the Welsh border. It is at the heart of the territory of the ancient Marcher Lords whose ruined abbeys and castles dot the surrounding countryside. Away from Hay take a look at the spectacular show caves at Dan-yr-Ogof, the priceless Mappa Mundi in Hereford or guided tours of the Royal Welsh crystal factory. Stay a little longer at The Swan - and who would not, given the opportunity, and you will have time to discover the hidden valley below nearby Hergest Ridge with its fabulous Rhododendron garden. Make The Swan your base for whatever reason and you will never regret it.

USEFUL INFORMATION

OPEN; All year
CHILDREN; Welcome
CREDIT CARDS; All major cards
LICENSED; Yes
ACCOMMODATION; 18 ensuite rooms
PETS; Dogs by arrangement

RESTAURANT; Superb a la carte menu
BAR MEALS; Wide range
VEGETARIAN; Yes, own menu
DISABLED ACCESS; No facilities
GARDEN; Yes, flowers, shrubs, 2 tiered Lawns

RUXTON FARM
*Kings Caple, Hereford
HR1 4TX*

Tel: 01432 840493

Within the glorious setting of the Wye Valley is located the 17th century Ruxton Farm, renowned for its Equestrian Centre. Here horses and their riders are trained in the expertise of Showjumping, Eventing and the demands of Dressage. This is the predominant enterprise of this 20 acre setting, but it is also a wonderful location for holiday accommodation, and here the owner Milly Slater, offers her guests an exceedingly warm welcome when they arrive. On entering the house of Ruxton Farm, one will be aware of the glorious exposed beams and a wonderful staircase, circa 1700, which leads up to the galleried landing. Throughout the furniture is of a very high standard and in harmony with the building. The bedrooms are bright and spacious and very tastefully furnished, and each with its personal ensuite shower and toilet, towels are supplied and each room has tea and coffee making facilities. Meals are served in the hall and are of traditional English fare, however if requested vegetarian and continental food will be provided. A lovely wood burning stove has been installed in the lounge and is a wonderful focal point along with the colour television for your relaxation. Close to the house is ample off road parking. Within half a mile is the local post office and public house. Local facilities for those who enjoy fishing are available along 80 yards or so of the River Wye, there are golf courses and riding conveniently situated close by. This is a wonderful area central to so many delightful and charming towns and villages each with its own history and many with eye catching thatched roofs and cottage gardens. The ancient Forest of Dean located as it is twixt the Rivers of the Wye and Severn, ideal for long idyllic walks and plenty of flora and fauna. Travel a little further and visit the Slimbridge Trust, the fascinating bird sanctuary founded by the late Sir Peter Scott. The olde worlde town of Tewksbury with its own special architecture is sure to impress, and the City of Hereford with its 11th century Cathedral, this city was once the Saxon Capital, and has many places of interest to visit including the Fragrant Gardens, Water Gardens and several museums. Stokesay Castle with a wonderful fortified Manor House on the A49 north of Hereford is well worth an inspection.

USEFUL INFORMATION

OPEN; *All year*
CHILDREN; *Welcome*
CREDIT CARDS; *None taken*
LICENSED; *No*
ACCOMMODATION; *3 ensuite rooms*

DINING ROOM; *Traditional English fare*
No evening meal
VEGETARIAN; *Catered for*
DISABLED ACCESS; *Not really*
GARDENS; *Yes, lovely lawns*

Chapter Four

MILL COTTAGE
Canon Frome, Ledbury,
Herefordshire HR8 2TD

Tel: 01531 670506

    Mill Cottage, which is part of Riverside Cottages situated in a most peaceful spot in the Frome Valley, away from the main roads, though within easy reach of Ledbury, Hereford and Malvern, is the main house of this small, delightful group and in it Julian and Lorna Rutherford offer bed and breakfast in two large en-suite bedrooms, each with colour TV's and tea and coffee making facilities. One has a four-poster bed and the other twin beds. There is a private guest lounge with a log fire in a self-contained spacious wing with views towards the river. No evening meal is served but breakfast is a meal to relish , freshly cooked and with a choice. The five-acre water gardens in which you are welcome to roam, are bisected by the River Frome. There are further streams and a mill pool. Footpaths, stepping stones and bridges lead around an interesting wooded garden with an abundance of wildlife.
    Two other cottages make up the group. These are both self-catering, superbly equipped and heated by modern night storage units supplemented by day-time electric heating. Both have colour TVs. The Swiss Cottage is situated on the bank overlooking a waterfall. From the balcony, which overhangs the river, a wide variety of wildlife can be seen, including the resident kingfishers and sometimes otters and leaping salmon if you are lucky. It is suitable for two people but probably not suitable or safe for some pets or children. Lime Cottage,which also sleeps two, is in a different part of the garden, overlooking fields at the front and a pool to one side.

USEFUL INFORMATION

OPEN; All year
CHILDREN; Welcome
ACCOMMODATION; 2 ensuite rooms
2 self-catering cottages sleeping 2
DINING ROOM; For bed & breakfast only
DISABLED ACCESS; No
GARDEN; 5 acres, beautiful
PETS; By negotiation

MOOR COURT FARM
Upper Egeleton, Nr Ledbury,
Herefordshire

Tel: 01531 670408

Home made cooking makes this country house a must. Elizabeth Godsall who runs it is a qualified cook who bakes all her own bread and cakes, and makes butter and cheese from her own Jersey cow. Don't even try to watch the waistline here! And if on a good summer evening you feel like sitting on the lawn and admiring the view then Elizabeth will serve you a Pimms just to round the evening off! Sounds like heaven! You are even welcomed on arrival with tea and cakes! Breakfast is a hearty farmhouse meal and there is a set English evening meal, again cooked by Elizabeth. Trying to get away from food, the house is beautifully furnished with antiques and dates back to 1500. It is a working traditional farm with a trout lake and duck pond and Elizabeth breeds Welsh ponies. It is surrounded by beautiful countryside with walks leading to spectacular views.

USEFUL INFORMATION
OPEN: All year
CHILDREN: Welcome
PETS: No
CREDIT CARDS: None taken
LICENSED: No
ACCOMMODATION: 3 rooms; all en suite.
RESTAURANT: Not applicable
BAR FOOD: Not applicable
VEGETARIAN: Yes
DISABLED ACCESS: No
GARDEN: Very pleasant

HIGHFIELD
Newtown, Ivington Road,
Leominster, Herefordshire HR6 8QD

Tel: 01568 613216

This elegant Edwardian accommodation is the home of Catherine and Marguerite Fothergill. Surrounded by a large garden, open farmland, and distant hills, the atmosphere is friendly and relaxed. All bedrooms are comfortable with tea and coffee. One twin room has a bathroom en-suite with W.C. The other two have wash basins and there is a shower and W.C. and a bathroom and W.C. just across the landing for the use of these two rooms only. You are asked not to smoke in the bedrooms. Residents have the use of two sitting rooms, one of which has a TV and French windows opening on to the patio, and the other has the 'tourist information library'. The two sisters enjoy cooking so all meals are a delight and they are happy to cater for everyone's taste. A wine list is available to compliment the food. Highfield is ideal for house parties of four to six people. Then they can feel really at home and the Fothergills will cater for their specific needs.

USEFUL INFORMATION
OPEN; All year
CHILDREN; By arrangement only
CREDIT CARDS; None taken
LICENSE; Residential
ACCOMMODATION; 3 pretty bedrooms
DINING ROOM; Delicious, interesting and plain fare
VEGETARIAN; Yes
DISABLED ACCESS; Not really
GARDEN; Beautifully maintained garden

Chapter Four

PRESTON PRIORY
*Ledbury,
Herefordshire HR8 2LL*

Tel: 01531 660247

You will find this imposing house on the Herefordshire-Gloucestershire border in the heart of the English countryside and near to the small and delightful market town of Ledbury. Preston Priory was formerly the rectory of Preston parish church and has the claim of being the church in which the local, famous Poet Laureate, John Masefield was baptised. It is an ideal place to stay because from here you can easily visit some breathtaking places including the MalvernHills, the Black Mountains, the Wye Valley and Cheltenham Spa - a paradise for shoppers. It is also near the historic Cathedral cities of Hereford, Worcester and Gloucester and there are many other places of historic interest.

Preston Priory was built in Victorian times and has the hallmark of the architects of those days who made the rooms light and spacious and the exterior dignified. It is a warm and friendly house in which guests are genuinely welcomed by the owner, Elizabeth Drew. There is a spacious drawing room and dining room, both for the exclusive use of guests. The bed and breakfast accommodation is in traditionally furnished rooms. One twin bedded room and one double room on the first floor, each with a wash basin, share a bathroom. On the ground floor there is a twin-bedded room with its own bathroom ensuite. This room is particularly suitable for those who have difficulty with steps and stairs as there are no steps into the house, nor on the ground floor. All the rooms have central heating, tea and coffee making facilities, hairdryers, radios and colour TV. Breakfast is a splendid meal with a choice of dishes. No evening meal is served but there are several pubs and eating places within a short driving distance.

The Priory has a wonderful garden, which is easily accessible from the house. Guests are very welcome to enjoy it and just relax taking in the peace of the countryside and admiring the pleasant views of the nearby hills. To find Preston Priory leave Ledbury on the A449 Ross road. At the roundabout take the left turn to Newent on the B4215. Preston Priory is the third house on the right after approximately half a mile.

USEFUL INFORMATION

OPEN;*All year*
CHILDREN;*Over ten years*
CREDIT CARDS;*None taken*
ACCOMMODATION; *3 rooms, 1 ensuite*
PETS; *By arrangement*

DINING ROOM;*Excellent breakfast*
VEGETARIAN;*Upon request*
DISABLED ACCESS;*Ground floor room*
GARDEN; *Extensive*

478

THE HOPTON ARMS
Ashperton, Nr. Ledbury,
Herefordshire HR8 2SE

Tel: 01531 670520

Centrally placed for a comprehensive touring holiday, Ashperton near Ledbury is the location of the 200 year old red bricked 'Hopton Arms' personally supervised by Marion Lustig. Adjacent to The Hopton Arms, is a recently converted coach house with tastefully furnished ensuite bedrooms offering comfortable and modern accommodation with colour television and radio. To the rear is a 2 ½ acre field just the place for the children to play ball and various games, equipment is supplied. There is also a childrens play area with swings, scramble net and climbing frames. In the attractive beamed and cosy bar there is an extensive menu, and the separate dining room offers a wide range of traditional dishes, special dietary needs are also catered for. The counties of Hereford, Worcester and Shropshire offer visitors a miscellany of interesting historical locations, charming thatched cottage villages, fashionable spa and market towns, and gracious cities with cathedrals dating back to the 11th century. Within driving distance is the Welland Animal and Bird Garden. Local outdoor pursuits include fishing either coarse or lake, horse riding, shooting, golf and leisurely country walks are extensive.

USEFUL INFORMATION
OPEN; All year
CHILDREN; Welcome
CREDIT CARDS; None taken
LICENSED; Yes
ACCOMMODATION; 5 ensuite rooms
GARDEN; Yes, with swings and slides
RESTAURANT; Traditional English fare
BAR FOOD; Extensive menu
VEGETARIAN; Catered for + special diets
DISABLED ACCESS; Yes
PETS; Yes

CALDEWELL,
Pershore Road, Stoulton,
Worcester WR7 4RL
Tel: 01905 840894.

Enjoy the friendly and warm hospitality of your hosts at this 19th century home known as Caldewell. The four bedrooms are delightfully furnished two having use of ensuite facilities, the other two have wash hand basins. All have central heating and a tea and coffee tray. A traditional English breakfast is served in the Victorian dining room. The 25 acre estate contains wonderful wildlif a small plant nursery and even a miniature railway. Fishing, walking and golf are available locally.

USEFUL INFORMATION
OPEN; All year
CHILDREN; Welcome
CREDIT CARDS; None taken
ACCOMMODATION; 4 rooms, 2 ensuite, 2 with wash hand basins
PETS; Welcome
DINING ROOM; Traditional English breakfast. No evening meal available
VEGETARIAN; By arrangement
DISABLED ACCESS; No
GARDEN; Very pretty

Chapter Four

WALL HILLS COUNTRY GUEST HOUSE,
Hereford Road, Ledbury,
Herefordshire, HR8 2PR.

Tel : 01531 632833

Nestling in the Herefordshire countryside, overlooking the old market town of Ledbury, you'll find this fine Georgian house. Approximately 250 years old, and still mirroring the graceful era of its past, this house exudes a warm, inviting presence to all its guests. A 15th century Cruck barn (which is Grade II listed) and Oast Houses from the 1600's are part of this property. Your hosts are David and Jennifer Slaughter, who's ambience gives you a welcoming feeling the second you step through the door. Every effort is made to ensure your stay is a delightful one and you will not be disappointed by the standards and cordiality David and Jennifer extend. There are three charming bedrooms, all with period furnishings and fine views over the surrounding countryside. Each has tea/coffee tray, clock radio and a TV is available on request. Food is prepared and cooked by David (a man of many talents!) using local meat, game, fish and home grown vegetables. His menus are inspiring and innovative and are not to be missed! Try; breast of pheasant stuffed with herbs and wrapped in bacon, with Damson Wine, or even; fillets of red mullet with tomato & fresh thyme! And the desserts!! Sticky date & walnut tart or home made nectarine and hazelnut ice cream! Doesn't your mouth just water at the thought! All these delectable choices are complimented by an extensive wine list - some of which is locally produced and highly recommended. The art of cider and perry making is still very much alive in this area. Coddington Vineyard is nearby, (where some of these delightful wines are made) and a visit must be on your list of 'things to do'. The Bacchus Wine of 1992 was the Silver Medal winner in the South West Vineyards 1995 Annual Competition and can be purchased at a very reasonable price. Wander round, enjoy the garden and 'sample' the wine on offer!

Ledbury Town is a pretty place with cobbled streets and half timbered houses and it is often used by the film and TV industry for its locations. The Malvern Hills are close by with breathtaking scenery, and walking here is a must for anyone wishing to enjoy the views. Photography, painting and drawing are all ways to capture the beauty of this region, but it will linger within your heart even without these reminders. For the 'shoppers' Worcester and Cheltenham are ideal, with national and quality shops on offer and for those perhaps more interested in history and architecture, the cathedral cities of Hereford and Gloucester are easily reached. Wall Hills Country House is a perfect location to enjoy all these activities.........and still come 'home' to a well cooked meal, a comfortable bed and congenial hosts. Ideal in every way!

USEFUL INFORMATION

OPEN : All year except Xmas & New Year
CHILDREN : Most welcome
PETS : No
LICENSED : Full
CREDIT CARDS : All major
DINING ROOM : Wonderful menu
VEGETARIANS : Catered for
DISABLED ACCESS No
BAR SNACKS : No
GARDEN : Yes
ACCOMMODATION : 3 rooms; 1 twin ensuite, 1 dbl en suite, 1 dbl private.

HEATH HOUSE
Stoke Prior, Leominster,
Herefordshire HR6 0NF

Tel: 01568 760385

Heath House, built before 1750 is the home of Margaret and Peter Neal who have become known for the beauty of their own gardens and knowledge of the gardens in the area, but they should be equally well known for their welcoming approach to the guests who come to stay in this nice old, house. You will find the house in a peaceful rural setting in the heart of the North Herefordshire countryside about twelve miles from Hereford and Ludlow and four miles from Leominster. Everything about the house is well done. It gleams with the love and care given to the furniture, the drapes and wallpapers are pretty and fit into the scheme of things quite delightfully.

There are two bedrooms with ensuite facilities, one with a shower and the other a bathroom. In the middle and probably the oldest part of the house there is another twin-bedded room which has a large private bathroom. When required this can be used as a family suite with an adjacent single bedroom. There is a large, comfortable lounge for the use of guests with a television if required. You will be extremely well fed both at breakfast, which is a full English traditional meal, and again at dinner if you so wish. All three rooms have a welcoming hostess tray well supplied with tea and coffee.

From Heath House it is easy to explore this splendid part of Herefordshire. Leominster, pronounced 'Lemster' is an ancient town with much of the past still to be seen. One of the features today is the busy mid-week furniture auction. Within an hour's drive there are the Cathedral cities of Hereford, Worcester, Gloucester and Brecon. Then there is Ludlow, one of the prettiest towns in the country, Hay-on-Wye well known for its dozens of bookshops, Church Stretton, Ross-on-Wye, Malvern and many others. The National Trust have several properties within easy reach and each small village you come across will delight you.

USEFUL INFORMATION

OPEN; Open Mar-Nov inclusive
CHILDREN; Over 9 years
CREDIT CARDS; None taken
ACCOMMODATION; 3 ensuite rooms
GARDEN; Beautiful gardens

DINING ROOM; Excellent breakfast. Dinner By arrangement
VEGETARIAN; Catered for
DISABLED ACCESS; No facilities
PETS; No

Chapter Four

THE COMPASSES HOTEL,
Wigmore, Nr Leominster,
Herefordshire HR6 9UN

Tel: 01568 770203 Fax: 01568 770705

The village of Wigmore lies in the quiet and beautiful Marcher Country, an area of particular interest to those who enjoy walking, local history, vernacular architecture or geology. It has the church of St James whose early features date from the Conquest and the picturesque ruin of Wigmore Castle one of the largest castles on the Welsh border. To the west of the village a network of footpaths leads upwards into the Wigmore Rolls and beyond, along forested rides with views as far as Central Wales. The new Mortimer Trail - a walk from Ludlow to Kington with loops off through Wigmore and other villages is a must for walkers of all levels. All of this endorses why you should visit this quiet village. The Compasses Hotel is a delightful, privately owned village inn and country restaurant of 19th century origin offers you an ideal base for exploring the hills, valleys and forests, the picturesque villages and market towns in the surrounding area. Ludlow is a few minutes away by car - claimed by some to be the most beautiful town in England.

No matter what time of the year you come to the Compasses you will find a warm welcome. The charming accommodation of 1 double, 2 twin and 1 single room is all centrally heated, each bedroom has hot and cold water, television and tea-making facilities. The restaurant which is open to non-residents serves beautifully cooked traditional English fare in an informal manner in the evenings and at Sunday lunchtime. Bar Meals are available every day with a good choice and several tasty Daily Specials. There is a well-stocked, friendly bar and a Functions Room for up to 80 persons. Frequently there is live entertainment ranging from Country and Western to Jazz and individual performers. The garden is lovely for a summer's day drink.

USEFUL INFORMATION

OPEN; All year
BAR MEALS; Daily, wide range
CREDIT CARDS; All major cards
LICENSED; Full On
ACCOMMODATION; 4 rooms
RESTAURANT; Good, traditional fare
VEGETARIAN; Catered for
DISABLED ACCESS; Yes. No special facilities
GARDEN; Yes.

CORNDENE,
Coreley, Ludlow,
Shropshire, SY8 3AW.

Tel & Fax : 01584 890324

Corndene is a lovely old 18th century village rectory, which has been refurbished and sympathetically restored by its owners, David and Clare Currant. Sitting in 2 acres of extensive, mature gardens, away from the main road, the house looks out over woods and farms. The site is peaceful and rural, and is ideal for relaxing and 'recharging the batteries'. There are three bedrooms, all en suite, with colour TV, tea/coffee tray and full central heating, and all are spacious and airy, with comfortable furnishings for a good night's slumber! All can be used as family rooms or singles, and two have French windows which open directly on to the garden. What a lovely way to start the day - opening the doors on to a sun drenched lawn and breathing the fresh, sweet perfumes of the flowers! Wonderful! The bedrooms are obviously on the ground floor, and this makes them accessible for the disabled, and with this thought in mind, the bathrooms and public areas are disabled friendly, and there are many extra facilities available on request. As well as being 2 Crown Commended by the English Tourist Board, Corndene has been inspected under the National Accessible Scheme for the disabled, and has a Category 1 bedroom, and two Category 2 bedrooms. Children are most welcome, and cots, high chairs are all available, and even baby sitting can be arranged if notice is given! Breakfast is served in the charming dining room, and the choice is anything from a boiled egg to a full English meal! Fruit juices, fruit, cereals are all there and vegetarians have quite a choice. Packed lunches are available on request but rather uniquely, Corndene has a 'visitor's kitchen'. This gives you the opportunity to cook your own lunches and evening meals if desired, with Clare supplying the basic things such as bread, milk, etc. for a small fee. This is a very generous idea : even down to the dish washing service which comes free of charge. If this does not appeal then David and Clare have compiled a list of local eating establishments, and will even help you with your choice! There is a sitting room with a log fire which is ideal for sitting and relaxing in the evening and perhaps working out the next day's entertainment! Talking of entertainment, this is one area of England where you will find ample diversion! Walking is a great pastime here with the beautiful South Shropshire Hills designated an area of outstanding beauty, and the Border Marches which offer a variety of scenery to please all. Apart from walking, there are castles, museums, great houses, steam railways, and shops, to mention but a few! David and Clare are very knowledgeable on the area and are only too pleased to help you with maps and any information you should require. A peaceful, charming location with lots of atmosphere, and friendly, amicable hosts to ensure a great time!

USEFUL INFORMATION

OPEN : March to November inc.
CHILDREN : Most welcome
PETS : Dogs by arrangement
LICENSED : No
CREDIT CARDS : None taken
ACCOMMODATION : 3 rooms en suite, 2 twin, 1 fml.
NON SMOKING ACCOMMODATION

DINING ROOM : Generous fayre
VEGETARIANS : Catered for
BAR SNACKS : Not applicable
DISABLED ACCESS : Total access
GARDEN : Mature

Chapter Four

LOWER HAYTON GRANGE
Lower Hayton,
Ludlow, Shropshire SY8 2AQ

Tel: 01584 861296 Fax: 01584 861371

Lower Hayton Grange has two roles. It is a delightful non-smoking 15th century house with 16th and 17th century additions, owned by Malcolm and Margaret Lowe in which they welcome you to stay in their two delightfully furnished bedrooms, both ensuite. One of these rooms has a splendid four-poster and glorious views over the gardens. The second bedroom is equally charming and also has an adjoining large private lounge with beautiful views over the Welsh hills. This apartment has its own front door entrance. Both rooms have TV, and a beverage tray. Breakfast is served in the magnificent conservatory, a meal which is delicious, and beautifully cooked to your choice. From here you look out onto the swimming pool. For the energetic there is also an all weather tennis court. Evening meals are by arrangement and wonderful value. Bald facts do not do justice to the charm of this house, the harmonious combination of furniture and coverings, all of which give it a great feeling of home, something which is enhanced by the friendliness of the owners.

The second role of Lower Hayton is its two charming holiday cottages within the grounds available for those who enjoy the freedom of self-catering and at the same time the benefit of the swimming pool and the tennis court. Pear Tree sleeps 2 adults + 2 children + cot or 3 adults + 1 child + cot. Equipped to the same standard as the main house, it is centrally heated as is Apple Tree Cottage which sleeps 4 adults. One small pet is allowed in the cottages only. Garden furniture is provided for the cottages' own private patios and there is parking for two cars for each cottage.

USEFUL INFORMATION

OPEN; All year   **DINING ROOM;** Excellent traditional breakfast
CHILDREN: By arrangement in main house   Evening meals by arrangement
CREDIT CARDS; None taken   **VEGETARIAN;** Catered for
LICENSED; No   **DISABLED ACCESS;** No
ACCOMMODATION; 2 ensuite rooms   **PETS;** Not in house. 1 small dog
GARDEN; Beautiful grounds, swimming pool, tennis court

Central England

THE BULL HOTEL
*14 The Bull Ring, Ludlow,
Shropshire SY8 1AD*

*Tel: 01584 873611
Fax:01584 873666*

Ludlow is certainly one of Britains loveliest towns, it is so often known as 'the perfect historic town', with its agreeable mixture of medieval Tudor, Stuart and Georgian buildings, nearly 500 of these are listed. In the 18th and 19th centuries it became a fashionable centre for socialising and county families had very elegant houses built in brick. The major industry was glove making, this was so successful the population grew and so did the town. Today Ludlow is ideal for touring this superb region, with its wonderful scenery and many places of interest. In the centre of the town is an old property once known as 'Peter the Proctor's House', it is now called The Bull Hotel and a very impressive black and white building it is too. The courtyard area is very much Tudor in style, the front however is more Georgian, this part having been rebuilt after a fire in 1795. Sally and Phillip Maile are the hospitable and welcoming hosts who make sure your stay is enjoyable whether it is just for a drink, a meal or a night or two.

Inside, the old world charm exists, with some original features still remaining. The bedroomsare warm and comfortable, there are 2 double and 2 twin, all are ensuite with colour television, clock radio and a complimentary tea and coffee tray. Breakfast is served in the dining room and here you can start the day off well with a hearty full English meal with all the trimmings. Evening meals are not available. The bar at the Bull is a great meeting place for visitors and locals, there is a fine selection of cask conditioned Marston's Ales, including Marston's Pedigree, Bitter and Head Brewer's Choice on draught. There is also a range of stout, ciders and premium lagers. The Bull offers a range of food including Bar Snacks, a Vegetarian Menu and 'Specials of the Day', these are served between 12.00 and 2.00pm. From Easter to September the courtyard has tables and chairs enabling you to sit outside.

Alongside the famous Ludlow Festival held every year in late June and early July are 15 days of fringe events, with 4 days of International Jazz held in the covered yard of The Bull Hotel. Something for everyone to enjoy. There are regular live music shows during the rest of the year.

USEFUL INFORMATION

OPEN; All year except Christmas eve- Christmas night, Boxing Day
BAR FOOD; for accommodation
CHILDREN; Welcome, not in the bar
CREDIT CARDS; Mastercard/Visa/Amex
DISABLED ACCESS; Limited to Bar areas
LICENSED; Yes, fine Ale selection
ACCOMMODATION; 4 ensuite rooms
PETS; By arrangement

DINING ROOM; Full English breakfast
Range of lunch time snacks and Specials of the Day

VEGETARIAN; Catered for

GARDEN; Open courtyard with chairs and tables from Easter to September

Chapter Four

BRICKBARN FARM,
Hanley Road,. Malvern Wells,
Worcester WR14 4HY

Tel: 01684 561775

This 300 year old farmhouse is everything that good farmhouse accommodation should be. The farm is run by the Morris family whilst Mrs Morris looks after the guests, something she does extremely well. The old house has that spacious, well-lived in, contented feeling that only somewhere which has been constantly occupied for centuries seems to achieve. The rooms are all furnished with traditional pieces, the house smells of polish and cleanliness. There are three bedrooms with private bathrooms, each of which has good, comfortable beds, pretty drapes and bedcovers, television, radio and a generously supplied beverage tray. Having slept peacefully you come downstairs for breakfast to the tantalising smell of freshly brewed coffee and sizzling bacon. It is a substantial, true farmhouse meal in which you can choose what you wish. Everything is freshly cooked. There are no evening meals available but Malvern is awash with good eateries so that poses no difficulty. Brickbarn Farm is opposite the Three Counties Showground and ideally situated for anyone who wants to walk in the Malvern Hills, play golf - just five minutes away, fish, ride or shoot. With endless attractive villages and small market towns within easy reach as well as the Cathedral Cities of Worcester, Hereford and Gloucester, one could never bored staying at Brickbarn.

USEFUL INFORMATION
OPEN; All year **DINING ROOM;** Excellent farmhouse breakfast
CHILDREN; Welcome **VEGETARIAN;** Upon request
CREDIT CARDS; None taken **DISABLED ACCESS;** No facilities
ACCOMMODATION; 3 rooms **GARDEN;** 200 acres, cattle, sheep, corn
PETS; Yes

WILLOW CORNER
Armscote,
Stratford-upon-Avon,
Warwickshire CV37 8DE
Tel: 01608 682391

Willow Corner is a luxurious country cottage nestling in the tranquil hamlet of Armscote seven miles from Stratford-upon-Avon. Built some 300 years ago this picture post card property is partially thatched and within are beams and glorious log fires. The bedrooms are beautifully appointed and furnishings are of a high quality being a blend of modern and antique. Colour television, tea and coffee making facilities, fruit and fresh flowers further enhance these cosy rooms. A delicious breakfast, including a choice of cereals and home-made preserves, is served as well as the traditional English cooked meal, with vegetarians catered for. There are many varied and interesting places to visit, including a Shire Horse Centre, Lily Farm, Hidcote Manor Gardens, Warwick Castle and Blenheim Palace.

USEFUL INFORMATION
OPEN; All year **DINING ROOM;** Good home-cooking
CHILDREN; Welcome **VEGETARIAN;** Catered for
CREDIT CARDS; None taken **DISABLED ACCESS;** No
LICENSED; No **GARDEN;** Yes
ACCOMMODATION; 3 rooms, 2 double, **PETS;** By prior arrangement only
1 Twin, 1 ensuite

LONGVILLE ARMS
Longville-in-the-Dale, Much Wenlock,
Shropshire TF13 6DT

Tel: 01694 771206 Fax: 01694 771742

Much Wenlock is a lovely old market town full of history. The ancient Tudor Guildhall is still in use as a Court House and Council Chamber. There are charming timber-framed buildings in the Bull Ring. You will find picturesque half-timbered cottages, a wealth of graceful Georgian houses and a 15th century house near St Owen's Well, which features an archway made from oak boughs. Much Wenlock Museum brings alive the social history of the area with special displays on local trades and crafts. Wenlock Priory was founded long ago in the 7th century, and is one of the regions most ancient religious foundations founded by the granddaughter of King Penda of Mercia. It was the site of the Olympic Games in 1850 and is the precursor to the Modern Olympics.

On the B4371 between Much Wenlock and Church Stretton is an attractive village called Longville-in-the-Dale, situated on the doorstep of Wenlock Edge, where you can follow the paths set out by the National Trust taking in some of the most wonderful scenery. It is in the village that the Longville Arms can be found, an old coaching inn which was built approximately 200 years ago, owned and run by Patrick and Madeline Egan. The accommodation provides five comfortable ensuite bedrooms, all attractively furnished with remote control television and a plentifully supplied tea and coffee tray including chocolates and home-made shortbread. A very generous breakfast is served to set you up for the day ahead. The public rooms, furnished in a country style with exposed oak beams, contribute to the restful atmosphere and natural character of the inn. The food at the Longville Arms is very good indeed, a comprehensive menu is available at lunch time and in the evening, except Tuesday evenings. It is all home-cooked using fresh local produce whenever possible. Children are well catered for with their own menu and a black board is available with 'Specials of the Day'. You will definitely not go hungry during your stay. The Longville Arms can also be found in the 'Good Pub Guide'. The pub also has a tastefully converted Barn used for self-catering accommodation, sleeping up to 6 persons. It is very well appointed with everything to make your stay comfortable and is centrally heated throughout. It is suitable for the partial disabled.

The Longville Arms is very well placed for visiting the many places of interest in the area, and you are assured that you will always be given a warm welcome by Patrick and Madeline.

USEFUL INFORMATION

OPEN; Pub: 12.00-3pm, 7.00-11.00pm
B & B: All year except Christmas Day
Self-catering: All year
CHILDREN; Welcome
CREDIT CARDS; None taken
LICENSED; Yes
GARDEN; Beer garden

ACCOMMODATION; 5 ensuite rooms.
Plus self-catering in converted Barn
DINING ROOM; Excellent home-cooked Comprehensive menu, Daily Specials
VEGETARIAN; Catered for
DISABLED ACCESS; Category C. Limited
PETS; By arrangement

Chapter Four

THE ALBYNES
Nordley, Bridgnorth,
Shropshire WV16 4SX

Tel: 01746 762261

Northwest of Bridgnorth not far from the A442 to Telford is Nordley a small village where Cynthia Woolley and her husband live in their beautiful home. The Albynes was originally built in 1823 by John Smallman, and is very impressive indeed with lovely stone work and large windows to look out across the open countryside, the front walls are clothed in trailing plants, a very pleasing sight as you approach up the gravel drive. It was once the home of the Burgher of Bridgnorth who named it after his son Albinius. The superb dining room was designed to accommodate fine carved panelling which was removed from a local Tudor house. There is also an elegant Oak staircase that spirals its way up to the bedrooms, three in all, one double ensuite, one twin with ensuite facilities and another twin with a private bathroom, which can be used as a single. The rooms are spacious and comfortable with matching drapes and bedding, colour television and a complimentary tea and coffee tray, they also have lovely views overlooking the lake or hills beyond. The furnishings are antique and period pieces which enhance the house immensely. There are steps and twisting passages, unusual curved wooden doors and alcoves with round arches all adding to the character. The sitting room has fine views, a colour television and a large open fireplace, and here you can rest or plan your day away. In the dining room you are served an excellent full English breakfast and a superb 3 course evening meal, if ordered in advance, at a time to suit guests. The Albynes is not licensed but you are more than welcome to bring a bottle of wine. Vegetarians and special diets are catered for by prior arrangement. Cynthia is a talented lady not only does she care for her guests exceptionally well, she is an expert flower arranger, growing the flowers and greenery she needs in her informal garden which surrounds the house. Her husband is also very busy, he farms the adjoining land which is a mixture of arable fields and pasture for cattle or sheep.

Explore historic Bridgnorth, take a nostalgic steam train trip on the Severn Valley Railway: visit National Trust properties and stroll in the gardens of Shropshire. Ironbridge is nearby, here the world's first ever bridge of iron was built in 1777-79, it spans the River Severn as a magnificent reminder of our industrial heritage. Enjoy the superbly presented museums within the beautiful Ironbridge Gorge, now recognised as a World Heritage site. With so much to do and see you will need to stay awhile and there is nowhere better than The Albynes the friendly home of Cynthia Woolley.

USEFUL INFORMATION

OPEN; All year except Christmas
CHILDREN; Over 12 years
CREDIT CARDS; None taken
LICENSED; May bring your own wine
ACCOMMODATION; 3 rooms,
1 double ensuite, 1 twin ensuite, 1 twin with private bathroom

DINING ROOM; Home-cooked fare. Evening meal by arrangement. Special diets with notice
VEGETARIAN; By prior arrangement
DISABLED ACCESS; No
GARDEN; Yes
PETS; No
NO SMOKING

LINE FARM,
Tunnel Lane, Orleton,
Nr. Ludlow,
Shropshire, SY8 4HY.

Tel : 01568 780400

This beautiful country house is only five years old and was built by the Lewis family. Carol, your hostess, actually designed the house and is to be congratulated on her perception; the rooms are all charmingly appointed and every possible comfort is taken care of. There are three bedrooms, all en suite, and all designed to relax in. Hairdryer, colour TV, tea/coffee tray, clock radio........the list goes on - a real home from home! All are furnished with pretty co-ordinating fabrics, and with the comfortable furniture, grant a soothing night's rest. The cosy sitting room is just the place to unwind in the evenings and plan your activities for the following day, and with the friendliness and helpfulness of Carol you are sure to enjoy your stay here. The wonderful gardens are really something special, and nothing could be more pleasant than to sit here on a warm summer's evening and enjoy the vista before you. Breakfast is full English or Continental, served in a welcoming and cordial environment, and with this cheerful start to the day, the remainder can be nothing short of agreeable! Sadly, an evening meal is not available, but there are three good pubs locally which serve excellent food both in the evening and at lunch time.

Line Farm is just the place to 'get away' and enjoy the peace and tranquillity of the countryside, but if you are looking for a little extra to do, you will not be short of entertainment! Ludlow on the River Terne, is only about five miles away and offers great interest in the way of architectural masterpieces, with buildings from medieval to Georgian times. At the side of the A49 is Stokesay Castle, a magnificent fortified manor house. The border between England and Wales is shown at Knighton, the Welsh name being Tref-y-Clawdd, meaning 'the town on the Dyke', which was an earthern barrier erected by King Offa of Mercia in the 8th century, and part of which can still be seen today. Enough of the history lesson! There is a host of activities here and you are sure to find something of interest! Walking is a great exercise, and with the farm just being off the Mortimer Trail, you could not wish for better. Fishing, golf, horse riding.....they are all available - what more could you ask for?

USEFUL INFORMATION

OPEN : End Feb-End Oct inc. **DINING ROOM** : Traditional breakfast
CHILDREN : Welcome **VEGETARIANS** : Catered for
PETS : No **BAR SNACKS** : Not applicable
LICENSED : No **DISABLED ACCESS** : No
CREDIT CARDS : None taken **GARDEN** : Delightful
ACCOMMODATION : 3 rooms en suite; 2 dbl, 1 twin.

NON SMOKING ESTABLISHMENT

Chapter Four

BRON HEULOG
*Waterfall Road,
Llanrhaeadr YM Mochnant,
Nr.Oswestry, Powys SY10 0JX*

Tel: 01691 780521

Karon and Ken Raines had spent some years coming to Wales at weekends and staying in bed and breakfast establishments so when they bought Bron Heulog (pronounced Bron Hilog) they knew exactly how people wanted to be treated and what was needed to provide the comforts to make guests want to come back again. Simple things really, like soft pillows, a welcoming smile and a hearty breakfast. Having found the large Victorian house standing in one and a half acres, they set about getting it ready for their guests and achieving what it is today - a beautiful house, tastefully decorated and lovingly restored without taking away any of it's character and charm. The Victorians would certainly have approved and from the enthusiasm of their guests, they do as well.

The three bedrooms are enchanting and each with a pretty name. Orchid is spacious, beautifully decorated in aquamarine and pale pink. This room has a fully draped four-poster bed in co-ordinating fleur-de-lys fabrics. Sunflower as it names suggests is decorated in sunshine yellow. A large bright room benefiting from the morning sun through dual aspect windows, one overlooking a weeping ash which is over a hundred years old. Both these rooms are ensuite in full Victorian style. Bluebell is a very pretty twin-bedded room decorated in sky blue with co-ordinating yellow fabrics. All the rooms offer every comfort including colour television, tea/coffee making and full ensuite facilities. Breakfast is delicious, with lots of choices and if you decide to dine in you will be given a three course meal which is equally good.

Llanrhaeadr is a typically Welsh village on the border of two counties marking the division between Mid and North Wales. It is a tranquil place with beautiful surroundings, pretty stone cottages follow the contours of the valley. Ideal for the energetic who want to climb, cycle, paraglide and do many other outdoor things. Pistyll Rhaeadr, the highest waterfall in Wales is a truly breathtaking sight. It is stunning countryside and Bron Heulog is everything anyone could want. Please note this is a strictly non-smoking house.

USEFUL INFORMATION

OPEN; *All year*
CHILDREN; *Welcome*
CREDIT CARDS; *All except Amex*
LICENSED; *No*
ACCOMMODATION; *3 ensuite rooms*

DINING ROOM; *Excellent breakfast*
First class evening meal optional
DISABLED ACCESS; *No facilities*
GARDEN; *Yes*
Bron Heulog is strictly non-smoking

THE LEEZE
63 High Street, Rocester,
Staffs ST14 5JU
Tel: 01889 591146

Ideally situated just 10 minutes drive from the fun world of Alton Towers is The Leeze, a well appointed comfortable and friendly guest house, dating from 1750 and having some exposed beams. The spacious bedrooms each have a wash hand basin, thermostatically controlled radiator, colour TV and tea/coffee tray. One room has ensuite facilities. On arrival you will be greeted with a welcoming cup of tea when Mike and Elizabeth Venn will be only too pleased to answer any of your questions and directing you to local places of interest. Vegetarian and dietary meals are prepared and presented to the same criteria as the delicious traditional English fare which is served using top quality ingredients and farmhouse recipes. There is wheelchair access with one bedroom on ground floor with adjoining toilet but unfortunately as yet, no ground floor shower room. The Roman village of Rocester nestles between the rivers Churnet and Dove, the Dove being the county boundary between Staffordshire and Derbyshire. This wonderful scenic area offers the visitor a whole host of attractions. Lovely Dimmings Dale has footpaths for all abilities, some being suitable for wheelchairs and prams. The long distance footpath, the Staffordshire Way passes close by. At the Gladstone Pottery Museum you can have a go at making a pot. Bargains are to be found at the factory shops.

USEFUL INFORMATION
OPEN; All year
CHILDREN; Welcome
CREDIT CARDS; None taken
LICENSED; No
ACCOMMODATION; 5 rooms, 1 double, 2 family, 2 twin, 1 ensuite
PETS; Yes, by arrangement
DINING ROOM; Genuine home-made Farmhouse fare
VEGETARIAN; Catered for
DISABLED ACCESS; Wheelchair access ground floor bedroom by arrangement
GARDEN; No

BURGAGE HOUSE
4 College Precincts,
Worcester WR1 2LG

Tel: 01905 25396

Janette Ratcliffe makes you feel really welcome to this comfortable guest house next to the Cathedral in Worcester. It is an absolutely beautiful home with a comfortable lounge for guests, with spacious well kept bedrooms and antique furniture throughout. Pay special attention to Janette's home-made marmalade of which she is justifiably proud and note that all meals are served on wonderful Spode china. The house sits in a little cobbled street overlooking the grounds of Worcester Cathedral. The Royal Worcester Porcelain Factory is within walking distance and there are many other things of interest to see and do. The river is only 3 minutes walk away and provides interesting riverside walks and boat trips.

USEFUL INFORMATION
OPEN; All year, except Christmas
CHILDREN; Most welcome
CREDIT CARDS; None taken
LICENSED; No
ACCOMMODATION; 4 rooms
DINING ROOM; Good home-cooking
VEGETARIAN; Catered for
DISABLED ACCESS; No
GARDEN; No
PETS; No

Chapter Four

HILLCREST GUEST HOUSE
Sherbourne Hill, Stratford Road
Nr Warwick, Warwickshire CV35 8AG

Tel: 01926 624386

Hillcrest stands as the name implies at the top of a hill and is a pretty cottage with a delightful garden. People come here to stay for several reasons, the main one being the friendly atmosphere and the genuine welcome Mick and Sue Twigger give to their guests whose welfare is very much their concern and their aim is to make sure that every one who stays wants to return. Another reason is the convenience of its situation. Warwick is close by with its imposing castle, Stratford is within easy distance, Blenheim Palace is not far away and the wealth of beautiful Warwickshire countryside is at the door.

The house is about 250 years old and has lots of nooks and crannies giving it a great deal of character and when you add that to the comfortable beds and pleasant rooms, it is a home from home. There are three bedrooms none of which are ensuite but this is overcome by the plentiful supply of hotwater in the well appointed bathroom. Each bedroom has a wash basin, television and a beverage tray. If you require an alarm call or an early breakfast you only have to ask. Every morning there is a choice for breakfast which is delicious and freshly cooked to your order. Vegetarians are catered for if required. No evening meals are served but there are plenty of eateries within easy reach; Mick and Sue will advise you on where to go. They are both keen gardeners and you are welcome to buy some of their home-grown vegetables. Supposedly many moons ago a vicar of the local church was buried just over the garden fence and it is said that his spirit haunts the garden - perhaps because it is a friendly spirit it is blessing the vegetables, flowers and shrubs - nice thought. The views from the rear of the cottage are beautiful and overlook the Avon Valley.

USEFUL INFORMATION

OPEN; All year
CHILDREN; No
CREDIT CARDS; Diners only
ACCOMMODATION; 2 dbl 1 tw not ensuite
PETS; No

DINING ROOM; Full traditional breakfast
No evening meal
VEGETARIAN; Upon request
DISABLED ACCESS; No facilities
GARDEN; Yes, beautiful

ASCOTT HOUSE FARM
Ascott, Whichford,
Shipston-on-Stour,
Warwickshire CV36 5PP
Tel: 01608 684655

Surrounded by countryside of outstanding natural beauty on the periphery of the Cotswolds is Ascott House Farm. Built 200 years ago this Listed building is set amidst 500 acres of arable and sheep pasture, and offers guests peace and quiet to enjoy this tranquil backwater. There is an outdoor solar heated swimming pool positioned within very attractive gardens and a snooker room. The property is centrally heated and is attractively furnished with traditional and antique effects. Bedrooms, some with ensuite facilities, have radio, colour television, vanity units and a tea and coffee tray. A delicious farmhouse style breakfast is served in the charming traditional dining room. Mrs. J Haines, the owner has been rewarded by the English Tourist Board with '2 Crowns'. Local facilities include golf where Ascott house guests enjoy special rates, horse riding, clay pigeon shooting and wonderful walks are readily available. There are several good inns within easy reach for evening meals. There are many fascinating and interesting places to visit, including Broughton Castle, Blenheim Palace, Bourton-on-the-Water, Stratford-upon-Avon and Warwick Castle. Burford Wildlife Park has an extensive variety of wild animals. Bibury a beautiful English village with a famous row of Cotswold cottages, called Arlington Row.

USEFUL INFORMATION

OPEN; *All year, not Christmas Day*
CHILDREN; *Welcome*
CREDIT CARDS; *None taken*
LICENSED; *No*
ACCOMMODATION; *3 ensuite rooms, 2 double, 1 twin*
DINING ROOM; *Home-cooked fare*
VEGETARIAN; *Catered for*
DISABLED ACCESS; *No*
GARDEN; *Yes*
PETS; *Yes*

DEARNFORD HALL
Whitchurch,
Shropshire SY13 3JJ
Tel/Fax: 01948 662319

Elegance and domestic comfort rarely go together. But from the moment you see the Steinway grand in the entrance hall of Dearnford Hall and the log fires in all reception rooms, you know that Charles and Jane Bebbington have carried it off with style. They have incorporated 20th century comforts into this beautiful house, built in the age of Purcell, Marlborough and Sir Christopher Wren. Huge baths and power showers in the new ensuite bathrooms. Central heating throughout. Gracious living has been preserved in the guests' own drawing rooms, the spacious bedrooms and the elegant dining rooms, where an English breakfast of local produce is served. Beyond the lawns and garden of a country house, their own 15 acre spring-fed trout pool beckons. Fly fishing from boat or bank for the angler and instruction for beginners. Dearnford is strategically placed for exploring Chester, Shrewsbury, the Ironbridge Gorge, Hawkstone Park Follies, Hodnet Hall, Bridgemere (Europe's largest garden centre), two race courses and several golf courses.

USEFUL INFORMATION

OPEN: *All year excluding Christmas*
CHILDREN: *By arrangement*
CREDIT CARDS: *None taken*
PETS: *By arrangement*
DINING ROOM: *Breakfast only*
VEGETARIAN: *Upon request*
DISABLED ACCESS: *No*
GARDEN: *Yes*

Chapter Four

NEWBOLD NURSERIES
Newbold-on-Stour,
Stratford-upon-Avon,
Warwickshire CV37 8DP
Tel: 01789 450285

Just outside Stratford-upon-Avon, the birth place of the Bard, is the small village of Newbold-on-Stour, here Mr. Everett has his businesses. Mr. Everett runs a successful nursery where he specialises in Hydroponically-grown tomatoes and cucumbers. He also looks after his guests in his lovely modern farmhouse. This very rural setting is peaceful and relaxing. There are 3 charming bedrooms all with colour TV and tea and coffee making facilities. There are reductions for children sharing a family room. The views are across open countryside and are truly lovely. Breakfast is a traditional meal and plenty of it, you will need it as there is an awful lot to do in this area. Newbold Nurseries is only 10 minutes from Stratford with its wonderful architecture, museums, gardens and of course the Shakespeare Centre. Another wonderful place to visit is Warwick here you will find the dominating 14th century castle with its magnificent state rooms, dungeons with gruesome torture tools and the waxworks depicting history. Closer to home there are lovely walks, golf, fishing, riding and shooting. With the heart of the Cotswolds on your doorstep you are sure to have an enjoyable stay.

USEFUL INFORMATION
OPEN; Closed Dec/Jan
CHILDREN; Over 12 years, reductions for children sharing a family room
CREDIT CARDS; None taken
LICENSED; No
ACCOMMODATION; 3 rooms
DINING ROOM; Good home-cooking
VEGETARIAN; Catered for
DISABLED ACCESS; No
GARDEN; Yes
PETS; Yes

THE OLD RECTORY
Churchside, Harlaston,
Tamworth, Staffordshire B79 9HE

Tel: 01827 383583/0973 756367

This pretty old house built in 1840 for a Victorian Rector is light and airy, with spacious rooms and interesting features. Rectories always seem to have a peaceful air about them and this one is no exception. The house is furnished with a pleasant mixture of modern and antique furniture which blends together well and produces a comfortable, friendly effect. The three bedrooms haveverycomfortable beds, a well-stocked beverage tray, Television and an excellent view. Christine King is your hostess and she has just the right touch in looking after her guests. Everything runs smoothly and without fuss. You are immediately made to feel at home and she will happily discuss with you the various places there are to visit within easy reach as well as directing you towards the many sporting activities available in the area. If you simply feel like relaxing you will find the large garden very appealing. Breakfast is a first class meal with as much or as little as you wish to eat and everything cooked freshly. Evening meals are by arrangement only.

USEFUL INFORMATION
OPEN; All year
CHILDREN; Welcome at any age
CREDIT CARDS; None taken
ACCOMMODATION; 1tw 1dbl/fam 1sgl
DINING ROOM; Great breakfast Evening meals by arrangement
DISABLED ACCESS; No
PETS; Welcome

THE CITADEL,
Weston-under-Redcastle, Nr Shrewsbury,
Shropshire SY4 5JY

Tel: 01630 685204

This splendid castellated dower house, built in the early nineteenth century by the famous Hill family, is to be found between Hodnet and Weston on the A49, 12 miles north of Shrewsbury, 8 miles south of Whitchurch. You follow the signs to Weston-under-Redcastle/Hawkstone Park and the house is on the right, a quarter of a mile after taking the Hodnet road out of the village. The Citadel stands in a spectacular position overlooking Hawkstone Park and the beautiful North Shropshire countryside with views of the Welsh Hills. Anyone who appreciates the glory of the English countryside will soon fall in love with the enchanting village and surroundings of Weston-under-Redcastle. In recent years people have travelled from far and wide to play golf at Hawkstone Park, made famous by Sandy Lyle. Today there is also the joy of exploring the magical paths, caves, monuments, grottos and obelisk which have been hidden by nature for so many years. For those lucky enough to stay at The Citadel, these delights are just a walk away.

The interior of the Citadel is striking, with guest rooms occupying two of the turrets, each with its own private bathroom. A third bedroom has en-suite facilities. There is a full-sized billiard table and a peaceful, elegant drawing room, where the French windows lead out into the rhododendron and azalea filled gardens. Dining at The Citadel is an occasion where the best home produce is produced in traditional ways. Guests are invited to join their hosts for a sherry before the meal. A choice of starters is offered, and the set main course is varied daily, followed by the owner, Sylvia Griffith's home made puddings and local cheeses, with coffee served in the lounge. If you have any special dietary requirements or preferences you are asked to let Sylvia know in advance. The Citadel is not licensed but you are very welcome to bring your own wine. Dogs are welcome, but not in the house, and you are asked to refrain from smoking in the dining room and bedrooms.

USEFUL INFORMATION

OPEN; April to October
CHILDREN; No
CREDIT CARDS; None taken
LICENSED; No
ACCOMMODATION; 1 ensuite room 2 with private bathrooms
DINING ROOM; Excellent breakfast and delicious home-cooked dinner
VEGETARIAN; With prior notice
DISABLED ACCESS; Not suitable
GARDEN; Wonderful rhododendron filled gardens

Chapter Four

DANALLY HOUSE HOTEL
*46-48 Lichfield Road,
Stafford ST17 4LL*

Tel/Fax: 01785 42533

This well maintained small family hotel sits quietly in a street of good looking houses only a quarter of a mile from the town centre and 5 minutes from Junction 13 and 14 M6. Not only is it easily reached but it provides an excellent base for visiting many places of interest such as Alton Towers, Drayton Manor Park and Zoo, Shugborough Hall, the ancestral home of the Earl of Lichfield, Isaac Walton Cottage, The Potteries, Gladstone Museum, Weston Park and the Black Country Museum, providing something to entertain everyone whatever their age.

Danally House is the home of the proprietors, David Oxley and his wife who named the hotel after their two sons, Daniel and Alastair. There is a genuine warmth in the Oxleys welcome, and you will find the whole establishment has a friendly atmosphere. Here you have quality and the Oxleys have been determined to ensure that the accommodation is at affordable prices. There are fifteen bedrooms, most of which are ensuite giving you a choice of family, double, twin or single rooms. There are 2 ground floor bedrooms especially suitable for disabled guests. Every bedroom has Colour and Satellite Tv as well as tea/coffee making facilities.

In the tastefully decorated restaurant, which is open to non-residents, you will enjoy a good range of home-cooked fare both at Breakfast and in the evening. Traditional Sunday Lunches are very popular but you do need to book in advance. The Oxleys cater for special diets including vegetarian and vegan. The hotel is a charming place in which to hold a small wedding reception or some other special occasion. Your wishes are of paramount importance and everything will be done to make sure the occasion is memorable.

On summer evenings the small beer garden at the back of the hotel is a quiet and attractive place in which to enjoy a drink and unwind before dinner. You will find Danally House is unpretentious and one of the most comfortable places in which to stay. At the time of writing the most expensive room is a double ensuite from thirty four pounds per night which includes an excellent English Breakfast and VAT.

USEFUL INFORMATION

OPEN; *All year*
CHILDREN; *Welcome*
CREDIT CARDS; *Master/Visa*
LICENSED; *Yes*
ACCOMMODATION; *15 rooms mainly ensuite*
RESTAURANT; *Good home-cooked fare*
VEGETARIAN; *Yes + Vegan & other diets*
DISABLED ACCESS; *Ground floor rooms*
GARDEN; *Small beer garden*
PARKING; *Car park*

HOLLINHURST FARM
Park Lane, Endon,
Stoke-on-Trent, Staffordshire ST9 9JB

Tel: 01782 502633

Sam and Sandra Clowes have a delightful 17th century farm house on this working stock farm and if you choose to stay here you will find yourself genuinely welcomed into the family home. The farm stands above the tranquil Cauldon Canal and is close to Endon village with its ancient well dressing ceremony - a fascinating spectacle to watch and a tradition that is kept up in Staffordshire and Derbyshire particularly. From the farm you are within easy reach of many interesting places to visit including The Peak District, The Potteries and Alton Towers.

If you stayed here a month you would never run out of something fascinating to do every day whatever the time of the year including some good walks through the farm. Part of the pleasure in a walk on the farm is watching the canal barges as they wend their way along the canal which winds its way through the farm.

There are four bedrooms, three of which are ensuite including one downstairs. Every room has central heating, shaver points, television and a tea and coffee welcome tray. The upstairs bedrooms have the bonus of stunning panoramic views. Breakfast is a delicious meal freshly cooked and with home-made Staffordshire Oatcakes and home-made preserves. No evening meals but Sandra will point you in the direction of several good eateries.

USEFUL INFORMATION

OPEN: All year except Dec/Jan
CHILDREN: Welcome
CREDIT CARDS: None taken
PETS: Not in the house
ACCOMMODATION: 4 rooms, 3 ensuite
DINING ROOM: Full English breakfast incl. Staffs Oatcakes & home-made preserves
VEGETARIAN: Upon request
DISABLED ACCESS: By arrangement

Chapter Four

HARDWICK HOUSE
1 Avenue Road,
Stratford-upon-Avon,
Warwickshire CV37 6UY

Tel:01789 204307 Fax: 01789 296760

Stratford-upon-Avon must be the most visited place in the whole of England and naturally has a number of good hotels and guest houses but high on the list of excellent accommodation must be Hardwick House, owned and run by Drenagh and Simon Wootton. It is a delightful Victorian building dating from 1887 and has all that one associates with good Victorian architecture; the rooms are spacious, high-ceilinged and the whole house has a light, airy feel about it. It is in a quiet mature tree-lined avenue, but within easy walking distance of all the Shakespearean properties and the Royal Shakespeare Theatre. Only 4 miles from the M40 it is well placed for anyone wanting a good base for a holiday or for those who want comfort and quiet after a busy working day. From here you can set off for Warwick Castle, Coventry Cathedral, the National Exhibition Centre, Blenheim Palace and a myriad of other places which would keep you more than occupied if you stayed here for a month!

The house is traditionally furnished throughout with an eye for detail and an understanding of the comforts that the modern day guest requires. The 14 bedrooms all of which are ensuite have excellent beds, pretty drapes and bed covers, TV and a generously supplied hostess tray. Breakfast, which is a substantial traditional English meal, is served in the spacious dining room. There are no evening meals but this is totally unimportant when you realise that Stratford has a vast number of eateries to suit everyone's taste and pocket.

USEFUL INFORMATION

OPEN; All year except Xmas
CHILDREN; Welcome
CREDIT CARDS; All major cards
ACCOMMODATION; 14 ensuite rooms
DINING ROOM; Full English breakfast
No evening meal
VEGETARIAN; Upon request
PETS; No

WINTON HOUSE
The Green,
Upper Quinton,
Stratford-upon-Avon,
Warwickshire CV37 8SX

Tel: 01789 720500
Mobile: 0831 485483
Email: lyong@ibm.net
Internet: http//www.stratford-upon-avon.co.uk/WINTON.HTM

The English Tourist Board has awarded Winton House '2 Crowns Highly Commended' and when you arrive you will see why. This delightful Victorian farmhouse built in 1856 of red brick is covered in red and green Ivy. The house is owned and efficiently run by Mrs. G Lyon. The furnishings here are very tasteful and in perfect keeping with the house. The 3 very comfortable bedrooms all have their own ensuite/private bathrooms with tea and coffee making facilities. 2 of the bedrooms have 4 poster beds for the romantic at heart, all the rooms have beautiful views over the countryside. There is an old pine staircase which leads to a private guest lounge with an original marble fireplace, and a television. The breakfasts here are wonderful and you can choose from a full English, vegetarian or a 'Winton House Special' which is an unusual dish that changes daily, there is also home-made jams, and fruit from the orchard. Winton House is ideally situated for touring around the famous Cotswold villages. There are cycle paths and walks. Bicycles are available and you can ride on a disused railway track to Stratford. This really is a charming, warm and friendly house to stay. Self-catering in romantic 4 poster is also available.

USEFUL INFORMATION

OPEN: All year
CHILDREN: Welcome
CREDIT CARDS: None taken
LICENSED: No
ACCOMMODATION: 3 rooms 2 ensuite, 1 private bathroom

DINING ROOM: Excellent home-cooked fare
VEGETARIAN: Catered for
DISABLED ACCESS: No
GARDEN: Yes with fruit trees
PETS: No

Chapter Four

TILTRIDGE FARM & VINEYARD
Upper Hook Road, Upton-upon-Severn,
Worcestershire WR8 OSA

Tel: 01684 592906 Fax: 01684 594142

Tiltridge Farm is about one mile outside the pretty riverside town of Upton-upon-Severn. The house itself is quite old, the original timber-framed building was built around the 17th century and over the next two hundred years a Georgian front was added and then a Victorian extension, culminating in the substantial country house of today. Set in approximately nine and a half acres of land, one and a half acres have been given over for two vineyards. Peter and Sandy Barker, your hosts, produce some very good wines and have even won the South West Vineyards Association 'Wine of the Year' award in 1994. Please ask for a tasting! The house is very comfortable, a real home from home. The three bedrooms all have the luxury of private bathroom, TV and a tea and coffee tray. Two of the rooms can easily take extra beds for a family. There is also a large sitting room with an inglenook fireplace, and a television and video for your use. Meals are served in the separate dining room where you can enjoy a bumper English breakfast with eggs from the farms chickens, and home-made preserves particularly grape and citrus marmalade using grapes from the vineyard. Tiltridge has a delightful garden with a south facing terrace where you can relax and enjoy a cup of tea or a glass of wine. The farm is a good base for visiting neighbouring areas such as the Wye Valley, the Forest of Dean, the Cotswolds and the Malvern Hills.

USEFUL INFORMATION

OPEN; All year
CHILDREN; Welcome
CREDIT CARDS; None taken
LICENSED; Residential
ACCOMMODATION; 3 ensuite rooms, 2 double, 1 twin
DINING ROOM; Delicious home-cooked fare
VEGETARIAN; Catered for
DISABLED ACCESS; No
GARDEN; Delightful south facing & vineyard
PETS; Yes

WESTWARD GUEST HOUSE
60 Carter Street,
Uttoxeter,
Staffordshire
ST14 8EU

Tel:01889 563096
Fax: 01889 568039

Westward Guest House is situated in the historic little market town of Uttoxeter near many places of interest and beauty, nestling in the countryside between Derby and Burton-on-Trent. Alton Towers, the most popular tourist attraction outside London is only fifteen minutes drive by car, and the Peak District, the factory shops of the Potteries, the cities of Nottingham, Derby, Birmingham, Stoke, Stafford and Lichfield are within very easy distance of the Guest House.

Uttoxeter Racecourse is 7 minutes walk. Westward is a charming little house which dates back to 1648, so some of the accommodation has a wealth of old beams and funny little nooks and crannies, as is usual with a property of this age. Despite its age the house has been upgraded to a very high standard, and offers every comfort to the most discerning traveller.

All of the six bedrooms are amazingly spacious and have been decorated in keeping with the character of the property. Four of the rooms are ensuite and each room has colour TV and tea and coffee making facilities. Ron and Dee make every effort to ensure that guests come first, and the high level of return visits is proof that guests are well satisfied. Westward breakfasts are a legend and should keep the hungriest of guests going for several hours. Ron is a keen cook and the dinners are wholesome, filling and prepared from only the best ingredients available.

Whether you require an overnight stay or wish to visit the area for a longer period, then the management and staff at Westward will ensure that your stay is a memorable one. The prices for 1997 are single room and breakfast twenty five pounds. Double or twin with breakfast thirty five pounds. Family room with breakfast fifty pounds. Dinner 1 course five pounds fifty, 2 courses six pounds fifty. 3 courses eight pounds.

USEFUL INFORMATION

OPEN; *All year*
CHILDREN; *Welcome*
CREDIT CARDS; *None taken*
LICENSED; *No*
DINING ROOM; *excellent breakfast and dinner*
VEGETARIAN; *Upon request*
DISABLED ACCESS; *No*
ACCOMMODATION; *6 bedrooms, 4 ensuite*
Ample parking

Chapter Four

THE OLD VICARAGE
Hanely Road,
Malvern Wells,
Worcestershire WR14 4PH

Tel: 01684 572585

In the last century Great Malvern was a fashionable spa town, the water here is still very popular. The church here is wonderful, built in the 11th century it has the most impressive stain glass, which is amongst the best in the country. Not far from this town is The Old Vicarage, an elegant Victorian residence overlooking the Severn Vale on the slopes of the Malvern Hills. The impressive looking property is very pleasing with large windows that look out onto the lovely cultivated garden full of trees, flower borders, shrubs and closely cut lawns up to 1 acre. The house itself is excellently furnished with antiques and country style furniture, it has a very comfortable feel about it where you know you can instantly unwind and relax. The six bedrooms all have ensuite bath or shower room, colour TV and tea and coffee making facilities, one of the bedrooms is situated on the ground floor. There is a residents lounge where you can enjoy a drink in the evening before you go out, or if you have arranged to have dinner in. If you have chosen the latter, you will be able to feast on such wonderful delights as Vegetable Soup followed by Beef with Kumquats and finish off with Gooseberry Crumble. All the food is fresh on the day, breakfast is another excellent meal to set you up for the day. The Old Vicarage is within walking distance of the Three Counties Agricultural Showground, and within easy reach of the Cotswolds, Tewkesbury and Cheltenham. A superb area for walking and golf is also available.

USEFUL INFORMATION

OPEN; All year
CHILDREN; Welcome
CREDIT CARDS; None taken
LICENSED; Yes
ACCOMMODATION; 6 ensuite rooms
3 double, 2 twin, 1 family
DINING ROOM; Excellent fresh on the day fare predominantly English
VEGETARIAN; Catered for
DISABLED ACCESS; Yes by arrangement
GARDEN; Lovely cultivated garden
PETS; Yes

THE CROWN INN
Wentnor, Nr Bishop's Castle,
Shropshire SY9 5EE

Tel: 01588 650613 Fax: 01588 650436

The Crown is a true country inn run in the best traditions of innkeeping by David and Jane Carr who richly deserve the Tourist Boards Listed Commendation . Built in the 17th century it has retained all the charm, the nooks and crannies, the low ceilings and exposed beams that one would expect. Log fires give it the warmth and welcoming appearance that is immediately noticed by visitors coming for the first time - there is a regular clientele who would not go anywhere else. Great attention has been paid to the standard of the food served both at lunchtime and in the evening. Everything is freshly prepared and local produce is used as much as possible. The menu will offer you 6 starters which will include a very good homemade Chicken Liver Pate. The main courses include tender steaks cooked to your choice, a Treble Fish Crumble - white fish and smoked fish with Prawns in a creamy parsley sauce, topped with breadcrumbs and cheese as well as the Specials of the day which are on a blackboard. The home-made puddings will tempt anyone who has a sweet tooth and for those who prefer cheese, the board always has a good selection. Vegetarians always have a choice of at least three dishes. Simple bar food is available as well including some excellent sandwiches and traditional Ploughmans Lunches.

The Crown has four comfortable bedrooms complete with tea/coffee making facilities, TV and Radio. They are not ensuite but there are two bathrooms between the four rooms and plentiful hot water. Apart from anything else staying here becomes a pleasure because you are so readily made part of the inn's extended family. For the energetic there are many sporting activities and for those who like history the area abounds with it.

USEFUL INFORMATION

OPEN; All year
CHILDREN; Welcome
CREDIT CARDS; All major
LICENSED; Yes. Full On
ACCOMMODATION; 4 rooms not ensuite
PETS; By arrangement
RESTAURANT; 30 Covers. Delicious food
BAR MEALS; Wide ranging, sensible prices
VEGETARIAN; Always three dishes
DISABLED ACCESS; Only public bar & eating
GARDEN; Yes

Chapter Four

RHYDSPENCE INN
Whitney-on-Wye,
Hereford HR3 6EV

Tel: 01497 831262 Fax: 01497 831751

No one who visits this enchanting 14th century Inn ever regrets having made the decision to do so. It is without doubt one of the prettiest and most interesting hostelries in this part of the world. Originally a Manor house before it became an Inn, it was a main assembly point on the 'Black Ox Trail' for Welsh drovers and Irish cowboys pushing cattle, sheep and geese to the English towns and cities, as far as London. The drovers are gone but the welcome at Rhydspence Inn is as strong and genuine as it ever was. Set in its own spacious gardens overlooking the Wye you could not find a more perfect spot for a holiday, a honeymoon, a break or for the businessman wanting to unwind after a hard day. The Inn combines, in the competent and professional hands of Peter and Pamela Glover, the resident proprietors, the friendly atmosphere of a country pub with the civilised comforts of a smart hotel. Within easy reach is much of interest for those who are fascinated by the history of the Marches. Twenty miles into Wales stands the town of Brecon, Hay-on-Wye, the 'town of Books' is the nearest town. Whether your passion is for watching nature or for sport you will find yourself within easy reach of a wide range of activities.

The 7 ensuite bedrooms are a delight with a mixture of the half-timbered and quaint to the traditional and spacious. Beautiful drapes, comfortable beds, colour television and tea and coffee making facilities as well as full central heating make any room a pleasure to sleep in. The bars, are warm and welcoming and the three dining areas can cater for anything from a simple bar snack to a banquet for 50 with private functions and small weddings. The food is sometimes traditional, sometimes exotic but whatever it is the ingredients will be of the highest quality. Rhydspence Inn is an unforgettable experience.

USEFUL INFORMATION

OPEN: All year except 2 weeks in January
CHILDREN: Welcome
CREDIT CARDS: All except Diners
LICENSED: Full on. Good wine list

RESTAURANT: Superb food
BAR FOOD: Traditional and unusual
VEGETARIAN: Always a choice
DISABLED ACCESS: Restaurant only

ACCOMMODATION: 7 ensuite rooms
PETS: No

GARDEN: Mature with stream

The Midshires

Chapter Five

THE MIDSHIRES

including **NOTTINGHAMSHIRE,
LEICESTERSHIRE, LINCOLNSHIRE
DERBYSHIRE & NORTHAMPTONSHIRE**

CHAPTER 5

THE MID-SHIRES

including NOTTINGHAMSHIRE, LEICESTERSHIRE, LINCOLNSHIRE, DERBYSHIRE & NORTHAMPTONSHIRE

INCLUDES

Ardel House	**Ashbourne**	p. 517
The Falcon Hotel	**Ashby**	p. 513
Throwley Hall Farm	**Ilam**	p. 514
Dale Cottage	**Millers Dale**	p. 514
Hill House	**Whitfield**	p. 516

Chapter Five

THE MIDSHIRES
including NOTTINGHAMSHIRE, LEICESTERSHIRE, LINCOLNSHIRE DERBYSHIRE & NORTHAMPTONSHIRE

Nottinghamshire brings back memories of childhood stories and games involving the famous Robin Hood. Nowhere is there more evidence of the history and heritage than in the main city of **Nottingham** itself. Nottingham Castle, high above, overlooking the thronging streets, is the home of the annual Robin Hood Pageant which is held each year in October. It is also a museum and art gallery with impressive collections of glass, silver and ceramics. A short walk along Maid Marian Way will take you to the 'Tales of Robin Hood', where you can relive the legend in sight, sound and smell. But Nottingham has much more on offer. Take the underground caves - 400 hand chiselled caves beneath the city that were used for numerous reasons - first as dwellings and later as air raid shelters, tanneries and wine cellars. Famous names are associated with this city; Jessie Boots opened his first chemist shop here on Goosegate in 1864 - I wonder if he could foresee the success 'Boots' would have. The cycle manufacturers Raleigh also began in this city, but the most famous of all her products is probably Nottingham Lace. The story is that this became so popular that country girls were brought from the fields to work indoors, giving rise to the reputation of Nottingham girls having the best complexions in England! The Lace Hall tells the fascinating story of lace, and the Lace Centre offers a floor to ceiling array of the products which you can admire and even buy.

The modern Nottingham is a great shopping centre having been voted the fourth best in the UK. It has two spacious shopping centres and many pedestrianised streets to browse round. Derby Road is for the antique enthusiasts, and there are lots of bistros, cafes and restaurants where you can take a break. The indoor market in the Victoria Centre is a must for bargain hunters, and much good local produce is sold here.

The surrounding countryside is full of things for the active and not so active. Cycling along quiet byways, self guided walks and horse riding for trekking round what they call 'Robin Hood Country'. There are plenty of golf courses, and archery is quite popular here - again probably due to the historic Robin. You can visit the birthplace of author DH Lawrence at **Eastwood**, or visit the Bramley Apple Exhibition at **Southwell**. At **Winthorpe**, the Newark Air Museum has more than 30 historic aircraft on show, including a Vulcan bomber. Sherwood Forest at **Edwinstowe** is not only famous for being the home of Robin Hood, but for it's natural history and fascinating wildlife. Rangers offer guided walks telling of the impressive stagheaded oaks and silver birch glades. The visitors centre has an excellent range of heritage shops and superb catering facilities. Edwinstowe village and the church of St. Mary is where Robin married Maid Marian, and the painted scenes and carvings in the church would seem to endorse this. For the serious walker the 'Robin Hood Way' is a charming manner in which to link and visit the many sites associated with this hero.

Nottinghamshire also has links with the Pilgrim Fathers as the leaders of the Mayflower Expedition were born at **Scrooby.** Babworth Church is the focus of many ancestral seeking visitors, as this was where the first sermons were preached by Richard Clifton. There are many places of interest in this fine county - **Wellow,** close to Rufford Abbey still has a maypole in the village green, **Scarrington's** blacksmith shop has a collection of over 50,000 horseshoes, and **Hawksworth** has a glorious church and manor house, along with a huge dovecote. Clumber Park at **Worksop** is high on my list as a place to visit. 3,800 acres of forest, countryside and beautifully landscaped gardens with an 80 acre lake at it's centre. This was once home to the Dukes of Newcastle, and includes a fine Gothic Revival Chapel, walled garden and the longest double lime tree avenue in Europe.

Tea is a popular pastime in Nottinghamshire, and in most towns and villages there are ample opportunities to sample many home made recipes in tea shops. The friendly people are only too anxious to make you feel welcome, and are justifiably proud of their Shire and it's background.

Derby is a particularly fine city. With over 2000 acres of parkland and green open spaces, the city has a spacious, roomy feel to it, and with so much parkland it is a simple task to get away from the hustle and bustle for a few hours. Derby is known for it's porcelain, and any visit must include a tour of the Royal Crown Derby Porcelain Company. Shopping is very good too, with modern and traditional blending well together, and with many areas being pedestrianised. The Markeaton Craft Village is where you will find a host of hand-made items, and you can watch many of the artists at work, practising their skills. The museums here are different, an example being Rolls Royce and the Industrial Museum. The Cathedral of All Saints has one of the highest perpendicular towers in the country, and houses the oldest ring of ten bells in the world.

To the north of the city, near **Ashbourne,** is Kedleston Hall. This is a neo-classical palace designed by the great Robert Adams in 1759 for the Curzon family. This beautiful house is set in handsome landscaped gardens, and features include the magnificent Marble Hall and Lord Curzon's Indian Museum.

Chapter Five

Sudbury Hall at Ashbourne is another fascinating place to visit, and includes intricate wood carvings by Grinling Gibbons and a magnificent carved staircase by Edward Pierce. Also here is the National Trust Museum of Childhood where you can take a bewitching look at childrens play in Edwardian and Victorian times. This appeals very much to children and there is a wonderful shrinking corridor and chimney climb for the bold (you must be sweep size!).

Outdoors you have the South Peak Estate at **Ilam** where the National Trust have an information centre giving details of the 3,800 acres. The green fields and drystone walls are very characteristic of this area furnishing a soft, undulating landscape which is gentle and tranquil. There are 84 acres of parkland with magnificent views, and a shop and tea room.

To the south of Derby at **Ticknall** lies Calke Abbey, known as 'the house that time forgot'. It is virtually unaltered since the death of the last Baronet in 1924 and is a fascinating place to visit. Crammed full of possessions, it portrays an English country house in decline and offers great insight into the life of an English upper class home.

Derbyshire with it's beautiful countryside has a host outdoor activities available, and many attractions which suit all the family. One of the most popular of these is Alton Towers which is travelled to from all parts of the country. The Midland Railway Centre is a great day out, or you can climb the heights in a cable car at the 'Heights of Abraham' in **Matlock Bath.**

Chesterfield is a charming market town which is famous for it's crooked spire, and which has a wonderful open air market where you can buy almost anything! Hardwick Hall, just outside, is one of the most spectacular Elizabethan homes in England and appears to have more 'glass than walls'. The inside is just as spectacular with wonderful tapestries and needlework, contemporary furniture and a striking frieze in the High Great Chamber.

Lincolnshire is a county of rich fertile lands with the gently rounded Wolds in the north and the lush farmland in the south. The great marshes of the south are a refuge for many birds and wildfowl that is unequalled anywhere in Britain. Saltfleetby-Theddlethorp dunes run over four miles along the North Lincolnshire coast and include a specially protected area for the rare natterjack toad. **Lincoln** is the main city and has over 2,000 years of history for you to enjoy. There are Roman remains, including Newport Arch, which is the oldest Roman archway still used by traffic. Lincoln was also an important centre in Viking times, and when the Norman invasion of William the Conqueror reached the city, they built a magnificent cathedral and castle. The cathedral was started in 1072 and some of the original church still exists, but some was destroyed by fire and earthquake in the 12th century, and the remainder of the existing structure is Gothic from the 13th and 14th centuries. It is a magnificent building and has many attractive features including the beautiful stained glass windows, and the splendid open nave. Lincoln Castle dates back to 1068 and is on the site of the original Roman fortress. Again, it is a glorious building with great architecture from various ages of our past - one of these being when it was used as a Victorian prison. One of the most interesting attractions for me was the Jewish quarter of the city. Jews House is thought to be one of the oldest domestic buildings in Britain, dating from around 1170, and nearby Jews Court is the site of an old synagogue. There are many black and white buildings around the city which date back to the prosperous times of the wool trade. Leisure and shopping are both catered for very well here with a multitude of shops both major and specialist, and a good cultural mixture for all tastes. Sport plays a big part with many top class sporting activities like city centre cycle rides, and of course Lincoln City Football Club, and Lincolnshire Cricket Club. The waterways offer boat trips, fishing, yachting, water skiing, while there are many excellent walks in and around the city.

Further afield there are many places to be explored, and I will mention just a few. Belton House at **Grantham** is a Restoration house built between 1685 and 1688, and has wonderful gardens and a superb orangery. The furnishings and decoration inside is breathtaking, and this house was used as the setting for 'Rosings', home of lady Catherine de Bourgh in the BBC's production of 'Pride and Prejudice'. **Tatershall** Castle was built for Ralph Cromwell, Lord Treasurer of England in 1440. Inside there are some very fine features but the views across Lincolnshire from the battlements is well worth the climb! The home of Sir Isaac Newton was Woolsthorpe Manor at**Woolsthorpe-by-Colsterworth.** This is a small 17th century farmhouse with an orchard - and perhaps having the descendant of that famous apple tree!

Gunby Hall near **Spilsby** is reputedly Tennyson's 'haunt of ancient peace' and is a red brick country house with a fine oak staircase, English furniture and pretty gardens. Nearby at **Bratoft** is Whitegates cottage which is a good example of mud and stud walling beneath a long-straw thatched roof. This has recently been restored using traditional methods proving that not all traditional crafts and arts have been lost.

At the heart of Leicestershire is a lively, cosmopolitan city - **Leicester**. This is a city at peace with the surrounding countryside and it's place in the bigger picture of things. It is environmentally conscious and offers the visitor a vibrant and entertaining stay. Historically it has been inhabited since before Roman times, and has a wealth of attractions to see. The museum and art

Chapter Five

gallery includes the famous dinosaur from Rutland, Egyptian artefacts, German expressionist painting, and a collection of important decorative arts. The massive walls built by the Romans still stand as a testament to their engineering skills, and a walk round Castle Park takes you through much of the city's rich and colourful history. Churches, buildings, ancient walls, gateways and museums are all together in this area and display a sumptuous record of the past.

Leicester is also unique in that it has the biggest proportion of residents of Indian origin in Great Britain. To sample some of this diverse culture try shopping along the Golden Mile, the busy centre of the Gujarati community. Leicester also boasts the only Jain Temple in Europe, and one of the largest saree shops outside India. Due to the diversity of the population there is a wealth of festivals and events to be celebrated, making for almost a daily carnival atmosphere, and one which all can enjoy.

The countryside is full of villages and towns waiting to be explored. Lincolnshire is cut almost equally in two by the River Soar which flows through the centre of Leicester to join the Nottinhampshire Trent, and there is a lot of history associated with the Grand Union Canal which is two hundred years old. At Foxton Locks, near **Market Harborough,** there is a canal museum, including the remains of an unusual Victorian steam powered lift designed to transport narrow boats up a set of ten canals - fascinating!

Northwards from the city lies **Melton Mowbray** (home of scrumptious pork pies) and one of the most beautiful parish churches in England. St. Mary's is quite wonderful with it's early 14th century Galilee Porch and majestic tower with it's perpendicular crown. **Loughborough** is a town famous for it's bells, and you can visit one of the world's leading bell foundries here. To the north east is **Ashby-de-la-Zouch**, a spa town in the 19th century, which has excellent shopping facilities and an indoor market. It takes it's name from the Breton la Zouch family who acquired Ashby Manor in 1160. **Coalville** is set on the edge of Charnwood Forest and takes it's name from the opening of the Colliery in the 1820s.

To the east, lovers of the countryside will delight in **Rutland Water.** This 3,300 acre man made lake has facilities for visitors of all ages, and you can enjoy the peace and tranquillity this beautiful oasis offers. There are Water Guides to help you explore, and you can sample anything from a lake cruise to visiting the exotic butterfly and aquatic centre. This is a lovely part of the country, and one which offers complete relaxation in the most serene surroundings.

THE FALCON HOTEL,
Castle Ashby,
Northampton NN7 1LF

Tel: 01604 696200 Fax: 01604 696673
E Mail: Falcon @ Castle Ashby.co.uk.

Just six miles south east of Northampton, this traditional 16th-century country cottage hotel is made for relaxation. Privately owned and managed by the resident proprietors Jo and Neville Watson it epitomises the best of England's cottage hotels. The Watsons have an eye for beauty which is apparent throughout the hotel. The overall atmosphere is cosy, warm and comfortable and enhanced in the winter with a blazing log fire. One of the ni cest things is the presence of fresh flowers everywhere lovingly arranged. Special weekend breaks are very popular and for those who have been fortunate enough to have a private party, wedding reception or small conference here, they will tell you with one voice that nothing seems to be too much trouble and the end result is perfect. The hotel is licenced for civil weddings.

All 16 bedrooms have private bathroom or shower ensuite, colour television, direct dial telephone, tea and coffee making facilities, hairdryer, bath robes and electric trouser press. Friendly faces greet you on arrival; French, Spanish and German is spoken. People come from far and wide for the restaurant alone. The food is outstanding but it is more than that. In summer the pretty restaurant seating 60, and pavilion marquee overlooks a luscious green lawn, surrounded by willow and walnut and in winter you can sit by the roaring fire, enjoying a drink whilst you peruse the exciting menu. Local asparagus during May and June is a speciality. As part of an extensivewine list, which includes well tried traditional varieties, Neville has introduced a good selection of interesting half bottles. For less formal meals the friendly Cellar Bar with its wealth of exposed beams and fine selection of real ales, has an excellent menu. The hotel is a member of the Best Western Consortium, a Relais du Silence and a member of 'The Great Inns of England'.

Situated minutes from Castle Ashby House, The Falcon is within easy walking distance of the magnificent grounds. The 10,000 acre estate has been owned by the Marquess of Northampton's family for over four centuries. There are many fun things to do close by including golf, riding, balloning, fishing, clay pigeon shooting and water sports, and a little further afield Silverstone, Stratford, Bedford, Woburn and Althorp.

USEFUL INFORMATION

OPEN; All year. Bar 12-3pm & 6.30-11pm. **RESTAURANT;** Renowned for its food Outdoor dining in the summer
CHILDREN; Welcome
BAR FOOD; Wide choice
CREDIT CARDS; Visa/Master/Amex/JCB
VEGETARIAN; Always a choice
LICENSED; Yes. Good wine list
DISABLED ACCESS; 1 room
ACCOMMODATION; 16 ensuite rooms
GARDEN; Yes, very pretty

Chapter Five

THROWLEY HALL FARM
*Ilam,
Nr. Ashbourne,
Derbyshire DE6 2BB
Tel: 01538 308202*

As you drive along the Calton to Ilam road within the Manifold Valley, the road rises and as you reach the top of the hill, you are greeted with the most stunning view, as you look down you will see Throwley Hall Farm a working beef and sheep farm, your destination. The superb Georgian built farmhouse is comfortably furnished with traditional furniture. The 4 bedrooms are well appointed with wash basins, colour television and a tea and coffee tray. 2 of the rooms, one double and the family room, have ensuite facilities. All the bedrooms have lovely views either of the farm or the spectacular countryside. There is a guests sitting/dining room where Mrs. Muriel Richardson, your host, will serve an excellent full English breakfast including oatcakes, cereals and fruit. The garden is large with plenty of room for the children to run about, there is even a climbing frame with swings and slides. There is a large area for parking. Throwley Hall Farm is popular with families and walkers, as it is situated at the gateway to the Peak District, it is also only a short drive from Alton Towers. You are sure to leave Throwley Hall refreshed and with a lasting memory of the wonderful scenery.

USEFUL INFORMATION
OPEN; All year
CHILDREN; Welcome
CREDIT CARDS; None taken
LICENSED; No
ACCOMMODATION; 4 rooms, 2 double, 1 family, 1 twin, 2 ensuite
DINING ROOM; Excellent choice of breakfast
VEGETARIAN; Catered for
DISABLED ACCESS; No
GARDEN; Yes large with climbing frame
PETS; By arrangement

HILL HOUSE
*Whitfield, Nr Brackley,
Northamptonshire
NN13 5TQ
Tel/ Fax: 01280 850332*

This late Georgian (1809) farmhouse with 12 acres is set in a quiet and peaceful location offering friendly and attentive service. The house is nicely furnished with comfortable and well decorated bedrooms. Tea or coffee and colour television are provided in the bedrooms on request. Breakfast is traditional and well presented, vegetarians are well catered for. Dinner is not available but the village pub, the 'Sun Inn', offers an extensive menu. Whitfield is a small village just off the A43 where the Victorian church contains some interesting stained glass windows from the school of William Morris. There are many outdoor and historic attractions to visit, such as the Waterfowl Sanctuary near Banbury, Grasshoppers Children's Farm in Bicester, Broughton Castle also near Banbury, Stowe Landscape Gardens which are only 5 miles away, the Canal Museum at Stoke Bruerne, Sulgrave Manor and other country houses. Mr. & Mrs. Digby, the owners of Hill House, have a large collection of informative brochures to point you in the right direction.

USEFUL INFORMATION
OPEN: All year
CHILDREN: Welcome
CREDIT CARDS: None taken
LICENSED: No
ACCOMMODATION: 3 rooms
DINING ROOM: Good home-cooking, no evening meal
VEGETARIAN: Catered for
DISABLED ACCESS: Not really
GARDEN: Yes
PETS: Dogs and horses by arrangement

DALE COTTAGE
Millers Dale, Nr Buxton,
Derbyshire SK17 8SN

Tel: 01298 872400

Originally part of the Railway Hotel built in 1840, today Dale Cottage is a very pretty cottage overlooking the River Wye and located in the Peak National Park at scenic Millers Dale. The owners Mike and Bev McAuliffe are most attentive hosts ensuring their guests are made very welcome. Bedrooms are situated on the ground floor and ideal for semi-disabled visitors, with the dining area on the first floor, taking advantage of the lovely views. Both rooms are tastefully furnished, modern and very comfortable each with coloured television, radio, tea/coffee facilities, while sharing a luxury bathroom. A splendid home cooked breakfast with several choices is served in true English style. Dinner is available, but must be ordered either on booking your room or by 10am on the day the evening meal is required. A first class pub is within 5 minutes walk. There are many impressive places of interest to visit such as, Chatsworth House the 17th century stately home, the gracious spa town of Buxton with its famous Opera House and Pavillion Gardens, or the market and tourist town of Bakewell the home of the Bakewell Pudding, all approx 7 miles away. Millers Dale is also the home of a Craft Centre for woodturning and related crafts. The area is a walkers paradise with rock climbing and cave exploring as additional pursuits, not forgetting the glorious views of the National Park and a variety of quaint villages to explore where the unique art of 'Well Dressing' during June to September takes place.

USEFUL INFORMATION

OPEN; All year
CHILDREN; Welcome
CREDIT CARDS; None taken
ACCOMMODATION; 2 rooms
1 double, 1 twin/family, centrally heated, luxury bathroom

DINING ROOM; Delicious breakfast, Evening meal available with prior notice
DISABLED ACCESS; Yes
GARDEN; Yes
PETS; No
Private car park

NO SMOKING

Chapter Five

THE OLD POST OFFICE
*Main Street, Lullington,
Swadlincote, Derbyshire DE12 8EG*

Tel: 01827 373314

Lullington is a quiet pretty village where time stands still. Set in the heart of the countryside, yet within easy reach of the Midland Motorway Network, which makes the Old Post Office an ideal base for both the business person and tourist. It is 30 minutes from East Midlands and Birmingham International Airports, also the N.E.C. National Conference Centre and National Indoor Arena. 40 minutes from Birmingham, Derby and Nottingham, and is 7 miles from the M42 junction 11, 15 mins from the A38 and 5 minutes from the A444 at Overseal. Lullington lies within a Conservation area and the National Forest, and is a winner of the 'Best Kept Village' and 'Britain In Bloom' awards. Other attractions include The Potteries at Stoke-On-Trent, with Stratford-on-Avon being only a 45 minute drive away. For the sportsperson there is the Dry Ski Slope at Swadlincote, the Snow Dome at Tamworth, Garlands Clay Pigeon Shooting grounds, Fly and Coarse Fishing within 2 miles and Golf at The Belfrey.

The Old Post Office dates back to approximately 1806 and was then two cottages. It is now a substantial family house with a warm atmosphere. Fresh flowers greet you leading to rooms with furnishings from the 19th and early 20th century. The owners Paul and Jenny Higgins ensure guests are made very welcome. There is one twin-bedded room with ensuite bathroom and a Garden Studio which is a pretty double bed-sitting room in its own separate building, and can be either part of the Bed and Breakfast accommodation or entirely self-catering. Both have TV and tea/coffee making facilities. A full English or Continental breakfast is served daily with a range of specialist teas and coffee.

USEFUL INFORMATION

*OPEN;*All year
CHILDREN; No
CREDIT CARDS; None taken
*ACCOMMODATION;*1twin 1 double bed-sitting room in Garden studio
NON-SMOKERS ONLY PLEASE

DINING ROOM; Traditional full Breakfast and Continental. No evening meal
*VEGETARIAN;*Yes
*DISABLED ACCESS;*Not suitable
PETS; No

ARDEL HOUSE
*41 Compton
Ashbourne
Derbyshire
DE6 1BX*

Tel: 01335 343203

Ashbourne is the attractive gateway to the Peak District, with its old Alms Houses and tall-spired church. Close to the town centre is Ardel House, a small friendly establishment, now in its 5th year as a Bed & Breakfast, owned and run by Mrs Hazel Waring with some assistance from her daughter. This attractive house opens up onto an enclosed courtyard ehich is full of flowers, vines, pots and hanging baskets. This warm and comfortable property is opular with families as is has 2 spacious en-suite family rooms with colour television and tea and coffee making facilities. The breakfasts are excellent and highly recommended, the visitors book proves it! Evening meals are not available. Ardel House is close to may major tourist attractions inclding Alton Towers, American Adventure and Gullivers Kingdom. With fishing, golf, cycling and of course superb walks in the Peak District National Park. A very pleasant place to stay and enjoy yourselves.

USEFUL INFORMATION

OPEN; *All year*
CHILDREN; *Most Welcome*
CREDIT CARDS; *None taken*
ACCOMMODATION; *2 ensuite family roms*
DINING ROOM; *Highly commended breakfast*
LICENSED: *No*
VEGETARIAN; *Yes, very popular*
DISABLED ACCESS; *No*
PETS; *By arrangement*

Chapter Five

Gloucester, Oxford & The Cotswolds

Chapter Six

GLOUCESTER, OXFORD & THE COTSWOLDS

CHAPTER 6

GLOUCESTER, OXFORD & THE COTSWOLDS

INCLUDES

Agdon Farm	**Banbury**	p. 529
The Old School House	**Berkeley**	p. 530
Farncombe	**Bourton-on-the-Water**	p. 531
Lansdowne Villa	**Bourton-on-the-Water**	p. 531
Rooftrees	**Bourton-on-the-Water**	p. 532
Windrush Farm	**Bourton-on-the-Water**	p. 533
Gilberts Bed & Breakfast	**Brookthorpe**	p. 534
Guiting Guest House	**Cheltenham**	p. 535
Upper Farm	**Cheltenham**	p. 536
Brymbo	**Chipping Campden**	p. 537
The Leauses	**Cirencester**	p. 538
Middle Fell	**Didcot**	p. 536
The Old Rectory	**Didmarton**	p. 536
Amervyn House	**Henley-on-Thames**	p. 539
Little Parmoor	**Henley-on-Thames**	p. 540
Cambrai Lodge	**Lechlade**	p. 541
The Ragged Cot Inn	**Minchinhampton**	p. 542
Blue Cedar House	**Moreton-in-the-Marsh**	p. 534
Fosseway Farm	**Moreton-in-the-Marsh**	p. 538
Windsoredge House	**Nailsworth**	p. 543
Rectory Farm	**Northmoor**	p. 544
Earlmount Guest House	**Oxford**	p. 545
Green Gables	**Oxford**	p. 546
Brookhouse Mill Cottage	**Painswick**	p. 547
Cardynham House	**Painswick**	p. 548
Manor Farm	**Poundon, Nr Bicester**	p. 545
Cromer Farm	**Staunton**	p. 546
Tethers End	**Steventon**	p. 549
The Grey Cottage	**Stonehouse**	p. 550
Courtleigh House	**Swindon**	p. 551
Corner Cottage	**Tewkesbury**	p. 552
Fords Farm	**Wallingford**	p. 553
Squires Guest House	**Wallingford**	p. 549
The Plaisterers Arms	**Winchcombe**	p. 554
Hawthorn Guest House	**Witney**	p. 551
Plane Tree House	**Woodstock**	p. 552

Chapter Six

GLOUCESTER, OXFORD & THE COTSWOLDS

Oxford, city of 'dreaming spires', is the oldest university city in the country, and holds a special charm in it's many colleges with their quadrangles and chapels. These are open to visitors each day and you can stroll alongside the undergraduates as they scurry to and fro on foot, or ride by, gowns flapping, on bicycles. At times like this you may feel that this city has not changed since the 12th century, (apart from the bicycles) and with the beautiful buildings on view it is a delight to wander this city. Great Tom, the bell in Wren's Tom Tower is tolled 101 times every night at 9.05pm, and is the old signal for the closing of the college gates. On May Day you will find the **Cherwell** packed with punts at 5am to hear the Choristers of Magdalen sing a Latin hymn to salute the day from Magdalen Tower.

A wonderful experience that will never be forgotten! A number of colleges have beautiful gardens including Wadham, New College, and Trinity. The Ashmolean Museum holds the lantern used by the famous Guy Fawkes and also the Alfred Jewel which is believed to have been made for King Alfred in the 9th century. Bodleian Library is one of the world's most important libraries and holds in excess of 4 million books and manuscripts. (I think I could happily spend the rest of my life here!) The Broad, the High, Cornmarket and the narrow lanes leading off them is the centre of University life, and is where you will find good shops, restaurants, public houses and the old colleges.

Radiating out from Oxford you will find many towns and villages well worth exploring. **Woodstock** is one of these, home of Blenheim Castle, built between 1705 and 1722, and presented to the 1st Duke of Marlborough by Queen Anne, after his victory over the French. This was the birthplace of Sir Winston Churchill, and includes many fine paintings, tapestries and furnishings. The gardens here are regarded as some of Capability Brown's finest works. Travelling further round we have **Witney, Abingdon,** and the pretty village of **Northmoor** which are all worth visiting. Witney has a working museum of Victorian rural life on a 20 acre site. This is a great day out with activities for all the family - Manor House, riverside walk, various breeds of animals, gardens and much more. Church Green has the beautiful church of St Mary with it's spire of 150ft soaring above the town. Again, there is a great deal of history in this town, and all just waiting to be explored!

Moving on to **Banbury** in the north takes us through Oxford Canal Country with it's pretty villages dotted adjacent to the canals, and with superb views of the gentle rolling countryside and open waterways. Banbury is in Ironstone Country with it's distinctive honey coloured stone cottages, sometimes thatched, and always pretty. It dates from medieval times and the Historic Town Trail will take you through the history of this busy market town.

Coming back down to **Bicester** we travel through Flora Thompson country, who immortalised the villages of **Fringford, Cottisford** and the hamlet of **Juniper Hill** in 'Lark Rise to Candleford.' Bicester is a busy thriving market town of Saxon origin, and is home of the purpose built Bicester Village - a New England style shopping attraction with many well known brands and shops, both designer and otherwise.

Again south of Oxford, we travel from **Wallingford** to **Henley on Thames**. Here the roads hug the riverside, but in late June and early July the area can become rather busy, as this is the time of the famous Royal Regatta.

Travelling across from Wallingford, takes you past **Didford** (the exciting home of Formula IRacing), and past **Steventon** (4 miles south of Abington), a picturesque village with a rather unique raised causeway in the village green, and on to **Swindon**. Here we are at the entry to Gloucestershire and in a town which is probably the only major one in the area. Swindon is known in it's relation to the Brunel Great Western Railway and the town that grew up around it, but in fact there has been a town here since at least the 11th century, and it is an interesting contrast of old and new. The Western Railway Museum is a must for enthusiasts, but there are plenty of other interesting spots and many leisure facilities. Swindon has been in the news lately because of its participation in the experiment of a cashless economy. This is where the pilot scheme for the 'Mondex' card is being tried; a card that can be loaded with money from your account and which can communicate with other electronic tills to lose or gain money.

Frankly I'm not sure what all the fuss is about, as we have been doing this through various cards such as Switch and Electron for some time now. I still like to have the reassuring 'wad' of *real* money in my possession - if only for a short period of time until I reach the check out and pay the shopping bill! Talking of shopping, Swindon has very good facilities - again it was a pioneer in pedestrianisation - closing its main street to traffic over 30 years ago. It has all the major shops in beautifully designed shopping centres which are modern yet tastefully reflecting the past of this town. The Brunel Shopping Centre has the feel of a Victorian railway station and is host to many of the chief names in shopping along with many individual, specialist outlets. Sports and leisure centres are plentiful, and you can enjoy swimming, ice skating, superbowl, golf and much more at any time of year.

Chapter Six

As Swindon is where the West Country meets The Cotswolds, this leads us very nicely into the next section. The Cotswolds are one of England's most beautiful areas; the charming medieval towns and villages built in the warm mellow stone of the district, and the soft rolling countryside with it's woodlands and grasslands. Nowhere else is man seen to be so in harmony with his surroundings; the buildings are a natural part of the countryside which blend in accord with the environment. The Cotswolds are a designated area of outstanding beauty (the largest in the country) and cover an area of nearly 800 sq miles. This is an area which has been inhabited for many thousands of years, and to keep and protect this 'living landscape' income from tourism, local crafts and shops is a very important part of the local economy. Visitors are made extremely welcome, and it is delightful to spend a night's rest in some of the most charming homes in the country. I cannot mention all the market towns and villages, but a few will give you a taste of the rich history and background that assails the senses in every hamlet visited. **Bourton-on-the Water** is one of the most popular and well known villages, due to the **River Windrush** running through the centre of the village and crossed by several bridges. It is likened to Venice, and is a very appealing place to visit. One unusual exhibition is the Perfumery Exhibition. There is a 'Smelly Vision' theatre which gives an explanation through audio and vision, of plant extracts used, and a beautiful perfume garden where the fragrances are wonderful. **Chipping Campden** is often thought of as the jewel of the Cotswolds, and is an extremely attractive town. It's traditional buildings have been carefully restored in the warm honey coloured stone that is reflective of the area. St.James' Church, built around the 15th century, is interesting with it's 120 ft tower and a superb collection of monumental brasses. The 'Cotswolds Olympics' are held in this town each year, and have been so since founded by Captain Robert Dover in the 17th century. This is a great place for local arts and crafts, and a day can be spent happily browsing round the delightful shops.

The **River Thames** begins it's journey in the town of **Lechdale**, and St John's Lock is where they shipped the local stone from to build St Paul's Cathedral in London. The lock is still working today, but is more likely to carry pleasure boats than working barges. This is a peaceful, tranquil spot, and one where you can enjoy the luxury of total relaxation!

One of my favourites is the small town of **Stow-on-the-Wold.** This may be rather coloured as I have a passion for antique shops, and this (to me) is the idea of heaven. Even to window shop is a dream, and the quality and novelty of the pieces will have you exclaiming in delight (and possibly emptying the bank account!). It is the highest town on the Cotswolds Hills, and presents a rather timeless quality with the elegant 17th and 18th century buildings. Definitely not to be missed!

Minchinhampton is another of those charming ancient towns with a great history of weaving, and situated on the hilltop between the Golden and Nailsworth valleys. **Nailsworth** is a busy town which stands at the junction of the road to Tetbury and Bath, and which has a rich history as a centre of the wool industry. The lovely Georgian and Jacobean houses are attributed to the wealth brought here by the industry. Another unspoilt Cotswold town is that of **Winchcombe** near Cheltenham, and St Peter's Church with it's marvelous, irreverent gargoyles can be seen from almost any part of the town. This is where you will find Sudley Castle, where Katherine Parr, the sixth wife of Henry VIII, made her home. It was also Charles I's headquarters for some time during the civil war. The castle today is home to Lord and Lady Ashcombe, and included in the impressive collection is the prayer book of Katherine Parr and the bed of Charles I. There are some fine paintings, furniture and tapestries here, and in addition there is a children's play park and a bird garden. It is surrounded by eight charming gardens with long avenues of majestic trees, shrubs, grand old yew hedges and wide expanses of still open water. The centrepiece of these fine gardens is the Queen's Garden, named after Queen Katherine Parr, and winner of the HHA/Christies Garden of the Year Award 1996.

Passing **Stroud** and **Stonehouse**, and on to **Berkeley** near the **Severn**, where stands Berkeley Castle, one of the oldest inhabited castles in England and site of the murder of Edward II in 1327.

Also here is the Jenner Museum which tells the fascinating story of Dr. Edward Jenner and his first vaccination in 1796. It is quite interesting to learn how a cow, a milkmaid and a small boy played their parts in this discovery.

Brookthorpe is a pleasant location outside **Gloucester** with good accommodation, which is an excellent base for visiting the various attractions in the surrounding area without actually staying in one of the busy towns. Gloucester is an extremely cultural city with a rich historical background and a strong tradition of welcome. The Norman Cathedral is one of the most beautiful in Britain and is a wonderful landmark for the surrounding countryside. The tomb of Edward II is here and the largest stained glass window in the country measuring 72 x 38ft depicting the Coronation of the Virgin. Step back in time and follow the monks through the fan vaulted cloisters, visit the crypt and the Cathedral Exhibition, and just enjoy this wonderful monument to Britain's history! There are lots of museums in this fine city, and the past is all around just waiting to be explored. For those interested, the Gloucester Docks is a must on the list of places to be visited. Fifteen Victorian Warehouses still stand as a reminder of the times when Gloucester was the gateway to waterbourne traffic reaching the Midlands, and you can envisage the tall ships and barges that once queued to enter this

Chapter Six

port. Nowadays it is full of museums and wonderful shops, furnishing a great 'day out' for all the family. One of the attractions is the National Waterways Museum which shows the development of the inland waterways over the last 200 years. This is a 'hands on' experience with you having the opportunity to drive a barge through a lock and see how families once lived on the barges. If you find all this just too much then there is a good variety of bars, cafes and restaurants where you can relax and enjoy a pleasant meal or snack. I cannot mention Gloucester without the dry ski slope, where I have spent many a full day at the Races. This is a fun event for the children, with parents being probably more involved than is good for their blood pressure!

Cheltenham with its impressive Regency architecture and tree lined avenues offers a rather special character and style to this spa town. Originally the spa was discovered 250 years ago, and the enterprising owner saw a future in the use of the waters. The story of this is very entertaining and although a bit incredible is ardently believed by the local people. The town became fashionable in 1788 when King George III and his family set up court here for five weeks, but was probably made more popular by the Duke of Wellington who found relief for a disordered liver and strongly recommended it to his officers and families. Along with the spa waters one of the main reasons that visitors flock to Cheltenham is for the horse racing at the Cheltenham course, one of the prettiest in the country. At times of meetings the town is full to overflowing and a wonderful atmosphere permeates the whole area.

On to **Tewkesbury** with it's old picturesque streets and interesting shops. On the edge of town, where the Severn is joined by the Avon, you will find the Benedictine monastery, Tewkesbury Abbey. This magnificent building is in wonderful condition with it's giant columns, painted and gilded ceilings and it's monuments. There are monuments to the Prince of Wales, Sir Edward Despenser, Standard Bearer to the Black Prince, and many more. Today the Abbey is a musical centre, and also has a series of tours and events which commemorates it's great history. This is where the decisive battle of the War of the Roses was fought in 1471 - a decidedly historical part of England! The Battle of Tewkesbury and the Medieval Fayre are re enacted each year, and make for a very exciting event. There are many more historic buildings such as the Old Baptist Chapel, the Little Museum and the Town Museum which are all worth a visit.

The rivers form quite a major part of Tewkesbury, and many cruises are available to take you into either Shakespeare country or down towards the Bristol Channel. A spectacular event is the Tewkesbury Water Festival with it's fireworks and displays, but at any time of year the rivers are to be enjoyed and are great for relaxing. Shopping here is a diverse activity with a variety of shops not only in Tewkesbury but in the surrounding towns and villages. Hand printed silks from **Beckford,** craft potteries at **Conderton, Bredon** and **Winchcombe** are just a couple of the interesting places that are easy to call on.

Another interesting activity in the area suitable for all ages is the Gloucestershire Warwickshire Railway. This steam railway is not only spectacular for enthusiasts, but runs a series of special events throughout the year aimed at children. Something else for the children is the Cotswold Farm Park where over 50 breeds of rare British livestock are reared. From Old Spot pigs to Shire horses, the children will be fascinated by seeing these animals in their natural habitat. For those children who may have a short attention span there is also a great adventure playground, and for the adults afflicted the same way, there is seasonal exhibitions, gift shops and a welcoming cafe.

The Forest of Dean will enchant you like no other place. King Canute in 1016 is to be thanked for this when he decreed that 27,000 acres should become a royal hunting ground. The area stretches from the River Wye on the western border to the River Severn on the eastern. It has many attractions revealing evidence of its industrial past, but the real beauty to me is in the changing landscape and wildlife which abounds in this haven of nature. At any time of year the beauty is breathtaking with autumn colours of red and golds , spring carpets of bluebells, summer tranquillity, and even the harshness of winter. Outdoor activities thrive here and you can enjoy walking, cycling, rock climbing, caving, abseiling to name just a few. Local crafts such as pottery, handmade glass and even organic foods are popular, and there are many exhibitions of local art and sculpture to entrance you. The history of the area includes coal mining and timber,and nowhere is this brought more forcibly home than at Clearwell Caves which show the dangerous and courageous lives that the miners must have lived. Eight caverns are open to the public, and although very beautiful with calcite, you can see the horrific labour involved in bringing ore to the surface. To think that small boys were used in these mines is quite unbelievable. Today one of the chambers is home to the Greater and Lesser Horseshoe Bats and the tour will take you through this - don't worry - they usually use it for hibernating through the winter months!

Nearby is Puzzle Wood, which was created out of some open cast iron workings which were left to gather moss. It was landscaped in the 19th century, creating a puzzle path with steps, bridges and seats, and is a very pleasant spot for a picnic.

Chapter Six

There are many other places of interest in this beautiful forest; the Dean Heritage Centre, the Dean Forest Railway, the Mohair Centre, and Westbury Court Gardens are just a few of the stimulating variety of options to the visitor. To spend some time here is to find yourself eager to return and explore the many beautiful sights and sounds of this entrancing forest.

AGDON FARM
Brailes,
Banbury,
Oxfordshire OX15 5JJ

Tel: 01608 685226

The village of Brailes not far from Banbury, has a fascinating history. Mentioned in the Domesday Book as being the second largest town in Warwickshire, next to Warwick and was called Berailes, a Saxon word meaning wood, as the village was surrounded by an expanse of woods. It later became a major wool producing area. Near Brailes is a large 500 acre working farm with an elegant Cotswold Stone built farmhouse known as Agdon Farm. Situated in a designated area of outstanding natural beauty, this substantial house is very pleasing to look at, and warm and comfortable to be in. The furnishings are a mixture of modern and traditional and compliment the house immensely.

There are 3 charming bedrooms, 2 double and 1 twin, all rooms have radio, colour television and tea and coffee making facilities. The rooms share a guests bathroom. A traditional farmhouse breakfast is served using fresh farm produce, what better way to start the day. Evening meals are available on request. The area is teeming with places to visit, such as Hidcote Manor a 17th century estate with its lovely gardens laid out by Major Lawrence Johnston. Upton House, a mansion dating from 1695 has a superb collection of paintings by Canaletto, El Greco and Stubbs. Horse riding, fishing, golf and walking are all close at hand. Agdon Farm is also a Registered Caravan Club Site and is 'Listed' with the English Tourist Board. So why not come and relax in the tranquil atmosphere of Agdon Farm.

USEFUL INFORMATION

OPEN; All year
CHILDREN; Welcome
CREDIT CARDS; None taken
LICENSED; No
ACCOMMODATION; 3 rooms, 2 double, 1 twin
DINING ROOM; Farmhouse cooking, using fresh farm produce, evening meals on request
VEGETARIAN; Catered for
DISABLED ACCESS; No
GARDEN; Yes
PETS; No

Chapter Six

THE OLD SCHOOL HOUSE
Canonbury Street,
Berkeley,
Gloucestershire GL13 9BG

Tel: 01453 811711

Berkeley lies in the centre of the Vale of Berkeley and is dominated by a magnificent 12th century castle. The castle is still inhabited by the Berkeley family and has played a pivotal role in English history. It was in a dungeon in the castle's keep that King Edward II was brutally murdered in 1327; a century earlier, 1215, the barons of England had foregathered in the great hall before forcing King John to sign the Magna Carta.

Open to visitors from spring to autumn, it is a fascinating place and is one good reason for staying at The Old School House which is surrounded by the grounds of the castle and enjoys an uninterrupted view across the vale to the Cotswold Hills.

There are many other very good reasons for making The Old Schoolhouse your base. You will find that once an old school and chapel, the hotel has been skilfully converted and the result is a harmonious, small unusually comfortable hotel which might well be likened to the best French auberges or continental inns. Family owned and run the emphasis is on high standards of personal service in a friendly informal atmosphere. There are seven, large double rooms, all individually decorated and offering everything one could wish for in comfort. All the rooms have either showers or bathrooms ensuite and each has colour television, radio, direct dial telephone and tea/coffee making facilities.

The restaurant is highly thought of locally. It seats 34 and has a delightful intimacy in which to enjoy the excellent cuisine which is both innovative and imaginative and at the same time producing some of the time-honoured favourites. There are conference facilities for up to ten individuals, and private dinner parties, company functions or celebrations of all kinds can be catered for by arrangement.

Four miles north of Berkeley is the Slimbridge Wildfowl Trust and a short drive to the east is the Westonbirt Arboretum where a vast collection of trees and shrubs grow in profusion. The spa towns of Bath and Cheltenham are also within easy driving distance of Berkeley, and across the Severn bridge, on the western bank of the Severn one can visit the old market town of Chepstow, the ruins of Tintern Abbey, the Forest of Dean, and the beautiful Wye Valley with its traces of Offa's Dyke, built in the 8th century to contain the Welsh.

USEFUL INFORMATION

OPEN; All year
CHILDREN; Welcome
CREDIT CARDS; All major cards, Not Amex
LICENSED; Yes
PETS; Yes

RESTAURANT; Superb food. Open to non-residents
VEGETARIAN; Several dishes daily
DISABLED ACCESS; Yes. 2 ground floor
GARDEN; Yes
ACCOMMODATION; 7 ensuite rooms

FARNCOMBE
Clapton-on-the-Hill,
Bourton-on-the-Water,
Gloucestershire GL54 2LG
Tel/Fax: 01451 820120

This pretty modern '2 Crown Highly Commended' house built with mellow Cotswold stone fits harmoniously into one of the most attractive hamlets in the Cotswolds. Just two and a half miles from the famous Bourton-on-the-Water it is completely peaceful and away from the normal tourist trail. For those who love walking Farncombe is ideal. It is surrounded by beautiful walks and for the less energetic a drive will take you through stunning scenery, into fascinating villages, small market towns and to Cheltenham with its magnificent architecture and fine shops. You will find Farncombe set in a large garden and the last house in the hamlet at the end of a No Through Road. It is a friendly, comfortable house, strictly non-smoking where Julia Wright will do everything she can to make your stay memorable and happy. Thoughtful touches like a selection of tourist informtion, maps and books and current menu's of local pubs and restaurants - Julia does not serve evening meals. A TV lounge off the dining room has tea & coffee makingfacilities. Breakfast is freshly cooked to order and offers a choice as well as plenty of toast, preserves, coffee and tea. There are three letting rooms, two doubles with showers and basins and one twin en suite.

USEFUL INFORMATION
*OPEN;*All year except Xmas & New Year   *DINING ROOM;*Delicious breakfast
CHILDREN; Over 12   *VEGETARIAN;*Catered for
*CREDIT CARDS;*None taken   *DISABLED ACCESS;*No
*ACCOMMODATION;*2dbl 1 twin ensuite   *GARDEN;*Yes   *PETS;*No

---

LANSDOWNE VILLA,
Lansdowne,
Bourton-on-the-Water,
Gloucestershire
Tel: 01451 820673

Bourton-on-the-Water is described as "A year round experience". A very fair description of somewhere that is as good in the depth of winter as it is in the height of summer. It is made even better if you stay in Lansdowne Villa, a large stone Victorian house set at the quiet end of this beautiful village - everyone's idea of the perfect place in the Cotswolds. Tony and Marie-Anne Baker are the resident proprietors who have both had immense experience in the hotel and catering trade in both the Seychelle Islands and other parts of the Cotswolds. Their ability to make their guests feel relaxed and at ease is apparent as soon as you enter the house. Each of the twelve bedrooms has an ensuite bathroom, colour TV, radio alarm, and tea/coffee making facilities. For your comfort there is also a TV Lounge. Breakfast, a memorable meal, is served in the pretty dining room where, if you wish, you can also enjoy a 3 course table d'hote meal between 6-7pm. Lansdowne is licensed for residents and their friends. The Guest House has its own car park. If you are thinking of taking a winter break Lansdowne Villa is ideal and there are frequently special offers.

USEFUL INFORMATION
*OPEN;*All Year   *DINING ROOM;* Memorable breakfast
CHILDREN; Welcome   3 course table d'hote evening meal
CREDIT CARDS; All major cards   *VEGETARIAN;* Catered for
LICENSED; Residential   *DISABLED ACCESS;* No special facilities
ACCOMMODATION; 12 ensuite rooms - Winter breaks

Chapter Six

Cotswold Bed & Breakfast
ROOFTREES,
Rissington Road,
Bourton-on-the-Water, Cheltenham,
Gloucestershire GL54 2DX

Tel: 01451 821943

Rooftrees in Rissington Road, is situated in a quiet part of Bourton-on-the-Water, and only 8 minutes level walk, part of which is a long the Windrush riverside, to the village frequently referred to as the "Venice of the Cotswolds'. It is a typical Cotswold stone house enhanced by mullioned windows and a frontage adorned with colourful flower baskets. Sylvia and Sean Farley are the resident owners who have spent some years in making this one of the most comfortable and attractive houses to be found in this part of the world. The standard of decor and furnishing is very high and is in keeping with everything that the Farley's provide for the well-being of their guests. Two bedrooms for example have handsome four-poster beds with beautiful drapes and frills and the same care has gone into the other rooms. All three of which are ensuite. An additional feature in this non-smoking house is the enchanting display of cuddly animals, all dressed in fine costumes and made by Sylvia. The house runs like clockwork but nonetheless has an informal and relaxed air about it. For anyone who has difficulty with climbing stairs, two of the bedrooms are on the ground floor.

A full English breakfast is served every day, with a choice of dishes and also a lighter breakfast if it is required. A delicious four course dinner is available upon request with a complimentary glass of wine because Rooftrees is not licensed. All the meals are prepared from fresh local produce. The glorious garden with its massive, colourful flowerbeds is a delight to behold. Rooftrees is the ideal base to tour all the Cotswold's attractions too many to name.

USEFUL INFORMATION

OPEN; All year
CHILDREN; Welcome
CREDIT CARDS; Visa/Mastercard
PETS; No
ACCOMMODATION; 3 dbl ensuite

DINING ROOM; Excellent breakfast
Optional four-course evening meal
VEGETARIAN; Catered for
GARDEN; Beautiful garden
DISABLED ACCESS; 2 ground floor rooms. No special facilities

WINDRUSH FARM
Bourton-on-the-Water,
Cheltenham,
Gloucestershire GL54 3BY
Tel/Fax: 01451 820419

Non smokers are appreciated in this very nice farmhouse which lies one and half miles west of the pretty village of Bourton-on-the-Water, in unspoilt countryside. Windrush is a working farm run by Jenny and David Burrough and their family, and a very welcoming place to be. The house is built of mellow, traditional Cotswold stone with mullioned windows and inside you will find the furnishings delightful. Every room has been decorated and furnished with taste including the comfortable, large lounge reserved for the use of visitors complete with colour television. The two double bedrooms both en-suite have firm, comfortable beds and a beverage tray that is plentifully supplied.

Breakfast is a meal you will not forget in a hurry! It is everything you imagine a hearty farmhouse meal would be. No evening meals are served but Jenny and David will point you in the right direction to find a good eating house. From Windrush Farm you are spoilt for choice in the number of places to visit or sporting activities to pursue. The village itself is charming with a selection of quality shops, tea rooms and other attractions. Cheltenham, Oxford and Stratford-on-Avon are easily accessible as well as the countless picturesque Cotswold villages. There are superb walks with numerous footpaths well signed. Fishing, golf, riding and shooting are available. In fact everything to make your stay enjoyable.

USEFUL INFORMATION

OPEN; March to December inc.　**DINING ROOM**; Great farmhouse breakfast
CHILDREN; No　　　　　　　　　　　No evening meal. Non-smoking
CREDIT CARDS; None taken　**VEGETARIAN**; Upon request
PETS; No　　　　　　　　　　**DISABLED ACCESS**; No
ACCOMMODATION; 2 ensuite rooms　**GARDEN**; Extensive

Chapter Six

BLUE CEDAR HOUSE
*Stow Road,
Moreton-in-Marsh,
Gloucestershire GL56 0DW
Tel: 01608 650299*

This is an attractive, modern detached house set in half an acre of pleasant garden, and within five minutes walk of the centre of the village. Moreton-in-Marsh is probably best known today for its Tuesday street market held on the wide Fosse Way on which the town is built. It is reputed to be the largest street market in Europe, it is certainly fascinating. This is only one of the reasons for choosing Moreton as a base for a holiday or short break. The whole of the glorious Cotswolds are within reach as well as a number of stately homes and other attractions. At Blue Cedar House you will find Sandra and Graham Billinger welcoming hosts. Everything about the house is spotless, the rooms are comfortably furnished and the ensuite bedrooms overlook the gardens. Each bedroom has TV, hairdryers and tea/coffee making facilities. In the pretty garden room, a freshly cooked breakfast is served every day with several choices and there is a good home-cooked optional evening meal. The Billinger's also have a self-catering bungalow which sleeps three.

USEFUL INFORMATION
OPEN;Feb-end Nov.   **DINING ROOM**;*Full English breakfast*
CHILDREN;*Yes. Cots & highchairs*   *Optional evening meal*
CREDIT CARDS;*None taken*   **VEGETARIAN**;*Catered for*
LICENSED;*No*   **DISABLED ACCESS**;*No special facilities*
ACCOMMODATION;*4 rooms, 2 ensuite* **PETS**;*No*

GILBERTS BED & BREAKFAST
*Gilberts Lane,
Brookthorpe,
Gloucester GL4 0UH
Tel/Fax: 01452 812364*

'Highly Recommended' by the English Tourist Board and 'Highly Acclaimed' by the RAC are accolades to be proud of, and visitors to Gilberts will assuredly concur with these descriptions. Built around 400 years ago this captivating Jacobean house has been lovingly restored and a reassuring atmosphere of relaxed, yet gracious living prevails throughout this country house. The guest bedrooms are stylishly furnished with ensuite bathroom, radio, colour television, telephone and a tea and coffee tray along with other thoughtful comforts. Breakfast is excellent prepared with organically grown produce from Gilberts very own orchard and garden and locally produced bacon and bread, a truly delectable way to start the day. The guest sitting room with its wood burning stove, is a cosy room in which to relax, brochures and additional reading material give information of various pastimes and pursuits within easy reach, as well as games and books. An excellent pub is close by serving evening meals. The glorious Forest of Dean, the Cotswold and Severn Vale provide great contrast in scenery and activities. Gilbert's Lane is opposite Brookthorpe filling station just north of the bridge over the M5 on the A4173.

USEFUL INFORMATION
OPEN; *All year*   **DINING ROOM**; *Excellent breakfast*
CHILDREN; *Very welcome*   *using locally grown organic produce*
CREDIT CARDS; *None taken*   **VEGETARIAN**; *Catered for*
LICENSED; *No*   **DISABLED ACCESS**; *No*
ACCOMMODATION; *4 ensuite rooms,*   **GARDEN**; *Very large and attractive*

GUITING GUEST HOUSE
Post Office Lane,
Guiting Power,
Nr Cheltenham GL54 5TZ
Tel: 01451 850470
Fax: 01451 850034

Guiting Power is one of the friendliest and most unspoilt villages in the Cotswolds and it is here that Yvonne and Bernie Sylvester invite you to stay in their pretty home. The house is a delightful, carefully restored 16th century Cotswold stone Farm House. Everywhere there are exposed beams, inglenook fireplaces, open fires and polished wooden floors that shine with the patina that only loving care and age can achieve. The attractive bedrooms ooze comfort with fully fitted carpets and central heating for chilly days. Some rooms have fourposters but all are either ensuite or have private facilities. Television is in each room and so is a generously filled hospitality tray. You are welcome to use the house all day if you wish or perhaps rest in the lounge after exploring the numerous public footpaths which give easy access to some of the most beautiful and peaceful countryside in England. Guiting Guest House is also within easy motoring distance of Stratford-upon-Avon, Stow-on-the-Wold, Bourton-on-the-Water, Blenheim Palace, Oxford and many other fascinating places. An excellent breakfast is served every morning and evening meals are available.

USEFUL INFORMATION
OPEN; All year. Closed Xmas & New Year **DINING ROOM;** Full English breakfast
CHILDREN; Welcome   Home-cooked evening meals
CREDIT CARDS; All major cards   **VEGETARIAN;** Upon request
LICENSED; No   **DISABLED ACCESS;** No
ACCOMMODATION; 5 ensuite rooms   **GARDEN;** Yes
PETS; By arrangement

MIDDLE FELL
Moreton Road,
Aston Upthorpe,
Didcot, Oxon OX11 9ER
Tel: 01235 850207

Middle Fell is a beautiful large red brick house in Aston Upthorpe a village not far from Wallingford. This lovely property is close to the River Thames, ideal for those who like messing about in boats, as well as those who like a peaceful, relaxing time away. You can be assured of that at Middle Fell, Christine and Tim Millin really make you feel so welcome. The 3 bedrooms are well appointed, 2 have ensuite facilities, all have television, radio and a tea and coffee tray. There is a guests lounge where you can plan your day or rest after a hard days sightseeing. Train enthusiasts will enjoy a stay here being so close to Didcot where old Great Western Railway engines are seen again at the 16 acre Didcot Railway Centre, where a wonderful Victorian Station has been recreated. This area certainly has many places of interest and activities to suit everyone. Golf, fishing, riding, shooting, boating and walking, your days will be constantly filled.

USEFUL INFORMATION
OPEN; All year   **DINING ROOM;** Full English breakfast, the
CHILDREN; Over 8 years   local pub serves excellent home-cooked fare
CREDIT CARDS; None taken   **DISABLED ACCESS;** No
LICENSED; No   **GARDEN;** Extensive
ACCOMMODATION; 3 rooms, 2 ensuite **PETS;** No

Chapter Six

UPPER FARM
Brockhampton, Swindon Village,
Cheltenham, Gloucestershire GL51 9RS
Tel: 01242 525923

You know sometimes instinctively that you have chosen the right place to stay and this is what happens when people arrive at Upper Farm. The whole place is relaxed and friendly and at ease with itself including your host, Carol Holder. This is a lady who is fun to be with and who genuinely cares about the well being of her guests. The house was built in the 16th century and is full of nooks and crannies, low ceilings and big fireplaces. It is furnished as a family home and this is what makes it so easy to become a temporary member of Carol's family. With the virtue of being almost a part of Cheltenham Upper Farm is equally as good for those who come to the area on business as it is for those who are enjoying a holiday or a break. There are 3 very comfortable bedrooms complete with TV, Radio, Tea and coffee making facilities. Breakfast is a meal to remember with fresh eggs from the farm and whole range of choices. There is plenty of eveything and no one could possibly leave the table hungry. From Upper Farm you are within easy reach of so many interesting and delightful places to see in the Cotswolds, including exploring Cheltenham which is fascinating in its own right. If you enjoy the sport of kings, the racecourse is close by and for those who like to ride, horse riding can be arranged as can clay pigeon shooting or golf. The Cotswold Way provides splending walking.

USEFUL INFORMATION
*OPEN;*All year
*CHILDREN;*Under 5 or over 12years
*CREDIT CARDS;*None taken
*LICENSED;*No
*ACCOMMODATION;*1dbl 1tw 1sgl
*DINING ROOM;*Super farmhouse breakfast
No evening meals
*VEGETARIAN;*Upon request
*DISABLED ACCESS;*No
*PETS;*No

THE OLD RECTORY
Didmarton,
Gloucestershire GL9 1DS
Tel: 01454 238233

Old Rectories always have a nice feeling about them and this one at Didmarton is no exception Built in the 18th century it is now a warm and comfortable home but one does wonder if the occupants in the 18th century enjoyed this cosiness. Furnished with care and good taste the rooms all have co-ordinated colour schemes and fabrics giving an all over appearance of elegance. Owned and run by Mrs Sayers who is always known as M.T. you will find yourself being welcomed by this very nice lady who will not fail to make you make sure your stay is a happy one.. There are three bedrooms either ensuite or with private facilities and all with TV and hairdryers. Breakfast is a delicious, freshly cooked meal with several choices. No evening meals but there is an excellent pub The Kings Arms a few doors away. The garden is a delight and very interesting and you can take some wonderful walks from here as well as set off to nearby Tetbury with its plethora of antique shops or to nearby Westonbirt Arboretum.

USEFUL INFORMATION
*OPEN;*All year except Christmas
*CHILDREN;*Over 12 years only
*CREDIT CARDS;*None taken
*LICENSED;*No
*ACCOMMODATION;*2dbl 1 tw
*DINING ROOM;*Excellent breakfast
No evening meals
*VEGETARIAN;*Upon request
*DISABLED ACCESS;*No
*GARDEN;*Large & interesting

BRYMBO,
*Honeybourne Lane,
Mickleton, Chipping Campden,
Glos., GL55 6PU.*

Tel : 01386 438890

In the heart of the beautiful Cotswold countryside, this charming country house offers a wonderful friendly welcome, and a home from home relaxed atmosphere. On arrival your hosts, Gene and Barry Jeffrey, greet you with a most welcome tray of tea, ready to share their wealth of information on the surrounding area. There are three comfortable bedrooms for guests, all on the ground floor, with full central heating, colour TV and that essential tea/coffee tray. A full English or vegetarian breakfast is served in the sunny breakfast room with its views of the countryside. The sitting room has a warming log fire for those cooler evenings spent chatting after a day's exploring. Gene and Barry offer a complimentary 4-wheel drive tour for those guests staying three nights or more, which is an ideal way of spotting those places you would like to return to and explore. Out of season special rates are sometimes available, so it is worth a phone call to see what is on offer.

This is a really central part of the country, and is ideal for those family get togethers, when you want to gather the members for a special occasion. Gene and Barry are only too happy to cater for special events and you are sure to enjoy the informal, congenial environment provided. There is easy access to Stratford upon Avon (Shakespeare country), Oxford and Cheltenham, and walking in the stunning Cotswolds must be one of life's greatest pleasures. Fishing, golf, and riding are all available, and at any time of year Brymbo offers the perfect haven for a relaxing and tranquil break.

USEFUL INFORMATION

OPEN : All year
CHILDREN : Welcome
PETS : By arrangement
LICENSED : No
CREDIT CARDS : None taken
ACCOMMODATION : 3 rooms: 1 dbl, 1 fml, 1 twin.

DINING ROOM : Good English breakfast
VEGETARIAN : Catered for
DISABLED ACCESS : By arrangement
GARDEN : Delightful
EVENING MEAL : No

Chapter Six

THE LEAUSES
*101 Victoria Road,
Cirencester,
Gloucester GL7 1EU
Tel: 01285 653643*

Beneath today's modern shopping centre of Cirencester lies Britain's second largest Roman city. It is on Victoria Road you will find a high quality town guest house. Owned and run by Janet Richens, The Leauses is a large attractive 112 year old house for non-smokers. It is ideally situated being only 5 minutes from the centre of town. The house is also covered by a full fire certificate, and has secure parking. There are 5 charming bedrooms, all have their own lovely ensuite facilities for that added touch of privacy, there is also colour television and a tea and coffee tray. There is also an attractive lounge for you to relax in. Janet will serve you an excellent large home-cooked traditional breakfast, with all the trimmings. The gardens here are lovely and very well kept with lots of flowers, shrubs and lawn. The surrounding area is teeming with things to do and places to visit, you will be spoilt for choice. Cricklade is the only Wiltshire village on the River Thames, and along its main street the houses are 17th and 18th century, a very pretty place. Another charming village is Lechlade with its lovely 15th century church, and wide Georgian streets. Along with other pastimes such as golf, walking, riding and shooting this is an excellent holiday location.

USEFUL INFORMATION
OPEN; *All year*
CHILDREN; *Welcome*
CREDIT CARDS; *None taken*
LICENSED; *No*
ACCOMMODATION; *5 ensuite rooms*
DINING ROOM; *Traditional English breakfast*
VEGETARIAN; *Catered for*
DISABLED ACCESS; *No*
GARDEN; *Yes, well kept*
PETS; *Yes*

FOSSEWAY FARM
*Moreton-in-Marsh,
Gloucestershire GL56 0DS
Tel: 01608 650503*

Anne de Rivaz and Jim Smith have that instinctive gift that tells them how to make people feel immediately at ease in their beautiful farmhouse. They have created a wonderful atmosphere and so relaxed and easy going that you are welcome to sit around the large farmhouse table with them if you wish or use the attractive dining room and comfortable lounge. Jim has always been a farmer and what goes with horses has always been his hobby. Anne, a farmer's daughter, bred Appaloosa Horses for many years and was known as 'The Spotted Lady' in equestrian circles. Their motto is 'We are here to please' and make you feel at home - this they seem to do without any effort providing not only charmingly appointed ensuite bedrooms but a superb breakfast. A four minute walk into the middle of Moreton in the heart of the Cotswolds, Fosseway Farm is an ideal base for exploring this magical part of England and Anne and Jim will be only too happy to give you the benefit of their local knowledge. Fosseway Farm was awarded '2 Crowns Commended' by the English Tourist Board.

USEFUL INFORMATION
OPEN; *All year*
CHILDREN; *No*
CREDIT CARDS; *None taken*
LICENSED; *No*
ACCOMMODATION; *3 ensuite rooms*
DINING ROOM; *Excellent breakfast*
VEGETARIAN; *Upon request*
DISABLED ACCESS; *No facilities*
GARDEN; *Yes*
PETS; *No*

AMERVYN HOUSE,
4 St.Marks Road,
Henley on Thames,
Oxon, RG9 1LJ.

Tel : 01491 575331 Fax : 01491 411747
Mobile : 0374 771513
Email:carterely@mcmail.com

This Victorian house, set in a charming tree lined road is home to Caroline and Terry Ely. Decorated and furnished with style, this house extends a friendly welcome to all its guests, and Caroline and Terry ensure that every comfort is catered for. The warm, inviting bedrooms are tastefully decorated and have colour TV, teasmade, tea/coffee tray, central heating and other little items to make you feel at home! Two are en suite while the other has access to a private bathroom. This property is English Tourist Board 1 Crown 'Commended'. Breakfast is a full traditional English affair and vegetarians can be cheerfully catered for.

Caroline and Terry are interesting people; Terry is an ex long haul airline pilot and can probably relate a hair raising tale or two,(Biggles wouldn't get a look in!) Both have lived abroad in Australia and the Far East, and again I imagine they have extensive stories of both! Spending some time in this home can only be described as informative!

Henley on Thames is just great for commuting to London: 45 minutes to Hyde Park by car and 55 minutes if you prefer to go by train. Oxford is 35 minutes away and the beautiful Cotswolds only a one hour drive. But even if you never leave Henley upon Thames there are some charming walks by the river, tennis , horse riding, painting, (the scenes would 'inspire' even the most trite of us!), wonderful galleries and many other activities just waiting for your pleasure! Don't miss the opportunity of staying with these congenial hosts and sampling the delights of a captivating town!

USEFUL INFORMATION

OPEN : All year
BREAKFAST : Traditional English
CHILDREN : Over 12 years welcome
VEGETARIANS : Catered for
PETS : By arrangement (NB:Dog lovers welcome) **BAR SNACKS** : Not applicable
LICENSED : No
DISABLED ACCESS : No
CREDIT CARDS : None taken
GARDEN: Yes, with covered patio
ACCOMMODATION : 3 rooms; 1 en suite dbl,(shwr & wash basin only) 1 en suite twin, 1 sgl with wash basin. Private bathroom.

Chapter Six

LITTLE PARMOOR
Frieth, Henley-on-Thames,
Oxon RG9 6NL

Tel: 01494 881447
Fax: 01494 883012

Situated in an area of outstanding natural beauty in the wonderful Chilterns is Frieth, a small charming village, convenient for the M40, M4 and within easy reach of Windsor, Oxford and only 40 minutes from Heathrow. Yet the peace and quiet that pervades this small village, you would think you were a million miles from anywhere. About three quarters of a mile outside Frieth is Little Parmoor, a perfect holiday retreat or stopping off oasis. It is idyllic. The pretty Georgian house was built in 1724 and just oozes peace and tranquillity, which is an atmosphere very much preferred by Wynyard and Julia Wallace your congenial hosts. The house is set in approximately an acre of mature and well tended gardens with trees, shrubs, old roses and herbs, all this is surrounded by superb farmland. The interior is delightful with an elegant panelled drawing room where during the winter months a log fire roars away. The guest rooms are beautifully appointed and very comfy. There are 2 double/twin with ensuite facilities and a single with wash hand basin, and its own private bathroom. All rooms have colour television and a tea and coffee tray. A full English or Continental breakfast is available and is served in the dining room, unless the weather is fine and then it is served on the patio under the vine. What a perfect way to start the day. A three course evening meal is available with prior notice, Julia prepares a delicious traditional meal using fresh local produce. If however you prefer to eat out then there are plenty of delightful pubs in the area serving good food.

Wynyard and Julia have travelled quite a bit around England and are keen members of the National Trust and The Royal Horticultural Society. With the knowledge they have gained, they are only too pleased to help their guests plan itineraries to historic houses, gardens and places of beauty and interest. Henley-on-Thames is worth a visit, this charming town is steeped in history with more than 300 buildings of architectural interest, the Church of St Mary dates back to the 16th century and the 18th century Five-arched bridge spans the river. The Regatta takes place in the first week in July and is one of Britains most famous boating events. The town is bulging at the seams, and the atmosphere is one of excitement.

An excellent holiday location in an excellent country house, Little Parmoor is not to be missed.

USEFUL INFORMATION

OPEN; All year
CHILDREN; Over 5 years
CREDIT CARDS; None taken
ACCOMMODATION; 3 rooms, 2 double/twin ensuite, 1 single with private bathroom
DINING ROOM; Excellent home-cooked fare using fresh local produce. Evening meal by arrangement
VEGETARIAN; Catered for
DISABLED ACCESS; No
GARDEN; Yes
PETS; By arrangement

CAMBRAI LODGE
Oak Street,
Lechlade,
Gloucestershire GL7 3AY

Tel: 01367 253173

Wool and stone have given the Cotswolds its own unique and distinctive character, long ago merchants built great manor houses and wonderful churches on the riches from the fleece of sheep, little villages sprung up along the streams that powered the mills which manufactured the lovely cloth, and the houses were built from the golden stone. In this delightful area is Lechlade an attractive village with wide Georgian streets, lots of fine buildings, antique shops, tea shops, restaurants and pretty gift shops. It is here the Rivers Leach and Coln meet to expand the Thames. Shelley was inspired to write 'Summer Evening in a Churchyard' after seeing the lovely 15th century church with its noble tower and spire. Within walking distance of the village in a quiet residential area is Cambrai Lodge, an attractive stone built house owned by John and Sue Titchener.

The house is very nicely furnished with a happy mixture of antique and modern making it a very comfortable place to stay. There are both twin and double rooms, with ensuite facilities or shared bathroom, one double has the luxury of a four poster bed. There is a ground floor bedroom with access for the disabled but it has no special facilities. Breakfast is served in the superb conservatory overlooking the garden where you will be treated to an excellent meal. With no evening available you will be able to choose from the many restaurants in the village or the surrounding area. An ideal location for getting out and about. A warm and friendly welcome is assured at Cambrai Lodge.

USEFUL INFORMATION

OPEN; All year
CHILDREN; Welcome
CREDIT CARDS; None taken
ACCOMMODATION; 4 rooms, ensuite facilities
DINING ROOM; Breakfast only
DISABLED ACCESS; Ground floor bedroom, but no special facilities
GARDEN; Lovely well kept. Parking
PETS; By arrangement

Chapter Six

THE RAGGED COT INN & RESTAURANT
*Hyde, Minchinhampton,
Nr. Stroud, Gloucestershire GL6 8PE*

Tel: 01453 884643/731333 Fax: 01453 731166

You would be extremely difficult to please if you did not fall for the charm of The Rugged Cot, half a mile away from the home of the Princess Royal at Gatcombe Park and set in the small hamlet of Hyde near Minchinhampton. Deep in the heart of the Cotswolds it is surrounded by a wealth of picturesque villages, 580 acres of National Trust open grassland on which cattle roam freely. It is tranquil, welcoming and ideal for a holiday, a short break or for business - a recently completed Function/ Conference room detached from the main buildings has full facilities for up to 50 people. It has everything that one could wish for in a country inn. Inside it is delightful and spacious furnished in the 'Olde Worlde' style that is perfect for this 16th century building. The bedrooms are individually decorated and designed to enhance the character of the inn. Pretty colour co-ordinated drapes set off the comfortable beds, the ensuite bathrooms are luxurious and each of the 10 rooms is equipped with TV, telephone and a hospitality tray. The Bridal Suite has a traditional Four Poster bed.

Downstairs the bar is welcoming and friendly, full of character and with open log fires that beckon on colder days. The Ragged Cot is a Free House so the bar stocks a wide range of Beers, Wines and Spirits. Here you can enjoy a meal chosen from the bar menu if you prefer a quick meal during the day. The beautifully decorated and colourful restaurant which is open to residents and non-residents is totally relaxing and the food delicious. All the dishes are prepared from the freshest market produce by a talented and inspired chef; the service is efficient without being obtrusive and the prices are realistic. It is not surprising that The Rugged Cot has won several awards for the standard of its food.

You are spoilt for choice in the number of places of interest within close proximity; anything from racing at Cheltenham to the Cathedral at Gloucester, Slimbridge Bird Sanctuary to the Royal City of Bath.

USEFUL INFORMATION

OPEN; *All year*　　　　　　**RESTAURANT**; *Award winning*
CHILDREN; *Welcome*　　　**BAR FOOD**; *Wide choice*
CREDIT CARDS; *All major cards*　**VEGETARIAN**; *Yes*
LICENSED; *Yes*　　　　　**DISABLED ACCESS**; *Bar & restaurant*
PETS; *Yes*　　　　　　　　**GARDEN**; *Yes*
ACCOMMODATION; *10 ensuite rooms*

WINDSOREDGE HOUSE,
Windsoredge Lane, Windsoredge,
Nailsworth, Gloucester GL6 0NP

Tel: 01453 833626

From this sturdy house built about 1650 there are stunning views of typical Cotswold scenery. It is situated one mile from the centre of Nailsworth on a prominent hillside. From Windsoredge House there are some wonderful walks and for those who enjoy fishing it is available on the five lakes in nearby Woodchester Park, the property of the National Trust. Golf, riding and shooting form part of the many activities within striking distance. A little more sedately one may choose to visit Westonbirt Arboretum, surely one of the finest in the country or perhaps explore the many pretty and fascinating Cotswold villages. Tetbury, for example is full of antique shops and is of course the home of Prince Charles who lives at Highgrove House.

Brian and Chris Butcher are the owners of this very nice English Tourist Board '2 Crowns Commended' house and it is their pleasure to share it with their guests. You have only to read the visitors' book to realise how much they are appreciated. Furnished with great taste it is also designed for warmth and comfort. You will find it both quiet and peaceful - a wonderfully relaxing place to stay if one wants to charge ones batteries. The three bedrooms are beautifully appointed and have the most luxurious bathrooms in which one can either relish a deep bath with plenty of hot water or be reinvigorated by a powerful shower after a day's exploration. Each room has Television, Radio and a hostess tray including bottled water. Laundry and drying facilities are available. Breakfast is a sumptuous meal and dinner, if you choose to dine in, is delicious and cooked using the Butcher's own garden produce. Windsoredge is a strictly non-smoking house.

USEFUL INFORMATION

OPEN; All year. Centrally heated
CHILDREN; No
CREDIT CARDS; None taken
LICENSED; No
ACCOMMODATION: 1dbl 2 twin
Either ensuite or private bathroom
DINING ROOM; Traditional English food, own garden produce
VEGETARIAN; Upon request
DISABLED ACCESS; No
PETS; No
GARDEN; Yes, beautiful flowers and wildlife pond

Chapter Six

RECTORY FARM
Northmoor, Nr. Witney,
Oxon OX8 1SX

Tel: 01865 300207
Fax: 01865 300559

    This whole area has gentle landscapes, market towns and small villages which nestle contently amongst this rural scene and none more so than Northmoor. Set in the upper Thames Valley, this attractive and friendly village can be found by taking the A415 from Witney to Kingston Bagpuize, turn off at Standlake, then follow the signs for Northmoor. In Northmoor is Rectory Farm, a working farm of over 400 acres with a superb Elizabethan Farmhouse, bearing a date-stone of 1629, but it was actually built before then, it formed part of an original endowment contained in a Charter of Sir Thomas White, the then Lord Mayor of London, dated 29th May 1555. The present owner Robert Florey, who's family has lived in this area since the 17th century and for 3 generations has farmed at Rectory Farm. The farm is situated in the Upper Thames Environmental Sensitive Conservation Area and has permanent pasture and river meadows used for grazing cattle and sheep. The farm also grows a variety of cereals, and recently established the Northmoor Herd of North Devon cattle. The farmhouse offers warm, comfortable and relaxing accommodation. All the rooms are centrally heated, there is a large guest's dining/sitting room with woodburner. The two guest bedrooms are attractive and comfy and have the luxury of ensuite facilities, a tea and coffee tray and stunning views. After an excellent nights sleep, Mary Anne Florey serves a sumptuous farmhouse breakfast to keep you going all day. Evening meals are not available, but there are a range of pubs and restaurants to suit all tastes, the village pub is only a two minute walk away.
    From the farmhouse are some lovely walks through open and unspoilt countryside, where you can take in the wonderful fresh air and beautiful scenery. Robert can also arrange trout fishing, or he can offer fishing on the Thames path which runs through the farm. In the area there is golf, water sports, swimming and horse riding and for the more energetic squash and tennis. There are many places of interest near and far so there will be plenty to keep you occupied during your stay at this superb English Tourist Board '2 Crown Highly Commended' property. Rectory Farm also has two self-catering cottages, recently converted from a traditional cart shed, sleeping up to 4 persons each. They are exceptionally well equipped with everything you need for todays modern living. Robert and Mary Anne look forward to welcoming you to their lovely home.

USEFUL INFORMATION

OPEN; 1st February-1st December
CHILDREN; In self-catering only
CREDIT CARDS; None taken
ACCOMMODATION; 2 ensuite rooms.
Plus two self-catering cottages sleeping up to 4 persons

DINING ROOM; Sumptuous breakfast. No evening meal
DISABLED ACCESS; No
GARDEN; Yes
PETS; No
NO SMOKING

EARLMONT GUEST HOUSE
322-324 Cowley Road,
Oxford OX4 2AF

Tel: 01865 240236
Fax: 01865 434903

Oxford is a beautiful city, it grew into a world famous seat of learning after the first colleges were founded in the 13th century. Just a 20 minute walk away from the centre of Oxford is the Earlmont Guest House, a 1930's built property. The Earlmont is a non-smoking Guest House where most of the 8 bedrooms are ensuite; all have colour TV, radio/alarm clocks, hair dryers and tea and coffee making facilities for your comfort. A resident's lounge is available where guests can relax in comfort after a days exploration of the quadrangles and immaculate gardens of famous Oxford colleges. The museums and riverside walks, cosmopolitan restaurants, theatres and a host of music venues ensure plenty to do during your evenings in Oxford. The breakfasts are a real treat with fresh fruit, cereals, fruit juices and a full English with all the trimmings. Vegetarians are catered for. Being so centrally placed Earlmont is ideal for touring and visiting the outlying area. With lovely walks, fishing and golf, the Earlmont Guest House is definitely the place to stay.

USEFUL INFORMATION
OPEN; Closed December
CHILDREN; 5 years plus
CREDIT CARDS; All major cards
LICENSED; No
ACCOMMODATION; 8 rooms in main house
DINING ROOM; Good English fare
VEGETARIAN; Catered for
DISABLED ACCESS; Not at all
GARDEN; No
PETS; No

MANOR FARM
Poundon,
Nr. Bicester,
Oxon,
Oxfordshire OX6 0BB
Tel: 01869 277212
Fax: 01869 277166

Manor Farm was built in the 17th century and is today a working farm, located in a tranquil and peaceful rustic setting. Spacious rooms are elegantly furnished in quality antiques. Bedrooms are light and airy and very comfortable, with tea and coffee making facilities and colour television. The menu for breakfast is exceedingly varied with local produce utilized where possible and served to perfection. The hospitality is warm and friendly and Andrew and Jeannette will be delighted for you to wander around the farm to see for yourselves the engaging workings of life on the farm. Andrew not only runs the farm but also flies a 4 seater light aircraft and is happy to provide sightseeing flights at cost sharing prices, something not to be missed. Places of interest worth visiting include the ancient market town of Buckingham, Broughton Castle and Blenheim Palace birthplace of Sir Winston Churchill.

USEFUL INFORMATION
OPEN; All year
CHILDREN; Welcome
CREDIT CARDS; None taken
LICENSED; No
ACCOMMODATION; 3 rooms, 1 double, 1 single, 1 family
DINING ROOM; Varied menu
VEGETARIAN; Catered for
DISABLED ACCESS; Not really
GARDEN; Yes, with quiet sitting areas
PETS; Yes, not in bedrooms

Chapter Six

GREEN GABLES
326 Abingdon Road,
Oxford OX1 4TE
Tel: 01865 725870
Fax: 01865 723115
email: ellis.greengab@pop3.hiway.co.uk

Set back and secluded from the road by trees and shrubs is a fine Edwardian house. Built 80 years ago for a local merchant, Green Gables is solid but elegant, with a comfortable, warm and friendly atmosphere. The 9 light and airy bedrooms are pleasant and well decorated; 6 of the bedrooms are ensuite and all have television, tea and coffee making facilities, and - a nice touch - a selection of books from which to choose and take away. On the ground floor a room has been specially adapted for the disabled with its own ramp and front door. Breakfast is served in the charming dining room overlooking the mature garden, the separate tables with fresh flowers. The full English traditional breakfast is served with fresh coffee. There is ample secluded parking at the front of the house. Green Gables has been 'Commended' by the English Tourist Board and 'Recommended' by the AA. Connie and Charles Ellis are a friendly couple who make you feel very welcome. There is easy access to all local facilities and surrounding places of interest. To help you spend your time in Oxford to best advantage, the Ellis's have prepared an excellent small guide to the city.

USEFUL INFORMATION

OPEN; All year
CHILDREN; Welcome
CREDIT CARDS; Visa/Mastercard
LICENSED; No
ACCOMMODATION; 9 rooms, 6 ensuite
DINING ROOM; Traditional English fare
VEGETARIAN; Catered for
DISABLED ACCESS; Yes, specially adapted room
GARDEN; No **PETS**; No

CROMER FARM
Staunton,
Gloucestershire EL19 3PG

Tel: 01531 650309

The scent of honeysuckle and roses fill the air. Geraniums in hanging baskets, poppies, foxglove, all set the scene. This charming country house is set in 40 acres, providing complete peace and privacy. There are two lakes on the grounds with waterfowl and an indoor heated swimming pool with Jacuzzi. The bedrooms are quaint with exposed beams and antique furniture and all have either private or ensuite bathrooms and showers. Facilities include TV, tea and coffee making facilities and an unusual touch, sherry. This is an area of outstanding beauty with the Malvern Hills, the Cotswolds and the Royal Forest of Dean surrounding you. A wonderful, peaceful location to relax.

USEFUL INFORMATION

OPEN; All year
CHILDREN; Welcome
CREDIT CARDS; Visa, Access
LICENSED; Yes
ACCOMMODATION; 3 rooms
GARDEN; Extensive, interesting and well maintained
DINING ROOM; Good food plus an excellent wine list
VEGETARIAN; Yes
DISABLED ACCESS; Some but not wheelchairs in bathrooms, lift to first floor
PETS; Welcome

BROOKHOUSE MILL COTTAGE
Tibbiwell Lane,
Painswick,
Gloucestershire GL6 6YA

Tel: 01452 812854

Converted from a 17th century Smithy this Cotswold stone cottage is an absolute delight, set amidst a 2 acre garden and bestriding a stream of trout and with its bubbling waterfall is the locale for this idyllic getaway, and yet only minutes away from the centre of Painwick with its famous spired church and 99 Yew trees and a host of shops and restaurants. Bedrooms are furnished in keeping with cottage style, Jean Hernen is a talented quilter and the results of her gift are displayed by the quilts on each bed, designed and individually made by her, these are available for sale. Furniture and soft furnishings are in first class order and each room is further complimented with ensuite facilities, colour television, a tea and coffee tray, and a clock radio. Meals are beautifully presented and served in tranquil surroundings, vegetarian and special diets are catered for, fresh local produce is used where possible. The piece de resistance must surely be the luxury of the indoor heated swimming pool and jacuzzi, which is open throughout the year. Castles, woodlands and rivers are an intrinsic part of this majestic area. History abounds and this is demonstrated by the number of diverse and interesting museums to be found at Cheltenham, Tewkesbury and Gloucester. Slimbridge is but a short distance away and is the home of the Wildfowl and Wetlands Trust, founded by Sir Peter Scott, numerous ducks, swans and geese live here, but migratory birds use Slimbridge in their thousands. Jean also has many varieties of ducks living on her lake and come to be fed at her call.

USEFUL INFORMATION

OPEN; All year
CHILDREN; Over 12 years
CREDIT CARDS; None taken
LICENSED; No
ACCOMMODATION; 3 ensuite rooms, 2 double, 1 twin.

DINING ROOM; Excellent home-cooking
No evening meal/ or by special arrangement
VEGETARIAN; Catered for plus special diets
DISABLED ACCESS; No
GARDEN; Yes, Millstream, Trout lake
NON-SMOKING HOUSE   **PETS;** No

Chapter Six

CARDYNHAM HOUSE
The Cross,
Painswick, Gloucestershire GL6 6XX

Tel: 01452 814006
Fax: 01452 812321

Carol Keyes is an American with the heart of an Anglophile! Fifteen years ago she came to the Cotswolds which was the beginning of her love affair with old English properties. Since then she has renovated three houses in the Cotswold village of Painswick, each one larger and more challenging than the last. The third is the 15th-16th century Grade 2 Star Cardyham House which is a tribute to her artistic and architectural brilliance. Formerly a manor house, it once belonged to a local wool merchant. Carol was unaware of its great historical significance until she started restoring it and found a wealth of original features which had been covered up. For example a grand Elizabethan fireplace and bread oven, magnificent ship's timbers covered by a false ceiling, and a Jacobean oak staircase was hidden under 15 layers of black gloss paint! The house is now exquisitely beautiful but very much a comfortable home that has been restored with loving attention to detail in order to make it so.

Enter through the little door and step back in time. All the bedrooms have four posters and are either ensuite or have private bathrooms. Each bedroom is individually decorated with antiques, murals, and garlands of dried flowers. Each has colour TV, telephone, clock radios, coffee-tea facilities and drinks, wine and spirits are available. The house has central heating and a full fire certificate. Charming names adorn the rooms; The Dovecot, The Highlands, Old Tuscany, Medieval Garden, New England and Palm Beach. Breakfast served by a large open fire in the winter, is a speciality at Cardynham House with an extensive menu including American pancakes, waffles and maple syrup. The March Hare is filled with antiques and collectables which are offered for sale. What is so special about Cardynham House is the superb atmosphere created by Carol through her painstaking efforts to fill the house with lovely things and set them in exactly the right place. One example for instance is the mass of blue amd white china displayed on a Georgian dresser. It includes Burleighware, turn-of-the-century American sectioned willow-pattern plates, 'Asiatic Pheasant' and a pale, floral china which was designed for Liberty by a friend of Carol's. A house not to be missed.

USEFUL INFORMATION

OPEN; All year
CHILDREN; Over 12 years
CREDIT CARDS; Yes
ACCOMMODATION; 6 rooms ensuite or private bathrooms
MARCH HARE; A memorable breakfast
DISABLED ACCESS; No
PETS; No

TETHERS END
Abingdon Road,
Steventon,
Oxfordshire OX13 6RW
Tel: 01235 834015

Oxfordshire is a wonderful mixture of market towns and villages situated in beautiful countryside of fields and woods. The building materials add to the character, the use of Cotswold stone, Northamptonshire ironstone, with brick, timber and tile. The historic town of Abingdon, built on the north bank of the River Thames, was an important river port and crossing place in years gone by and boasts many handsome old houses and 17th century Town Hall housing the local history museum. Tethers End is a large, comfortable house situated in the village of Steventon some 4 miles south of Abingdon. The property is close to the imposing village green and the unique, mile long, raised causeway which is a feature of the village. The owners of the house, Mr. & Mrs. Miller, have created a totally separate unit from the main house, a twin bedded room with ensuite facilities, a lounge complete with bed settee, television, refridgerator and a tea and coffee tray. It is here you are served a delicious breakfast of your choice. The furnishings have been carefully chosen and are excellent throughout the whole house. There is a garden where you can sit and relax This whole area has so much to offer, with something for all the family from fishing and golf to museums, country houses and steam engines.

USEFUL INFORMATION
OPEN; All year
CHILDREN; Welcome
CREDIT CARDS; None taken
ACCOMMODATION; 1 twin bedded separate unit with ensuite facilities
DINING ROOM; Breakfast only
DISABLED ACCESS; Check suitability
GARDEN; Yes with furniture
PETS; No

SQUIRES GUEST HOUSE
The Cottages, St Johns Green,
St Johns Road, Wallingford,
Oxford OX10 9ER
Tel: 01491 837707
Fax: 01491 652037

Wallingford is a small quiet old market town with lovely old buildings dating from medieval times which has been tastefully converted into todays well known chain stores and these inturn blend in well with the locally owned shops, many antique shops and restaurants, catering for all tastes. Squires Guest House is to be found in St Johns Road, this 17th century property is delightful with exposed beams, antique and old furniture which give the house a lovely welcoming feeling. There are 5 ensuite rooms, two of which have a 4 poster beds. There is a ground floor room suitable for a disabled person without a wheelchair. All the rooms have colour television and a tea and coffee tray. A guests sitting room is available for you to relax in. There is plenty to do in the area with lots of places to visit, and with golf, fishing and plenty of walking, especially along the Ridgeway and Thames Path, you are sure to enjoy yourselves. Oxford is 30 minutes away by car.

USEFUL INFORMATION
OPEN; All year
CHILDREN; Not really
CREDIT CARDS; None taken
LICENSED; No
DINING ROOM; Continental breakfast
DISABLED ACCESS; Yes ground floor room
GARDEN; Small
PETS; No

Chapter Six

THE GREY COTTAGE,
Bath Rd., Leonard Stanley,
Stonehouse,
Glos. GL10 3LU.

Tel/Fax : 01453 822515

   Prior booking is essential to enjoy the Grey Cottage and the good company of your hosts, Andrew and Rosemary Reeves. Mentioned in several guides, this is charming accommodation, with very high standards in food, and equally high standards in the solicitude of your hosts. Every possible thought has gone into the comfort and well being of their guests, and it is through personal recommendation that this country house has retained it's reputation. This Cotswold stone house, was built circa 1807 with many of the original features having been preserved. The sitting and dining rooms have open log fires to give that wonderful sense of warmth and friendliness, but are backed up by full central heating throughout the house. Each bedroom is individual in it's decor and furnishings, and gives one the impression of being a family guest, rather than a paying one. All have tea and coffee trays, colour TV, trouser press, and large bath towels! Andrew and Rosemary do not have a license but they do run an 'honesty' bar for your comfort, and are quite happy to sit down with you to discuss your day. Food is another delight here and breakfast can be taken in the sunny conservatory which overlooks the bright garden. You will appreciate the quality, and dinner is possible if arranged at time of booking. There is no choice, but your preferences will have been 'discussed' and you will not be disappointed.
   The house sits at the top of a hill which overlooks the surrounding fields, giving a peaceful, rural outlook. But it is not really that rural - it is quite close to Stroud and there are many things of interest in the neighbourhood, including the Priory Church in the village which dates back to 1178. There are lots of outdoor pursuits around, including some very good walking - Cotswold Way, 1 mile. A pleasure indeed, as you will find out for yourself!

USEFUL INFORMATION

OPEN : All year except Xmas
CHILDREN : No
CREDIT CARDS : None taken
LICENSED : No
PETS : No
ACCOMMODATION : 3 rooms; 1 dble, 1 twin, 1 sgle.

DINING ROOM : Very high standards
VEGETARIANS : Catered for
BAR MEALS : Not applicable
DISABLED ACCESS : No
GARDEN : Very nice

COURTLEIGH HOUSE
40 Draycott Road,
Chisledon,
Swindon
Wiltshire SN4 0LS
Tel: 01793 740246

    Swindon is the largest town in Wiltshire, and was built on the prosperity of the Great Western Railway, the Railway Museum is housed in a former Wesleyan Chapel, and here you can feast your eyes on the wonders of steam up to the present day. There are lovely shops to wander around, a few pubs and restaurants where you are sure to have a pleasant meal or two. It is just outside Swindon in the village of Chisledon, that Ruth Hibberd has her country house where she welcomes her guests. Ruth is a very friendly person who goes out of her way to make you feel at home. On arrival you are welcomed with tea, coffee and home-made biscuits and cakes. The furnishings are a Regency style and compliment the house. The bedrooms are delightful being light, airy and very comfortable, with the added privacy of ensuite facilities, colour TV, a tea and coffee tray, and fruit. The views from the rooms are of beautiful open countryside. The breakfast at Courtleigh House is plentiful including delicious fresh eggs. Evening meals are not available, however the local pub serves good food. The garden is very large and well kept, there is even a hard tennis court if you feel a little energetic. Courtleigh House is convenient for the M4, Marlborough, historical Avebury, Bath and the Cotswolds, making it ideal for business and pleasure.

USEFUL INFORMATION
OPEN; *All year*   **DINING ROOM;** *Breakfast only*
CHILDREN; *Welcome*   **DISABLED ACCESS;** *Not really*
CREDIT CARDS; *None taken*   **GARDEN;** *beautiful, large. Hard tennis court*
ACCOMMODATION; *2 ensuite rooms*   **PETS;** *Not really*

HAWTHORN GUEST HOUSE
79 Burford Road,
Witney,
Oxen OX8 5DR
Tel: 01993 772768

    Pamela and Roland Schall own this lovely modernised Victorian family home. Hawthorn is situated on a quiet residential road overlooking the beautiful Windrush Valley. There are 4 light and airy bedrooms all of which are ensuite with colour TV and a tea and coffee tray. Hair dryers and irons are available on request. The house is centrally heated, and is excellently furnished. Breakfast is a traditional meal, with vegetarians being well catered for. Hawthorn is a non-smoking house. A 2 minute drive will find you in Witney a pleasant town with shops, fine restaurants and public houses. Oxford and Blenheim Palace are all within easy reach by car. With fishing, golf and walking you couldn't spend your holiday in a better place.

USEFUL INFORMATION
OPEN; *All year*   **DINING ROOM;** *Excellent English fare*
CHILDREN; *Welcome*   **VEGETARIAN;** *Catered for*
CREDIT CARDS; *Most taken, Visa/Mastercard*   **DISABLED ACCESS;** *Not really*
LICENSED; *No*   **GARDEN;** *Beautiful, with garden furniture*
ACCOMMODATION; *4 double ensuite rooms*   **PETS;** *No*

Chapter Six

CORNER COTTAGE
Stow Road, Alderton,
Tewkesbury, Gloucestershire GL20 8NH

Tel: 01242 620630

This pretty house built in the early part of this century is ideally situated for anyone either on business or pleasure. For the former it is convenient for Gloucester, Cheltenham or Worcester and for those on holiday Tewkesbury itself is a delightful town full of architectural interest and with an Abbey that is stunningly beautiful and full of history. From Corner Cottage one can explore The Cotswolds, go fishing having acquired a day ticket, play golf, ride or shoot and above all enjoy walking in the lovely countryside. Within easy reach also is Cheltenham Racecourse, one of the best courses in the country. Keith and Caroline Page own Corner Cottage and they clearly enjoy their guests. It is not a big house but charmingly furnished, warm and comfortable. They have three bedrooms for their guests; 1 double, 1 twin and 1 single. The twin room is ensuite and the other two share a bathroom. Each room has Television and Radio and a generously supplied tea and coffee tray. Breakfast served in the light, attractive dining room is a delicious meal with several choices and freshly cooked to order. You can either have a full English breakfast or enjoy a lighter Continental meal. Keith and Caroline do not provide evening meals but they will happily recommend you to a variety of eateries within easy distance.

USEFUL INFORMATION
OPEN; All year
CHILDREN; Welcome
CREDIT CARDS; None taken
ACCOMMODATION; 3 rooms
PETS; No
DINING ROOM; Excellent breakfast
No evening meal
VEGETARIAN; On request
DISABLED ACCESS; No facilities
GARDEN; Yes

PLANE TREE HOUSE
15 High Street,
Woodstock,
Oxford
Tel: 01993 813075

Located within a quiet square and in a central position close to excellent shops and restaurants is Plane Tree House offering guests warm and comfortable accommodation. Bedrooms are aesthetically pleasing and offer colour television and a tea and coffee tray. Breakfast is served in traditional fashion. Evening meals are not catered for but Steve and Jane will certainly recommend a restaurant to suit your taste. They are also keen fly fishermen and welcome like-minded souls. Facilities on offer locally include fishing, golf and walking. Blenheim Palace built in 1704 is well worth a visit. There are many picturesque villages, country parks or museums just waiting to be explored.

USEFUL INFORMATION
OPEN; All year
CHILDREN; Welcome, but bring your own highchair and cot for very young
CREDIT CARDS; None taken
LICENSED; No
ACCOMMODATION; 3 rooms, 1 twin, 1 double, 1 family
DINING ROOM; Traditional home-cooked fare
VEGETARIAN; Catered for
DISABLED ACCESS; Not really
GARDEN; No
PETS; No

FORDS FARM
Ewelme,
Wallingford,
Oxfordshire OX10 6HU

Tel: 01491 839272

Ewelme is one of the Chiltern's most attractive villages with some wonderful buildings dating back to the 15th century. It is also the home of the Chaucer family, infact the tomb of Chaucer's grand-daughter, the Duchess of Suffolk, is in the church. It is close to the village you will find Fords Farm with a most attractive stone and brick 15th century farmhouse, together with stables and a tithe barn surrounding a lawned courtyard. The house, which is '2 Crowns Highly Commended by the Southern Tourist Board, is very comfortable, and full of character - the beamed kitchen still has the original fireplace with bread oven and the original spit. The hallway has a flagstone floor.

The 2 twin bedrooms have colour television, tea and coffee making facilities and both have wonderful views - one looking over to the oldest church of England School in the country and the other looks over the rambling countryside. There is a traditional breakfast served in the tastefully decorated dining room. Evening meals are not available, however there are some good local pubs in the area. Oxford, Henley, Windsor and London are all within easy reach. There are other activities such as fishing, golf, riding and some lovely walks including the Rideway or you can just take in the beautiful scenery. You will certainly get a warm and friendly welcome from Marlene Edwards when you stay at Fords Farm.

USEFUL INFORMATION

OPEN; *All year*
CHILDREN; *Over 12 years*
CREDIT CARDS; *None taken*
LICENSED; *No*
ACCOMMODATION; *2 twin rooms*

DINING ROOM; *Excellent traditional breakfast*
VEGETARIAN; *Catered for*
DISABLED ACCESS; *No*
GARDEN; *Yes*
PETS; *No*

Chapter Six

THE PLAISTERERS ARMS
Abbey Terrace,
Winchcombe,
Gloucestershire GL54 5LL

Tel: 01242 602358

The Cotswolds is not only a beautiful part of the country with delightful villages, well tended gardens and thatched roofs, it is also steeped in history, no more so than Winchcombe, former capital of Mercia in the Middle Ages. It is here you will find The Plaisterers Arms an 18th century Cotswold Stone Inn, which first became a Beer House around 1830, and is unusual in that the bars are arranged in a split level design. The bedrooms are comfortable and are well appointed, the 5 rooms, 3 double, 2 twin and a family room, all with the privacy of ensuite facilities, radio, television and a tea and coffee tray.

The food at The Plaisterers is simply delicious and all freshly prepared to order. So much to choose from with Home-made Soups, Hot Platters, Home-made Pies, Curries and Sandwiches. Children are well catered for with their own menu serving all their favourites and there is at least one vegetarian dish. Mouthwatering desserts followed by tea or coffee. Not forgetting the Daily Specials listed on the blackboard. A traditional Roast lunch is served every Sunday. At the rear of the Inn you will find a lovely garden and terraced patio area also a separate children's play area. There is plenty of free parking available outside the pub. One is definitely assured an enjoyable stay.

USEFUL INFORMATION

OPEN; *All year*
CHILDREN; *Welcome*
CREDIT CARDS; *All major cards*
LICENSED; *Full*
ACCOMMODATION; *5 ensuite rooms, 3 double, 2 twin, 1 family*
PETS; *Welcome*

RESTAURANT; *Excellent traditional English fare, Bar meals available*
VEGETARIAN; *Catered for*
DISABLED ACCESS; *No*
GARDEN; *Delightful with patio and children's play area*

The North West Counties

Chapter Seven

THE NORTH WEST COUNTIES

including **LANCASHIRE, CUMBRIA, CHESHIRE, MERSEYSIDE, GREATER MANCHESTER**

The North West Counties

CHAPTER 7

THE NORTH WEST COUNTIES
including **LANCASHIRE, CUMBRIA, CHESHIRE, MERSEYSIDE, GREATER MANCHESTER**

INCLUDES

Betley Court Farm	**Betley, Nr Crewe**
Pool Farm	**Bickerton**
Oak Bank House	**Bowness-on-Windermere**
New Mills	**Brampton, Nr Carlisle**
Broadlea Guest House	**Carlisle**
Marchmain Guest House	**Carlisle**
Skiddaw Grove Hotel	**Keswick-on-Derwentwater**
The Paddock Guest House	**Keswick-on-Derwentwater**
Laurel Farm	**Malpas**
Albany House	**Penrith**
Bridge End Farm	**Penrith**
Tudor Farm	**St Michaels-on-Wyre, Nr Preston**
Roughlow Farm	**Tarporley**
Firgarth	**Windermere**
Holly Park House	**Windermere**

Chapter Seven

THE NORTHWEST COUNTIES
including **LANCASHIRE, CUMBRIA, CHESHIRE, MERSEYSIDE, GREATER MANCHESTER**

Cheshire is a county that could almost be swallowed up by Merseyside and Greater Manchester, but on the whole it is an interesting and varied county in it's own right. **Chester** is the main city, and the first thing you will notice is the steps. There are steps up to houses, to the gates in the walls,.... to everywhere. It seems to have been founded by the Romans, who took advantage of it's position at the mouth of the River Dee, and the walls still standing around the city are spectacular in their completeness. The famous walls of red sandstone are nearly 2 miles long, and make a raised walk from which to see many of the sights of the city.

The cathedral which is partly 11th century and partly restored in the 19th century, contains beautifully carved 14th century choir stalls, and the Chester Imp, a famous gargoyle, leers out from the north side of the clerestory in the cathedral nave. The 13th century castle contains an interesting military museum, and the Grosvenor Museum has a splendid collection of Roman remains and Anglo Saxon coins. The unique and world famous 'Rows' is a group of 13th century shops, and amongst the interesting buildings is the 17th century Bishop Lloyd's House. Nearby is God's Providence House, the only building untouched by the Black Death as it rampaged through the city. This is a lovely old city and one which you will find enjoyable. The racecourse attracts many people, while the magnificent zoo has 110 acres of natural enclosures, some of which can be toured by waterbus.

Nantwich is the most important town after Chester, and is a delightful place to visit. The Welsh were always trying to get their hands on the town because of the brine-pits which were the locals livelihood, but they didn't succeed! In 1604 the plague hit and killed nearly 500 people before it abated in March 1605. Nantwich has several attractive places to visit including Stapley Water Gardens, the world's largest water garden centre.

Up the A51 from Nantwich is the village of **Tarporley,** built of brick, and with a famous pub The Swan, a meeting place of the Torporley hunt. Onwards to Beeston Castle, a 12th century fortress above the Cheshire Plains which has wonderful views. Peckforton Castle, a medieval fortress, is also worth a visit if only for the views!

Congleton's prosperity was once linked with gloves, lace and ribbons. It has fine houses and from the streets, hill climbers can recognise in the distance their favourite Mow Cop. Canals are very much a part of life in

Cheshire and close to the M6 **Crewe** to **Middlewich** road is the pretty village of **Wheelock**, where the Trent and Mersey Canal runs through. The old silk town of **Macclesfield** is one that should not be missed. Even although it is a busy market town, it's full of quaint cobbled streets that add to the charm and character.

Merseyside, and you immediately think of **Liverpool**. Famous for many names such as The Beatles, Cilla Black, and many, many more, this is a city that exudes talent. It also has a colourful and interesting past - it was first settled in the 1st century, and it's position has made it a great port for all manner of trade. It was the point of massive immigration by the starving Irish in the famine of the 1840s, and Liverpool docks were known the world over. Part of them have become redundant today, but have been put to good use in telling the history of the city. It is an interesting city with a diversity of interesting people who are forthright, friendly and cheerful. **Aintree** is home of the Grand National, reputedly the best horse race in the world, and attended by thousands of spectators each year. 1996 saw them staying a little longer than anticipated, but the wonderful hospitality of the local people came to the forefront and won the day!

Albert Dock in Liverpool has lots of museums, wonderful art galleries and The Beatles Story in the Britannia Vaults. The famous Mersey Ferries are there for you to travel on and you will probably know the words to the immortal song....'So ferry, cross the Mersey'.....

Manchester has a good motorway system to hand and an international airport on it's doorstep. It is a busy cosmopolitan city, rich in life and with very good shopping facilities. There is actually quite a lot of history here with the 15th century castle, the 19th century Gothic tower which has a carillon of 23 bells, and which houses the Tourist Information Office - close to hand for all the facts! The City Art Gallery has a wonderful collection of drawings, paintings and sculptures by various artists; Stubbs, Gainsborough, Turner, Duccio and Canaletto, and also the Pre-Raphaelites. Castlefield Gallery has a changing exhibition of contemporary paintings and sculptures, and Heaton Hall is a superbly restored 18th century house. These are just a few of the attractions, and there are many more for you to discover.

Lancashire is famous for that seaside town **Blackpool** which has all the thrills and excitement of a traditional family seaside holiday. Apart from the autumn illuminations, adventure playground, aquarium and circus hall, Blackpool has a fine art gallery with a good collection of works by 19th and 20th century British artists. **Fleetwood** along the coast is just the place for bargain hunters with it's large indoor market. **Lancaster** is the capital of Lancashire and has a wonderful Norman castle on the site of a Roman fort.

Chapter Seven

Since the 18th century it has housed a prison and the countycourts. The Priory Church of St Mary is a 15th century Perpendicular on the site of a Saxon church, and has some splendid 13th century carved choir stalls; among the finest in Britain. The 18th century Customs House contains an interesting maritime history of the area.

Southport is another charming resort with large sandy beaches and a lovely wide open front. It has gained a reputation as being the floral capital of England's north west, and the Southport Flower Show is a major event in any horticulturist's diary. The formal Victorian parks and gardens in Southport are many, and you can spend a delightful day at either Heskith Park or the Botanic Gardens. There are plenty of golf courses with the most famous being the Royal Birkdale Course, and the 'Open' will be coming to Southport again in 1998. Another feature of the north west is brass bands, and during the season Southport has it's share. This is something that delights both young and old, and you will soon be clapping along in time to the music.

Moving into Cumbria and the beautiful Lake District brings us to one of the prettiest parts of the British Isles. Apart from the stunning scenery, the towns and villages are a delight to the eye with their quaint streets, curio and antique shops, and picturesque cottages of granite.

The M6 takes you to **Kendal**, home of Mint Cake, and birthplace of Katherine Parr, sixth wife of Henry VIII. The castle where she was born is 12th century, and Abbot Hall nearby is an 18th century house with a museum of local industry. Another museum here tells of the natural and human history of the Lake District and has a World Wild Life Gallery. Truly worth a visit. **Grange-over-Sands** is the next stop, and although not safe for bathing, is more than compensated by the promenade and extensive gardens.

This place became fashionable with the coming of the Furness Railway which linked it with Lancaster, and with the unusually mild climate giving rise to sub tropical plants and alpines, it has stayed one of the most perfect places in the district. Walking is wonderful here, and no more so than on the path which leads to Hampsfell Summit and The Hospice, a small stone tower with superb views of Morcambe Bay and of the rolling foothills climbing to the majestic peaks of the Lake District. The historical 'Cistercian Way' starts it's 37 mile journey here, travelling through Furness to Barrow.

Coniston is an unspoilt village nestling in the heart of the mountains, and even with the notoriety it received when Donald Campbell used the lake for his record speed attempts, it has managed to stay that way. The village is still a working one with many locals employed in the slate quarries and hill farms. It is an absolute haven for walkers and ramblers, with quiet walks through woodland, and climbing routes in Dow Crags for the more experienced climber. Brantwood House at Coniston was the home of painter John Ruskin for many years until his death in 1900, and contains much of his work. **Windermere** is always a beautiful spot whatever the time of year; the lake is 10 miles long, and the biggest in England. It is a wonderful place with the mood of each season taking you over completely and losing you in the loveliness and serenity of the setting. Winter with it's white coat takes your breath away (sometimes literally), while a summer evening cradles you in the warmth of the setting sun shimmering over the water. You can tell that I like this place! **Grasmere** was home to Wordsworth for a period of time, and his tiny cottage is almost as he left it. You can see where his great inspiration came from - living in this sanctuary with beauty all around him. He is buried in the churchyard here, and Wordsworth Museum contains manuscripts and first editions of his works.

Travel on to the northern lakes and half a million acres of some of the most breathtaking landscapes in England, with rolling fields and sandstone villages just waiting to be discovered. **Alston**, the highest market town in England is a thousand feet above sea level, and is delightfulwith it's steep cobbled streets. Surrounded by the wonderful North Pennines, Alston and nearby villages like **Nenthead** and **Garrigill** became prosperous with the lead mining.

Penrith is the main northern gateway to the Lake District and the North Pennines. With it's good rail links and closeness to the M6, it is an ideal base for touring the area. It is a popular shopping town with it's excellent arcades and traditional markets. The town is dominated by Beacon Hill, which dates back to the Border Wars, and there are many other interesting historical places to visit. **Appleby** is another market town in the north, and one of the finest. It is justifiably proud of it's Royal Charters dating from 1174. Sitting on the River Eden it is also within easy reach of the wonderful scenery of the Pennines.

The Settle Carlisle Railway makes it's way to it's highest point below Wild Boar fell at the head of Mallestang Dale. Nearby are the villages of **Brough** with a castle built by the Normans, and **Ravenstonedale.** Here at gallows Hill in Lord Park there are traces of Ancient Britons.

Onward to **Keswick** which has some interesting historical places to visit. The Cumberland Pencil Museum is really quite fascinating (am I glad we now use computers!), and the Keswick Museum and Art Gallery contains original manuscripts by Wordsworth, Southey and Walpole.

Chapter Seven

My last stop must be **Carlisle** (this is frequently my last stop on the train journey to Scotland!). Travelling by train you do not see much of the city, and what you do see does not do it justice. The castle here was a border stronghold, and remains include a 12th century keep, a maze of vaulted chambers and passages, and Queen Mary's Tower, the enforced home of the sad Mary Queen of Scots in 1568. The tower now houses an fascinating collection of the Border Regiment. The Guildhall Museum is a 15th century town house which is now a museum of civic and local history, and a lovely silverware collection. The cathedral is 12th to 13th century, with a fine 14th century east window, and a Renaissance screen. Carlisle is a important city with good road and rail links, and it's own airport. It has some very good shopping facilities and caters well for sporting interests.

The trip through this part of England has been a lovely one, with a diversity and medley of scenery to soothe the soul and tantalise the spirit. These are the places that make me yearn to be able to paint, draw or even make some recognisable mark on paper that could capture the memory of the journey, or that special moment when the scene in front of you takes your breathe away.

BETLEY COURT FARM
Betley,
Nr Crewe,
Cheshire CW3 9BH

Tel: 01270 820229

Betley is a charming, historical village and in its centre is Betley Court Farm, a mixed farm of some 226 acres and with a delightful farmhouse in which Jayne Speed offers three beautifully appointed ensuite bedrooms complete with central heating, colour TV, a generously supplied beverage tray and delicious full English breakfasts. The house, built in Victorian times, is warm and comfortable and splendidly relaxed. Children are very welcome and the garden is secure and enclosed making it ideal for the very young. An evening meal can be arranged with notice and if you are lucky enough to sit down to this meal you will find everything is home-made and the produce fresh.

Betley Court Farm includes the picturesque 'Betley Mere' a 26 acre lake. It is renowned for its unusual plant and wildlife and gives much pleasure to visitors. The panoramic views are stunning and within the farmland there are some superb walks and exceptional fishing. In fact Betley Court Farm is great for people who are either on holiday or business. It is convenient for Keele University, The Potteries, Alton Towers, Crewe Business Park, Bridgemere Garden World and many other places. Golf courses abound and horse riding is available. Betley Court Farm is also the host of the Betley Show in August and Betley Bonfire in November - two great occasions.

USEFUL INFORMATION

OPEN; All year
CHILDREN; Welcome
CREDIT CARDS; None taken
ACCOMMODATION; 3 ensuite
PETS; By arrangement only
PARKING; On site
DINING ROOM; Traditional English breakfast
Evening meals by arrangement
VEGETARIAN; Yes
DISABLED ACCESS; No
GARDEN; Yes. Secure & enclosed

Chapter Seven

POOL FARM
*Goldford Lane,
Bickerton,
Nr Malpas,
Cheshire SY14 8LN
Tel: 01829 782411
Fax: 01829 782108*

Set in one of the Cheshire's beauty spots is Pool Farm, a 600 acre working dairy/arable and beef farm. The farmhouse was built approximately 300 years ago and was once used to manufacture Cheshire cheese, infact the 'Old Cheese Room' is now the snooker room. There are wonderful exposed beams and some low ceilings and the whole house is surrounded by open fields and is very peaceful and relaxing. The pretty bedrooms, one of which is ensuite, have tea and coffee making facilities. There is an attractive guests lounge with a colour television. Breakfast is a hearty meal indeed, it is full English including various home-made jams, and really sets you up for the day. You will need a good start to the day as there is so much to do in this area, with easy access for Chester, North Wales, The Potteries and Lake District. With fishing, golf, riding and wonderful National Trust area walks on the doorstep, you are sure to enjoy yourselves.

USEFUL INFORMATION
OPEN; January-November
CHILDREN; By arrangement
CREDIT CARDS; None taken
LICENSED; No
ACCOMMODATION; 4 rooms, 2 double, 1 twin, 1 single, 1 double is ensuite
DINING ROOM; Very hearty breakfast, home-made jams, no evening meal
VEGETARIAN; Catered for
DISABLED ACCESS; No
GARDEN; Yes
PETS; By arrangement
NO SMOKING

BROADLEA GUEST HOUSE
*25 Broad Street,
Carlisle, Cumbria CA1 2AG
Tel/Fax: 01228 24699*

Built in 1875 and pleasantly situated in a peaceful tree lined street, sits Broadlea Guest House a comfortable home with lots of friendly atmosphere, and attentive service. Attractive bedrooms with high quality modern fabrics and tasteful furnishings, offer ensuite or private bathroom facilities, with colour TV, clock radio, hair dryer, also a tea and coffee tray with biscuits. Trouser press, iron and ironing board are available on request. An appetizing and tasty traditional English breakfast is served or for those requiring something lighter Mrs. Hullock, offers a Continental menu with hot croissants. Well presented evening meals are provided by prior arrangement. Broadlea makes the perfect base from which to visit the stunning scenic areas which surround Carlisle, and being so close to Scotland and the wonderful Lake District.

USEFUL INFORMATION
OPEN; All year
CHILDREN; No
CREDIT CARDS; Access/Visa/ Delta/Switch
ACCOMMODATION; 3 rooms, 1 ensuite, 2 with private bathroom
DINING ROOM; Full English or Continental breakfast. Evening meal on request
VEGETARIAN; Catered for
DISABLED ACCESS; No
GARDEN; No
PETS; Yes

564

OAKBANK HOUSE
Helm Road,
Bowness-on-Windermere,
Cumbria LA23 3BU

Tel: 015394 43386

In the heart of the Lake District, the poet William Wordsworth did his wandering and Beatrix Potter wrote her delightful childrens books, they were both inspired by the serenity and natural beauty of this wonderful part of the country, with its steep, uneven fells and tranquil lakes. Nestling in all this is Bowness-on-Windermere, a resort on Lake Windermere, England's largest lake which measures 10 $\frac{1}{2}$ miles from north to south and 1 $\frac{1}{2}$ miles east to west, and is surrounded by mountains that rise with dignity at the northern end of the lake. Bowness is primarily a Victorian village with charming narrow streets, which in summer are bustling with visitors, sailors, walkers and anglers. Just off the main street is Oakbank House, a superb guest house, owned and efficiently run by the Sidwell family, who have totally refurbished the house to create a very comfortable and relaxing home, which they graciously share with you. The whole house has been tastefully decorated with high quality furnishings, drapes and carpets. The bedrooms are delightful with colour co-ordinated bed linen, comfy beds and the privacy of ensuite facilities. Each room is well appointed with colour television, intercom telephones, a tea and coffee tray and complimentary shampoo and soap. The attractive and spacious dining room is where you will be served a hearty Lakeland breakfast, the Sidwell's are of farming stock so are used to starting the day well, their traditional English breakfast will certainly keep you going all day. There are superb views from all the rooms, as Oakbank overlooks the village, Lake Windermere and the mountains beyond. It is a place you can feel totally at home, where you can unwind and enjoy yourself. With so much to do and see in this area you will find it hard to fit everything in. Nearby is a children's play park with swings, slides and roundabouts, then there is the World of Beatrix Potter Exhibition, who actually lived in Bowness, here you can see how Peter Rabbit and his friends were created and adults can become children again. Take a cruise around the islands or the full length of the lake or stroll around the quaint shops mingling with the rest of the holiday makers. You cannot possibly fail to be enchanted by this wonderful area of outstanding naturalbeauty.

USEFUL INFORMATION

OPEN; *All year*
CHILDREN; *Yes. Cot & Highchair available*
CREDIT CARDS; *Yes*
LICENSED; *Residential*
ACCOMMODATION; *11 rooms, 4 double, 6 family, 1 twin, 10 ensuite, 1 private bathroom*

DINING ROOM; *Excellent hearty breakfast Evening meal is not available*
VEGETARIAN; *By arrangement*
DISABLED ACCESS; *No*
GARDEN; *Yes with fish pond*
PETS; *Yes, well behaved, must be on a lead*

Chapter Seven

NEW MILLS HOUSE
*Brampton, Nr. Carlisle,
Cumbria CA8 2QS*

Tel: 016977 3376

Brampton is a market town with old cobbled streets and brick buildings with slate roofs. In 1745 Bonnie Prince Charlie had his headquarters in a shop in High Cross Street. Brampton is also the home of Mrs. Boon, who owns a very impressive 19th century stone built Country House known as New Mills House. This charming property was once part of the estate belonging to the Lords of Carlisle, and is set in the wilds of Border country. The house is very warm and comfortable with a very homely atmosphere, created by Mrs. Boon, to help you feel relaxed and happy in her lovely home. The furnishings are comfy and traditional. There are 3 bedrooms, all double, 2 of the rooms are separate from the house and are situated in a delightful courtyard setting, where pots abound, full of lovely flowers making a superb show of colour in the summer months. These rooms have ensuite facilities, fridge, shaver points, they also have their own key. The third room is in the house with its own adjacent bathroom. All the rooms have a tea and coffee tray. A hearty full English breakfast with all the trimmings, and plenty of toast with home-made preserves and tea or coffee. An evening meal is by arrangement only. Mrs. Boon uses the best fresh local and home-grown produce. The large garden is a particular feature, it is beautiful and very well tended.

Hadrian's Wall is only 2 miles away, built by the Roman Emperor between AD122 and 136 to protect Roman Britain, extends for 73 miles. The wild and rugged vastness of the Northumberland National Park is a few miles drive, here wildlife is plentiful from the lovely piping cry of the curlew, which is the emblem of the Park, to the rare merlins, the noblewoman's hunting bird of the Middle Ages. This bleakness has a beauty all of its own, in the north of the Park is Kielder Forest, the largest man-made forest in Europe. The Castle has a visitor centre, and Duke of Northumberland's Hunting Lodge, where many forest walks start from. The forest drives are very popular, Kielder is famous for being a stage in the Lombard RAC Rally. Within the forest is Kielder Water, a huge man-made reservoir, wonderful for fishing, sailing and windsurfing, and very scenic for your picnic. In the opposite direction is the Lake District with all it has to offer, is just a 45 minute drive away, and the lovely gently pastureland of the Eden Valley. New Mills House is the perfect place to stay, either for a short break or a long holiday, whatever you choose you will receive a warm and hospitable welcome.

USEFUL INFORMATION

OPEN; All year except Christmas
CHILDREN; Welcome
CREDIT CARDS; None taken
ACCOMMODATION; 3 double rooms
2 ensuite, 1 private bathroom
PETS; Yes, well behaved
DINING ROOM; Full English breakfast
Evening meal by arrangement
VEGETARIAN; Catered for
DISABLED ACCESS; Good
GARDEN; Large and beautiful

'MARCHMAIN' GUEST HOUSE,
*151 Warwick Road, Carlisle,
Cumbria, CA1 1LU.*

Tel : 01228 29551

This traditional, comfortable house dates from 1880 and is owned by Bill and Marion Bertham. As your hosts, Bill and Marion ensure a high degree of comfort with all the necessities being thought of. Each bedroom is equipped with colour TV, tea/coffee facilities, hair dryer, shaving facilities, shampoo & soap, and a welcome tray. Although not en suite, there are three toilets and two private bathrooms which cater for the seven charming guest rooms. Breakfast caters to all, with a choice of continental, vegetarian or full English, and evening meals can be arranged on request.

Marchmain is the ideal location for seeing some of the wonderful sights in this part of the world. Carlisle itself is a very historic city with guided walks and many tours available. As a bordertown the history is quite unique with the remains of the grim castle where many battles were fought, a 12th century keep with a maze of vaulted chambers and passages, Queen Mary's Tower, where she was kept imprisoned in 1568, and much more. Museums, galleries and churches are all represented here in this fine city. Tullie House is such an art gallery and museum, which tells the story of Carlisle and the Borders in excellent detail through vision and sound. From Marchmain all this is within easy distance and is not to be missed. Further afield you have Hadrian's Wall, which again has many organised tours. Discover the Roman heritage of Britain as you gaze upon the hills of Scotland and marvel at the scope and audacity of our Roman ancestors. Housteads Roman Fort is one of the most complete examples to be found in Britain and lets one see just how the Roman soldiers would have lived. In addition there is Chesters Roman Fort and Corbridge Roman Site, each fascinating in it's own way.

Not only is there great history in this area, but the scenery is wonderful too! With easy access to the North Pennines (known as England's last wilderness) there is superb scenery and remoteness about this once industrial part of England. It was at one time the wealthiest lead mining centre in Europe and was where schooling first became compulsory, leaving behind a myriad of villages and towns which combined farming and mining into their lives. Nowadays these villages and towns cater for the local and tourist alike, but the moors still have that remoteness and haunting quality which no amount of 'civilisation' can change. This is a great area to visit to see the forces of man and nature together, and how they can compliment each other. Don't miss the opportunity of good food, comfortable accommodation and a kaleidoscope of entertainment and history all on the doorstep of Marchmain Guest House!

USEFUL INFORMATION

OPEN : *All year*
CHILDREN : *Welcome*
PETS : *No*
LICENSED : *No*
CREDIT CARDS : *All major*
ACCOMMODATION : *7 rooms; 3 fml, 1 twin, 1 dbl, 2 sgl.*

RESTAURANT : *Evening meal by request*
VEGETARIANS : *Catered for*
BAR SNACKS : *Not applicable*
DISABLED ACCESS : *No*
GARDEN : *No*

Chapter Seven

SKIDDAW GROVE HOTEL
Vicarage Hill,
Keswick-0n-Derwentwater,
Cumbria CA12 5QB
Tel: 017687 73324

    Built about 1820 as a Gentleman's residence, Skiddaw Grove has happily adapted to being an hotel. To begin with the situation is delightful. It is set in its own private gardens with a heated outdoor swimming pool, which is usually open between May and mid-September. It has a sun terrace on the secluded southern side of house - an ideal place to sit whilst enjoying a gin and tonic or simply relaxing. The garden offers magnificent mountain views and there is private parking for all cars. Vicarage Hill is a quiet lane on the fringe of Keswick, yet only 10 minutes walk (via Fitz Park) from the town centre. It is a great place for a holiday or for a break. Owned by Jonathan and Audrey Brooks it is run with that degree of informality that only comes when those in charge are totally professional. Over the years Skiddaw Grove has been skillfully modernised to provide ten comfortable, en-suite bedrooms. There is a choice of double, twin or single bedded rooms and one family room. Every room has colour TV,tea andcoffee facilities, hair dryers and clock radios. The spacious dining room and separate residents lounge both have superb views over open countryside towards Skiddaw, one of Lakelands highest mountains, and to Bassenthwaite Lake.
    The generous Breakfast menu offers everyone a choice. Whatever you choose will be freshly cooked and accompanied by piping hot tea or freshly brewed coffee, as much toast as you could wish for and a selection of preserves. Dinner is optional. It is served every evening except Sunday and is a four course meal with an interesting choice of starters, main courses and sweets, followed by a cheeseboard with coffee and mints being served in the lounge to finish. Special diets are always catered for and vegetarian meals are available. Emphasis is placed on ensuring that all the food is freshly prepared and cooked using locally purchased ingredients. The friendly bar is well stocked and you will find a carefully chosen wine list to suit both taste and pocket. Smoking is not permitted within the house except the bar. Children are very welcome but pets are strictly forbidden - not even if they sleep in the car. There are excellent boarding kennels nearby. Keswick itself is a thriving market town and holiday centre near Derwentwater in the northern part of the Lake District. The views are stunning. It is a well loved and cared for town and has featured regularly in the finals of Britain in Bloom. One of the enchanting things about staying in the Lake District is the ability to use the regular launch service around the lakes. You will find the town interesting to explore, it has good exhibitions, excellent shops and activities for all ages, all weather and all times of the year. There is live theatre during the summer months. There are many fascinating places within easy reach. Skiddaw Grove makes an ideal base from which to enjoy all that this part of Britain has to offer. If you prefer a self-catering holiday do ring and enquire about High Meadow, a modern, three bedroomed house owned by the Brooks.

USEFUL INFORMATION

OPEN; All year except Christmas week

CHILDREN; Very welcome
CREDIT CARDS; None taken
LICENSED; Yes
ACCOMMODATION; 10 en suite rooms
Private parking

DINING ROOM; Bbreakfast
                               & dinner
VEGETARIAN; Catered for
DISABLED ACCESS; Difficult, ring
GARDEN; Yes + heated pool
PETS; Not permitted. Boarding
                               kennels closeby

THE PADDOCK GUEST HOUSE,
Wordsworth St., Penrith Rd.,
Keswick-on-Derwentwater,
Cumbria CA12 4HU.

Tel : 017687 72510

The Paddock Guest House, run by Pauline and Geoff Brown, dates back to the mid 1800s and offers good quality, traditional English accommodation. The house is charmingly furnished, and offers a great deal of character to the visitor. There are six bedrooms, three of which are en suite, and all have colour TV, tea/coffee facilities, central heating and wash basins. Pauline and Geoff are solicitous of your requirements and are anxious that your stay is a pleasant one, and with their courteous friendliness you could hardly do otherwise! Children of any age are welcome and there are cots available if required. Pets can also be accommodated, as long as you have made prior arrangements. The residents lounge is a warm inviting room with an open log fire situated in a fascinating surround made from local lakeland slate and mineralstones. A more pleasant way to spend a relaxing evening is difficult to imagine: a glass of something warming in one hand and your feet toasting in front of the fire, discussing the next day's adventures or those you have just had! Breakfast is full English with a variety of cereals, juice and cooked choices, and with plenty of tea or coffee and toast to finish off! Continental or vegetarian are both available on request. An evening meal is not offered but there are plenty of pubs and restaurants to choose from in the surrounding area.

Keswick itself is in the heart of the mountains: Skiddaw immediately north, and Grisedale Pike just one of the stunning array of peaks on the western skyline. This is a great place for scenery of all varieties, with the A66 leading to Keswick being just on the north side of the Lake District, stretching farmland views of Cumbria on one side, and miles of beach and sand dunes not too far away on another. Just imagine the beautiful views from the sand dunes of the West Cumbria coast, as you fill your lungs with healthy fresh air - sure to revitalise and invigorate! There is plenty of choice of activities with golf, trout fishing, cycling and walking. The Paddock Guest House is ideally suited for all these places and is a quiet haven of peace and tranquillity to return to at the end of the day. Fitz Park, Derwentwater and Keswick town centre are all within level walking distance of the house; Keswick has plenty to offer in the way of shopping, museum and art gallery (containing original manuscripts by Wordsworth), and at the site of the oldest original factory in the world dating from 1832, a delightful display of pencils and their history. A rather unusual exhibition but well worth the visit! Pauline and Geoff enjoy their visitors and you are sure to want to return again and again to this retreat in this charming part of the country.

USEFUL INFORMATION

OPEN : All year except Xmas & Boxing Day **RESTAURANT :** English breakfast
CHILDREN : Welcome **VEGETARIANS :** Catered for
PETS : By arrangement **BAR SNACKS :** Not applicable
LICENSED : Residential **DISABLED ACCESS :** Limited
CREDIT CARDS : None taken **GARDEN :** No
ACCOMMODATION : 6 rooms : 3 en suite, 2 fml, 4 dbl, 2 twin.

Chapter Seven

LAUREL FARM
*Chorlton Lane,
Malpas, Cheshire SY14 7ES*

Tel/Fax: 01948 860291

In an outstanding, peaceful situation, surrounded by acres of glorious countryside, yet only minutes from the attractive market village of Malpas, Laurel Farm is set off by a large landscaped duck pond to one side of the drive, (a bevy of cheeky ducks may greet you!). You stand momentarily before entering the front door and take the pure air into your lungs and looking about you see some truly lovely views. A good start but when you enter the house the ambience just jumps out at you. It is warm and welcoming and a perfect place to stay. Anthea Few is your hostess and this lady has a great eye for colour and detail, something she has given to the furnishings of Laurel Farm. Her taste is exquisite, not only is the furniture a mixture of antique and traditional, it gleams with the patina of age. Warmth, welcome and comfort are the hallmarks of this elegant house which dates from the 17th century. The atmosphere is very relaxed - something guests always remark on at Laurel Farm. Sympathetically restored, it retains all its original character and charm enhanced by exposed beams, old doors, mellow Welsh quarry tiled floors and much more besides.

There are stunning views from each individually furnished bedroom - here again comfort is the key - a well stocked hot drinks tray, remote colour TV, hairdryer and the many personal touches finish the rooms off beautifully. Never over the top however! To one side of the house there is a private suite of two bedrooms plus a sitting room - excellent for parties of four to five people. Here guests have their own keys and are most welcome to come and go at their own leisure. A lovely, very English dining room awaits you in the morning. An excellent variety of food and splendid cooked breakfasts - always freshly cooked when you arrive - a friendly affair which will be a highlight of your visit

Situated on the North Wales/Shropshire borders, the area offers a wealth of interesting places to visit - Chester, Shrewsbury, some glorious countryside, a bit of 'hidden' England and the dramatic and spectacular scenery of North Wales together with castles, fine houses, some magnificent gardens and wonderful walks on the Sandstone Trail. Close by are numerous golf courses and the excellent sporting and leisure facilities at Carden Park. Locally there is an excellent range of good pubs and restaurants. In all Laurel Farm makes an ideal base for a break, or for those on business who prefer a more restful stay in quality surroundings. To reach Laurel Farm from the attractive village of Malpas, go down the High Street and in the centre of the village take the B5069 towards Bangor-on-Dee. One mile take the first right to Chorlton. After one mile turn right opposite the red telephone kiosk. The farmhouse is less than a 1/4 mile on the right hand side

USEFUL INFORMATION

OPEN; All year
CHILDREN; Over 12 years
CREDIT CARDS; None taken
LICENSED; No
ACCOMMODATION; 4 ensuite rooms
PETS; No

DINING ROOM; Traditional breakfast. Dinner by arrangement. (Min. 4 guests-48hrs notice) Light suppers
VEGETARIAN; Upon request
DISABLED ACCESS; Ground floor bedroom. Not suitable for wheelchairs
GARDEN; Lovely with ducks & pond
A NON-SMOKING HOUSE

ALBANY HOUSE
5 Portland Place, Penrith,
Cumbria CA11 7QN

Tel: 01768 863072

Penrith is a very interesting place with plenty going on and is closely associated with William Wordsworth, who lived in a house here which is now the Town Hall, and was educated at Dame Birkett's School which today is a restaurant. The Castle is very old, early 14th century, and Beacon Hill Tower was used during border wars, when fires were lit to warn the people of invaders. No need for that these days, in fact you couldn't ask for a more friendlier welcome than you receive at Albany House. Owned and expertly run by Mrs. Cath Blundell, this mid-Victorian Guest House is a few minutes walk away from the town centre, and conveniently placed for the M6 and A66. The 5 guest rooms are attractively furnished, spacious, light and airy, with colour/satellite television, in-house movies, central heating, wash hand basin and a plentiful tea and coffee tray. There is a bathroom with shower, a separate shower room and 2 separate WC. The large family room has ensuite facilities. After a good nights sleep, a delicious full English breakfast is served in the breakfast room. Cath can also cater for special diets, and with notice she will prepare a packed lunch for your day away. Your days here will be overflowing with outings and activities, the area has so much to offer, the Lake District, Eden Valley, Scottish Borders and Hadrian's Wall. This English Tourist Board 'Commended' and AA '3Q' Guest House is definitely an excellent place to stay, where the atmosphere is warm and relaxed.

USEFUL INFORMATION

OPEN; All year
CHILDREN; Yes
CREDIT CARDS; None taken
ACCOMMODATION; 5 guest rooms, 1 ensuite
PETS; No
DINING ROOM; Traditional breakfast. Evening meal not available. Packed lunches on request
VEGETARIAN; Catered for + special diets
DISABLED ACCESS; No
GARDEN; No

Chapter Seven

BRIDGE END FARM
Kirkby Thore, Penrith,
Cumbria CA10 1UZ

Tel: 017683 61362

The landscape around the Westmorland fells and dales is breathtaking, with salt marshes, quiet valleys interspersed with glistening lakes and the peace and tranquillity it pervades. It is a place where you want to explore or you can just sit and admire its beauty. The area is large and it will take you a while to travel through, so you will require a good base to start from, and there is nowhere better than Bridge End Farm in Kirkby Thore just off the A66 and 8 miles form Penrith. Situated in the heart of the Eden Valley overlooking the Pennines hill, this substantial 18th century farmhouse is a working farm specialising in pedigree Holstein dairy cows. The decor in the house is delightful, with antique furniture, the Residents Sitting Room has been newly furbished but has retained the original plaster cornice with decorated plaster work, it also has a colour television and large open fire, where in winter logs crackle away. The guest bedrooms are superb, spacious with the luxury of ensuite facilities, the comfortable beds display wonderful hand-made patchwork quilts enhancing the antique furniture. The rooms all have hair dryer, clock radio, television and a complimentary tea and coffee tray. Farmers wives are renowned for their excellent cooking and Yvonne Dent is no exception, here breakfasts are a real treat, with a large full English meal with all the trimmings to get you off to a good start, and an evening meal to rush back for. Yvonne uses all local freshly prepared ingredients wherever possible, she is well known for her Sticky Toffee Pudding. Bridge End Farm is not licensed but you are more than welcome to bring your own wine to compliment the meal. The garden is very spacious with a large lawn, trees, shrubs and flower borders. Take a stroll along the River Eden, where private fishing is available.

For your days away why not visit Alston, the highest market town in England. Gardeners will love this area with Hartside Nursery Gardens and Acorn Bank Gardens whish has the most comprehensive herb garden in the North of England. There is also Wetheriggs Country Pottery, Lowther Leisure Park, Appleby Castle Rare Breeds Conservation Centre and - BroughamHall. There are also beautiful walks, fishing, golf and horse riding. If you want a 'get away from it all' holiday, then Bridge End Farm is the place for you, you will not be disappointed.

USEFUL INFORMATION

OPEN; All year
CHILDREN; Welcome
CREDIT CARDS; None taken
LICENSED; May bring your own wine
ACCOMMODATION; 3 rooms,
2 double, 1 twin, 2 ensuite, 1 private bathroom
DINING ROOM; Excellent farmhouse cooking
VEGETARIAN; By arrangement
DISABLED ACCESS; No
GARDEN; Spacious
PETS; By arrangement

TUDOR FARM
*Sowerby Road,
St.Michaels, Garstang, Nr.Preston,
Lancashire, PR3 0TT.*

Tel : 01995 679717

Set in the beautiful Lancashire countryside, Tudor Farm is a charming 1995 built house with stunning views and a peaceful position. This is a working farm, with sheep and calves, but the main concern is the growing and supplying of 'Turf'. Dave and Barbara Brennand are the owners, and while Dave deals mainly with the business of the turf cultivation, Barbara acts as your hostess with the aid of her 'little helper' Sarah. All bodies are required when it comes to the animals! - you might even find yourself lending a hand in times of need! This is a friendly household where being part of the family is natural and everybody is afforded the same welcome. It is listed 'commended' by the English Tourist Board. Accommodation is on the ground and first floors, with a twin en suite room being available for the disabled. The doorways on the ground floor level are accessible to wheelchairs with the twin room having some disabled facilities. All rooms have TV, and that essential tea/coffee tray, and Barbara also welcomes her guests with refreshments. Breakfast is a traditional English affair in the ground floor dining room, which has panoramic views over the farm. There is a cosy lounge on the first floor where you can relax and plan your activities for touring the area! Children are most welcome and there is even a reduction for those under 10 years.

With good access from the M6 at junction 32/33, this is a excellent centre from where to visit the many things around you, with Bowland Fells being only 10 minutes away, and the dizzy rides of Blackpool Fun Beach only 20 minutes away! Obviously there are many other pursuits and places of interest within easy distance and I am sure Barbara and Dave will be only too happy to help you 'enjoy your stay'.

USEFUL INFORMATION

OPEN : All year
DINING ROOM : Home cooked breakfast
CHILDREN : Most welcome (cot available)
VEGETARIANS : By arrangement
PETS : By arrangement
BAR SNACKS : Not applicable
LICENSED : No
DISABLED ACCESS : yes
CREDIT CARDS : No
GARDEN : Views over farm
ACCOMMODATION : 3 rooms; 1 dbl, 1 twin, 1 fml. Bathroom/shower each floor.

Chapter Seven

ROUGHLOW FARM
Willington, Tarporley,
Cheshire CW6 0PG

Tel/Fax: 01829 751199

Roughlow Farm is a delightfully converted farmhouse built about 1800 and situated 450ft above sea level with magnificent views to Shropshire and Wales. The total peace which surrounds it makes it a wonderful place in which to stay, relax and unwind from the cares of every day life. It is quite hard to believe when you are within its welcoming doors that it is only 15 minutes away from Chester with the M6 and M56 25 minutes away and Manchester Airport 35 minutes. It is easy to drive into Wales or go to the Lakes. In fact ideal for either those in pursuit of pleasure of those with business in mind.

You will find Roughlow is very much a family home, friendly and informal. The whole house is furnished with beautiful antique furniture and the walls adorned with delightful and interesting paintings. There are three bedrooms, one of which is a suite with bathroom and sitting room. The other two rooms are ensuite and all of them have hospitality trays and hair dryers. Breakfast, served in the elegant dining room, is a delicious meal complete with free range eggs and home-made jams and marmalades. It is possible to arrange an evening meal providing there is a minimum of 4 people to enjoy it. Roughlow has a very attractive garden with a cobbled courtyard and a tennis court. With plenty of places to visit within easy distance it is also wonderful walking country and blessed with three golf courses close by as well as riding stables. There are good, reasonable pubs, wine bar and hotels in Willington and Tarporley. A strictly non-smoking house.

USEFUL INFORMATION

OPEN: *All year*
CHILDREN: *Over 6 years*
CREDIT CARDS: *None taken*
ACCOMMODATION: *1 suite with bathroom, 2 ensuite rooms*
DINING ROOM: *Full English breakfast*
VEGETARIAN: *Yes*
DISABLED ACCESS: *No*
GARDEN: *Yes + tennis court*

574

THE FIRGARTH,
Ambleside Road, Windermere,
Cumbria LA23 1EU.

Tel : 015394 46974

Just around the corner from the stunning Lake Windermere lies this elegant Victorian house which opens its doors in friendly welcome to visitors from near and far. The house is ideally suited for visiting the Lake District, and with this in mind, your hosts Mary and Brian Lucking, organise tours in luxury mini coaches which collect and return you to the Firgarth.

If you desire something a bit more individual there are plenty of maps and selected walks in the area, and at any time of year you will be captivated by the spectacular vistas all around you. Each season has its own beauty, whether it be the spring awakening with its pull on the heartstrings or the white blanket offered by the winter when you can spend time in front of blazing fires sampling local hospitality and the warmth of the people.

The Firgarth offers much in the way of comfort to its guests. The eight bedrooms are all en suite, have colour TV, central heating and tea/coffee trays. Each is individual and beautifully appointed, and are a delight on the eye. There is a residents lounge, again very comfortably furnished, and breakfast is a full English affair with vegetarians catered for on request. A wonderful location, with superb accommodation and benign hosts to complete the picture!

USEFUL INFORMATION

OPEN : All year except Xmas & Boxing Day
CHILDREN : Most welcome
PETS : No
LICENSED : No
CREDIT CARDS : All major
ACCOMMODATION : 8 rooms en suite: 7 dbl, 1 fml.

RESTAURANT : Full English breakfast
VEGETARIANS : Catered for
BAR SNACKS : Not applicable
DISABLED ACCESS : No
GARDEN : No

Chapter Seven

HOLLY PARK HOUSE,
*1 Park Road, Windermere,
Cumbria, LA23 2AW.*

Tel : 015394 42107.

The name of Windermere immediately conjures a picture of the beautiful Lake District. Sleepy little hamlets with elegant houses gracing the streets, antique shops and craft fayres, all together in a most charming fashion! Many people come to the Lake District to walk, and admire the beauty of the scenery, and for them there is no need for any other form of entertainment - but there is much more! Stately homes, museums, pretty villages, you have it all - and you can return again and again for the wealth of variety in the locality.

Holly Park House is one of those elegant homes, dating back to 1880, it is built of Lakeland stone and is a graceful building inside and out. It is situated just five minutes from the railway station and is really central for tours and other excursions. Roger Wallis and James Peters are your hosts, and extend a warm welcome to all their guests. There are six bedrooms, all en suite, very comfortably furnished, and all having TV, and tea/coffee trays.

The lounge is a charming room with a lovely marble fireplace, just the place to relax after a day's activities! Breakfast is a full traditional affair, and vegetarians are catered for. An evening meal is available from a superb a la carte menu, and there is a bar to have a pre dinner drink in (or after if you prefer, or, dare I say, even in between!). Roger and James are the perfect hosts and endeavour to ensure that your stay is a pleasant and memorable one!

USEFUL INFORMATION

OPEN : *All year*
CHILDREN : *Most welcome*
PETS : *By arrangement*
LICENSED : *Residential*
ACCOMMODATION : *6 rooms en suite; 6 dbl, 4 able to take fml.*
DINING ROOM : *A la carte menu*
VEGETARIANS : *Catered for*
DISABLED ACCESS : *No*
GARDEN : *Yes*
CREDIT CARDS : *All major*

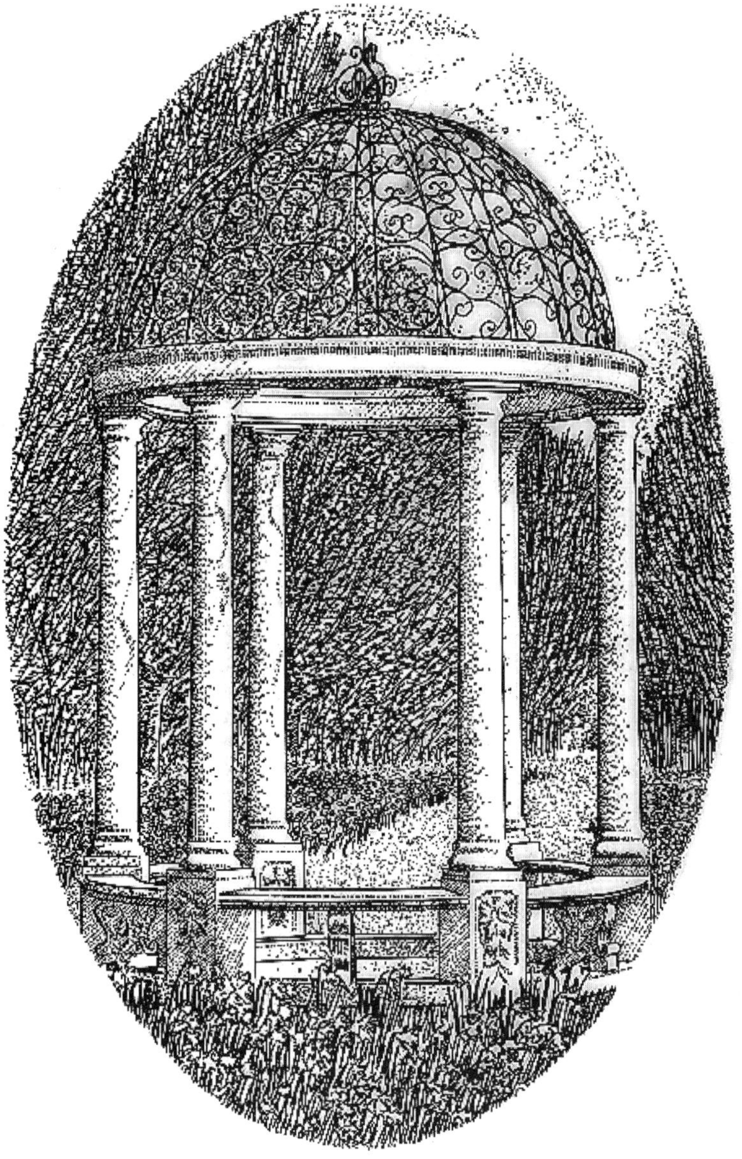

Chapter Eight

THE NORTH EAST COUNTIES
including YORKSHIRE, NORTHUMBERLAND, DURHAM & CLEVELAND

CHAPTER 8

THE NORTH EAST COUNTIES
including YORKSHIRE, NORTHUMBERLAND, DURHAM & CLEVELAND

INCLUDES

Highfield House	**Asenby**	p. 587
East Mellwaters Farm	**Barnard Castle**	p. 588
Upsland Farm	**Bedale**	p. 589
Southfields	**Bedale**	p. 590
The Green Dragon Inn	**Bedale**	p. 590
Beric West Cottage	**Brayton**	p. 591
Grange Farm	**Bulmer**	p. 591
Lower Barn	**Castle Howard**	p. 592
Beacon Guest House	**Cleveland**	p. 593
Holly Bush Hotel	**Cleveland**	p. 594
Old Chapel	**Cotterdale Hawes**	p. 588
Grimston House	**Deighton**	p. 595
37 Nevilledale Terrace	**Durham**	p. 596
Castle View Guest House	**Durham City**	p. 597
Miners Arms	**Eyam**	p. 614
Sea Brink Hotel	**Filey**	p. 598
Whitfield House Hotel	**Goathland**	p. 599
Crescent Lodge	**Harrogate**	p. 600
Laskill Farm	**Hawnby**	p. 601
Barnclose Farm	**Helmsley**	p. 602
Buckingham House	**Helmsley**	p. 603
Sproxton Hall Farm	**Helmsley**	p. 604
Forest Farm	**Huddersfield**	p. 592
The Mallow Guest House	**Huddersfield**	p. 605
Gracefield	**Ilkley**	p. 606
Clyde House	**Leyburn**	p. 607
Manor Farm	**Little Barugh, Nr Pickering**	p. 608
Coney House	**Riccall**	p. 596
West Cottage	**Richmond**	p. 597
Wilson House Farm	**Richmond**	p. 609
Harmony Country Lodge	**Scarborough**	p. 612
Studley House	**Scarborough**	p. 613
Grange Farmhouse	**Skelton**	p. 615
Beech Tree House Farm	**Slingsby**	p. 610
Fawn Lea	**Standrop**	p. 611
Hambleton House	**Thirsk**	p. 616

Chapter Eight

Spital Hill	**Thirsk**	**p. 617**
Herriots Hotel & Restaurant	**Wensleydale**	**p. 618**
Whitfield	**Wensleydale**	**p. 619**
Andra's Farm	**Wharfedale**	**p. 620**
Postgate Farm	**Whitby**	**p. 621**
Sneaton Hall Hotel	**Whitby**	**p. 622**
The Beacon	**Whitby**	**p. 623**
Hammer & Hand Country Guest House	**York**	**p. 624**

The North East Counties

Yorkshire, Northumberland, Durham & Cleveland

They say that beauty is in the eye of the beholder, but I believe that all who 'behold' this wild, untamed land can only wonder at the loveliness and splendour of these cherished Dales, and enjoy the history and heritage preserved for our appreciation. This is an area unspoilt by time or by man's avarice (for which we can be truly thankful), and where we can enjoy nature, and all she has to offer, at her very best. For the outdoor types there are lots and lots of activities, with to my mind, the best being just walking. This way you can appreciate the ever changing colours of the landscapes, and be stimulated by the sounds and smells all around you. But don't be misled by this - for those who enjoy a more 'animate' stimulation there is plenty in the way of history, local crafts, pleasant towns and picturesque villages to be found. The tales and folklore of this great area could fill a book and more, but I will try to give you a little information - just to give you a taste!

Starting with the Northern Dales we have **Swaledale** which lies along the course of the **River Swale** in the north east, and which lends it's name to a hardy breed of sheep whose fleece are used in the local woollen industry. **Reeth**, the capital of the vale, is a delightful centre for crafts, sculpture and painting. **Richmond** is a busy market town with plenty of historical interest, including three museums and a lovely Georgian theatre. Richmond Castle has wonderful views from it's 30 metre high, 12th century keep.

To the far north east is the **River Tees**, and the rich farmland of **Lower Teesdale**. Lewis Carroll, the author, lived here, and you can understand the inspiration he must have gained from this peaceful landscape. Today, **Croft**, where he was born, is home to an exciting motor racing circuit which holds many events all year round. **Wensleydale** is a particular fine area with it's stunning fells and rich pastures. The main market towns are **Hawes, Leyburn** and **Masham**, each very individual, but with charm and presence that will delight the visitor. Masham is very proud of it's annual Sheep Fair in September, and also the Steam Engine and Fair Organ Rally in July - great for enthusiasts! Just outside Leyburn is Middleham Castle, a splendid example of an English keep and childhood home of Richard III. Between Leyburn and **Bedale** is Crakehall Watermill, which was restored in 1977, and which in 1980, ground corn for the first time in 50 years. This is a fascinating process to watch and the interesting machinery dates from the 18th and 19th centuries. Wensleydale is probably best known (apart from the cheese!)

Chapter Eight

for it's waterfalls, and fine examples of this can be seen at **Aysgarth** and **Hardraw.** Aysgarth also has an interesting Yorkshire Carriage Museum which is worth visiting. There are many varied and interesting sites on these vast moors, with charming towns and villages peeping between the hills, and all with a wealth of culture and history just waiting to be explored. To name all the Dales, towns and villages would fill the pages of this chapter, leaving nothing but facts to bore the pants off you! So, I will choose just some of the places that may be of interest, but leaving much, much more to be delightfully discovered on your travels.

The southern Dales include **Wharfedale, Airedale** and **Ingleborough.** Wharfedale is an area of breathtaking scenery such as Kilsney Craig with the Kilsney Park and Trout Farm nestling beneath it's stern rocky face. Even if you are not an angler this is a pleasant place to visit as youcan feed the fish as well as catch them - or if even that is too much effort then just buy them fresh from the local shop! **Grassington** is the main town, and with it's cobbled streets and quaint shops, you will have a delightful day out. Malharn Tarn is one of England's largest mountain lakes, and is a very popular local to visit. Artists of all abilities (including Turner) have painted this area, and it apparently was a favourite spot of Charles Kingsley the author who wrote his classic 'The Water Babies' here.

Skipton in Airedale is known as the Gateway to the Dales, and has the splendid Skipton Castle guarding the town. The Leeds-Liverpool Canal also runs through the centre of the town, and you can spend a pleasant day exploring the waterway on one of the many barges. One other place I would like to mention is **Lothersdale,** as it was here that Charlotte Bronte found inspiration for the house in that wonderful novel 'Jane Eyre'. Stone Gapp is actually a private residence, but the description of 'Gateshead Hall' in her book marries very well!

Ingleborough is part of the legendary country known as the Three Peaks, and with it's unyielding landscape of peaks, caves and rocks it is a haven for walkers and ramblers. **Settle** is the main town in the heart of the area, and is a pretty, charming place with a good market and much local history. The great Victorian railway, Settle to Carlisle, runs from here and for enthusiasts the architecture and especially the viaduct is a must.

Nidderdale is in the east and has rather a unique landscape in it's rock formations at Brimham Rocks. The unrelenting elements have formed fascinating shapes and forms over the years, and the National Trust have undertaken the preservation of this intriguing native display. Fountains Abbey and Studley Royal Water Gardens must be on your list of places to visit. This is a great day out - the Abbey dates from around 1132, and has recently gained World Heritage status, and the Water Gardens are a delight of temples, ponds and immaculate lawns. In addition the medieval park is home to Red, Fallow and Sika deer, and you can see them roam freely amongst the oak, chestnut and lime trees. The Abbey and Water Gardens unite to provide an interesting variety of activities (if wished) for all the family; from 'Flower Power' where you can discover the uses of wildflower and herbs, to 'Sleepers Awake', a 'Hunters and Gatherers Challenge' for wiggly worms! Ugh! That one wasn't for me - but those delightful little beings we call 'children' love it! A very good day's entertainment.

Moving outwards to the coastal towns we visit **Scarborough**, closely followed by **Whitby** and **Filey**. Scarborough has been a holiday destination for the British tourist from as early as 1735! Today it offers a wealth of attractions for young and old making it a platform for all types of holidays from golfing to windsurfing, with beautiful gardens and excellent walking, and with a variety of nightlife to suit all. Midsummer finds the attraction of Scarborough Fair (much notoriety gained through the canticle by Simeon & Garfunkle) when you will find a multitude of entertainment and a gay time is on every street corner. One thing of note is the beautifully restored steam railway which winds it's way to York from this pleasing town. There is a fascinating assortment of architecture down by the harbour where chapels, cafes, and curio shops sit side by side with stands selling whelks, cockles and all types of sea life. It is an interesting place, and one which should definitely be experienced. Whitby has some fine beaches and quaint streets which you will enjoy strolling around. The ruins of the Abbey here date back to the 13th century and was home of Caedmon, the first English poet. Brams Stoker was impressed by the eerie atmosphere, and set part of the blood curling novel 'Dracula' in the town. There are no vampires today (not that I met anyway), and this is a pleasant spot to spend some time. The North Yorkshire Railway passes here too, and stops at **Pickering** on it's way to York. This is a lovely market town with a medieval castle and church, and many fine shops to browse round. Just west of Pickering it would be remiss of me not to mention **Helmsley,** and the nearby castle. This is a spectacular 12th century fortress, and an excellent exhibition of the more modern Tudor living. A little further takes you to Rievaulx Abbey, the remains of one of the first Cistercian monasteries in northern England. The site of this abbey is one of beauty and serenity in the valley of the River Rye, and the terrace and temples are magnificent   Away from York the other railway stops are at Levisham, Newton Halt and **Goathland** which you may recognise as the famous 'Aidensfield' in that engaging programme 'Heartbeat'. Filey carries on the tradition of these fine seaside towns, but with a quieter more traditional air. Six miles of safe, sandy beaches, and the quaint olde-worlde fishermens cottages make this a delightful, quiet relaxing holiday spot. The Parish Church of St Oswald (the patron saint of fishermen), is set aside from the town by a

Chapter Eight

deep ravine, and dates from the time of King Stephen. It is a fine building, and at one time had a music gallery and an organ at it's west end. There is an interesting stained glass window which is dedicated to fishermen, and it is thought that St Oswald once passed through Filey on his gospel calling. It is also said that Charlotte Bronte worshipped here whilst on holiday. Filey is a great place for souvenir hunting with hand-made chocolates, shell boxes or even authentic fishermen's jumpers.

From here we jump to **Castle Howard,** rather an eccentric house with a mixture of periods from Egyptian, Roman, Tudor, and Medieval that at first confuse the eye. But this is a castle built upon the ruins of another, and as such lends a rather unique image. This house was made famous by the highly popular 'Brideshead Revisited' and you are probably familiar with the delightful interior and furnishings used in the filming. On to **Thirsk** and it's attractive setting by the river. Thirsk Church is often referred to as the Cathedral of the North and is a very handsome building. It was started in 1430 and took 70 years to complete. Thirsk is also famous for it's racing and offers some of the finest in Yorkshire, with people travelling from all over the country just to spend the day here. Thirsk Museum houses the original manuscripts of James Herriot, the real life vet who became so famous with his tales of a country vetenary practice. Having read his works you can see the warmth and fondness he had for this enticing county and it's hardy people.

On to the magnificent city of **York,** the great northern capital of Roman Britain. Clifford Tower is the place to visit to get unparalleled views over the city, and to learn the history of York's past. Not all of the history is pleasant as this is the site of the massacre of York's Jewish community in 1190. There is a good visual display of a model of the original castle and there is an additional Braille text. This city has a lot of history to offer in it's architecture and with the art galleries, museums and York Minster, which is a wonderful example of a Gothic Church with fine stained glass windows.

The Five Sisters window has 100,000 pieces containing grisaille glass; the Rose window commemorates the end of the War of the Roses; the Great Western window with it's tracery in the shape of a heart is often regarded as the heart of Yorkshire, and the Great East window in the Lady Chapel is one of the most important in the world, as it depicts the beginning and end of created things in the world. There are many churches in York; somewhere in the region of 40, and many worth visiting. One of the best ways to see York is to travel the medieval walls. This is a walk of about 2 ½ miles but a glorious way to see the city. Before leaving York I would like to mention the exciting excavation area between York's two rivers where a sunken treasure house was found preserved in the peaty soil. Travelling in electric time cars, the voice of Magnus Magnusson takes you back to a time where people conversed in Old Norse, where ships unloaded their exotic cargoes, and the people of the time went about their daily business. This is probably one of the most important insights into our past and one which all can enjoy.

Across from York is **Harrogate**, traditionally a spa town, and now one of the most important conference centres in the country. It is a very attractive town with it's Regency buildings and treelined streets. There are some good shopping facilities here, and as a 20th century town it has a lot to offer the visitor. The Royal Pump Museum offers the spa waters which once made the town famous, and the art gallery has some very fine examples of English paintings. Coming down the A64 we pass the great city of **Leeds, Bradford** and one which I shall mention **Huddersfield.** This town's reputation was built round the textile industry, and today it's fine wools are still a part of it's industry. There is splendid Victorian architecture here which in recent years has benefitted from much refurbishment and stone cleaning. Much of the town is pedestrianised, so this is a pleasant way to wander around and see for yourself all on offer. The railway station, St George's Square, is reputed to be one of the finest facades in England and has been described as a 'stately home with trains in'. The Church of St. Peter is in the Gothic Revival style and is a most imposing building. Huddersfield has plenty of parks and green spaces, and in addition you are only a fews minutes from the lovely Pennines and stunning scenery. A very good location for touring the area, with a very pleasant base to return to.

Returning back up the way takes us through **Ilkley** (the name may bring back a few scouting memories), where the walking is wonderful and the vista difficult to surpass, back over the moors and on to **Barnard Castle, Darlington** and **Cleveland**. Barnard Castle is a charming historic market town with plenty of character and a delightful array of history. It is known as one of the 51 most important historical and architectural towns in Britain, and you will not be disappointed. The ruins of the castle are 12th century with a 14th century round keep, and there are some wonderful riverside walks in what once were the hunting grounds round the castle. The Church of St. Mary is interesting, and Bowes Museum is a 19th century house created in the Fench chateau style, housing collections of European art and paintings, including some by Goya and El Greco.

Darlington is mostly associated with the 'Age of Steam' and is famous for the Stockton and Darlington railway. Darlington's Railway Centre and Museum has one of the finest collections to be found, and is a joy for enthusiasts. Today, this is a thriving market town with something for all in the way of culture, shopping, and splendid architecture. It has a wealth of leisure activities including a good golf course and an outdoor bowling green.

Chapter Eight

Taking the train from here to **Durham** is a pleasant journey, and brings you to a lovely city with a lot to give to those interested in the history of the area. Durham Castle is a magnificent Norman cathedral which was founded in 1093, and together with the adjacent castle is a World Heritage Site. The Oriental Museum is unusual in that it is the only museum in the country dedicated solely to oriental art, and covers all major cultures and periods of the East from Ancient Egypt to India, Tibet, China and Japan. **Beamish** is one of the largest tourist attractions in the area with it's turn of the century working town, where shop staff greet you costumed in the dress of the period, and guided tours are given to the underground mine in the Colliery Village. There are many more attractions in the beautiful County of Durham, and the scenery and landscape makes any type of outdoor activity a great pleasure.

HIGHFIELD HOUSE
*Asenby, Thirsk,
North Yorkshire YO7 3QT*

Tel: 01845 577857

    In the small village of Asenby 5 miles from the market town of Thirsk and 7 miles from the cathedral city of Ripon is the most impressive, Grade II listed Georgian residence. Highfield House is set in secluded gardens of approximately 3 acres on the banks of the River Swale with private fishing rights. Highfield is listed for historical and architectural reasons, it retains many of the original features including picture rails, shuttered windows and brass door furniture. This charming property is very pleasing to the eye, with ivy adorning part of the front of the house. The garden is mainly laid to lawn with lovely shrubs, trees and flower borders, also a summer house, paddock and stables. The interior is just as beautiful, the excellent standard of decor is very tasteful and has been carefully chosen to compliment the house, which is furnished with antiques. A grand piano adorns the guest's sitting room, where large comfy sofas and chairs invite you to relax and unwind, and on chilly days a log fire roars away in the large open grate. The bedrooms are stylish and spacious, bright and airy and offer colour television, clock radio and a tea and coffee tray, with views across the garden. One of the rooms has ensuite facilities, the other two each with wash basins, share a delightful bathroom. Hair dryer, trouser press and laundry facilities are available on request. After a peaceful nights sleep in the extremely comfortable beds, you are served one of the best breakfasts in Yorkshire. Susan Millard your capable host, is Cordon Bleu trained, the food is all fresh and locally produced as much as possible, all this is served in the beautiful dining room which has a lovely feature open fire place. Evening meals are by prior arrangement only. Alternatively, the local Inn, The Crab and Lobster is only a 3 minute walk away with it's award winning restaurant, serving a varied and interesting menu.

    Highfield House is an excellent base for touring North Yorkshire and all it has to offer. There are many visitor attractions in this region including Kilburn, where Robert Thompson the famous woodcarver, well known for his 'mouse' trademark had his workshop, he died in 1955 but his craft is still continuing today. Thirsk is 'Herriot' town, here you can see James Herriot's surgery and museum. The Cathedral City of Ripon and World Heritage site of Fountains Abbey are only a 15 minute drive away. The town of Helmsley is where you can visit the lovely Duncombe Park which was built in 1713 and here you can see terraces, temples and have wonderful riverside walks. Of course walkers will be in heaven as the North York Moors is very close by. If you are coming to this area then you cannot possibly stay anywhere else but Highfield House.

USEFUL INFORMATION

OPEN; All year
CHILDREN; Over 10 years
CREDIT CARDS; None taken
ACCOMMODATION; 3 rooms, 2 double, 1 twin, 1 ensuite
PETS; No

DINING ROOM; First class traditional fare
    Evening by prior arrangement
VEGETARIAN; Upon request
DISABLED ACCESS; No
GARDEN; Beautiful leading to river fishing

Chapter Eight

EAST MELLWATERS FARM
Bowes, Nr Barnard Castle,
County Durham DL12 9RH
Tel: 01833 628269

East Mellwaters has been farmed for 2000 years and owned by the Milner family since 1947, and is a very busy working farm. This does not detract from the friendly and warm welcome guests receive. Within minutes of arrival one will very soon be sitting down to a cup of tea and home-made biscuits. Bedrooms are decorated and furnished to a high quality and are warm and cosy with ensuite shower or bathrooms, colour TV, a tea and coffee tray are standard. There is a pay phone in the lobby. Residents can enjoy the luxury of an open fire and countryside views from the lounge. An appetizing and traditional farmhouse breakfast is prepared with local produce. Dinner is served using organically reared beef and lamb, together with fresh garden vegetables and herbs. Special diets are catered for with prior notice. Camping is offered for groups or individuals. Mrs Trish Milner is a mine of information with regard to the Dales and will be delighted to point you in the right direction of the many and varied tourist attractions. A three minute walk gives you the opportunity to fish for trout, which will be frozen and stored until you depart of Trish will cook it for your dinner. There are wonderful walks, along gurgling rivers, through woodlands or along the Pinnine Way. East Mellwaters is a non smoking house.

USEFUL INFORMATION
OPEN; February-November   **DINING ROOM;** Excellent traditional fare
CHILDREN; Welcome   using fresh local and garden produce
CREDIT CARDS; Yes   **VEGETARIAN;** Catered for
ACCOMMODATION; 5 ensuite rooms   **DISABLED ACCESS;** No
GARDEN; Yes   **PETS;** No   NON SMOKING

THE OLD CHAPEL,
Cotterdale, Hawes,
North Yorkshire, DL8 3 LT.
Tel : 01969 667605

The Old Chapel quite literally was....... and served the local community until the mid 60s. Old tombstones can still be found peeking through the flower borders and bushes, and it really is an interesting place. It is now the home of Norma Lynn and is a comfortable, traditional house with beamed ceilings, old stone fireplaces, and rough cast walls that fit in very nicely with the surroundings. Norma will cheerfully arrange packed lunches, afternoon teas and evening meals, if given advance warning! The village itself is at the end of a 1.5 mile valley and is ideal for exploring the wonderful Yorkshire countryside and the nearby Lake District. This is a great place from which to pursue all those outdoor activities and enjoy the scenery around you.

USEFUL INFORMATION
OPEN : All year   **DINING ROOM :** Evening meal by arrangement
CHILDREN : Welcome   **VEGETARIANS :** Catered for
PETS : No   **BAR MEALS :** Not applicable
CREDIT CARDS : None taken **DISABLED ACCESS :** No
LICENSED : No   **GARDEN :** Pleasant
ACCOMMODATION : 2 rooms; 1 dbl, 1 twin.

UPSLAND FARM,
Kirklington, Bedale,
North Yorkshire, DL8 2PA.

Tel : 01845 567709.

Upsland Farm was rebuilt by its owners in 1994 and has won a design award. This stunning farm sits on a historic moat site dating back to pre 1086, and is ideal for any visitor wishing to see some of the beautiful open countryside in Yorkshire. Breakfast is home cured bacon cooked on the Aga, and the drawing and dining rooms have beautiful antique furniture. The bedrooms, although thoroughly modern in their facilities, have brass bedsteads and are furnished charmingly. Each has it's own en suite bathroom and every comfort has been thought of. Does this set the scene? A more welcoming home would be difficult to find and Constance Hodgson, your hostess, will bake her way into your heart! An evening meal is available, and food is a mixture of French and English with the addition of Constance's home made pies, preserves and variety of sweets. The menu is quite extensive and you will not be disappointed in your choice. The drawing room is cosy, with T.V. and a log fire, which is ideal for relaxing in the evening and talking over the events of the day, or planning your next excursion.

This is a beautiful location and is convenient for visiting the Moors, the Dales and the various country towns around you. There is plenty in the way of sports with fishing, riding, even gliding being available. There are stately homes, castles and fine gardens to visit, and you would find it difficult to have a boring day in this area! On the other hand, if what you require is peace and solitude away from the hustle of city life - then you have found it! There is something about the moors and the dales that bring a peace to the soul, and with the physical comforts looked after by Upsland Farm..........well, it is just idyllic.

USEFUL INFORMATION

OPEN : *All year except Xmas Day*
CHILDREN : *Welcome*
PETS : *Welcome*
CREDIT CARDS : *None taken*
LICENSED : *No*
ACCOMMODATION : *3 rooms; 3 dbl en suite.*
DINING ROOM : *English & French cuisine*
VEGETARIANS : *Catered for*
BAR SNACKS : *Not applicable*
DISABLED ACCESS : *No*
GARDEN : *Pretty water garden*

Chapter Eight

SOUTHFIELDS,
96 South End, Bedale,
North Yorkshire, DL8 2DS.

Tel : 01677 423510

A 'hearty' English breakfast is the trademark of this fine family guest house run by Marjorie Keighley. Marjorie believes in satisfying the tummy to match that of the spirit, which is captivated by the scenery in this wonderful part of the country! Breakfast is one of those meals that lasts the morning, through lunch, and up to tea time! Having been in the business for nineteen years, Marjorie is well aware of the needs and desires of her guests, and this comfortable family home supplies them all. Furnishings are traditional and the bedrooms have all that is necessary to ensure a good night's rest. Each room has a tea & coffee tray, radio alarms, and hair dryers and a trouser press can be supplied on request. The charming lounge has colour T.V. and is a comfortable room to spend the last hours of the day, resting the weary body for the next day's activities!

USEFUL INFORMATION

OPEN : All year (bar Xmas & New Year) **DINING ROOM :** Traditional breakfast
CHILDREN : Welcome **VEGETARIANS :** Catered for
PETS : No **BAR MEALS :** Not applicable
LICENSED : No **DISABLED ACCESS :** No
CREDIT CARDS : None taken **GARDEN :** Yes
ACCOMMODATION : 4 rooms; 2 with private bathroom, 1 dbl, 1 fml, 1 sgl, 1 twin.

THE GREEN DRAGON INN,
Bedale,
North Yorkshire, DL8 2HA.
Tel : 01677 422233

The Green Dragon Inn is a country establishment built in 1630 with a good sized restaurant seating 65 persons, and of course the public bar. It is finely furnished in traditional style and offers a great deal of comfort to the traveller. The food is home cooked English fayre and a good variety is available on the menu. There are three guest rooms, all en suite, which are pleasantly appointed and have tea/coffee trays, clock radios and hair dryers. Richard Fawcett is your host and ensures that your stay is comfortable. This is a relaxing rural setting from where you can explore the surrounding beautiful countryside and perhaps enjoy a spot of fishing, golf or walking on the scenic moors. There is plenty to see and do, but if you just wish to sit back and appreciate the quiet of the country, and perhaps chat to a few of the locals in the bar, you are sure to hear a good tale or two!

USEFUL INFORMATION

OPEN : All year **RESTAURANT :** Good English food
CHILDREN : Welcome **VEGETARIANS :** Catered for
PETS : No **BAR SNACKS :** Variety
LICENSED : Full **DISABLED ACCESS :** No
CREDIT CARDS : All major **GARDEN :** Pleasant
ACCOMMODATION : 3 rooms; 2 dbl, 1 sgl, all en suite.

BERIC WEST COTTAGE
Mill Lane, Brayton,
Selby, Yorkshire YO8 9LB
Tel: 01757 213318

A cordial welcome is assured by your hostess Mrs. Betty Fletcher at Beric West Cottage. Built in 1904, this friendly, warm and attractively furnished property extends to visitors a home from home atmosphere. Pretty bedrooms have ensuite bathrooms, tea and coffee making facilities and colour television. A most comfortable lounge with colour television overlooks the extensive and well kept gardens, plus a grass tennis court, which guests are encouraged to enjoy. Breakfast is a most pleasurable experience, with a fine selection to suit all tastes. Evening meal is not served, but there are several good eating places within easy reach. Beric West Cottage is placed in a superb location close to many and varied places of interest, including the historical and fascinating City of York. The area is also well known for its links with business and commerce, making Beric West Cottage ideal for the business person.

USEFUL INFORMATION
OPEN; All year
CHILDREN; By arrangement
CREDIT CARDS; Visa/Access
ACCOMMODATION; 2 ensuite rooms
PETS; No
PARKING; Good off road
DINING ROOM; Traditional full English breakfast. No evening meal
DISABLED ACCESS; No
GARDEN; Yes, extensive and well kept plus a grass tennis court
NO SMOKING

GRANGE FARM
Bulmer,
York YO6 7BN
Tel: 01653 618376

Castle Howard is the magnificent Country House where they filmed 'Brideshead Revisited'. It is on this estate that Mrs. Janet Foster and her family have their working farm. The farmhouse has spectacular uninterrupted views across open countryside and woodlands. The farmhouse is centrally heated, spacious and has much to offer the visitor. There is a sitting room with a television and a games room, where you can play table tennis and pool. The 3 guest bedrooms, the double/family and twin with vanity units and a single. All rooms have tea and coffee making facilities. Guests have their own bathroom complete with shower. In the morning you are served an excellent farmhouse breakfast in the attractive dining room. There is a large secluded garden making it safe and ideal for children. Baby sitting is also available. The farm is in an ideal location for touring this superb area, there is easy access to the east coast, the North Yorkshire Moors and the lovely historic City of York with its museums, galleries and charming shops. There are castles, country houses and friendly market towns to explore. For walkers there is 'Ebor Way'. Fishing and horse riding are also available close by. Janet and her family are waiting to extend a very warm Yorkshire welcome to you.

USEFUL INFORMATION
OPEN; All year
CHILDREN; Welcome
CREDIT CARDS; None taken
ACCOMMODATION; 3 rooms, shared bathroom
DINING ROOM; Farmhouse breakfast only
DISABLED ACCESS; No
GARDEN; Yes, large and secluded
PETS; Yes

Chapter Eight

LOWER BARN
Wandales Lane, Bulmer,
Nr. Castle Howard,
York YO6 7ES
Tel: 01653 618575

When the corn is fully ripened, and waving in the breeze, the view from Lower Barn is rather like looking across a sea of gold. The seclusion enjoyed by this converted 200 year old barn makes this the perfect setting for a relaxing holiday. On arrival guests are immediately made to feel at home with tea and home-made biscuits. Bedrooms are very attractively furnished with antique pine furniture, and the most comfy beds. Tea and coffee making facilities are supplied. Guests have the use of a private lounge, which is relaxing and has beamed ceilings with a cosy and warm woodburning stove plus colour television. The first class food is home-made including jams and marmalade, and a hearty Yorkshire style breakfast is guaranteed to set you up for the day. There is a meal served in the evenings and bringing your own wine is very acceptable. This is an ideal base for visiting Castle Howard, York and the North Yorkshire Moors. The stunning scenery will delight everyone, and with so many historical venues to explore this make an ideal area to enjoy. The east coast is an easy drive away offering golden beaches and all seaside attractions.

USEFUL INFORMATION
OPEN; All year
CHILDREN; Over 5 years
CREDIT CARDS; None taken
LICENSED; May bring your own wine
ACCOMMODATION; 3 rooms, 2 double, 1 twin
DINING ROOM; Excellent breakfast, Evening meal by arrangement
VEGETARIAN; By arrangement
DISABLED ACCESS; No
GARDEN; Yes
PETS; No   NO SMOKING

FOREST FARM
Mount Road, Marsden,
Huddersfield, West Yorkshire
HD7 6NN
Tel: 01484 842687

In the heart of the Pennines set amidst the beauty of the moorland sits Forest Farm, formerly a weavers cottage and working farm, it has been fully restored retaining much of the original character. All bedrooms are most comfortable, well decorated with tea and coffee making facilities. There is a separate lounge where you can sit and read or watch the television. Great care is taken in the culinary department to provide good wholesome food, and May and Ted Fussey, the owners offer pure spring water, free range eggs, fresh garden produce and delicious cream teas. Special diets and packed lunches are available by prior arrangement. Separate accommodation providing sleeping facilities for up to 19 people is housed in the Forest Farm Bunk House. There are many varied and interesting places to visit, and sporting activities abound in the area, including rock climbing, hang gliding, windsurfing, fly and coarse fishing to name but a few. For walkers there is the wonderful Pennine Way. Forest Farm has an arrangement with the local golf club, providing there are no competitions guests may use the course.

USEFUL INFORMATION
OPEN; All year
CHILDREN; Welcome
CREDIT CARDS; None taken
ACCOMMODATION; 3 rooms,
DINING ROOM; Good wholesome fare
VEGETARIAN; By arrangement
DISABLED ACCESS; No
GARDEN; Yes

BEACON GUEST
Chop Gate, Bilsdale,
Cleveland, North Yorkshire TS9 7JS

Tel/Fax: 01439 798320

The North York Moors is a veritable paradise for walkers and ramblers, the scenery is marvellous, the air is fresh and clean, what more could you want. Artists will be inspired to put pencil or paint to paper and create a masterpiece. For total peace, rest and relaxation this is definitely the place to come. The moors and surrounding scenery changes by the day, the purple clad uplands dotted here and there by farms and villages. Not far from this vast and rugged wilderness, and in total contrast, is the coast with charming fishing villages and sea side resorts.

Nestled amongst the moors, Val and John Clark have their home which they very kindly share with their guests. Beacon Guest was built around 1637 and is delightful indeed, it is situated high on a hill giving it impressive views of Bilsdale from all rooms. Furnishings are traditional and in keeping with the house which is centrally heated throughout. All rooms are linked together along a colourful conservatory where guests are able to sit and enjoy the peace and quiet. This superb house offers excellent accommodation with double and twin rooms. They are delightfully decorated with attractive bed linen and drapes, all have ensuite or private facilities, hair dryer, tea and coffee making facilities and extremely comfortable beds. There is a guest's sitting room with television, where you can plan your day out, get to know the other guests, or just sit and relax, in the winter this room has a wonderful roaring log fire. The dining room is where you will be served a delicious full traditional English breakfast, large enough to keep you going for most of the day. In the evening, Val serves a dinner to remember, it comes highly recommended, using fresh local produce as much as possible and all home-cooked. Beacon Guest has a table licence, so you will be able to enjoy a glass or two of wine with your meal. The garden is delightful with a lawned area surrounded by trees, shrubs and flower borders, all this is encompassed by a wooden fence. There is a patio area where you can sit, enjoy a cup of tea and drink in that wonderful fresh air.

There are a mass of stately homes including the famous Castle Howard, where the filming of 'Brideshead Revisited' took place, gardens and museums, especially the folk museum at Hutton-le-Hole. Rievaulx Abbey, founded in 1131 by Cistercian Monks is worth a visit for the peace and quiet alone. In Kilburn is Robert Thompson's workshop, a wood caver who's famous trademark was a mouse, he died in 1955, but his workshop is still in working order. A stay at Beacon Guest is a must.

USEFUL INFORMATION

OPEN; April-November **DINING ROOM**; Traditional home-cooking
CHILDREN; Welcome   Excellent evening meal
CREDIT CARDS; None taken   **VEGETARIAN**; Yes with prior notice
LICENSED; Table licence   **DISABLED ACCESS**; Limited
ACCOMMODATION; 6 ensuite rooms   **GARDEN**; Yes, delightful
PETS; Welcome

Chapter Eight

HOLLY BUSH HOTEL
Station Lane, Skelton,
Cleveland,
North Yorkshire
TS12 2LP

Tel: 01287 650736

The Holly Bush Hotel is situated in a quiet area off the main road in the town of Skelton, five miles from the North Yorkshire Moors. It is owned and very well run by Stewart and Denise Fraser. The hotel was built around 1969 and the Frasers are hoping to completely refurbish the establishment in time, and bring a family atmosphere back to a well known and much loved establishment. The accommodation is basic but comfortable, there are five rooms altogether, one double and four single. Each with a welcome tea and coffee tray. The restaurant seats approximately 100 and here you can enjoy your meal, or you may just require a bar meal, Stewart and Denise can cater for your needs. On Sundays you can sit down to a delicious roast lunch. A large function room is also available for up to 60 people, just right for small conferences. A large car park holds 100 cars, and caravans are welcome to stay overnight for a nominal charge.

This is an ideal hotel for those who love walking, the North York Moors are teeming with wonderful walks and places to visit, and only 15 minutes away is the Captain Cook Trail. Apart from walking there is horse riding at the stables across the road, fishing and golf. The popular resort of Redcar is only 7 miles away, famous for it race course, the museum here houses the world's last remaining lifeboat 'Zetland' which was built in 1800. Along the promenade fishing boats add to the colour and life of this town. For more serious shopping, then Middlesborough is only 14 miles away, this city is also full of museums and galleries. The Captain Cook Birthplace Museum tells the story of James Cook and a heritage trail departs from here. Three miles away from the Holly Bush is the Victorian town of Saltburn-by-the-Sea where 'Victorian Week' is celebrated every year in August. A lovely village where you can climb a path to the cliff top and take in the wonderful views. This really is the most delightful area to have a holiday, with something to suit everyone.

USEFUL INFORMATION

OPEN: All year
CHILDREN: Over 5 years, under by arrangement
CREDIT CARDS: None taken
LICENSED: Yes
ACCOMMODATION: 5 rooms, none ensuite
RESTAURANT: Good food, open to non-residents
BAR FOOD: Yes
VEGETARIAN: Catered for
DISABLED ACCESS: Limited, in bar, not accommodation
GARDEN: Small
PETS: No

GRIMSTON HOUSE,
Deighton, York YO4 6HB

Tel:01904 728328

Built in the nineteen thirties, Grimston House is an attractive place standing within a well kept garden in the village of Deighton which is within very easy reach of York. The house, owned by Alan Wright is comfortably furnished in a style in keeping with its age. The first impression is of light and space and a friendly ambience which becomes more apparent when you realise how welcoming it is. There are 7 bedrooms, 5 of which are ensuite and each, in addition to its pretty drapes and very comfortable beds, has colour television and a plentifully supplied beverage tray. The Dining Room, where breakfast is served looks out onto the garden and it is wonderfully peaceful to start ones day here enjoying a perfectly cooked breakfast which is freshly prepared to your order. No evening meals are served but that does not pose a problem; the area is full of good restaurants, pubs and other eateries. York itself abounds with almost every form of ethnic cooking.

Grimston House makes a good base for anyone wanting to enjoy the magnificence of York and its glorious Minster. It is a city full of history, with fascinating streets, a plethora of shops, museums, galleries. The River Ouse wends its way through the city and many visitors find that boat trips provide them with a completely different view of this splendid city. York Race course has horseracing several times a year. From Grimston House you can go fishing within one mile, play golf within half a mile, enjoy horseriding or take some delightful walks in the countryside.

USEFUL INFORMATION

OPEN; *All year*
CHILDREN; *Welcome*
CREDIT CARDS; *None taken limited*
LICENSED; *No*
ACCOMMODATION; *7 rooms 5 ensuite*

DINING ROOM;*Excellent breakfast*
VEGETARIAN;*Upon request*
DISABLED ACCESS; *Yes, but*
GARDEN; *Large and beautiful*
PETS; *By arrangement*

Chapter Eight

MRS. BYRNE
*Castledene,
37 Nevilledale terrace,
Durham City DH1 4QG
Tel: 0191 3848386*

The City of Durham was founded when the Vikings invaded this part of the country and forced the Monks of Lindisfarne to find themselves somewhere else to live. This delightful city is immersed in history, from 1072 to 1837 the castle was the palace of bishops, today it is used by the students attending the University as a residence. The Durham Light Infantry has it's museum here depicting artifacts from several battles, there is also the Museum of Archaeology. It is close to the city centre that Mrs. Byrne has her guest house, a lovely old Victorian terraced house with lots of character. This English Tourist Board 'Commended' property is warm, cosy and very pleasant to stay in. There are 2 guest bedrooms, both twin, which are light and airy and well appointed with television and tea and coffee making facilities. The shared bathroom has a bath with a separate shower cubicle, toilet and basin. Breakfast is a traditional full English meal with all the trimmings and plenty of it. The rest of the house is very comfortable and traditionally furnished giving a welcoming feeling and a sense of being able to relax. There is no such word as boredom here with the area jam packed with attractions, places to visit, museums and country houses not forgetting the coast with all it has to offer. Fishing, golf and walking are all plentiful in supply.

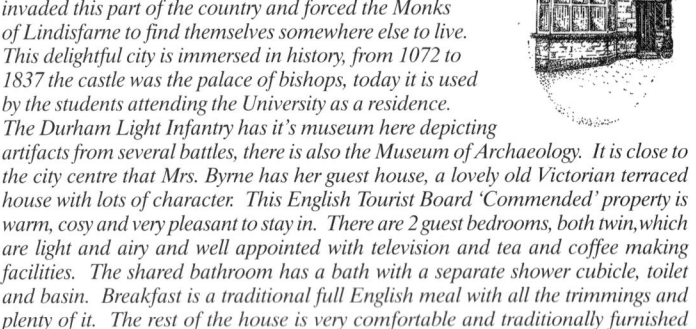

USEFUL INFORMATION

OPEN; *All year*
CHILDREN; *Welcome*
CREDIT CARDS; *None taken*
ACCOMMODATION; *2 twin rooms*

DINING ROOM; *Breakfast only*
DISABLED ACCESS; *No*
GARDEN; *Yes, small*
PETS; *No*

CONEY HOUSE,
*48 Main Street, Riccall,
York, YO4 6PZ.
Tel : 01757 248283*

This charming 1830s house is built from handmade bricks and is of delightful character. John and Dorianne Latimer are your hosts, and extend a most hospitable welcome to all who stay under their roof. The bedrooms are pleasant and traditionally furnished with the welcome addition of tea/ coffee tray, bottled water and T.V. on request. Dorianne prides herself on the quality of her breakfast and you will not be disappointed. 'Coney' comes from the Scandinavian and is a derivative of the word meaning 'King'. The history is interesting as King Harold of Norway (no, not 'our 'arold'!) passed this way in 1066, and many Scandinavian names are to be found in this area. There is a Norman Church in the centre of the village not to mention three restaurants and two pubs. This is all without leaving the village! Further afield you have plenty with the Dales, the Moors, York, Selby and many others, giving you unlimited choices in entertainment and places to see!

USEFUL INFORMATION

OPEN : *All year*
CHILDREN : *Welcome by arrangement*
PETS : *No*
LICENSED : *No*
CREDIT CARDS : *None taken*
ACCOMMODATION : *2 rooms; 1 dbl, 1 sgl.*

DINING ROOM : *Quality breakfast*
VEGETARIANS : *Catered for*
BAR SNACKS : *Not applicable*
DISABLED ACCESS : *No*
GARDEN : *Yes*

WEST COTTAGE
Victoria Road, Richmond,
North Yorkshire DL10 4AS
Tel: 01748 824046

The glorious unspoilt dales and moors lures many visitors to this area, walkers explore the many facets and thrill to the stunning scenery. Richmond is an excellent centre to be based with its many historical attractions and delightful town centre. West Cottage was built in 1830 and conveniently situated for all local amenities, and offers charming bedrooms with ensuite facilities, colour television, hair dryer and tea and coffee making facilities. The furnishing are a mixture of modern and antique which blend well together. A truly traditional English breakfast offering a wide choice of dishes. An evening meal is not served but Mrs. Kay Gibson, the owner will be pleased to assist you in selecting a suitable restaurant or pub. Fishing, golf and of course, walking are a selection of the outdoor pursuits on offer. Along with many castles and historical houses, not forgetting the working village of the Beamish Museum, there is plenty to keep you occupied.

USEFUL INFORMATION

OPEN; March-October
CHILDREN; Well behaved, 10 years and over
CREDIT CARDS; None taken
ACCOMMODATION; 2 ensuite rooms
PETS; No

DINING ROOM; Full English breakfast
Evening meal is not available
VEGETARIAN; Catered for
DISABLED ACCESS; Difficult
GARDEN; Yes
NO SMOKING, Private Parking

CASTLE VIEW GUEST HOUSE
4 Crossgate,
Durham City DH1 4PS
Tel: 0191 3868852

Durham is a city that no one should ever miss from their visiting list. It is steeped in history and the icing on the cake, apart from the imposing Castle is probably the magnificent cathedral which appears to hang over the river. Inside it is magical, and if for no other reason, you should stay in Durham to witness the majesty and spiritual beauty of this wonderful building. Of course there are many other things to do here. Plenty of interesting walks, fishing, golf for the energetic, shopping perhaps for others. Mrs Williams in her very nice, Grade II Listed house, Castle View in Crossgate, is a welcoming hostess to those who want to stay in Durham. There is little formality about the house but everything is kept spotlessly clean, the rooms are charmingly decorated, the beds extremely conducive to a good night's sleep. Every one of the 6 spacious bedrooms is centrally heated and all are ensuite. Every room has television and a welcoming hostess tray - there is nothing nicer than being able to make a cup of tea whenever you wish. When you come downstairs in the morning it will be to enjoy a classic, North Country breakfast with several choices and each meal cooked freshly to order. You will certainly not leave the table hungry! There are no evening meals served here but there is a wealth of eating places in Durham and Mrs Williams is happy to recommend you to one which will suit your taste and your pocket.

USEFUL INFORMATION

OPEN; All year, except Xmas
CHILDREN; Welcome
CREDIT CARDS;None taken
ACCOMMODATION; 6 ensuite rooms

DINING ROOM; Excellent breakfast
VEGETARIAN; Upon request
DISABLED ACCESS; No facilities
GARDEN; Small patio garden

Chapter Eight

SEA BRINK HOTEL,
The Beach,
Filey, North Yorkshire YO14 9LA

Tel: 01723 513257

To stay in a seaside hotel that is so close to the beach that on a windy day the spray of the North Sea comes over you as you walk along the sand, is exciting and exhilarating. This is so of the Sea Brink Hotel which is a traditional hotel of character and charm. Whilst it does remind one of the days of one's childhood when a fortnight by the sea was de riguer, the Sea Brink has moved with the times and provides all that the modern holiday maker requires. The atmosphere is a contented and happy one with a smiling staff who truly want you to enjoy your stay.

All nine bedrooms are ensuite, individually decorated, have central heating, colour television, continental quilts, hospitality trays, direct-dial telephones, radio and clock alarms.. Breakfast is a meal which will set you up for the day. You can choose from a traditional Yorkshire Breakfast, Scrambled, fried or boiled eggs or grilled kippers. At night the food is predominantly English with a menu that changes daily. It is of excellent quality and only the finest fresh produce and locally caught sea food are selected to create the wide variety of dishes on offer. There is a good choice of wines selected both for taste and pocket! Non-residents are always welcome to dine.

The 'Brink Coffee Shop' is open from February to November inclusive and here you can have morning coffee, enjoy a light lunch, have a hot or cold snack and in the afternoon indulge in a Yorkshire afternoon tea. The well-stocked bar is a meeting place in the evenings both to enjoy a drink and natter with newly made friends about the day. Filey is one of the few remaining unspoilt resorts and it appeals to all ages. The attractions contrast from the Nature Trail on Brigg to angling parties from the famous Coble landing. The long flat promenade provides an enjoyable walk, yachtsmen relish the sailing in Filey Bay and the glorious sandy beach invites anyone who just wants to laze or swim. A great place for a holiday.

USEFUL INFORMATION

OPEN; February to December
CHILDREN; Welcome
CREDIT CARDS; All major cards
LICENSED; Yes
ACCOMMODATION; 5dbl 4 fam ensuite
DINING ROOM; Good, traditional fare
'Brink Coffee Shop' open Feb-Nov inclusive
VEGETARIAN; Catered for
DISABLED ACCESS; Difficult
PETS; By arrangement

WHITFIELD HOUSE HOTEL,
Goathland, North Yorkshire YO22 5LA

Tel: 01947 896215

The description a 'Hotel for all Seasons' really fits this friendly, comfortable establishment owned and run by John and Pauline Lusher. First it is so well situated for everyone to enjoy the staggering beauty of this part of North Yorkshire. You will find it on the fringe of the hamlet of Darnholm, near Goathland in the heart of the North York Moors National Park. It is located almost at the end of a 'No through road' where traffic is minimal and peace and quiet assured. It is just 300 metres from the stepping stones at Darnholm and the open moors. The North York Moors National Park is one of the lesser known National Parks and remains a region of unspoilt and outstanding natural beauty. Secondly the time of the year that you choose to come is almost immaterial, there is always something beautiful upon which to feast your eyes. In August it is the miles of purple heather and in the Autumn the brilliant colours. Whenever you come you will find Whitfield House is a place in which to recharge your batteries, unwind and totally relax. You can be as energetic or as lazy as you feel. There are endless places to visit from the fun of the coast perhaps at Whitby, Scarborough or the smuggler's haunt, Robin Hood's Bay to the Museums which abound. Castle Howard and other stately homes are within easy reach and so too are the Abbeys of Whitby, Rievaulx and York Minster. It is superb walking country with scenery to delight the eye.

Whitfield House is warm, friendly and comfortable and the ideal base for anyone wanting to enjoy a holiday or break. The house, part of which is 17th century in origin was once a farmhouse and is full of old world charm. There is a nice Lounge Bar, a cosy lounge and a charming dining room in which the food is of a very high standard. Smoking is permitted only in the Lounge and Bar. The 9 ensuite bedrooms are all furnished in a cottage style and have tea and coffee making facilities, colour television, direct dial telephone, hairdryer and clock-radio-alarm. The hotel is centrally heated throughout. Whitfield House deserves its three crowns commended from the English Tourist Board as it does its other accolades. Certainly somewhere for all seasons.

USEFUL INFORMATION

OPEN; Feb-Nov inclusive
CHILDREN; Welcome over 5 years
CREDIT CARDS; All major cards
LICENSED; Yes. Residential
ACCOMMODATION; 9 ensuite rooms
DINING ROOM; Full English breakfast
4 course dinner
VEGETARIAN; Catered for
DISABLED ACCESS; Difficult
PETS; Dogs by arrangement

Chapter Eight

CRESCENT LODGE,
20 Swan Road, Harrogate,
North Yorkshire, HG1 2SA.

Tel & Fax : 01423 503688

  The setting for this lovely early Victorian house is a quiet part of central Harrogate. Grade II listed, it is approximately 150 years old, and is 2 crowns commended by the English Tourist Board. Mrs Humphris is your hostess and emphasises the comfort of her guests as being of paramount importance. Each bedroom has fresh flowers and fruit as well as the usual comforts of tea/coffee making trays, wash basins and shaver points. Some bedrooms are ensuite and if not, there are ample additional bathroom facilities. This is a charming house, with elegant, good taste showing in all furnishings, and the warm personality of your hostess adding to the copious welcoming feeling you have upon arrival. Breakfast is a delight with a variety of food on offer, from cereals, yoghurts and warm croissants to a perfectly cooked English breakfast, all served in a graceful dining room which can only add to the ambience of this warm household. Again, the drawing room is cosy and welcoming, and is a pleasant place to spend the evening, after a 'day out' exploring the surrounding attractions.

  Harrogate itself has a lot to offer. Just a short distance away from Crescent Lodge is the Royal Pump Room Museum with its sulphur well, where you can taste the waters if so desired! There are also displays here pertaining to local history which make some very interesting reading. Harrogate's own art gallery has some very fine exhibits of English paintings and watercolours, and if this is not to your taste then a day spent wandering round the shops can be just as fulfilling! It is a good centre for business with the Conference Hall and Exhibition Centre, and there are many tours that will show you the wonderful countryside just a few minutes away. Travel just a little further to visit the Yorkshire Dales National Park and bask in some of the most scenic views in England. Walking is a joy here, as well as climbing and many other outdoor activities. Harrogate's picturesque neighbour, Knaresborough has the ruins of a 14th century castle and is an appealing place to visit. Crescent Lodge is in an ideal position for all these amenities and a short stroll will have you in the heart of a first-class town. Restaurants are again within walking distance, and Mrs Humphris actually displays some of the menus in the room folders, to give you the opportunity to see for yourself what is on offer. This lady has thought of everything, and her hospitality matches her exquisite taste and comfortable home.

USEFUL INFORMATION

OPEN : All year
CHILDREN : Over 14yrs welcome
PETS : No
LICENSED : No
CREDIT CARDS : None taken
ACCOMMODATION : 4 rooms; 3 twin, 1 sgl, 2 en suite

DINING ROOM : Excellent fayre
VEGETARIAN : Catered for
BAR SNACKS : Not applicable
DISABLED ACCESS : No
GARDEN : Small, neat & walled

LASKILL FARM
Hawnby, Nr Hemsley,
York YO6 5NB

Tel: 01439 798268

This attractive 18th century farmhouse owned by Sue Smith is just 45 minutes from York and 30 minutes from the market and racing town of Thirsk. It is in the North York Moors National Park, near Rievaulx Abbey and is ideal for anyone wanting to explore the many surrounding places -of interest and scenic beauty. Two interesting places to visit, amongst many, are Ryedale Folk Museum and Beck Isle Museum which give you an idea of life in this awesome and fantastically beautiful part of the world. Stately homes and castles are also within easy reach for you to enjoy. For walkers it is a paradise and for those who just want to relax, the lovely walled garden of Laskill Farm with its own lake and summerhouse will bring you peace and contentment. There is also fishing on their own stretch of the river.

Inside this 18th century listed farmhouse you will find a warm welcoming atmosphere, traditional furnishings and comfortable rooms. The spacious lounge is there for you to enjoy and you will be served breakfast in a large breakfast room leading to the conservatory. It is all charming and guests rapidly feel at home - Sue manages to achieve this without any effort. Having spent a peaceful night in one of the pretty bedrooms, two of which were completed in 1992 having been converted from the old dairy still with its original Oak beams - all of the bedrooms are either ensuite or have private facilities and are equipped with TV, a beverage tray, telephone etc -, you come down to breakfast and find it is one of the best meals you have ever had. Everything is freshly cooked to your order, the coffee smells and tastes delicious and the tea is always piping hot. Evening meals of an equal standard are available by arrangement.

Sue Smith also has some very attractive and well equipped self catering accommodation. The Smithy and the Forge were converted from an old stable in 1996, both retaining the old beamed ceiling and both benefitting from Inglenook fireplaces, both have large french windows opening on to a patio and they are on one level, very suitable for partially disabled people. The other accommodation is in houses and cottages in nearby villages plus one in Helmsley. If you are interested ring Sue and she will send you all the information.

USEFUL INFORMATION

OPEN; *All year*
CHILDREN; *Welcome*
CREDIT CARDS; *None taken*
LICENSED; *No*
ACCOMMODATION; *6 rooms ensuite*
PETS; *Self-contained accommodation only*

DINING ROOM; *Excellent breakfast*
Evening meal by arrangement
VEGETARIAN; *By arrangement*
DISABLED ACCESS; *Not for B & B but in The Smithy & the Forge*

Chapter Eight

BARN CLOSE FARM
*Rievaulx, Helmsley,
North Yorkshire YO6 5LH*

Tel: 01439 798321

Barn Close Farm is ideal for those wanting to get away from it all. Situated in a hidden valley, the warm and friendly atmosphere guarantees guests the peace and tranqillity they crave. This is a working farm with cattle and sheep and is surrounded by glorious countryside and wooded hills with panoramic views down the Rievaulx Valley. Both bedrooms are furnished and decorated in very good taste with tea and coffee making facilities. There is an ensuite shower/WC room to the double room. The family room has the use of a private bathroom.

For young children a cot and high chair are available, as well as baby sitting. There is a Shetland pony for the children. Special emphasis is placed on providing imaginative and tasty menus. Breakfast is traditional with various choices. The evening meal is optional but recommended. Mrs. Milburn bakes her own bread and uses organically grown vegetables and fresh meat and eggs from the farm. Guests are most welcome to supply their own wine. A cosy lounge with an open fire and colour television is very restful. Pony trekking and excellent walking terrain is nearby. There are many wonderful attractions to discover including the regal and splendid Castle Howard. Barn Close Farm has been awarded '3Crowns' by the English Tourist Board and has been 'Recommended' by the Daily Telegraph, both accolades are well deserved.

USEFUL INFORMATION

OPEN; All year
CHILDREN; Yes, cot, high chair, and baby sitting available
CREDIT CARDS; None taken
LICENSED; May bring your own wine
ACCOMMODATION; 2 doubles, one can be made into a family, 1 is ensuite
DINING ROOM; Delicious home-cooking using home grown vegetables, fresh meat, fresh bread
VEGETARIAN; Catered for
DISABLED ACCESS; No
GARDEN; Yes
PETS; No

BUCKINGHAM HOUSE
33 Bridge Street, Helmsley,
York YO6 5DX

Tel: 01439 770613

The North York Moors is a vast wilderness, rugged and breathtaking, with deep valleys where villages and farms are gathered together, and the uplands are clothed in heather. On the edge of this walkers paradise is Helmsley, a small town where the 11th century Castle has the original earthworks. It is here also that Mrs. Wood has her Georgian Grade II Listed guest house. Buckingham House was built in 1776 and is very impressive, the soft stone and large windows enhance this lovely property. The inside is just as charming with comfortable furnishings, and central heating. The bedrooms are delightful with colour co-ordinated drapes and bedding, a vanity unit, television and a tea and coffee tray. The double and twin rooms have views overlooking the Castle. The bathroom has a bath, shower, WC and wash hand basin. There are lots of books and games for your use. The artwork you see adorning the walls of Buckingham House are by Mrs. Wood, a talented lady whose hobby is textile art. An excellent home-cooked breakfast, with choices, is served in the morning, using fresh local produce. A packed lunch is also available on request. Evening meals are not served, so you have a chance to try out the local hostelries and restaurants. Children are welcome, cot and high chair are available. Duncombe Park is close by where you can enjoy a riverside walk. The well-preserved ruins of Rievaulx Abbey are beautiful, it was founded in 1131 by Cistercian Monks, and is well worth a visit just for the peace. There are plenty of outdoor pursuits including riding, cycling, gliding, fishing, golf and of course walking and bird watching.

USEFUL INFORMATION

OPEN; All year except Christmas Day
CHILDREN; Welcome
CREDIT CARDS; None taken
ACCOMMODATION; 3 rooms, 1 double, 1 twin, 1 single

DINING ROOM; Breakfast only.
Packed lunches are available
DISABLED ACCESS; No
GARDEN; Yes
PETS; Yes

Chapter Eight

SPROXTON HALL
*Sproxton, Helmsley,
York YO6 5EQ*

*Tel: 01439 770225
Fax: 01439 771373*

For wonderful breathtaking views one could not go wrong with a visit to the North York Moors. The upper regions are shrouded in heather, creating a carpet of colour. Villages nestle amongst all this beauty, there are valleys cut deep into the moors with rivers and streams cascading downwards. It is a place to get away from all the hustle and bustle of everyday living, to enjoy the peace, tranquillity and marvellous fresh air. One of the villages tucked away on the edge of the moors is the attractive market town of Helmsley set in the Rievaulx Valley close to the Cleveland Way. The area here has much to offer the visitor with several places of interest including Helmsley Castle which dates back to the 11th century. To the south of the town is the village of Sproxton and the magnificent 17th century Grade II Listed property Sproxton Hall. It is owned and run by Margaret Wainwright and her family. This superb farmhouse oozes warmth and friendliness, you can feel it as soon as you walk through the door. There are exposed beams and the house has been lovingly and tastefully furnished and decorated in a traditional way, providing an elegant country home. The guest's drawing room is extremely peaceful, where one is able to relax and unwind in the cosy surroundings of deep chinz sofa and chairs, here you can read, plan your day or rest after a busy one. The bedrooms are charming, decorated in colour co-ordinating Sanderson or Laura Ashley prints. The double rooms have half-tester or coronet drapes over the bed, absolutely delightful. All the rooms have a vanity unit, shaver point, remote control colour television and tea and coffee making facilities. Some rooms are ensuite, some with private bathroom. After an excellent peaceful nights sleep, you make you way to the attractive dining room where you can enjoy a hearty full English breakfast. An evening meal is not available at Sproxton Hall, however, there are many interesting Inns in the surrounding area, serving a variety of meals to suit all tastes and pockets.

The Wainwright family are kept very busy as this is a working farm consisting of 300 acres, with sheep, pigs, cereals and silage, visitors are welcome to take an interest in any aspect of the farm. There are plenty of outdoor activities on offer including fly and reservoir fishing, golf and of course walking. For the more adventurous you could try gliding or hang gliding, what a marvellous way to see the beauty of this astonishing area.

USEFUL INFORMATION

OPEN; *All year*
CHILDREN; *Over 10 years*
CREDIT CARDS; *None taken*
ACCOMMODATION; *4 rooms, 2 double, 2 twin, 2 ensuite. Plus 5 self-catering cottages sleeping 4-8*

DINING ROOM; *Hearty full English breakfast. No evening meal available*
DISABLED ACCESS; *No, only in self-catering*
GARDEN; *Yes*
PETS; *No*

THE MALLOWS GUEST HOUSE,
55 Spring Street, Springwood,
Huddersfield, HD1 4AZ.

Tel : 01484 544884

'Welcome to Huddersfield' is what you would expect on the front of a brochure of the town, but this is the warm greeting afforded you at this pleasant guest house. Mrs Chantry is your hostess, and shows the hospitality native to this part of the world. The house is Grade II listed and is approx.150 years old. The traditional furnishings further enhance the rooms, which are very comfortably furnished, and have all modern facilities including T.V. and tea & coffee trays. Three of the bedrooms are en suite, while the other three have wash basins and access to a bathroom. All the rooms are of a very high standard and are tastefully decorated. The dining room is charming, with a feature marble fireplace and a large picture window. Breakfast is traditional English with a vegetarian menu available. There is a large comfortable lounge where you can relax after a day's activities; whether it is pleasure or business!

Mallows Guest House is ideally suited for the businessman or tourist, as it is really central for everything. You are just five minutes from the centre of Huddersfield with its shops, restaurants, cinemas and business premises. It is a lovely Victorian town having recently seen a great deal of refurbishments, which has restored its former glory, and with a lot of the town now pedestrianised, it is a joy to explore. Along with national shops, there are many smallstores and markets which offer an exciting mix of memorabilia and high class shopping. Due to Huddersfield's background in the weaving industry, there are many mill shops selling quality, and value for money goods. There is much more than just shops to this fine town. Historically, it has a lot to offer with the canals being restored, the railway station, which has been described as 'a stately home with trains in', and much more architecture being refurbished. This is a town that recognises conservation.

If on the other hand, you only wish to use this as a base to explore the surrounding countryside, then again it is ideal. 'Last of the Summer Wine' country is only 15mins away whilst Bronte country is 30mins away. Walking and climbing in the beautiful Yorkshire Dales is just one way to spend your days, but there is also hang gliding, fishing, golf and many other outdoor sports to be found here. This is a location to suit all, with every kind of entertainment possible, and what better way to finish your day than relaxing in the lounge of this superb accommodation!

USEFUL INFORMATION

OPEN : All year
CHILDREN : Over 12yrs welcome
PETS : No
LICENSED : No
CREDIT CARDS : None taken
ACCOMMODATION : 6 rooms; 3 en suite.
DINING ROOM : Breakfast only
VEGETARIANS : Catered for
BAR SNACKS : Not applicable
DISABLED ACCESS : No
GARDEN : No

Chapter Eight

GRACEFIELD
133 Bolling Road, Ilkley,
West Yorkshire LS29 8PN

Tel: 01943 600960

This Edwardian end terraced house has been charmingly refurbished throughout in the traditional French style. Dr and Mrs Weinert, your hosts, speak both French and German, and converse easily in both languages (in addition to English). They are friendly, amiable people who enjoy the company of guests and endeavour to ensure your stay is a pleasant one. There are three double warm and cosy bedrooms, and a private bathroom and shower room for guests use. The residents lounge leads to a large raised patio with overlooks the Wharfe Valley, giving a stunning view over the countryside. It is a pleasant place to sit in the evenings and is equipped with deck chairs and a parasol for those lazy afternoons snoozing in the sun.

Ilkley is home to that famous song, sung by scouts the world over. Here is Ilkley Moor with all the outdoor activities; walking, fishing, riding, golf and much more, (you can just see the scouts marching over the dales in their uniforms!). The ancient market town of Skipton is nearby and is ideal for a quiet day shopping in this unique part of the world. There are many 'olde worlde' villages and quaint textile towns in this area alongside the rugged and wild beauty of an untameable moor, all of which is sure to capture the heart of those who visit. Gracefield is just the place to find yourself conveniently positioned to visit all these attractions, and to come home to in the evening after a satisfying day exploring the wealth and beauty of the vista surrounding you.

USEFUL INFORMATION

OPEN: All year
CHILDREN: Welcome
CREDIT CARDS: None taken
LICENSED: No
ACCOMMODATION: 3 double rooms
DINING ROOM: Excellent breakfast, evening meal not available
DISABLED ACCESS: No
GARDEN: Raised garden/patio
PETS: No

CLYDE HOUSE,
Railway Street, Leyburn,
North Yorkshire
DL8 5AY

Tel: 01969 623941

Monica and Adrian Morris are your gracious hosts at Clyde House, a listed building dating from 1750, just off the market square. Formerly a coaching inn, it is believed to be one of the oldest buildings in town. It is 'commended' by the English Tourist Board, and belongs to the Board's 'Welcome Host' Scheme. Monica and Adrian have thought of most things in their large, comfortable rooms, as well as today's necessities like TV and a tea and coffee tray. There are easy chairs, adjustable heating, lashings of hot water, a hair dryer, even a corkscrew! Occasionally a third person has been known to 'appear', adding a touch of mystery to this fine house, although obviously she is as pleasant as your hosts, otherwise Clyde House might not have such a good reputation as it has! A full English breakfast is served which can be varied to suit each individual taste, including that of vegetarians. Packed lunches can be arranged for those wanting to disappear in the Dales for a day, and there is a variety of excellent eating places within walking distance offering a wide choice of evening meals.

During the summer your hosts also open their small tearoom to the public and it has become known far and wide for the quality of Monica's home baking, and her delicious specials including warm ginger cake with cream and luscious fruit crumbles. The mouth waters at the thought doesn't it! It is featured in the Yorkshire Dales Teapot Trail and has a high reputation.

The Yorkshire Dales is an area of spectacular beauty, with much of it being a National Park. If you are a walker then this is ideal (you will probably need to after some of Monica's teas!); the scenery is unsurpassed anywhere, and the clean, fresh air is sure to bring that bloom back to your cheeks. Leyburn itself is the perfect town from which to visit the many interesting and historic sites in the surrounding area, and there are many outdoor pursuits like golf, fishing and sailing nearby. The town regularly holds fascinating antique and general auctions, and there is a maket in the Square each Friday. You will feel at home in Clyde House, and are sure to enjoy the hospitality of the friendly Yorkshire people.

USEFUL INFORMATION

OPEN; All year
CHILDREN; Welcome
PETS; Welcome by arrangement
LICENSED; No
CREDIT CARDS; None taken
ACCOMMODATION; 4 rooms all En suite 1fml, 2dbl & 1 twin

DINING ROOM; Breakfast only
VEGETARIANS; Catered for
TEA ROOM; Summer only - delicious
BAR MEALS; Not applicable
DISABLED ACCESS; No
GARDEN; Secluded and south facing

Chapter Eight

MANOR FARM
Little Barugh, Malton,
North Yorkshire YO17 0UY

Tel: 01653 668262

Streams spill down from the moors through the Vale of Pickering and into the River Derwent, where visitors can enjoy long rambling walks. Manor Farm was built in 1780 and extends a warm and friendly welcome, where guests can unwind and enjoy the hospitality of Judith Murray. The bedrooms are spacious and bright, furnished and decorated with style. There are two twin bedded rooms one which has a lovely ensuite bathroom, and the other a private bathroom which is adjacent. Recently the single bedroom has been totally refurbished and would make an ideal room for an accompanying child or relative. A welcome tray with tea and coffee is afforded. A spacious conservatory is being added for the 1997 season which will incorporate a breakfast room with lovely views, and overlooking the garden. For the use of guests is a comfortable sitting room with an open fire and a good selection of books. Breakfast is guaranteed to set you up for the day with a wide choice, prepared with flair using fresh produce. An evening meal is available with prior arrangement only. There are plenty of outdoor activities to be had locally with include fishing, golf and cycling and there are very few places which offer such wonderful walks amidst stunning scenery. Flamingo Land, Eden Camp and the splendour of Castle Howard are just a few of the many places for visitors to enjoy.

USEFUL INFORMATION

OPEN; All year
CHILDREN; Welcome
CREDIT CARDS; None taken
ACCOMMODATION; 3 rooms, 2 twin, 1 single, 1 twin is ensuite
DINING ROOM; Excellent large breakfast
Evening meal by prior arrangement only
DISABLED ACCESS; No
GARDEN; Yes plus tennis court
PETS; Yes by arrangement

WILSON HOUSE FARM
*Barningham, Richmond,
North Yorkshire DL11 7EB*

Tel: 01833 621218

In glorious country surroundings barely a mile from the A66, stands Wilson House, a 475 acre working farm, and ideally situated for a touring holiday of Yorkshire and the Durham Dales. Helen Lowes considered every aspect when transforming the property into accommodation to suit all family sizes and to offer guests the thoughtful extras not usually found. For instance there is a kitchenette with fridge and microwave, very handy for preparing picnic lunches and beverages. Bedrooms are light and airy and prettily furbished. Two have adjoining smaller rooms for either relatives or young children. Ensuite facilities are available. Rooms include colour television and a tea and coffee tray.

A pay phone is available. Tasty and appetising meals in true farmhouse style are presented, making use of fresh local produce with a choice of menu, including vegetarian dishes. Helen also bakes her own bread and the aroma pervades the farmhouse on baking days. Richmond with its cobbled market square is overlooked by the Norman Castle, visit the beautifully restored Theatre Royal or meander alongside the River Swale. For stunning views of the Pennines and Teesdale then the Stang is well worth a visit, with walks through the forest which open out into lovely picnic areas.

USEFUL INFORMATION

OPEN; March-October
CHILDREN; Welcome
CREDIT CARDS; None taken
ACCOMMODATION; 5 rooms 2 ensuite
DINING ROOM; Traditional farmhouse cooking using fresh local produce
VEGETARIAN; Catered for
DISABLED ACCESS; Yes, wheelchair users with assistance
GARDEN; Yes

Chapter Eight

BEECH TREE HOUSE FARM
South Holme, Slingsby,
York YO6 7BA

Tel: 01653 628257

    Built in 1878 Beechtree House Farm is surrounded by well manicured lawns and majestic trees, and features comfortable and restrained furnishings. Guest rooms are spacious with a choice of double or family rooms. Linen and drapes are most attractive and enhance the well presented decor. The residents lounge features the warmth and cosiness of an open log fire, with colour television, video and books. There is a playroom for children and a very thoughtful touch by the owners Richard and Carol Farnell, has been to supply bikes for use around the 260 acre farm and they are quite happy for the guests to walk their friendly dogs.

    Overlooking the garden is the lovely dining room and here you will find the standard of cuisine very acceptable, dishes are produced using home produced vegetables and meat. Guests are most welcome to supply their own wine. Beechtree would make an ideal centre from which to tour the North Yorkshire Moors with its stunning scenery and quaint cobblestoned villages. The area is renowned for its scenic walks and attracts visitors from far and wide, who come to marvel al the landscape. The beautiful City of York is a short drive away, steeped in history and well worth a visit.

USEFUL INFORMATION

OPEN; All year except Christmas
CHILDREN; Yes, at reduced rates
CREDIT CARDS; None taken
LICENSED; May bring your own wine
ACCOMMODATION; 4 guest rooms, 3 with private bathrooms
DINING ROOM; Delicious home produced vegetables and meat.
VEGETARIAN; By arrangement
DISABLED ACCESS; No
GARDEN; Yes
PETS; No

FAWN LEA
10 Winston Road, Standrop,
Co. Durham DL23 NN

Tel: 01833 660356

About 14 miles from the historic City of Durham in the village of Standrop, Mrs. Joy Robson has her English Tourist Board '2 Crown Commended' guest house. This lovely house was built around 1900 and is very nicely appointed with traditional and comfortable furnishings. In the 3 bedrooms, 2 double and 1 twin, you will find ensuite facilities, colour television, hair dryer, shaver points, a teas maid and very comfy beds. There are rooms on the ground floor, which make it convenient for a disabled person. The dining room is very pleasant, and it is here you are served an excellent full English breakfast including black pudding and Cumberland sausages, absolutely delicious, just what you need to set you up for the day.

Vegetarians are catered for if required. An evening meal is not available at Fawn Lea, but don't worry there are a number of restaurants and inns within easy reach. Packed lunches are available, on request, for your day out, and what a lot there is to do. A visit to the Beamish Open Air Museum is a must, 200 acres of nostalgia, an old town has been re-created with cobbled streets, old houses, a working farm, shops stocked with goods of the time, a working pub and tram rides, an excellent day out. The coast is not to far away either. There are museums, country houses, gardens and shops. Golf, fishing and plenty of wonderful walks.

USEFUL INFORMATION

OPEN; All year
CHILDREN; Yes
CREDIT CARDS; None taken
ACCOMMODATION; 3 ensuite rooms
GARDEN; No, there is a patio

DINING ROOM; Delicious breakfast
No evening meal. Packed lunches available
VEGETARIAN; If required
DISABLED ACCESS; Ground floor
PETS; By arrangement

Chapter Eight

HARMONY COUNTRY LODGE
Limestone Road, Burniston,
Scarborough,
North Yorkshire YO13 0DG

Tel: 01723 870276

The unusual octagonal design of Harmony Country Lodge is quite unique and eye catching. A tree lined approach opens out to extensive well tended grounds and ample car parking space. Standard or ensuite bedrooms are comfortably furnished, central heated, with colour television, and complimentary tray. Guests can relax in the residents' lounge or admire the stunning panoramic coastal and country views from the spacious conservatory. The house is totally non-smoking for which the owners, Tony and Sue Hewitt were granted the 'Roy Castle Good Air' Gold Award. Regrettably there are no facilities for young children or babies. However, a large and comfortable static caravan sleeping up to 6 persons, situated amongst trees and gardens, within the perimeter of Harmony Country Lodge is available on a self-catering basis. Good honest traditional fare is served in attractive surroundings with an alternative choice should a vegetarian meal be requested. Arrangements can be made for evening meals but there are plenty of restaurants locally. The wonderful coastline of North Yorkshire extends to the visitor; stunning coastal walks, rugged headlands, sandy beaches and charming hamlets, whilst inland, the scenery is simply breathtaking.

USEFUL INFORMATION

OPEN; All year
CHILDREN; Over 7 years
CREDIT CARDS; None taken
LICENSED; Yes
ACCOMMODATION; 6 rooms, 4 ensuite plus self-catering caravan sleeping up to 6 persons
Bicycle hire

DINING ROOM; Good wholesome cooking, Evening meal by arrangement
VEGETARIAN; Catered for
DISABLED ACCESS; No
GARDEN; Yes, large 1 ½ acres
PETS; By arrangement only
NON SMOKING
Aromatherapy massage

STUDLEY HOUSE
67 Main Street, Ebberston,
Scarborough,
North Yorkshire YO13 9NR

Tel: 01723 859285

On the east coast of Britain is the resort, spa and fishing town of Scarborough with its twin bays. This historic town has many theatres, art galleries and museums, and is well known for its attractive parks and gardens, and lively amusement park. Moving away from Scarborough, as you drive along the A170 towards Pickering, you enter a small village by the name of Ebberston, it is here that Jane and Ernie Hodgson live in their charming early 1800's country house. They have been in business for 13 years and offer a range of accommodation, bed and breakfast, a self-catering cottage and a small caravan site for touring vehicles only.

Studley House is where they offer superior bed and breakfast lodgings. The 3 light and airy bedrooms are well appointed with wash hand basin, colour television, alarm clocks, hair dryer, shaver point, toiletries and a complimentary tea and coffee tray. The two main bedrooms, one double and one double/twin, have the privacy of ensuite facilities. The single room has a private bathroom with a shower. Breakfast is a real treat, a full English with all the trimmings including home-made marmalade and local honey made from the heather flower. Guests have their own sitting room, for planning your day away or just relaxing. Studley House is strictly non-smoking.

Cow Pasture Cottage is a delightful self-contained property on one level, making it suitable for the partially disabled. Originally a milking parlour, it has been lovingly converted by local craftsmen to provide accommodation for 4 people. The bedrooms, one double and one twin which has a vanity unit and shaver point. The bathroom is well appointed. The kitchen has every modern convenience including a microwave oven, fridge, electric cooker, iron and ironing board. The lounge/diner is comfortable and has a colour television, comfy seating, an 'open' gas fire and storage heater. All bed linen and towels are included in the price as is the electricity. A cot and highchair are also available. There is a patio with garden furniture.

And last but certainly not least is the caravan site, originally an old apple orchard which is beautifully kept for eight touring caravans. It is grassed and level, with hook-ups, hot and cold water, razor points, chemical disposal and battery charging. There is a toilet adjacent to the site but guests should bring their own. Dogs are welcome, but must be kept on a lead. However you decide to stay here, you are assured a wonderful welcome and an excellent holiday. Your days will be filled to overflowing.

USEFUL INFORMATION

OPEN; All year. Caravan site Apr-Oct
CHILDREN; Welcome over 10 years in B & B
CREDIT CARDS; Yes
ACCOMMODATION; Bed & Breakfast: 3 rooms, 1 double, 1 double/twin, 1 single 2 bedroomed self-catering cottage, caravan site for 8 touring vehicles.
B & B is NON-SMOKING
DINING ROOM; Breakfast only
VEGETARIAN; Catered for
DISABLED ACCESS; Suitable for partially disabled in self-catering cottage
GARDEN; Yes
PETS; Must be kept on a lead at the site. No dogs in B & B or cottage

Chapter Eight

THE MINERS ARMS
*Water Lane,
Eyam, Nr Sheffield,
Derbyshire S30 1RG*

Tel: 01433 630853

When Nicholas and Ruth Cook took over the 17th century Miners Arms in November 1991, it was a homecoming for Ruth; she was raised on a farm nearby. Nicholas, previously, was the General Manager of the Greenhouse Restaurant in Mayfair, London.

This charming couple wanted to enhance the good reputation for food that The Miners had before they came here, and this they most certainly have achieved. In addition to the excellence of the food you will find yourselves in a building which has been an inn since 1630, before the Great Plague of 1665 which made the village of Eyam, where the Miners Arms is situated, legendary after their noble and self-imposed isolation to prevent the spread of the fatal disease. The Inn, as you can well believe, is inhabited by several ghosts, the most infamous being Sarah and Emily who perished in a fire many years ago. In the days of lead mining, the inn was a meeting place of the Great Barmote Court which upheld the ancient and unique lead miing laws. The lead miners depended entirely on this court to settle their disputes.

Eyam is an ideal spot to use as a base for exploring the Peak District. The Miners has delightful bedroom accommodation comprising 6 twin or double bedrooms and one single, all ensuite. The menu in the restaurant which opens in the evenings from Tuesday to Saturday, reflects the skill of the chef. His homemade bar meals served every lunchtime from 12-2pm include Braised Oxtail, a Roast of the Day and a selection of puddings. On Sundays the traditional roast is excellent value for money. The secret of success is the use of fresh food using local produce whenever possible. There is no food on Sunday evening.

USEFUL INFORMATION

OPEN; Bar Meals: 12-2pm Tues-Sat
Rest: Tues-Sat 7-9pm Sun: 12-2pm
CHILDREN; Welcome
CREDIT CARDS; Access/Visa
LICENSED; Full Licence
ACCOMMODATION:6 twin or double
1 single, all ensuite

RESTAURANT;Quality English/French Cuisine
BAR MEALS; Traditional
VEGETARIAN; On request
DISABLED ACCESS; Level entrance
Accommodation difficult
GARDEN; Beer Garden at rear

THE GRANGE FARMHOUSE,
Skelton,
York YO3 6YQ.

Tel : 01904 470780

The Grange Farmhouse is Grade II listed, and commended by the English Tourist Board. just 3.5 miles from the centre of York, it has five very high standard rooms on the ground floor, which are perfect for the disabled, and are furnished beautifully. It was a former milking parlour and a great deal of thought has gone into this conversion, offering all modern conveniences but removing none of the charm of a bygone age. Each room is en suite, has colour T.V., and facilities for tea & coffee. The family suite has two bedrooms; one double, with two single beds in the other room. The house opens on to the green of a quiet private village, and for further privacy the house is located in a walled garden with seating for guests. This is the place to unwind and relax, with the solitude of the surrounding countryside to admire and soothe away 'your worldly cares.' Mr Spencer, your host will ensure a pleasant stay with a traditional hearty breakfast, and good advice regarding eating out and sampling some local ale!

There is plenty to do in the area with the usual country pursuits of fishing, golf and walking, and the historic city of York is within easy driving distance. There is a fine gothic church here and even the 13th century keep of a ruined castle, along with an art gallery and museum and much more. This is a lovely city, and for those of you interested, shopping is a joy (Good sturdy shoes are a must!). Walking in Yorkshire must be one of the chief delights, as there are so many wonderful views to admire and so many places to see. There is an individuality about this place that is beyond words and must be seen to be appreciated!

USEFUL INFORMATION

OPEN : All year
CHILDREN : Welcome
PETS : By arrangement
LICENSED : No
CREDIT CARDS : None taken
DINING ROOM : Traditional breakfast
VEGETARIANS : Catered for
BAR FOOD : Not applicable
DISABLED ACCESS : Yes
GARDEN : Walled with seating area
ACCOMMODATION : 5 rooms all en suite 4 dbl, 1 fml.

Chapter Eight

HAMBLETON HOUSE,
*78 St.James' Green, Thirsk,
North Yorkshire, YO7 1AJ.*

*Tel : 01845 525532
Mobile: 0976 215453*

Think of country vets, and especially that great series, All Creatures Great & Small, and you will have it! Thirsk is more commonly known as Herriot Town, the place where James Herriot lived and worked, and as well as practising his profession, wrote his famous books. You are probably visualising this town already, and Hambleton House with it. But the similarity does not end there, as your hosts, Mike and Christine Bourner, are both classic car enthusiasts, so you may well think that you are slightly back in time in this quiet, relaxing corner of the world! This is a restored Victorian house, overlooking a peaceful village green and the perfect setting to rest and unwind. The rooms are large and comfortable, with charming decor, T.V., and the ever essential tea & coffee tray. All are en suite or with private bathroom and have the added bonus of being non smoking. The dining room is traditional in it's furnishings with exposed beams adding flavour to a delightful room.

The location of Thirsk is ideal as it sits between the North York Moors and the Dales, and is therefore the best possible place from which to tour. For many overseas visitors travelling from England to Scotland, Thirsk is exactly ½ way (4 hours driving time from London- the perfect stopping point!) Mike and Christine have detailed motoring maps of the area and will be delighted to help you choose and plan your routes, so that no part may lie undiscovered. York and Harrogate are a comfortable drive away if you should get withdrawal symptoms for city life, and there are a lot of local activities to keep you busy. Cod Beck river runs through Thirsk, so fishing is popular along with other country pursuits such as golf, bird watching and cycling. A great place to stay to sample the hospitality and beauty of Yorkshire!

USEFUL INFORMATION

OPEN : All year
CHILDREN : Over 10yrs welcome
PETS : No
LICENSED : No
CREDIT CARDS : None taken
ACCOMMODATION : 3 rooms; 2 dbl, 1 twin.
DINING ROOM : Breakfast only
VEGETARIANS : Catered for
BAR SNACKS : Not applicable
DISABLED ACCESS : No
GARDEN : Yes

SPITAL HILL
York Road, Thirsk,
Yorkshire YO7 3AE

Tel: 01845 522273

The cares of the world fall away on entering the peaceful and secluded gardens of Spital Hill, and once inside this elegant and genteel Victorian country house, one soaks up the atmosphere. Rooms are discriminating and sophisticated with furnishings which reflect the era in which it was built. Bedrooms subtly adorned offer style and comfort, private bathroom or ensuite facilities are available. Imagination and flair are also evident in the excellent cuisine, utilising home grown produce and fresh home-made breads complimented by a modest but none-the-less discerning range of wines. You will be welcomed by your hosts Ann and Robin Clough who will ensure your stay is one to remember. There is also a roaring log fire to curl up by. Within the spacious grounds is a former Grooms Cottage which has been superbly and skilfully restored and is now available as a luxury self-catering holiday home. Accommodation includes 2 double bedrooms with private facilities, sitting room, dining room and kitchen. Golf, gliding and fishing are within easy reach. Thirsk was the home of the late James Herriot and if you watched the television series you will know what dramatic and stunning countryside await you. The National Trust and English Heritage own many historical houses and abbeys which are within this area, as well as museums reflecting the crafts of days gone by.

USEFUL INFORMATION

OPEN; All year
CHILDREN; Over 12 years
CREDIT CARDS; Access/Visa/ Mastercard/Amex
LICENSED; Fully
ACCOMMODATION; 3 rooms 2 double ensuite, 1 twin with private facilities plus 2 bedroomed self-catering cottage

DINING ROOM; Excellent cuisine using home grown produce and fresh vegetables
DISABLED ACCESS; Yes in self-catering for partially disabled, 2 steps up to get to front door. All doors are too narrow for a wheelchair
GARDEN; Yes
PETS; No

NO SMOKING

Chapter Eight

HERRIOT'S HOTEL & RESTAURANT,
Main Street, Hawes,
Wensleydale,
North Yorkshire, DL8 3QU.

Tel : 01969 667536

Sitting in a cobbled street, in the picturesque market town of Hawes, is Herriot's Hotel & Restaurant. Formerly the only shoe and clog shop in the area, this 18th century building has been tastefully renovated to incorporate the 20th century, whilst losing none of the charm of the 18th. Joanne Wright is your hostess, and runs a friendly, cheerful establishment, with staff who provide the best of Yorkshire hospitality. There are seven bedrooms, all en suite, with the necessities of a tea/coffee tray, colour TV, and all decorated and furnished in a pleasing antique style. There are panoramic views over Wensleydale, and a more delightful sight upon wakening after a good night's rest, is difficult to imagine. The restaurant serves an excellent variety of locally produced meat and vegetables, and sea food is something of a speciality. Try the 'broccoli and Wensleydale cheese tart' as a starter, followed by 'pan fried Tuna in rosemary and lime'. Delicious! Finish off with a home made sweet and you are sure to have enjoyed a satisfying meal! The bar is well stocked, so you can enjoy a pre dinner drink in the welcoming atmosphere, and choose an appropriate wine to compliment your meal from the well selected wine list.

This is the heart of the Dales, and as such is ideally suited for those wishing to enjoy the peace and tranquillity of this magnificent part of the country. Walking is one way to enjoy the vistas before you, but even driving round the area will convey some of the balance and serenity of nature which encompasses these hills and vales. The Lake District is just a short drive over the hills, and there are many places of historical interest within easy reach. Richmond, with its 11th century castle ruins is just one place to visit, while Kendal has a 12th century castle to visit, among many other delightful places. York is easily reached, and this beautiful city has a great deal to offer. Whether it is a day's shopping that draws you here, or the fine Gothic architecture, or the reconstructed Viking centre, you will certainly relish a day spent in this glorious haven of English heritage. Herriot Hotel is certainly well placed for a host of activities and offers the perfect retreat for those wishing to 'get away from it all' but at the same time being comfortably close to those places you would wish to visit. Have a break here at any time of the year, sample the Yorkshire friendliness and wonder at the beauty of nature which is available to us all in these idyllic surroundings.

USEFUL INFORMATION

OPEN : All year (except January)
CHILDREN : Welcome
PETS : By arrangement
LICENSED : Residential
CREDIT CARDS : All major
RESTAURANT : Excellent local fayre
VEGETARIANS : Catered for
BAR SNACKS : No
DISABLED ACCESS : No
GARDEN : No
ACCOMMODATION : 7 rooms en suite; 4 dbl, 1 twin, 1 fml, 1 sgl.

WHITFIELD
Helm, Askrigg,
Nr. Leyburn, Wensleydale,
North Yorkshire DL8 3JF

Tel/Fax: 01969 650565

When you mention Wensleydale most people think of the cheese, but once you have stayed at Whitfield, when someone mentions that name you will instantly remember an excellent bed and breakfast. Whitfield is a superb 350 year old converted barn and is situated 285 metres above sea level in Upper Wensleydale, giving uninterrupted views that are stunning. This charming house is very comfortable and warm and is owned by Kate Empsall, who makes her guests feel at home as soon as they walk through the door. All rooms and the garden face south and overlook the Dale. The guests bedrooms are light and airy with spectacular views, the double has ensuite facilities, the twin has a wash hand basin, both have hair dryers, television and a tea and coffee tray. The sitting room has comfy chairs, television and a large open fire, there are also books, maps and guides here, so you can relax and plan your day. A full cooked English breakfast is served with delicious home-made preserves. Whitfield is close to Whitfield Fell and a wooded gill where you can see 2 high waterfalls. Surrounded by all this wonderful peace and tranquillity it won't take you long to unwind, once you have done so it is time to get those walking boots on, or hire a bike, and explore the Dales. The English Tourist Board has awarded Whitfield '2 Crowns Commended', and it is not difficult to see why.

USEFUL INFORMATION

OPEN; All year except Christmas
CHILDREN; Welcome
CREDIT CARDS; None taken
ACCOMMODATION; 1 double ensuite, 1 twin with wash hand basin
DINING ROOM; Breakfast only
DISABLED ACCESS; No
GARDEN; Small with pond
PETS; Yes
NON SMOKING

Chapter Eight

ANDRA'S FARM
*Appletreewick,
Nr. Skipton,
North Yorkshire BD23 6DA*

*Tel: 01756 720286
Fax: 01756 720241*

North Yorkshire is full of beautiful places and wonderful scenery and none more so than the Dick Whittington's birthplace, the village of Appletreewick which is surrounded by some of the most beautiful scenery in Wharfedale much beloved by artists and walkers alike with Simon's Seat to the east, and the majestic Burnsall Fell visible from most points in the village. Appletreewick today boasts a thriving local community in the village and enjoys the benefit of St John's Church, a village hall, two public houses - the New Inn and Craven Arms, a cricket team, darts and domino teams and various other local activities. It is an excellent village in which to make your base if you want to enjoy all that it has to offer as well as the wondrous beauty of Wharfedale. From here one can Pot Hole, go Hot Air Ballooning, Pony Trekking and Rock Climbing as well as fish for brown trout or play golf at Skipton. Superb walking country; the first leg stop on the Dales Way Walk.

Where to stay? You will find Andra's Farm is the answer. This delightful 17th century farmhouse owned by Judy Jackson and her husband, is warm and comfortable. Judy is a great hostess and has that wonderful ability to make you feel that you have known her for years. The house is furnished throughout in a cottage style which suits the old house admirably. It is obviously a well loved home and has that sort of atmosphere that is created by the centuries gone by and the ambience built up by the present owners. The three bedroms, two of which can be family rooms if required, either have ensuite facilities or a bathroom and private shower. Each room is attractively and individually decorated and complete with a generously supplied beverage tray which has the addition of biscuits if you are peckish. Breakfast is a traditional meal for which Judy uses fresh produce. You may choose whatever you wish to eat. There are no evening meals but Cream Teas are served at the weekends in the garden, weather permitting, with home-baked scones, lashings of butter, preserves and cream. The garden is stunning with over 250 varieties of fuschia.

USEFUL INFORMATION

OPEN; *All year. Apart from Xmas & January* **DINING ROOM;** *Excellent breakfast*
CHILDREN; *Welcome*   **VEGETARIAN;** *By arrangement*
CREDIT CARDS; *None taken*   **DISABLED ACCESS;** *Not accommodation*
ACCOMMODATION; *3 rooms ensuite .   Yes to garden for Cream Teas*
or private bathroom
PETS; *Guide dogs only*   **GARDEN;** *Delightful*

POSTGATE FARM
Glaisdale,
Whitby,
North Yorkshire YO21 2PZ

Tel: 01947 897353

Visitors to this small working farm may well be interested in the history relating to the area and Postgate Farm which has been collated and put into print, and retained by your hostess Mrs. Mary Thompson. Situated in the beautiful Esk Valley and surrounded by stunning open moorland, Postgate Farm built circa 1600, is an excellent centre from which to explore and appreciate the wonder of this diverse area. Bedrooms are furnished to an exacting standard and offer ensuite facilities, a tea and coffee tray and colour television. Early booking is advisable if you wish to have the use of the four poster bed, for that special occasion.

Guests also have the use of a small kitchen which is equipped with a microwave, fridge, freezer and electric kettle. A private sitting room with colour television, a dining room and a games room for the sole use of guests. Breakfast is in the traditional English style, an evening meal is not served. Special midweek rates and off season reductions are obtainable. Apart from walking there are many outdoor activities to be enjoyed, sea and river fishing, horse riding and golf. Situated near the coast it is a short drive to Whitby and Robin Hood's Bay, each with its own history. Nearby is the North York Moors Steam Railway, and the award winning Ryedale Folk Museum.

USEFUL INFORMATION

OPEN; All year
CREDIT CARDS; None taken
ACCOMMODATION; 3 ensuite rooms one room has a four poster bed
DINING ROOM; Breakfast only
DISABLED ACCESS; Not good
GARDEN; Yes
PETS; No

NON-SMOKERS PREFERRED

Chapter Eight

SNEATON HALL HOTEL
Sneaton, Whitby,
North Yorkshire YO22 5HP

Tel: 01947 605929

    Sneaton is a small North Yorkshire country village just outside the coastal town of Whitby. It has the delightful Sneaton Hall Hotel with superb gardens that overlook the busy fishing town which is three miles away. Staying at Sneaton Hall is a joyous experience. Di and Robin Halliwell own and run it aided by a friendly, well trained staff. The whole ethos of the hotel is to ensure that for guests it is a haven of content allowing them to be entertained at a leisurely pace. As you see the rooms in the hotel you realise that there is great attention to detail everywhere. The eight en-suite bedrooms have been charmingly and comfortably furnished complete with colour TV and a hostess tray that always has sufficient of everything on it. The public rooms have big armchairs into which one can sink and relax or curl up with a book, preferably with a gin and tonic alongside. The candlelit Restaurant, which is open to non-residents, is strictly non-smoking which is always a blessing but the focus is on the unique carved fireplace. The food is delicious and prepared from fresh local produce by a chef who is both imaginative and artistic. If you do not want to dine in the restaurant the well stocked lounge bar has a good selection of bar meals available every day.

    From Sneaton Hall it is easy to get into Whitby with its working port and historic Abbey. Two such diverse characters as Captain Cook and 'Count Dracula' have great associations with the town. Then there is Robin Hood's Bay with its history of smuggling, narrow streets and houses that cling to the cliffside, and a beach where rock pools at low tide thrill every inquisitive child. The North Yorkshire Moors Railway runs the magnificent 18 miles from Pickering to Grosmont and nearby Goathland - better known to Television viewers as 'Adensfield' in the series 'Heartbeat'. Permits are available for salmon & trout fishing on the River Esk. There is boating, pony trekking and fossil and jet hunting on the beaches for those who want to be energetic. Having enjoyed all that this glorious area has to offer it is splendid to know that you can return to Sneaton Hall for an excellent dinner and a perfect night's sleep. It is much more than just a hotel and Restaurant. Certainly not to be missed if you want to stay in this part of Yorkshire.

USEFUL INFORMATION

OPEN; All year
CHILDREN; Welcome
CREDIT CARDS; All major cards
LICENSED; Yes
ACCOMMODATION; 8 ensuite rooms
PETS; Yes
RESTAURANT; Open to non-residents
Delicious food. Closed Mon/Tues lunch
BAR MEALS; Excellent choice daily
VEGETARIAN; Daily choice
GARDEN; Yes. Quoits team
DISABLED ACCESS; Difficult

THE BEACON
Goathland, Whitby,
North Yorkshire YO22 5AN

Tel: 01947 896409

    The coast line that stretches from the resort, spa and fishing town of Scarborough to Whitby, the former whaling port set on the Esk Estuary, is associated with the explorer and navigator Captain James Cook, who lived in the town from 1746-49. The Cook Museum is dedicated to him and charts his life. Taking the A169 out of Whitby, heading towards the North York Moors, you will see a sign post for Goathland, a small village consisting mainly of 19thcentury houses. It is in this village, which the television company used to film 'Heartbeat', that Mrs. Ursula Katz has her country guest house. This lovely old property is about 100 years old and is sturdily built of Yorkshire stone. Beacon Guest House has a lovely warm and friendly atmosphere created by Ursula, a very amiable person, who goes out of her way to cater for your every need. The decor has been carefully chosen and enhances the house immensely, there is antique furniture everywhere. There are 6 bedrooms in all, 3 are ensuite, the other rooms share a very pleasant guest's bathroom. All the rooms have a well stocked complimentary tea and coffee tray. Most of the bedrooms have lovely wood panelling, 2 of them have panelling made from the original wood believed to have come from the Manor House in Helmsley, which was built in 1631. All the beds are either half testers or have canopies and are extremely comfortable. After an excellent nights sleep you make you way down to the dining room, where Ursula serves a delicious home-cooked full English breakfast with several choices, to really set you up for the day. An evening meal is available and here again it is all home-cooked using fresh local produce.

    Being so ideally situated in the middle of the North Yorkshire Moors, walkers will be in their element, in fact Goathland is the centre for moorland and woodland walks and waterfalls. This area has so much to offer everyone, the North Yorkshire Moors Railway is wonderful, an 18 mile stretch of track, built by George Stephenson in the 1830's, runs from Pickering to Grosmont, where you will travel through the grounds of Pickering Castle, and you may even catch a glimpse of a deer or two. Golf, fishing and many other outdoor pursuits are available. The coast is but a short drive away. Ursula looks forward to meeting you and welcoming you to her lovely home.

USEFUL INFORMATION

OPEN; All year except Christmas Day and Boxing Day
CHILDREN; Welcome
CREDIT CARDS; None taken
ACCOMMODATION; 6 guest rooms, 3 ensuite

DINING ROOM; Excellent home-cooking using fresh local produce. Evening available
VEGETARIAN; Upon request
DISABLED ACCESS; Full facilities
GARDEN; Yes, 1 ½ acres
PETS; Yes

Chapter Eight

HAMMER AND HAND COUNTRY GUEST HOUSE,
Hutton-le-Hole York,
North Yorkshire YO6 6UA

Tel: 01751 417300 Fax: 01751 417711

'By Hammer and Hand All Arts Do Stand' is the motto of this delightful house with its door knocker designed as a hammer with a hand wrapped around it. To stay here is a privilege. The house and its owner Ann Willis are welcoming. No one could fail to enjoy the 1784 building with its mellow York Stone and few would guess that its original role was as the village Beer House. It stands in a sheltered spot on the east side of the pretty village of Hutton-le-Hole, facing the green and beck within the North York Moors National Park. It is such a beautiful area and there is so much to do. Glorious walks and touring routes abound - Castle Howard, North Yorks Steam Railway, Dalby Forest Drive, to name but a few. Hutton is the home of the Ryedale Folk Museum. York and the famous coastal resorts of Scarborough and Whitby are within easy striking distance. All sorts of sporting activities can be arranged for you.

The interior of the house lives up to one's expectations. It contains many original features; old stone fireplaces, cruck beams, panelled doors, antique and reproduction furniture providing character accommodation and a wonderful olde worlde atmosphere. There is a comfortable sitting room with beamed ceiling and superb Georgian fireplace with an open log fire. The house makes one feel relaxed and be happy to absorb all it has to offer. The delightfully named bedrooms, The Fitzherbert, The Snug and The Hutton are all individually furnished with beautiful fittings and luxury ensuite bathrooms. Fitzherbert has an ornate Kingsize bed and The Hutton a double, canopied bed whilst The Snug is the prettiest of country bedrooms with double sized oak bedstead. Each room has TV, Tea/coffee making facilities and hairdriers with a lot of other nice touches. Breakfast is a delicious meal of five courses served in the oak panelled Old Tap Room and Dinner is memorable with every evening becoming a great occasion.

USEFUL INFORMATION

OPEN; All year
CHILDREN; By arrangement
CREDIT CARDS; None taken
LICENSED; Yes
ACCOMMODATION; 3 ensuite rooms
DINING ROOM; Memorable food
VEGETARIAN; Yes + diets by arrangement
DISABLED ACCESS; No
GARDEN; Yes with seats front & back
PETS; Yes

East Anglia

Chapter Nine

EAST ANGLIA

including **NORFOLK, SUFFOLK & CAMBRIDGESHIRE**

East Anglia

CHAPTER 9

EAST ANGLIA
including NORFOLK, SUFFOLK & CAMBRIDGESHIRE

INCLUDING

Ounce House	**Bury St Edmunds**
Twelve Angel Hill	**Bury St Edmunds**
The Plough Inn	**Clare**
South Elmham Hall	**Harleston**
Edgehill	**Ipswich**
Tudor Rose Hotel	**Kings Lynn**
The Great House	**Lavenham**
Almond Tree Hotel	**Norwich**
The Norfolk Mead Hotel	**Norwich**
Welbeck House	**Norwich**
Malthouse	**Palgrave**
Barn Court	**Rackheath**
Sutton Straith Hotel	**Sutton Staithe**
The Red Lion	**Swaffham**
College Farm	**Thetford**
Rose Cottage	**Thetford**
Briarfields Hotel	**Titchwell**
Quayside Cottage	**Waldingfield**
Grange Farm	**Woodbridge**
Cobweb Cottage	**Wymondham**
Kimberley Home Farm	**Wymondham**

Chapter Nine

EAST ANGLIA

Norfolk, Suffolk & Cambridgeshire

East Anglia is the epitome of that rural England we all visualise and love, with its gently rolling countryside and slow, easy pace of life. It is easily recognised as the bump on the east side of England, and although time seems to have passed this little corner by, it is easily within reach of major cities and good travelling facilities.

King's Lynn in West Norfolk is a historic port on the **River Great Ouse**. This is a beautiful town with a labyrinth of tiny streets, and history oozing out of every pore. There are medieval buildings, Georgian buildings, and many monuments to it's seafaring history. The Custom House, built by Henry Bell in 1683, is splendid and houses a special display of the maritime history of the town. 'Tales of the Old Gaol House' was opened by HRH Prince Charles in 1993, and is a delightful visionary experience of the lives and tales of some of the prisoners incarceratedwithin these cells. It is not difficult to imagine the horror and terror that some of these 'not so nice' characters installed in the local community! There are many, many more places of historical interest in this fine town, and if such is your inclination you will not be disappointed! For those who are interested in the art of shopping then you too will have plenty of opportunity - the elegant Tuesday Market Place hosts a large market on Tuesdays and Fridays where lots of interesting local produce and crafts can be found, whilst the smaller Saturday Market Place hosts another market on - yes you've guessed- Saturday. Alongside these markets is the modern, charming Vancouver Centre where all manner of shops, cafes and snack bars (where you can rest those aching feet!) can be found. King's Lynn is also excellent for antique shops, and a stroll along King's Staithe Lane, St James' Street, and Chapel Street may leave your pocket just a little lighter!

There is plenty of entertainment in the way of theatre and the arts; local and international performers can be seen at the King's Lynn Art Centre, and also in the fabulous Corn Exchange. There are any number of discos and night clubs for the more energetic, and a lot of the hotels hold dinner dances and cabaret evenings during the summer months. This is a fun place for all age groups, and with a diversity and charm that will capture each member of the family.

Inland, in the heart of Norfolk is **Swaffham**. There are many splendid Georgian buildings here, including Montpelier House and the Assembly

Rooms. The Church of St Peter and St Paul which is 15th century, is well worth visiting. There is also a good museum with a varied interesting display of artefacts.

Just along the coast is **Hunstanton**, the only west-facing resort on the east coast. The wondrous golden sands make it the ideal location for that family seaside holiday, and there is a wealth of entertainment and attractions ensuring that boredom gains no roots! Further north it becomes much quieter with curving sand dunes and clear horizons, providing the ideal habitat for much wildlife. The picturesque village of **Dersingham** is on the Hunstanton road, and has a view over the **Wash** on one side, and the lovely woods of the **Sandringham** border on the other. Here you will find one of Norfolk's many fine churches; this one from the 14th century, and with a beautifully carved wooden chest dating from the same period.

Wells next the Sea is the delightful name of a rather charming coastal port still in use, but combining rather well with a thriving tourist trade. With its Edwardian and Victorian fronted shops, a good browse is the order of the day! Before moving on, it is important to mention the Wells & Walsingham Light Railway which is just outside Wells. This runs the course of the old Great Eastern Line and is the longest 10" narrow gauge railway in the world. Even if you are not an enthusiast, the journey between Wells and **Walsingham** is a beautiful one, travelling over five bridges and through countryside renowned for its wild flowers and butterflies, with halts at **Warham St Mary** and **Wighton**. Walsingham has a great deal of history on offer, and the journey allows ample time for exploration.

Holkham Hall at Wells next the Sea, is one of Britain's most majestic stately homes, sitting in 3,000 acres on the north Norfolk coast. It is a classic 18th century Palladian style mansion, and is an absolute must on the list of places to be visited. It is full of artistic and architectural riches, and is a wonderful experience for all the family. Apart from the house, there is a museum, a history of farming exhibition, pottery, garden centre, gift shop, art gallery, tea rooms, not to mention the deer park, lake and beach. As I said; something for everyone!

Eastward, along the coast from **Sheringham** is the fishing village of **Cromer**. Although it now has a good tourist trade, the locals still depend very much on the sea for their livelihood, and a meal of fresh crab in this part of the world is a very worthwhile experience! This is great walking country, with views to stun from the clifftops, and walks of any length to suit all. The coastal road then skirts the **Broads,** which is probably what most people associate with Norfolk. This is a network of rivers and lakes, formed by flooded medieval peat diggings. There is 125 miles of lock free waterway,

Chapter Nine

and is an idyllic way to spend a holiday. I can think of no better pastime than idling the day away in these peaceful waterways, and finding a nice riverside pub in which to have an evening meal and a quiet drink. Heaven! (If only I was a good sailor!)

Wroxham considers itself the unofficial capital of the Broads, and here you will find Barton House Railway, a riverside miniature railway. Also here is Hoveton Hall, 10 acres of woodland and beautiful lakeside gardens, with herbaceous borders and kitchen gardens. Wroxham is linked to **Hoveton** by means of a hump backed bridge over the **River Bure**. This is a lovely area, throbbing with vitality and active with the numerous, colourful boats busy by the river's banks. If you just fancy a day trip on the adjacent broads, then the Marina has a choice of motor launch or paddle steamer for you to enjoy. **Rackheath** is a village just outside Wroxham, and again there is one of those interesting little Norfolk churches here, this one dating from the 14th century.

Coming round the coast leads us to **Great Yarmouth**, a well known resort for all ages. This is a town with attractions from racing to fun fairs, and with marvellous long sandy beaches first discovered by the Victorians as a great holiday destination. As the local economy relied heavily at that time on the fishing industry, they quickly 'caught on' and the town has thrived ever since! But alongside the sometimes overwhelming 'attractions' there is great history in this town. The medieval stone wall is only one of a number of interesting items, along with many museums and heritage sites. The quayside is lined with fine buildings, and the maritime heritage is visible in a variety of historical buildings, including the 13th century Tollhouse which is supposedly the oldest civic building in the country. The Maritime Museum for East Anglia is at 25 Marine Parade, previously the home of a shipwrecked sailor, it now is home to Norfolk's maritime history. There are many displays from life-saving to shipwrecks, and obviously Nelson who plays a big part in the history of this area. Nelson's monument is again worth a visit - but be warned - after you have climbed the 217 steps to the viewing platform you may have to wipe the sweat from your brow to appreciate the stunning views! The monument was built 14 years after his death at Trafalgar, and shows how proud Norfolk was of their famous son, who was born at the rectory in **Burnham Thorpe**. The parish church in Great Yarmouth has a 12th century foundation and a 13th century west front. Although it was gutted during World War II, it has come some way towards it's former glory and now boasts some wonderful stained glass windows.

The more modern side of the town has many temptations of a different nature. The Living Jungle and Butterfly Farm is an indoor centre where you can walk among beautiful tropical gardens surrounded by humming birds and exotic butterflies. This is a wonderful experience for children, and you can take as many photographs as you desire to remind you of this novel event. Next door is the Sea Life Centre and further along is Wally Windmills Giant Indoor Children's Adventure Playground. (I think a shorter name may have been more memorable!) There is plenty for the family's entertainment, and a good way to spend an evening may be at the Royalty Centre which holds live family shows in the summer months. With it's long sandy beaches, unspoilt surrounding countryside and varying interests, Great Yarmouth makes for a very entertaining location for any holiday.

Norwich is the county town and regional shopping centre of the area. It is an extremely exciting place with it's modern facilities and easy access to the continent. This may account for the cosmopolitan air you find here, although the specialised shops and good quality department stores also help this image. It is an extremely cultured city with fine concert halls and theatres, and the history is all around you in every step you take. A medieval merchant's hall holds a cinema, while a charming church is used as a puppet theatre or an arts centre. This preserves the history, whilst making the money to keep it in order. The city centre is best explored on foot as some of it's network of streets are closed to traffic. It is enclosed by the old city walls, and has a substantial number of medieval buildings which tell of the wealth based on the wool and cloth trade of the Middle Ages. It was once the second largest city in England and has a grand Cathedral and Norman castle, which is a restored 12th century castle with museum and art gallery. If churches are your passion then this is the place to be - there seems to be one around every corner - the last count was 35 medieval churches - I would suggest more than one day touring these! This is a great base for exploring the Norfolk Broads, it's wildlife havens and idyllic lakes.....and still have the comfort of top quality city life and all it has to offer.

Taking the A11 out of Norfolk brings you to **Wymondham,** where the Abbey ruins have a charming story to tell. The Abbey was founded in Norman times by William D'Albini, whose desire it was that the monks and townsfolk could worship together. This was not to be, and the medieval church was almost divided in two by the factions who could not agree, and who built their own towers at each end of the church. Neither of these was ever completely finished but the size is most impressive. All was finally settled by the erection of a solid wall separating the parish at the west end from those at the east! The monastic tower is now in ruins, but a visit here is still a worthwhile experience, to see the hammerbeam roof arrayed with angels and bosses above the magnificent Norman nave. One of the Abbey's rare treasures is the 13th century Corporas Case, and along with the 16th century Renaissance monument and the superb gilt reredos, makes this a special place.

Chapter Nine

There was a great fire in the town in 1615 when at least 300 houses were destroyed. As a result there are not many houses from before this date, and today is a mixture of styles of 18th century, Victorian and more modern. One thing they all have in common is that they are all simple two storey buildings. The lovely Market cross was rebuilt almost immediately after the fire, and is octagonal and timber framed. The ground floor is open on all sides, with the building crowned by a pyramid roof and the emblems of the town, a wooden spoon and a spigot crossed, on the wood carving around the building. The Green Dragon, a 15th century pub, is one of the oldest in England.

Bungay is on the border of Suffolk, and the boundary on three sides is the **River Waveney.** Because of this it is an excellent place for walking, with delightful paths next to the river. You can see how the town developed round the 12th century castle, which is now in ruins, but the 13th century tower of St Mary's Church is definitely the centrepiece of the town.

The A143 travels through **Harleston** to the town of **Diss**. This town is an attractive mixture of Tudor, Georgian and Victorian houses, and has a weekly corn market on Fridays. Diss has been described by Betjeman as the archetypal English country town.

The last place in Norfolk I will mention is **Thetford**. South Norfolk is rural, tranquil and peaceful, dotted with pretty villages and bustling market towns. Whether you wish to cycle, walk or travel by car, the beauty and charm of the countryside will captivate and enchant you. Thetford is one of those lovely little towns, and in addition has a wonderful Forest Park of 50,000 acres of pine forest, with picnic sites, paths and trails. The town itself has some historical interest with a Norman priory and Castle Hill where earthworks, Norman motte and bailey with iron age ramparts can be found. Warren Lodge is the interesting ruin of a small two storey hunting lodge built around 1400.

Straight over the border to Suffolk, into the town of **Bury St Edmunds** and our next stop on the list. This town was named after Edmund, Anglo-Saxon King of East Anglia, who was killed by the invading Danes in 869, and who was eventually declared a saint. The town grew around the Abbey from the 11th century, which was one of the largest and influential in England. The Barons of England are reputed to have met here to swear they would force King John to sign the Magna Carta. The Abbey was mostly dismantled following its dissolution by Henry VIII, but the remainder, in the Abbey Gardens, are interestingly explained at the visitor centre. The town did well at the height of the medieval cloth making industry, but many of the buildings were later given new facades in the Georgian period which gives this town it's charm and elegance. The Theatre Royal is one building which has been beautifully restored, and there are many other places of historical interest to visit. Ickworth House and Park is an unusual 18th century stately home with fine paintings, whilst Manor House Museum has some choice paintings and clocks in an elegant Georgian town house. Moyses Hall is a 12th century house now containing an excellent display of local antiques. St Mary's Church has a magnificent roof and Mary Tudor is buried here. St Edmundsbury Cathedral was the mother Church of Suffolk and dates from around the 16th century. This is a wonderful church with a fine hammer-beam roof and a wonderful display of over 1000 embroidered kneelers. On the more modern side Bury St Edmunds has an excellent leisure centre with 3 swimming pools, giant water slides, saunaworld and good sports facilities. Activity World is an adventure playground for children under 5ft tall, and there is also a roller skating centre. As they say, 'something for all the family' in this traditional yet active country town.

Just up country from **Stowmarket** in the area of inland East Sussex is the small country town of **Eye.** This charming town's name means 'island', and although nowhere near the coast, in times gone by it was surrounded by marches and the River Dove. Again we have a ruined castle, and a great church tower with fantastic decoration. Head east from Eye and you will come to another market town with a castle; **Framlingham.** But in this case the castle is far from ruined - the views from the battlements of the town and surrounding countryside are breathtaking. Originally built in 1190, it has now been partially restored with towers, parapet walk and lower court beside an artificial lake. This is where Mary Tudor was proclaimed Queen of England in 1553 - a fascinating place.

Several miles from the open sea seems a strange place to have a port, but that is what **Woodbridge** is! The quays, boat yards, and tide mill and the tang of the salt air that comes along the **River Deben,** all add to the feeling that you are by the sea. The narrow streets and medieval buildings are worth exploring, and there are many interesting shops in the town. There is an interesting museum here; the Suffolk Horse Museum, which tells the history of the Suffolk Punch, the oldest breed of heavy working horse in the world. This is housed in a beautiful Elizabethan building and has displays of how the horse was worked, the blacksmiths, harnessmen and horseriders, and also the story of how the breed was rescued in the 1960s.

Felixtowe, on the coast is probably known as being a container port, but it is also an excellent family holiday resort. With it's south-facing beaches, charming gardens, and entertainment it has a lot to offer the tourist. Onward to **Ipswich,** again a port, but one which was founded in the6th/7th century by the Anglo-Saxons for trading with continental Europe. This is still it's role

Chapter Nine

today but combined with being an important regional centre and country town. It is well equipped with good quality hotels and facilities, and is excellent for touring the surrounding area. There is a variety of good architecture both old and new including the internationally acclaimed Willis Corroon insurance building. I must admit to preferring Christchurch Mansion, a 16th century house in a historic park. The rooms are furnished in various styles from Tudor to Victorian, and there is the best collection of Constable and Gainsborough paintings outside London.

The **Stour Valley** is birthplace of two of Britain's finest painters - a few miles and half a century apart. Thomas Gainsborough was famous for his paintings of the rich and famous in Ipswich, London and Bath, although some of his writings indicate that his first love may have been landscape painting, and many of his portraits contain recognisable local scenes. John Constable was supposedly influenced by some of Gainsborough's early landscapes, and his most famous and inspired paintings were of where he grew up and spent his youth. **Flatford**, where Constable's father was the miller, has changed little in the passing of time, and even today you can understand the inspiration that Constable could have received in the sparkling river and the rustling trees.

At this stage I should just like to pop over the border into Essex and visit **Colchester.** This is Britain's oldest recorded town, and has a wealth of history and fascinating stories within it's walls. It was the first capital of Roman Britain, and William the Conqueror's 11th century castle which was built here, is the largest surviving Norman keep ever built. It was recently discovered that the keep was built on the remains of a Roman temple, and today you can visit the 'murky deeps' below the Castle Museum. The town has over a dozen museums and galleries, and there is a fascinating profusion of architecture throughout. Stop in at Hollytrees, an elegant Georgian house which has a wonderful collection of costume, pottery, toys and dolls. The Minories Art Gallery holds a wide variety of 20th century art exhibitions, with a delightful garden where sculpture exhibitions are held in the summer months. Apart from the many historical interests that this town holds, it is also a great cultural centre, with it's lively network of music, cabaret and theatre. Shopping is a delight in the narrow alleyways and lanes, while the larger shopping centres hold all the large company names. There are lots of traditional delicatessens and English tea-rooms where you can 'break' from the spending to watch the world go by. Antiques and bric-a-brac are obviously very popular here (after all, Lovejoy has picked up a few bargains here), and in addition there are excellent shopping facilities for people with disabilities. A lovely town, and one which should not be missed!

East Anglia

Back over the border South Suffolk is probably what we epitomise rural England to be, with its medieval towns, villages and pretty countryside. **Lavenham** is one of the best of these with its timbered, white-washed buildings crowding the hilly narrow streets, and its perfect market place (it could almost be from a film set). The Guildhall, Priory and Little Hall are good examples of medieval buildings, and all have interesting displays within.

Going towards **Haverhill** we reach the town of **Clare**. This town gets it's name from one of our most ancient families; the Earls of Clare. This is a well known name in Cambridge as Elizabeth, fathered by the ninth Earl of Clare, became the founder of the second oldest college in the university. It is a beautiful town of handsome houses with wonderfully patterned plasterwork, one of which, The Ancient House, now serves as a museum of Clare's history. The Country Park, just off the High Street, has as an attractive feature the **River Stour,** and a stroll along the riverside path is a pleasant way to spend a couple of hours. Kingfishers, swans and many other birds can be seen here, and birdwatchers will most certainly enjoy it. The path leads you to the remains of the Austin Friars priory which was originally founded in 1248, and after a lapse of many years is now once again in use by the Augustinian order. In the town is the Church of St Peter and St Paul, with it's fine 13th century tower. This is a lovely church with it's rood-stair turrets with crocketed spirelets, Jacobean gallery pew, and the chancel that was practically rebuilt in the 16th century.

Travelling through **Stumer** brings you to Haverhill which is well situated on the A604 between Cambridge and Colchester. It is an excellent stopping place being about mid way between the two. It has a fine shopping centre which is mostly pedestrianised and there are many interesting shops to browse through. In addition there is a fine old church which is well worth a visit.

On up to **Newmarket** and you will find that you are seeing sleek thoroughbreds grazing in paddocks, or going through the streets to the clatter of hooves. This is nothing unusual as since the 17th century Newmarket has been a centre for horse racing in Britain. Everywhere you go, you will either see horses or hear people speaking about them, and it is nothing unusual to see strings of horses in the High Street. Many of the finest race horses have been born, bred and trained in this fine town. The National Horse Racing Museum will give you an insight into the history, and the paintings of famous racehorses by local artist Alfred Munnings will show you the beauty and elegance of these wonderful animals. Many of the stables provide tours, and watching the horses in their exercise areas you cannot help but become involved and interested in what is going on around you.

Chapter Nine

Cambridgeshire is a beautiful county with **Cambridge** (probably the best known city in Britain), as it's pride and joy. It was established as a teaching centre for the nearby monasteries, and by the 13th century the University was established. Peterhouse, the oldest college was founded in 1284, with many others such as Trinity, Magdalene, and King's to follow. The representation of architectural styles is magnificent, and to see some of the students scurrying along, robes billowing, almost takes you on a medieval journey through some of these wonderful buildings. King's College Chapel is the city's 'Crowning Glory' with it's smooth lawns, formal gardens and large open spaces, and Henry VIII's Trinity, and can best be viewed from the 'Backs'(a punt along the river). These punts are normally 'chauffeured' by students who can give you a lively insight into the background and sights, and also a bit about life as a student! It is a lovely way to see Cambridge, and very relaxing too! Because of the history and architecture in this great city there are many tours organised by the Tourist Information Centre. These are worthwhile as you may otherwise miss some of the more interesting places that you may find difficulty in accessing. During the school year it swarms with academics, and it may be advisable to plan your trip well in terms of accommodation and access, as various parts may only be open during the academic terms.

Apart from the very obvious historical interest, Cambridge is a very lively city, from classical recitals to jazz concerts and various theatrical performances. In July there are festivals of classical music, art, theatre and film, the Cambridge Folk Festival and a huge carnival and fireworks. The city has many excellent shops, especially it's book shops, and I suppose some thanks may be given to the University for this. It is a city to be enjoyed at any time of the year, and one to which many visitors return as they often find that one visit is not enough!

Cambridge is surrounded by the rural countryside of South Cambridgeshire with many attractive villages and historical buildings. One such is Wimpole Hall, an 18th century country house with a colourful history of owners! This is a charming house with interiors by celebrated architects, an interesting collection of furniture and pictures, and lovely formal gardens in the landscaped park grounds. The Imperial War Museum at **Duxford** contains the finest collection of civil and military aircraft in Britain.

Huntingdonshire is centred around the **River Great Ouse,** and is the land of Oliver Cromwell, and Queen Catherine of Aragon. It is charming, gentle countryside with fascinating market towns and small villages nestling in the vales. Oliver Cromwell was born and lived in this area. The Falcon Inn at **Huntingdon** was at one time his headquarters, and you can see his statue in St Ives Market Square and visit the Cromwell museum. Queen

Catherine of Aragon was sent to Buckden Castle near Huntingdon before her death. **Godmanchester** was, in Roman times, a major settlement and is still separated from Georgian Huntingdon by water meadows which are criss-crossed with footpaths, and rivulets from the River Great Ouse. A beautiful 13th Century road bridge still links the two towns over the river. **St Ives** boasts only one of four surviving medieval bridge chapels, while **St Neots'** history dates back to the 10th century. It's 15th century church has a splendid roof with carvings of animals, birds and angels. Visit **Ramsey** and the Abbey Gatehouse and St Thomas A Becket church which was originally used as a hospital for the Abbey.

There are some wonderful places to visit and it is a gentle, quiet area with over 600 miles of public footpaths and bridleways to explore. The Ouse Valley Way is a 26 mile distance footpath that takes you through several of the old attractive villages, offering you a rich tapestry of the history and culture of the area.

Moving on to **The Fens** we can see a unique landscape - vast areas of artificially drained land that was reclaimed from it's marsh like state. The Romans, to their credit, made the first attempt at drainage, but it was Cornelius Vermuyden in 1630 who successfully completed the job! The landscape gives us wide open views, exposed skyscapes and breathtaking sunsets. Examples of fen drainage include Stretham beam Engine, built in 1831 and preserved today.

Ely was where the family home of Cromwell was located, and today you can visit this Cromwellian style house which has a visual presentation about the man's life. The house sits in the shadow of Ely Cathedral, a wonderful architectural achievement of the Middle Ages. Wonder at the Octagonal Tower; over 400 tons suspended in space without visible support! The Cathedral is located in a close containing the largest collection of medieval domestic architecture in England. The Cathedral can be seen for miles around Ely; a beacon of beauty in the rich dark landmass of the Fens.

To the north is the Georgian market town of **Wisbech.** This is probably one of the finest examples of Georgian architecture in the country, and you cannot leave without visiting The North Brink, the Crescent and Museum Square. Peckover House is of particular interest with its fine Georgian plaster and wood rococo. The Victorian gardens are notable for their unusual trees, orangery, stables, thatched barn, and summer house. Incidentally, this is where Barclay's bank first came into being in 1896, and at one time 'Peckover' notes were looked upon with greater favour than the Bank of England notes! Elgoods historic brewery is another must, but tours are by appointment only.

Chapter Nine

March and **Whittlesley** are two other places to be visited. March has St Wendrera's Church, with it's splendid double hammer beam roof, and Whittlesley has a variety of very well preserved architecture including some unusual mud walls. Both towns are tranquil, peaceful havens, with the old course of the River Nene flowing through both, making it a fisherman's heaven, or the perfect place for a stroll along the riverbank with lunch at a riverside inn.

Peterborough is classed as a 'new city' but really has history dating back thousands of years. The Norman Cathedral has been there for over 750 years and is the burial place of Queen Catherine of Aragon (Henry VIII's first wife), and was for a short time, that of Mary Queen of Scots. The architecture is magnificent, the West Front with it's three soaring Gothic arches is said to be one of the finest in Europe, and the medieval painted ceiling is not to be missed! The city museum has a fine collection of mainly local material, showing how life has changed since the time of the dinosaurs, and there are also two excellent paintings by Turner. One of the most exciting attractions to me was Flag Fen, a fairly recent archaeological discovery of artefacts from the Bronze Age. Visitors can actually watch the uncovering of a large 3,000 year old bronze age timber platform.

The Nene Valley Steam Railway travels from **Wansford** through Nene Park; a 2,000 acre park of lakes, woodland and watermeadows, to Peterborough. This is great for steam enthusiasts, but for anyone it is a very pleasant way to see the countryside. Historic buildings include Longthorpe Tower, with a superb collection of medieval wall paintings, Burghley House, a grand example of an Elizabethan stately home, and Elton Hall, home of the Proby family since 1660. There is plenty to see and do in this fine city, and the new is combined very tastefully with the old, taking nothing away from the rich cultural history this city has to offer. Many of the old streets are now pedestrianised so you can enjoy shopping and admiring the architecture at the same time, while the newer shopping centres are attractive with household names at your fingertips!

This is a very short trip round an exquisite county, but I hope you may find it useful and add to the extensive memorable places yourself!

OUNCE HOUSE
Northgate Street, Bury St Edmunds,
Suffolk IP33 1HP

Tel: 01284 761779 Fax: 01284 768315

Bury St Edmunds is one of the most delightful and splendid of Suffolk towns. The charm has got something to do with the way the streets were laid out in the 11th century, this enables you to see the wonderful varied architecture. Ounce House was built in 1870 as a merchant's house, this fine Victorian property is now a superb guest house. Situated on 2 floors, this impressive house is warm and inviting with lovely drapes, soft decor and antique furniture. The Guest's Lounge is elegant with comfy chairs, pictures and dried flowers. The Dining Room is just as elegant with lots of dark wood, a magnificent dining table at which you sit to partake in a delicious breakfastall served on Spode. There is a choice in the mornings including cereals, fruit juices and a full English meal. The bedrooms are large, light and airy and decorated in pastel colours with matching bed linen, they all have their own bathroom, hair dryer, trouser press, telephone, television and tea and coffee making facilities. Ounce House is fully licenced. Being only 5 minutes walk from the town centre, you have plenty of restaurants to choose from for your evening meal. Bury St Edmunds is a wonderful centre for touring the area including Cambridge, Norwich, and Newmarket to name a few, the east coast ports are also within easy reach. The M11 gives speedy access to London. A truly exceptional guest house where Simon and Jenny Pott look forward to welcoming you.

USEFUL INFORMATION

OPEN; All year
CHILDREN; Welcome
CREDIT CARDS; All major cards
LICENSED; Full
ACCOMMODATION; 4 ensuite rooms
DINING ROOM; Delicious breakfast
DISABLED ACCESS; Not really
GARDEN; Yes
PETS; No
NON SMOKING

Chapter Nine

TWELVE ANGEL HILL
12 Angel Hill, Bury St Edmunds,
Suffolk IP33 1UZ

Tel: 01284 704088
Fax: 01284 725549

Twelve Angel Hill
... A MOST EXCLUSIVE ADDRESS

    In the delightful medieval town of Bury St Edmunds is where you will find a rather nice Hotel. Twelve Angel Hill is 'Highly Acclaimed' by the RAC, and '5Q Premier Selected' by the AA, Which? County Hotel of the Year 1996 and BTA Jewel of Britain 1997. It is richly furnished to an exacting standard, with many antiques. The house was built in the 19th century, but some parts date back to the 1500's, many of the original features still remain. This warm, comfortable and centrally heated house is owned and excellently run by Bernie and John Clarke, who extend a friendly welcome to all their guests. There are 6 bedrooms all ensuite with either bath or shower, TV, radio, trouser press, hair dryer, telephone and tea and coffee making facilities. They are opulently decorated with matching soft furnishings and are all named after a French wine. One room has a magnificent dark wood four poster bed. Breakfast is served in the lovely dining room, where you are treated to a first class meal. For your evening meal Bernie and John will gladly book a table for you at one of the many restaurants in the town. The Hotel is centrally positioned close to the Cathedral, 14th century Abbey remains and gardens, and the shops. Being a market town there is a lively Street Market on Wednesdays and Saturdays. The cities of Cambridge, Norwich and Colchester with their many attractions are all within easy reach.

USEFUL INFORMATION

OPEN; Closed January
CHILDREN; No
CREDIT CARDS; All major cards
LICENSED; Yes
ACCOMMODATION; 6 ensuite rooms
PETS; No

DINING ROOM; Traditional English breakfast
Evening meal is not available
VEGETARIAN; Catered for
DISABLED ACCESS; Not really
GARDEN; Yes
Totally NON-SMOKING Hotel

THE PLOUGH INN
Brockley Green, Hundon,
Sudbury, Suffolk CO10 8DT

Tel: 01440 786789
Fax: 01440 786710

A traditional country inn is always a delightful find but seldom does it have the quality and style of a 4 star hotel. Tucked away in the Suffolk countryside this is exactly what you will discover at The Plough Inn. It stands in 5 acres of ground with superb views over the Stour Valley in the quiet rural hamlet of Brockley Green. Originally it was the local for the farming community and it was not until 1982 when it was bought by David and Marion Rowlinson that it blossomed into what you see today. They have spent considerable time, loving caring and dedication to achieve the effect of an 18th century hostelry with all the comforts of a 20th century 4-star hotel and lose none of its old charm.

In the beamed bar with its welcoming log fire, locals still gather to enjoy a chat and especially to savour the well-kept traditional ales and the guest beers - The Plough is a Free House and David chooses a different beer each week, with some prompting from the customers! Six years ago a new restaurant was added and is now one of 'the' places to eat. Although it is capable of seating eighty it is none the less a warm, intimate place with quiet corners - just right for a special evening. People dine here knowing that the food will be superb and that if they wish they can stay overnight with an inclusive price which provides an English breakfast as well. Seafood has become one of the specialities of The Plough including an enormous Seafood Platter whilst the rest of the menu has all sorts of exciting and traditional dishes. Sunday lunches are another popular event as well as the excellent value Bar Meals. Wine lovers will enjoy the opportunity to select from an interesting list. The Plough does not have a dart board or a pool table but you can play Petanque and Boules or try your hand at croquet.

The 8 luxury ensuite bedrooms are delightful and add another reason why one should visit this very nice establishment. For people on business or pleasure it is well situated with a plethora of places to visit including Cambridge, Bury St Edmunds, Lavenham, the most resplendent of Suffolk towns, and Newmarket for anyone who loves the sport of kings.

USEFUL INFORMATION

OPEN; *All year*
CHILDREN; *Welcome*
CREDIT CARDS; *All cards*
LICENSED; *Yes*
ACCOMMODATION; *8 luxury en suite rooms*

RESTAURANT; *Traditional, imaginative food Seafood a speciality*
BAR FOOD; *Wide range, excellent value*
VEGETARIAN; *Always a choice*
DISABLED ACCESS; *By arrangement*
PETS; *By arrangement*
GARDEN; *Yes, Boules, Petanque, Croquet*

Chapter Nine

SOUTH ELMHAM HALL,
St.Cross, Harleston,
Norfolk, IP20 0PZ.

Tel : 01986 782526

    Where to begin is probably the most difficult decision when looking at this exquisite country house. There is so much to see and do here, without the added attractions of the surrounding area. The house was built in the 13th century by the Bishop of Norwich and was originally a hunting lodge for the bishops, who kept a large deer park. It sits within a moated area of 4 acres alongside the ruins of one of its gate houses. There are wall paintings in the hall from the same era and many old stone and brick archways throughout the house. It is absolutely fascinating and 'if only walls could talk' I am sure the tales would be riveting! The accommodation consists of three rooms; two double and one twin, all en suite. Each room has a refreshment tray, hair dryer and individual central heating, and are beautifully furnished with co-ordinating bed linen and drapes. Breakfast is a delightful English farmhouse meal, with locally smoked bacon and sausages, free range eggs and an array of choices to please the most discerning palate! An evening meal is available, if warning is given. Jo Sanderson is your hostess and whilst leading a busy life, has ample time for her guests and their comfort. She welcomes children and can cater for cots, highchairs, even baby sitting. There is a cosy dining room, and the lounge is a large inviting room, which is ideal for relaxing after a days exploring.
    South Elmham Hall is part of a 450 acre farm which consists of arable and permanent pasture. There are beef cows here who rear their own young: one of the breeds being the rare British Whites with their distinct black ears, noses and feet. There is a network of pathways over the farm which take you on a historic and naturalistic journey through this weave of old pasture and parkland trees. A late Saxon ruin can be seen, along with an abundance of wildlife and their habitats. There is a brochure detailing these farm walks and you can choose from a 45 minute to a 2 hour stroll. We still haven't left the farm grounds and you will certainly have not become bored! Horse riding is available in the village. On a different track the city of Norwich is within a short distance, and boasts a wonderful array of shops alongside many historic and interesting buildings. Southwold, Dunwich and Lowestoft are all within easy reach with their restaurants and shops, and there are four pubs within 3 miles of the farm where a reasonably priced evening meal can be savoured. If you eventually want to travel further afield from the peace and tranquillity of the farm, then the local area will provide many attractions from wildlife trust to transport to theme parks to pleasure beaches! Whatever your choice is, you are sure to find it here, and why not relax at the same time, in the ultimate accommodation at South Elmham Hall.

USEFUL INFORMATION

OPEN : All year
NON-SMOKING ACCOMMODATION
CHILDREN : Most welcome
PETS : No
LICENSED : No
CREDIT CARDS : None taken
ACCOMMODATION : 3 rooms en suit; 2 dbl, 1 twin.

DINING ROOM : Evening meal by arrangement
VEGETARIAN : Catered for
BAR SNACKS : Not applicable
DISABLED ACCESS : No
GARDEN : 4 acres bounded by moat

EDGEHILL,
2 High Street,
Hadleigh, Ipswich,
Suffolk, IP7 5AP.

Tel : 01473 822458

    Edgehill Country House is the paramount in style and taste. Dating back to 1590, with rebuilding work in the 1700s, this house stands pretty much as it was, with it's Georgian frontage, elegant staircase and flagstoned hallway. All the decor and furnishings enhance the era of this house, except those chosen to add to the ultimate comfort and solace of guests. There are seven bedrooms, en suite, with high quality fittings all colour co-ordinated, TV, tea/coffee tray, and each room has either easy chairs or settees to relax in. (Much preferable to perching on beds!) One room even has a 19th century four poster bed, wonderful for that romantic weekend away - a little bit of self indulgence! Angela Rolfe is your hostess and ensures the 'pleasantest of pleasant' stays with friendly, amicable ways and ever cheerful company. Quality is of the upmost importance here and you will certainly find it in the breakfast on offer! A full traditional English meal with fruit and optional choices - plenty of scope for the vegetarian among you. An evening meal can be arranged and with the good home grown vegetables, this is a delight. The varied set menu is complimented by a good selection of fine wines, and you are sure to enjoy the ambience created. There is an extremely attractive walled garden which is ideal for those balmy summer evenings, or perhaps a game of afternoon croquet is to your liking! - It can be arranged! Afternoon tea served on the lawn, is another of those delightful English traditions that must be preserved, and can still be enjoyed at Edgehill.

    This country market town is perfect in every way for seeing the pretty Suffolk countryside. Villages and coastal towns are all within easy reach, and you can even visit the cities of Norwich or Cambridge. There are plenty of local walks which take in the scenic beauty of this part of England, you will find plenty of inspiration in your travels. Half timbered houses adorn the towns and a wealth of antique shops will certainly take up some of your time! Part of the TV series 'Lovejoy' was filmed in the towns of Hadleigh & Long Melford, which has a street over a mile long full of antique shops! This is also Constable and Gainsborough country, and you may even recognise scenes from these great painters, as little has changed in the years that have passed. Without even leaving Hadleigh itself you will find a host of activities to keep you amused. The architecture for one is most impressive, and there is a charming riverside walk alongside the River Brett which is easily accessible. Fishing, golf and horse riding are all abundant and many a pleasant day can be spent idling in this delightful haven of rural England.

USEFUL INFORMATION

OPEN : All year (except Xmas)
CHILDREN : Welcome
PETS : Welcome in some rooms
LICENSED : Residential restuarant
CREDIT CARDS : None taken
ACCOMMODATION : 7 rooms en suite; 3 dbl, 2 twin, 2 fml.

RESTAURANT : Excellent fayre
VEGETARIANS : Catered for
BAR SNACKS : Yes
DISABLED ACCESS : No
GARDEN : Mature shrubs & lawn

Chapter Nine

THE TUDOR ROSE HOTEL
*St Nicholas Street,
Kings Lynn, Norfolk PE30 1LR*

Tel: 01553 762824

 Dating back to 1500 this atmospheric hotel is steeped in the history of Kings Lynn. We are told that number 11 St Nicholas Street, now the hotel, is part of a complex of buildings whose history can be traced back to the 12th century, with many ghostly stories attached to it. One in particular is of a lady who was murdered on her wedding night and now haunts the restaurant mostly around Christmas time. Her bridegroom was her killer. Whilst the hotel today has a wonderful feeling of contentment about it there is still the lingering presence of these sad people.

 Whilst the Tudor Rose Hotel has delightful, mainly ensuite bedrooms all with tea and coffee making facilities, hair dryers, TV and direct dial telephones, it nonetheless has the feeling of a good Inn. Indeed there are two bars which are very popular with local people and oddly enough they have become naturally divided by age groups - the 'crumblies' in one and the youngsters in the other. It works very well and either is a welcoming place to enjoy a drink or a bar meal. Throughout the furnishings are of a very high and comfortable standard and especially in the pretty 28 seater restaurant in which one can enjoy a relaxed and beautifully cooked meal from a menu that offers everything from the traditional to specialities. Vegetarians are catered for and other dietary needs can be arranged. In the summer months the attractive beer garden is a splendid place in which to meet friends and enjoy the well kept ale.

 Kings Lynn is an excellent base for anyone coming to this part of Norfolk either for business or pleasure. Close by one can get sea fishing, play golf, walk, ride, windsurf or take off to explore the many interesting places including Sandringham. If cathedrals interest you Norwich, Ely and Peterborough are not too far distant.

USEFUL INFORMATION

OPEN; *All year*
CHILDREN; *Welcome*
CREDIT CARDS; *All major cards*
LICENSED; *Yes*
PETS; *Yes*
ACCOMMODATION; *14 rooms 11 ensuite*

RESTAURANT; *Wide choice*
BAR FOOD; *Excellent choice*
VEGETARIAN; *Yes*
DISABLED ACCESS; *No*
GARDEN; *Beer garden*

THE GREAT HOUSE,
Market Place, Lavenham,
Suffolk, CO10 9QZ.

Tel : 01787 247431

Deep in the heart of Suffolk, in one of England's choicest medieval towns, is the Great House Restaurant and Hotel. This charming building dates back to the 15th century, with additions in the 18th century, and more recently in the 1980s, when it was turned into this magnificent hotel. Sitting beside the market square in a quieter part of the town, this hotel offers supreme comfort and cuisine. There are four rooms beautifully furnished (look out for the antiques!), all en suite, and each with a separate lounge or sitting area. The furnishings and drapes make these rooms cosy and inviting, and with their beamed ceilings and added personal touches in paintings and greenery, this makes for a home from home! Martine and Regis Crepy are your French hosts, and bring a little touch of France to this charming part of England. The service and attitude of the staff is impeccable and the beaming French faces and friendly disposition of these people all add a little 'something' to your stay here! The food is superb as Regis is the chef, and brings great knowledge of French cuisine to his menus. Most are traditional foods, served in sauces to make your mouth water (not for the 'watching your figure' type!) and are reasonably priced, with smaller portions for the children. The dishes are exciting with such starters as veal and pork pate flavoured with Cognac and baked in a pastry crust, served with pickled Victorian plums. Follow this with something from the main menu; Duck Magret stuffed with chicken livers and pistachios, before being baked and served with a slightly spicy green peppercorn sauce! Regis has great pride in his wonderful recipes....with justification! Little ones are most welcome; in that indomitable French way, families are loved and a crowd of all ages (from baby to Grandma!) around a table, seems to delight the staff! The restaurant is a wonderful place, with its large inglenook fireplace and carved historic bressemer beam above, to the delightful tables with their linen and sparkling glassware all reflected in the warm glow of the fire. There is a courtyard outside for those sunny lunches or 'al fresco' evening meals enjoyed on warm balmy summer evenings. The hotel is fully licensed and you can enjoy some of the superb wines on offer (even take some advice!) with your meal.

Martine and Regis are also the owners of 'Il Punto', a delightful 'floating brasserie' at Neptune Quay in Ipswich. Again this is a glorious setting with lots of polished wood and gleaming brass staging the scene for a wonderful meal in relaxing surroundings. The menu here is simple but delicious, and inevitably with a French flavour, and again, children are most welcome.

USEFUL INFORMATION

OPEN : All year
CHILDREN : Most welcome
PETS : With own bedding
LICENSED : Full
CREDIT CARDS : All major
ACCOMMODATION : 4 rooms en suite; 1 dbl, 2 twin, 1 fml.

RESTAURANT : Wonderful French cuisine
VEGETARIANS : Catered for
BAR SNACKS : Excellent range
DISABLED ACCESS : Restaurant, with help
GARDEN : Patio for summer meals

Chapter Nine

THE ALMOND TREE HOTEL
*441 Dereham Road, Costessey,
Norwich, Norfolk NR5 0SG*

Tel: 01603 748798 Fax: 01603 749114

    This pretty hotel has been furnished in keeping with its name, The Almond Tree. It is almost as if every colour scheme and every piece of furniture has been acquired to enhance the lightness and freshness that one associates with almond. The whole is a delightful effect and add that to the genuine welcome you will receive from the owners Chris and Caroline Foster, and you have discovered somewhere to stay that is just 10 minutes away from the beautiful and historic Norwich with a wealth of things to see and do; Norwich Castle, the Cathedral, Elm Hill and the new Castle Mall Shopping Centre.

    After sightseeing, shopping or exploring the countryside, or perhaps a strenuous day of business, you will find the Almond Tree's new bar a friendly relaxed place. Light meals are available here and in the lounge. The hotel has a high reputation for its food and the non-smoking restaurant has a first class menu and wine list. Each of the 8 bedrooms have beenindividually designed and furnished. The honeymoon suite boasts a sumptuous draped four poster bed. All the rooms have en-suite bathrooms, tea and coffee making facilities, remote control colour TV with Teletext and direct dial telephones.

    The Almond Tree is a hotel which it is a pleasure to rcommend both as a place in which to stay or to enjoy a super meal in the very pretty restaurant.

USEFUL INFORMATION

OPEN; All year
CHILDREN; Welcome
CREDIT CARDS; All cards
LICENSED; Yes
ACCOMMODATION; 8 ensuite

RESTAURANT; Highly recommended
BAR MEALS; Available in bar & Lounge
VEGETARIAN; Catered for
DISABLED ACCESS;No special facilities
PETS; No

THE NORFOLK MEAD HOTEL & RESTAURANT
Church Loke, Coltishall,
Norwich, Norfolk NR12 7DN

Tel: 01603 737531

The Norfolk Mead Hotel and Restaurant is very impressive indeed, this elegant Georgian manor house stands in 12 acres of gardens and lovely lawns which lead down to the River Bure that flows gently by. The house was built in 1740, then in 1985 it was lovingly restored and converted into the charming property it is today. The 10 bedrooms are very attractive with co-ordinating drapes and bed covers, the decor is very restful, and the beds extremely comfortable. The ensuite bathrooms are very stylish with complimentary toiletries. All rooms have colour television, telephone and tea and coffee making facilities. The Guest Lounge is delightful with comfy chairs and sofas again with matching drapes, in the winter a large log fires burns brightly, in the summer the French doors are open to let in the warm sun. The lounge is perfect to relax with your drink as you peruse the mouthwatering A La Carte and Table D'Hote menus. There is also a comprehensive wine list carefully chosen by Jill and Don Fleming the proud owners of Norfolk Mead. The Dining Room is very pleasant with matching table linen, and looks out across the attractive garden. Why not take a stroll down to the river where you may catch sight of a Kingfisher or the many other birds that congregate here. A well stocked fishing lake, off-river mooring and outdoor swimming pool are all here for your use. For those with the energy then rowing dinghies are available for messing about on the river! The Norfolk Mead Hotel is superb, you are sure to have a very enjoyable and memorable stay.

USEFUL INFORMATION

OPEN; All year
CHILDREN; Welcome
CREDIT CARDS; All cards
LICENSED; Restaurant & **Residential**
ACCOMMODATION; 10 ensuite

RESTAURANT; Varied and interesting menus
VEGETARIAN; Welcome
DISABLED ACCESS; With help
GARDEN; Superb lawns leading down to river, walled rose garden
PETS; By arrangement - please phone

Chapter Nine

WELBECK HOUSE
Brooke, Norwich,
Norfolk NR15 1AT

Tel: 01508 550292

The secluded setting of Welbeck House positioned well back from a quiet country road within 5 acres of grounds, mostly woodland, is an ideal peaceful and relaxing location. This charming old farmhouse is 300 years old. Rooms are spacious with modern and traditional furniture to an exacting standard. Soft furnishings and bed linen are of quality, and central heating ensures a warm and cosy atmosphere. A welcome tray and colour television are supplied. Children over 12 years are most welcome as are well behaved pets. This is a non smoking property. The cuisine is carefully prepared using specially selected ingredients and caters to the needs of particular diets should prior notice be given. Dinner however is not served, but there is within walking distance an excellent pub serving good food. The Norfolk Broads are renowned for their waterways and are a haven for boating aficionado's. Wildlife enthusiasts will be enthralled by the variety of waterfowl, animals and bird life found in and around this area. East Anglia's flourishing capital Norwich, only 7 miles away, is steeped in history and is home to one of the country's most beautiful Cathedrals. The city centre is dominated by Norwich Castle, which houses an excellent museum. The east coast is half an hours drive away with the holiday resort of Lowestoft with its sandy beach and coastal walks.

USEFUL INFORMATION

OPEN; All year
CHILDREN; Over 12 years
CREDIT CARDS; None taken
ACCOMMODATION; 3 rooms
GARDEN; Yes, cultivated
DINING ROOM; Traditional home-cooking
VEGETARIAN; By arrangement
DISABLED ACCESS; No
PETS; Yes
NON SMOKING

THE MALT HOUSE,
Denmark Hill,
Palgrave, Nr Diss,
Norfolk IP22 1AE

Tel: 01379 642107 Fax: 01379 640315

Marj and Phil Morgan bought this delightfully converted house on their return to this country after 24 years in the Orient. Their intention was to have guests occasionally but because they have entirely the right approach to guesthouse keeping, they have found that their rooms are much in demand. The house is charming, beautifully and interestingly furnished with nice pieces brought from their home in the East - many of them with fascinating stories attached which the Morgans are happy to tell you about. The acre of garden is full of colour and interest and landscaped with many varieties of Conifer, Heather and roses. The large walled garden provides much of the fruit for the table. The garden is a delight to sit in. Phil and Marj have discovered that many of their guests are keen gardeners who have come from far afield to visit the world renowned Bressingham Gardens 2 miles away. The Morgans have made lots of friends among their guests who enjoy swapping hints and tips on 'How to make it grow'!

Inside, the house has three de-luxe ensuite bedrooms charmingly furnished and with Interior Designer fabrics. Each room has Colour TV, Radio and Coffee/Tea making facilities. The beamed Lounge is a restful place in which to sit at the end of a day's exploration. Breakfast is a delicious meal, freshly cooked to your order. There are no evening meals but there are many good places to eat locally which Marj and Phil will tell you about. The house is totally non-smoking, well behaved children over two years of age are welcome, but pets are definitely taboo! Awarded a 2 Crown de Luxe by the Tourist Board and holding a 'Good Room Award from Guestaccom, the Morgans are also members of 'A Break with Tradition', a group of people who all have interesting houses in which you can stay.

USEFUL INFORMATION

OPEN; All year except Dec 20th-Jan 3rd   **DINING ROOM;** Super breakfast
CHILDREN; Over 2 years   No evening meals
CREDIT CARDS; Most major cards   **DISABLED ACCESS;** No
LICENSED; No. Guests welcome to bring their own wine
ACCOMMODATION; 3 de luxe ensuite rooms - A non-smoking house

Chapter Nine

BARN COURT
6 Back Lane, Rackheath,
Norfolk NR13 6NN

Tel: 01603 782536

About 5 miles from the city of Norwich and two miles from the heart of the Norfolk Broads at Wroxham on the A1151 is the village of Rackheath and here you will find a very delightful bed and breakfast which goes by the name of Barn Court. The bungalow is a converted 17th century stable block and provides a warm and friendly place to stay. There are 3 very pretty bedrooms, all of which are on the ground floor suitable for the elderly, and for the romantic, one room has a four poster bed, they are colour co-ordinated and very tastefully decorated. Each room has colour television and a tea and coffee tray.

The lounge and dining area are large and extremely well furnished with lovely exposed beams enhancing the character. A traditional full English breakfast is served between 7.00-9.30am so there is no need to rush. Evening meals are by prior arrangement, if you would like to eat out, then Julie Simpson your host can recommend plenty of excellent local pubs and restaurants. There is a Norfolk pub within walking distance and serves reasonably priced meals. Packed lunches are also available, with notice, for your day out. Norwich is East Anglia's capital and is a flourishing city with lovely shops, leisure facilities, the market, museums and the castle. Whether you stay for business or pleasure Barn Court is the ideal location.

USEFUL INFORMATION

OPEN; All year
CHILDREN; All ages welcome
CREDIT CARDS; None taken
ACCOMMODATION; 1 double ensuite, 1 dble private bathroom
1 twin shared bathroom

DINING ROOM; Traditional home-cooked fare. Packed lunches and evening meal by arrangement
VEGETARIAN; Catered for
DISABLED ACCESS; All ground floor rooms
GARDEN; Extensive garden available
PETS; Dogs allowed by prior arrangement

SUTTON STAITHE HOTEL
Sutton Staithe, Nr. Stalham,
Norfolk NR12 9QS
Tel: 01692 580244

One hundred feet from the waters edge stands the 17th century Sutton Staithe Hotel. Recently refurbished and under new management this friendly and family run hostelry is the perfect base for discovering the joys and delights which have made the Broads so popular. Extensive gardens surround the property, with plenty of car parking space and most importantly ample free moorings. Accommodation is comfortable and well appointed with private bathrooms and includes a tea and coffee tray and colour television. Particular attention is paid to the quality and variety of food served in the La Carte Restaurant. Bar meals are served in the Lounge Bar with a fine selection of ales. A comprehensive wine list is available to compliment any meal. Your host, John Holmes, offers good old fashioned personal service and will be only too happy to assist you in every way. There is a multitude of outdoor activities to enjoy. Hire a bike from Sutton Staithe Boatyard and explore the picturesque village of Sutton or take a leisurely stroll to the Sutton Windmill Museum, which is most enlightening. This waterside Hotel is highly recommended.

USEFUL INFORMATION
OPEN; All year
RESTAURANT; Varied menu, home-cooking
CHILDREN; Welcome
BAR FOOD; Bar snacks
CREDIT CARDS; All cards
VEGETARIAN; Catered for
LICENSED; Yes
DISABLED ACCESS; Yes
ACCOMMODATION; 10 ensuite rooms
GARDEN; Yes, with river
PETS; Yes, limited space

COLLEGE FARM
Thompson, Thetford,
Norfolk IP24 1QG

Tel: 01953 483318

College Farm has had quite a history, it begins in 1349 when two brothers Sir Thomas and Sir John Shardelow founded Thompson College for a Master and five priests to serve the chantry chapel. In 1400 it was rebuilt. Between then and 1975 it had a variety of owners who added to the property, but unfortunately, by that year, it had become a dilapidated farm. It was then lovingly and carefully converted into the attractive home it is today, owned by Lavender Garnier. There are three double ensuite rooms, all tastefully decorated and comfortable with television and fresh flowers to add that special touch. The dining room has wonderful panelling, there is lovely antique furniture everywhere. Breakfast is a full traditional meal. With no evening meal you can try the local pub, where they serve an excellent varied menu. The walled garden is a feature with ponds where the priests kept their fish. Tea and coffee is served free at any time - in the garden in fine weather. In Thetford you can visit the ruins of the 12th century priory and the Local History Museum is accommodated in the 15th century Ancient House. Bicycles for hire. A stay at College Farm is both interesting and very enjoyable.

USEFUL INFORMATION
OPEN; All year
DINING ROOM; Breakfast only
CHILDREN; Over 7 years
VEGETARIAN; Catered for
CREDIT CARDS; None taken
DISABLED ACCESS; Not really
ACCOMMODATION; 3 double
GARDEN; Yes

Chapter Nine

THE RED LION,
Market Place, Swaffham,
Norfolk, PE37 7AQ

Tel : 01760 721022

The Red Lion is a former 1700 coaching inn and used to be a stop off point for the Royal Mail. You can imagine the clatter of horses hooves, the white plumes of their breath as the coach rolled into the yard, and the agent dismounted to take some welcome food and ale at this hostelry! But back to the present! George and Ronnie Hoare are the proprietors of this fine establishment. There are eleven guest rooms, all fully self contained, eight of which are the former coach garage, stable and coachman's accommodation. All are very comfortable and furnished to extremely high standards, and George and Ronnie are to be commended on the relaxing comfort with which they supply their guests! Four of the rooms are double, six are twin and one is a family room. Each has a TV and a refreshments tray. Breakfast is a traditional meal and vegetarian meals are also available. There are two bars, very pleasantly laid out and here you can have morning coffee if desired, lunch time snacks, full lunches or evening meals. George and Ronnie also cater for meetings and parties, and this is the ideal spot to cater for that special family occasion with the excellent, attentive staff ensuring you are well looked after! The food is good traditional English fayre with a fine selection of options to cater to any taste. Anything from jacket potatoes with various fillings, to Narborough Trout is available, and are served either with a fresh salad garni or choice vegetables. The food is wholesome with ample quantities, and all for very reasonable prices.

This comfortable inn is suitably positioned for visiting many of the interesting, surrounding landmarks. Swaffham itself has many splendid Georgian buildings including the Montpelier House and the Assembly Rooms. Fishing, golf, walking and many more outdoor sports are available nearby and there is a Saturday Market which is prolific in memorabilia and definitely worth a visit! King's Lynn is a drive away, with its rich, historic buildings, dating from medieval to Georgian times, and the Guild Hall and Town Hall are of special interest with their unusual flint chequered design. Still on the history trail, a day out in Norwich will leave you exhausted but fulfilled! Here you can please everyone with the Cathedral, the Castle, museum and art gallery, and a host more......and for those who find this all rather stuffy.......the shops are good too! Come back to a pleasant meal and a quiet drink, followed by a good night's sleep and you will thank your lucky stars you decided to stay at The Red Lion Motel!

USEFUL INFORMATION

OPEN : All year
CHILDREN : Not in pub
PETS : No
LICENSED : Full
CREDIT CARDS : All major
RESTAURANT : Good English Fayre
VEGETARIANS : Catered for
BAR SNACKS : Good variety
DISABLED ACCESS : By arrangement
GARDEN : No
ACCOMMODATION : 11 rooms all fully self contained: 4 dbl, 6 twin, 1 fml.

ROSE COTTAGE
Butters Hall Lane, Thompson,
Thetford, Norfolk IP24 1QQ
Tel: 01953 488104

Thetford is surrounded by lovely countryside in an area offering visitors a wide range of attractions, so where better to make you base than Rose Cottage. This period house was built 300 years ago and is set within an acre of gardens. Kevin and Yvonne Fickling make their guests feel very much at home. Kevin rears and trains gun dogs, whilst Yvonne concentrates her time providing the very best for her guests. The bedrooms are spacious with high quality furnishings and tasteful linen and drapes. There is a pretty private bathroom, colour TV, and tea and coffee making facilities. One room has a King size bed. Special attention is given to the preparation and presentation of meals, which affords a comprehensive choice. An evening meal is available with interesting and varied dished. Dogs are welcome. Encompassing Thetford visitors can enjoy a wealth of historical venues, including museums, manors and one or two castles. The largest Pine Forest in Britain is here at Thetford with a most interesting bird trail. Just along the road is a Nature Reserve and Sanctuary. A little further afield is Bressingham Gardens and most unusually a Narrow Gauge Railway running across the Waveney Valley and a collection of steam locomotives.

USEFUL INFORMATION
OPEN; All year
CHILDREN; Welcome
CREDIT CARDS; None taken
ACCOMMODATION; 2 double room, private bathroom
PETS; Dogs welcome
DINING ROOM; Traditional home-cooked fare Evening meal available
VEGETARIAN; Catered for
DISABLED ACCESS; No
GARDEN; Yes, spacious

QUAYSIDE COTTAGE
The Quay, Waldringfield,
Woodbridge, Suffolk IP12 4QZ
Tel: 01473 736724

Quayside Cottage is '3 Key Highly Commended' by the English Tourist Board and is quietly situated on the banks of the River Deben, in the delightful village of Waldringfield. In the village, about 150 yards from the cottage is a store, post office and the Maybush Inn, a favourite watering hole for locals and visitors alike. The cottage itself is very comfortable indeed and is equipped with everything you could possibly need. The kitchen has all the modern day facilities including microwave and fridge/freezer. The one double bedroom has a ensuite shower room. Separate WC. All linen and towels are provided. The patio doors lead to the conservatory where you can sit and watch the boats on the river and relax. There is off-road parking adjacent to the property. Whilst staying in the cottage you are asked not to smoke and animals are not permitted. If you are a sailor or you like golf and wonderful walks then Quayside Cottage is the place for you.

USEFUL INFORMATION
OPEN; All year
CHILDREN; No
CREDIT CARDS; None taken
LICENSED; Not applicable
ACCOMMODATION; Self-catering
1 bedroom cottage. Weekly bookings are from Friday to Friday. November-March weekends and midweek bookings available
DISABLED ACCESS; No
GARDEN; Very attractive overlooking the river
PETS; No
PARKING; In drive by cottage
NON SMOKING COTTAGE

Chapter Nine

BRIARFIELDS HOTEL
*Main Street, Titchwell,
Hunstanton, Norfolk PE31 8BB*

*Tel: 01485 210742
Fax: 01485 210933*

    The north coast of Norfolk has many features, none more so than the exposed sandy coastline teeming with wildlife. Great prosperity grew here during the agricultural revolution, bringing wealth to the great houses, towns and villages. There are some attractive resorts, where you can wander and browse around the shops. Along this coastline is the small village of Titchwell where the delightful country hotel, Briarfields, overlooks the sea. There are 17 bedrooms, 10 doubles, 5 twin and 2 family rooms, all individually furnished and with the added privacy of ensuite facilities. Each room also has a colour television, direct dial telephone and a plentiful supply of tea and coffee. For the romantic amongst you, two of the bedrooms have wonderful four poster beds. Guests have their own large sitting room where one can relax in congenial surroundings and meet others, or plan your day away. The dining room is very pleasant and it is here you are served delicious home-cooking. Briarfields is renowned for its extensive menu and dessert trolley, all the food is prepared from daily fresh ingredients. You will definitely not go without here with breakfast, morning coffee, the bar, afternoon tea, evening bar meals, and dinner.
    Briarfields is in a perfect location and if you are a birdwatcher then this is paradise. The RSPB Nature Reserve at Titchwell Marsh, is within easy walking distance, here you will find an area rich in bird life. The salt and freshwater marshes and reed beds are ideal for reed buntings, red warblers, water rails, wigeons to name but a few, with viewing hides, an information centre and a lovely picnic area you are sure to be in your element. There are other Nature Reserves in the area including, Snettisham RSPB Reserve, from Brancaster Straithe it is possible to catch a ferry out to Scolt Head Island, and a few minutes drive away is the National Nature Reserve at Holkham. There is definitely something here for everyone in the family, the superb cathedral cities of Norwich, Cambridge and Ely are all within easy reach, there are fascinating market towns and lovely sandy beaches. It is no wonder that the AA has awarded Briarfields with '2 Stars' and the English Tourist Board '3 Crown Commended', it is an excellent hotel where you are invited to stay awhile and relax in it's peaceful and charming atmosphere.

USEFUL INFORMATION

OPEN: *All year, 24 Hours*
CHILDREN: *Welcome*
CREDIT CARDS: *Mastercard/Visa/Switch*
LICENSED: *Yes*
ACCOMMODATION: *17 ensuite rooms*
PETS: *On request*

RESTAURANT: *Extensive menu, delicious home-cooking. Open to non-residents*
BAR MEALS: *Yes*
VEGETARIAN: *Catered for*
DISABLED ACCESS: *Yes*
GARDEN: *Yes*

GRANGE FARM
Dennington,
Woodbridge, Suffolk IP13 8BT

Tel: 01986 798388

Imagine having a meal beside the moat, with swallows swooping over the water? It sounds idyllic doesn't it? This is what happens in warm weather at Grange Farm, the moated home of Elizabeth Hickson which dates back to the 13th century. The moat is medieval and is fascinating to watch in the evenings when the reflections thrown off the water stretch the imagination and increase ones sense of rural peace. Everywhere you go in this enchanting house there is another discovery to make. Every room is beamed and in winter the Aga burns in the kitchen and log fires throw out a wonderful heat in the sitting-rooms where you are welcome to do nothing at all or perhaps watch television and play the occasional game of billiards. It is such a relaxed home and perfectly run without fuss which allows guests to unwind completely. In the dining room where meals are served the runners for wooden shutters can still be seen which were used before the days of glass. It really is a privilege to stay here.

All the rooms look out over the extensive and beautiful gardens which teem with bird life. An all weather tennis court is there if you feel energetic. There are three beautifully appointed bedrooms . Guests have their own bathroom with individual towels, mats and soaps provided. Breakfast is delicious and has the additional pleasure of home-made bread, marmalade and local honey. An evening meal is available by arrangement when home grown vegetables are used whenever possible.

The surrounding countryside is excellent for walking, cycling and riding. There are good stabling facilities for horses. You will be spoilt for choice in the number of places one can visit including Framlingham Castle, Sutton Hoo-burial ground of the Anglo-Saxon Kings. Nearby lies Hoxne, site of King Edward's martyrdom and of the recently discovered treasure. Snape Maltings, the RSPB Bird Sanctuary at Minsmere and the coast are all within easy reach. If you wish Elizabeth will arrange tours for you. You will never regret staying here, it is so delightfully different.

USEFUL INFORMATION

*OPEN;*All year
CHILDREN; Over 12 years
*CREDIT CARDS;*None taken
ACCOMMODATION; 3 rooms not ensuite
PETS; No
DINING ROOM; Traditional breakfast with variations. Evening meal by arrangement
VEGETARIAN; Yes & other diets
DISABLED ACCESS; No
GARDEN; Delightful. Parking

Chapter Nine

COBWEB COTTAGE
Queens Street, Spooner Row,
Wymondham, Norwich,
Norfolk NR18 9JU

Tel: 01953 604070

Rory and Donna McAllister have created an enchanted world within the walls of the 18th century Cobweb Cottage. They have done it with imagination, loving care and a feeling for the age of the building. It has a true cottage feel about it. The furniture is a happy mix of antique and modern aligned to very pretty drapes and matching soft furnishings. The three bedrooms are warm and comfortable with everything within them designed to be restful and relaxing. Two of the bedrooms are ensuite and the third has a private bathroom. All three rooms have colour television and a well supplied beverage tray. Breakfast is a delicious meal with a full, traditional English menu with options. Everything is freshly cooked to order. The aroma from the coffee tantalises the taste buds, the tea is piping hot, toast is constantly supplied and the preserves are home-made. Vegetarians are catered for by arrangement. No evening meals are served but there are any number of excellent places to eat within easy distance. The McAllister's will be happy to point you in the right direction.

Cobweb Cottage has a charming garden, a sun lounge area which guests are welcome to enjoy. For those who want to be energetic there is a golf course closeby and fishing is also available. The historic city of Norwich is nearby and here you can spend hours exploring the fascinating places like the cobbled Elm Hill, the centre with its good shops, the castle and the magnificent cathedral. The coast is not far off and The Broads an easy drive. Cobweb Cottage really is an ideal base if you wish to take advantage of all that is on offer.

USEFUL INFORMATION

OPEN; All year
CHILDREN; By arrangement
CREDIT CARDS; None taken
ACCOMMODATION; 3 doubles
2 ensuite 1 bathroom
PETS; By arrangement

DINING ROOM; Excellent breakfast
No evening meal
VEGETARIAN; By arrangement
DISABLED ACCESS; No
GARDEN; Yes with sun lounge area

KIMBERLEY HOME FARM,
Wymondham,
Norfolk, NR18 0RW.

Tel : 01953 603137
Fax : 01953 604836

Mike and Jenny Bloom are the owners of this working farm, which is situated well away from the 'rat race', very deep in rural Norfolk. Kimberley Home Farm forms part of what once was the 'old Kimberley Estate', it has 500 acres with sheep, cattle and cereal crops. But.....during the winter months race horses are trained here, so if you've a mind for a flutter and an eye for form, you could pick a few of next season's winners! It might even inspire you to have a go at riding which can be arranged (though sadly not one of the thoroughbreds!) Then again, if you are not the horse type, there is a hard court tennis. Golf, fishing and walking are nearby. 'Peddars Way' from coast to Breckland.......just imagine a lung full of clean country air and the added touch of ozone!

So after a full day's activities come 'home' to a very warm welcome and (if you've made prior arrangements with Mike and Jenny!) a delicious 3 course evening meal. Retire to your room which is delightfully furnished in the antique style and all to very high standards. Awake in the morning feeling relaxed and refreshed, and prepare yourself for breakfast. (A renowned farmhouse affair with various options and all farm produce - you'll probably skip lunch!) The emphasis here is on quality, comfortable surroundings, pleasant company and very good food!

Wymondham itself is of some interest with the splendid remains of the Abbey Church. Here you can see the hammerbeam roof with carved flying angels, the high altar and the towers at each end of the church. The scenery is such that anyone interested in painting or sketching will find it a delight to be here and see the different colours and textures of the landscape and skies. This is a peaceful location and with the help of your hosts Mike and Jenny you will have a wonderful time! Norwich is only 9 miles away and this historic city has a lot to offer. The Norman cathedral, the 12th century castle, and even the origins and history of Colmans Mustard! Just 1 hour away you have all parts of the Norfolk and much of the Suffolk coasts, and also the famous 'Norfolk Broads' You will not be bored here whatever your tastes - a great place to stay, with warm people and a host of activities!

USEFUL INFORMATION

OPEN : March to Nov.   **DINING ROOM** : Evening meal by arrangement
CHILDREN : Welcome   **VEGETARIANS** : No
PETS : No   **DISABLED ACCESS** : No
LICENSED : No   **BAR SNACKS** : Not applicable
CREDIT CARDS : None taken   **GARDEN** : Spacious grounds
ACCOMMODATION : 3 rooms; 2 dbl, 1 twin   Hard tennis court
& 1 fml suite.

Chapter Nine

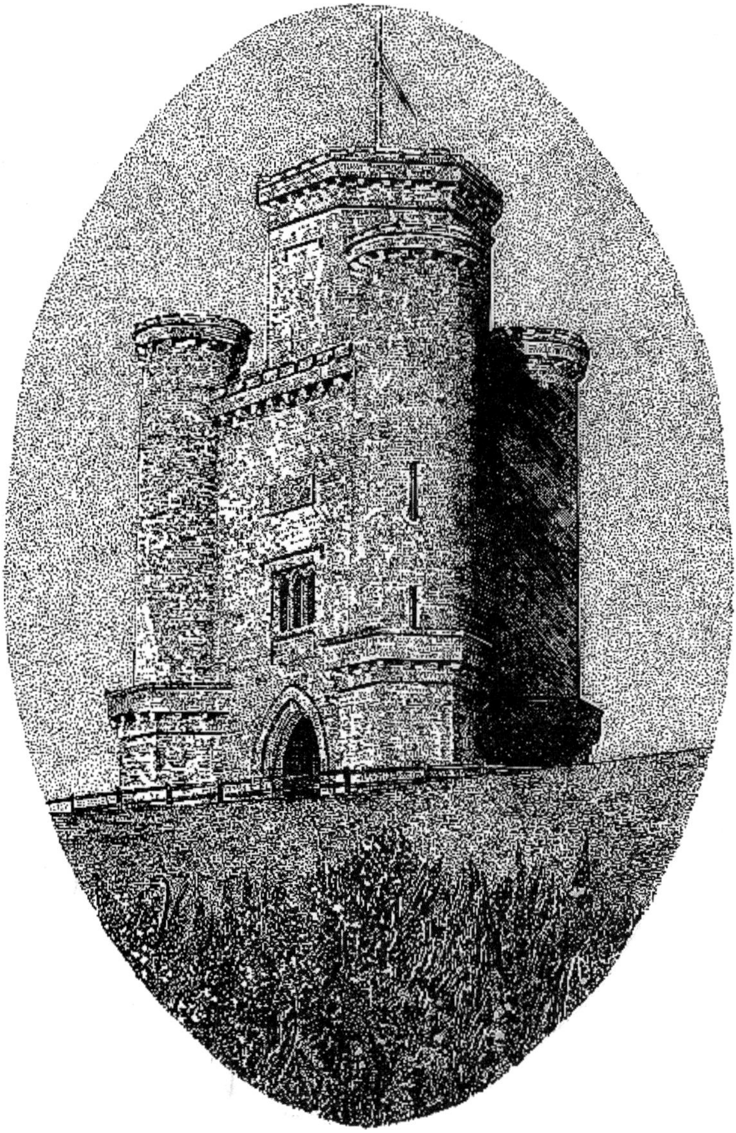

Chapter Ten

WALES

Wales

CHAPTER 10

WALES

INCLUDING

The Harbour Hotel	**Aberdovey**	p. 709
Maes Glas	**Abergavenny**	p. 710
Abercelyn	**Bala**	p. 711
Wavecrest Hotel	**Barmouth**	p. 712
Bryn Llewelyn Guest House	**Betws-Y-Coed**	p. 713
Church Hill Hotel	**Betws-Y-Coed**	p. 714
Glasfryn Guest House	**Brechfa**, Carmarthen	p. 715
Belvedere	**Brecon**	p. 716
Lansdowne Hotel & Restaurant	**Brecon**	p. 717
Maeswalter	**Brecon**	p. 718
Dol-Llyn-Wydd	**Builth Wells**	p. 719
Orchard Cottage	**Builth Wells**	p. 720
The Cedars Guest House	**Builth Wells**	p. 721
Pantgwyn Farm	**Carmarthen**	p. 722
Craig-Y-Mor Guest House	**Criccieth**	p. 723
Borthwnog Hall Country House Hotel	**Dolgellau**	p. 724
The Ivy House	**Dolgellau**	p. 725
Guest House Gwynfa	**Dyffryn Ceiriog**, Llangollen	p. 726
Einion House	**Fairbourne**	p. 727
The Wenallt	**Gilwern**, Nr Abergavenny	p. 728
Crossways House	**Glamorgan**	p. 729
Gwestry Fferm	**Glynarthen**, Nr Cardigan	p. 730
Fairfield Cottage	**Gower**	p. 731
Tregynon Country Farm House Hotel	**Gwaun Valley**	p. 732
Plas Tirion Guest House	**Gwynfryn**, Wrexham	p. 733
The Black Lion Royal Hotel	**Lampeter**	p. 734
Ffaldu Country House	**Llandegley**	p. 735
Maerdy Cottages	**Llandeilo**, Nr Carmarthen	p. 718
Cwmgwyn Farm	**Llandovery**	p. 736
Llwyncelyn Guest House	**Llandovery**	p. 737
Bwlch Farmhouse	**Llandrindod Wells**	p. 738
Holly Farm	**Llandrindod Wells**	p. 739
Hotel Commodore	**Llandrindod Wells**	p. 740
The Severn Arms Hotel	**Llandrindod Wells**	p. 741
St Tudno	**Llandudno**	p. 742
Glyngwernen Farm	**Llanelli**	p. 716

Chapter Ten

Pengrug	**Llangadog**	**p. 743**
Cae Crwn Farm	**Llangollen**	**p. 744**
The Glyn Valley Hotel	**Llangollen**	**p. 745**
Bryn Hyfryd	**Llanstysilio, Llangollen**	**p. 747**
Glanrannell Park Hotel	**Llanwrda**	**p. 746**
The Riverside Hotel	**Monmouth**	**p. 748**
The Dragon Hotel	**Montgomery**	**p. 749**
Tides Reach Guest House	**Mumbles**	**p. 750**
Cwmtwrch Hotel	**Nantgaredig**	**p. 751**
Pen-Y-Gelli	**Newton**	**p. 752**
Dyffryn Farm Holidays	**Newtown**	**p. 753**
Wychwood House	**Penally**	**p. 754**
The Old Rectory	**Ruthin**	**p. 755**
Harbour Light	**Sandersfoot**	**p. 756**
Sant-Y-Nyll House	**St Brides-Super-Ely**	**p. 757**
Ramsey House	**St Davids**	**p. 758**
Hurst Dene Guest House	**Swansea**	**p. 759**
Windsor Lodge Hotel	**Swansea**	**p. 760**
The Olde Masons Arms Hotel	**Talgarth**	**p. 761**
The Tower Hotel	**Talgarth**	**p. 762**
Maes-Yneuadd Hotel	**Talsaenau**	**p. 763**
The Fountain Inn	**Tintern**	**p. 764**
The Old Rectory	**Tintern**	**p. 765**
Valley House	**Tintern**	**p. 766**
Wye Barn	**Tintern**	**p. 767**

WALES

To attempt to describe Wales in a chapter, albeit a lengthy one, is ludicrous. To do it justice in a large volume would still be difficult but as this option is not open to me I hope you will find the tales of my journeying an appetiser encouraging you to delve into, and enjoy the beauty, the splendour, the warmth and the people of this wonderful Principality.

I decided to start by embracing Anglesey, Snowdonia and the Lleyn Peninsula which allows me a choice between the sea and land, with a breathtaking diversity of scenery and activities. Firstly, I used **Bangor** as a base. Here is a city of impressive religious and historic heritage. A place in which to enjoy the natural beauty of the area and to be drawn to the many old buildings which have been carefully maintained or restored. **The cathedral** was founded by St Deiniol in 575Ad - 70 years before Canterbury - and is built on one of the oldest Christian sites in Britain. Its turbulent history has included sacking by the Vikings and destruction by King John's forces when they burnt Bangor in 1210, and it is the resting place of Prince Owain of Gwynedd. Work was begun on the present Cathedral in the mid 13th Century, and was finished with the completion of the Central Tower in 1967.

The City of Bangor is dominated by the academic towers of the **University of Wales** - the 'college on the hill' - which celebrated its centenary in 1984. Apart from good shopping in pedestrianised streets I wandered down to the waterfront intent on visiting the Pier. It stretches a full 1500feet into the Menai Straits, and has recently been restored to its Victorian splendour.

As I moved away from the coast and drove into the mountains the scenery became truly spectacular. Dyffryn Ogwen - the Ogwen Valley - delights artists and photographers. My route took me through **Bethesda**, a village with a Hebrew name which means 'a house of mercy', and along the shores of Llyn Ogwen. The landscaped was dominated by the mountain ranges of Carnedd Llywelyn, Carnedd Dafydd, Tryfan, Glyder Fach and Glyder Fawr. Salmon and sea-trout ascend the River Ogwen as far as the falls below Llyn Ogwen, and many of the lakes in the area - Ogwen, Bochlwyd, Ffynnon Lloer - provide excellent sea-trout fishing, for which permits are available locally.

And so to **Llanberis**. With a history going back to the Iron Age, the town is one of the oldest settlements in Wales and a bastion of the Welsh language and tradition. Old Roman forts lie to the east and west, and the uplands behind Llanberis are reputed to be linked to the legends of King

Chapter Ten

Arthur. Although perhaps best known as the lower terminus of the **Snowdon Mountain railway**, Llanberis is also renowned as a centre for climbers.

The views across the twin lakes to the mountains are stunning, and from here their grandeur contrasts sharply with the softness of lush green meadows and the beauty of the lower wooded slopes. You may well opt for the Mountain Railway, as I did, as the favoured way of reaching Snowdon's summit - climbing up tracks is no longer for me! The Mountain Railway is Britain's only public rack and pinion railway. It was opened in 1896 and climbs more than 3,000 feet, the journey lasting approximately an hour. Views on the way up are spectacular, and from the summit, on clear days, you can see the Isle of Anglesey, the Wicklow mountains in Ireland, and the Isle of Man. First train of the day is usually at 9am from Llanberis - much depends on the weather.

Two places to visit in Llanberis - **The Piggery Pottery** and **The Snowdon Honey Farm** which are right in the centre of town. **The National Museum of Wales** has its Northern branch in Llanberis, and the Power of Wales Exhibition is particularly well-presented.

To most people, at least since 1969, **Caernarfon** means ' castle'. It was then that the Investiture of HRH Prince Charles as Prince of Wales took place, although what is not quite such common knowledge is that Caernarfon was also the scene for the Investiture of Prince Edward in 1911 - later to be Edward VIII and then Duke of Windsor, after his abdication. The setting of the castle is superb. The King's Gate is said to be the mightiest in the land; the Eagle Tower houses an exhibition and audio visual programme; the Royal Welch Fusiliers have their museum in the Queen's Tower; the Prince of Wales' exhibition is in the North-East Tower; and in the Chamberlain Tower there is an exhibition of the Castles of Edward I.

But Caernarfon is much more than a magnificent castle. In the past the landscape artist, Turner, came here, and marvelled at the quality of the light and sunsets. At the turn of the century so many famous newspaper men had connections with the town that it was known as the Fleet Street of Wales. The River Seiont flows past the castle walls into the Menai Strait. There can surely be no finer way of viewing both town and castle than from a boat on one of the regular trips run from the quayside.

The lovely, quiet part of Britain that is the Lleyn Peninsula is full of rare, natural treasures, whether it is the Peninsula's own breed of sheep, the abundant wild flowers, the hedgerows abounding in honeysuckle, rosehips and blackberries, or the overwhelming sense of history. It is a very Welsh heartland.

The journey down the Peninsula is dominated by the two peaks of Yr Eifl (The Rivals) mountains, proof surely that nowhere in North Wales can you ever be far from high ground! Going along the B4417 one comes to **Nefyn**, a coastal resort which was once a halt for pilgrims on their way to **Bardsey Island** (Ynys Enlli - the island of tides, where 20,000 saints are said to be buried.) Now, the village's church of St Mary houses a maritime museum, and if you have time to pause take a look at the fine, sweeping bay formed by Nefyn, Morfa Nefyn and Porth Dinllaen. The 'Whistling Sands' at **Porthoer** is one of the area's outstanding beaches, an ideal spot to take the folding chairs out of the car boot and relax for a while. It is fact that the golden sands whistle mysteriously as one picks one's way across the picturesque bay.

Churches in the Lleyn Peninsula are among the most attractive in Wales. There is a stunningly simple example at **Llangwnnadl**, which lies to the north-east of Porthoer, and a mile or so inland at **Bryncroes** is St Marys on the site of St Mary's Well, an important watering place on the Pilgrim's Route. By taking a minor road across country I came to **Llangian** where, in the churchyard of St Gian's, one of the earliest known doctors from the 16th century is buried.

The final point of interest on the southernmost tip of the Lleyn Peninsula is **Aberdaron**, which was always the last port of call for pilgrims on their way to Bardsey. The place is steeped in history. At least one Prince of Wales has sheltered in the 6th-century church of St Hywyn which nestles on the seashore, as have Cromwell's soldiers. It is said that the marks still visible on the door pillars were made by those same soldiers as they sharpened their swords.

Next to **Abersoch**. This is best done by taking the A499, which together with the A497, is a most attractive road following the southern coastline of the Peninsula as far as Porthmadog. Thissection of the coast is stunningly beautiful and has the weather to match. It is a mecca for sailing enthusiasts and sometimes referred to as ' Cowes of the North'. Ideal conditions mean that Abersoch and nearby Pwllheli are frequent locations for major British, European and World sailing championships, and for the casual sailor the waters offer some of the very best sheltered sailing facilities in Britain.

Until the earlier part of this century **Porthmadog** was a bustling shipping port. It served the international Welsh slate trade which was brought down from **Blaenau Ffestiniog** by the Ffestiniog Railway, now a major tourist attraction. The full round trip takes about 2 hours, and is well worth taking because of the wonderful scenery. Much of the town is flat - it is recognised as a model of 18th century town planning.

Chapter Ten

Whatever you do, do not leave this beautiful coast without visiting **Portmeirion**. This unique village was created by Sir Clough Williams-Ellis between 1925 and 1972 in what he calls his 'light opera approach'. It is located on a secluded peninsula which juts out into Traeth Bach. It consists of fifty buildings arranged around a central Piazza, all predominantly Italianate in style, and is surrounded by the sub-tropical woodlands of Y Gwyllt. I love the place for its beauty, its escapism and the totally peaceful atmosphere. To stay here either in self-catering accommodation in one of the villas or houses or to enjoy the superb hotel is a never to be forgotten
experience. It is equally pleasureable for day visitors to wander round the village, have a meal in one of the restaurants, sit a while on the Piazza and dream dreams. Portmeirion Pottery is available in the shop - seconds in the Portmeirion shop and others in one of the delightful little shops.

Leaving the Lleyn Peninsula I took the A498 which led me to the A4085 and a spectacular, if slightly tortuous journey through the Snowdon mountain range to **Beddgelert**. There is a tradition here, and romantic legend, which suggests that the village's name (Geldert's Grave) comes from Prince Llywelyn's heroic dog Gelert, slain by the Prince who mistakenly thought the dog had killed his son. Later the prince realised a dead wolf was to blame, and the blood-spattered dog had been killed defending the boy. The village which won the Queen Mother's Birthday Award 1992 - Keep Wales Tidy Campaign, is vastly different from those I visited on the Lleyn Peninsula. There the sea was always evident, the small hamlets bright and airy, a feeling of space all around. In the Aberglaslyn Valley lushness prevails. Paths close by lead to Snowdon, Moel Hebog, Moelwyn and the Cnicht, and the Rivers Glaswyn and Colwyn merge to flow through the glorious beauty of the Aberglaslyn Pass. Other beauty spots not to be missed include the Nant Gwynant Pass, and Cwm Pennant, where the River Dwyfor flows through one of Britain's most lyrical valleys.

Conwy is, literally, a fortress city by the sea. As you swoop down from the Sychnant Pass you will see that it is dominated by the castle built by Edward I as part of his master plan to subdue the Welsh. That was between 1283 and 1289 and today the castle is perhaps the most picturesque in Wales, the town walls with 22 towers and 3 original gateways the most complete of any in Europe. To make room for his castle, Edward moved Cistercian monks from their Abbey to Maenan in the Conwy Valley. Of the Abbey all that remains is the Abbey church which is still in use after seven centuries - a haven of peace in the very centre of the busy town.

Thomas Telford's graceful suspension bridge is one of three crossing the river Conwy. It was opened in 1826 and in use until the modern road bridge was completed in 1958. As you drive east out of Conwy you will see alongside both bridges the tubular railway bridge, built by Robert Stephenson in 1846. A superb technical achievment, it is still a vital link on the railway line between Chester and Holyhead. Odd, how even in those days, care was taken in building themock-medieval towers so that they harmonised with the castle. We are surely wrong to believe that our generation is the first to care about the environment!

From **Llandudno Junction** the A470 goes through another area famed for its scenery. The Vale of Conwy is more usually referred to locally as the **Conwy Valley**, and the road winds up the eastern bank of the river. This really is a lovely area to explore, and I suggest a drive as far as **Betws-y-Coed** where you can cross the river by bridge and so return to Conwy.

Llanrwst is an old market town and famed for its bridge built by Inigo Jones in 1636. Pont Fawr is narrow and humped, and until traffic lights were installed it was frequently the scene of heated arguments as drivers claimed right of way! If you walk to the centre of the bridge you will see a group of standing stones on the far bank. These are the Gorsedd Stones, and they are closely connected with the ceremonies associated with the bards who attend the National Eisteddfodau. At Llanrwst the stones are frequently marooned when the River Conwy breaks its banks during the winter months.

Betws-y-Coed is four miles further on. It is just 50 feet above sea level and entirely surrounded by hills of an average height of 1,000 feet. 'Y Coed' is the Welsh for 'the wood', and as you drive in over Telford's cast-iron Waterloo Bridge you must be captivated by the surrounding woodlands - native hardwoods, and many species of conifer. This famous little village has four churches, of which St Michael's is the most venerable. The old part of the building dates back to the 14th century, while the large transept at the northern end and the vestry at the south-east were added in 1843.

Three rivers - the Conwy, the Lledr and the Llugwy - pass through or very close to Betws-y-Coed. This means there are several old bridges in the area. The Waterloo bridge I have mentioned already, and the other one that attracts tourists is Pont-y-Pair - the Bridge of the Cauldron. The River Llugwy passes beneath it, cascading out of the foaming waters of the upstream 'cauldron' formed by masses of black rock.

That water has already had a tumultous passage before it reaches Pont-y-Pair. The Swallow Falls are the most famous of several in the area, and these are found but a short drive up the A5. Steps lead down to the water's edge, and during the rainy season they are a truly spectacular sight as the waters of the Llugwy thunder down the rocky gorge, drenching the unwary.

Chapter Ten

High up in the hills there are the most beautiful lakes you could imagine, at altitudes ranging from 600 feet to almost 1500 feet. Lead pollution from old mines means that there are no fish in Llyn Gerionwydd, but it is a superb sailing and water-skiing venue. Llyn-y-Parc is shallow and also dead, but it is reachable from Pont-y-Pair and can be exceedingly beautiful, particularly when bracken and larches change colour in the autumn. There are gentle river walks along the banks of the Llugwy from Pont-y-Pair.

You will probably know of **Harlech** for its castle, again the work of Edward I, and from hearing those magnificent Welsh male voice choirs singing the rousing 'Men of Harlech'. The Castle does dominate the town. It was the stronghold of Owain Glyndwr, and was the last castle to fall in the Wars of the Roses. The town is charming with narrow streets and a wonderful golf course at Royal St Davids with International Class facilities. If you are a walker you will

delight in the Rhinog range of mountains which form a grand backdrop to all these coastal towns and villages. You can reach them through the valleys of Cwm Bychan and Cwm Nantcol.

Barmouth is famed for its two miles of golden sands and is hard to beat for a family seaside holiday in Wales. You simply cannot get away from the sight of sleek sailing boats in this part of the world, and at Barmouth they look a picture. Moving inland from Barmouth on the A496 which hugs the wooded banks of the Afon Mawddach is no hardship. The route is one followed by the art critic Ruskin and the poet Manley Hopkins. Wordsworth too loved this magnificent walking country.

At **Bontddu** is **The Clogau Gold Mine** - the Old Clogau - situated in a fold eight hundred feet up in the hills alongside the Hirgwm stream which tumbles downhill to Mawddach. It sounds extraordinary to those who do not know the story, but it is one of many in the area - so many that a ring round the Rhinog mountains has been called 'the Dolgellau Gold Belt'. Princess Margaret, the Princess Royal and the Princess of Wales all wear wedding rings fashioned from Clogau's Welsh gold.

15th-century **Dolgellau** was the Welsh Parliament capital of Owain Glyndwr. It is built of Welsh granite and roofed with grey-blue Welsh slate, yet what might be an unremittingly bleak scene is overwhelmed by the majesty of Cader Idris range of mountains, and further relieved by the softer beauty of the Mawddach Estuary.

Penmaenpool is on the south bank of the river at the point where the Mawddach estuary opens out. An ideal place to watch a wide variety of birds in their natural habitat from the RSPB Observatory and afterwards to call at **Penmaenuchaf Hall** for one of their famous afternoon teas. The Hall was built as a summer house for the Leigh-Taylor family in 1860, a Lancashire family with cotton connections, and has since housed two High Sheriffs of Meirionnydd. A delightful spot.

Bala, a pleasantly flat, market town makes a wonderful base for a holiday. Here there is a lake which when the water is low may allow you to see the remains of Pentre Celeyn, the tiny village which was flooded to create what is now a reservoir supplying water for Liverpool. It seems always that progress has its down side, doesn't it? Yet filled with crystal-clear water from the mountains, stocked with lake trout and perch, this man-made lake is beautiful, hides its secrets well, and serves many useful purposes.

The town is best known as an international centre for watersports, with the five mile long Llyn Tegid judged by many to be the finest sailing lake in Britain. So you will head here if you are a yachtsman, and turn to the River Tryweryn if you are keen to hone your canoe slalom skills or try the wild white waters that make the river one of Europe's finest venues for canoeists. Llyn Tegid will also attract you if you intend to pit your wits against the perch, pike and roach. The deep water gwyniad fish has been unique to the lake since the Ice Ages.

Bala is famous too for its Sheepdog Trials. They began here and the town has been associated with television's 'One Man and his Dog'.

Finally in this section, **Anglesey**. You cross one of the two bridges over the Menai Strait. The Menai Suspension Bridge was built by Telford in 1826, with graceful arches of Pemmon limestone and a central span suspended high above the water by massive chains. The nearby Britannia Bridge was once a tubular structure built by Stephenson, but while his similarly constructed bridge at Conwy is still in use in its original state, this one was destroyed by fire in 1970. It has since been remodelled, and is now a twin road and rail link with its new road deckcarrying the A5. You cannot fail to notice that each bridge carries a large sign which reads 'Mon Man Cymru'. It is the Welsh for 'Anglesey, Mother of Wales'. For centuries this island's mild climate and rich farmland has made it the provider of grain for the harsher highlands of the Welsh interior. So you will find windmills here too, Llynnon Mill at **Llanddeusant** near Holyhead was built in 1775 and has recently been restored.

Anglesey is wonderful. It has a tremendous sense of freedom. Gone are the immensity of the mountain ranges, so much a part of this journey and instead there are gently rolling hills, low white cottages, and skies which seem endless. The whole of the island is criss-crossed with enticing small

Chapter Ten

roads although there are two or three excellent A roads. I made for **Menai Bridge** with the intention of making my way up the east coast.

You will reach **Beaumaris** along a delightful wooded section of the A545 which follows the coast past the landscaped gardens of elegant Victorian mansions. The town was Edward I's 13th-century English garrison borough, which later became a busy seaport and fashionable Victorian resort. There is a castle, of course, and the one at Beaumaris was the last and largest of those Edward built to contain the Welsh.

Llansadwrn off the B5109 has a gem of a Victorian church which is home for the oldest memorial stone in Wales. It is dedicated to St Saturnius and his wife, and you will find it set into the wall of the chancel.

Anglesey is famed for its sheltered beaches. **Red Wharf Bay** is a snug cove that reveals fifteen square miles of sand at low tide. Bathing only advisable on the incoming tide - the soft sands can be a trap for the unwary. Charles Dickens came here to report on the wreck and called in at **The Panton Arms** at **Pentraeth** for refreshment.

At **Moelfre** you will be able to take a headland walk to the site of the 'Royal Charter' shipwreck in 1859.

There are so many ancient sites on Anglesey, it is impossible to mention them all. At **Din Lligwy** between Moelfre and Amlwch, for example, there are the remains of six foot thick hut walls that were once part of an iron age village.

Llaneilian has a 15th-century church with Norman tower - passageways link the church to an old chapel with well-preserved carvings and decorative features. To the east of **Llangadrig** lies the site of an oratory or chapel established by a female recluse in the 7th century. At **Valley** I rejoined the A5. This wonderful old London to Holyhead road has been with us since the time of Elizabeth I - England's link with Ireland. A causeway carries it across from the mainland of Anglesey to Holy Island, and after a mile or so it reaches **Holyhead** and swings sharply right towards the inner harbour.

Holyhead was founded in the 3rd century AD, when the Romans built a fortress. St Cybi's Church is named after a Celtic saint who settled here in the 6th century, and dates from the 13th century to the 17th century. Holyhead mountain is a modest 220 metres high, but Celtic warriors once stood watch on the ramparts of the Iron Age hillfort, and Roman soldiers lit beacons from a watchtower.

From these heights if you look down and a little way to the west you will see South Stack, a lump of rock joined to Holy Island by a precarious suspension bridge. Unfortunately the bridge is closed to the public. Nevertheless there is a fine view of the lighthouse, built in 1909 and nowautomatic. This is where wildlife really flourishes. The RSPB confidently expect about 3,000 guillemots, 400 razorbills and 100 puffins each year. The best time to come is during the breeding season in late May or June.

If the weather is fine and sunny there is no finer spot to spend an hour or so than **Trearddur Bay**. Slip down to one of the rocky coves and inlets for a quiet picnic, or if you want to stay, there is plenty of excellent holiday accommodation ranging from simple caravans to the finest hotels. The journey back across the island along the A5 will take you through **Gwalchmai** where the Anglesey Agricultural Show is held each August. Electricity there now comes from the national grid, which is no doubt an improvement on the supply - the first on Anglesey - which was once generated by a watermill.

No one should miss **Plas Newydd**. This elegant 18th-century house by James Wyatt, is the home of the Marquess of Anglesey, and is set in a landscaped garden on the banks of the Menai Strait. It contains an exhibition devoted to the work of Rex Whistler, and a military museum with relics of the Battle of Waterloo. You will find it open from April to late September, and it will be one of the fond memories you take with you as you retrace your route across the Britannia Bridge.

My next adventure took me to the north-east coast and to **Llandudno**. This elegant 19th-century purpose built holiday resort retains its character and the local council lays down strict guidelines which ensure that the many hotels on the sea front perpetuate the old world charm. The curved promenade stretches for two miles between Great Orme to the west and the slightly less impressive bulk of the Little Orme to the east. A visit to Llandudno must always include a trip to the summit of the Great Orme, and there are two excellent ways of getting there. The Great Orme Tramway was opened in 1902, and is the longest cable-hauled tramway in Britain. From Victoria Station in Church Walks the climb is at first steep, the views spectacular. Yet, even that experience is surpassed by the breathtaking exhilaration afforded by the alternative route - The Cable Car. This, too, is reputed to be the longest in Britain.

The Great Orme has a history dating back some 300 million years. The newest tourist attraction in this designated Country Park, the Great Ore Copper Mine, is also of a great age, and is opening the eyes of visitors and experts alike.

Chapter Ten

Over recent years the discovery of rib and thigh bones which once served as scrapers and picks suggest that mining was carried out here more than 4000 years ago. Now it is possible to go on a short guided tour through candlelit Bronze Age tunnels, and one can only marvel at the work that was done by native Britons in a mining complex that went out of business 2000 years ago!

From **Llandudno Junction** it is easy to pay a visit to **Glanwydden** where **The Queen's Head** in the capable hands of Robert Cureton has won many awards for its imaginative food. The A55 will take you to **Rhos-on-Sea**. Here lie the dried-up beds of three long-dead creeks that once carried small timber ships inland from the coast. But for many years now Rhos-on-Sea has been a delightful backwater where holidays proceed at a leisurely pace.

Colwyn Bay next. The Welsh mountains form an impressive backdrop to the wonderful crescent of golden sands. The whole stretch of coastline is a combination of its Victorian ancestry and modern times. The town's Victorian architecture delights the historian, while Theatr Colwyn will provide for the lover of music and drama, a programme of productions that has included a visitby the Welsh National Opera.

The arrow straight road into **Abergele** will take you past Gwyrch Castle, a romantic 19th-century folly which was built to a medieval design by Lloyd Bamford Hesketh. Nestling against wooded hills the castle looks in excellent condition, yet closer examination will reveal broken windows and other signs of neglect. Many ambitious plans for its use have been mooted, sadly, none so far has reached fruition.

Abergele is an historic market town, with some splendid walking country in the hills behind the excellent golf course. Nearby **Pensarn** is its seafront suburb. As well as fine sandy beaches there are long walks here too, along grassy dunes which afford an alternative view of Gwrych Castle.

There is a landmark familiar to all regular visitors to this area; the graceful spire of St Margaret's Church, **Bodelwyddan**. You can reach this wonderful building - popularly known as the Marble Church - by taking the A55 out of Abergele until you reach the first exit. The foundation stone was laid in 1856, and the church was built of native limestone to a design by John Gibson. There is a marvellous hammer-beam roof with arched principals and collars and cusped spandrils together with beautiful stained glass windows by Burne-Jones, T.F. Curtis and Michael O'Connor. Four traceried windows, portraits on the four finials, and finely worked flying buttresses, all combine to make the 202 foot spire unique.

The tiny city of **St Asaph** has a beautiful and superbly appointed cathedral. The site at the top of the narrow, gently sloping High Street has a history dating back to a monastic community founded by St Kentigern, Bishop of Strathclyde, in 560AD. Associated with him are the Kentigern Window in the North Aisle, and the emblem of Salmon and the Ring on the carving in the Choir ceiling. His successor was Asaph who gave his name to the City and Diocese in 570AD.

In passing it is worth mentioning that archaeological treasures abound in this part of the world. There are hundreds of prehistoric burial grounds and a site in a cave close to St Asaph dates back some 250,000 years.

My journey towards Rhyl brought me within sight of **Rhuddlan Castle**, which dates back to 1277 - again courtesy of Edward I - but it is built on the site once occupied by other castles dating back to the 10th century. **Rhuddland** itself is a deceptively sleepy little town hugging the banks of the River Clwyd. If you take a diversion of two miles or so along the A5151 you will reach **Dyserth**, where you must see the spectacular 60 foot waterfalls located in a delightful wooded glen.

Rhyl is a totally different kettle of fish from the resorts I have seen. It is brash, vibrant, unashamedly a traditional seaside playground where life is lived to the full. Undoubtedly the liveliest resort in North Wales.

The A548 runs straight into **Prestatyn**. A very popular resort but without the overt brashness that characterises its close neighbour. Here the attractions are less blatant, yet once sought out they are immensely varied, and again a blend of the modern and traditional. Offa's Dyke was, or is, the defensive earthwork along the Welsh Border and it stretches from Prestatyn to Chepstow. A great walk but not for me, however there are many intrepid walkers who tackle its beautiful length.

The attractions to be reached from the A55 as it makes its way to the English border are of a very different nature from what I have just seen. There is always a new discovery like Pont Dafydd -David's Bridge - at the village of **Waen**. This very old bridge spans the River Clywd, in 1630 it replaced an even older bridge. **Pantasaph** is quite close to the larger market town of **Holywell**, and is the home of an ancient Franciscan Friary.

It came into being in 1852 when Rudolph Viscount Fielding and his wife Louisa invited Capuchin friars to accept a missionary opportunity. As a result, Italian and Flemish friars created an oasis of prayer, and today it offers residence to retreatants of both sexes.

Chapter Ten

Naid Y March, between Pantasaph and **Brynford**, is the name given to a pair of Bronze Age standing stones. The name - The Horse Leap - recalls a legend which tells how Thomas ap Harri jumped the stones on his horse. **Llanasa** lies to the south of the A55, and is well worth a visit because of the delightful stone cottages which in colour are similar to those found in the Cotswolds.

Compared to some major roads the A55 is relatively calm. Nonetheless I was quite pleased to leave it for a while to take a look at **Holywell**, a town with an absorbing history. St Winifred's Well has been a place of pilgrimage for 1300 years and the legend behind this Holy well tells of the fair maid, Winefride. She was the daughter of a local prince, and became a martyr in 660AD. Apparently she was pursued by a young nobleman called Caradoc, whose intentions were far from honourable. He caught her, and in his anger, cut off her head. Where her head came to rest, a spring flowed from the earth. Later, she was brought to life by St Beuno, while Caradoc sank to the ground never to be seen again. The Chapel and Well buildings - erected circa 1500 - are open to visitors. The Cistercian monks of Basingwerk were in possession of the Well from 1240 to 1537, so a drive down the steep hill to Basingwek Abbey makes a neat historical link.

You may remember the name of Master James of St George from Beaumaris Castle on Anglesey. At **Flint** you will come across one of the most unusual fortresses built under his direction. **Flint Castle** was one of four to be built by Edward I after his first campaign against Llywelyn ap Gruffydd. Construction work on the castle and town began in 1277, and quickly involved some 2,300 diggers. Historically the castle is remembered for the imprisonment of King Richard II in 1399 who was then transported to London where he abdicated. A unique feature is the Great Tower of Donjon, which is outside the main structure and from which you can get a wonderful view of the Dee Estuary.

Driving into **Mold** down a steep hill brought me past a modern complex which many feel is the cultural heart of the town, if not the whole of North Wales. Within neatly-lawned landscaped grounds overlooking the town is the Civic Centre - Mold is the county town of Clywd - the studios of HTV, and Theatr Clwyd. This is a marvellous venue which stages the very best in theatre, dance, film and music, plus a variety of exhibitions. Entertainment here is of a standard rarely found outside London - indeed, Theatr Clywd is the only regional theatre to have transferred ten shows to the West End in three years.

The parish church is 500 years old. Stanley, Lord of the Manor of Mold, and his second wife, Margaret Beaufort, were learned, and devout, and they also had considerable wealth. They undertook the rebuilding of the 'Stanley churches' of which Mold is a fine example. There is a stunning window portraying the Patron Saints of Britain. It commemorates the landscape painter, Richard Wilson, whose tomb is outside the window. The town is delightful and has lively street markets on Wednesday and Saturdays. There are many features of historical interest within a few miles, all of them in glorious unspoilt countryside.

The quickest way to learn about Wrexham is in The Heritage Centre in King Street, where a permanent exhibition traces the story of the town since the Bronze Age. Wrexham is often described as the 'Capital of North Wales', and has grown from a small market town into a major shopping centre. There have been many changes in recent years, including pedestrianisation of part of the town centre, and the opening of The People's Market.

The Parish Church of St Giles was built in the late 15th and early 16th centuries, and is one of the 'Seven Wonders of Wales'. Incidentally all seven are mentioned in the 19th century rhyme which goes:

Pistyll Rhaeadr and Wrexham Steeple,
Snowdon;s Mountain without its people,
Overton Yew Trees, St Winefride's Well,
Llangollen Bridge and Gresford Bells.

You reach the church by strolling through Church Walks, a gentle little backwater with quaint half-timbered buildings. The church is at least the third to be built on the site - there was one already standing in 1220. It is a church full ofinterest and one or two surprises.

Before I set off to explore the border country starting at Chirk, I went to **Holt** taking the A534 out of Wrexham. Apart from its beautiful Norman church,Holt is so closely linked with **Farndon** that you proceed from one to the other without noticing the difference. There is the ancient, narrow bridge crossing the River Dee, a brief wait if the traffic lights are against you, but no matter which direction you are taking, if the prominent signs are ignored then, logically, there should be nothing at all to say that one town has been left behind and another entered. Yet, each town has its own, distinctive character and charm. Each has developed quite differently - and the reason is that Holt and Farndon, not only straddle the beautiful River Dee, but also the border between England and Wales.

I love **Bangor-on-Dee** (Bangor-is-y-Coed) with its superb medieval bridge spanning the River. Racegoers will already know of the racecourse

Chapter Ten

which provides an excellent mix of steeplechasing, hurdle races, and the occasional National Hunt Flat Race. South east of Bangor lies the village of **Hanmer** - you can reach it by taking the A525 and the A539 - where in the 15th century the legendary Welsh leader Owain Glydwr married Margaret Hanmer. Close by is **Penley**, which is believed to be the only thatched school in Britain. **Overton** is a mile or so further on. In St Mary's Churchyard you will find the glorious yew trees mentioned as one of the 'Seven Wonders of Wales.'

Chirk from the south is the Gateway to Wales and for many years it was a bottleneck on Thomas Telford's London to Holyhead A5 road. Thankfully, the heavy traffic now bypasses the town, and conditions are much improved for residents and visitors.

Chirk Castle has been continuously occupied since it was built by a Marcher Lord, Roger Mortimer, in the early 14th-century, and the elegant staterooms with Adam-style furniture, tapestries and portraits bear testimony to the loving care bestowed on it over the years. On a more sombre note, there is also a nightmare dungeon which reminds us all of the violence and cruelty that once ravaged the Welsh Marches. Now looked after by the National Trust, the castle is located one and a half miles west of the town, set in beautiful gardens amid fine parkland. Offa's Dyke traverses the grounds. In the 12th century St Mary's Church you will see monuments to theMyddleton family occupiers of Chirk Castle for almost 400 years.

Two immense structures are famous landmarks hereabouts: a wonderful viaduct constructed in 1848 to carry the former Great Western Railway, and running alongside and below it Telfords Shropshire Union Canal aqueduct, built in 1801. Both of these are best viewed on foot - and you will be able to see a quarter mile long canal tunnel, which lies immediately to the north. Along the A5 and within a few miles you will pass close to yet another spectacular aqueduct, this one an iron trough, 1006 feet long which soars 121 feet above the River Dee between Froncasyllte and Trevor. It is the Pontcysyllte Aqueduct, again the work of Thomas Telford.

If you remain on the A5 you can easily pass through Llangollen and feel that you have not missed a great deal. That would be a pity. You must turn right at the traffic lights and proceed down Castle Street, and at once you will see that this is a little town of great character. There is a large car park, and you will find that many of the attractions here are within easy walking distance. Trevor Bridge is one of the ' seven wonders' dating back to the 14th century. Beneath it the waters of the River Dee tumble wildly over black rocks. Here, white water canoeing championships have been held, on a testing and hazardous course.

Wales

A handsomely converted Baptist Chapel in Castle Street is now the European Centre for traditional and Regional Cultures, and reflects Llangollen's stature as the home of the International Music Eisteddfod.

The Llangollen Steam Railway is of standard gauge and was restored by volunteers. It will enthrall steam buffs, while others will simply sit back and enjoy the five and a half mile trip through beautiful countryside. Along the route there are stations, halts and restored workshops, all open to visitors throughout the year. The trips start from Trevor Bridge, and continue up the Dee Valley as far as **Glyndyfrydwy**.

Plas Newydd must be seen although it is a bit of a climb up Hill Street. This is a wonderful half-timbered building with ornate woodwork and a lovely interior filled with rare medieval oak carvings. Inside and out it is beautiful. It was the home of Lady Eleanor Ponsonby and Miss Sarah Butler, two Irishwomen who eloped from Waterford in 1778 and became known as the 'Ladies of Llangollen. In Sarah's words, the area is 'the beautifullest countie in the world.'

You can view Llangollen Canal by taking a more gentle climb up Wharf Hill. There is an information museum for canal enthusiasts, and wonderfully relaxing trips on horse-drawn barges. Many of the local walks are very strenuous but keen walkers will delight in the views from the Panorama Walk - another section of the Offa's Dyke National Trail - Llantysilio Mountain, and Geraint's Hill.

From Llangollen you will have a drive of no more than fifteen or sixteen miles to **Ruthin** which has been a seat of administrative and commercial importance for more than 700 years, and recent discoveries suggest a Roman connection. It has St Peter's Square in a lovely elevated position with splendid old buildings put to excellent modern use. The half-timbered old Courthouse of 1401 is now the National Westminster Bank. Exmewe Hall is now in the hands of Barclays. Outside its doors is the Maen Huail Stone, said to be where King Arthur had a rival beheaded.

As you wander across the Square your eyes will be drawn to the Myddleton Arms, which is at it should be. For gazing back at you will be the 'Eyes of Ruthin', an extraordinary multi-dormer roof in the Dutch style whose seven windows flash in the bright sun. It was built in the 16th century. In CastleStreet is Nantclwyd House, a fine Elizabethan town house built around an earlier medieval structure. A little further along is the pillared entrance to a long, shaded drive which will bring you to Ruthin Castle. Now a gracious hotel, it was built between 1277 and 1282 by Edward I.

Chapter Ten

During the Civil War the garrison at Ruthin capitulated to Cromwell's forces after a severe bombardment, and in 1646 the castle was demolished. The ruins and land were owned by the Myddleton family from 1677, and remained in a sorry state until 1826, when a castellated, two storey, double block of limestone was built on the south-east corner of the ruined site. Then, in 1849, part of that building too was demolished, and the present building designed by Henry Clutton, was erected on the same site.

Eight miles north-west of Ruthin along the A525 is **Denbigh**, also set on a hill, with a castle that dominates the town. Denbigh has ample free parking, most of it close to the town centre. This is important, because although High Street itself is well elevated, there is a stiff walk to the castle - and it is best approached on foot.

You will reach it through the impressive Burgess Gate, or by passing Leicester's Church (intended to supplant St Asaph Cathedral) and St Hilary's Church tower, which will bring you to the green where the medieval Denbigh once stood. This is another of the strongholds Edward I built as part of his plans for subjugating Wales.

Construction under the direction of Henry de Lacy was begun in 1282 - and there is a strong gatehouse with a trio of towers. The town walls are almost complete. The castle is sited on a limestone bluff, and there are splendid views. The town is delightful with an exceptionally wide High street flanked by colonnades. If you are here on any Wednesday you will be able to wander among the stalls in the small but lively street market. If perchance your visit includes Boxing Day you will see a strange happening - a barrel race that takes place on a straw-lined course up and down the High Street.

Having travelled through Anglesey, Denbighshire and Caernarvonshire, and touched on Merioneth. Now for Montgomeryshire and a final tour of the southern part of Merioneth.

There is a wonderful scenic route out of Dolgellau, up a steep, winding road past Cader Idris, which at almost 3,000 feet is an attraction to both walkers and climbers. Charles Darwin once said that 'Old Cader is a grand fellow' but my own recent memories of that road are of descending it and experiencing some shock as an RAF jet came screaming up towards me from somewhere far below!

Eventually the road begins to tumble down towards less giddy heights, and before taking the B4405 towards **Trwyn** it's worth going on the couple of miles into **Corris**. You will first pass through **Corris Uchaf**, along a stretch of road lined with pine, beach and oak, and picturesque cottages once used by quarry workers. The craft centre at Corris is open all year. In summer you will appreciate the splendid picnic area, while in winter the warmth of the restaurant will beckon after you have watched various craftspeople at work.

Almost as soon as you turn onto the B4405 you are on the shores of Lake Tal-y-Llyn. For a mile or so the southern bank of a stretch of water is breathtakingly beautiful, and especially popular with fishermen in season.

At **Abergynolwyn** there is a small slate museum and here too is the inland terminus of the Tallyn railway. This 'Great Little train of Wales' - there are eight of them altogether - was bought and rescued in 1951, and now travels the six miles or so from Tywyn through wild hills and thickwoodland around **Nant Gwernol** and Abergynolwyn. On the way it passes close to the rushing waters of Dolgoch Falls.

Tywyn is a popular seaside resort which has six miles of firm sands. At the right time of the year the conditions are perfect for swimming, sailing and windsurfing.

Before you drive into **Aberdovey** on the A493 you will see on the right the lush greens of Aberdovey's championship golf course, whose two mile long links occupy an enviable position twixt hills and sea. Aberdovey is almost Mediterranean in character, with the proximity of the Gulf Stream ensuring that temperatures are always higher than further inland. Its pleasures are unashamedly of the sea, with fishing, windsurfing and waterskiing favoured sports, and private yachts of all sizes making splashes of bright colour in the waters of the pretty harbour. Many of its fine hotels and guesthouses were built during the Edwardian era when it was at the height of its popularity.

The drive inland towards **Machynlleth** is along an exceptionally pretty stretch of the A493 that hugs the cliffs as it takes one through an area of the Dovey Estuary rich in rhododendrons. The town has an impressive broad main street and a wonderful old clock tower with needle sharp spire and arched openings.

In 1991 Machynlleth celebrated the 700th anniversary of its market charter. It was granted in 1291 by Edward I to Owen de la Pole, Prince of Powys, and enabled two fairs in Spring and Autumn and a weekly street market ' to be held in perpetuity'. The midweek market has been held ever since, and has grown to become one of the largest and liveliest street markets in Wales.

Chapter Ten

It would be strange to visit any part of Wales without hearing mention of Owain Glyndwr, and Machynlleth does not disappoint. The great man held a Welsh parliament here in 1404. An old stone building in Maengwyn Street is now the Owain Glyndwr Centre, and home to an absorbing heritage exhibition that displays his campaigns and charts his contribution to Welsh history.

Newtown is the commercial capital of Montgomeryshire, and like Machynlleth it has a well-known street market held on Tuesdays with one in the Market Hall on the same day. The town has a delightful situation in a loop of the River Severn, and as the home of the Welsh flannel industry it was at one time known as the 'Busy Leeds of Wales'. One of the original hand-loom weaving factories
is now the Newtown Textile Museum on Commercial Road. You will find in Newtown a bewildering mixture of architecture with Tudor, Gothic, Jacobean, Georgian, Victorian and modern buildings standing cheek by jowl so that scarcely two blocks are alike. The Royal Welsh Warehouse is the tallest building in the town. It was built in 1861 by Sir Pryce-Pryce Jones. His mail order company was the world's first - so now you know where all those catalogues originated! Queen Victoria was one of the company's customers, and the warehouse is still open to the public to this day.

Montgomery, a delightful border town is a wonderland of Georgian architecture, perhaps the finest example of which is the imposing Town Hall with its white clock tower. The ruins of the old Montgomery Castle stand on a rocky promontory overlooking the town, a position which made it virtually impregnable until the Civil War. For once Edward I had no hand in it; it was built at the command of Henry III in 1223.

The garrison Parish Church of St Nicholas contains the chapel of the poet, George Herbert, and in the graveyard you will find an odd grave. John Davies was convicted of murder in 1821. Before he died he swore his innocence, and declared that as proof nothing would grown on his grave for one hundred years. When you visit the Robber's Grave you can judge for yourself whether he was innocent or not!

Not many people know that **Welshpool** was originally called Poole. It is built on the banks of the River Severn, and long ago the flatlands were criss-crossed by a network of creeks known as 'pills'. These were frequently devastated by flash floods from the river, hence the town's original name. But they have long since been drained, and the name of the town was eventually changed to Welshpool to distinguish it from the English town of Poole.

You will see a wide diversity of attractive buildings and as well as having the river close by, Welshpool is also a canal town. The Montgomery Canal passes through the town. It was part of a grand scheme to link the rivers Mersey and Severn. Work finished in 1821, and it was a busy inland waterway until long decline led to its closure in 1944. Volunteers are valiantly bringing it back to life, and at the Powysland Museum situated in a restored canal warehouse you can see some important local collections covering the archaeology and social history of Montgomeryshire **Powys Castle** stands on a dramatic, rocky outcrop one mile south of Welshpool. It was built by the medieval Princes of Upper Powys in the 13th century, and has been occupied continuously for 700 years. In 1587 it was bought by Sir Edward Herbert, and has been the family's ancestral home ever since. That family, and later the Clives - descendants of Clive of India - continually laboured to create a jewel of a building set in the most beautiful gardens. These are thought to have been planted by William Wilde. Dating from the 17th-century, they are laid out in four formal terraces influenced by French and Italian styles. Those hanging, terraces are the most famous in the world. Each is 200 yards long, falling away towards the Severn Valley. In the 18th-century an informal wilderness was added. The extensive parklands were landscaped by Capability Brown in the 19th-century. The castle is full of atmosphere and crammed with treasures. In particular are those brought from India by Clive and his son, and on display in the Clive Museum since 1987: relics of Tipu, Sultan of Mysore, Moghul jades, textiles and ivories, and a wonderful array of Chinese and Indian bronzes.

Amongst the many wonderful sights to be seen there is one just eight miles or so from **Llangedwyn**. It is well off the beaten track but take the B4396 towards **Llanrhaedr-ym-Mochnant** onto a minor road into stunning countryside. Cadair Berwyn lies ahead of you as you approach the Berwyn Mountains beyond which lies Corwen and the Dee Valley. It is **Pistyll Rhaeadr** I wanted to see, one of the highest waterfalls in Britain, cascading over a narrow ledge with delicate trees on all sides. George Burrows found this an enchanting place, and said of Pistyll Rhaeadr 'I never saw water falling so gracefully, so much like thin beautiful threads, as here'. There is a legend which relates how giants were disturbed while building a bridge and dropped the huge rocks which now lie scattered at its base.

Driving south-west along the A487 from Machynlleth will immediately transport you into an area with an astonishingly rich history. I was not aware that the lands belonging to the Welsh once stretched as far north as Strathclyde in Scotland. They did and in 451 AD the chieftain Cunedda and his sons marched an army south to the area we know as Wales, where they succeeded in freeing those lands from seaborne invaders. A district known as Tyno Goch was awarded to Cunedda's son, Ceredig. Today Ceredigion -

Chapter Ten

the land of Cerig - stretches from the Dovey Estuary to Cardigan in the south, with its inland boundary following a semi-circular path.

My route took me along the south side of the Dovey Estuary where I visited the Ynis-Hir Reserverun by the RSPB. The easiest way to find it is to follow the signposts from the village of **Eglwysfach**. The reserve attracts some 67 species of bird to its salt and fresh water marshes, reed beds, peat bogs, woodland and open hillside.If you are a keen bird-watcher you will be reaching for your field-glasses at the mere mention of the pied fly-catcher, wood warbler, blacktrap and treecreeper.

Borth has three miles of virtually unbroken sands. It also has an interesting legend. Stumps in the sand, which you will see if the tide is right, are said to be the vestigial remains of an ancient forest - the last reminder of the drowned Welsh lowlands of Cantre'r Gwaelod.

The last village before Aberystwyth is **Clarach**, where the fine beach is sheltered by steep shale cliffs along which there are magnificent coastal walks. This was my first visit to **Aberystwyth**. It is one of Wales' favourite seaside towns, and for the academic it provides unrivalled facilities with the University of Wales and the National Library of Wales on the one site off Penglais Road. There are three good beaches. Tanybwlch Beach to the south of the harbour, while North and South beaches are separated by the wind driven headland which is the site of Aberystwyth Castle. Its history has a familiar pattern. Built by Edward I in 1277, damaged and rebuilt in 1282, captured by
Prince Owain Glyndwr in 1404. Uniquely coins from the local silver mine were minted here between 1637 and 1646. The castle was doomed to fall to the enemy soon after: Cromwell's army overcame its defences, and it was blown up in 1649.

An interesting and unusual attraction can be found on the 450 foot summit of Constitution Hill which stands at the north end of North Beach. Equally unusual is the manner in which you can reach the apex. **The Aberystwyth Electric Cliff railway** is the longest in Great Britain. It dates back to Victorian times and once again demonstrates how much we owe to the people who lived and worked in that imaginative age.

The ride to the summit is nothing short of spectacular, and once there you will find, in a fascinating octagonal tower, the **Great Aberystwyth Camera Obscura**. The very name spells out that it was a popular Victorian amusement, and it consists of a massive 14 inch lens which focusses detailed views onto a screen in a darkened viewing gallery. The outside viewing balconies will reward you with a beautiful panorama.

The Vale of Rheidol Railway runs from Aberystwyth to **Devil's Bridge**. It is a narrow gauge steam railway and there are conflicting theories about why it came into being. One suggests that it was opened in 1902 to serve the lead traffic of the valley. Another says that it is the only one of the 'little trains' to have been built to satisfy the tourist trade. At any rate, now it is British Railway's last operational link with the 'age of steam' and is an exciting ride. the line clings to the hillside as it climbs towards Devil's Bridge, affording views of the broad river valley, thickly wooded hillsides, and the wonderful open moorland of Plynlimon. The train is pulled by the engines 'Owain Glyndwr', 'Llewlyn' or 'Prince of Wales' on a journey through a natural wonderland.

Devil's Bridge (Pontarfynach)is a village set amid scenery which needs to be explored at length on foot. There are three bridges over the River Mynach, built one on top of the other. The first dates back to the 11th century, probably built by Cistercian monks. The second bridge was built in 1708, the third in 1901. You can take an easy path to visit the bridges but it is an area of such charm that you will almost certainly opt to do some energetic scrambling. There are 94 steps of Jacob's Ladder to be descended, the 300 foot cascade where the Mynach tumbles through spectacular chasms carved in the rock to join the River Rheidol, and nature trails and footpaths. Not suitable for the disabled or the infirm and please do wear sensible shoes.

You will get a different view of Devil's Bridge after turning right onto the A4120, but you must then turn smartly onto the B4343 which will take you south along a lovely, winding route to the village of **Pontrhydfendigaid**. The Cistercian Abbey of Strata Florida was founded in 1164 and by 1184 had acquired thye patronage of Rhys ap Gruffydd, the last independent native prince of South Wales. Here at Ystrad Fflur, in 1238, Llywelyn the Great called together the Welsh Princes to swear allegiance to his son, Dafydd. Later, hard on the trail of Owain Glyndwr (the last native prince of a fully-independent Wales), Henry IV expelled the monks, and took the abbey as his headquarters. The building fell into disrepair after the Dissolution, but you can still see the magnificent Norman arch. In the abbey grounds are buried some of the princes and princesses of old Ceredigion, while Dafydd ap Gwilyn, the amorous medieval Welsh poet - still popular to this day - is buried under the spreading yew tree in the adjacent churchyard. Once the Westminster of Wales, the Abbey's name means 'Vale of Flowers'.

Tregaron lies at the junction of several roads, in countryside which is now a Natural Nature Reserve and famous for the variety and numbers of wild birds. George Borrow was reminded of 'an Andalusian village overhung by its sierra', and the mile upon mile of heathered upland to the east was once the haunt of Twm Sion Cati, the Robin Hood of Wales.

Chapter Ten

Before leaving this stunningly beautiful area and making my way towards the coast, I continued along the B4343 as far as **Llanddewi Brefi**. Ceredigion was the birthplace of St David, Patron Saint of Wales, and the church at this tiny village is dedicated to his name.

In **Llandiloes** we are back in Montgomeryshire, and this bonny little town is the first the River Severn encounters as it flows down from its source in the high moorlands of Plimlumon. History here in full measure with a Market Charter granted in 1280 and a 16th-century Market Hall of black and white timber which is the only one in Wales to survive on its original site. The town owes much of its prosperity to the lead mining which took place in the surrounding hills. Relics of the woollen trade can still be seen in the neat row of weaver's cottages, and there is a fine, half-timbered merchant's house on Llangurug Road.

Natural and man made lakes abound in the Montgomeryshire countryside, and Llyn Clywedog, between Llandiloes and Machynlleth is one of the more recent of the latter. The dam was built in the 1960s, and is the tallest in Britain. From Llandiloes you can reach the lake by taking the B4518; it is a short and very pleasant drive. LLyn Clywedog is used to control flooding on the River Severn, but wherever there is an expanse of water you will find sailors of one kind or another. This is also ideal walking country in the green pastureland and sweeping open hills that surround it. The three mile route of the Llyn Clywedog Scenic Trail has been carefully designed to reveal the best features of the reservoir and the wooded slopes flanking the deep valley. An alternative walk pays more attention to the engineering feats involved in the dam's construction. The Clywedog Gorge Trail is self-guided, and also takes in the abandoned lead mine.

There are two rivers of note as you travl south along the A470. One is the River Wye, and the other is the River Elan whose course follows another wonderful valley.

The gateway to the Elan Valley is **Rhayader**, a town dating back to the fifth century and the setting for one of the most important markets of the area. For a small town it also has an extraordinarily violent past: in Tudor times the assize judge was murdered and the town razed, the castle was destroyed during the Civil War, and more recently it was the scene of the Rebecca Riots which were protests against toll gates. Like Machynelleth, the town centre features a fine clock tower, and in Rhayader the main streets radiate from this focal point.

There are five reservoirs quite close by and no shortage of Information Centres for those wishing to explore this wonderland of lakes and hills. The main one to note is the Elan Valley Visitor Centre which is located on the B5418 south-west of Rhayader. Interesting to note that it was these dams Barnes Wallace used when trying out the famous bouncing bomb.

Although **Llandrindod Wells** is not an old town, the chalybeate springs there have been used from time immemorial. The first reference to the Saline Spring was in 1694. The town was built to fulfil the Victorian's increasing demand for healing waters. They came for sulphur for their complexions, magnesium to aid their digestion, chalybeate for the blood and saline for 'inner cleanliness' - all were available and still are at the restored Pump Room in Rock Park. There is a good leaflet available from the Memorial Gardens in Temple Street which proves to be an excellent guide around the town.

Hundred House Village has a splendid inn of the same name and it is possible that when the Shire was divided into 'hundreds' and courts were held, they might well have used the Inn as well as the Vicarage. The Hundred House Inn was used by cattle drovers, who, because of the distance between West Wales and London, would provide their cattle with shoes - and ducks and geese had their feet dipped in tar!

Builth Wells is another example of a town that grew up around a spa, although the saline and sulphur springs are no longer used. Ask a farming Welshman - there for the Monday sheep and cattle markets - about the town and he will immediately lift his head and tell you with pride of the Royal Welsh Agricultural Show which is held here each year. It is the biggest agricultural show in the country, and is held on a permanent site alongside the River Wye.

Llandovery is quite charming with Town Hall and Market Square and a feeling of history which comes from being a former cattle collection point for drovers about to make the long walk to the English cities. Stock markets are still held two or three times weekly, and market stalls make a splash of colour under the Town Hall each Friday.

I found the task of exploring the peninsula to the south of Cardigan Bay - the area now known as Dyfed - quite daunting. It takes in most of the coast in a great sweep from Aberaeron right round to Carmarthen plus a whole lot of inland areas of special interest.

Aberaeron does not immediately spring to mind as a place likely to attract lovers of history but how wrong can one be. I soon discovered that in this corner of Wales one house in every four in Aberaeron is designated of special architectural interest and it is one of Wales' first planned towns. August

Chapter Ten

1807 seems to be the recognised starting point of any study of the town's history. On that date Royal Assent was given to an 'Act to enable the Reverend Alban Thomas Jones-Gwynne, his Heirs and Assigns, to repair and enlarge the Harbour and Port of Aberaeron...and to regulate the mooring of Ships and Vessels there'. The good Reverend carried out his task well providing money for design and construction which involved the eminent engineer John Rennie, and takingthe advice of John Nash on the layout and design of the fledgling town.

The town is now a gracious, picturesque place, with well laid out streets and squares, and a charming, stone-walled harbour. It is very worthwhile spending some time here.

From Aberaeron to **Newquay** is just a short distance even on the minor roads. Establishing New Quay's origins is difficult, though an admiralty survey undertaken in 1748 does mention the name, albeit with a different spelling (New Key). It is a lovely little town, thoroughly deserving its reputation as the 'jewel of the Welsh Coast'. It is built on terraced slopes which fall steeply to a crescent of sand and a sheltered harbour, and is thought to be the town Dylan Thomas used as a model for Llareggrub in'Under Milk Wood'. He spent some time in new Quay between 1944 and 1945.

Aberporth is another wonderful seaside gem with a snug little bay and a wedge of clean sand that will delight all children and many adults. Moderately high cliffs on either side make fine natural boundaries, a comforting situation. It is a place well known for its cliff-top walks and one in particular is very popular. It links Aberporth with the neighbouring village of **Tresaith** - no more than a mile to the east - and at low tide you can then go on to reach the golden beach at **Penbryn**. If you take that path you are moving back towards New Quay. Penbryn beach, once beloved by smugglers, can also be reached by road from **Sarnau** on the A487. The name Tresaith is said to derive from the landing of seven banished Irish princesses, who settled in the area and married local Welshmen. If you have no romance in you then you are more likely to believe that the name comes from the local river - the Saith!!

Llangrannog is a little further on in the same direction, another village bounded by rocky headlands. One of them, which I believe is known as Ynys-Lochtyn, is worth exploring more fully for it has the remains of a prehistoric fort.

The correct name for **Cardigan** is Aberteifi - the mouth of the Teifi - and the word Cardigan is a derivation from a word already familiar to us: Ceredigion, for which Aberteifi was once the county town. Today the town is of strategic importance to visitors, not invaders, for its position makes it an ideal base for those wishing to explore the spectacular Pembrokeshire countryside. Cardigan is famous for staging the very first competitive National Eisteddfod, which was held in the castle under the patronage of Rhys ap Gruffudd in 1176. That event was commemorated in 1976 when the Eisteddfod came back to the town to celebrate the eight hundredth anniversary of Rhy's original event.

Cilgeran an be found by driving a little way south of Cardigan, and on a crag overlooking a deep gorge of the River Teifi the two powerful towers of Cilgerran Castle dominate a romantic scene. The castle was begun in 1220 and was the subject of a well knwon painting by Richard Wilson. No finer setting could have been chosen for any fortress - both beautiful and unassailable - and in August each year it is all enhanced with the staging of the annual coracle races.

A glance at any good map will show you that Cardigan is the start of the Pembrokeshire Coast Path which wriggles its tortuous way around the jagged coastline and is almost unbroken until it reaches distant Milford Haven. Heading south from Cardigan you will find the village of **St Dogmaels** by taking the B4546 especially taking a look at the ruins of the Benedictine Abbey. The story is interesting. TheBenedictine Abbey was founded by monks of the French order of Tiron in 1113. The Sagranus Stone now in the parish church dates from the 6th century, and the Latin inscriptions on its face provided the key to the interpretation of the ogham alphabet of the ancient Giodelic language.

The church at **Nevern** - quite hard to find, best off the A487 and B4582 - was founded by St Brynach. A dark avenue of yews leads to the church door and one of them exudes a blood-red stain from a sawn branch. This is the bleeding Yew. The ogham alphabet is again encountered on the Vitalianus Stone which stands beside the church porch: it commemorates a prominent man who died around 500 AD. This one I found absolutely charming: there is a carved cross some 13feet high standing in the churchyard, and from it, each year on April 7th (St Brynach's Day), the first cuckoo sings.

Another interesting church can be found at Eglwyswrw which lies on the A487. This one is an early foundation that may have been built within a pre-Christian earthwork. Roughly between Nevern and Eglwyswrw you will find Pentre Ifan, which was one of the finest burial chambers in the country. A massive capstone is supported by three tall pillars, and George Owen once described it as 'one of the wonders of Pembrokeshire'.

Chapter Ten

Newport is an Ancient Borough with its own Mayor, Burgesses and Court Leet. It lies on the slope of a hill beneath a Norman castle, and below the town the River Nevern meanders across a wide estuary to enter the sea in Newport Bay, the Welsh name for Newport is Tredraeth Edrywy, and it is said not only that the original settlement stood near the shore, but that it was 'swallowed by the sands, like another Peranzabuloe'.

Not far from the old trading quays there is a beautiful sandy beach, with the shallow surf of **Newport Sands** offering safe bathing for all. If you intend staying here for any length of time, you will find plenty to do, with sailing, pony-trekking and golf - on a pleasant, nine hole course adjoining Newport Sands. Fishermen of all temperaments will find sport here. Salmon, sea trout and brown trout are found in the Nevern, and surf fishing from Newport Sands will often bring good catches of bass. During the season there is also salmon fishing from those same sands, using seine-nets.

In 1191 the Lord of Cemais, William Martin, was driven out of Nevern, and he established his stronghold at Newport where he built a castle. The castle was captured by Llywelyn the Great in 1215, and by Llywelyn the Last in 1257; during the revolt of Owain Glyndwr it suffered heavily, and was reckoned to be worth no more than £33!. By 1583 the castle had been in ruins for many years, and it was not until 1859 that the gatehouse was converted into a residence by Sir Thomas Lloyd, and the ruins substantially restored. You can still see what remains of the Hunter's Tower, the Kitchen Tower and the Great Tower, and the site on a spur standing over the estuary is most impressive.

Cwym-yr-Eglwys is tucked away at the eastern curve of Newport Bay, and this 'valley of the church' is one of the loveliest little bays in Wales. Most road atlases will show you Dinas Head, but only the larger Ordnance Survey maps will show the tiny peninsula bearing the name **Dinas Island**. In fact this small promontory was once cut off from the mainland by the Pwllgwaelod - Cwmyreglwys depression, and was once known as Ynys Fach Lyffan Gawr - ' the little island of Lyffan the Giant'. The Pembrokeshire Coastal Path leads around it, and there are two interesting books by R.M. Lockley -Island Farmers and The Golden Year - which tell of the author's life on Dinas Island Farm.

I was eager to visit **Fishguard**. With its wonderful harbour and fascinating town, it demands attention, but beyond that it also holds a unique place in the history of our islands; it was the scene of the last invasion of Britain. In 1797, French troops led by Colonel William Tate, an American, landed in a rocky bay beneath Carresgwastad Point, with the intention of rousing the population against George III. Popular legend tells us that the attack ended when the troops mistook Welsh women wearing traditional red cloaks for British soldiers. They advanced no further than Goodwick Sands, where they laid down their arms. Today a stone marks their landing place at Carregwastad.

The eastern coast of Dyfed has several fair-sized islands of the kind which are always formed as exposed coastlines are gradually eroded by the hungry seas. Ramsey Island and Skomer Island are the two largest, and from Fishguard I took the A487, this time towards **St Davids**. I knew that it is quite easy to get from the town to the coastal path, from which Ramsey is clearly visible - but my main intention was to spend some time at St David's Bishop's Palace, which I had briefly visited once before. It was built largely by Henry de Gower (1328-47). The richly decorative building stands within the Cathedral Close, among a group of buildings unique in Wales. The arcaded parapets of Bishop Henry extend along both main wings of the palace, and are decorated with some of the finest medieval sculptured heads and animal figures in Wales. The entrance to the Great Hall is also impressive, and the other great joy is the piscina in the Palace Chapel - a stone basin which carries away water used in rinsing chalices. Supposedly the presence of the Cathedral makes St David's the smallest city in Britain. The people of St Asaph will tell you differently!

Skomer Island can be rached by taking the A487 for six or seven miles in a south-westerly direction, then switching to a delightful minor road that hugs the coastal path. Skomer is included in the Marine Nature Reserve which takes in the island and the coastline around the Marlowe Peninsula - the only one of its kind in Wales, and only the second in the UK. Over 150 seals are born regularly making it the second largest pupping site in South West Britain. In addition, it is home to the largest concentration of sea birds such as puffins, guillemots and 5 razor bills in England and Wales, and over half the world population of the Manx Shearwater.

To get to Pembroke I meandered, quite intentionally, and found the easiest way, having got quite lost en route, was to take the B4327 and follow that to **Haverfordwest**. This market town of narrow streets which overlooks the River Cleddau is attractive, and like many others all over Wales is overlooked by an ancient castle. Built in 1100 it was part of a chain of fortifications erected across Pembrokeshire by English invaders to pen in the Welsh to the north. Later modifications strengthened the walls which are between six and twelve feet thick, and although Cromwell ordered the castle's destruction during the Civil War, much of it was left intact. It is now an appropriate site for the area's Information Centre, and it also houses a museum.

Chapter Ten

The road into Pembroke passes conveniently close to **Carew** with its castle built between 1280 and 1310, and considerably enlarged in the 15th century. It is particularly interesting because it has a long window and large galleries which illustrate the transition from the original stronghold to a charming Elizabethan country residence. Also in Carew there is a tidal mill -**Carew French Mill** - which is one of only three restored tidal mills in Britain, and the only one remaining intact in Wales. This grand, four-storey building dates back to 1558, and almost all its original machinery has been retained. Restoration of the huge south wheel has taken place in recent years.

Whilst there is no apparent direct route from Carew to **Upton**, although the distance is no morethan a mile, it is somewhere worth seeking out. Upton Castle grounds offer hours of enjoyment. The 35 acres contain almost 200 different species of trees and shrubs. Woodland and formal gardens are thoughtfully provided with all weather footpaths. There is also an interesting 11th-century family chapel.

Pembroke did not begin its development until the late 11th century although there is ample evidence, with standing stones and burial mounds, of an earlier, prehistoric occupation. Not surprisingly the development was around the splendid castle, the oldest in West Wales. It is certainly one of the best preserved Norman castles in Britain. It was founded by the Montgomerys in 1093, and around the year 1200 work was started on the Great Tower. This enormous structure is 75ft high and has walls at the base up to 19ft thick. Its circular shape is unusual, and it is also roofed, which was not common practice. Other claims to fame include the birth within the castle walls of the founder of the House of Tudor - Henry VII. It was held by both Royalists and Parliamentarians during the Civil War, and the siege that led to its final surrender was led by Cromwell himself. You may visit the castle on any day of the year except Christmas Day, Boxing Day and New Year's Day. From the end of May to the end of August guided tours are available.

The town experienced a period of decline until about 1814, when the Royal Naval Dockyard was moved from Milford Haven to Pembroke Dock, and brought prosperity with it. Since that date over 250 warships have been built at Pembroke Dock, as well as three Royal yachts for Queen Victoria. If nautical history interests you there are boat trips which will take you to see Warrior, the first iron-clad warship, which was launched in 1860 and is now at Pembroke Ferry. From there they continue the short distance to Milford Haven.

Milford Haven is both the name of the town and the stretch of water it overlooks, which was fittingly described by Nelson as ' one of the finest natural harbours in the world'. In fact the town was founded in 1793 - by Sir William Hamilton, husband of Nelson's mistress, Emma - and was a whaling port before becoming a dockyard. Milford Haven was used by Henry II to launch his invasion of Ireland in 1172, and Henry Tudor, Earl of Richmond landed there in 1485 on his was to defeating Richard III at the Battle of Bosworth Field. Since 1960 Milford Haven has gradually expanded to become a major oil port, its huge refineries fed by supertankers from all over the world.

Daniel Defoe described **Tenby** as ' the most agreeable town on all the south coast of Wales, except Pembroke', and since then thousands of visitors have echoed those words in one way or another. It is sheer delight, a compact little town with shops and houses almost touching across the narrow streets packed inside the town walls. Appropriately, the remains of a 13th-century Norman castle overlook the old fishing harbour, standing on the site occupied by a Welsh fort called Dinbych-y-Pysgod - Little Fort of the Fish. The town is also the birthplace of the portrait painter Augustus John, and of Robert Recorde, the mathematician who invented the = sign.

In Tenby you cannot escape the wonderful beaches, four of which encircle the headland. But they can be boisterous or placid as the fancy takes you, with quiet picnic spots always available to those who will venture away from the crowds.

Carmarthen shares with **Caerleon** the title of the oldest town in Wales, and settlement in the area can be traced back almost 2,000 years. There are remains of a large hill fort at Abergwili, three miles to the east, and a local bastion of Roman rule that was built near the centre of the present town survives in the modern name: Moridunum (mor dinas, or sea fort) became Caer-mori-dunum, and then Carmarthen! A Roman ampitheatre that once seated 5,000 people was identifiedin the 1930s on a site at the east end of Priory Street, and saved for posterity by the quick thinking of a former Borough Engineer, George Ovens. The arena wall has been reconstructed, and adjacent gardens cover still more remains.

Life is nothing without legend to intrigue and inspire, and here Welsh folklore tells how King Arthur's wizard, Merlin, was born near the town in 480AD. The story is given further credence by the decayed stump of an oak that stood at the end of Priory Street and apparently carried his spell: 'When Merlin's oak shall tumble down, then shall fall Carmarthen town'. But a more likely story is that it was planted at Priory Street's junction with Oak Street to commemorate the accession of Charles II to the throne - and what is absolutely certain is that it was removed in the interests of road safety in 1978. Carmarthen is fascinating to explore and demands attention.

Chapter Ten

South West Wales has its own charm. I proceeded along the A40 in the direction of **Llandeilo** with the intention of branching off to view two nearby attractions. The first, **Dinefwr Castle**. This is not one of the country's better known ruins, yet for all that it has an air about it, a certain brooding presence that on gloomy days can set the imagination racing. It was built on the site of an older castle, and its position has a lot to do with its undoubted attraction, for it is poised on the edge of a precipice. Its moats were carved from the rock and, like the keep and parts of the curtain wall which are all that remain, were designed to keep out the enemy in the long struggles with the Anglo-Normans. From 877 AD it was the principal residence of the princes of South Wales. I'm told the castle can be reached by walking through Castle Woods, where there are fine nature trails and superb parkland landscaped by Capability Brown. The paths are waymarked, and easily followed, though if you are going to be brave enough to walk from Llandeilo, you have a long walk ahead of you. En route you will come across the church of Llandyfeisant, which is within the park and is reputed to be built on the site of a Roman temple. The second is **Paxton's Tower**, a mile or so south of Dinefwr Castle, and surely one of the finest follies ever. Designed by Samuel Pepys Cockerel, it is triangular and crenellated, and was apparently erected in honour of Lord Nelson. It dates from the 19th century, and affords magnificent views of the Tywi valley. National Trust owned, it is open all the year round, whereas Dinefwr Castle is open only on appointed days.

There is yet another castle a few miles further west. **Dryslwyn** is again in a magnificent position, and was the scene of a three week siege in 1287 at the beginning of a revolt led by Rhys ap Meredudd. Some among you may know that Sappers are soldiers in the Royal Engineers and that their name comes from work they once did which involved the 'digging of saps for the purpose of moving towards the enemy, being under cover at all times'. The reason I bring that up is because Dryslwyn Castle had its defences quite literally undermined when what must have been the distant forerunners of those Sappers dug tunnels under the walls, which led to their collapse. There is a car park and a picnic site at Dryslwyn.

Llandeilo is a pleasant market town, built on a hill, and you will notice that most of the buildings in the main part of the town are early Victorian. the bridge over the river was built in 1848 - a splendid structure. The restored Church is mainly Victorian but has an interesting 13th-century tower. If you turn from the A40 onto the B4302, after a few miles you will reach the skeletal ruins of **Talley Abbey**. It dates back to the late 12th century when Rhys ap Gruffydd founded a House of Premonstratension Canons, which was severely handled in uprisings and revolts during the Middle Ages. Although once protected by Edward I it was again much abused, and after the rebellion of Owain Glyndwr there was little left of it. Nevertheless the site in the Carmarthenshire hills is a pretty one, and what is left is impressive - part of the central tower of the church has survived and there are two, high-pointed arches and several lancet windows.

If by now you have a nodding acquaintance with the Welsh language you will know that **Pumsaint** means 'five saints'. The name of this pleasant little village comes from the quintuplets born to Cynnyr Farfdrwch ap Gwron ap Cunedda. However my real reason for driving up the A482 was to visit the Roman gold mines at **Dolcaucothi**, which were actually worked as recently as 1938 - though not by the Romans! They were exploiting it almost 2000 years ago, and although you will now have difficulty interpreting the site on your own, there are self-guided trails which you can follow using the explanatory leaflets. As proof of the advanced techniques used so long ago, there is a fragment of a timber waterwheel - used to drain the galleries - in the National Museum at Cardiff.

Back tracking a bit along the A482 and then the A40 my intention was to seek out the village of **Bethlehem**. Not surpisingly this is a popular posting place for Christmas mail. Near it lie the ancient earthwork remains known as Carn Goch. This is well known as the largest Iron Age hill fort in Wales. It is enormous with its two forts spread over 800 metres. The views from here were breathtaking. Stay on the minor roads and you will see **Carreg Cennen**. This one outdoes most castles you will ever see! Its limestone eyrie must be seen to be believed - and if you intend taking a closer look you must be prepared for a stiff climb from the farmyard beneath its walls. The remote, timeless air which pervades appealed to artists during the Romantic Revivial, and it is not hard to understand why. The building dates back to the 13th and 14th centuries, but there was a castle on the site long before then. There is an inner ward with a fine gatehouse, and this is the earliest part of the castle. The arrow slits in the gatehouse walls are of the cross-slit variety, which apparently gave cross-bows more freedom of movement, and thus a greater arc of fire. The castle fell to Edward I in 1277 and seems to have remained in English hands from that date. Edward I gave it to John Gifford and another owner was John of Gaunt. Lancastrian supporters during the Wars of the Roses overcame the defence and the castle was demolished in 1462 to prevent its use as a robbers' refuge. That work was accomplished by 500 men armed with picks and crow bars - a task of monumental proportions!

You will certainly head towards **Trapp** when you leave Carreg Cennen. The latter is isolated and it is really hard to imagine why the village ever came about. There is a good Arts and Crafts Centre here with a charming tea-room. There is also a splendid working Welsh hill farm with a 17th century longhouse and a number of rare and unusual farm animals. Here too you can eat in the converted 18th-century barn. On the menu good home-made

Chapter Ten

farmhouse cooking. Either before or after your meal you can enjoy walking along riverside or hill footpaths. and there is every chance that you will see many of Britain's rarest birds of prey.

Whilst I am aware that from here **Swansea** is close by, I want to leave it for now and tell you about the Gower Peninsula. Gower has long been an Area of Outstanding Natural Beauty, and most of it is protected by the National Trust

and the Gower Society. It is a peninsula but its extreme isolation brought about by the flanking estuaries and the sandstone scarp at its eastern or inland border has enabled it to escape the industry that has mushroomed close by. There is just one major road (the A4118), a sparse network of byways - and that is it. The rest is sheer beauty, an area to explore until intoxicated.

The A4067 comes to an abrupt end just before Mumbles Head which marks the eastern end of the Gower. The name Mumbles actually refers to the two rounded rocks at the entrance to the bay, but has gradually come to cover the whole area from the pier to the shopping centre.

Mumbles is just five miles along the shore from Swansea, but it has established a unique reputation for itself while managing to retain a delightful village atmosphere. I knew Mumbles from details of the lifeboat tragedy, when the entire crew of the Mumbles lifeboat perished during rescues from the merchant ship Tampana. So the images I bore with me were of stormy seas and jagged rocks, and while those conditions do exist, Mumbles boasts wonderful sandy beaches, quaint coves just around the headland, and waters that are ideal for the staging of international yachting events.

Oystermouth is of interest for several reasons, not least the restored church which has a low tower often seen in this corner of Wales. The three bells came to the Mumbles from the burned cathedral of Santiago, Chile, and part of the aisle consists of fragments of Roman paving stones which were found nearby. Oystermouth Castle stands above the A4067; it was constructed in the late 13th century by the infamous Norman lord, de Breos, a member of a family noted for their villainous deeds. The drum towers that once flanked the main gateway leading to the single courtyard have long since disappeared, but there is doubt about Cromwell being instrumental in their destruction for the castle was not involved in the Civil Wars. Oystermouth Castle is full of interest. the keep has fine domestic apartments with beautiful windows, and there is a romantically named room - the White Lady's Chamber. The chapel adjoins the banqueting hall on the second floor, and here you can see a piscina, and more elaborate windows.

I like **Bishopston**. Such a tranquil place with a small church containing an interesting font, and earthwork remains on nearby Pwlldu Head. There are also delightful little coves nearby with firm, sandy beaches.

Oxwich National Nature Reserve and Centre is an area of dunes, marshes and woodlands above the sweeping curve of Oxwich Bay, and you will find here a wonderful concentration of wildlife. Information is readily available at the Centre, though opening times vary. But much of the Reserve is there for you to explore, and it is always open.

You will find **Oxwich** church on a rocky ledge near the sea. The Tudor Mansion known as Oxwich Castle is on a hill above the village. In the 16th century the Mansel family abandoned Penrice Castle to move into their new home, and there is still an impressive crested gateway leading into the courtyard. From Oxwich Bay you can see the medieval castle at **Penrice** that was abandoned in favour of Oxwich; as you would expect, it was built round about the 12th century, and is now in ruins.

Port Einon is just beyond Oxwich and is a fishing hamlet overlooking its own small bay. Tales of smuggling and piracy abound, and at the base of a reef known as Skysea you will come across the ruins of the Salthouse, which once had contrband wine stored in its cavernous vaults. The bay is often stormy, and evidence of this can be found in the churchyard where there is a statue commemorating a lifeboat hero. From Port Einon there is a wonderful cliff-top walk as far as **Rhossli**, but even keen and experienced walkers will need to take care on the rocky paths. It is well worth the effort, for the caves here are large enough to be marked on maps; both Culver Hole and Paviland Cave can be reached, but it is difficult. Of the two it is Paviland (actually a number of caves) that has a tale to tell. The 'Red Lady of Paviland' was a red-stained, human skeleton - minus skull - that was discovered in the Goat's Hole in 1823. A hundred years later, research resulted in a change of sex, for the remains turned out to be those of a youth who had been buried some 18,000 years ago. The gory stains were red ochre.

If you are still full of energy you can continue walking beyond Rhossli, Rhossisli Downs are quite desolate but they have more than their fair share of secret places, and budding archaeologists will pick their way quite happily through the rough grass around two Neolithic chambered tombs. These are Sweyne's Houses (or Swine Houses'), and date from around 2500BC. Beneath the Downs there is probably the finest beach on the Gower, with sands stretching for three miles in a graceful curve between Worm's Head and Burry Holms, a tiny island with the remains of a ruined church and a teeming bird population.

Chapter Ten

Llandewi is where you will find the **Gower Farm Museum** in a cluster of old farm buildings in which the owners have recreated rural life as it was at the turn of the century. The farm courtyard is stocked with many animals - chickens and ducks, goats, even rare breeds such as Gloucester Old Spot pigs - and there is a pets corner where children can gently handle guinea pigs and rabbits. The Gower Farm Museum is open May to September.

Another minor road off the A4118 would bring you to **Reynoldston**, which is considered to be the central point of the Gower. It is a pretty village with a green, and if you make the stiff walk to the summit of nearby Cefyn Bryn, a clear day will allow you to see across the Channel to South West England. It is worthwhile continuing your walk from there, for you will soon come across Arthur's Stone, a prominent landmark backed by interesting legends. It is actually four stones supporting a mighty capstone, and this is rumoured to have been split by Arthur.

There are conflicting historical details about **Weobley Castle** which you will find near **Cheriton**. It seems that all or part of this late medieval fortified house was built towards the end of the 13th century, probably by Henry Beaumont, Earl of Warwick. Later, it was occupied by the de la Bere family. Other sections were added in later centuries, and of the substantial remains perhaps the biggest difference you will notice between Weobley and other castles is the sheer variety of towers. Some have six or eight sides, some are square, yet all come together to form a complete square. If you visit on any day of the year you will be able to see the hall, kitchens and cellar, and an interesting exhibition on the history of the castle and of the Gower through the ages.

Llanrhidian is worth an hour of your time. Among the sights to be seen is St Rhidian's church, which has a curiously carved stone in the porch for which no-one can offer an explanation. As you stroll through the village you will see two standing stones on the green, and the old village stocks. Nearby Cil Ifor Top is the site of an Iron Age fort of considerable size, with terraces which can still be clearly seen.

Once upon a time you would have seen the cockle-women of **Penclawdd** in their bonnets and flannel dresses crossing the sand at low tide, their donkey carts ready to be loaded with the fresh harvest of shellfish. Things have changed but the sprawling village is still the centre of the cockle industry.

I left The Gower with reluctance but the history of **Kidwelly** beckoned me. It is a fine example of a town that has grown around a Norman castle. The estuary location at the mouth of the river Gwendraeth again demonstrates how the rulers and military commanders of the day recognised the importance of access from the sea. The earthwork defences of Kidwelly date back to the reign of Henry I, when they were raised by Roger, Bishop of Salisbury. The semi-circular moat is early 12th century, the inner ward was constructed by Payn de Chaworth late in the 13th century, and the cliffside chapel - it juts out over a scarp which formed a natural defence to the east - was added around 1300. In fact most of the existing building is the work of castle builders who were active in the 13th and 14th centuries.

Even before that period was reached, the castle had changed hands several times. One notable battle involved Maurice de Londres, Lord of Kidwelly, who in 1136 was faced by an army led by a woman - Gwenllian, the wife of Gruffydd ap Rhys. The Normans won the day in a fierce, bloody fight, and both Gwenllian and her son, Morgan, were beheaded.

Centuries later, Kidwelly Castle suffered severe damage in the Glyndwr rebellions. Concentric castles, of which Kidwelly is a fine example, had two rings of defences. The inner bailey or ward would have high walls with their own gateway. This would be encircled by the outer bailey protected by exterior walls with towers and - in Kidwelly's case - a massive gatehouse. You can see that three-storey structure to this day, and several of the towers are complete to their turrets. The old town of Kidwelly would have been completely walled; now, although it has lost its medieval buildings, the roads almost certainly follow their original lines and you can still see the early 14th-century town gate, which lies to the south.

If you continue on the A484 out of Kidwelly you will come to Ferryside, a little village with wonderful views and super sands with the sheltered waters of the estuary making it a lovely spot to spend a lazy afternoon.

Swansea makes a wonderful starting point from which to set out on the next stage of my travels, a remarkable journey which includes the two largest cities in Wales - one of which is the capital - and the astonishing contrast between vast urban industrial complexes and the breathtaking beauty of the Brecon Beacons. Cardiff may be the capital, but Swansea is justifiably proud to be the second largest city in Wales. Its name has buccaneering undertones, too, for it reached its present form from the original Sweyn's Ea (the island of Sweyn). Sweyn was a Viking pirate who used the site on the River Tawe as a base from which he could plunder the south coast. The docks at Swansea were established in 1306 for the purpose of ship building, but by the 18th century a change was underway as the exporting of Welsh coal, copper and iron ore became big business. The city is full of interest with an excellent market on Oxford Street, an exciting Maritime Quarter which has a marina with berths for 600 craft, a waterfront village, restaurant, art gallery, theatre, sailing and sea angling schools, and an unusual floating restaurant. The centrepiece of the Maritime Quarter is the Maritime and Industrial Museum with Wales' largest collection of historic vessels; the lightship Helwick and steam tug Canning can be boarded.

The Glynn Vivian Art Gallery on Alexander Road should not be missed. Among its static displays is one of the largest collections of Swansea porcelain and an outstanding collection of European ceramic and glass. These and many other displays which are constantly changing bring to the people of Swansea and visitors, the best in art from around the world.

The Brangwyn Hall is a mile from the city centre and just off the A4067 as you head back towards Mumbles. It could actually be called two buildings in one, for it was built in 1934 as the Guildhall and now comprises Swansea's civic offices, and the Brangwyn Concert Hall. The latter was named after Sir Frank Brangwyn, who designed the murals of the British Empire which were intended for the House of Lords but now adorn the walls of this splendid building. They did not get there without some difficulty - the 18 panels are so big that in order to accommodate them adjustments had to be made to the building! Brangwyn Hall is the focal point for the Swansea Festival of Music which is held each Autumn. International orchestras and soloists perform there, while opera is staged at the Grand Theatre.

The Vale of Neath is renowned for its own natural beauty and a number of major attractions that draw visitors in their thousands. **Neath** town centre is fully-pedestrianised, and as in Swansea, there is a thriving Victorian covered market. The Neath Borough Museum is housed in a beautifully refurbished Grade II listed building. Neath has a castle too, which was built in 1284 on a promontory guarding the approach to the town. It is currently being restored. Neath Abbey was founded in 1130 by the Norman Baron Richard de Granville.

Today it can be found on the edge of the Tennant Canal in an industrial area just off the A465. It does not sound like the ideal position for an Abbey that became Cistercian in 1147, and was considered by the Tudor historian, John Leland to be, 'The fairest Abbey in all Wales.' In fact the site is still tranquil and haunting and now in the care of CADW: Welsh Historic Monuments. The substantial ruins are open all year.

Aberdulais Falls and Ironworks will interest people with disparate tastes. I was intrigued to learn the natural waterfalls are not just beautiful to behold: a new water wheel will soon harness the natural energy source to produce electricity in a wooded gorge that contains the remains of 400 years of industrial activity. There is an interesting exhibition which deals with history and displays works of art by famous painters, and guided tours are available at this important National Trust site.

On the A4109 you will find the Cefyn Coed CollieryMuseum. So much of this part of the world is inextricably linked to the production of coal that a brush with the reality of the industry, however brief, is a must. The museum is located a little way south of **Crynant**, and is next to an operational mine. Most of the surface buildings remain from the former active colliery, and in the museum there are simulated underground workings, a huge steam winding engine, and massive boilers that once powered the pithead winding gear. There is also a good display of photographs which vividly trace the history of the workings, and round about there are lovely forest walks and picnic sites. An unusual and fascinating attraction.

On the same subject, it is worth going to Afon Argoed Country Park where there is the Welsh Miners Museum. Best reached by returning to Neath and taking the B4287 and then the A4107. You can look at this as confirmation that here the countryside and industry have always been uncomfortable bedfellows, or as an example of how two different natural resources complement each other - the one never complete without the other.

Afon Argoed Country Park has wonderful facilities on a beautiful steep sided valley that can be explore in several ways. Cycle tracks run along both banks of the River Afan (bikes can be hired), there are waymarked walks fanning out from the Countryside Centre, which is situated to the west of Cynonville, and landrover tours operate from the main car park during the summer season. My own reason for taking a look was to add to the coalmining information I had picked up at Cefyn Coed. Here, the story is by miners, from their point of view: there is a traditional miner's cottage scene, historic photographs, the story of children underground and a lot of mining equipment in realistic settings. Quite absorbing and always there is the knowledge that it can be tempered with the beauty of the Country Park waiting to embrace you when you tire of your research.

The Neath Canal deserves a mention. Some sections of it have recently been restored and now offer delightful diversions. Head for **Resolven** on the A465 where there is a tea room and gift shop in an 18th century cottage, and the 'Thomas Dadford' waiting to transport you along the placid waterways through idyllic scenery. Good towpath walks, too.

Porthcawl is regarded as the leading resort in South Wales - no doubt some would argue that it is not but what is certain is that it grew up as a coal port in the 19th century, and with the declineof that industry turned naturally to the holiday trade. Brochures will tell you of the seven beaches and coves

Chapter Ten

of the district, in particular Sandy Bay which is overlooked by the massive Cony beach entertainment complex. However, at the risk of being dubbed an old stick in the mud, I'd like to draw your attention to the dunes to the north west where the lost city of Kenfig lies buried by the sand. It was apparently engulfed in the Middle Ages, and today you may still see the ruins of Kenfig Castle poking through the sands. Kenfig Pool is also something of an oddity. Scarcely a mile from the sea, it is locked in by the dunes and is the county's largest freshwater lake.

Porthcawl is famous for golf. The Royal Porthcawl Club will be known to most people, if only by name, for it has hosted many international events including in recent years the Coral Classic. But there is also Pyle and Kenfig Club, the Southerndown Club and the Maesteg Club, the last two having wonderful views which could possibly result in ruined handicaps (or better handicaps, depending on how you view these things!) A word of warning - letters of introduction from your own club are usually required before you can tee off.

This is an outstanding stretch of coast for castles. The three main castles of Ogwr - all clustered around **Bridgend** - bear testimony to the ruthlessness of Prince Llywelyn, who partially destroyed them to prevent their being used by invaders. Ogmore Castle guarded a river crossing on the River Ewenny. It was constructed of undressed boulders, and probably dates back to the 12th century. Stepping stones lead across the river to the tiny village of **Merthyr-Mawr**, perhaps the most attractive in Ogwr. **New Castle**, paradoxically, controlled a ford on the River Ogmore.

The third castle is Coity, and this one can be traced back to the days of the Norman Lordships. Those of you who have read Thomas Hardy will recognise the name when I tell you that Coity Castle was held by the Turbevilles. Legend has it that the family acquired the castle through marriage, but certainly their descendants were one of Glamorgan's most powerful families. The castle was rebuilt in the 14th century, and added to in Tudor times.

Bridgend straddles the River Ogmore where three valleys meet - the Ogmore, Garw and Llynfi, and as well as being the traditional market town of the area it is now an industrial centre. The A48 from Bridgend will take you to **Cowbridge** whose origins lie in the first century AD and its location is on the important Roman road between Carmarthen and Caerleon. Modern thought also suggests that it is the sight of a missing Roman fort - Bomium - though nothing has been found to support the theory. It is now largely Georgian in character with many of the buildings listed. Charming place to be and full of interest.

Wales

The Vale of Glamorgan next with its plethora of places to see. **Llantwit Major** was once known as Llanilltud Fawr - 'Great Church of Illtud' - and as such was the first Christian College in Britain. It is also mentioned in the Guiness Book of Records as the site of the oldest school in Britain, and in legend St David, St Gilda and St Patrick are said to have been educated in this little town.

Barry or the old Port of Barry was first mentioned in 1276, and went on to flourish in the 16th and early 17th centuries. The larger, more modern town of Barry grew up as a port in the 1880s, like Porthcawl there to serve the needs of the South Wales coal industry. Now this bustling town is an excellent shopping centre, with good leisure facilities and a varied night life. It is also the location of Glamorgan Borough Council's head office, a fact worth noting as they can supply a wealth of information on accommodation, and places to see in the Vale of Glamorgan. Barry Island is linked by road and rail, and is a flourishing holiday resort. Its situation is ideal, for as apeninsula it has sea on three sides and all road and rail communications in the centre. There are two very large sandy beaches, plenty of rock pools to explore, and promenades and landscaped gardens ideal for strolling or lazing in the sun.

The B4267 is the road you need to take you towards Cardiff, and there are several interesting places to visit en route. Cosmeston Lakes Country Park has all the attractions you would expect, and in addition a Medieval Village which is not a reconstruction. Archaeologists are excavating and restoring, and a personal guide is there to introduce you to the history of Comeston Village.

Like Llandudno on the north coast, **Penarth** has a fine Victorian esplanade that provides a touch of old world charm. It is a pleasant resort on high ground to the west of Cardiff, which has been in turn fishing village and coal-exporting port. This is probably not the place for those who like sea swimming, for there are strong currents running off the shingle beach that is backed up by cliffs up to 100 feet high. There are, however, several swimming pools which make ideal alternatives. From Penarth pier you can embark on The Waverley, the world's last, sea-going paddle steamer. Five miles offshore - almost midway between Penarth and Weston-Super-Mare - Flat Holm island is reputed to be the burial place of the knights who murdered Thomas Becket.

We must go back to 75AD to learn of the first settlements where **Cardiff** stands today, for it was then the Romans built a fort by the River Taff to control Welsh tribesmen. It was extended in 300 AD, this time as a defence against pirates from across the Irish Sea. The town grew up around a fort

Chapter Ten

built by Robert FitzHamon - which can still be seen in the grounds of Cardiff Castle -and it was given its first Royal Charter by Elizabeth I in 1581. Coal played a big part in the town's prosperity, leading to the construction of docks which in 1794 were linked by canal to Merthyr Tydfil.

Shirley Bassey fans will know of **Tiger Bay**, a region of sprawling quays to the east of the Taff where seamen frequented taverns with names such as The Bucket of Blood and the House of Blazes. A once tough area, now developed into a modern city suburb with up to date docks.

It is almost impossible to know where to start exploring Cardiff, and you will be guided by preferences. Sports fans are certain to head for Cardiff Arms park, others will go first to the waterfront, while the Castle will for many be the magnet that first attracts. **The National Museum of Wales** is located at Cathays Park. Permanent exhibitions here cover an enormous range of subjects such as geology, botany, zoology, archaeology - surely enough 'ologies' to keep Maureen Lipman happy for months! Other sections feature industry and art, and there are temporary exhibitions, holiday activities for children, lunchtime and evening concerts and regular lectures and readings.

The Welsh Industrial and Maritime Museum is on Bute Street and, appropriately, the site is adjacent to the Bute West Dock Basin. It was opened in 1977 so is comparatively new, but its comprehensive coverage of industrial and maritime matters in Wales over the past two centuries is staggering. This is very much an open air site too; the steam tug 'Sea Alarm', a pilot cutter and a canal boat, a number of cranes and industrial locomotives as well as a railway footbridge and a lifeboat, will have people from all walks of life enthralled.

The Welsh Folk Museum is some distance away at St Fagans - about five miles west of the city centre. This is a museum packed with fascinating exhibits, and I found it wonderful because it reflects everyday life in Wales, which of course is of interest to absolutely everybody. The settingis super - an Elizabethan mansion standing within the walls of a medieval castle.

Cardiff Castle is different in several respects from others we have seen. It is for a start, in the very centre of this capital city, and it is also the creation of a Victorian Architect. The castle was considerably extended in the 13th century, but the ornate 150 foot clock tower, the Guest Tower, the guest rooms and Octagonal Tower are all the work of William Burges, who rebuilt the castle in the 1870s to fulfil the dreams of John Patrick Crichton-Stuart, the third Marquess of Bute.

There are mixed opinions about this castle, some love it, some think it to be so lavishly decorated that it is vulgar in parts and yet the design and construction of other parts approaches perfection. The Entrance Hall has elegant stained glass windows showing the monarchs who have owned the castle. The Library also has lovely stained glass windows - this time with a Biblical theme.

St David's Hall is the National Concert and Conference Hall of Wales and was completed in 1982. I always associate it with that wonderful television programme 'Cardiff - Singer of the World' - which appears every two years and allows me to listen to truly wonderful voices every night for a week. It is centrally located alongside the St David's Shopping Centre, and as well as an auditorium seating 2000 there are numerous meeting rooms and dressing rooms. Excellent bar facilities and an in-house catering department.

What can one say of **Cardiff Arms Park**? An ideal situation alongside the River Taff, minutes away from the town centre and Cardiff Central railway station, and of course known to millions of Rugby Union fans all over the world. If you are there on the day of an international - perhaps Wales versus England -the singing may well move you to tears.

Singing of a different kind can be heard at the New Theatre, which opened in 1906 and is Cardiff's sole surviving traditional theatre. The Royal Shakespeare Company, London Contemporary Dance Theatre and Sadlers Wells Royal Ballet have all appeared here, plus West End Musicals, and, of course, the Welsh National Opera for which the new Theatre provides a fitting home.

Probably one of my favourite locations in Wales is **The Brecon Beacons**. The scenery is stunning and varied as are the villages. Along the A470 for just five miles and you come to Castell Coch. This is the first fairy-tale castle

I have seen in Wales. A marvellous jumble of round towers and conical turrets. Yet, like Cardiff, it is the physical representation of a Victorian dream - and the same two people are responsible: William Burges, and John Patrick Crichton-Stuart. The work on Castell Coch ran in parallel with the work five miles down the road, and if anything Burges gave even freer rein to his imagination. All is lavishly decorated with murals, carvings, paintings and figures taken from Aesop's Fables and Greey mythology - yet there is a sombre note, too, for a flight of stone steps lead down to a gloomy dungeon.

I suggest the simplest way of tackling the Brecon Beacons National Park is to drive slowly through to **Brecon** and then pause to catch your breath

Chapter Ten

and take stock. You are in exhilirating mountain country all the way and some six miles from Garwnant you will come abreast of the three peaks of the beacons: Pen-y-Fan (2907 ft), which is flanked by Cribyn (2608 ft) and Corn Du (2863 ft). They are the highest mountains in South Wales, and it is very easy to see why this daunting terrain is ideal training ground for elite army units, and the haunt of mountaineers.

Brecon is situated at the junction of the rivers Usk and Honddu, and is one of the oldest Welsh towns. It was granted its first charter in 1246 and a second granted in 1366 gave it the right to hold a fair. That right is never taken lightly in Wales, and pleasure fairs are still held in the Brecon streets for three days each May and November. The town has a bewildering mixture of architectural styles - Medieval, Georgian, Jacobean and Tudor, as well as excellent modern buildings. There was a castle, but all that remains now are a tower and battlemented wall.

If you are tired of driving yet determined to see more of this beautiful part of Wales, all is not lost. Brecon and Beyond is the name of a firm running luxury landrover tours, and they offer the ideal way to get off the beaten track without ruining the family car's suspension. Drovers' tracks criss-cross a 12,000 acre private estate, and there are super views, rugged mountains, waterfalls and limestone gorges.

It was a great disappointment to me to discover that **Caerphilly** cheese is mainly made in Somerset today and not in this small town where until 1910 there used to be a bustling cheese market. Caerphilly has experienced enormous changes, as have most towns and villages in this land with an unusually turbulent history. In the hills around the town the Welsh held out against the Norman invaders for 200 years after 1066. Later, around 1268, Gilbert de Clare, the Red Earl of Gloucester, began the construction of Caerphilly Castle, which is the largest in Wales and the second largest in Britain. It was destroyed just two years later by Llywelyn ap Gruffydd, Prince of Wales, when it was still only partially built. A second attempt at construction was begun - again by the Earl - in 1271, and this time it was successful. The site is right in the middle of the town and very impressive. The concentric ground plan and huge encircling moat rendered normal siege methods ineffective, and even in mopdern times it's easy to visualise the attackers' abortive attempts to break through. A magnificent sight!

One of the first things a visitor notices is a tower that leans almost 12 feet off the perpendicular, and not for the first time I came across conflicting stories when I tried to root out an explanation. The first suggests that during the Civil War - in 1646 - the Royalists attempted to blow up the castle to prevent the Roundheads from using it, and in so doing badly damaged the tower. The other theory is that the lean is caused by subsidence. The first appeals to me infinitely more than the second!

Caerphilly Castle has a ghost. Known as the Ghost of the Green Lady, it is said to be Alice of Angouleme, bride of Gilbert de Clare, who fell for a Welsh Prince called Griffith the Fair and was immediately banished to her home in France. Since then her spirit has looked out from the grey ramparts, waiting for the return of her prince....

The ruins of Newport Castle stand close to the bridge over the River Usk. It was built in the 15th century and has a wonderful Gothic arch on which can still be seen the grooves of the original portcullis. By the 16th-century Newport was already known for its excellent harbour; three hundred years later that came to good use when the Industrial Revolution brought coal pouring down from the Monmouthshire valleys. **Newport** is now the foremost shopping and commercial centre in Gwent, with a heritage dating back three thousand years and a character moulded by Celts, Romans, Saxons, Normans, Plantagenets and Tudors.

You will need to take the B4236 to reach old **Caerleon,** which today is an attractive village, of interest in its own right. Visitors flock to see Caerleon Isca, a fortress laid out beside the River Usk in about 74AD which became one of the three principal military bases in Roman Britain, headquarters of the 2nd Augustan Legion. The aerial photographs I had seen clearly show the shape of these wonderful remains, but actually walking through them left me with the uncanny sensation of having stepped a long way back in the past - obviously true, yet I felt it here stronger than anywhere else (except perhaps canterbury cathedral).

The Barracks at Caerleon are the only Roman legionary barracks on view anywhere in Europe. It is an extraordinary feeling to see the buildings that once housed 80 men, and realise you are walking down a Roman street. Broadway is the course of the Via Principalis, and a sign on a farm wall to the left marks the site of the sout-west gateway - Port Dextra. The Fortress Baths are if anything more impressive. They served as the main leisure centre for the soldiers, and the building once stood 60 feet high. There is an open air swimming pool - now displayed under cover - that was discovered as recently as 1964.

The Ampitheatre stands outside the fortress walls. It once seated 5,000 spectators - the whole garrison. Today it is still a superb setting for open-air theatrical events and festivals. All the separate parts of this wonderful site are brought together and thoroughly explained in the spacious Legionary Museum.

Chapter Ten

From Caerleon I had intended to go straight to Caldicot. But there is no M4 junction there so instead I took the A48, which allowed me to call at Penhow and Caerwent.

Penhow Castle is the home of the Seymour family, and the oldest lived-in castle in Wales. It was restored in 1973 by the owner, who still lives there. An interesting way of touring the building is provided: audio cassettes in handy 'walkman' players act as guides, providing an acommpaniment of authentic period music.

Caerwent is just a few miles further on, a peaceful village that is built on the site of the Roman walled town of Venta Silarum. Excavations here have revealed houses, shops and a temple, and in places the well-preserved walls stand 15 feet high. All of this interests me tremendously, because it is not something I have delved deeply into yet in the space of a few short miles I have come across a Roman fortress, a Roman town, and a little further on is **Portskewett,** a tiny village close to the River Severn, which centuries ago was an important landing stage for the Romans when they first came to Wales. The landing point at Black Rock is now a delightful picnic site.

From Caerwent it is a short drive down a minor road to **Caldicot,** a lovely town which was mentioned in the Domesday Book in the 11th century. Rich in history - in particular that relating to the Roman occupation. At nearby Mount Ballan, Crick - home of showjumper David Broome - the Wales and the West Showjumping events are held.

Caldicot Castle was built in stages during the 12th and 14th centuries, but unlike others that were left to decay it was restored by a wealthy Victorian and converted into a family home. The castle is the focal point of a delightful country park and also renowned for its medieval banquets. Large parties must be booked but quite often there are tables available for smaller numbers.

Chepstow marks the western edge of my tour through Wales. It is delightfully situated in a loop of the River Wye and has streets that slope down to the river. There are many tea-houses, antique shops, galleries and craft shops on the way down to the riverbank which is the spectacular setting for, among other things, the fine new bandstand.

The castle dominates the town and is the earliest Norman stone castle in Wales. William Fitzosbern, Earl of Hereford, built it on limestone cliffs at the water's edge, and it was greatly enlarged in the 12th and 13th centuries. It is one of the few sites where it is possible to follow the many phases of castle building in Britain. It was considered impregnable until the walls were breached by Cromwell's guns during the Civil War.

Several grand walks are waymarked from Chepstow. one of them beginning on the Welsh side of the river, is the Wye Valley walk, which starts at the castle and passes through glorious countryside. For the other you will need to cross to the English side; it is Offa's Dyke.

You must look out for the signs to the village of **Tintern**. This is an attractive hamlet with a south-facing hill overlooking the Abbey where Welsh table wines are produced from a fine vineyard. But it is Tintern Abbey that folk come to see and it really is a wonderful sight.

The original abbey was a Cistercian house founded by Henry I in 1131, but the existing remains are much larger, and date from the late 13th century. The setting is superb, with the river flowing through grassy banks dotted with white cottages, and all around thickly wooded hills. Wordsworth was impressed while on a walking tour, and indeed the abbey ruins are among the most beautiful and best preserved in Britain.

Monmouth is a splendid town. It stands at the confluence of the Wye, Monmnow and Trothy rivers, and this former county town of Monmouthshire boasts many well-preserved Tudor and Georgian buildings. Agincourt Square is elegant, bordered by a cluster of fine inns and the Shire Hall and library, and a statue there is itself a tribute to a man who helped bring elegance to the motor industry: Charles Stewart Rolls, co-founder of Rolls-Royce, who was born at nearby Rockfield.

I am sure you will be smitten by Usk. It is a wonderfully picturesque town that has sveral times been voted 'Best Kept Small Town in Wales'. It has also won the small town category in the 'Britain in Bloom' competition, and in the summer months you will find it ablaze with masses of flowers in beds, window boxes and hanging baskets. July and September are good months to visit Usk. The Usk Festival is held in midsummer, and in recent years jousting tournaments have been added to the traditional music and drama. The Usk Agricultural Show takes place at summers end, and is held in Trostrey on the outskirts of the town.

Abergavenny was my last port of call on this tour of Wales. If I were asked to name my favourite spot in this old market town then I would certainly plump for Castle Meadows alongside the River Usk. On a summer's day there can be no more idyllis place to be and a picnic beneath tall trees on the gently sloping banks is certainly my idea of heaven.

This has been a wonderful journey for me, and I hope you have found something along the way to inspire you and room in your heart to forgive my ommisions. Some have been deliberate, giving me the excuse to return.

Chapter Ten

Wales

THE HARBOUR HOTEL,
Aberdovey,
Gwynedd LL35 0EB

Tel: 01654 767250
Fax 01654 767792

This small conservation, coastal village is one of the prettiest to be found in Britain with an unrivalled combination of beach, estuary, sea, countryside and excellent local amenities.It is a very close knit community of some four hundred people who take pride in everything about their village. Surprisingly for somewhere so small the amenities are excellent with a championship eighteen hole links golf course, five miles of sandy beaches and dunes, an estuary suitable for all water sports and a good range of shops. Inland is equally interesting and the whole provides a perfect place for a holiday at anytime of the year. People who have come here for a holiday or a break will tell you that the classic Victorian Harbour Hotel is the place to stay for many reasons.

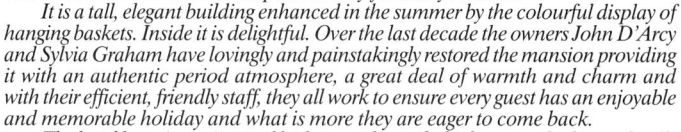

It is a tall, elegant building enhanced in the summer by the colourful display of hanging baskets. Inside it is delightful. Over the last decade the owners John D'Arcy and Sylvia Graham have lovingly and painstakingly restored the mansion providing it with an authentic period atmosphere, a great deal of warmth and charm and with their efficient, friendly staff, they all work to ensure every guest has an enjoyable and memorable holiday and what is more they are eager to come back.

The hotel has nine suites and bedrooms three of which are two bedroom family suites, three are double or twin bedrooms with sea views, and three are standard double or single bedrooms. One of each category is designated non-smoking and no pets. All nine suite and bedrooms have ensuite bathrooms, direct dial telephones, television and radio, tea and coffee making facilities, irons and ironing boards and hair dryers. Cots and high chairs are available and there is a variety of baby listening systems.

Three restaurants are designed to suit everyone. Rumbles is a coffee shop, tea rooms and popular family restaurant. During the summer months residents breakfasts are served here and it is open all day and evening. Wellies is a bistro style restaurant in the hotel basement which opens at seven o'clock every evening during the summer. The very attractive Harbour Restaurant, is a traditional hotel dining room with limited choice table d'hote menu and is a non smoking area. Wherever you eat the food is of a very high standard, home-cooked and both Vegan and Vegetarian dishes are always available. Other diets can be accommodated with notice. The two sitting rooms are elegantly furnished, one which is for adults only has a well-stocked bar and the smaller one is a non smoking area and is suitable for children. You will never regret choosing to stay in this exceptionally good seaside hotel.

USEFUL INFORMATION

OPEN; All year
CHILDREN; Welcome, cots,
CREDIT CARDS; All major cards
LICENSED; Yes
ACCOMMODATION; 9 suites & bedrooms
VEGETARIAN; Yes + Vegan
PETS; By arrangement

RESTAURANT; Rumbles Coffee shop open all day and evening. Wellies bistro restaurant opens from 7pm in summer. Harbour Restaurant serves limited choice table d'hote menu

DISABLED ACCESS; No special facilities

Chapter Ten

MAES GLAS,

Raglan Terrace,
Monmouth Rd.,
Abergavenny,
Wales,
NP7 9SP.

Tel : 01873 854494

This is probably one of the few names in Wales I can pronounce. These delightful, lilting place names tie my tongue in knots, and I get much further by just pointing silently to them on a map!

Abergavenny is a little market town and as such is a delight to the senses. Maes Glas is about 10 minutes walk from the town and is a charming detached bungalow furnished in a traditional way. Mrs Haynes, your hostess, greets you on arrival with a welcoming cup of tea or coffee, and so heralds the beginning of your stay with her.

Children are most welcome and Mrs Haynes will supply everything from cot to toys for the comfort of youngsters! The bedrooms are extremely comfortable with hot & cold water, T.V., and more tea and coffee! Breakfast is a traditional hearty meal and evening meals can be arranged.

Walking in the area is a must as the views are wonderful, and there are various walks for all. Other popular activities are painting, (I always envy painters their ability to convey a sense of something to canvas!) pony trekking, freshwater fishing and much more. Maes Glas is listed by the Welsh Tourist Board and does credit to Welsh hospitality.

USEFUL INFORMATION

OPEN : *All year but Xmas (non smoking)*
CHILDREN : *Most welcome*
PETS : *No*
LICENSED : *No*
CREDIT CARDS : *None taken*
ACCOMMODATION : *2 rooms; 1 dbl, 1 fml.*

EVENING MEAL : *By arrangement*
VEGETARIANS : *Catered for*
BAR MEALS : *Not applicable*
DISABLED ACCESS : *Limited*
GARDEN : *Pleasant*

Wales

ABERCELYN COUNTRY HOUSE,
Llanycil, Bala,
Gwynedd LL23 7YF

Tel: 01678 521109 Fax: 01678 520556

This charming Welsh stone country house is wonderfully set overlooking Bala Lake in the Snowdonia National Park. Built in 1729 as a Georgian Rectory it has retained many of its original features; the Georgian staircase, marble fireplaces, panelled doors, shuttered windows and window seats. The bedrooms are spacious, bright and comfortably furnished with traditional and antique furnishings, en suite or private facilities, and all with tea/coffee trays, electric blankets, hair dryers and full central heating. The sitting room is a cosy, comfortable room with an open log fire for those chilly winter evenings; somewhere with a library where you can sit and read, or chat about your day's activities and plan your next excursion! A good wholesome country breakfast cooked on the Aga, with fresh bread, home-made jams and freshly laid eggs, is sure to guarantee a great start to the day, and if you require a special diet it is not a problem. Judy Cunningham, who owns Abercelyn, is a friendly person who is happy to cater for most requirements. The dining room overlooks the splendid gardens which have a stream running alongside, and with views over the lake, this is the perfect beginning to any day - especially with some of Judy's home-cooking having satisfied the more earthly requirements! Off season, Judy will supply an evening meal if arranged in advance, but during the summer the local pubs and restaurants cater for your every need in food and beverages!

Snowdonia is an area of great beauty and calls to the artist in all of us. Whether you wish to paint or just take a photograph you will feel the swell of emotion that outstanding perfection brings to us all. Abercelyn is ideally placed for touring this magnificent area and enjoying the many sports available. Bala Lake is the largest natural lake in Wales, and has sailing, wind surfing and other water activities, which can all be enjoyed in the prettiest of settings. There is golf on one side of the lake, and fishing is obviously a firm favourite here. But walking is the answer - to see and appreciate the colours and moods of the mountain slopes and valleys and feel the fresh winds on your skin, - this is the only way to do it! The Cunninghams organise very good walking tours called 'Celtic Trails' which show you the splendour, history and mystical beauty of this area. Each walk is graded to accommodate different abilities and there is something for everyone; from mountain tops to golden sandy beaches totally wild and uninhabited, this compact country offers great adventures from coast to coast. Castles, country houses, National Trust properties and gardens, standing stones, druid circles and monasteries, are all within easy distance of this perfect Welsh home.

USEFUL INFORMATION

OPEN; All year excluding Christmas
CHILDREN; Welcome
PETS; No
CREDIT CARDS; All major cards
LICENSED; No

DINING ROOM; Good country food
VEGETARIANS; Catered for
DISABLED ACCESS; No
GARDEN; Landscaped
ACCOMMODATION; 2dbl en suite
1 twin with private facilities

Chapter Ten

WAVECREST HOTEL
8 Marine Parade, Barmouth,
Gwynedd, Wales LL42 1NA

Tel/Fax: 01341 280330

Snugly settled at the mouth of the beautiful Mawddach Estuary is the unique town of Barmouth, which is rich in history and enjoys a mild west coast climate. Overlooking the harbour is the headland called Dinas Oleu which means 'Fortress of Light' and is the birthplace of the National Trust, which was bestowed to the Trust by Mr. John Ruskin and a Mrs. Talbot. This delightful harbour is a haven for pleasure craft and fishing boats, yet years ago was very busy with ships from the Americas loading and unloading their cargoes. Within metres of the sandy beach sits the Wavecrest Hotel, this charming family run hotel offers all that is best about a traditional holiday. With a welcome as fine as you will receive anywhere, where nothing is too much trouble, and the service most attentive. Throughout Wavecrest the standard of decor and furnishings is very high, with special attention to detail, for instance there are fresh floral arrangements, attractive pictures and ornaments all adding to that special homely feel. Bedrooms are well appointed with most enjoying the privacy of ensuite facilities, colour TV, a tea and coffee tray, clock radio and hair dryer, some with superb sea views. Mr. and Mrs. Jarman have earned themselves an established reputation for good food and have been recognised as a 'Taste of Wales' hotel, also a 'Food Rosette' by the AA. The French guide 'Guide de Routard' also adds their recommendation. The dining room is attractively furnished and adjacent to the cosy and intimate bar, which boasts 40 Irish and Scottish whiskies and a comprehensive selection of specially chosen wines to compliment any meal. Locally produced Welsh beef and lamb, wild local salmon as well as fresh vegetables are used to produce delicious and imaginative dishes. Special diets are catered for.

A veritable wealth of outdoor activities and attractions awaits visitors; golf, pony trekking, climbing and water sports, which includes boating, fishing, surfing and swimming. There are 15 miles of lovely beach with stunning coastline and breathtaking scenery, and views of the mountains of Snowdonia, famous for its walks or for the more energetic the steeper climbs. Quaint villages with glorious waterfalls, shady valleys and beauty spots offer ideal walking and picnic areas. The Portmeirion Italianate Village is fascinating and well worth a visit. For nature lovers there are forestry centres with nature trails, offering an ideal opportunity to enjoy the local habitat.

USEFUL INFORMATION

OPEN; March-November
CHILDREN; Welcome
CREDIT CARDS; All major cards
LICENSED; Yes
ACCOMMODATION; 10 rooms,
4 double, 4 twin/family, 2 single, 7 ensuite

DINING ROOM; Traditional fare, using fresh local produce
VEGETARIAN; Yes and special diets
DISABLED ACCESS; Limited access
GARDEN; At the front with seating
PETS; By arrangement

Wales

BRYN LLEWELYN,
Betws-Y-Coed, Gwynedd,
North Wales, LL24 0BN.

Tel or Fax : 01690 710601

This attractive 1870, stone built, Victorian house is in the perfect location for seeing the beautiful country of Wales. Naomi and Steve Parker who own and run this guest house, are friendly, warm people who extend the hospitality of their home, making sure their guests have every comfort required! This non smoking house itself has great character and is furnished in a traditional manner in keeping with its age. There is a total of seven rooms, all highly appointed, with colour TV, tea/coffee trays, and hot & cold running water. The two family, and two of the double rooms have en suit facilities. Breakfast is a traditional meal but variations can be catered for.

Betws-Y-Coed is a mountain village, and sits at the foot of Mynydd Griball; looking out your bedroom window this is very obvious. The views are stunning, as the village nestles between the hills with their ever changing, seasonal colours. From the purple hues of the heathers and the shaded greens of the trees in summer, to a white overcoat in winter, this is a scene from a postcard! (And it probably is!) Steve knows all about the local walks, and can give you advice on forest, riverside and mountain walks that lead from the very doorstep of this guest house! Walks that would include Swallow Falls, Miners Bridge and Fairy glen, all of which are recognised beauty spots, and then of course (I mean we are in Wales!) Conwy Falls and Nature Trail, spectacular water falls and salmon leaps! It almost takes your breath away! A wonderful location! Snowdonia National Park is all but a stone's throw away. But not only walking can show the beauty of this country - pony trekking or horse riding is another ideal way to see the countryside, and both are available here. Anybody who is interested in the arts will not be disappointed either because the landscape is such that it inspires the painter, poet or even photographer in all of us! Betws-Y-Coed is also the home of the Conwy Valley Railway Musem, which houses comprehensive displays of the LNWR period, with working models and a steam locomotive that has a ¾ mile scenic ride. The village has its own railway station and is quite a thriving little community. There are plenty of shops in the village and various eating establishments that Naomi and Steve will surely recommend.

USEFUL INFORMATION

OPEN : *All year*
CHILDREN : *Welcome*
PETS : *By arrangement*
LICENSED : *No*
CREDIT CARDS : *None taken*
ACCOMMODATION : *7 rooms; 4 en suite, 3 dbl, 2 fml, 1 twin, 1 sgl.*
NON SMOKING

DINING ROOM : *Traditional fayre*
VEGETARIANS : *Catered for*
BAR SNACKS : *Not applicable*
DISABLED ACCESS : *No*
GARDEN : *No*

Chapter Ten

CHURCH HILL HOTEL
Vicarage Road, Betws-y-Coed,
Gwynedd, Wales LL24 0AD

Tel: 01690 710447

Slightly elevated and overlooking the village green at the foot of tree clad hills stands Church Hill Hotel, stone built in 1910. This licensed Hotel is located in an attractive and scenic area, much visited by tourists. Accommodation is comfortable, warm and extremely well presented, offering guests ensuite bedrooms, with tea and coffee making facilities and colour television. There is also a family suite and a ground floor bedroom, suitable for those unable to use the stairs. The cuisine offered is traditional home-cooked fare, with fresh local produce used where possible. There is a cosy Resident's Bar and a comfortable lounge to relax in. Mr. & Mrs French offer a very warm and hospitable welcome, in time honoured Welsh fashion.

Various outdoor activities such as fishing, riding, canoeing and trekking can be arranged locally. Extensive walking through glorious countryside, is guaranteed to delight those interested in the indigenous flora and fauna, or for the more energetic there are mountainous climbs, in and around Snowdonia. The coastline of Cardigan Bay affords glorious beaches with windsurfing, sail boarding and boating, and a visit to Portmeirion Fantasy Village is a must and shouldn't be missed.

USEFUL INFORMATION

OPEN; *All year except Christmas Day and Boxing Day*
CHILDREN; *Welcome, family available suite*
CREDIT CARDS; *Visa/Mastercard*
LICENSED; *Residents*
ACCOMMODATION; *13 rooms*

DINING ROOM; *Traditional home-cooked fare, using fresh produce. Set evening meal*
VEGETARIAN; *Catered for*
DISABLED ACCESS; *Limited, one ground floor bedroom*
GARDEN; *Yes*
PETS; *By arrangement*

Wales

GLASFRYN GUEST HOUSE
Brechfa, Carmarthen,
Wales SA32 7QY
Tel: 01267 202306
Fax: 01267 202306

Renowned for its welcome and comfort Glasfryn is, a large turn of the century property built of Welsh stone and situated in the heart of the Brechfa Forest area, which is home to many species of trees, including conifer plantations. Personal attention is assured at all times by your hosts, Joyce and Derek Hart, and you can look forward to a warm welcome. Bedrooms are tastefully decorated and soft furnishings are in pastel shades.

Private bathroom or ensuite facilities, central heating and a welcome tray are afforded to each room. An attractive feature of the dining room is the conservatory which makes an ideal setting in which to sample the excellent cuisine whether it is a hearty satisfying breakfast or a scrumptious dinner. Fresh local trout and salmon is served when available, as well as a wide choice of delicious dishes served with specially selected vegetables. The Guests Lounge is inviting and comfortable where one can relax, read, listen to music or play board games, which are supplied, or watch television. Wild life abounds, and can be seen on the many walks which visitors can traverse through woods or alongside rivers. Pony trekking can be arranged locally and is highly recommended as is fishing, mountain biking and golf.

USEFUL INFORMATION

OPEN; All year
CHILDREN; Welcome
CREDIT CARDS; None taken
LICENSED; Small restaurant bar
ACCOMMODATION; 3 rooms, 2 double-1 ensuite, 1 ensuite twin
RESTAURANT; A La Carte menu, excellent cuisine
VEGETARIAN; Catered for
DISABLED ACCESS; Into restaurant
GARDEN; Yes
PETS; By arrangement

Chapter Ten

BELVEDERE
Station Road, Talybont-on-Usk,
Brecon, Powys LD3 7JE
Tel: 01874 676264

Situated between the Brecon Beacons, which rise to 2907ft, and the Black Mountains is Belvedere designed and built 20 years ago by Pat and John Price. This area is a walkers paradise the scenery is breathtaking. The centrally heated house has a warm and homely atmosphere. There are 3 guest bedrooms, one double, one twin and a family room, all have colour television and tea and coffee making facilities. The furnishings are traditional and compliment the house, the Welsh Tourist Board agree and have awarded Belvedere with 'Highly Commended', no wonder guests return year after year. Belvedere is within walking distance to a selection of excellent restaurants. There are other activities apart from walking such as golf, fishing, pony trekking, climbing and cycling. Or if you would rather, you can visit the lovely towns and villages, also the Brecon to Monmouth canal, there is definitely something for everyone.

USEFUL INFORMATION
OPEN; All year except Christmas
CHILDREN; Welcome
CREDIT CARDS; None taken
LICENSED; No
ACCOMMODATION; 3 rooms
1 double, 1 twin, 1 family, 1 ensuite
DINING ROOM; Full English breakfast, evening meals are not available
VEGETARIAN; Catered for
DISABLED ACCESS; No
GARDEN; Yes
PETS; No

GLYNGWERNEN FARM
Felinfoel, Llanelli,
Wales SA1 4QD
Tel: 01554 821372

3 miles from junction 48 off the M4 you will come across a very large modern farmhouse, thisis Glyngwernen Farm. This working sheep farm is set amongst acres of wonderful hills and fields, and is an excellent location for ramblers. Mrs. Brenda Rees is your host, extends a very warm and friendly welcome to her guests. The are 3 ensuite rooms, all have colour TV, tea and coffee making facilities and personal items such as soaps and tissues to add that special touch. The furnishings are a mixture of French Georgian and modern. The food is good home-cooked fare with breakfast and an evening meal. The Welsh Tourist Board have awarded Glyngwernen with '2 Crowns'. The farm is close to Pembrey Country Park with 7 miles of sandy beach which boasts a 'Blue Flag'. With plenty of activities such as fishing, golf, riding and walking. You are also close to the wonderfully named Kidwelly, also Carmarthen and Swansea. You certainly won't have time to get bored here you'll be to busy enjoying yourselves.

USEFUL INFORMATION
OPEN; All year except Christmas
CHILDREN; No
CREDIT CARDS; None taken
LICENSED; No
ACCOMMODATION; 3 ensuite rooms
DINING ROOM; Good home-cooked fare
VEGETARIAN; Catered for
DISABLED ACCESS; No
GARDEN; Yes
PETS; No

THE LANSDOWNE HOTEL & RESTAURANT
The Watton, Brecon,
Powys LD3 7EG

Tel: 01874 623321

Gone are the days when this hotel used to be a famous tea shop for which there were always queues and a cobblers shop which did a brisk trade. Now we have a delightful, warm and relaxed hotel in the stonebuilt 18th century Georgian building. Everything has been done to make the hotel welcoming and friendly. The furnishing is comfortable and reminiscent of the 30s. John and Pamela Nancarrows capabilities as hoteliers and restauranteurs is recognised in Brecon and beyond. They are well known local personalities and involved in many local organisations and clubs including the golf club for which playing arrangements can be made at the hotel. In addition to golf there are many sporting activities available including coarse and freshwater fishing and some wonderful walks. For those who like exploring, The Brecons are wonderful and so too are the many villages and towns within easy reach. Brecon itself is fascinating and has a busy market as well as a beautiful cathedral.

The Lansdowne has ten bedrooms, eight of which are ensuite and all have television, direct dial telephone and tea/coffee facilities. Breakfast is a sumptuous affair with a good choice and ample portions to set one up for the day. The Restaurant is well known locally for its delicious dishes and is a charming place in which to dine at your leisure. The menu is changed daily and is a mixture of traditional and continental and is all home-cooked using fresh local produce wherever possible. There are several dishes every day for vegetarians.

USEFUL INFORMATION

OPEN; All year
CHILDREN; Over 8 years
CREDIT CARDS; All major cards
LICENSED; Yes
ACCOMMODATION; 10 rooms, 8 ensuite
RESTAURANT; Renowned for its food
VEGETARIAN; Several dishes daily
DISABLED ACCESS; To restaurant only
PETS; Well behaved small dogs by arrangement

Chapter Ten

MAESWALTER
Heol Senni, Nr Brecon,
Powys LD3 8SU
Tel: 01874 636629

This friendly 17th century non-working farm house situated in the quiet and picturesque valley of Heol Senni 9 miles south west of Brecon, is ideal for anyone wanting to unwind, enjoy the uplifting fresh air of this spectacular countryside and delight in the excellent, beautiful cooked breakfast served every morning by our smiling hostess Joy Mayo who, with her husband Haydn owns this attractive establishment. The three bedrooms are furnished in a traditional cottage style with taste and an eye for colour one of the bedrooms is ensuite, the other two rooms share separate bathroom and shower rooms with all the hot water you could possibly require. Each bedroom has remote control, colour television, razor points and vanity units as well as a beverage tray which not only has coffee and chocolate but a selection of teas as well. The house has an air of well being and tremendous character highlighted by the exposed beams. From here you can explore the National Park, go hang gliding, boating, pony trekking, cycling, canoeing and rock climbing, as well as play golf or fish. Rare Bird spotting is a favourite pastime and that has brought many would be artists to the area to capture the stunning scenery and the birds on canvas for posterity.

USEFUL INFORMATION
OPEN; All year
CHILDREN; Welcome
CREDIT CARDS; None taken
PETS; By arrangement
ACCOMMODATION; 1 room ensuite, 2 standard
DINING ROOM; Super breakfast and evening meal by arrangement
VEGETARIAN; Upon request
DISABLED ACCESS; No

MAERDY COTTAGES
Taliaris, Nr Llandeilo,
Carmarthenshire SA19 7DA
Tel: 01550 777448
Fax: 01550 777067

Strictly speaking Maerdy should appear only in 'Joy David's Choice - Self-Catering' but the service in these wonderful cottages includes an outstanding catering service supplied by the owner Mrs M.E. Jones - always known to her friends as M.E. You can have all the benefits of a self-contained, beautifully appointed and historically interesting cottage and at the same time not even have to cook breakfast in one cottage. The evening meals are outstanding and in keeping with the incredibly high standards of the buildings. There are six cottages, each one different but in every case furnished with everything you could possibly require to make your holiday a perfect one - even the weather would not mar your pleasure, log fires and plenty to see and do plus superb meals, including delicious home-made cakes, would assuredly take your mind off the possible lack of sunshine. That is why Maerdy is so popular all the year round. One of these cottages is particularly suitable for the disabled, elderly or for those with young children. The Maerdy is wonderfully situated for enjoying the glorious countryside whatever the time of year. Ideal family bed and breakfast facility.

USEFUL INFORMATION
OPEN; All the year
CHILDREN; Welcome. Cots etc
ACCOMMODATION; 6 cottages,
Very high standard
GARDEN; Yes & courtyard or patio plus furniture
CATERING; Superb catering service brought To your door if required
DISABLED ACCESS; Yes, details on request
PETS; By arrangement

DOL-LLYN-WYDD
Builth Wells, Powys,
Wales LD2 3RZ

Tel: 01982 553660

Mrs. Biddy Williams is the proud owner of this delightful traditional 17th century farmhouse on the families working beef and sheep farm. The house is very attractive set in a pretty garden with a lawn, herbaceous borders and climbing roses around the front portico. The inside is very comfortable with oak beams and on those chilly days a large log fire. The bedrooms are warm and cosy, one being ensuite the other two have private facilities.

Biddy is an excellent cook and will serve a delicious breakfast, using fresh local produce including meat and free range eggs. Evening meals are available by prior arrangement. The Wales Tourist Board has awarded this delightful property '2 Crowns'. Dol-Llyn-Wydd is situated in a very quiet area beneath the Eppynt Hills, an outstanding region for walking, bird watching, riding, and golf. Salmon and trout fishing can be arranged. The town of Builth Wells is approached by an elaborate 18th century bridge across the River Wye.

It was once a fashionable 19th century spa town but today it is the headquarters for the Royal Welsh Show, held here every summer, when the whole town erupts into a colourful display. This is a very beautiful area and with the comfort of Dol-Llyn-Wydd what more could you ask for.

USEFUL INFORMATION

OPEN; March-December
CHILDREN; No
CREDIT CARDS; None taken
ACCOMMODATION; 3 rooms, 2 with private facilities, 1 ensuite
DINING ROOM; Breakfast and evening meal
VEGETARIAN; Upon request
DISABLED ACCESS; No
GARDEN; Yes, with chairs
PETS; No

Chapter Ten

ORCHARD COTTAGE
Erwood, Builth Wells,
Powys LD2 3EZ

Tel: 01982 560600

The River Wye meanders through some of the loveliest countryside, towns and villages in Powys, one of these is Builth Wells, the once fashionable spa town of the early 19th century, it is now the headquarters of the Royal Welsh Show, held here every summer. The river continues its journey through Erwood, where it flows past Orchard Cottage, an 18th century stone cottage owned by Alan and Pat Prior. The cottage is delightful with a wonderful garden which leads down to the river, the garden is well stocked with plants, shrubs, flowers, lots of trees and a well kept lawn. There is even a private stream for fishing.

Artists will be in their element as early morning mists rise from the fields to leave them fresh and green, the air is clear and the skies are blue, just perfect. Inside the cottage are oak beams, traditional and country style furniture. The bedrooms, 2 double, one of which is ensuite, and 1 twin, have colour television and tea and coffee making facilities. On arrival guests are greeted with tea, coffee, home-made cakes and a wonderful warm welcome. Breakfast is full English, evening meals can be taken next door in the pub, an old coaching and drovers inn which serves excellent food. Orchard cottage is an ideal base for touring Mid Wales, Elan Valley, Upper Wye Valley and the Brecon Beacons. Alan and Pat are more than willing to help you plan your day, getting the most out of it. You cannot possibly go wrong when you stay at this most desirable residence.

USEFUL INFORMATION

OPEN; All year
CHILDREN; Welcome
CREDIT CARDS; None taken
ACCOMMODATION; 3 rooms,
2 double one of which is ensuite, 1 twin,

DINING ROOM; Breakfast only
DISABLED ACCESS; No
GARDEN; Beautiful overlooking the river with lots of flowers
PETS; By arrangement

THE CEDARS GUEST HOUSE,
Hay Road,
Builth Well, Powys LD2 3BP

Tel: 01982 553356

The front garden of this friendly guest house overlooks the Royal Welsh Showground and the River Wye. It is a welcoming house where the owners, Mr and Mrs Morris strive to make it a real 'Home from Home' and succeed admirably. Recently refurbished throughout, every room is attractively decorated and the bedrooms have comfortable beds, colour TV, a generously supplied Beverage Tray with hair dryers, shoe cleaning materials and an iron and board being readily available. The house has the Welsh Tourist Board 3 Crowns and is Acclaimed by the RAC. Food is all important at anytime and seems to take on special importance when one is staying away from home.

The meals here are delicious and traditional using vegetables fresh from the garden most of the time. It is a regularly changing menu and if you have special Dietary needs all you have to do is ask. Breakfast is a sustaining meal with a choice and plenty of toast and marmalade as well as freshly brewed coffee and tea. After a busy day either on business or holiday, the bar may well beckon you for a pre-dinner drink or you may prefer the comfortable relaxed atmosphere of the lounge to discuss the day and plan for the tomorrow.

Builth Wells dates back to Roman times and is a traditional Welsh market town, rich in tradition and history. It provides a perfect base for an outdoor holiday, with the River Wye for fishing or canoeing the hills and countryside for walking or riding or just having fun in the sports centre. You could never be bored in this beautiful part of Wales.

USEFUL INFORMATION

*OPEN;*All year
CHILDREN; Welcome
*CREDIT CARDS;*None taken
*LICENSED;*Yes. Residential
*ACCOMMODATION;*7 rooms 5 ensuite
PETS; Yes

RESTAURANT; Good, traditional fare
Using fresh vegetables from the garden mainly
*VEGETARIAN;*Yes & other Dietary needs
*DISABLED ACCESS;*No facilities
*GARDEN;*Yes

Chapter Ten

PANTGWYN FARM,
Whitemill,
Carmarthen,
Carmarthenshire
SA32 7ES

Tel: 01267 290247
Fax: 01267 290880

Nestling in the hills above the beautiful Towy Valley, just 10 minutes from the end of the M4 and 4 miles from Carmarthen, lies the 17th century Farmhouse, Pantgwyn. Owned and run by Tim and Sue Giles, it is a quiet haven where guests are welcome to roam the farm and explorethe local byways. In the spring you will see the sheep with their lambs. The pet goat will be found munching in some quiet corner, Chloe the dog will be happy to take you for a walk while Thomas, the donkey and Bobby the Shetland Pony will oblige with rides by prior arrangement, and along the farm lane to the house you will undoubtedly encounter the farm's free range chickens. It is a very happy place to stay with so much to occupy one that you could almost have a holiday without leaving the farm! Wildlife abounds, foxes can be seen crossing the newly mown meadows where rabbits play. At dusk bats flit across the farmyard in search of insects or watch for the Barn Owl on the old cowshed. It is a truly delightful place.

In the Farmhouse there is very comfortable bed and breakfast accommodation and in the converted barn there are family suites and self-catering accommodation. The ground floor suite has been specially designed for the disabled or the less mobile visitor. There are no steps and all doors are wide enough for wheel chairs. The Farmhouse has been renovated to a very high standard whilst not losing its original features. In the Resident's Lounge you will find a huge inglenook fireplace and bread oven and a log fire in the colder months. Meals at Pantgwyn are very special whether it is Breakfast or Dinner. You eat in an attractive dining on delicious farmhouse food using traditional Welsh recipes and cooked with produce. Non residents are welcome to dine here on Friday and Saturday nights and all guests staying in suites can take meals in the farmhouse if they choose. Non-residents must book in advance. The Resident's Lounge is a friendly meeting place after the day's exploration which might have taken you bird watching, pony trekking or perhaps sketching or painting the glorious countryside. Sea and Freshwater fishing is available and there is both an 18 and a 9 hole golf course in the vicinity.

USEFUL INFORMATION

*OPEN;*All year except Christmas   *RESTAURANT;* Super food. Welsh produce
CHILDREN; Welcome   *VEGETARIAN;* Catered for
CREDIT CARDS; All major cards   *DISABLED ACCESS;* Special suite
LICENSED; Yes   *GARDEN;* Yes + farm
ACCOMMODATION; 3 ensuite rooms   *PETS;* Not in farmhouse
And suites in converted barn, self-catering   No Smoking in Farmhouse. Smoking allowed In Family Suites & Self-catering accommodation

CRAIG-Y-MOR GUEST HOUSE
West Parade, Criccieth,
Gwynedd LL52 0EN

Tel: 01766 522830

The views from Craig-y-Mor are stunning indeed, across Tremadog Bay, one can even see Harlech. This delightful Guest House where Arlene and Brian offer a very warm and friendly welcome to their home. The house was built approximately 100 years ago, situated overlooking West Beach at Criccieth a quiet picturesque town. The quality of accommodation is high with very comfortable bedrooms. All have ensuite shower facilities, colour television, radio, telephone and a tea and coffee tray. There is also a guests bathroom with bath for your use. The lounge is very relaxing complete with an open fire for those chilly days. There is aseparate dining room where you are served a choice of delicious breakfasts including a full English, evening meal is optional.

All the fare is excellent home-cooking using fresh local produce. Special diets and vegetarians are catered for. Craig-y-Mor is ideally situated for exploring the unspoiled beauty of Snowdonia and the Llyn Peninsula, there is also a wide range of attractions all within easy reach, along with golf, fishing, and wonderful walks. The Wales Tourist Board has awarded Craig-y-Mor with '3 Crowns Highly Commended' and it is no wonder, it really is a delightful place to stay.

USEFUL INFORMATION

OPEN; March-October
CHILDREN; Welcome
CREDIT CARDS; None taken
LICENSED; No
ACCOMMODATION; 6 ensuite rooms, 2 double, 4 family
DINING ROOM; Tradition Welsh and English fare, optional evening meal
VEGETARIAN; Catered for and Special Diets
DISABLED ACCESS; No
GARDEN; Yes and Car Park
PETS; Yes by arrangement

Chapter Ten

BORTHWNOG HALL COUNTRY HOUSE HOTEL
Bontddu, Dolgellau,
Gwynedd, Wales LL40 2TT

Tel: 01341 430271 Fax: 01341 430682

Borthwnog Hall Country House Hotel and Restaurant is a most impressive property, the elegant facade is inviting indeed. Borthwnog was built in the late 17th century and is an excellent example of a preserved Regency country house, and is situated on the breathtaking Mawddach Estuary, with stunning views. The house oozes peace and tranquillity, and you have a feeling of being able to totally relax once you have unpacked. The decor is superb, the walls are clothed with wonderful pictures, in fact the Hotel has an Art Gallery containing original watercolours, oils, embroidered pictures, sculpture and pottery. The gallery is recognised by the Welsh Arts Council. The Guest's Sitting Room is delightful, with large comfy chairs and a roaring log fire in the winter, there are lovely display cabinets full of intricate china and porcelain. The bedrooms are individually furnished and decorated in keeping with the house, with ensuite bathroom or shower, colour television, telephone, radio/alarm and tea and coffee making facilities. In the evenings you can dine in the intimate little restaurant with its varied A La Carte and Table D'Hote menus, there is an excellent wine list to compliment your meal. The Hotel is ideally placed for walking and touring around the Snowdonia National Park and Mid-Wales. With awards such as '4 Crown Highly Commended' by the Wales Tourist Board, AA '5Q' and RAC 'Highly Commended', a stay in this beautiful Country House, where you will be among friends, is highly recommended.

USEFUL INFORMATION

OPEN; All year except Christmas
CHILDREN; Welcome
CREDIT CARDS; Mastercard/Visa
LICENSED; Residential bar
ACCOMMODATION; 3 ensuite rooms
PETS; By prior arrangement
RESTAURANT; Varied A La Carte and Table D'Hote menus
VEGETARIAN; Yes. Special diets by request
DISABLED ACCESS; To the restaurant
GARDEN; 3 $\frac{1}{2}$ acres

Wales

THE IVY HOUSE
Finsbury Square,
Dolgellau Gwynedd LL40 1RF

Tel: 01341 422535 Fax: 01341 422689

Dolgellau nestles happily at the foot of Cader Idris in the valley of the River Wnion. It is a contented country town built mostly of granite and local Welsh slate. Ivy House is just out of the main square on the Twywn Road. What an interesting house it is, proclaiming that it was built in 1829, yet the focal point of the pretty dining room is a fine fireplace which is almost an inglenook and must show that part of the building is considerably older. Every one of the 6 letting rooms, some of which are en-suite, is attractively furnished with every facility. Children are very welcome and highchairs are available. Everywhere is centrally heated and guests are encouraged to enjoy the comfort of the lounge and the fun of the cellar bar.

Non-residents are very welcome at Ivy House for meals which are an enjoyable experience, cooked by Margaret Bamford, who with her husband James, owns the establishment. They have been here 14 years, gradually bringing the house to its present standard. With the exception of ice cream and sorbet everything on the menu is home-made and produced in Margaret's sparkling and well-planned kitchen. The range of dishes is certain to provide something to suit everyone no matter what the age. One starter is especially good. Anglesey Egg - a baked egg on sauteed leeks topped with cream and cheese. There are vegetarian dishes and a Welsh Supper which is quite delicious.

USEFUL INFORMATION

OPEN; All year. Dinner 5pm-9.30pm
CHILDREN; Very welcome
CREDIT CARDS; Visa/Master/Euro/Amex
LICENSED; Residential & Restaurant
ACCOMMODATION; 6 rooms 3 ensuite

RESTAURANT; Home-made food at its best
BAR FOOD; Not applicable
VEGETARIAN; 6 dishes + omelettes
DISABLED ACCESS; Level entrance
GARDEN; Small garden for pre-dinner drinks

Chapter Ten

GUEST HOUSE GWYNFA
*Llanarmon Dyffryn Ceiriog,
Llangollen, North Wales LL20 7LF*

Tel: 01691 600287

Glen and Goff Oldaker own and run this small, friendly Guest House which lies very near to the centre of the picturesque village of Llanarmon Dyffryn Ceiriog, which is set high in the Ceiriog Valley amongst the lovely uncrowded Berwyn Mountains. The house is welcoming and relaxed, the comfortable, centrally heated bedrooms with private WC, basin, have beverage facilities and towels. The double bedded family room is entirely en-suite. You will be extremely well fed both at breakfast and for a picnic lunch and dinner if you require it. Everything is home-cooked with a great choice at breakfast for both vegetarians and non-vegetarians. The four course evening meal you will find tasty and satisfying - something to look forward to at the end of the day. There is always time to relax in the garden or sample the near-by hostelries.

The Oldaker's offer much more than the normal hospitality. Because walking is the perfect way to absorb the beauty of the region, many guests walk the hills and valleys and if you wish they will plan your walks for you or you may decide to come here on one of their planned Walking Holidays which are normally two to six days. The area offers a varied choice of walking from deep-cut valleys to high moorland and craggy ridges. The walks are in the Berwyn, Aran and Arenig mountain ranges. Each day they offer personally guided walks. These can either be easy, moderate or strenuous, to suit your requirements. Alternatively borrow detailed walk sheets for your use. Paths are generally not waymarked and some navigating ability is needed. Or try Goff's Map and Compass weekends and never get lost again!

There is more! 'Joy through Flowers' is a relaxing option. Glen will take you on easy explorative walks, discovering flowers in hedgerows, meadows, hillsides and colourful gardens, and lead you in refreshing 'tension-relieving' mini workshops. For the walking, map-reading and flowers, you will need walking boots and waterproof jackets. Combining the comfort of 'Gwynfa' with the options of peace and relaxtion, or participation in the activities, makes for a stunning holiday.

USEFUL INFORMATION

OPEN; *February 1st- 3oth November* **DINING ROOM;** *Delicious home-cooked fare*
CHILDREN; *Welcome* **CREDIT CARDS;** *None taken*
DISABLED ACCESS; *No* **VEGETARIAN;** *Catered for with prior notice*
ACCOMMODATION; *Comfortable rooms*

EINION HOUSE
Friog, Fairbourne,
Gwynedd, Wales LL38 2NX

Tel: 01341 250644

North Wales has such diverse scenery with wonderful craggy mountains, rugged and wild landscape, windy roads and narrow gauge railways. Then there are quaint villages and castles and finally the sea, there is everything here for the complete holiday for the whole family and where better stay than a family orientated guest house. There is an excellent one in Friog, a unspoilt small hamlet set between the sea and the mountains on the periphery of the beautiful Snowdonia National Park. Einion House is situated near the A439 coast road between Dolgellau and Tywyn, so is very easy to find. The house has the most stunning views across the Rhinogs and Cardigan Bay. Mr and Mrs Waterhouse own this delightful guest house, a very warm and friendly couple, who welcome you to their home, and treat you as friends. The house itself was built around 1750 and is comfortably furnished and totally centrally heated. There are 7 guest bedrooms altogether, 5 doubles, 3 being ensuite, 1 ensuite twin and an ensuite single. All the rooms have wash hand basin, clock/radio, hair dryer, colour television and a complimentary well stocked tea and coffee tray. The guest's sitting room is very comfy, where you can meet the other guests, plan you days outing or just relax, with such a happy atmosphere that is not hard to do, on chilly days a log fire roars away adding to the ambiance. Being such a family based guest house, children and dogs are especially welcome, but dogs must not enter into the public rooms. Einion is renowned for its good wholesome home-cooked fare, breakfast is a real treat and will set you up for the day, with several choices including a traditional full English meal. An evening meal is available where you may feast upon such sumptuous delights as Minestrone Soup, then Roast Ham with Mustard Sauce, Roast Potatoes, Sprouts and Mixed Vegetables, followed by Rhubarb Crumble and Custard Sauce, finishing with coffee served in the Lounge Bar. There is a good choice of wine for you to partake with your meal. One of Britain's finest and safest sandy beaches on the west coast is but a few minutes walk away, it is also good for windsurfing and surfing. Fairbourne has its own narrow gauge railway running along the coast. This is excellent walking terrain, and with golf, fishing and pony trekking is a superb area, and where better to enjoy it from than Einion House.

USEFUL INFORMATION

OPEN; All year except Christmas
CHILDREN; Welcome
CREDIT CARDS; Diners
LICENSED; Residential
ACCOMMODATION; 7 rooms,
5 doubles-3 ensuite, 1 ensuite single,
1 ensuite twin

DINING ROOM; Excellent home-cooking, Delicious evening meals
VEGETARIAN; Upon request
DISABLED ACCESS; Limited
GARDEN; No
PETS; Dogs by arrangement

Chapter Ten

THE WENALLT,
Abergavenny, Montmouthshire,
Gwent,
South Wales, NP7 0HP.

Tel : 01873 830694

Nestling in the hills of the Brecon Beacons National Park, this 16th century converted longhouse is perfectly charming. Owned and run by the Harris family, much care has been taken with the refurbishment, ensuring the character and qualities of the property have not been lost. There are lots of oak furniture, some of it hand made, oak beams, inglenook fireplaces and log fires adding to the ambience and warmth of this home, all tied together by the friendly, sincere feelings of this family towards their guests. Bedrooms are large and comfortable with all the necessities; TV, tea/coffee tray and central heating. Some are in the Ty-Bach annexe, a mere 15 yards from the house, and are all en suite. The TV room is cosy, and there is an elegant Drawing Room with original oak beams and an inglenook fireplace. You can relax here in front of a warm log fire in great comfort, and perhaps discuss your activities and plans for the next day. (Even more ideal is a glass of something warming in your hand whilst doing so!- This can be obtained from the bar!) Food is of good quality, all beinghome cooked and local produce where possible; it is served in the traditional dining room where the service and friendliness are outstanding, and there is a comprehensive wine list to compliment your meal. Breakfast is traditional fayre and vegetarians can be catered for. Dogs are allowed in the house but not in the public rooms, if only for other guests comfort! The house stands on a hillside, in 50 acres of farmland, with views over the Usk Valley and surrounding area. It is a magnificent setting and the views alone will make you want to return here again and again! It is rumoured that Cromwell stayed here on one of his marches and the house would certainly have had the comfort for a guest of his standing!

Gwent is a lovely area with many activities available if desired. The magic and history of the mountains and valleys are all there to be investigated and a more pleasurable pastime cannot be envisaged! Walking these areas and breathing the clean, fresh air will bring a bloom to your cheeks that no city air could! Wales is one of those places with the mystery of the Celt races in its blood, and much of its history incorporates Celtic stones and the Druids of times past. At some of these sites you can almost see the swirl of the robes and hear the cries of the worshippers as they called upon their gods to favour them. There are castles and great houses, gardens and abbeys to visit and digest the stories and history. The old market towns offer great interest too; Abergavenny, Monmouth or Brecon are all within a drive away and offer a great day out. There is sailing on Llangorse Lake, pony trekking over the Black Mountains and a wealth of other activities, all within easy distance of The Wenallt!

USEFUL INFORMATION

OPEN : All year
CHILDREN : Welcome
PETS : Dogs welcome
LICENSED : Full
CREDIT CARDS : None taken
ACCOMMODATION : 10 rooms, 8 en suite.

DINING ROOM : Good home cooking
VEGETARIAN : Catered for
DISABLED ACCESS : Accessible
BAR SNACKS : No
GARDEN : 1 acre lawn

Wales

CROSSWAYS HOUSE
Cowbridge,
Vale of Glamorgan CF71 7LJ

Tel: 01446-773171

Crossways House built by the shipping magnate Owen Williams in 1921 is both beautiful and Gothic. It has played host to princes and been occupied by a Maharajah. During World War II it was a hospital but settled back peacefully to use as a stately home after the war. There is an impressive turret, superb wood panelling, a magnificent staircase and a stunning barrel-vaulted ceiling in the living room. The house is set in 6 acres of landscaped grounds with a tennis court and a clutch of chickens who wander freely and assure you of fresh, newly laid eggs for breakfast! Warm and welcoming you cannot fail to enjoy staying here.

You will find the house situated just one mile outside the historic and picturesque town of Cowbridge, which is known for its many smart shops, pubs and restaurants - there are also some excellent hostelries which will provide you with good evening meals - two pubs are within walking distance of the house. For the energetic there are any number of outdoor activities within easy reach.

Within the house, which is beautifully appointed, Anne Paterson, the owner, has created a delightful home in which she has two double-bedded rooms, one with en-suite shower-room and one with private bathroom, and a twin-bedded room with en-suite bathroom. They are such pretty rooms and each is equipped with TV and a hospitality tray which includes Hot Chocolate and biscuits. There is also the Ballroom Flat which is self-contained, very comfortable and will sleep up to four people. Breakfast is a feast with a full Welsh or English platter or any number of other choices even down to home-made Glamorgan Sausages.

USEFUL INFORMATION

OPEN;*All year*   **DINING ROOM;***Full English or Welsh*
CHILDREN;*Welcome*   **VEGETARIAN;** *Catered for*
CREDIT CARDS;*None taken*   **DISABLED ACCESS;***No special facilities*
LICENSED;*No*   **GARDEN;***6 acres*
ACCOMMODATION;*2 ensuite rooms*   **PETS;***By arrangement*
and one with private bathroom + self-catering apartment sleeps 4.

Chapter Ten

GWESTY FFERM PENBONTBREN FARM HOTEL
Glynarthen, Nr Cardigan,
Ceredigion SA44 6PE

Tel: 01239 810248 #
Fax: 01239 811129

Situated in the secluded valley of the River Dulais, this must be one of the most interesting hotels in Wales. No wonder it has won so many awards. Built in early Victorian times it is a well established farm hotel especially planned for those who wish to enjoy a holiday with a true Welsh flavour. For the last 5 generations it has been in the capable hands of the Humphreys family and it is their imaginative, creative skills which one notices everywhere. The Victorian farmhouse overlooks the complex which is set in 90 acres of livestock raising farmland in the Ceredigion countryside and within 3 miles of sandy beaches. You can sleep in a stable, a granary or a threshing barn in family rooms that have been converted from original stone outbuildings. The character remains, with beams and exposed stone work everywhere. Everything conforms to the highest national standards and at the same time every room is charmingly furnished with pretty drapes and covers. All the rooms have private bathrooms, colour TV and tea making facilities. Two of the ground floor suites can cater for the disabled. Across the courtyard from the bedrooms is the restaurant with a bar and a lounge. Furnished in period pine it is both delightful to see and extremely comfortable. Penbontbren is renowned for the quality of its food and the carefully compiled menu makes sure that the wide range of fresh food produced locally is used. Traditional Welsh fare features largely of course but the overall menu covers a range of exciting dishes. People come from a distance to enjoy both the atmosphere and the cuisine.

There is so much to do that one can never be bored for a moment. On the farm there is a Countryside Museum displaying a collection of restored items from a rural past, including old tools, the original farm tractor, authentic Welsh costume and much more. The Nature Discovery Trail is a mile long signposted walk which takes in a river, ponds and wildlife. Sandy beaches abound and there are tiny villages to explore as well as a number of flour mills where you watch the miller at work. The famous falls of the River Teifi at Cenarth cannot be missed and St Davids is another must. The list is endless and add to this fishing, riding and golf and you must have everything for a perfect holiday. For the business man there are full conference facilities.

USEFUL INFORMATION

OPEN; All year except Xmas week
CHILDREN; Welcome
CREDIT CARDS; All major cards
LICENSED; Yes
ACCOMMODATION; 6 family rooms 1 dbl 3tw
PETS; By arrangement

RESTAURANT; Excellent food using local Produce + Welsh traditional dishes
VEGETARIAN; Catered for
DISABLED ACCESS; Fully accessible
GARDEN; Yes

730

FAIRFIELD COTTAGE
Knelston, Gower,
Swansea SA3 1AR

Tel: 01792 391013

This enchanting cottage was built in the 18th century and apart from the modern comforts one demands today it has the same character and warmth that it must have had when it was first occupied. The walls are thick, the floors slightly uneven and a host of nooks and crannies delight the eye. It even has friendly ghosts! Knelston is a hamlet just 12 miles west of Swansea with its Marina, Theatres and excellent shopping and entertainment facilities. The Gower Peninsula which has been designated an area of outstanding natural beauty has fine beaches and splendid coastal paths for walkers, riding and golf are also available locally.

Fairfield Cottage has a very beautiful garden with a mass of ornamental shrubs and flowers surrounding the lawns. This typical Gower cottage has a comfortable lounge with an inglenook fireplace from which the wood fires throw out warmth and fill the air with that tantalising smell that only logs can produce - something that enhances the country cottage atmosphere. The three pretty double bedrooms with hot and cold water and full central heating provide a relaxing night's sleep and in the morning you come down to the attractive dining room to enjoy a beautifully cooked breakfast of your choice. Caryl Ashton, the owner, is a skilled cook and produces delicious food of a very high standard with locally produced vegetables and fruit when in season.

USEFUL INFORMATION

OPEN; All year except Christmas
CHILDREN; Over 5 years old
CREDIT CARDS; None taken
PETS; No
ACCOMMODATION; 3 double rooms not ensuite

DINING ROOM; Delicious home-cooked food. Dinner is available
VEGETARIAN; By arrangement
DISABLED ACCESS; No
GARDEN; Beautiful with lawns, shrubs and flowers

Chapter Ten

TREGYNON COUNTRY FARMHOUSE HOTEL
Gwaun Valley, Nr Fishguard,
Pembrokeshire SA65 9TU

Tel: 01239 820531
Fax: 01239 820808

However beautifully compiled and illustrated no brochure could ever do justice to Tregynon. It is one of those places that one dreams of finding and seldom does. In the heart of the Pembrokeshire Coast National Park just over 2 hours drive from the Severn Bridge, the hotel is an attractive 16th century farmhouse approached by its own half mile drive. Total peace surrounds you the moment you step out of your car and enter this magical world. Tregynon is in a unique situation overlooked by Carn Ingli, Mountain of Angels, and perched on the edge of the spectacular Gwaun Valley with its banks carpeted with ancient oaken forests. This forgotten ice-age valley where time seems to stand still has been designated a 'Site of Special Scientific Interest'. No one could ever get tired of watching the 'resident' badgers, buzzards, herons and ravens whilst red kites, peregrine falcons, polecats and otters are also seen from time to time. Apart from forest walks which lead down from Tregynon to the valley floor some 200ft below, there are spectacular walks from the head of Tregynon's drive to the peaks of the Preseli range. There are also 180 miles of National Park coastal footpath to explore, all of which is within easy reach by car in under an hour. Excellent sea and river fishing for salmon, trout and sewin is available at Newport whilst fly fishing enthusiasts will delight in the richly stocked waters of the nearby reservoirs. Boat trips, sandy, safe bathing beaches, sailing, windsurfing are among the many activities on offer. For those who like exploring towns and villages the choice is endless
  Only a few miles away is the impressive Neolithic burial chamber of Pentre Ifan with its huge pillars and capstone. This is the land from which came the famous blue stones of Stonehenge and parts of Tregynon are built with this stone. Although the farmhouse is known to date back to 1594, surrounding earthworks indicate the site was inhabited well before the Roman invasion. Inside the farmhouse, the sense of age and history are apparent and the atmosphere is wonderful. The Heards, whose home it is, have furnished it with loving care to ensure both comfort and a sense of harmony. The massive stone inglenook provides an attractive feature in the beamed lounge. The dining room is charming and it is here you will be provided with a wonderful breakfast with a choice of starters, followed by a varying choice of cooked main course, such as their own oak-smoked bacon, additive-free sausages, kippers and vegetarian cutlets. Dinner is an unforgettable occasion - children are fed separately around 6pm to enable parents and other guests to savour their meal in a relaxed and peaceful atmosphere. Tregynon offers award winning cusine with wholefood and vegetarian dishes a speciality. The centrally heated bedrooms have been converted from a range of old stone cottages adjacent to the farmhouse. They are beautifully appointed, all en suite and equipped with colour television and tea-making facilities. The Heards personally run Tregynon and pride themselves on the excellent reputation that has been gained. One could not fail to enjoy a holiday or a 'Great Little Break' in which Tregynon specialises, at any season of the year. Come and escape from the outside world.

USEFUL INFORMATION

OPEN; All year
CHILDREN; Welcome
CREDIT CARDS: All major cards
ACCOMMODATION; All ensuite rooms

DINING ROOM; Imaginative, exciting food
VEGETARIAN; A speciality
DISABLED ACCESS; Yes
PETS; Yes, but not in bedrooms

PLAS TIRION GUEST HOUSE
Ffordd Bryn Madoc,
Gwynfryn, Wrexham LL11 5UP
North Wales

Tel: 01978 757497

With panoramic views, located in the solitude of lovely countryside stands Plas Tirion Guest House, a very warm and friendly home. This Wales Tourist Board '1 Crown Commended' property was built in 1979, is owned and excellently run by Mrs. Evelyn Jones, a very welcoming and most helpful lady, who has a wide and varied knowledge of the surrounding area. There are 2 guest rooms which are attractively presented with vanity unit, colour television, fridge and a complimentary tea and coffee tray. Guests have their own bathroom.

A good wholesome and delicious farmhouse style breakfast is served, starting the day off well. An evening meal is provided by prior arrangement. The garden is lovely, the front has wonderful views overlooking the valley. Walkers will be in paradise staying here, with extensive walks and organised footpaths. Other activities include fishing, golf, cycling, painting and drawing. If you are looking for somewhere off the beaten track then Plas Tirion Guest House is just the place.

USEFUL INFORMATION

OPEN; All year
CHILDREN; Welcome, under 10 years by arrangement
CREDIT CARDS; None taken
ACCOMMODATION; 2 guest rooms, 1 double, 1 twin
DINING ROOM; Traditional home-cooking, using fresh produce. Evening meal by arrangement
DISABLED ACCESS; No
GARDEN; Yes, front overlooking the valley, panoramic views
PETS; By arrangement

Chapter Ten

THE BLACK LION ROYAL HOTEL
High Street, Lampeter,
Dyfed SA48 7BG

Tel: 01570 422172
Fax: 01570 423630

Dyfed is a mixture of moorlands and fine beaches, the Cambrian Mountains where desolate moorlands rise and the uncultivated and infertile hills reach up to a height of over 2000ft in some places, and rapid flowing streams and rivers plummet through densely wooded vales to the sea. Some of the finest beaches in Britain are along the 40 mile stretch of Cardigan Bay, here they are sandy, safe and secluded, and standing at the gateway of river estuaries are peaceful seaside towns. Close to this wonderful setting is the small market town of Lampeter. The town itself has lovely Georgian and Victorian properties that stand either side of the main street, it has a good range of shops, most are old established family businesses. The St Davids University College, built around 1822 stands in the centre of the town as does The Black Lion Royal Hotel. Originally an old Coaching Inn it is very comfortable indeed, Barbara and David Bennett work extremely hard and have created a first class establishment where guests are made to feel at ease, to relax and enjoy their stay. The bedrooms, 15 in all, have colour co-ordinated bedding and drapes, the luxury of ensuite facilities, either a bath and/or shower. Therooms have colour television incorporating satellite TV and radio, direct dial telephone with alarm and baby listening facility and a plentifully supplied tea and coffee tray. The whole Hotel is centrally heated, creating a warm and cosy atmosphere. There are several public rooms including a Reception Lounge, friendly Resident's Bar, comfortable Lounge Bar and a function room, making it an ideal location for the business person as well as the holiday maker. All this is complimented by a good Restaurant seating around 40. The food is excellent with a fine selection of starters including Escargot with Garlic Butter, the main course has 3 sections; Fish, Poultry and Beef. Vegetarians are very well catered for with a large selection of mouthwatering dishes. Desserts are delectable, all finished off with tea or coffee.

A stay here would not be complete without a visit to those wonderful Cambrian Mountains, for those who love walking this is paradise but there are plenty of little places to explore by car or bike. A super Hotel in a delightful setting and one not to be missed.

USEFUL INFORMATION

OPEN; All year
CHILDREN; Welcome
CREDIT CARDS; All cards
LICENSED; Yes
ACCOMMODATION; 15 ensuite rooms
PETS; By arrangement
RESTAURANT; Fine A la carte menu
BAR FOOD; Available
VEGETARIAN; Catered for + special diets
DISABLED ACCESS; Restaurant only
GARDEN; Yes

THE FFALDU COUNTRY HOUSE
Llandegley, Powys LL1 5UD

Tel: 01597 851421

It is almost impossible to believe that this charming country house built about the turn of the 16th century could have been virtually derelict when the present owners, Leslie and Sylvia Knott bought it in 1985, Today it has the tranquil ambience of a well loved house, beautifully furnished that has spanned the centuries contentedly. It has been lovingly and carefully restored and is now the pride of Llandegley village. Imagine the scene; the picturesque Ffaldau Country House stands in its own landscaped gardens with a variety of flowers, shrubs and trees, nestling amongst rolling hills in one of the most scenic parts of Wales, just 10 minutes drive from Llandrindod Wells. You step inside the house into a comfortably furnished lounge with a welcoming log fire. Oak beams are everywhere, family heirlooms in every corner and charming floral decorations. The resident's bar overlooks the lounge and it is here you can relax after dinner with coffee and chocolates. Smoking is only allowed in the downstairs bar. In the summer a gentle stroll around the garden before or after dinner allows you to enjoy the profusion of floral colour from the many hanging baskets and window boxes. Neat lawns blend with the scenic backdrop of the rolling Radnor hills. A delightful upstairs sitting room nestles under exposed cruck beams and provides television, board games and an impressive collection of books, many on railways - Leslie's passion.

If ever anyone needed tempting to eat one of the delicious meals served at The Ffaldau then the romantic charm of the dining room with its Welsh slate floor, low oak beams and log fire must be the catalyst. It is enchanting. The breakfast selection is extensive and dinner is memorable. Sylvia Knott, the chef is extremely talented and produces superb food. Dinner can be 2/4 courses and most menus include organic meat supplied by Graig Farm, Dolau. Sylvia's daughter, Sara destroys anyone's determination not to eat desserts - hers are irresistible. However special diets can be catered for as well as alternatives to the menu should you prefer it. A light supper is also available on request. The small wine list has a well chosen number of quality wines. The 4 centrally heated bedrooms are all different although furnished with country cottage charm, three are ensuite and the fourth has private facilities. Each has a tea/coffee making facility, hairdryer, shampoos, shoe cleaning and in two rooms there is colour TV. Having read this you will not be surprised to know that The Ffaldau has many accolades including Welsh Tourist Board 3 Crowns Highly Commended, AA Premier Selected 5Q's and The Taste of Wales, AA 1996 Guest House of the Year for Wales, 1997 'Which Hotel Guide' as one of their Welsh Hotels of the Year. No one would ever regret staying here and most people leave with a promise to themselves to return as quickly as possible.

USEFUL INFORMATION

OPEN;All year
CHILDREN;Over 10 years
CREDIT CARDS;Visa/Master/Euro
LICENSED;Yes
ACCOMMODATION;4 ensuite rooms

DINING ROOM;Superb food, home produce
VEGETARIAN;Catered for
DISABLED ACCESS;No facilities
PETS;Dogs by prior arrangement
GARDEN;Beautiful gardens

Chapter Ten

CWMGWYN FARM
Llangadog Road, Llandovery,
Carmarthenshire, Wales SA20 0EQ

Tel: 01550 720410
Fax: 01550 720262

A characterful 17th century farmhouse with exposed beams and plenty of atmosphere awaits and welcomes you to Cwmgwyn Farm. It is admirably situated with splendid views across the River Towy which runs through the farmland. Guest bedrooms enjoy good quality decor, furnishings and linens, colour television, a tea and coffee tray and hair dryer, and for your privacy an ensuite bathroom. Mrs. Lewis your able hostess, offers traditional farmhouse cooking prepared and served using fresh locally produced ingredients. Residents can enjoy the relaxing comfort of the oak beamed lounge with its inglenook fireplace and exposed stonework. The garden is a feature with a picnic area that overlooks the river.

Cwmgwyn has been awarded the Wales Tourist Board '2 Crown Highly Commended' accolade, reflecting the high standard to be found here. Visitors to this area can enjoy the many interesting and varied beauty spots, forest areas offer lovely walks and to enjoy the local flora and fauna. Fascinating villages and towns steeped in history, country houses and castles just wait to be explored. You are always assured a warm and friendly welcome at Cwmgwyn Farm.

USEFUL INFORMATION

OPEN; Easter-End of October
CHILDREN; Welcome
CREDIT CARDS; None taken
ACCOMMODATION; 3 ensuite rooms
PETS; No
DINING ROOM; Traditional farmhouse cooking. No evening meal
DISABLED ACCESS; No
GARDEN; Yes with picnic area

Wales

LLWYNCELYN GUEST HOUSE
Llandovery,
Carmarthenshire SA20 0EP

Tel: 01550 720566

Discover the glorious scenic and outdoor attractions of Mid and South Wales, returning at the end of each exciting day to the comfort and warmth of the Llwyncelyn Guest House. This lovely house stands within its own grounds, where the neat and well kept lawns sweep downto the River Tywi, where one can relax whilst indulging in an alfresco afternoon tea served by the owners. Personal and attentive service is most evident and Mr. & Mrs. Griffiths, who have run the Guest House for well over 28 years, are delighted to boast of how their guests return time and time again, to soak up the peaceful ambience and good wholesome home cooking. Bedrooms have full central heating and for extra comfort electric blankets are supplied for cooler nights. There is a wash basin with hot and cold water, a shaver point and tea and coffee making facilities. Furnishings are traditional with good quality fabrics. The 2 guest bathrooms are close to the bedrooms. A welcoming and comfortable lounge with colour TV is available. There is a separate dining room and here one can take advantage of the residential licence and indulge in a bottle of wine or a glass of ones favourite tipple.

Llandovery is a very pretty place with its cobbled market square and the remains of a medieval castle and can be found in grid square 760-340. Just off the A40 is Llwyncelyn Guest House close to the river bridge, the grid reference is SN 761-347 Within the surrounding area is the chance for visitors to satisfy themselves in one of the many pastimes available. A 9 hole golf course is situated locally. Pony trekking or cycling and for those wishing to while away the hours fishing, look no further than the owners private stretch of river, or the local Fishing Association water where trout and salmon abound. Extensive walks are many and varied, through lush forests or on the hills, where rare birds and unusual flora and fauna pervade. The Brecon Beacons has magnificent views and the town of Brecon affords the visitor fascinating narrow streets where craft and antique shops lay side by side.

USEFUL INFORMATION

OPEN; All year except Christmas week
CHILDREN; Welcome. Cot, highchair and baby-sitting available
CREDIT CARDS; None taken
LICENSED; Residential
ACCOMMODATION; 6 rooms, 1 double, 3 twin, 1 family, 1 single, 2 bathrooms

DINING ROOM; Good wholesome fayre. Evening meal by arrangement
DISABLED ACCESS; No
GARDEN; Beautiful lawns, hedges, mature borders, all lead down to the river
PETS; No

Chapter Ten

BWLCH FARMHOUSE
Llananno, Llandrindod Wells,
Powys, Wales LD1 6TT

Tel: 01597 840366 Fax: 01597 840366

Bwlch is a beautiful old cruck farmhouse, a 'cruck' being a pointed timber arch forming the framework of a house from ground to gable. Bwlch is a wonderful example. The house is very old and has cruck beams dating from 1522. Some of the stone walls are original, there are still stone floors, but modern comforts have been added including central heating. The farmhouse has 3 guest rooms, 2 of the rooms having ensuite shower facilities, the other a private bathroom. Each has a radio/alarm and a tea and coffee tray. Breakfast is served in the dining room, which houses a beautiful carved beam over the fireplace.

While you are here why not arrange with your hosts, Mr. & Mrs. Taylor, an excellent 3 course evening meal, to be eaten by candlelight. Set amidst the hills of mid-Wales and overlooking the Ithon Valley, Bwlch Farmhouse is the ideal location for taking wonderful walks, especially along the 'Glyndwr's Way' and by the Elan Dams. There is also fishing, golf and riding nearby and Bwlch can offer basic stabling for 2 horses, by arrangement. A short drive away is Knighton where you can visit Powys County Observatory and Offa's Dyke Heritage Centre. The elegant Victorian spa town of Llandrindod Wells is only 12 miles away. The Wales Tourist Board has awarded Bwlch Farmhouse '2 Crowns Highly Commended'. A farmhouse not to be missed.

USEFUL INFORMATION

OPEN; Easter-October
CHILDREN; Welcome
CREDIT CARDS; None taken
LICENSED; No
ACCOMMODATION; 3 rooms,
2 double, 1 twin, 2 ensuite, 1 private bathroom

DINING ROOM; Excellent home-cooked fare, 3 course evening meal by arrangement
VEGETARIAN; Catered for
DISABLED ACCESS; No
GARDEN; Yes
PETS; Yes

Wales

HOLLY FARM
Howey, Llandrindod Wells,
Powys LD1 5PP

Tel: 01597 822402

Holly Farm dates back to Tudor times and has the happy atmosphere that is created over centuries. Today it has been carefully modernised with full central heating and mainly ensuite bedrooms beautifully appointed with soft relaxing colours, some with exposed beams and all the bedrooms have lovely views over the farm and surrounding woodlands. Guests sit in the comfortable lounge with its fine stone fireplace in which a log fire is lit on chilly evenings. Here too you can watch TV if you wish. In the Dining Room you will be served a full cooked English breakfast and if you dine in you will relish the delicious home grown Beef and Lamb. Traditional cooking using all home produced vegetables is the speciality of the house. Holly Farm is a delight to stay in and you can be assured of the courteous and caring attention of Ruth Jones and her family.

The superb countryside around Holly Farm is easily reached and it is close to the village of Howey on the A483 only one and a half miles away and south of the fascinating spa town of Llandrindod Wells. As well as walking one can go pony-trekking or fish by the lake. There is golf, tennis, bowls and swimming to complete the activities. Builth Wells is 6 miles away on the banks of the River Wye. Here you will find some lovely river walks. Apart from being an interesting town it is also home to the Royal Welsh Show. The Elan Valley Reservoirs with their breathtaking views and spectacular mountain scenery offer a wealth of bird life. Red Kite, Buzzards and many more. Powis Castle is fascinating; in fact there is so much to do one is spoilt for choice.

USEFUL INFORMATION

OPEN: *April-November. Winter by request*
CHILDREN: *Welcome*
CREDIT CARDS: *None taken*
LICENSED: *No*
ACCOMMODATION: *5 rooms mainly ensuite*
PETS: *No*

DINING ROOM: *Excellent home-cooked fare*
VEGETARIAN: *Yes, by request*
DISABLED ACCESS: *No*
GARDEN: *Yes*

Chapter Ten

HOTEL COMMODORE
Llandrindod Wells,
Powys LD1 5ER

Tel: 01597 825737
Fax: 01597 822288

The Hotel Commodore is one of the most imposing buildings in this part of Wales. Built as a Vicarage in 1893 it became a hotel in 1900. One wonders why it was ever a vicarage. It would have needed a wealthy man to maintain and heat it, let alone furnish it, and one cannot suppose vicars were any better off then than they are now. As a hotel it found its metier. The spacious, gracious rooms lend themselves perfectly to the business of innkeeping. It has always had a good reputation but under the new and inspired ownership of Ian Watkins it has undergone a complete and skilful transformation. Everything that was good about it has been highlighted and the improvements in keeping with the age of the building are superb. The end product is a Victorian style establishment with the theme carried throughout. The only anomaly is the intriguing American Nostalgia Bar.

Within the hotel, which has 50 ensuite bedrooms perfectly appointed with colour TV,Direct Dial Telephone and a Hostess Tray, there is a Leisure Complex available to residents consisting of a heated swimming pool, Jacuzzi, Sauna, Gym with State of the Art Equipment. The Ballroom provides four nights a week of live entertainment including a Dinner Dance. You can choose to eat in the elegant Fountain Restaurant, in which the food is imaginative, innovative and delicious either from an a la carte menu or from the Carvery. The Bar is welcoming and a variety of meals are available from a traditional menu at lunchtime.

Llandrindod Wells is a delightful place and surrounded by glorious countryside which will appeal to the walker. Here one can fish, play golf, bowls, tennis or go pony trekking and go-karting. The town itself will give you hours of pleasureable exploration. At the end of the day returning to the Hotel Commodore in the certain knowledge that you are going to be very welcome, well fed, offered wine from an exceptional list, entertained and finally retiring to a room with a supremely comfortable bed, there is little more one could ask for.

USEFUL INFORMATION

OPEN; All year
CHILDREN; Welcome
CREDIT CARDS; All major cards
LICENSED; Yes
ACCOMMODATION; 50 ensuite rooms
GARDEN; Yes + Leisure Complex

RESTAURANT; A la Carte & Carvery
BAR FOOD; Traditional
VEGETARIAN; Several choices
DISABLED ACCESS; Totally accessible
PETS; By arrangement

THE SEVERN ARMS HOTEL
Penybont, Llandrindod Wells,
Powys LD1 5UA

Tel: 01597 851224 Fax: 851693

This pleasing late-Georgian Style inn stands at the centre of village life at Penybont, as it always has done down the centuries though not always on the same site. It was moved from its site west of the river in 1840 and it is that building that give so much enjoyment to so many people today in the capable, experienced and friendly hands of Geoff and Tessa Lloyd. Over the years the hotel has been modernised to a very high standard. All the well furnished and very comfortable bedrooms are ensuite, the rooms centrally heated and with colour television, tea/coffee making facilities, telephone, hair dryers, trouser presses, and a welcoming glass of sherry..

Staying here you will rapidly realise that The Severn Arms is the focal point of village life. The friendly Olde Worlde Bars always have a sprinkling of regulars talking about local matters with good humour and not infrequent banter. The great thing about it is that they do not make newcomers feel unwelcome, quite the reverse. The Lloyd's have a great reputation for food and whether you eat in the restaurant or enjoy a bar meal, the food is always well-cooked and presented and includes many traditional favourites as well as other dishes. The specialities of the house are Grills, Roasts, Home-made Steak and Kidney Pie and Cottage Pies. If you would prefer something simple like a freshly cut sandwich or a Ploughmans, they are readily available as well as interestingly filled Jacket Potatoes. There is a special Children's Menu and for the sweet toothed a delectable home-made fruit pie, Sherry Trifle or a variety of ice creams. Vegetarians are catered for. The food is sensibly priced and served by a friendly, welcoming staff.

From the Severn Arms one can indulge in many sporting activities including golf at five courses, Bowls, Climbing, Canoeing, Shooting, Horse Riding and Mountain Biking. The shops in the nearby towns are fascinating and most of them have lively market days. Hay-on-Wye is for the book lover.

USEFUL INFORMATION

OPEN; All year except Xmas & New Year
CHILDREN; Welcome
CREDIT CARDS; All major cards
LICENSED; Yes
ACCOMMODATION; 10 ensuite rooms
PETS; By arrangement

RESTAURANT; Good, food Home-cooked.
BAR FOOD; Great choice.
VEGETARIAN; Yes, catered for
DISABLED ACCESS; None special

Chapter Ten

THE ST. TUDNO HOTEL,
Promenade,
Llandudno,
North Wales LL30 2LP

Tel: 01492 874411
Fax: 01492 860407

If one were to list all the accolades that this most delightful small hotel has been awarded it would require almost as much space as we have to tell you why it is so good. Firstly it has one of the prime positions on Llandudno's promenade opposite a Victorian Pier, gardens and the beach. It is sheltered by the nearby Great Orme headland and even if you do not wish to sit outside and soak in the sun you can still enjoy the views from the Bar Lounge across the Bay, whilst sipping a gin and tonic or perhaps the Sitting Room which also provides delightful views of the seafront. This room is set aside for those guests who wish to relax and enjoy the ambience of the house in a smoke-free atmosphere. It is this caring thoughtfulness for guests that is evident throughout this excellently run hotel. The owners Martin and Janette Bland have made the St Tudno one of the most luxurious seaside resort hotels in Great Britain by progressively refurbishing it over the 25 years they have been there and constantly ensuring that the welfare and happiness of their guests is paramount. Within their brochure they quote Lewis Carroll 'One of the deep secrets of life is that all that is really worth the doing is what we do for others". This is evident. Lewis Carroll's real Alice stayed at the St Tudno with her family in 1861 when she was eight years old.

The centrally heated, ensuite bedrooms are charming. Each has been individually designed and what strikes one most is the harmony of the colour schemes. Colour and Sky TV as well as a beverage tray complete with home-made biscuits, hair dryer, bath robes and a bottle of sparkling wine are to be found in every room. In the Garden Room Restaurant, again furnished in keeping with the hotel's individual character, you will breakfast and dine on delicious food which has made it acknowledged as one of the best restaurants in Wales and, not surprisingly, has 3 Rosettes awarded by the AA. Open to non-residents it has to be visited to realise how very good it is and worthy of the many prestigious awards. Joint Head Chefs David Harding and Ian Watson use only the finest fresh ingredients available, local whenever possible. They are also understanding of peoples individual needs for diets or simpler foods.

If one wants to visit Snowdonia, or the many other places of interest in this part of Wales, perhaps enjoy some sea or freshwater fishing or play on any one of the three 18 hole golf courses, go pony trekking or practice skiing on Llandudno's Dry Ski Slope, as well as enjoying the sun, the sand, the sea, and the hotel's heated indoor swimming pool, you will certainly do no better than to stay at The St. Tudno.

USEFUL INFORMATION

OPEN; All year
CHILDREN; Welcome. Awards for Welcome of children
CREDIT CARDS; All major cards
LICENSED; Yes. Excellent wine list
ACCOMMODATION; 20 ensuite rooms Passenger lift. Indoor heated swimming pool

RESTAURANT; Award-winning. 3 AA Rosettes. Open to Non-residents
VEGETARIAN; Catered for
DISABLED ACCESS; Limited access
PETS; By arrangement
PARKING; Car Park & Garaging

PENGRUG
Gwynfe, Llangadog,
Carmarthenshire,
Wales SA19 9RP

Tel: 01550 740686

Built in the 17th century Gwynfe farmhouse offers home from home comforts. Carefully tended household plants are placed throughout. Lovely gardens laid mostly to lawn surround the property and seasonal hanging baskets adorn the exterior. Panoramic views extend across the lovely scenic valley adding to the peaceful setting. Guest bedrooms are attractive and well furnished with wash hand basin, a welcome tray with tea and coffee and a radio. The private residents lounge is very comfy where one can take ones ease. An inglenook fireplace with the original oven and fire enhances this room where a colour television is situated. A delicious farmhouse style breakfast is served with a selection of home-grown produce. An evening meal will be quite happily catered for by prior arrangement. Children are made very welcome.

Should you wish your pet to accompany you, then make your request known at the time of booking. There is ample car parking space. The Gower Peninsula within driving distance has lovely scenery, golden beaches with wild surfing and plenty of local interest. Carmarthen Bay offers ideal conditions for boating, fishing or scenic coastal walks. Or maybe a day out at Gwili Railway with its steam train which passes through pretty rural countryside. There is also a nature trail and picnic area.

USEFUL INFORMATION

OPEN; All year except Christmas
CHILDREN; Welcome
CREDIT CARDS; None taken
ACCOMMODATION; 3 rooms with wash hand basins
DINING ROOM; Traditional breakfast. Evening meal by arrangement
DISABLED ACCESS; No
GARDEN; Yes, laid to lawn
PETS; By arrangement

Chapter Ten

CAE CRWN FARM
*Bryneglwys, Nr Llangollen,
Denbighshire LL21 9NF*

Tel: 01490 450243

Bryneglwys is on the A5104 near Corwen, a market town on the River Dee, well known for its salmon and trout. The village of Bryneglwys is where you will find a rather delightful bed and breakfast owned and expertly run by Mrs. Reed, Cae Crwn Farm. The farmhouse was built around 1910 of good solid Welsh stone, the thick walls makes the house warm and cosy. The accommodation is very comfortable, there is a residents sitting room with a colour television and roaring log fire on chilly evenings, here you can sit and relax, or plan your days away. There are 3 attractive bedrooms, one family/double with a vanitory unit, one twin and a single. Each having a clock/radio and a tea and coffee tray.

The farmhouse benefits from central heating. Mrs. Reed presents you with a true farmhouse breakfast, including freshly home-baked bread and rolls, a divine aroma to wake up to, all this is served in the separate dining room. Evening meals are by arrangement and include such delights as home-made soup followed by chicken casserole with fresh vegetables, then apple crumble to finish, simply delicious. There are an assortment of animals on the farm including a dog, ducks, goats and horses. If you have your own horse why not bring him along, stabling and grazing can be arranged. There may also be an opportunity for you to have a pony ride and horsedrawn carriage rides. This Wales Tourist Board 'Commended' farmhouse is also Cyclist and Walker Friendly. There is something for the angler and golfer as well. A superb location.

USEFUL INFORMATION

OPEN; All year
CHILDREN; Welcome
CREDIT CARDS; None taken
ACCOMMODATION; 3 rooms, all have private facilities
PETS; By arrangement
DINING ROOM; Excellent home-cooked fare, fresh baked bread, evening meals by arrangement
VEGETARIAN; Catered for
DISABLED ACCESS; No
GARDEN; Yes
NON SMOKING

Wales

THE GLYN VALLEY HOTEL
Glyn Ceiriog, Llangollen,
Clwyd LL20 7EU

Tel: 01691 718896

This small family run hotel has much to recommend it especially the reasonable room rates and charges for meals. The hotel was built in 1835 and has the graciousness that was so much a part of the architecture of the time. Mike and Janet Gilchrist, the owners have spent a great deal of time and money in bringing it up to date in keeping with its period charm. Situated in the village of Glyn Ceiriog, it is only six miles off the A5 and stands in the Ceiriog Valley which is an area of outstanding beauty. Wonderful place to stay because there is so much to do within easy reach of the hotel whether you are keen on sporting activities, enjoy a gentle ramble rather than a arduous walk or are as fascinated as so many people are by the varying towns and villages. Chirk Castle stands at the entrance to the valley and the superb Pystyll Rhiadar waterfall, a few miles away from the other end. The scenery is stunning, the air invigorating and the hospitality of the Glyn Valley Hotel second to none.

The hotel is attractively furnished with a mixture of traditional and antique pieces. The three Bars each have their own character: The Lounge Bar which has a roaring log fire on chilly days leads into an annex which houses a Pictorial Railway Museum of the former Glyn Valley Tramway. It also has a piano and many a Friday evening is spent listening to and joining in when the local Choir use the room after rehearsals and are more than happy to have a Sing-Song. The Sports Bar with its real ale, darts, dominoes and electronic games has wall covered with a collection of sports prints and photographs. The quiet elegance of the Cocktail Bar is the place to be for an enjoyable, relaxed drink before dinner. Many people have discovered that a meal in the pretty Restaurant is something to remember. The choice is wide and the food expertly cooked. The Glyn Valley also is a popular place for Wedding buffets, receptions, annual dinners and can be used for dancing with the hotel disco equipment or piano. Totally self-contained with its own bar and toilet facilities, it is ideal for any of these occasions.

There are nine bedrooms with all but one single being ensuite. They are warm, comfortable, equipped with colour TV and tea/coffee making facilities. The Honeymoon Suite has a curtained Brass Four Poster Bed, there are two large Family Rooms with no charge for children in carry cots and reduced rates for the under 12's. Relax in the warmth of the Resident's Lounge which has a colour TV. The whole hotel is centrally heated.

USEFUL INFORMATION

OPEN; All year
CHILDREN; Welcome
CREDIT CARDS; None taken
LICENSED; Full On
ACCOMMODATION; 9 rooms, 8 ensuite

RESTAURANT; Good food
BAR FOOD; Wide choice. Daily Specials
VEGETARIAN; Yes + Special Diets
DISABLED ACCESS; Restaurant only

Chapter Ten

**GLANRANNELL PARK
COUNTRY HOUSE HOTEL,**
Crugybar, Llanwrda,
Carmarthenshire, SA19 8SA.

Tel : 01558 685230
Fax : 01558 685784

'Croeso' is the Welsh word for welcome, and this is definitely what you receive at this beautiful country hotel. Set in 23 acres of parkland, surrounded by lawns and overlooking a small lake, this is the ideal refuge from the busy outside world. Whether you want to relax and just enjoy the scenery, or partake of some of the outdoor sports available, then Glanrannell Park is just the place! Built in 1852 this wonderful house is home to Dai and Bronwen Davies, who present a warm, informal atmosphere and an outstanding quality of service. All staff are local people who extend that well known, friendly Welsh hospitality and ensure that your holiday is memorable. There are 8 bedrooms, all with colour TV, that ever essential tea/coffee tray, and all are ensuite, apart from the single room which has its own private bathroom. They are all charmingly furnished in a mixture of traditional and modern country house style, and are warm and inviting rooms with views over the lawns and paddocks of the estate. There are two comfortable lounges, one with a small library, where you can relax and enjoy the cosy mood of this great house, the bar is well stocked, as are the cellars where there is a variety to suit all tastes. The restaurant caters for up to 25 people and offers local, fresh produce cooked in a traditional Welsh style. Try *'BWCHADANYS MELYNLLYS'* (I may not be able to pronounce it but I certainly could eat it!): braised venison steak served on a red wine and honey sauce. (To save embarrassment pointing to the menu may be a good choice) The selections are delicious and special diets and vegetarians are cheerfully catered for. Morning coffee, bar lunches, teas and picnic lunches are all available on request.
Wales is a land of intrigue and mystery, with it's Celtic heritage and wonderful folklore. Situated in West Wales, Glanrannell Park is perfect for visiting ancient castles, forts and various National Trust properties and gardens. Cardigan Bay is only a short car journey, and here you can walk the rugged cliffs and enjoy the spectacular views of the craggy coastline. Dai Davies is a very enlightened host and obviously takes a great interest in the surrounding countryside. He produces various interesting leaflets telling of the history, the sports available, and the wildlife to be found in the vicinity. The hotel organises a range of excursions from riding to a *'Magical History Tour'* which takes you through some of the history in the area, and there is always something of interest to see and do......on the other hand......sit back and watch the activity around you in the serenity and calm of a beautiful establishment where the guest is of prime importance and luxury is commonplace. What more could you possibly ask for?

USEFUL INFORMATION

OPEN : Easter to end Oct.
CHILDREN : Welcome
PETS : By request
LICENSED : Full
CREDIT CARDS : All major
DINING ROOM : Wonderful Welsh fayre
VEGETARIANS : Catered for
BAR SNACKS : Available
DISABLED ACCESS : Restaurant only
GARDEN : Yes
ACCOMMODATION : 8 rooms: 3 dble, 3 twin, 1 fml, all en suite, 1 sgl with private bathroom.

746

BRYN HYFRYD GUEST HOUSE
Llantysilio, Llangollen,
Clwyd LL20 7YU

Tel: 01978 860011

This charming bed and breakfast accommodation has wonderful views of the Dee Valley from each of it's bedrooms. There are three traditionally furnished rooms with private bathrooms and facilities include a courtesy tray of tea and coffee. Mrs Davies is your hostess and provides a warm Welsh welcome for her guests. Breakfast is a traditional affair, and if required, a good evening meal can be had at the local 16th century inn which is just a few minutes walk from the guest house.

This is a wonderful area for walking, and the countryside encroaches on all sides of this tiny hamlet. You only have to step out of the house in the morning to be on your way to explorethe beautiful valleys, and meet the friendly, local people. Mrs Davies organises four wheel drive breaks (great for seeing this part of the world) with planned routes, which allows you to cover quite a large area and see the sights!

Llantysilio is just over two miles from Llangollen which is home of the International Music Eisteddfod since 1947. One of the Seven Wonders of Wales is here too - the 12th century bridge with it's four pointed arches.

The roads in this area are minor but often lead to wonderful views in the heart of the hill country. One road near Llangollen leads south to Glyn Ceiriog where the peace and tranquillity, combined with superb mountain views, will have you reaching for your camera or sketch pad, to keep forever a record of this delightful part of the country.

USEFUL INFORMATION

OPEN: All year
CHILDREN: Welcome
CREDIT CARDS: None taken
ACCOMMODATION: 3 rooms, 2 dbl, 1 twin. All with private bathroom
DINING ROOM: Traditional breakfast, No evening meal available
VEGETARIAN: Catered for
DISABLED ACCESS: Not really
PETS: Yes

Chapter Ten

THE RIVERSIDE HOTEL
Cinderhill Street,
Monmouth, Gwent NP5 3EY

Tel: 01600 715577
Fax: 01600 712668

This one time 18th century coaching inn is in one of the most beautiful and spectacular parts of Wales which makes it a particularly good place for visitors to stay, although even if it were not surrounded by so much beauty, The Riverside Hotel would be most people's choice because of its warm welcome, the quality of its rooms, its friendly efficient staff and a restaurant which has food to die for. All the 17 immaculately furnished bedrooms are ensuite and have everything for one's creature comfort including a hospitality tray, hair dryers and complimentary satellite programmes on the colour television. Four of the rooms are designed for families with cots and a baby listening service available. For the disabled there are special facilities as well.

The Long Bar is a popular local meeting place where strangers rapidly become friends and it is here in addition to the well-stocked bar that one can find a very good bar meal from an extensive menu which includes traditional favourites and some very appealing daily specials. Residents can find a peaceful retreat in the Conservatory Lounge away from the madding crowd. One of the highlights of The Riverside Hotel is the award winning Lady Hamilton's Restaurant which offers an A La Carte menu with dishes both traditional and from around the world. Whatever you choose will be cooked to perfection and will have the highest quality fresh local produce.

People come to Monmouth for all sorts of reasons and whether your visit is for business or pleasure The Riverside Hotel is a perfect base. From there you can explore the historic town with its famous 13th century fortified gatehouse over the River Monnow. It is within easyreach of all that the beautiful Wye Valley has to offer. There are golf courses including the world class Rolls of Monmouth Club and the St Pierre course at Chepstow. You can be adventurous and go ballooning, dry skiing, clay pigeon shooting, horse riding, canoeing, shooting and many other sporting pastimes. For the artistic, painting is another option.

USEFUL INFORMATION

OPEN; All year
CHILDREN; Yes. Cots & beds
CREDIT CARDS; All except Amex/Diners
LICENSED; Yes
PETS; By arrangement
ACCOMMODATION; 17 ensuite rooms

RESTAURANT; Superb A La Carte
BAR FOOD; Wide choice
VEGETARIAN; Daily choice
DISABLED ACCESS; Totally accessible
GARDEN; Patio

THE DRAGON HOTEL
Montgomery,
Powys SY15 6PA

Tel/Fax: 01686 668359

Built in about 1630 but today with a late Victorian timbered frontage, the elegant Dragon Hotel is highly recommended. It holds the Welsh Tourist Board's '4 Crown Commended', AA '2 Star', it has the Good Beer Award from the Good Pub Guide and is also in Michelin and the Taste of Wales. Sometimes when a hotel has all these accolades it does not live up to the image the awards paint but in the case of The Dragon Hotel you will not be disappointed.

Montgomery itself is a small town with established character, charm and a feeling of tranquillity. It provides an ideal base for touring, fishing on the Wye and the Severn and for golfers the local courses welcome visitors. Situated on Offa's Dyke, it also provides an ideal centre for the serious walker, or happy rambler. There are also opportunities for riding, shooting and even a rally school. Powis Castle and other sites of historic interest are nearby.

With all this to recommend Montgomery you cannot do better than enjoy the hospitality of The Dragon which is as welcoming today as it was when it as a Coaching Inn and greeting tired travellers from the Stagecoaches. Mark and Sue Michaels are your hosts; two friendly people whose skills in running this delightful inn are widely appreciated.. Sue supervises personally the kitchen from which delicious dishes are brought to table. Welsh lamb features prominently as well as fresh fish, tender steaks and a wide range of fresh local produce. The extensive menus include vegetarian dishes. Mark you will find in the lounge bar greeting old friends and rapidly making new ones. The bar and the lounge contain beams and masonry reputed to have been taken from Powis Castle after its destruction by Oliver Cromwell. Despite the age of the building you will find that all the double and twin rooms are ensuite with bathrooms whilst the small number of singles have shower rooms. Every room has colour television, central heating, direct dial telephones and a plentifully supplied hostess tray.

USEFUL INFORMATION

OPEN; All year
CHILDREN; Welcome
CREDIT CARDS; All except Diners
LICENSED; Yes
ACCOMMODATION; 15 ensuite rooms
PETS; By arrangement

RESTAURANT; Good food, local produce
BAR FOOD; Traditional, sensible prices
VEGETARIAN; Provided for
DISABLED ACCESS; No
GARDEN; Yes

Chapter Ten

TIDES REACH GUEST HOUSE
388 Mumbles Road,
Mumbles, Swansea SA3 5TN

Tel: 01792 404877

There is something innately elegant about Victorian town houses and this definitely applies to the Tides Reach Guest House which since 1979 has been in the capable hands of Mrs. Jan Mayberry. With an unerring eye for colour, comfort and detail, she has made this once 'Bath House Hotel' become one of the most sought after bed and breakfast establishments in Mumbles. The objective was to create a cosy, old world atmosphere without sacrificing modern comforts and this has definitely been achieved. All the 5 pretty, well appointed ensuite bedrooms and the three standard rooms have central heating, television and tea making facilities. The delightful dining room, furnished with great care to harmonise with the age of the house, is where you will be served a delicious, traditional Welsh breakfast with several choices and all freshly cooked to order. There are many good places to eat locally about which Mrs. Mayberry will be pleased to give you information.

You will find Tides Reach on the sea front and about five minutes walk from the centre of the beautiful village of Mumbles. Ideally situated for anyone wanting to tour the magical Gower Peninsula. Mumbles itself has plenty to offer the visitor from disco dancing to a gentle stroll on the promenade, exploring Oystermouth Castle or just lazing on the nearby glorious beaches. Swansea is only five miles away. Tides Reach has won many independent recommendations which are well deserved. You could not fail to have a happy holiday here.

USEFUL INFORMATION

OPEN; All year
CHILDREN; By arrangement
CREDIT CARDS; None taken
ACCOMMODATION; 5 ensuite rooms 3 standard

DINING ROOM; First class breakfast
DISABLED ACCESS; No special facilities
2 ground floor rooms
PETS; Welcome

CWMTWRCH HOTEL & FOUR SEASONS RESTAURANT
Nantgaredig,
Carmarthenshire SA32 7NY

Tel: 01267 290238
Fax: 01267 290808

Until you have actually visited Cwmtwrch Hotel you cannot possibly appreciate how delightful it is. Converted from a Georgian farm house and its outbuildings, it is set, with its restaurant, in 30 acres of Carmarthen's most beautiful countryside. That in itself gives it charm but it is so much more than that. The buildings create an 'L' shape and in so doing provide all sorts of charming areas to sit and relax, read a book or enjoy quiet conversation. The hotel is furnished throughout in traditional country cottage manner which is absolutely right and creates such a cosy atmosphere. There are six ensuite bedrooms, four at ground level, all individually furnished and complete with TV and a hospitality tray. Comfortable beds provide a good night's sleep and in the morning the day starts with a true Welsh breakfast served in the old farm house.

The Four Seasons Restaurant offers dinner in very pleasant surroundings and has achieved a great reputation locally for its distinctive menu. The emphasis is on home-cooking and everything is cooked in house including bread. Fresh ingredients and local produce are always used. The menu varies according to the seasons and to the chef's choice but frequently includes local smoked salmon with avocado salad, or fresh tomato and basil soup amongst the many starters. Few people can resist Welsh lamb, especially when it is roasted with Redcurrant jelly and rosemary or perhaps local sewin with hollandaise sauce. Breast of Pembrokeshire Duck with Oranges and Caramelised Onions is another firm favourite. The desserts are irresistible and the cheese board is tempting. There is a comprehensive and sensibly priced wine list as well as mineral waters, aperitifs and beers in abundance. Live jazz evenings take place occasionally.

The Four Seasons Leisure Club which opened in 1992 has a 50ft indoor swimming pool with Jacuzzi and multigym. Drinks can be served at the poolside. The garden is large and it is a treat to wander through the extensive planting of trees and shrubs to compliment the existing Oaks and Ash. Fishing, pony trekking, beaches & craft shops are all within easy travelling distance.

USEFUL INFORMATION

OPEN; All year
CHILDREN; Welcome
CREDIT CARDS; None taken
LICENSED; Yes
ACCOMMODATION; 6 ensuite rooms
GARDEN; Extensive

RESTAURANT; Imaginative menu and all fresh ingredients. Home-made bread
VEGETARIAN; Daily choice
DISABLED ACCESS; Limited
PETS; Yes, by arrangement

Chapter Ten

PEN-Y-GELLI
Newtown, Powys SY16 3AH

Tel: 01686 628292

The warm, friendly, relaxed atmosphere is what strikes you first about this mid-19th century house built for a mill owner and now a home from home for many visitors both those on holiday and those who have come here to Newtown on business. Pen-y-Gelli stands in 20 acres of its own grounds and in recent years it has been extensively renovated adding all the comforts that this modern age demands. The accommodation is of a very high standard and furnished in a traditional country house style with pretty Laura Ashley colour co-ordinated drapes and covers. The comfortable guest lounge with its log fire is a great place for chatting or curling up with a good book. All the bedrooms have en suite bathrooms, colour television, tea-making facilities and the Laura Ashley style decor is continued here. The use of an indoor heated swimming pool adds to the very considerable benefits of staying at Pen-Y-Gelli. The house holds the Welsh Tourist Board's Garde 3 Crown Commended deservedly.

Breakfast, which is a hearty farmhouse affair, is delicious and sustaining with a choice which finds something to suit everyone. Farmhouse dinners are also available upon request. You will find Newtown is within easy reach and is a busy market town sitting astride the River Severn in the heart of Mid-Wales. There are plenty of sporting activities for the energetic including fishing, golfing, trekking, walking and farm trails. There is an excellent local theatre and Powis castle with its magnificent gardens. Pen-y-Gelli is an ideal place to stay.

USEFUL INFORMATION

OPEN; *All year except Xmas* **DINING ROOM;** *Traditional breakfast and*
CHILDREN; *Welcome*   *Farmhouse dinners*
CREDIT CARDS; *None taken*   **VEGETARIAN:** *Upon request*
ACCOMMODATION; *1dbl, 1tw, 1fam all ensuite*
GARDEN; *Yes with stream & duckpond*   **DISABLED ACCESS;**
                                                                                    Grade 3 minimum

DYFFRYN FARM HOLIDAYS,
Aberhafesp,
Newtown, Powys SY16 3JD

Tel: 01686 688817
Fax: 01686 688324

Dyffryn, just 3 miles from Caersws on the right down the farm lane, is a lovingly restored half-timbered barn on the banks of the Nant Rhyd Rhoslan, part of the 100 acres of a Welsh Hill farm where sheep and beef cattle are the main enterprises. The setting is superb. Wildlife abounds along the streams and in the small woodland copses - you may be lucky enough to see badgers at play in the evening. It is a place in which one can re-charge ones batteries before returning to the exigency of every day life, in a house that is beautifully, yet informally run and where your hosts, Sue and Dave Jones clearly love people. It is a traditional farmhouse in many ways especially when it comes to the attractive country pine furniture and the exposed oak beams in every room. The three luxury ensuite bedrooms are individually furnished and have pretty drapes and bed covers as well as colour TV and a plentifully supplied beverage tray. You will find that the guests' lounge looks out over the stream and adjoining farmyard where there is always some form of interesting seasonal activity. You are very welcome to sit in the garden alongside the stream or walk the farmland acres. Traditional farmhouse fare including vegetarian and special diets is served in the guests' dining room both at breakfast and in the evening if you require a meal.

You will never be short of something to do if you base yourselves at Dyffryn. Two miles away are the upland lakes of Llyn Mawr Nature Reserve, Llyn Du and Llyn Tarn, where kites, buzzards merlin and other wildlife may be seen. Pony trekking is available at a farm nearby. For the golfer there is a driving range at Caersws and an 18 hole course at Newtown, 5 miles away. The list is endless and your hosts will be happy to help you plan your day. Dyffryn is a strictly non-smoking house.

USEFUL INFORMATION

OPEN; All year except Xmas   **DINING ROOM;** Traditional farmhouse fare
CHILDREN; Welcome. Cot, high chair,   Breakfast & Evening Meal
CREDIT CARDS; None taken   **VEGETARIAN;** Catered for + other diets
ACCOMMODATION; 3 luxury ensuite rooms   **DISABLED ACCESS;** No
Non-smoking house

Chapter Ten

WYCHWOOD HOUSE
Penally,
Pembrokeshire SA70 7PE

Tel: 01834 844387

There is something very special about Wychwood House, highly commended by the Wales Tourist Board. Not only is it a warm and welcoming house which makes you feel relaxed the moment you walk over the front doorstep, it also has an intangible charm probably created by the attractive mixture of traditional and antique furniture and something far more tangible in the genuine welcome you will receive from you hosts Lee and Mherly Ravenscroft. Wychwood is a large country house with superb sea views, a beautiful garden surrounded by lawns, shrubs and trees and from the rear garden there is a public footpath to the beach and walled town of Tenby 2 miles away. Inside the house is fitted throughout with English Oak which not only gives an aura of graciousness but also of warmth. The elegant and spacious bedrooms, some with fourposter beds and some with a balcony, are beautifully appointed, one is ensuite, one has a private bathroom and all three rooms have colour TV, a beverage tray furnished with tea, coffee, hot chocolate and biscuits. Incidentally on arrival you will be regaled with a very welcome pot of tea and some freshly made, mouthwatering Welsh cakes. In the colder months open fires add to the general feeling of well being.

Lee is a superb cook and it is he who will provide you with one of the best breakfasts in Wales and then go on to serve a delectable afternoon tea, which is available to non-residents, and a memorable four course candlelit dinner with a menu that ranges from the traditional to tastes of the Far East. Wychwood is not licensed but you are more than welcome to bring your own wine. For the benefit of guests there is restricted smoking in the house.

There is plenty to do in this attractive part of Wales as well as the nearby excellent beach. Wychwood House is located in between two full size golf courses, one of which can be see from the bedrooms, together with glorious sea views. The old walled town of Tenby is charming to explore and boat trips are available to visit the monastic Island of Caldey.

USEFUL INFORMATION

OPEN; All year
CHILDREN; Welcome
CREDIT CARDS; None taken
LICENSED; No, welcome to bring your own
ACCOMMODATION; 3 rooms,
1 ensuite, 1 private bathroom

DINING ROOM; Delicious food breakfast, afternoon teas, dinner
VEGETARIAN; On request
DISABLED ACCESS; No
PETS; By arrangement
GARDEN; Yes

THE OLD RECTORY
Clocaenog, Ruthin,
Denbighshire, Wales LL15 2AT

Tel: 01824 750740

The Old Rectory is a rather lovely house built in 1832 and has attractive windows overlooking the well kept garden with its lawn, trees, shrubs and flowers. Your hosts are Mr. & Mrs. Buxbaum, a very friendly and warm couple who make you feel at home at once. Gill Buxbaum is a talented lady and, in the 1970s when the Buxbaums hired out narrow boats to holiday makers on the Llangollen canal, she decorated them in that distinctive style used by the people who lived and worked on them years ago. She now decorates a wide range of items in her studio attached to the house, using the traditional designs and colours, selling them through Museum and canalside shops, rallies and craft fairs in the Midlands and Wales. As well as her painting she also has time to look after her guests which she does impeccably. This '2 Crown Highly Commended' property is spacious and comfortably furnished in a mixture of period, pine and country which gives it a real homely feeling. There are 4 bedrooms, including 2 ensuite, one a family room.

All rooms have a tea and coffee tray. There is also a bathroom for guests. The residents sitting room is comfy with a colour television, radio and lots of books for you to peruse. Breakfast is traditional and delicious. Children are most welcome, a cot, high chair and baby listener are available. This area is a walkers paradise, wonderful views, peace and fresh air. Mr. and Mrs. Buxbaum are very knowledgeable and can help plan your days out with you, so you take in as much of the beautiful countryside as possible. You can be assured a warm and friendly welcome and a relaxing stay. You are sure to come away refreshed.

USEFUL INFORMATION

OPEN; All year except Christmas
CHILDREN; Welcome
CREDIT CARDS; None taken
ACCOMMODATION; 4 rooms,
2 ensuite, 2 (1 family) with own facilities, shared bathroom

DINING ROOM; Breakfast only
DISABLED ACCESS; No
GARDEN; Yes
PETS; No

Chapter Ten

THE HARBOUR LIGHT
2 High Street,
Saundersfoot, Pembrokeshire SA69 9EJ

Tel: 01834 813496

Saundersfoot is a delightful holiday resort within the Pembrokeshire Coastal National Park. A quiet friendly place, the village has been sympathetically modernised without losing any of its important historical features such as the thriving 17th century harbour, used for the export of coal, which had been mined in the area since the 13th century. It is a place of beautiful safe, sandy beaches and an abundance of wildlife - watch the fulmars nestling on the cliffs. The harbour is a place of fascination, always busy with fishing boats and pleasure craft jostling for moorings. The uncrowded Glen Beach is a place of peace and tranquillity, somewhere to enjoy the scenery, absorb the sound of the sea and recharge your batteries.
Situated in the heart of Saundersfoot is The Harbour Light, a friendly house built by a carpenter in 1864 as his family home and converted today into a charming and comfortable Guest House owned and run by Hazel Wadey and John James whose easy informality makes everyone feel at home. They run the house beautifully making sure of everyone's comfort. Some of the ten bedrooms are ensuite and all rooms have TV, radio, heating, tea and coffee making facilities and a hand basin. There are non-smoking rooms available. The food is so good that you will want to linger over your meals. Everything is home-cooked and the menu is imaginative. Served in the attractive dining room, breakfast offers lots of variety and the evening meal which is served at 6.30pm always has an abundance of fresh vegetables. The Harbour Light is licensed and the cosy bar with its nautical flavour is the hub of the house in the evenings although the comfortable lounge is relaxing. There is a spacious garden with views over Carmarthen Bay to the Gower Peninsular. The shops, beaches and harbour are only a stones throw away so you can leave your car in the car park and simply relax and enjoy yourselves.

USEFUL INFORMATION

OPEN; All year except Christmas   *DINING ROOM;* Good, home-cooked food
CHILDREN; Welcome   *VEGETARIAN;* Catered for
CREDIT CARDS; Visa/Access/Master/Diners *DISABLED ACCESS;* No facilities
LICENSED; Yes   *PETS;* Yes by arrangement
ACCOMMODATION; 10 rooms 4 ensuite   *GARDEN;* Yes
Self catering flat available - ask for details

SANT-Y-NYLL HOUSE
St Brides-Super-Ely,
South Glamorgan CF5 6EZ

Tel/Fax: 01446 760209

One would never suppose that Sant-Y-Nyll House was a product of this century. It has the elegance of yesteryears and a dignity that impresses. This is enhanced by the splendid grounds in which it stand surrounded by the picturesque Vale of Glamorgan countryside. Paul and Monica Renwick have furnished it beautifully with pieces that they have collected over the years on their worldwide travels. The result is one of harmony, charm and graciousness that will be long remembered by anyone fortunate enough to stay here.

Each bedroom has pretty drapes and furnishings that enhance the elegance of the rooms. The beds are so comfortable that one would not dare to have a bad night's rest! Whilst only the master bedroom is ensuite the others all have hand basins and shaver points and share facilitiesthat provide lashings of hot water and sufficient room for everyone. Each room is centrally heated and has television and tea/coffee making facilities. Breakfast is served in the spacious dining room and is a meal that will long stay in your memory. Everything is freshly cooked, the smell of the coffee tantalises ones nostrils whilst waiting for your choice from the varied menu. There are no evening meals but there are many places locally where one can enjoy a good meal - the Renwicks will be happy to point you in the right direction. Sant-Y-Nyll House is licensed for residents so one can return after dinner to enjoy a friendly nightcap and perhaps talk over the day's explorations with your fellow guests.

Within easy reach are many fascinating places to explore including the Welsh Folk Museum at St Fagan's. Dyffryn Gardens and historic Cardiff Castle. The coast, M4 and Cardiff Airport are also close at hand.

USEFUL INFORMATION

OPEN; All year
CHILDREN; Welcome
CREDIT CARDS; Amex only
LICENSED; Yes
ACCOMMODATION; 6 rooms, 1 ensuite
DINING ROOM; Breakfast only
VEGETARIAN; Upon request
DISABLED ACCESS; No
GARDEN; Yes
PETS; By arrangement

Chapter Ten

RAMSEY HOUSE
Lower Moor, St David's,
Pembrokeshire SA62 6RP

Tel: 01437 720321
Fax: 01437 720025

Catering exclusively for adults, the non-smoking Ramsey House is very special. There would be few people who, once having savoured the unique informal, relaxed but totally professional standards, would not want to return speedily. One might be convinced already that the St David's Peninsula was the ideal place for a holiday but the icing on the cake must be the enjoyment to be found at Ramsey House. The owners, Mac and Sandra Thompson, do everything in their power to make your visit memorable. The en-suite rooms are furnished to a very high standard and the food is delicious. Ramsey House specialises in providing the best in Welsh food, combining quality local produce with quality cooking. In addition to its famous lamb and beef, Wales has a bountiful larder of fresh vegetables, superb seafood and cheeses to rival the world's best. These ingredients are used to produce both traditional dishes and fresh imaginative ones. Ramsey House has a string of well deserved accolades including the Wales Tourist Board 3 Crown Highly Commended and Dragon Awards. RAC Highly Acclaimed, AA 4Q Selected and Les Routiers Corps d'Elite Wine Award, and is a member of the 'Taste of Wales' Hospitality Scheme.

USEFUL INFORMATION

OPEN: All year including Christmas New Year
VEGETARIAN: Yes
CHILDREN: No children
CREDIT CARDS: Mastercard/Visa/JCB
LICENSED: Yes
ACCOMMODATION: 7 en-suite rooms

DINING ROOM: Traditional and imaginative
DISABLED ACCESS: Ground floor bedrooms, but not suitable for wheelchairs
GARDEN: Yes. Private parking
PETS: Welcome

NON-SMOKING ESTABLISHMENT

HURST DENE
10 Sketty Road,
Uplands,
Swansea SA2 0LJ

Tel: 01792 280920

If you want somewhere to stay that is welcoming and friendly whether you come to Swansea on business or for the pleasure of discovering not only what the town has to offer but also the outstandingly beautiful Gower Peninsula which is closeby then staying at Hurst Dene is ideal. Built in Victorian times, the house has that solid structure one expects from the era and is also blessed with large windows and high ceilings which makes all the rooms seem spacious and light. From Hurst Dene you can go fishing, play golf, enjoy some splendid walks. The house is only ten minutes from the M4 and offers easy access to the City Centre, Grand Theatre, Brangwyn Hall, University and the St Helen's Rugby and Cricket ground.

The Guest House is family run and has recently been refurbished. The bedrooms are attractively appointed and most are ensuite. Each room has colour television, a beverage tray and also available are cots, hairdriers and ironing facilities. In the pleasant dining room a substantial full Breakfast is served or if you prefer it, a lighter Continental breakfast. Evening meals are available and cooked to order. The menu is entirely home-cooked and changes daily. Vegetarians are also catered for with prior notice. Hurst Dene emphasises quality with a warm welcome and that is endorsed by the Three Crowns Highly Commended Award for food, hospitality and service.

USEFUL INFORMATION

OPEN; 24 hours 365 days a year
CHILDREN; Welcome. Cots
CREDIT CARDS; All major cards
LICENSED; Yes
ACCOMMODATION; 10 rooms 5 ensuite
PETS; No

DINING ROOM; Excellent breakfast
Home-cooked evening meal to order
VEGETARIAN; On request
DISABLED ACCESS; No
GARDEN; Yes

Chapter Ten

WINDSOR LODGE HOTEL & RESTAURANT
Mount Pleasant,
Swansea SA1 6EG

Tel: 01792 642158/652744
Fax: 01792 648996

This is the only 2 star hotel in Swansea and must also be the only one that creates the atmosphere of a country house hotel within the city's confines. It is charming and gracious, welcoming and relaxed, small enought to be intimate and in which the service is second to none. Owned by Ron and Pam Rumble Windsor Lodge is in its 26th year as a hotel but the building is 200 years old and grade II listed, The emphasis everywhere is on comfort and you will find the modern furniture completely at home in its older setting. The 19 bedrooms, all of which are ensuite, have been beautifully appointed, the beds designed to ensure a good night's sleep. Each room has TV, Radio. Direct Dial telephone and a welcome beverage tray. The reception rooms are equally attractive and if you read the visitor's book you will discover that a host of famous names, including ex U.S. President Jimmy Carter, Cilla Black, Ned Sherrin, have all found their way here. One of its great advantages is its easy access. It is less than 5 minutes walk to the station, 10 minutes drive to the M4 and within easy reach of Swansea's business centres. Cardiff is 40 minutes to the East and Carmarthen 40 minutes to the West. Swansea is Wales' maritime city and offers much of interest to the visitor. It is quite near to Gower, Britains' first Area of Natural Beauty, Brecon and Pembrokeshire National Parks.

Windsor Lodge also has a first class, elegant and delightful, award winning restaurant which has developed from the original dining room of the hotel and become one of Swansea's favourite eating places. Its style is one of simplicity based on fresh and local ingredients. British and French influences in the menu tantalise the taste buds and change with the seasons. Vegetarians are especially welcome. Naturally the wine list lives up the standard set by the menu. The hotel is ideal for parties, conferences and weddings for about 60 people. The restaurant is open for dinner Monday to Saturday, booking by telephone, and for lunch by arrangement.

USEFUL INFORMATION

OPEN; All year. 24hrs Closed Xmas & Boxing Day
CHILDREN; Welcome
CREDIT CARDS; All major cards
LICENSED; Yes

RESTAURANT; Award winning
VEGETARIAN; Choice of menu
DISABLED ACCESS; No special facilities
ACCOMMODATION; 19 en suite rooms

Wales

THE OLDE MASONS ARMS HOTEL,
Talgarth, Powys,
Wales, LD3 0BB.

Tel : 01874 711688

The Olde Masons Arms Hotel has been an inn since as long ago as the 16th century. Now run as a small hotel by Pat Banford, it offers first class accommodation and excellent cuisine in pleasant surroundings, and at affordable prices. It is very tastefully decorated in a country cottage style, and has log fires and exposed beams to add to the character. There are various 'special offers' for weekend breaks, mid week breaks and reductions for children under 10 years. It is worth phoning to check these offers as you may find the prices are very tempting. The six bedrooms are all en suite and have colour TV, radio, tea/coffee tray and are centrally heated throughout. Each is cosy and comfortable, and with Pat as your hostess, you feel as if you are in a 'home from home'. The visitor's book adds credence to this statement with a wealth of statements on the hospitality and friendliness of this house. Also you may find the resident white cat, Suky, curled up anywhere, totally oblivious to the different people coming and going! The lounge bar has a wide selection of wines, spirits and beers, and nothing could be nicer than to curl up with a warming drink in front of the log fire and relax. There are even various home made bar snacks to 'keep you going'! Planning the next day's activities may take some time (so a few drinks may be required!) as there is a host of things to do in this area! Planning your menu may take some time also, as there is a delightful choice of food, and trying to 'eliminate' various options may be difficult. Vegetarians and those on special diets need have no worries, as Pat will cheerfully cater for all! The restaurant holds a 'Taste of Wales' certificate and Pat is justifiably proud of the culinary skills required to gain this merit. Intimate and warm is the character of this establishment making your stay and your meals just that bit more enjoyable.

The pretty town of Talgarth (where the BBC TV series 'Morgans Boy' was filmed) is in the Brecon Beacons National Park. The whole area is of outstanding beauty, with a wealth of activities for all! Whether you enjoy fishing, golfing, horse riding or just walking this is the ideal spot. The scenery and landscapes of mountains, streams and waterfalls will take your breath away, and have you reaching for your camera to record this holiday forever! Explore the history of Wales with its castles, abbeys, and standing stones, and hear the folklore of these mysterious Welsh mountains and valleys - you cannot but be impressed with this compact country and its friendly welcoming people!

USEFUL INFORMATION

OPEN : All year
CHILDREN : Welcome
PETS : By arrangement
LICENSED : Full
CREDIT CARDS : All major
RESTAURANT : A la carte/ Table de hote
VEGETARIAN : Catered for
BAR SNACKS : Varied
DISABLED ACCESS : No
GARDEN : Large array of flowers
ACCOMMODATION : 6 rooms en suite; 2 dbl, 2 fml, 1 twin, 1 sgl.

Chapter Ten

THE TOWER HOTEL & RESTAURANT
The Square, Talgarth,
Brecon LD3 0BW

Tel/Fax; 01874 711253

For one hundred years The Tower Hotel has been a part of the life of Talgarth. Set in the heart of the Brecon Beacons and Black Mountains, the area is oustandingly beautiful. Cascading water has shaped the lush green land, where you can explore meandering rivers and stunning waterfalls. The dramatic open spaces, rich in widlife attract walkers, the Bridle ways offer an escape for pony trekkers, while Talgarth itself is on the Offa's Dyke Route. Lakes and rivers provide watersports fun in scer... locations. Theres golf, para gliding and mountain biking. Castles and gardens. Celtic remains and folk museums, light railways and traditional woollen mills, the Centre for Alternative Technology and the Welsh Whisky Experience are all within easy reach.

With all this to whet your appetite for this glorious part of Wales then staying at The Tower Hotel must be your destination. This perfectly run establishment has recently been carefully and lovingly refurbished by its owners, Mr and Mrs Hamilton. What they have done is to enhance what was already a good hotel. It is now the epitome of comfort. The ten ensuite rooms have been charmingly decorated and equipped with colour TV, hair dryers andtea/coffee making facilities. The furniture is a harmonious mixture of traditional and period pieces throughout the hotel. Fresh flowers abound in all the public rooms. Food is of the utmost importance and in the small, intimate, 20 cover restaurant you will be fed on some delicious dishes. Starting at breakfast with a scrumptious traditional Welsh meal with choices or a Continental breakfast for those who prefer something lighter. Dinner is a feast with all sorts of exciting things on offer. The menu changes regularly, is never vast but always has sufficient choices to make sure everyone is happy including vegetarians. The cosy bar has Real Ale and Guest Beers and is well-stocked with every other sort of drink. The wine list has been carefully chosen to include wines from around the world; all chosen for their excellence and with a regard for ones pocket. You will be difficult to please if you do not enjoy The Tower Hotel.

USEFUL INFORMATION

OPEN; *All year*
CHILDREN; *Welcome*
CREDIT CARDS; *All major cards + Switch*
LICENSED; *Yes.*
ACCOMMODATION; *10 ensuite rooms*

RESTAURANT; *Excellent, imaginative menu*
VEGETARIAN; *Always a choice*
DISABLED ACCESS; *No special facilities*

GARDEN; *Yes*
PETS; *By arrangement*

HOTEL MAES-Y-NEUADD,
Talsarnu,
Nr. Harlech,
Gwynedd
LL47 6YA

Tel:01766 780319

Guests from all over the world make a beeline for Hotel Maes-Y-Neuadd which must be one of the finest in Wales. Everything about it is delightful, there are fascinating corners to be explored and enjoyed. Sheltered corners of the beautiful grounds and old trees provide welcome shade during the summer months. A pre-dinner drink on the terrace on warm summer nights allows you to enjoy the magnificent spectacle of the sun setting over the Lleyn Peninsula. You will find the house nestling into a wooded mountainside and situated amongst some of the most beautiful scenery in Britain, with spectacular views across the Snowdonia National Park. The oldest part of the house was built less than a century after Edward I's mighty castle at Harlech. 16th, 18th and 20th century additions to this gracious house, blend harmoniously. It is a much loved house and since 1981 has been in the personal care of the Horsfall and Slatter families who have sympathetically restored their home to provide the highest standards of comfort and luxury. Evenings draw guests to the oak-beamed bar with its ancient inglenook and recesses full of interesting curios. On cooler days a cheerful log fire burns. Dinner, in the gracious and elegant dining room is a truly memorable experience. Delicious dishes are created by talented chefs, using fresh produce for which Wales is renowned. The wines have been chosen with great care and offer choices from all over the world. There are sixteen bedrooms and suites, twelve in the main house and four in the adjoining Coach House. Many have fabulous views of the mountains or Tremadoc Bay and the distant Lleyn Peninsula. Each room is imaginatively designed and furnished with its own very individual style.

There are a wealth of fascinating places to visit, magnificent walks, numerous drives and interesting pursuits to follow. Above all you will experience the special Welshness of the area. Maes-Y-Neuadd has joined forces with the world famous Ffestiniog Railway to create 'Steamand Cuisine' - a unique experience in Fine Dining. Imagine a gentle journey by narrow gauge steam train through some of the most spectacular scenery in the country and at the same time sipping champagne and enjoying a superb dinner. Wonderful for parties of 30-100.

USEFUL INFORMATION

OPEN; All year
CHILDREN; Welcome
CREDIT CARDS; All major cards
LICENSED; Yes. Fine wines
PETS; By arrangement
ACCOMMODATION; 16 rooms & suites
DINING ROOM; Superb food. Welsh produce
BAR MEALS; Not applicable
VEGETARIAN; By arrangement
DISABLED ACCESS; Limited
GARDEN; Delightful grounds

THE FOUNTAIN INN
Trellech Grange, Tintern,
Chepstow, Gwent NP6 6QW

Tel: 01291 689303

There can be few better places that offer you accommodation in a 17th century inn which is tucked away from the hustle and bustle of the seasonal visitors to the Wye Valley and yet from which it is so easy to explore the magic and delight in this designated area of Outstanding Natural Beauty. Apart from the glorious scenery there are the ravishing ruins of Tintern Abbey and many other exciting places to visit. For walkers Offa's Way and The Wye Valley Trail are carefully signposted and allow you to be as leisurely or as adventurous as you wish. Within the Fountain Inn you will find a tremendous welcome and an atmosphere that has remained since it was first built inspite of a disastrous fire in 1964 which would have completely destroyed the inn had it not been for the very thick walls. It was rebuilt and somehow has managed to retain its character and charm. The 5 bedrooms, 2 of which are ensuite are warm and comfortable and the food either in the bar or the restaurant, is memorable. A delightful place in which to stay.

USEFUL INFORMATION

OPEN; All year
CHILDREN; Welcome
CREDIT CARDS; Visa/Master/Amex
LICENSED; Yes
ACCOMMODATION; 5 letting rooms 2 ensuite
RESTAURANT; Excellent, home-cooked fare
BAR FOOD; Wide choice
VEGETARIAN; Daily choice
DISABLED ACCESS; Not suitable
GARDEN; Yes

THE OLD RECTORY
Tintern, Chepstow,
Monmouthshire NP6 6SG

Tel: 01291 689519 Fax: 0374 570395

The delightful 19th century Old Rectory Guest House used to belong to the ancient Church of Wales, but for the past 15 years it has been a very comfortable guest house with stunning views of the beautiful Wye Valley. Wendy and Kevin Taylor your hosts, specialise in a relaxed and friendly atmosphere. The centrally heated bedrooms are well furnished, having television and tea and coffee making facilities. Four of the rooms have wash basins and lovely river views, 2 ensuite shower rooms are to be installed early in 1997. Children under 12 and sharing the parents room have special rates and children under 2 are free, baby sitting is also available by prior arrangement. The food at The Old Rectory is rather special, all home-made using local produce with a wide choice of breakfasts, the optional 3 course evening meal is a real treat with a choice of starters, main courses and sweets, and all concluding nicely with coffee and mints. A snack menu and children's meals are also available. There is nothing better than drinking fresh water from a natural spring and The Old Rectory is lucky enough to have its own. There is a cosy guests sitting room with a log fire. The Old Rectory has a non-smoking policy. Beautiful scenery makes this a very popular area for walking, climbing and exploring the rivers and forests or you could just relax and admire the views. Horse riding, canoeing and golf are all within easy reach.

USEFUL INFORMATION

OPEN; All year except Christmas
CHILDREN; Welcome, Special rates available
CREDIT CARDS; None taken
LICENSED; No
ACCOMMODATION; 5 rooms, 2 double, 2 twin, 1 single
DINING ROOM; Delicious home-cooked fare optional 3 course evening meal, local produce
VEGETARIAN; Catered for
DISABLED ACCESS; No
GARDEN; Yes
PETS; Yes, by arrangement
NO SMOKING

Chapter Ten

VALLEY HOUSE
Raglan Road, Tintern,
Monmouthshire NP6 6TH

Tel: 01291 689652 Fax: 01291 689805

Mrs. A Howe certainly has got the professional touch when it comes to running her excellent guest house, and she has been rewarded for her efforts with a host of awards AA 'QQQ', RAC 'Acclaimed' and the Welsh Tourist Board '2 Crown Commended'. Valley House was built in 1762 and is an impressive 3 storey building, it is furnished in a Regency/Victorian style which is in total keeping with the house. The 3 ensuite rooms, 2 double and 1 twin, are delightful indeed with colour TV, direct dial telephone and tea and coffee making facilities. The Breakfast Room, which is in the lower ground floor, is unusual in that it features a 'Stone Arch', breakfast itself is traditional English with all the trimmings and plenty of it. Valley House is 800 yards from the village of Tintern, where you will find numerous places to eat and Tintern Abbey one of Britain's finest relics of the monastic age, founded in the 12th century by Cistercian monks, the history is told in an exhibition. There is plenty to do and places to visit, the nearby Angiddy Ironworks, is an interesting 16th century scene of one time iron making. On the banks of the River Wye is Chepstow with its winding medieval streets, Norman castle and graceful bridge, the museum covers the history of the area. Golf, fishing, pony trekking and walking are all within easy reach and for the more adventurous there ishang-gliding.

USEFUL INFORMATION

OPEN; All year except Christmas
CHILDREN; Yes by arrangement
CREDIT CARDS; Amex only
LICENSED; No
ACCOMMODATION; 3 ensuite rooms

DINING ROOM; Places to eat nearby
VEGETARIAN; Catered for
DISABLED ACCESS; No
GARDEN; Yes
PETS; Yes by arrangement

Wales

WYE BARN
*The Quay, Tintern,
Chepstow, Monmouthshire NP6 6SZ*

Tel: 01291 689456

Wye Barn is a 400 year old converted Bark House and is situated on the banks of the River Wye, and only 200 yards from Tintern Abbey. The house is very warm and friendly and features furniture by modern designers of the John Makepiece School in Dorset. The bedrooms are very attractive and centrally heated in season, with television, a tea and coffee tray, hair dryer and shaver point, there is also comfortable seating in the rooms. The views from all the rooms are beautiful, there is also a pretty walled garden with many cottage garden flowers. Breakfast and evening meals are traditional English and Welsh, packed lunches are also available on request. Wye Barn is owned and excellently run by Miss Judith Russill, a local historian who has written a book on Tintern, a small village some 6 miles from Chepstow. Walkers will be delighted by all the wonderful walks so close to Wye Barn, including Wye and Usk Valleys and the Brecon Beacons. Excellent stately homes and gardens and places to visit, plus golf, riding and fishing, Wye Barn is a super holiday location.

USEFUL INFORMATION

OPEN; *All year except Christmas*
CHILDREN; *No*
CREDIT CARDS; *None taken*
LICENSED; *No*
ACCOMMODATION; *3 rooms, 2 twin, 1 single, 1 ensuite*

DINING ROOM; *Traditional English and Welsh*
VEGETARIAN; *Catered for*
DISABLED ACCESS; *No*
GARDEN; *Yes, pretty walled garden*
PETS; *No*

Chapter Ten

Scotland

Chapter Eleven

SCOTLAND

Scotland

CHAPTER 11

SCOTLAND

INCLUDES

Palace Hotel	**Aberfeldy**	791
The Old Aberlady Inn	**Aberlady**	792
Pagani's Restaurant	**Annan**	793
Allt-Na-Craig	**Ardishaig**	794
Auchendarroch Hotel	**Ardishaig**	795
Gleneagles Hotel	**Auchterarder**	796
The Green Inn	**Ballater**	797
Kinnoul Guest House	**Balloch**	795
Birnam House Hotel	**Birham by Dunkeld**	798
Caiplie Guest House	**Caiplie**	799
Gart House	**Callander**	800
Hetland Hall Hotel	**Carrutherstown**	801
Long Acre Manor	**Castle Douglas**	802
Ardgairney Farm	**Cleish**	803
Todhall House	**Darsie by Cupar**	804
Dunduff Farm	**Dunure**	805
Drummond House	**Edinburgh**	806
Allt-Nan-Ros Hotel	**Fort William**	807
Beinn Ard	**Fort William**	808
The Grange	**Fort William**	808
Malin Court	**Girvan**	809
Kelvingrove Hotel	**Glasgow**	810
Torwood House Hotel	**Glenluce**	811
Blackswater Inn	**Glenshee**	812
Ardmore Guest House	**Helensburgh**	813
East Bank	**Helensburgh**	813
Ravenswood	**Helensburgh**	814
Traquair Arms Hotel	**Innerleithen**	815
Kilmeny Farmhouse	**Isle of Islay**	816
Clachaig Hotel	**Killen**	817
Morenish Lodge Hotel	**Killen**	818
Muirhouse Farm	**Kilmarnock**	819
Selkirk Arms Hotel	**Kirkcudbright**	820
Stonehaven	**Largs**	814
Whin Park	**Largs**	821
Leslie Castle	**Leslie by Insch**	822
Monachyle Mhor	**Lochernhead**	823
Sheildale Farm	**Loch Lomond**	812

771

Chapter Eleven

Kings Arms Hotel	**Lockerbie**	**824**
Lockerbie Manor	**Lockerbie**	**825**
Ravenshill House Hotel	**Lockerbie**	**826**
Burts Hotel	**Melrose**	**827**
Moffat House Hotel	**Moffat**	**828**
Burnside House Hotel	**Newburgh**	**829**
Kildonan Lodge	**Newington**	**830**
Corsemalzie House Hotel	**Newton Stewart**	**831**
Lerags House	**Oban**	**832**
Parsons Lodge Restaurant	**Patna**	**833**
Smithston Farm	**Patna**	**834**
Cringletie House Hotel	**Peebles**	**835**
Buttonboss Hotel	**Pitlochry**	**836**
Moulin Hotel	**Pitlochry**	**837**
Fernbank	**Prestwick**	**834**
Dryburgh Abbey Hotel	**Roxburghshire**	**838**
The Philipburn House Hotel	**Selkirk**	**839**
Brownlees Guest House	**St Andrews**	**840**
Achray House Hotel	**St Fillans**	**841**
Queens View Hotel	**Strathtummel by Pitlochry**	**842**
Springside	**Tarbert**	**843**
Drumcruilton	**Thornhill**	**844**

SCOTLAND

Dumfries & Galloway, Borders, Lothian, Strathclyde, Central, Fife, Tayside, Grampian, Highlands & Islands.

Land of majestic mountains, velvety glens, icy waterfalls, and a fiercely independent people. This describes the Scotland I know and love, and one which captures your heart, bringing you back time and time again. Scotland covers an area of approximately 30,000 square miles, surrounded on three sides by water, and influencing the climate of this wonderful country. At any time of year the scenery and beautiful landscape will leave you breathless; whether it is the snow covered peaks and frozen waterfalls with their myriad of colours, or when the glens and mountains are covered in a purple and yellow hue from the wild heathers and gorse.

Scottish culture has been strongly influenced by the varying settlers, from Picts and Celts, and to a much lesser degree the Romans (who had great difficulty with these 'wild' Britons). The border with England was frequently disputed, and many of the recent American films such as Rob Roy and Braveheart give a vague idea of the troubles. (Not too accurate I might add!) The fierce independence of these proud people have led to many a fight, and even today their voices are loudly heard in clarifying their rights and heritage.

Dumfries & Galloway is an area that I hold a great deal of affection for. There are memories here, good and bad, but poignant in their recollection. **Lockerbie** is probably the saddest of these, as it is now known throughout the world for the horrific act of terrorism that devastated so many peoples lives. But I also have happy memories of a little town with a beautiful campsite beside the river, where I spent many happy weekends just 'pottering'. People will always remember Lockerbie for what I think are the wrong reasons, but this is a pleasant place with a lot to offer and a community to match. There is a very good 18 hole golf course with the only pond hole in Dumfriesshire, and visitors are made most welcome. And of course we have **Gretna Green** which is just a short way from **Annan**! For those romantic hearts, this is where all those young lovers who could not get permission to marry, used to elope to in days gone by! Nowadays, the same rules as the rest of the land governs here, but the church and the romantic notion is still there! Just think of all those British Romeos and Juliets who pledged their love at this spot! An experienced guide is on hand to take you through 200 years of history and tell you some of the stories connected with this fascinating location! There is a great souvenir shop - all that is Scottish is probably sold here - from haggis to oatcakes, and from kilts to pottery! A great place to ferret around.

Moving away from the border, I would straight away like to visit the coast, and one of my very favourite places. Just up from **Stranraer**, the main ferry link to Ireland, is **Portpatrick**. On a clear day you can see the Irish coast, the **Mull of Kintyre**, and the **Isle of Man**, and this may give you an inkling as to why it was a great smuggling port! Apparently in war time when there was rationing, there was much 'toing and froing' between these coasts - if you couldn't get it in Scotland then you might in Ireland, and vice versa. The history of smuggling goes back a long time here, and the people still have that devilish twinkle! This is an attractive place and has some wonderful walks along the cliffs, giving you access to little hidden coves with golden sands and sheltered waters. The golf course runs along the top of the cliff too, so watch where you hit those balls! **Dunskey Castle,** the ruins of which also sit on the clifftops, is in a dramatic setting, and lends itself to vivid flights of fantasy when you stand within these ruined walls and visualise the history that was made here. The village does cater very well for the visitor, and there are bed & breakfast places as well as a variety of camping facilities. The pubs are great! One in particular on the harbour front has a gorgeous dog that will take a coin in it's mouth, deposit it behind the bar, and help itself to a packet of crisps! The only downfall is that you have to open them for him! Not completely trained, eh! There is usually music and jovial banter from the locals, who seem intent on having a good time whenever you visit. I cannot emphasise enough the beauty and pleasure this place has given me, and it would be remiss of me if I didn't encourage you to visit and enjoy it for yourself.

Moving up to Stranraer there are many gardens, castles and places of historical interest to visit. One of the most beautiful is the site of Soulseat Abbey at **Castle Kennedy,** where the **Meadowsweet Herb Garden** is located. The herb garden is the attraction, but the position of the remains of the Abbey, of which there are only a few mounds left, is quite outstanding. It sits on a 'tongue' which juts out into **Loch Soulseat** and is really spectacular. The herb garden is Galloway's original and has over 150 herbs set in beds. The shop sells both fresh and dried varieties, and the interesting uses of these can come as quite a surprise. Some lovely teas can be sampled, and I came away with a new knowledge of the uses of everyday herbs that I had previously only used in flavourings and colour! Again at Castle Kennedy *is* Castle Kennedy! The original castle was burnt down in 1716 and **Lochinch Castle** was built to replace it. This is the home of the present Earl and Countess of Stair. The ruins of Castle Kennedy sit on a peninsula between two lochs, and the gardens are renowned world wide for their displays of rhododendrons, azaleas, magnolias, and embrothriums. As the coastline along here is warmed by the Gulf Stream, a surprising variety of plants can be grown - this may account for the number of gardens on show in this part of Scotland. One of the most spectacular are those at **Logan.** The Botanic Gardens here show a really remarkable display of southern hemisphere plants which flourish outdoors in the unusually mild climate.

Travelling along the A75 brings us to the charming market town of **Newton Stewart.** Founded by the youngest son of the Earl of Galloway in the mid 17th century, the 'New Town of Stewart' was just a few cottages on the banks of the River Cree. Eventually it became a Burgh and was granted the right to hold markets and fairs, and grew into this engaging town we see today. This is the perfect location from which to see the countryside of Galloway: it has everything on offer with a good choice of restaurants and pubs, shops and many leisure activities. **The Galloway Forest Park** with its mountains, rivers and waterfalls, offers a wonderful panorama to explore. Wildlife is abundant, and with trails through heather covered hills, and alongside sparkling streams, you cannot fail to appreciate nature in all it's glory. This is 300 square miles of 'God's Country' with wild deer and lots of bird life. Nearby is the Bird Reserve at the **Wood of Cree** where woodpeckers, sparrowhawks and tawny owls are but a few of those to be found.

To the south of Newton Stewart lies an area known as '**The Marchars**'. This takes you through a profusion of country lanes with fishing villages hugging the shoreline, or to **Wigtown** which is the country town of the seat. Chance upon hidden lochs and stretches of deserted beaches, or admire the rich pastureland which is ideal for dairy farming. History has its share here too, with standing stones, castles, abbeys, and especially the archaeological dig at **Whithorn.** This gives a great insight into early Christianity in Scotland. It was only fully begun in 1986, and shows 1500 years of Scottish history, with the discovery of an abandoned town from Anglo Saxon times. Everything is exhibited in the nearby **Whithorn Discovery Centre**, where you can see the artefacts unearthed and actually take part in your own dig! A really worthwhile experience -especially for those of us who romanticise with the 'Indiana Jones' of the world! There is much more to this site with the famous Bishop Ninian who converted the Southern Picts to Christianity, and the cult that surrounded his shrine...............but this is for you to discover! Enjoy this great piece of history and be fascinated by the knowledge unearthed so recently.

Round the coast to **Kirkcudbright,** which has been known for a long time as an artists colony. One look at the architecture and the picturesque location will give you the reason why this has been such a haven for anybody with an artistic leaning, and today it is very popular with visitors. There is a good range of shops and facilities, and there is an excellent marina should

Chapter Eleven

you wish to sail into this charming harbour. Further inland, visit **Castle Douglas,** with its art gallery and deliciously bleak **Threave Castle** dating from the 14th century. Built on an island on the River Dee it was once home of the Black Douglases, including Archibald the Grim. Visiting this is quite an adventure as you have to ring for the ferryman to carry you across the water to the island. This is the point where the imagination runs riot, and you wonder if the ferryman is going to appear in black cowled cloak with ghoulish features!

Dumfries is the major town of this area and has plenty on offer for the visitor. Whatever your forte, you are sure to find something of interest in or surrounding this welcoming town. History is there for all, from Mary Queen of Scots to Robert Burns, there is a wealth of sites, castles folklore and just local legend which will fascinate and truly surprise you with its depth and intrigue. **Caerlaverock Castle,** just eight miles from Dumfries, is probably one of Scotland's finest castles, and is everyone's idea of how a medieval castle should look, with its moat and beautiful setting. Inside is a wonderful Renaissance residence, squeezed around its triangular courtyard. The ownership of this fine residence and surrounding landscape dates back to the time of the Norman Conquest, and honestly looks as if it hasn't changed since! The saltmarches of the **Solway Firth** are a haven for wildlife, and at any time of year there is something of interest, from natterjack toads in the summer, to thousands of geese, duck and wading birds in the winter. There are hides, towers and a heated observatory from which to observe this wonderful animalscape, and the friendly wardens are always on hand to answer your questions and help you enjoy your visit.

Dumfries as a town has a great array of hotels and hostelries which cater for all. The warmth of the Scottish welcome is genuine and the saying 'Haste ye back' is always on the lips of these friendly people. The town has many delightful craft, gift and memorabilia shops, along with some really good historical sites. One of these is the **Church of St.Michael** which houses the mausoleum where Robert Burns and his family are buried. Another is **Lincluden College**, where remains are to be found of some of the best medieval stonework in Scotland. Entertainment in this part of the world is something which happens all year round - I suppose that with some of the winter weather which can block the roads with snow and ice, it is wise to have an agenda that allows for boredom to be kept at bay! This is good news for the visitor, which means there is always something going on, even if the snowdrifts are preventing you from travelling further afield!

Moffat is a spa town leading into the **Borders,** the road climbing up through the Southern Uplands, past the famous 200ft **Grey Mare's Tail** waterfall, and round the spectacular scooped out **Devil's Beef Tub.** The

Scotland

Borders, has as it's spine, the Cheviot Hills, and with the magnificent hills, deep forests and tempestuous rivers, it is an area of extreme beauty. The Berwickshire east coast is a ragged one with substantial cliffs, and it is at **St Abb's Head** where one of the most important Scottish wildlife reserves can be found. The beautiful **Eildons** were Sir Walter Scott's favourite hills and his house, **Abbotsford,** was built nearby. He lived here until his death in 1832 and the house now stands as a museum to his life with everything very much as it was. Three of the great ruined Border abbeys lie in this area; **Melrose, Kelso** and **Dryburgh** where Sir Walter Scott chose to be buried. The A7 to the east takes you through **Langholm, Hawick** and **Selkirk** on a very picturesque and pleasant journey. This is home of the Border Common Ridings; probably in memory of historical border incidents, when each year around June cavalcades of horsemen parade through the town centres and everyone enjoys the ceremonies and processions. Further on, towards Lothian, is the most beautiful part of the **Tweed Valley**, where high above **Neidpath Castle** guards the wooded valley. The road meanders on through **Peebles** and **Innerleithen** and really is a most scenic vista.

The city of **Edinburgh** is known world wide for its Festival in the autumn months. This is a spectacular show and whether your forte are plays, music or comedy there is something for everyone. Every street corner, every pub, every soap box has a performance going on and it is definitely one of the gayest cities in Europe at this time. Seeing the Military Tattoo is a memory to be cherished, and I have never met anyone who did not enthuse about this spectacular event. The city offers some very fine shops, theatres and hotels to its visitors, and the wide main streets are a delight. The back cobbled streets hold some very interesting pubs and clubs, and it really is an active, enthralling city. In the way of history and architecture there is too much to mention, but the castle is a definite with its bird's eye view over the city, and the Crown Room where the Scottish Regalia can be seen. It is well worth the climb to see this magnificent building and the panoramic view. **Holyroodhouse Palace,** official Scottish residence of the Queen can also be visited, and a favourite of mine is the **Museum of Childhood** where as a child I was told all dolls and broken toys go 'to get better'.

East Lothian is well known for its great conservation work and this can be seen in the villages of **Aberlady, Athelstaneford** and **Tyninghame**, and nestled along the foothills of the **Lammermuirs**, the villages of **Gifford, Garvald** and **Stenton.** This is some of the best arable land in the country, and the fields of crops lend a colourful patchwork to the landscape. The **Pentlands** between Edinburgh and **Glasgow,** although being a very busy road area, still offers some lovely countryside. The network of country roads allows you to take your time and see some of this beauty. The thing I always find amazing is the difference in weather between Edinburgh and Glasgow

Chapter Eleven

- this I am told, is apparently because of an east-west divide rather than a north-south divide - all I know is that in winter Glasgow could make a good skiing resort at times! Don't let this put you off! Glasgow has a great deal to offer, and has played an important role in the history of Scotland since medieval times. On one side it had access to the Highlands and Islands, and on the other to Ireland and the Americas. It also played an important role in tobacco trading, shipbuilding and linen production. This city has had a great impact on me, and with the facelift it has undergone in the last few years, it is hardly recognisable as the unsociable, gang run, dreary place written about in such books as 'No Mean City'. The people are friendly and curious, and take a justifiable pride in the wellbeing of this great city. The tenement buildings have all been sandblasted and restored, and the lovely red colour lends a warmth to the overall picture. There is much architecture to see here. Being home of Charles Rennie MacKintosh the architect and designer, means there are many interesting places to visit. **Glasgow School of Art** and **Queen Margaret Medical School** are both of his design, but the most enthralling for me is his reconstructed house which is at **Glasgow University.** This dates back to 1914, but even by todays standards it is ultra modern with its white carpets and white furniture. There is a kind of reverence here which inspires the visitor to think of words such as avant-garde, innovation and inspired! Whilst others were living with the fashionable heavy Victorian furnishings of the day,here was a man creating light and pastels through his use of metals and paints and coloured glass. This was a very talented man 'well ahead of his time'.

Pollok Estate is 361 acres of beautiful woodland walks and open spaces where children play and families picnic. This was donated to the people of Glasgow and is today one of the most popular parks in the city. Pollok House, an 18th century Adam house, which was and still is owned by the Maxwell family, is open for viewing, and here you can see the accommodation and lifestyle of a wealthy family as it was in the 19th century. Also in the grounds is a purpose built building which houses the famous **Burrell Collection.** This was donated to the city by the Burrell family, and has more than 8000 pieces of oriental art, French paintings, medieval tapestries, and English stained glass.

Again on the grounds of Pollok Estate, the coup de grace for me was the handsome if not grand highland cattle sombrely chewing the grass and receiving my attention as if it were their due!

On the entertainment side, Glasgow has catholic tastes. It is home to Scottish Opera, Scottish Ballet, and the Royal Scottish National Orchestra. In May, Glasgow holds it's own art festival, which is a programme of events from dance and music to theatre, from community art projects to the culmination in an open air event over the River Clyde. Each year portrays a different theme and is known as Mayfest.

Theatres in Glasgow are numerous, and one of my favourites is **Citizens Theatre** in the infamous Gorbals. The atmosphere and electricity in this small original 600 seat Victorian auditorium is inspiring, and I have not seen a production here that I haven't enjoyed; whether it was the atmosphere or the players I know not. I confess that part of my affection for this theatre is that it was the 'peoples theatre' and prices were always kept to a minimum to allow ordinary working class the opportunity of enjoying the classics and the arts. Often productions were totally free to schoolchildren, and this was a wonderful chance for those who may otherwise have grown up without the wonders of live theatre.

Glasgow has a great array of shops and specialised arcades, and along with these very individual shops are all the well known, high quality names available in the major European cities.

What makes Glasgow an excellent base for any holiday, is the easy access to neighbouring towns and countryside. **Inverclyde** for example, is great for outdoor pursuits and cruises on the River Clyde. You can take a trip and see the islands, perhaps visit **Arran** and climb 'Goat Fell' or wander round the castle, former seat of the Dukes of Hamilton. **Brodick Castle** is 13th century and has some wonderful rooms with fine examples of silver, porcelain and paintings. The gardens here are famous for their rhododendrons, or perhaps you would like to just gaze at the rugged wild beauty of the landscape. Arran is the epitome of Scottish beauty with its glens, peaks and miles of beautiful coastline dotted with picturesque villages. The pace of life is slow and you can wander heather covered moors, quiet roads and sandy beaches at your leisure and enjoy the freshly caught seafood or local venison in any number of friendly local inns.

A trip round the islands here is a delightful experience, the **Isles of Jura and Islay** just a bit further north, with the **Island of Mull** just off the coast from **Oban.**

The **Rosneath Peninsula** juts far out into the Firth of Clyde, giving panoramic views of the surrounding hills and lochs, and due to it's location the villages of **Clynder, Rosneath, Kilcreggan** and **Cove**, have managed to hold on to their charm of a previous age. These villages, like **Helensburgh** and **Dunoon** and other Clyde resorts, were used as retreats from the smoky city of Glasgow, and are still used today as great holiday resorts by the sea. They have lost none of their charm, and can still take you to a delightful seaside paradise of peace and relaxation.

Chapter Eleven

There are many walks and cycleways from Glasgow, taking in much beauty and historical interest. The Clyde walkway follows the course of the River Clyde through **Cambuslang,** while the Highland Way starts in **Milngavie**, travelling via **Loc Lomond, Rannoch Moor** and through **Glencoe** to **Fort William** where if you feel the urge you can finish in style by climbing **Ben Nevis!** Needless to say this is not something to be done in a day (it would probably take me a month!) But it is a marvellous walkway if you have the stamina and are not too blinded by the sweat of exertion to take in the breathtaking views! This is an extremely scenic part of the country, and along with walking and climbing, there are great facilities for skiing and snowboarding.

Any visit to Scotland must incorporate a scotch whiskey distillery. I think this is the question most asked upon returning from any length of stay in this country of mist and heather (and occasional whiskey fumes). The ideal place for this is **Glengoyne Highland Malt Whiskey Distillery** which is at **Dumgoyne**, near **Killearn** on the A81. Spend a delightful 50 minutes on the tour and tasting at this distillery where traditional skills and crafts are still used. Something that really fascinated me was the 'tutored nosing lesson' available each Wednesday evening at 7.30pm. Sadly I did not get the chance to partake of this, but am determined to make the time if the opportunity should arise again!

Travelling from Glasgow to Arran takes you through the scenic county of Ayrshire. This is Rabbie Burns country and some trace of the poet's touch can be seen almost everywhere. Lovers of the 'Bard's' poetry travel from all parts of the world to visit the home of this great man and the many sites of his famous poems. Just on the outskirts of the seaside town of **Ayr** is **Alloway**, where the original 18th century cottage Burns was born in, is now a museum containing relics of the poet. Visit '**Auld Brig o' Doon**', the 13th century bridge where Tam o' Shanter of the famous poem, escaped the witches.

Ayrshire has much to offer and the friendly hospitality will encourage you to return. A day at the famous **Ayr Racecourse** is just one of the fun attractions on offer along with a wealth of ancient castles and country parks. The rolling countryside with its myriad of colours, from the purple hues of the heathers to the velvety greens of the ferns, imprint a lasting memory to take home with you, leaving something of yourself forever in these gentle hills.

Largs in Ayrshire, is one of those delightful seaside towns with an attractive promenade and a stimulating display of shops, restaurants and cafes. This is the home of the world famous Nardini ice cream which is a

Scotland

must for those connoisseurs of this rapturous confectionery! It is also a great sailing port which is ever expanding, with the Largs Yacht Haven where yachtsmen come to take advantage of some of the best sailing waters in Europe. Largs has been named as Scotland's top tourist town, and there is certainly a flush of activities for those of all ages who visit the area.

Just across the water is the **Great Cumbrae Island.** This small island is definitely the home of the bicycle with all types, from doubles to tandems, and from large wheels to small. It seems to be quite the thing to come here for the day, hire a bike and torture yourself with cycling round the whole island! Don't worry! This is a slight exaggeration when I tell you that the complete track only measures 14 miles! With it's sandy beaches and charming resort town, this has been a popular holiday centre for over a century.

The **Firth of Clyde** is one of the most scenic areas of Britain where you can still sail on a paddle steamer. This is truly an experience and you can visit the engine room to see the massive 2100 horsepower steam engine in operation. The Waverly paddle steamer is a lovely way to travel the Firth of Clyde and see its variety of scenery, with stretches of open water and sea lochs surrounded by towering mountains, and a diversity of islands. My favourite is the **Isle of Bute** with the Mount Stuart House and gardens. Here you enter a world of fantasy in this Victorian Gothic house, which was built by the 3d Marquess of Bute (1847 to 1900). His interests in the arts, astrology and religion are all reflected in the building, giving a breathtaking panorama to the visitor. The combination of stained glass and marble is quite remarkable and swathes one in the history and mystique of the house.

Kilmarnock is a pleasant town to visit. It has a good variety of shops and there are many historical buildings to be viewed. The monument to Rabbie Burns here encases a statue by W.G.Stevenson, and there is a good view of the surrounding countryside from the top. **Dean Castle** and **Country Park** is a beautiful site, and the Visitor Centre gives great insight into the past of the area and also the natural history.

Loch Lomond is probably the best known and most beautiful part of Scotland that visitors from all over the world recognise instantly and flock to. By car, you can travel the A82 which runs alongside nearly the full length of the loch. Just driving along here slowly, gives you a marvellous view of the loch and it's backdrop of mountains. You can understand why the songs were written about this exquisite setting and why people are inspired by the landscape. **Ben Lomond,** which stands guard over the loch, and its magnificent peak, sometimes swirled in clouds, juts high into the heavens. The beauty here is ravishing at any time of year. Whether it is at the height of summer, with cotton wool clouds and green patchwork mountains, with

Chapter Eleven

fields of wild flowers colouring the horizon, or autumn with its distinct shades of orange and reds giving a warm golden glow to the landscape. Even winter gives its own domain to the scenery, softening the rough edges under a blanket of white powder and producing frozen waterfalls of iridescent colours that hang suspended in the winter sunshine.

Another enthralling way to visit this area is by the **West Highland Railway**. This was originally opened in 1894 and served the lochside communities on its way to the **West Highlands**. The scenery is quite stunning as it takes you above the rooftops of **Helensburgh** and winds its way up into the mountains. The line travels up above the **Gare Loch** where the view is of the full length of the loch, and then continues up to the summit of **Glen Douglas** at 560ft before descending back down the hillside. The next mountain to be seen is **The Cobbler**, unmistakable in its rugged silhouette. The train then dips into the valley between **Loch Long** and Loch Lomond, and Ben Lomond comes into view. Across the loch is **Inversnaid** where Rob Roy once lived, the hero of many a Scottish battle. At the head of Loch Lomond the train pulls into **Ardlui** and catches its breath before continuing on up to **Crainlarich** where the line splits for **Oban** or **Fort William**

The hamlets and villages around the banks of Loch Lomond are many, and each is individually charming. **Luss**, for example, is a delightfully preserved estate village which caters very well for tourists. There are a variety of eating establishments from an inn to a milk bar, and if you would like to sample some malt whiskies then the Ben Lomond Whiskey Shop has over 200 varieties for you to try! **Balloch Castle** in Loch Lomond Park is set in 200 acres of woodland, park and gardens.

From conifers, azaleas and other bushes, to a walled garden and even a fairy glen. The visitor centre at the site of the old castle has plenty of information on nature trails and guided walks. Park Authority Rangers organise various events for the whole family on a daily basis. The centre at Luss has exhibitions on the landscape, wildlife and cultural history of the area, and a slide presentation lets you see the wonders of Loch Lomond in all the changing seasons.

Balloch itself, is home of the many coloured vessels that sail on the loch. In the town are boat yards and a pier, and from here you can take a boat trip and cruise round the loch for either a pleasant day sail or a romantic evening sail! Many people and many types of vessels are found here, from sailing boats to houseboats, and there can be a great sense of peace found on these calm waters. Travel through the islands and enjoy a spot of fishing in the deep waters, or if you are terribly brave then perhaps with a coating of grease you could have a quick dip and relish the cool depths! Brrrr!

Close to the edge of the Highlands are the towns of **Bridge of Allan, Dunblane** and **Doune**. Each is interesting in it's own right. Bridge of Allan could almost be a suburb of **Stirling**, but it is soon apparent that it's not, and it is worth a visit with it's spa waters and local history. Dunblane has a magnificent cathedral, whilst Doune is home to one of Scotland's medieval castles. Stirling is a beautiful clean city, with a vast array of shops to browse round, and of course another castle! The monument to William Wallace is here, and with wonderful audio-visual technology, you can actually meet Wallace in his 'battle tent'. Further north are **Callander** and **Lochearnhead** which has a beautiful setting at the head of **Loch Earn**.

The **Kingdom of Fife** covers a large area, from **St Andrews** to **Dunfermline**, and across almost to **Perth**. Dunfermline is one of the major towns, and sadly, in the eyes of the tourist, it is very underrated, but this is to the advantage of those who choose to visit. It is a critical spot in Scotland's heritage, with history oozing out of every building. This is Scotland's ancient capital and as such, deserves more attention. It is more than 1000 years old, and was part of the Kingdom of the Picts. It is also the birthplace of Andrew Carnegie who built Carnegie hall in New York. Everywhere there are streets and halls named after the famous man, and with a justifiable pride. It was something my mother used to say when I was little. As all children, I never tired of asking for everything in sight, and my mother's favourite saying was, "Do you think my name's Carnegie?" implying that, as all parents do, she was not made of money! I have always remembered that man's name! This is a lovely city, with lots of history and excellent buildings for those architectural enthusiasts.

Cupar was the county town of Fife until 1975, when local government reorganisation made it the administrative centre for North East Fife. It is one of the oldest burghs in Scotland and is certainly central of all the roads in the area. Places of interest include the Mansion House and Gardens designed by Sir Robert Lorimer, Duffus Park, and the Scottish Deer Centre - all worth a visit.

How can I possibly talk about St Andrews and not mention golf? Impossible! One conjures up a picture of the other! Anyone who is interested in golf does not need me to tell them about the golf courses here, but I will say just a little. This is the location of the world's number one golf course 'the famous Old Course'. Golf has been played in St Andrews since 1547, and these traditions are carried on by the citizens of today. There are 20 golf courses in the district and reasonable green fees make this a most enjoyable pastime. But this is not all St. Andrews is about! I have a soft spot, as this is where I received my proposal of marriage many moons ago! I suppose due to that I will always find it a rather romantic sort of place with

Chapter Eleven

pretty streets and lovely moonlight walks. Even today, although I am not so starry or cross eyed and need specs for any close inspection, I still find it a lovely town. A beautiful clean beach, historical landmarks, cluttered antique shops, impressive architecture, and even the weather seems that bit better! The people are friendly, with that unhurried style of living that makes one envious of the amount of spare time they seem to have!

Leaving St Andrews I would like to tell you about the **East Neuk**. This is the coastal area that runs between St Andrews and **Kirkcaldy**, and history tells that these little ports were used in medieval times as trade links with France and the Scandinavian countries. Later they were the epitome of the fishing villages that made their living through the colourful herring fishing. Today, they are peaceful 'wee' villages that carry the seafaring atmosphere in their very being. Each one is distinct, yet all have a common heritage in their unchanged character that has been bypassed by time. One of these villages that I will mention is **Lower Largo**. This place has a very famous son Alexander Selkirk. I expect you are saying "Who is Alexander Selkirk?". Well, this man had a great interest in the seafaring life, and upon reaching age ran away to sea to sail on the ship Cinque Ports across the Pacific Ocean. Any bells ringing yet? He had a disagreement with the captain which resulted in him being put ashore on the island of Juan Fernandez, where he was to remain for four years and four days. "Aha" I hear you say, "this sounds familiar". When he returned to Britain, a novelist was captured by his story and decided to write a book on his life. The novelist was Daniel Defoe and that's right, the book was called Robinson Crusoe! Another village is **Anstruther**, where there is a great fishing museum displaying the lifestyles and histories of the fishing communities of a bygone era. There is also a collection of boats, and a herring boat launched in 1900 lies at anchor in the harbour. This place also has a claim to fame as Robert Louis Stevenson stayed here as a boy, and who knows, it may even have been inspiration for some of his work. There is a house here which has been restored by the National Trust and is completely covered in shells! The 'Buckie House' stands on the corner of the High Street and is quite something to see!

Tinkerbell, as a character, was the product of a great imagination, and I like to think the product also of a heritage of folk stories, the surrounding freedom and space, and a sense of mystery that surrounds us all in nature, even today. J.M.Barrie, the author of the classic Peter Pan, was born in a little cottage just outside **Kirriemuir** in the county of **Angus**. To produce a work of this calibre, in my opinion, conjures up a happy and secure childhood, and a confidence and belief in the beauty of all around one. Angus is just the place to give one those ideals. This beautiful county has scenery to make you weep, and a variety to ensure the captivity of even the most sceptical.

Scotland

The **Angus Glens** range from romantic and haunting, wild and grand, soft and undulating, and above all, soothing enough to the artist in all of us. **Glen Esk** has beauty in the tumbling waters of the **North Esk**, and the winding roads through the pastures below. In **Glen Cova** the road ends below the crags, and many people start here on a voyage of discovery both of themselves and wild and wonderful terrain laid out before them. The myriad of settings arouse sentiments beyond belief. **Glen Prosen** has the most stunning views that will have you reaching for your camera, to keep for ever that moment of beauty. **Glen Isla** is wild and natural, it's haunting virtue astounds the senses in its intensity. The colours, smells and even the taste, distinctive in it's freshness and will bring back some of that forgotten bloom to your cheeks, that some of us 'city dwellers' seem to have lost.

Forfar is where you will find **Glamis Castle,** a royal residence since 1372. This was the childhood home of the Queen Mother and the birthplace of Princess Margaret, and has magnificent rooms decked with furniture, porcelain, tapestries and historic paintings. In the Angus Folk Museum close by you will find the domestic and farming history of Angus going through the last 200 years. This is especially interesting, to see the various farming methods used, and just how 'easy' life has become in this century.

Arbroath is another great place in this county. I really like this place; the harbour, the town itself, it's pubs and people. There is a real mixture here as Britain's own Royal Marines have a base here and have done so for a long time - probably about 25 years, prior to which it was a naval airstation. Families have come here with a draft to the area........and stayed. There is a real cosmopolitan feel to the town and over the last few years a progressive one. This is the site of some of the best nightspots in Scotland and the young travel from all over for 'a night on the town!' Don't let this put you off! - You can still have a 'jig' in one of the hotels , or even a quiet drink in a pub, but it is nice to see the younger generation catered for!

Arbroath goes back a long way in the history of Scotland. The Abbey was founded in 1178 by William the Lion, King of Scots, and the monks were allowed a port and weekly market in the forming of the Burgh. It was in this Abbey that the Nobles of Scotland swore their independence from England, in the Declaration of Arbroath. The Stone of Destiny which recently came back to Scotland after 700 years, to be placed in Edinburgh castle, was stolen from London in 1951 and interestingly enough, was discovered in Arbroath Abbey some months later - someone knew their history!

Brechin is probably the smallest city in Scotland, but this does not take away from it's interesting history. The cathedral its Round Tower which date back as far as the 11th century is only one of two in Scotland. The

Chapter Eleven

graveyard has tombstones dating back to the plague and has some really good inscriptions! This city is also the home of **Caledonian Railway Co.,** and for any enthusiast the station here is a must. It is all run by volunteers, and steam trains run between May and September from Brechin to the **Bridge of Dun**, a lovely journey. Even if you go out of season do not miss the fantastic station which is open all year round! On the way from Brechin to **Montrose** you come across the **House of Dun**. This Georgian house was designed by the famous William Adam and built in 1730. It is a wonderful place with many royal mementos and some great plasterwork by Joseph Enzer. There is a miniature theatre, Victorian walled garden, woodland walks and imposing parkland, all to be visited on the grounds. The courtyard buildings show various displays including a handloom weaving workshop, and there is a national trust shop and restaurant. A great day out (and you will spend the day!), and there is a vintage coach service and steam train from Brechin during the season.

Montrose is a lovely place with its open aspect overlooking the bay. In **Montrose Basin** there is now a Wildlife centre, this enclosed estuary has been virtually untouched by industrialism or pollution, and is a rich feeding ground for thousands of birds, both resident and migrant. Montrose itself, has a host of little shops, with galleries, crafts and antiques being a speciality. There are some lovely walks just outside the town and you are never far from spectacular scenery (or a golf course for that matter!), and open countryside. Talking of golf, **Carnoustie**, on the other side of Arbroath, which obviously has a golf course; the British Open was played here in 1931......but if you like golf you'll know of Carnoustie, so I'll say no more!

Dundee is one of the oldest Royal Burghs in Scotland, and could tell many tales of the Vikings and the English plundering and pillaging the city! William Wallace attended Dundee grammar School, and during the occupation in 1288 he slew the English Governor's son in a fight, and had to flee for his life. It might well have been this that started him on his quest to free Scotland and write the history we all know today. Dundee is definitely linked to the sea, and the great shipbuilding skills of times gone by were what led Captain Scott here, to build his famous ship Discovery. It is said that Dundee is built on the three 'J's; jute (cloth), jam and journalism, but there is a host of other things you could add to this. What about Dundee Cake! Shipbuilding, linen and much more attributed to this fine city's wealth. Because of it's strategic position, it was well positioned to receive the raw jute from India, and became wealthy through the industry it promoted. Today, the city concentrates on the expansion of micro-technology and the service industries - specifically the tourist industry. Dundee is very good at this; it caters very well to it's visitors tastes and needs, and there is always a friendly welcome from a people who recognise where their 'living' comes from.

We could not mention Dundee without the **Tay Rail Bridge**. This bridge was the longest when built, at a length of 2 miles and 73 yards, and is still the longest bridge in Europe today. Sadly, the first bridge collapsed in a storm in 1879 with the loss of 75 lives, but was rebuilt in 1887. This is a spectacular sight at night when lit up, and adds quite a romanticism to the city. The highest point overlooking the city is **The Law**, Dundee's War Memorial, with beacons which are lit four times a year. The view from here is fantastic, not only of Dundee but across to distant mountains in the north and west, and deep into the Fife countryside on the south. This is how I like to remember Dundee and Angus; from this stunning vantage point overlooking a kingdom that has seen much strife and warring, but that has retained it's wild, rugged beauty both in it's landscape and it's people.

The central **Grampians** is home to two of the major tourist attractions of **North Perthshire;** the holiday resort of **Pitlochry** and **Blair Castle**. Beside Pitlochry is the **Fascally Dam**, where you can view the spawning salmon struggling upstream from an observation chamber, and the wooded walks high above **Loch Tummel** offers extensive pictures of the surrounding lochs and countryside. The Grampians were much loved by Queen Victoria, who spent a lot of time in this haven, away from the hustle and bustle of court society. She bought the castle at **Balmoral** in 1848 and immediately fell in love with the area. This love affair has continued with succeeding monarchs who, thanks to Queen Victoria, have managed to maintain this holiday retreat ever since. Much pride surrounds this area where the Royal family holiday, and the Royal warrant coat of arms is visible on many, of even the smallest, shops in the area. The **River Dee** is in a beautiful valley and many of the villages like **Ballater, Banchory** and **Aboyne**, that hug the borders of the river have the most wonderful settings. One of Queen Victoria's favourite places was **Glen Muick**, near Ballater, where the vista is exceptional, rugged and wild with that stern Scottish terrain that is quite unique. When Prince Albert died she had a cottage built at the far end of the glen to give her solitude from the increasing number of tourists in the area, and it was known as Widow's House. Today, Glen Muick is a nature reserve with remarkable walks through the forest, and a trail that leads to the top of **Lochnagar.** Red deer are quite common here and can be seen rutting during the season.

Beyond Balmoral, is **Braemar,** where the famous Highland Games are watched each September by visitors from near and far. If you approach Braemar from **Glen Shee** in the south, you are travelling the highest main road summit in Scotland - nearly 2000ft above sea level. The Highland Games is something that happens in many parts of Scotland, and if you perchance happen upon this event then do not miss the opportunity to watch! Young dancers compete in a pirouette of flashing kilts and exacting footwork, while giant brawny men contend to find the champion of the games. Tossing the

Chapter Eleven

caber, the hammer event and the tug o' war are all designed to find the strongest as was done in days of auld. In the background are the sounds of the pipe bands and the solitary pipers as they too compete in their class. The colour and sounds of these events, the fierce determination of the competitors, the smiles and tears of the young dancers as they win or lose, will stay with you to bring back fond memories of an exhilarating experience.

The distinction of a good malt whiskey is the purity of the water, and this is the area where you can see frothy clean water cascading down rocks and rushing through channels cut into the hillside by the force of the water. Hence, the number of malt whiskey distilleries in the area! More than half of those in Scotland are located here, and the **Malt Whiskey Trail** is a singular experience! (From what I can remember!) There are at least ten distilleries where you can watch the whiskey-making process, combining the barley with the sweet water, yeast and peat, culminating in this delicious amber nectar! Most distilleries are more than keen to let you sample a 'dram' of their own specialised elixir!

Archaeologically, we know that people have lived and worked in the Grampian Region for at least 8000 years, and today, this leaves an impressive account for us to enjoy. From Stone circles to Hillforts to Pictish Stones, we can see the history of the area and build up a picture of this heritage. The fascinating record is there for us all to see, and is well documented in the area with maps and brochures easily available, and a simple series of signposts to follow.

And so to the scenery. What can I say? Words seem inadequate to describe the scenery that you come across in this part of the world. There is something very individual about Scottish scenery; the mountains and glens give you a great sense of peace and tranquillity, and at the same time it stirs emotions todays 'civilised' society thought lay dormant.

It's as if all the history is still there; the battles fought, the ancient Celt's harmony with the earth, the people's struggle to abide in this sometimes inhospitable landscape, you can see it all. It instills a feeling in the chest unlike any other, and when you are standing atop a windswept hill with the heather murmuring round your feet and rays of sunlight shining through the ever moving cloud cover, highlighting glens and sparkling burns, then you will know exactly what I mean. This is walking country with delights over every mound, and displays that are breathtaking. Wildlife is bountiful with the courtly Red Deer gracing the glens and forests, and the birds of prey, kestrel and sparrowhawk, soaring majestically over the hillside. Here, nature's true force is recognised and makes one feel just how insignificant we are.

On the coastal side of the district, the benefits of conservation coupled with leisure facilities is very much in evidence. The craggy cliffs and golden fringed beaches have something for everyone, with marvellous scenery, historical castles, smugglers villages, rolling sand dunes and thousands of sea birds nesting on the cliffs. Visit Lawrence of Arabia's holiday destination at **Celestine**, a perfectly charming village renowned for fishing and of course, smuggling. Visit the site of an early lighthouse at **Fraserburgh**, where you can learn the history at an exhilarating museum, and imagine the lonely vigil kept by those keepers of our ships. If you have a vivid imagination the history, sights and smells of these places will invoke a tapestry of bygone days, that will unravel with each and every attack on the senses.

Mention **Aberdeen** and you immediately think of 'black gold'; oil! This does not inspire, as our vision is immediately filled with ugly tankers, oil drums, noise, pollution and all manner of nasty things. But, just a minute! This impression would be very wrong and unfair to the Aberdonians who, over the last 25 years, since the discovery of oil off their shores, have done a magnificent job of marrying the old with the new. This is a wonderful city, which has used the boom in its economy in a very sensible and mature fashion. It has been awarded the title of 'Britain's Cleanest City', and has won the 'Britain in Bloom' title 10 times. Due to it's position, Aberdeen has always been an important port. Situated on the mouth of the **Rivers Dee and Don,** it is the main gateway to the **Northern Isles** and has regular shipping services to the continent. Obviously with advent of oil, the harbour and docks have been improved immensely to cope with the influx of larger and more frequent cargoes for the oil industry. It is also a member of the Cruise Europe promotional organisation, and cruise ships are often seen in the harbour due to its convenience to the scenery of the **Highlands.** It has an international airport, and links with Europe and other parts of the UK are excellent. This is a thriving city with a quality of life amongst the best in the country. Yet Aberdeen has a rich cultural heritage; alongside the new buildings and shopping malls stand the original granite faced structures whose sparkling facades gave rise to the name 'Silver City'. This locally quarried stone was used in some of the finest architecture built, which can still be seen today shimmering in the sunlight. There is something very fine about granite which gives an elegant, smooth finish to the buildings and lends majesty to their age. Much has been done in the way of conservation and much thought has gone into the new constructions seen alongside the old.

Because of the cosmopolitan lifestyle which now envelops the city, there is something for every age and every degree of energy. The nightlife throbs, whilst the international hotels cater to your every whim, and any type of food from traditional Scottish to any of the foreign cuisines are on offer in any number of restaurants, cafes and inns. The history and culture

Chapter Eleven

are magnificent, and whatever your choice, there is certainly no problem finding somewhere to satisfy your needs or desires. Aberdeen has certainly found wealth in the discovery of oil, but I think these people always had it in their culture and hospitality towards others. The fact that oil enriched their economy only ensured that it was perhaps more visible to a visitor, but the distribution of the wealth shows us that these people are rich in happiness and in sharing their good fortune.

Scotland as a whole, is a great place to visit, and caters very well to the tourist industry. These friendly, curious people, with their lilting accents and 'Scottish pride', welcome you with open arms into their homes and to the warmth of their hearths. You will return home feeling you have made a whole new set of friends, and perhaps left just a little of your heart in these glens and valleys.

THE PALACE HOTEL
Breadalbane Terrace,
Aberfeldy,
Perthshire PH15 2AG

Tel: 01887 820359

The Palace Hotel has been a recent acquisition for Clare and George Robertson but in less than a year they have brought the sturdy, typically Scottish, Palace Hotel into the 1990's with careful refurbishment that does not detract from the original building. Every room is furnished with an eye to tradition and with an emphasis on comfort and it is an hotel in which children are genuinely welcome, pets too. In fact kennel service is available on request if required. It is ideally situated for anyone wanting to enjoy shooting, fishing or walking. The Robertsons will arrange shooting and fishing for you. It is good fun too to return in the evening and join in the Pool and Darts in the Public Bar. If you prefer to be quieter, the invitingly large sofas and armchairs in the Residents Lounge, are waiting for you.

The Palace has 21 bedrooms, all equipped with TV and a generous beverage tray. 17 of the rooms are ensuite including two family rooms. In the Dining room which seats 30 easily, the food served is delicious. Breakfast is a true Scottish feast, although a lighter breakfast is available if that is your preference. The Dinner Menu is well chosen with interesting dishes. For example Tomato, Orange and Walnut Soup or Avocado Pear with Mimosa Salad for Starters followed by Sauted Supreme of Chicken filled with a herb mousseline and wild mushroom sauce or traditional Roast Sirloin of Beef with Yorkshire Pudding - the beef defies description. For the sweet-toothed there are several choices.

This is a hotel with a growing reputation for both its accommodation and its food and above all for its welcoming atmosphere.

USEFUL INFORMATION

OPEN; All year
CHILDREN: Welcome
CREDIT CARDS; Access/Visa/Master
LICENSED; Full Licence
ACCOMMODATION; 21 rooms, 17 ensuite
DINING ROOM; Traditional & imaginative
BAR FOOD; Good, sensibly priced choice
VEGETARIAN; Catered for
DISABLED ACCESS; No
GARDEN; Not at present

Chapter Eleven

THE OLD ABERLADY INN
Main Street,
Aberlady,
East Lothian, EH32 ORF

Tel: 01875 870503
Fax: 01875 870209

This interesting and friendly hostelry came into the hands of Murray and Karen Georgeson in October 1995 and in a very short time they have carried out major refurbishments, and stamped their own personalities on the inn without detracting from its existing charm. These two very professional people have been involved in the catering business for some time, running the successful Kings Walk Restaurant/Bistro in Leith which is still in their care. You will find more about Kings Walk in the back of this book in the 'Where to eat' section.

The Bar is a lively place and much used by local people who are enjoying the changes made by the Georgesons. For example the bar has been 'aged' to suit the new ambience and has a delightful little separate 'pre-dinner' bar at the rear and a Bistro style restaurant with an excellent selection of wines from around the world. Murray runs the kitchen together with his talented chef, Billie. Between them they create deliicious dishes and will always use fresh local produce and game. The menu is not large but it does offer an adventurous choice. The success is proven by the ever increasing number of people who come here just to eat. Imagine dining on Steamed Mussels with a mild curry sauce followed by Chicken, Leek, Ginger and Cashewnut Casserole. The charmingly furnished bedrooms are all ensuite and have TV, telephone and tea/coffee making facilities. If you prefer self catering there is a chalet villa which will sleep up to 8 adults and still allow you to have full use of the hotel for the bar and restaurant. The prices are right, the area is full of interest and abounds with golf courses. Historic buildings, a famous bird sanctuary and many bracing walks will delight anyone who stays and for those who wish to explore Edinburgh, Scotland's Capital is only 20 minutes away.

USEFUL INFORMATION

OPEN; All year
CHILDREN; Welcome
CREDIT CARDS; All major cards
LICENSED; Yes. Good wine list
ACCOMMODATION; 9 ensuite
Self catering chalet for 8 adults

RESTAURANT; Adventurous, concise menu
BAR MEALS; Daily variety
VEGETARIAN; On request
DISABLED ACCESS; No
GARDEN; Yes, large
PETS; Permitted

Scotland

PAGANI'S RESTAURANT
95 High Street,
Annan,
Dumfries & Galloway DG12 6DJ

Tel: 01461 201999

John Pagani has made 95 High Street into one of the best Italian restaurants in Scotland. His menu embraces both Italian and Scottish dishes using the finest ingredients and combining them to make a unique eating experience. At Pagani's it is not only the cusine which is Italian but the restaurant has captured the true, amenable atmosphere which is found in many of Italy's country restaurants. The latest menu, which changes frequently, is based on dishes from Livorno, a coastal city with miles of beach umbrellas sporting the colours of the local football teams on one side and the foothills of the Appenines as a backdrop. Well placed in Tuscany it has an abundance of fresh frutta dimare and, of course, fruit of the vine. Imagine yourswelf there and settle down to study the menu in order to choose from the delights of its traditional delicacies. Everything is freshly prepared and served by a smiling, friendly staff who want you to enjoy both the restaurant and the delicious food. Prices are sensible and the wine list, whilst not vast, has been chosen by John Pagani, who has a true love of Italian wines. For example you will find three wines made from the Montepulciano grape and a dry white with a little fizz called Pignarello which the italians love drinking on lazy warm evenings. There are other classic Italian wines, some French and some from the New World. In fact something for everyone and to suit every pocket.

If you have insufficient time to dine in the restaurant Pagani's Coffee Shop is open for Breakfast, Lunch and Tea and serves a whole range of dishes from Starters and Snacks to Jacket Potatoes with numerous fillings. There are fresh salads and Pagani's Platters including anything from Chicken to Macaroni Cheese. Excellent value for money, the service is quick and efficient. There is a Childrens' Menu and the Coffee Shop is licensed.

USEFUL INFORMATION

OPEN; Coffee Shop 9-6pm **RESTAURANT;** Italian & Scottish
CHILDREN; Welcome. Childrens menu   dishes, changing menu
CREDIT CARDS; Access/Master/Visa/Switch **COFFEE SHOP;** Wide range
LICENSED; Yes. Restaurant & Coffee Shop **VEGETARIAN;** Yes, several
ACCOMMODATION; Not applicable **DISABLED ACCESS;** Yes
GARDEN; Not applicable

Chapter Eleven

ALLT-NA-CRAIG GUEST HOUSE
Tarbert Road,
Ardrishaig, Argyll PA30 8EP

Tel: 01546 603945

This elegant Victorian mansion with breath-taking views over Loch Fyne stands in beautifully maintained grounds on the outskirts of Ardishaig. An ideal base from which to explore the surrounding area which is steeped in history, or simply to relax and enjoy the fine food and hospitality. Ardishaig stands at the southern end of the Crinan Canal, the gateway to the Western Isles. From here you can take a boat trip to the many islands including Arran, Mull and Islay. Waiting to be explored are Bronze Age burial cairns, standing stones and the remains of old forts including Dunadd Hill, where the ancient Kings of Scotland were crowned. Hill walking, bird watching, fishing, golf, riding, diving, wind surfing and many other outdoor activities are available in the area. There are gentle walks and stunning scenery, the delights of Inverary, whose picturesque castle is home to the Duke of Argyll. To enjoy all this what better than making Allt-na-Craig your base.

The Bed and Breakfast accommodation consists of six guest rooms all with their own modern en suite shower or bathroom and facilities to make tea and coffee. The famous Allt-na-Craig breakfast makes a perfect start to a day's exploring, with choices as varied as a full Scottish breakfast, Loch Fyne kippers or a lighter offering of Scotch pancakes, tea and toast. Evening meals are available by arrangement and feature home cooking with a distinctly Scottish flavour. You can choose between a set menu and a la carte, with a wine list to accompany both. The lounge, with its open fire and splendid views, is fully equipped with colour TV, piano, games and tourist guides. The house is fully centrally heated and has ample parking space within its ground. Situated within the grounds is The Coach House, which has recently been refurbished for up to six self-catering guests. Self-catering guests are welcome to join other guests for meals in the main house.

USEFUL INFORMATION

OPEN; All year except Christmas and New Year
CHILDREN; Welcome
CREDIT CARDS; None taken
LICENSED; Residential Licence
ACCOMMODATION; 6 en suite rooms
Self Catering Coach house available

DINING ROOM; Super Scottish breakfast. Evening meals by by arrangement
VEGETARIAN; Catered for
DISABLED ACCESS; No
GARDEN; Yes
PETS; Yes

AUCHENDARROCH HOTEL
Tarbert Road, Ardishaig,
Argyll, Scotland PA30 8PE

Tel: 01546 602275

An attractive hotel owned by Alistair and Mary MacVicar. Attractively furnished ensuite bedrooms, with colour TV and Tea and coffee making facilities. The International menu includes a number of favourites and is keenly priced. Open to non-residents. Bar Meals are also available daily from 12-2pm and between 6-8pm. Ideal hotel for short breaks for which there are special offers.

USEFUL INFORMATION

OPEN: All year
CHILDREN: Welcome
CREDIT CARDS: Mastercard/Access
LICENSED: Yes
ACCOMMODATION: 2 double, 2 TWIN, all ensuite
PETS: Welcome

RESTAURANT: Excellent comprehensive menu. Open to non-residents
BAR FOOD: Yes
DISABLED ACCESS: For meals and toilets only
GARDEN: Yes

KINNOUL GUEST HOUSE
Drymen Road,
Balloch,
Loch Lomond,
Scotland G83 8HS

Tel: 01389 721116

As the song goes 'on the bonnie bonnie banks of Loch Lomond' for that is where you will be if you stay at Kinnoul Guest House, only 2 minutes from the shores of the famous Loch itself. This Highly Commendable Guest House offers the perfect choice for a holiday and an ideal base for touring this stunning and dramatic part of Scotland. The house itself is very attractive, with 5 tastefully decorated bedrooms, 3 are ensuite the others having private facilities. All the rooms have television and a tea and coffee tray. There is a cosy residents lounge, a lovely garden and a patio for barbecues. In the evening a traditional 3 course dinner is served, you may bring your own wine. The morning starts with a full Scottish breakfast before you set off sight seeing, packed lunches are available with prior notice.

USEFUL INFORMATION

OPEN; All year
CHILDREN; Welcome
VEGETARIAN; Catered for
CREDIT CARDS; Access/Visa subject to 3% surcharge
LICENSED; No, bring your own
ACCOMMODATION; 5 rooms, 3 ensuite 2 double, 2 family, 1 twin

DINING ROOM; Traditional and Scottish fare

DISABLED ACCESS; Not really
GARDEN; Yes + patio for barbecues
PETS; Yes, prior arrangement only

Chapter Eleven

THE GLENEAGLES HOTEL
Auchterarder,
Perthshire PH3 1NF

Tel: 01764 662231
Fax: 01764 662134

'There are many beautiful places in the world. There are many great hotels. There are many famous golf courses and sporting centres. There's only one Gleneagles.' This appears in the front of the brochure for this magnificent hotel and really says everything. For those who know nothing about it except perhaps its name, prepare yourselves for an unforgettable experience. Ever since it opened its doors in time to become one of the celebrated venues of the Jazz Era people have come here from all over the world. From maharajahs to millionaires, the rich and the famous and those with absolute taste. It was not just to idle away their time in sumptuous surroundings but to see world class golf, play their own matches and sometimes replay them far into the night in the Dormy clubhouse and the hotel bars. Whilst Gleneagles means golf it also offers much more. There are walks and rides, tennis, billiards, croquet and mountain biking to mention just a few of the activities. The Equestrian Centre is one of the best equipped in the world and provides facilities for every discipline of horsemanship and at every level of experience. The British School of Falconry at Gleneagles is just another facet of this glorious place.

Gleneagles may well be one of the most luxurious hotels in the world but it prides itself on the warmth and friendliness of its staff. It is relaxed and unstarchy. The Taste of Scotland is always to be enjoyed here from morning kippers or a fresh egg from a nearby farmhouse, scones and cream or Dundee cake for afternoon tea in the Drawing Room to superb dinners. There are three main restaurants or you may eat simple salads or lighter meals in one of the bars or grills. Each has its own charm and everyone offers very high standards.

USEFUL INFORMATION

OPEN; All year
CHILDREN; Welcome
CREDIT CARDS; All major cards
LICENSED; Full. Fine vintage wines
ACCOMMODATION; Superb ensuite rooms and suites
PETS; By arrangement
RESTAURANT; 3 main restaurants serving exquisite cuisine
BAR FOOD; Excellent choices
VEGETARIAN; Always a choice
DISABLED ACCESS; Yes
GARDEN; Wonderful grounds
Golf, Equestrian Centre, Falconry etc.

THE GREEN INN RESTAURANT AND ROOMS
9 Victoria Road,
Ballater,
Aberdeenshire AB35 5QQ

Tel: 013397 55701

'Good Food is like a good human relationship enjoyed by both chef and diner alike.' This comment you will read on the front page of the menu of this charming Award winning Restaurant with Rooms - one of the few in Scotland. Owned and run by Jeff and Carol Purves, they have worked at that relationship and quite rightly have achieved an enviable reputation fo their cuisine - freshly cooked local and regional dishes, attractively presented and based on healthy eating disciplines - Jeffrey is the chef and he never uses clarified butter or deep frying, for example.

The attractive dining room has 32 covers and is run with a friendly informality that nonetheless ensures the diner is quietly well cared for. It is relaxing and entirely the rightsetting in which to enjoy the dishes put in front of you. Jeffrey is a master at traditional Scottish Specialities and equally at home creating exciting new dishes, inspiration for which he draws from other traditions, Oriental for example.From exquisite starters to sumptuous main course and rich desserts, this is a gastronomic experience. If you prefer food served in a simpler style he is only too happy to accommodate your request. A set vegetarian menu is available but you are asked to pre-book to allow the restaurant time to do justice to your needs.

Food fashions change but the basic preparation skills remain the same and it is on those skills that Jeffrey Purves has built his experience and reputation. The Green Inn in the centre of Ballater through his efforts has gone a long way to establishing Ballater as the gastronomic capital of the north-east. Staying here is an added bonus and not to be missed.

USEFUL INFORMATION

OPEN; All year. 7-9.30pm
CHILDREN; Well behaved welcome
CREDIT CARDS; All major cards
LICENSED; Yes. Fine wines, malts
ACCOMMODATION; 3 en suite rooms
GARDEN; Yes
PETS; In bedrooms only

RESTAURANT; Award winning. Taste of Scotland winner. Traditional & innovative dishes. Sunday lunch April-October
BAR FOOD; Not applicable
VEGETARIAN; Yes, Pre-book please
DISABLED ACCESS; Restaurant

Chapter Eleven

THE BIRNAM HOUSE HOTEL
Birnam,
Dunkeld,
Perthshire PH8 0BQ

Tel: 01350 727462
Fax: 01350 728979

This outstanding and impressively decorated hotel stands on the south bank of the river Tay opposite Dunkeld, the ancient capital of Scotland. Steeped in history, the driveway leads to the Birnam Oak, the last remnant of Birnam Woods, made famous in Shakespeare's Macbeth. From the great fire in 1912, the huge wrought iron gates leading to the Tay, to the visit by the King of Spain and the French Empress, at different times though. The French Empress stayed when the railway terminus was at Birnam. The hotel was much patronised by the nobility and gentry during the second half of the last century and it was said that if a young man wished to enter society he should first spend a month here to observe its manners! To observe Birnam House today is a pleasure, to stay in it a rare treat. The 26 bedrooms all with ensuite facilities are furnished in the unique style of the hotel - there is nothing historic about the appointments! There are special facilities for disabled and elderly guests. Prime Angus Beef and salmon from the Tay features largely on a superb menu prepared by the chefs from all the finest local produce including fresh home grown vegetables. You dine in the elegant, pannelled Shakespeare Room and meals have the enhancement of a selection of fines wines from around the world. The Oak Room Cocktail Bar is a relaxed and friendly place supported by many local people which adds to the atmosphere. Furnished in Rennie Mackintosh style decor with an open fire it is the perfect spot to enjoy your evenings entertainment with either a quiet drink or one of the extensive choices of bar meals. Potters Lounge named after the famous Beatrix Potter gardens which can be viewed from the east side of the lounge, is an ideal location for small private parties or maybe an executive conference. The Baronial Hall Function Room has a large dance floor and can comfortably accommodate 120 guests. Ideal for weddings, conferences, seminars, exhibitions. Birnam House is an ideal centre for touring, Edinburgh, Glasgow, Aviemore, Braemar or Loch Lomond are within one hour. The historic trail of stately homes includes Glamis Castle, Balmoral, Scone Palace, Blair Castle. The hotel offers a range of outdoor activities such as fishing, shooting, climbing, golfing and hill walking.

USEFUL INFORMATION

OPEN; All year
CHILDREN; Welcome
CREDIT CARDS; All cards
LICENSED; Full - fine wines
ACCOMMODATION; 26 ensuite rooms

RESTAURANT; Superb food, local produce
BAR FOOD; Delicious selection
VEGETARIAN; A daily choice
DISABLED ACCESS; Yes + facilities
GARDEN; Splendid grounds and the Beatrix Potter gardens.

THE CAIPLIE GUEST HOUSE
53 High Street North,
Crail,
Anstruther KY103RA
Tel: 01333 450564

Crail is a beautiful place with its picturesque harbour, beaches and coastal walks. It has everything to make it a perfect place for a holiday. Artists love it because of the strong light and the enchanting scenery, families enjoy the clean beaches and for others the superb walks along the coastal paths bring total contentment. Leave your car and wander through the quaint streets and narrow wynds which lead down to one of the most photographed harbours in Scotland. Here the old stone harbour walls embrace the boats that shelter there. On a Summer Sunday you can take a guided walk from the town's fascinating little Museum, on other days play a round of golf on the historic 18 hole course. There are many good pubs, antique shops and of course places to stay. It is part of East Neuk an area of Scotland that is renowned for its beauty and spectacular scenery.

We can heartily recommend Caiplie Guest House as the place to stay. Owned and run by Sandy and Sandra Strachan, it is very informal, has no restrictions and somewhere you can treat like home but also be pampered. Sandy delights in talking to anyone who shares his interest in golf and he is also a keen naturalist and ornithologist. Sandra is the cook and provides wonderful traditional Scottish food with a great breakfast and evening meals by arrangement. Caiplie is licensed. Within this Victorian house there are 7 letting rooms, none of which are ensuite at present, which is obviously reflected in the reasonable price. Each bedroom has a tea and coffee tray and for those who do not want to miss television there is a special TV Lounge. The standard of the house is high and it is mentioned in 'Taste of Scotland' as well as being AA and RAC listed and 1 crown commended by the Scottish Tourist Board.

USEFUL INFORMATION

OPEN; March to November
CHILDREN; Welcome
CREDIT CARDS; None taken
LICENSED; Residential
ACCOMMODATION; 4 dbl, 2tw 1 sgl
PETS; By arrangement
DINING ROOM; Traditional Scottish
BAR MEALS; Not applicable
VEGETARIAN; Upon request
DISABLED ACCESS; No
GARDEN; No

Chapter Eleven

GART HOUSE
Callander,
Perthshire FK178LE

Tel: 01877 331055

This superb stone built mansion house built in 1835 with its round turrets and imposing entrance stands in 12 acres of beautifully maintained grounds. The house is protected by magnificent conifers fringed with colourful shrubs. In the centre of splendid countryside for sports pursuits, Gart House has its private fishing rights on the River Teith. Golf features high on the list of activities nearby which include some excellent walks.

This is essentially a home and not an hotel. You are welcomed to the house by the charming owner, Coral Frerichs, who is delighted to share this happy house with you. It is furnished superbly with period furniture gleaming with the patina of age and pretty drapes that grace the tall windows adding an additional focal point to the rooms. For the energetic, the Snooker Room has a full sized table. The very comfortable bedrooms all have Colour TV, Direct dial telephones and electric blankets for cold winter nights. There is a stair lift, a bath hoist and a shower with a chair for those who need special facilities. Breakfast is served in the elegant dining room and is a sumptuous meal although a lighter meal is available.

Gart House is ideal for anyone wanting a totally relaxing break, yet in easy reach of so many fascinating places ripe for exploration. It is one of those houses you will always remember for its warmth friendliness and because it is so very Scottish.

USEFUL INFORMATION

OPEN; All year
CHILDREN; Welcome
CREDIT CARDS; Visa/Access
LICENSED; No
ACCOMMODATION; 4 double rooms ensuite Bath hoist. Shower with chair
PETS; Not allowed

DINING ROOM: Delicious, traditional
BAR FOOD; Not applicable
VEGETARIAN; On request
DISABLED ACCESS; Yes. Stair lift
GARDEN; 12 acres. Private fishing rights

HETLAND HALL HOTEL,
Carrutherstown,
Dumfries & Galloway, DG1 4JX

Tel: 01387 840201
Fax: 01387 840211

Hetland Hall is a stylish and elegant Georgian style country mansion set in 45 acres of wooded parkland between Carlisle and Dumfries, easily accessible off the A75 Annan - Dumfries road. Over the years the house has been carefully and sympathetically refurbished, decorated and extended. The result today is a hotel which is a peaceful haven for guests on holiday and a super Conference Centre for those who wish to conduct seminars and meetings in surroundings conducive to achieving the best results from their delegates - Meeting rooms for two people or conference halls for up to 200 persons are available. It is equally a wonderful setting for weddings and for private functions. Not only is the hotel beautifully appointed, it has a cheerful and hard working staff who unobtrusively make sure that the service provided is efficient and friendly, whilst maintaining an atmopshere of enjoyable informality.

The comfortably furnished public rooms look south over lawns to the Solway beyond. The bar is a great meeting place for pre and after-dinner drinks, coffee and liquers, whilst if you wish to be quieter, the spacious lounges are ideal to relax with a newspaper or have discussions with colleagues. The 'Copper Beech' restaurant is highly regarded locally and has menus reflecting the chefs' imaginative use of seasonal produce from the area. The wine list has a good choice of thoughtfully selected vintage wines at sensible prices. The individually designed ensuitebedrooms have recently been re-decorated and each has a direct-dial telephone with alarm call and baby monitoring facilities, colour TV with satellite and radio channels. A hairdryer, trouser press and tea/coffee facilities are also there. For disabled guests there is a specially designed bedroom on the ground floor. Hetland has many leisure facilities to offer. Within the hotel there is a badminton court, full sized billiard/snooker table and a solarium. Within the Swiss Chalet style complex you will find a heated and well insulated swimming pool, sauna, steam room and fitness area.

USEFUL INFORMATION

OPEN; All year
CHILDREN; Welcome
CREDIT CARDS; All cards
LICENSED; Full Licence
PETS; By arrangement
ACCOMMODATION; 26 ensuite bedrooms

RESTAURANT; Imaginative menus
BAR FOOD; Available at lunch and dinner
VEGETARIAN; Daily choice
DISABLED ACCESS; Yes. Purpose built ground floor room
GARDEN; 45 acres wooded parkland

Chapter Eleven

LONG ACRE MANOR
Ernespie Road,
Castle Douglas,
Dumfries & Galloway,

Tel: 01556 503576

Elma and Charles Ball have made Long Acre Manor into the most beautiful and relaxed of homes into which they are happy to welcome guests. Everywhere has the gleam and polish that only a well loved house acquires. Furnished with a fine mixture of furniture, mainly antiques, every room has a superb view as far as the Galloway Hills. This is somewhere to come if you want total relaxtion but with sufficient things and places of interest within easy reach. The house is within a short distance of the hills, bird watching will delight the twitcher, castles and abbeys will satisfy those interested in things temporal and spiritual.

Members of 'The Taste of Scotland Scheme' set up in 1973, Elma and Charles are well known for the high standard of their food. For Dinner, served in the Wedgwood Dining Room, there is a set price menu and needs to be ordered in advance. There is an excellent choice and all home-cooked. Imagine starting with a delicious Orkney Crab Pate and following it with Supreme of Chicken stuffed with Haggis, Mushrooms and White Wine Sauce. Naturally the selection of vegetables is fresh and beautifully cooked. For those with a sweet tooth Nectarines Chatelaine or Strawberry and Rhubarb Pie with mouth-watering pastry and cream, are hard to resist. A selection of Cheeses is available for those who prefer it.

You are welcome to bring your dog but children need to be over ten years unless a special arrangement has been made. Long Acre Manor is ideally suited for a house party and for special occasions. One can see perhaps a family gathering or a few friends enjoying themselves hugely in this very happy environment.

USEFUL INFORMATION

OPEN; All year
DINING ROOM; Delicious, home-cooked food
CREDIT CARDS; Access/Visa/Euro/Delta **BAR MEALS;** Not applicable
CHILDREN; Over 10 years   **DISABLED ACCESS;** No special facilities
LICENSED; Residential   **VEGETARIAN;** By arrangement
PETS; Welcome   **GARDEN;** Yes, lawns and woodland
ACCOMMODATION; 2 double & 2 twin all ensuite

Scotland

ARDGAIRNEY FARM GUEST HOUSE
Cleish-Kinross KY13 7LG

Tel: 01577 850305

It would be difficult not to enjoy staying with Colin and Mary Laird at Ardgairney which is a fully working farm of some 500 acres - Colin may well invite you to join him for milking their 150/180 cows at 6am! The house is a true farmhouse with an ever open door and the hospitality and welcome are irresistible. Alongside the house what was the old coach house has been superbly converted and refurbished to a very high standard - hard to imagine that this was once used for horses and carts on their way to market. From every angle there are wonderful views overlooking Ben Arty, The 'Bishop' and the Ochill Hills. It is very close to Loch Leven, near Kinross and handy for Brown Trout fishing and shooting geese. Loch Leven, of course, is where May Queen of Scots was imprisoned on the island in the middle. Easy reach of Edinburgh, (20 miles) Stirling, St Andrews and East Fife coast, Craig St Monance Anstruther.

The meals are memorable. Mary is an accomplished cook and produces real farmhouse dishes. Breakfast is a meal which will certainly set you up for the day. The evening meal, at which you will be offered a drink on the house, is absolutely delicious. Mary uses as much farm and local produce as possible. There are no ensuite bedrooms but this is unimportant in such a friendly establishment where the pretty bedrooms all have electric blankets, radios and plentifully supplied tea/coffee from the kitchen. The house is centrally heated and also has a cheerful open log fire in the lounge. The price for dinner, bed and breakfast as we go to print is just £28. When you stay with people who have as much knowledge of the area as the Lairds you can be sure that you will get the very best suggestions of where you should go each day. The countryside is staggeringly beautiful, walks abound and there are many places of historic interest within striking distance.

USEFUL INFORMATION

OPEN; All year
CHILDREN; Welcome
CREDIT CARDS; None taken
LICENSED; No
ACCOMMODATION; 1 dbl 2 twin not ensuite. Wash hand basins

DINING ROOM; True farmhouse cooking
BAR FOOD; Not applicable
VEGETARIAN; On request
DISABLED ACCESS; No
GARDEN; On farm
PETS; Permitted

Chapter Eleven

TODHALL HOUSE
Dairsie,
By Cupar,
Fife KY15 4RQ

Tel/Fax: 01334 656344

In a very central position in the Kingdom of Fife is Dairsie by Cupar, a quiet village set amidst farmland which extends through the fertile Howe of Fife to the Lomond Hills in the West and to the estuary of the River Eden and St Andrews Bay in the East. Todhall House is near the village and situated between Cupar and St Andrews. This traditional, non-smoking Scottish country home with its fine bow windows and extensive lawns and pretty walled garden, is the most welcoming of places. Owned and run by John and Gill Donald it is an excellent place to stay. You will find it just off the A91 2 miles east of Cupar and three quarters of a mile from Dairsie. Look for the sign for Todhall on the left beside a single tall beech tree at the road end. The house is half a mile from the main road.

There are so many places to visit within easy reach with an abundance of unspoilt picturesque villages, the coast and small towns like the busy market town of Cupar which has many buildings of considerable architectural interest and merit. For golfers, St Andrews - the home of golf and Scotland's oldest University. You can explore the quaint East Neuk fishing villages, walk in the Lomond Hills, forests or on the beaches and headlands. Discover the Scottish Deer Centre and Falconry near Cupar or the delights of 3 National Trust properties Kellie Castle, Hill of Tarvit Mansionhouse and Falkland Palace.

Comfortably furnished, Todhall House has 3 ensuite bedrooms, each well appointed and with TV, Toiletries, Hairdryer and a Tea/Coffee Tray. Both the Donalds are excellent hosts. Gill enjoys cooking and produces a hearty traditional Scottish breakfast. She will also cook an evening meal if requested. The house is not licensed so you are invited to bring your own wine although you may well be invited to have a drink with your hosts. The price at £25 per person for Bed and Breakfast is very reasonable.

USEFUL INFORMATION

OPEN; Mid- March-October inclusive
CHILDREN; Welcome over 12 years
CREDIT CARDS; None taken
LICENSED; No
ACCOMMODATION; 3 rooms ensuite
PETS; No

DINING ROOM; Traditional Scottish breakfast. Evening meal on request
BAR FOOD; Not applicable
VEGETARIAN; On request
DISABLED ACCESS; No
GARDEN; Large and very pretty

Scotland

DUNDUFF FARM
Dunure,
Ayrshire KA74LH

Tel: 01292 500225

Dunduff is a 660 acre working farm with cattle and sheep including 36 Rare Breeds plus a Vietnamese pot bellied pig! Agnes Gemmell, a cheerful and warm-hearted lady has run the accommodation side of the farm for 11 years and has become well known for the standard of care and for the superb Scottish breakfasts every morning. If you have an enormous appetite you might care to choose the 'Dunduff Grand' which includes local smoked kippers as well as the full Scottish breakfast! Indeed she was featured on the BBC 'Food and Drink' programme because she serves the cholestrol free Auracana Eggs (Green shelled).

This large, 15th century strongly built farmhouse is extremely well furnished. Every bedroom is spotlessly clean and shines with the polish of ages. Each room is ensuite and equipped with Colour TV and that blessing to travellers a tea/coffee tray. Agnes does not serve evening meals but she recommends her guests to try the Dunure Anchorage which sits on the picturesque harbourside.

In addition to the farmhouse accommodation there is also Bothy Cottage which has 2 bedrooms and is fully equipped and ideal for those who enjoy self-catering. There is access here for the disabled which is not available in the farmhouse. Special breaks available.

You will find Dunduff Farm approximately 5 miles south of Ayr, 1.5 miles from Dunure village on the A719 coast road, 1 mile from the village shop, pub and restaurant and half a mile from the nearest public transport. It has views over the Isle of Arran. There are sandy beaches at Ayr and Croy shore and it is convenient for golfing, fishing and touring in the area.

USEFUL INFORMATION

OPEN; All year except December & January
CHILDREN; Welcome
CREDIT CARDS; None taken
LICENSED; No
ACCOMMODATION; 3 rooms ensuite Self-catering cottage

DINING ROOM; Breakfast only
BAR FOOD; *Not applicable*
VEGETARIAN; *Upon request*
DISABLED ACCESS; In Bothy
GARDEN; 660 acre farm
PETS; By arrangement

Chapter Eleven

DRUMMOND HOUSE
17 Drummond Place,
Edinburgh EH3 6PL

Tel/Fax: 0131 557 9189

This distinguished and elegant house forms part of a handsome residential square overlooking the trees of Drummond Place Gardens. Built in 1819 with the grace and style of the finest of Georgian architecture, it is one of the few remaining complete and original Town Houses. Drummond House stands on the North West corner of Drummond Place, quarter of a mile North of St Andrew Square at the East End of Great King Street. Princes Street and Waverley station are a ten minute walk. Edinburgh airport is approximately twenty minutes by car.

Strictly a No Smoking House, this is an exceptional place in which to stay. From the outside it is impressive but inside this is enhanced by a wonderful, sweeping stone staircase that spirals its way with great style to the upper floors. Spacious rooms with high ceilings and tall windows are elegantly decorated with antiques and sumptuous furnishings in keeping with the age of the house, and the atmosphere is redolent of a house that has been lived in and loved for almost two hundred years. The ground floor Sitting Room is perfect for relaxing after a pleasant stoll around Edinburgh's many artistic and historic attractions.

The three delightful guest bedrooms on the upper floors are individually designed with canopied beds and antique furniture. Each has its own bathroom which blends with the period style combining character with modern comforts. Breakfast is the only meal served and this is eaten in the fine bow-ended Dining Room. The traditional 'full' Scottish breakfast is a memorable meal but if you prefer something lighter there is a tempting selection of cereals, fruits and yoghurt, homemade preserves and breads. The owners Josephine and Alan Dougall have the great ability to make guests feel they are staying in a private house rather than a hotel.

USEFUL INFORMATION

OPEN; All year except Christmas
CHILDREN; 12 years and over
CREDIT CARDS; Mastercard/Visa
LICENSED; No
ACCOMMODATION; 3 double ensuite
PETS; No

DINING ROOM; Breakfast only
BAR FOOD; Not applicable
VEGETARIAN; On request
DISABLED ACCESS; No
GARDEN; No. Key available for Drummond Place Gardens.

Scotland

ALLT-NAN-ROS HOTEL
Onich, by Fort William,
Inverness-shire PH33 6RY

Tel: 01855 821 210/250
Fax: 01855 821 462

Once a Victorian shooting lodge and summer residence, this Lochside Hotel with its truly panormaic mountain view is very special. The Macleod family, Lachlan, his son James and daughter-in-law, Fiona, welcome you to their country house hotel in which you will find total relaxation. It is set in 4 acres of award winning gardens, streams and wooded walks and has that intangible air of wellbeing that is achieved when a hotel is run with total professionalism and in which the guest's pleasure and comfort is the prime purpose of the owners and the staff. Allt-nan-Ros is Gaelic for 'the burn of the roses', an apt name for a hotel whose gardens offer a colourful display especially in the early Spring and Summer with rhododendrons and azaleas aplenty. There is no need to go farther than the front lawns to enjoy wonderful scenery. In the warmer months, teas, coffees, lunches and drinks on the lawns around the pond are popular with guests. In the evenings the lounge/bar has a roaring log fire and is just the place for a quiet drink before or after dinner. The hotel cuisine is unashamedly French in style - with that special Scottish touch in keeping with the entente cordiale of the 'auld alliance' betweeen Scotland and France! From the Restaurant, the eveningcascade of colour over the mountains and loch is quite breathtaking. And so to bed. The Macleods have ensured that all the ensuite bedrooms are furnished with charm and colour to a very high standard and share, with the restaurant and lounge/bar, the same spectacular view sweeping south, down the spacious tiered gardens and across Loch Linnhe, to Appin and the hills of Ardgour and Morvern. Open all year, Allt-Nan-Ros is one of the finest hotels in the Highlands and Islands. This is a land of mountains and moors. The village of Onich lies on the northern shore of Loch Linnhe, 5 miles from spectacular and historic Glencoe and 10 miles from Fort William. It is also midway between the ski resorts of Nevis Range and Glencoe's White Corries. Access to the mountains and hills is only a short drive or slightly longer walk away. Ben Nevis, Aonach Mor, Bideannam Bian, Buachaille Etive Mor, Aonach Eagach - magnificent mountains. A visit to Mull, Skye, Eigg, Rum, Muck or Canna will be a treasured memory. All this is within easy reach from the Allt-nan-Ros.

USEFUL INFORMATION

OPEN; *All year*
CHILDREN; *Welcome*
CREDIT CARDS; *All cards*
LICENSED; *Yes*
ACCOMMODATION; *All rooms ensuite*
PETS; *By arrangement*

RESTAURANT; *Superb French cuisine in the Scottish style. Award winning*
BAR FOOD; *Not applicable*
VEGETARIAN; *Always a choice*
DISABLED ACCESS; *Yes*
GARDEN; *Award winning grounds*

Chapter Eleven

BEINN ARD
*Argyll Road,
Fort William,
Scotland PH33 6LF
Tel: 01397 704760*

This unusual, attractive wooden house stands in a quiet street in an elevated position just above the town with panoramic views of Loch Linnhe and surrounding hills. It is only five minutes walk from the town centre, station and pier. Fort William is one of the most interesting places in Scotland and surrounded without doubt by some of the most spectacular scenery that Scotland in all its glory, has to offer. The house is charming and its owner, Patricia Jordan very welcoming. She offers not only comfortable bedrooms which are either ensuite or have private facilities but a breakfast which will be long remembered. Every bedroom has TV and tea/coffee making facilities. Beinn Ard has drying facilities for skiers and walkers and a secure outside shed for ski's, mountain bikes etc. Patricia can arrange fishing, golf and other outdoor pursuits as well as directing you towards the best walks. No evening meals but there are plenty of excellent restaurants and cafes in the town.

USEFUL INFORMATION

OPEN; All year
CHILDREN; Welcome
CREDIT CARDS; None taken
LICENSED; No
ACCOMMODATION; 1dbl, 1family ensuite
1 dbl & 2 sgl with wash hand basins

DINING ROOM; Super breakfast
VEGETARIAN; Catered for
DISABLED ACCESS; No
PETS; Yes
GARDEN; Yes

THE GRANGE
*Grange Road,
Fort William,
Inverness-shire PH33 6JF
Tel: 01397 705516*

This enchanting, late Victorian house, complete with turret looks out over Loch Linnhe and is within ten minutes walking distance of Fort William. It not only has the spacious rooms of the Victorian era but also has rooms with distinctive shapes like The Turret bedroom which is a large room complete with a small turret window which overlooks the garden and loch. Furnished with a brass bedstead and furniture of the period, it is a favourite for honeymoons. The Garden Room is the most peaceful and equally pretty whilst The Rob Roy Room is furnished in the Colonial style and has fine views of the loch and the hills beyond. Jessica Lange chose this room whilst making the film 'Rob Roy'. All the bedrooms are ensuite and well appointed with TV, tea and coffee making facilities and hair dryers etc with the addition of a complimentary Sherry decanter. It is a lovely place to stay and has an unsurpassable breakfast menu. The Grange is a wonderful base for anyone wanting to explore the delights of this part of Scotland. No one would leave disappointed. Awarded the Thistle Award for 'Best Bed & Breakfast 1996' by the Scottish Tourist Board.

USEFUL INFORMATION

OPEN; Easter until late October
CHILDREN; Over 12 years

CREDIT CARDS; None taken
LICENSED; Yes
ACCOMMODATION; 3 ensuite rooms

DINING ROOM; One of the best in breakfast in Scotland. No evening meal
VEGETARIAN; Catered for
DISABLED ACCESS; With care
GARDEN; Delightful garden

Scotland

MALIN COURT HOTEL
Turnberry,
Ayrshire KA26 9PB

Tel: 01655 331457
Fax: 01655 331072

Malin Court is situated in the heart of Burns Country close by Culzean Castle and Country Park and has breathtaking sea views of the Isle of Arran and the Firth of Clyde. It is also only a few miles from Alloway where the poet Robert Burns was born and schooled and where the new Burns National Heritage Park has recently opened, including the exciting Tam O'Shanter Experience. It is also near to Souter Johnnie's cottage, the Bachelor's Club and Mount Oliphant and Mossgiel Farm where Burns composed many of his most famous poems. If you wish leisure and recreational pursuits, hunting, fishing, horse-riding and sailing can be arranged. There are also twelve local golf courses including the famous Open Championship courses at Troon, Prestwick and Turnberry.

Malin Court, itself, offers a perfect blend of informality, congeniality, the best of local produce, cooked to perfection, and the warmest of Scottish welcomes. All 17 bedrooms are en-suite and are fully equipped with all modern facilities, while the eye-pleasing public areas include a hairdressing salon, a choice of welcoming lounges and a restful and well-stocked bar which has been considerably enhanced by recent refurbishment. The Carrick Restaurant, which offers a daily-changing fixed price menu for both lunch and dinner, and which serves an excellent traditional Scottish High Tea, is an appropriate setting for Chef Andrea Beach's honest, modern style of cooking which brings an innovative approach to the best of local Scottish ingredients.

Winner of the 1995 Scottish Tourist Board's Thistle Award for Company Training, Malin Court's staff take great care to ensure that their guests' wishes are met with a warm efficiency which seems to pervade the entire operation. All in all, Malin Court, in this Burns Bi-centenary year, is the ideal location for soaking up the history and heritage of Burns Country and the picturesque Clyde Coast and, of course, for tasting Scottish cooking at its best.

USEFUL INFORMATION

OPEN; All year round
CHILDREN; Free accommodation for those under 14 when sharing with adults
CREDIT CARDS; All major cards
LICENSED; Full on licence
PETS; Welcome
ACCOMMODATION; 17 ensuite Court bedrooms all with sea views

RESTAURANT; Mouth watering food by one of Scotland's most talented young chefs
BAR FOOD; Lunch and high tea
VEGETARIAN; All menus have vegetarian starters & main course, changing daily
DISABLED ACCESS Yes - Malin also has a Residential & Nursing Home

Chapter Eleven

THE KELVINGROVE HOTEL
944 Sauchiehall Street,
Glasgow G37TH

Tel: 0141 3395011

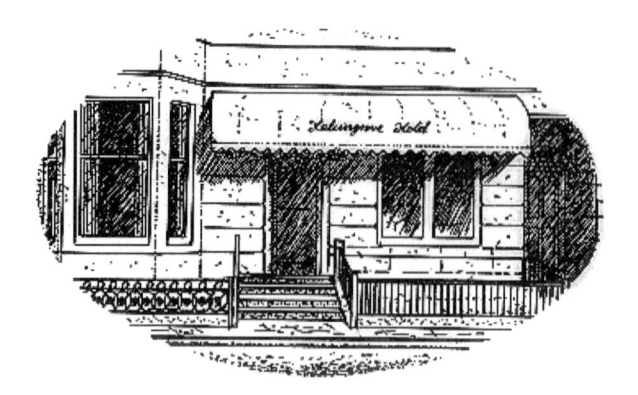

Seldom do you find a really good hotel in the centre of a city which is not only excellent value for money but also has easy parking. This rarity is to be found at the Kelvingrove Hotel in Sauchiehall Street. It stands two minutes from Charing Cross and the city by bus amd from the M8 motorway. It is also just a walk away from Art Galleries, Kelvin Hall, Transport Museum, Scottish Exhibition and Conference Centre and Glasgow University.

The house is Victorian and is part of a Conservation Area. As with all Victorian houses it is gracious, high ceilinged and spacious. Robert Wills, the owner refurbished it throughout in 1990 and it is a welcoming and comfortable establishment. The 20 bedrooms, 18 of which are ensuite, are all furnished attractively, the beds are well sprung, centrally heated and haveColour TV, Direct dual telephones and tea/coffee trays. Whilst there are no facilities for the disabled, children are welcome and pets as well.

Within the Kelvingrove Hotel is The Grove Tearoom which serves breakfast, at very reasonable prices, all day. There is always a wide selection of filled rolls, filled sandwiches, savoury toasties, cakes and biscuits, all priced at under £1. This is ideal for anyone who really only wants a bedroom and the freedom to choose whether to breakfast or not. There is a separate entrance from the courtyard for non-residents. The Grove Tearoom is not licensed at present and does not serve evening meals.

USEFUL INFORMATION

OPEN; All year
CHILDREN; Welcome
CREDIT CARDS; All except Diners
LICENSED; No
ACCOMMODATION; 20 rooms, 18 ensuite
PETS; Yes

RESTAURANT; Not applicable. Grove Tea room serves breakfast and snacks throughout the day
VEGETARIAN; Upon request
DISABLED ACCESS; No
GARDEN; No. Tearoom extends to open courtyard

TORWOOD HOUSE HOTEL
Gass, Glenluce,
Newton Stewart,
Wigtownshire DG8 0PB

Tel/Fax: 01581 300469

This late 19th century Sporting Lodge is the home of the 'Taste of Burns Award Winning Restaurant and, much, much more than just an hotel. Standing in 40 acres of grounds which include lakes, it offers guests the opportunity to relax totally in a peaceful environment much as it would have done a century ago. Within the sturdy house there are 8 comfortable ensuite rooms, each with hairdryer and a beverage tray and in the grounds is a delightful, well equipped log cabin. The public rooms are comfortably furnished and both the restaurant and the supper room are attractively laid out. Here you may eat good Scottish fare, sensibly priced. The extensive Bar and Supper menu ranges from simple sandwiches served with Crisps and Salad to a splendid 12oz Sirloin steak or an enormous Mixed Grill. Every Friday Night the covered Barbecue area caters for 150 with live music varying from easy Listening to Folk Music - definitely no Disco or Karaoke! Every Saturday Afternoon from 3pm-6pm there is a Family Barbecue.

Sporting activities are one of the main reasons for coming to Torwood House. Clay Pigeon Shooting is very popular. There are guns for hire and beginners are welcome. Fishing plays an important part as well. Torwood holds the Scottish Tench Record but you can also fish for pike, trout and salmon. Sea Fishing too is available with boats for hire. Arrangements can also be made for Pony trekking, Golf, Go-karting, Sailing, Bird watching, Rough shooting, Wildfowling, Walking, Cycling, Stalking and Photographic safaris. Something for everyone in fact. The proprietor, David Canning, is a personable and likeable man who sets out to make sure his guests enjoy every minute of their stay.

USEFUL INFORMATION

OPEN; 365 days a year
CHILDREN; Welcome
CREDIT CARDS; Access/Visa
LICENSED; Yes
ACCOMMODATION; 8 rooms. 1 log cabin, 4 log cabins

RESTAURANT & SUPPER ROOM: Good, reasonable prices.
BAR MEALS; Extensive range available
VEGETARIAN: On request - wide variety
DISABLED ACCESS; Assistance available
GARDEN; 40 acres
PETS; Welcome

Chapter Eleven

THE BLACKWATER INN
Glenshee PH10 7LH

Tel: 01250 882234

This friendly inn is an hotel which has a plant market and a Craft Shop. It makes it a gathering place for many local people and certainly for visitors who come to the ski slopes close by or to enjoy the golf, fishing and pony trekking. It is also central for anyone wanting to visit Blairgowrie, Braemar, Pitlochry or Dundee. What makes it special is the relaxed atmosphere created by the hospitable owners Tom and Ivy Bailey who have been here for eleven years. During that time their lively personalities and keen sense of humour have endeared them to many people who come here regularly to enjoy the comfort afforded by the eight ensuite bedrooms or the simplicity of one bedroom with five bunks designed for walkers etc, the knowledge that the food is going to be wholesome, traditional and sustaining, and that their stay will be memorable for all sorts of reasons. In addition to all this there is regular live entertainment to be enjoyed at night, and Vintage and Modern day Motorcycle rallies during the season.

Various dishes created in the kitchen of The Blackwater Inn, have become popular over the years. What is on offer varies according to the season and is subject to what local produce is available. They are known to have the best Haggis in Scotland, serve a splendid Steak Sandwich and are winners of 'The Cheese Board of Scotland'. Everything is home-cooked and served all day including a truly traditional Scottish High Tea in the Restaurant. The Plant Shop specialises in herbs and Alpines and the Craft Shop in all things Scottish. It would be difficult not to enjoy The Blackwater Inn. Everything about it is right and it is essentially good vale for money.

USEFUL INFORMATION

OPEN; All year
CHILDREN; Welcome
CREDIT CARDS; No
LICENSED; Yes
ACCOMMODATION; 8 ensuite rooms plus one bunk room
PETS; By arrangement
RESTAURANT; Good traditional fare, high Teas
BAR FOOD; Served all day
VEGETARIAN; On request
DISABLED ACCESS; Yes
GARDEN; Yes

ARDMORE GUEST HOUSE
98 West Clyde Street,
Helensburgh,
Dunbartonshire G84 8EE

Tel:01436 673461/675739
Fax: 01436 675739

Christine Walkers comfortable and friendly Ardmore Guest House on the banks of the Clyde has stunning views across the river. The house is ideal for those of us who are getting slightly older and would enjoy the peace and quiet the house has to offer. There are nine well furnished and spotlessly clean bedrooms each of which has a Television. Renowned for the quality and quantity of her splendid Scottish breakfasts, Christine also provides traditional evening meals with a choice at every course. Ardmore is licensed and it is very pleasant to enjoy a quiet drink with ones fellow guests before and after the evening meal. Helensburgh is an attractive place in its own right and from here there are so many exciting places to visit quite easily.

USEFUL INFORMATION
OPEN; All year
CHILDREN; Welcome
CREDIT CARDS; Yes
LICENSED; Residential
ACCOMMODATION; 9 rooms
1 ensuite. Showers and bathroom

DINING ROOM; Excellent breakfasts and Traditional evening meals
VEGETARIAN; Catered for
DISABLED ACCESS; No special facilities
GARDEN; Yes with BBQ

EASTBANK
10 Hanover Street,
Helensburgh,
Scotland G84 7AW

Tel/Fax: 01436 673665

This quiet Victorian house built in 1832 has three comfortable letting rooms for bed and breakfast on the first floor of the house. Dorothy Ross, the owner, delights in taking care of people and ensures that everyone of whatever age is made to feel welcome and at home. Only the twin bedded room is ensuite but the bathroom provides plentiful hot water to service the other two rooms. Breakfast is a sumptuous meal in the best Scottish tradition. No evening meals are available but eateries are plentiful in Helensburgh. The house is within easy reach of the shopping area and the shore and the views of the Clyde are stunning. It is also no distance from some very beautiful countryside. If, perchance, you are a keen machine knitter you will find Dorothy an expert who runs knitting courses. The premises have been inspected by the Scottish Tourist Board Grading and Classification Scheme and awarded Commended and Listed also Dorothy and her husband have attended both 'Welcome Host' and 'Scotland's Best' courses and awarded cerificates for both.

USEFUL INFORMATION
OPEN; All year

CHILDREN; Welcome
CREDIT CARDS; None taken
ACCOMMODATION; 1tw.1 sgl 1 fam

DINING ROOM; Traditional full breakfast
VEGETARIAN; Upon request
DISABLED ACCESS; No
GARDEN; Patio

Chapter Eleven

RAVENSWOOD
32 Suffolk Street,
Helensburgh,
Dunbartonshire G84 9PA
Tel: 01436 672112

Helensburgh, a unique seaside town on the Firth of Clyde is architecturally fascinating in its own right, particularly including the domestic commission of Charles Rennie Mackintosh, The Hill House belonging to the National Trust, and is also the centre for exploring much of the West and Central Scotland and only ten minutes from Loch Lomond, the gateway to the Highlands and Islands. For that reason it is all important to find somewhere special to stay and this is without doubt, the friendly, welcoming home of Margaret and Bryan Richards at Ravenswood, a Victorian red sandstone villa situated in a quiet setting in the west end of Helensburgh with an attractive garden. The house is a strictly non-smoking establishment which enhances the health and comfort of guests. There are four pleasant bedrooms, two of which are ensuite. Every room has colour television, a hospitality tray and clock radio/alarm. A Scottish traditional breakfast, with many choices, is served every day between 7am and 9am and in the evening a delicious, home-cooked evening meal is available at 6.30pm providing you order before 5pm. Everything is done for your comfort; there is a large drying room for wet boots, sailing gear etc, an iron and ironing board as well as hair dryers on request plus shoe cleaning facilities in the cloakroom.

USEFUL INFORMATION

OPEN;All year
CHILDREN;Welcome
CREDIT CARDS;None taken
LICENSED; No. Welcome to bring your own
ACCOMMODATION;4 rooms;2 ensuite

DINING ROOM;Excellent breakfast and Optional evening meal
VEGETARIAN;Catered for
DISABLED ACCESS;No facilities
GARDEN; Yes
PETS;No

STONEHAVEN GUEST HOUSE
8 Netherpark Crescent,
Largs, Ayrshire KA30 8QB
Scotland
Tel: 01475 673319

Overlooking Largs Bay and the islands beyond, within 300 yards of the sea front and beach, and set within carefully tended and colourful gardens in the yachting centre of Largs is Stonehaven Guest House. Owners Isabel and Stanley Martin offer a relaxed and informal atmosphere, which has been awarded '2 Crowns Highly Commended' by the Scottish Tourist Board. Accommodation is in tastefully styled bedrooms, each with a complimentary tea and coffee tray and colour television. Ensuite facilities are limited, so early booking is advised. A wonderful hearty breakfast is served in real Scottish tradition. This is truly an area of outstanding beauty located as it is on the coast, walkers will be in awe of the scenery both coastal or on hill walks. Fishing can be arranged and there are several good golf courses, one being only 100 yards away.

USEFUL INFORMATION

OPEN; All year
CHILDREN; Welcome
CREDIT CARDS; None taken
LICENSED; No
ACCOMMODATION; 3 rooms.

DINING ROOM; Large Scottish breakfast.
No evening meal
VEGETARIAN; Catered for
DISABLED ACCESS; Not really
GARDEN; Yes, with swings etc for children

TRAQUAIR ARMS HOTEL AND RESTAURANT
Innerleithen,
Peebleshire EH44 6PD

Tel: 01896 830229
Fax: 01896 830260

The Scottish Borders has rich rewards for anyone who wishes to discover them either in the comfort of your car or on foot. It is a soft, pleasing landscape interlaced with characteristic towns and villages, historic churches, monuments and magnificent stately homes. The Traquair Arms on the outskirts of the village of Innerleithen is the ideal base from which to explore and for keen walkers it is a good starting point for the Southern Upland Way. Innerleithen was made famous by Sir Walter Scott in his Waverley novels, who called it 'St Ronan's Well'. It is a friendly place and renowned for its unique water-powered Printing Works and Stationers which is owned and run by the National Trust for Scotland, and also for its much sought after cashmeres and tweeds. Private Salmon and Trout fishing on the River Tweed is available from the hotel, whilst the golfer has no less than eighteen first class, uncrowded golf course available.

Traquair Arms, built in 1836 as a coaching inn, sits in the peaceful Tweed valley with splendid hills rising on either side. Anyone who has stayed here will tell you that it emanates peace and tranquillity and a cosy, friendly warmth which is created not only by the comfortable and stylish way in which it is furnished but also by the owners and their staff who maintain the traditional Scottish coaching inn hospitality. Open fires, soft lighting and subtle decor simply add to the sense of well being. Here one can sample local ales, including Bear Ale from Traquair House brewery, only available in two places in Scotland. Lovers of Malt whiskies will find it much to their taste. The attractive bedrooms are all en suite and equipped with everything the modern day traveller requires. In the non-smoking restaurant, which is open every day from 12 noon until 9pm, delicious food is served. Prepared and cooked by the Chef/Proprietor, the menu is imaginative and wide ranging with something for everyone's tastes and pocket. Special Breaks are available for most of the year.

USEFUL INFORMATION

OPEN; All year
CHILDREN; Welcome
CREDIT CARDS; All cards
LICENSED; Full licence
ACCOMMODATION; 2 family 3 dbl, 2 twin, 3 sgl, all ensuite

RESTAURANT; Imaginative food at sensible prices
BAR MEALS; Good value
VEGETARIAN; Catered for
DISABLED ACCESS; No special facilities
GARDEN; Yes. Parking facilities
PETS; Allowed but not in public rooms

Chapter Eleven

KILMENY FARMHOUSE
Ballygrant,
Isle of Islay,
Argyll PA45 7QW

Tel: 01496 840668

Kilmeny farmhouse lies 4 miles west of Port Askaig and 17 miles from Port Ellen terminal. Look out for the sign at the end of the road. If the sign had room to tell you more than you are approaching Kilmeny Farmhouse, it would be bound to tell you that this delightful, and very special, establishment has always rested on quality and above all personal attention. Speak to anyone who has stayed here, and there are many who return year after year, you will hear only praise.

Margaret and Blair Rozga for over twenty years have been providing dinner, bed and breakfast in their, strictly non-smoking 19th century farmhouse which over th years has undergonea tasteful conversion of adjoining stables to create an elegant home-from-home on Islay. Everything about the house speaks of loving care. It is beautifully furnished with fine quality furniture, decor and fabrics, and superb colour co-ordination. Bedrooms have en suite facilities, and nice little touches to make visitors feel at home. The dining room is intimate with a special atmosphere and the splendid sitting room has a sumptious elegance usually found only in a country house setting. The food is wonderful, from the afternoon tea on arrival to home-cooked dinners prepared with care for the succulence of Islay meat, fish and game.

Islay is home to a great array of wildlife including eagles, choughs, otters, deer and, for 6 months of the year, geese. The geese during their Islay stay feed on the grasslands of Kilmeny where, in co-operation with 'Scottish National heritage' they are protected from disturbance. Kilmeny also works in association with the R.S.P.B whose reserve is nearby. Islay has a number of sights of historical interest and nearby is Finlaggan, seat of the Lords of the Isles for almost 400 years.

USEFUL INFORMATION

OPEN; All year
CHILDREN; Over 8 years
CREDIT CARDS; None taken
LICENSED; No, please bring your own
ACCOMMODATION; Beautiful en suite rooms
PETS; By arrangement

DINING ROOM; Superb home-cooked using Islay meat, fish and game
BAR FOOD; Not applicable
VEGETARIAN; On request
DISABLED ACCESS; No

Scotland

THE CLACHAIG HOTEL
Falls of Dochart,
Killin,
Perthshire FK21 8SL

Tel: 01567 820270
Fax: 01567 820731

The Clachaig is a small hotel, owned and run by John and Maureen Mallinson, offering guests comfort in a relaxed atmosphere. It is set in Clan McNab country and as a listed building of some 200 years still retains its original charm. Beside the small village of Killin in the heart of Perthshire, it is ideally placed for day trips to destinations such as Oban, Glencoe and Pitlochry - all within a radius of 50 miles. The hotel is more frequently known as 'The Salmon Lie'! due to its excellent angling location beside the River Dochart and close to Loch Tay. It overlooks the magnificent Falls of Dochart which have an elusive quality compelling visitors to stop and take a longer look. The hotel specialises in short stays and longer holidays, particularly to suit active people. You can stroll or take a strenuous hike with mountains such as Ben Lawers, Ben Vorlich and Ben More within easy reach. There are 20 Munros within 15 mile radius of Killin. The hotel has its own salmon beat on Loch Tay, one of the finest salmon lochs in Scotland, and its own beat on the river Dochart. Killin has a picturesque and demanding 9 hole golf course and a day at other courses close by can also be organised. The hotel can also offer arrangements for all shooters. Loch Tay and Loch earn are renowned for their water sport activities.

Each of the nine bedrooms is comfortably furnished with privatebathroom/ shower, tea making facilities and TV (Sky Movies). There is also a spearate residents lounge area. The charming candle lit dining room seats approximately 40 people, Les Routiers Recommended and is renowned for its local specialities such as venison, salmon and smoked trout. The hotel was the Scottish regional winner of the calor gas spnsored 'Pub Meal of the Year' competition and the Egon Ronay Recommended Salmon Lie Bar, which was formerly a smithy's cottage, serves meals daily. If you are a Malt whisky drinker you will appreciate the wide range available in the bar. The Clachaig hotel has four self-catering cottages, all of which are newly converted or renovated and close to the Falls of Dochart.

USEFUL INFORMATION

OPEN; All year
CHILDREN; No restrictions
CREDIT CARDS; All cards
LICENSED; Yes
ACCOMMODATION; 9 ensuite
PETS; By arrangement

DINING ROOM; Renowned for its specialities such as venison, salmon
BAR FOOD; Egon Ronay Recommended
VEGETARIAN; Choice of dishes
DISABLED ACCESS; Yes
GARDEN; Yes

Chapter Eleven

MORENISH LODGE HOTEL
Loch Tayside, By Killin,
Perthshire FK218TX

Tel: 01567 820258

It would be hard to find a more tranquil setting than the Morenish Lodge. This delightful highland house was originally built as a shooting lodge for the Earl of Breadalbane around 1750. Its setting is superb, nestling in the shadow of Ben Lawers, two and a half miles outside the picturesque village of Killin on the A827 to Aberfeldy, and looking down over rolling farmland onto unspoilt Loch Tay. The area is beautiful and provides excellent opportunities to participate in most outdoor activities. Centrally situated it really is ideal for touring or finding alternatives on the occasional 'Scotch Mist' day.

Lorna and Carew Thomas are skilled in the art of catering for guests. They spent a number of years abroad running luxury yachts in many parts of the world and now bring this very high standard to Morenish Lodge. It is their ability to create an air of relaxation everywhere which makes staying here so attractive. Beneath the apparent informality, the hotel is run with great professionalism. The service is friendly, the delicious Scottish and international cuisine superb. Wherever possible local products such as trout, salmon, venison and prime Scottish beef form the basis for the innovative menu. The lovely dining room has panoramic views across the loch and in the cosy 'Laird's Bar' one can sample a selection of wines and some of the finest malt whiskies to be had anywhere. The thirteen bedrooms - 12 ensuite and one with private facilities - are furnished charmingly. Two bedrooms are on the ground floor and there is also a two-bedroom family suite available - equally ideal for two single persons travelling together. Special weekend and Midweek Breaks are available in Spring, Autumn and Winter.

USEFUL INFORMATION

OPEN; All year except January February
CHILDREN; Welcome over 3 years
CREDIT CARDS; Access/Visa/Delta Mastercard/Eurocard
LICENSED; Yes

ACCOMMODATION; 12 en suite + one with private facilities
PETS; Welcome, but not in the house

DINING ROOM; Scottish and and International cuisine
BAR MEALS; Not applicable
VEGETARIAN; Catered for upon request
DISABLED ACCESS; Yes. Ground floor rooms
GARDEN; 4 acres overlooking Loch Tay

Scotland

MUIRHOUSE FARM
Gatehead,
Kilmarnock,
Ayrshire KA2 0BT

Tel: 01563 523975

This is a traditional Scottish farmhouse pleasantly situated in the Ayrshire countryside by the village of Gatehead. To reach it from Kilmarnock (A759) you enter the village and turn right at the Cochrane Inn onto the country road. Muirhouse Farm is approximately a quarter of a mile ahead on your right. The Love family own Muirhouse Farm which is a working dairy farm of 170 acres. You will be more than welcome to see around the farm during your stay. In the house Martha Love, a friendly and hospitable lady, makes sure that all her guests are comfortable and contented. Do take notice of the pictures around the house which incorporate a fascinating selection of little sayings, poems and 'homilities'. Comfortably and practically furnished there are 3 bedrooms, 2 of which are ensuite and the third has private facilities. Each room has a plentiful supply of tea and coffee and is equipped with a hairdryer, Radio Alarm, TV and Central Heating.. Martha is a splendid cook and her full Scottish breakfasts are renowned. There is always a choice of menu and she uses the farm's own produce. A perfect start to the day. An evening meal can be arranged.

Apart from being close to Kilmarnock, with all it has to offer including Loudon Castle Country Park, Ayr is not far away nor Glasgow for that matter. You can cross the water by ferry from Ardrossan to the Isle of Arran and local fishing can be arranged. For golfers Ayrshire is paradise with over 30 courses. Within a few miles of Muirhouse Farm is Royal Troon and Old Prestwick. One thing not to miss is the recently restored Laigh Milton Viaduct - the world's oldest surviving railway viaduct, which is almost adjacent to the farm.

USEFUL INFORMATION

OPEN; *All year*
CHILDREN; *Welcome*
CREDIT CARDS; *None taken*
LICENSED; *No*
ACCOMMODATION; *3 rooms, 2 ensuite 1 with private facilities*

DINING ROOM; *Superb Scottish Breakfast. Choice of menu*
VEGETARIAN; *Catered for*
DISABLED ACCESS; *Yes. No special facilities.*
GARDEN; *Farm of 170 acres*
PETS; *Yes*

Chapter Eleven

SELKIRK ARMS HOTEL,
High Street,
Kirkcudbright DG6 4JG

Tel: 01557 330402
Fax: 01557 331639

This is arguably the most historic hotel in the Stewartry and where Robert Burns is believed to have written his famous 'Selkirk Grace'. Always a delightful place to visit, it has recently undergone a major refurbishment and remodelling of the ground floor public rooms. The result is a charming 70 seater Garden restaurant, a bistro, probably unique in this part of Scotland, which holds about 20, a comfortable lounge bar where forty people can enjoy a drink in a totally relaxed atmosphere, and an attractive coffee lounge/sitting room, which features original works depicting Kirkcudbright's harbour and the closes of High Street. This room is frequently used for seminars and meetings. In addition there are 16 ensuite bedrooms all furnished and equipped to the same high standard as the ground floor. An ideal place to stay whilst enjoying the colourful area. Shooting, Golf, Sea Fishing, Birdwatching and some splendid walks offer something for everyone.

With a hotel of this standard one would expect the food to be exceptional - and it is. Emphasis is placed on using fresh and local produce, especially fish which is cooked in a hundred and one different creative ways. For example The Selkirk buys the best king scallops from the town's harbour and other favourites include bass, halibut, turbot and monkfish. John and Sue Morris own and run the hotel and take a 'hands on' approach to management which inspires their friendly and willing staff. John Morris trained as a brewer and worked for 10 years in breweries in Edinburgh - surely a guarantee that the beer served at The Selkirk will take a lot of beating.

USEFUL INFORMATION

OPEN; All year. 11am-midnight.
Lunch 12-2pm Dinner 6-9.30pm

CHILDREN; Well behaved welcome
CREDIT CARDS; Access/Visa/Amex/Diners
LICENSED; Full Licence
ACCOMMODATION; 16 ensuite rooms
PETS; Not allowed in public areas

RESTAURANT; Well known for its creative menu. Specialises in fish
BAR MEALS; Wide variety
VEGETARIAN; Yes. Special diets with prior notice
DISABLED ACCESS; Yes. Disabled toilet
GARDEN; Not applicable. Car park

Scotland

WHIN PARK
16 Douglas Street,
Largs,
Ayrshire KA30 8PS
Scotland
Tel: 01475 673437

A friendly informal atmosphere pervades this comfortable red roofed villa which is situated in a residential area close to the sea front. The bright hall opens to reveal a spacious house whose bedrooms, which have been comfortably furnished in modern style, offer quality ensuite facilities as well as all the expected amenities, while the pleasant lounge invites peaceful relaxation. Your choice of breakfast is served at individual tables in the elegant dining room. Within easy reach of the promenade and town centre Whin Park is free of parking problems and being off the main thoroughfare you will not be disturbed by traffic noise. It is convenient for access to the islands of the Clyde and to Argyll. Within easy reach of many other attractive areas of West Central Scotland, Glasgow International and Prestwick Airports.

USEFUL INFORMATION
OPEN; All year
CHILDREN; Welcome
CREDIT CARDS; Access/Visa
LICENSED; No
ACCOMMODATION; 4 ensuite rooms, 1 Double, 1 Family, 1 Twin, 1 Single
DINING ROOM; Traditional fare
No evening meal
VEGETARIAN; Catered for
DISABLED ACCESS; Not really
GARDEN; No
PETS; No

SHEILDAIG FARM
Upper Stoneymollen Road,
Loch Lomond,
Scotland G83 8QX
Tel: 01389 752459
Fax: 01389 753659

The tranquil and scenic beauty surrounding Sheildaig is quite outstanding, nestling in the hillside overlooking Loch Lomond. Your hosts Jeanette and Bill Wilson, offer a standard of hospitality and sheer comfort difficult to better. Bedrooms are spacious and delightfully furnished with ensuite bathrooms, colour television, trouser press, hair dryers and tea and coffee making facilities. Jeanette is meticulous with regard to her culinary art, and prides herself in presenting the finest cuisine, making use of fresh and tasteful local produce, to be appreciated in tandem with a fine selection of wines or spirits. Spectacular walks are endless. Fishing can be arranged and golf is available locally.

USEFUL INFORMATION
OPEN; All year
CHILDREN; Welcome
CREDIT CARDS; All major cards
LICENSED; Yes
ACCOMMODATION; 5 ensuite rooms
PETS; Yes
DINING ROOM; Excellent home-cooking
VEGETARIAN; Catered for
DISABLED ACCESS; Yes, but restricted
GARDEN; Yes

Chapter Eleven

LESLIE CASTLE,
Leslie, By Insch,
Aberdeenshire AB52 6NX

Tel: 01464 820869
Fax: 01464 821076

Leslie Castle is personally managed and run by David Leslie and Leslie Leslie, the Baron and Baroness of Leslie and their family, and guests are welcomed into and become part of a living heritage which dates back to the eleventh century. Leslie Castle is the original seat of Clan Leslie and caput of the Barony of Leslie. The present castle is the third fortified building on the site. By the time David and Leslie acquired the castle in 1979 it was a decaying, roofless ruin. Ten years of careful, painstaking, detailed restoration has resulted in the transformation of the ruin into a fairy-tale turreted, 17th century fortified house. Including Baronial Hall and large spacious comfortable rooms affording fine views of the surrounding countryside.

The Baronial Hall with timber beamed ceiling, large fireplace and stone flagged floor creates a fitting atmosphere to enjoy splendid Scottish and international cuisine prepared personally by the Baroness. She is renowned for her food and especially for the smoked and fresh Fish, Game, Lamb and Aberdeenshire Beef. Vegetables are varied and always fresh. A restricted licence is operated for residents and non-residents using the castle and facilities, offering a wide selection of wines, beers and spirits. The Hall and adjoining Withdrawing Room make an excellent setting for small receptions for up to 20 guests or private dinner parties for 12 with crystal and silver place settings. Alternative dining facilities are available in the Kitchen Dining Room, the original kitchen of the castle. This barrel vaulted, smaller room with groined ceiling, large arched fireplace and stone flagging is very special. The bedroom accommodation includes two four-poster bedrooms, one double bedroom and one twin bedroom all ensuite with colour TV, telephone, trouser press, alarm clock/radio, courtesy tray facilities, fresh fruit, sherry, sweets and flowers. All bedrooms are large and suitable for family use and furnished in hand made furniture in the Jacobean style. Reductions are available for stays over five nights and special rates for children sharing a room with parents. 2 night short breaks are also available.

USEFUL INFORMATION

OPEN; All year
CHILDREN; Welcome
CREDIT CARDS; All major cards
LICENSED; Yes
ACCOMMODATION; 4 rooms ensuite
PETS; No

DINING ROOM; Superb food
BAR FOOD; Not applicable
VEGETARIAN; On request
DISABLED ACCESS; No
GARDEN; Yes

MONACHYLE MHOR
Balquhidder,
Lochearnhead,
Perthshire FK19 8PQ

Tel: 01877384 622
Fax: 01877384 305

This enchanting, characterful, family run Farmhouse Hotel is set in a land of hills and in its own 2,000 acres, in the heart of the staggeringly beautiful Braes O' Balquhidder. Open all the year it offers private Salmon and Trout fishing with Red Deer Stalking and Grouse shooting in season. The Hotel has magnificent views over Lochs Voil and Doine, one of the many reasons for staying here. Throughout the hotel there is evidence of the tasteful and loving care that the owners, Rob, Jean and Tom Lewis have taken to make Monachyle Mhor one of the best small hotels in Scotland. Each room is beautifully appointed, the ensuite bedrooms have pretty drapes and every comfort, the restaurant and cosy bar have been designed to enhance ones appetite and to help one relax whilst having a quiet drink. In addition to the rooms in the hotel there are also some stunning self-catering cottages available on request. Deservedly Monachyle Mhor has won several accolades including 'Taste of Scotland', an AA 2 rosette for the restaurant as well as being Three Crown's commended.

The restaurant has a pretty enclosed, extension with rough stone hewn walls, an abundance of hanging plants, pine and attractively set tables, looking out over the patio onto the grounds. This leads from the elegant dining room with its polished furniture. The food is sensational whether you have the three or five course set menu or choose from the a la carte menu. Elect to have a starter perhaps of roasted boneless Quail on buttered cabbage with a red currant dressing followed by Mallaig scallops poached in ginger and spring onions on a bed of squid ink tagliatelle. And then a selection of mouth watering home-made puddings or Scottish cheeses. Wonderful food complemented by a well chosen wine list.

USEFUL INFORMATION

OPEN; All year
CHILDREN; Welcome
CREDIT CARDS; All major cards
LICENSED; Yes
ACCOMMODATION; En suite rooms self-catering cottages

RESTAURANT; Superb food
BAR FOOD; Not applicable
VEGETARIAN; Always a choice
DISABLED ACCESS; Yes
GARDEN; 2,000 acres
PETS; By arrangement

Chapter Eleven

KINGS ARMS HOTEL
*High Street,
Lockerbie,
Dumfries-shire DG11 1JL*

*Tel;01576 202410
Fax: 01576 204464*

Dumfries and Galloway is a region that just cries out to be explored. It is blessed with magnificent scenery, steeped in history, gifted with supremely varied flora and fauna and above all it is an area of peace with miles of gloriously quiet country roads. Primarily agricultural country with a strong emphasis on dairy and livestock-breeding, it also has 200 miles of unspoilt coastline. Wonderful for walkers, ornithologists, yachtsmen, golfers - there are 24 courses - and fishing for salmon on the Nith, brown trout from secluded hill-lochs or sea fishing on the Solway.

The 17th century old coaching inn, The Kings Arms, in the heart of Lockerbie, is the ideal place to stay to enjoy everything the area has to offer. It is equally useful if you are wanting a halfway stop over en route to the north of Scotland. The old inn is full of atmosphere with oak beams in the bars and in the pretty dining room. It has the air of well being that only comes from centuries of loving care. You walk through the main entrance with its sturdy doors straight into a great welcome. Run by the resident proprietors, Aoirig and Mike Carry, you will be cossetted, shown to one of the 10 well furnished and decorated bedrooms - the bedrooms are mainly ensuite - each has colour TV, direct dial telephone and a hospitality tray. You can eat either in the restaurant or in the bar; the latter is where the locals gather. The food is all home-cooked and fresh, local produce is used whenever possible. The menu is imaginative and has one or two surprises as well as the true and trusted favourites.

USEFUL INFORMATION

OPEN; All year
CHILDREN; Welcome
CREDIT CARDS; All cards
LICENSED; Full Licence
ACCOMMODATION; 10 rooms mainly ensuite

RESTAURANT; Good, imaginative home-cooked fare.
BAR FOOD; Wide range, home-cooked
VEGETARIAN; Catered for
DISABLED ACCESS; No special facilities
GARDEN; Not applicable

LOCKERBIE MANOR COUNTRY HOTEL
Boreland Road,
Lockerbie,
Dumfries & Galloway DG11 2RG

Tel: 01576 202610/203939
Fax: 01576 203046

Just north of the border this has to be one of the finest country hotels in southern Scotland. It has a grace and a grandeur that combines to give the visitor a great sense of wellbeing and security. Built in 1814 for Sir William Douglas and Dame Grace Johnstone, the great grandparents of John Sholto Douglas, the 8th Marquis of Queensbury, who was responsible for formulating the present day 'Queensbury' boxing rules, believed to have been completed in this house. In 1920, it became the smart country house hotel it is today.

Set in 78 acres of tranquil park and woodland, the interiors have retained their traditional charm. The elegant Lounge has an original Adam fireplace, lovingly cared for antique furniture and walls lined with some fine oil paintings. Each of the 30 bedrooms arranged on 2 floors, all with private bathrooms, coffee making facilities, colour television, direct-dial telephones, trouser presses and 4 crown comforts. No two bedrooms are alike but each is delightful and full of character. There is a choice of regular, deluxe and 4-poster rooms - there are five beautifully adorned four poster suites and a prettily decorated Bridal Suite. The Queensbury Dining Room, with its wood panelled wall, ornate chandeliers and magnificent views is a wonderful background in which to enjoy a delectable meal. The cuisine is of an international nature, where eastern flavours and cooking style blend with western recipes. The Douglas Room offers a choice of intimate dining amidst an air of graceful elegance, or a formal private dining area for corporate or personal parties. Lockerbie Manor is known for the excellence of its conference, private parties and special events facilities. Weddings too are exceptional. A perfect romantic setting for weddings. There are Golf Courses close by, Fishing for Salmon and trout on the River Annan and Milk, Shooting on the numerous large estates around Lockerbie as well as Ice skating, Race meetings, Woodland walks, Sailing, Green bowling, Farm buggy trails, Pony trekking and Putting.

USEFUL INFORMATION

OPEN; *All year*
CHILDREN; *Welcome*
CREDIT CARDS; *All major cards*
LICENSED; *Yes, full. Fine wines*
ACCOMMODATION; *30 ensuite rooms 4 posters. Pets by arrangement*

RESTAURANT; *Superb food with an international flavour*
BAR FOOD; *Bar menu available*
VEGETARIAN; *Catered for*
DISABLED ACCESS; *Yes*
GARDEN; *78 acres.*

Chapter Eleven

RAVENSHILL HOUSE HOTEL
12 Dumfries Road,,
Lockerbie,
Dumfriesshire DG11 2EF

Tel & Fax: 01576 202882

Set in 2.5 acres of mature gardens with private car park, Ravenshill House is just half a mile west of Lockerbie town centre, with easy access from the motorway. Ideal for businessor for pleasure, Ravenshill House, is owned and run by Norman and Sheila Tindal, whose sheer professionalism shows in everything that they do but never loses the warmth and hospitality which is so much the ethos of this friendly hotel.
    All the 8 ensuite bedrooms are indivdually and attractively furnished with warm and restful colour schemes. Each room has tea/coffee making facilities, direct dial telephone and colour television. There's even a four poster bed for a special occasion or honeymoon - the house is only 15 minutes from Gretna Green after all! The non-smoking dining room can seat up to 48 and is ideal for small weddings and private dinner parties or for company meetings. The french doors give direct access onto the lawns bordered by mature trees - wonderful for wedding photographs. Food features high on the list of reasons for staying in this excellent hotel. Norman Tindal is an inspired chef who conjures up exciting and innovative dishes as well as producing one of the best Sunday lunches in Scotland. He specialises in steaks but never forgets the vegetarians who come to eat here. For them he prepares special dishes often prepared with fresh produce from the garden. The garden is Sheila Tindal's province, a place of tranquillity where one can sit and have a drink in preference to frequenting the cosy bar on a summer's evening. The bar also offers good bar meals with 'Daily Specials'. For those with sporting inclinations, Golf and Fishing can be arranged.

USEFUL INFORMATION

OPEN; All year
CHILDREN; Welcome
CREDIT CARDS; All cards
LICENSED; Full Licence
ACCOMMODATION; 8 ensuite rooms
PETS; By arrangement

RESTAURANT; Home-cooked, innovative
BAR MEALS; Varied. Daily Specials
VEGETARIAN; Several dishes
DISABLED ACCESS; No special facilities
GARDEN; 2.5 acres mature garden.

Scotland

BURTS HOTEL
Market Square,
Melrose,
Roxburghshire TD6 9PN

Tel: 01896 82285
Fax: 01896 822870

    The Burts Hotel has an unusual history, built in 1722 as a town house for an important dignitary, it then became Anderson's Temperance Hotel! Guests will be pleased to note that with a change of ownership in the 1930's the Temperance Hotel was changed to Burts Hotel with a full 'On Licence'. Today you may enjoy wine from an excellent list or sup a first class Malt Whisky, if that is your preferrnce. The building is listed and reflects much of the period of charm of bygone years.
    Graham and Anne are the proprietors and Nicholas, their son, is the resident manager. Together they and their loyal staff have created a cheerful and relaxing hotel in which the well being of the guests is of paramount importance. The hotel has 21 delightful bedrooms, all en-suite, and equipped with colour tlevision, radio, telphone, tea/coffee making facilities and hairdryers. Residents have a private lounge. There is also a lounge bar open to the general public; a very popular meeting and eating place for locals and visitors.
    The talented chef, Gary Moore, has been at Burts for 8 years. He prepares the most exquisite cuisine using only the very best local, fresh produce. Many of his dishes are a little different, such as 'Potted Spiced Rabbit set in a Ramekin with seasonal leaves and toasted brioche' or 'Quails Eggs laid in a green nest of spinach.' Of course he prepares more traditional fare for those who are not quite so adventurous. The Burts Hotel has justly been awarded AA 3 star, RAC 3 star, STB 4 crowns commended, Egon Ronay, Michelin, Les Routiers, Taste of Scotland recommendations as well as an AA Food Rosette.

USEFUL INFORMATION

OPEN; All year except Boxing Day.
Eating & drinking: 12-2pm & 6-11pm
CHILDREN; Children's certificate
Allowed in bar.
CREDIT CARDS; Amex/Visa/Access/
Mastercard/Diners
LICENSED; Full On
ACCOMMODATION; 21 en-suite bedrooms
PETS; By arrangement

RESTAURANT; A taste of Scotland
with a touch of French Cuisine
BAR FOOD; Popular, traditional
wholesome, extensive menu
VEGETARIAN; 2 dishes. Can cater
for special dietary requirements.
DISABLED ACCESS; Level entry
GARDEN; 1 acre with large
rose garden

Chapter Eleven

MOFFAT HOUSE HOTEL
High Street, Moffat,
Dumfriesshire DG10 9HL

Tel: 01683 220039
Fax: 01683 221288

This gracious three-storey John Adam mansion built in the 1750's as a private house for the Earl of Hopetoun did not become an hotel until 1950 and even today the building is, to a great extent, unaltered. Twenty one years ago it came into the hands of the Reid family who have carefully modernised the hotel within the framework of the main house and its two wings, retaining all the charm of an old country house together with the quality and efficiency of a modern hotel. Moffat House has 20 ensuite bedrooms: 14 twin/double, 3 single, 2 family and one honeymoon suite with an antique four-poster bed. Every room is attractively and comfortably furnished and has colour television, tea and coffee maker, direct-dial telephone, radio and hair drier. For those with young children, a baby listening service is available. All the public rooms have a pleasant welcoming air. The Adam lounge, where a log fire blazes on chilly evenings, is where many people gather to enjoy a drink or to savour some of the delicious bar food on offer - it is served throughout the year, both at lunch-time and in the evening, and there is an extensive choice, including vegetarian dishes. Curling up with a book becomes an enhanced pleasure in the comfort of the coffee lounge whilst in the spacious dining room home-cooked dishes made from the freshest of Scottish produce make meal times a particular delight. You will find the menu is a splendid blend of Scottish Fare, French cuisine and traditional cooking, using local Solway salmon, sea trout, venison and Galloway beef. The wine list complements the food. Moffat House Hotel is AA/RAC 3 stars and Scottish Tourist Board Four Crowns Highly Commended.

USEFUL INFORMATION

OPEN; All year. 7am-midnight
CHILDREN; Yes. Baby listening Service
CREDIT CARDS; Amex/Visa/Diners
LICENSED; Full
ACCOMMODATION; 20 ensuite rooms

RESTAURANT; Extensive menu. Scottish French, traditional.
BAR FOOD; Wide choice of starters main courses and sweets
VEGETARIAN; Always at least 6 Masters/dishes
DISABLED ACCESS; Yes, ground floor
GARDEN; 2.5 acres plus picnic tables

THE BURNSIDE HOUSE HOTEL

Cupar Road,
Newburgh,
Fife KY14 6EP

Tel: 01337 840013

This Victorian house was built as a Manse for the local minister but since then it has had well constructed additions and enabled Bernie Kerrigan, the chef proprietor and his wife

Linda to run it as a successful hotel as well as a venue for many functions small and large which can provide comfortable accommodation for up to one hundred people in the attractive function room which has its own dance floor. It stands next to a Burn by the River Tay fed from Loch Lindones, where there is good trout fishing. In fact The Burnside has excellent contacts for Fishing, Shooting, Golf and Sailing.

The functions do not intrude onto the hotel itself which has a nice restaurant with 30 covers plus a cosy Bar. Every room in the house has that feeling of spaciousness so beloved by the Victorians. It allows for tall windows and high ceilings. The food is all home-cooked and is generous in portion and very reasonably priced. There are dishes to suit every taste including Vegetarians and children.

The four large ensuite bedrooms which include a family room, are equipped with Television, hairdryers and that boon to travellers, a tea/coffee tray. Guests staying at The Burnside find that the atmosphere is friendly and welcoming and without petty restrictions. Bernie is happy to adapt his menu if there is something you would particularly like to eat.

The fact that the rooms are so economically priced in 1996 at £25 for a single bed and breakfast and £40 double per night is helpful to many families.

USEFUL INFORMATION

OPEN; All year
CHILDREN; Welcome. Childrens menu
CREDIT CARDS; All cards but Diners
LICENSED; Yes. Full Licence
ACCOMMODATION; 2dbl, 1 sgl 1 family
PETS; Permitted
PRICE BAND A/B

RESTAURANT; Good range, freshly prepared to order
BAR FOOD; Excellent snacks
VEGETARIAN; Always a choice
DISABLED ACCESS; No
GARDEN; Yes, very large

Chapter Eleven

KILDONAN LODGE
27 Craigmillar Park,
Newington,
Edinburgh EH16 5PE

Tel; 0131 667 2793
Fax: 0131 667 9777

Built in 1874 by a wealthy Edinburgh businessman, Kildonan Lodge is an outstanding example of Victorian elegance. Its position makes it ideal for anyone wanting to explore Scotland's Capital. Princes Street is about one and a half miles away and easily accessible using the frequent bus service which takes you into the heart of the city - a marvellous opportunity to park and forget your car.

The owners, Maggie and Bruce Urquhart, have spent time and loving care in restoring the house, recapturing the atmosphere of a bygone era. Beautiful ceilings, vast windows gracefully draped, polished furniture, shining with the patina of age, and an open fire give the house a wonderful air of well-being. The splendid residents' lounge provides a tranquil haven in which guests can relax by the fire whilst enjoying a dram from the 'Honesty Bar'. Well appointed non-smoking bedrooms with ensuite bathrooms, direct dial telephone, colour television, radio alarm, hair dryers and a tea and coffee tray plus some other nice little touches make guests feel at home. Family rooms are available and children are very welcome. The hotel only serves breakfast which is a delicious wholesome Scottish meal served in the spacious and elegant dining room. This rooms is also used for small weddings and functions which the Urquharts and their staff handle efficiently and with a great understanding of people's needs. Edinburgh has a host of wonderful restaurants, the choice of which Kildonan Lodge will be pleased to help you. Kildonan Lodge has a large private car park.

USEFUL INFORMATION

OPEN; *All year*
CHILDREN; *Welcome*
CREDIT CARDS; *All cards*
LICENSED; *Yes. Residential*
ACCOMMODATION; *Non-smoking ensuite*
PETS; *By arrangement*

DINING ROOM; *Super Scottish Breakfast only*
BAR FOOD; *Not applicable*
VEGETARIAN; *Upon request*
DISABLED ACCESS; *No special facilities Ground floor bedroom available*
GARDEN; *Yes. Large Car Park*

CORSEMALZIE HOUSE HOTEL
Port William,
Newton Stewart,
Wigtownshire DG8 9RL

Tel: 01988 860254
Fax: 01988 860213

Corsemalzie House is the epitome of a Scottish Country Mansion. Built during the 19th century the hotel has retained all the elegance of the era yet the careful restoration over the years has ensured that every facility is provided for guests without altering the intimate atmosphere of the original house. Set in forty acres of garden and woodland, the hotel provides peaceful seclusion, with an abundance of wild life in the environs. The colourful backdrop to the house changes with the seasons, as the snowdrops, daffodils, rhodendrons and azaleas blossom against the verdant green of the woodland. The hotel is within easy reach of many historical castles and sites. Golf is a favoured pastime of many guests and a wide range of courses are within easy reach of the hotel. A Putting Green and Croquet Lawn have been laid out on the lawns in front of the hotel. Shooting is available over 8,000 acres of neighbouring woods and estates where a variety of game is to be had in season. The quality of Salmon and Trout fishing on the Rivers Bladnoch and Tarff is renowned within the area. First class sport can be experienced on the hotel's private waters. Tuition and a gillie are available. Leisurely walks amidst unspoilt countryside or dramatic coastline, an array of wildlife and famous gardens await the visitor looking for a memorable holiday.

Inside the hotel there is a sense of tranquillity and comfort which is very welcoming. It is probably the views over the lawns and putting green from the elegant Drawing Room which you will notice first but looking round the room you will see how beautifully it is appointed. It is the Cocktail Bar that tends to attract guests in the evening before dinner. Stocked with an extensive range of carefully selected wines and malt whiskies, it could not be a better place in which to unwind and mull over the events of the day. Peter McDougall, the resident proprietor, has a great love and understanding for food. Under his personal supervision delicious Scottish fayre, locally produced, enhances the excellent cuisine. At night you will go to your very well furnished ensuite bedroom to enjoy a good night's sleep and look forward to a superb Scottish breakfast in the morning. A Member of Logis Great Britain and of Scotland's Commended Hotels.

USEFUL INFORMATION

OPEN; All year
CHILDREN; Welcome
CREDIT CARDS; All cards
LICENSED; Full
ACCOMMODATION; Ensuite rooms
GARDEN; 40 acres garden & woodland

RESTAURANT; Scottish fayre, wide range of superb dishes
BAR FOOD; Wide choice
VEGETARIAN DISHES; Several every day
DISABLED ACCESS; Yes but not bedrooms

Chapter Eleven

LERAGS HOUSE
Lerags,
By Oban,
Argyll PA34 4SE

Tel: 01631 563381

This charming Georgian country house stands in almost two acres of mature gardens with the property boundary reaching down to the tidal mark on the shores of Loch Feochan. Lerags House is set in the tranquil and picturesque Lerags Glen; a truly wonderful place to stay for anyone, but for those who paint or sketch, write orphotograph, it must seem like paradise. For those of us who do not have these talents there is much else to do. Oban, four and a half miles away with its town facilities, shopping and terminal for the Islands is worth exploring. There are many delightful walks in the vicinity and the scenery is breathtaking.Boat trips on Loch Etive and Loch Awe make a superb outing and the regular CalMac ferries to Lismore, Colonsay, Mull and the more distant islands leave directly from Oban's Railway Pier. Scottish Country Dancers may like to know that Lerags House offers special rates during the dancing season. Your hostess Margaret is an RSCDS qualified teacher.

Lerags House is the family home of Norman and Margaret Hill and their aim is to provide good quality accommodation, food and service at value for money prices in a warm and relaxing country house atmosphere. There are seven spacious and charmingly furnished ensuite bedrooms. They are all on the first floor and most have views overlooking the grounds towards the loch. Both the Guest Lounge and Dining Room, which overlooks the grounds, have open fires for the cooler seasons. Good food is high on the list of priorities. Breakfast is a sumptuous repast and evening meals are served by prior arrangement. The emphasis is on traditional recipes using only the best locally purchased produce, cooked by Margaret and Norman to a high standard. A range of carefully chosen wines is available. Lerags House is a strictly non-smoking establishment.

USEFUL INFORMATION

OPEN; March-October. Christmas and Hogmanay
CHILDREN; By arrangement
CREDIT CARDS; Yes
LICENSED; Yes
ACCOMMODATION; 7 ensuite rooms
PETS; By arrangement

DINING ROOM; Traditional dishes using local produce.
Dinner by prior arrangement
BAR FOOD; Not applicable
VEGETARIAN; Upon request
DISABLED ACCESS; No
GARDEN; 2 acres mature gardens

PARSONS LODGE HOTEL AND RESTAURANT
15 Main Street,
Patna,
Ayrshire KA67LN

Tel: 01292 531306

Parsons Lodge sits in the middle of the main street of the old mining village of Patna. Architecturally it is probably the most interesting building here. No one would ever call Patna the prettiest of Scottish villages but it has a great deal to offer nonetheless. It is a terrific centre for walks, clay pigeon shooting, pony trekking and fishing. Indeed, the owner, Sheila Campbell takes walkers on guided tours and also holds permits for fishing on the River Doon. The hotel is ideally suited for sporting groups.

Parsons Lodge has one double and 2 twin bedrooms all ensuite or with private bathroom. Each room has TV and a tea/coffee tray. The house built of Ballochmylesandstone in 1918 is comfortablyand attractively furnished and extremely welcoming. There is no doubt that you would be very well cared for here. It is equally a good place to stop for food. The menu is simple, well chosen, traditional food at sensible prices. You can have anything from a Scrambled egg roll and a pot of tea to roast chicken with bacon and French fries or a choice of several fish dishes, salads and grills. Everything is freshly cooked to order. A lot of people find their way here for Sheila's renowned High Teas. Children are very welcome and pets by arrangement. There is access for the disabled into the restaurant but not the accommodation. In the summer months the pretty garden attracts visitors.

USEFUL INFORMATION

OPEN; All year
CHILDREN; Welcome
CREDIT CARDS; All except Diners/Amex
LICENSED; Yes
ACCOMMODATION; 1 dbl, 2twn all ensuite
PETS; By arrangement
GARDEN; Yes

RESTAURANT; Open to non-residents
Good traditional food, reasonable
Well known for High Teas
BAR FOOD; Not applicable
DISABLED ACCESS; For food only

Chapter Eleven

SMITHSTON FARM
Patna,
Ayr
Scotland KA6 7EZ
Tel: 01292 531211

The relaxed and congenial atmosphere is evident on arrival at Smithston Farm. Well presented and traditional food is served in the dining room, which is furnished in a modern style. The bedrooms are very comfortable with attractive soft furnishings. To ensure your privacy the rooms are ensuite, with a complimentary tea and coffee tray. A ground floor room has been set aside for the disabled. The farm has its own stretch of river and anglers will relish the ideal fishing conditions and the hope of catching trout or salmon. Local facilities include golf and glorious walks are many. Situated close to the coast of The Firth of Clyde. A visit to the castle of Culzean will certainly be of interest.

USEFUL INFORMATION
OPEN; *All year*
CHILDREN; *Welcome*
CREDIT CARDS; *None taken*
LICENSED; *No*
ACCOMMODATION; *4 ensuite rooms*
DINING ROOM; *Good home-cooked fare*
VEGETARIAN; *Catered for*
DISABLED ACCESS; *Good, ground floor bedroom*
GARDEN; *Yes*
PETS; *Yes*

FERNBANK
213 Main Street,
Prestwick,
Ayrshire,
Scotland KA9 1LH
Tel/Fax: 01292 475027

Ayrshire is Robert Burns' countryside; it benefits from the warm currents of the Gulf Stream which bring a mild climate to this part of Scotland. Prestwick has a lovely promenade and several sandy beaches running round the curve of Ayr bay. Fernbank Bed and Breakfast Guest House, which has several awards to its name, stands only 300 metres from one of these beaches. There are 7 bedrooms all of which have wash hand basins and four of them are fully ensuite. The other three share the use of a bathroom and separate shower room. All rooms have TV, tea and coffee making facilities, radio alarms and hair dryers. The house is excellently furnished in a modern style which compliments the surroundings. It is owned by Linda and David Catterson, a very pleasant couple who treat their guests as friends. Breakfast is a good traditional meal, and for lunch and dinner there are a wide range of restaurants to choose from. There are many local golf courses and if requested, golfing holidays can be arranged. As well as golf there is fishing, walking, swimming, sailing, bowling, ice skating and tennis.

USEFUL INFORMATION
OPEN;*All year*
CHILDREN;*Not under 5 years*
CREDIT CARDS;*None taken*
LICENSED;*No*
ACCOMMODATION;*7 rooms, 4 ensuite*
PETS;*No, except guide dogs by arrangement*
DINING ROOM;*Traditional, home-cooked breakfast*
VEGETARIAN;*Catered for*
DISABLED ACCESS;*No*
GARDEN;*Yes*

CRINGLETIE HOUSE HOTEL,
Peebles, EH45 8PL

Tel: 01721 730233
Fax: 01721 730244

Cringletie, designed by the renowned Scottish architect David Bryce, was built in 1861 for the Wolfe Murray family (of Quebec fame). The warm sandstone building is set in its own extensive grounds well back from the main Edinburgh/ Peebles road, in the gently rolling hills of the Scottish Borders. It makes a perfect hotel enhanced by the delightful Maguire family who have run it for almost a quarter century. They combine professional hotel-
keeping with good food, comfortable surroundings and a friendly service which makes one feel as though you are staying in a country house for a holiday.

Every room in Cringletie, public rooms and bedrooms enjoy fine views of the surrounding countryside as well as glimpses of the 28 acres of gardens and woodlands which provide very pleasant walks. There is a croquet lawn, putting green and an outdoor all-weather tennis court. After a day exploring the Borders, shopping in Edinburgh or even walking in the grounds you will come back to a crackling log fire in the lounge and perhaps have a drink before dinner. There are two lounges on the first floor - the drawing room and the smaller no-smoking lounge. The friendly bar is on the ground floor. Throughout the house, decoration and furnishings reflect the traditional atmosphere of this historic country house incorporating the highest standards of modern comforts. The bedrooms all have ensuite facilities, and also colour television and direct-dial telephones.

Cringletie is proud of its reputation for good food and has consistently won accolades from the leading hotel and restaurant guide books for its delicious freshly-cooked dishes. The menus change daily and include both traditional and innovative dishes created by Aileen Maguire and her kitchen team who use the fruit and vegetables from the hotel's two-acre walled garden, and honey from the hives, as well as other fresh local ingredients. Every menu includes a vegetarian dish. The well chosen wine list complements the cuisine.

USEFUL INFORMATION

OPEN; All year
PETS; Yes. Not in public rooms
CHILDREN; Welcome.
CREDIT CARDS; Visa/Access/Amex
LICENSED; Yes. Good wine list
ACCOMMODATION; En suite bedrooms

RESTAURANT; Menu changes daily. Freshly cooked dishes.
BAR FOOD; Not applicable
VEGETARIAN; Always 1 dish/day
DISABLED ACCESS; Ground floor only
GARDEN; 28 acres gardens & woodlands

Chapter Eleven

THE BUTTONBOSS LODGE
25 Atholl Road,
Pitlochry PH16 5PX

Tel: 01796 472065 or 473000

Colin and Marleen Mackay never fail to make evryone of their guests feel at home at Buttonboss Lodge. This sturdy, greystone house has weathered well in the hundred and fifty years or so that it has stood in Atholl Road. It looks welcoming and the interior does nothing to detract from this feeling. Comfortably furnished with the sort of furniture that is there to enjoy and relax in rather than a showpiece, the house is an ideal place for anyone wanting to explore the Strathmore area which includes Pitlochry. This is countryside that is just right for the walker or for anyone wanting to cycle -mountain bikes are available. The Mackay's have sensibly provided a drying room to deal with wet clothes if the Scottish weather decides not to be kind. There are excellent Golf Clubs closeby including Taymouth Castle where Colin is a PGA Professional to help the needy. In fact Buttonboss Lodge can arrange combined Golfing and Fishing Holidays. There are many places of historic interest within easy reach including Glamis Castle, steeped in history and the birthplace of the Queen Mother and Princess Margaret.

There are nine, attractively appointed bedrooms, four of which are ensuite. Warm in winter they are cool in the heat of the summer largely because of the thickness of the outer walls. The bedrooms all have Colour TV and beverage trays and in the Lounge, Sky TV is available. In true Scottish tradition, the food is excellent and home-cooked using as much in the way of local produce as possible. Vegetarians are catered for and special diets can be dealt with upon request.

USEFUL INFORMATION

OPEN; February-Mid-December
CHILDREN; By arrangement
CREDIT CARDS; None taken
LICENSED; No
ACCOMMODATION; 9 rooms, 4 ensuite

RESTAURANT; Not applicable
BAR FOOD; Not applicable
VEGETARIAN; Catered for + other
DISABLED ACCESS; Yes
GARDEN; Yes

Scotland

MOULIN HOTEL
Kirkmichael Road,
Pitlochry,
Perthshire PH16 5EW

Tel: 01796 472196
Fax: 01796 474098

It is the character of the Moulin Hotel which strikes one first. Here is an old inn established in 1695 which has been added to over the centuries but has never lost its charm. It is open all day every day and is a mecca for local people as well as visitors. The area is renowned for its wonderful countryside and many of the local walks start at Moulin. The village boasts an historic kirk and Crusaders Graves. There are golf course and fishing readily available. You will find the hotel situated in the Village Square of Moulin which is just three quarters of a mile from Pitlochry.

The Moulin is always busy, apart from anything else it has its own brewery which brews Ale of Atholl, Braveheart and Commemorative Ales as well as others. As a party you can book a tour which will include either High Tea and Sample Brew or an Evening Tour which offers Pie and Chips plus 4 pints of ale.

In the hotel you will find 15 very comfortably furnished ensuite bedrooms complete with TV and a beverage tray. The price is incredibly reasonable. The rooms in 1996 are from £20 per person per night. Spring, Autumn and Winter Breaks offer even greater value at £15 per person per night for a minimum of 4 nights. The food is equally sensibly priced and includes a wide range of dishes. For Daily Specials you are asked to see the Blackboard at the Bar. You can eat at antyime between 11am-9.30pm. Lunch and Afternoon Snacks finish at 6pm. The lovely Garden Restaurant overlooks the pretty grounds and the burn.

You can eat outside in warm weather if you wish. It is a tranquil and comfortable setting with attentive, friendly service. In fact you could not find a happier or more friendly place in which to stay.

USEFUL INFORMATION

OPEN; All day every day
CHILDREN; Welcome
CREDIT CARDS; All cards
LICENSED; Yes
ACCOMMODATION; 15 ensuite rooms
PETS; By arrangement

RESTAURANT; Wide range, well-cooked interesting dishes, inexpensive.
BAR FOOD; Wide range
VEGETARIAN; Always a choice
DISABLED ACCESS; Rest and /bar
GARDEN; Yes, seating &

Chapter Eleven

THE DRYBURGH ABBEY HOTEL
St Boswells,
Roxburghshire,
Scottish Borders TD6 ORQ

Tel: 01835 822261
Fax: 01835 823945

One of the most beautifully situated hotels in the Scottish Borders, it stands next to the historic ruins of Dryburgh Abbey on the banks of the River Tweed. It is the most tranquil of places and an ideal venue for Salmon or Trout fishing. One might think that the peacefulness is reminiscent of the past but Dryburgh Abbey is certainly up to date - it is the first hotel in Scotland to offer a free computerised availability and booking service covering 14 beats. The hotel can also arrange a variety of shooting for parties or individuals. The indoor swimming pool is yet another dimension of this excellent establishment and for the more energetic there are 14 golf courses most of which are within half an hour's drive of the hotel. Alternatively, you can simply explore the beautiful countryside in this delightful part of Scotland.

The hotel was acquired in 1991 by the Grose family who also have the Four Star Thurlestone Hotel in South Devon, which they have owned and managed since 1896. Whilst they take a very keen and personal interest in the hotel, it is the skilled professionalism of John Sloggie, the General Manager, and his very well trained staff, who make staying here memorable. The Hotel has undergone a complete restoration since 1991 and now offers guests a warm welcome and the peace and calm of a Scottish Country House Hotel. The bedrooms are delightful and have been designed with an eye to detail and comfort. From the smaller Garden View rooms to the sumptuous Four Poster rooms and Suites, they all have hairdryers, trouser presses, direct dial telephones and teletext remote control TV's. Dining is an experience. The kitchen under the supervision of Patrick Ruse who is supported by an enthusiastic and skilful team, prepare and cook the locally produced fresh ingredients with care and imagination using both traditional and modern recipes. David Grose is responsible for the very special wine list - a lover of fine wines he has provided a superb selection for guests. The Tweed Restaurant is a perfect setting for dinner but a simpler meal in the bar is equally attractive.

USEFUL INFORMATION

OPEN; All year
CHILDREN; Welcome
CREDIT CARDS; All major cards
LICENSED; Yes. Fine wine list
ACCOMMODATION; All ensuite. 4 posters suites

RESTAURANT; Scottish & international cuisine
BAR MEALS; First class, wide range
VEGETARIAN; Several dishes daily
DISABLED ACCESS; Yes
GARDEN; On banks of River Tweed

PHILIPBURN HOUSE HOTEL
Selkirk, TD7 5LS

Tel: 01750 20747

Philipburn, in former times the Dowager House to Philiphaugh Estates was built in 1751, not long after Covenanters and Royalists fought the bloody battle of Philiphaugh a few yards from the now tranquil and peaceful lawns, flowers and woodlands amidst which the lovely old house lies. Now, as it has done for over two centuries, Philipburn looks over the historic Border market town of Selkirk with commanding views of its rich and colourful gardens and woodlands, changing with the season from the orange and coppery shades of Autumn to the glistening buds of Spring.

The hotel has the accolade of many awards both as a hotel and restaurant and is a member of the prestigious Scotland Heritage Hotels, but whilst the enormously high standards are always maintained Philipburn House prefers the friendly Austrian 'Gemutlich' atmosphere to the often vacant grandeur and opulence of other baronial-style country hotels. The Hill family own and run the hotel with a passion for everything that is good in hotel-keeping. Everywhere there are fresh flowers, wonderful food comes out of the kitchens where Jim presides as Chef Patron, producing a dazzling array of dishes which embrace Haute Cuisine and Classical old Scottish, while all the time relying on the wonderful supply of Game from the surrounding hills, Salmon from the nearby rivers Tweed, Teviot and Ettrick and of course the finest Border Lamb. Philipburn's Garden and Poolside restaurants are pretty, leafy places, where old, mellow pine panelling combines with delightful table settings. In winter Souters bar is always alive with talk and laughter and here you can enjoy rich fish soups, bacon roasted local partridge or traditional bubbling Swiss cheese Rosti' being served to you from the pan. The wine list is a legend in its own right. Each bedroom is markedly different from the others with pretty chintz fabrics and old Pine furniture. Cottage apartments close to the hotel have breathtaking panoramic views and there are exclusive poolside suites. Or there is the Scandinavian Pine Lodge, straight out of Hans Christian Anderson. At whatever time of year you visit there is much to do with everything from fishing to a matchless menu of museums, woollen mills, castles and historic abbeys. In Winter, Spring & Autumn, Philipburn offers deliciously relaxing Midweek & Weekend breaks, spiced frequently with gastronomic theme nights.

USEFUL INFORMATION

OPEN; All year
CHILDREN; Welcome
CREDIT CARDS; All major credit cards
LICENSED; Yes. Fine wine list
ACCOMMODATION; 17 ensuite + cottage
GARDEN; 5 acres + sporting activities

RESTAURANT; Superb, creative food
BAR FOOD; Wide variety. Excellent
VEGETARIAN; Selection daily
DISABLED ACCESS; Cottage only with ramp for disabled
PETS; By arrangement

Chapter Eleven

BROWNLEES GUEST HOUSE
7 Murray Place,
St Andrews,
Fife KY16 9AP

Tel:01334 473868

St Andrews is world famous for its golf links which was first played on around 1400AD! Times have changed and there are now five 18 hole courses and one 9 hole course at St Andrews Links, giving a total of 99 holes of golf. With this in mind no hotel or guest house in St Andrews could not have an interest in the game and this is certainly true of Janet Smith who owns and runs the comfortable and homely Brownlees Guest House in Murray Place. She takes a keen interest in golf and is very knowledgeable. The location is excellent, it is in the middle of the town and very close to the links, the shops and the beaches. People who have stayed here over the years will tell you that Brownlees is welcoming and friendly and unrestricting. It is purely for bed and breakfast but Janet will always recommend somewhere for an evening meal.

This is a Victorian Town House with high ceilings and big windows lending it a gracious air. In side it is furnished with an eye to comfort and colour. There are pretty drapes at the windows and every one of the six bedrooms has a different decor. There are four ensuite rooms and each has colour TV and that boon to the traveller, a tea and coffee tray. In the lounge you will find Satellite TV. Smoking is permitted. Breakfast is a sumptuous meal, cooked to order and will include home made Scotch pancakes, potato cakes, scones, home made preserves as well as bacon, sausages, eggs, tomatoes etc. Vegetarians can be catered for upon request. Children are welcome but no pets please.

USEFUL INFORMATION

OPEN; All year   **DINING ROOM;** Full Scottish breakfast
CHILDREN; Welcome   **BAR FOOD;** Not applicable
CREDIT CARDS; None taken   **VEGETARIAN;** Upon request
LICENSED; No   **DISABLED ACCESS;** No
ACCOMMODATION; 6 rooms 4 ensuite   **GARDEN;** No
PETS; No.

ACHRAY HOUSE HOTEL
Loch Earn, St Fillans,
Perthshire PH6 2NF

Tel: 01764 685231
Fax: 01764 685320

The whole ethos of Achray House is to ensure that guests are never happy to stay just for one visit; they always want to return as quickly as possible. There may be many hotels offering just as many superb views, great comfort and good food but there is something intangible about the hospitality shown here which makes Achray House outstanding and memorable.

Set in the stunning scenery of the southern central Highlands and overlooking Loch Earn, Achray House is off the beaten track and is recognised as one of Scotland's finest small hotels. It is situated in the peaceful village of St Fillans, itself within a designated 'area of outstanding natural beauty', yet it is only seventy minutes from the cities of Edingburgh and Glasgow. There are a host of major tourist attractions for the visitor: Blair, Glamis and Stirling castles, Scone Palace, and the coastal towns of Oban and St Andrews are all within easy reach. There are many local attractions too, as well as walks, gardens, glens and lochs to enjoy with an abundance of wildlife. The hotel has its own foreshore and jetty and there are a number of watersports available on the loch, including trout fishing, sailing and wind surfing. For golfers, there are fourteen courses within half an hour's drive. One of the most scenic is St Fillans' own course half a mile away.

Most bedrooms have a loch view and private facilities. The accommodation comprises new, and more traditional bedrooms with some of the best views, whilst the newer rooms offer a very high standard of modern facilities. All bedrooms have tea and coffee making facilities, colour television, and direct-dial telephone. Achray House is renowned for its fine food with an extensive choice of dishes, generous portions and value for money. Lunch and supper can be ordered from the bar menus which feature traditional fare with a good vegetarian selection. In the restaurant a wide choice of dishes go to make the overall choice very special.

USEFUL INFORMATION

OPEN; All year
CHILDREN; Welcome
CREDIT CARDS; All major cards
LICENSED; Yes
ACCOMMODATION; En-suite rooms
GARDEN; Lovely gardens. Own jetty and foreshore

RESTAURANT; Wide choice. Excellent
BAR FOOD; Available at lunch & supper
　　　　　　　Traditional fare
VEGETARIAN; Good selection
DISABLED ACCESS; Yes. No special
PETS; By arrangement

Chapter Eleven

THE QUEENS VIEW HOTEL
Strathtummel by Pitlochry,
Perthshire PH16 5NR

Tel: 01796 473291
Fax: 01796 473515

Even in a land with outstanding scenic beauty,there are probably not many hotels in Scotland with such a stunning location as The Queens View. It stands 150 feet or more above Loch Tummel, five miles from the A9 at Pitlochry halfway between Edinburgh and Inverness within reach of all the good things which Scotland has to offer. It took Norma and Richard Tomlinson a long time to find just the right place for their first venture into hotel keeping but having found it they have transformed it. In the space of twelve months The Queens View has been renovated, redecorated and centrally heated staying open most of the year.

The Tomlinsons are natural hosts and they welcome residents and non residents alike. You will be invited to stay in beautifully appointed ensuite bedrooms with outstanding views, offered food which is definitely out of the ordinary whether it is the bar menu at lunch time or the dinner menu at night. A three course dinner is offered, preceded by savouries whilst pre-dinner drinks are taken and followed by coffee or tea and mints. The selection of dishes changes frequently. Often it changes daily. Much depends on what fresh local produce is available to the talented chef. Maybe it will be a starter of Puff Pastry Horns with a melange of Mushrooms,Caps, Morels and Chestnuts in Madeira followed by Marinated Breast of Duck with a Red Wine and PruneSauce with Lardons and Red Cabbage. You will find it quite hard to choose. Delicious puddings complete the meal although you may have Cheese and Biscuits if you do not have a sweet tooth. The hotel does have trout fishing rights on Loch Tummel but it is surrounded by opportunities for the sportsman, the walker and the sightseer. Theatre goers will have heard of the Festival theatre at Pitlochry at which it is possible to see a different play each night before or after supper at the hotel or indeed both!

USEFUL INFORMATION

OPEN; All year
CHILDREN; Welcome
CREDIT CARDS; All major cards
LICENSED; Yes. Fine wine list
ACCOMMODATION; 10 ensuite rooms
PETS; Yes

RESTAURANT; Outstanding dishes
BAR FOOD; Definitely different
DISABLED ACCESS; Not really
VEGETARIAN; By arrangement
GARDEN; Yes

SPRINGSIDE
Pier Road,
Tarbert,
Argyll PA29 6UE

Tel: 01880 820413

Tarbert is almost one of Scotland's best kept secrets! It is at the top of the Kintyre Peninsula and quite often missed by people who travel north from Inverary. Those who discover it are well rewarded for Tarbert is a beautiful fishing village with access to two stunning lochs and within one hour of the Mull of Kintyre. A super place to stay for the sheer scenic beauty of the area, there are some wonderful walks and for birdwatchers it is especially attractive. Tarbert even has a small golf course, but the well known Machrihanish Links course is only 40 minutes away.

Donald Marshall, a Chartered Architect, and his wife Alison, own and run Springside providing a relaxed and friendly atmosphere in which to stay. The house is situated at the harbour entrance and is within five minutes walking distance of the village amenities. Open all year, there are five rooms, one single, one double and two family, all with central heating and tea and coffee making facilities. Donald and Alison are currently obtaining planning permission for ensuite facilities in the bedrooms and this it is hoped will be ready by the end of June 1996. The attractive guests lounge has colour television and is just the place to sit in and plan your day's outing. Breakfast is a truly Scottish feast and evening meals are available by arrangement. Special attention is paid to the needs of vegetarians. There is ample parking and arrangements can be made for early and late ferry crossings. Guests wishing to bring pets are welcome to do so. The house has a fire certificate and is commended by the Scottish Tourist Board.

USEFUL INFORMATION

OPEN; All year
CHILDREN; Welcome
CREDIT CARDS; None taken
LICENSED; No
ACCOMMODATION; 5 rooms
PETS; Welcome

DINING ROOM; Excellent Scottish Breakfast. Dinner by arrangement
VEGETARIAN; Catered for
DISABLED ACCESS; Yes. No special facilities
GARDEN; Yes

Chapter Eleven

DRUMCRUILTON
Thornhill,
Dumfriesshire DG3 5BG
Tel: 01848 500210

This fine Victorian, pink sandstone, listed farmhouse set in beautiful Drumfriesshire countryside is the home of George and Dorothy Hill and their family. It is a working stock farm which includes pure bred Charollais sheep and Salers cattle. It is an out of the ordinary place because of the skillful manner in which Dorothy Hill has set about transforming the interior of the rather solid, 150 year old building. Inside the house radiates warmth and colour. Every nook and cranny has been highlighted with deft touches. Log burning fires emit that wonderful smell and heat all at the same time. The furnishings are a splendid mixture of antiques and good furniture set off beautifully by the fantastic colours of the walls and patterns of the drapes. The house is a delight and no one can possibly not feel welcome and at ease.

Drumcuilton House has two double bedrooms (one with en-suite shower room, one with private bathroom) and a twin room. There is also a single room available on the ground floor. All the rooms are comfortably furnished and have hospitality trays, hairdryers, access to ironing and shoe cleaning facilities, with ample areas for drying clothes. A sitting room with colour television is provided for guests and the house has full central heating. Dorothy is an accomplished cook and she places great emphasis on the quality of food served. A full Scottish breakfast is served every day and Dinner is available on request. Fresh local produce and produce from the farm is used whenever possible. Drumcuilton is not licensed but you are welcome to bring your own wines.

From Dumfries, take the A76 north to Thornhill and continue north for two miles to Carronbridge. Turn right on the A702 Edinburgh Road. After 1 3/4 miles Drumcuilton is signposted on the left. The countryside has abundant wild life, scenic drives and walks, old castles and much more. Fishing, shooting, rough shooting, deer stalking, and riding are all available in season.

USEFUL INFORMATION

OPEN; May to November
CHILDREN; Welcome
CREDIT CARDS; None taken
LICENSED; No. Do bring your own
ACCOMMODATION; 2 dbl, 1tw 1sgl

RESTAURANT; Not applicable
BAR FOOD; Not applicable
VEGETARIAN; On request
DISABLED ACCESS; Ground floor bedroom
GARDEN; Delightful garden

Where to Eat

Chapter Twelve

WHERE TO EAT

Where to Eat

AVON

BATH
LE BEAUJOLAIS, 5 Chapel Row, Queens Square.
Tel: 01228 423417.
A charming, informal French restaurant with red checked table cloths and fresh flowers on the tables. Food is a mixture of classic French styles prepared by French chefs. An excellent range of wines and liqueurs. Garden area has seating. Open: lunch Mon-Sat 12-2.30pm. Dinner Mon-Sat 7-11pm. Children welcome. All major cards. Vegetarians catered for. Disabled access.

CORNWALL

BODMIN
WAFFLES COFFEE HOUSE, 14 Market House Arcade.
Tel: 01208 75500.
A self-catering coffee shop and licensed restaurant, popular with locals and visitors alike. Superb range of food which is all home-made and prepared daily. Cordial staff and efficient service. Open 6 days from 8am-5pm. Children welcome. No credit cards. Take away service.

THE OLD INN, St Breward, Bodmin Moor.
Tel: 01208 850711.
The classic Cornish Moorland pub is a great find for any visitor. Warm friendly atmosphere with stone walls, flagged floors, beamed ceilings and even a bar built from solid granite. An amazing selection of 80 Malt Whiskies. The food is excellent and extremely reasonable and served in an intimate restaurant. A wide range of Bar meals. Open: 12-3pm & 6.30-late. Children welcome. No credit cards. At least 5 vegetarian dishes. Pets welcome.

BUDE
THE BRASSERIE RESTAURANT, Lower Wharf Centre.
Tel: 01288 355275.
A facinating conversion of a 19th century warehouse, beautifully decorated with paintings and works by local artists. The areas inside the restaurant are totally 'non-smoking'. A very comprehensive menu, serving lunch and evening meals, and always a 'Dish of the Day' for vegetarians. Open: Mar-Oct 10-8.30pm 7 days a week. Children welcome. All major cards not Amex. Alcohol is served as a supplement to meals.

FALMOUTH
THE GEM FISH BAR & RESTAURANT, 6 Quarry Hill.
Tel: 01326 313640. This is a pleasant no nonsense eating establishment with attractively laid up tables and bench seating. The emphasis is on delicious food at reasonable prices and you can have anything form a cup of tea to a full blown 3 course meal with wine. The fish is especially good. Open daily 11.30-2pm & 4-7.30 Mon-Wed. 4-9pm Thurs-Sat. Children welcome. Good choice os vegetarian dishes. No credit cards.

Chapter Twelve

THE PEAR TREE, 2 Bank Place.
Tel: 01326 312566.
This fine, unassuming, brick built Georgian house is home to a restaurant of outstanding choice and service. There are 2 rooms available, one is non-smoking. The menu is mouthwatering and offers a choice of superb food, catering for vegetarians and special diets, with some notice. Comprehensive wine list. Open summer 7 till late. Winter 7-9pm Mon-Thurs,7pm till late Fri & Sat. Open sun in July and August. All major cards. Children welcome.

HELSTON
THE COFFEE BEAN, 32 Coinagehall Street.
Tel: 01326 572970.
This very nice family restaurant is not only warm and welcoming, it is quaint, small and has a wonderful atmosphere. Every month there is a 'Specials List'. You can drop in for a cup of coffee or a specialist pot of tea and indulge in a jam doughnut, oozing with home-made preserve, split and filled with cream!. Gourmet food at inexpensive prices. Open Mon-Sat 9-5pm Fri-Sat evening from Easter-Autumn. Children welcome, own menu. No credit cards. Vegetarians catered for.

THE YARD BISTRO, Trelowarren, Mawgan.
Tel: 01326 221595.
Situated in the converted carriage house of Trelowarren, a 1000 acre estate on the baks of the Helston River. Trevor Bayfield is your host and chief chef, and ensures a delectable range of dishes for all palettes. The choice is anything from delicious local fresh fish to lamb or guineafowl. You will not be disappointed in either the food or the standard of service. Open through quiet periods; weekends only by booking. Closed Sun & Tues evenings, all day on Mon. Vegetarians very well catered for. Visa/Master.

LOSTWITHIEL
TREWITHEN RESTAURANT, Fore Street.
Tel: 01208 872373.
If you like to eat in a relaxed unhurried cottagey atmosphere then this is the place for you. Nestled in the Fowey River Valley. Excellent food, specialises in Steak, Duckling, lobster and local fish. The menu is supplemented by a 'Specials Blackboard'. Open all year. Closed Sun & Mon in winter and Sun in summer. Visa/Master/Diners/Switch/Delta. Children welcome. At least 2 dishes for vegetarians.

MOUSEHOLE
CORNISH RANGE, 6 Chapel Street.
Tel: 01736 731488.
18th century licensed restaurant situated in a wonderful setting in the picturesque harbour village of Mousehole. Excellent food, specialising in the finest seafood, with chargrilled steaks and vegetarian dishes. Choice of wines. Served in attractive surroundings. Open all year. All major cards. Children welcome.

Where to Eat

ST AGNES
SCHOONERS BISTRO, Trevaunance Cove.
Tel: 01872 553149.
The murmur of the waves lapping the beach, the smell of the tangy salty air, the cries of the seagulls, fishing the shallows, - all this and superb food too! The Bistro is situated on the beach, in the cove, and is unique both in its position, and its quality and service. Wide and varied menu from traditional to more continental dishes. Open: Easter-Sept, daily 10.30-4pm. Evenings 7pm till late. All major cards. Children welcome. Vegetarians and special diets catered for. Excellent wine list.

ST CLEER
THE STAG INN
Tel: 01579 342305.
Believed to be 250 years old and complete with ghost, theis friendly pub has stories of lights falling, glasses chinking and bar stools moving! Stone walls and simple furnishings go well with the local produce and real ales. Good value pub food, intimate dining room for the evening. Extensive menu catering for every taste. Open 12-11pm. Children welcome in dining room, own menu. No credit cards. Vegetarians catered for.

ST IVES
THE GARRACK HOTEL, Burtallan Lane.
Tel: 01736 796199 Fax: 01736 798955.
For those wanting a special meal in delightful surroundings, The Garrack Hotel has everything. Wonderful, locally produced food whenever possible, nearby Newlyn supplies fresh fish and fine seafood. The Garrack has its own storage tank for live lobsters The unique pricing policy on wines offers exceptional value for more expensive wines. Open All year except January 1st. Children welcome. Coffee Shop. Vegetarians catered for. Disabled access.

THE LIZARD
MOUNTS BAY INN, Churchtown, Mullion.
Tel: 01326 240221 Fax: 01326 240249.
This 100 year old pub is home ot Barrie and Crystina Petterson, who extend their hand of hopsitality to all their customers. Having the charm and atmosphere of a good country inn, you can enjoy a pleasant drink in good company, and smaple the menu of classic English pub food. The menu is stimulating and enticing with a varied choice and price range for all. Open: summer-pub hours plus all day Sat & Sun. Winter-normal pub hours. Children in restaurant and childrens room. All major cards. Bar snacks. Accommodation. Pets welcome.

TRURO
FODDERS, Pannier Market, Back Quay.
Tel: 01872 71384.
Fodders is quite unique and has a steady following of local people which always bodes well for any restaurant. Situated in an 18th century hayloft featuring much of the original stonework and beams. It is a friendly, informal establishment. Restaurant serving delicious wholefood menu. Tea room serving a wonderful 'teatime' spread. Open 10-5pm Mon-Sat inc. Not Bank

Chapter Twelve

Holidays. Children welcome. Wines and beers only. Vegetarian and special diets catered for.

KINGS ARMS, Tregony.
Tel: 01872 530202.
A 16th century Inn with a welcoming, friendly atmosphere where you can relax and enjoy a drink and the good home-cooked fare from the wide ranging menu which caters for all tastes. Specials Blackboard. Bar food. Open all year. All major cards. Children welcome, own section on menu. At least 2 vegetarian dishes.

CLEVELAND

SALTBURN-BY-SEA
THE ELLERBY HOTEL, Ellerby, Hinderwell.
Tel: 01947 840342.
Offers a wide range of meals both at lunchtime and in the evening every day of the week plus traditional Sunday lunch. Comprehensive menu. For the really hearty appetite the 'Farmhouse Supper' is a winner, and they also have an extensive 'Specials Board'. Rest: Sun-Thurs 12-2pm 7-9pm. Fri-Sat: 7.15-9.30pm. Children welcome. Games provided. All major cards. Always dishes for vegetaians. Price Band: B
GRINKLE PARK HOTEL, Easington.
Tel: 01287 641278.
Emphasis on quality and presentation in Restaurant. Good value bar food. Open all year. All major credit cards. Children welcome. Vegetarians catered for.
Price Band: B

DEVON

BLACKAWTON
THE SPORTSMAN'S ARMS, Henborough Post.
Tel: 01803 712231.
This interesting pub is rapidly making a name for itself for its food and especially for the speciality of the house - fish. The steaks are also excellent along with lamb, duck, chicken and delicious local ham. This pub has a happy atmosphere and is well worth a visit. Open all year. Children welcome to eat. All major cards. Vegetarians catered for.

BOVEY TRACEY
INDIA COTTAGE, 38 Fore Street.
Tel: 01626 833111.
An excellent Indian restaurant and take-away. This high quality establishment serves traditional Indian cuisine in pleasant and comfortable surroundings. Comprehensive menu, well stocked bar. Open summer 6-11.30pm 7 days a week. Winter 6-11.30pm (closed Mon) 6 days a week. Excl. Bank Holidays. Children welcome. All major cards except Amex/Diners. Vegetarians catered for.

Where to Eat

BUDLEIGH SALTERTON
MARIO AND FRANCO, Italian Restaurant, 1A High Street.
Tel: 01395 443330.
The reputation of Mario and Franco's has grown rapidly and spread far and wide people come from quite long distances to take part in the gastronomic experience. The menu is full of delicious dishes, everything is prepared and cooked on the premises including the bread. Superb Italian food Mario and Franco's is a great find. Open all year. Children welcome. All major cards. Vegetarians catered for. Award winning wine list.

CHAGFORD
WHIDDONS COFFEE HOUSE & ANTIQUE SHOP, High Street.
Tel: 01647 433406.
The timeless town of Chagford is home of the delightful establishment named Whiddons. This thatched 16th century cottage in the heart of the town specialises in good old fashioned courtesy and service. Sandwiches, home-made cakes, strawberry jam, freshly baked scones and lashings of clotted cream! Wonderful. Open all year except Christmas Day. Children welcome. No credit cards.

EXETER
THE COWICK BARTON, Cowick Lane, St Thomas.
Tel: 01392 274011.
Built in the late 16th century you enter Cowick Barton through a four-foot wide door and walk straight into an amazing interior. The Great Hall has a remarkable Tudor fireplace modernised by the Victorians by a facing of coloured tiles. It is gracious and welcoming and here you may dine extremely well, looked after by a well-trained courteous staff. Well presented good value menu, wide choice. Open every day. Last orders Lunch 2pm. Evening 9.30pm. Children welcome. All major cards. Always a vegetarian choice.

HOLSWORTHY
THE WHITE HART HOTEL
TEL: 01409 253475.
This 400 year old inn is very special, especially to the people of Holsworthy and those who stream into the busy town on market days. You will always feel comfortable here, the locals are friendly and cheerful chatter makes a happy atmosphere on its own. Food is all important and there is great emphasis on local produce. Good, wholesome and imaginative menu. Wide ranging bar food meals. Separate menu for vegetarians. Open all year 11-3pm & 6-11pm. Children welcome. Visa/Mastercard. Accommodation.

ILFRACOMBE
THE HELE BAY HOTEL, Hele.
Tel: 01271 867795.
The Hele bay is a comfortable establishment, run along the lines of a friendly 'local pub'. It offers good service in a warm, imformal atmosphere. There is a childrens games room, a skittles rooms and a large car park. The restaurant covers between 35 and 40 persons, and there are special meals for children, all are at very reasonable prices. Open all year. Children welcome. Visa. Vegetarians catered for. Bar snacks. Accommodation.

Chapter Twelve

KINGSBRIDGE
CYDER PRESS RESAURANT, Stancombe Farm, Sherford.
Tel: 01548 531151.
If you thought it was impossible to find total peace, quiet and tranquillity then you have not visited Stancombe Farm in the glorious South Hams of Devon. At the beautiful 17th century thatched Cyder Press Restaurant you will receive the warmest of welcomes, offering the best of West Country fare and traditional Sunday lunches (booking advisable). Open evenings all year. Daily Apr-Oct (light lunches, cream Teas etc). Children welcome. All major cards. Licensed. Vegetarians catered for.

JOURNEY'S END INN, Ringmore.
Tel: 01548 810205.
Nestling very comfortably in the beautiful and unspoilt, thatched village in the heart of the South Hams countryside, Journey's End is one of the oldest pubs in Devon. There are open log fires in all the bars and in the intimate dining rooms which seats 30. The menu at the Inn is interesting and varied and there are regular 'Food Feature' weekends. Fresh local produce used whenever possible. Open weekdays: 11.30-3.30pm & 6.30-11pm. Open all day Sunday. Children welcome, games room and garden, own menu. Mastercard/Visa. Vegetarians catered for. Accommodation.

LYDFORD
LYDFORD HOUSE HOTEL
Tel: 01822 820347.
This award winning hotel is 'One of Britain's Great Little Hotels', situated just outside the historic village Lydford on the edge of Dartmoor. You are invited to enjoy leisurely meals served by an efficient and unobtrusive staff, the table d'Hote dinner is a three course meal of generous proportions with a wide choice at each course. Afternoon tea served in the Tea Room during the season. Traditional Sunday lunch. Open all year. Children over 5 years. Visa/Mastercard. Licensed. Accommodation.

OKEHAMPTON
PLYMOUTH INN, 26 West Street.
TEL: 01837 53633.
16th century coaching inn in the small market town close to Dartmoor. Excellent home-cooking using local produce, Mexican, English and French. Lovely family room has been attractively furnished, children may eat in the restaurant where they have their own menu. Full bar menu. Take-away pizza service. Open all year. Children welcome. All major cards except Amex & Switch. Vegetarians catered for.

THE BARTON, Belstone.
Tel: 01837 840371.
This is the quintessential Dartmoor village tea shop, situated in an idyllic position in the heart of Belstone Village. Renowned for it's cream teas and delicious home-made cakes. It is recommended by the 'Ramblers Association' and featured in the 'Teapot trail'. Sunday lunches available but must be booked in advance. Open all year summer 2-6pm, winter2-5pm. Children welcome. Licensed for Sunday lunch. Accommodation.

Where to Eat

OTTERY ST MARY
OSWALDS, 25 Silver street.
Tel: 01404 812262.
Oswalds is an old stone building, lying adjacent to the magnificence of St Mary's, the parish church. A congenial French restaurant offering a wide ranging menu enhanced by an interesting use of sauces, many flavoured with fruit and other original ingredients. The result is memorable eating. Open Mon-Sat 7pm Lunch by appointment. Children welcome. Visa/Master/Diners/Amex. Vegetarian on request.

PLYMOUTH
PIERMASTERS RESTAURANT, The Barbican.
Tel: 01752 229345.
Just 10 minutes from the city centre, on the historic Barbican, is this charming restaurant and bistro. Excellent cuisine, you will not be disappointed either in the service provided, or the food consumed. Open all year, lunch and evening meal. Children welcome. All major cards. Vegetarians catered for.

ROCKBEARE
ORIENTAL PROMISE, Old London Road.
Tel: 01404 823323/823328 Fax: 01404 823203.
Wonderful oriental restaurant serving the most delicious food, Peking, Szechaun, Cantonese and Far East. You can have a set meal which can be varied to suite individual taste, or simply choose from the extensive menu. Superb. Open for luch & evening meal except Tuesday. Children welcome. All major cards. Vegetarians catered for. Good take-away service.

SEATON
THE KETTLE RESTAURANT & BED AND BREAKFAST, 15 Fore Street.
Tel: 01297 20428.
This very homely restaurant was built around 1800 and is situated on the main street. Traditional English fare and Continental dishes. Open all year. Children welcome. No credit cards. Several dishes for vegetarians. Licensed. Accommodation.

SIDMOUTH
DI PAOLO'S RESTAURANT, Radway Place, Vicarage Road.
Tel: 01395 578314.
The finest Italian restaurant in East Devon is housed in a late 1800 Victorian building. The food is just superb, with a Tuscan influence. Being so close to the sea the seafood dishes are wonderful. Local produce is used as much as possible including fresh fish, meat and vegetables. Open lunch 12noon-2pm. Evenings 6.30-10pm(last order), Fri-Sat 6.30-10.30pm. Closed Mon. Children welcome. All major cards except Amex/Diners. Vegetarians catered for.

Chapter Twelve

TAVISTOCK
THE HARVEST HOME, Gulworthy.
Tel: 01822 611022.
This is such a welcoming pub in a delightful setting near Tavistock. A glassroofed, non-smoking family rooms with exposed beams. Best described as high quality, traditioan West Country Pub Fare. The menu changes daily and there are always very tasty Daily Specials. Open summer 11-11pm Sun 12-10.30pm. Oct-Apr 12-3pm & 6-11pm Sun 7-10.30pm no food Sun/Mon evenings in winter. Children welcome. All major cards. Bar food. Wide range of vegetarian dishes.

THE PETER TAVY INN, Peter Tavy.
Tel: 01822 810348.
A 15th century inn set on the Western fringe of Dartmoor just two milesnorth of the delightful market town of Tavistock. The food served is rapidly acquiring a fine reputation. Everything from fish to venison and cheese is local and the vegetables are grown in the South Hams. The menu is mouthwatering and delicious. Open all year summer Mon-Thurs 11.30-2.30pm, Fri & Sat 11.30-3pm, Sun 12-3pm. Eve Mon-Sat 6.30-11pm Sun 7-10.30pm. Winter Mon-Thurs 12-2.30pm, Fri-Sun 12-3pm. Children accompanied by adults. All major cards except Diners/Amex. Vegetarian and other diets catered for. Accommodation.

THE ROYAL STANDARD, Mary Tavy.
Tel: 01822 810289.
The Royal Standard has stood since the 16th century and at one time had a miners' cottage attached to it. It is a comfortable, popular pub with chunky pine tables, a roaring log fire and an attractive bar. The reputation for taditional pub fare grows steadily, there is an extensive vegetarian selection and everyday the Specials Board announces one or another of ones favourite dishes. Open 11-2.30pm & 6.30-11pm. Children welcome. No credit cards. Garden. Disabled access.

TOTNES
ANNE OF CLEVES LICENSED TEA ROOMS & RESTAURANT,
56 Fore Street.
Tel: 01803 863186.
Originally an ex-sea captains house built about 400 years ago it still retains the exposed beams and timber joists. When you walk in you are welcomed by the restful ambiance created by the antique furniture and fresh flowers. Wide selection of delicious dishes catering for all tastes. Home-made cakes and scones for cream teas. Traditional Sunday Roasts. Open Mon-Sat 9.15-5.30pm Sun 10.30-5.30pm. Children welcome, own section in menu. No credit cards. At least 5 vegetarian dishes. Licensed.

COPPA DOLLA INN & RESTAURANT, Bradhempston, Nr Totnes.
Tel: 01803 812455.
The charm of this delightful inn is undoubted but it is enhanced by the blissful absence of any form of machine or pool table. The bars are alsways busy and welcoming. It is a perfect atmosphere in which to enjoy the top of the range cuisine, including an A La Carte menu, varied home-cooked bar meals, snacks and a choice of six excellent vegetarian dishes. Open 11.30-2.30pm

& 6.30-11pm. Children in dining areas only. Visa/Master. Lovely garden. 2 luxury apartments.

THE RED SLIPPER, Stoke Gabriel.
Tel: 01803 782315.
The Red Slipper is situated in the heart of the charming, unspoilt village of Stoke Gabriel, and is pleasing guest house and restaurant. Serving traditional English fayre and is open for morning coffee, lunch, afternoon teas, evening meals and Sunday Lunches, (booking is essential for evening meals and Sunday lunch). Open all year. Children welcome. No credit cards. Vegetarians catered for. Garden. Accommodation.

DORSET

BLANDFORD FORUM
TANNERS RESTAURANT, 13/15 West Street.
Tel: 01258 453233.
Situated in West Street close to the English Tourist Board stands Tanners Restaurant, where fodd has been served since 1906. Margaret and David Bunch offer a pleasant and friendly atmosphere, where the service is attentive. All dishes are traditionally British, and offer a set luncheon, all day breakfasts, a wide and tasty choice of grills and vegetarian dishes. Home-made cakes and a Dorset Cream Tea. Open 9.30-6.30. Closed Mondays. Sun 10.30-6.30pm. Children welcome. No creadit cards. Licensed.

DURHAM

BARNARD CASTLE
THE MORRITT ARMS HOTEL, Greta Bridge, Rokeby.
Tel: 01833 627232.
Charles Dickens stayed here when he was researching 'Nicholas Nickleby'. Reomantic and unspoilt, the food is imaginative both in the restaurant and the bar. Open 24 hours. Children welcome. All major cards. Always several choices for vegetarians.
Price Band B

DARLINGTON
THE COACHMAN HOTEL & LAS CAROZZA RESTAURANT,
Victoria Road.
Tel: 01325 286116.
Charming hotel with a restaurant that is renowned in the area. Open all year. Children welcome. All major cards. Vegetarians catered for. Price Band B

WALWORTH CASTLE HOTEL
Tel: 01325 485470.
Unique hotel in 12th century castle. Excellent food, bars, entertainment. Open all year. Children welcome. All major cards. Vegetarians catered for. Price Band: B

Chapter Twelve

DURHAM
CENTURION INN, Firs Terrace, Langley Park.
Tel: 0191 373 1323.
3 miles from Durham, this is an interesting inn which is very different. Converted from a large house, it is welcoming and friendly and has two talented chefs who produce delicious and imaginative food both in the restaurant and bar. Open 12-3pm & 6-11pm. Mastercard/Visa/Barclaycard. Vegetarian dishes. Children welcome - half portions. Price Band: A

MIDDLETON-IN-TEESDALE
THE TEESDALE HOTEL, Market Square.
Tel: 01833 640264.
Located in the heart of the majestic and colourful High Pennines, possessing the highest and perhaps most dramatic peaks of the whole Pennine range. Family run hotel that once was a coaching inn. Delicious food, tasty Bar Meals, Daily Specials, Morning Coffee, Afternoon Tea. Open all hours. Children welcome. All major cards. Several dishes for vegetarian. Price Band A

STRATHMORE
ARMS INN, Holwick.
Tel: 01833 640362.
Attractive inn in an old lead mining hamlet. Wonderfully remote but easily accessible in an area of the North Pennines of outstanding beauty. Home-prepared food, local ingredients. A little different to normal. Open 12 noon-11pm. Children welcome in room at side of bar. No credit cards. 2-3 vegetarian dishes daily. 2 bedrooms not ensuite. Ideal for families. Price Band: A

GLOUCESTERSHIRE

BIBURY'
THE SWAN
Tel: 01285 740695.
17th century Cotswold stone coaching inn. Attractive gardens by the river. Fishing. Beautifully cooked and presented food both at lunch and dinner. Children welcome. All major credit cards. Open all year. Vegetarians catered for. Price Band: B/C
BOURTON-ON-THE-WATER
THE MOUSETRAP INN, Lansdowne.
Tel: 01451 20579.
This old fashioned pub has a major plus - a car park, something that is like gold dust in Bourton. Good, well kept beer and home-cooked food including the specialities 'Desperate Dans Cow Pie' and Rabbit Pie. Friendly, unpretentious and sensible prices. Bed and Breakfast available. Children welcome. No credit cards. Open: 12-3pm & 6.30-11pm. Vegetarians dishes. Price Band: A

THE OLDE CHARM, 1, The Chestnuts.
Tel: 01451 20244.
Charming 300 year old restaurant with unobtrusive, friendly service. Food is available all day, the hours depending on the time of the year. Excellent

Where to Eat

home-made soups, fresh salads, succulent roast meats and a selection of desserts. Cotswold Cream Tea very popular. The bedrooms are beautifully appointed and en suite. Access/Visa/Amex/Diners. Children welcome but no under 5 facilities. Open: approx 10.30am-9.30pm. Price Band: A/B

CHEDWORTH
THE SEVEN TUNS, Queen Street.
Tel: 01285 720242.
Small 17th century pub - the small lounge bar only seats 16-18. Charming walled water garden. Simple, good pub fare with the emphasis on steaks at night. Great value for money. Open: 12-2.30pm 6.30-11pm. Closed Monday lunch in winter. No credit cards. Well behaved children welcome. Usually 2 dishes for vegetarians. Price Band: A/B

CHELTENHAM
THE KINGS HEAD, Church Road, Bishops Cleeve, Cheltenham
Tel: 01242 673260. 3 miles from Cheltenham on the A435 Evesham road, this wonderful old thatched 16th century inn is a listed building standing next tot a tithe barn and believed to be the oldest inhabited building in the village. No restaurant but delicious 'Daily Specials' and snacks served in the busy bar. Open: 11-2.30pm & 6-11pm. Children not allowed in bar area. Beer garden. No credit cards. 2 dishes for vegetarians. Price Band: A

CHIPPING CAMDEN
THE SEYMOUR HOUSE HOTEL, High Street.
Tel: 01386 840429.
Lovely mellow building, with all sorts of interesting shapes in the beautifully appointed rooms. Delicious food at all times, morning coffee and afternoon tea. Open all year. Children welcome. All major credit cards. Vegetarians catered for. Price Band: B

FRAMPTON MANSELL
THE CROWN HOTEL, Frampton Mansell, Nr Stroud.
Tel: 01285 760601 Fax: 01285 760681.
Parts of this fascinating building date back to 1595. It is tucked away in the corner of the village looking out over a magnificent valley. You would bedifficult to please if you did not enjoy the traditional home-made food which includes Pan Fried Liver and Onions, Gloucester Sausage served with Bubble and Squeak and Poached Fillet of Salmon with Hollandaise Sauce. Bread and Butter Pudding is another favourite with diners. Children welcome. All major cards except AMEX. Price Band: A/B

GLOUCESTER
FLEECE HOTEL, 19 Westgate Street.
Tel: 01452 522762.
Modernised Tudor coaching inn with 12th century vaulted crypt. Good food, sensible prices. Access/Visa/AMEX. Children welcome. Vegetarians catered for. Price Band: A

Chapter Twelve

MORETON-IN-MARSH
THE MARSHMALLOW RESTAURANT, High Street.
Tel: 01608 651536.
This charming restaurant has many accolades one such being the Good Food Guide and another being voted tea shop of the year 1993/4. It is open for morning coffee, lunches, afternoon teas, candlit suppers and traditional Sunday lunch. The food is superb quality and meticulously prepared. Open 7 days & 5 nights. Children welcome. No credit cards. Vegetarian and special diets catered for. Licensed.

NEWLAND
THE OSTRICH, Nr Coleford.
Tel: 01594 33260.
Charming village pub, no juke boxes, no one armed bandits but superior quality food with normally a choice of ten dishes including local specialities Venison Pie and Game Casserole. Wide choice of bar snacks. Attractive walled garden. Open: Mon-Sat 11.30-3pm &6-11pm. Sun 12-3pm & 7-10.30pm. Children welcome in the restaurant and garden. No credit cards. Vegetarian dishes. Price Band: A/B

NORTH NIBLEY
THE BLACK HORSE INN
Tel: 01453 546841 Fax: 01453 547474.
16th century true village inn which opens its welcoming doors with the same friendliness to strangers as it does to those who come in regularly for a pint and a chat, a good meal or a game of dominoes. You will find it on the B4060 midway between the old market towns of Dursley and Wotton-under-Edge. Full of old world charm the pub offers an extensive lunchtime and evening menu from good home-cooked dishes to light bar snacks. Try their home-made mushroom soup - it will be hard to find its equal. Children permitted if eating. All major cards. Price Band: A/B

STOW-ON-WOLD
OLD STOCKS HOTEL, The Square.
Tel: 01451 830666 Fax: 01451 870014.
A Grade II Listed 16th-17th century building enhanced by the mellow Cotswold stone of the period. The restaurant offers a wide variety of dishes including those for vegetarians which will tempt even the most jaded palate. The chef is always happy to produce something special for a child. Good range of bar food. Children welcome. Visa/MasterCard. Price Band: A/B

THE ROYALIST, Digbeth Street.
Tel: 01457 830470.
The oldest building in Stow and features in the Guinness Book of Records as the oldest inn in England dating from 947AD. It is a Grade II Listed building of both architectural and historical interest. The 'Coffee Shop' is open from 10am-5.30pm serving tasty home-made bar food. Children welcome. Visa/MasterCard.
Price Band: A/B

Where to Eat

GRAPEVINE HOTEL, Sheep Street.
Tel: 01451 830344 Fax: 01451 832278.
Delightful award winning hotel where nothing is too much trouble. Dinner 7pm-9.30pm, Bar Meals 12-2pm & 7-9pm. Closed Christmas Eve - January 12th. English and French haute cuisine. Daily changing menu. The bar serves a delicious selection of unusual dishes. Children welcome. No dogs. Afternoon teas. No smoking restaurant. All major credit cards. Vegetarian dishes. Price Band: C

TETBURY
THE TROUBLE HOUSE INN, Cirencester Road.
Tel: 01666 502206. 17th century inn with fascinating history plus a friendly ghost. Traditional and friendly. Serves good casserole and Indian curries at night. No cooked meals on Sundays. Open: 11-2.30pm &6-11pm. Children welcome. Large garden and field to play in. No credit cards. 4 dishes for vegetarians. Price Band: A/B

TEWKESBURY
THE ABBEY MILL, Mill Street.
Tel: 01684 292287.
Originally built in the 8th century, The Abbey Mill belongs to the past but today it still has the same charm even though the interior has given way to a modern comfortable restaurant. The food is wonderful with many themed nights including Medieval Banquets!. It is beautifully run and will never disappoint. Open all year for banquets & restaurants, Tea Shop & Patio Easter-September. No credit cards. Children welcome. Vegetarians catered for. Disabled access in summer only via Tea Shop.

UPPER ODDINGTON
THE HORSE AND GROOM, Upper Oddington, Nr Stow-on-the-Wold. This 16th century inn is as charming inside as it is out. Very much the focal centre of the village - you will find regulars at the bar every day. Everyone is made to feel welcome. Good traditional food comes out of the immaculate kitchen which offers everything from fresh fish to game in season. The bar menu suggests home-cooked daily. Specials as well as the simpler freshly cut sandwich. Children welcome. All major cards except AMEX and Diners. Price Band: A/B

HAMPSHIRE

BARTON-ON-SEA
THE VENTANA, Marine Drive.
Tel: 01425 610309.
This friendly pub run by the Blanksby family stands literally on the edge of a cliff giving it one of the best pub views in England. To the east is Hurst Castle, to the south east the Isle of Wight and the Needles, on the west is Hengesbury Head and Swanage. The emphasis is on a warm welcome and quality products and value for money. Home-cooked traditional but slightly adventurous food is on the menu. There are always vegetarian dishes and small meals for children. There is a Play Area and a Barbecue which seats 40. Visa/Mastercard only. Price Band A

Chapter Twelve

BROCKENHURST
THE THATCHED COTTAGE HOTEL & RESTAURANT,
16 Brookley Road.
Tel: 01590 623090 Fax: 01590 623479.
This very pretty hotel has a charming Tea Garden where in summer the tables have lace tablecloths and napkins and are protected by umbrellas. The hotel specialises in a complete English Breakfast and their famous afternoon teas, complete with a three tier cake stand. It has the accolade of being voted by the English Tourist Board, one of the best cream teas in the south of England. In the evening exquisite culinary delights are freshly prepared by 'Chefs on Show' in thier open kitchen. A gourmet table d'hote menu complimented by a selection of fine wines and beverages, is set in a unique and casual atmosphere by romantic cnadlelight. Children welcome. Visa/Mastercard. Price Band: A/B

THE SNAKE CATCHER, Lyndhurst Road.
Tel: 01590 622348.
Interesting pub with strange tale about the name. Wide range, exciting dishes, value for money. Open all year. Visa/Mastercard. Children welcome. Vegetarians catered for. Price Band A

CHERITON
THE JOLLY FARMER, Petersfield Road.
Tel: 01962 771252.
Next to National Trust property, Hinto Ampner on the A272 Winchester to Petersfield Road, 6 miles outside Winchester. Hospitalbe, small tasty menu which includes a Beef stew and a Hot Pot that would be hard to equal for miles around. Accommodation available. No credit cards. Children to eat only. Vegetarian dishes on request. Price Band: A

DAMERHAM
THE COMPASSES INN, Nr Fordingbridge.
Tel: 017253 231. Friendly 16th century coaching inn on the village green. Damerham is a Conservation Area on the edge of the New Forest. An extensive, beautifully cooked and presented menu makes food a must here. Real fires in winter, large garden for summer. Accommodation. Open 11-2.30pm & 6-11pm. Sat 11-11pm. Visa/Mastercard. Well behaved children welcome. Vegetarian choice. Price Band: A/B

EAST MEON
YE OLDE GEORGE INN, Church Street.
Tel: 01730 87481.
Freehouse with origins dating back to the 13th century. From May-September open all day and in addition to the bars and restaurant, both serving fresh and imaginative food, you can call in for a Cream Tea. Mastercard/Visa. Children in play area. 6 plus dishes for vegetarians. Ensuite accommodation. Price Band: A/B

EMSWORTH
THE BLUE BELL INN, 29 South Street.
Tel: 01243 373394.
This delightful inn is within 100 yards of Emsworth Harbour and Mill Pond

Where to Eat

and is a Mecca for many people who live in the area and who have discovered the warm, genuine welcome offered by Tom Babb and his partner Jackie. Fish is the main dish in various formshowever, there are plenty of good tried and trusted favourites included in the menu. Daily Specials Blackboard. Open all year. Well behaved children welcome. No credit cards. Limited wine list. Vegetarians catered for.

THE CROWN HOTEL, High Street.
Tel: 01243 372806 Fax: 01243 370082.
Jester's Restaurant, with it's comfortable and pleasant surroundings, offers an exciting International menu and comprehensive wine list. For a more informal meal or snack the buffet bar has outstanding reputation for serving home-made quality fayre at inexpensive prices. The hotel is situated in the idyllic harbourside village of Emsworth whcih encompasses a wealth of fishing, boat building, sailmaking and leisure pastimes and experiences. Children welcome. Major credit cards. Price Band: A/B

36 ON THE QUAY, South Street.
Tel: 01243 375592.
This is probably the best restaurant between Birghton and Southampton. The dining room of this yachting village cottage is full of surprises. What appears to be a bookcase opens to reveal a door to the wine cellar - with over 200 excellent wines from eleven pounds to one hundred and fifty pounds. The very grand cooking is executed with an ease that speaks of the true professional. There are courses of amuse-bouches and friandises and between them lightly fried scallops and bacon with herb noodles, salmon with olive oil dressing, and potato souffle with superb smoke salmon. If you enjoy sauces there are no better in the county especially with meat dishes. You really should try the Grand Marnier souffle afterwards. The service is perfection though a trifle pretentious - but who can fault this standard of excellence. Price Band C

FACCOMBE
THE JACK RUSSELL INN, Faccombe, Nr Andover.
Tel: 01264 737315.
Friendly pub 1,000ft above sea level on a privately owned estate. Opposite the manor house overlooking the village pond. Attractive food at affordable prices. Freehouse. Open all year. Children welcome to eat in conservatory. BBQs & Pig Roasts in summer. All major cards. Vegetarians catered for. Price Band: A

FORDINGBRIDGE
LIONS COURT RESTAURANT & HOTEL, 29-31 High Street.
Tel: 01425 652006.
Fine food and accommodation in a classic. 17th century English setting with gardens extending down to the River Avon. The area around Lions Court is rich in interest and activities. Delightful place. Children welcome. Visa/Amex/Diners/Mastercard. Price Band: B

Chapter Twelve

GREATHAM
THE SILVER BIRCH INN, Petersfield Road, Nr Liss.
Tel: 01420 538262.
The food is plentiful, tasty and true good pub food. Friendly, welcoming landlords. For Golfers there are three courses nearby. Open 11-2.30pm & 5.30-11pm. No credit cards. Children to eat and in garden. Vegetarian dishes on request. Price Band: A

HAMBLE
THE VILLAGE TEA ROOMS, High Street.
Tel: 01703 455583.
The present owner, Christina Pullen, is a skilled and enthusiastic cook whovirtually cooks or bakes everything she serves. Her pastry is melt in the mouth and her cakes are irresistible and the scones are freshly baked served either with jam and cream or jam and butter or just butter. Delicious. It is AA recommended and also by the 1993 'Lets Stop for Tea' and the 1995 'That Tea Room'. Open all year. Children welcome. No credit cards.

HIGHCLERE
THE YEW TREE, Hollington Cross, Andover Road, Nr Newbury.
Tel: 01635 253360.
Highclere Castle is a mile away. For over 350 years travellers have been beating a path to this good inn. It is full of character and the food is superb. In the Restaurant the menu is fresh, cosmopolitan and traditional fare. In the Bar there are sandwiches and a range of Platters etc. It is a place that delights all who visit it. Open: 11-3pm &5.30-11pm. Children welcome. Visa/Euro/Mastercard. Vegetarian dishes. Price Band:A/B

HORDLE
ORDLETON MILL HOTEL & PROVENCE RESTAURANT,
Silver St, Nr Lymington.
Tel: 01590 682219.
This privately owned hotel is a 17th century water mill house which has been sympathetically restored, extended and refurbished. The riverside location is spectacular with grounds that extend to five and a half acres on the banks of the River Avon Water. The nationally acclaimed Provence style dining room serves superb meals. During the summer months, breakfast and luncheon are served from the terrace, whcih also makes the perfect spot in which to take evening aperitifs whilst watching the fish jump. Children over 10 years. All major credit cards. Price Band: B

LYNDHURST
THE NEW FOREST INN, Emery Down.
Tel: 01703 282329.
Delightfully situated in the heart of the New Forest, the Inn has an unusual history, in the early 1700s, before a licence to sell beer was necessary, the story goes that a caravan stood on this site having claimed squatter's rights. The caravan now forms all of the front lounge porchway and the inn has been extended on either side. Open all year for Bed and Breakfast and has excellent food at sensible prices. Price band: A

Where to Eat

THE CROWN STIRRUP, Clay Hill.
Tel: 01703 282272.
Mark & Kim Pycroft welcome you to this historic 15th century inn. The name relates to the King's law regarding the size of dogs. During Tudor times only the King and his entourage went into the forest to hunt. The Commoners were allowed only if their dogs were small enough to fit through the 'Verderers Stirrup'. Very popular pub, good fun and excellent food. Regular theme evenings are well attended and you should make sure you book in good time. Tuesday Music evenings are also a great hit. Please ask for a programme of events. Children welcome. This is essentially a value for money pub. Price Band: A

FOX AND HOUNDS INN, 22 High Street.
Tel: 01703 282098.
15th century coaching inn. Black and white building full of charm. Open all year. Children welcome. Visa/Mastcard. Vegetarians catered for. Price Band: A

LYMINGTON
THE RED LION INN, Boldre.
Tel: 01590 673177.
This pretty black and white, flower bedecked inn is as welcoming inside as it appears on approach. Attractively furnished it is a good place to make for if you want a meal in the New Forest. Children welcome. Price Band: A/B

THE TOLLHOUSE INN, 167 Southampton Road.
Tel: 01590 672142.
Charming 17th century country pub serving some of the best pub food in Hampshire. Freshly cooked, reasonable. Open 11-3pm & 6-11pm. Visa/Mastercard. 4 dishes for vegetarians. Children welcome. Price Band: A/B

MINSTEAD
HONEYSUCKLE COTTAGE, Minstead, Nr Lyndhurst.
Tel: 01703 813122.
A thatched cottage in the heart of the New Forest conjures up a delightful picture and the reality is greater than the anticipation! Honeysuckle Cottage restaurant stands in one and a half acres of lovely grounds which also house the Honeypot Tea Rooms with seating for 40 inside and 40+ in the garden. The delicious varied menu which changes every ten weeks to allow for seasonal food, incorrorates all that is good in English cooking. The cakes and scones are wonderful. The Honeysuckle Cottage Restaurant has a set price for the three and four course menu, both of which are extremely good value for money. Children are welcome. Visa/Master. Price Band: B

NETLEY MARSH
THE WHITE HORSE, Ringwood Road, Woodlands, Southampton.
Tel: 01703 862166.
Traditional village pub about 200 years old. Good atmosphere and serves freshly prepared home-cooked food at reasonable prices. Sunday lunch is recommended. Vegetarian dishes. Children welcome. Visa/Master. Price Band: A

Chapter Twelve

RINGWOOD
THE LAMB INN, 2 Hightown Road.
Tel: 01425 473721.
250 year old inn where the landlords are quite prepared to rise early to give fishermen a substantial breakfast before they make for the first rise. Golf and horse racing vie with fishing in this friendly establishment. Bar food is available at all times; it is true pub grub, plentiful and inexpensive. Open: 11-3pm & 6-11pm. Children welcome. No credit cards. Vegetarian dishes on request. Price Band: A

ROMSEY
THE ABBEY HOTEL, Church Street.
Tel: 01794 513360 Fax: 01794 524318.
Bar meals daily except Sunday evenings. Sold by Henry VIII to the townspeople for one hundred pounds, Romsey Abbey was of some importance. Naturally there was an inn to service the many visitors, and the one you see today was built in 1880 on the site of its medieval predecessor. The original cellars and an underground passage to the Abbey are still there; it seems this may still be used by a spectral nun who likes to turn off the gas! The atmosphere upstairs is, however warm and convivial. After a good meal of home-cooking from a varied menu, relax by an open fire or in the colourful garden, watching the dragonflies over the stream. Children welcome. Car park. Visa/Master. Price Band: A

STROUD
THE SEVEN STARS INN, Winchester Road, Stroud, Nr Petersfield.
Tel: 01730 264122.
Owned by two welcoming and experienced publicans, Jake and Barbie Cable, this delightful inn has much to offer. Wonderful views, a designated area of 'Outstanding Natural Beauty', it is close to a number of tourist and leisure activities. Golfers will think they are in paradise! There are 15 golf courses within a 20 mile radius of the pub. Ther A La Carte menu and bar meals both offer a wide choice and everything is freshly cooked on the premises. Your choice extends from steak and grouse to moussaka and fish pie. Real ales come straight from the cask. Children welcome within the law. Mastercard/Visa/Switch. Price Band: A/B

WEST LISS
THE SPREAD EAGLE, Farnham Road.
Tel: 01730 892088.
Set in 3 acres it has a superb view of the 13th century church. The Grade II listed building dates partly from the 15th century. Even if the food here was not as good as it is and very reasonable the pub would still be a must for people visiting the area. Open: 11-3pm & 5-11pm. No credit cards. Children welcome. Always dishes for vegetarians. Price Band: A

WEST WELLOW
THE RED ROVER, Salisbury Road, Nr Romsey.
Tel: 01794 22266.
400 year old coaching inn. Full of character and impedimenta. Simple bar food, no restaurant. Master/Visa. Children allowed in the garden. 6 dishes for vegetarians. Open: 10.30-3pm & 6.30-11pm. Price Band: A

Where to Eat

WHITSBURY
THE CARTWHEEL INN, Nr Fordingbridge.
Tel: 017253 362.
Cosy pub with beams and open fires. Horseracing and training is the basic conversation in the bar - Whitsbury was the home of Desert Orchid. Extensive menu in restaurant and bar. Daily Specials. Crab, lobster and fish. Summer barbecues. Open: 11-2.30pm & 6-11pm. No food Tuesday evenings. Children in restaurant and garden only. Visa/Mastercard/Amex. 10 dishes for vegetarians. Price Band: A/B

WINCHESTER
THE ELIZABETHAN RESTAURANT, 18 Jewry Street.
Tel: 01962 853566.
Table d'hote, A La Carte, fixed price menu. Exciting food. Children welcome. All credit cards. Vegetarians catered for. Price Band: A/B

WOODLANDS
BUSKETTS LAWN HOTEL
Tel: 01703 292272.
Delightful family run country house hotel is near the village of Lyndhurst, eight miles west of Southampton. You eat either in The Crystal Room with its beautiful Italian chandeliers or in The Francis Room with its delightful garden aspect. An excellent table is offered, with fine homely cuisine served by cheerful and helpful staff. You are invited to take tea on the Terrace and snacks, teas and drinks are always available around the heated swimming pool, while poolside lunches, buffets and barbecues are held during summer. Children welcome. Al major credit cards. Price Band: Restaurant B Teas etc A

HEREFORDSHIRE

BISHOPS FROME
THE GREEN DRAGON.
Tel: 01885 490607.
If you are a traditionalist when it comes to pubs, this one you will enjoy. In the heart of hop farming country it has an oddly cosmopolitan air which blends in well with the past traditions of the area. Oak beams, flagstone floors and large fireplaces with roaring fires in winter. Real Ale and home-cooked food, especially pies. Open: 12-3pm & 5-11pm. Children welcome. Access/Visa. Several dishes for vegetarians. Price Band: A/B

GLEWSTONE
GLEWSTONE COURT HOTEL, Nr Ross-on-Wye.
Tel: 01989 770367 Fax: 01989 770282.
Spacious, elegant, Listed Country House in 3 acres. Half a mile off the A40 and 3 miles from the centre of Ross-on-Wye. Georgian Restaurant offers food of a very high standard. Bar meals would outshine most restaurants. All major credit cards. Price Band: B

Chapter Twelve

HEREFORD
GILBIES BISTRO, 4, St Peters Close, Commercial Street.
Tel: 01432 277863.
Modelled in many ways on the kind of Bistro you might find in any of the lager French of Spanish cities, the hours are flexible. Somewhere you can go early for breakfast if it is pre-arranged - have coffee, maybe a snack or a full meal throughout the day. The proprietor describes his food modestly as 'good but not great, at reasonable prices, eaten in a completely relaxed atmosphere'. The menu changes hour by hour and covers all styles of cuisine from steaks to kebabs - from fish to sea-food or simple snacks like bacon sandwiches through to New Zealand mussels. Open: 10am-11pm every day. Good children welcome. Visa/Access. At least 3 vegetarian dishes.
Price Band: A/B

KENTCHURCH
THE BRIDGE INN
TEL: 01981 230408.
Wonderful 400 year old building lying on the banks of Monnow River with a delightful riverside restaurant and a large geer garden. Nothing pretentious about the menu in the restaurant or the bar, just good, imaginative, home-made fare. Open: 11-2.30pm & 6-11pm. No credit cards. Always 4 dishes for vegetarians. Children welcome. Price Band: A/B

LEOMINSTER
THE BLACK HORSE COACH HOUSE, 74, South Street
Tel: 01568 611946.
This Listed building has its own brewery attached producing very good Real Ale. Excellent choice of home-made food at very reasonable prices. Open: 11-2.30pm & 6-11pm, sat 11-11pm. No credit cards. Several dishes for vegetarians. Children welcome. Price Band: A

MICHAELCHURCH ESCLEY
THE BRIDGE INN
Tel: 01981 23646. One of those story book places, situated at the foot of the Black Mountains between Hereford and Hay-on-Wye right by Escley Brook, surrounded by fields. In summer, customers can drink and dine outside watching the trout in the river. Some parts date back to 14th century. Tremendous atmosphere. Home-cooked fare by the Jean Draper, who is a talented chef using many of her own recipes, vegetarian ones in particular. Her Leek Croustade is a mega favourite. Open: 12-2.30pm & 7-11pm. Closed Mon lunch. Well behaved children welcome. No credit cards.
Price Band: A

PEMBRIDGE
THE NEW INN, Pembridge, Nr Leominster
13th century, all black and white painted brick on a massive stone base. Enchanting place with uneven stone floors, low beamed ceilings, roaring fires plus two ghosts!. Traditional home-made fare using local produce and as much game as possible in season. Bar food offers a wide range with Daily Specials including vegetarian dishes. No credit cards. Food available lunch and evening everyday. Price Band: A/B

Where to Eat

THE CIDER HOUSE RESTAURANT AT DUNKERTONS, Luntley
Tel: 01544 388161.
Described as 'the best restaurant between Chester and the Channel Islands'. Warm, friendly and beautiful with the emphasis on revival British Cooking. Lunch: everyday except Sunday. Open for coffee, tea, home-made cakes and biscuits, local ice cream and...Dunkertons delicious cider and perry on draught. 10am-6pm. Dinner: from 7.30pm Friday and Saturday evenings. Booking for dinner is essential.
Price Band: B

WEOBLEY
YE OLDE SALUTATION INN, Market Pitch
Tel: 01544 318443.
On the outside it is a black and white timber-framed building which dates back over 500 years. Inside it is delightful with a large inglenook fireplace, a comfortable lounge bar leading into 40 seater Oak Room restaurant. The food is of a very high standard and you can stay here in great comfort. Open: 11-3pm & 7-11pm. Children in eating area, lounge conservatory. MasterCard/Visa. 3/4 dishes daily for vegetarians. Price Band: B

ROSS-ON-WYE
THE CHASE HOTEL, Gloucester Road
Tel: 01989 763161 Fax: 01989 768330.
Handsome Regency Country House standing in own grounds, a few minutes walk from town centre. The chef favours a modern British approach with a continental influence and takes full advantage of the fine local produce. Bar snacks, cold buffet, vegetarian dishes. All major cards.
Price Band: B

PHEASANTS RESTAURANT, 52, Edde Cross Street
Tel: 01989 65751.
Once a tiny pub building this has now become an acclaimed testaurant with a Victorian style dining room with no more than a dozen tables, fronted by a dispense bar and a fireside lounge. Intimate dining both at lunch and in the evening on old English recipes makes this special. You can stay here, there are two rooms. A 10% discount on evening meals is offered to those staying. Open: Tues-Sat 12.30-2pm & 7-1-pm. Well behaved children welcome. AMEX/Access/Visa. Vegetarians catered for. Walled courtyard garden with pond in summer. Price Band: B

CLOISTERS WINE BAR, 24, High Street
Tel: 01989 67717.
This 18th century building stands out in the High Street because of the golry of its stained glass windows. The wealth of exposed beams and nooks and crannies make it a truly secluded and intimate restaurant full of olde worlde charm. The menu is full of gastronomic delights including some unusual fish, such as Parrot Fish, Sweet Lips, Monkfish and Groupa, if you are not adventurous there are steaks of all kinds with or without sauces. Wide selection of wines & beers. Open: Mon-Sun 6-11pm, Sat/Sun lunchtimes. No credit cards. 6 dishes for vegetarians. Difficult for the disabled. Price Band: A/B

Chapter Twelve

THE CROSS KEYS INN, Goodrich
Tel: 01600 890650/890203.
Traditional village pub complete with a resident ghost. Two friendly bars offering good simple Pub Fare. The pub has 5 double and 2 single rooms, not en suite. Price Band: A

NORFOLK

BRANCASTER STAITHE
THE LOBSTER POT, Main Road.
Tel: 01485 210262.
Charming fishing village with this very nice pub from which there ar stunning views. The restaurant overlooks the harbour, the salt marshes and Scuit Island. Specialise in sea food and fish but there are many other dishes always using fresh produce. Open: Summer 11-3pm & 6.30-11pm, Winter 11-2.30pm & 7-11pm. Children welcome. No credit cards. Several dishes for vegetarians. Price Band: B

BURNHAM MARKET
FISHES RESTAURANT, Market Place
Tel: 01328 738588.
Standing on the village green this 18th century building is a restaurant of great charm and character. Two simply furnished dining rooms have a vast open fire and bookcases full of the sort of books one might have at home. Specialising in fish, Gillian Cape, the owner, makes one of the best crab soups you will ever taste. It is a very special place. Children welcome. No credits cards. Several dishes for vegetarians. Price Band: B

THE LORD NELSON
Tel: 01328 738321. Friendly pub run by two talented people - Peter Jordan is a keen fungus hunter which provides the pub with some exciting offerings in the autumn when his findings become part to the menu. Valerie Jordan is a skilled artist and regular art exhibitions are held in the stables. Children welcome. Open: Mon-Sat 11.30-3pm & 7-11pm, Sun 12-3pm & 10.30pm. No credit cards. Price Band: A/B

COLKIRK
THE CROWN, Crown Road,Colkirk, Fakenham
Tel: 01328 862172. A pub for over 300 years but rebuilt after a fire. Friendly, comfortable and with a reputation for good food. The portions are generous and it is value for money. Open: 11-2.30pm & 6-11pm, Sun 12-2.30pm& 7-10.30pm. Access/Visa. Children welcome. Vegetariandishes. Price Band: A

DICKLEBURGH
THE KINGS HEAD, Norwich Road, Nr Diss
Tel: 01379 741481.
Welcoming, unpretentious pub with a ghost!. Three letting rooms. Probably the best Steak and Kidney Pie in the country. Surrounded by open ground which is available for 5 caravans and 10 tents. Open: 12-2pm & 7-10pm. Children welcome. No credit cards. Vegetarian dishes on request. Price Band: A

Where to Eat

GORLESTON
THE CLIFF HOTEL, Cliff Hill
Tel: 01493 662179 Fax: 01493 653617. Attractive 3 star hotel is open to non-residents and offers good quality traditional dishes. Children welcome. All major cards. Price Band: B

THE PIER HOTEL, Harbourmouth
Tel:01493 662631 Fax: 01493 440263.
Overlooking sandy beach, open to non-residents. A la carte and table d'hote. Fish a speciality. Wide range of bar meals and for vegetarians. Children welcome, high chairs and childrens menu. All major cards. Price Band: B

GT RYBURGH
THE BOAR INN, Gt Ryburgh, Fakenham
Tel:01328 829212.
Sitting on the suntrapped patio of the delightful inn looking out on the garden, enjoying a good lunch on a summer's day, is one of life's great pleasures. Inside the 300 year old pub is full of warmth and character. Food of an International flavour is served at lunch and in the evening 7 days a week. Well known locally it has a deserved repution. Childrens meals. Access/Master/Visa/Barclaycard/Euro. Always five dishes plus salads for vegetarians. Price Band: A/B

GT YARMOUTH
THE GALLON POT, 1-2 Market Place
Tel: 01493 842230.
Amusing pub offering good food at sensible prices plus afternoon tea which far exceeds most. Children welcome. No credit cards. Limited dishes for vegetarians. Price Band: A/B

THE IMPERIAL HOTEL, North Drive
Quite seafront location. The intimate Rambouille Restaurant offers table d'hote and a la carte menus with wide range of dishes to appeal to the gourmet and the more traditional diner. Bar food available for those who want quick service and tasty dishes. All major cards. Children welcome. Dishes for vegetarians. Price Band: B

HAPPISBURGH
THE HILL HOUSE
Tel: 01692 650004. Friendly old coaching inn dating back to the 16th century. It was a favourite retreat of Sir Arthur Conan Coyal. Full of character, oak beams, large fireplaces. Here you can relish Real Ales at their best, good home-cooked meals which are substantial and reasonablypriced with a sea view thrown in. Children welcome. Visa/Access/AMEX. 2 dishes for vegetarians. Price Band: A/B

HEVINGHAM
THE MARSHAM ARMS HOTEL
Has a newsletter of its own edited by the inn's proprietor, Nigel Bradley. Anyone unfamiliar with this excellent hostelry cannot fail to pick up some of the enthusiasm as you read its humourous message. The food in the bar or in Bradley's Restaurant is excellent with a wide choice and sensibly priced.

Chapter Twelve

There are 8 self-contained study bedrooms, all en suite and beautifully furnished. Open: 11-3pm &6-11pm. Children allowed in certain areas. Visa/Access. Many varied vegetarian dishes. Price Band: B

HORNING
PETERSFIELD HOUSE HOTEL
Tel: 01692 630741 Fax: 01692 630745.
Elegant, comfortable, family run 18 bedroomed hotel, open to non-residents. Impressive restaurant overlooking the garden. High standard of cuisine both a la carte and table d'hote. Saturday night Dinner Dances a major attraction. Children welcome. All major cards. Several dishes for vegetarians. Price Band: B

KINGS LYNN
THE PARK VIEW HOTEL, Blackfriars street
Tel: 01553 775146 Fax: 01553 766957.
Unfussy 47 bedroom hotel. The bar is welcoming and serves both traditional ale and good, inexpensive bar snacks and meals. The 52 seater Edwardian restaurant offers a wide range of dishes, beautifully presented and at sensible prices. Children welcome. All major cards. Several dishes for vegetarians. Price Band: A/B

THE ROCOCO RESTAURANT, 11 Saturday Market Place
Tel: 01553 771483.
Situated next to the Guildhall, the building is 300 years old and has panache. The food is of the highest quality as are the wines. Comfortable lounge for morning coffee, light lunches and afternoon teas. Dinner is a gastronomic delight. It is not cheap but it is money well spent. Open: Mon Dinner 7pm, Tues-Sat 10-3pm Dinner 7pm, Sun 12-3pm. Booking advisable. Afternoon teas May-September. Price Band: B

LODDON
THE LODDON SWAN INN, Church Plain
Tel: 01508 20239.
Fascinating history here. Good home-made food. Unpretentious. Book for Sunday lunch - one of the best in Norfolk. Open: 11-3pm & 6.30-11pm, Sun 12-3pm &7-10.30pm. Children welcome. Visa/Access/JCB. 2 dishes for vegetarians. Price Band: A/B

NEATISHEAD
BARTON ANGLER COUNTRY INN, Irestead Road
Tel: 01693 630740. 500 years old and once a rectory, this is a welcoming, informal establishment. Menu best described as 'English Country House Cuisine with a slight French influence'. It is certainly delicious food. Children welcome. AMEX/Visa/Master. 2 dishes +salads for vegetarians.

NORTH WALSHAM
SCARBOROUGH HILL HOUSE HOTEL, Old Yarmouth Road
Tel:01692 402151 Fax: 01692 402151.
Open to non-residents and set in a 4 acres of gardens this is a charming spot and within easy reach of The Broads and sandy beaches. The menu is varied and encompasses a range of dishes, mainly English at its best but with a

Where to Eat

touch of French and the East. Everything is freshly cooked. Bar meals are prepared daily. Vegetarians will find at 2 dishes. Children welcome. Access/Visa/Diners/AMEX. Price Band: A/B

NORWICH
BEECHES HOTEL & VICTORIAN GARDENS, 4-6 Earlham Road
Tel: 01603 621167 Fax: 01603 620151.
Restaurant offers an interesting menu with an Italian bias but using mostly fresh local produce and cooked to order at modest prices. Children welcome. High Chairs. All major cards. 2 dishes for vegetarians. Price Band: B

BRASTEDS RESTAURANT, St Andrews Hill
Tel: 01603 625949 Fax: 01603 766445.
Here John Brasted will invite you to enjoy what can only be described as a culinary experience. Customers will tell you that part of the pleasure of eating here is to experience the peculiarly welcoming and friendly atmosphere that emits from the ghost who has haunted 8-10 St. Andrews Hill since the 17th century. Children welcome. Visa/Access/AMEX/Diners. Good selection for vegetarians. No lunch Saturdays. Closed Sundays. Price Band: B/C

ST BENEDICTS RESTAURANT, 9 St Benedicts Street
Tel: 01603 765337.
Busy city centre restaurant in a bustlin street full of atmosphere. You sit on church pews, choose your food from a blackboard, changed daily which temps the most jaded palate. Well chosen wine list. All at affordable prices. Closed Sunday & Monday. Children welcome. All major cards. Vegetarian choice.

REEDHAM
REEDHAM FERRY INN
Tel: 01493 700429.
Well maintained late 16th century inn alongside working car ferry. The pub is full of fascinating memorabilia. Varied menu including game in season, prime meats, fresh produce and home grown herbs. Open: Summer 11-3pm & 6.30-11pm, Sun 12-3pm, Winter 11-2.30pm & 7-10.30pm. Access/Visa. Children in Sun Lounge or restaurant until 9pm. 3 dishes for vegetarians. Wide doorways for the disabled. Price Band: A/B

WELLS-NEXT-THE-SEA
THE GLOBE INN, The Butlands
Tel: 01328 710206.
Busy, much sought after pub run with efficiency and charm. Steaks are the speciality of the house but there is a good choice. Full bar menu and snacks. Open: 10.30-11pm. No credit cards. Several dishes for vegetarians. Children welcome in Pool room. 4 letting rooms. Price Band: A

WROXHAM
THE BROADS HOTEL, Station Road
Tel: 01603 782869 Fax: 01603 784066.
Much used by local people, the bars are fun and the a la carte and carvery restaurant is of a very high standard. Children welcome. All major cards. 5 vegetarian dishes daily. Price Band: A/B

Chapter Twelve

OXFORDSHIRE

BLEDINGTON
THE KINGS HEAD INN, The Green.
Tel: 01608 568365 Fax: 01608 658365.
This is one of the most picturesque village in The Cotswolds on the Oxford/Gloucester border 4 miles from Stow-in-the-Wold. It is everything that a 15th century inn should be facing the village green, complete with brook and friendly ducks. It has a high reputation for its excellent cuisine. Game of all kinds features largely on the menu. The starters are imaginative, delicious fish simply cooked is very popular and for those who want a simple meal in the bar there is a wide choice at sensible prices. A cosmopolitan selection of good quality wines, competitively priced is the icing on the cake. A marvellous base for a meal, a holiday or a short break. Children welcome. Mastercard/Switch/Visa. Price Band: B/A

BURFORD
THE ANGEL INN, Witney Road.
Tel: 01993 822438.
In just a few inspired years Jean Thaxter has become recognised as the owner of one of the most atractive and exciting small inns in the Cotswolds. Its charm lies in the atmospheric interior which will not have changed much in the 400 years it has been in existence. Low ceilings, a roaring log fire, beams, nooks and crannies make it a delightful meeting place for those who want to enjoy good wine in old world surroundings or to cross the stone flagged floor to eat in the small, intimate restaurant which is run rather like a good bistro than a stuffy dining room. Fish and Game are the specialities of The Angel. Children over 7 years. Mastercard/Visa. Price Band: B

CHARLBURY
THE BULL, Sheep Street.
Tel: 01608 810689.
16th century coaching inn tastefull restored. Traditional home-made English food comes to the table in a whole range of dishes, sometimes the expected and sometimes innovative. Children welcome. Visa/Mastercard. Price Band: B/A

CHIPPING NORTON
THE WHITE HART HOTEL, High Street.
Tel: 01608 642572 Fax: 01608 644143.
Behind the 18th century facade lies an inn with 13th century origins. The whole atmosphere is one of friendliness and a desire to please. The bar and restaurant are popular with people who live locally. Good food which you choose from colourfully chalked blackboards, offering a range of dishes and well chosen wines from around the world, make eating a pleasure. It is the perfect place for morning coffee or afternoon tea. Children welcome. All major cards. Price Band: B/A

CLIFTON
THE DUKE OF CUMBERLAND'S HEAD, Clifton, Nr Deddington.
Tel: 01869 338534.
Over 300 years old this atmospheric establishment is wonderful. Walk through the main entrance and the smell of logs burning in the big fireplace plus the

air of well being that pervades the inn, and you will recognise that you have found somewhere that will remain in your memory as one of the good things of life. The food is very French with international overtones. Beautifully cooked and presented at sensible prices, you may eat in the candlelit restaurant or in the low, beamed bar. Lunchtime Blackboard Specials and a traditional Sunday lunch. No food Sunday evenings and the restaurant is closed on Monday evenings. Well subscribed Themed evenings attract people from as far away as Wales and the Fens to enjoy the fun and the feast. Children welcome. Visa/Master. Price Band: B/C

DUNSTEW
THE WHITE HORSE INN
Tel: 01869 40272 Fax: 01869 47732. 17th century quiet inn off the beaten track. Excellent, sensibly priced and freshly prepared food. Ideal venue for a weekend away or an evening out; a business lunch or a simple drink with friends. Children welcome. Master/Visa. Price Band: B

KINGSTON LISLE
THE BLOWING STONE INN
Tel: 01367 820288.
Friendly, charming establishment with the most welcoming of landlords, David and Ann Fearn. Pretty conservatory restaurant, two attractive lounges and lively public bar. The food in the restaurant is very special with imaginative dishes on offer according to the season and availablity. Peace and fun just fifteen minutes off the M4. You take the B4507 between Ashbury and Wantage where a left turn will take you into the village. Children welcome in restaurant. All major cards except Diners. Price Band: B/A

LOWER BRAILLES
THE GOERGE HOTEL
Tel: 01608 685223.
Much has happened at The Goerge throughout 7 centuries and as one dines on good food and drinks fine wines it is wonderful to dwell on the past whilst savouring the food of the present. Fresh home-cooked food is served all the year round. Fresh fish is prominent on the menu. Children welcome. No credit cards. Price Band: B

SHROPSHIRE

BISHOP'S CASTLE
TROTTERS RESTAURANT, At the Boars Head Hotel, Church Street.
Tel: 01588 638521.
This elegant, beautifully appointed restaurant was opened at Whitsun 1995 within the doors of the historic Boars Head Hotel. Delicious food is served in the Dining Room or if you wish to eat less formally there is a dining area in the main bar. Open 12.00-2pm & 6.30-9.30pm, Sun 12.00-2pm & 6.30-9.30pm. Children welcome. Vegetarians catered for.

Chapter Twelve

SOMERSET

CREWKERNE
GEORGE HOTEL, Market Square.
Tel: 01460 73650.
A much loved hostelry in the town that has been here for centuries, full of local people frequenting both its bars and restaurant. Whilst there is an excellent restaurant you may choose to eat wherever you like from the same wide ranging menu. Open all year. Restaurant: lunch 12-2.30pm Dinner 6.30-9.30pm. Children welcome. All major cards. Bar food. Vegetarian choice. Accommodation.

FROME
LA BISALTA, 6 Vicarage Street.
Tel: 01373 464238.
Everything an Italian restaurant should be, from the moment you step through the door, the itimacy and ambience will make you feel as if you've gone to a good friend's for dinner. The food is delicious with lovely cheeses, vegetables and a variety of sauces to tantalise. Open 6 days-closed Sun 12-2pm & 7pm till late. Children welcome. All major cards. Vegetarians catered for. Licensed.

GLASTONBURY
ABBEY TEA ROOMS & RESTAURANT, 16 Magdalene Street.
Tel: 01458 832852.
Probably best known for the excellence of its home-made cakes which make afternoon tea so special, a delightful place to rest awhile after exploring Glastonbury. Lunch, Sunday roasts and on Friday and Saturday evening meals are served. You will be extremely well fed at extremely reasonable prices. Open 7 days a week and Fri & Sat evenings from 7pm. Children specially well catered for. Vegetarian & vegan menus. Visa/Master/Amex. Disabled access. Licensed.

PORLOCK
CAMELLIA TEA & COFFEE HOUSE, High Street.
Tel: 01643 862266.
Excellent home-made fare. Ligh lunches, savouries, afternoon teas are all available. Open Dec-Jan: weekends 1-4pm, Feb-Apr: Thurs-Sun 1-5pm, summer: 7 days 12-5pm. Children welcome. No cards. Pets welcome. Vegetarians catered for. Licensed with full meals. Accommodation.

SUFFOLK

ALDEBURGH
NEW AUSTINS HOTEL, 243 High Street
Tel: 01728 453932 Fax: 01728 453668.
Close to the sea, good food both in restaurant and the bar. All major cards except AMEX. Children welcome. Vegetarains catered for. Open all year. Price Band: B

Where to Eat

BATTISFORD
THE PUNCH BOWL, Bildeston Road
Tel: 01449 612302.
Pretty village with thatched cottages. Pub has oak beams, open fires, plenty of gelaming brass and a wonderful welcome. Simple home-cooked fare. Garden for children. Traditional Sunday lunch. Open: 11-3pm & 7-11pm. No credit cards. 2-3 vegetarian dishes. Children welcome in the restaurant and garden. Price Band: A

BECCLES
WAVENEY HOUSE HOTEL, Puddingmoor, Beccles
Tel: 01502 712270 Fax: 01502 712660.
Friendly, beautifully run small hotel with excellent restaurant. Riverside frontage & moorings. Lively bar serves good bar food. Children welcome. Access/Visa/AMEX/Diners. 6 dishes for vegetarians. Open all year. Dogs not permitted in bar or restaurant. Price Band: A/B

BENTLEY
THE CASE IS ALTERED, Caple Road, Nr Ipswich
Tel: 01473 310282.
Nothing pretentious about this oddly named pub but it does offer good home-cooking. The spicy curry and the cauliflower cheese are particularly good. Inexpensive and value for money. Open: 11.30-3pm & 6-11pm, Sat 11-11pm. No credit cards. Dishes for vegetarians. Children welcome. Price Band: A

BLAXHALL
THE SHIP INN, Nr Woodbridge
Tel: 01728 88316.
If you are a lover of bird life, a rambler or a devotee of music then Blaxhall and this inn are just the place for you. The village is well known to the people who come to the concert hall at Snape, a mile away. 17th century inn much used in BBC productions. Simple pub food at sensible prices. 4 well equipped twin chalets converted from the old stables. Open: 11-3pm & 7-11pm. Not open Monday lunchtime. No credit cards. Children welcome if eating. One or two dishes for vegetarians. Price Band: A

BRANDESTON
THE QUEENS HEAD, The Street, Nr Woodbridge
Tel: 01728 685307.
Set in picturesque countryside near the Deben. Over 400 years old but has been modernised. Letting rooms. Good home-cooked traditional fare is available every day lunch and evenings, except Sunday evenings. Traditional Sunday lunch. Warm and friendly. Certified as camping and Caravan Club accommodaion for 5 touring vans and 15 tents. Open: Mon-Sat 11.30-2.30pm & 5.30-11pm, Sun 12-3pm & 7-10.30pm. Children welcome in restaurant and Family Room. No credit cards. Vegetarian dishes. Price Band: A

BURY ST EDMUNDS
GRILLS AND GILLS, 34, Abbeygate Street
Tel: 01284 706004.
You will find this restaurant as unique in name as it is in its food and Mediterrannean style interior. The food is exciting and beautifully cooked,

whether meat or fish. A daily changing Fish Board which also features an extension to the lunch menu with Pies, Cromer Crab, Mussels, Liver and Bacon and a host of other dishes. It is a sister restaurant to 'Somewhere Else' at 1 Langton Place, Hatter Street which is equally good. Open daily. Children welcome. Visa/Access/Master. 10 vegetarian dishes. Price Band: A

CLAYDON
CLAYDON COUNTRY HOUSE HOTEL, 16-18, Ipswich Road
Tel: 01473 830382.
Small enough to ensure that every guest receives individual attention. Traditional English and French menu. Children welcome. Garden. Visa/Access/AMEX. 5/6 choices for vegetarians. Price Band: B

EAST BERGHOLT
THE RED LION, The Street, Nr Colchester
Tel: 01206 298332.
15th century inn in historic village. Ideal place from which to explore Constable country. First class interesting food. Try Pidgeon in Elderberry Wine or Chicken, Cheese and Mustard Pie. Wide variety of dishes. Bar meals. Children welcome in dining room and garden. 4 letting rooms. No credit cards. Vegetarian choice. Open: 12-3pm & 7-11pm. Price Band: A/B

FELIXSTOWE
THE FERRY BOAT INN, Felixstowe Ferry
Tel: 01394 284203.
Pub dates from 1450. Recently renovated - we have not seen it since. The hospitality is renowned and the food is good home-cooked fare with a blackboard menu that changes regularly. Open: 11-2.30pm & 6-11pm. No food Sunday evening. Access/Visa. Children in dining area only. Price Band: A/B

GILLINGHAM
THE SWAN MOTEL, Loddon Road
Tel: 01502 712055 Fax: 01502 711786.
78 cover restaurant serving freshly prepared English home-made fare. Blackboard specials and snacks. Children welcome. All major credit cards. Vegetarians catered for. Price Band: A/B

HARKSTEAD
THE BAKERS ARMS, The Street, Nr Ipswich
Tel: 01473 328595.
You will find this friendly pub on the Shotley Peninsula, 6 miles from Ipswich and five minutes walk through fields from the charming tidal River Stour. Amazing value home-cooked food. Just the thing after a walk and no one minds muddy boots, wellies or dogs. Open: 11.30-3pm & 7-11pm. Children welcome in games room. 3-4 dishes for vegetarians. No credit cards. Price Band: A

IPSWICH
THE SINGING CHEF, 200, St Helens Street
Tel: 01473 255236.
Not to be missed, this very different and refreshing establishment provides a touch of France. Ken and Cynthia Toye are les patronnes, the food is regional

Where to Eat

French and quite wonderful. Very much a family restaurant, they close when the customers go. Ken lives up to his name, the 'Singing Chef' and at the end of the evening he sings like an angel. Most customers stay for the whole evening. This is a gastronomic and personal experience to be enjoyed. Price Band: B

KERSEY
THE BELL INN, The Street, Nr Hadleigh
Tel: 01473 823229.
This 1,000 year old village is almost like a stage set and has been used by film makers time and again. The bell is a Grade II Listed building, the second oldest in Kersey. You can now stay as well as eat and drink here. Wonderful food produced by an imaginative chef. The bar food is definitely above average. Kersey will put a spell on you and so too will TheBell. Open: Mon-sat 10.30-2.30pm & 6.30-11pm, Sun 10.30-3pm & 7-10.30pm. Children if well behaved to eat. Visa/Access/Diners/AMEX. Vegetarian choice in bar and restaurant. Price Band: A/B

KETTLEBURGH
THE CHEQUERS INN, Nr Woodbridge
Tel: 01728 723760.
Super site with a garden that runs down to the banks of the Deben. Good choice of food at realistic prices. Try the Kettleburgh Ploughman with a choice of cheese, ham Mackerel or pate. Childrens menu. Access/Visa. Vegetarian dishes. Open: Mon-Sat 11-2.30pm & 5.30-11pm, Sun 12-3pm & 7-10.30pm. Price Band: A

LEISTON
THE WHITE HORSE, Station Road
Tel: 01728 830694.
The village dates back before the Norman Conquest. Purpose built in 1770 by the family Gildersleeves, a well known inn-keeping family who supplemented their regular income by a heavy involvement in the smuggling trade. Comfortable hotel provideng first class French/English fare in the restaurant and a wide range of food in the bar. Childrens menu. Sunday lunch. Access/Visa. Vegetarian dishes. Open all day weekdays, Sun 12-3pm & 10.30pm. Price Band: A/B

PIN MILL
THE BUTT AND OYSTER INN, Pin Mill, Chelmondiston
Tel: 01473 780764.
A very special, traditional inn right on the river's edge, with old Thames barges tied up alongside. The ale is superb, the food traditional and interesting, and the company unbeatable. Dick Mainwaring is the jovial landlord whose warmth of character spills over onto all the people he welcomes into this, one of Suffolk's nicest pubs. Children allowed in to eat and in smoke room. No credit cards. Dishes for vegetarians. Price Band: A/B

SAXMUNDHAM
THE BELL HOTEL, High Street
Tel: 01728 602331.
Renovated carefully since 1991, this early 17th century building is comfortable and charming. Good food, good hospitality and well equipped bedrooms.

Strong emphasis on Italian cooking and wines. Open: Mon-Sat 11-11pm. Normal Sunday hours. Children welcome. Choice for vegetarians. Access/Visa/Diners. Price Band: B

THE WHITE HORSE, Darsham Road, Westleton
Tel: 01728 73222.
This is a pretty and well kept village with a thatched church just outside Saxmundham. The partially 16th century inn is on the green. It is cosy with lots of brass and paintings on the walls. Excellent home-cooking using local produce and locally caught fish. Probably the largest Mixed Grill you will ever see. Sunday lunch, Daily Specials, cream teas in the summer plus what is best described as a Scottish High Tea served from 6-7pm, in which for an all inclusive price, you can feast on a main meal, bread and butter, scones, cakes, jam, cream and a pot of tea. Comfortable bedrooms and you will certainly be well fed. Open: winter 12-3pm & 7-11pm, summer 11-3pm & 5.30-11pm. Children welcome. No credit cards. Vegetarian choice. Price Band: A/B

SOUTHWOLD
THE RED LION INN & RESTAURANT, 2 Southe Green
Tel: 01502 722385.
Good, sensibly priced food in a pleasant atmosphere. Open all year. Price Band: A

STOKE-BY-NAYLAND
THE ANGEL INN
Tel: 01206 263245.
All fresh international cuisine. Welcoming, beamed bars, nice atmosphere. All major cards. No children. Open all year. Vegetarians catered for. Price Band: A/B

WOODBRIDGE
THE CAPTAIN'S TABLE, 3Quay Street
Tel: 01394 383145.
For 25 years Tony and Jo Prentice have owned and run this excellent restaurant in what was once a farmhouse with land going down to the Deben. The Tudor buildings are painted Suffolk pink, and in summer the small patio in front of the restaurant is a suntrap protected from the world by the outer brick wall. The extensive menu specialises in fish and sea food. 'Starters from the Net' include Moules Mariniere, hald a dozen oysters from Bentley Creek or a Mousse of Avocado with a fresh tomato and herb dressing. Main courses maybe local Dover soles, or Scallops tossed in butter with bacon and garlic. There is an alternative selection for those not keen on seafood. A fixed price menu which is value for money. 'All dishes are offered subject to wind and tide, fisherman's fancy, farmer's whim and gardener's back'!. If you only desire a bar snack you will still be very welcome. Price Band: B

Where to Eat

SUSSEX

BOGNOR REGIS
THE CAMELOT HOTEL & RESTAURANT, 3 Flansham Lane, Felpham.
Tel: 01243 585875 Fax: 01243 587500.
Situated on eht A259 Bognor Regis to Littlehampton main coastal road in the village of Felpham, ten minutes walk to the sea. 70 seater restaurant and King Arthur's Room with unique round table for twelve people. Good food catering for the trencherman as well as more delicate eaters. Sensible prices. Price Band: B

BRAMBER
THE OLD TOLLGATE RESTAURANT & HOTEL,
The street, Bramber Steyning.
Tel: 01903 879494 Fax: 01903 813399.
This has been a renowned and popular 'eating spot' for over twenty years. The 'visual A La Carte' menu features The Tollgate's famous cold table as the first course, with some 30 different starters. The carvery is laden with at least four different roasts plus pies, casseroles, curries and vegetarian dishes. Sumptuous sweets and a cheeseboard will delight if you are still hungry! Children welcome. Visa/Diners/Master/Amex. Price Band: B

CHICHESTER
THE WHITE HORSE INN, Chilgrove.
Tel: 01243 535333.
This award winning inn offers some of the finest food in the county and boasts a superb wine cellar. Alongside it Forge Cottage which opened in the spring of 1995 offers first class accommodation. Visa/Diners. Children welcome to eat. Price Band: B

SUFFOLD HOUSE HOTEL & RESTAURANT, No 3 East Row.
Tel: 01243 778899 Fax: 01243 787282.
Stylish Georgian building, privately owned and run quite beautifully. Excellent bar and restaurant open to non-residents. Dine on Cordon Bleu Cuisine with imaginative and innovative dishes. Children welcome. Vegetarian dishes to order. All major cards. Pets are permitted. Price Band: B

COWDEN
THE COWDEN CROWN, Market Square.
Tel: 01342 850477.
Everything about this pub is charmingly different. The Inglenook fireplace is a major attraction on which pheasant and other game, steaks and fish are cooked, all over apple logs. Wide menu with additional Daily Specials. The restaurant features French cuisine and is renowned for its sauces. You can stay overnight if you wish in authentically decorated bedrooms. Open: 11-3pm & 6-11pm. Closed Monday evening. Visa/Mastercard. Children welcome in restaurant and garden. Notice required for vegetarian dishes. Price Band: B

Chapter Twelve

CUCKFIELD
THE KINGS HEAD, South Street, Nr Haywards Heath.
Tel: 01444 454006.
A personal favourite of the Prince of Wales, later, George IV, it is beautifully appointed and offers everything expected from a coaching inn of the modern era. A popular intimate restaurant serves great value home-cooked food at lunchtime plus Tues-Fri evenings. Bar food is always available. 9 ensuite rooms. Open: normal pub hours. Children welcome. Garden and games room. Vegetarian dishes daily. Mastercard/Visa/Amex. Price Band: B

EASTBOURNE
BROWNINGS HOTEL, 28 Upperton Road.
Tel: 01323 724358 Fax: 01323 731288.
Dignified Victorian mansion on the main A22 from London. Wonderful homely atmosphere. Small intimate dining room open to non-residents. Good food at realistic prices. Children welcome. One vegetarian dish daily. No pets allowed. All major credit cards. Price Band: B

LANDOWNE HOTEL, King Edward Parade.
Tel: 01323 725174 Fax: 01323 739721.
High standard, delicious food in gracious surroundings. There are 125 ensuite rooms. Open all year except New Year and the first two weeks in January. All major cards. Children's menu. Vegetarians catered for. Price Band: B

FISHBOURNE
THE WOOLPACK, Fishbourne Road.
Tel/Fax: 01234 782792.
Known for its culinary delights. The steaks melt in your mouth. Simple bar fare also available. Children are welcome - adults tolerated! Large garden. No pets. Visa/Master/Switch. Price Band: A/B

LITTLEWORTH
THE WINDMILL, Partridge Green, Nr Horsham.
Tel: 01403 710308.
Attractive pub that was once three cottages. 'Rural Memorabilia' adorns the walls and every corner that can be found for it. Whilst good, traditional food is served, the landlords, John and Gill Booth, are determined that it remains a pub that serves food rather than a restaurant serving ale! Open: 11-3pm & 5.30-11pm. No credit cards. Children welcome. One dish always available for vegetarians. Price Band: A/B

MIDHURST
THE CROWN, Edinburgh Square.
Tel: 01730 813462.
16th century inn behind and below the church, in the old part of the town. Opposite the famous 14th century Spread Eagle Hotel. Good value, home-made food, imaginative and chip free. Open: Mon-Sat 11-11pm. Sun: 12-3pm & 7-11pm. Children welcome in a limited area. No credit cards. 3-4 vegetarian dishes. Price Band: A/B

Where to Eat

SLINDON
THE SPUR INN
Tel: 0124365 216/635.
Charming 17th century coaching inn. Roaring fires and mulled wine in winter. The food is memorable covering every possible tastes both in the restaurant and the bar. Open: 11-3pm & 6-11pm. Sun 12-3pm & 7-10.30pm. Children welcome. Visa/Mastercard. 7+ dishes for vegetarian. Price Band: A/B

SOUTH HARTING
THE SHIP INN
Tel: 01730 825302.
17th century traditional village pub in picturesque South Harting. Recommended in The Good Beer Guide and renowned for high quality food all home-prepared at sensible pub prices. Well worth seeking out. Children over 14. Dogs permitted. All major cards. Price Band: A

TANGMERE
THE BADER ARMS, Malcolm Road, Nr Chichester.
Tel: 01243 779422.
Built at the end of the runway at this once famous airfield, and named after Sir Douglas Bader, this friendly pub is a fitting tribute to the 'The Few'. Food at luchtime and evenings both in the bar and restaurant. Restaurant closed Monday and Sunday evenings. Traditional Sunday Lunch. Theme evenings are very popular. Good value. Open all year, pub hours. Children welcome. Master/Visa. Always at least 4 dishes for vegetarians. Price Band: A

RYE
THE FLACKLEY ASH HOTEL, Peasmarsh.
Tel: 01797 230651 Fax: 01797 230510.
This hotel has everything including a Health and Leisure complex. Wonderful gardens and a charming restaurant with an English/French menu specialising in Rye Bay fish. Special menu for vegetarians. Children permitted. All major cards. Price Band: B

WEST WITTERING
THE LAMB INN, Chichester Road.
Tel: 01243 511105.
This Freehouse is a traditional pub and a friendly place. No background music or amusement machines. Fifteen wines, including champagne are available by the glass. The emphasis is on home-made food whether a toasted sandwich or a full meal. Fish is the speciality of the house. Open 11-2.30pm & 6-11pm. Children welcome if eating. Mastercard/Visa. Usually 2 dishes for vegetarians. No accommodation. Price Band: A/B

TYNE AND WEAR

NEWCASTLE
THE PLOUGH INN, Mountsett, Nr Burnopfield.
Tel: 01207 570346.
The Plough stands 800ft above sea level with magnificent views up the Derwent Valley and on a clear day you can see the glory of the Cheviot Hills. Traditional country inn with a great deal of charm. Fresh food, high quality,

home-cooked served daily in the bar. Open Mon-Sat 11.30-11pm. Sun 12-3pm & 7-10.30pm. Children's menu. Master/Visa. 3 dishes always for vegetarians. Price Band: A

WARWICKSHIRE

KENILWORTH
CLARENDON HOUSE, Old High Street
Tel: 01926 57668.
Old building in the heart of Kenilworth. Full of atmosphere. Cromwells bistro restaurant, partially housed in the original kitchen of the Elizabethan Castle Tavern, offers an extensive menu of fine foods and wines in a relaxed and informal setting. Royalist Retreat Bar has an extensive range of bar snacks available at lunchtime. Open all year. Children allowed. Visa/Access/Switch. Vegetarian dishes. Price Band: A/B

SHIPTON-ON-STOUR
GEORGE HOTEL, High Street
Tel: 01608 661453.
In historic small town, this delightful inn dates back to the 15th century. Has an unbelievable air of the past. Delicious food in the restaurant and a varied and exciting bar menu. Open all year 10.30-11pm. Children welcome, special space. Visa/AMEX. Vegetarians catered for. Price Band: A/B

STRATFORD-UPON-AVON
THE FALCON, Chapel Street
Tel: 01789 205777 Fax: 01789 414260.
16th century inn beautifully extended. Restaurant renowned for its friendly service and the culinary skills of the chef and his team. Good food in the lounge and Oak Bars. Coffee or afternoon tea in the 'covered walkway' overlooking the garden. Open all day, all year. Children welcome. All major credit cards. Vegetarians catered for. Price Band: A/B/C

ETTINGTON PARK, Aldminster
Tel: 10789 450123 Fax: 01789 450472.
There can be few hotels in this country more grand orbeautiful that Ettington Park. Dine here in the spectacular Oak Room on the very finest of English and French cuisine and it will be never forgotten. Everything about the hotel is superb. Price Band: C

WORCESTERSHIRE

ARLEY
THE NEW INN, Pound Green
Arley is three and a half miles from the historic riverside town of Bewdley. A pub in which Acoustic Musicians are especially welcome - the landlord Malcolm Gee publishes the international magazine 'The Accordion News' and runs high profile accordion concerts. The pub is essentially a 'conventional' one and caters for families although children are not allowed to roam the lounges. The 40 cover restaurant is provided over by a Head

Where to Eat

Chef who has an excellent reputation for good traditional food,generous portions and modest prices. Godd bar food is available. Several vegetarian dishes. No credit cards. Price Band: A

ECKINGTON
THE ANCHOR INN & RESTAURANT, Cotheridge Lane
Tel/Fax: 01386 750356.
On the edge of the Cotswolds, Eckington, close to Pershore, is a quiet village dating back to Saxon times. The 18th century Anchor Inn, full of character is famous for the excellence of its restaurant. Fish and Steaks are the speciality but there is an excellent, varied menu which includes dishes for vegetarians as well as Daily Specials. The bar food is exciting and home-made. Cheildren welcome. All major cards within Cardnet. Price Band: A

LITTLE MALVERN
HOLDFAST COTTAGE HOTEL
Tel: 01684 310288 Fax: 01684 311117.
This is a charming 17th century hotel set in its own grounds surrounded by orchards and open farmland; far removed from traffic noise although it is less than 15 minutes drive from the M5 and M50 and only 4 miles from Malvern and Upton-Upon-Severn, offers dinner to non-residents. The delicious food is cooked by the owners Stephen and Jane Knowles whose love of food is reflected in the varied choice and the delicate use of herbs from the hotel's Victorian Herb Garden. Visa/Access/Master/Euro. Licensed. Price Band: B

MALVERN WELLS
THE COTTAGE IN THE WOOD HOTEL, Holywell Road
Tel: 01684 575859 Fax: 01684 560662.
Excellent hotel with stunning views perched high on the Malvern Hills. The Daily Mail calls it 'The best view in England'. Delightful restaurant open to non-residents. At lunchtime choose from the Light Bite menu which reflects the modern trend for healthy eating. Dinner is a gastronomic dream, essentially English at heart, but influenced by styles and flavours of the world. Children and vegetarians welcome. Access/Visa/Amex/Switch. Price Band: B

FLYFORD FLAVELL
THE RED HART INN, Kington, Flyford Flavell
Tel: 01386 792221.
Over 400 years old and much of the original black and white building remains. You will find it on the A422 halfway between Worcester and Stratford-upon-Avon. Over the years it has become known as the 'Sportsmans Pub' because of its great cricketingconnections. A la carte restaurant serving traditional food. Sunday carvery lunch. Good bar meals. From Easter to September breakfast and a super afternoon tea are available. Open: Sat 11-2.30pm & 6-11pm, Sun 12-3pm & 7-10.30pm, longer Easter-Sept. Price Band: A/B

PERSHORE
THE OLD CHESTNUT TREE, Manor Road, Lower Moor
Tel: 01386 860380.
This Grade II Listed building has a gently flowing river behind it, along whose banks is a delightful walk. Black and white with ancient leaded

Chapter Twelve

windows, it was built in 1547 as a Granary for the Manor House. Heavy beams, open fireplaces, ghosts!. Good, traditional food at reasonable prices. 2 letting rooms not en suite. Open: Mon-Fri 11-2.30pm & 6-11pm, Sat 11-11pm, Sun 12-3pm & 7-10.30pm. Children welcome. No credit cards. Vegetarians catered for. Price Band: A

THE ANGEL INN & POSTING HOUSE, High Street
Tel: 01386 552046.
In the heart of the town, welcoming, family run. Extensive bar food. Imaginative meals. Price Band: A

ST MICHAELS
CADMORE LODGE
Tel/Fax: 01584 810044.
Situated 2 miles west of the market town Tenbury Wells, and lying in its own secluded valley with 60 acres of woodland with a nine hole golf course and 2 shimmering lakes. The skilled chefs offer a tempting menu whether it is the set price dinner, dishes taken from the a la carte selection or the good value bar food. Vegetarians catered for. Children welcome. Access/Visa/Master. Price Band: B

SEVERN STOKES
THE OLD SCHOOL HOUSE HOTEL & RESTAURANT
is only 35 miles from the centre of Birmingham and is a popular venue for diners who come to enjoy 'School Dinners' - gastronomic feasts that bear no resemblance to those we remember!. The only similarity is the superb range of old fashioned steamed puddings with custard. The menu is imaginative, beautifully presented and the price is reasonable. Snacks and Daily Specials are available served in the Study. During the summer one can enjoy drinks and meals on the terrace overlooking the garden with its swimming pool and marvellous views of the Severn Vale. Vegetarians & children welcome. All major cards. Price Band: B

UPTON-ON-SEVERN
THE WHITE LION HOTEL, High Street
Tel/Fax: 01684 592551.
Famous old inn on banks of the River Severn, in the centre of this historic Tudor town. Surrounded by a wonderful pastoral landscape leading to the majestic Malvern Hills. Charming restaurant serving interesting English fare with a French influence. Busy bar offering good meals with an emphasis on fresh fish. Open all year. Access/Visa/Amex/Diners. Vegetarians catered for. Price Band: B

YORKSHIRE

AINTHORPE
THE FOX AND HOUNDS INN, Ainthorpe, Danby.
Tel: 01287 660218.
Nice village pub in a wonderful setting. Good, home-cooked food. Open normal pub hours. Children welcome. Vegetarians catered for. Price Band: A

Where to Eat

DONCASTER
THE DUKE WILLIAM, Church Street, Haxey.
Tel: 01427 752210.
Close to the Lincolnshire Wolds and historic Lincoln. Pretty and very ancient village, the old capital of the Isle of Axholme. Popular village pub with great food using local produce, restaurant and bar food. Children welcome. Open 11-11pm. Mastercard/Visa. 6 dishes for vegetarians. Price Band: A/B

EGTON BRIDGE
THE POSTGATE, Egton Bridge, Whitby.
Tel: 01947 895241.
Pretty creeper covered inn on the North Yorkshire Moors close to the sea. Popular with television companies. High quality traditional fare in restaurant and bar with Blackboard Specials. Open normal pub hours. No credit cards. Children welcome. Vegetarians catered for. Price Band: A/B

GOATHLAND
THE MALLYAN SPOUT HOTEL, The Common.
Tel: 01947 896486.
Yorkshire Television filmed the successful series 'Heartbeat' in Goathland. On the village green is The Mallyan Spout Hotel which is open all day from 8am-12 midnight. Good wholesome Englsih food in the restaurant and freshly cooked fare in the bar every day. Children welcome in lounge only. Master/Diners/Visa. Several dishes for vegetarians. Price Band: A/B

HARROGATE
THE RUSKIN PRIVATE HOTEL & GALLERY RESTAURANT
Tel: 01423 502045 Fax: 01423 506131.
Charming private hotel. French/English cuisine. Table d'hote and A La Carte. Children over 3 years. Master/Visa. Always 4+ dishes for vegetarians. No disabled access. Price Band: A/B

HEMINGBROUGH
HEMINGBROUGH HALL HOTEL, School Road.
Tel: 01757 630393.
Close to York and Selby and set in 7 acres of rural countryside. Peaceful and undisturbed by the outside world. Delicious food prepared by Classical French chef. Bar food between 12-2pm daily. Open every day. Children welcome. Visa/Amex. Vegetarian dishes on request. Price Band: A/B

HUTTON-LE-HOLE
THE FORGE TEA SHOP.
Tel: 01751 417444.
Once and old smithy it is now a very attractive tea room serving delicious home-cooked food. Simple or sophisticated snack or a meal, delectable home-made cakes, sconeswith lashings of butter, jam and cream. Nothing could be better. Open Mar-Oct 10-5pm 7 days in summer, Nov-Feb: weekends only 10-4pm. Children welcome. No cards.

Chapter Twelve

KNAREBOROUGH
THE YORKSHIRE LASS, High Bridge, Harrogate Road.
Tel: 01423 862962 Fax: 01423 869091.
Filming of 'Emmerdale' goes on around here. The pub sits on the banks of the River Nidd opposite Mother Shipton's Cave. Quite often see TV and Film stars plus their film crews here lunching on the home-cooked food. Open 11-3pm & 5.30-11pm. Children to eat only. Visa/Master/Amex. Always 5 dishes for vegetarians. Price Band: A/B

LEYBURN
KINGS ARMS HOTEL, Market Place, Askrigg in Wensleydale.
Tel: 01969 650635.
Totally delightful - known throughout the world as The Drovers at Daroby in the television series 'All Creatures Great and Small'. Wonderful food both in the bar and restaurant. Open all year. Children welcome. All major cards. Vegetarians catered for. Price Band: A/B/C

MIDDLEHAM
THE RICHARD III HOTEL, Market Place.
Tel: 01969 232240.
Set in the heart of 'Herriot Country' in the smallest town in the country. This double fronted building backs onto the original boundary wall of Middleham Castle. Intimate 'olde worlde' restaurant with a home-cooked menu. Bar food served daily with a variety of 'Daily Specials' 4 choices for vegetarians. Open 11-3pm & 6-11pm and Fri-Sat 11-11pm. Sunday normal pub hours. Visa/Master. Children welcome in rear bar area. Price Band: A

OTLEY
CHEVIN PARK COUNTRY LODGE HOTEL, Yorkshire.
Tel: 01943 467818.
Unique hotel with a difference set in glorious grounds. The lakeside restaurant forms the centrepeice of what is the largest log building in Britain and has a cosy and intimate atmosphere. The cuisine is recognised and commended by all the major guides. Open all year. Children welcome. All major cards. Vegetarians catered for. Price Band: B

PETELEY BRIDGE
HAREFIEDL HALL HOTEL, Ripon Road.
Tel: 01423 711429.
Superb hotel and leisure complex nestling deep within its own grounds in the Nidderdale Hills. Full A La Carte and Table d'hote served every evening from 7pm. Bar meals on scenic patio with views over Pateley Bridge or in lounge bar both lunchtime and evenings. Open all year. All major cards. Children welcome. Vegetarians catered for. Price Band: A/B

SCARBOROUGH
KAM SANG CHINESE RESTAURANT, 3-3A North Marine Road.
Tel: 01723 501718.
A superb Chinese restaurant. All food is cooked to order, and where possible good local produce is used. Excellent choice. Open lunch: Mon-Sat 12-2.30pm, dinner Mon-Sat 6pm to midnight. Children welcome. Vegetarians catered for. All major cards. Disabled access.

Where to Eat

SKIPTON
BIZZIE LIZZIES FISH & CHIP RESTAURANT, 36 Swadford Street.
Tel: 01756 703189.
It would seem that there is no doubt the North Country produces the best fish and chips in the whole of England. This is confirmed by the excellence of Bizzie Lizzies. Seats up to 76 people in comfort with special non-smoking and smoking areas. Open all year Mon-Sat 11.30am (last orders 10pm), Sun Noon-last orders 10pm from 1st Oct until Easter last orders will be 9pm. Children welcome. Licensed. Vegetarian upon request. No credit cards.

SINNINGTON
THE FOX AND HOUNDS COUNTRY HOTEL, Main Street.
Tel: 01751 431577 Fax: 01751 432791.
Sinnington demonstrates what a true Englsih village should look like. The Fox and Hounds offers good food both in the restaurant and at the bar. Daily Specials. Open 12-2.30pm & 6.30-11pm. Children welcome. Master/Visa/Euro. Dishes for vegetarians. Price Band: B

WHITBY
THE MAGPIE CAFE, 14 Pier Road.
Tel: 01947 602058/821723.
The accolades of this fine licensed restaruant immidiately tell you that there is something special about the establishment. Excellent fayre fresh fish is a great speciality here with 12 to 15 varieties being available at any time. Children are most welcome here with high chairs, toy boxes and a special menu. Open Feb to Dec, Easter-Oct 11.30-9pm daily, Feb-Easter & Nov-Dec 11.30-6.30pm Sun-Thurs, 11.30-9pm Fri & Sat. All major cards. Vegetarians catered for.

YORK
LASTINGHAM GRANGE, Lastingham.
Tel: 01751 417345/402.
If you leave the A170 at Kirby Moorside and follow the road north to Hutton-le-Hole, you will find the historic village of Lastingham, five miles away. Relaxed friendly atmosphere in a house that has a justifiable reputation for good food and personal, courteous service. Open to non-residents. Open all year. Children welcome. No credit cards. Vegetarians catered for on request. Price Band: B

WALES

BRECON
SELAND NEWYDD, Pwllgloyw, Brecon, Powys.
Tel: 01874 690282.
One of Wales's most exciting eating experiences is to be found on the 'old road' from Brecon to Builth Wells. The restaurant is sufficiently small with 35 covers to be intimate and ideal for a special evening out. Wonderful food at affordable prices. Not to be missed. Open 11-3pm & 6-11pm Mon-Sun. Children - yes cooked to order! All cards except Amex. Bar food Mon-Fri lunch and evenings meals Fri & Sat lunchtimes, and Sun Lunch. Accessible disabled access.

887

CARDIFF
BENEDICTO'S, 4 Windsor Place, Cardiff.
Tel: 01222 371130.
This attractive Continental style restaurant has a great atmosphere, delightfulfurnishings and a welcoming host, Ben Lado. The food is superb you will certainly have a problem deciding what you would like form this imaginative and beautifully compiled menu. Open 12-2.30 & 7-11.30pm all year except Christmas Day and Boxing Day. All major cards. Children welcome. Good wine list. Daily vegetarian choice.

GOYCHURCH
THE WHITE HORSE INN, Goychurch, Mid-Glamorgan.
Tel: 01656 652583.
This attractive inn which was once an hotel has something for all ages. The food is delicious with home-made pies being the speciality of the house. The pastry melts in your mouth and there are a whole variety of different, tasty fillings. Excellent A La Carte menu. Open Mon-Thurs 11-4pm & 5.30-11pm Fri/Sat 11am-11pm Sun 12-3.30pm & 7-10.30pm. Children welcome. All cards except Amex/Diners. Wide range of Bar Food with Daily Specials. Always a vegetarian choice. Award winning Beer Garden.

SWANSEA
WINDSOR LODGE HOTEL & RESTAURANT, Mount Pleasant, Swansea.
Tel: 01792 642158/652744 Fax: 01792 648996.
Within the confines of the elegant, comfortable Windsor Lodge Hotel, right in the heart of Swansea's city centre, is a restaurant which has become one of the best known and most popular in South Wales. The dishes have a British and French influence using fresh ingredients allowing the menu to change with the seasons. Award winning food. Open all year 24 hours except Christmas and Boxing Day. All major cards. Children welcome. Good vegetarian choice. Good wine list. Accommodation

Visitor Attractions

Chapter Fourteen

VISITOR ATTRACTIONS

Visitor Attractions

BEDFORDSHIRE

BEDFORD DISCOVER THE BEDFORDSHIRE COUNTRYSIDE
Tel: 01234 228671
Discover the wonderful landscape and varied heritage by taking a family day out to visit one of the many country parks and cyclewalks that Bedfordshire has to offer. Throughout the year there is plenty to do. Visitor Centres and Country Parks are open all the year round.

BEDFORD MUSEUM
Tel: 01234 353232
This lively museum is set in attractive surroundings close to the River Great Ouse. Excellent displays interpret the human and natural history of the region. Open Tues-Sat 11-5pm Sun & Bank Holidays 2-5pm. Closed Mondays. Admission free.

PRIORY COUNTRY PARK
Tel: 01234 211182.
This Country Park is a tranquil countryside area just a stone's throw from Bedford town centre. The park, with lakes surrounded by trees and grassland, is a great place to see wildlife. Prioiry Water Sports offer sailing, sail boarding and canoeing. Open all year round.

CECIL HIGGINS ART GALLERY & MUSEUM
Tel: 01234 211222.
A Victorian mansion, original home of the Higgins family, is furnished in authentic style, with an adjoining modern gallery displaying fine collections of watercolours, prints, drawings, ceramics, glass and lace. Open all year Tues-Sat 11-5pm Sun & Bank Hols 2-5pm. Admission free.

THE BUNYAN MEETING FREE CHURDH & MUSEUM
Tel: 01234 358870.
Scenes from The Pilgrim's Progress are depicted on the bronze entrance doors, presented to the church in 1876 by the 10th Duke of Bedford, and on the five stained glass windows. The museum contains most of the known possessions of Johm Bunyan, many editions of his 60 recognised works, including The Pilgrim's Progress in 168 foreign languages. Open Apr-Oct Tues-Sat 2-4pm & Jul-Sept 10.30-12.30pm.

BROMHAM MILL
Tel: 01234 824330.
Built in 1695, Bromham Mill is an attracive stone building set by the River Great Ouse. Now restored to its former working glory, the enormous revolving water wheel is the focal point.

Chapter Fourteen

DUNSTABLE WHIPSNADE ANIMAL PARK
Tel: 01582 872171
Location: 20 miles from the M25 junction 21 following elephant signs from Dunstable. Europe's largest conservation centres offering 2,500 rare and endangered species in 600 acres of beautiful parkland, including all the family favourites - elephants, tigers, penguins, bears, rhinos and many more. Free daily demonstrations of Elephant Encounters, Californian Sea Lions and free flying Birds of the World will keep all the family entertained. Open daily 10-6pm.

HARROLD-ODELL COUNTRY PARK
Tel: 01234 720016.
Tufted duck, great crested grebe, Canada and greylag geese, coots, moorhens, swans, mallards and kingfishers are just some of the birds that visit the landscaped lake of Harrold-Odells' 144 acre country park. Open Apr-Sept Tues-Sat 1-4.30pm Sun & Bank Holidays 1-6pm. Oct-Mar Sat-Sun & Bank Hols 1-4pm.

LEIGHTON BUZZARD RAILWAY
Page's Park Station, Billington Road (A4146) Tel: 01525 373888
This is one of England's foremost narrow gauge preservation sites; home to over fifty engines. It provides a great day out. Page's Park Station is situated alongside a large public recreational area offering grassy open space, children's play equipment and sports facilities. The station has a souvenir shop and buffet serving hot and cold snacks and refreshments at most times when trains are running. There is a picnic area, free car parking and space for coaches. The five and a half mile return journey by historic steam train takes just over an hour. A museum project display is open to visitors and much of the railway's historic locomotive and wagon fleet is based here. Steam locomotive viewing, a working quarry display and the demonstration sand trains are planned throughout the year. Industry Train Displays are live demonstrations of authentic locomotives and wagons which represent the major industries served by narrow gauge railways. Another form of heritage transport can be enjoyed on your day out to the railway. Cruises on the 19th century Grand Union Canal can be combined with your historic steam train ride. Ring or write for details. Although the trains mainly operate on Sundays from April-October, there are Festive Specials in December complete with Father Christmas, mince pies etc.

LEIGHTON BUZZARD GREBE CANAL CRUISES
Pitstone Wharf, Pitstone, Nr Leighton Buzzard LU79AD Tel: 01296 661920.
Rod and Margaret Saunders founded this business some 20 years ago and operate passenger vessels on the Grand Union Canal on a most beautiful length of the Canal where it climbs up the Chiltern escarpment from the

Vale of Aylesbury into the Chilterns themselves. Built 200 years ago, the passage of time has seen the canal mellow into the beautiful countryside, it's quaint hump-back bridges and locks complimenting the scene. The fleet of passenger vessels operate from the purpose built base, Pitstone wharf, near to the village of Cheddington (of 'great train robbery fame') and there is a regular service of one and a half hour trips run during the peak summer months via the Chiltern Summit level of the canal at Tring, the highest point of the waterway, 396 feet above sea level. Passengers have the opportunity to leave the boat in the lock flight and view Marsworth reservoirs and nature reserve and to picnic ashore if they wish. The boats are mainly wide-beam, offer all weather protection, and provide considerable comfort for the passengers. There are bars on all the boats and for pre-booked parties meals can be served while cruising - try the very popular afternoon cream teas. At Pitstone Wharf the Saunders have developed a boat yard which is open to everyone, where the non-boat owner can come and enjoy the canal and if so wished, can hire a self-steer boat, from a single day hire to a week or fortnight's holiday. Tuition is available for the beginner. Superbly run, with efficient professional crews, you can relax aboard and enjoy Grebe Canal Cruises.

LUTON WOODSIDE FARM & WILD FOWL PARK
Tel: 01582 841044.
At Woodside Farm Shop and Wild Fowl Park, there are over 160 different breeds of animals and birds to see and feed with special feed from the Farm Shop. Large picnic areas, pony rides, tarzan trails, birds of prey displays and daily tractor and trailer rides are available. Open all year round Mon-Sat 8-5.30pm. Closed Sunday.

THE WERNHER COLLECTION
Tel: 01582 22955
The works of the Russian Court Jeweller, Carl Faberge are part of the finest private art collection in Great Britain. There are many paintings, costumes and other personal possessions of the Russian Imperial Family Romanov. Treasures include old master paintings, magnificent tapestries, English and French porcelain, sculpture, bronzes and renaissance jewellery. Open to the public 29th Mar-16th October Fri-Sun 1.30-5pm.

RSPB NATURE RESERVE & GARDENS
Tel: 01767 680551.
Enjoy a day out and discover a wealth of wildlife when you visit The Lodge nature reserve set in the beautiful Bedfordshire countryside. A great day out will include woodland walks and nature trails, observation hides and wildlife garden and picnic area. Open all year round 9-9pm.

Chapter Fourteen

SILSOE WREST PARK HOUSE AND GARDENS
Tel: 01525 860152
The history of English gardening from 1700-1850 is set out in acres of stunning delights at Wrest Park. In the Great Garden, water catches the eye in every direction, while intersecting alleys provide splendid vistas of the many garden buildings and ornaments. West Park House was inspired by an 18th century French chateaux. the delightful intricate French Garden, with statues and fountains, enhances any view of the house from The Great Garden. Open 1st April-30th Sept weekends & Bank Holidays only 10-6pm.

THE SWISS GARDEN
Tel: 01767 627666.
Regarded as one of the top ten gardens in the country, though still under restoration, the secret of The Swiss Garden's romantic charm lies in its unique landscape design of the early 19th century. Shubberies and ponds, intricate ironwork bridges, an award-winning fernery and grotto, in a variety of follies and tiny Thatched Swiss Cottages are all contained within just ten acres. Open Mar-Jul & Sept, Sat, Sun & Bank Hols 10-6pm. Oct-Jan & Feb Sun 11-4pm.

WOBURN ABBEY
Tel: 01525 290666
Home of the Dukes of Bedford for over 350 years, Woburn Abbey is now lived in by the Duke's heir, the Marquess of Tavistock and his family. The house contains one of the most important collections and works of art in the world and is surrounded by a 3,000 acre deer park with nine species of deer. Open 1st Jan-26 Mar weekends only 27th Mar-30th October everyday.

WOBURN SAFARI PARK
Tel: 01525 290407.
Britain's largest drive through safari park with lions, tigers, rhinos, wolves, bears, hippos, monkeys and many more are all part of the attractions which make the safari park a great family attraction. New attractions include: The Adventure Ark, Penguin World and Great Woburn Railway. Open 5 Mar-30 October everyday.

BUCKINGHAMSHIRE

AYLESBURY AYLESBURY BREWERY COMPANY
Tel: 01296 395000
The company has been part of Buckinghamshire since 1895. It has some 200 Public houses most of them in the county, but you can see the ABC sign in parts of neighbouring Bedfordshire and Oxfordshire too. In addition to its

own wide range of beers and lagers, you'll find a number of outstanding products from several other breweries. Visit Aylesbury and sample for yourself.

THE CHILTERN BREWERY
Tel: 01296 613647 Location: A413 Aylesbury.
The ancient and revered art of the English Brewer can still be discovered flourishing in the beautiful countryside of Buckinghamshire. Completely independent and family run since its inception in 1980, this unique small brewery specialises in the production of high quality, traditionally brewed English beers with a real local flavour. Included in the large selection of home brewed ales is a 300 year old ale available in imperial pint bottles. Open Mon-Sat 9-5pm.

BUCKS RAILWAY CENTRE
Tel 01296 75440
Home to the private collection of steam locomotives. The centre boasts vintage carriages, signal box, station and gift shop. Throughout the year the centre holds special events and steaming days including regular visits by Thomas the Tank Engine, steam train rides and the extremely popular Victorian afternoon cream teas.

BUCKINGHAMSHIRE RAILWAY CENTRE
Tel 01296 75720
The centre's 25 acre site is at Quainton Road station and exchange sidings, the last remaining Metropolitan Railway county station. On display is one of the country's largest collection of historic steam and diesel locomotives as well as a comprehensive collection of coaching and freight rolling stock. Open 11-6pm daily.

BEACONSFIELD BEKONSCOT MODEL VILLAGE
Tel: 01494 672919
The oldest model village in the world is a charming minature covering over one and a half acres. Included in the many things to see are beautifully landscaped gardens, miniature houses, castles, churches, shops and railway stations, through which runs the finest outdoor model railway (Gauge One) open to the public in the United Kingdom. The 'country' of Bekonscot is planted with 8,000 conifers, 2,000 minature shrubs, and 200 tonnes of stone used for the rockeries alone.There are no less than one hundred and sixty buildings icluding churches, hotels, shops and private houses constituting Bekonscot and the outlying villages. Souvenir Shop. Refreshment Kiosks, 2 Picnic Areas, Childrens Playground, Miniature Tramway and many other scenes. It is a paradise for photographers, a fascination for model-makers, an admiration for gardeners, 'Heaven' for small children. In fact a must for

Chapter Fourteen

the whole family. OPEN; Every day from 10am-5pm from 17th February to 3rd November.

BUCKINGHAM SILVERSTONE MOTOR RACING CIRCUIT
Tel: 01327 857271.
Home of the internationally famous British Grand Prix, Silverstone is the centre of the British motor racing industry. Throughout the year there are regular national and internationalrace meetings featuring all shapes and forms of motor vehicles.

STOWE LANDSCAPE GARDENS
Tel: 01208 822850.
These beautiful gardens are placed in an impressive 18th century mansion set in over 500 acres of landscaped gardens inspired by William Kent and Capability Brown. The gardens feature a multitude of follies, ornate lakes, temples and monuments. Once home of the Dukes of Buckingham it is now home to one of the nation's premier independent schools, whose old boys include jazz singer George Melly and entrepreneur Richard Branson. During the summer months a series of musical events are regularly organised including music and firework concerts and the famous Stowe Opera.

CLAYDON HOUSE
Tel: 01296 730349.
Famous as the home of the Verney Family and a house which Florence Nightingale often visited, Clayon House has impressive rococo state rooms, and a Chinese tea-room. Florence Nightingale's bedroom and a museum of her nursing work from the Crimean Wars are also open to the public.

THE ROTHSCHILD LEGACY
Tel: 01296 662183.
The wealthy and influential Rothschild family were drawn to Buckinghamshire during the 19th century creating vast estates and building impressive mansions throughout the Vale of Aylesbury. These mansions are still open to the public. Mentmore Towers, designed by Sir Joseph Paxton for the Barone Meyer de Rothschild offers panoramic views of the Chilterns. Nearby Ascott House was built mainly in the 19th cnetury and set in elegant Victorian gardens. The house, originally a Jacobean Hunting Lodge can boast a fine collection of French and Chippendale furniture alongside important works of art by Rubens, Hogarth, Gainsborough and Stubbs. Open to the public daily.

HADDENHAM OAK FARM RARE BREEDS PARK
Tel: 01296 415709.
Aylesbury is perhaps best known for its association with ducks. In the 18th

and 19th century many people in the town kept the distinctive pure white ducks considered to be a delicacy by the rich and famous in London. The ducks became known as the Aylesbury. By the 20th century tastes changed and duck breeding died out in Aylesbury. Nowadays, one of the few remaining breeds can be seen at Oak Farm Rare Breeds Park at Broughton. The park which opened in 1993 is a traditional livestock farm featuring a variety of farm animals including sheep, goats, cattle, pigs and poultry, many of which are rare breeds.

BUCKS GOAT CENTRE
Tel: 01296 612983.
One of the most comprehensive collections of goats in Britain as well as a fine selection of other livestock. The centre can also boast a farm and gift shop, plant nursery and Naughty Nanny Tea Rooms making it ideal for a family or educational visit. Open daily.

GRAND UNION CANAL
Tel: 01296 661920.
A branch of the Grand Union Canal connects into Aylesbury offering a variety of waterside walks and excellent course fishing. Picnic sites can be found beside the canal at Pitstone Wharf and at the three Locks of Soulbury. Grebe Canal Cruises run regular scheduled services into the Chiltern Hills from Pitstone Wharf.

CAMBRIDGESHIRE

CAMBRIDGE OLIVER CROMWELL HOUSE
Tel: 01353 662062.
Standing almost in the shadows of Ely Cathedral this was the home of Oliver Cromwell and his family for some ten years. Several rooms have been refurbished in Cromwellian style to show features of the house which Cromwell would have known in his time. Displays tell the story of the house's history, for although Cromwell was still the most famous occupant, the house itself has medieval origins and a fascinating past. Built in the early 14th century for the collection of tithes, it was used as a brewery and inn during the 19th century. Open 1st Apr-30th Sept 10-6pm daily including Sat, Sun and Bank Holidays 1st October-30th April 10-5.15pm.

DUXFORD AEROPLANE MUSEUM
Tel: 01223 833376 Location:
Duxford is next to junction 10 off the M11 motorway, 48 miles from London. A day at Duxford is a day you'll never forget. You'll find Europe's biggest collection of historic aircraft, over 130, displayed in the giant exhibition

Chapter Fourteen

hangers. Flimsy biplanes that fought over the trenches of the First World War through to Gulf Jets are on show at this preserved wartime airfield. See the legendary Spitfire, Lancaster and B-17 Flying Fortress. Marvel at the U-2 Spyplane that flew on the edge of space and climb aboard Concorde. Look at the only F-111 supersonic swing-wing bomber on show in Europe and be amazed by the Harrier jump-jet. Open everyday except 24,25 & 26 December. Summer 26-Mar-16 October 10-6pm. Winter 10-4pm.

ELY CATHEDRAL
Tel: 01353 667735. Location: A10 from Cambridge.
In 673 St Ethelreda, Queen of Northumbria, founded a monastery in the centre of the Fens on the Isle of Ely where she was Abbess until her death in 679. Some 400 years later in 1081, work on the present building was begun, under the guidance of Abbot Simeon. It was completed in 1189 and the cathedral now stands as a remarkable example of Romanesque architecture. Undoubtedly, the most outstanding feature of the cathedral is the octagon, built to replace the Norman tower which collapsed in 1322. The regular free guided tours will help you appreciate all that is special about the cathedral. The Cathedral Shop in the High street offers an imaginative selection of beautiful greetings cards, pottery, glassware, and jewellery. Open daily all year round. Summer 7-7pm and in the winter 7.30-6.30pm. Sun 5pm.

LINTON ZOO
Tel 01223 891308 location:
Ten miles east of Cambridge on the B1052 just off the A460. All set in 16 acres of beautifully landscaped gardens. Find time to visit the zoo and you will find lots to interest the whole family from Sumatran Tigers, African Lions, Snow Leopards, Lynx, Wallabies and Toucans and many exciting and unusual wildlife to be found at Cambridgeshire's Wildlife Breeding Centre. The zoo is continually expanding as more of the world's threatened species are taken on board. Open all year round every day including Bank Holidays.

CORBY KIRKBY HALL
Tel: 01536 203230 Location: Off A43, four miles North East of Corby.
Begun in 1570 and completed by Sir Christopher Hatton, an Elizabethan courtier who built on a scale matching his ambition to entertain the Queen. The ruins of this marvellous country house show the dawning influence of the renaissance on more traditional Tudor forms. Impressive in its sheer grandeur, the house is still partially roofed and glazed with many rooms to explore, and a wealth of richly carved stonework to discover. Kirby's Great Garden is the scene possibly of the most important formal garden restoration project in England. Open daily 10-6pm 1st April-31st October 10-4pm.

LYDDINGTON BEDE HOUSE
Tel: 01572 822438 Location: 6 miles north of Corby.
Amidst the picturesque golden stone of the Leicestershire village of Lyddington, next to the handsome medieval parish church, stands Bede House. For more than 300 years, since 1602, the building was used as an almshouse, but its beginnings were less humble. It was once part of the rural palace of the Bishop's of Lincoln. Many fine details from beautiful 16th century wooden ceilings, 15th century painted glass and a grand fireplace remain to remind us of the original purpose. Open daily 10-6pm 1st April-30th September.

HUNTINGDON HAMERTON WILDLIFE CENTRE
Tel: 01832 293362.
Location: 20 minutes away on the A1 from Peterborough.
Set in lovely rolling countryside, Hamerton's fifteen acres are home to a fascinating array of beautiful creatures from around the world. Opened in June 1990, the centre was established as a Wildlife Conservation Sanctuary. The families and colonies of animals, some virtually extinct, can be found at the wildlife sanctuary. Over 120 species including owls, parrots, wallabies, kookaburras, meerkats and small cats can be seen here. The centre is open every day all year from 10.30-6pm in the summer and 10.30-4pm in the winter.

HINCHINGBROOKE COUNTRY PARK
Tel: 01480 451568.
At Hinchingbrooke Country Park you can wander freely through beautiful, unspoilt Cambridgeshire countryside, through woodland glades and meadows or along river banks and lakesides. Set in 156 acres of woodland, there is a natural habitat home to a suprising variety of wildlife. Here you can see herons, woodpeckers, snipe, foxes and even deer, especially on a peaceful early morning walk. Terns and dragonflies hunt over the lakes in the summer and butterflies drift effortlessly over the meadows. As dusk falls bats emerge and you may even hear a nightingale sing. Open all the yearround.

THE OLD HUNTINGDON CAR TRAIL
Tel 01480 425831
This wonderful car trail has been designed to allow motorists or cyclists to join at any point, journeying around until you return to your starting point. Travelling through all parts of Cambridgeshire taking in all the major sights and attractions, the trail is a great way to travel. Open throughout the year Mon-Fri 9.30-5.30pm Sat 9-5pm. Closed Bank Holiday Mondays.

Chapter Fourteen

BUCKDEN TOWERS
Tel: 01480 811868.
Former Palace of the Bishops of Lincoln. Splendid 15th century gatehouse and tower, catherine of Aragon was imprisoned here. Open Wed 1.30-5.30pm Thurs-Sat 9-5pm Sun 9-12.30pm. Admission free.

RUTLAND WATER RUTLAND NATURE RESERVE & BIRDWATCHING CENTRE
Tel: 01572 770651.
Within easy reach of Peterborough. The Nature Reserve lies at the western end of Rutland Water, and consists of a narrow strip of land stretching for seven miles around the perimeter of the reservoir and covering an area of 350 acres between Lyndon and Egleton. Anglian Water's new Birdwatching Centre at Egleton offers superb views across the lagoons where huge flocks of waterfowl can be seen at close range. More than 200 different species of birds have been recorded at Rutland Water including ospreys and Great Northern Divers. Open all year round.

CORNWALL

BODMIN AND WENFORD RAILWAY.
Bodmin Station just south of town centre on B3268 to Lostwithiel.
Tel: 01208 73666.
Bodmin General Station is a typical Great Western Railway terminus connected by three and a half miles of line to Bodmin Parkway. (British Rail main-line) The railway passes through lovely Cornish countryside and gives access to walks and other attractions. Most trains are steam hauled. For timetables ring or write. Open April-1st week in November plus Christmas and New Year.

LANHYDROCK, National Trust.
Two and a half miles south east of Bodmin-Liskeard or B3268 Bodmin-Lostwithiel roads. Tel: 01208 73320. The finest house in Cornwall, superbly set in wooded parkland of 450 acres and encircled by a garden of rare shrubs and trees, lovely in all seasons. Allow time ot view the 42 rooms. Through the crenellated gatehouse (1641) an idyllic walk on to the River Fowey and back through the woods should not be missed. Open 30th March-31st October daily except Monday when the house only is closed, garden, shop and restaurant remain open. Open Bank Holiday Mondays 11-5.30pm, 5pm in October.

Visitor Attractions

PENCARROW HOUSE AND GARDENS
Pencarrow, Washaway, Bodmin. Tel: 01208 84369.
Georgian House belonging to the Molesworth-St Aubyn Family. 4 miles north-west of Bodmin, signed off the A389 and B3266 at Washaway. Mile long drive through an Ancient British Encampment, flanked by huge rhododendrons, blue hydrangeas, and specimen conifers. Historic Georgian house and Grade II listed garden; still owned and lived in by the family. Superb collection of pictures, furniture, china and some antique dolls. Marked walks through beautiful woodland gardens. Imaginatibve children's play area. Dogs welcome in grounds. Craft centre, picnic area, plant shop, self-pick soft fruits, facilities for the disabled. Open: house, tea rooms & craft centre open daily except Friday and Saturday. Easter to 15th October 1.30-5pm (1st Jun to 10th Sept and Bank Holiday Mondays open 11am) gardens open daily during season.

COLLIFORD LAKE PARK
Bolventor, Bodmin Moor. Tel: 01208 82469.
3 miles south of Bolventor.
On the north-shore of Colliford Lake, a man-made reservoir completed in 1988. The 50 acre moorland park is dedicated to pleasure, education and conservation to suit all age groups and contains rare breeds of birds, cattle, poultry and sheep; many unusual and endangered species as well as more common domestic and household animals. Covered walkways. Indoor and outdoor play areas. Wide range of activities. Undercover assault course and museum. Sheltered nature walks. Open Easter until end of October 10.30am daily

JAMAICA INN
... just off A30 at Bolventor.
Made famous by Daphne du Mauriers novel of the same name. For 400 years it has stood high on Bodmin Moor welcoming smugglers, highwaymen and travellers of all descriptions. It is an experience and in addition to the bars, restaurant and accommodation there is MR POTTERS MUSEUM OF CURIOSITY - showing the remarkable work of Walter Potter the famous Victorian Taxidermist who created the most imaginativeanimal scenes with loving care. Jamaica Inn is open all year and so too is Mr Potter's Museum except January. Tel: 01566 86250.

CAMBORNE SCHOOL OF MINES
GEOLOGICAL MUSEUM & GALLERY.
Pool on the A3047 between Camborne and Redruth
Tel: 01209 714866.
Display of rocks and minerals from all over the world - colourful and interesting as well as educational. Added to this a backdrop of pictures by

artist living in Cornwall. Coffee corner.shop. Open Mon-Fri 9-5pm except Bank Holidays. Admission free.

NORTH CORNWALL MUSEUM
The Clease. Tel: 01840 212954.
Opened in 1974. Privately owned and covers many aspects of life in North Cornwall from fifty to a hundred years ago. Changing exhibitions throughout the season of crafts and paintings. Open 1st Apr-30th Sept 10-5pm daily except Sundays. Free Council car park opposite.

MUSEUM OF HISTORIC CYCLING
The Old Station. Tel: 01840 212811.
One mile north of Camelford on the Boscastle road. Over 250 examples of Cycles. Old cycle repair workshop. A history of cycling from 1818. Fascinating. Open Sundays to Thursday 10-5pm all year.

DOBWALLS FAMILY ADVENTURE PARK
Tel: 01579 20578
Look for signs at Dobwalls on the A38.
Wonderful day out for the whole family with one admission fee allowing you to travel ont eh Rio Grand Miniature Railroad and The Union Pacific Miniature Railroad. Access to Locomotive sheds with their 6 steam and 4 diesel locomotives including the famous 'Big Boy'. Unlimited use of Adventureland. Mr Thorburn's Edwardian Countryside. Beautiful picnic areas and Woodland Walks. Open 30th March-30th September 10-6pm. October weekends only but daily durning Devon and Cornwall Half Term holidays.

CORNWALL MARITIME MUSEUM
Bell's Court, up alley opposite Marks and Spencers in Market Street.
Tel: 01841 520413.
Cornwall's Maritime History, new 'Cornwall and the Sea' exhibition. Marine paintings, ship models, navigation and marine instruments etc. Open Easter-31st October 10-4pm daily. 1st Nov-Easter 10-3pm not Sundays.

TREBAH GARDEN
Mawnwn Smith, Nr Falmouth
Tel: 01326 250448.
This magical old Cornish garden is listed by the Good Gardens Guide as being one of the eighty finest gardens in the world. The twenty five acre, steeply wooded ravine garden falls 200 feet from the 18th century house down to a private beach on the Helford River. It is truly wonderful. The garden is undergoing a major replanting and the beach which is open to visitors to the gardens, is a secluded haven with superb views. Visitors are

welcome to use the beach for swimming and picnics. Open every day of the year 10.30-5pm.

GLENDURGAN GARDENS

.. adjoining Trebah on the Helford River, the steep, sheltered valley garden harbours a gloriously lush display of trees and flowers. The famous cherry laurel maze of 1833 reopened in July 1994 after three years of restoration. Open 1st Mar-31st Oct Tues-sat (closed Good Friday) open Bank Holiday Monday 10.30-5.30pm.

TRELISSICK

National Trust.
4 miles south of Truro on both sides of the B3289 above King Harry Ferry. A garden which offers both peace and tranquillity and splendid panoramic views across the River Fal to the Carrick Roads and Falmouth harbour. Trelissick has been planted with an abundance of those tender shrubs so characteristic of Cornish gardens. Fine woodlands encircle the gardens through which a varied circular walk can be enjoyed all year round. The house is not open. Open 1st Mar-31st Oct wed, Thrus, Fri, Sat & Bank Holiday Mondays 10.30-5.30pm (5pm in Mar and Oct).

THE TAMAR VALLEY DONKEY PARK

St Ann's Chapel, Gunnislake. Tel: 01822 834072.
14 acres for children to explore. The donkeys enjoy it as much as the visitors and so do the loved and well cared for tame cuddly animals. Donkey rides, cart rides, rabbit warren, goat mountain, adventure play ground and much more. Picnic area, cafe, disabled facilities. Good fun for everyone and not expensive. Open every day Easter to end October 10-5.30pm. Weekends from Nov-Mar. Closed January.

THE CORNISH SEAL SANCTUARY

Gweek. Tel: 01637 872822.
Located on the upper reaches of the Helford River by the creekside village of Gweek, approximately 6 miles from Helston. Europe's largest rescue centre for seals and occasionally even rarer sea creatures including dolphins and turtles - specially equipped hospital. Feeding time is the highlight of any visit, when the resident seals and sea lions each have their own amusing techniques and tactics for trying to steal more than their fair share. It is a different adventure every time you come here. Open all year except Christmas Day from 9am. Feeding times twice daily.

Chapter Fourteen

LAND'S END
... where the land meets the mighty Atlantic.
It is still spectacular, standing majestically, dramatic and defiant. A powerful Celtic mixture of heritage, mystery, legend and sheer natural beauty. A day out for the whole family with every concievable attraction from Moghar's Lair to the Lobster Pot Maze and The Land of Greeb and Little Cornwall bo Blackbeard's Drop. Restaurants, cafes, an hotel make this unique. 9 miles from Penzance. Open every day except Christmas Day from 10am. Tel: 01736 871501.

LANREATH FOLK AND FARM MUSEUM
Nr Looe.
Village Tithe Barn - home of hundreds of vintage exhibits, craft workshops, local crafts and bric-a-brac shop. Farmhouse Kitchen, Pets corner, play area. Open daily except Saturdays Easter-June 11-5pm June to September 30th 10-6pm October 11-5pm.

LAUNCESTON STEAM RAILWAY
Station car park on Launceston's Newport Industrial Estate.
Tel: 01566 775665.
Runs through the beautiful Kensey valley from Launceston to the hamlet of New Mills. Locomotives built in Victorian times are among the oldest in regular use. The teminus also provides a buffet, book and gift shop and a transport museum. Trains run at frequent intervals from 11-4.30pm. Open Easter to end of October (closed Saturdays) Santa Specials in December.

LAWRENCE HOUSE MUSEUM
9 Castle Street. Tel: 01566 773277.
1993 Gulbenkian Award Winner. The house built in 1753 was scheduledas a building of special historical and architectural interest in April 1950. Wide diversity of exhibits about Launceston and its history. Run by voluntary helpers, you receive a warm welcome and willing answers to any of your questions. Open 1st Apr-30th Sept including Bank Holidays 10.30-4.30pm Mon-Fri inclusive.

LAUNCESTON CASTLE
English Heritage.
Tel: 01566 772365.
Launceston is crowned by the ruins of its castle, set high on a grassy mound above the town with commanding views of this beautiful corner of England. Built in the years after the Norman Conquest, it became a symbol of the power of the Earls of Cornwall. The remains of a mighty keep, high tower and surrounding walls testify to their authority and status. Parts of the castle are currently inaccessible due to essential conservation work. Access for

Visitor Attractions

visitors in wheelchairs to outer bailey; picnics welcome. Open 1st Apr-31st Oct daily 10-6pm. English Heritage members free admission.

TAMAR GLASS
Units 2C North Petherwin Workshops, North Petherwin.
Tel: 01566 785527.
Easy access from the B3254 six miles north of Launceston. Take Week St Mary turning at North Petherwin village cross roads, then 200 yards past church. Watch the Glassmakers blowing beautiful, original 'Tamar Glass' designs. Mon-Fri 10-1pm, 2-5pm. Showroom also open Sundays 2-5pm. Closed saturdays. Open Apr to end Sept, including Bank Holidays. Free entry. Ample Free parking. Tableware and gifts for all. Quality 'Seconds' available. Commissions welcomed.

COLD NORTHCOTT WIND FARM
.. on the A395 between Launceston and Camelford.
Come and see modern technology working to produce electricity enough to supply 5,500 homes. Set amid farmland with scenic views of North Cornwall countryside. The Windmill Tea Room serves delicious homemake cakes, pasties and light refreshments. Open daily 10-6pm 7 days a week.

TREDIDON TRAILS
Tredidon Barton, St Thomas, Nr Launceston.
Tel: 01566 86288.
Signposted one mile off the A395 approximately one mile from the A30 Kennard's House junction, down a country lane. Tredidon Trails welcomes you to a new exciting countryside experience. Here are a series of different trails designed to challenge all ages and provide both fun and education, set in a beautifully landscaped area of natural beauty, with woodland, lakes and wildlife. Open Mon-Sat 9.30-5pm Easter until the end of October. Special opening in December.

PAUL CORIN'S MAGNIFICENT MUSIC MACHINES
.. just off the B3254 at St Keyne Station, near Liskeard.
Tel: 01579 343108.
Come to the Old Mill in the lovely Looe valley, for an unforgettable nostalgic Musical entertainment - Fair Organs, Orchestrions, Player Pianos, and the Might Wurlitzer Theatre Pipe Organ. A great experience. Free car park, picnic area by the river, light refreshments, books and recordings, photography welcome, also dogs on leads. Open 10.30-5pm Easter: Good Friday for 10 days inclusive. Daily May 1st until last Sunday in October. Spring: Sundays and Thursday in April.

Chapter Fourteen

THE CHEESE FARM
.. between Upton Cross and Rilla Mill.
Tel: 01579 62244.
Discover the secrets of Yarg nettle Cheese. Visit theworking Cheese Farm, Wild Boar Paddock. Entertaining Guided Tours. Barn Shop and restaurant. Drop in between 10-4pm Mon-Sat Easter to October.

THE MONKEY SANCTUARY
.. is signposted on the B3253 at No Man's Land between East Looe and Hessenford. From Liskeard or Plymouth take the A38 to the Trerulefoot roundabout then follow the signs for Looe.
Tel: 01503 262532.
Beautiful woodland setting overlooking Looe Bay. For 25 years the Victorian house and gardens have been the home of a natural colony of woolly monkeys. Extensive grassed enclosures, heated indoor rooms and access to trees provide an environment in which these monkeys can thrive. Three generations of these beautiful monkeys, all born in Cornwall, may now be seen at the Sanctuary. The special relationship between monkeys and Sanctuary staff can be observed both inside and outside their territory talks are given throughout the day explaining monkey life at the sanctuary as well as how to behave if you meet a woolly monkey in the gardens. Open Easter: Sunday before till Thursday after inclusive. Summer: Beginning of May to end of September, Sunday to Thursday 10.30-5pm (closed Friday and Saturday). Allow at least 2 hours for your visit.

MARAZION ST MICHAEL'S MOUNT,
Marazion, Penzance. National Trust.
Tel: 01736 710265.
This magical island is the jewel in Cornwall's crown, a national treasure which is a must for every visitor to the far west. The great granite crag which rises from the waters of Mount's Bay is surmounted by an embattled 14th century castle, home of the St Aubyn family for over 300 years. On the water's edge there is a harbourside community, an ancient trading place for tin and other Cornish goods which today features shops and restaurants. Open: 30th March-31st October Mon-Fri (shop and restaurant open daily) 10.30-5.30pm November - 29th March. Guided tours as tide, weather and circumstances permit.

NEWLYN ART GALLERY.
Approaching Newlyn, the gallery is the first building on the sea-side of the coast road from Penzance.
Tel: 01736 63715.
Presents an exciting and varied programme of contemporary art and related events throughout the year. The Gallery is a dynamic artistic activity. One of

the most important visual arts resources in the South West. Open: Mon-Sat 10-5pm Admission free.

NEWQUAY TRERICE
National Trust.
Tel: 01637 875404.
An architectural gem - a small Elizabethan manor house, built before the Armada in 1571. The summer-flowering garden is unusual in content and layout and there is an orchard planted with old varieties of fruit trees. A small museum traces the history of the lawn mower. Open: 30th Mar-31st October daily except Tuesday 11-5.30pm Closes 5pm in October.

SPRINGFIELDS PONY CENTRE AND FUN PARK
St Columb Major. Well signposted from the St Columb Major roundabout.
Tel: 01637 881224.
All wather attraction. Friendly Shetland ponies, pony rides. Pets Corner. Enjoy feeding lambs, calves and goats and hand feed the ducks fish and Sika deer. Springfields is a paradise for children. Burger Bar. Lake View restaurant. Dogs not allowed. Open: 31st March-30th October, 7 days a week 9.30-5.30pm October 10-4.30pm.

NEWQUAY SEA LIFE CENTRE
Towan Promenade. Tel: 01326 22361.
Experience the thrill of a deep sea dive without getting wet as you journey through a wondrous watery world with a surprise around every corner. Fascinating and extraordinary experience. Open: All year except Christmas Day 10am.

PRIDEAUX PLACE
Tel: 01841 532411/532945. F
ollow brown tourist signs from A389 Padstow Ring Road. Free parking in grounds. Dogs welcome in grounds on leads. For 400 years, Prideaux Place has been the home of the Prideaux family, an ancient Cornish clan who can be traced to Prideaux Castle, Luxulyan at the time of the Conquest in 1066. Completed in 1592 the Grade I Listed building has been embellished and extended by successive generations. Filled with treasures, including royal and family portraits, porcelain and fine furniture, this beautiful Cornish mansion is still very much a family home with the majority of rooms still in regular use. Open: Easter-Sept 30th 1.30-5pm Sundays to Thursday inclusive. Easter, Whit and late summer Bank Holidays from 11am.

GEEVOR TIN MINE
Beside the B3306 coast road from St Ives to Land's End, at Pendeen, St Just. Tel/Fax: 01736 788662. The last tin mine in Penwith, in spectacular coastal

setting. A unique Cornish Mining Museum, with a video showing surface and underground working. Personal guided tour of surface plant, the most complete historic mining/processing plant in Britain. Open: Easter to October daily 10.30-5.30pm November-Easter Mon-Fri 10.30-4pm.

PENZANCE AND DISTRICT MUSEUM AND ART GALLERY.
Off Morrah rd.
Tel: 01736 63625.
New Interactive Multimedia computer technology which has been istalled in the new Archaeoloty gallery. Discover the shops of the 1890s and 1030s and use the new computer image data- bank to discover what the area looked like in times past. The Art Galleries contain the largest collection of Newlyn School paintings in public ownership. Open: Mon-Fri 10.30-4.30pm Sat: 10.30-12.30pm.

TRINITY HOUSE NATIONAL LIGHTHOUSE CENTRE
The Old Buoy Store, Wharf Road.
Tel: 01736 60077.
One of the few national museums outside London, it houses the finest collection of lighthouse equipment in the world. Audio-visual. Open: Daily April-October.

TRENGWAINTON GARDENS
Nr. Penzance. In the far west, the uncommonly mild climate encourages the most tender and exotic shrubs and trees to flourish. A unique feature is the complex of walled gardens with west-facing raised beds, built c1820 for the gorwing of early vegetables. Open: 1st March-31st October, Wed, Thurs, Fri, Sat and Bank Holiday Mondays 10.30-5.30pm (5pm in March and October) National Trust.

THE EGYPTIAN HOUSE c.1835.
Built to contain a Geological Museum. After years of neglect was artistically restored by the Landmark Trust in 1973. The Royal Arms are of the period George III,IV and William IV.

PERRANPORTH NANSMELLYN MARSH RESERVE
.. is to be found where the stream flows into the outskirts of Perranporth - here there isthe remnant of a large reed bed which used to occupy the valley floor. The reeds provide shelter and food for Sedge Warblers and Reed Buntings, whose songs can be heard all night in May. Several species of the very local Wainscott moths are also well established in the reserve. A hide on the east side of the reserve provides a good vantage point from which to observe the birds. Keys from Perranporth Information Centre.

Visitor Attractions

PORTHCURNO THE MINACK THEATRE
Tel: 01841 540147.
The theatre is on the south coast about 3 miles from Land's End and 9 miles from Penzance. At the seaward end of the Porthcurno valley go up the winding hill. The Theatre is on your left. Wonderful open air theatre. Audience are admitted one and a half hours before 'curtain up'. The earlier you arrive the closer you will be to the stage. The sun can be very hot at matinees and it is advisable to wear warm clothes in the evening. The seats are very hard but they do hire cushions! If you are disabled, please bring a t least one able bodied person with you and try to let the management know in advance. Parking is free. Sandwiches and confectionery, hot and cold drinks are available pre-show and during the interval. There is an Exhibition Centre. Hours 10-5.30pm daily from 1st April-31st October (closing at 4.30pm in Oct). On days when there is a matinee, the Centre will be closed from 12-2.30pm, and viewing of the Theatre will be restricted durning the performance. A fabulour experience and unlike any other theatre in the world.

REDRUTH CORNISH ENGINES,
National Trust, Pool, Redruth.
Tel: 01209 216657.
In the heart of Cornwall's richest mining district there is a rare opportunity to see two fine Cornish beam engines preserved in their imposing houses. One can be seen in action. Open: 30th Mar-31st Oct daily 11-5pm (or sunset if earlier) 11-6pm July and August.

SALTASH COTEHELE.
National Trust.
On the west bank of the Tamar 1 mile west of Calstock by footpath, 8 miles south west of Tavistock, 14 miles from Plymouth visa Saltash Bridge.
Tel: 01579 50434. Recorded Information 01579 51222.
Enchantingly remote, perched high above the wooded banks of the Tamar. For nearly six centuries the home of the Edgcumbe family. The manor house gives the impression of having been woven through time. It retains a medieval atmosphere. Cotehele today is a romantically unique estate - the terraced garden with its pools and dovecote, a working watermill and adjoining ciderpress, the Quay with its evocation of Victorian bustle. Now the home berth of the Shamrock, one of the last surviving Tamar sailing barges. Worth spending a day here. Open: 30th Mar-31st Oct. House, restaurant and mill daily except Friday (open Good Friday) House 12-5.30pm. Tearoom on Quay, shop and garden daily 11-5pm. Quay gallery daily 12-5pm.

Chapter Fourteen

ST AUSTELL WHEAL MARTYN CHINA CLAY GERITAGE CENTRE.
Follow the signs to Carthew on the B3274, 2 miles north of St Austell.
Tel/Fax: 01726 85362.
Historic trail - discover the history of this important Cornish industry. Open air historic clay workings, indoor exhibitions, displays and audio-visual show, 1899 locomotive working water wheels and 1916 Peerless lorry. Nature Trail - mile long walk through the beautiful wooded site andspectacular views of a moder day working clay pit. Childrens Adventure Trail - picnic area, mineral displays, gift and pottery shop. Open: daily April to October 10-6pm.

LOST GARDENS OF HELIGAN,
Pentewan, St Austell.
Tel: 01726 844157/843566.
Award winning gardens, asleep for more than seventy years, are the scene of the largest garden restoration project in Europe. Most exciting, must be seen. Open: every day of the year 10-4.30pm.

KIDS KINGDOM
Albert Road, St Austell.
Tel: 01726 77377.
Indoor Adventure Play Centre for the under 12's who must be accompanied by a responsible adult. Great fun, plenty to do. Open: 7 days a week Easter-end September 10-9pm. October-Easter 10-6pm.

ST IVES SOCIETY OF ARTISTS,
Old Mariners Church, Norway Square adjacent to Sloop car park. Exhibits representational work. Gallery overlooks harbour that was the inspiration for so much of their work. Open: March-early November Mon-Sat. 10-12.30 & 2-4.30pm Mid-December-Mid January sam hours. Closed Christmas Day and Boxing Day. Tel: 01736 795582.

BARBARA HEPWORTH MUSEUM
Barnoon Hill,.
Tel: 01736 796226.
Sculptures in wood, stone and bronze can be sen in the late Barbara Hepworth's house, studio and sub-tropical garden where she lived and worked form 1949-75.

TATE GALLERY,
Porthmeor Beach. Tel: 01736 796226.
Presents changing displays of 20th century modern art in the context of Cornwall. Displays are drawn from the Tate Gallery collection. Open: all year. Closed 24,25,26 Dec and 1st Jan.

Visitor Attractions

ST KEW THE CORNWALL DONKEY & PONY SANCTUARY.
Lower Maidenland. Tel: 01208 84710.
Plenty to do. Help groom the donkeys and ponies. Play area. Adventure Swamp. Cart rides for children. Picnic by the stream. Under cover: The Eeyore Club for younger children. Bouncy Castle. Meet the baby animals. Coffee Shop and Tea Garden. Just off the A39 Wadebridge to Camelford road, 3 miles form Wadebridge. Open: daily one week before Easter-October 10-5pm. Telephone for winter opening hours.

TINTAGEL OLD POST OFFICE
Tel: 01840 770024.
National Trust.
One of the most characterful buildings in Cornwall, and a house of great antiquity, this small 14th century manor is full of charm and interest. Tumble-roofed and weathered by the centuries, it is restored in the fashion of the Post Office it was for nearly 50 years. Open: 30th Mar-31st Oct daily 11-5.30pm. Closes 5pm Oct.

TINTAGEL CASTLE
Tel: 01840 770328.
Off Tintagel Head, half a mile along a track from Tintagel (no vehicles). Throughout the ages Tintagel has exerted a profound fascination for writers, artists and travellers. Even today this wild and windswept corner of the Cornish coast preserves its mystery. Associated in legend with Merlin and King Arthur it remains an enigma. Clearly it was occupied long before the medieval castle, whose ruins you can see, was laid out in the 13th century. Whatever the truth, Tintagle Castle, clinging to its lonely island, with the surfthundering against the cliffs below and the waves breaking over the threshold of Merlin's Cave, remains one of the most spectacular and romantic spots in the British Isles. Toilets on site. Land Rover service from village to castle. Open: 1st Apr-31st Oct open daily 10-4pm. English Heritage members free admission.

TORPOINT ANTHONY,
National Trust. Torpoint 01752 812191.
A superb example of an early 18th century mansion. The main block is faced in silver grey stone, with red brick wings. Set in parkland and fine gardens overlooking the Lynher River, home of the great Cornish family of Carew. Anthony contains a wealth of paintings, tapestries, furniture and embroideries. An unusual Bath House in the grounds can be viewed by arrangement. Open: 30th Mar-31st Oct Tues, Wed, Thurs and Bank Holiday Mondays plus Sundays in June, July and August 1.30-5.30pm. Tea room opens 12.30pm.

TRESCO ABBEY GARDENS,
Isles of Scilly. Tel: 01720 422849.
The garden flourishes on this small island only two miles long. Nowhere else in the British Isles does such an exotic and exciting collection of plants grow in the open. Within its 14 acres, palms shoot skywards; stately echiums resemble burning rockets. Quite wonderful to see. From its early days Tresco has welcomed visitors; the effect is so stunning that even the non-gardener cannot fail to be impressed. Open: everyday of the year. 10-4pm.

TRURO ROYAL CORNWALL MUSEUM,
River Street. Tel: 01872 72205.
Superb collections of Cornish history and archaeology, paintings, ceramics, silver and gold. Examine a genuine Egyptian mummy of the world famous collection of Cornish minerals. Shop and cafe. Open: Mon-Sat 10-5pm except Bank Holidays.

TREWITHEN GARDENS,
Grampound Rd, Nr Truro. Tel: 01726 882763/4.
Adjoining Probus Gardens on A390. Covering some 30 acres and created in the early years of this century, the gardens are outstanding and internationally famous. Renowned for the magnificent collection of camellias, rhododendrons, magnolias and many rare trees and shrubs. Extensive woodland gardens surrounded by traditional landscaped parkland. Teas and light refreshments. Plants and shrubs for sale. The house goes back to the 17th century and has been cared for and lived in by the same family since 1715. Open: Gardens: 1st Mar-30th Sept Mon-Sat 10-4.30pm Nursery: All year Mon-Fri 9-4.3-pm House: Apr-Jul Mon and Tues only and August Bank Holiday Monday 2-4pm.

PROBUS GARDENS,
Probus. Tel: 01726 882597.
A garden with a difference; a true centre of excellence. Here you can enjoy literally thousands of specimen plants and shrubs growing in superb settings - and find new ways to get more out of your garden. Whether you live in Cornwall or are visiting, a real enthusiast or an enthusiastic amateur you'll find something here to inspire you. Open: every day 1st April-30th Sept 10-5pm and Mon-Fri in the winter from 10-4pm

THE ORIGINAL CORNISH SCRUMPY CALLESTOCK CIDER FARM,
Penhallow. Tel: 01872 573356.
Traditional Cider farm with a Jam Kitchen.Shire Horses and other friendly farm animals. Free samples of all their products. Signposted off the A3075 Newquay road at Penhallow. Designated as being of outstanding natural beauty and listed as being of special historical interest. Open: Easter-Dec

Mon-Fri 9-6pm and Saturdays form Easter-end Oct. July/August Mon-Fri until 8pm. Sundays: shop only 12-3pm.

WADEBRIDGE SHIRE HORSE ADVENTURE PARK,
Tredinnick, Wadebridge. Tel: 01841 540276.
8 miles from Newquay, 6 miles Wadebridge. Take A39. Bigger every year this provides a fantastic day out. 6 major attractions in one. Magnificent Shire Horses, unique owl sanctuary, the thrilling world of Adventure, amazing Playhouse for younger children, Old McDonald's Barn, full of baby animals to pet and feed. Jungle Fantasy, 9,000ft of ropes, balls, nets and slides. The whole family will be entertained for hours on end - regardless of weather and all for one all-inclusive entry price. Dogs welcome on a lead. Opem daily 1st Apr-28th Oct 10-5pm. Closed Saturdays in October.

MELLINGEY MILL WILLOW CRAFT CENTRE,
St Issey. Tel: 01841 540604.
Basket Workshop, Willow Beds, Nature Walks, Willow Walks with play houses. Illustrated history and nature displays. Photographic Exhibitions. Basket Showroom. Picnic and play area, tearoom and terrace, waterwheel, gift shop. Ample parking. Open: Easter-October 10-5pm. Admission fee redeemable on basket sales over £10.

ZENNOR THE WAYSIDE MUSEUM
B3306 St Ives to St Just coast road. Tel: 01736 796945.
A unique private museum, founded in 1935, covering every aspect of life in Zennor from 3,000 BC to 1930s. Waterwheels, Millhouse, Wheelwrights, Blacksmiths, a Miller's cottage with kitchen and parlour etc. nearby is the famous Mermaid Chair in the village church. Open: Easter to October 31st daily from 10am plus evenings in high season.

DEVON

ASHBURTON THE RIVER DART COUNTRY PARK,
Holne Park. Tel: 01364 652511.
Country fun for everyone. Adventure Playgrounds, Bathing, Picnics, Woodland Walks, Pony Riding, Ananconda Run and more. Suitable for any age. Open: Easter to September.

ASHBURTON MUSEUM,
1 West Street. Tel: 01364 63278.
Attractive small town museum displaying local artifacts and items of local history, geology and social customs. The home of the Paul Endacott North

Chapter Fourteen

America Indian Collection. Open: Tues, Thurs, Fri & Sat. 2.30-5pm, mid-May to end of September.

AXMINSTER THE MINSTER CHURCH OF ST MARY.
Tel: 01297 32264.
There has been a church in Axminster for over 1200 years. Open all day.

BABBACOMBE THE MODEL VILLAGE
Tel: 01803 328669.
Unique reproduction of the English countryside often featured on TV. A Masterpiece of miniature landscaping. Press Button information in English and French. Illuminated every evening from dusk (Easter to October). Buses direct from Brixham, Paignton, Torquay, Teignmouth, Dawlish and Exeter. Open: every day except Christmas Day. Easter to September 9am-10pm. October 9am-9pm. November 9am to dusk.

BARNSTAPLE ARLINGTON COURT.
N.T. Tel: 01271 850296.
Houses one of the country's finest collection of carriages in the stables. Walk through peaceful woods, a haven for birdlife. See Shetland ponies and Jacob sheep in the park. The Regency House has fascinating Victorian collections of model ships, animals, exotic shells, pewter and snuff boxes, and the history of a 600 year old Devon family. Open: Mar 30th-Oct 30th daily except Sat 11-5.30pm. Dogs in park only on short leads. Refreshments and Shop.

MARWOOD HILL GARDENS
4 miles north of Barnstaple, signed from the A361 (Barnstaple-Braunton road). Beautiful gardens with many RHS Awards for plants.

GREEN LANES SHOPPING CENTRE
- at the heart of the town. Excellent shopping centre. Every Wednesday afternoon there is the sound of live music. Thrpughout the week, the Centre plays host to a wealth of displays and exhibitions. So whether shopping, dining, or just enjoying the experience - make a day of it in Green Lane.

BICKINGTON GORSE BLOSSOM MINIATURE RAILWAY PARK
Tel: 0162682 361.
Off old A38 near Bickington, 3 miles north-west of Newton Abbot. The 7 1/4 inch guage trains, carring all the family, run for nearly 3/4 mile, twisting and turning through acres of gardens and natural woodland, in cuttings on high banks, recapturing the great days of steam in miniature. Unlimited train rides for an all inclusive admission price. Large car park. Adventure play ground. Picnic area, restaurant and shop. A great family attraction. Open Easter daily to first Sunday in October 10am-4.30pm.

BICKLEIGH BICKLEIGH MILL
Tel: 018845 419.
Mid-Devon's largest and most popular award winning centre. Craft Centres, Farm & Fishing Centres, Picnic, Leisure and Bird Garden. Special events. Don't come without a camera or with less than an hour to spare. Open: Easter to Christmas 10-6pm (5pm in Nov & Dec).

BICKLEIGH CASTLE
Tel: 01884 855363.
Ancient Royalist stronghold spanning 900 years of history and architecture - and still lived in! The 11th century detached Chapel with pre-tudor furnishings, the Armoury including Cromwellian arms and armour, the Guard Room, The Great Hall, 'Tudor' Bedroom, and the 17th century farmhouse - are all shown. Excellent Museum. Picturesque moated garden. A great tome for the whole family - and educational too! Open: Easter week and then Wednesdays, Sundays and Bank Holidays to late May Bank Holiday; then to 2nd October daily. (Except Saturdays) 2-5.30pm. Refreshments and Shops.

BIDEFORD THE BIG SHEEP
Tel: 01237 477916.
2 miles west of Bideford on the A39 North Devon link road. Look for the big flag! A working farm turned wacky tourist attraction. Combining traditional rural crafts, such as cheesemaking and shearing, with hilarious novelties such as sheep racing and duck trialling. An amusing programme of events throughout the day. Hours of entertainment for all ages whatever the weather. The main programmes start at 10.30am and 2pm. Phone for details. Shop and restaurant. Open: daily 10-6pm all year.

BLACKAWTON WOODLANDS LEISURE PARK
Tel: 01803 712598.
60 acres of indoor and outdoor fun for a full day of variety for the whole family. Experience 12 challenging Play-Zones for every age and ability plus great Entertainment Days. Go walk-about round the seven acre Animal park then linger by the exotic Waterfowl Collection. Take time to relax by a woodland pool; enjoy that cream tea on the Rose Terrace or a delicious meal in the cafe. Browse round the Gift Shop for that souvenir of a fantastic day out. Discount Ticket for 2 adults and 2 children. Open daily March until the beginning of November 9.30am until dusk. Winter opening at weekends and School Holidays except December 24,25 & 26.

BOVEY TRACEY THE DEVON GUILD OF CRAFTSMEN
Riverside Mill. Tel: 01626 832223.
Constantly changing series of exhibitions of the finest craftsmanship in Britain today. There is a shop where members of the Guild sell a wide range of top

quality goods, and an attractive Granery Coffee Shop serving light meals including imaginative vegetarian dishes throughout the day. Open 10am-5.30pm seven days a week all year.

PARKE RARE BREEDS FARM.
N.T. Haytor Rd. Tel: 01626 832093.
Over 200 acres of parkland in the wooded valley of the River Bovey, forming a beautiful approach to Dartmoor. Lovely walks through woodlands, beside the river and along the route of the old railway track. National Trust and Dartmoor Park information centre and National Park headquarters. A private collection of rare farm animals. An interpretation centre and farm trail helps people to discover yesterday's farm and bring it to life. National Trust members must pary the admission charge. Open: parkland all year. Rare Breeds Farm, April to October daily 10-5pm.

HOUSE OF MARBLES,
The Old Pottery, Pottery Rd. Tel: 01626 835358.
At the House of Marbles they have been manufacturing their unusual range of games, toys, marbles and glassware for many years. Visitors are welcome to view the old pottery buildings with their listed kilns. Watch the glass blowing work in progress and browse in the factory showroom/seconds shop. Coffee Shop/Restaurant. Museum area. Open: Shop. Mon-Sat 9-5pm. Sundays (easter-September). Glassmaking can be viewed Mon-Fri 9-5pm. Sundays and Bank Holidays 10-3pm (Easter-Sept).

BRENTOR ROWDEN GARDENS,
Nr Tavistock. Tel: 01822 810275.
Rare, unusual and aquatic plant specialists. Open: 1st Apr-30th Sept. Sat, Sun and Bank Holidays 10-5pm.

BRIXHAM BRIXHAM MUSEUM,
New Road. Tel: 01803 856267.
Brixham is Torbay's oldest town, and the museum has been created by the local community to portray its own unique history. A history close to the sea and rich in fishing, trawling, shipbuilding, the dangers of life at sea, and reliance on the lifeboat. Enjoy a charming historical insight into the lives of Brixham people, from early times to the present day. Open: April-October Mon-Sat 10am-5pm.

BUCKFAST ABBEY
Tel: 01364 43723.
The Abbey is a living Benedictine monastery and the only fully restored medieval monastery in Britain. The church contains many internationally known works of art. Shops, refreshments, ample car park and caravan park.

An audio-visual and exhibition tells you about the Abbey from its foundation in AD 1018 to the present day. Church open daily. Exhibition: Easter to end October.

BUCKFAST BUTTERFLY FARM,
Buckfastleigh Steam & Leisure Park. Tel: 01364 42916.
Wander through the tropical landscape gardenwith its ponds, waterfalls and bridges and see exotic butterflies and moths from many parts of the world - live - flying around you. An all weather educational attraction for all the family. Free parking for cars and coaches. Gift Shop. Picnic area. Open: daily Apr-1st Nov from 10-6pm.

SOUTH DEVON RAILWAY
Tel: 01364 642338.
Buckfastleigh Steam and Leisure Park takes you right back into the steam age with a seven mile Great Western branch line alongside the beautiful River Dart to Totnes, a museum, other attractions and extensive riverside picnic grounds, putting, maze, pets corner and much more. Trains run at Easter and daily during the summer season. For other days, exact dates and train times see timetable or telephone.

PENNYWELL DEVON'S FARM & WILDLIFE CENTRE
Tel: 01364 642023.
Take your most direct route to the A38 between Exeter and Plymouth. Follow the brown signs for Pennywell near the town of Buckfastleigh. Traditional farming mixes easily with modern tourism here. Christopher and Nicola Murray, with their team of helpers, show tremendous skill at introducing even the youngest child to all the animals. Great value for the whole family. A wonderful day out. Excellent meals, snacks and drinks at realistic prices. Family ticket for 2 adults and 2 children. Opendaily 10am-5.50pm from the end of March until the end of October. 10am-5.30pm. Discount for group bookings.

BUCKLAND MONACHORUM THE GARDEN HOUSE,
Nr Yelverton. Run by the Fortescue Garden Trust, the walled garden has been discribed as the 'most beautiful 1½ acres in England'. It is certainly a very beautiful garden from March to October, with an enormous range of plants and colour. Teas and light lunches are served in the main rooms of the elegant house. There is also a well-stocked plant centre, which has an enviable reputation as a source of well-grown unusual plants. Open every day March-October 10.30am-5pm.

Chapter Fourteen

CHUDLEIGH THE WHEEL CRAFT WORKSHOPS & RESTAURANT
Tel: 01626 853255(Rest) 01626 852698(Workshops).
Workshops producing high quality craft/designer goods in and around restored mill. Items always for sale. Large working backshot wheel with extensive interior machinery. Licensed restaurant. Home-made food. Open in the evenings. Open 1-am-5.30pm 7 days a week all year. Admission free.

SILVERLANDS,
Stokelake. Tel: 01626 852872.
The exciting new all-weather family attraction set in the heart of the beautiful Teign Valley. Delightful model displays, fascinating exhibitions, craft workshops, animal meadow, special events. Cafe, gift shop, free parking. Direct access from A38 Exeter/Plymouth road, take Teign Valley exit on to B3193. Open daily 1-am-6pm Easter to late October.

CANONTIEGN FALLS,
Nr Chudleigh. Tel: 01647 52434.
Set in the heart of a private 100 acres estate, it is a joy to visit in any season, with its waterfalls, lakes and abundant wildlife. Lady Exmouth Falls has a sheer drop of 220ft, making it the highest fall in England. Clampitt Falls and Secret Garden Falls must also be seen. Canontiegn Nature Trails about one mile in length take in the woods, waterfalls and lakes. Licensed restaurant and cafe plus all weather barbecue offers a wide range of meals and snacks including delicious cream teas. Turn off the A38 at Teign Valley Cudleigh junction. Follow the brown tourist signs for 3 miles on the B3193. Open 10-5.30pm mid March-mid November. Winter: Sundays only and school holidays. One overall charge.

CLOVELLY THE MILKY WAY,
Downland Farm, Nr Clovelly. Tel: 01237 431255.
Offers one of th largest undercover attractions in the South West. It is a family run countryside experience, featuring shows, demonstrations, train rides, play areas, history and much more. The North Devon Bird of Prey Centre is part of the Milky Way. Wonderful day out. Inside and outside picnic areas. Tea garden. Free parking. Dogs allowed on leads. No need for wellies. Open Mar 31st-31st Oct 10.30-6pm. On the main A39 Bideford-Bude road, 2 miles from Clovelly.

COMBE MARTIN WATERMOUTH CASTLE
Tel: 01272 867474.
Between Ilfracombe and Combe Martin. One price covers all attractions except coin operated machines, catering and shop goods. One of the UK's most exciting and unique all weather attractions. Enter the castle and experience nostalgic displays, brilliant sights and sounds, breathtaking

Visitor Attractions

beautiful coloured waterfalls, haunteddungeons, magical fairy tales that come to life before your very eyes. And that's not all. Open from end of March until end of October. Sunday-Friday generally. Ring to confirm dates and times.

DALWOOD   BURROW FARM GARDENS,
Nr Axminster. Tel: 01404 831258.
Beautifully landscaped gardens extending to over 5 acres. Superb views. The fascinating woodland garden, created in an ancient Roman clay pit, features wild flowers and an array of moisture loving plants including candelabra primulas. These provide a wonderful compliment to the rhododendrons and azaleas. This area is particularly beautiful early in the season. Gardens open daily 1 Apr-30th Sept 2pm-7pm. Home-made Cream Teas Sundays, Wednesdays and Bank Holidays. Ample parking with picnic area.

DARTINGTON   THE DARTINGTON CIDER PRESS CENTRE,
Skinners Bridge. Tel: 01803 864171.
The Cider Press Centre just 2 miles from Totnes on the A384 Buckfastleigh road offers a complete day out for all the family. Well known for its exhibitions, the centre also house some unusual shops including Tridas Toys and Dartington Glass. There are two restaurants and lots of special events throughout the summer. Plenty of free parking. Open 9.30-5.30pm Mon-Sat and on Sundays during school summer holidays.

DARTMOUTH CASTLE,
Tel: 018043 3588.
Guarding the narrow entrance to the Dart estuary - one of the loveliest in England - the Castle was one of the first to be built for artillery. Dates from 15th century. It says much for the foresight of the burgesses of Dartmouth that the site of the fortress has not been bettered. Guns were mounted there in the Second World War. Open: all year round except for Dec 24/25/26 and Jan 1st. Car park. Toilets. Refreshment facilities nearby.

DAWLISH   DAWLISH MUSEUM
... is open to and for the benefit of the public for the display of exhibits relating to the history of the Town of Dawlish, and of the South West of England in general. Open daily May-Sept 10-12.30pm, 2-5pm. Sunday 2-5pm.

THE CRAWSHAW GALLERY
Priory Road. Tel: 01626 862032.
Talented artist family led by Alwyn Crawshaw. The gallery houses his paintings, fine art prints, his many books on learing to paint and also general

Chapter Fourteen

artisic memorabilia. The work on show for sale varies greatly from small sketches through to large paintings in all mediums. Car park. Open Tues-Sat 9.30-1pm & 2-5.30pm.

DREWSTEIGNTON   CASTLE DROGO
Tel: 01647 4333306.
Perched on a crag overlooking the Teign Valley, the castle is a marvel of the ingenuity of the architect Sir Edwin Lutyens. The house was built during the early part of this century and not fully completed before the Second World War. It is full of fascination; magnificent craftsmanship combines with the grim splendour of a medieval castle. There are magnificent views from the castle standing above the wooded gorge of the Teign to Dartmoor. Beautiful secluded garden containing a circular croquet lawn. Equipment may be hired from the Administrator. Open daily, except Friday, 30 Mar-30 Oct 11-5.30pm. Tearoom in car park.

EXETER   CREALY COUNTRY PARK
Sidmouth Road, Clyst St Mary. Tel:01395 233200.
Fun for everyone. Buzzard's Swoop Freefall Slide. Archery, Animal Farmand Barnyarn. Bug Club Corner, Games Meadow, Discovery Trails, Milk-a-Cow and many more attractions. Open every day 10-6pm mid-Mar until 23rd Dec. Dogs welcome in most of the park.

MARITIME MUSEUM
Tel: 01392 58075.
The World's biggest and best collection of World's Boats. This is a 'Please Touch' Museum where you go where you like, when you like. There are boats of every kind from Canoes to Coracles, Row Boats to Steamers. Super place. Free parking. Tea room. Summer Boat Hire. Open daily all year except Christmas and Boxing Day 10-5pm (6pm in summer).

TOPSHAM MUSEUM
25 The Strand, Topsham. Tel: 01395 873244.
Late 17th century merchants house with period rooms and sail loft. The Exe Estuary story of shipbuilding and maritime trade of Topsham. 1900 model of Topsham. Honiton lace and lace making. Open 2-5pm Mar-Oct Mon, Wed, & Sat. Sundays in July, Aug & Sept. Tearoom Shop and garden.

ROYAL ALBERT MEMORIAL MUSEUM
Queen Street. Tel: 01392 265858.
One of the finest Victorian buildings in Exeter holds outstanding collections of local and national importance. Fine Art includes Devon artists of the 18th and 19th centuries. Open East-October. Mon-Sat. Nov-Easter Tues-Sat 10-5.30pm Coffee Shop & Gift Shop. Admission Free.

Visitor Attractions

GUILDHALL,
High Street. Tel: 01392 265500.
Earliest reference contained in a deed of 1160. One of the oldest municipal buildings in the United Kingdom still regularly used for council meetings and civic functions. The City Silver and Regalia, and an interesting portrait of Princess Henrietta, sister to Charles II is on display. Open Tues-Sat subject to Civic requirements. Ring first.

ST NICHOLAS PRIORY
The Mint, off Fore Street. Tel: 01392 265858.
Originally the guest wing of a Benedictine Priory, St Nicholas Priory is now displayed as it later became, the house of a rich, Elizabethan merchant. Splendid 15th century guest hall with period furniture and fine plaster ceilings. Open Easter-October Mon-Sat. Ring for opening times.

UNDERGROUND PASSAGES
off High Street. Tel: 01392 265887.
Unique medieval water supply of the city and an amazing experience. The passages are very narrow and are not suitable for anyone prone to claustrophobia.

THE CATHEDRAL
Open daily. Cathedral shop. Licensed refectory. Somewhere that deserves your time.

KILLERTON
Broadclyst. Tel: 01392 881345.
A National Trust property. Wonderful house the home of the Acland family. There are 15 acres of beautiful hillside gardens which sweep down to wide lawns and formal herbaceous borders. The garden and park offer delightful walks through rare trees and shrubs. Ice house and bear hut. The Pauline de Bush collection of costume is displayed in the house in a series of rooms furnished in different periods, ranging from the second half of the 18thcentury to the present day. Licensed restraurant. Light refreshments in the Coach House. Shop including plant sales. Fresh home-baked bread and cake sales. Open April-end of October, daily 11-6pm. You will find Killerton 2 miles north of Broadclyst on the west side of the B3181 Exeter to Cullompton road. The entrance is off the B3185.

POWDERHAM CASTLE
Kenton. Tel: 01626 890243.
In a tranquil and beautiful setting beside the picturesque estuary of the River Exe lies the medieval Castle of Powderham. Visit a succession of magnificent Halls and State Rooms filled with lavish furnishings, tapestries and historic

Chapter Fourteen

portraits of the fascinating Courtenay family. The castle has been their home for over 600 yeas and the present Earl of Devon is a direct descendant of Sir Philip Courtenay who built the Castle between 1390 and 1420. It was extensively damaged during the Civil War and considerable restoration and alterations followed during the 18th and 19th centuries. Open every day except Saturday from 10-5.30pm (last guided tour 5pm) April to September inclusive. Cream teas, light lunches available in the Courtyard Tea Rooms. Gift Shop.

GREAT TORRINGTON   DARTINGTON CRYSTAL
Tel: 01805 624233.
A unique working factory where you can watch skilled craftsmen at work blowing and shaping beautiful crystal. A superb exhibition 'Glass the Incrdible Liquid' reveals glass in a new light - its history fashion, colour and science from Egyptians to spacecraft - with 'hands-on' exhibits for the young. Open all year. Visitor Centre including Factory Visit Mon-Fri 9.30am-3.30pm except Bank Holidays. Visitor Centre only - Glass the Incredible Liquid Mon-Sat 9.30am-4.30pm (open Sundays during July & August). Factory Shop and Pavilion Restaurant Mon-Fri 9.30am-5pm (Sundays from June-Dec 10.30am-4.30pm).

ROSEMOOR GARDEN,
.. one mile south-east of Great Torrington on the B3220 Exeter Road.
Tel: 01805 624067.
Visit this famous garden, beautiful in all seasons and now being expanded by the Royal Horticultural Society to 40 acres. The year round display from Lady Anne's internationally renowned 8 acres garden is now complemented by a variety of exciting plantings in the new garden. Herb garden. Ornamental vegetable garden. Cottage garden and foliage garden. New in 1994 a fruit and vegetable garden. Open: Garden all year, April to September 10-6pm. March and October 10-5pm. November-February 10-4pm. Closed Christmas Day. Visitors Centre March 1st to 4th December. Licensed Restaurant. Shop and Plant Centre.

KINGSBRIDGE MINIATURE RAILWAY
.. gives a half-mile return ride for the length of the quay alongside the estuary. The track guage is only 1 1/4 inches, yet the train is robust enough to take the whole family. The miniature railway is right by the quay car park, ideally placed for rides to keep the children amused while shopping in Kingsbridge or on the way to and from the beaches. Trains run at Easter, then daily mid-May to mid-Sept. 11-5pm weather permitting.

Visitor Attractions

KINGSBRIDGE TO SALCOMBE RIVER CRUISES.
Tel: 01548 3607 or 3525.
Weekday scheduled Kingsbridge to Salcombe Ferry service, evening cruises, Sunday estuary and coastal cruises. The ferry operatesfrom its boatyard and the quay, Kingsbridge and from Ferry pier, Salcombe. It takes about half an hour each way. The scenic beauty and maritime activity provide estuary and land views of unrivalled magnificence. Boats run daily from May to end of Sept. For details ring.

COOKWORTHY MUSEUM OF RURAL LIFE
108 Fore Street. Tel: 01548 3235.
A lively, local museum housed in a beautiful 17th century school building. Children particularly love the miniature world of the dolls house and toys while parents enjoy costumes, porcelain, craft tools, old local photographs, Victorian kitchen, dairy and the farm machinery gallery, plus a complete Victorian pharmacy. Open 1st Apr to 30th Sept 10-5pm Mon-Sat. Oct 10-4.30pm Mon-Fri.

LODDISWELL VINEYARD & WINERY,
Lilwell, Loddeswell, Nr Kingsbridge. Tel: 01548 550221.
Six-acre vineyard growing traditional and new varieties for commercial wine production, including the use of polthene tunnels. Wines prodiced have received the coveted Gold Seal of Quality. An opportunity to taste the wines and buy a bottle to take home. Video films of planting, harvesting and wine-mak8ing. Large picnic area and tea room. Open 2pm-6pm Mon to Thurs 1st Apr to 30th Oct and Sundays during July and August. Guided tours start 2.30pm and 4pm. May to September.

LYDFORD   LYDFORD GORGE NT
At Lydford village half-way between Okehampton and Tavistock, 1 mile west of A386. Tel: 0182282 441 or 320.
This famous gorge is one and a half miles long, providing enchanting riverside walks leading to the spectacular 90ft White Lady Waterfall. The walk then enters a steep sided, oak-wooded ravine scooped out by the River Lyd as it plunges into a series of whirlpools including the thrilling Devil's Cauldron. A home to a wide variety of animals, birds and plants. Visitors must wear stout footwear and take care at all times. There may be delays at the Devil's Cauldron during busy periods. Open: 30th Mar-30th Oct daily 10-5.30pm. Nov-Mar 10.30am-3pm. Dogs on leads only. Light refreshments daily in July and August. Sundays and Bank Holidays during the remainder of the season.

Chapter Fourteen

LYNMOUTH EXMOOR BRASS RUBBING AND GOBBYCRAFT CENTRE,
Woodside Craft Centre, Watersmeet Road. Tel: 01598 52529.
Well established family attraction with an exciting collection of over one hundred facsimiles of Monumental Brasses and special Rubbing Plates for small children. Choose from Knights dating from 1277, Ladies and Clergy, the Nobility, animal footrests and even a skeleton. The aim is to help visitors discover an easy and rewarding craft. Open: Easter Holidays, Spring, Half-term, Summer Holidays (from 3rd weekend in July to end of August) and Autumn Half-term. 10.30-5pm. At all other times from Monday to Friday 11-4.30pm. The Public are asked to note that due to school visits they are sometimes closed during term time. Visitors are advised to check first by telephone.

MANATON   BECKY FALLS
On the B3344 Bovey Tracey to Manaton Road.
Nature Trails, 70ft Waterfall in a private estate of 50 acres, set in a beautiful deep wooded valley. Safe attended car park. Restaurant and Tea Rooms. Gift Shop, Picnic areas. Super family day out at a reasonable inclusive price - car including all occupants. Open 10-6pm Easter to October.

MORETONHAMPSTEAD   THE MINIATURE PONY CENTRE
Tel: 01647 432400.
Acres of fun in this beautiful country park. Tiny cuddly ponies, rare miniature donkeys and many other animals. Pony rides. Action packed adventure playground - indoors and out. Lakes, birds and giant trout. Licensed restaurant. Gift shop. Open end of March to 31st October 10.30-5pm. Closed Fridays except Easter.

NEWTON ABBOT   TUCKERS MALTINGS,
Teign Road, Osborne Park. Tel: 01626 334734.
England's only working Malthouse open to the public. This spectacular unique Victorian building is one of Devon's most fascinating family days out. Become a maltster and help produce malt for over twenty five West Country breweries. There is a 19th century street, with audio and video effects. Open: Easter to 30th October. (Closed Saturdays) 10-4pm (July & August 10-5pm). Follow the brown and white signs from Newton Abbot railway station. Allow at least three hours for your visit.

OKEHAMPTON   FINCH FOUNDRY, NT.
Sticklepath. Tel: 01837 840046.
Fascinating early 19th century forge, powered by three water wheels, which produced sickles, scythes and shovels for both agriculture and mining. The forge is situated in the centre of this picturesque village with attractive

countryside and river walks adjoining. Picnic area, refreshments available. Open: Apr to Oct, daily except Tuesdays 11-5pm.

MUSEUM OF DARTMOOR LIFE.
Tel: 01837 52295.
The galleries tell the story of the people who have lived and worked on Dartmoor from pre-historic times to the present day. Displays also examine issues such as the environment and the effects of social change. Open Easter to October 10-5pm Monday to Saturday plus Sundays from June to September. Weekdays only through winter.

OKEHAMPTON CASTLE
.. half a mile south west of Okehampton signed from the old A30.
Tel: 01837 52844.
Established by the Normans as the seat of the first Sheriff of Devon. It was largely rebuilt in the 14th century as a lavish country home for the Courtenays, Earls of Devon. Beautiful woodland setting. Inclusive Soundalive personal stereo tours. Picnic area. Free car park. Open: 1st April-30th September, 10-6pm daily. October to 31st March, 10-4pm, Tuesday to Sunday (closed Christmas and New Year).

OTTERY ST MARY CHADHAY,
1 mile northwest of Ottery St Mary. Tel: 01404 812432.
Mentioned in the reign of Edward I. The main part of the present house was built about 1550. An Elizabethan Long Gallery was added at the end of the 16th century, thereby forming a unique and lovely courtyard. Some alterations in the 18th century. The house is occupied by the present owners. It is viewed by conducted tours. Open: Spring Bank Holiday, Sunday and Monday and then each Tuesday, Wednesday and Thursday during July and August. Also Late Summer Holiday Sunday and Monday.

PAIGNTON ZOO
Tel: 01803 527936.
Tucked away in a lush green valley Paignton Zoo has 75 acres of botanical gardens and one of England's largest zoos with over 1,300 animals. Excellently laid out and informative. Children love the hands-on activity centre. Meet zoo keepers and hear how they care for the animals. Allow 3-5 hours. Open: Every day except Christmas Day from 10am. Close 6pm summer and 5pm in winter. Restaurant. Picnic lawns and indoorpicnic area. Shops.

PAIGNTON & DARTMOUTH STEAM RAILWAY.
Queen's Park Station, Paignton.
Tel: 01803 555872.
Steam trains run for seven miles in Great Western tradition along the

Chapter Fourteen

spectacular Torbay coast to Churston and through the wooded slopes bordering the Dart estuary to Kingswear. The Boat Train circular journey from Paignton to Kingswear by steam train, by ferry to Dartmouth, then a river cruise or the Round Robin tour which includes the river trip to Totnes and return by bus to Torbay. Services run from April to October with Santa Special trains in December. Ring for times.

OLDWAY MANSION.
Tel: 01803 529914.
Guided tours round this imposing mansion, set in 17 acres of beautiful, landscaped gardens, which was built as the home of Isaac Merritt Singer of sewing machine fame, and made even more impressive by his son, Paris. Open: Daily from 9.30-5pm during the week and from 9.30-12.00 noon on Saturdays and Sundays. Refreshments are available

PLYMOUTH DOME.
On Hoe overlooking Plymouth Sound.
Tel: 01752 600608.
Since the days of Drake, Cook and Darwin, Plymouth has been associated with adventure and discovery. Today, visitors can embark on their own adventures and discover the rich heritage and fascinating history of this great seafaring City in the award-winning Plymouth Dome. Atmospheric reconstructions and high-tech equipment take you on an extraordinary journey through time, through the sights and smell of Elizabethan Plymouth; on dramatic voyages across the world; and through the tragic devastation wrought by the Blitz on Plymouth. Full access and facilities for people with disabilities. Its a great adventure for all the family come rain or shine. Open: daily at 9am. Closed Christmas Day. Cafe. Shop.

SALTRAM HOUSE,
Plympton. Tel: 01752 336546.
A magnificent George II mansion complete with its original contents, set in a lovely landscaped park overlooking the estuary. There is superb plasterwork and decoration including two important rooms designed by Robert Adam. The house contains fine period furniture and pictures, including many portraits by Sir Joshua Reynolds. There is an Orangery and the woodlands run down to the river. Beautiful stables. Restaurant. Shop. Saltram is three and a half miles from Plymouth City Centre and 2 miles west of Plympton, between the A38 and A379. Open: House - April to end of October Sundays to Thursday, but open Good Friday and Bank Holiday, Saturdays from 12.30-6pm. Garden: daily from 11am-6pm.

SOUTH MOLTON   QUINCE HONEY FARM,
North Road. Tel: 01769 572401.
Signposted from A361. Free parking and picnic area. Home to a million honey bees, this unique world famous exhibition is acknowledged by experts to be the best in the world. Fascinating place. Open: end of March-end of September 9am-6pm daily. October 9am-5pm daily. Cafeteria serving breakfast, lunch, afternoon tea and light refreshments. Shop: open all year. Sells Devon Honey in jars, combs and pottery, beeswax candles, honey and beeswax cosmetics.

SPARKWELL   DARTMOOR WILD LIFE PARK.
Nr Plymouth. Tel: 01752 837209.
The park is situated on the South Western edge of Dartmoor in thirty acres of beautiful Devon countryside, three miles from Plymouth and one and half miles from the A38. It has one of the most comprehensive Big Cat collections in the South West, a Falconry Centre second to none and a very successful animal breeding programme. Daily Events: Flying Displays 12 noon-4pm. Animal Encounters 2pm-3.30pm. Big Cat Feeding Time 3.30pm. Seal Feeding Time 4.30pm. Open every day of the year.

TAVISTOCK   MORWELLHAM QUAY
.. off A390 between Tavistock and Gunnislake.
Tel: 01822 832766.
Award winning 'Leading West Country Day Out'. 150 acres of family fascination and fun with The Copper Mine, Wagonette Rides - shire drawn carriages. Try on Costumes from the 1860's wardrobe (bring your camera). Guided tours of port and ships, village school, workshops, farm. Open 10am-5.30pm daily. Winter: 1st November-Easter, Copper Mine and grounds only 10am-4.30pm (closed Christmas week). Licensed restaurant. Pasty House. In winter light refreshments only. Shop.

COUNTRYMAN CIDER,
Felldownhead, Milton Abbot.
Tel: 01822 87226.
Located in the 15th century stables of a former coaching inn, on the Devon side of the lovely Tamar Valley. You are welcome to visit all the year round to see how their traditional Farmhouse Ciders are made. Countryman Cider is available on Draft. Opening hours: Mon-Fri 9am-6.30pm all year round. Saturdays 9am-6.30pm from May to September.

TIVERTON   GRAND WESTERN HORSEBOAT
7 miles from M5 J27. On approaching Tiverton follow brown signs for 'Grand Western Canal'.
Tel: 01884 253345.

Chapter Fourteen

From Tiverton's historic Lime Kiln Wharf, traditionally painted barges are gently pulled along by heavy horses wearing colourful harness and brasses, as you travel the same journey as their predecessors 100 years ago. At the Wharf there is a permanently moored Restaurant Barge, picnic area and car park. Enjoy a quiet stroll along the towpath or hire an electric or rowing boat. Open: Easter-mid October. Two and a half or three and a quarter hour return trips. General Departure Times: 11am-2.15 pm approximately. May. Wed-am. Tues-Thurs, Sunday - pm. June once daily. July and Aug twice daily (except Saturday). Other months vary.

TORQUAY KENTS CAVERN SHOWCAVES.
Off Babbacombe Road. Tel: 01803 215136.
A masterpiece of nature which cannot be copied. Spectacular formations. Stalagmites, stalactites and limestone naturally sculptured and coloured over 2,000,000 years. A natural underground world. Accompany a member of the team who will help you discover the mystery of prehistory on a 40 minute stroll. Open: all year. July and August 10am-8.15pm (Sat 5.15pm). April, May June and September 10am-5.15pm. October 10am-4.15pm, November to March - winter timetable applies, please enquire. Refreshments Easter to October. Well stocked shop.

TORQUAY MUSEUM,
529 Babbacombe Road.
Tel: 01803 293975.
Here you will find exhibits that are unimaginably ancient. Discoveries from Kents Cavern which helped unravel the antiquity of man and how he lived. The evidence of animals that lived 400 million years ago. As well as these early exhibits you can see the quaint bygones and pictures which trace the history of Torquay from the Victorian Age to Agatha Christie in our own century. Open: allyear round. Mon-Fri 10am-4,45pm Sunday afternoons 1.30pm-4.45pm. Easter to October Mon-Sat 10am-4.45pm Closed Christmas Week and Good Friday.

TORRE ABBEY,
The King's Drive.
Tel: 01803 293593.
History comes alive at Torbay's most historic building. Built in 1196 you can trace the 900 years of development from monastery, imposing home of wealthy families to Mayor's official residence of modern day. Eight galleries house stunning collections of pictures and works of art, twelve historic rooms, the Agatha Christie Memorial Room, and refreshments in the Victorian Kitchen. Outside the colourful gardens, gatehouse and the magnificent 'Spanish Barn' of Armada fame. Open: easter to October daily 9.30am-6pm. November-March parties only by appointment.

Visitor Attractions

BYGONES,
Fore Street, St Marychurch.
Tel: 01803 326108.
Wander back in time, explore an olde worlde street with over 20 life size shops and period rooms including a forge and pub with authentic smells and sounds. Allow at least one hour for your visit. Summer opening June to end of August. Sunday to Friday 10am-10pm Winter opening March, April, May, September, October. Daily 10am-6pm January, February, November, December, Monday to Friday 10am-2pm. Saturday & Sunday 10am-5pm.

TOTNES   BOWDEN HOUSE,
1 mile west of Totnes off A381.
Tel: 01803 863664.
Photographic Museum. Fascinating. Guided tours - allow one hour. Family in Georgian Costume - welcomed by the footman in the courtyard. Tudor and Queen Anne architecture. Movie memorabilia coffee bar. Licensed cafe, cream teas - served by wenches. Picnic area - enjoy the grounds with farm views. Open: Tuesdays, Wednesday and Thursday plus Bank Holiday Sundays and Mondays. From first Tuesday in April to last Thursday in October. Grounds and Museum 11am. House 2pm. Open all year for coaches by appointment.

TOTNES MOTOR MUSEUM
500 yards from Town Centre on the Paignton side of the river.
Tel: 01803 862777.
Exciting with live and changing exhibitions of Historic Grand Prix cars, Vintage Sports cars and Sports Racing cars, old models and toys, motorbikes, engines, a 1920's picinc scene and a 1930' workshop. From Austin 7 to Alfa Romeo, Frazer Nash and D Type Jaguar, Scott and Velocette, a cross-section of motoring history from the 20's to the 60's is on show for your enjoyment. Open: every day, Easter to October 10am-5pm. Shop.

WIDECOMBE-IN-THE-MOOR   THE CHURCH HOUSE,
NT. Tel: 0136 41321.
Originally a brewhouse dating back to 1537, this former village school is now leased as a village hall and occasionally open to the public. The adjacent Sexton's Cottage is a National Trust and Dartmoor National Park information centre and gift shop. Open: Information Centre and shop, mid-February to Christmas daily 10am-5pm.

YEALMPTON   NATIONAL SHIRE HORSE CENTRE.
Tel: 01752 880268.
A big day come rain or shine. Get close to the gentle Giants, watch the unique Parade of the Shires. See thrilling Birds of Prey flying displays. Try

Chapter Fourteen

the excitement of the Adventure Playground. Restaurants. Open every day 10am-5pm. Winter opening mid-Novemberto March. Stables and Restaurant 10am-4pm. Closed 24th-26th December.

KITLEY CAVES.
Tel: 01752 880202.
The cave research team based here is continually extending the known limits of the caves and adding to the information on their formation. Visitors are free to wander through the illuminated cave passages where information panels are set amongst the strange and spectacular rock formations. Surrounded by pretty countryside and close to the River Yealm, this makes a very pleasant outing. The caves, gift shop, museum and children's play area are open for Easter weekend and daily from the Spring Bank Holiday until the end of September 10am-5.30pm.

YELVERTON BUCKLAND ABBEY
N.T. 11 miles north of Plymouth and 6 miles south of Tavistock to the west of A386 at Yelverton. Buckland's peaceful atmosphere belies its fascinating past. Once inside, the story of this 13th century monastery, which later became home to Sir Francis Drake, and his descendants, unfolds through exhibitions on monastic life, the Battle of the Armada and Drake memorabilia including his famous drum. The Tudor Great Hall features beautiful plasterwork and the Kitchen has a range of cooking utensils, open hearth and 'hams' hanging form the ceiling. Wonderful grounds. Open: 30th Mar-10th Oct daily except Thrus 10.30-5.30pm. Nov, Mar, Sat and Sun 2pm-5pm. Dogs in car park only, on leads. Licensed restaurant. Light refreshments in tea room at peak times. Shop.

YELVERTON PAPERWEIGHT CENTRE.
Tel: 01822 854250.
Houses the famous 'Broughton Collection' of antique and modern glass paperweights. Both the casual visitor and the serious collector are fascinated by the beautifully handcrafted milleriori and abstract designs. Open: 2 weeks before Easter to end of October Mon-Sat. 10am-5pm. Sundays end of May-mid September Sun 10am-5pm. All winter Wed 1pm-5pm. Sat 10am-5pm. December 1st-24th Mon-Sat 10am-5pm. At Leg O'Mutton Corner, large car park, toilets, restaurant, pub, post office, corner shop, moorland for picnics.

DORSET

ABBOTSBURY TITHE BARN COUNTRY MUSEUM
Tel: 01305 871817.
This fascinating collection of farm tools, machinery and rural bygones is housed in one of the largest thatched barns in the country. Exhibits include, a farm workers kitchen, game keeping, 17th century working Dovecote, Monastic Remains, and rare poultry. Open daily in the summer Apr-Oct 10-6pm. Winter Sun only Children free entry.

SUB TROPICAL GARDENS
Tel: 01305 871387.
These magnificent gardens are famed for their stunning magnolias, ancient camellias and rhododendrons. Set in over 20 acres of woodland valley with 18th century walled garden, peacocks, ponds and streams, the gardens are home to many rare and record breaking plants from all over the world, thriving in its own unique micro-climate. The Sub Tropical Gardens include a woodland trail, Victorian Garden, children's play area and guided tours. Open daily in the summer mid Mar-Nov 10-5pm and in the winter Nov-mid Mar 10am-dusk. Free admission for children.

SWANNERY & THE FLEET
Tel: 01305 871684.
Famous as the home for the only managed colony of mute swans in the world that can be visited during nesting time. Situated on the shore of the fleet, separated from the sea by the Chesil Bank, it is a place of great beauty, teeming with wildlife, where you can watch the family life of swans at close quaters. Little changes since 1400AD. Attractions include children's Ugly Duckling activity trail, gift shop and Ancient Duck Decoy. Open daily in the summer from Apr-Oct 9.30-5pm and in the winter Sunday only 10-dusk.

BEAMINSTER PARNHAM HOUSE
Tel: 01308 863130.
Location: Exit 25 from M5 in Taunton. Parnham House is a restored manor house and gardens that are the focal point for a renaissance in English furniture design. A whole day can be enjoyed exploring the extensive gardens, playing croquet, picnicking and paddling. See the spacious interiors where the leading artists and craftsmen show their work and then discover the innovations in a working woodland. The magnificent Great Hall with heraldic stained glass is the heart of the house, the major staircase is embellished with anotable trompe l'oeil, the delight of many visitors. Open 10-5pm Wed, Suns & Bank Holidays from Apr-Oct.

Chapter Fourteen

BOURNEMOUTH   THE BOURNEMOUTH BEARS. T
el: 01202 293544.
Explore the cuddly world of the teddy bear. Old bears, new bears, famous bears and designer bears. A fluffy wonderland for the young, a nostalgic journey for the not so young. Open daily all year round 9.30-5.30pm.

MUMMIES & MAGIC
Tel: 01202 293544.
An amazing exhibition featuring Royal Mummies and Ancient Egypt from the earliest sand-dried bodies to the majestic mummy of Rameses the Great. Discover the secrets of mummification and the magic that protected them. Open daily all year round9.30am-5.30pm.

DINODAUR SAFARI
Tel: 01202 293544.
Bournemouth's great hands-on indoor adventure of discovery. See life-size dinosaurs, bones, fossils and computers that let you experiment with dinosaurs. A great day out for all the family. Open daily 9.30-5.30pm.

BOVINGTON   THE TANK MUSEUM.
Tel: 01929 403463.
Six large exhibition halls includefascinating displays including World War I, Inter War Years, World War II, Post War, Experimental Tanks and carriers. They all make for an exciting and enjoyable day out for the whole family. Many of the 270 plus armoured fighting vehicles are permanently on show, but there is always something new and exciting to be seen. There are permanent attractions including video theatres, Costume Collection, Challenger Tank Ride, Simulator and much more. Open daily.

CHARD   FORDE ABBEY & GARDENS
Tel: 01460 20231.
Location: four miles south of Chard on the B3167. Founded by Cistercian Monks over 800 years ago, the monastery still stands transformed by the architecture of the 16th and 17th centuries into a splendid Country House. The gardens extend to 30 acres with origins in the early 18th century. They are landscaped around this great building. There are lakes, magnificent trees and shrubs and in the kitchen garden there is an extensive nursery specialising in rare and unusual plants. Open daily throughout the year 10-4pm. The Abbey is open from 1st April-end of October Wed, Sun and Bank Holidays 1-4.30pm.

DORCHESTER ATHELHAMPTON HOUSE & GARDENS
Tel: 01305 848363.
A visit to Athelhampton will attract you to one of the fines examples of 15th

century donestic architecture in the kingdom. Enjoy the lived in family house with its Great Hall, Great Chamber, Wine Cellar and King's Room all exquisitely furnished. Wander through 20 acres of beautiful grounds including eight walled gardens, fountains, pavillions and topiary pyramid all encircled by the River Piddle. Home-made cream teas, gift shop and free car park. Open daily 27th Mar-30th Oct, Wed, Thurs, Sun and Bank Holidays.

TUTANKHAMON - THE EXHIBITION
Tel: 01305 269571.
An unforgettable experience can be had by all at Tutankhamon's Tomb and Treasures exhibition. Walk into the past to recapture the mystery and magnificence of ancient Egypt. Open daily all year round 9.30-5.30pm.

POOLE   COMPTON ACRES
Tel: 01202 700778.
Location: Three miles to the south of Bournemouth.
Compton Acres is a wonderful set of international gardens. There is a delightful Herbaceous Border, Italian Garden, Palm Court, Woodland Walk and Glen, Rock and Water Garden all of which are separate and distinct gardens. The Japanese Garden opened in 1986 and is reputed to be the only completely genuine Japanese Garden in Europe. Open daily from 1st Mar-end of October from 10.30am-6.30pm.

NATURAL WORLD
Tel: 01202 686712.
The Natural World is one of Poole's biggest attractions, housing the widest collection of fish, insects, amphibians and reptiles in the area providing all year-round indoor entertainment. Watch the reptiles being fed on Saturdays and for a big thrill see the sharks being fed on Wednesdays, Fridays and Sundays. Open daily ghroughout the year. Summer 9.30-9pm and Winter 10-5pm.

WAREHAM   MONKEY WORLD
Tel: 0800 456600.
Monkey World was opened in 1987 to rescue chimpanzees and rehabilitate them into natural surroundings. See the baby chimps playing in their nursery or visit some of the other monkeys having fun in the natural habitat. Apart from visiting the monkeys test your skill on the new 15 stage obstacle course and enjoy the three outdoor play areas, including mini motor bikes, swings and slides. Open every day from Apr-end of October 10-5pm.

CORFE CASTLE
Tel: 01929 481294.
Location: on 351 Wareham to Swanage Road. Corfe Castle is one of the

Chapter Fourteen

most impressive ruins in England. An important medieval Royal fortification commanding a cleft in Purbeck hills. Bought in 1635 by Sir John Bankes, Attorney General to Charles I; in 1646 his wife Lady Bankes withstood two long sieges in the Civil War, only surrendering the Castle to the Parliamentary Forces after treachery. The Castle was then systematically demolished. Today it stands ruined on a hill and the only natural route is through the Purbeck hills. Open from Feb-end of Oct daily. 10-5.30pm and Nov-Feb Sat & Sun only 12-3.30pm.

WEYMOUTH SEALIFE PARK
Tel: 01305 788255.
Location: short walk from Weymouth town centre on A353 towards Wareham. Don't miss the chance to voyage to the bottom of the sea, take a wildlife trek through a tropical rain forest and brave the jaws of a giant shark in Captain Kid's World......all on the same day! In Neno's Discovery you'll experience the spine-tingling sensation of peering through the windows of a sunken wreck whilst special outdoor rock-pools provide 'hands on' encounters with a host of sturdy rockpool creatures like hermit crabs and starfish. With regular talks and feeding displays adding to the entertainment, along with a challenging quiz trail to test the fishy knowledge of young and old alike, the day is sure to be a fun-filled memorable adventure for everyone. Open from 10am seven days a week.

BREWERS QUAY
Tel: 01305 788255.
Brewers Quay is an amazing complex of so many interesting and exciting attractions it is difficult to know where to begin. From the Famous Timewalk with its Brewers Tale, free entry to the shopping village, craft centre and 'Grannys Attic' antiques loft, through to the hands on Discovery experience, magnificent Shire Horse Centre and Boat Trips, not to mention the town museum, exhibitions and regular festivals, to the wonderful cafes, bars and restaurants. Brewers Quay is a treasure just wating to be discovered. Open seven days a week 9.30-5.30pm except Christmas Day and Boxing Day.

THE DEEP SEA ADVENTURE
Tel: 01305 760690.
Come and explore for yourself the undersea world and experience the story of underwater exploration and maritime exploits through the ages. As you enter the scene is set. You pass through a creaking, rusty shipwreck, and travel back to the 17th century discovering the ancient means used to explore the oceans. Follow the diver signs around this 9,000 square foot maritime adventure story and you will descend through three floors of exciting displays. As you pass through the sights, sounds and smells of the deep, the story is one of underwater discovery, shipwreaks and survival exploits brought to

life by the use of animation and interactive displays covering over 300 years. Open 10am-10pm July and August and 10-4.30pm Nov-Feb.

WIMBORNE MERLEY BIRD GARDENS
Tel: 01202 883790.
Location: 15 minute drive from Bounremouth along A35.
Visit this fascinating combination of exotic birds, formal gardens, shrubberies and water gardens all set in one of the largest and most beautiful historic walled gardens in the country. Walk through aviaries and see an extraordinary variety of birds or visit the herb gardens or children's pets corner. Open daily throughout the year.

KINGSTON LACY
Tel: 01202 883402.
Location: on B3082 Wimborne to Blandford Road.
17th century house designed for Sir Ralph Bankes by Sir Roger Pratt. It was altered by Sir Charles Barry in the 19th century. Houses one of the finest picture collections in the country with paintings by Titian, Rubens and Velasquez. Fine collection of Egyptian artefacts collected by William John Bankes in the 19th century. The house is set in 13 acres of formal gardens and woodland walks surrounded by a park of 254 acres with a fine herd of Red Devon cattle. Open 26th Mar-30th Oct daily except Thurs and Fri, 12-5.30pm.

ESSEX

COGGLESHALL THE SECRET GARDEN OF ESSEX
Tel: 01376 563796.
Visit the estate of Marks Hall and stroll around the beautiful parkland and unspoilt countryside, little changed in 100 years. See the ornamental lakes, cascades and wall garden or have a longer walk through the ancient woodlands and enjoy the peace and tranquillity of this historic estate. Open Easter-31st October 10.30-4.30pm weekdays. 10.30-6pm weekends and Bank Holidays.

COLCHESTER ZOO
Tel: 01206 330253.
Award winning Colchester Zoo, set in 40 acres of beautiful grounds is home to 150 species of animals from around the world including Snow Leopards, Siberian Tigers, Orangutans, Elephants and breeding Chimpanzees. Children will enjoy the chance to stroke the animals in the centre's Children's Paddock and can also play amoung a menageries of rescued animals and birds, open: daily from 9.30.

Chapter Fourteen

COLCHESTER LEISURE WORLD
Tel: 01206 766500.
A fun-filled exercise day out for the whole family can be enjoyed. Get wet in the split level leisure pool with two stunning flume rides, outside river rapids and water cannons or relax in the Agna Springs with saunas, thermal hydro massage pool, spa pools, steam rooms, solaria and plunge pools. Open daily every day of the year.

COLCHESTER CASTLE MUSEUM
A day which will allow you to be a Roman and take a step back into their way of life. Visit the vaults of a Roman Temple, try on a toga, touch genuine Roman pottery or dress up as a Roman Soldier. Discover the secrets of the Castle Prisons and learn the story of the Colchester martyrs and find out about the prisoners themselves and the prison conditions over the centuries. Open daily 10-5pm Mon-Sat all year round and 2-5pm on Sundays from Mar-Nov.

STANSTEAD HOUSE ON THE HILL TOY MUSEUM.
Tel: 01279 813237.
This interesting place is one of the largest toy museums in the world covering 7,000 square feet and housing a vast collection of toys, games and books from the late Victorian era, right up to the 1970s. The Museum offers a nostalgic trip back to childhood with a wealth of displays, some of them animated, there is apuppet theatre, moving Meccano fairground, military displays, space toys, books, comics, games and much, much more. Open: daily 13th Mar-13th Nov 10-4pm.

MOUNTFICHET CASTLE & NORMAN VILLAGE
Tel: 01279 813237.
Why not wander through the mists of time and visit this historic castle, the only Norman motte and baily Castle in the world, re-constructed on its original site, steeped in 900 years of history. From 1215, the castle lay forgotten and overgrown for over 750 years until its re-creation today and the site now offers the visitor an opportunity to be transported back through the centuries. Open daily 13th March-13th November 10-5pm.

SAFFRON WALDEN   AUDLEY END HOUSE & PARK
Tel: 01799 522399.
Location: one mile west of Saffron Walden on B1383.
The facade of Audley End, glimpsed across the superb landscaped parkland that surrounds it, is one of the great sights of East Anglia. From the columns of the elaborate twin porches to the distinctive turquoise copper caps of the turrets, the whole beautiful sight of the building speaks of the ambitions of the Jacobean Lord, the Earl of Suffolk. The richly decorated interiors of the

house are arranged to show how they would have appeared in particular periods in history. Amongst the highlights of a tour of the house - with 30 rooms -are the Great Hall with its massive wooden Jacobean screen, the decorative little Drawing Room designed by Robert Adam. Visits to the house can be taken daily. Open 1st April-30th September Wed, Sun and Bank Holidays.

THE FRY ART GALLERY
Location: 15 miles north of Cambridge.
This art gallery which could be called 'The Gallery in the Garden' houses a unique collection of works brought together during the lidetime of many of the artists who were part of the artistic community which flourished in and around the nearby village of Great Barfield before and after World War II. The Fry Gallery exhibits examples of work by George Chapman, Sheila Robinson, Marianne Straub and Kenneth Rowntree to name but a few, and demonstrates the continuing artistic tradition of north-west Essex by including a number of works of other artists who have local connections. Open on Sat and Sun afternoons 2.45-5.30pm from Easter Sunday to the last Sun in October. Free admission.

SAFFRON WALDEN MUSEUM
Tel: 01799 510333.
From moccasins to mummy cases and woolly mammoths to Wallace the Lion, there is something to please everyone. The Museum is close to the parish church of this lovely medieval market town and the ruins of Walden's 12th century castle stand in the grounds. Displays include fine ceramics, glass, furniture and woodwork, costume, needlework, dolls and toys. The Museum also hosts The Worlds of Man Gallery showing objects of international importance from the peoples of Africa, Australia and the Pacific, mainly collected in the 19th century. Open Mon-Sat 10-5pm Mar-Oct. Mon-Sat 11-4pm Nov-Feb.

SOUTHEND ON SEA SEALIFE CENTRE
Tel: 01702 462400.
Visitors to this new underwater attraction can journey beneath the ocean waves and discover thousands of amazing sea creatures. A dramatic walk-through tunnel creates the illusion of a walk on the sea bed with sharks, rays and many others gliding silently by, inches above your head. Open daily from 10am all year round.

THE LYNN TAIT GALLERY
Tel: 01702 471737.
This wonderful gallery can be found in the heart of the historic old town of Leigh. In this lovely atmosphere of times gone by you can discover unusual

gifts, local paintings and early local photographs from the turn of the century, all displayed on delightful arefacts from yester-year, including a magnificently restored Southend Pier Train. Open from 11am till dusk.

GLOUCESTERSHIRE

BERKELEY   BERKELEY CASTLE
.. off A38 Tel: 01453 810332
Perfectly preserved 800 year old castle. Keep, dungeons, staterooms, Great Hall kitchen, tapestries, furniture, silver. Ornamental gardens and Butterfly house. Open Apr-Sept Tues-Sun. October Sundays only.

BIBURY   BIBURY TROUT FARM
Tel: 01285 740215.
A working farm which breeds Rainbow Trout. Visitors can see developing trout in 20 ponds and may feed the fish. Gift shop, picnic area, fishing. Open all year daily.

BOURTON ON THE WATER   COTSWOLD MOTOR MUSEUM
Tel: 01451 21255.
30 motor vehicles and the largest collection of vintage advertising signs in Britain. Also Village Life exhibition. Open daily Feb-Nov.

BIRDLAND
Rissington Road.
Tel: 01451 20689
Bird garden on the banks of the River Windrush. Penguins, waterfowl, tropical and sub tropical birds, many at liberty. Open daily all year.

BOURTON-ON-THE-WATER THE MODEL VILLAGE
Situated behind the Old New Inn, this is an incredible piece of work which delights and intrigues people of all ages from childhood upwards. The idea of building came from the late Mr C.A.Morris, landlord of the inn who in 1935 decided to turn his vegetable garden into something more decorative. It was not his intention to build a miniature model village but gradually the idea evolved and the model village was born. Every building and every feature of the landscape was built carefully to a scale of one ninth of the original and everything was erected exactly in position with the sole exception of the Church of St Lawrence, which stands at the far end of the model from the inn. One of the most fascinating aspects of the village is the miniature River Windrush, which is an artifical stream about three feet wide flowing from the working model of the mill through the whole length of the village. It is spanned by five little stone bridges, all of which are precise replicas of the

Visitor Attractions

famous bridges of Bourton. Now that the Model Village has been standing for some years the Cotswold stone of which all the buildings are constructed has begun to mellow. Each year it looks more and more like the original. OPEN; Summer 9-6pm. Winter 10-dusk. Not Christmas Day. Pets on leads. No access for disabled.

FOLLY FARM WATERFOWL
Off A436 near Bourton-on-the-Water.
Tel: 01451 20285.
Collection of rare poultry breeds and waterfowl including endangered species, in natural Cotswold farm surroundings. Open daily all year.

BROADWAY   SNOWSHILL MANOR
NT. Tel: 01386 852410.
Location: 3 miles south west of Broadway, off A44, the Cotswold manor house is full to the brim with Charles Wade's collection of craftmanship from all over the world. Each room has a theme from Samurai armour to navigation, from musical instruments to carts and bicycles. The cottage garden is charming. Open Easter Sat,Sun and Mon 1-6pm. Closed Good Friday. April-October: Sat and Sun 1-5pm. May to end September: daily except Tues 1-6pm.

CHELTENHAM CHEDWORTH ROMAN VILLA
Yarnworth. Tel: 01242 890256
Location: 10 miles south east of Cheltenham.
One of the best exposed Romano-British villas in Britain. Open March-end October Tues-Sun and Bank Holiday Monday 10-5.30pm Closed Good Friday. 2nd November -4th December: Wed-Sun 11-4pm. National Trust.

CHELTENHAM ART GALLERY & MUSEUM
Clarence Street.
Tel: 01242 237431.
Important arts and crafts collection, including furniture, pottery and silver inspired by William Morris. Also local history and archaeology, rare Oriental porcelain and Dutch and British paintings. Admission free. Open all year. Mon-Sat plus Sunday afternoons in summer.

HOLST BIRTHPLACE MUSEUM
4 Clarence Road.
Tel: 01242 524846.
Regency house where the composer of 'The Planets' was born, showing the 'upstairs-downstairs' way of life in Victorian and Edwardian times. Admission free. Open Tues-Sat. Closed Bank Holidays. Open all year.

Chapter Fourteen

PITTVILLE PUMP ROOM MUSEUM
Pittville Park. Tel: 01242 512470.
Housed in the magnificent Pump Room overlooking its own beautiful lake and gardens, the Museum imaginatively uses original costumes to bring to life the history of Cheltenham from its Regency heyday to the Swinging Sixties. Jewellery showing changing taste and fashion from Regency to Art Nouveau, and a spectacular collection of tiaras are also included. Open end of May-September Tues-Sat 10-4.20pm. Sunday 11-4.20pm. Bank Holiday Mondays 11-4.20pm.

CHIPPING CAMDEN   HIDCOTE MANOR GARDENS
Hidcote Bartrim
Tel: 01386 438333
Location: 4 miles east of Chipping Camden off B4632, Internationally renowned, this memorable garden is, in reality, a series of smaller gardens. Each has its own special atmosphere and leads on to the next surprise. Open: April to end of Oct daily except Tues and Fri. 11-7pm. Closed Good Friday. Shop. Restaurant. Plant Sales Centre. National Trust.

WOOLSTAPLERS HALL MUSEUM
High Street. Tel: 01386 840289.
Constructed in 1340 for merchants to buy the staples of Cotswold fleece; the Hall, with its superb roof carving, is now a museum. It houses an interesting collection of town and country bygones. Open: daily 1st April-31st October 11-6pm.

RIFTSGATE COURT GARDENS
Tel: 01386 438777.
A magnificently situated house with fine views and trees. The garden, created over three generations, has many unusual shrubs and a good collection of old fashioned and specie roses including RosaFilipes Kiftsgate, the largest rose in England. Open: Wed, Thurs and Sun 2-6pm. Also Bank Holiday Mondays and Saturdays in June and July 2-6pm. 1st April-30th Sept.

CINDERFORD   DEAN HERITAGE CENTRE
Camp Mill, Soudley on B4227. Tel: 01594 822170.
The museum of the Royal Forest of Dean interpreting the natural and man-made environment. Nature trails, shop, picnic/barbecue sites, art and craft exhibitions. Open daily all year.

CIRENCESTER   CORINIUM MUSEUM
Park Street. Tel: 01285 655611.
One of the finest collections of antiquities from Roman Britain. Full scale reconstructions of kitchen, dining room and mosaic craftsman's workshop

Visitor Attractions

bring Corinium (Roman Cirencester) to life. New Cotswold pre-historic gallery. Special exhibitions of local history and archaeology. Award winning museum and one of the Good Museums Guide 'Top Twenty'. Open daily all year, Sunday afternoons and all Bank Holidays. Closed Mondays from November to March and Christmas. Facilities for the disabled.

BREWERY COURT
Tel: 01285 657181.
The Cirencester Workshops and the Niccol Centre are housed in a converted Victorian Brewery and comprise a specialist craft centre where 20 professional craftworkers run their businesses, a shop selling the best of British craft work, a theatre, studios where courses are held in a wide range of disciplines, a gallery showing exhibitions in applied and fine art and a Wholefood Coffee House. Open: Cirencester Workshops - Mon-Sat 10-5pm. Niccol Centre - Mon-Fri 9.30-5.30pm and Sat 9.30-1pm. Admission free. Open all year.

COTSWOLD WATER PARK
Tel: 01285 861459.
It lies to the south of Cirencester and offers exciting and varied activities based on a network of lakes formed as a result of 60 years gravel extraction. In addition to the variety of water-based activities including angling, windsurfing, sailing, water, skiing and power boat racing, there are lakeside walks and picnic sites provided at two country Parks. The area is recognised as being nationally important for nature conservation. A number of public and private nature reserves provide an opportunity to study the enormous variety of its wetland flora and fauna. Open all the year. Facilities for the disabled.

BARNSLEY HOUSE GARDEN
The Close Tel: 01285 740281
Spring bulbs, autumn colours. Mixed borders, climbing and wall shrubs. Knot garden, herb garden, laburnum walk (early June). Decorative vegetable potage. 18th century summer houses. House (not open) 1697. Interesting plants for sale. Carpark. Pub lunches available in Barnsley at the village pub.

COLEFORD   CLEARWELL CAVES
Royal Forest of Dean.
Tel: 01594 32535.
Superb caverns and tunnels stretching far under the Forest of Dean. Worked for iron ore over 2,000 years until 1945. Open daily Mar0Oct. 1-24 December Christmas fantasy.

Chapter Fourteen

PUZZLEWOOD
Lower Perrygrove Farm on B4228.
Tel: 01594 33187.
Open Roman iron mines in 14 acre woodland setting. Paths arranged in apuzzle, landscaped in 1800s. Open Easter-October Tues-Sun and Bank Holidays.

GLOUCESTER GLOUCESTER CITY MUSEUM
Brunswick Road Tel: 01452 524131
Famous Iron Age mirror, Roman sculptures and mosaics. Also Georgian silver, barometers, furniture and exhibitions. Admission free. Open Mon-Sat & Bank Holiday Mondays all year.

GLOUCESTER FOLK MUSEUM
Westgate Street.
Tel: 01452 526467. Socialhistory folklore, crafts and industries of Gloucester, housed in Tudor timber framed buildings. Special exhibitions. Admission free. Open Mon-Sat & Bank Holiday Mondays all year.

HOUSE OF THE TAILOR OF GLOUCESTER
9 College Court. Tel: 01452 422856.
The building chosen by Beatrix Potter to illustrate her famous story. Now a gift shop and exhibition. Admission free. Open Mon-Sat all year.

NATURE IN ART
On A38 2 miles north of Gloucester. Tel: 01452 713422.
Unique collection of wildlife art from all parts of the world and all periods. Specially commended in National Heritage Museum of the year awards. Nature gardens and outdoor sculptures. Full programme of artists in residence. Open Tues-Sun and Bank Holidays all year.

REGIMENTS OF GLOUCESTERSHIRE MUSEUM
The Docks, Tel: 01452 522682
Museum of the Year Award for the Best Small Museum 1991. New displays tell the story of Gloucestershire's soldiers in peace and war. Gift shop. Open Tues-Sun & Bank Holidays all year.

ROBERT OPIE COLLECTION MUSEUM
OF ADVERTISING AND PACKAGING
Albert Warehouse, Gloucester Docks. Tel: 01452 302309.
Memories of childhood brought to life. Goods which since Victorian times have crowded the shelves of Britain's grocers, confectioners, chemists, tobacconists, pubs and corner shops. Vinage TV Commercials. Open all year but closed winter Mondays.

Visitor Attractions

GLOUCESTER SKI CENTRE
Robinswood Hill. Tel: 01452 414300.
240m, 200m nursery slopes. Full length ski lifts. Beginners to experts. Full tuitions and equipment. Ski shop. Open daily all year.

GLOUCESTER ANTIQUES CENTRE
Severn Road, Gloucester Docks Tel: 01452 529716
Collections of all kinds of antiques taking up four floors of a magnificent restored warehouse. Admission free. Open daily all year.

CRICKLEY HILL COUNTRY PARK
6 miles east of Gloucester on B4070. Tel: 01452 863170.
145 acres of grassland, woodland and parkland with panoramic views. Site of archaeological interest. Visitor centre and 5 self-guided trails. Admission free. Open daily all year.

ROBINSWOOD HILL COUNTRY PARK
2 miles south of Gloucester. Tel: 01452 412029.
250 acres of countryside with walks and views. Waymarked trails. Visitor centre. Gloucester Trust for Nature Conservation centre. Admission free. Open daily all year.

GUITING POWER COTSWOLD FARM PARK RARE BREEDS CENTRE
off B4077. Tel: 01451 850307.
The country's most comprehensive collection of rare breeds of farm animals. Adventure playground, farm trails, pets corner. Open daily Easter-September.

MORETON-IN-THE-MARSH BATSFORD ARBORETUM
Batsford. Tel: 01608 50722.
Fifty acres of garden containing over 1200 different species of trees, many rare with superb views over the vale of Evenlode. Springtime carpets of bulbs, magnificent magnolias, flowering cherries and a spectacular 'Handkerchief' tree. Laterin the year the large collection of maples and sorbus provide wonderful autumn colour. Refreshments. Open 1 Mar-early Nov 10am-5pm daily.

COTSWOLD FALCONRY CENTRE
Batsford Park. Tel: 01386 701043.
Located adjacent to Batsford Arboretum, eagles, hawks, owls and falcons are flown throughout the day giving you a chance to see their grace, speed and agility and the close relationship with the falconer. The emphasis here is on the breeding and conservation of these magnificent birds. Open: Mar-Nov daily 10.30 to last admission at 5pm. Facilities for the disabled.

Chapter Fourteen

LECHLADE COTSWOLD WOOLLEN WEAVERS
Filkins.
Tel: 01367 860491.
Working woollen mill showing traditional skills in 18th century buildings. Permanent exhibition areas. Large mill shop. Admission free. Open Mon-Fri and Sat am. Restricted opening Christmas, Easter, Bank Holidays.

NEWENT THE NATIONAL BIRDS OF PREY CENTRE
Tel: 10531 820286.
A full day out for the family is offered plus the chance to experience Birds of Prey at close quarters. The Daily Flying Demonstrations are undoubtedly the highlight of the day but there is so much more to see and do. Coffeeshop. Book and Gift Shop. Children's Play Area and Picnic sites. No pets. Free parking. Open: 7 days a week 10.30-5.30pm Closed December-January. Facilities for the disabled.

THE SHAMBLES
16-20 Church Street.
Tel: 01531 822144.
A staggeringly large collection laid out as a complete Victorian town of shops, cobbled streets, gas lamps and alleyways, rural and town trades and crafts. All approached through a fully furnished four storey house, in an unexpectedly spacious location behind the main streets of this attractive market town. Open: 10-6pm mid March-December Tues-Sun and Bank Holiday Mondays. Facilities for the disabled.

THREE CHOIRS VINEYARD
Welsh House Lane.
Tel: 01531 890555
Production of English Wine reviving the ancient tradition of Gloucestershire wine making. Admission free (Charge for tours) Open daily all year.

NEWENT BUTTERFLY & NATURAL WORLD CENTRE,
Birches Lane off B4215
Tel: 01531 821800
Tropical Butterfly house, Nature Exhibition, Menagerie and Water Life. Spiders, snakes, rabbits, guinea pigs, rare breed fowl, waterfowl, pheasants, peacocks, parakeets and other small birds. Open daily Easter-October.

LYDNEY DEAN FOREST RAILWAY
Norchard Steam Centre B4234 Nr. Lydney. Tel: 01594 843423.
Full size railway engines, coaches and wagons. Admission free to site. Open daily all year. Admission charge for steam rides (certain days throughout the year).

Visitor Attractions

NORTHLEACH   COTSWOLD COUNTRYSIDE COLLECTION
Tel: 01451 60715.
Fine collection of agricultural history, set in former 'House of Correction'. Restored cells and courtroom. Special exhibitions. Open daily Apr-Oct.

KEITH HARDING'S WORLD OF MECHANICAL MUSIC
Oak House. Tel: 0145160181.
A museum of antique clocks, musical boxes, automata and mechanical musical instruments in an old wool merchant's house. Restorers of clocks and musical boxes. Gift shop. Open daily all year.

PAINSWICK   PAINSWICK ROCOCO GARDEN,
The Stables, Painswick House. Tel: 01452 813204
18th century, 6 acre Rococo garden with garden buildings. Vistas and woodland paths. Open Feb-mid Dec. Wed- Sun.

PRINKNASH ABBEY
Nr. Painswick. On A46. Tel: 01452 812455.
Benedictine Abbey with world famous pottery worked by local craftsmen. Adjoined by Bird Park. Open daily all year.

SLIMBRIDGE   THE WILDFOWL AND WETLANDS TRUST.
Off A38 Tel: 01453 890065.
World's largest collection of wildfowl in 73 acres of grounds. Tropical house. Permanent exhibition. Open all year. Closed Dec 24th & 25th.

STANWAY   STANWAY HOUSE,
Near Cheltenham. Tel: 01386 73469
The jewel of Cotswold manor houses is very much a home rather than a museum. The mellow Jacobean architecture, the typical squire's family portraits, the exquisite Gate House, the old Brewery and medieval Tithe Barn, the extensive pleasure grounds and formal landscape contribute to the timeless charm of what Arthur Negus considered one of the most beautiful and romantic manor houses in England. Open: June, July, August Tuesdays and Thursdays 2-
5pm.

TETBURY CHAVENAGE
Tel: 01666 502329.
Elizabethan Manor House (1576). Tapestry rooms, furniture and relics of Cromwellian period. Chapel and Edwardian Wing. Personal tours by the owner. Spacious gardens for visitors to the house to enjoy. See where Agatha Christie's 'Hercule Poirot' was filmed. Open: May-Sept, Thurs, Sun, Bank Holidays 2-5pm. Also Easter Sunday and Monday.

Chapter Fourteen

WESTONBIRT ARBORETUM
.. on the A433 nr Tetbury. Tel: 0166 880220.
600 acres containing one of the finest collections of temperate trees and shrubs in the world. Open all year. Visitor Centre open daily Easter-mid November.

WESTBURY COURT GARDEN
Tel: 01452 760461
Location: 9 miles south west of Gloucester on A48. Laid out between 1696 and 1705, this formal Dutch water garden is a rare survival of its type in England. Historical varieties of apple, pear, plum, along with many other species of plants introduced to England before 1700, make this a fascinating study for any gardener. Open: April-end October: Wed to Sun and Bank Holiday Monday 11-6pm. Closed Good Friday. National Trust.

WINCHCOMBE   HAILES ABBEY
Tel: 01242 602398
Location: 10 miles north east of Cheltenham off B4632. Picturesque ruins of great Cistercian Abbey and centre of pilgrimage. English Heritage. Open: April 1st- end September daily 10-6pm. Oct-March Tues-Sun 10am-4pm. Closed 24-26 December and New Year Bank Holiday. Museum may be closed on certain days from October-end of March for staffing reasons. Ring first.

SUDELEY CASTLE AND GARDENS
Tel: 01242 602308.
Once the residence of Queen Katherine Parr, Sudeley is now the charming home of Lord and Lady Ashcombe. Sudeley houses many fine antiques, civil war relics and old-master paintings. The gardens with the Queen's garden as their centrepiece, are quite magnificent and are complemented by 'Sudeley Castle Roses' a specialist plant centre. Also available: craft workshops, adventure playground, castle shop, licensed restaurant. Calendar of special events throughout the year.
OPEN: Apr 1st-31st October. Grounds 11am-5.30pm. Castle apartments 12 noon - 5pm. Sudeley Castle Roses; 10am-5.30pm. Free parking for cars and coaches.

GLOUCESTERSHIRE - WARWICKSHIRE RAILWAY,
Toddington, at intersection of B4632/A438.
Tel: 01242 621405.
Restored GWR Station. Mainline steam rides. 8 miles round trip. Large rail complex, rolling stock under restoration. Admission free to site. Open daily. Admission charge for steam rides (Easter-October Sat, Sun & Bank Holidays) Open all year.

Visitor Attractions

HAMPSHIRE

ALDERSHOT MUSEUM OF AIRBORNE FORCES
Browning Barracks.
Tel: Aldershot 24331 Ext 619.
Briefing models of World War II (Normandy, Arnhem and Rhine Crossing) post war operations including Suez and the Falklands campaigns. Open all year. Mon-Fri 9-12.30pm & 2-4.30pm. Sat/Sun 10-12.30pm & 2-4.30pm.

ROYAL ARMY MEDICAL CORPS HISTORICAL MUSEUM
Tel: 24431 Ext 212.
Items of medical interest from 1660. Over 2500 items on display including Falkland Islands War. Horse drawn and motor ambulance. Open 9-4pm.

AMPFIELD   SIR HAROLD HILLIER GARDENS AND ARBORETUM
Jermuns Lane, Nr Romsey.
Tel: 01794 368787.
See the trees of the world in a glorious setting. In the grounds of 160 acres grow some 40,000 plants originating from every Continent. This unique collection is attractive throughout the year to both the plantsman and novice gardener, and those who just like to be amongst lovely things. Light meals and teas available in Jermyns House Testaurant. Open all year 10.30-6pm April-31st October. 10.30-5pm or dusk 1st November-31st March. Closed Christmas Day, Boxing Day and New Year's Day.

ANDOVER   CHOLDERTON RARE BREEDS FARM PARK.
Just off A303/338 9 miles west of Andover.
Tel: 0198064 438.
Superb collection of rare and young alike. Many under cover attractions. Water gardens, Toddler's and adventure playgrounds. Picinc areas, restaurant and shop. Open daily mid-March-30th October 10-6pm.

THE HAWK CONSERVANCY.
4 miles west of Andover just off the A303
Tel: 01264 772252.
This is the largest and most comprehensive collection of Birds of Prey in Southern Englsnd. You can see and photograph Birds of Prey from all over the world, these include Hawks, Falcons, Eagles, Owls Vultures and Kites. The Flying Demonstrations could be the highlight of your visit. These take place at 12 noon, 2-3pm & 4pm. (Weather permitting, as flying is not possible on wet days). Open: 1st March to last Sunday in October. 10.30-5pm spring and autumn. 10.30-5pm summer. Refreshments available. Children are not permitted unless accompanied by an adult. No dogs or pets allowed.

Chapter Fourteen

FINKLEY DOWN FARM PARK
.. situated 1 ½ miles north of the A303, 2 miles east of Andover.
Tel: 01264 352195.
The farm has a comprehensive selection of rare and not so rare breeds of all farm animals including ponies, shire horses, cattle, sheep, pigs, goats and poultry. Always many baby animals. Barn of 'Bygones'. Romany encampment. Adventure playground. Picnic under spreading chestnut trees of enjoy the Barn Cafe. Open mid-Mar to end Sept approximately, 10.15-6pm. Large free car park.

ALRESFORD   THE WATERCRESS LINE,
Mid-Hants Railway PLC. The Railway Station.
Tel: 01962 733810/734200.
Talking timetable 01962 734866. This historic steam railway runs over ten miles through Hampshire's rolling countryside between Ropley, where a variety of steam locomotives can be seen at various stages of restoration. Open Sundays in February Weekends and Bank Holidays March-October. Mid-week running beginning of June-mid July. Daily running during school holidays (check for details).

ASHURST
A must for animal lovers young and old. A modern working farm, it combines thehustle and bustle of a busy dairy unit with all the fun of children's farm. You can watch the herd being milked and find out how a modern farm is managed, get to know lots of friendly animals and even test your knowledge on the farm's computer. Video room, picnic area, playground and farm shop. Free car parking. Open 7 days a week. Easter to 30th October 11-5pm. Just off the A35 between Lyndhurst and Southampton.

NEW FOREST BUTTERFLY FARM,
Longdown. Tel: 01703 292166.
Just beyond the outskirts of Southampton you will find one of Hampshire's most popular attractions. The main attraction is a huge indoor jungle where butterflies and moths from all over the world live and breed in temperatures of up to 80 degrees. It is very much a wildlife attraction with its woodland walk, aquarium tanks and aviaries. Picnic area. Adventure playground. Restaurant and shops. Open: 7 days a week 10-5pm from end of March until 31st October.

BASINGSTOKE   STRATFIELD SAYE HOUSE
AND WELLINGTON COUNTRY PARK
.. signposted off A33 between Basingstoke and Reading. The House is still the home of the present Duke and Duchess and retains, with many of his personal belongings, much of the atmosphere created by the Great Duke.

Visitor Attractions

The Wellington Exhibition shows the life and times of this famous soldier and statesman, also a special display of his magnificent funeral carriage. In the grounds are gardens and the grave of Wellington's horse Copenhagen. Three miles away the Wellington Country Park has something for everyone. Tel: House 01256 882882. Country Park: 01734 326444. House open: daily (except Fridays) from May 1st to last Sunday in September 11.30-4pm. Country Park daily from 1st March to 31st October and at winter weekends 10-5.30pm.

THE VYNE
Sherborne St John, 4 miles north of Basingstoke.
Tel: 01256 881337.
National Trust. A splendid Tudor Mansion with fine stained glass in the Chapel. The first English country house to acquire a portico (1654). Peaceful garden with lawns sloping to lake. Open 30th March-30th September. Daily except Monday and Friday (open Good Friday and Bank Holiday Monday but closed Tuesday following). Garden 12.30-5.30pm House 1.30-5.30pm Garden only: weekends in March and October 12.30-4pm. Light refreshments and home-made teas.

BEULIEU THE NATIONAL MOTOR MUSEUM.
Tel: 01590 612123.
One of the world's most famous attractions. Inclusive admission covers The National Motor Museum, a superb exhibition of over 250 historic vehicles dating from 1895 to the present day and including Donald Campbell's 'Bluebird'. 'Wheels' an amazing journey throughout the history of motoring. Palace House, the ancestral home of the Montagu family since 1538 and former Gatehouse to Beaulieu Abbey, founded in 1204 by Cistercian monks, it lies mainly in ruins today. It is a fantastic and thrilling outing. Open: Every day except Christmas Day. Easter to September 10-6pm. October-Easter 10-5pm.

BRAMDEAN HINTON AMPNER
.. on the A272 west of Bramdean, 8 miles east of Winchester. Tel: 01962 771305. A Georgian style Hampshire Manor. Fine Regency furniture, pictures and porcelain. The gardens are a tribute to their former owner who conceived the delightful walks with many prospects and unexpected vistas. Open: April-end September. Gardens: Sat, Sun, Tues & Wed only, also Sat & Sun in August 1.30-5.30pm Tearooms sam days as gardens 1.30-5pm. National Trust.

BREAMORE BREAMORE HOUSE
.. on the A338 between Salisbury and Ringwood. Tel: 01725 512468. Breamore is a beautiful and unspoilt village on the edge of the New Forest.

Chapter Fourteen

The Countryside Museum is designed to explain the development of village life from a self-containedunit to the post-war period. At the house, the stables which were built about 1700, have been used to show the vehicles of the orse era. A fine collection includes the Red Rover, which was the London to Southampton Stagecoach. The house in 1538 has a splendid collection of pictures and furniture contributed by ten generations. The trees in the park must be admired and a visit to the Saxon church should be included. Open Easter, Bank Holidays and 1st Apr-end of Sept 2-5.30pm (Countryside 1pm) April: Tues/Wed/Sun. May, June, July, Sept : Tues/Wed/Thurs/Sat/Sun and all Bank Holidays. August: every day.

BUCKLERS HARD
Historic 18th century village, maritime museum, display cottages, river cruise and riverside walks.
Tel: 01590 616203. Open every day except Christmas Day.

FARNBOROUGH ST MICHAELS ABBEY,
.. the Empress Eugenie built the abbey, adjacent to Farnborough Hill in 1886 in memory of her busband and son. A year later she also had built an impressively flamboyant and colourful mausoleum for herself, Emperor Napoleon and their son. Below the dome and reached by an imposing staircase is the vaulted crypt. Both crypt and mausoleum can be visited by prior arrangement. Treasures in the Abbey include several personal relics of the Imperial family. With the status of a Priory, St Michaels Abbey is now a community of Benedictine Monks. For further information and details of guided tours ring: 01252 372822.

FORDINGBRIDGE   ROCKBOURNE ROMAN VILLA,
Rockbourne. Tel: 017253 541.
The villa nestles in the bottom of a wide chalkland valley about 3 miles north of Fordingbridge. It was discovered in 1943 and excavations revealed it to have been one of the largest Roman villas in the country. Open Easter to 1st October. April-June and September: weekdays from 12 noon until 6pm. Saturday/Sunday 10.30am until 6pm.

KEYHAVEN   HURST CASTLE,
South of Keyhaven on pebble spit, best approached by ferry from Keyhaven.
Tel: 01590 642344.
Built by Henry VIII to counter the threat of invasion from Europe and then added to in Victorian times. See the immense and formidable fire power it possessed from its battlements using 38 ton guns. A site exhibition explains the running and history of the fort and spectacular views over the Solent, Isle of Wight and South Coast must be seen. Open 1st April-31st October daily 10-6pm 1st November-31 March weekends 10-4pm.

Visitor Attractions

LYNDHURST NEW FOREST MUSEUM & VISITOR CENTRE.
Tel: 01703 283914.
There's so much more to the story of the New Forest than ponies and deer and you can discover it all at the New Forest Museum and Visitor Centre. Open daily from 10am.

MIDDLE WALLOP MUSEUM OF ARMY FLYING,
Nr Stockbridge. Tel: 01264 384421.
It houses a unique and award winning collection of aircraft World War II gliders and helicopters depicting the role of Army Flying since the late 19th century. Next to the Army Air Corps active airfield visitors can experience 100 years of history and watch the pilots of tomorrow training on Lynx and Gazelle helicopters. On A343 between Andover and Salisbury. Open 10-4pm daily. Restaurant. Coffee shop. Pcinic area. Free parking.

MILFORD ON SEA LYMORE VALLEY HERB GARDEN,
Braxton Courtyard, Lymore Lane. 1 mile from Milford.
Tel: 01590 642008.
These beautiful gardens set around attractive Victorian farm buildings have now become well established. A tranquil courtyard leads into a walled garden overflowing with aromatic herbs. The nursery produces a comprehensive selection of plants. Good shop. Open daily 9-5pm. Closed December 25th to end February.

MINSTEAD FURZEY GARDENS,
Nr Lyndhurst.
Tel: 01703 812464.
Set in the heart of the New Forest, Furzey Gardens can offer you a peaceful time away from the rush and hurry of our world. It has eight acres of delightful, informal landscape. Visit the ancient cottage, believed to have been built in the 16th century. The gallery displays and sells the work of local crafts people. Gardens open daily throughout the year 10-5pm (earlier in the winter). Cottage and Gallery open daily in the summer and on weekends in the winter.

NEWBURY HIGHCLERE CASTLE,
4 miles south of Newbury, off the A34 road to Winchester.
Tel: 01635 253210.
Home of the Earl and Countess of Carnarvon, Victorian splendour at its very best. Stunning interiors, grounds of Capability Brown. The 5th Earl discovered the tomb of Tutankhamun. An exhibition of his Egyptian antiquities is on display. The present Earl is the Queen's Racing Manager and recently opened his own racing exhibition. Location of many TV and Film productions. Open: Easter Sunday and Monday, May Bank Holiday,

Chapter Fourteen

Sunday and Monday, Whit Sunday and Monday, July, August and September. Open Saturday, Sunday, Wednesday, Thursday 11-6pm.

PORCHESTER CASTLE
.. off A27, south of Porchester. Surprisingly perhaps, the impressive outer walls of the castle, unbroken and standing to their full height were built as a fortress in Roman times. Within these walls you will find plenty of evidence of the use of Porchester as a prisoner of war camp in the 18th and 19th centuries. Many of the walls of the castle keep are scratched with the names of the inmates. The exhibition of the history of the castle will provide a fascinating conclusion to your tour of 2,000 years of history. Open: daily 10-6pm 1st Apr-31st Oct. 10-4pm 1st Nov-31st Mar. Closed 24-26 Dec and 1st Jan. Tel: 01705 378291 for further details. English Heritage.

ROMSEY MOTTISFONT ABBEY,
.. 4 ½ miles north west of Romsey 3/4 mile west of A3057.
Tel: 01794 340757.
This tranquil garden beside the River Test contains magnificent rees, walled gardens and the Trust's National collection of old fashioned roses. The Abbey contains a drawing room decorated by Rex Whistler and the cellarium of the old priory. Open: Garden; Apr to end Oct Sat-Wed 12 noon-6pm. Jun Sat-Wed 12 noon-8.30pm House (Whistler Room only) Apr to end Oct Tues, Wed, Sun 1-5pm.

WELLOW WINE CENTRE AND VINEYARD,
Tanners Lane, East Wellow.
Tel: 01794 830880.
A taste of the Test Valley awaits you at Hampshire's largest vineyard. A refreshingly new experience in an outstandingly beautiful setting. Wine centre and licensed bar. Meals, free parking for cars and coaches. Unguided vineyard and woodland walks. Open daily from 11-10.30pm. Mon-Sat 12-3pm & 7-10.30pm Sundays. Winter opening times may vary.

BROADLANDS
.. located on the A31 at Romsey.
Tel: 01794 516878.
Famous as the home of Lord Mountbatten. Braodlands is an elegant Palladian mansion in a beautiful landscaped setting on the banks of the River Test. Visitors may view the house with its art treasures and mementoes of the famous, enjoy the superb views from the Riverside lawns or relive Lord Mountbatten's life and times in the Mountbatten Exhibition and spectacular Mountbatten A-V Presentation. Open: Easter to last Sunday in September, 12 noon-5.30pm. Closed Fridays except Good Friday and in August. Self service tearoom. Gift shop. Free parking.

Visitor Attractions

PAULTONS PARK,
Ower, between Romsey and Cadnam.
Just off Exit 2 M27 junction A36/A31.
Hotline 01703 814455.
A great day out for all ages. Over 40 attractions included in admission price. Thrilling rides on Runaway train, Bumper Boats and Astroglide. Kids Kingdomis a paradise of play activities. Visit land of Dinosaurs, Pets Corner and Magic Forest where nursery rhymes come to life. See Romany and Village Life Museums and take a ride on the Rio Grande Railway. See over 1,000 exotic birds, wildfowl and animals in beautiful gardens, parkland and Japanese garden. Restaurant, Tearooms, Picnic areas. Speciality shops. Open daily 10-6.30pm mid-Mar to the end of Oct. Earlier closing spring/ autumn. No dogs allowed.

SELBOURNE GILBERT WHITE'S HOUSE & GARDEN AND THE OATES MUSEUM,
The Wakes, High Street, Selbourne.
Tel: 01420 511275.
Historic house and glorious tranquil five acre garden, home of famous 18th century naturalist Gilbert White, author of 'The Natural History of Selborne'. Furnished rooms, original manuscript and beautifully embroidered bed hangings. Charming garden with many fascinating old plants, a ha-ha rose and herb gardens, topiary and laburnum arch. The Oates Museum celebrates the lives of Frank Oates, a Victorian explorer in Africa and Captain Lawrence Oates, hero of Scott's Antarctic Expedition. Picnic area. Open: daily from Easter to end of October then weekends during November and December 11-5pm.

SHEDFIELD WICKHAM VINEYARD,
Botley Road, on the A334 halfway between Botley and Wickham.
Take J7 or J10 off M27. Find out all about grape growing and the amking of the award winning wines of Wickham. Highly acclaimed self-guided tour. Picnic garden. Nature Trail through ancient woodland and conservation area. Wine tasting. Open all year 10.30-5.30pm Mon-Sat. Sun Noon-3pm.
Tel: 01329 834042.

SOUTHHAMPTON EXBURY GARDENS
(Beaulieu 3 miles). Tel: 01703 891203.
These 200 acres landscaped woodland gardens include an outstanding collection of Rhododendrons, Azaleas, Camellias and Magnolias. In addition to many other notable trees and shrubs they feature a Rock Garden, Heather Gardens, Daffoldil Meadow, Iris Garden, Ponds, cascades and unlimited walks. Lunches and cream teas. Free parking. Plant Centre. Gift shop. Open: March to October 10-5.30pm.

Chapter Fourteen

HISTORIC SOUTHAMPTON
Why not spend the day in medieval town Southampton. Walk the walls around the Old Town, and visit historic sites including three museums. This is a self-guided walk with signposts, panels and historic characters to help you find your way around the medieval town.

TUDOR HOUSE MUSEUM,
Bugle Street. A fascinating 16th century house with unique Tudor Garden and exhibitions of domestic and social life in Southampton from the Tudors to today.

MARITIME MUSEUM,
Bugle Street/Town Quay. The story of the port of Southampton from the age of steam to the modern docks, with popular exhibits including the Titanic story.

MUSEUM OF ARCHAEOLOGY,
Winkle Street. Visit Roman, Saxon and medieval Southampton with a rich display of finds from archaeological excavations.

SOUTHAMPTON HALL OF AVIATION,
Albert Road South. Tel: 01703 635830.
The official and the Supermarine Company. The museum dipicts the story of some 26 aircraft companies, the legendary Spitfire and the history of the biggest flying boat operation in the world. Fascinating. Open: 10-5pm Tues-Sat. 12 noon-5pm Sundays. Open 10-5pm Mondays during School Holidays.

WINCHESTER CITY MILL,
.. foot of High Street beside City Bridge.
Tel: 01962 870057. Positioned over River Itchen the mill was rebuilt in 1744 using materials dating back to the 15th century. There is a delightful island garden and an impressive millrace. Open: 1st April to end Sept daily 11-4.45pm. Open Sat and Sun in October 12 noon-4pm. Shop open April-31 Dec daily 10-5pm.

MARWELL ZOOLOGICAL PARK, Colden Common.
Tel: 01426 943163. Marwell is world famous for its dedication to the conservation of Endangered Species. There are nearly 1000 animals and some are the rarest on earth. Its 100 acres of beautiful parkland are ideal for a relaxing day out with all the family. Open: every day except Christmas Day. 6 miles south east of Winchester.

Visitor Attractions

HEREFORD AND WORCESTERSHIRE

DROITWICH HANBURY HALL
Tel: 01527 821214
Location: Off M5 Junction 5 to Droitwich, 4 miles east of Droitwich off B4090. William and Mary style brick house, notable for the famous Thornhill staircase. Fine collection of porcelain. Re-creation of formal 18th century garden. Open: Easter to end October; Sat, Sun and Mon 2-6pm. Closed Good Friday. Aug: also open Tues and Wed 2-6pm. Shop, Tearoom, National Trust.

HEREFORD CITY MUSEUM & ART GALLERY,
Broad Street. Full of interest. Open: Tues, Wed, Fri 10am-6pm. Thurs & Sat 10-5pm 10-4pm in winter.Sunday May-September 10-4pm.Open Bank Holiday Mondays.

THE OLD HOUSE
17th century museum open Monday 10-1pm Tues-Sat 10-1pm & 2-5.30pm Sat (winter) 10-1pm. Sunday May-December 10-4pm open Bank Holiday Mondays

CHURCHILL GARDENS MUSUEM & THE HATTON GALLERY,
Venns Lane. Furniture and costume. Open Tues-Sat 2-5pm Sunday(summer) 2-5pm. Open Bank Holiday Mondays. Visit the Fragrant Garden open daily throughout the year until dusk. Admission free. Suitable for visits by blind persons and the disabled.

DINMORE MANOR AND THE COMMANDERY OF THE KNIGHTS HOSPITALLER OF ST JOHN OF JERUSALEM.
6 miles north of Hereford on A49. Tel: 01432 830322.
Spectacular hillside location. A range of impressive architecture dating from the 12-20th century. Chapel, Cloisters, Great Hall(Music Room) and extensive roof walk giving panoramic views of the countryside and beautiful gardens below. Large collection of stained glass. Open 9.30-5.30pm daily all year. Refreshments available most afternoons during summer.

LEDBURY EASTNOR CASTLE
Tel: 01531 633160.
Splendid Georgian Castle in fairytale setting with Deer Park, lake and arboretum. Inside this family home tapestries, fine art, armour and furniture from the Italianate and Gothic in richly decorated interiors, many recently restored to critical acclaim. Home-made cream teas and ice cream. Open Sundays Easter to end September, Bank Holiday Mondays. Sunday to Friday during August 12 noon-5pm.

Chapter Fourteen

LEOMINSTER BERRINGTON HALL
Nr. Leominster.
Tel: 01586 780246
Location: 3 miles north of Leominster. Signposted off A49.
A classical elegant 18th century mansion by Henry Holland, set in a gracefully landscaped park by 'Capability' Brown. Park walk open July to end October only. Open Easter to end September; Wed-Sun (open Bank Holiday Mon. closed Good Friday) 1.30-5.30pm. October Wed-Sun 1.30-4.30. Grounds open from 12.30pm. Shop. Licensed restaurant. Dogs on leads in car park only. National Trust.

CROFT CASTLE
Tel: 01586 780246
Location : 5 miles north west of Leominster. Signposted off A49 and A4110. Just 5 miles from Berrington Hall, this Marcher Castle has been the home of the Croft family since Domesday (with a short break of 170 years).Ancient walls and castellated turrets house an interior shown as it was in the 18th century with fine ceilings and Gothic staircase. The surrounding parkland is open all year. Open: Easter Sat, Sun & Mon 2-6pm. Closed Good Friday. April and October Sat & Sun 2-5pm. May to end Sept: Wed-Sun and Bank Holiday Monday 2-6pm. National Trust.

LYDE KENCHESTER WATER GARDENS
Church Road.
Tel: 01432 270981.
Largest and perhaps best stocked aquatic centre in the South Midlands. More than two hundred tropical fish tanks, fresh and saltwater, are filled with some of the most fascinating, colourful and eye-catching sea and fresh water creatures. The best view of these beautiful gardens is from the Tea Rooms. On the A49 Hereford to Leominster Road - two miles north of Hereford. Free admission. Carpark. Disabled access. Open every day of the week.

BRINGSTY LOWER BROCKHAMPTON
Tel: 01885 488099
Location: 2 miles east of Bromyard on A44.
A 14th century half timbered moated farmhouse with a very unusual gatehouse. Only the medieval hall and parlour are shown. Open: House; April-end September; Wed-Sun and Bank Holiday Monday. 10-5pm. Closed Good Friday. Oct: Wed-Sun 10am-4pm. Estate open all year.

ROSS-ON-WYE   THE BUTTON MUSEUM
Kyrle Street.
Tel: 01989 566089
Unique award winnng Museum of Dress and Uniform Buttons, worn by ladies and gentlemen over the last two hundred years. Museum shop. Open 7 days a week 1st April-31st October 10-5pm.

SWAINSHILL   THE WEIR
Location: 5 miles west of Hereford on A438.
Fine views of the River Wye and the Welsh Hills from a steep bank studded with trees, shrubs and plants. Beautiful, particularly in springtime, with drifts of flowering bulbs. Open: Mid-February to end October; Wed to Sun (including Good Friday) and Bank Holiday Monday 11am-6pm. National Trust.

TENBURY WELLS -BURFORD HOUSE GARDENS
Tel: 01584 810777 Fax: 01584 810673.
Burford House is an early Georgian House built on the ancient site of Scrob's Castle, at the confluence of the River Teme and Ledwych Brook. It was acquired by the late John Treasure in 1954 as the ideal setting for his new garden. Since then and until his death in 1993 John Treasure transformed the grounds of this austere Georgian red brick house from a scattering of a few good trees and an elegant summerhouse into an eloquently defined twentieth century garden. Contrasting its spare symmetry on the north front with curving vistas and beds on its south side, he elegantly described the setting of the house in the fertile alluvial loam of the River Teme which weaves around the garden. As an architect by training he brought that all too rare combination of the positive discipline of design to a passion for plants and the result is a garden of quiet serenity and fascination. John Treasure's high standards of discipline are revealed in the crisply edged and well groomed beds. This is a plantsman's garden, laid out to display myriads of forms and species in ordered frameworks. There are special combinations and ideas which gardeners of all kinds will be inspired to study and copy.harmonising combinations of colour have been brilliantly achieved throughout the garden, and especial use made of clematis, a favourite of John Treasure. The garden now boasts over 150 varieties and is home to the National Collection. There are so many kinds of plants to be seen especially those that grow on neutral to limey soils, and many marginal plants that grow along the stream gardens. Of the genera that are well represented there are, Hosta, Hydrangea, Philadelphus, grasses, hellebores, shrub roses, penstemons, birches, irises, astilbes, agapanthus, daylilies and hosts of bulbs and rarities, all grouped beautifully and new ideas and plants are finding homes here in this dynamic and graceful garden. Many of the unusual plants in the garden can be found in Treasures Plant Centre adjacent, who specialise

in clematis, herbaceous, shrubs, trees and climbers. There is a Gallery open in the House and a new Craft Shop in the grounds. The Burford Buttery serves hot and cold meals together with home-made cakes, tea and continental coffee throughout the day. Coach parties are welcome and The Buttery is happy to cater for special occasions. OPEN: Monday-Sunday 10am-6pm (Dusk if earlier).

WELLINGTON QUEENSWOOD GARDEN CENTRE
Wellington HR4 8BB
Tel: 01432 830880. Fax: 01432 830833.
The Milne Family - Tony, Frank,Kathleen, Eric and Alexi own and operate this attractive garden centre which is far more than somewhere one comes just to buy plants. It is an outing that is thoroughly enjoyable and one from which you can gain gardening advice from an expert and helpful staff. The plants are second to none. The company offers all its customers a unique plant and gardening equipment ' finder service'. If they do not have a product in stock they will make every attempt to source it for their customers to collect or have sent to them by post. To help gardeners and those interested in horticulture a joint venture with Pershore College of Horticulture has been set up resulting in Pershore setting up a lecture hall at Queenswood and offering courses/qualifications to local people. All of this demonstrates how dedicated the Milne family and their staff are to the centre. A large pet shop on the site offering small domestic pets such as rabbits and guinea pigs and a huge selection of tropical and cold water fish attracts many people. Here too advice is top notch from PTIA trained staff. The Tea House is a favourite place for customers. Not only does it serve excellent tea but lunches and evening meals are available including cakes and specialities made on the premises. OPEN; Mon-Sat 1st April-30th June & 1st Dec-23rd Dec. 9am-8pm. 27th Dec-31st March & 1st July -30th Nov 9am-6pm. Sundays. Teahouse & Outdoor Plant Area 9am-5pm. Main Building and Pet Shop 11am-5pm. Easy parking - 500 spaces. Coaches welcome.

WHITNEY ON WYE   CWMMAU FARMHOUSE
Brilley. Tel: 01497 831251.
Location: 4 miles south west of Kingston between A4111 and A438. Attractive early 17th century timber-framed and stone-tiled farmhouse. Open: Easter, May, Spring and Summer Bank Holiday weekends only and Weds in August 2-6pm. National Trust.

WORCESTER THE GREYFRIARS,
Friar Street. Tel: 01905 23571
Still surviving in the heart of Worcester, this medieval timber-framedhouse has been carefully restored. Delightful walled garden. Open: April-end October. Wed, Thurs and Bank Holiday Monday 2-5.30pm. National Trust.

Visitor Attractions

HERTFORDSHIRE

BARNET RIDING CENTRE
Tel: 0181 449 3531.
Location: Situated only 25 miles from Central London ideally situated off the A1 and on the border of Hertfordshire junction 23 off the M25. Away from the hustle and bustle of inner-city life children and adults alike can take time off to spend some time amongst nature and take horse riding lessons. Amateurs and professionals can spend one hour or more learning how to ride and hack through the Hertfordshire countryside. Open Tues-Sat all year including Bank Holidays.

BROXBOURNE PARADISE WILDLIFE PARK
White Stubbs Lane, Broxbourne EN10 7QA
Tel: 01992 468001.
Paradise Wildlife Park is unique! As Britain's most interactive Wildlife Park it is an ideal place to touch, feed and meet many animals - both domestic and exotic. You can learn a great deal during the 'meet the animals' session where experienced keepers impart information about the wonderful creatures and answer visitors questions. The 'Meet the Animals' experience includes: foxes, birds of prey, reptiles, chinchilla, camels, llamas and zebras.
There are many other daily events including Dr Do and Dr Little amazing animal facts show, the Sweetie man, the feeding of the lions and tigers and lion and tiger cub talks. The friendly family run Park is very compact and is set in the wonderful backdrop of Broxbourne woods. Other attractions on the site comprise a Woodland Railway, Crazy Golf, Children's rides and Tractor Trailer rides for which there is a fee of 50p per ride. FREE facilities include 3 superb adventure playgrounds, Fantasy Land, Adventureland and Fun Land plus a woodland walk. There is a wide range of catering from Mannings Snack Cabin, The Pembridge Cafeteria to a Barbecue and Bar area and The Pembridge Restaurant. There are also ample picnic areas spread across the park.
Paradise Wildlife Park also offers the public the chance to meet their lion or tiger cubs. This is literally the opportunity of a lifetime and is available outside the normal opening hours of the park. The money raised goes to Project Life Lion, a registered charity which helpe to save African lions in the Serengeti from Canine Distemper. The sessions last up to 30 minutes and are for a group of up to 4 people. Priced at forty pounds a session - numbers are strictly limited. For further details or to book ring 01992 470490.
The Park is located 6 miles from Junction 25 off the M25. Brown and White tourist signs direct you to the Park from the A10 at the Broxbourne/Turnford Junction. Admission prices are as at January 1996 £4.50adults, £4.00 senior citizens and £3.50 children (3-15_. Opening times are 10am-6pm (Summer) and 10am-dusk (Winter). Paradise Wildlife opens every day of the year.

Chapter Fourteen

Information line 01992 468001. Paradise Wildlife Park is a truly wonderful place with something for everyone - whatever your age!

HATFIELD MILL GREEN MUSEUM
Tel: 01707 271362.
This local museum is housed in what was for centuries the home of the millers who worked in the adjoining water mill. Mill Green Museum has twopermanent galleries where local items from Roman times to the present day are on show - everything from pottery and craft tools to underwear and school certificates. Open throughout the year Tues-Fri 10-5pm and Sat,Sun and Bank Holidays 2-5pm Admission free.

MILL GREEN MILL
Tel: 01707 271362.
Adjoining the museum is the water mill which has been restored to its full working order, as it would have been during the 18th and 19th century. Visitors can take a look at how a mill used to work, with the reconstruction of a new water wheel. Mill Green Flour freshly ground from organically grown wheat is on sale. Open throughout the year Tues-Fri 10-5pm and Sat, Sun and Bank Holidays 2-5pm. Admission free.

WELWYN ROMAN BATHS
Tel: 01707 271362.
Preserved under the A1(M) in a steel vault, Welwyn Roman Baths are the remains of a bathing suite which was originally part of a country villa. The site was evacuated during the 1960s and early 70s by the Welwyn Archaeological Society and the vault installed to save the bathing suite from deconstruction when the motorway was built. The layout of cold room, warm room, hot room, cold and hot baths and furnace room can be clearly seen together with the remains of the hypocaust. Also on show are related archaeological finds from the Welwyn area and an explanatory exhibition on Roman baths and the history of the site. The site is open on Thurs-Sun and Bank Holidays from 2-5pm.

HATFIELD HOUSE;
Tel: 01707 262823.
Location: 21 miles north of London on the Great North Road (A1), seven miles from M25. This celebrated Jacobean house, which stands in its own great park, was built between 1607 and 1611 by Robert Cecil, the first Earl of Salisbury and Chief Minister to King James I. It has been the family home of the Cecils ever since. The State Rooms are rich in world famous paintings, fine furniture, rare tapestries and historic armour. The beautiful stained glass in the chapel is original. Within the delightful gardens stands the surviving wing of the Royal Palace of Hatfield (1497) where Elizabeth I spent

much of her childhood. Open 25th Mar-9th October weekdays from 12-4pm, Sun 1.30-5pm.

HATFIELD GARDEN
Tel: 01707 262823
Connected to Hatfield House, the West Gardens date back to the late 15th century when the Palace of Hatfield was built. Keeping in line with the manner of the garden of the 17th century, the garden has been planted with a great variety of sweet smelling flowers, bulbs, trees and shrubs for every season of the year. Although the West Garden is planted with mainly herbaceous plants, roses, irises and peonies, with a considerable number of rare and unusual plants. The West Gardens are open daily except Good Friday 11-6pm.

THE OLD PALACE, HATFIELD PARK
Tel: 01707 262055
Location: 31 miles north of London AI (M) junction 4.
Take an exciting trip back to Elizabethan times by visiting The Old Palace for an authentic Banquet. Set in the Great Hall people enjoy a magnificent five course meal of royal proportions including red or white wine and mead. From the moment you take your seat you are under the spell of a troop of costumed minstrels and players.Singing songs from the period, performing some of the picturesque ceremonies and customs of the Elizabethan era, they move from table to table serenading you as you dine. The authentic setting, the cuisine, the atmosphere and spectacle combine to make this not just a feast of entertainment but an unforgettable experience too. The Banquets are held every Tues, Thurs, Fri and Sat evenings.

KNEBWORTH   KNEBWORTH HOUSE & GARDENS
Tel: 01438 812661
Location: entrance direct from Junction 7 of the AI (M) at Stevenage.
Hours of fun can be had by all the family at the historic home of the Lytton family since 1490. The house contains many beautiful rooms, and magnificent paintings, fine furniture and objects d'art. As well as a visit to the historic house children can enjoy hours of fun at the giant Adventure Playground which includes a fort, suspension slide, bouncy castle and miniature railway, or a trip around the 250 acres of Parkland to see the herds of Red and Sika deer. Open daily 26th March-17th April and 28thy May-4th September. 11-5.30pm.

ROYSTON   WILLERS MILL WILD ANIMAL SANCTUARY
Tel: 01763 262226
Moulded out of a wilderness of nettles, rubbish, and an old deserted cottage, between the railway line and the village cricket pitch of Shepreth, Terry and

Chapter Fourteen

Gill Willers have created a wonderful setting for their animal sanctuary. Here between a duck pond and in a totally enclosed environment, young children are able to come into direct contact with a variety of animals, often for the first time, and are able to touch and handle all species, much to their obvious enjoyment. It is a place for unwanted or injured animals to live in safety and to be well cared for, just as homes exist for unwanted cats and dogs. The animals come from a variety of sources, such as road, gun and gassing casualties, unwanted pets, research centres, zoos, safari parks and meat markets. Some even arrive by themselves! The majority of the animals have the run of the sanctuary and can indeed leave at any time if they wish to. However, some have to be kept in enclosures for their own protection as their injuries prevent them from leading a normal life. The more exotic species require special diets and a heated environment to keep them healthy. Willers Wildlife Park receives no form of government grant or other help. Entrance fees are its sole source of revenue so please do go and visit. OPEN; Summer 10am-6pm every day. Winter: 1st Nov-28th Feb 10-5pm every day. Closed Christmas Day.

ST ALBANS   BOWMANS OPEN FARM
Tel: 01462 424055.
Bowmans Farm is open daily throughout the year and provides both an entertaining and educational day out for the whole family. It will allow you to see both the livestock and arable enterprises, see the herd of pedigree Freisian cows being milked every afternoon, see the new born piglets and calves, visit the pets corner and take a stroll around the lake to observe the nature and wildlife. Or why not visit the farm shop and restaurant and sample a wide selection of fresh vegetables, home-made yoghurt and award winning ice-cream. Open throughout the year 9-5.30pm.

STEVENAGE   STEVENAGE MUSEUM
Tel: 01438 354292.
When you step inside you enter another world. Fascinating collections of everyday objects tell the story of Stevenage from pre-history tothe present. There are hundreds of objects for you to see including a 1950s living room, a perfect 1930s dolls house, gas masks, old farm tools and a Roman silver coin hoard. Open Mon-Sat 10-5pm. Free admission.

ROGER HARVEY GARDEN WORLD
Tel: 01438 814687.
A 400 year old complex of farm buildings has been converted into a Garden Centre. Seasonal displays of plants, bulbs and Christmas Wonderland decorations means that there is something special for everyone including tropical fish, children's adventure playground, pets corner, gift hall and houseplant conservatory. Open daily 9.30-5.30pm. Admission free.

Visitor Attractions

WELWYN GARDEN CITY   PANSHANGER GOLF COMPLEX
Tel: 01707 333350.
Set in some of Hertfordshire's most delightful countryside this offers one of the most popular 'Pay as you Play' courses in the country. The Herts Golf Academy offers men, women and children of all ages the opportunity to learn to play golf or improve their skills. The golf course offers a scenic and challenging eighteen hole par 72 golf course, nine hole pitch and putt, putting green and cafe open from 9am providing excellent refreshments. Open daily.

WHITEWELL   WATERHALL FARM & CRAFT CENTRE
Tel: 01438 871256.
Open all year round this farm and craft centre offers adults and children the opportunity to take a step back to nature to see how many farm animals live today. A wide range of quality gifts and souvenirs is always available from the craft shop including antiques, bric-a-brac and pine furniture. A visit can also be made to the tea-room which serves a selection of light lunches, delicious cream teas and home-made cakes. Open Wed-Sun 10-5pm March-October and all Bank Holidays.

HUMBERSIDE

SCUNTHORPE   ELSHAM HALL COUNTRY PARK
Tel: 01652 688698.
Elsham Country Park was opened in 1970 by Captain and Mrs Elwes because they wanted visitors to enjoy the Park and appreciate wildlife, Rural Crafts and Arts. The award-winning facilities now include the Granary Restaurant and Tea-Rooms, the 'Haybarn Centre', the new Garden Centre; Monk's Wood Arboretun; Children's Animal Farm and Pets Corner. There are also many special events and Arts Exhibitions throughout the year. Why not take a look for yourself. Open Easter Sat- mid Sept 11-5pm and mid-Sept-Easter Sun 11-4pm. Closed Good Friday and Winter Bank Holidays.

LEICESTERSHIRE

CASTLE DONNINGTON   AEROPARK AND VISITOR CENTRE
Tel: 01332 810621
See the action from this 12 acre park next to the taxiway at the eastern end of the airport. Aircraft exhibitions in the Aeropark include a Lightning jet fighter, Vulcan bomber, Canberra bomber, Argosy freighter and Whirlwind helicopter. There is also a viewing mound, themed children's play area and picnic tables. Open Easter-October Mon-Fri 10-5pm Sat 11-4pm Sun 11-6pm.

Chapter Fourteen

COALVILLE SNIBSTON DISCOVERY PARK
Tel: 01530 510851
Built on the 100 acre site of a former colliery, Snibston Discovery Park is Leicestershire's largest attraction where finding out is a great day out for everyone. The Exhibition Hall contains five galleries exploring the Industrial Heritage of Leicestershire including transport, engineering, extractive industries, textiles and fashion. Follow fashion through the ages, travel through time from 1600 until the present day or see what it was like for a miner in the mid 19th century. Open daily all year round from 10-6pm.

HINCKLEY ASHBY CANAL
Tel: 01455 232789
The Ashby-de-la-Zouch Canal was a relative latecomer being completed in 1804 but had many of the attributes of the earliest navigations. It follows the contours of surrounding countryside and has no locks throughout its lengths. The Canal is home to a wonderful variety of creatures and plants, including ducks, fish, dragonflies, waterlilies, kingfisher and many more. Open daily it is a great escape from the hustle and bustle of everyday life.

THE GUILDHALL
Tel: 01533 532569
The Guildhall is within five minutes walk of the City Centre. From the Clock Tower, turn into East Gate, and turn left onto Silver St. The Guildhall is on Guildhall Lane, the continuation of Silver St. It is a unique Grade I listed building and has been the scene of many significant events in Leicester's history. The Building comprises the following rooms: THE GREAT HALL: The timber framed Great Hall is the original Guildhall of the Gild of Corpus Christi dating back to c1390 and evokes a wonderful sense of space and time. As well as direct promotions, the Hall, outside museum hours, is available for public hire. THE MAYOR'S PARLOUR; The ground floor of the West Wing c1490 contains the Mayor's Parlour, a smaller civic room, remodelled in 1563. The room is oak panelled with a beautifully carved and painted overmantle above the fireplace.
THE JURY ROOM; The west wing also contains The Jury Room, above the Mayor's Parlour and was originally the retiring room for the Jury after Quarter Sessions. It now houses the Library of the Leicestershire Archeological and Historical Society founded in 1855. The room is available as a study and meeting room and seats 30 people. THE LIBRARY; The upper floor of the East Wing houses the Town Library. The Library is the third oldest public library in the country and was established in 1632. THE POLICE STATION; Leicester's first police force was established in 1836 and is the third oldest in Great Britain. The Borough Police Force was based at the Guildhall, and originally had 3 cells. The Cells have 2 replica criminals based on real criminals of the Victorianperiod. THE RECORDER'S

BEDROOM; The office of Recorder was established in 1464 and the Recorder was required to visit the borough at least 4 times a year to preside over the Quarter Sessions. A bedroom was granted to the Recorder and it's fitting out is recorded in the Chamberlain's records for 1581-82. THE CONSTABLE'S HOUSE: The brick built house off the side of the courtyard was built in 1836 for Leicester's first Chief Constable and is now the administrative base of the Guildhall and will shortly be converted into a new exhibition hall. GUIDED TOURS; Available on request. PUBLIC HIRE; Available for both community and commercial hire. PERFORMANCES AND CONCERTS; Magical atmosphere with its audience capacity of 100 people. SPECIAL EVENTS;Throughout the year. OPEN; Mon-Sat: 10am-5.30pm Sundays:2-5.30pm. Admission Free.

THE CATHEDRAL
Tel: 01533 625294
The Church of St Martin's was one of six parish churches recorded in Leicester in 1086. Extended in the 14th and 15th centuries and restored in the 19th century it was hallowed as the Cathedral of Leicester in 1927. Visitors are invited to tour the building and see its impressive roof, stained glass windows and stone and wood carvings. Inside the chancel is a memorial to King Richard III. Outside the graveyard has been laid out as a garden containing many interesting slate headstones. Open every day.

CASTLE GARDENS & CASTLE MOTTE
This used to be a low-flying marshy area of reeds and willows. At the end of the 19th century the land was drained and used for allotments before being opened as public gardens in 1926. The Motte is a man-made mound built by Leicester's first Norman Lord in about 1070. It may originally have been several metres higher and would have had timber fortification on the top. The Motte is open to the public and in the gardens is the statue of Richard III which commemorates his links with Leicestershire. Garden open daily during daylight hours.

RIVERSIDE PARK
This eight mile stretch of footpaths along the banks of the River Soar and Grand Union Canal passes through Castle Park and allows an insight into Leicester's early industrial history. The dominant Pex Building was originally a worsted spinning factory providing yarn for the knitting trade. Goods were brought to and from the City by the major waterway network. Flood alleviation work to the river in the late 19th century formed the 'Mile straight' on which rowing regattas are held annually. The line of the Great Central Railway has now been developed as a pedestrian walk and cycleway.

Chapter Fourteen

FARMWORLD,
Stoughton Farm Park, Gartree Road, Leicester LE22FB.
Tel:01162 710355
This is an exciting day out for every age group. You will find it 3 miles SE of Leicester City Centre and 6 miles off the M1/M69 Junction 21. Follow the southerly ring road. Signposted 'Farm Park' from A6 and A47. It is a real working Dairy Farm with acres of Parkland for pleasure and play. There are Shire horses and cart rides, rare farm animals, lakeside and woodland walks, a picnic area, Toy Tractor park and indoor sandpit. A special Children's Farmyard and Playground. You are invited to the Milking Parlour to watch the herd being milked and to try your hand at operating a milking machine. The Craftworkshops are fascinating and quite frequently there are demonstrations. Add to this lots of lovable pets, an Edwardian Ale House, Audio Visual Theatre and Exhibitions and displays featuring the countryside at work and it becomes very clear why Farmworld is so popular. In keeping with Leicester's innovative and go ahead thinking, Farmworld also offers a unique Conference venue. It is housed in beautifully restored and converted 18th century farm buildings and equipped with a wide range of modern facilities to provide for every business requirement. For further details please ring 01162 710355 or Fax: 01162 713211 FARMWORLD IS OPEN; Daily 10am-5.30pm (Winter 5pm) except December 25th &26th and January 1st. Dogs cannot be admitted. (Except Guide dogs) Disabled access. Gift Shop. Wheatsheaf Cafe.

MARKET BOSWORTH TWYCROSS ZOO
Tel: 01827 880250
This is an ideal day out. There is a wide variety of animals including gorillas, chimps, orangutans, gibbons, elephants, lions and giraffes. There is also an adventure playground, pets corner and penguin pool. Open daily from 10-6pm all the year round.

OAKHAM RUTLAND FARM PARK
Tel: 01572 756789
In 18 acres of beautiful parkland Rutland Park Farm has a wonderful selection of farm animals, goats, poultry and wildfowl for the whole family to see. Apart from visiting the animals and old farm vehicles why not stroll through the countryside and look at the fern, bamboo and wildflower meadow. Open 3rd April-18th Sept 10-5pm.

RUTLAND WATER ANGLIAN WATER BIRD WATCHING CENTRE AND RUTLAND WATER NATURE RESERVE.
Egleton, Oakham, Rutland, Leicestershire LE15 8BT
Tel: 01572 770651
Rutland Water has become one of the most importnt wildfowl sanctuaries in

Visitor Attractions

Great Britain, regularly holding in excess of 10,000 waterfowl of up to 28 species. It is a Site of Special Scientific Interest and has received recognition of its international importance by the European Community and has been designated as a globally important wetland. It covers an area of 450 acres and the wide variety of habitats ensures that many species of birds are present throughout the year, but the reserve is best known for the thousands of wildfowl which flock to spend the winter on the lagoons and open water. Gadwall shoveler, teal, tufted duck, pochard and shelduck are present all year round; in winter they are joined by pintail, goldeneye, goosander, wigeon and other, rarer ducks, such as smew, red-breasted merganser and long-tailed duck. Rare grebes and divers are frequent visitors. In summer common terns and cormorants breed communally on the lagoons. During spring passage, little gulls, Arctic terns and black terns pass through, often in their hundreds, while rare Caspian and white-winged black terns have been recorded. Wader passage may bring up to 19 species in a single day. Birds of prey include breeding kestrel and sparrowhawk; osprey and harriers during migration; regular sightings of peregrine and merlin in winter; and spectaculr views of hobbies in summer as they feed on insects over the lagoons. Three lagoons and 9 miles of shore and open water are overlooked by a total of 17 hides. Other attractive wildlife habitats contain species rare elsewhere; wildflowers, butterflies and dragon flies. Old hay meadows, rough grassland, hedges, plantations and woodland invite wildlife and visitor alike. On both reserves, trails lead to the hides throughall these habitats. Car parking is provided free to reserve visitors at Egleton and Lyndon. There are toilets in both reserves. Disabled facilities at Egleton. Dogs not allowed at Egleton. At Lyndon they must be on a lead. Disabled visitors access is available at Egleton at the Anglian Birdwatching Centre and Shoveler hide and at Lyndon Centre using Teal and Swan hides.

LINCOLNSHIRE

GRANTHAM   BELVOIR CASTLE
Tel: 01476 870262
Location: Near Grantham signposted off A607.
Home of the Duke and Duchess of Rutland, Belvoir Castle is superbly situated overlooking the Vale of Belvoir. The house has magnificent staterooms, containing notable pictures, tapestries and fine furniture. The Queen's Royal Lancers Museum is also situated within the Castle. Open April 1st -29th Sept. Tue, Thurs, Sat, Sun & Bank Holidays 11-5pm.

LINCOLN LINCOLN CATHEDRAL
.. is one of the largest in England and has many attractive features including the magnificent open nave, St Hugh's Choir, the Angel Choir and beautiful

Chapter Fourteen

stained glass windows including the 14th century 'Bishop's Eye'. The Chapter House Cloisters, Wren Library and Treasury are other interesting features and all visitors are invited to seek out the Lincoln importance... Services are held daily and there are generally guided tours and tower tours.

LINCOLN CASTLE
.. is on the site of the original Roman fortress and the present castle dates back to 1068. Interesting architectural features include the keep known as the Lucy Tower, Cobb Hall which was the site of the public gallows, and the Observastory tower which offers tremendous views of the cathedral and city as a whole. The Victorian prison includes a unique prison chapel with separate pews like upright coffins. This building also houses an original version of the famous Magna Carta from 1215, and an exhibition interpreting the history of this document and its importance to modern freedoms and democracy. Guided tours and wall walks are available.

MIDDLESEX

EPPING LEE VALLEY PARK.
Tel: 01992 700766.
Location: along M25 from Potters Bar.
The Lee Valley is Britain's first regional park devoted entirely for the enjoyment of leisure and recreation and the conservation of countryside and natural environment. Only a walk or boat trip away is splendid countryside, a Wildlife Oasis and Sporting Paradise along with the fascinating history and secrets of the Lee Valley industrial heritage. Admission free. Open throughout the year.

NORTHUMBERLAND

BAGPIPE MUSEUM
Tel: 01670 519466.
Location: Morpeth Chantry.
This unusual museum specialises in the history and development of Northumbrian small pipes and their music from India to Inverness. Small admission charge. Open Mon-sat 9.30-5.30pm Mar-Dec, Mon-Sat 9.30-5.30pm Jan-Feb. Closed between Christmas and New Year.

Visitor Attractions

BATTLEFIELDS CASTLE.
Tel: 01670 514343.
English Heritage battlefields and castles which display the roots of history in Northumberland from the Battle of Heavenfield in 635 and the Battle of Carham in 1018. Many of the Castles are owned by Englsih Heritage and are open daily from 10-6pm Apr-30th Sept and 10-4pm 1st Oct-31st Mar.

BELSAY AHLL & GARDENS.
Tel: 01661 881636.
Location: 14 miles NW of Newcastle on A696.
Belsay Hall, Castle and Gardens is one of the most remarkable estates in the border country. Set admist beautiful gardens and occupied continuously by the same family for nearly 600 years the medieval hall and castle encapsulate much of the history of this often turbulent region. Open daily 10-6pm 1 Apr-30Sept Tues-Sat 10-4pm 1 Oct-31 Mar.

KIELDER WATER CRUISES.
Tel: 01434 240398.
Enjoy a 10 mile cruise in comfort on Europe's largest man-made lake in a covered ferry with commentary, licensed bar and light refreshments on board. Take a round trip calling at places of interest or use the ferry as access to self-guided walks on the north side of the lake. Open throughout mid-Mar to 31st Oct, weather permitting.

NORTHUMBRIA CRAFT CENTRE.
Tel: 01670 511217.
Location: Just off the A1 15 miles north of Newcastle.
Take a day out to browse around a selection of high quality, reasonably priced crafts including pottery, jewellery, knitwear and stained glass. Choose from a variety of goods produced by over 40 Northumbrian craftsmen. Open Mon-Sat 9.30-5.30pm Mar-Dec. Mon-Sat 10-4pm Jan-Feb.

CHANTRY SILVER.
Tel: 01670 511323.
Location: Just off the A1 15 miles north of Newcastle. Housed within the Chantry Court Yard one can purchase hand-made jewellery and silver from Chantry Silver. Also on view and for sale are original paintings, tapestries and glass engravings by many local artists. Admission free. Open Mon-Sat 9.30-5.30pm.

THE NORTHUMBERLAND WILDLIFE SHOP.
Tel: 01670 519001.
Location: Just off the A1 15 miles north of Newcastle. The friendly atmosphere of the Trust shop staffed by Trust members is the ideal place for

Chapter Fourteen

the unusual gift or souvenir or for information about Northumberland Wildlife. Admission free. Open Mon-Sat 10-4pm.

THE NORTHUMBERLAND COASTAL ROUTE.
Tel: 01670 511323.
A 35 mile signed Coastal Route from Druridge Bay to the village of Belford, on the A1, 5 miles south of Holy Island. Attractions along the route include a Country Park at Druridge Bay, a marina at Auble, castles at Warkworthy, Dunstanburgh and Bainburgh, fishing harbours at Auble, Craster and Seahouses, and delightful sandy beaches all along the coast.

NORTHUMBERLAND NATIONAL PARK.
Tel: 01434 605555.
The NorthumberlandNational Park stretches for over 40 miles from Hadrian's Wall in the south and round the Cheviot Hills which form the border of Scotland. Its 398 square miles also contain delightful wooded valleys and some of the finest stretches of moorland in the country.

ENGLAND'S LAST WILDERNESS.
Tel: 01434 605225.
South of Hexham is the North Pennines, the most recent part of the country to be officially declared an 'Area of Outstanding Natural Beauty'. It spans 3 counties: Northumberland, Durham and Cumbria and comprises magnificent moorlands, wooded valleys and small unspoilt villages.

WALLINGTON HOUSE.
Tel: 01670 74283.
Location: 12 miles west of Morpeth (B6343).
Built in 1688 and altered in the 1740s, the house features exceptional plasterwork; fine collections of porcelain and dolls houses and the Museum of Curiosities. The house is set in 100 acres of lakes, lawns and woodland with a beautiful Walled Garden. Admission to House, Walled Garden and Grounds £4.00. Open daily 1st Apr-31st Oct, except Tues 1-5.30pm. Last admission 5pm.

OXFORDSHIRE

BURFORD   COTSWOLD WILD LIFE PARK
Tel: 01993 823006
Situated in 180 acres of gardens and woodland around an old English manor house, a large and varied collection of animals from all over the world can be seen in spacious grassed enclosures. There is also a reptile house, aquarium, tropical house, exhibition of fruit bats, picnicking areas, narrow

Visitor Attractions

gauge railway (Apr-Oct), adventure playground, bar, restaurant, children's farmyard, insect house and gift shops. Special events during summer months. Open; Daily (except Christmas day) from 10-6pm or dusk (whichever is the earlier).

OXFORD   THE OXFORD STORY
6 Broad Street
Tel: 01865 790055
Created by Oxford University and the people behind York's 'Jorvik' Viking Centre, this is an extraordinary exhibition about Oxford's 800 years past. Now recognised as the best short introduction to Oxford. The Oxford Story uses a ride through the streets from the past, from medieval Oxford to Inspector Morse Magnus Magnusson or Timothy Mallett (for children) provide the commentary. Open: April-October 9.30-5pm. July-August 9.30-7pm. Nov-March 10-4pm. Closed Christmas Day.

WITNEY   COGGES MANOR FARM MUSEUM
Church Lane. tel: 01993 772602
A working museum of Victorian rural Life on a 20 acre site, close to Witney town centre. The historic site includes the manor house with room displays, walled garden, orchard, riverside walks, farm buildings housing traditional breeds of animals, exhibitions in the barns, daily demonstrations of cooking on the kitchen range and special weekends and activities. Buttery serving light lunches and teas, gift shop and car park. Open: April-end October, Tues-Friday abd Bank Holiday Mondays 10.30-
5.30pm. Saturday and Sunday 12 njoon- 5.30pm.

WOODSTOCK BLENHEIM PALACE
Tel: 01993 811091
Home of the 11th Duke of Marlborough, birthplace of Sir Winston Churchill. A visit to Blenheim is a wonderful way to spend a day. An inclusive ticket covers the Palace tour, and Gardens, Butterfly House, Motor Launch, Train, Adventure Play Area and Nature trail. Optional are the Marlborough Maze and Rowing Boat hire on Queen Pool. Car parking is free for Palace visitors. Shops, Cafeterias and Restaurant. Special events include the Blenheim Audi International Horse Trials. Mid- March- 31st October daily 10.30-5.30pm.

Chapter Fourteen

SUFFOLK

ALDEBURGH MOOT HALL,
Sea Front.
Town history and maritime affairs including prints, paintings, relics of Snape Anglo-Saxon ship burial. In 16th century timbered town hall. Open: April, May Sat & Sun 2.30-5pm. Jun-Sept daily 2.30-5pm. Jul, Aug daily 10-12.30pm & 2.30-5.30pm.

BURY ST EDMUNDS MANOR HOUSE MUSEUM,
Honey Hill. Tel: 01284 757072.
A new museum of art and horology in refurbished Georgian Mansion. Colliection of clocks, watches, paintings, furniture, costumes and ceramics. 'Hands On' Gallery. Cafe & shop. Open all year Mon-Sat 10-5pm Sun 2-5pm. Closed Good Friday, Christmas Day and Boxing Day.

SUFFOLD REGIMENTAL MUSEUM,
The Keep, Gibraltar Barracks, Out Risbygate. Tel: 01284 752394 ext 6.
Military uniforms, weapons, medals, photographs, drums etc, illustrating history of the Suffolk and Cambridgeshire regiments from 17th century. Open all year. Mon-Fri 10-12, 2-4pm. Closed Bank Holidays. Admission free.

ST EDMONDSBURY CATHEDRAL
Angel Hill 11th century Mother church of Suffolk with fine hammer beam roof and a display of 1,00 embroidered kneelers. Open Jun-Aug 8.30-8pm Sept-May 8.30-6pm. Exhibitions in the Cloisters.

BURY ST EDNUNDS ABBEY.
Ruins of St Edmunds Abbey church. 12th century Norman Tower and magnificently restored Abbey Gate. Set in attractive gardens. Guide from TIC. Open daily. Admission free.

EUSTON HALL.
Tel: 01842 766366.
18th century house, set in Evelyn and Kent landscaped park. Paintings by Lely, Van Dyck and Stubbs. 17th century church with Wren style interior. Jun-Sept Thurs 2.30-5pm. Tea room.

CHARSFIELD ARKENDIELD,
1 Park Lane.
Half an acre cottage garden in village made famous by Ronald Blythe's book. Orchard/picnic area. Mid Apr-Oct 1st daily 10.30-dusk.

Visitor Attractions

CHEDBURGH REDE HALL FARM PARK
.. off A143 near Chedburgh. Tel: 01284 850695. Working farm based on agricultural life of the 1930s-1950s. Suffolk Punch horses working with agricultural implements and wagons. Rare breeds of cattle, sheep and pigs. Working displays of seasonal farm activities. Children's pet area. Tearoom. Gift shop. Open Apr-Sept inc daily 10-5.30pm

CLARE PRIORY.
Ruins of 13th century Monastery and Monastic Church. Open: daily.

COTTON MECHANICAL MUSIC MUSEUM
.. off B1113 south of Diss. Tel: 01449 613876. Extensive collection, includes organs, street pianos, polyphones, gramophones, music boxes, musical dolls, fruit bowls and even a musical chair. Also the mighty Wurlitzer Theatre pipe organ in specially reconstructed cinema. Open: Jun-Sept 2.30-5.30pm.

DUNWICH MUSEUM,
St James' Street. Tel: 0172 873796.
History of the town of Dunwich from Roman times, chronicling its disappearance into the sea over the centuries. Open: Mar Sat&Sun 2-4.30pm. Good Friday-Sept 30th daily 11.30-4.30pm. Oct daily 12-4pm. Admission free.

EAST BERGHOLT BRIDGE COTTAGE,
Flatford. Tel: 01206 298260. 16th century cottage in Dedham Vale close to Flatford Mill (Mill not open to public). Easter, Apr, May Oct: Wed-Sun. Jun-Sept daily 11-5.30pm. Free, but fee for car park. National Trust.

EAST BERGHOLT CHURCH.
Impressive perpendicular exterior. Tower never completed. Unique 16th century timber framed bell cage. Open in daylight.

FLIXTON NORFOLK AND SUFFOLK AVIATION MUSEUM.
On B1060 Homersfield Road. 17 historic aircraft; toher aviation material. 446th Bomb Group Museum. Royal Observer Corps Museum. Open: Apr-Oct Sundays and Bank Holidays 10-5pm. Also summer school holidays, Tues, Wed & Thurs 10-5pm. Free.

FREMLINGHAM CASTLE.
Tel: 01728 724189.
Built in 12th century by the Bigod family. One of the finest examples of a curtain walled castle. Open Apr-30th Sept daily 10-6pm. Oct1st-Mar 31st daily but closed Mon, Dec 24-26 and Jan 1st. 10-4pm. English Heritage.

Chapter Fourteen

FREMLINGHAM CHURCH.
Outstanding hammer-beam roof/monuments. Open in daytime.

HARTEST   GIFFORD'S HALL.
Tel: 01284 830464.
'A small country living', 33 acres with vineyard/winery (free tastings), wild flower meadows, organic vegetables, rare breeds sheep/chickens. Flowers Rose Garden. Shop and Tea room. Children's pet and play areas. Open: Easter-Sept 30th daily 12-6pm.

IPSWICH   TOLLY COBBOLD BREWERY & BREWERY TAP,
Cliff Road.
Tel: 01473 281508.
Taste the malt, smell the hops and enjoy a complimentary glass of beer at one of the country's oldest breweries. A must for those interested in beer, heritage and history. Artefacts from 1723. Guided tours. Open: Easter & May-Sept daily 12 noon. (Extra tours weekends). Oct-Apr: Fri, Sat, Sun 12 noon. Min age 14. Public bar/food.

KETTLEBURGH   EASTON FARM PARK.
Tel: 01728 746475.
Victorian model farm with many breeds of farm animals including rare breeds. Modern milking unit with viewing area. Unique Victorian Laundry and Dairy. Early farm machinery, rural bygones. Green Trail. Food and Farming Exhibition. Tea room. Gift shop. Open Easter-beginning of October 10.30-6pm.

LAVENHAM   THE GUILDHALL OF CORPUS CHRISTI.
Tel: 01787 247646.
History of the wool, cloth and horsehair industries, historic Lavenham and its timber-framed guildhall. Open Easter-31 Oct daily 10-5pm. Closed Good Friday.

LITTLE HALL.
15th century 'hall' house with crown post roof. Rooms furnished with gayer-Anderson collection of furniture, pictures, sculptures and ceramics. Walled garden. April-October Wed, Thurs, Sat, Sun, Bank Holidays 2.30-5.30pm.

THE PRIORY.
Tel: 01787 247003.
14th-16th century timber-framed house. Paintings. Herb garden. Gift shop. Restaurant. Easter-October daily 10.30-5.30pm.

Visitor Attractions

LAXFIELD BIRDS OF PREY CONSERVATION CENTRE,
St Jacobs Hall.
Tel: 01986 798844.
On B1117 from the A140 Stowmarket-Norwich road. The Centre is in the heart of ruralSuffolk, just one and a half miles from the delightful village of Laxfield. You can spend time studying a wide variety of Birds of Prey in their large aviaries, or walking amongst the newly planted woodland trees covering around 4 acres of the 12 acre site. There are 3 flying displays every day, at 11.30, 2pm and 4pm. Open all year 10.30am-5.30pm every day.

LONG MELFORD MELFORD HALL.
Tel: 01787 880286.
Turreted brick Tudor mansion. Rooms in various styles. Chinese procelain collection. Gardens. Apr: Sat, Sun & Bank Holidays. May-Sept 30th Wed, Thurs, Sat, Sun & Bank Holidays. Oct: Sat, Sun 2-5.30pm. NT.

KENTWELL HALL
Elizabethan manor house with moat and gardens. Unique mosaic Tudor rose Maze. Rare breeds farm animals in park. Home-made teas. House, moat house, gardens and farm open 12-5pm (except for Re-creations) Late Mar to mid Jun and Oct: Sun only and Bank Hiliday weekends. Mid-Jul-end Sept daily. Ring for details of re-creations and other times. Tel: 01787 310207.

LOWESTOFT EAST ANGLIA TRANSPORT MUSEUM,
Chapel Road, Carlton Colville. On B1384.
Working trams, trolley buses in reconstructed 1930s street scene. Also narrow gauge railway, battery powered vehicles, commercial vehicles, steam rollers etc. Open Easter Sun & Mon, other Bank Holidays and Sundays from May to the end of Sept 11-5pm. Sats first week in Jun to end of Sept. Weekdays mid-Jul-beginning of Sept 2-4pm.

SOMERLEYTON HALL.
Tel: 01502 730224.
Rebuilt in Anglo-Indian style in 1840s. Fine state rooms, period furnishings and paintings. Superb gardens with famous maze. Deer Park. Tea Room. Picnic area. Hall open: Easter-Sept, Thurs, Sun and Bank Holidays. Also July & August: Tues, Wed 2-5pm. Gardens and tea room open from 12.30pm. Miniature railway Sun, Thurs, Bank Holidays from 3pm Guided tours of house, gardens, Luncheons, suppers, by prior arrangement. Lord and Lady Somerleyton hope that you will enjoy your day here and also that you will pay a visit to Fritton Lake Countryworld, part of the Somerleyton Estate, which is only a 10 minute drive and is open from 10am every day during the season.

Chapter Fourteen

NEWMARKET NATIONAL HORSE RACING MUSEUM,
High Street.
Tel: 01638 667333.
Story of the development of horse racing over 300 years, house in Regency subscription rooms. Arts, bronzes, development of the rules, institutions and the great men of the sport. Also British Sporting Art Trust Vestey Gallery. April-end of November Tues-Sat 10-5pm Sun 2-5pm except July, Aug 12-5pm. Also Bank Holiday Mondays and July, August Mondays 10-5pm. Various guided tours of the gallops, training grounds. National Stud, Jockey club, musuem and historic town by prior arrangement.

OXFORD CASTLE.
Tel: 01394 450472.
Built in 12th century for coastal defence by Henry II. Near perfect example of Norman Keep with panoramic views. Opening times as Framlingham Castle.

SNAPE MALTINGS.
Converted Maltings beside River Alde. Home of world famous Aldeburgh Festival in June and other concerts/master classes during year. Tel: 01728 452935. Riverside centre includes six unusual shops and galleries, tea shop, pub and restaurant. Open all year daily 10-6pm (5pm in winter). River trips in summer. Tel: 01728 688303/5.

STOKE-BY-NAYLAND.
Tower brasses, tombs. Open in daytime, but closed on wet days.

STOWMARKET MUSEUM OF EAST ANGLIAN LIFE,
Iliffe Way.
Tel: 01449 612229.
Fine collectikons of East Anglia's rural past on attractive 70 acre site. Displays on gypsy caravans, domestic life, farming etc. Working watermill and wind pump. Craft workshops smithy, tithe barn etc. Suffolk Punch horses. An exciting outing. Refreshments, picnic area. Open April, May, October Tues-Sun and Bank Holiday Mondays June-Sept daily 10-5pm.

SUDBURY GAINSBOROUGH'S HOUSE
Gainsborough Street. Tel: 01787 372958.
Birthplace of Thomas Gainsborough RA 1717-88. Georgian fronted town house, with attractive walled garden, displays more of the artist's work than any other British Gallery. 18th century furniture and memorabilia. Open: Easter-Oct Tues-Sat 10-5pm Sun & Bank Holiday Monday 2-5pm Nov-Easter Tues-Sat 10-4pm Sun 2-4pm. Closed between Christmas and New Year, Good Friday.

Visitor Attractions

SUTTON HOO
.. archeological site, burial ground of Anglo Saxon Kings of East Anglia. Access by foot from B1083 at Hollesley turn. Open: Easter, Sat, Sun, Mon. May-early Sept Sat, Sun & Bank Holidays. Guided Tours at 2 & 3pm.

WEST STOW ANGLO SAXON VILLAGE.
6 buildings reconstructed on original sites. Open daily 10-4.15pm. Access via Visitor Centre in West Stow Country Park.

SHROPSHIRE

BRIDGNORTH   RAYS COUNTRY MATTERS.
Tel: 01299 841255.
Enjoy a warm welcome at this farm set in the heart of unspoilt Shropshire countryside and spend a relaxing day delighting in the many varieties of animals at this traditional English farm. A great selection of unusual animals include Martha, the famous pot-bellied pig and sevastian the Llama, along with Rufus the Red Deer Stag, or why not take a stroll around the farm and look at the many attractions, or take a woodland walk strolling along the well marked paths past many different varieties of trees, shrubs and wild flowers. Open every day 10-6pm.

CHURCH STRETTON   ACTON SCOTT WORKING FARM
Tel: 01694 781306.
A visit to Acton Scott will enable visitors to experience life on an upland farm at the turn of the century. The waggoner and his team of shire horses work the land with vintage farm machines. Daily demonstrations of rural crafts complete the picture of estate life 100 years ago. There are weekly visits from the wheelwright, farrier and blacksmith and children will love the cows, pigs, poultry and sheep in the farmyard and fields. Open 29th Mar-3oth Oct Tues-Sat 10-5pm Sun and Bank Holidays 10-6pm.

IRONBRIDGE JACKFIELD THE MUSEUM
Tel: 01952 433522
One of the several museum sites within the famous Ironbridge Gorge which no one should miss. . Within the Gorge you will find hours of pleasure and fascinating features to absorb. Jackfield the Museum was a world centre of the decorative tile industry. The museum houses an impressive collection of wall and floor tiles ranging from the Victorian era, through the art deco periods, to a range of attractive silk-screened designs from the 1950s. Open daily all year round.

Chapter Fourteen

IRONBRIDGE TOY MUSEUM
Tel: 01952 433926
Overflowing with toys, games and childhood memorabilia from magic lanterns to Bayko building sets, clockwork trains to Rupert Bear can all be seen at this wonderful museum. See how toys reflect our lifestyle from houses, cars, fashion and TV culture. Also visit the well-stocked shop selling high quality traditional toys, collectors' models, dolls and teddies, children's books and greeting cards. Open daily from 10am.

IRONBRIDGE
Tel: 01952 433522
This is one of Britain's 11 World Heritage Sites, where the modern world began over 250 years ago. This was the birthplace of the Industrial Revolution, and here were made the first iron railing the first iron wheels and even the first high pressure steam locomotive. Today the Ironbridge Gorge Museum shows 20th century visitors how and why these events took place and how people lived during those momentous years. Open daily through the year 10-5pm.

KIDDERMINSTER   WYRE FOREST NATURE RESERVE.
Tel: 01562 827800.
The Wyre Forest Area offers many excellent examples of nature and man-made habitats for everyone to enjoy. Whether you want to picnic with the family, take a gentle stroll or enjoy a natureramble, there are plenty of lacations to visit including the Springfield Nature Reserve which is an important habitat for many species of plants and wildlife. Or why not visit Burlish Top Heathland Nature Reserve which gives you an excellent opportunity to enjoy a habitat which is now scarce both nationally and internationally. Open daily throughout the year.

MUCH WENLOCK   MUCH WENLOCK MUSEUM
Tel: 01952 727773
Interesting local museum, housed in former market hall. It contains new displays on the geology and natural history of Wenlock Edge, local history, exhibits including the Wenlock Olympics and information about Wenlock Priory. Open Apr-Sept Mon-Sat.

WENLOCK PRIORY
Tel: 01952 727466
Much Wenlock is a picturesque market town lying between Wenlock Edge and the Ironbridge Gorge in some of the most attractive countryside in Shropshire. Set amongst smooth lawns and ornamental topiary, are the magnificent remains of Wenlock Priory. A prosperous and powerful monastery in its time and a place of pilgrimage, Wenlock is an inspiring

place to visit. There is plenty to explore and the Priory church still dominates the scene. The Norman Chapter House has some superb decorative arcading and you can also see the remains of the Cloister, once the bustling hub of daily life. Open daily 1st April-31st October 10-6pm 1st November-31st March Sun & Wed 10-4pm

THE AEROSPACE MUSEUM
Tel: 01902 374112
Locaton: On A41 just one mile from junction 3 on the M54.
One of the largest aviation collections in the UK with over 70 aircraft on display, including many unique examples, together with missiles, engines, uniforms and aviation memorabilia. Open all year round.

WYRE FOREST
Tel: 01299 266302
This magnificent 6000 acre forest nature reserve is home to a variety of wildlife, including deer, butterflies and wild flowers. A visitor centre includes forest information, exhibitions and a shop and cafe. Explore the forest on a range of way-marked paths, including a special wheelchair route. Open daily all year round. Visitor Centre open 11-4pm.

MARKET DRAYTON   HODNET HALL GARDENS
Tel: 01630 685202
Over 60 acres of brilliantly coloured flowers, magnificent forest trees, sweeping lawns and a chain of ornamental pools which run tranquilly along the cultivated garden valley to provide a natural habitat for waterfowl and other wildlife are just some of the many attractions on offer. No matter what the season, visitors will always find something fresh and interesting to ensure a full and enjoyable days outing. Open from 1st April-end September Mon-Sat 2-5pm. Sun & Bank Holidays 12-5.30pm.

SHREWSBURY ATTINGHAM PARK
Tel: 01743 709203.
Attingham Park is one of the finest houses in the country, set in its own grounds of 250 acres, and offers the whole family a wealth of things to see and do. Explore the landscaped park, take a gentle stroll by the river or through the woods, discover the estate history at the Bothy exhibition, enjoy the elegant house and its beautiful furnishings, learn about the Berwick family and end your visit with home-made refreshments in the tea-room or purchasing a gift or souvenir from the shop. The Park and Houseare open throughout the year from the end of March until the end of September. 1.30-5pm, last admission 4.30pm.

Chapter Fourteen

BUILDWAS ABBEY
Tel:01952 433274
Founded in the 12th century Buildwas Abbey was largely untouched by the great events of history though periodically attacked by raiders from across the Welsh border. Its simple, sturdy buildings give a powerful impression of both grandeur and the austerity of monastic life, with its fine vaulted roof and unusual medieval floor tiles, depicting birds and animals. Open 1st April-30th September 10-6pm daily.

WROXETER ROMAN CITY
Tel: 01743 761330
To visit Wroxeter today is to step back in time to the heyday of Roman Britain. The centrepiece is the remains of the extensive bath complex, one of the best preserved in England. The enormous hill which divided the baths from the exercise area still stands, and whilst walking around you can recreate the everyday activities of the thriving Roman City. Open; April 1st - 31st October 10-6pm.

TELFORD   BOSCOBEL HOUSE
Tel: 01902 850244.
A visit to Boscobel House will take you to the scene of one of the most romantic stories in English history. King Charles II sought refuge in an oak tree at Boscobel House when he was chased by Cromwell's soldiers after the Battle of Worcester in 1651. The Royal Oak can be seen to this day painted on signs outside countless pubs all over the country, and you can still see a direct descendant of the famous oak itself now nearly 300 years old, in fields surrounding the house. A visit to the house will show that it has retained its romantic character. There are panelled rooms and hiding places, including the 'sacred hole' in the attic where Charles is said to have stayed at night. Open daily from 1st April-31st October 10-6pm. 1st Nov- 31st Dec & 1st Feb - 31st March Wed 7 Sun 10-4pm.

WEST MIDLANDS

BINLEY   COOMBE ABBEY PARK COUNTRY FAIR.
Tel: 01336 411285.
Location: Brinklow Road, Binley, Nr Coventry.
Coombe Abbey Park is a major new outdoor events and entertainment centre for the Midlands. Already famous for its beautiful parkland and teeming wildlife, Coombe Abbey Park is the ideal place for a Country Fair which brings the past to life and explores the way forward. Open all year round 10-6pm.

COOMBE ABBEY PARK FOLK FESTIVAL.
Tel: 01336 411285.
A non-stop weekend of first class folk music in an idyllic setting takes place in September each year. Two performance marquees plus tents for dancers, singers and musicians will ensure non-stop music and entertainment from Friday evening to Saturday afternoon.

COOMBE ABBEY COUNTRY PARK.
Tel: 01203 453720.
Come and explore the splendid beauty of Coombe Abbey Country Park with its beautiful gardens, woodland and lakeside walks and drink in the historic surroundings. There are plants, animals and birds in abundance and everyone has the chance to get close to nature. Most of the parkland is classified as a Site of Special Scientific Interest in recognition of its importance to wildlife. Country Park open every day 7.30am-dusk.

COVENTRY KENILWORTH CASTLE.
Tel: 01926 52078.
Location: Off the M40 near Warwick.
Great and gaunt against the Warwickshire sky, Kenilworth Castle rises up to doninate the surrounding town and peaceful countryside. Kenilworth is the finest and most extensive castle ruin in Britain. As you survey the soaring walls of the Great Hall and the elegance of the Earl of Leicester's additions to the castle for the visit of Queen Elizabeth I in 1575, you can almost recreat the pomp and pageantry of life here in the past. Open: 1st April-October 10-6pm, 1 Nov-31 Mar 10-4pm.

LUNT ROMAN FORT.
Tel: 01203 832381.
In AD 60, seventeen years after the Roman invasion, the Britains rebelled against foreign rule. It took more than a year for the Roman Army to put down the revolt by the East Anglian Iceni tribe. As a result forts were rebuilt, and the army moved to new strategic locations. The lunt is the only reconstructed Roman Fort of this type in Britain and provides valuable evidence about life in a Roman Cavalry fortification. Situated on a spur of high ground overlooking the River Sowe, the lunt was in an ideal location, typical of rural Roman forts. Museum shop, free parking, picnic area and toilets. Open 2 Apr-30 Oct 10-5pm and everyday from 16th Jul-31st Aug inclusive.

CATHEDRAL LANES SHOPPING CENTRE.
Tel: 01203 632532.
Cathedral Lane provides an ideal setting for shopping, meeting and eating in the heart of Coventry. Browse in a wide range of shops selling books,

Chapter Fourteen

fashion, beauty, sportswear, gifts and much much more. Relax over a drink or meal in the light, airy brasserie, or just sit and watch the regular, fun entertainment.

SHOPMOBILITY.
Tel: 01203 832020.
Location: The Shopmobility Unit, Upper Precinct, Coventry.
Shopmobility is a service which provides powered and unpowered wheelchairs and scooters for people who have either permanent or temporary limited mobility. It will allow them greater independence to use the pedestrianised shopping areas in the City Centre. The opening hours ar Mon-Sat 9-5pm.

MUSEUM OF BRITISH ROAD TRANSPORT.
Tel: 01203 832425.
At the Museum of British Road Transport you'll delight in the largest display of Bitish made road transport in the world. All under one roof. With more than 150 cars, 75 motorcycles and 200 cycles, the Museum tells the fascinating story of Coventry's contribution to Britain's road transport history, as seen through the famous Marques of Alvis, Daimler, Hillman, Jaguar, Riley, Rover, Standard, Triumph and many more. Open: daily all year round from 10-5pm.

WARWICK ARTS CENTRE.
Tel: 01203 524524.
Warwick Arts Centre - a resource provided by the University of Warwick - attracts over 250,000 visitors a year to the artistic programme and provides a vital link between the local and regional community. Entertainment facilities include the arts, dance, exhibitions and a selection of International Celebrity Concerts. Open daily throughout the year.

THE HERBERT ART GALLERY & MUSEUM.
Tel: 01203 832381.
Introduction to Weaving is a Crafts Council exhibition which takes an intriguing and delightful look at woven textiles from the Crafts Council Collection, with weaving by local maker Susan Wright. Admission free Mon-Sat 10-5.30pm, Sun 2-5pm.

Visitor Attractions

WALES

BEDDGELERT   SYGUN COPPER MINE,
Beddgelert, LL55 4NE
Tel: 01766 890595 24 hour info/line: 01766 890564.
Sygun is one mile from the village of Beddgelert on the A498 road to Capel Curig. Sygun Copper Mine is one of the wonders of Wales - a remarkable and impressive example of how part of our precious industrial heritage can be reclaimed, restored and transformed into an outstanding family attraction. The mine provides an excellent and informative experience of the underground world of the Victorian miner.The mine, a unique modern day reminder of 19th century methods of ore extraction and processing is situated in the glorious Gwynant Valley - the heart of the stunning Snowdonia National Park - and on probably the most popular tourist route in Wales. The incomparable scenery captured the imagination of movie-makers, who turned the mountainside surrounding Sygun into a Chinese village in 1958 for the filming of 'The Inn of the Sixth Happiness' which starred the late Ingrid Bergman. Sygun offers a rare opportunity for those with a sense of adventure and curiosity, from the young to the elderly, to discover for themselves the wonders it still shelters after being abandoned in 1903. Audiovisual tours allow you to explore the old workings on foot in complete safety. there are winding tunnels and large chambers, magnificent stalactite and stalagmite formations and copper ore veins which contain traces of gold, silver and other precious metals. It usually takes about 40 minutes to complete the quarter mile route which rises 140feet via stairways to emerge at the Victoria level for a breathtaking view of the Gwynant Valley and surrounding Snowdonia mountain range. A shorter, less demanding tour can be arranged. Refreshments and a wide range of souvenirs are available in the visitors centre. **OPEN;** All year. Oct, Nov, Feb, March 10.30am-4pm. (11am Sunday) Dec, Jan 11-3.30pm. Main season: Easter or late March - Sept inc. 10am-5pm (11am Sun. & 4pm Sat.) Visa/ Access/Switch. Flat soled shoes advisable. Dogs not permitted underground.

BLAENAU FFESTINIOG LLECHWEDD SLATE CAVERNS,
Blaenau Ffestiniog,LL41 3NB
Tel: 01766 830306 Fax:01766 831260.
This is a day out to remember. Winner of all Britain's top tourism awards, Llechwedd Slate Caverns have been visited by five million people, including Edward VIII when he was Prince of Wales, the Princess Margaret, the Duchess of Gloucester and the Crown Prince of Japan. The spectacular underground lake has been used for a Walt Disney film set. Other sites have endeavoured, unsuccessfully, to copy the magic of Llechwedd - where the tourist operation has the benefit of historic authenticity while also remaining part of the biggest working slate mine in Wales. Here you can take two quite

Chapter Fourteen

different rides, one exploring the complexities of old slate mining skills, the other the triumph, humour, religious fervour, and the pathos of the Victorian miner. Visitors are at liberty to take either or both. Add to that an exploration of the Victorian Village, and some refreshment at one of the wide selection of catering facilities, and there is no reluctance to spend at least a day at Llechwedd. A very interesting and informative little book about Llechwedd writtenby Ivor Wynne Jones, a Director, is well worth acquiring. Not only does it tell you about the mine but also about the history of slate, and relates Llechwedd Slate Caverns' unexpected contribution to the conservation of Wales' endangered wild life. Choughs' Cavern which visitors see while the Miners' Tramway, was named after the shy crow-like birds which nested there for many years,returning in 1969, disappearing in the 1970s but rediscovering the same unlikely spot in 1991, since when annual nesting has been re-established.

On the surface hovering kestrels are a common sight and buzzards nest on the northern rock face. One of nature's most beautiful contributions is rhododendron ponticum which bursts into flower each spring. An interesting highlight of a visit to Llechwedd is the facility for spending Victorian coins, at Victorian prices, in the village shops and the ever popular Miners Arms. This journey back in time begins at the Old Bank of Greenway & Greaves. This is a banking museum, preserving the appearance of a small country branch early in the last century.

The Llechwedd 'bank' has a shop counter where five pre-decimal coins may be purchased. They show correct designs on the reverse, but with modern dating. All prices in the Victorian Village -Pentre Llechwedd - are shown in old and new currencies, enabling such experiences as buying a 'pennorth' of sweets or a 3d pint at the Miners' Arms. In 1972 when a half-mile level section of the Miners' Tramway was opened to the world revealing the vast workings, it was immediately given the top awards of both the British Tourist Authority and the Wales Tourist Board. Boarding a train in a corner of the original slate slabbing mill of 1852, visitors now ride into an 1846 tunnel, hauled by battery-electric locomotives. Entering through the side of the mountain, this journey into the early Victorian past remains on the level, and traverses some spectacular caverns. Passengers alight at various points to learn something of the strange skills needed to extract slate. There is a sound and light tableaux deep underground and guides describe the other chambers.

OPEN: Daily 10am including Sundays. (Closed on Christmas Day, Boxing Day and New Year's Day) Last tours into mines: 5.15pm March to September 4.15pm October to February. Access, Visa, Switch. Special terms for parties of 20 or more. Free car parking, free surface exhibitions. Dogs not allowed on either ride. Separate cafe. Victorian Pub and Licensed restaurant.

Visitor Attractions

CAERNARFON   CAERNARFON AIR WORLD,
Museum and Pleasure Flights   Caernarfon Airport, Dinas Dinlle, Nr Caernarfon, Gwynedd LL545TP
Tel: 01286 830800.
In the great hangar here you can see planes and helicopters in landscaped settings, aircraft engines, ejector seats and over two hundred model aircraft. If you enjoy the history and nostalgia associated with planesand flying,this is the place for you and it is 'Hands On'. You can sit in cockpits, take the controls in the Varsity Trainer and wander round full size planes. There are also exhibitions featuring Local Aviation History, the story of the Dambusters, Welsh Flying V.C's, the first RAF Mountain Rescue Service, fascinating wartime newspapers and historic First Day Covers. There is a cinema where you can watch aviation shorts and full length films. The well stocked museum shop has been extended, and for small children there is a themed adventure playground, built around a Dragonfly helicopter. Pleasure Flights will provide you with a unique experience in North Wales. Take a bird's eye view of mountains,castles and coastline in a Cessna or the Vintage de Havilland Dragon Rapide. There are three standard flights, but you can always plan your own. The first is a ten minute flight over the Menai Strait around the 13th century Caernarfon Castle and back over the 18th century Fort Belan. The second flight is a breathtaking 25 minute experience flying over the mountains of Snowdonia, over the summit of Snowdon, the highest peak in England and Wales, over Crib Coch and the Llanberis Pass, then back to the airport taking in Caernarfon Castle and Fort Belan. The third is another 25 minute flight that is offered if weather conditions do not favour a mountain trip. This one flies over the Menai Strait and the lovely island of Anglesey, taking in the foothills of Snowdonia and Caernarfon Castle on the return journey.
OPEN; MUSEUM Daily 1st March -31st October 9am-5.30pm. PLEASURE FLIGHTS Daily, weather permitting throughout the year. Check by phone prior to visit. RESTAURANT Open daily all year. Coffee Shop open from Easter to 31st October.

COLWYN BAY   EIRIAS PARK,
Colwyn Leisure Centre, Colwyn Bay LL29 8HG
Tel: 01492 533223
Here you will find something for all the family. With over half a million visitors annually to Eirias Park its popularity as a tourist and recreational attraction cannot be questioned. Set in 50 acres of beautiful parkland, the facilities on offer provide a unique recreational experience and offer an outstanding day out for all ages. Facilities available all year round include: Leisure Pool/Waterchute, Sports Halls, Squash Courts, Sauna/Solarium Suite, Function Room, Fitness Room, Lounge Bar/Cafe, Athletics Stadium, Indoor/Outdoor Tennis Courts and Synthetic Pitch. Facilities available throughout

Chapter Fourteen

the summer season include: Crown Green Bowling Greens, Boating Lake with small and large pedaloes, Model Yacht Pond, Mini Golf Par Putting, Children' Play Area, Picnic Areas and Dinosaur World. From a promotional point of view, the facilities within Eirias Park, serve as an ideal location for the hosting of a corporate day and last year such days were organised on behalf of the Inland Revenue for Wales and the Post Office, North West. Simply choose from the available facilities or allow the competent, friendly staff to arrange a programme of activities to suit your company's personal needs. To complement the days activities, the Catering Manageress will be delighted to arrange a buffet with a wide selection of menus to choose from. From its commanding position overlooking the promenade and beach, the park is easily accessible by road via the A55 Expressway which links North Wales with the UK Motorway network and by rail with regular inter-city services from all parts of Britain. Easy access for the disabled. Free Car Parking.

CWMBRAN   GREENMEADOW COMMUNITY FARM,
Green Force Way, Cwmbran NP44 5AJ
Tel: 01633 862202
In the early 1980's a group of local people formed an action committee in a bid to protect one of the last green spaces in Cwmbran from further development. The group came up with the exciting prospect of establishing a Community Farm. Today, the original, fully refurbished c17th farmstead with 150 acres of land throughout Cwmbran, offers a magnificent rural retreat in an urban setting. It is a place full of excitement where you will see traditional farm animals and Rare Breeds, a well-stocked aviary, an Exhibition Barn with ever changing exhibits. On the woodland trails you will see a surprisingvariety of wildlife and the Pets Corner is a place in which children have a chance to make friends with the smaller animals. All visitors are encouraged to feed and handle selected farm animals. The Farm House Tea Room offers traditional home-made fare. The Sheep Dip Bar is open every evening and the 16th century Cordell's Restaurant is ideal for an intimate meal. It opens every evening 7-10pm and for Sunday lunch. Special events are organised throughout the year. OPEN; All year except Christmas Day Summer 10-6pm Winter 10-4.30pm. Disabled people welcome. Pets allowed. Licensed. Conference facilities.

DOLGELLAU   GWYNBFYNYDD GOLD MINE,
The Marian, Dolgellau, Gwynedd LL40 1UU
Tel: 01341 423332 Fax: 01341 423737
To get to the mine take the courtesy bus from Welsh Gold in Dolgellau and enjoy the short guided journey through some of the most beautiful countryside in Wales. Here you will see the place where a huge bonanza of gold was found a century ago: worth £5 million if found today. As far as one

Visitor Attractions

can tell Gwynfynydd Gold mine is the only working gold mine open to the public. Gold ore is mined daily but actual gold is very rare ; the mine yields about 25g per month on the whole but most times it can be less. 8 full time miners work here with additional staff to guide people through the mine during the summer season. Once you arrive at the mine you are presented with protective clothing which include a hard hat, waterproof jacket and boots. (It is advisable to take a sweater with you as it can be quite cold underground.) On the tour itself you can experience the roar and thunder of modern machinery, the blast of explosions, and take away your own free sample of a Welsh Goldmine ore. You will also see how they mined in the olden days, by candle light. After being underground for around one hour you will see the Gold Smelting room, where gold is melted down to a small gold bullion. At the end of your tour you may pan for gold, should you find any, which is normally found in small pieces of rocks, you may take it home!! The retail shop sells Welsh Gold Jewellery which is displayed amongst other crafts from Wales. It is advisable to book in advance for tours throughout the year. The gold centre is open throughout the year 9.30am until 5.00pm, later on some occasions in the summer. It is open 7 days from Easter to September and closed on Sundays during the winter.

HOLYWELL   HOLYWELL LEISURE CENTRE
Fron Park, Holywell CH8 7UZ
An exciting Leisure Centre offering something for every age. The 6 lane swimming pool incorporates broad shallow steps for easy access. Contained within the pool hall is a small shallow water area where toddlers can play in safety and a splash pool which provides a safe landing area to the 42 metre corkscrew water slide. The swimmng pool is open from 10am each day but closes each weekday between 3.45pm and 5.15pm for junior swimming classes. Indeed there is a whole range of classes for swimmers of all ages and all stages. The Silhouette Fitness Centre and the Silhouettes Health Suite are both excellent for anyone and supervised by an experienced and caring staff. Both open from 10am-10pm seven days a week. The Sports Hall has five a side football, basketball, volleyball and four badminton courts, bookable from 10am-10pm each day. The Dance Studio has a comprehensive range of dance classes and some popular aerobic and step aerobic sessions. This multi use area is excellent forsmall theatrical productions, drama workshops, film shows, seminars and training courses. The Hall is also used for Karate, Thai Boxing, Kung Fu, 50+ Exercise classes and children's birthday parties. Open from 10am-10pm seven days a week. The Snooker Room has 6 tables. For Bowling, two crown greens, one of which is floodlit are available for casual use from the beginning of April to the end of October. There is an Outdoor Area, two floodlit tennis courts, and a Synthetic Pitch for soccer. The Cafeteria is open from 9.30am-9.30pm each day and there is a comfortable lounge bar which opens from 7.30pm each evening. For further details please ring 01352 712027.

Chapter Fourteen

LLANDRINDOD WELLS THE RADNORSHIRE MUSEUM,
Temple Street, Llandrindod Wells, LD1 5LD
Tel: 01597 824 513
Situated in the centre of Llandrindod Wells, the museum houses exhibits relating to the history of the old mid-Wales county of Radnorshire. Displays illustrate the largely rural farming lifestyle of the area as well as the development of Llandrindod Wells as a country Spa Resort during the Victorian and Edwardian Era. The museum also displays material relating to Fine Art, costume and the Prehistoric,Roman and Medieval history of the area: including the Roman Fort of Castell Collen. New for 1995 was the Red Kite Centre: set on the museums first floor, this exhibition highlights the lifestyle and successful fight back from the edge of extinction of Britons most beautiful bird of prey. The exhibition also includes a thirty minute video on the Red Kite and computer information station on the birds of Europe.
OPEN; 10-12.30 and 2-4.30. Closed Wednesday (all year) and Saturday afternoon and Sunday (winter only).

TEIFI VALLEY RAILWAY,
Henllan Station, Henllan, Nr Newcastle Emlyn SA44 5TD
Tel/Fax: 01559 371077
The only Famous Little Trains of Wales in West Wales gives hours of pleasure to people of all ages. A 40 minute train ride experience for which you pay once and ride all day (if seats available). Facilities include Woodland Theatre (Phone for details), Woodland Trails, Cafe. Shop, Pictorial Museum, Crazy Golf/Quoits/Skittles, Childrens'Play Areas, Picnic and Barbeque Areas. W.C's, large Car Park, Coaches Welcome. Usual Coach Driver Facilities. OPEN; Easter-Oct inc 10.30am-6pm. Closed: Saturdays. Apr 13/20/27 May 4/11/18 Oct 5/12/19. TRAINS: Apr. May. June Oct. 10.30,11.30, 12.30, 2pm, 3pm, 4pm. July, Aug-Sept Last train 5pm + Bank Holidays. SPECIAL EVENTS: April 6th, Aug 17th, 25th and 26th, Oct 26th, December - SANTA SPECIALS Entrance/Parking 50p (Adults) £3.50 (Children) £1.50(OAP) £3 Dogs 50p. Opending hours: daily Easter -26th October.

LLANGOLLEN MODEL RAILWAY WORLD & DR WHO EXHIBITION,
Lower Dee Mill Llangollen LL20 8SE
Tel: 01978 860584.
These two exciting attractions opened in the summer of 1995 and rapidly drew attention from visitors to the area as well as curious locals! The Model Railway World Museum is based around the original Hornby Dublo Factory from Binns Road, Liverpool. You will see 24 large superb layouts with 1000s of models on display. You can try shunting in the hands-on section and watch and talk to expertsabout building these models. Fascinating and educational. Dapol Ltd design and manufacture precision model railways and a wide range of toys including Dr Who models. The move to Lower Mill not only

Visitor Attractions

enabled Dapol to improve its manufacturing but also to realise the life-long dream of its Managing Director, David Boyle - to establish a National Model Railway Museum. Over the years David has amassed a huge collection of model railway artefacts and memorabilia including the original design drawings, art work, photographs, lathes, jigs, etc from Hornby, Dublo, Mainline,Wrenn. Airfix. All these are displayed together with the working layouts resulting in a unique exhibition relating to the history of model railways from the very beginning to the present day. The DR WHO exhibition adds yet another fascinating dimension at Lower Dee Mill. It was opened by former Dr Who actor, Colin Baker on the 17th June 1995 and has been mounted in association with the BBC who have provided the original costumes, Daleks, Cybermen monsters, visual effects (many of which are priceless).In consultation with BBC Dr Who producer, John Nathan-Turner the exhibition, covering three huge rooms, has been designed more as an experience than an exhibition with a full size working TARDIS and original sound effects give a fascinating insight into how the longest running science fiction series in the world was made for television. Please ring 01978 860584 for opening times.

LLANGOLLEN   LLANGOLLEN HORSE DRAWN BOAT TRIPS
Llangollen Wharf, Llangollen
Tel: 01978 860702 for general enquiries. 0169 175322 for Group bookings, Day Boats and Holiday Hire.
To take a trip on one of these boats eases you back to the days of leisure as you glide noislessly through the spectacular scenery of the Vale of Llangollen. You may find yourself being pulled along by one of five horses who are all friendly and have names. Spot is the old boy who only works occasionally and then there is Fred, Sam, Stan and Arthur. They seem to enjoy their work as they go slowly along the towpath. In this timeless setting, the horse-drawn canal trips are as relaxing today as they were when the first pleasure boats slipped away from the Wharf in 1884. On the Wharf, you will find the Canal Exhibition Centre, telling the Canal Story with words, pictures and models. It is good to wander among the gaily painted canal ware in the gift shop and delightful to take tea on the terrace overlooking the town. Llangollen Wharf is a fascinating place for a day out. The popular cruise on the luxury narrowbat Thomas Telfrod includes a crossing of the Pontcysllte Aqueduct. OPEN; Daily for 45 minute horse-drawn boat trips and exhibition visits from Easter to September with limited opening in October.

LLANGOLLEN   LLANGOLLEN RAILWAY,
Abbey road, Llangollen LL208SN
Tel:01978 860979
Llangollen is at the junction of the A5 and A539. The railway station is by

Chapter Fourteen

the bridge over the River Dee. The nearest car parks are in Market Street in the town and at Lower Dee Mill on the A539 approaching from Ruabon. The nearst British Rail station is 5 miles away at Ruabon. Bryn Melyn buses operate hourly to Llangollen from Wrexham and Ruabon, two hourly on Sundays. The Llangollen Railway Society rescued this delightful line and have spent years bringing the track, thestation and the trains back to their original beauty and splendour.

The Railway you see at Llangollen today is a direct result of the dreams and aspirations of the former Flint and Deeside Railway. The work has been done mainly by volunteer enthusiasts who removed masses of undergrowth and rubble from the trackbed and vandalised buildings without water or supplies to be restored. The journey in the restored carriages through the countryside with the River Dee appearing constantly, is both beautiful, exciting and relaxing. Thrilling for youngsters and an outstanding experience for steam railway enthusiasts. There are opportunities for people to spend two hours on the footplate on 14 miles of firing and driving. Full hot meals for the trainee and light refreshments for up to six guests. Try the Llangollen Steam Driving Course - something you will never forget or regret. There are special dining opportunities and Sunday Lunches aboard the Berwyn Belle. Friends of Thomas Events, Santa Specials and much more. Ring for further information 01978 860979.

COWBRIDGE TASKFORCE PAINTBALL GAMES
(147 Ynysddu, Pontyclun CF7 9UB office)
Tel:01443 227715 Fax:01443 225803
Situated just off the A48 west of Cowbridge, part of a large three and a half thousand acre estate at Penllyn. With easy access from the M4, just 10 minutes away, it can be reached with ease from most of the south west's major towns via the motorway network. Task Force is set in 30 acres of woodland within a deep undulating valley.

It has been a venue for Paintball games since 1989 and during this period has had many special features added to it to create an exciting and varied site to play. Amongst its many varied features and scenarios are numerous bunkers, dugouts, a helicopter, bridges and a HUGE 'woodland village'. Your day will begin with a comprehensive briefing, followed by the issuing of all the equipment you will need for the day. Then once you are all kitted up and have had a practice on the firing range, you are ready for battle to commence. During the day you will play approximately 12 games. You do not need a special amount of players to book. There is an excellent Junior Paintball Game exclusively for 11-16 year olds. Open; Saturday and Sunday or during the week if you have a group of 15 or more people. Credit Cards: Visa/Delta/Access/Master .

Visitor Attractions

LLANDYSUL   TY HEN FARM
Llwyndafydd, Nr New Quay, Llandysul SA44 6BZ West Wales.
Tel: 01545 560346
Approached by a bumpy lane and set on a sheep farm in peaceful countryside close to the Cardigan coast, near Cwmtudu, this attractive Guest House which also offers delightful, converted self-catering cottages is wonderful for people who want to relax, be well cared for and within easy reach of a whole host of exciting places. The main house has well appointed en suite bedrooms, the self-catering cottages and apartments are around the farmyard and so too is The Pits Centre which houses the restaurant and leisure facilities which comprise an indoor heated pool, well equipped gymnasium, sunbed, sauna, changing rooms, toilets, bowls/skittle alley, coin operated washing machine and drier. Good food is part of the reason this excellent place was awarded 3 Crowns and the farm-house award. **OPEN;** Mid-Feb - Mid-Nov. Residential & Table Licence. Pets by prior arrangement. Disabled Access. Visa/Mastercard. Children welcome

MACHYNLLETH   KING ARTHUR'S LABYRINTH
Corris, Machynlleth, SY20 9RF
Tel: 01654 761584 Fax: 01654 761575
King Arthur's Labyrinth is a fairly recent visitor attraction which has delighted people since it opened in 1994. An underground boat takes visitors deep into the spectacular caverns under the Braichgoch mountain at Corris. As visitors walk through the caverns, Welsh tales of King Arthur are told with tableaux and stunning sound and light effects. The journey ends with a return trip along the beautiful subterranean river into the grounds of the Corris Craft Centre. This exciting centre is the starting point for King Arthur's Labyrinth and home to six craft workshops at which visitors are invited to see at first hand the skills of the craft workers and, if they wish, to buy from the displays of woodcraft, toy making, jewellery, leather work and hand-made candles, while the Labyrinth shop provides a range of souvenirs, books and gifts on the Celtic Arthurian theme. The Crwbyr Restaurant provides full meals, teas and refreshments throughout the day. There is also a picnic area in the gardens and an extensive children's play area. Visitors to the Labryinth are advised to wear warm clothing as the underground caverns are cool. The 45 minute tour of the caverns involves a walk of about half a mile along level gravel paths unsuitable only for the very frail. However the variety of craft shops, gardens and refreshments within the Corris Craft Centre and the stunning scenery of the Corris valley provide ample enjoyment for everyone. Group bookings are welcome. OPEN; 10-5pm daily from April to October.

Chapter Fourteen

MACHYNLLETH   MEIRION MILL,
Dinas Mawddwy, Nr Machynlleth SY20 9LS
Tel: 01650 531311
In a wonderful setting in the mountains of the Snowdonia National Park, shopping becomes a sheer delight when you see what wonderful goods, clothing, crafts and gifts are on offer.There is a tremendous range of wool products all under one roof: traditionally woven tweeds and rugs, skirt lengths, wool jackets, knitwear from black sheep, warm jumpers, subtle blended colours in ties and hats, sheepskin slippers, hats and gloves and of course, sheepskin rugs. The shelves are full of locally produced honey and jams, slate gifts, Celtic jewellery, lovespoons, jumping sheep and small items for children to collect. They also stock Portmeirion Pottery. Meirion Mill has everything going for it; parking couldn't be simpler nor the access easier. The Old Station Coffee Shop has a restaurant licence and serves delicious home-cooked fare. There is a level entrance to the shop and all areas are accessible by wheelchair. You will find Meirion Mill situated on the Powys/Gwynedd border at the southern end of the National Park. The Mill site was originally the terminus for the old Mawddwy railway which ran for six miles down the valley to join the main railway at Cemmaes Road. The double arched Pack Horse Bridge spans the River Dyfi next to the entrance gate. Heavily laden donkeys were led across this narrow bridge transporting bolts of flannel to be sold over the border. OPEN: Daily early March to late November. Mon-Sat 10am-5pm. Sun: 10.30am-5pm. Times do vary in the early and late season. Current times can be obtained by phoning 01650 531311. Normally closed during winter months. Amex/Visa/Access/Mastercard/Delta/Switch. Childrens Play Area. Picnic area. Dogs not allowed in play area, shop or coffee shop.

CENARTH   THE NATIONAL CORACLE CENTRE,
Cenarth Falls, Newcastle Emlyn

NEWCASTLE

EMLYN
SA389JL Tel: 01239 710980
Rescued from decay by Mr and Mrs Martin Fowler in 1983, Cenarth Mill was re-roofed in 1991 and the National Coracle Centre stands in the grounds of the 17th century flour mill where the mill pig stys and workshops once were. The mill is included in your visit here. An organised tour of the Centre takes you back to one of the earliest forms of transport, and presents a unique display of Coracles from many parts of the world. As well as nine varieties of Welsh Coracle and those from other British rivers, you can see

examples from Iraq, Vietnam, India and North America. The workshop is an important part of the Centre and the ancient craft of Coracle making is displayed here. Coracles can be seen on the river during the summer holidays, and trips in one can sometimes be arranged. Viewing areas and pathways allow easy access for disabled people and provide wonderful views of the falls, salmon leap and 200 year old bridge. OPEN; Easter-October Sunday to Friday 10.30am-5.30pm and other times by appointment. Gift Shop. Tea rooms.

PORT DINORWIC - Y FELINHELI   THE GREENWOOD CENTRE
Tel: 01248 671493 Fax: 01248 670069
Indoors and outdoors the Award Winning Greenwood Centre is all about discovering the fascinating World of Trees. It is an enjoyable and educational experience for all ages. You can find out how trees work, how they clean the air, visit the Rainforest and hear its sounds, see a banana plant and find stick insects. Try out your sense of smell at the scent boxes and see if you can identify the fragrances. Find out about the history of forestry in Wales. Explore the rhododendron maze, tree nursery, root circle. See the wildlife pond and make friends with the rabbits in pets corner, and in the main holiday season, watch forest craft demonstrations and try out a Welsh Longbow from May to September.Enjoy a picnic outdoors or sample some of the tasty snacks and light lunches in the Tea Room. OPEN; Daily 10am-5.30pm March to October inclusive. Winter visits by arrangement. Dogs on leads welcome. Free car & coach park. Disabled and baby changing facilities.

PORTMEIRION,
Gwynedd LL48 6ET Tel: 01766 770228
One single word, Portmeirion, conjures up a magical place, somewhere that everyone should visit at least once in a lifetime. It is the realisation of a dream by its creator Sir Clough Williams-Ellis who had long nurtured the idea of one day building his own ideal village on some romantic coast. Eventually he was offered the Aber la peninsula, only five miles from his ancestral home- a perfect place to prove that the development of a naturally beautiful site need not necessarily lead to its defilement. Work began when he ws 42 in 1925 and when Sir Clough died in 1978 at the age of 95 he was content in the knowledge that his dream had become a reality. For people like myself the sheer beauty, colour and charm of Portmeirion is enough to make me want to just stand and stare. There are different vistas at every turn and each one you think cannot be more beautiful than the last, but it always is. Portmeirion is a world apart and you may come here as a day visitor - not the best way because you cannot see and absorb all it has to offer. Portmeirion has six different shops including the Seconds Warehouse, which is the only place in Wales selling second quality Portmeirion Pottery, designed by Susan Williams-Ellis. The Ship Shop sells best quality Portmeirion

Chapter Fourteen

Pottery plus a wide range of design led gifts for all ages. There is also a Papur a Phensal for cards, the Golden Dragon bookshop, and Pot Jam selling Portmeirion preserves and confectionery. The Six of One shop specialises in The Prisoner TV series. The village has a licensed self-service restaurant with a pleasant terrace for meals outside. There is an ice-cream parlour and several ice-cream kiosks. The Hotel restaurant on the quayside welcomes non-residents and provides reasonably priced two and three course lunches.

RHAYADER WELSH ROYAL CRYSTAL,
5 Brynberth, Rhayader LD6 5EN
Tel: 01597 811005
Winner of Wales Tourism Awards 1995 'Highly Commended' Welsh Royal Crystal is the Principality's own complete manufacturer of hand-crafted lead crystal products in tableware,stemware, presentation trophies and gift items. All production processes are undertaken on the one manufacturing site situated in Rhayader in the heartlands of Wales. Welsh Royal Crystal melts glass containing a lead content in excess of 30% (known as Full Lead Crystal) which is considered to be the best quality glass from which fine quality crystal glass products are made - weight and feel, definition of cutting and polishing brilliance are very much enhanced. Welsh Royal Crystal's range of products is traditional and the decoration combines classic florals (intaglio) with straight diamond cuts.
A unique range of Celtic themes reflecting the design images of the Welsh Celtic heritage has been successfully introduced. The design and supply of presentation trophies and gifts is an expanding area of the Company's business. Welsh Royal Crystal can number within its customer portfolio important corporate customers in Wales and is pleased to be associated with the Cardiff Singer of the World Competition sponsored by British Petroleum, the Young Welsh Singer Competition sponsored by the Midland Bank and more recently, the Welsh Women of the Year sponsored by the Western Mail and HTV. In addition to supplying our fine Welsh crystal to over 100 retail accounts in Wales, sales are increasing acrossthe borders of the Principality into England, Scotland, Saudi Arabia, North America, Australia and Canada.
Time spent in the Welsh Royal Crystal Visitor Centre provides an opportunity to see the WELSH MASTERS OF FIRE AND GLASS handcraft full lead crystal products to the finest quality. A visit to the Welsh Crystal Shop presents an enviable opportunity to purchase quality crystal manufactured in Wales, whether it be a valuable centre piece or small gift item.
OPEN; All year round 9am-12.30pm and 1.30-4.30pm. Glass blowing demonstrations may not be available on some weekdays, Saturdays and Sundays.

Visitor Attractions

MUMBLES   THE LOVESPOON GALLERY
492 Mumbles Road, Mumbles, Swansea SA348X
Tel: 01792 360132.
You will find this unique gallery located on the right opposite the 1st Car Park just before the mini-roundabout in Mumbles. Do not miss the opportunity of visiting The Lovespoon Gallery. It is the world's first gallery devoted entirely to Welsh Lovespoons. Until you have seen the astonishing range you will have no idea that there are literally hundreds of designs made by some of the very best carvers in Wales. The Lovespoon has a well earned reputation for having only genuine carved Lovespoons and is known world wide. A Lovespoon makes a wonderful gift for special occasions like weddings, anniversaries christenings, birthdays and any important event. For 400 years this has been a Welsh tradition which is another good reason for buying one. When you examine the spoons you will see what wonderful artistry is employed when they are carved. They are certainly collectors' items.
OPEN: 10am-6pm Sunday opening in August. Children welcome. Credit cards: Visa.Mastercard. Suitable for the disabled, just one small step. Assistance given. Amex and Diners.

SCOTLAND

ABERDEEN
STORYBOOK GLEN, Maryculter.
Tel: 01224 732941.
Children will be in their element in this 28 acre children's fantasy land. There are nursery rhyme and fairytale characters everywhere. Adults will also enjoy the chance to become children again. A delightful area surrounded by trees, flowers and waterfalls. Open 1st Mar-31st Oct, daily 10-6pm. Nov-end Feb, Sat and Sun only 11-4pm.

BALLETER
DEE VALLEY CONFECTIONERS, Station Square.
Tel: 013397 55499. Delicious traditional hand-made sweets. Free viewing area. Open: Sweet Factory, all year Mon-Thurs 9-5.30pm. Shop open daily 9am-9pm.

BANCHORY
CRATHES CASTLE. Scottish National Trust.
Tel: 01330 844525.
Beautiful Castle and Gardens with a Castle Visitor Centre, adventure

Chapter Fourteen

playground, restaurant and shop. You may also like to purchase some plants from the plant sales, to transform your garden. Open: all year round daily 9.30-sunset.

DUFFTOWN
THE GLENFIDDICH DISTILLERY.
A good point at which to start of the Malt Whiskey Trail which stretches for 70 miles and takes in seven distilleries and the Speyside Cooperage at Craigellachie. All the distilleries have gift shops, audio-visual, exhibitions and picnic areas, some have tea rooms. A wonderful experience to view whiskey in the making. Make sure there is someone to do just the driving.

GALSTON
LOUDOUN CASTLE PARK.
Tel: 01563 822296.
This wonderful visitor attraction is set in the most magnificent parkland and woods. The imposing castle ruin is surrounded by farm livestock, aviary, playgrounds, adventure playground, and picnic area. There is also a Coach House restaurant and gift shop for those important souvenirs. It holds Britain's largest carousel. Open: from Easter daily 10.00-dusk.

GRETNA GREEN
THE FINE ARTS GALLERY,
Headless Cross. Tel: 01461 338066.
Beautiful ceramics figurines all hand painted. Daily painting demonstrations throughout the summer. Open: daily.

HUNTLY
LEITH HALL, Kennethmont. Scottish National Trust.
Tel: 01466 831216.
A 17th century mansion house. Inside it contains a military collection belonging to the Leith family. Wonderful gardens, picnic area tea room and disabled toilet. Open: House: 14th Apr-1st Oct daily 1.30pm-5.30pm (last admission 4.45pm). Garden and grounds: all year daily 9.30-sunset.

IRVINE
SCOTTISH MARITIME MUSEUM.
Tel: 01294 275059.
Here you can see quite a unique collection of machinery, craft and buildings all from the 19th century. For visitors there is 'hands on' where you are encouraged to climb aboard the different vessels including the world's oldest clipper ship the 'Carrick'. In the main hall is an exhibition. Open: 1st Apr-31st Oct 10-5pm.

Visitor Attractions

KILLIN
THE BREADALBANE FOLKLORE CENTRE.
TEL: 01567 820254.
In the heart of Scottish mountain territory is the beautiful village of Killin, where legend has told of giants, saints, sinners, soothsayers spirits and warrior clans populated the area. A Celtic monk, SaintFillan an early Christian missionary and Irish prince, settled here by the roaring waters of the Falls of Dochart, where he performed his wonders. Robert the Bruce gave credit to the Saint for the victory at Bannockburn, and stones which he blessed are said to heal different parts of the body. All this can be seen in the Centre, along with videos and artefacts from the past and wonderful stories from Gaelic folk tradition. A restored water wheel, Tourist Information Centre and a souvenir shop. Open: Mar-Jun and Sept-Oct daily 10-5pm. Jul-Aug daily 9-6pm. Nov-Dec and Feb weekends only 10-4pm. Closed January.

KILMARNOCK
DEAN CASTLE AND COUNTRY PARK.
TEL: 01563 522702/534580.
The Castle is set in some 200 acres and is surrounded by woodland with rivers, nature trail, children's corner, picnic areas adventure playground, a riding centre and tea room. The Castle has the most fascinating array of medieval arms, armour, tapestries, musical instruments from an early European era, and a display of manuscripts belonging to Robert Burns. Open: all year round. Daily 12 noon-5pm.

MAYBOLE
CULZEAN CASTLE AND COUNTRY PARK.
National Trust of Scotland.
Tel: 01655 760274/760269.
The Castle was designed by Robert Adam in 1777, and is magnificently furnished. A special presentation explains General Eisenhower's part in European History. Not so long ago the Country Park was named as the 'most beautiful country park in Britain'. It has a deer park, swan pond, walled garden, aviary, and a ranger service with guided walks. Restaurant and tea room. Open: all year.

MOFFAT
THE MOFFAT POTTERY,
Gerry Lyons, 20 High Street.
Tel: 01683 220793. See the 'Singing Potter' at his wheel and listen to the fine selection of songs from the operas. Once of the Scottish Opera Company, he now spends his time crafting beautiful item from clay. Take your time and peruse the individual designs in the studio. Open: Mon-Sat 9.00-5pm.

Chapter Fourteen

MOTHERWELL
BARON'S HAUGH NATURE RESERVE. RSPB.
Adele Street.
Tel: 0131 5573136.
The marsh meadowland has been flooded to give ideal conditions and habitat for the many species of birds. Here you can quietly watch the different wildlife from special hides which look out over the lake. A visit here will be an enchanting experience whether you are an expert bird watcher or just a beginner. The disabled have not been forgotten and certain parts of the reserve are accessible for wheelchair users. Also available are expert staff to offer help and information. A super day out.

ORKNEY
The are 18 inhabited islands, and on all of them history abounds. There are many Stone Age tombs where the communities buried their dead. There are underground earth houses where Iron Age families lived. The Farm and Folk Museum, here you can see the evolution of farm buildings with traditional breeds of sheep and poultry. The Wireless Museum has exhibits of early crystal sets to the present day radio, and much more. In 1850 a Stone Age Mainland village was discovered having been buried by sand for over 4000 years, a wonderful piece of history.

SKARES
DOON VALLEY RARE BREEDS CENTRE.
Tel: 01290 421553.
With over 60 different breeds of waterfowl, poultry and animals to see, this is a wonderful experience and very educational too. Tea room and car park. Open: 1st mar-31 Nov. Daily 10-6pm. Dec-Feb by appointment only.

Joy Davids Choice

A	
Abbotsbury	239
Aberaeron	685
Aberdaron	665
Aberdeen	789
Aberdovey	679
Harbour Hotel	709
Aberfeldy Palace Hotel	791
Abergavenny	707
Maes-Glas	710
Abergele	672
Abergynolwyn	679
Aberlady	777
Old Aberlady Inn	792
Aberporth	686
Abersoch	665
Aberystwyth	682
Abinger Hammer	522
Abingdon	522
Adderbury	
Airth	
Albury	341
Stream Cottage	379
Alcombe	33
Alfriston	369
Alresford	263
Alstonfield	442
Alton	264
French Horn	233
Alton (Staffs)	455
Hansley Cross Cottage	
Amberley	361
Amesbury	253
Ampfield	273
Amport	278
Broadwater	278
Amwell	341
Andover	267
Lains Cottage	
Angelsey	669
Angus	784
Annan	793
Paganis Restaurant	793
Anstruther	784
Ansty	248
Anthony	62
Appledore	51
West Farm	135
Ardishaig	
Alt-na-Craig	794

Auchendarroch Hotel	795
Arundel	362
Arran	779
Ascot	335
Asenby Highfield House	587
Ashbourne	509
Ardel House	517
Ashburton	48
Ashby Falcon Hotel	513
Ashby de la Zouch	512
Ashwater	49
Renson Mill	136
Blagdon Manor	147
Athelney	22
Auchterarder	
Gleneagles Hotel	796
Avebury	256
Aviemore	
Axminster	39
Granary Cottage	127
Lea House	137
Manor House	138
Ayr	780
Ayot St Lawrence	340
B	
Badminton	19
Bala	669
Abercelyn	711
Ballater The Green Inn	795
Ballindolloch	
Balloch	782
Kinnoul Guest House	798
Bampton	49
Banbury	522
Agdon Farm	529
Bangor	663
Bangor-on-Dee	675
Banstead	342
Bardsey Island	665
Barmouth	712
Wavecrest Hotel	712
Barnard Castle	585
East Mellwaters	588
Bath	16
Della Rosa	140
Oakleigh	141
Parkside GH	142
Redcar Hotel	144
Siena Hotel	145

Joy Davids Choice

Bathford	10	Bishops Tawton	51
The Old School	146	Downrew House	151
Battle	375	Bishopston	695
Baydon	257	Bishopswood	152
Beaconsfield	337	Hawthorn House	152
Beaminster	237	Swaynesfirs Farm	280
Beaulieu	271	Blackdog	140
Beaworthy	49	Oaklands	142
Blagdon Manor	147	Blackdown	238
Bedale	581	Blackpool	559
Upsland Farm	589	Black Torrington	49
Southfields	590	Blaenau Ffestiniog	665
Green Dragon Inn	590	Blandford	244
Beddgelert	666	Blagdon	20
Beech	279	Blue Anchor	33
Glen Derry	279	Hele House	143
Beer	38	Boddinnick	60
Garlands	140	Bodelwyddan	672
Benoath Cove	54	Bodieve	54
Berkeley	525	The Mowhay	154
Old School House	530	Bodmin	61
Berrynarbor	51	Loskeyle	155
Langleigh House	148	Skisdon	156
Betchworth	342	Bognor Regis	363
Gadbrook	380	Westholme GH	
Bethesda	663	Boldre	270
Bethlehem	693	Boltonsborough	26
Betley	563	Bontddu	668
Betley Court Farm	563	Borth	682
Betws-y-Coed	667	Boscastle	53
Bryn Llewelyn GH	713	Lower Meadows Hse	155
Church Hill Hotel	714	Westerings	158
Bewdley	449	Bosham	357
Bexhill	373	White Barn	382
Bickerton	564	Bosinney Cove	54
Pool Farm	564	Botley	273
Bickleigh	49	Bournemouth	235
Bideford	52	Woodside Hotel	281
Lane Mill Farm	141	Bourton-on-the-Water	524
Burscott House	143	Farncombe	531
Newbridge Hotel	229	Lansdowne Villa	531
The Old Mill	149	Rooftrees	532
Biggleswade	338	Windrush Farm	533
Birnam by Dunkeld	798	Bovey Tracey	46
Birnam House Hotel	798	Bovington Heath	245
Birmingham	451	Bowness-on-Windermere	565
Bishops Castle	435	Oak Bank House	565
Boars Head Hotel	455	Bradford	585
Bishops Frome	415	Bradford-on-Avon	261
Bishops Stortford	340	Bradworthy	50

Joy Davids Choice

High Park	158	Brynford	674
Brampton	566	Buckerell	39
New Mills House	566	Splatthayes	161
Bransford Croft G H	455	Buckfastleigh	159
Bratton Clovelly	49	Globe Inn	159
The Old Rectory	159	Buckland in the Moor	47
Braunton	51	Bucklers Hard	271
Brayton	591	Bude	52
Beric West Cottage	591	Brightlands Apts	162
Brecon	703	Longfield Manor	163
Belvedere 7	16	Lopthorne	164
Lansdowne Hotel	717	Stratton Gardens	163
Maeswalter	718	Inn on the Green	166
Brechfa Glasfryn		Trebarn	167
Guest House	715	Treworgie Barton	168
Brent Knoll	22	Winswood	169
Bridford Bridge Farm	282	Budleigh Salterton	38
Bridgend	700	Builth Wells	685
Bridgnorth	434	Dol-Llyn-Wyn	719
Hannigans Farm	458	Orchard Cottage	720
Hampton House	457	Cedars Guest House	721
Oldfield Cottage	459	Bulmer	591
Bridgwater	23	Grange Farm	591
Bridpt	238	Bungay	632
Lanscombe House	280	Burbage	255
Bristol	15	Burcombe	250
Britford	45/ 252	Manor Farm	285
Brixham	40	Bures	354
Broadchalke	248	Burghclere	266
Broadhalfpenny Down	275	Burlesden	274
Broadhempston	41	Burnham-on-Sea	22
Coppa Dolla	160	Bury St Edmunds	632
Broadmead	15	Ounce House	639
Broadstairs	350	Twelve Angel Hill	640
Broadway Barn House	460		
Brook House	461	**C**	
Leasow House	462	Caerleon	705
Tudor Cottage	463	Caernarfon	664
Broadwindsor	237	Caerphilly	704
Brockenhurst	269	Caerwent	706
Brockham	341	Caiplie	799
Bromsgrove	449	The Caiplie G H	799
Bromyard	415	Caldicot	706
Brookthorpe	525	Callander	783
Gilberts	534	The Gart House	800
Broseley	433	Calne	259
Broughton Yewtree House	283	Camborne	58
Brownsea Island	246	Halgarrock Cottage	161
Bruton	26	Cambridge	636
Braunton	51	Cannock Chase	441

Joy Davids Choice

White House	464	Chesterfield		510
Canterbury	349	Chew Magna		20
Carbis Bay	55	Chew Stoke		20
Tregorran Hotel	170	Chideock		236
Cardiff	701	Chideock House		286
Cardigan	686	Chilmark		248
Cary Fitzpaine	31	Chippenham		259
Cary Fitzpaine Farm	166	Bramleys		284
Carew	690	Fairfield Farm		287
Carlisle	562	Chipping Camden		524
Marchmain	567	Brymbo		537
Broadlea	567	Chipping Sodbury		19
Carmarthen	722	Chirk		437/676
Pant Gwynn Farm	722	Christchurch		246
Carreg Cennen	693	Ashbourne		288
Carrutherstown	801	Hazeldene		286
Hetland Hall Hotel	801	Number 19		288
Castle Cary	27	The Homestead		289
Horse Pond Motel	227	Three Gables		291
Castle Combe	258	Churchstow		42
Castle Douglas		Home Farm		171
Longacre Manor	802	Church Stretton		435
Castle Howard	584	Belvedere		463
Lower Barn	592	Court Farm		465
Cawsand Bay	35	Cilgerran		687
Halfway House	171	Cirencester		538
Cerne Abbas	241	The Leauses		538
Chagford	44	Clarach		682
The Mews	167	Clare		635
Chalfont St Giles	337	The Plough Inn		641
Chard	31	Clawton		49
Hornsbury Mill	172	The Hollies		
Charminster	241	Cleveland		585
Charmouth	236	Beacon Guest House		593
Chacewater	58	Holly Bush Hotel		594
Chatham	353	Clifton		15
Chawton	266	Clovelly		33
Cheltenham	526	Coalpit Heath		16
Guiting G H	535	Box Hedge Farm		174
Upper Farm	536	Coalville		512
Chelwood Gate Holly House	383	Cobham		343
Chepstow	706	Cedar House Rest.		389
Cheriton	696	Cockington		40
Chichester	356	Colchester		354
Cottage G H	384	Thorington Hall		391
Easton House	385	Ryegate House		390
Hatpins	386	Cold Ashton		259
Riverside Lodge	387	Whiteways		287
St Andrews Lodge	388	Colwyn Bay		672
Chester	558	Combe Martin		51

Joy Davids Choice

Rone House	174	Knowles House	103
Combewich	173	Cwyn-yr-Eglwys	688
Moxhill Farm	173		
Combe Raleigh	175	**D**	
Windgate Farm	175	Danebury	267
Congleton	558	Darlington	585
Coniston	560	Darsie by	
Conwy	666	Cupar Todhall House	804
Cookham	335	Dartmeet	47
Corfe	245	Dartmoor	47
Corfe Castle	245	Dartmouth	41
Corfe Mullen	290	Ford House	104
Coventry Lodge	290	Dawlish	41
Corris	678	Deal	351
Corsham	259	Deighton	595
Pickwick Lodge	293	Grimston House	595
Cotheridge	467	Denbigh	678
Little Lightwood Farm	467	Derby	509
Cotterdale Hawes	588	Devil's Bridge	683
The Old Chapel	588	Deviock	62
Coventry	452	Cair Farm	105
Coxley	26	The Barn	106
Amber House	175	Devizes	254
Cranborne	246	Castle Hotel	295
Cranborne Chase	247	Orchard Cottage	296
Craswall	418	Didcot	535
Craven Arms	468	Middle Fell	535
Hesterworth Holidays	468	Didmarton	536
Crawley	365	Old Rectory	536
Crediton	48	Din Lligwy	670
Bostona	176	Ditchling	367
Copper Oak Cottage	176	Longcroft House	392
Great Leigh Farm	177	Dittisham	43
Crewkerne	31	Cott Farm	106
Beverly Farm	178	Doccombe	45
George Hotel	102	Dolcaucothi	693
Cricket St Thomas	24	Dolgellau	668
Cricklade	258	Borthwnog Hall	724
Criccieth	723	The Ivy House	725
Craig-y-Mor		Dorchester	240
Guest House	723	The Old Farmhouse	297
Cromer	629	Dover	349
Croyde	51	Downderry	62
Combas Farm	103	Treliddon Farm	107
Crudwell	294	Drewsteignton	45
Crudwell Court	294	Old Inn	108
Crynant	699	Droitwich	448
Cuckfield	366	Droxford	272
Culborn	28	White Horse Inn	298
Cullompton	48	Dryslwyn	692

1003

Dudley	450	Etchingham	375
Dulcote	26	King John's Lodge	393
Manor Farm	109	Eton	335
Dulverton	29	Evesham	424
Dunsford	45	Church House	471
Dunstable	338	Exeter	36
Dunster	30	Channel Vista	112
Woodville House	110	Hill Farm	113
Dunure	805	Exmoor	23
Dunduff Farm	805	Exmouth	37
Durham	586/37	Sunnymead	114
Nevilledale Terr	596	Eyam	614
Durham City	597	Miners Arms	614
Castle View G H	597		
Durlston	245	**F**	
Duxford	636	Fairbourne	727
Dyffryn Ceiriog	726	Einion House	727
Gwynfa Guest House	726	Falmouth	57
Dyserth	673	Camelot	115
		Farnham	342
E		Highwray	394
Eardisland	419	Mill Lane Lodge	395
Eastbourne	373	Felton	472
East Budleigh	37	Felton House	472
Sir Walter Raleigh Inn	111	Felixstowe	633
East Cornworthy	42	Findon	362
Black Ness Cottage	112	Filey	583
East Grinstead	364	Seabrink House	598
East Knoyle	248	Fishbourne	357
East Looe	62	Fishguard	658
East Manley	48	Fittleworth	361
East Meon	264	Flash	442
Combe Cross	233	Fletching	370
Dunvegan Cottage	300	Flint	674
East Portland	301	Folkestone	351
Alessandra	301	Fordingbridge	289
East Portlemouth	43	Sandy Corner	289
Ebbesbourne Wake	248	Fort William	780
Eccleshall	469	Allt-Nan-Ross Hotel	807
Slindon House Farm	469	The Beinnard	808
Edinburgh	777	The Grange	808
Drummond House	806	Fovant	248
Eckington	470	Fowey	60
Sandrene	470	Fremlingham	51
Eglwysfach	682	Framlington	633
Ellesmere	436	Fyfield	256
Ellesmere Port	436		
Emsworth	276	**G**	
Newnham House	302	Gillingham (Dorset)	243
Erlstoke	254	Girvan	809

Joy Davids Choice

The Malincourt	809
Gilwern	728
The Wenalt	728
Gittisham	39
Glamorgan Crossway House	729
Glanwydden	672
Glasgow	777
Kelvin Grove Hotel	811
Glastonbury	24
Ashcombe	225
Dennis & Edna	116
Wick Hollow	117
Glencoe	780
Glenluce	812
Torwood Hse Hotel	812
Glenshee Blackwater Inn	812
Gloucester	525
Glynarthen	730
Gwestry Fferm	730
Glyndebourne	370
Glyndyfrydwy	677
Gnosall	438
Goathland	583
Whitfield Hse Hotel	559
Godney	26
Goodrich	414
Golant	61
Golberdon	119
Swallows Rest	118
Gorran Churchtown	60
Gosport	275
Gower	731
Fairfield Cottage	731
Grasmere	561
Great Charfield	261
Great Hampden	336
Great Torrington	49
Great Yarmouth	630
Gretna Green	773
Grimley	429
Guildford	341
Gwain Valley	732
Tregynon Country Farmhouse Hotel	732
Gwalchmai	671
Gwynfryn	733
Pas Tirion Fford Bryn	733

H

Hackett	473
Broughton Manor	473
Halstead	355
Timbers	396
Hamble	274
Hambledon	265/337
Hampton-in-Arden	452
Handcross	366
Hanmer	676
Harbertonford	43
The Hungry Horse	118
Hardham	361
Harlech	668
Harleston	642
South Elmham Hall	642
Harmans Cross	
Downshay Farm	233
Harrogate	585
Crescent Lodge	600
Hartlake	24
Hartlake Farm	119
Hartland	52
Hartland Quay Hotel	213
Hastings	374
Hatherleigh	49
Haverfordwest	689
Hawkeridge	261
Hawnby	601
Laskill Farm	601
Hay Bluff	418
Hay-on-Wye	418
The Swan	474
Hayle	55
Godolphin Bridge Hotel	119
Hayling Island	275/16
Charleston Cl	292
Haywards Heath	366
Helensburgh	779-782
Ardmore Guest House	813
Eastbank	813
Ravenswood	814
Helmsley	583
Barn Close Farm	602
Buckingham House	603
Sproxton Hall Farm	604
Helston	56
Boak House	120
Cobblers Cottage	120

Joy Davids Choice

Henley-on-Thames	523		Ipplepen	40
Amervyn House	539		Ipswich	633
Little Parmoor	540		Edgehill	643
Hereford	415		Ironbridge	432
Hickstead	366		Isle of Islay	
Highclare	266		Kilmeny Farm Hse	816
Higher Halstock	31		Isle of Man	774
Sydney Farm	121		Ivybridge	35
High Wycombe	337			
Hilperton	303		**J**	
Paxcroft Cottages	303		Jordans	337
Hinton Ampner	264			
Hindhead	342		**K**	
Hodnet	438		Kenilworth	446
Holbeton	36		Kendal	560
Mildmay Colours	122		Kentisbury Ford	51
Holcombe Rogus	49		North Patchmole	126
Holford	28		Kentisbeare	48
Alfoxton Cottage	123		Keswick	561
Holsworthy	49		Keswick-on-Derwentwater	561
Court Barn	124		Skiddaw Grove Hotel	568
Holt	675		The Paddocks	569
The Coppers	293		Keyhaven	270
Holyhead	670		Kidderminster	449
Holywell	670		Kidwelly	696
Honiton	39		Killen Clachaig Hotel	817
Pheasantry	224		Morenish Lodge Hotel	818
Yard Farm	104		Kilmarnock	781
Horsham	365		The Muir House Fm	819
Hoveton	630		Kilmeston	264
Huddersfield	585		Kilpeck	417
Forest Farm	592		Kingsbridge	41
The Mallow G H	605		Centry Farm	127
Hundred House Village	685		Holmfield	128
Huntingdon	636		Lower Grimpstonleigh	129
Hythe	351		Marsh Mills	130
			Seamark Apartment	131
I			Hope & Anchor	132
Icklesham	375		The Sloop Inn	133
Ilam	441		Kingsclere	266
Throwley Hall Farm	514		Kingsteignton	41
Ilfracombe	51		Attworth	134
Combe Lodge Hotel	226		Kingswear	42
Seven Hills Hotel	125		Coleton Barton Farm	195
Ilkley	585		Kings Caple	475
Gracefield	606		Ruxton Farm	
Ilminster	31		Kings Lynn	628
Innerleithen	815		Tudor Rose Hotel	644
The Traquair Arms	815		Kirkby-in-Ashfield	775
Instow	51		Kirkcudbright	820

Joy Davids Choice

Selkirk Arms Hotel	820	Lerryn	61
Knowle	452	Leslie By Insch	822
		Leslie Castle	822
L		Lesnewth	53
Lacock	260	Courtyard Farm	200
Lambourne Downs	257	Letchworth	339
Lamorna	56	Lewes	398
Lampeter	734	Nightingales	398
The Black Lion		Leyburn	581
Royal Hotel	734	Clyde House	607
Land's End	55	Lifton	54
Langport The Old Mill	196	Milford Farm Cotts	200
Langton Matravers	295	Lilleshall	430
Maycroft	295	Lindfield	366
Lanlivery	62	Liskeard	62
Lynwood B & B	197	Crylla Farm	202
Lanteglos-by-Fowey Hall Fm	198	Linden Cottage	202
Largs	780	Lower Trengale	203
Stonehaven	814	Rosecraddoc Lodge	204
Whinpark	821	Shenstone	208
Launceston	54	Old Rectory	206
Chelsfield Farm	197	Tredinnick Farm	204
Glencoe Villa	199	Tregondale	207
Hurdon Farm	200	Littlehampton	362
Lavant	359	Little Barugh	608
Lavenham	635	Manor Farm	608
The Great House	645	Little Malvern	427
Laverstock	267	Little Stretton	435
Lechlade	541	Littleton	263
Cambrai Lodge	541	Liverpool	559
Ledbury	414	Llanasa	674
Kilmory	467	Llanberis	663
Mill Cottage	476	Llanddeusant	669
Moor Court Farm	477	Llandegley	735
Preston Priory	478	Ffaldau Country Hse	735
Hopton Arms	479	Llanddewi Brefi	684
Wall Hills	480	Llandeilo	692
Leeds	585	Maerdy Cottage	718
Leek	442	Llandewi	696
Leicester	511	Llandiloes	684
Leigh	234	Llandovery	685
Carpenters Arms	234	Cwmgwyn Farm	736
Leighton Buzzard	338	Llwyncelyn Guest House	737
Lelant	55	Llandrindod Wells	685
Leominster	415	Bwlch Farm Hse	738
Heath House	481	Holly Farm	739
Highfield	477	Hotel Commodore	740
Ladymeadow Farm	469	Severn Arms Hotel	741
Compasses Hotel	482	Llandudno	671
Leonardslee	364	St Tudno	742

Llandudno Junction	667, 672	Lundy Island		51
Llaneilian	670	Lustleigh		46
Llanelli	716	Cleavelands St Mary		219
Glyngwernen Farm	716	South Harton		220
Llangadog	743	Lydford		44
Pengrug	743	Lydford House		209
Llangedwyn	681	Lyme Regis		236
Llangian	665	Cliff Cottage		305
Llangollen	744	Devonia Guest House		306
Cae Crwn Farm	744	Coombe House		297
Llangrannog	686	St Michaels Hotel		307
Glyn Valley Hotel	745	Lymington		270
Llanrhaedr-ym-Mochnant	681	Pennavon		308
Llanrhidian	696	Lyndhurst		271
Llanrwst	667	Lynmouth		50
Llantwit Major	701	Lynton		50
Llanstysilio	747	Ingleside Hotel		210
Bryn Hyfryd	747	Sandrock Hotel		212
Llanwrda	746			
Glanrennell Pk Hotel	746	**M**		
Lochernhead	783	Machynlleth		679
The Monachyle Mhor	823	Maidenhead		335
Loch Lomond	780	Malmesbury		258
Sheildaig Farm	821	Malpas		570
Lockerbie	773	Laurel Farm		570
Kings Arms Hotel	824	Malvern Link		427
Lockerbie Manor	825	Malvern Wells		427
Ravenshill House	826	Brickbarn Farm		486
London	343	Clevelands		470
Durrants Hotel	399	The Old Vicarage		502
11 Cadogan Gardens	400	Manaccan		56
Number Sixteen	401	Manaton		46
Goring Hotel	402	Manchester		559
Portobello	403	Marazion		56
Uptown Reservations	404	Marden		473
London Colney	339	Vauld House Farm		473
Longleat	249	Margate		350
Longnor	442	Market Drayton		436
Looe	62	Market Harborough		512
Windermere House	208	Marlborough		255
Lostwithiel	60	Paddocks		309
Lower Beeding	364	Marlow		337
Ludgershall	255	Marshfield		19
Ludlow	434	Mary Tavy		44
Corndene	483	Matlock		510
Lower Hayton Grange	484	Melcombe Bingham		244
Bull Hotel	485	Melksham		259
Lullington	516	Longhope Guest Hse		306
The Old Post Office	516	Mells		22
Lulworth Cove	245	Melrose		827

Joy Davids Choice

Burts Hotel	827	Guest House	750
Melton Mowbray	512	Mullion	57
Mere	249		
Meltone House	309	**N**	
Peacehaven G H	304	Nailsworth	525
Merthyr-Mawr	700	Windsoredge	543
Mevagissey	59	Nanpean	61
Treleaven Farmhouse	208	Nant Gwernot	679
Michaelchurch Escley	418	Nantwich	437, 558
Middlewich	559	Neath	698
Midhurst	360	Nantgaredig	751
Millers Dale	515	Cwmtwrch Hotel	751
Dale Cottage	515	Nefyn	665
Milford Haven	690	Nether Wallop	267
Milton Keynes	337	Nevern	687
Milford-on-Sea	270	Newhaven	368
Milton Abbas	244	Newburgh	829
Milverton	28	Burnside Hse Hotel	829
Lovelynch Farm	214	Newcastle-under-Lyme	443
Minchinhampton	525	Newington Kildonan Lodge	830
Ragged Cott Inn	542	Newlyn	56
Minehead	33	Newmarket	635
Penny Hill Farm	113	Newport	430, 688
Alcombe House	211	Newton Stewart	775
Dollons House	215	Corsemalzie	
Stockleigh Lodge	216	House Hotel	831
Minstead	271	Newquay	55
Minster	53	Cotehele Lodge	210
Minterne Magna	241	Trenance Lodge	218
Modbury	41	Fairhavens	217
Moffat	776	Newton	752
Moffat House Hotel	828	Pen-Y-Gelli	752
Mold	674	Newton Abbot	40
Monksilver	33	Warmhill Farm	211
Monmouth	707	Newton Ferrers	35
Riverside Hotel	748	Newtown	680
Montacute	24	Dyffryn Fm Holidays	753
Montgomery	680	Nordley	488
Dragon Hotel	748	Albynes	488
Moretonhampstead	45	North Leigh	222
Mortehoe	51	Smallicombe Farm	222
Moreton-in-Marsh	534	North Malvern	427
Blue Cedar House	534	North Petherton	5
Fosseway Farm	538	Lower Clavelshay Fm	220
Mounts Bay	56	North Petherwin	54
Much Marcle	414	The Sunday School	64
Much Wenlock	433	North Tawton	50
Longville Arms	487	Lower Nichols	
Mumbles	694	Nymet Farm	64
Tides Reach		Northam	52

Yeolden House	221	Cringletie	835
Northmoor	544	Pelynt	63
Rectory Farm	544	Trenderway Farm	69
Norwich	631	Pembridge	420
Almond Tree Hotel	646	Pembroke	690
The Norfolk		Penally	53
Mead Hotel	647	Wychwood House	754
Welbeck House	648	Penarth	701
Noss Mayo	35	Penbryn	686
Slade Barn	65	Pendclawdd	696
Nottingham	508	Penhow	706
		Penley	676
O		Penmaenpool	668
Oban	779	Penrith	571
Lerags House	832	Albany House	571
Okehampton	44	Bridge End Farm	572
Easterbrook Farm	65	Pensarn	672
Olney	337	Pentargen	53
Orleton	489	Pentraeth	670
Line Farm	489	Penzance	56
Oswestry	436	Lynwood G H	71
Bron Heulog	490	Wymering G H	71
Ottery St Mary	37	Perranorworthal	58
Pitt Farm	66	Perranporth	55
Overton	676	Pershore	425
Overwallop		Perth	783
Oxford	522	Peter Tavy	44
Earlmount G H	545	Petersfield	265
Green Gables	546	Petworth	361
Oystermouth	694	Pevensey	373
		Pickering	583
P		Piddlehinton	245
Padstow	54	Piddletrenthide	245
Trevone Bay Hotel	67	The Poachers Inn	310
Old Mill	68	Pitlochry	837
Painswick	547	The Moulin Hotel	837
Brookhouse Mill		The Buttonboss Hotel	836
Cottage	547	Pitminster	32
Cardynham House	548	Queens Arms	72
Palgrave	649	Plas Newydd	671
The Malt House	649	Plymouth	34
Pantasaph	673	Imperial Hotel	73
Parracombe	51	Polperro	63
Patna Parsons Lodge		The Watchers	66
Restaurant	833	Polzeath	74
Smithston Farm	834	Seaways G H	74
Paul	56	Pontrhydfendigaid	683
Peaslake	341	Poole	235
Hurtwood Inn	405	Lewina Lodge	311
Peebles	772	Porchester	274

Joy Davids Choice

Port Einon	695	Rhuddlan	673	
Port Isaac	54	Rhyl	673	
Fairholme	75	Riccall	596	
St Andrews Hotel	76	Coney House	596	
Portesham	238	Richmond	581	
Porthcawl	699	West Cottage	597	
Porthcurno	56	Wilson House Farm	609	
Porthmadog	665	Ringmore	42	
Porthoer	665	Journey's End	79	
Portland	239	Rocester		
Portmeirion	666	Leeze Guest House	491	
Portpatrick	774	Rochester	353	
Portskewett	706	Rock	54	
Portsmouth	274	Cant Farm	80	
Postbridge	46	Rode	24	
Poundon	545	Irondale House	81	
Manor Farm	545	Rodhuish	82	
Poundsgate	47	Higher Rodhuish Fm	82	
Powerstock	238	Romney Marsh	348	
Prestatyn	673	Romsey	272	
Prestwick	834	Pyesmead Farm	313	
Fernbank	834	Ross-on-Wye	413	
Princetown	46	Roxburgh	838	
Duchy House	77	Dryburgh Abbey	838	
Puddletown	245	Royal Leamington Spa	447	
Pulborough	361	Royal Tunbridge Wells	352	
Pumsaint	693	Runnymede	341	
Purbeck	245	Ruthin	677	
Purse Caundle	243	The Old Rectory	755	
Pycombe	367	Rutland	512	
		Rye	376	
R		Fiddlers Oast	407	
Rackheath	650	Rye Foreign		
Barn Court	650			
Radstock	19	**S**		
Melon Cottage	78	Salcombe	43	
Ratford	312	Salisbury	251	
Hazeland Wood	312	Castleaven G H	314	
Redruth	58	Farthings	310	
Holmehurst	78	The Gallery	315	
Ramsgate	351	Websters	316	
Abbeygail G H	384	Salisbury Plain	249	
Reading	335	Sandersfoot	756	
Windy Brow	397	Harbour Light		
Redruth	58	Sandringham	629	
Reigate	342	Sandwich	349	
Barn Cottage	406	Saunton	51	
Reynoldston	696	Sayers Common	367	
Rhos-on-Sea	672	Scarborough	583	
Rhossli	695	Harmony Lodge	612	

Joy Davids Choice

Studley House	613	Spilsby		511
Scilly Isles	56	St Agnes		87
Seaford	368	Grange Farmhouse		87
Seaton (Devon)	38	St Albans		339
The Harbour House	76	St Andrews		783
Seatown	236	Brownlees G H		840
Selborne	265	St Austell		59
Selkirk	839	St Brides-Super-Ely		757
Philipburn Hotel	839	Sant-Y-Nyll House		757
Sennen	56	St Davids		689
Shaftesbury	243	Ramsey House		758
Mitre Inn	317	St Dogmaels		687
Old Forge	318	St Fillans		841
Wodonga	318	Achray House Hotel		841
Shaldon	41	St Germans		61
Shebdon	439	St Ives		55
Sheepwash	49	Boskerris Hotel		88
Shepton Mallet	26	Cobbles		224
Shrubbery Hotel	83	Rivendell		87
Sherborne	242	Surfside Yellow House		89
Sherborne Hill	492	The Count House		89
Hillcrest	492	The Willows		90
Sheringham	629	St Just-in-Roseland		58
Shipston-on-Stour	447	St Keverne		56
Ascott House	493	St Levan		56
Skelton	615	St Mary		31
Grange Farm	615	Pheasant Hotel		91
Skomer Island	689	St Mawes		57
Shrewsbury	436	St Michaels-on-Wyre		573
The Citadel	495	Tudor Farm		573
Sidmouth	38	St Neot		63
Groveside G H	84	Dye Cottage		90
Pinn Barton	84	London Inn		92
Southern Cross G H	85	St Winnow		61
Willow Bridge	86	Stafford		440
Silsoe	338	Donally House		496
Sixpenny Handley	247	Standrop		611
Slingsby	610	Fawn Lea		611
Beechtree House Fm	610	Starcross		41
Slough	336	Staunton		546
Somerton Still Cottage	85	Cromer Farm		546
South Brent	36	Steep		265
Hollymount Cottage	86	Steeple Ashton		321
South Harting	358	Spiers Piece Farm		321
South Molton	50	Steventon		523
Southborne	246	Tethers End		549
Southampton	272	Stirling		783
Southsea	275	Stockbridge		267
Mallow Guest House	320	Stogumber		34
Southwell	508	Stoke Gabriel		43

1012

Joy Davids Choice

Little Paddocks	93	T	
Stoke Gregory	22	Talgarth	761
Stoke Poges	337	Olde Masons Arms	761
Stoke-in-Teignhead	41	The Tower Hotel	762
Stone-on-Trent	443	Tamworth	453
Hollinhurst Farm	497	Old Rectory	494
Stone	440	Taplow	335
Stonehenge	253	Tarbert	843
Stonehouse	525	Springside	843
Grey Cottage	550	Tarporley	558
Stopham	361	Roughlow Farm	574
Stourhead	24, 249	Talsaenau	
Stourpaine	244	The Hotel	
Stourport-on-Severn	449	Maes-Y-Neuadd	763
Stowey	28	Taunton	31
Apple Tree Hotel	230	Longaller Mill	150
Stow-in-the-Wold	524	Forde House	228
Stowmarket	633	Tavistock	44
Stoulton	479	Teffont Evias	248
Caldewell	479	Teffont Magna	248
Stratford-upon-Avon	444	Teignmouth	41
Hardwick G H	498	Bonrose	93
Newbold Nurseries	494	Telford	430
Willow Corner	486	Tenbury Wells	415
Winton House	499	Tewkesbury	422, 526
Strathtummel-By-Pitlochry	842	Corner Cottage	552
Queens View Hotel	842	Thetford	651
Street	31	College Farm	651
Studland	245	Rose Cottage	653
Sturminster Newton	243	Thirsk	584
Lower Fifehead Fm	322	Hambleton House	616
The Deer Park	307	Spittal Hall	617
The Old Post Office	317	Thorncombe	237
Yew House Farm	324	Thorngrove	429
Sutton Staithe	651	Thornhill	844
Sutton Staithe Hotel	651	Drumcruilton	844
Swaffham	628	Thruxton	325
Red Lion	652	May Cottage	325
Higher Western		Tichborne	264
Restaurant	97	Tiger Bay	702
Little Holwell	97	Timberscombe	33
Swallowcliffe	248	Knowle Manor	94
Swanage	245	Tintagel	53
Swansea	694	Tintern	707
Hurst Dene G H	759	The Fountain Inn	764
Windsor Lodge Hotel	760	The Old Rectory	765
Swindon	257	Valley House	766
Courtleigh House	551	Wye Barn	767
Symonds Yat	414	Titchwell	654
		Briarfields Hotel	654

Joy Davids Choice

Tolpuddle	240	**W**	
Tonbridge	352	Wadebridge	54
Tong	432	Waen	673
Torbay	39	Waldingfield	
Torquay	39	Quayside Cottage	653
Suite Dreams Hotel	98	Wallingford	523
Totnes	42	Squires Guest House	549
Durant Arms	95	Fords Farm	553
Old Hazard	99	Walsall	451
Springfield House	101	Ware	341
School House	100	Wareham	245
Trearddur Bay	671	Ashcroft	313
Trebarwith Strand	54	Bradle Farm	323
Port William	179	Warminster	249
Tregaron	683	Washaway	61
Trerice	55	Watchet	33
Trerulefoot	62	Welcombe	52
Tresaith	686	Mead Barn Cottages	185
Trowbridge	261/26	Wellington	32
The Beeches	323	Greenham Hall	184
Herons Knoll	321	Wells	26
Trull	32	Bekynton House	186
Higher Dipford Farm	177	Home Farm	187
Truro	57	Ancient Gatehouse	188
Amarallas	180	Wells-next-the-Sea	629
Pengelly	181	Welsh Newton	417
Ventongimps Mill	178	Welshpool	680
Trwyn	678	Wem	436
		Wendover	336-7
U		Wensleydale	581
Uckfield	371	Herriots	618
Ugborough	36	Whitfield	619
Hillhead Farm	181	Wentnor	503
Upavon	253, 255	Crown Inn	503
Upper Beeding	364	Weobley	419/696
Upper Milton	26	Westbury	253/261
Milton Manor Farm	182	Westgate on Sea	350
Upton	690	Westhay	25
Upton-upon-Severn	426	West Bay	326
Tiltridge Farm	500	Westpoint Tavern	326
Uttoxeter	441	West Dean	369
Westward G H	501	West Firle	370
		West Grinstead	364
V		West Kennet	256
Venterdon	182	West Looe	62
Venterdon House	182	Anchor Lights	183
Virginstow	54	Westcliffe Hotel	185
Percys Restaurant	183	West Malvern	427
		West Wittering	359
		Weston-Super-Mare	20

Joy Davids Choice

Weston-under-Lizard	431	Alpine House	192
The Citadel		Woburn	338
Weymouth	239	Wolfhall	255
Premier Hotel	327	Wolverhampton	450
Wharfedale	582	Wolverton	336
Andra's Farm	620	Woodbridge	633
Wheelock	559	Grange Farm	655
Whipsnade Heath	338	Woodlands Glen Rest	329
Whitby	583	Woodstock	522
Postgate Farm	621	Plane Tree House	552
Sneaton Hall Hotel	622	Woolacombe	51
The Beacon	623	Worcester	422
Whitchurch (Shrops)	436	Burgage House	491
Whitchurch Canonicorum	237	Worthing	363
Whitfield Hill House	514	Wroxham	630
Whiteley	341	Wylye	250
Whiteparish	328	Wymondham	656
Brickworth Farm	328	Cobweb Cottage	656
Whitney-on-Wye	504	Kimberley Home Farm	657
Rhydspence Inn	504		
Whitstable	350	**Y**	
Whittington	436	Yarnscombe	51
Wichenford	429	Netherne	188
Widecombe-in-the-Moor	47	Yelverton	36
Widegates, Looe,	62	Lydgate House	193
Coombe Farm	189	The Forge	191
Trevana Farm	190	Yeovil	31
Wilmington	369	Seeburg	194
Wilton	250	York	584
Wimborne Minster	246	Hammer & Hand	
Thornhill Holt	327	Country Guest House	624
Twynham	328		
Wimborne St Giles	247	**Z**	
Wincanton	27	Zennor	55
Winchcombe	525		
The Plaisterers Arms	554		
Winchelsea	375		
Winchester	262/32		
Hyde Street	329		
Clovelly	326		
Windermere	561		
Hollypark House	576		
Windsor	334		
Winsford	29		
Kemps Farm	191		
Winterbourne	21		
Wisbech	637		
Witney	522		
Hawthorn G H	551		
Wiveliscombe	29		

Joy Davids Choice

DON'T DELAY

SEND FOR YOUR

JOY DAVID
ADVANTAGE CARD
TODAY

MEMBERSHIP IS ABSOLUTELY
FREE
TO PURCHASERS OF THIS BOOK

THE ADVANTAGE CARD..
..enables members to take advantage of the
many special offers;
Discounted Accommodation, Entrance Fees,
Food and Wines -
a more enjoyable time for less outlay.

*Save yourselves £££ whenever you visit
participating venues
featured in this book as well as receiving
a chatty newsletter
and an up date on special offers
three times a year.*

JOY DAVID'S CHOICE

If you would like to have any of the other titles currently available in this series, please complete the coupon and send to:

JOY DAVID'S CHOICE
4, St. Andrews Street, Plymouth,
Tel: 01752 220774

I would like to receive the following (please tick as appropriate):

- ❒ An Invitation to Plymouth — £12.00 inc p&p

- ❒ *Joy David's Choice -
    England Second Edition — £15.95 inc p&p

- ❒ Joy David's Choice -
    Wales, Central England
    & East Anglia — £12.00 inc p&p

- ❒ Joy David's Choice - Great Britain — £15.95 inc p&p

- ❒ Joy David's Choice -
    Eat Out, Eat Well in Britain — £16.25 inc p&p

- ❒ Joy David's Choice - Self-Catering in Britain — £12.00 inc p&p

- ❒ *Joy David's Choice -
    Classic Choice in Britain — £15.95 inc p&p

- ❒ *Joy David's Choice - Ireland — £15.95 inc p&p

- ❒ **Joy David's Choice -
    Castles, Cathedrals
    & Country Houses — £12.95 inc p&p

*Due out in late 1997
**Due out in 1998

Please tick to receive more information about future titles

NAME..
ADDRESS..
....
....

Tel. No. (Daytime)...
Please make cheques payable to 'Joy David's Choice'

Joy Davids Choice

ADVANTAGE CARD - JOINING FORM

TITLE....................INITIALS..
SURNAME...
SEX   M............   F.................
NATIONALITY...
AGE GROUP   18-30.................. 31-49................. 50+.................
ADDRESS...
TOWN................................ COUNTY..................................
POSTCODE..
HOW MANY HOLIDAYS DO YOU TAKE A YEAR?........................
HOW MANY OF THESE IN THE UK?............ EUROPE.............
OTHER..
HOW MANY OF THESE ARE SHORT BREAKS?.......................
                                   W/ENDS..........................
PLEASE STATE YOUR INTERESTS
i.e. Fishing, Golf, antiques etc..
DO YOU NORMALLY BOOK IN ADVANCE?..................Y..........N
WHICH OF THESE DO YOU NORMALLY STAY IN?
HOTEL................... INNS................ COUNTRY HOUSE.................
HOW DO YOU SETTLE YOUR ACCOUNT?
CREDIT CARD ....CHEQUE ....CASH ....
HOW OFTEN FO YOU EAT OUT?..
WHERE DID YOU BUY THIS BOOK?
....

SIGNATURE..
DATE...

Please note that this is not a credit card and is provided for the use of the applicant only at the venues included in the quarterly list which will be sent to you. The publishers cannot be held responsible for any changes in the offers made by establishments. Information is sent out in good faith and is believed to be correct at the time issued to Advantage Club members.

Please return your application form to: JOY DAVID'S ADVANTAGE CARD, FREEPOST, 4 St. Andrews Street, Plymouth, and allow 28 days for delivery.

JOY DAVID'S CHOICE

4, St Andrews Street, Plymouth
Tel: (01752) 220774

Dear Reader,

I hope you have enjoyed my choice of places of all kinds - I have certainly enjoyed researching them in order to write this book.

It would make the next edition much easier if you would help by suggesting places that could be included and your comments on any establishment or attraction you have visited, would be much appreciated.

I enjoy corresponding with my readers and look forward to hearing from you.

Yours sincerely,

Joy David

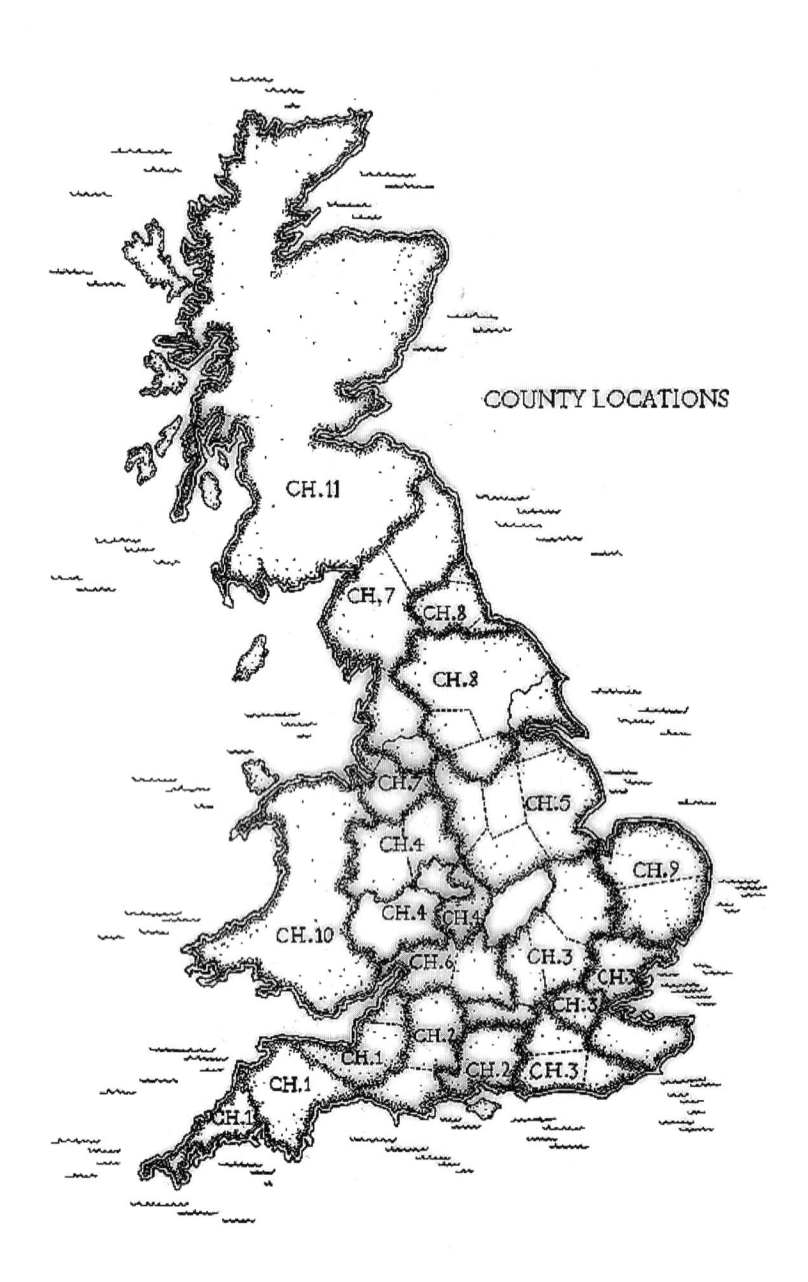

Joy Davids Choice

COUNTY LOCATIONS

CH.11
CH.7
CH.8
CH.8
CH.7
CH.5
CH.4
CH.9
CH.4 CH.4
CH.10
CH.6 CH.3
CH.3
CH.2
CH.1
CH.2 CH.3
CH.1
CH.1